FOURTH EDITION

HOTEL Housekeeping

OPERATIONS AND MANAGEMENT

G. Raghubalan
Hospitality Consultant & Trainer
Partner- SRJ Services

Smritee Raghubalan
Hospitality Educator & Consultant
Former Professor of Accommodation Management

OXFORD
UNIVERSITY PRESS

OXFORD
UNIVERSITY PRESS

Oxford University Press is a department of the University of Oxford. It furthers the University's objective of excellence in research, scholarship, and education by publishing worldwide. Oxford is a registered trade mark of Oxford University Press in the UK and in certain other countries.

Published in India by
Oxford University Press
22 Workspace, 2nd Floor, 1/22 Asaf Ali Road, New Delhi 110002

First Edition published 2007
Fourth Edition published 2023
Second impression 2025

ISBN-13: 978-93-5497-138-9
ISBN-10: 93-5497-138-5

eISBN-13: 978-93-5497-553-0
eISBN-10: 93-5497-553-4

Typeset in Adobe Garamond Pro and Eurostile Lt Std
by B2K-BYTES 2 KNOWLEDGE, Tamil Nadu
Printed in India by Thomson Press India Ltd.

Cover image: © natu /Shutterstock

For product information and current price, please visit www.india.oup.com

Preface to the Fourth Edition

Welcome to the remarkable world of hospitality! Working in this industry is both exhilarating and challenging. Hotel housekeeping is an area where each day brings a new challenge due to which learning is a 'work in progress' for housekeepers.

The department is responsible for the décor, cleanliness and upkeep of the front as well as the back of the hotel areas. Typically called the 'backbone of the hotel', the housekeeping department is increasingly being referred to as the 'heart of the hotel' because it freshens up and invigorates the entire hotel day in and day out, keeps it aesthetically appealing, and is responsible for the long and healthy life of the hotel.

Housekeepers have proved their mettle and are today a force to reckon with in the hospitality industry. Many of them have gone on to become general managers at various properties around the world.

Since the publication of the last edition, there has been a paradigm shift in hoteliering due to conscious prioritization by the industry for adoption of UN Sustainability Development Goals, advances in pathbreaking technology solutions and above all, the pandemic. All departments, more so the housekeeping, are following the tenets of sustainability, innovative technology adoption and clinical standards of cleaning. Thus, the fourth edition of the textbook, incorporating developments in hotel housekeeping in these arenas, is the need of the hour. Also included in this revised edition are certain topics received through valuable feedback both from the industry and academia.

The fourth edition of this well-accepted textbook continues to provide an exhaustive yet lucid coverage of the various aspects of hotel housekeeping. We sincerely hope that this edition will further aid students in understanding the basic concepts and applications of this subject.

About the Book

Hotel Housekeeping: Operations and Management is specially designed to meet the needs of students of undergraduate and diploma courses in hotel management, certificate courses in housekeeping, and postgraduate courses in accommodation operations. Students of home science will also find the book useful. This book can act as a reference for all issues related to housekeeping for managers and supervisors in the hotel industry.

New to This Edition

Apart from updated content in all chapters, readers can look forward to:

- New features
  - 150+ curated SOPs, formats, exhibits and videos ready to use for housekeeping operations
  - User friendly scan codes for complete reference on topics, new case studies developed in collaboration with industry experts introduced in all chapters & chapter-end exercises and projects.
  - Insights in specific chapters for additional knowledge
- New chapters on
  - Infection prevention and control protocols for hospitality accommodation facilities
  - Sustainability concepts in hospitality properties
- New sections on
  - Career and entrepreneurship in housekeeping for students and young professionals
  - Role of housekeeping in guest satisfaction, wowing the guests
  - Resources managed by housekeepers, making training calendars, minibar management, vendor management, managing cultural diversity, work study, and quality management

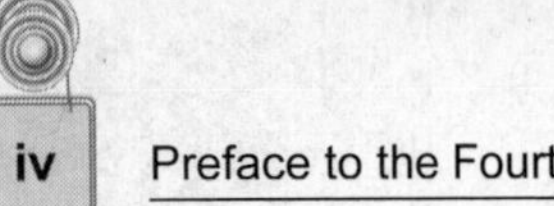

- Sample layouts of king room with balcony & room for differently abled guests, features of a smoking room
- Safety and hygiene factors in cleaning, recycling used amenities, façade cleaning, cleaning of discotheques, pubs and nightclubs
- Creating mood boards, ethnic textiles of India, themed decorations in hotels, rangoli
- Garden styles, horticulture equipment, hydroponics and terrariums, artificial plants
- Personal Protective Equipment (PPE), Hazard Identification and Risk Assessment (HIRA)
- Staff uniform specifications, uniform room layout
- Applications of nanotechnology, artificial intelligence, robotics, and latest software in housekeeping operations in hotels
- Sleep science and enhancing guest sleep experience, environmental factors in human comfort, indoor air quality (IAQ), the five senses concept in guest experience
- Sustainability concepts such as net zero, carbon neutral, responsible procurement, life cycle costs, certification of eco-sensitive hospitality properties, energy and water efficiency ratings
- Managing housekeeping budget in Covid times, clinically clean standards, operational and hygiene audits
- Rethinking hospitality design to facilitate infection control and use of technology to facilitate infection prevention and control

Online Resource Centre

For Faculty

- PowerPoint Slides

For Students

- Multiple Choice Questions
- Flashcard
- PowerPoint presentations on flower arrangements, mechanical cleaning equipment, uniforms, laundry equipment, types of windows, sanitary fittings and fixtures, interior design elements, lighting fixtures, types of guestroom accessories

The faculty of hospitality institutes and hotel housekeepers will find the revised book an essential tool in training students and staff respectively.

Smritee Raghubalan
G. Raghubalan

Praise for Previous Editions

A comprehensive ready reckoner for budding hospitality professionals- helps facilitate learners in developing their cognitive skills, critical thinking and in-depth subject knowledge.

–Prof. Sudipta Saha Gure, Senior Lecturer, IHM Kolkata

This book is a stepping stone for any Housekeeping professional or student who wishes to advance in the industry.

–R. Vigneshraj, Executive Housekeeper, Conrad, Bengaluru

This is an excellent book that covers all aspects of accommodation operations and management in a comprehensive manner in accordance to the Hospitality Industry needs and standards.

–Dr. Bhuvan G.M., Principal, Apeejay Institute of Hospitality, Navi Mumbai

Acknowledgements

All endeavours undertaken with passion achieve success with the right advice and cooperation of well-wishers.

The authors would like to mention the contribution of people and organizations who have either directly or indirectly contributed towards the conceptualization and compilation of this book. The students of the various hotel management colleges where we have worked deserve special mention. It was their queries that helped in the realization of the fact that there is a need for a quality housekeeping text in India. Also placed on record is our appreciation towards those who have provided constructive reviews and suggestions to elevate the content of revised edition.

We gratefully acknowledge the support of the Management of CGH Earth Group of Hotels, Kochi; The Orchid hotel, Mumbai; The Paul Hotel, Bengaluru; Hotel Kohinoor Continental, Mumbai; Karcher Cleaning Systems Pvt. Ltd.; Roots Multiclean Limited, Kochi; Oracle Hospitality; Diversey India Hygiene Pvt. Ltd.; Ecolab Food Safety & Hygiene Solutions Pvt. Ltd.; Jaquar and Company Pvt. Ltd.; and Dusters Total Solutions Services Pvt. Ltd. for providing inputs in diverse ways.

We would like to make a special mention of Mr. Rakshith Shetty, General Manager, Mr. Amith Shetty, Executive Housekeeper, and the housekeeping team at The Paul, Bangalore who facilitated video shoots for the book at the beautiful property. Our sincere thanks are due to Ms. Asha Premkumar, Housekeeping Consultant; Mr. Kingshuk Chakraborty, Senior Housekeeping Associate, Oberoi Bangalore; Mr. Shivakumar V., Manager - Housekeeping, Prestige Property Management & Services Bangalore; Ms. Nirupama Patra, HoD, IHM Shri Shakti, Hyderabad; Ms. Elizabeth Ngoruh, Senior HoD- Rooms Division, IIHM Bangalore; Mr. Sanju Samuel, Hospitality Consultant & Entrepreneur, Tecxotic; Mr. Kiran Kumar, General Manager, Rosetta by Ferns, Sakleshpur; Mr. Shamsher Puri, Director, SIS Group; Mr. Soban Nair, Partner, SRJ Services; and Mr. Dinesh, Director, Raenco Mills Pvt. Ltd. for their valuable inputs.

We would like to offer an appreciative word of thanks to Ms Namitha Suresh, an exceptional florist based at Bengaluru, who helped with the pictures of flower arrangements. Our sincere thanks are also due to Mr. R.S. Ganesh Naarayanan, Founder & Media Director, RSG Media Productions for professional videography to produce videos for our book. A big thank you to our daughter, Aditi Raghubalan, for painstaking drawing of some newly incorporated illustrations for the revised book.

We would like to thank the team at Oxford University Press, India for their persistence and support in bringing out this revised edition.

Finally, we would like to thank all our well-wishers—housekeepers, housekeeping consultants, academia, friends and family—for having in some way influenced the development of this revised edition.

Smritee Raghubalan
G. Raghubalan

Contents

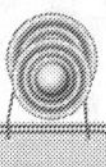

Scan code for the detailed Table of Contents

Scan code for the Index

1 The Hotel Industry—An Overview

Learning Objectives

After reading this chapter, you should be able to
- claim an insight into the history of the hotel industry
- understand the classification of hotels based on different criteria
- appreciate the placement of housekeeping as an important support department in the organization of hotel departments

Introduction

The term 'hospitality' refers to the cordial and generous reception and entertainment of guests or strangers, either socially or commercially. Indians are known the world over for their hospitality—*atithi devo bhavah* ('the guest is like God') has been our adage from time immemorial. It is because of this heritage that India, with its numerous hotels, is considered one of the world's leading hospitality venues. With the tourism and hospitality industry earning substantial foreign exchange and generating employment for lakhs of people across the country,[1] it has gained popularity as a profession and this popularity is expected to only increase in the future.

In ancient times, travellers relied on roadside homes for meals. Later travellers, mostly pilgrims, were cared for in temples or monasteries. In India, various universities also provided accommodation to pilgrims and religious scholars. Chandragupta Maurya built inns and guesthouses that were referred to as *sarais* and *dharmashalas*. During the British Raj, circuit houses and *dak banglas* came into being in India.

The first passenger-carrying stagecoach started operating in England in 1658. This was the time when inns started mushrooming along the route of the stagecoach. In the early 1700s, the accommodations available in the form of inns and restrooms were crude, but offered the basic necessities of food, shelter, meeting space, and security. Soon, more demand and competition led to the growth of motels and hotels. The first building especially designed as a hotel was the City Hotel in New York.

In India, the first commercial hotel, the Taj Mahal, Mumbai, was built in 1903. With the growth of transportation—roadways, railways, waterways, and airways—people became even more mobile. Inns, motels, hotels, resorts, and the like have kept pace with the developments, and have been refurbished to

---

[1] As per the *Indian Tourism and Hospitality Report 2021*, brought out by Indian Brand Equity Foundation (IBEF), Ministry of Commerce and Industry, Government of India, the sector in financial year 2020 accounted for 39 million jobs and this statistic is expected to rise to 53 million by 2029.

meet the quality demands. According to the Ministry of Tourism, Government of India, the inventory of approved hotel rooms stood at about 1,05,292 by mid 2021.[2] If rooms inventory of unbranded hotels, new-age hotels and alternate accommodations too are considered with branded hotels, research by Hotelivate estimates that by 2018, there were 2.72 million accommodation rooms operating in the country and by 2023, this inventory is anticipated to rise to 3.33 million.[3]

A hotel may be defined as a place that offers accommodation, food, and beverages at a cost that enables it to make a profit.

The *Concise Oxford Dictionary* defines a hotel as a 'house for accommodation of paying travellers, etc'.

According to the Webster's Dictionary (1978), 'a building or institution providing lodging, meals and service for the people' is termed a hotel.

Classification of Hotels

Hotel industry is so diverse that many hotels do not fit into a single well-defined category. Hotels can be classified in various ways, based on the criteria for classification. These criteria could be:

- Location
- Type of ownership and affiliations
- Size of property
- Length of stay
- Target market
- Level of service
- Theme
- Star categorization

Table 1.1 gives a detailed classification of hotels.

Based on Location

The classification of hotels on the basis of their location is discussed here.

City-centre/downtown hotels These are located in the heart of the city, within a short distance of the shopping areas, theatres, public buildings, business centres, and such. Rates in these hotels are normally high due to their locational advantage. Example: The Taj Mahal Palace, Mumbai.

Suburban hotels Located in the suburbs, these have the advantage of quieter surroundings. Rates here are moderate to low. Such hotels are ideal for budget travellers. Example: Evoma Hotel, Bengaluru

Motels This term is derived from the phrase 'motor hotels', being located primarily on highways (that is, motor ways). They provide modest lodgings to highway travellers. The length of stay is usually overnight. Most motels provide ample parking space, and may be located near a petrol station. Example: The Kamat Yatri Nivas chain found all over Karnataka.

Airport hotels These are hotels set up near airports. They cater to mainly transit guests, who might have to stay over at the hotel between flights. Example: Taj Bangalore, adjoining Kempegowda International Airport.

Resort hotels These cater to people who want to relax and enjoy themselves at a hill station, near the seashore, and so on, as well as to people who are looking for a change for health reasons. Therefore, resort hotels may be variously called health resorts, hill resorts, beach resorts, summer resorts, winter resorts, and so on, depending on their location and positioning. Most resorts, particularly those in hill stations,

[2] *India Tourism Statistics 2021*, Ministry of Tourism, Government of India

[3] *The Ultimate Indian Travel & Hospitality Report*, Vol. 1, 2019, Hotelivate

Table 1.1 Classification of hotels based on different criteria

Location	Target market	Type of ownership and affiliations	Size and number of properties	Level of service	Length of stay	Themes	Star categorization
• City-centre/ downtown hotels • Suburban hotels • Motels • Airport hotels • Resort hotels • Forest hotels • Floatels • Boatels • Underwater hotels • Ice hotels • Rotels	• Commercial /Business hotels • Convention hotels • Resort hotels • Suite hotels • Capsule/ Pod hotels • Yotels • B&B hotels • Extended-stay hotels • Casino hotels • Pet-friendly hotels • Apartment hotels/ Service apartments/ corporate lodgings	• Independent hotels • Chain hotels • Hotels under management contract • Hotel Franchise • Referral group properties • Timeshares • Condominiums/ Condo hotels	• Small hotels • Medium sized hotels • Large hotels • Very large hotels • Mega hotels	• Economy/ Limited-service/ budget hotels • Mid-scale/ mid-market hotels • Luxury hotels	• Transient hotels • Residential hotels/ apartotels • Semi-residential hotels	• Heritage hotels • Legacy vintage hotels • Eco-sensitive/ Green hotels • Boutique hotels • Spas	• One-star • Two-star • Three-star • Four-star • Five-star • Five-star deluxe

work to full capacity only during the clement seasonal periods and hence undergo fluctuations in sales revenue from season to season. Examples: Bangaram Island Resort (a beach resort in Lakshadweep); Ananda in the Himalayas (a spa resort); Coconut Lagoon (a backwater resort in Kerala); and Spice Village (a wildlife resort).

Forest hotels These are located within a forest range and cater to tourists visiting the forest area. Example: Kabini River Lodge in Karnataka; Ranthambore Forest Resort in Rajasthan.

Floatels (floating hotels) As the name implies, these are hotel establishments on luxury liners or ships and also those built on water bodies. Rivers, big lakes, and seas are ideal spots for such hotels. Example: Polo Floatel, Kolkata.

Cruise ships These are passenger ships intended as destination holidays. The luxuries aboard the ship as well as the various destinations along the way help create a unique experience for travellers. The furniture onboard such ships is heavier than usual furniture used in hotels and resorts to lend more stability on a moving ship. Example: Royal Carribbean Cruises.

Boatels A houseboat hotel is referred to as a boatel. The *shikaras* of Kashmir and the *kettuvalams* of Kerala are houseboats that offer small but luxurious accommodations to travellers in midst of lakes and waterways.

Underwater hotels These hotels have accommodations located many feet under large water bodies, usually seas. At least one of the walls is typically made of glass for guests to appreciate the underwater flora and fauna. Eg: Poseidon, Fiji; Jules' Undersea Lodge, Florida, the first such hotel built.

Ice hotels These unique temporary hotels are hand-sculpted in ice and snow, reincarnated every winter in sub-zero temperature venues. Guests can expect in-room ice sculptures by dedicated artists and there usually are exhibits and gallery experiences provided. Snowmobile tours, skiing, dogsledding, ice fishing are other activities offered. Example: Icehotel Winter in Sweeden is the world's first and largest ice hotel. Igloo hotels also fit into this category. Manali Igloo hotel is India's first such hotel.

Rotels These novel variants are rolling hotels or hotels on wheels. Our very own Palace on Wheels and Deccan Odyssey are trains providing a luxurious hotel atmosphere. Rotels also include some large buses and trucks with the interiors done up like hotel rooms. They are normally used by a small group of travellers to visit various places by road. Example: Das Rollende Hotel tour buses of Germany, LuxeCamper launched in partnership with Karnataka Tourism.

Based on Target Market

The classification of hotels on the basis of their target market is discussed in this section.

Commercial/Business hotels These hotels cater mostly to businessmen and are typically designed on the European plan. They are situated in the heart of the city in busy commercial areas so as to get increased business. Example: The Oberoi Towers, Mumbai.

Convention hotels These hotels have a large convention complex and cater to people attending a convention, conference, or similar event. Examples: Renaissance Mumbai Convention Centre Hotel, The Retreat Hotel & Convention Centre, Mumbai, and Novotel Hyderabad Convention Centre are hotels that cater mainly to MICE (meetings, incentives, conventions, and exhibitions) customers.

Resort hotels These leisure hotels are mainly patronized by vacationers who want to relax and enjoy themselves. Guests may stay for a week or upto even a month. The numbers vary with the season. There are peak seasons and off seasons. In order to boost business during the off season, special off-season packages are offered. The atmosphere is more relaxed and laidback. Since resorts are usually spread out over a large area, commuting from one room/cottage to another and transporting amenities take more time and effort. Hence, the time taken to clean rooms, for instance, is longer. Many resorts have mechanized, solar-powered carts for the transport of guests, cleaning supplies, and amenities.

Suite hotels These hotels offer rooms that may include a compact kitchenette, complete with utensils, refrigerator, and microwave oven, as well as a wet bar. They have fewer guest services than other hotels. They cater to people who are relocating, act as a home away from home for frequent travellers, and are suitable for professionals such as lawyers, accountants, and executives during a longer business stay. Where most conventional hotels have a few rooms that can be classified as suites, suite hotels have all their rooms as suites. Example: The Paul, Bengaluru.

Capsule/Pod hotels Originating in Japan in late 1970s, capsule hotels offer most affordable, no-frills accommodation for travellers on the go, typically in the form of cubicles, about 6–7 ft. long and 3 ft. high. These technologically advanced hotels offer a TV and wi-fi access apart from a comfortable bed. Guests are allocated lockers for luggage and restroom facilities are located in common area. Example: UrbanPod at Mumbai Central Railway Station.

Yotels These hotels are aimed at independent tech-savvy travellers who lay great value on their time and efficiency. Inspired by first-class airline cabins, accommodations here boast of luxury hotel experience with hi-tech, design-led smaller smart spaces offered to modern-day travellers at affordable prices. Yotels also offer a sense of community with areas for co-working, social gatherings and exercise. Example: Yotelair London at Gatwick Airport, the first Yotel.

B&B hotels A European concept, bed-and-breakfast hotels range from houses with a few rooms converted into overnight facilities to small commercial buildings with 20–30 guestrooms. The owner usually lives on the premises and is responsible for serving breakfast to guests. Most B&Bs offer only lodgings and limited board, or, as the name implies, only breakfast and the price is generally lower than that at a full-service hotel.

Extended-stay hotels These hotels are similar to suite hotels, but usually offer many kitchenette amenities in the room, which suite hotels usually do not. They are designed for travellers who intend to stay for five days or longer, and require reduced hotel services. Extended-stay hotels usually do not provide uniformed services and often do not provide food, beverages, or guest laundry services. Room rates here are determined by the length of stay.

Casino hotels Hotels with predominantly gambling facilities may be categorized as a distinct group. Although the guest rooms and the food and beverages (F&B) operations in these hotels may be quite luxurious, their function is secondary to and supportive of the casino operations. These hotels tend to cater to leisure and vacation travellers. Gambling activitiaes at some casino hotels operate 24 hours a day and 365 days a year. They also provide extravagant floor shows and chartered flights for guests. Las Vegas in the United States is famous for casino hotels. Example: SLS Hotel & Casino in Las Vegas.

Pet-friendly hotels These are hotels that allow their guests' pets (specific species) to stay with them. Such hotels provide services and amenities for the pets too. Example: Four Seasons Hotel, Bengaluru; J.W. Marriott hotels.

Apartment hotels/Service apartments/corporate lodgings These are designed for guests wishing to stay for longer periods of time, often upto six months or longer. Guests often include business executives moving from one city to another as well as consultants on temporary assignments, corporate training programmes, and special projects connected with movie or sporting events. Corporate lodgings usually provide fully furnished apartments for guests. Example: Halcyon Residences and Melange Astris in Bengaluru.

Based on Ownership and Affiliations

Independent hotels These are standalone hotels with sole ownership, usually family holdings. They do not have contract or management affiliations with other groups or properties. These hotels are hence under no obligation to other hotels regarding policies, procedures, finances, and so on.

Chain hotels These are groups that administrate a number of hotels in various locations in India and International venues. They can be under total or partial ownership, management contract or franchise. There are typically centralized administration, marketing, purchasing, processes, policies and procedures. Renowned Indian hotel chains are The Taj Group of hotels (Taj Hotels Resorts and Palaces), the Oberoi Group (Oberoi Hotels and Resorts), and the ITC hotels. Some of the foreign chains such as Marriott, Hyatt, Accor, IHG, and Sheraton have their presence in India as tie-ups with local partners or as self-operated properties.

Hotels under Management Contract These are properties that are operated by management contract firms under an agreement with the hotel owner or investor to operate the property under an internationally recognized brand. The management contract firm assumes full responsibility of managing and operating the hotel and is usually a renowned hotel chain such as Hilton, IHG, Best Western International, Sarovar Hotels, and so on.

Franchise Under a franchise, the hotel owner operates as a member of the franchisor hotel chain, thereby cashing upon its brand image, name, goodwill, and also receives marketing and operating services. Examples of hotel brands that offer franchises are, IHG, Choice Hotels International, Hilton, Marriott International, and so on.

Referral Group properties These consist of several independent hotels or small hotel chains that affiliate under a common identity, maintaining their autonomy at the same time. The member hotels recommend guests to other hotels in the referral group. The referral association fee is considerably lower than in the hotel franchise system. The referral group hotels typically have a common logo, share a reservation system, have standardised quality and joint advertising campaigns. Example, Best Western International and Choice Hotels International operate referral groups.

Timeshares These are sometimes referred to as 'vacation-interval' or 'vacation-ownership' hotels. Timeshare resort properties involve individuals purchasing the ownership of accommodations for a specific period of time – usually one or two weeks a year. These owners then occupy the unit during that time. Owners may also have the unit rented out by the management company that operates the hotel. Example: Club Mahindra Holiday Resorts across India.

Condominiums Condominiums or Condo hotels are similar to timeshare hotels; the difference between the two lies in the type of ownership. Units in condominium hotels have only one owner instead of multiple owners, each for a limited amount of time each year. In a condominium hotel, an owner informs the management company of when he or she wants to occupy the unit. The management company is free to rent the unit for the remainder of the year and this revenue goes to the owner. Example: Tuscany Terraces, Neral, India.

Based on Size of Property

The capacity of a hotel in terms of the number of rooms is the main yardstick for the categorization of hotels by size.

Small hotels In India, hotels with 25 rooms and less may be termed small. However abroad, hotels with less than a 100 rooms are considered small.

Medium-sized hotels Hotels with 25–100 rooms may be called medium-sized in India. Abroad, hotels with 100–300 rooms are termed medium-sized.

Large hotels In India, hotels with 101–300 rooms are called large hotels. Hotels with 400–600 rooms are termed large hotels abroad.

Very large hotels These hotels in India have more than 300 rooms. Abroad, hotels with 600–1,000 rooms may be considered very large.

Mega hotels Hotels with more than 1,000 rooms are called mega hotels.

Based on Level of Service

Hotels may be classified into economy, mid-scale, and luxury hotels on the basis of the level of services they offer.

Economy/budget/Limited service hotels These properties focus on meeting the most basic needs of guests by providing clean, comfortable, and inexpensive rooms. Economy hotels appeal primarily to budget-minded travellers who want rooms with all the amenities required for a comfortable stay, but without the extras they do not really need or want to pay for.

Mid-scale/mid-market hotels Hotels offering mid-market services appeal to the largest segment of the travelling public. Mid-market services are modest but sufficient and the staffing level is moderate but not huge.

A fast-growing segment in the mid-market category is that of suite hotels that offer a small living room or parlour area with a grouping of appropriate furniture (often including a sofa bed) and a small bedroom with a king-size bed. Some guest suites include a compact kitchenette, complete with cooking utensils, refrigerator, microwave oven, and wet bar.

Luxury hotels These offer world-class services, providing upscale restaurants and lounges, exquisite décor, concierge services, opulent meeting rooms, and dining facilities. Bath linen is replaced twice daily (unless linen reuse card is opted for by guest) and a nightly turndown service is usually provided. In addition, these guestrooms contain furnishings, décor, and artwork that are more expensive than that of guestrooms in the mid-market service category. Primary markets for these hotels are business executives, celebrities, and high-ranking political figures. Example: Hyatt Regency Delhi; ITC Maurya, New Delhi.

Based on Length of Stay

Hotels may be classified into transient, residential, and semi-residential hotels, depending upon the period for which a guest can stay.

Transient hotels These are hotels where a guest can register for a day or even less. They are usually situated near airports and seaports. They are usually five-star hotels. They may have travel agencies and offer car rentals. The occupancy rate is usually very high, going up to more than 100%, since each room can sometimes be sold more than once each day! Since room rentals are back to back, the housekeeping department works in teams to clean rooms in the shortest possible time.

Residential hotels/apartotels These are hotels where guests can stay for a minimum period of one month and upto two years, and the hotel signs a detailed lease agreement with the customer. The rent is paid either monthly or quarterly, but never on a daily basis. The guestrooms include a sitting room, a bedroom, and a kitchenette. They cater to clients staying away from home for long periods for various purposes.

Semi-residential hotels These are hotels that incorporate the features of both transient and residential hotels.

Based on Theme

Depending on the theme, hotels may be classified into heritage hotels, eco-sensitive or green hotels, boutique hotels, and spas.

Heritage hotels Among tourism's significant gains in India has been the launch of unique heritage hotels. The country's rich and distinguished cultural past has bequeathed on it a number of feudal estates that are in the form of small forts, palaces, or *havelis*, the mansions of erstwhile aristocratic families. A hotel qualifies for classification as a heritage hotel provided a minimum of 50% of the floor area was

built before 1950 and no substantial change has been made in the façade. Further subdivisions of the heritage hotels category are given in Table 1.2.

Table 1.2 Heritage hotels

Category	Description
Heritage	This category covers hotels in residences/havelis/hunting lodges/castles/forts/palaces built prior to 1950 but after 1935. The property should have minimum 5 rooms (10 beds).
Heritage Classic	This category covers hotels in residences/havelis/hunting lodges/castles/forts/palaces built prior to 1935. The property should have minimum 15 rooms (30 beds) and atleast one of the specified sporting facility mentioned in guidelines.
Heritage Grand	This category covers hotels in residences/havelis/hunting lodges/castles/forts/palaces built prior to 1935. The property should have a minimum of 15 rooms (30 beds) with 50% of them having air-conditioning (except in hill stations, where heating arrangements should be present).

Source: *Guidelines for Classification of Heritage Hotels*, Ministry of Tourism, Government of India.

In a heritage hotel, a visitor can expect to be extended a gracious welcome, to be offered rooms that have their own history, to be served traditional cuisine toned down to the requirements of international palates, to be entertained by folk artistes, to participate in activities that allow a glimpse into the heritage of the region, and to bask in an atmosphere that lives and breathes of the past. Example: Jai Mahal Palace in Jaipur.

Legacy Vintage hotels These are hotels constructed with at least 50% of materials sourced from heritage properties, i.e. those built prior to 1950. Their façade, architectural features, construction style and techniques have a distinctive ambience reflecting the culture and heritage of the region. The subdivisions of legacy vintage hotels with their main features are given in Table 1.3.

Eco-sensitive/Green hotels Green hotels are environment-friendly hotels. The phrase 'environment-friendly', however, is now being replaced with 'environmentally sensitive'. This is so because no hotel can be friendly to the environment, since in one way or the other they will be, though in a small way, harming the environment; hence, the use of the term 'environmentally sensitive'. The Orchid, Mumbai, is Asia's first and most popular five-star ecotel. Other ecotels are Rhodas, Mumbai and The Raintree, Chennai. ITC Gardenia, Bengaluru is Asia's first LEED Platinum certified hotel. Refer Chapter 32 for Ecotel and LEED certification.

Table 1.3 Features of legacy vintage hotels

Category	Material sourcing	Min. no. of rooms & facilities
Legacy Vintage (Basic)	Materials sourced from heritage properties built prior to 1950 but after 1935.	5 rooms (10 beds), Rooms: 130 sq. ft. & Bathrooms: 36 sq. ft.
Legacy Vintage Classic	Materials sourced from heritage properties built prior to 1935.	15 rooms (30 beds), Rooms: 140 sq. ft. & Bathrooms: 36 sq. ft.
Legacy Vintage Grand	Materials sourced from heritage properties built prior to 1935.	15 rooms (30 beds), Rooms: 200 sq. ft. & Bathrooms: 45 sq. ft.

Source: *Guidelines for Classification/Reclassification of Legacy Vintage Hotels, 2018,* Ministry of Tourism, Government of India.

Boutique hotels These hotels provide exceptional accommodations, furnished in a themed and stylish manner, along with personalized services and facilities. They cater to corporate travellers and discerning travellers who place high importance on privacy, luxury, and service delivery. Boutique hotels target customers who are in their early twenties to mid-fifties and are in the middle to upper income bracket. Example: La Villa, Puducherry; RAAS Jodhpur.

Spas The word 'spa', derived from the name of the famous mineral springs in Spa, Belgium, has become a common noun denoting any place with a medicinal or mineral spring. The term also refers to a tub for relaxation or invigoration, usually including a device for raising whirlpools in the water.

A spa resort is a resort hotel providing therapeutic baths and massages along with other features of a luxury hotel. A medical spa is a facility that operates under the full-time, on-site supervision of a licensed health-care professional. Ananda in the Himalayas and Angsana Oasis Spa & Resort, Bengaluru are popular spas.

A couple of novel concepts in hotels are lotels and metels. Hotels with helipad facilities are termed lotels. Hotels which are completely mechanized are called metels. These are regular hotels with only the special features mentioned rendering them unique.

Star Rating of Hotels

The Indian hotel industry follows the star rating system, which indicates the number and standard of facilities and services offered by the hotel. The Hotel and Restaurant Approval Classification Committee (HRACC), with its headquarters in New Delhi, comprises representatives chosen from the government and the trade. It takes on the task of rating hotels against set criteria of standards brought out as 'Guidelines for classification/Re-classification of hotels' issued by the Ministry of Tourism, Government of India, and available on its website. An extract is presented in Exhibit 1.1.

Operational hotels in India are classified under this system into three categories:

Star category hotels One-star, Two-star, Three-star, Four-star, Five-star, and Five-star deluxe (See Exhibit 1.1 for rating criteria)

Heritage category hotels Heritage Basic, Heritage Classic, Heritage Grand (refer classification based on theme)

Legacy Vintage category hotels Legacy Vintage Basic, Legacy Vintage Classic, Legacy Vintage Grand (refer classification based on theme)

There is no common international hotel rating system. Ratings of hotels in different countries, if they exist, come from the government or from quasi-government sources, independent rating agencies, or sometimes the hotel operators themselves.

Exhibit 1.1 Accommodation-related facilities and services Necessary (N) and Desirable (D) to be provided by all-star category hotels (one-star – five-star deluxe)

General

Full time operation; 24-hour elevator for ground + two floors & easy access for differently-abled guests; daily-serviced guestrooms, public areas and kitchen; floor surfaces maintained clean & in good condition; hotel website to display the facilities and amenities provided complimentary and on loan and the website to display the classification status prominently on home page.

Guestrooms & Bathrooms

Minimum 10 lettable rooms, all with windows facing outside/ventilation; good quality guest linen with change of clean bed and bath linen daily and between each check-in; minimum bedding of 2 sheets, pillow with case, blanket, night spread or bed cover; complimentary drinking water- 2 sealed bottles 500 ml/person/day with minimum one glass per guest; shelves and drawer space; wardrobe with minimum 4 cloth hangers/bedding; sufficient energy-saving lighting – 1 lamp/bed, ; 2 multipurpose, 5 amp earthed power sockets; multi-socket adapter plugs provided on request; bedside table and drawer- 1/twin bed and 2/double bed; chairs – 1/bed; waste paper basket; ; iron and ironing board facility; opaque curtains or screening at all windows, blackouts in 4☆, 5☆ & 5☆ Deluxe categories; a mirror of minimum 3 ft.; a DND signage facility; a well-ventilated linen room; bathrooms with non-porous walls & floors attached with all guestrooms; 24 hours hot and cold running water; water conserving faucets; a western WC, water spray or bidet and shower area with shower curtain/ shower cubicle in all bathrooms; 1 bath towel, 1 hand towel, 2 clothes hooks, 1 toilet paper roll, 1 covered sani-bin and guest toiletries of good quality with minimum 1 new soap/guest.

Public area & back of the house areas

Lounge/seating area with requisite furniture in lobby; reception facility with availability of accommodation, F&B and other tariff; acceptance of credit cards and facility for digital payments; wake-up call service; delivery of guest messages; facilitation of doctor's availability; an on-premises public telephone; assistance with luggage; travel desk facilities; public restrooms for ladies and gents; staff uniforms; English-speaking staff at Front Office; restroom facilities for staff; display of pledge in back area, orientation and in-house training for 'Code of Conduct and Honourable Tourism'.

Safety & security

Security arrangements at entrance; CCTV at strategic location; staff and supplier verification; fire drills; manuals for disaster management, fire safety and first aid; smoke detectors; fire and emergency alarms with visual & audible signals; first aid kit at front desk; fire exit signages on guest floors with emergency power backup.

Facilities for differently-abled guests

At least one guestroom with attached bathroom with requisite features for differently-abled guest; ramps at entrance; minimum 1 m door width at entrance with free accessibility to all public areas; 1 public restroom with requisite features for such guests; provision of complimentary wheelchair.

Eco-friendly practices

Sewage Treatment Plant; Rain-Water Harvesting; waste management; air and water pollution control methods; non-CFC based refrigeration and AC and other eco-friendly initiatives.

Accommodation-related facilities & services Necessary (N)/Desirable (D) for star classification of hotels (one-star – five-star deluxe)

Facilities/ services	One-star	Two-star	Three-star	Four-star	Five-star & Five-star Deluxe	Remarks
Guestroom						
Minimum bedroom size, excluding bathroom & balcony	120 sq. ft.	120 sq. ft.	130 sq. ft.	140 sq. ft.	200 sq. ft.	

(Contd.)

Exhibit 1.1 *Contd.*

Facilities/ services	One-star	Two-star	Three-star	Four-star	Five-star & Five-star Deluxe	Remarks
Air conditioning	25%	25%	50%	100%	100%	Temperature between 20–28°C depending on climatic conditions
Minimum bed width for single 90 cm and double 180 cm	D	N	N	N	N	
Minimum mattress thickness 10 cm	D	D	N	N	N	Coir, foam or spring foam
Minimum 1 suite room	D	D	D	N	N	

Hotel Departments

The number of departments varies from one hotel to the other. All departments may have their own manager, reporting to the general manager and the assistant general manager. Figure 1.1 shows the various departments in a large hotel.

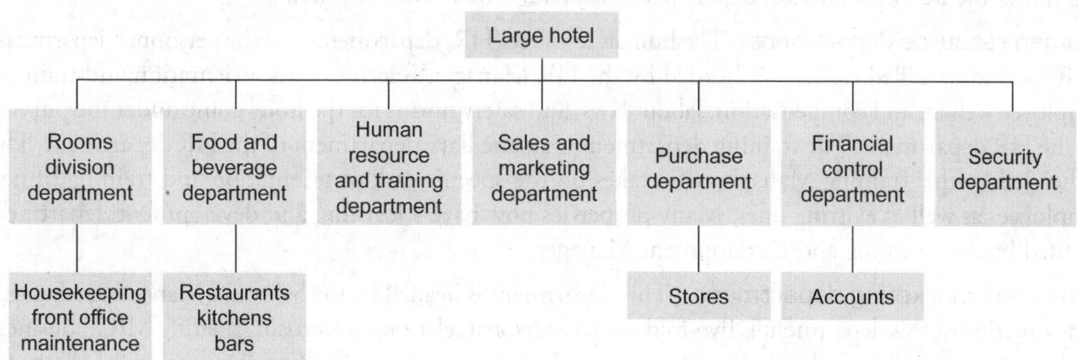

Fig. 1.1 Departments at a large hotel

Hotel departments fall under the category of either revenue-earning departments or support departments. Revenue-earning departments are operational departments that sell services or products to guests, thus directly generating revenue for the hotel. Revenue-earning departments include front office, food and beverage, and hotel-operated shops. Support departments, on the other hand, help to generate revenue indirectly by playing a supporting role to the hotel's revenue-earning departments. Support departments include human resources, maintenance, purchase, housekeeping, and so on.

Housekeeping is a major support department, engaging the largest workforce and handling responsibilities spread over a vast area in the hotel. The various departments in a hotel are discussed here in brief.

Rooms division department In a large hotel, the housekeeping, front office, and maintenance departments come under the rooms division. These departments together are responsible for managing, maintaining, and selling the rooms in a hotel. In most hotels, these are the departments that directly or indirectly generate more revenue than any other department. The rooms division is headed by the Rooms Division Manager, to whom the Front Office Manager, Executive Housekeeper, and very often the Chief Engineer report.

Housekeeping department This department is responsible for the cleanliness and upkeep of the front of the house areas as well as back of the house areas, so that they appear as fresh and aesthetically appealing as on the first day the hotel property opened for business. This department is headed by the Executive Housekeeper or, in chain hotels, the Director of Housekeeping.

Front office department Headed by the Front Office Manager, this is an operational department that is responsible for welcoming and registering guests, allotting them rooms, and helping guests checking out. The concierge, bell desk, EPBAX operators, and other uniformed services are part of the front office department.

Maintenance department Also called the engineering and maintenance department, this is headed by the Chief Engineer or the Chief Maintenance Officer. The department is responsible for all kinds of maintenance, repair, and engineering work on equipment, machines, fixtures, and fittings.

Food and beverage department The food and beverage (F&B) department includes the restaurants, bars, coffee shops, banquets, room service, kitchen, and bakery. This department is headed by the Director—F&B. While the restaurants, bars, coffee shops, banquets, and room service may be grouped specifically under the F&B service department, headed by the F&B Manager, the kitchen and bakery fall under the F&B production department headed by the Executive Chef.

Human resource department The human resource (HR) department—or the personnel department, as it used to be called earlier—is headed by the HR Manager. Recruitments, orientation and training, employee welfare and compensation, labour laws, and safety norms for the hotel come under the purview of the HR department. The training department is an ancillary department of the HR department. This is headed by the Training Manager, who takes on the specific task of orientation and training of new employees as well as existing ones. Many properties now have a learning and development department headed by the Learning and Development Manager.

Sales and marketing department This department is headed by the Sales and Marketing Manager. The function of this department is five-fold—sales, personal relations, advertising, getting MICE business, and market research. All these functions lead to the common goal of selling the product of the hotel, that is, rooms, and the services of the hotel by 'creating' customers.

Purchase department The purchase department is led by the Purchase Manager, who in some properties may report to the Financial Controller. The procurement of all the departmental inventories is the responsibility of the purchase department. In most hotels, the central stores is part of the purchase department.

Financial control department Also called the controls or accounting department, this is headed by the Financial Controller, who is responsible for ratifying all the inventory items of the operational departments.

Inventory control procedures are the responsibility of this department. The Financial Controller, along with the General Manager, is responsible for finalizing the budgets prepared by the heads of other departments. The hotel's accounts are also maintained by the controls department. Accounting activities include making payments against invoices, billing, collecting payments, generating statements, handling bank transactions, processing employee payroll data, and preparing the hotel's financial statements.

Security department Headed by the Chief Security Officer, the security department is responsible for safeguarding the assets and employees of the hotel. Their functions include conducting fire drills, monitoring surveillance equipment, and patrolling the property.

SUMMARY

The hotel industry provides primary support in the development of the country's economy by providing employment in the food and accommodation sector, which is growing rapidly. The hotel sector not only helps in generating greater employment opportunities, but also in developing remote and industrially backward areas, promoting and developing folk art and culture, and earning foreign exchange for the country. In this chapter, we have briefly traced the origins of the hotel industry. We have then defined the term 'hotel'. Hotels are classified in various ways and many hotels do not fit into any single, well-defined category. We have tried to give an exhaustive classification of hotels, but as new concepts keep emerging in this ever-changing industry, certainly a few more types could be added on. We have also discussed the star classification of hotels. The criteria that lead to hotels being classified in the various star categories have been described in brief. This chapter concludes by placing housekeeping as an entity in the complex organization of hotel departments. The functions and responsibilities of each department have been dealt with in brief, so that beginners reading this book may get an insight into the functioning of a hotel property. Readers must understand that the departments discussed in this chapter are the basic, most important ones and that they may come across other names and designations for the same departments across different properties.

KEY TERMS

Amenity A service or item offered to guests or placed in guestrooms for convenience and comfort, at no extra cost.

Back of the house The functional areas of the hotel in which employees have little or no guest contact, such as the engineering and maintenance department, laundry room, and so on. Also called 'heart of the house'.

Back to back Describes a heavy rate of check-outs and check-ins on the same day, so that as soon as a room is made up, a new guest checks into it.

Banquet A term used to describe catering for specific numbers of people at specific times, in a variety of dining layouts.

Bath linen Includes bath towels, bath sheets, hand towels, face towels, washcloths, and fabric bath-mats.

Bell desk A part of the front office department, responsible for handling the luggage of guests.

Boutique hotel A term referring to hotels designed with the same attention to detail that one would find in a specialized store or boutique offering customized services and products.

Chain hotels Groups that have hotels in a number of locations in a given country or across international venues.

Checking out An American term adopted by hotels in India, meaning the departure of a guest from a hotel.

Cleaning supplies Cleaning agents and small cleaning equipment used in the cleaning of guestrooms and public areas in the hotel.

Coffee shop A restaurant in a hotel that serves a limited menu to guests, normally functioning round the clock.

Concierge French terminology referring to a member of the hotel staff who assists guests by handling the storage of luggage, making reservations, arranging tours, procuring certain articles or services (such as bookings and tickets for plays and operas), and providing information about the city, activities, and experiences in and around the hotel as well as sightseeing options.

Condominiums Hotels similar to timeshare hotels. The difference between the two lies in the type of ownership. Units in condominium hotels have only one owner instead of multiple owners, each for a limited amount of time each year.

Continental breakfast This is a European breakfast comprising a choice of juices, choice of breads (toast, rolls, croissants, muffins, and so on) served with preserves, jams, honey, marmalade, and butter, plus tea or coffee.

Convention A formal assembly of representatives sharing a common field of interest, coming together to air their views.

Cuisine A country's, region's, or establishment's particular style of cooking.

EPABX operators Electronic private automatic branch exchange operators. These are the hotel switchboard operators who answer calls and connect them to the appropriate extensions.

Floatels Hotel establishments being operated on large water bodies such as seas and lakes. Cruise liners and some houseboats are typical examples of these.

Front of the house The functional areas of the hotel in which employees have extensive guest contact, such as food and beverage outlets and front office areas.

Hospitality The cordial and generous reception and entertainment of guests or strangers, either socially or commercially.

Hotel A place that offers accommodation, food, and beverages at a cost that enables it to make a profit.

Inventory Stocks of merchandise, operating supplies, and other items held for future use in a hotel. For example, linen, cleaning supplies, and so on are important housekeeping inventories.

King-size bed The largest size of bed available, with dimensions of 78 inches × 80 inches (Eastern king) or 72 × 80 inches (California king).

LEED certification LEED stands for Leadership in Energy and Environmental Design. The certification programme is offered by US Green Building Council.

Legacy Vintage hotels Hotels constructed with at least 50% of materials sourced from heritage properties, i.e. those built prior to 1950.

Lounge A place in the hotel lobby or floor areas where guests can sit back and relax. It is a public area, suitably furnished for relaxation.

MICE Meetings, incentives, conventions, and exhibitions. This segment is now a big revenue generator for the hotels. Certain hotels cater specifically to the MICE customer.

Mid-market service A modest but sufficient level of service. Properties offering this may provide uniformed service, room service, a speciality restaurant, a coffee shop, lounge, and special rates for certain guests.

Motels Hotels that are located primarily on highways. They provide modest lodgings to highway travellers. Most motels provide ample parking space and may be located near a petrol station.

Operational departments These are departments where actual guest interaction takes place or products and services are put together in a hands-on manner for guests. These departments have a very short cycle, in the sense that a room or dish made up on a particular day has to be sold on that day itself. The operational departments in a hotel are the front office, house-keeping, and food and beverage departments.

Orientation Orientation is the guided adjustment of a new employee to the organization, his or her work environment, and the job.

Parlour A sitting room usually having a concealed bed.

Refurbish To give a 'new' look to a room by redecorating, renewing soft furnishings, and possibly changing the carpet and 'touching up' the furniture.

Sofa bed Furniture that converts from a sofa into a bed, usually after the removal of cushions. A small handle in the centre of the seat unit releases the bed, which unfolds to reveal a double-size mattress.

Speciality restaurant A restaurant that serves a specific cuisine; has the entire interiors, uniforms, music and other accoutrements reflecting the same; and offers a formal style of service.

Surveillance equipment Equipment such as CCTVs (closed-circuit televisions) that help to closely observe suspicious activities and persons.

Timeshares 'Vacation-interval hotels'. These involve individuals purchasing the ownership of accommodations for a specific period of time, usually one or two weeks a year. These owners then occupy the unit during that time. Owners may also have the unit rented out by the management company that operates the hotel.

Turndown service A special service provided by the housekeeping department in which a room attendant enters the guestroom early in the evening to re-stock supplies, tidy the room, and turn down the covers on the bed in preparation for the night.

Uniformed service A hotel's uniformed service staff includes hotel cab drivers, parking attendants, door attendants, and bellboys. Uniformed service staff meet and greet guests and assist them on their arrival and departure.

Wet bar A bar where the sale of alcoholic liquor is allowed.

World-class service A level of service that stresses the personal attention given to guests. Hotels offering this kind of service provide upscale restaurants and lounges, exquisite décor, concierge service, opulent rooms, and abundant amenities.

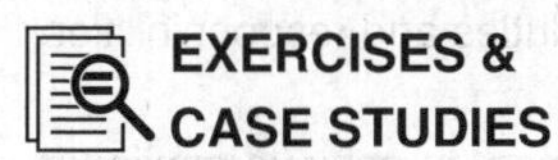

2 The Housekeeping Department

Learning Objectives

After reading this chapter, you should be able to

- understand the importance of housekeeping in hotels and grasp the responsibilities of the department
- figure out the organizational structure of the housekeeping department in various-sized hotels
- know about the various personnel in a housekeeping department and their duties and responsibilities
- list the personal attributes required in housekeeping personnel
- appreciate the importance of a functional layout for a housekeeping department to achieve maximum efficiency in providing guest services
- understand the coordination between housekeeping and other hotel departments
- enumerate the requirements to be met in order that the housekeeper be called a 'professional housekeeper'
- assess the scope of housekeeping in establishments other than hotels
- get insight into the career path in housekeeping in hotels
- learn about the scope of entrepreneurship in the field of housekeeping

Introduction

The aim of all accommodation establishments is to provide their customers with clean, attractive, comfortable, and welcoming surroundings that offer value for money. Nothing sends a stronger message than cleanliness in a hospitality operation. No level of service, friendliness, or glamour can equal the sensation a guest has upon entering a spotless, tidy, and conveniently arranged room. Both management and guests consider the keeping of the place clean and in a good order a necessity for a hotel to command a fair price and get repeat business. In a 2015 online survey of 2,065 customers, carried out by laundry equipment firm Miele Professional, nearly eight in 10 respondents (79%) stated that cleanliness is the main factor that influences their perception of a hotel's values, and almost two-thirds (59%) said a clean hotel would be a main factor in encouraging them to return again in the future.

According to a 2017 Procter & Gamble online poll of 1,008 US consumers, how clean and fresh a hotel, restaurant, salon or office is what matters most for 92% of consumers when deciding if they will become a repeat customer.

The housekeeping department takes pride in keeping the hotel clean and comfortable, so as to create a 'home away from home'.

 Importance of Housekeeping

Housekeeping may be defined as 'provision of a clean, comfortable, safe and aesthetically appealing environment'. By another definition, 'housekeeping is an operational department in a hotel, which is responsible for cleanliness, maintenance, aesthetic upkeep of rooms, public areas, back areas and the surroundings'.

The housekeeping department is typically called the 'backbone of the hotel', but now it is increasingly being referred to as the 'heart of the hotel' because just as the heart pumps the life sustaining pure blood to reach all parts of the body, the housekeeping department freshens up and invigorates the entire hotel day in and day out, helps eliminate unwanted waste, and is responsible for a long and healthy life of the hotel.

A hotel survives on the sale of rooms, food, beverages, and other minor services such as the laundry, health club, and so on. The sale of rooms constitutes a minimum of 65% of these sales. Thus, the major part of a hotel's margin of profit comes from room sales, because a room once made can be sold over and over again. On the other hand, an unsold room leads to considerable loss of revenue and rooms in fact are considered the most perishable commodity in a hotel.

The housekeeping department not only prepares clean guestrooms on a timely basis for arriving guests, but also cleans and maintains everything in the hotel so that the property is as fresh and attractive as the day it opened for business. Housekeeping, thus, is an ancillary department that contributes in a big way towards the overall reputation of a property.

It is rightly said that housekeeping is a 24 × 7 × 365 operation. Imagine the stacks of linen needed to make up all the beds in a hotel; the huge amounts of bath soap, tissue, and other amenities such as shampoos, colognes, and so on that must be placed in the guestrooms; the miles of carpeting, floors, walls, and ceilings to be cleaned and maintained; the countless pieces of furniture that must be dusted and polished, and the barrels of cleaning compounds along with special tools and equipment needed in order to clean these. Scientific housekeeping demands the employment of the most effective cleaning materials and procedures, attention to purchasing the most suitable linen and supplies, maintenance of decorative areas under the housekeeping department's purview, and proper organization and supervision.

The Role of Housekeeping in Guest Satisfaction

Guest satisfaction is sure to result as a state of mind when the guest's needs and expectations have not only been met but exceeded, leading to him/her becoming brand loyal and a repeat customer. A well-satisfied guest will not only develop brand loyalty but also bring in new guests to the hotel through word of mouth.

Creating favourable first impression As guests ride in through the neatly maintained driveway of a hotel, surrounded by the manicured lawns and landscaping, arriving into the welcoming porte-cochère with its impressive façade, entering the lobby with opulent, awe-inspiring décor and expensive breadth of brilliantly polished flooring, their minds already make a first impression – an impression which is favourable because of efficient housekeeping operations.

Creating a 'home away from home' Guestrooms are the heart of the hotel. Unless its décor is appropriate, the air odour-free, and furnishings and upholstery spotlessly clean, the hotel may lose the

guest as a potential repeat customer. Most General Managers agree that providing a superlative 'bed and bath experience' is their priority when it comes to satisfying guests. Today's guests also expect in-room cleanliness, décor, safety, facilities, amenities, and services to match and exceed those available to them at their homes and workplaces. The effort that housekeepers make in giving a guest a desirable room with these attributes has a direct bearing on the guest's experience in a hotel.

Creating and maintaining aesthetics and functionality of facility The feel of the hotel, as perceived by guests with five senses, is created by housekeeping. Whether it is the signature fragrance of the property, the visually aesthetic appeal of the décor of exterior and interior of the hotel, evidently high standards of cleanliness at all public areas, the indulgence of sound-less sleep in a luxurious bed or the intangible quality of caring the guests perceive at a hotel, this feel is created by housekeepers.

Thus, housekeeping from a customer's perspective, represents the core benefit of a hotel. In corollary, hotel guests prioritize satisfaction with housekeeping while making up their minds to return to the hotel, recommend it to friends and family and demonstrate loyalty to the hospitality brand.

Responsibilities of Housekeeping Department

The aims, objectives, and responsibilities of the housekeeping department are to

- achieve the maximum possible efficiency in ensuring the care and comfort of guests and in the smooth running of the department.
- coordinate with the front office department for efficient sale of rooms.
- establish a welcoming atmosphere and ensure courteous, reliable service from all staff of the department.
- ensure a high standard of cleanliness and general upkeep in all areas for which the department is responsible.
- provide linen in rooms, restaurants, banquet halls, conference venues, health clubs, and so on, as well as maintain an inventory for the same.
- provide uniforms for all the staff and maintain adequate inventories for the same.
- cater to the laundering requirements of hotel linen, staff uniforms, and guest clothing.
- provide and maintain the floral decorations and maintain the landscaped areas of the hotel.
- select the right contractors for jobs such as pest control, façade cleaning, etc. and ensure that the quality of work is maintained as at the onset of the business.
- coordinate with the maintenance department for timely redressal of maintenance-related issues and servicing of under repair rooms.
- coordinate renovation and refurbishing of the property as and when, in consultation with the management and with interior designers.
- coordinate with the purchase department for the procurement of guest supplies, cleaning agents, equipment, fabrics, carpets, and other items used in the hotel.
- ensure updation of records, forms, and formats for systematic operations and for auditing purposes.
- deal with lost-and-found articles.
- ensure training, control, and supervision of all staff attached to the department.
- establish a good working relationship with other departments.

- ensure that safety and security regulations are made known to all staff of the department.
- keep the general manager or administrator informed of all matters requiring attention.

Most housekeeping departments are responsible for the care and cleaning of the areas listed in Table 2.1. These areas are categorized as:

Front of the House (FOH) areas Functional areas of the hotel, in which employees have extensive guest contact.

Back of the House (BOH) areas Functional areas of the hotel in which employees have little or no guest contact.

Table 2.1 Areas under the purview of housekeeping

Front of the house areas	Back of the house areas
• Guestrooms	• Management offices
• Corridors	• Storage areas
• Lobbies and public restrooms	• Linen, uniform and sewing rooms
• Pool and patio areas	• Laundry room
• Meeting rooms	• Employee locker rooms
• Dining rooms/restaurants	• Administrative offices
• Banquet halls	• Employee entrance and clock/time room
• Convention halls	• Floor pantries
• Hotel-operated shops	
• Games rooms/recreation rooms	
• Exercise rooms/gymnasium	
• Building exterior	
• Landscaping and gardens	

Organizational Structure

Organization is the process of identifying and grouping the work to be performed, defining and delegating responsibility and authority, and establishing relationships for the purpose of enabling people to work more effectively in accomplishing objectives. If the whole establishment has to work as one unit, it is important that there are clear lines of authority and good lines of communication. The organizational structure of a housekeeping department—whether in a small, medium, or large hotel—is depicted using an organization chart. An organization chart is a schematic representation of the relationships between positions within an establishment, showing where each position fits into the overall organization and illustrating the divisions of responsibility and lines of authority.

The housekeeping department in a hotel is headed by the executive housekeeper. He/she reports to the general manager, or to the resident manager, or the rooms division manager in a larger hotel. In the case of a chain of hotels, the executive housekeeper also reports to the director of housekeeping, who heads the housekeeping departments in all the hotels of that chain. The deputy housekeeper assists the executive housekeeper and, depending on the size of the property, there can also be assistant housekeepers

who look after the various areas of responsibility in the hotel, that is, floors, public areas, the linen room, and desk control.

Then there are supervisors in each of these sections, who report to the respective assistant housekeepers. The floor and public area supervisors are responsible for getting the guestrooms and public areas cleaned. The linen room supervisor is in charge of the linen and uniform-room operations. The desk supervisor is responsible for coordinating all the housekeeping activities and liaising with the other departments of the hotel. Associates and housepersons (also referred to as housemen) report to the supervisors.

The horticulturist has gardeners reporting to him/her. He/she reports to the executive housekeeper. Normally, this area is farmed out on contract.

The laundry manager also reports to the executive housekeeper. He has laundry workers reporting to him. Laundry may also be given out on contract.

The organizational structure varies to some extent with different hotels. Therefore, organization charts are presented here for small (Figure 2.1), medium-sized (Figure 2.2), and large (Figure 2.3) hotels.

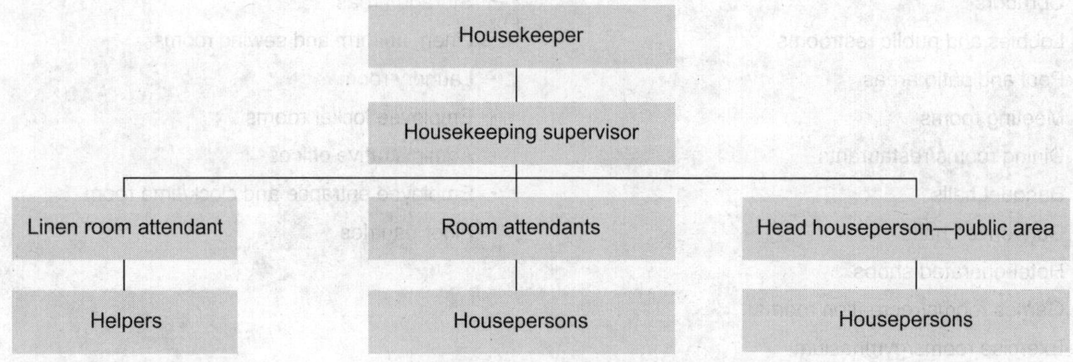

Fig. 2.1 (a) Organization chart of a housekeeping department in a small hotel—Sample 1

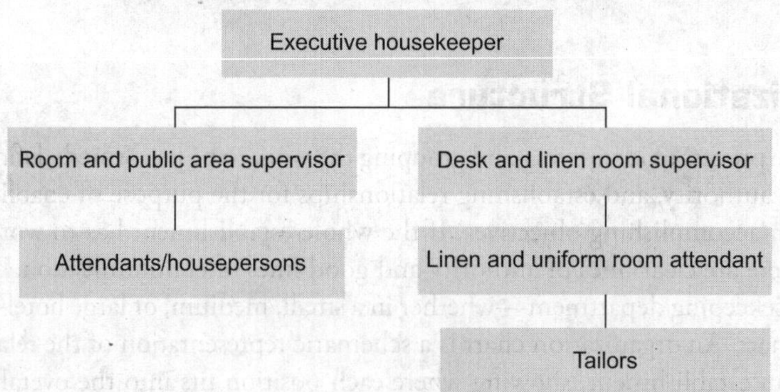

Fig. 2.1 (b) Organization chart of a housekeeping department in a small hotel—Sample 2

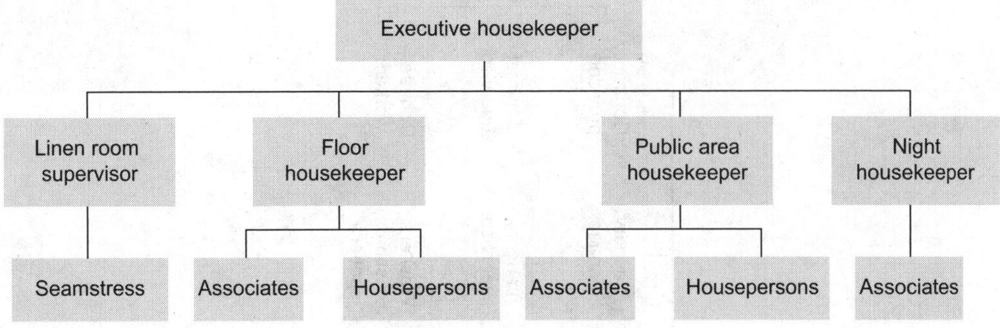

Fig. 2.2 (a) Organization chart of a housekeeping department in a medium-sized hotel—Sample 1

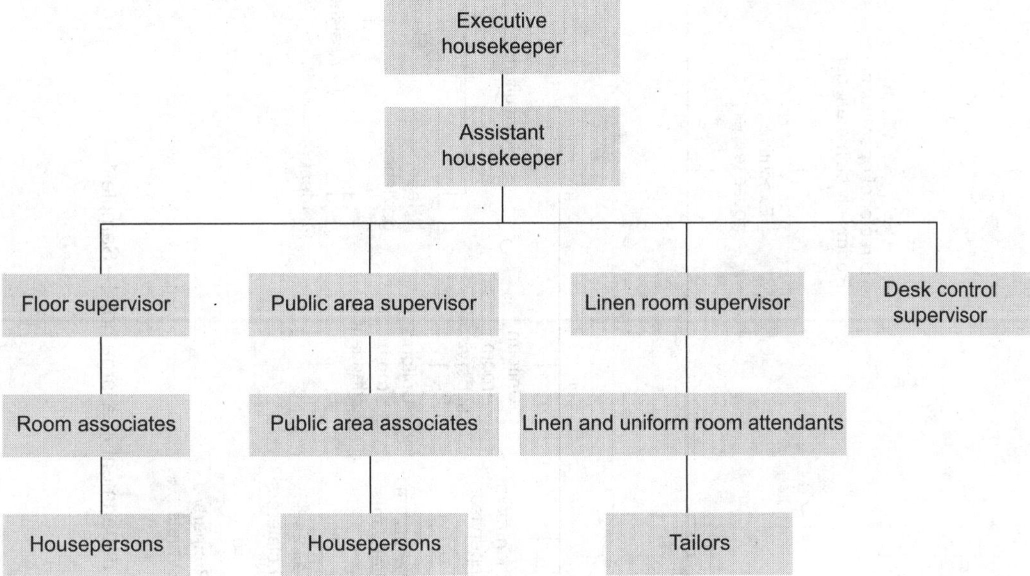

Fig. 2.2 (b) Organization chart of a housekeeping department in a medium-sized hotel—Sample 2

Housekeeping Personnel

Housekeeping staff can be divided into three categories:

Managerial Executive housekeeper, head housekeeper, corporate housekeeper, director of housekeeping

Supervisory Assistant housekeeper, floor housekeeper, linen room supervisor, public area supervisor, and so on

Semi-skilled and Unskilled Guestroom associates, public area associates, housemen, etc.

Executive Housekeeper/Director of Housekeeping

The executive housekeeper reports to the general manager, or the resident manager, or the rooms division manager/director of rooms. She/He is responsible and accountable for the total cleanliness

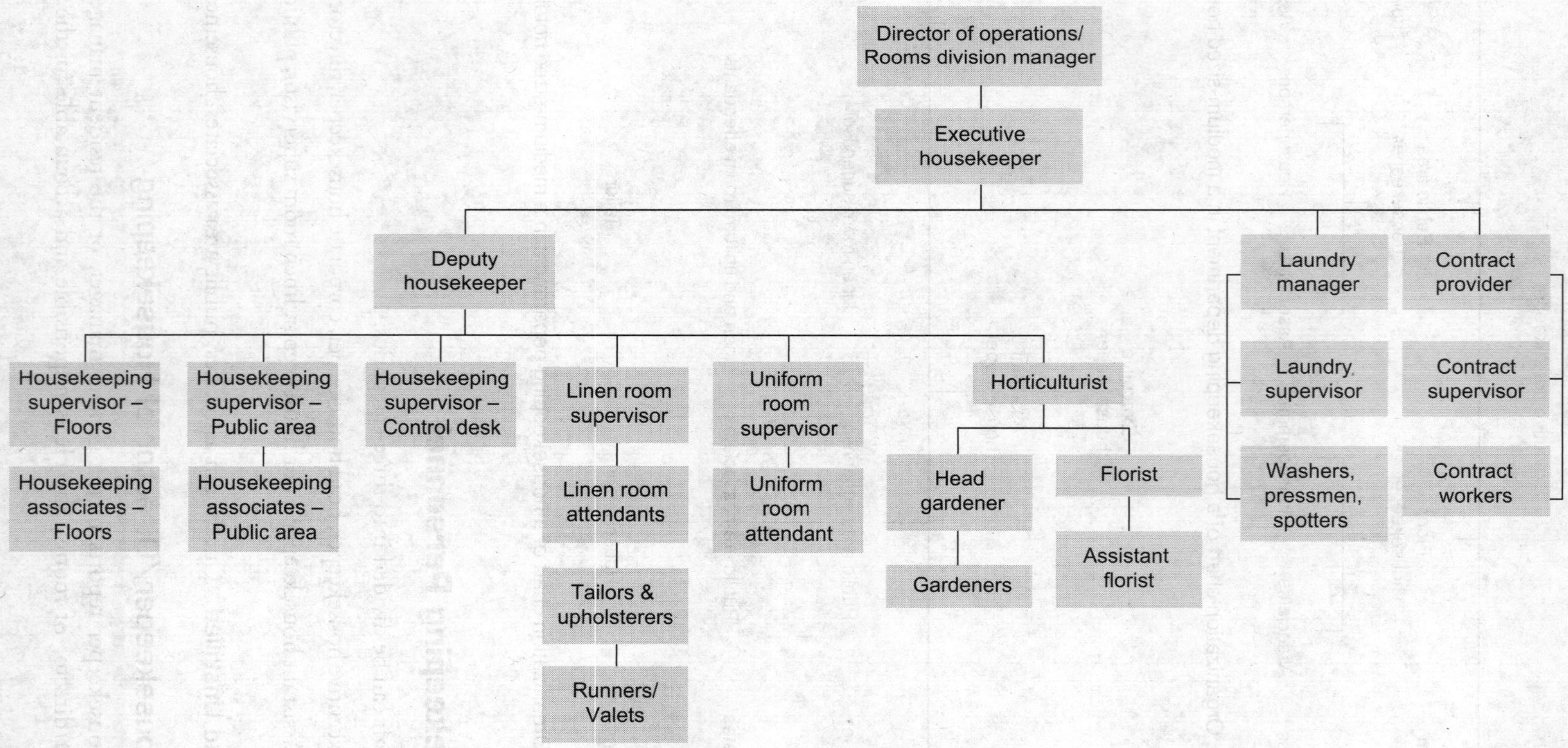

- Director of operations/ Rooms division manager
  - Executive housekeeper
    - Contract provider
      - Contract supervisor
        - Contract workers
    - Laundry manager
      - Laundry supervisor
        - Washers, pressmen, spotters
    - Horticulturist
      - Florist
        - Assistant florist
      - Head gardener
        - Gardeners
    - Deputy housekeeper
      - Uniform room supervisor
        - Uniform room attendant
      - Linen room supervisor
        - Linen room attendants
          - Tailors & upholsterers
            - Runners/ Valets
      - Housekeeping supervisor – Control desk
      - Housekeeping supervisor – Public area
        - Housekeeping associates – Public area
      - Housekeeping supervisor – Floors
        - Housekeeping associates – Floors

Fig. 2.3 (a) Organization chart of the housekeeping department in a large hotel—Sample 1

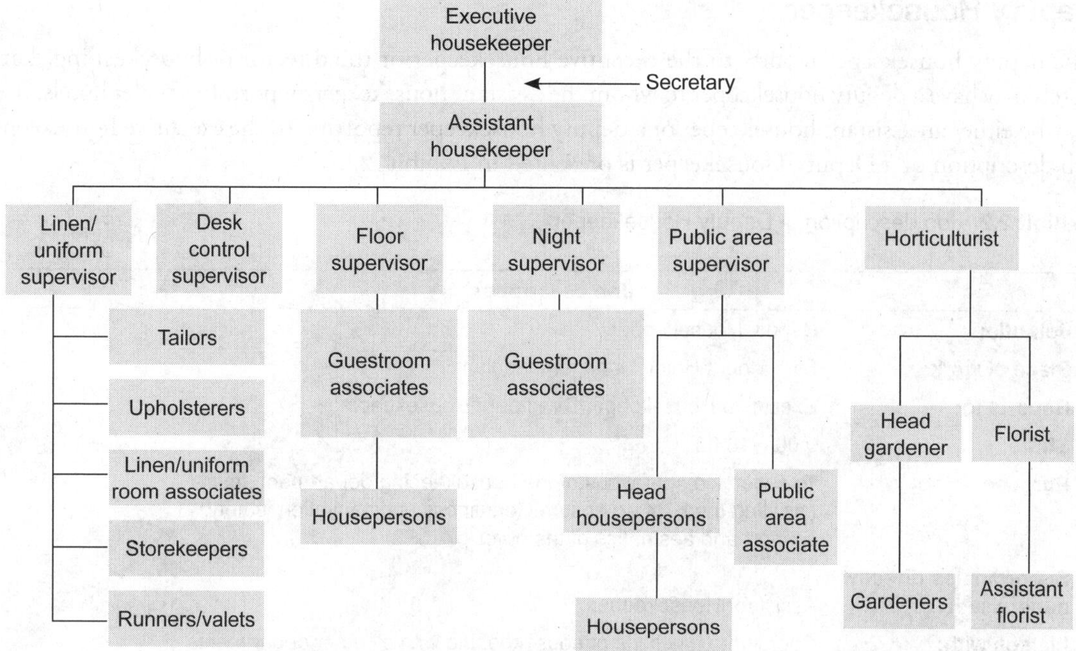

Fig. 2.3 (b) Organization chart of a housekeeping department in a large hotel—Sample 2

and aesthetic upkeep of the hotel. She/He supervises all housekeeping employees, has the authority to hire or discharge subordinates, plans and assigns work assignments, informs new employees of property regulations, inspects completed assignments, and requisitions supplies. The position description of an executive housekeeper is presented in Exhibit 2.1.

Exhibit 2.1 Position description of Executive Housekeeper

Position description	
Position title:	Executive Housekeeper
Company:	Blue Mount Hotel, Udhagamandalam
Reports to:	Rooms Division Manager/Director of Rooms/General Manager
Shifts:	9.00 – 18.00
Purpose of position:	To assume complete direction, operational control, and supervision of the housekeeping department; to ensure cleanliness and sanitation, safety, comfort and aesthetics of the hotel
Scope of work:	The incumbent must operate the department in the most efficient manner possible through effective application and enforcement of company policies, the use of methods devised in SOPs, and the use of sound management principles. The incumbent must accomplish tasks through proper training, motivation, and supervision of all employees assigned to the housekeeping department.

Deputy Housekeeper

The deputy housekeeper reports to the executive housekeeper or the director of housekeeping. Large hotels may have a deputy housekeeper to whom the assistant housekeepers report. In smaller hotels, there may be either an assistant housekeeper or a deputy housekeeper reporting to the executive housekeeper. Job description of a Deputy Housekeeper is presented in Exhibit 2.2.

Exhibit 2.2 Job description of Deputy Housekeeper

Job description	
Job title:	Deputy Housekeeper
Place of work:	Blue Mount Hotel, Udhagamandalam
Reports to:	Executive Housekeeper/Director of Housekeeping
Shifts:	9.00 – 18.00
Purpose of job:	To supervise operations of the housekeeping department, thus assisting the EHK; to ensure cleanliness and sanitation, safety, comfort and aesthetics of the hotel
Subordinates directly supervised:	Assistant Housekeeper
Liaison with:	Coordinate functions of housekeeping with all other departments
Scope of work:	Maintain set standards of work, manage stocks, plan and implement work to be carried out, train staff

Assistant Housekeeper/Housekeeping Manager

The assistant housekeeper usually reports to the executive housekeeper. In hotels where an additional senior position of deputy housekeeper exists, the assistant housekeepers may report to the deputy housekeeper. Generally hotels employ one assistant housekeeper per 50–60 rooms. There may be just one assistant housekeeper under the executive housekeeper in a medium-sized hotel or one for each shift in a large hotel. In large hotels, the responsibilities for the floors, public areas, linen room, and control room are divided among assistant housekeepers. Essentially, the assistant housekeeper manages the resources provided by the executive housekeeper to achieve the objectives of cleanliness, maintenance, and attractiveness during a given shift. His/her responsibility involves the daily supervision of specific areas within the hotel. In the absence of the deputy housekeeper, all the aforementioned duties and responsibilities are taken over by the assistant housekeeper. Job description of an assistant housekeeper is presented in Exhibit 2.3.

Exhibit 2.3 Job description of Assistant Housekeeper

Job description	
Job title:	Assistant housekeeper/Housekeeping Manager
Place of work:	Blue Mount Hotel, Udhagamandalam
Immediate supervisor/ Reports to:	Executive Housekeeper/Deputy Housekeeper

(Contd.)

Exhibit 2.3 *Contd.*

Shifts:	7.00 – 16.00 13.00 – 22.00
Purpose of job:	To implement operational standards and ensure compliance to SOPs, systems and policies in maintenance of cleanliness and sanitation, safety, comfort and aesthetics of the hotel
Subordinates directly supervised:	Housekeeping Supervisors
Liaison with:	All departments, especially, front office, maintenance, security and purchase
Scope of work:	Assist EHK and deputy housekeeper to maintain set standards of work, manage stocks, train staff, plan and implement work to be carried out and report any issues to EHK

Floor Housekeepers/Floor Supervisors

The floor housekeeper reports to the assistant housekeeper and executive housekeeper. Floor housekeepers have final responsibility for the condition of guestrooms. Each floor housekeeper is assigned three or more floors. She gives the room associates their room assignments and the floor master keys, which are returned at the end of the day. She checks, supervises, and approves the associates' work and makes periodical inspection of the physical condition of all rooms on the floor. Job description of a Floor supervisor is presented in Exhibit 2.4.

Exhibit 2.4 Job description of Floor Supervisor

Job description	
Job title:	Floor Supervisor
Place of work:	Blue Mount Hotel, Udhagamandalam
Immediate supervisor/ Reports to:	Assistant housekeeper
Shifts:	06.00 – 15.00 13.00 – 22.00 22.00 – 07.00
Purpose of job:	To ensure that all guestrooms and sundry areas are maintained to company standards, supervise the GRAs assigned to his/her team, relay information concerning the status of rooms to and from the housekeeping office and achieve maximum efficiency and guest satisfaction.
Subordinates directly supervised:	GRAs, Housepersons
Liaison with:	Other supervisors, receptionists, maintenance staff, laundry manager, linen room staff, valet, in-room dining staff, storekeeper
Scope of work:	Train staff, maintain set standards of work, maintain stocks, plan work to be carried out on floors, report any issues to immediate supervisor

Public Area Supervisors

The public area supervisor reports to the assistant housekeeper. Public areas are the 'front of the house' areas such as the entrance, lobby, guest corridors, and so on. Since much of the public-area cleaning is done at night, good coordination with the night supervisor is essential in this role. Job description of a public area supervisor is presented in Exhibit 2.5.

Exhibit 2.5 Job description of Public Area Supervisor

Job description	
Job title:	Public area supervisor
Place of work:	Blue Mount Hotel, Udhagamandalam
Immediate supervisor/ Reports to:	Assistant housekeeper
Shifts:	06.00 – 15.00 13.00 – 22.00 22.00 – 07.00
Purpose of job:	To ensure that all front and back of the house areas are maintained to company standards, supervise the public area associates and achieve maximum efficiency and guest satisfaction.
Subordinates directly supervised:	Public area associates
Liaison with:	Other supervisors, receptionists, maintenance staff, horticulturist, florist, store-keeper, cleaning contractors, pest control contractor, security personnel
Scope of work:	Maintain set standards of work, train staff, plan work to be carried out in public areas, report any issues to immediate supervisor

Night Supervisor

The night supervisor reports to the assistant housekeeper. He supervises all night staff engaged in the cleaning of public areas and guestrooms in the hotel. Job description of a night supervisor is presented in Exhibit 2.6.

Exhibit 2.6 Job description of Night Supervisor

Job description	
Job title:	Night Supervisor
Place of work:	Blue Mount Hotel, Udhagamandalam
Immediate supervisor/ Reports to:	Assistant housekeeper
Shifts:	22.00 – 07.00
Purpose of job:	Be responsible for night shift housekeeping activities

(Contd.)

Exhibit 2.6 *Contd.*

Subordinates directly supervised:	Guestroom associates, public area associates and housemen
Liaison with:	Front office, maintenance, IRD and security
Scope of work:	Ensure that all housekeeping tasks to be accomplished in night shift are carried out to company standards, supervise night shift housekeeping staff, achieve maximum efficiency and guest satisfaction

Evening Shift Supervisor

Evening shift supervisors are required for the floors, public areas, and control room. They report to the assistant housekeeper. Job description of an evening shift supervisor is presented in Exhibit 2.7.

Exhibit 2.7 Job description of Evening Shift Supervisor

Job description	
Job title:	Evening shift supervisor
Place of work:	Blue Mount Hotel, Udhagamandalam
Immediate supervisor/ Reports to:	Assistant housekeeper
Shifts:	13.00 – 22.00
Purpose of job:	Be responsible for afternoon/evening shift housekeeping activities
Subordinates directly supervised:	Guestroom associates, public area associates, housemen
Liaison with:	Front office, maintenance and security
Scope of work:	Ensure cleaning of rooms not serviced in morning shift and provision of turndown service

Linen Room Supervisor/Linen Keeper

The linen room supervisor reports to the assistant housekeeper. He/She supervises the work of the linen room and may have several linen attendants to assist her in providing clean, presentable linen throughout the house. Job description of a linen room supervisor is presented in Exhibit 2.8.

Exhibit 2.8 Job description of Linen Room Supervisor

Job description	
Job title:	Linen room supervisor/Linen keeper
Place of work:	Blue Mount Hotel, Udhagamandalam
Immediate supervisor/ Reports to:	Assistant housekeeper

(Contd.)

Exhibit 2.8 *Contd.*

Shifts:	7.00 – 16.00
Purpose of job:	Management and control of linen room activities
Subordinates directly supervised:	Linen room associates
Liaison with:	Laundry, health & recreation outlets, F&B and housekeeping supervisors
Scope of work:	Provision of clean, presentable linen to floors, spa, health & recreation outlets, and F&B.

Uniform Room Supervisor

A uniform room supervisor reports to the assistant housekeeper. He/she is responsible for the maintenance of hotel staff uniforms. Job description of a uniform room supervisor is presented in Exhibit 2.9.

Exhibit 2.9 Job description of Uniform Room Supervisor

Job description	
Job title:	Uniform room supervisor
Place of work:	Blue Mount Hotel, Udhagamandalam
Immediate supervisor/ Reports to:	Assistant housekeeper
Shifts:	7.00 – 16.00
Purpose of job:	Management and control of uniform room activities
Subordinates directly supervised:	Uniform room associates and attendants
Liaison with:	Laundry and all departments
Scope of work:	Provision of clean, serviceable uniforms as per company standards to all employees

Linen Room Attendant

Linen room attendants report to the linen room supervisor. Job description of a linen room attendant is presented in Exhibit 2.10.

Exhibit 2.10 Job description of Linen Room Associate/Attendant

Job description	
Job title:	Linen room associate/attendant
Place of work:	Blue Mount Hotel, Udhagamandalam
Immediate supervisor/ Reports to:	Linen room supervisor
Shifts:	6.00 – 15.00 13.00 – 22.00
Purpose of job:	Carry out linen room activities as per company standards
Subordinates directly supervised:	Linen room helpers
Liaison with:	Laundry, health & recreation outlets, F&B and housekeeping supervisors
Scope of work:	Process linen to provide clean, presentable linen to floors, spa, health & recreation outlets, and F&B.

Uniform Room Attendant

A uniform room attendant reports to the uniform room supervisor. He/she is in actual contact with the staff for the issue of uniforms. Job description of a uniform room attendant is presented in Exhibit 2.11.

Exhibit 2.11 Job description of Uniform Room Attendant

Job description	
Job title:	Uniform room attendant
Place of work:	Blue Mount Hotel, Udhagamandalam
Immediate supervisor/ Reports to:	Uniform room supervisor
Shifts:	6.00 – 15.00
Purpose of job:	Carry out uniform room activities
Subordinates directly supervised:	Uniform room helpers
Liaison with:	Laundry, health & recreation outlets, F&B and housekeeping supervisors
Scope of work:	Process uniforms to provide clean uniforms to all staff.

Storekeeper

A storekeeper reports to the deputy housekeeper. In large hotels, a storekeeper may be appointed to a full-time position. Job description of a storekeeper is presented in Exhibit 2.12.

Exhibit 2.12 Job description of Storekeeper

Job description	
Job title:	Storekeeper
Place of work:	Blue Mount Hotel, Udhagamandalam
Immediate supervisor/ Reports to:	Deputy Housekeeper
Shifts:	7.00 – 16.00
Purpose of job:	Control stocks of tools, equipment, guest supplies and cleaning agents
Subordinates directly supervised:	Store helpers
Liaison with:	Floor supervisors, public area supervisors, guest room associates and public area associates
Scope of work:	Provide stocks of supplies on regular basis to floors and public areas

Control Desk Supervisor

The control desk supervisor reports to the assistant housekeeper. The control room or control desk is the nerve centre of the housekeeping department. The desk is manned 24 hours a day. Since the control desk is the hub of information dissemination in housekeeping, the control desk supervisor is a critical person in housekeeping operations. Job description of a control desk supervisor is presented in Exhibit 2.13.

Exhibit 2.13 Job description of Control Desk Supervisor

Job description	
Job title:	Control desk supervisor
Place of work:	Blue Mount Hotel, Udhagamandalam
Immediate supervisor/ Reports to:	Assistant housekeeper
Shifts:	6.00 – 15.00 13.00 – 22.00
Purpose of job:	Manage and coordinate housekeeping control desk activities
Liaison with:	Front office, maintenance, security, floors, laundry
Scope of work:	Efficient management of housekeeping operations through coordination with relevant departments

Guestroom Associates/Guest Service Associates/Housekeeping Associates - Rooms

Guest room associates (GRAs) or Guest Service Associates (GSAs) as they are generally designated now, report to the floor supervisor (or the night supervisor, in case of night room associates). In small hotels, they may report to the assistant housekeeper directly. Generally hotels employ one room associate per 12–16 rooms. The room associates' work is of great importance because it contributes in a big way to the comfort of guests and hence, their impression of the hotel. Their day consists of servicing each room to the required standard of the hotel, and this includes making beds, coping with linen supplies, and general cleaning. Job description of a guest room associate is presented in Exhibit 2.14.

Exhibit 2.14 Job description of Guestroom Associate

Job description	
Job title:	Guestroom associate
Place of work:	Blue Mount Hotel, Udhagamandalam
Immediate supervisor/ Reports to:	Floor supervisor
Shifts:	6.00 – 15.00 13.00 – 22.00 22.00 – 7.00
Purpose of job:	Ensure guest satisfaction through providing in-room cleanliness and comfort as per company standards
Liaison with:	Housemen, IRD, Laundry valet
Scope of work:	Carryout servicing of guestrooms as per property standards

Butler

In luxury hotels offering world class service, a VIP guest may be provided with a butler, an associate who is exclusively responsible for servicing and looking after the guest in the VIP suite. The duties include maintaining high standards of guestroom suite and service, unpacking and packing guest belongings, managing guest laundry collection and receipt, providing shoe shine service, coordinate with IRD for guest meals, resolving any housekeeping or maintenance issues pertaining to the room in coordination with control desk and maintenance, and so on.

Head Houseperson

He/she reports to the public area supervisor. In some organizations, he/she may report directly to the executive housekeeper or assistant housekeeper, and is in charge of the housemen/housepersons. Job description of a head houseperson is presented in Exhibit 2.15.

Exhibit 2.15 Job description of Head Houseperson

Job description	
Job title:	Head Houseperson
Place of work:	Blue Mount Hotel, Udhagamandalam
Immediate supervisor/ Reports to:	Public area supervisor, Assistant housekeeper

(Contd.)

Exhibit 2.15 *Contd.*

Shifts:	6.00 – 15.00 13.00 – 22.00
Purpose of job:	Taking charge of cleaning, upkeep and maintenance of public areas
Subordinates directly supervised:	Housepersons
Liaison with:	Reception staff, maintenance staff, horticulturist, storekeeper
Scope of work:	Be responsible for cleanliness and upkeep work carried out by housepersons

Public Area Associates/Housekeeping Associates - Public Area/ Housepersons

The public area associates report to the public area supervisor. Their job involves heavy physical work as assigned, such as carpet cleaning, window cleaning, carrying heavy pieces of furniture, cleaning public areas, garbage clearance, and also complementing the work of room associates on guest floors. Job description of a public area associate is presented in Exhibit 2.16.

Exhibit 2.16 Job description of Public Area Associate

Job description	
Job title:	Public area associate
Place of work:	Blue Mount Hotel, Udhagamandalam
Immediate supervisor/ Reports to:	Public area supervisor
Shifts:	06.00 – 15.00 13.00 – 22.00 22.00 – 07.00
Purpose of job:	Cleaning, upkeep and maintenance of public area
Liaison with:	Reception staff, maintenance staff, horticulturist, storekeeper
Scope of work:	Clean and maintain public areas as per company standards

Tailors, Seamstresses, and Upholsterers

They report to the linen room supervisor. They are responsible for mending and stitching uniforms, linen, and upholstery, respectively. The upholsterers also replenish upholstery that require replacement. Job description of these personnel is presented in Exhibit 2.17.

Exhibit 2.17 Job description of Tailors, Seamstresses, and Upholsterers

Job description	
Job title:	Tailors/Seamstresses/Upholsterers
Place of work:	Blue Mount Hotel, Udhagamandalam
Immediate supervisor/ Reports to:	Linen room supervisor
Shifts:	7.00 – 16.00
Purpose of job:	Mending, stitching, monogramming linen items, uniforms, soft furnishings and upholstery

Cloakroom Attendant

In a hotel that hosts many events and receives many non-resident guests, it is usual to have someone on duty in a ladies' powder room during lunch and dinner time to attend to the requirements of guests, guard their belongings, and keep the powder room neat and tidy. The cloakroom attendant reports to the public area supervisor. Job description of a cloakroom attendant is presented in Exhibit 2.18.

Exhibit 2.18 Job description of Cloakroom attendant

Job description	
Job title:	Cloakroom attendant
Place of work:	Blue Mount Hotel, Udhagamandalam
Immediate supervisor/ Reports to:	Public area supervisor
Shifts:	06.00 – 15.00 13.00 – 22.00
Purpose of job:	Ensure cleanliness, upkeep and maintenance of public area restrooms at all times as per company standards
Liaison with:	Linen room attendant, storekeeper
Scope of work:	Cleaning and maintenance of public area restrooms

Hat Checker

A hat checker provides his services in some superior hotels in cold climates. His domain is the hat check room, where hats and heavy overcoats are deposited by guests as soon as they enter the hotel lobby, so as to spare them the inconvenience of carrying these articles around in the hotel. The hat checker carefully labels these guest articles, and hangs or stores them correctly so as to return them to the guests when they are leaving the hotel.

Horticulturist

Many large hotels have their own horticulturist, who reports to the assistant housekeeper. He/she leads a team of gardeners in maintaining the landscaped gardens of the hotel as well as in supplying flowers from the gardens for flower arrangements in the hotel. Flowers are used largely by the housekeeping department to aesthetically enhance various areas of the hotel. Flower arrangements may be used in banquet functions, guestrooms, restaurants, lobbies, offices, and so on. Job description of a horticulturist is presented in Exhibit 2.19.

Exhibit 2.19 Job description of Horticulturist

Job description	
Job title:	Horticulturist
Place of work:	Blue Mount Hotel, Udhagamandalam
Immediate supervisor/ Reports to:	Assistant housekeeper, public area supervisor
Shifts:	6.00 – 15.00 9.00 – 18.00
Purpose of job:	Be in-charge of upkeep and aesthetics of hotel's gardens and landscaped areas

Head Gardener

The head gardener reports to the horticulturist. He is required to maintain landscaped areas and gardens in a hotel, keeping in mind their cleanliness, aesthetic appeal, and freshness all the year round through a well-motivated team of gardeners. Job description of a head gardener is presented in Exhibit 2.20.

Exhibit 2.20 Job description of Head Gardener

Job description	
Job title:	Head Gardener
Place of work:	Blue Mount Hotel, Udhagamandalam
Immediate supervisor/ Reports to:	Public area supervisor, Horticulturist
Shifts:	6.00 – 15.00 9.00 – 18.00
Purpose of job:	Ensure upkeep and aesthetics of hotel's gardens and landscaped areas as per company standards
Subordinates directly supervised:	Gardeners
Liaison with:	Florist, maintenance staff, storekeeper
Scope of work:	Keep the gardens and landscaped areas optimally functional and aesthetically pleasing

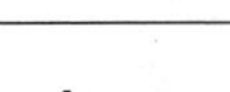

Gardeners

Gardeners (*maalis*) report to the head gardener or the horticulturist. They keep landscaped areas, lawns, and gardens clean, aesthetically beautiful, and fresh through the daily schedules of tasks assigned to them. Job description of a gardener is presented in Exhibit 2.21.

Exhibit 2.21 Job description of Gardener

Job description	
Job title:	Gardener
Place of work:	Blue Mount Hotel, Udhagamandalam
Immediate supervisor/ Reports to:	Head Gardener
Shifts:	6.00 – 15.00 9.00 – 18.00
Purpose of job:	Maintain gardens and landscaped areas

Florist

Many luxury hotels employ their own florist nowadays. Providing attractive flower arrangements for the entire hotel is his/her responsibility. A florist may report to the horticulturist or to the assistant housekeeper. He/she may have an assistant florist to help. Job description of a florist is presented in Exhibit 2.22.

Exhibit 2.22 Job description of Florist

Job description	
Job title:	Florist
Place of work:	Blue Mount Hotel, Udhagamandalam
Immediate supervisor/ Reports to:	Assistant Housekeeper
Shifts:	7.00 – 16.00
Purpose of job:	Enhancing the aesthetic appeal of public areas and VIP rooms with floral decorations
Liaison with:	Public area supervisor, reception staff, storekeeper, flower vendors
Scope of work:	Provide traditional and innovative floral decorations as per demand

Laundry Manager

The laundry manager reports to the director of housekeeping. He/she is responsible for the entire functioning of the laundry and dry-cleaning unit. A laundry manager must have organizational ability as well as technical knowledge of chemicals and their effect on fabrics. Figure 2.4 shows the laundry organization chart. Job description of a laundry manager is presented in Exhibit 2.23.

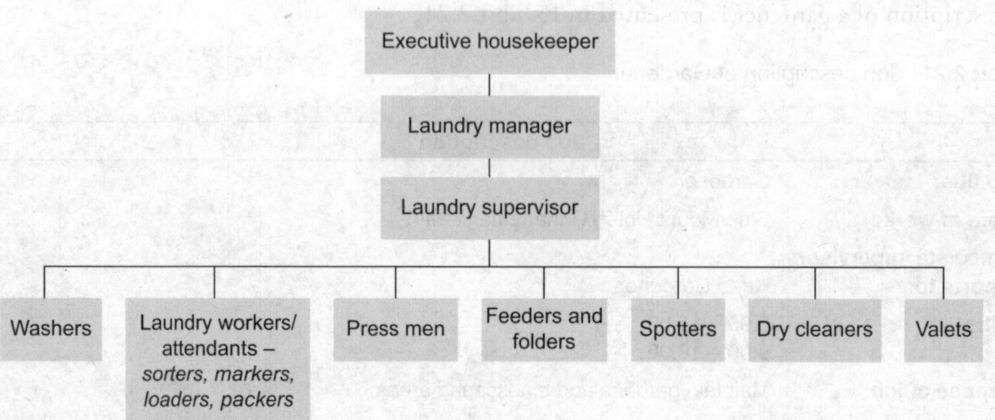

Fig. 2.4 Laundry organization chart

Exhibit 2.23 Job description of Laundry Manager

Job description	
Job title:	Laundry Manager
Place of work:	Blue Mount Hotel, Udhagamandalam
Immediate supervisor/ Reports to:	Rooms division manager, Executive housekeeper
Shifts:	8.00 – 17.00
Purpose of job:	Efficient management of in-house laundry as per company standards
Subordinates directly supervised:	Laundry supervisor
Liaison with:	Laundry equipment dealers, cleaning chemical suppliers, floor supervisor, linen room supervisor, uniform room supervisor, F&B department
Scope of work:	To ensure cleanliness and timely processing of linen, guest clothes and employee uniforms

Laundry Supervisor

He/she is in charge of the functioning of the laundry in the absence of the laundry manager. A laundry supervisor must have a good understanding of all aspects of the laundry equipment, chemicals, and fabrics. Job description of a laundry supervisor is presented in Exhibit 2.24.

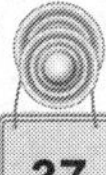

Exhibit 2.24 Job description of Laundry Supervisor

Job description	
Job title:	Laundry supervisor
Place of work:	Blue Mount Hotel, Udhagamandalam
Immediate supervisor/ Reports to:	Laundry Manager
Shifts:	7.00 – 16.00
Purpose of job:	Smooth daily operations of the in-house laundry
Subordinates directly supervised:	Laundry workers, washers
Liaison with:	Floor supervisors, linen room supervisor, uniform room supervisor, F&B department
Scope of work:	Ensure timely processing of soiled linen and clothes to provide clean, finished linen, uniforms and guest clothes

Dry-cleaner

The dry-cleaner is in charge of the dry-cleaning of hotel linen and guest clothing.

Washer

A washer is the person who actually does the laundering of linen, uniforms, and guest clothing. Job description of a washer is presented in Exhibit 2.25.

Exhibit 2.25 Job description of Washer

Job description	
Job title:	Washer
Place of work:	Blue Mount Hotel, Udhagamandalam
Immediate supervisor/ Reports to:	Laundry Supervisor
Shifts:	7.00 – 16.00 13.00 – 22.00
Liaison with:	Laundry workers
Purpose of job:	Operate washers as per the wash programme

Laundry Workers

They are the lower rung of staff in the laundry, carrying out a variety of duties. Proper training is essential to ensure they function smoothly and efficiently. Job description of a laundry worker is presented in Exhibit 2.26.

Exhibit 2.26 Job description of Laundry worker

Job description	
Job title:	Laundry worker
Place of work:	Blue Mount Hotel, Udhagamandalam
Immediate supervisor/ Reports to:	Laundry Supervisor
Shifts:	7.00 – 16.00
Purpose of job:	Carry out tasks of transporting, sorting, weighing and loading linen and marking and packing guest laundry and uniforms

Pressmen

Pressmen are responsible for ironing linen, uniforms, and guest clothing using hand irons, calendering machines, steam presses, and so on.

Valets/Runners

'Valet service' means that the hotel will take care of the guest's laundry. Valets report to the linen room supervisor. They are responsible for collecting soiled guest laundry and delivering fresh guest laundry. In many hotels, a valet is not charged with the task of delivering guest laundry only. Here the valet shares a service room with the GRAs; the room is complete with iron and ironing board, needles, cotton and string, shoe-cleaning necessities, and so on. He may also perform the less tedious functions of a houseman.

Personal Attributes of Housekeeping Staff

The housekeeping department in a hotel may easily have the largest workforce. No matter how luxurious the décor or how aesthetic the guestroom may be, grumpy, poorly trained, and unhelpful staff can destroy any potential customer satisfaction with the hospitality product. Being a service industry, the personal projection of staff to guests enhances the image of the hotel. It is also essential to know the qualities that a housekeeping staff must posses for the purpose of recruitment, induction, training, and self-development programmes. These attributes sometimes override the importance of skill, as skills can be taught but these personal traits (Figure 2.5) should be inherent in a member of the staff.

Pleasant personality A pleasant personality is the result of good grooming and good presentation in front of guests. The way a staff looks is the first impression he/she creates, and this reflects on the quality of service and standards in an establishment. It is good to remember that 'your last look in the mirror will be the guest's first look'. All the supervisory housekeeping staff and the associates should be especially well groomed, as they come into close contact with the guests. Grooming standards for female and male housekeeping employees are presented in Exhibits 2.27 and 2.28 respectively.

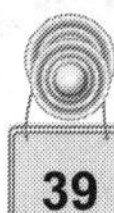

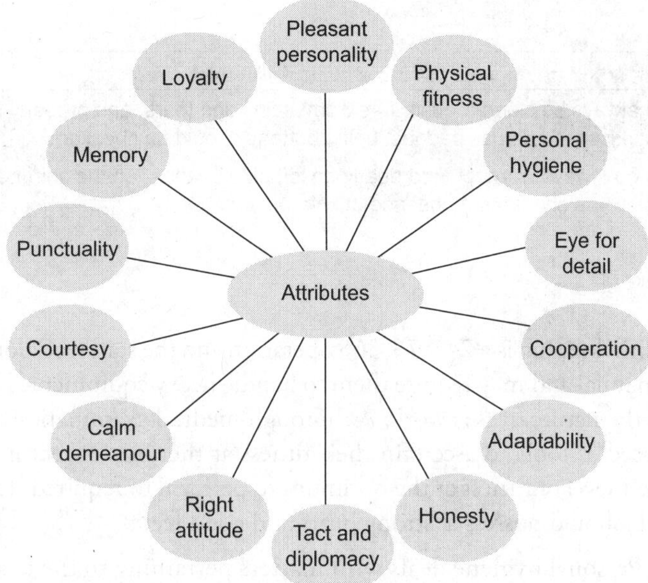

Fig. 2.5 Personal attributes of housekeeping staff

Exhibit 2.27 Grooming standard for female employees in housekeeping department

SOP Name:	**Grooming standards for female employees in housekeeping department**		
Effective Date:	**23.12.2019**	**SOP Author:**	**Shefali Shyam**
SOP No. :	**101**	**SOP Approver:**	**Vijay Dewan**
For Job title:	**Female HK staff**	**SOP Owner:**	**Hotel Sundown, Coorg**

Objective: To ensure that staff are presentable at all times in grooming standards set by the company.

Particulars	**Standard**
Uniforms	To always be clean, free from stains and tears, and properly ironed; uniform accessories such as badges, belts, buttons should be checked.

Exhibit 2.28 Grooming standard for male employees in housekeeping department

SOP Name:	**Grooming standards for male employees in housekeeping department**		
Effective Date:	**23.12.2019**	**SOP Author:**	**Shefali Shyam**
SOP No. :	**102**	**SOP Approver:**	**Vijay Dewan**
For Job title:	**Male HK staff**	**SOP Owner:**	**Hotel Sundown, Coorg**

Objective: To ensure that staff are presentable at all times in grooming standards set by the company.

(Contd.)

Exhibit 2.28 *Contd.*

Particulars	Standard
Uniforms	To always be clean & crisp, free from stains and tears, and properly ironed; uniform accessories such as badges, belts, buttons should be checked.
Name badge	To be always worn, pinned neatly on left side of attire, on the shirt pocket flap or 4 in. below the shoulder in absence of shirt pocket.

Physical fitness Housekeeping is a 24 × 7 × 365 operation and the staff work long hours on their feet. Most of their work is manual and may require them to handle heavy equipment. Hence, physical fitness is a must to cope with the nature of this work. A thorough medical examination and a medical history of candidates can be used as tools to ascertain their fitness at the time of recruitment. Housekeeping staff must maintain their level of fitness at the optimum to perform to required standards. It is said that ideal housekeeping staff should possess a 'strong heart and good feet'.

Personal hygiene Personal hygiene deals with matters pertaining to the health of the individual for the maintenance of which the responsibilities lie with him alone. Elements of personal hygiene include:

- Good and healthy habits
- Cleanliness of the skin
- Cleanliness and care of hair, eyes, ears, teeth, and nose
- Cleanliness of the nails and fingers
- Cleanliness, tidiness, and condition of clothes and footwear

Housekeeping staff must maintain a high standard of personal hygiene, as it reflects on the hygiene standards of the hotel. They must take a bath daily to avoid body odour. Their hair must be well combed, their nails clean and clipped. Their mouths should be free of any offensive odour. Any infection should be reported and attended to immediately. Cuts and burns should be covered with the correct dressings.

Eye for detail This is one of the foremost attributes that housekeeping staff must possess. They must be able to take into consideration minute details that a layman may let go unobserved. The power of critical observation is what distinguishes good service from average. Associates need to have an eye for detail in order to make up a flawless guestroom and housekeeping supervisors need to have a keen sense of observation to inspect these rooms for perfection. Furthermore, the whole property must be continually scrutinized by the housekeeping department for proper care and maintenance.

Cooperation Housekeeping staff must cooperate not only with each other, but also with the staff of other departments. This is absolutely essential, since housekeeping involves a lot of teamwork for efficient functioning. If there is any lack of cooperation and coordination, it indirectly affects the guests and hampers efficiency.

Adaptability This is an important quality in housekeeping staff. They should be willing to try out and experiment with new ideas. The entry of foreign hotel chains into India has brought about an immense sense of competition, due to which hotels in India are now trying out more innovative methods and materials in housekeeping. The staff should accept and adapt to change willingly and should welcome such innovations.

Honesty This quality is all-important to the staff in dealings with both guests and the management. Housekeeping staff have direct access to guestrooms. Guests' belongings are often left lying around the room and temptations are great. Housekeeping staff also deal with various kinds of guest amenities that may tempt them. It is inherent discipline and integrity that checks these temptations. If there is trust and respect across the triangle of staff, guests, and management relationships, then there will be a work atmosphere that encourages efficiency and a good team spirit.

Tact and diplomacy Housekeeping staff come into close contact with various kinds of guests. Some guests may make unusual requests or complaints. Sometimes guests may be fussy and demand services that override the management's policies. It requires a lot of tact and diplomacy on the part of housekeeping staff to handle such guests at their level, since under no circumstances can they be rude to a guest or hurt his/her sentiments. Staff need to be trained in handling guests who make such requests.

Right attitude Most managers agree that a candidate with the right attitude is more of an asset to them than a candidate who has the skills but the wrong attitude. The candidate with good attitude displays an even temper, courtesy, and good humour, and does not betray displeasure even in the most difficult of times. They learn from their mistakes and are always optimistic. The employee with the right attitude is proactive and anticipates the guest's needs and wishes.

Calm demeanour Housekeeping staff may be faced with various kinds of emergency situations, and it is essential that they remain calm so as to do their best in coping with the problem in hand. If they panic during an emergency, their anxious demeanour could become contagious and be passed on to guests and colleagues. A calm demeanour helps employees to think rationally themselves and to display their presence of mind.

Courtesy A housekeeping employee should extend courtesy to both guests and colleagues. It is essential that while dealing with guests, the staff be humble and polite. Housekeeping staff should never argue with a guest and, if they cannot deal with the situation, it should be referred immediately to a senior member of the team. Guests will always remember pleasant and charming staff, as this adds to the guest's positive experience in a hotel.

Punctuality This too is crucially important. If an employee is continually late for duty, it shows lack of interest in the work and a lack of respect for the management and guests. Respect for time during working hours will reflect on the employee's work and help to create an impression worthy of appreciation.

Good memory This is an essential asset in housekeeping staff, particularly when dealing with regular guests and repeat customers. A staff member who remembers a regular guest's name, likes, dislikes, needs, and wishes will be a tremendous asset to the hotel.

Loyalty An employee's first obligation and loyalty are to the establishment in which they are employed and to its management. A situation should never arise when employees use guests as their sounding board. They should respect the policies and decisions of the management.

Sub-Sections and Layout of the Department

The layout of the housekeeping department is the physical demarcation of areas in the department. When the layout is well-planned, it enables the smooth functioning of the department. The layout is dependent on the size of the hotel as well as physical space restrictions. Normally, the layout is decided by the executive housekeeper, at the facility-planning stage in setting up the hotel. The following factors are taken into consideration when deciding on the area and layout.

- Total number of guestrooms
- Number of function rooms and number of food and beverage outlets
- Amount of manpower required
- Volume of business anticipated
- Number of jobs contracted out
- Flow of traffic (people and equipment)

Figures 2.6 and 2.7 show the layout of the housekeeping department in a budget hotel and a large hotel, respectively.

The following areas constitute the layout of a housekeeping department.

Executive housekeeper's cabin The executive housekeeper should have an independent cabin, since it is the administrative centre of the department. A glass-panelled office with blinds to provide privacy at times, such as when meetings are conducted and confidential issues are discussed, is most appropriate. The cabin should have one entrance-cum-exit door where entry is controlled by the secretary. Ample built-in shelves and cupboards with locks should be provided to store files and records.

Assistant housekeeper's cabin A smaller cabin should be provided for the assistant housekeeper, preceding the executive housekeeper's cabin. Storage area for documents is essential in the AHK's cabin.

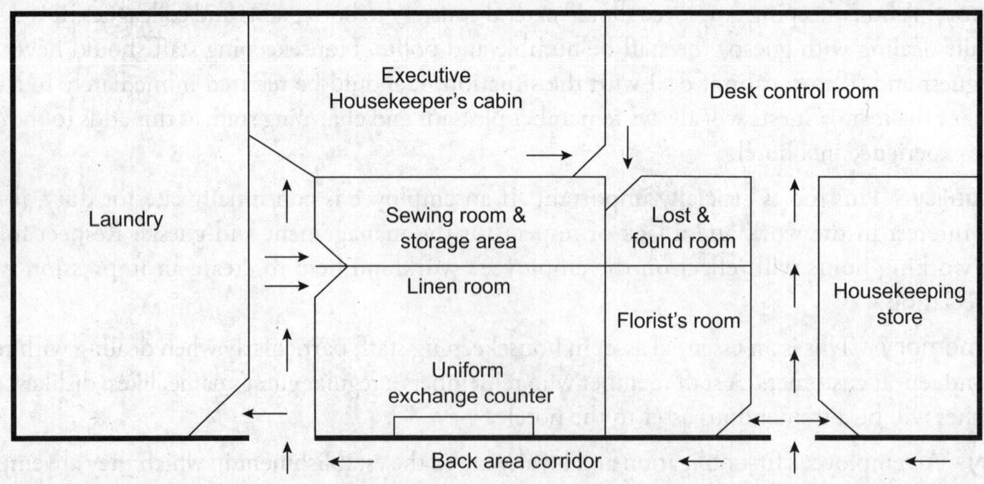

Fig. 2.6 Layout of housekeeping department in a budget hotel

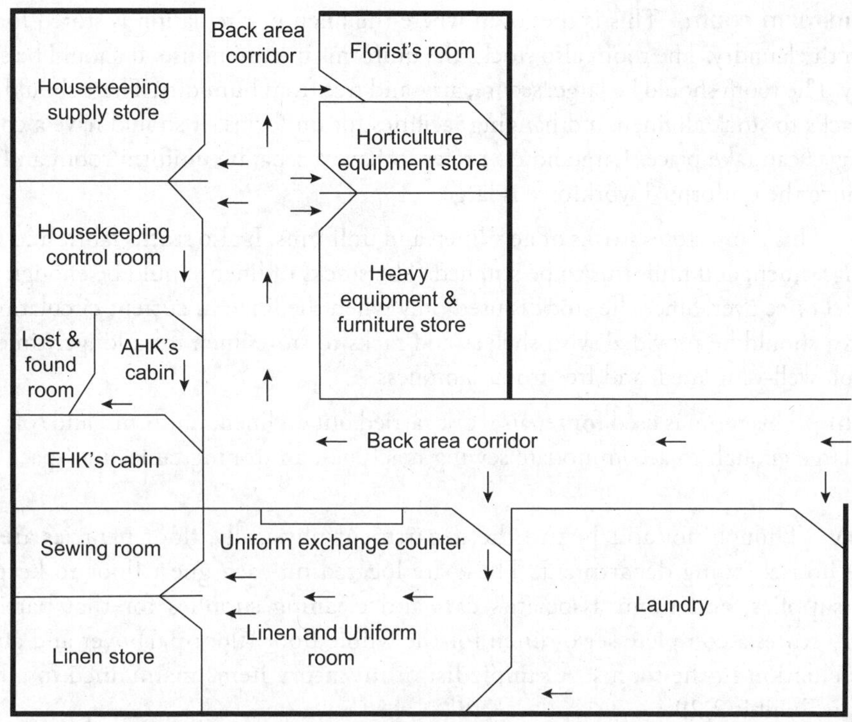

Fig. 2.7 Layout of a housekeeping department in a large hotel

Desk control room This is the communication hub of the housekeeping department and this desk is manned 24 hours a day. It should normally adjoin the executive housekeeper's cabin, as this is the point where all staff report for duty and sign out at the end of their shift. It should have a large notice board to pin up information for staff. It should also have more than one telephone connection as well as storage shelves for registers and files.

Lost-and-found section This is usually an area set aside in the desk control room, away from high-traffic areas. A cupboard with a good locking mechanism should be provided here for storing the lost-and-found articles so that they may be claimed later.

Housekeeping stores This is a room to store items such as cleaning supplies, guest supplies, and so on, which are issued on a daily basis. It should ideally be clean, dry, and securely locked.

Heavy equipment store This is a room to store bulky equipment and items such as vacuum cleaners, carpet shampoo machines, ladders, roll-away beds, and mattresses. It should be a clean, dry, and cool room that can be locked when not in use.

Horticulture equipment store This room is used for the storage of gardening implements such as rakes, spades, lawn mowers, pots, pails, water hoses, and seeds. It should be near to the garden area and should have its doors kept locked. The size of the room depends on the landscaped area to be tended.

Florist's room This should be an air-conditioned room to keep flowers fresh for the flower arrangements required by the hotel. It should have a work table, counters, a sink, adequate water supply, and cupboards to store equipment, containers, wire cables, and other accessories.

Linen and uniform room This is the room where the linen in circulation is stored for issue when received from the laundry. The room also stocks the uniforms in current use. It should be situated next to the laundry. The room should be large, secure, airy, and free from humidity. There should be adequate shelves and racks to stock all linen and hanging facilities for uniforms. It should have a counter across which exchanges can take place. Large hotels prefer to have a separate uniform room and a dedicated linen room since the uniformed workforce is large.

Linen store This room stores stocks of new linen and uniforms. It also stocks fabric and materials for soft furnishings, linen, and uniforms to be stitched. The stocks of linen should be enough to replenish the entire hotel once over. Since the stock is used only when the linen in current circulation falls short of par, the area should be provided with shelves and racks to store linen for a longer time. The room should be cool, well-ventilated, and free from dampness.

Sewing room This room is used for repair work carried out on linen, uniforms, and soft furnishings. It should be large enough to accommodate sewing machines, an ironing table, and space for items to be repaired.

Floor pantry Though not attached to the department physically, floor pantries are very much a part of the housekeeping department. These are located on each guest floor to keep a stock of linen, guest supplies, and room associate's cart and cleaning supplies for that particular floor. A floor pantry stores a complete set of linen for the whole floor (floor par) over and above what is already in circulation in the rooms. A sample list of inventory items maintained in a floor pantry is presented in Exhibit 2.29.

Exhibit 2.29 A sample list of inventory items maintained in floor pantry for a 20-room section

FLOOR PANTRY PAR STOCK					
Sl. No.	Particulars	PAR	Sl. No.	Particulars	PAR
1.	Soap (40 g)	20 nos.	7.	Shower cap	15 nos.
2.	Soap (25 g)	30 nos.	8.	Loofah	15 nos.
3.	Shower gel (35 ml)	20 nos.	9.	Comb	15 nos.
4.	Hair cleanser (35 ml)	20 nos.	10.	Dental kit	20 nos.
5.	Conditioner (35 ml)	20 nos.	11.	Shaving kit	20 nos.
6.	Body lotion (35 ml)	20 nos.	12.	Vanity kit	15 nos.

The floor pantries should be tucked away from guests' view and should be situated near the service elevators. It should store all housekeeping items so that the housekeeping staff do not have to keep going back to the housekeeping department or linen room for any item. It should have shelves and cupboards for linen and supplies, and sufficient area to park a room associate's cart. It should have a sink with water supply. A sample layout of a floor pantry is shown in Figure 2.8.

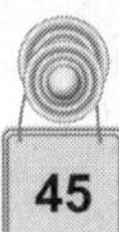

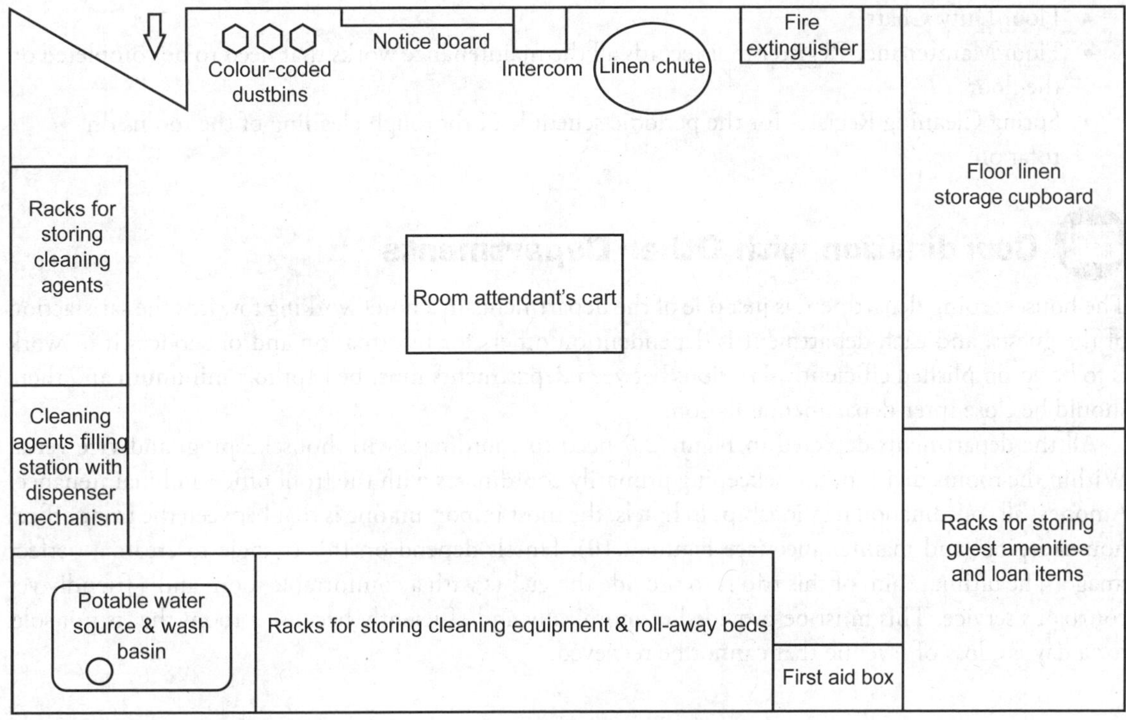

Fig. 2.8 Sample layout of a floor pantry

Since the floor pantry is used to stock expensive items such as linen, it should remain locked at all times when not in use. The key to the floor pantry is kept by the GRA of that floor and a duplicate is kept with the floor supervisor. The following should be provided in a floor pantry:

- Cupboards to store guest supplies, cleaning agents, and equipment.
- Shelves and racks to store fresh room linen.
- Linen trolleys to store fresh and soiled linen and for transporting/dispatching the same to the linen and uniform room.
- A notice board to display information regarding expected arrivals, VIPs in the house, extra beds, and guest loan items given to guests.
- A sink with hot and cold water facilities to wash or disinfect glasses, fill drinking water in flasks, and for flower arrangements.
- Guest loan items such as rollaway beds, cribs, and bed boards.

The forms and records maintained in the floor pantry are as follows:

- Room Linen Control Form (Refer Chapter 19, Exhibit 19.1) filled by the floor supervisor daily and sent along with soiled linen to the linen room. The signed copy is received back and filed.
- Copy of Room Linen Exchange Form (Refer Chapter 19, Exhibit 19.4) sent from the linen room
- Room Linen Inventory Form (Refer Chapter 19, Exhibit 19.9)
- Stores Requisition Form (Refer Exhibit 2.33) for requisitioning guest supplies, cleaning supplies, and stationery items

- Floor Duty Chart
- Floor Maintenance Register that records all the maintenance works that need to be completed on the floor
- Spring Cleaning Register for the periodic schedule of thorough cleaning of the rooms on rotation

 Coordination with Other Departments

The housekeeping department is just one of the departments in a hotel working towards the satisfaction of the guests, and each department is dependent on others for information and/or services if its work is to be accomplished efficiently. Frictions between departments must be kept to a minimum and there should be close inter-departmental liaison.

All the departments depicted in Figure 2.9 need to coordinate with housekeeping, and vice versa. Within the rooms division, housekeeping primarily coordinates with the front office and maintenance. Amongst all coordination relationships in hotels, the most important one is that between the front office, housekeeping, and maintenance (see Figure 2.10). Hotels depend on this triangle to create a perfect image. The ultimate aim of this trio is to provide the guests with a comfortable room and a friendly yet courteous service. This must be provided economically and efficiently because a room that is not sold for a day is a loss of revenue that cannot be retrieved.

Fig. 2.9 The various departments with which housekeeping coordinates

Coordination with Front Office

One of the most crucial coordination in hotels is that between the housekeeping department and front office. Both departments coordinate in the following aspects:

i. **Rooms management:** Rooms are of chief concern to the front office and housekeeping department. Hence, together, along with maintenance, they are called the 'Rooms division department'.

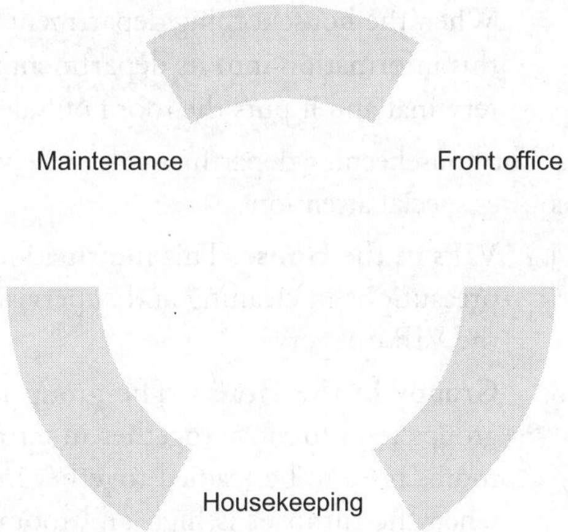

Fig. 2.10 Coordination between housekeeping, front office, and maintenance

- It is important for both the departments to continuously exchange information on room status. The front office must provide the list of expected arrivals and departures for the day in advance, and notify housekeeping of actual arrivals and departures as and when they occur.
- The front office is not allowed to assign guestrooms until the rooms have been cleaned, inspected and released by the housekeeping department.
- A front office assistant produces an occupancy report also called the 'night report'. It is prepared during night. This report lists rooms occupied that night and indicates guests who are expected to check out the following day.
- The executive housekeeper processes and consults this list early the next morning and schedules the rooms for cleaning. As guests check out, the front office notifies housekeeping. Housekeeping ensures that these rooms are given top priority in servicing, so that clean rooms are available for sale.
- To ensure efficient rooming of guests, both housekeeping and the front-office must inform each other of changes in a room's status. Knowing whether a room is occupied, vacant, on change, out of order (OOO) or under repair, is important for proper rooms management.
- If a guest checks out before the stated departure date, the front office must inform housekeeping that the room is no longer a stayover but is now a check out.
- The front office must be informed about rooms that are ready for occupation and those which are out of order or under repair.
- The housekeeping room status report is compared with front office's occupancy report and discrepancies are brought to the attention of the front office manager. A room status discrepancy is a situation in which the housekeeping department's description of a room's status differs from the room status information being used by the front office to assign guestrooms. The format of a discrepancy report is given in Chapter 6.
- As unoccupied rooms are cleaned and inspected, the floor supervisors call the housekeeping desk attendant, who in turn informs the front office of rooms ready. The front office then updates the room's status to 'vacant and ready'. Keeping room status information up-to-date requires close coordination between the front office desk and housekeeping.
- Now days all hotels have computerized room status information system, where, as soon as guest checks out, the front desk enters the departure into the computer. This information is received by housekeeping via the computer terminal located in the housekeeping department.

When the housekeeping department is done with cleaning and inspection of the room, it enters this information into its departmental terminal. This information is received on the front-office terminal and it puts the room on sale.

The housekeeping department also receives other important information from the front office, which requires special attention.

ii. **VIPs in the House:** This information is essential so that the staff can take a little extra care and precautions in cleaning and supervising VIP rooms and also in placing special amenities as per the VIP category.

iii. **Groups in the House:** The group room's list must be provided before the group's arrival as groups tend to move together in terms of arrival, departure, sightseeing tours and meals. Their rooms need to be readied together in view of strict time parameters. This is particularly crucial when the turnover is high and rooms are experiencing back-to-back occupancy.

iv. **Crew in the House:** Under normal circumstances, airlines crews are allotted a given set of rooms on a particular floor. However, sometimes, the arrival of a crew and the departure of another crew from the same airline may overlap. In such circumstances, it is important for the allotted rooms to be cleaned within a short period of time. Also, because of odd timings of international flights, these crew rooms may display a 'do not disturb' card (DND) at times when other guests are normally out, which the housekeeping schedule must take into account.

v. **Flowers:** Sometimes the management extends its compliments to a guest with a special gesture of flower arrangement in the room or a garland at arrival as recognition of the importance of the person. This requirement of floral decorations for certain guests is conveyed to housekeeping by the front office on a daily basis.

vi. **Uniforms:** Apart from the communications mentioned, the front office staff depends on housekeeping for the provision of clean uniforms.

Coordination with Maintenance Department

The maintenance department is responsible for the provision of engineering facilities that contribute to the comfort of guests and increase the efficiency of staff. The housekeeping department depends on maintenance to keep things in order. While carrying out their scheduled work, housekeeping employees may find some deficiencies in the hotel facilities, such as faulty electrical plugs, dripping faucets, leaking pipes, or malfunctioning air-conditioning units, or WC cisterns. The housekeeping department often takes the first steps in maintenance functions for which the maintenance department is ultimately responsible. However, these deficiencies and faults should be immediately reported to maintenance. A need for urgent repairs is reported to maintenance over telephone and these requests are usually dealt with promptly if the rapport between the two departments is good.

There are various heads under which maintenance work is done:

Electrical work Faulty air conditioning and heating; fused bulbs; lights and lamps that are not functioning; defective plugs and plug points; short circuits; and faulty geysers, refrigerators, and mini bars fall under this category.

Boiler work This is necessary to maintain a supply of hot water to guestrooms.

Mechanical work This entails repair or replacement of any faulty equipment, such as vacuum cleaners, ice-cube machines, and so on.

Plumbing work This deals with faulty faucets, showers, drainage systems, water closets, and so on.

Masonry work This involves construction and civil work using materials such as bricks, mortar, cement, stone, and paint.

Carpentry work Broken or shaky furniture, mirrors and cupboards in less than peak condition, and fresh woodwork are all part of this.

To look at it another way, in terms of frequency, urgency, and complexity of the job, there are three levels of maintenance work.

Routine maintenance This involves maintenance activities that relate to the general upkeep of the hotel. They occur on a regular basis, daily or weekly, and require minimal training or skills. These activities do not call for the making out of a formal work order, and no records are maintained for them. Most of these routine maintenance activities are carried out by housekeeping. Proper care of many surfaces and materials by housekeeping personnel is the first step in the overall maintenance programme for the property. Examples of such activities are replacement of fused light bulbs, polishing of furniture, cleaning of windows and floors, and so on. The maintenance department, in coordination with housekeeping, follows a routine maintenance schedule in which an all-purpose engineer, referred to as the Ken Fix It man, is assigned to handle all the routine maintenance tasks on all the floors, usually at a frequency of three months. This ensures that all rooms go through Ken Fix It four times annually. The room is blocked for 3–4 days to carry out Ken Fix It tasks along with thorough cleaning. The maintenance Ken Fix It tasks include painting and polishing, carpet shampooing, heavy pest control, dry cleaning of curtains, replating all chrome fixtures, servicing of electrical appliances such as minibar, AC and television, servicing of electrical points and wires, and so on. A sample Ken Fix It checklist is presented in Exhibit 2.30.

Exhibit 2.30 Sample Ken Fix It maintenance checklist

Ken Fixit maintenance checklist							
Sl. No.	Punch-list	Date: .... Room No.	Attended by	Remarks of Maintenance Supervisor	Signature of Maintenance Supervisor	Remarks of Housekeeping Supervisor	Signature of Housekeeping Supervisor
A.	Doors & peripheral areas						
1.	Frame						
2.	Hinges						
3.	Knob						
4.	Handle						
5.	Safety latch						
6.	Peep hole						
7.	Double lock						

Preventive maintenance This is a systematic approach to maintenance in which situations are identified and corrected on a regular basis to control costs and keep larger problems from occurring. It involves inspections, minor corrections, and initiation of work orders.

Inspections During the normal course of their duties, housekeeping personnel carry out inspections of most areas. Housekeeping associates and supervisors regularly check for leaking faucets, chipped caulking around bathroom fixtures, fused bulbs, AC malfunctions, and so on.

Minor corrections Problems of a greater magnitude are avoided if minor repairs are attended to promptly. If communication between housekeeping and maintenance is efficient, minor repairs will be rectified by the maintenance department even as the associate is cleaning the guestroom.

Initiation of work orders Preventive maintenance sometimes identifies problems that are beyond the limited scope of minor corrections. The necessary work is then referred to the maintenance department through a formal work-order system. The chief maintenance officer or the chief engineer then schedules this maintenance work to be done. A sample SOP for preventive maintenance in guestrooms is presented in Exhibit 2.31.

Exhibit 2.31 Sample SOP for preventive maintenance procedure for housekeeping department

SOP Name:	**Preventive maintenance procedure for HK department**		
Effective Date:	**23.12.2019**	**SOP Author:**	**Shefali Shyam**
SOP No. :	**108**	**SOP Approver:**	**Vijay Dewan**
For Job title:	**EHK, Floor Supervisor**	**SOP Owner:**	**Hotel Sundown, Coorg**

Objective: To ensure timely maintenance of guestroom furniture, fixtures & fittings and standard contents.

Procedure	Standard
1. Preparation of snag list	• Floor supervisor to prepare snag list for rooms on particular floor, raise a work order and inform EHK.

Scheduled maintenance This involves maintenance work initiated by a work order. Work orders are key elements in the communication and coordination between housekeeping and maintenance.

The procedure for scheduled maintenance is described in this section. The moment a housekeeping personnel detects a problem that requires attention from maintenance, she calls the housekeeping control desk, stating the nature of the problem, the kind of assistance required, and the location where it is required. The control desk fills out a work order form (see Exhibit 2.32) in triplicate, each copy being of a different colour. One copy is sent to the executive housekeeper and two copies to maintenance. The chief engineer keeps one of these copies and gives the other to the tradesperson assigned to do the repair. When the job is completed, a copy of the tradesperson's completed work order is sent to the executive housekeeper for acknowledgement of work satisfactorily completed. If this copy is not sent to the executive housekeeper within an appropriate period of time, housekeeping issues another work order, which signals maintenance to provide a status report on the requested repair.

Exhibit 2.32 Sample work order form

Hotel Spring Leaves International

MAINTENANCE WORK ORDER FORM

Time.............Date.........................
By...
Location.......................................
Problem..
....
....
....
....
Assigned To.......................................
Date Compl.......................................
Time Spent.......................................
Completed By.......................................
Remarks.......................................
....
....

Check (X) indicates unsatisfactory condition
Explain Check in Remarks section.

Bedroom

( ) Walls	( ) Woodwork	( ) Doors
( ) Ceiling	( ) Television	( ) Light
( ) Floors	( ) AC Unit	( ) Blinds
( ) Windows		( ) Drapes

Remarks.......................................
....

Bathroom

( ) Faucets	( ) Drains	( ) Shower
( ) Lights	( ) Wallpaper	( ) Paints
( ) Tiles	( ) Glass	( ) Door
( ) Accessories	( ) Window	

REMARKS.......................................

Nowadays, most hotels install a computerized maintenance management system (CMMS) to catapult them from the strategy colloquially called 'bust n' fix' to one of proactive maintenance. Job orders in such hotels are generated through the computerised system.

Engineering and maintenance departments in most hotels keep records of all equipment operated by housekeeping personnel. Equipment data cards contain basic information about these pieces of equipment. The purpose is to provide documentation of all maintenance activity on a given piece of equipment.

On the part of the housekeeping department, its personnel should cooperate with maintenance by getting room doors unlocked promptly when repairs are being done. Housekeeping should also have maintenance rooms already stripped when renovation, restoration, refurbishment or redecoration is to take place and should have furniture to be removed for repair appropriately labelled.

Coordination with Security Department

The coordination here is mainly concerned with the prevention of fire and thefts and the safekeeping of keys and lost property. There are so many security hazards on the floors that this liaison is particularly important, and the housekeeper cooperates by endeavouring to see that housekeeping staff are aware of the hazards. Housekeeping personnel should also report anything of a suspicious nature immediately to the security staff. A hotel guestroom should be the most private of places and the hotel staff must ensure their guests' privacy and security. However, a guest may take advantage of this privacy and may be engaged in certain illegal activities such as gambling, smuggling, and so on. Housekeeping personnel have to be alert to this risk and seek the security department's intervention if necessary. Situations such as room thefts, damages by guests, disturbances caused by in-room guests, or guest fatalities too call for coordination with security. The security department is responsible for conducting training sessions on handling emergency situations for the staff. For example, they conduct fire drills to train staff to gear up in a fire emergency.

Coordination with Food and Beverage Department

The food and beverage (F&B) department consists of both the service staff as well as the kitchen staff. The coordination of housekeeping with the restaurants and banquet halls is mainly concerned with the provision of linen and uniforms. The linen room supervisor, under the supervision of the executive housekeeper, needs to have sufficient stock of clean napery to meet the demands of the F&B department's restaurant and banquet functions. On his/her part, the restaurant manager should ensure that the time set for the exchange of linen is respected; that linen is not lost or misused; and that intimation of forthcoming banquet functions is conveyed to housekeeping well in advance. Besides extra/special linen, housekeeping may also have to arrange for flower decorations for banquets.

Coordination between the two departments becomes particularly necessary in the case of room service, so that friction does not arise over matters such as waiters not collecting trays from guestrooms or room service staff leaving soiled trays in the corridors or causing extra work through careless spills on the carpet.

In many hotels, housekeeping also looks after pest control in restaurants, kitchens, and stores attached to them. Special cleaning of these areas calls for coordination with the housekeeping department. Both restaurant and kitchen staff require clean uniforms on a daily basis, for which too they need to communicate with housekeeping. Provision of staff meals for housekeeping personnel, on the other hand, is the responsibility of the kitchen staff.

Coordination with Stores

Coordination with stores ensures the availability of day-to-day necessities of house-keeping. Larger hotels have a store attached to the housekeeping department that stocks linen, supplies, and so on. Smaller hotels may stock them in the general store, except for linen, which is sent to the housekeeping department on purchase. Communication with stores is by way of a requisition/indent form, which housekeeping sends to stores when it requires certain items. The format shown in Exhibit 2.33 may be used.

Coordination with Human Resources Department

Housekeeping coordinates with the human resources department for recruitment of housekeeping staff; managing their salaries and wages; addressing indiscipline; following through grievance procedures; issuing identity cards for employees; running induction programmes; maintaining locker facilities; completing income tax formalities; effecting transfers, promotions, appraisals, and exit formalities; procuring trainees; and organizing training sessions.

Coordination with Purchase Department

The purchase department procures out-of-stock items for housekeeping, such as guest supplies and amenities, stationery, linen, cleaning materials and equipment, and so on. Housekeeping should convey their requirements to purchase by way of advance notice in the form of a purchase requisition (Exhibit 2.34).

Exhibit 2.33 Sample stores requisition form

Hotel Snowflakes

STORES REQUISITION FORM

Date: ....

Items required on: .... Items indented on: ....

S. no	Ledger folio no	Name of item	Unit	Stock in hand	Quantity indented	Quantity issued	Rate	Amount

Signature of housekeeper: .... Signature of storekeeper: ....

Exhibit 2.34 Sample purchase requisition form

Hotel Greenwoods Continental

PURCHASE REQUISITION FORM

No. 3456 Date: ....

S. No.	Items required	Unit	Specification	Cost	Reorder level	Quantity in stock	Quantity to order	Remarks

Signature of HOD:...................... Approved by: Finance controller...................

Coordination with Sales and Marketing

The sales and marketing department informs housekeeping of the occupancy forecast for the entire year, which is broken up monthwise. This enables housekeeping to budget for the necessary expenses. An important contribution of the housekeeping staff to hotel sales is ensuring that repeat business is obtained by providing the level of cleanliness and service that meets or exceeds guest expectations. The sales and marketing team also has to depend on housekeeping for their uniforms. Two things are certain in the hotel business: no matter how many guests a salesperson brings in the door, if housekeeping does not execute its function with excellence, the guests will not be coming back. Vice versa, no matter how well-kept the rooms, if the sales staff do not bring potential guests to the hotel, occupancy falls. Coordination also takes place between the two departments when there are media shoots and property showcasing tours to be organized.

Coordination with Laundry

This applies when the laundry is under the supervision and control of a laundry manager. Without clean linen, the room associates simply cannot operate. During periods of full occupancy, the housekeeper needs a fast turnaround of linen from the laundry, but should not always be making an 'emergency' demand for them. As far as possible, the housekeeper should stick to the schedule for the laundry. In return, the laundry should provide an acceptable standard of service with regard to laundering. Housekeeping also needs to coordinate with the laundry with regard to housekeeping employees' uniforms and those of other departments as well.

The Professional Housekeeper

A professional housekeeper is one who contributes to the organizational goals directly or indirectly by guiding the efforts of her personnel, keeping in mind the vision, mission, values, objectives, and culture of the organization. A successful housekeeper is one who learns the art of inspiring others to accomplish goals with concern for and commitment to efficiency, quality, and cost control. The housekeeper today needs to be not only technically sound but also a good manager with conceptual abilities. The job profile of the housekeeper nowadays includes not only operational responsibilities, but also management processes such as planning, organizing, coordinating, staffing, directing, and controlling. Management may be defined as 'the art of getting things done through people', and this is what a professional housekeeper does.

The Management Process

Figure 2.11 presents the management process the housekeeper has to follow.

Planning Planning is the specification of goals and the means to accomplish those goals by the housekeeper. It involves seven basic activities:

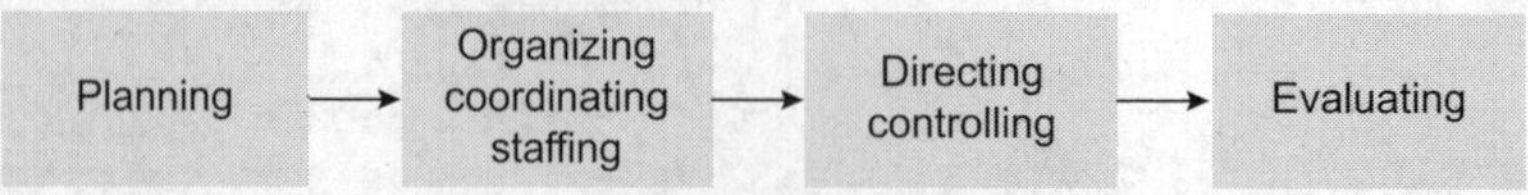

Fig. 2.11 The management process

Forecasting Establishing where present courses will lead.

Setting objectives Determining desired results.

Developing strategies Deciding how and when to achieve goals.

Programming Establishing priorities, sequence, and timing of steps to be taken.

Budgeting Allocating resources.

Setting procedures Standardizing methods of execution.

Developing policies Making standing decisions on important recurring matters.

Organizing and coordinating Organizing involves arranging and delegating work for the accomplishment of an objective. Coordination involves activities designed to create a relationship among all of the organization's efforts to accomplish a common goal. The activities here are as follows:

Establishing an organizational structure Drawing up an organization chart.

Delineating relationships Defining liaison lines to facilitate coordination.

Creating position descriptions Defining the scope, relationships, responsibilities, and authority of each member of the organization.

Establishing position qualifications Defining the qualifications for people in each position.

Staffing Staffing involves people. Leadership now comes into play and communication is established to ensure that understanding takes place. There are four activities:

Selecting employees Recruiting qualified people for each position.

Orienting employees Familiarizing new people with their environment.

Training Making people proficient at their tasks through instruction and practice.

Developing Improving their knowledge, attitude, and skills.

Directing The earlier processes of management might be performed before an operation gets underway. The following management activities are carried out when the operation is in process. There are five activities in the directing of operations:

Delegating Assigning responsibility and accountability for results.

Motivating Persuading and inspiring people to take desired action.

Coordinating Relating efforts in the most efficient combination.

Managing differences Encouraging independent thought while resolving conflict.

Managing change Stimulating creativity and innovation in achieving goals.

Controlling This process involves the control of operations and activities to ensure progress toward the desired objectives. The basic activities in controlling are:

Establishing a reporting system Determining what critical data are needed.

Developing performance standards Setting conditions that will exist when key duties are well done.

Evaluating Evaluating is the management function of assessing the extent to which planned goals are in fact attained. The activities here are:

Measuring results Ascertaining the extent of deviation from goals and standards.

Taking corrective action Adjusting plans, counselling to help attain standards, re-planning, and repeating the several management functions as necessary.

Rewarding Praising, remunerating, or administering discipline.

There has thus been a tremendous change in the job description and job specifications of the professional housekeeper.

Minimum Requirements

The following are the minimum requirements for a person applying for an executive housekeeper's post:

Educational qualifications An executive housekeeper should be a graduate in hotel management with postgraduate qualifications in management, which could be either business administration or human resources management. Knowledge of computers would be compulsory; an additional qualification in interior designing would be an advantage.

Age limit The age limit used to be a criterion for the post of executive housekeeper, but this factor may no longer be significant. Today there are successful executive housekeepers as young as in their mid-20s. Importance is given, rather, to an individual's performance, efficiency, effectiveness, and productivity.

Equipment skills The shift from manual to mechanical equipment is already underway. Technology is penetrating the housekeeping department rapidly. Efficient, low-noise, and cost-effective equipment of high quality is being manufactured, keeping ergonomics in mind as well. Executive housekeepers need to understand the working principles of all such equipment and train their team members accordingly.

Physical characteristics Physical fitness is a critical attribute of the housekeeper since housekeeping in a hotel is a physically demanding job that includes varied tasks and some of these could affect one's health. The main risk factors are a heavy physical workload and excessive bodily motion, which may leave the individual vulnerable to back injuries. Excessive walking, stooping, squatting, kneeling, stretching, bending, twisting, and crouching can have their ill effects. Studies have shown that an executive housekeeper in a five-star hotel walks more than 8 kilometres per day.

Mental traits A skill is an individual's ability to translate knowledge into action. Skills are not inborn. They can be developed through practice and experience. The mental skills and traits of a housekeeper would encompass conceptualization and human relations skills and technical proficiency. Conceptualization encompasses ideas, technical ability, and skill with people. While both conceptual and technical competence are needed for good decision-making, human relations skills are essential for a good leader.

Personality The personality of a person is an innate quality that directs all their activities. Besides being a good manager, a housekeeper should be an effective leader who can motivate and inspire his/her personnel. The emphasis is on the housekeeper's intelligence, emotional, and spiritual quotients. Since housekeeping is a work-intensive department, an insight into the complexities of human behaviour is vital.

Language skills With the world becoming smaller and progressing towards a global village, the movement of international tourists has increased. Language and communication skills have thus become an integral part of the hospitality industry. Housekeepers should not only be adept in English and the local languages, but also in a few foreign languages. They should also be familiar with the culture, values, and traditions of not only their own country but also of tourists who come from different countries.

Special requirements As an executive housekeeper, one should:

- Derive maximum job satisfaction even though housekeeping is considered a thankless job.
- Be an effective leader and a good team player.
- Update and implement the latest trends in the hospitality industry.
- Innovate and experiment with new concepts.
- Accept and welcome change.
- Maintain good human relations in the organization.
- Handle stress effectively.

A professional housekeeper needs to be a knowledge manager. New concepts are being experimented with every day, throughout the world, and the housekeeper should keep pace in order to meet new challenges and competition.

Skills of an Ideal Housekeeper

An ideal housekeeper possesses specific skills to manage smooth housekeeping operations.

Technical An EHK is expected to resolve any technical problems better than the supervisors. The EHK should train the supervisors and the room attendants too if needed on technical aspects of the job. For instance, training associates in dilution and usage of chemicals.

Managerial skills To be a manager means leading people to achieve their given objectives. The EHK should lead and motivate the entire housekeeping team to achieve work related goals. For this, the housekeeper must possess good communication skills and serve as a role model to the subordinates. The EHK is the link between the top management and her employees.

Conceptual Conceptual skills relate to vision and ability to imagine and anticipate events and ideas. Housekeepers should be able to anticipate events and emergencies during their daily routine and make decisions to meet eventualities. For example, renovation of a room. The EHK will visualize when renovation should happen, what resources and funds will be required and the time by which it will be completed.

Resources Handled by Housekeepers

The main resources handled by housekeepers can be categorised as the 5 M's – men, machinery, material, minutes and money. As an individual rises in rung in housekeeping, he/she becomes adept in handling these resources and achieves success as a manager.

Men The resource, 'men' encompasses the housekeeping team, irrespective of gender. The housekeeping team is typically the largest workforce in an accommodation property and a professional housekeeper must have excellent man-management skills to keep together a highly motivated and efficient team.

Machinery Housekeeping has come a long way from being a manually intensive operation to a hybrid one where the workforce relies heavily on cutting edge equipment and technology to achieve clinically clean standards and smooth operations leading to guest satisfaction.

Material Housekeepers now have scientifically designed solutions by enterprising vendors at their disposal, whether it is microfibre mops and dusters, efficient one-step green cleaning chemicals or nanotechnology enabled materials. There is constant research being carried out globally in making better cleaning materials and linen and housekeepers must keep abreast of the latest developments in this field.

Minutes Time is of great essence to a housekeeper as any delays in releasing rooms leads to loss of revenue, rooms being the most perishable commodities in a hotel.

Money Housekeeping has an immense role in a hotel earning profits through loyal repeat customers but it is erroneously considered a department which is cost incurring rather than revenue earning. Hence, housekeepers are always cautious while budgeting their operations. Intelligent budget formulation is an art they need to be adept in, so that essential resources for ensuring smooth operations are allocated to the department.

Housekeeping in Other Institutions

While hotels operate on a commercial basis, other institutions such as hostels, hospitals, and residential homes are establishments that satisfy social needs. In such welfare sectors, a reasonable standard of cleanliness and comfort is expected at the lowest cost. Dealing with patients in hospitals or with students in hostels is very different from dealing with hotel guests. Housekeeping is carried out in various types of institutions, the important ones among them being hospitals, hostels, residential homes, offices, and art galleries, museums, libraries, and archives. This is referred to as institutional housekeeping.

Hospitals

In hospitals, hygiene and cleanliness are of particular importance in reducing the threat of cross infection, with the result that housekeeping here is highly organized. It extends to wards, laboratories, administrative areas, doctors' chambers, lecture rooms, treatment rooms, waiting areas, mortuaries, kitchens, dining areas, and high-risk areas—operation theatres, intensive care units (ICUs), transplant units, premature baby units, and isolation wards. The organizational structure of a housekeeping department in a hospital (Figure 2.12) varies according to the type and size of the hospital.

The scope of hospital housekeeping is enormous. Here, control of dust and germs is so important that the cleaning equipment may have features that are not to be found in other establishments, such as:

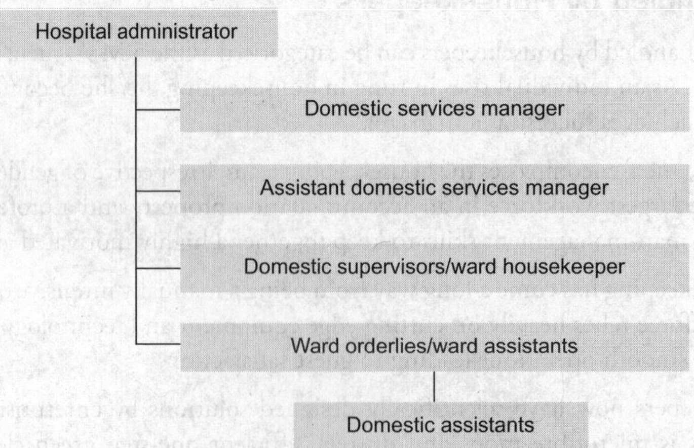

Fig. 2.12 Organizational structure of a housekeeping department in a hospital

- Electrical equipment fitted with extra filters to reduce the risk of dust distribution.
- Electrical equipment fitted with silencers to minimize irritation to patients.
- Colours used to identify equipment for certain jobs, for example, green cloths, buckets, mops, gloves, and so on, for toilet areas; pink for kitchen areas; and so on.

Cleaning methods may also differ slightly. For example:

- Dusting is carried out with damp cloths only, so that dust is better controlled.
- Sweeping is carried out using mops with heads that can be sterilized or disposed of after each cleaning session.
- Spray cleaning is carried out regularly using high-speed machinery that perform in such a way that highly resistant finishes are obtained on floorings.
- Dust-control mats are used extensively and surfaces tend to be non-absorbent, making them easy to clean and less likely to retain dust.

The responsibilities of a hospital housekeeping team may include:

- Maintaining a high degree of cleanliness and hygiene with a focus on health.
- Ensuring safety and security.
- Pest control.
- Control over contracted cleaning agencies.
- Providing staff uniforms.
- Laundering hospital linen, uniforms, and surgical suits. This involves sterilization of linen in autoclave too.

In the wards, responsibilities also include:

- Cleaning and bed-making, which must be done with the least amount of disturbance to the patients.
- Arranging flowers.
- Delivering and collecting patients' mail.
- Caring for clothes and personal belongings.
- Terminal cleaning of rooms, which must be done soon after a patient is discharged and before a new patient is admitted to the room. This includes total disinfection of the room, including all furniture and fixtures. Linen is subjected to a high-temperature wash, which is called a 'terminal wash'.

Precautions All employees working in high-risk areas must wear protective clothing and be gowned and masked if required. Gowns may be of the disposable variety or made of cotton. Once used, they should be treated as infected items and will require specific disinfection. Hands must be washed before entering, before cleaning, and after leaving a unit to prevent spreading of infection. Cleaning materials and agents must be suitably coded and, after use, they must be disinfected or changed. Waste arising in isolation areas must be disposed of separately and appropriately. Syringes and sharp articles must be disposed of appropriately.

Hostels

Hostels for young people and university halls of residence are medium- to long-stay establishments. In order to cater for the longer periods of stay, hostels must provide considerably more storage space than is found in hotels. The typical study-bedroom will contain a wardrobe, a desk, shelves, a washbasin,

a bed, drawers, and either a pin board or walls designed in such a way that the occupant can put up posters and such without causing any damage. Hostels are provided by the YMCA, YWCA, various universities, working women's associations, and so on. Room letting and allocation are usually carried out by an administrator, otherwise called a warden or bursar. This person takes overall responsibility and the day-to-day running of the establishment is delegated to managers with specialized knowledge in individual areas such as catering and housekeeping. Staff are kept to a minimum, simple work procedures are adopted, and students/occupants may be expected to make their own beds, keep their rooms tidy, and so on. Rooms may be cleaned weekly and, apart from public areas, there may be little or no cleaning at weekends. As a result, cleaning staff may be part-time, with most of their work being concerned with the maintenance of public areas (game rooms, TV lounges, the student's mess, and so on), dealing with linen, and vacuuming or buffing of corridors. Periodic heavy cleaning, repairs, and maintenance are carried out during the vacation period. The organization chart of a hostel of about 500 rooms is shown in Figure 2.13:

The responsibilities of the housekeeper here will be

- maintaining cleanliness and hygiene.
- reporting and checking on maintenance work.
- managing staffing.
- managing catering.
- undertaking budgetary control.
- ensuring the well-being and discipline of students.
- managing room keys and handling students' mail.
- providing security.
- undertaking pest control.
- maintaining and providing linen.
- handling lost property.
- undertaking stock control.

An inventory of all items must be taken at the time of a student vacating the hostel. Usually some amount of money is taken as a caution deposit at the time of allotting a student to a room, to cover the costs of any damage or pilferage. This deposit must be processed accordingly at the time of his/her vacating.

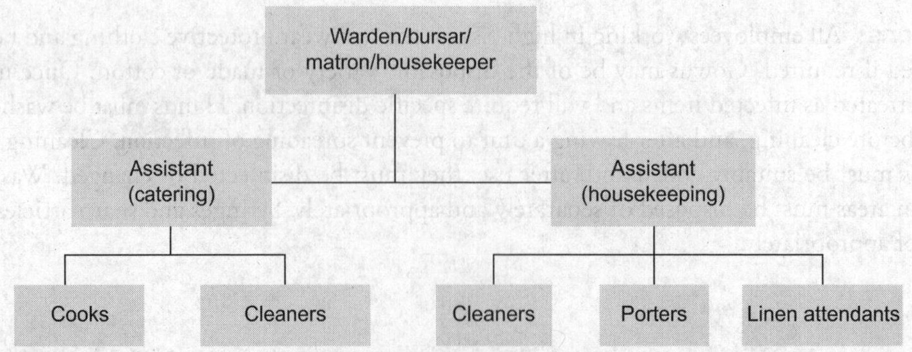

Fig. 2.13 Organization chart of a 500-room hostel

Universities

In large universities, low-cost housekeeping may be undertaken, with the number of staff varying according to the area of the campus, but with certainly not as large a workforce as in hotels of a comparable size. Although some universities do get government grants, they are largely self-financing organizations and they must at least break even at the end of any financial year though revenues are often not as high as in the hospitality industry. This consideration can dictate the employment of more modest resources towards housekeeping. The organizational structure of housekeeping staff at a university may be as shown in Figure 2.14.

The university's housekeeping staff may consist of the following roles:

- The estate manager is in charge of building maintenance and repairs.
- The catering manager is in charge of the food and beverage outlets, including their cleaning.
- The service manager is in charge of all public areas, lecture rooms, and other teaching areas.
- The accommodation manager is in charge of the cleanliness and organization of all student, staff and guest accommodations.

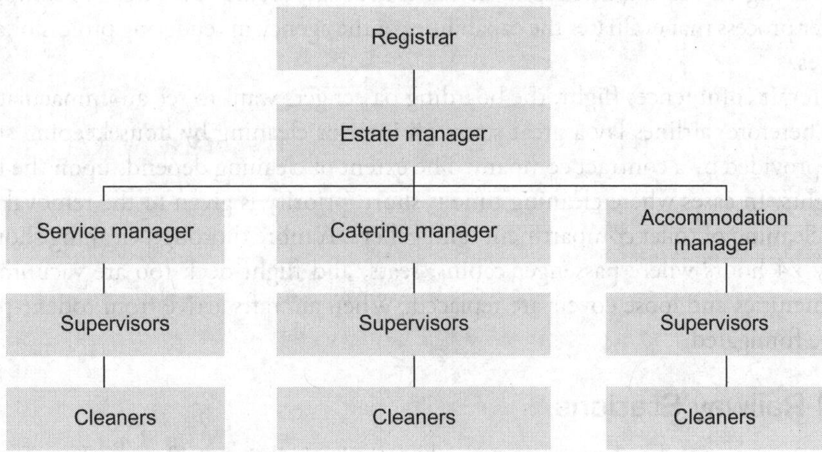

Fig. 2.14 Organization chart of university housekeeping staff

Residential Homes

These establishments include old-age homes, nursing homes, convalescence homes, destitute children's homes, hospices, and homes for the mentally or physically challenged. They may be privately owned or run by a local authority. The key word here is 'homes'—it is essential to create a happy, homely atmosphere. The residents here could themselves be involved in housekeeping activities, according to their capabilities. People working on the staff here require dedication and a generous, patient temperament. In many of these places, the staff in charge are usually trained nurses, with only a limited knowledge of cleaning, and standards therefore, depend very much on the common sense of the cleaning staff.

Airports and Aircrafts

Airports serve as hub to millions of passengers who travel in and out of a country or state. Airports are constructed with huge investments in interiors and enhancing the life of these assets by applying the right cleaning methodology and products is the onus of housekeeping; thus, the selection of cleaning agents & preparation of cleaning plan plays a vital role. Airports being large structures with dynamic environment subjected to constant usage, must have the right balance of manpower and machinery to ensure consistency in standards throughout the operations. Since airports cater to huge footfalls, housekeepers must have enough backup in terms of resources and materials to ensure uninterrupted operations. To ensure effectiveness of cleaning and hygiene operations, it is vital for housekeepers to make sure they are implemented as per defined protocol.

It is important that housekeeping operations at the airports are well defined and meet international standards. Most airports are operational round the clock, hence the cleaning activity is planned keeping in mind the passenger flow. Moreover, being public spaces, they are in line of scrutiny by passengers. Ensuring that the vast number of touch points (ticketing kiosks, escalator & travellator railings, luggage trays used by passengers during security check, washrooms, seating areas, etc.) are cleaned and sanitized regularly to inhibit bacterial growth and dedicated housekeeping teams carry out this job seamlessly throughout the day ensuring safety of passengers. Sophisticated cleaning machines are also used to achieve efficiency. The housekeeping team at airport leads the way in making air travel safe, reinstating confidence in passengers. Most housekeeping activities at an airport are outsourced to competent agencies through a tender process that evaluates the capabilities of the agency in rendering professional commercial cleaning services.

When an aircraft commences flight, the boarding passengers want to see an immaculately clean and safe interior. Therefore, airlines lay a great stress on interior cleaning by housekeeping staff, which in most cases are provided by a contract company. The extent of cleaning depends upon the time available in between flights. In cases where cleaning time is short, priority is given to the removal of refuse and dry waste and cleaning of toilet compartments and galleys. A more thorough cleaning should be carried out once every 24 hours where passenger cabins, seats, and flight deck too are vacuum-cleaned and disinfected. Amenities and loose covers are replaced. When aircrafts arrive from rodent-prone regions, they need to be fumigated.

Metro and Railway Stations

Metro and railway stations must be kept clean and hygienic at all times. The number of travellers using trains as modes of transport is huge and hence the cleaning standards at the platforms, concourse, restrooms and circulation areas around the stations must conform to international standards. At both metro and railway stations, housekeeping operations are outsourced based on tenders. Metro stations have hi-tech machines to carry out cleaning of large areas. Touchpoints are cleaned and sanitised regularly. Sustainable, hygienic waste management is important at stations.

Cruise Ships

Housekeeping work on cruises is similar to what housekeeping responsibilities are in a hotel. Housekeepers here are responsible for making cabins or staterooms comfortable for the guests apart from laundry pickups and delivery and general cleaning of common areas in the ship. Cleaning of cruises is to be done in compliance with Hazard Analysis and Critical Control Point (HACCP) regulations as hygiene is of utmost importance. Personalized butler service for suite guests is also provided by the housekeeping department.

Art Galleries, Museums, Libraries, and Archives

The scope of housekeeping at these establishments includes maintaining display areas, exhibits, old books, documents, and manuscripts. Particular problems include dust control across extensive areas of shelves and a quantity of books and also control of UV-ray exposure to prevent deterioration of documents. The organization and supervision of cleaning and maintenance form part of the curator's or librarian's job description.

Offices

Additional housekeeping factors here, apart from routine cleaning, include the following:

- Deep cleaning must be completed before or after office hours.
- Maintenance of indoor plants and flower arrangements must be regularly attended to.
- Disposal of confidential waste must take place by way of a shredder and/or incineration.

Facilities Management Companies

Facilities management companies ensure that buildings, including the infrastructure and services, meet the needs of people who work there and provide the most suitable working environment for their employees and their activities. These companies provide services such as housekeeping, security, and parking, and building management services such as maintenance of heating, ventilation, and air conditioning (HVAC) on contract basis. Many institutions have a facilities manager and his team on rolls. Facilities management is discussed in further detail in Chapter 28.

A Career in Housekeeping

A person who decides to take up housekeeping as a career, has several options. Housekeepers find lucrative avenues and are in high demand not only in the hotel industry but many other institutions and establishments. Listed below are avenues open to a person who has passion for housekeeping.

- Hotels and resorts
- Service apartments
- Private hospitals
- Corporate and government guest houses
- Airlines, airports
- Cruise liners
- Metro stations
- Malls, food courts and multiplexes
- Stand-alone restaurants
- Commercial offices
- Convention centers, entertainment centers, exhibition centers, museums & theme parks
- Residential apartments
- Universities, schools & hostels
- Defence establishments

- Celebrity and VIP homes
- Facilities management companies

In an hotel, the entry level designation is that of a room attendant and responsibilities mainly include cleaning of guest rooms and public areas. There is no short cut to higher rung as it is at this level that one learns to work in a team to ensure smooth operations leading to guest satisfaction. Based on merit, a student can also get in as Hotel Operations Trainee (HOT) in Housekeeping or as Management Trainee (MT). The 12 – 18 months HOT programme entails thorough hands-on training in rooms division operations. The 18 – 24 months of MT programme leads to management positions in front line housekeeping operations and entails intensive training in rooms division and opportunity to perform team leading tasks, leadership training sessions and management assignments. For a persevering individual, the rise on ladder to the higher rung is rapid in this field.

The middle level consists of supervisors. It is very important for someone who wishes to make a career in housekeeping to have a thorough knowledge and hands on experience of the work at the entry and middle levels, as that gives one a complete insight into what a typical housekeeping day is about and shapes an individual's personality to tackle new challenges effectively every day, with suaveness. A good manager in accommodation operation is one who can put systems in place and execute cleaning routines so as to ensure cleanliness, hygiene and safety before the necessity to clean the establishment is observable.

To achieve these goals, within the budget and resources that have been allocated and without any adverse staff issues, is a skill that makes one a valuable asset to the hotel. This has to be developed

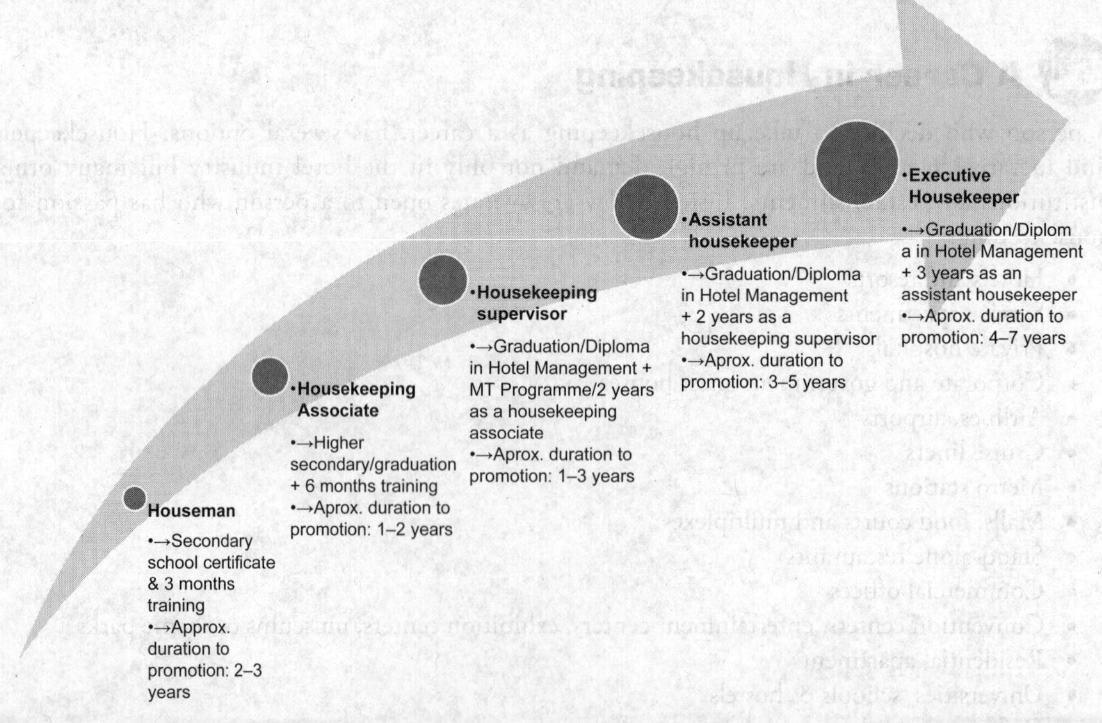

Fig. 2.15 Career path in housekeeping in hotels

through one's own efforts, education, help of mentors, past data and guidance from the management and a successful working model for that property is then synthesized. Once this is mastered, one can help train and produce more such managers.

Moving on to higher levels of the rung, one can become an Executive Housekeeper of a property, Director of Housekeeping for a chain of hotels and later, after gaining some experience as a leader, Rooms Division Manager (RDM) of a stand-alone property. Many housekeepers are now elevated to General Managers or Vice President-Operations of properties as they are familiar with every nook and corner of the hotel and are efficient resource managers. A typical career path to become an executive housekeeper is traced in Figure 2.15. A housekeeper can also take up consultancies or start his/her own company, delivering housekeeping services or branch into facilities management. Seasoned housekeepers are in high demand in sectors such as hospitals and airports to head their facilities management.

Entrepreneurship in Housekeeping

Many housekeepers, applying their resource management skills, go the entrepreneurship way and start their own cleaning businesses. The main inducement for the change in career path towards entrepreneurship is that one gets complete control of operation and despite risks, a successfully run cleaning business earns good profits. The scope is immense and the start-up costs are comparatively lower than other businesses. Housekeepers turned entrepreneurs are largely successful since they have inherent traits that make for an ideal entrepreneur – hardworking, disciplined, punctual, perfectionist, creative, organised, intensely committed, persevering, taking challenges head-on, finding practical solutions to problems, and so on.

Concept of Entrepreneurship

As per the Oxford dictionary, entrepreneurship is an individual undertaking to supply a good or service to the market for a profit. An entrepreneur sees new opportunity in an idea and is willing to take a risk. Where an employee is certain to be paid for their service, an entrepreneurial undertaking is a venture in which the outcome of the endeavour is not certain.

Making Business Plans

Before chalking out a business plan, one must decide what type of cleaning business they want to start, whether domestic cleaning, commercial cleaning, institutional cleaning or specialised cleaning. Domestic cleaning would entail cleaning people's homes; commercial cleaning involves cleaning offices, shops and other business premises. Institutional cleaning includes cleaning schools, hostels, libraries, museums and such places. Specialised cleaning involves a range of technically advanced cleaning activities such as carpet cleaning, façade cleaning, dome-roof cleaning and so on. This decision will depend on the regional requirement of the locality and would need market research to be done. Once the target market is established, business plans can be tailored.

A successful business is backed by a focused business plan. A business plan is a concise document that spells out aims and objectives of the business and how they are to be achieved. The outline of a business plan consists of the following:

Company details		**Mission statement**	
proposed name, address and contact details of the business, information on the management of the business		a one-line summary of the goal of the business	
Need/Problem and solution	**Competitors**	**Unique value proposition/USP**	**Target market**
defining a need in the locality that requires solution being fulfilled by the business idea proposed	list of local market players offering similar services, their strengths and weaknesses	the unique offering of the business that sets it apart from competitors	the demographics and size of the market being served by the business
Expenses	**Financials**	**Pricing strategy**	**Payment terms**
start-up costs and running costs which would include registering the business, insurance, licenses, rental, and so on	source of funding to start the business, self-financed or loan; projected profits/loss for the starting month and prediction for a year	how the services would be priced – hourly rate, square footage rate or flat rate	decision on payment options for clients, raising invoices for daily payments or monthly subscriptions
Team	**Revenue stream**	**Marketing activities**	**Timeline and new product roadmap**
key people of the business, partners and suppliers	Sources of revenue as per the business model	outlining the strategy to promote the business	a general timeline of growth of the business and introduction of new product to capture a larger market

Developing SOPs

Standard operating procedures ensure that all employees onboard the cleaning business perform the tasks systematically, as per company standards. All employees joining the company must be trained on the SOPs if expectations are to be met.

The first step in developing SOPs for the business is to list down tasks, however small, for which SOPs need to be written. The date of implementation of SOP and the developer, owner and approver of the SOP should be listed down. Next is to take up each procedure at a time and list down the objective/s of the procedure. Also put down the equipment and supplies needed to accomplish the task. Follow this up with writing down the actual procedure step by step, clearly, in simple language. Each and every step needs to be detailed with how-to's and it is practical to write down the steps while it is being performed so that nothing is missed out. It is important to test the procedure after the steps are written to fine tune the SOP. An employee should be made to follow the SOP to do the task to check its efficacy and modifications must be made accordingly. Take feedback from employees to keep improving the SOPs. The SOPs must be updated as there are changes in norms, software, equipment and so on. A template for an SOP for a cleaning business is presented in Exhibit 2.35.

Exhibit 2.35 Sample template for an SOP for cleaning business

SOP Name:	
Effective Date:	**SOP Author:**
SOP No. :	**SOP Approver:**
For Job title:	**SOP Owner:**
Objective:	

(Contd.)

Exhibit 2.35 *Contd.*

Equipment, tools & PPE needed:	Supplies needed:	
What is to be done	**How-to do**	**Additional information**

Investment

Investment is required in the business for rentals, legalities such as company registration, insurance policies and licenses, wages of workers, overheads, cleaning supplies and equipment, transport and logistics, advertising, technological interventions such as web and social media platforms and so on. Though the list seems exhaustive, the initial investment in a cleaning business is lower than most others. Self-financing, funding from investing partners, funding from government schemes for small businesses, bank loans are options to explore. In India, entrepreneurs can approach institutions such as SIDBI (Small Industries Development Bank of India), NABARD (National Bank for Agriculture and Rural Development), NSIC (National Small Industries Corporation Limited) and NCEUS (National Commission for Enterprises in the Unorganised Sector) for assistance.

Registration, Licensing and other Legalities

Some registrations and licenses are a legal requirement while others are optional and hence it is a good practice to take assistance of a law firm. Important registrations and licenses are GST (Goods and Services Tax), PAN (Permanent Account Number) and TAN (Tax Account Number) registration, company name and trademark registration, labour license and licenses for handling heavy machinery, tools, and chemicals. The entrepreneur must run the business in compliance with Minimum Wages Act and Occupational Safety, Health and Working Conditions (OSH) Code.

Insurance

The right type of insurance for the company is a necessity in cleaning business. It is a legal requirement and will also help to establish the credibility and professionalism of the business. The types of licenses involved are public liability, bonding, workers' compensation, business insurance covering building and equipment, business vehicle, and property damage insurance.

Pricing and Marketing

Pricing of services in the cleaning business can be done in any of the following ways:

Hourly rate charging per hour.

Square footage charging based on cleaning area covered in terms of square foot, a common pricing strategy for commercial cleaning.

Flat rate Specific standard rate quoted based on labour and time.

If the cleaning business is started with passion, backed by a systematic approach and proactive service, its success would be accomplished through word of mouth. It still helps to keep making an impact through social media and web platforms especially when they do not cost much. The advertising should be memorable, not intrusive. For instance, the website can offer valuable maintenance tips and have a platform where queries may be answered and feedback of services taken. Flyers too are economical ways of spreading the word about the business in the target client locality. Creative advertising would go a long way in keeping the company name in peoples' mind.

SUMMARY

The housekeeping department has often not been given its due importance in hotels, particularly in the Indian hotel industry. The volume of work undertaken by this department can easily be gauged by the fact that in a commercial hotel, the department easily employs the largest workforce. Just picture the vast expanse of area to be cleaned and maintained, the cartloads of linen to be washed, the huge amount of supplies and amenities to be handled, and one can easily understand why this department is referred to as the backbone of a hotel.

In this chapter, we have defined the term 'housekeeping', discussed its importance in hotels and its role in guest satisfaction. We have then chalked out the aims and objectives of the housekeeping department. The organizational hierarchy in the housekeeping department (at small, medium-sized, and large hotels) has been depicted in organization charts. The job descriptions listing duties and responsibilities of all housekeeping employees have been presented. The personal attributes of housekeeping staff have been discussed in detail, as this helps in the recruitment process. Ideal layouts have been outlined for the department; though many other layouts are also functional and successful. The all-important aspect of coordination and cooperation of the housekeeping department with the other hotel departments has been discussed vividly. The section on the professional housekeeper covers the managerial aspects of a housekeeper's work and the job specifications of the future-ready housekeeper. Resources handled by them are described. Housekeeping in institutions other than hotels—such as hospitals, hostels, residential homes, art galleries, and museums—has been discussed. The career path in housekeeping is discussed and in the last section a brief account of entrepreneurship in housekeeping is given.

KEY TERMS

Amenity A service or item offered to guests or placed in guestrooms for convenience and comfort, at no extra cost.

Autoclave An oven like equipment using steam under pressure in which supplies are subjected to intense heat for a specific period of time to disinfect them.

Back of the house The functional areas of the hotel in which employees have little or no guest contact, such as the engineering and maintenance department, laundry, and so on.

Back-to-back Heavy rate of check-outs and check-in activities on the same day, so that as soon as a room is made up, a new guest checks into it.

Check-in The arrival and registration of a guest at the hotel. The term is also used for a guest who has arrived and taken possession of a room and used the hotel services.

Check-out An American term adopted by hotels in India to mean a guest's departure from the hotel.

Chief engineer/Chief maintenance officer The person in charge of the engineering and maintenance department. He/she maintains a crew of plumbers, electricians, and other specialized personnel.

CMMS A 'computerized maintenance management system', installed in hotels to make sure that maintenance activities take place before the point of breakdown is reached.

Commercial cleaning A cleaning business that involves cleaning offices, shops and other business premises.

Deep cleaning Intensive or specialized cleaning undertaken in guestrooms or public areas, often conducted according to a special schedule or on a special project basis.

Departure room A room from which the guest has departed, settled the account, returned the room keys, and left the hotel. It is also called a check-out room or vacated room.

Desnagging The process of a housekeeper physically inspecting completion of snag list tasks of an area or guestroom, carried out by a maintenance worker or a project contractor and bringing up pending issues or further snags, if present; else ratifying the completion of job. Also see snag list.

DND card A 'do not disturb' card is hung outside the room to inform hotel staff or visitors that the occupant does not wish to be disturbed.

Double locked (DL) An occupied room in which the deadbolt has been turned to prohibit entry from the corridor. Only a grandmaster key or an emergency key can open it.

ELCB Electric Leakage Circuit Breaker. A safety device to protect against electric shock. It is used to protect the circuit from the electrical leakage.

Ergonomics The study of people in relation to their working environment.

Façade The exterior, front face of large buildings.

Faucets Another term for taps.

Floor pantry A service room provided on each floor for GRAs to store cleaning agents, equipment, guest supplies, guestroom linen, and maid's carts.

Floor par The quantity of each type of linen that is required to outfit all rooms serviced from a particular floor pantry.

Front office The department that handles check-ins and check-outs and where information regarding the guests is maintained.

Front of the house The functional areas of the hotel, in which employees have extensive guest contact, such as food and beverage facilities and the front office.

GRA Guestroom attendant/associate.

GSA Guest Service Associate

Hat checker A hat checker provides his services in superior hotels in cold climates. His domain is the hat check room, where hats and heavy overcoats are deposited by guests as soon as they enter the hotel lobby, so as to spare them the inconvenience of carrying these articles around in the hotel. The hat checker carefully labels these guest articles and hangs or stores them correctly so as to return them to the guests when they are leaving the hotel.

Housekeeping Housekeeping is defined as the provision of a clean, comfortable, safe, and aesthetically appealing environment.

IRD In-room dining. A part of F&B department that caters to in-house guests' in-room F&B orders.

Institutional housekeeping It involves maintenance and upkeep of institutions such as hostels, hospitals, art galleries, libraries, museums and so on. In such sectors a reasonable standard of cleanliness and comfort is expected at the lowest cost.

Inventory Stocks of merchandise, operating supplies, and other items held for future use in a hospitality operation.

Job description A job description is a detailed document identifying all the likely duties of a job position as well as reporting relationships, additional responsibilities, working conditions, and any know-how necessary about equipment and materials.

Job specification This document stipulates the minimum qualities and traits required by an individual to perform a particular job as defined by its job description.

Ken Fix It A routine maintenance schedule in which the maintenance department in the hotel assigns an all-purpose engineer to handle all the routine maintenance tasks on all the floors; and the engineer is known as the Ken Fix It man.

Linen Material woven from fibres of the flax plant; the term 'linen' is also used loosely to denote daily launderable articles in the linen room. Actual linen

material (derived from flax) is less elastic and more absorbent than cotton, which is now typically the material of choice.

Monogramming Embroidering or printing the hotel logo and/or name or initials in brand colours, as a combined motif on hotel linen, stationery and other amenities.

Nanotechnology Science of application of extremely minute particles of matter. 1 nanometer = 1 billionth of a meter.

Occupancy report A report prepared each night by the front office, which lists the rooms occupied that night and indicates guests who are expected to check out the following day.

OOO 'Out of order' is the status of a guestroom that is not rentable because it is being repaired or redecorated.

Organization chart A schematic representation of the relationships between positions within an organization, showing where each position fits into the overall organization and illustrating the divisions of responsibility and lines of authority.

Par stock/par number A multiple of the standard quantity of a particular inventory item that must be on hand to support daily, routine housekeeping operations.

Porte-cochère Covered porch at the hotel's entrance where guests alight from their vehicles and are welcomed by uniformed staff.

Preventive maintenance A systematic approach to maintenance in which situations are identified and corrected on a regular basis to control costs and keep larger problems from occurring.

Resident manager Person having accommodations on the hotel premises; usually the in-charge of hotel operations exclusive of food and beverages and principal assistant to the general manager.

Room rack An array of metal file pockets designed to hold room-rack slips arranged by room number. The room rack summarizes the current status of all rooms in the hotel.

Room status discrepancy A situation in which the housekeeping department's description of a room's status differs from the room status information with the front office.

Rooms division manager The rooms division manager is the person who heads the department responsible for the allocation of guestrooms—including the front office and the housekeeping department.

Room status report A report that allows the housekeeping department to identify the occupancy or condition of the property's rooms. It is generated daily through a two-way communication between housekeeping and the front office.

Routine maintenance Activities related to the general upkeep of the property that occur on a regular basis and require relatively minimal training or skill to perform.

Scanty baggage A room status indicating a room assigned to a guest with small, light, and few pieces of luggage that could be carried away without obviously indicating a departure, should a guest walk out with them.

Scheduled maintenance Activities related to the upkeep of the property, which are indicated through a formal work order or similar document.

Section par The quantity of each type of linen and supplies that are required to outfit all rooms that are part of a section serviced from a particular floor pantry.

Snag list A detailed list prepared on the basis of a physical inspection, in which all possible maintenance requirements in a room are mentioned. It is normally prepared by the housekeeper during takeover of a renovated area from the contractor handling renovation or of a new property from the project team.

Stayover A room status indicating a room occupied by a guest who is not checking out today and will remain at least one more night.

Upholstery Textiles, padding, springs, and other materials used for decorating furniture and rendering it more comfortable.

Water closet (WC) cistern A resevoir to hold the right amount of water required to flush the toilet. It is also called waste water preventer (WWP).

Water closet Sanitary fitting consisting of the toilet bowl and the cistern.

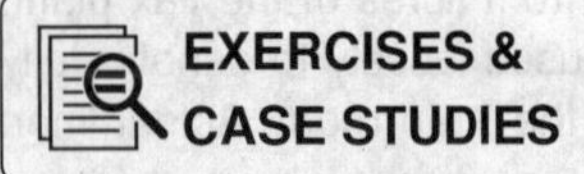

Please scan QR code to access All Exhibit & Tables

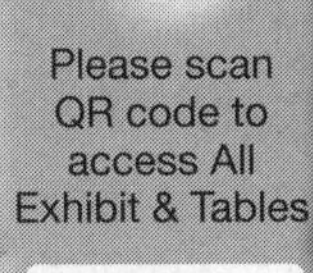

3 Managing Housekeeping Personnel

Learning Objectives

After reading this chapter, you should be able to

- describe the documental tools used in managing housekeeping personnel
- calculate the staff requirement using the staffing guide
- gain an insight into the processes of recruitment, selection, hiring, orientation, and training
- discuss various aspects of scheduling housekeeping staff
- understand the concept and management of workplace diversity
- appreciate the importance of motivating employees
- list the methods of appraising employee performance
- understand the techniques and importance of work study, time and motion studies and of job analysis
- appreciate the benefits of teamwork in housekeeping and realize the importance of good leadership in the department
- understand the need for employee welfare and discipline
- comprehend the importance of quality management and learn about its tools and techniques

Introduction

In a hospitality establishment, the housekeeping department undoubtedly has the largest workforce. Employees are the biggest and most challenging resource an executive housekeeper has to manage. Hospitality managers who treat their employees as internal customers reap the benefits as this gets translated to the employees satisfying the needs of their external customers, i.e, the guests, better. Managements must realise that satisfied employees create satisfied customers. A happy employee makes for a happy customer, and a happy customer brings ten new customers. Since happiness is always best spread inside out, internal customer's satisfaction and welfare must be a priority for hospitality companies. A happy workforce translates to employee retention and leads to savings in terms of decreased requirement for new recruitment and consequent training costs.

The functions of human resource management are presented in Figure 3.1. The organization chart (see Figures 2.1–2.3 in Chapter 2) is a useful but limited tool. It identifies tasks, job titles, and the planned relationships between these tasks. Organization charts do not, however, show the informal communication channels, cliques, and actual activities performed in the organization.

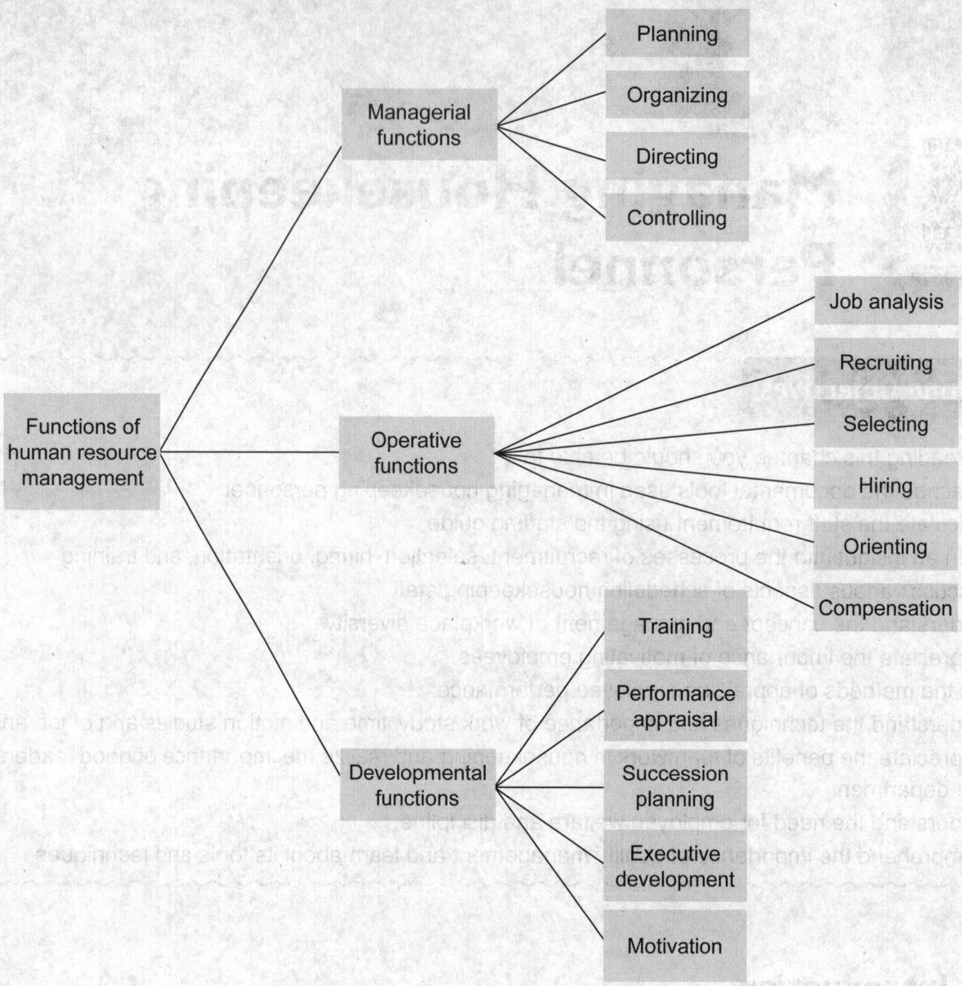

- Functions of human resource management
  - Managerial functions
    - Planning
    - Organizing
    - Directing
    - Controlling
  - Operative functions
    - Job analysis
    - Recruiting
    - Selecting
    - Hiring
    - Orienting
    - Compensation
  - Developmental functions
    - Training
    - Performance appraisal
    - Succession planning
    - Executive development
    - Motivation

Fig. 3.1 Functions of human resource management

There are certain other documents, though, that are effectively used as tools by the management and/or the executive housekeeper in communicating responsibilities and other information to the employees. These documents not only help the executive housekeeper in efficient management, but also ease employee anxiety by putting forth a clear picture of all aspects of their work and the expectations from them. Some of these tools are discussed in this chapter.

Documents for Personnel Management

A variety of documents, such as job descriptions, position descriptions, job specifications, lists, assignments, breakdowns, and procedures are used to detail various aspects of the jobs of different personnel in an establishment.

Job Description

A job description is a detailed document identifying all the likely duties appertaining to a job position as well as reporting relationships, additional responsibilities, working conditions, and any specific know-how necessary about equipment and materials.

Job descriptions must be tailored to the specific operational needs of individual properties. A well-defined job description brings about greater certainty of what is expected in terms of performance, and when actual results match expected ones, both morale and efficiency are raised. A job should not be too narrowly stipulated, as it leaves no scope for individual creativity. On the other hand, too vague a description makes it difficult to understand and handle the job. This may lead to frustration and loss of focus. Job descriptions are also excellent tools for training.

A job description covers the following aspects:

- Job profile
- Supervisory relationships
- Scope of job
- Reporting relationships
- Coordination details
- Hours of work

Job descriptions are written for unskilled, semi-skilled, and skilled employees as well as for supervisors, managers, and executives. In the organizational structure, as one proceeds down the chain of authority towards the operative levels, job descriptions need to be more detailed, clear-cut, and expressed in a way that can be understood by less-educated workers. A sample job description for a floor supervisor in a five-star hotel is presented in Exhibit 2.4 given in Chapter 2.

The advantages of a job description are as follows:

- Newly recruited employees know exactly what their job is all about.
- Job descriptions set a basic foundation for achieving the standards of performance.
- The document ensures that the supervisor and the subordinate have a clear understanding of their role in the common work; else there may be a misinterpretation of the job, leading to friction.
- A job description serves as a legal document for any disputes arising from a lack of definition of roles.
- A job description may come to the employees' aid when dealing with an unreasonable superior who overburdens them with tasks not in their purview.

At higher levels, people are expected to have a higher mental calibre, and often the results of their work are not immediately evident (unlike in the case of the operating staff). In large hotel chains and luxury hotels, for employees at 'high management' levels, a position description is written out instead.

Position Description

Position descriptions are written for employees with management prerogatives, who hire, fire, set wages, and make policies. Each position description gives the basic function, scope, and specific responsibilities of the occupant of this position. Relationships of responsibility that they have with other members of the organization are also listed. There is usually a statement referred to as 'work emphasis', outlining how a manager should allot his/her time and efforts. A sample position description is presented in Exhibit 2.1 given in Chapter 2.

Job Specification

A job specification is a document detailing the minimum qualities or traits required by an individual to perform a particular job. A job specification would include the following:

- Educational qualifications
- Equipment skills
- Mental traits
- Personality
- Age limit
- Physical characteristics
- Language skills
- Special requirements

Job specifications are generally used as tools for the selection of the right employee for a particular job, as defined in the job description. The job specification for an executive housekeeper has been drawn up in Chapter 2 in the section 'the professional housekeeper'.

Job List

A job list identifies all the key tasks that must be performed, in the order of their importance, by an individual occupying a specific position within the department. The job list should reflect the total job responsibility of the employee. The job list, sometimes called a 'task list', should be brief and to the point; it should not be a detailed breakdown of the procedures to be followed in carrying out each task. Samples of job lists are given in Exhibit 3.1.

Exhibit 3.1 Sample job lists

Job list for a laundry manager

- Record laundry costs.
- Make reports and recommendations when requested.
- Approve distribution of linen to guestrooms and F&B outlets.
- Direct all 'on premises laundry' (OPL) staff.
- Prepare the OPL budget.
- Hire and train new OPL employees.
- Develop methods for increasing OPL efficiency.
- Coordinate all maintenance and repairs of machinery.
- Supervise the OPL safety programme.
- Evaluate OPL staff performance.

Job list for a room attendant

- Collect guest amenities for the assigned guestrooms.
- Collect cleaning supplies for the assigned guestrooms.
- Organize the cart.
- Enter the guestroom and prepare it for cleaning.
- Begin to clean the bathroom.
- Clean the tub and the shower area.
- Clean the toilet.
- Clean the sink and vanity area.
- Clean the bathroom floor.
- Finish cleaning the bathroom.
- Make the bed.
- Dust the guestroom.
- Replenish supplies and amenities in the guestroom and bathroom.
- Clean windows, tracks, and sills.
- Vacuum the guestroom.
- Empty the wastepaper basket and the sani-bin into the trash bag on the cart.
- Exit the guestroom.
- Correct cleaning problems found during guestroom inspection.
- Perform all closedown activities for the shift.
- Hand over and sign for the keys.

Job Assignment

A job assignment is a list of tasks to be performed by an individual. For example, the job assignment for a guestroom attendant would list out the tasks he/she has to perform in a specific area or section of rooms on a specific day as an individual assignment.

A job assignment differs from a job list in that it may not assign the routine tasks of the employee and does not list all the job responsibilities of the employee. Job assignments are usually prepared for lower-rung staff. Job assignments lead to greater pride in work, a competitive spirit between employees, and easier supervision as the supervisor knows exactly what and where to inspect.

Job Breakdown

This is a form that details how the technical duties of a job should be performed. The best job breakdowns are developed by those who actually perform the tasks regularly. The executive housekeeper should delegate a group comprising supervisors and some experienced room attendants for the task of developing job breakdowns. Job breakdowns are excellent tools for the training of new employees. Figure 3.2 shows how a job breakdown can be developed, while Exhibit 3.2 shows a sample job breakdown for vacuuming carpets.

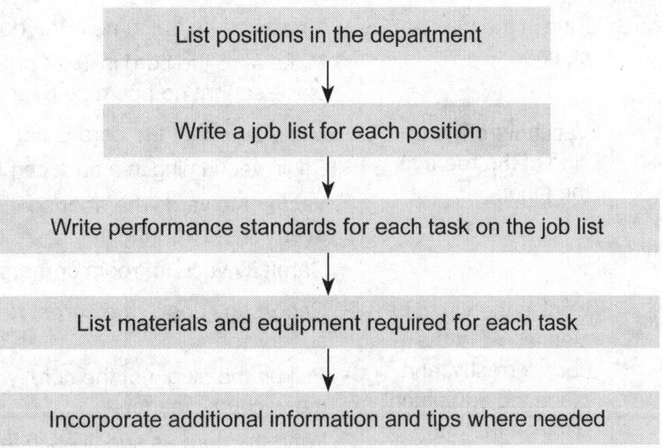

Fig. 3.2 How to develop job breakdowns

Job Procedures/SOPs

A job procedure specifies the way in which a task is to be performed. A job procedure for cleaning windows is shown in Exhibit 3.3. Job procedures should be used during induction and training sessions and ought to be incorporated into the department's procedure manuals. Updating job procedures is necessary as and when changes in equipment, cleaning materials, and so on, occur. They are most popularly called 'SOPs' or standard operating procedures. They are also referred to as 'work cards' or 'order of work' documents. SOPs comprise the following information:

- The job to be done
- Equipment and materials required
- Time required to do the job
- Procedure of work
- Safety factors

The goals in establishing SOPs are as follows:

- To aid standardization.
- To preserve surfaces and materials.
- To effect a saving on cleaning equipment and agents.
- To prevent accidents.
- To help in training.
- To ensure the completion of a task successfully.
- To aid the compiling of work schedules and help in staffing requirements.

Exhibit 3.2 Sample job breakdown for vacuuming carpets

Job breakdown

Material required: A small, stiff broom; a vacuum cleaner with a carpet-cleaning attachment; and caution signs, if necessary.

Steps	How tos	Tips
1. Remove dirt from room corners and carpet edges.	• Use a small, stiff broom to brush dirt from room corners and carpet edges to a carpeted area that the vacuum can reach. • Push down on the broom and pull it toward you—away from the wall.	• Place caution signs if necessary • Beating of a carpet is not advised unless extremely soiled.
2. Plug in the vacuum cleaner.	• Try to use an outlet near the door. • Make sure the cord is in an out-of-the-way place so that no one trips over it.	• Periodically check and empty the vacuum bag.
3. Vacuum from one side of the room to the other.	• Make sure that the cord is not coiled. • Begin vacuuming in a back corner of the room. • Vacuum towards the door so that you vacuum over your footprints. • Carefully vacuum room corners and edges.	
4. Unplug the vacuum cleaner, wind the cord correctly, and place the equipment back on the cart.	• Report any rips in the carpet to your supervisor. • Pull on the plug, not the cord, while unplugging the vacuum cleaner. • Wind the cord as specified in the equipment manual.	

Exhibit 3.3 SOP/Job procedure for cleaning windows (without branded cleaning products)

SOP Name:	**Procedure for cleaning windows**		
Effective Date:	**23.12.2019**	**SOP Author:**	**Shefali Shyam**
SOP No.:	**123**	**SOP Approver:**	**Vijay Dewan**
For Job title:	**Housekeeping associates**	**SOP Owner:**	**Hotel Sundown, Coorg**

Objective: To clean windows to a gleaming shine

Equipment & tools needed:	Two buckets, a window squeegee, polishing cloths (such as chamois leather), and newspaper	**Supplies needed:**	18 ml ammonia in half a bucket of warm water, or 18 ml vinegar in half a bucket of warm water, or warm synthetic detergent solution; warm water

Procedure	How-to do	Additional information
1. Get cleaning agents ready	Fill one bucket with cleaning solution and one with warm water for rinsing.	

Procedure Manual

Procedure manuals are developed by the organization for all employees, and departmental procedure manuals are developed in common for employees of a particular department. A procedure manual gives information about standard procedures to be followed for various activities. In housekeeping, these activities relate to the organization and procedures of cleaning activities, safety and security measures, human resource issues, and so on. These manuals are necessary in maintaining uniform standards even when managers and employees change. In order to be effective, these manuals must be updated whenever there are changes incorporated in these systems. SOPs should be part of procedure manuals.

Determining Staff Strength

Compared to other hotel departments, the housekeeping department employs the largest workforce in most hotels. Manpower thus becomes a major operating expense. Good management of the housekeeping department depends on achieving a balance between the workload and the staff strength. When calculating staff strength, it must be remembered that each property will have its individual requirements. The factors to be considered here are:

- The type of hotel it is
- The location of the hotel
- Traditions and customs of the locality
- The size of the hotel (in terms of number of rooms)
- The occupancy rate of the hotel
- Management needs
- Company policies
- The quantity of work to be done
- The quality of work expected, that is, the standards to be met
- The time needed to do the work
- The frequency with which the work needs to be done
- The time when the work area is available
- The amount of traffic in the area

The staff strength of the housekeeping department mainly depends on the size and structure of the hotel, that is, whether it has a compact structure with clusters of rooms, the number of rooms per cluster or floor, the expanse of the public areas and landscaped areas, and so on. The general guidelines for determining staff strength in the housekeeping department are presented in Exhibit 3.4.

Each hotel needs to develop its own staffing guide, which should help in scheduling the right number of staff for every positional level in the housekeeping department at various occupancy levels of the hotel.

The Staffing Guide

A staffing guide is a documental tool that specifies the positions within a department and the number of people required to fill these positions at various occupancy levels of the hotel.

Procedure for developing a staffing guide

Let us understand how a staffing guide is put together with a hypothetical example. Let's say there is a property called Hotel Coral Island, a 500-room luxury hotel, and that we need to have a staffing guide for the position of guest room attendant. How do we proceed?

Exhibit 3.4 Guidelines for determining staff strength

Managers & Supervisors	
Executive housekeeper	1 per property
Deputy/Assistant housekeeper	1 per property
Floor supervisor	1 per 50 rooms in morning shift 1 per 100 rooms in afternoon shift 1 in night shift
Public area supervisor	1 per 10,000 sq. ft. public area per shift
Desk supervisor	1 per shift
Linen room supervisor	1 in morning shift
Uniform room supervisor	1 in morning shift
Housekeeping Attendants	
Guest room attendant	1 per 14–16 rooms in morning shift (Area-wise: 1 per 5,000 sq. ft./shift)
Guest room attendant	1 per 50 rooms in evening shift
Guest room attendant	1 per 100 rooms in night shift
Public area attendant	1 per 7,000 sq. ft. public area per shift
Horticulturist	1 per property
Gardeners	1 per 4,500 sq. ft. of landscaped area

Step 1 Determine the work hours to be scheduled at various occupancy levels of this 500-room hotel, using the productivity standards for the hotel's room attendants (refer 'Productivity Standards' in Chapter 5). Assume that the productivity standard for guestroom attendants is 30 minutes (0.5 hours) to clean one guestroom. Using this productivity standard, we can calculate the work hours required for room attendants at various occupancy levels of the hotel. For example, at 100% occupancy,

Rooms to clean next day = 500 × 1.0 = 500 rooms
Work hours to clean 500 rooms = 500 × 0.5 = 250 hours

At 90% occupancy,

Rooms to clean next day = 500 × 0.9 = 450 rooms
Work hours to clean 450 rooms = 450 × 0.5 = 225 hours

At 85% occupancy,

Rooms to clean next day = 500 × 0.85 = 425 rooms
Work hours to clean 425 rooms = 425 × 0.5 = 213 hours

Thus, a staffing guide table can be developed for all occupancy levels, ending at a zero base, where no room attendants will be required since the occupancy is nil.

Step 2 Now determine the number of full-time employees (FTE) who must be scheduled to work when the hotel is at specific occupancy levels. Since the productivity standard is 0.5 hours to clean 1 guestroom, a room attendant is expected to clean 16 guestrooms during a 9-hour shift (for calculations, refer 'Productivity Standards' in Chapter 5). Given this information, the number of full-time room attendants who must be scheduled at different occupancy levels can be determined by dividing the number of occupied rooms by 16.

For example, at 100% occupancy,

Rooms to clean next day	= 500 × 1.0 = 500 rooms
No. of full-time GRAs needed	= 500 ÷ 16 = 31.25
	= 31 (rounded off)

At 90% occupancy,

Rooms to clean next day	= 500 × 0.9 = 450
No. of full-time GRAs needed	= 450 ÷ 16 = 28.12
	= 28 (rounded off)

At 85% occupancy,

Rooms to clean next day	= 500 × 0.85 = 425
No. of full-time GRAs needed	= 425 ÷ 16 = 26.56
	= 27 (rounded off)

The actual number of room attendants scheduled by the executive housekeeper will finally depend on the number of full-time and part-time room attendants available to her. For example, at 90% occupancy, 28 full-time room attendants may be scheduled; or 20 full-time room attendants, each working 8 hours, and 16 part-time room attendants, each working 4 hours, may be scheduled.

Step 3 Ideally, the executive housekeeper should also incorporate into the staffing guide table, the employee expenses required at each occupancy level. This helps in zero-base budgeting. Whether the executive housekeeper schedules only full-time or some part-time employees as well, the total employee expense for the room attendants should not exceed the calculated amount at a specific occupancy level.

The employee expense is calculated for room attendants by multiplying the work hours by the average hourly rate for room attendants. Assuming that the average hourly rate for room attendants is ₹10, the next day's employee expense will be calculated as follows:

At 100% occupancy,

Work hours of GRAs	= 250 hours
Employee expense for GRAs per day	= 250 × ₹10
	= ₹2,500

The staffing guide table should be completed for all positions and all occupancy levels in a similar way, taking productivity standards for the various positions into account. A sample staffing guide for Hotel Coral Island, a five-star luxury hotel, is presented in Exhibit 3.5.

Let us look at the calculation of the number of guest room associates (GRAs) required at Hotel Spring Leaves International, a 430-room property at occupancies of 100% and 76%, presented in Exhibits 3.6 and Exhibit 3.7 respectively. The hotel has the typical 3-shift system of 9 hours each. The productivity standards may be assumed as given in Chapter 5 Planning Housekeeping Operations, Exhibit 5.4.

Exhibit 3.5 Staffing guide for the housekeeping department, Hotel Coral Island (for variable positions)

Percentage of occupancy	No. of rooms occupied	GRAs (morning shift) (P. S. 0.5 hours)			GRAs (evening shift) (P. S. 0.2 hours)		
		No. of GRAs	GRA work hours/day	GRA employee expense/day	No. of GRAs	GRA work hours/day	GRA employee expense/day
100	500	31	250	₹2,500	17	100	₹1,000
95	475	30	238	₹2,380	16	95	₹950
90	450	28	225	₹2,250	15	90	₹900
85	425	27	213	₹2,130	14	85	₹850
80	400	25	200	₹2,000	13	80	₹800
75	375	24	188	₹1,880	13	75	₹750
70	350	22	175	₹1,750	12	70	₹700
65	325	20	163	₹1,630	11	65	₹650
60	300	19	150	₹1,500	10	60	₹600
55	275	17	138	₹1,380	10	55	₹550
50	250	16	125	₹1,250	9	50	₹500
45	225	14	113	₹1,130	8	45	₹450
40	200	13	110	₹1,000	7	40	₹400
35	175	10	88	₹880	6	35	₹350
30	150	9	75	₹750	5	30	₹300
25	125	8	63	₹630	5	25	₹250
20	100	6	50	₹500	3	20	₹200
15	75	5	38	₹380	3	15	₹150
10	50	3	25	₹250	2	10	₹100
5	25	2	13	₹130	1	5	₹50
0	0	0	0	₹0	0	0	₹0

Supervisors (morning shift) (P. S: 0.1 hours)			Housemen (P. S: 0.8 hours)		
No. of supervisor	Work hours/day	Employee expense	No. of housemen	Work hours/day	Employee expense/day
8	50	₹1,000	8	400	₹3,200
8	48	₹960	8	380	₹3,040
8	45	₹900	8	360	₹2,880
7	43	₹860	7	340	₹2,720
7	40	₹800	7	320	₹2,560
6	38	₹760	6	300	₹2,400
6	35	₹700	6	280	₹2,240
6	33	₹660	6	260	₹2,080
5	30	₹600	5	240	₹1,920
5	28	₹560	5	220	₹1,760
5	25	₹500	5	200	₹1,600

(Contd.)

Exhibit 3.5 *Contd.*

4	23	₹460	4	180	₹1,440
3	20	₹400	3	160	₹1,280
3	18	₹360	3	140	₹1,120
3	15	₹300	3	120	₹960
2	13	₹260	2	100	₹800
2	10	₹200	2	80	₹640
2	8	₹160	2	60	₹480
1	5	₹100	1	40	₹320
1	3	₹60	1	20	₹160
0	0	₹0	0	0	₹0

Notes: 1. P.S. stands for productivity standard; GRAs (morning shift): 1 per 16 rooms; GRAs (evening shift): 1 per 30 rooms; housemen: 1 per 60 rooms; supervisors (morning shift): 1 per 60 rooms

2. Employee expenses calculated on the following basis: GRAs ₹10 per hour, housemen ₹8 per hour, and supervisors ₹20 per hour

3. The total number of working hours per shift is taken as 9 hours, of which 1 hour is reduced by way of a break, hence only 8 hours are available for work.

Exhibit 3.6 Calculation of GRAs at 100% occupancy

Step 1	*List details given*	
	No. of rooms	**430 rooms**
	Occupancy level (i.e., all 430 rooms are to be serviced)	100%
Step 2	*List details of productivity standards*	
	Time taken to service one guestroom by GRAs in morning shift	**30 min.**
	Time taken to service one guestroom by GRAs in afternoon shift	**12 min.**
	(as per performance standards set using time and motion studies)	
	Total shift time of a GRA	9 hours = 9 × 60 min. = **540 min.**
	Total time available for guestroom servicing [subtract non-work productive time such as start & end-shift & break times from total shift time; 540 – (10 + 15 + 45 + 10)]	540 – 80 = **460 min.**
Step 3	**No. of rooms serviced by one GRA in morning shift**	460 min. ÷ 30 min. = 15.33 = **15 rooms** (rounded off)
	No. of GRAs needed in morning shift	430 rooms ÷ 15 rooms = **28.66 GRAs**
Step 4	**No. of rooms serviced by one GRA in afternoon shift** (mainly turndown service)	460 min. ÷ 12 min. = 38.33 = **38 rooms**
	No. of GRAs needed in afternoon shift	430 rooms ÷ 38 rooms = **11.218 GRAs**

(Contd.)

Exhibit 3.6 *Contd.*

Step 5	**No. of GRAs needed in night shift (@ 1 GRA per 100 rooms)**	430 rooms ÷ 100 rooms = **4.3 GRAs**
Step 6	**Total no. of GRAs in 3 shifts**	28.66 + 11.218 + 4.3 = **44.178 GRAs**
Step 7	**Allocating relievers for GRAs** (@ 1 reliever per 6 employees)	44.178 ÷ 6 = **7.363 Relievers**
Step 8	**Total no. of GRAs needed at 100% occupancy**	44.178 + 7.363 = 51.541 = **52 GRAs** (rounded off)

Exhibit 3.7 Calculation of GRAs at 76% occupancy

Step 1	*List details given*	
	No. of rooms	**430 rooms**
	Occupancy level	**76%**
	No. of rooms to service	430 × 0.76 = 326.8 = **327 rooms**
Step 2	*List details of productivity standards*	
	Time taken to service one guestroom by GRAs in morning shift	**30 min.**
	Time taken to service one guestroom by GRAs in afternoon shift (as per performance standards set using time and motion studies)	**12 min.**
	Total shift time of a GRA	9 hours = 9 × 60 min. = **540 min.**
	Total time available for guestroom servicing [subtract non-work productive time such as start & end-shift & break times from total shift time; 540 – (10 + 15 + 45 + 10)]	540 – 80 = **460 min.**
Step 3	**No. of rooms serviced by one GRA in morning shift**	460 min. ÷ 30 min. = 15.33 = **15 rooms** (rounded off)
	No. of GRAs needed in morning shift	327 rooms ÷ 15 rooms = **21.8 GRAs**
Step 4	**No. of rooms serviced by one GRA in afternoon shift** (mainly turndown service)	460 min. ÷ 12 min. = 38.33 = **38 rooms**
	No. of GRAs needed in afternoon shift	327 rooms ÷ 38 rooms = **8.605 GRAs**
Step 5	**No. of GRAs needed in night shift (@ 1 GRA per 100 rooms)**	327 rooms ÷ 100 rooms = **3.27 GRAs**
Step 6	**Total no. of GRAs in 3 shifts**	21.8 + 8.605 + 3.27 = **33.675 GRAs**
Step 7	**Allocating relievers for GRAs** (@ 1 reliever per 6 employees)	33.675 ÷ 6 = **5.6125 Relievers**
Step 8	**Total no. of GRAs needed at 76% occupancy**	33.675 + 5.6125 = 39.2875 = **39 GRAs** (rounded off)

Functions of Human Resource Management

The executive housekeeper works in close coordination with the human resource department to manage housekeeping personnel. The functions of human resource management are threefold, as depicted earlier in Figure 3.1.

Recruiting, Selecting, Hiring, Orienting, and Training

In this section, we shall discuss the process of recruiting, selecting, hiring, orienting, and training of employees in a housekeeping department.

Recruiting Employees

Recruiting is the process of actively seeking, selecting and hiring the most suitable employees for a particular job position. Even before publicizing job vacancies, there are sub-processes to be carried out and these are categorized under the pre-recruitment phase which comprises reviewing job descriptions to define the requirements of the job, assessing job specifications to know the expected attributes of a candidate, previewing the company's pitch to potential candidates, developing a strategy to guage the competitor market through potential recruits, identifying sources of potential employees, outlining the standard criteria of evaluating potential candidates and finalizing the mode of job publicizing.

Identifying potential employees

Various sources can be tapped for the purpose of recruitment, as depicted in Figure 3.3. These sources could be external or internal.

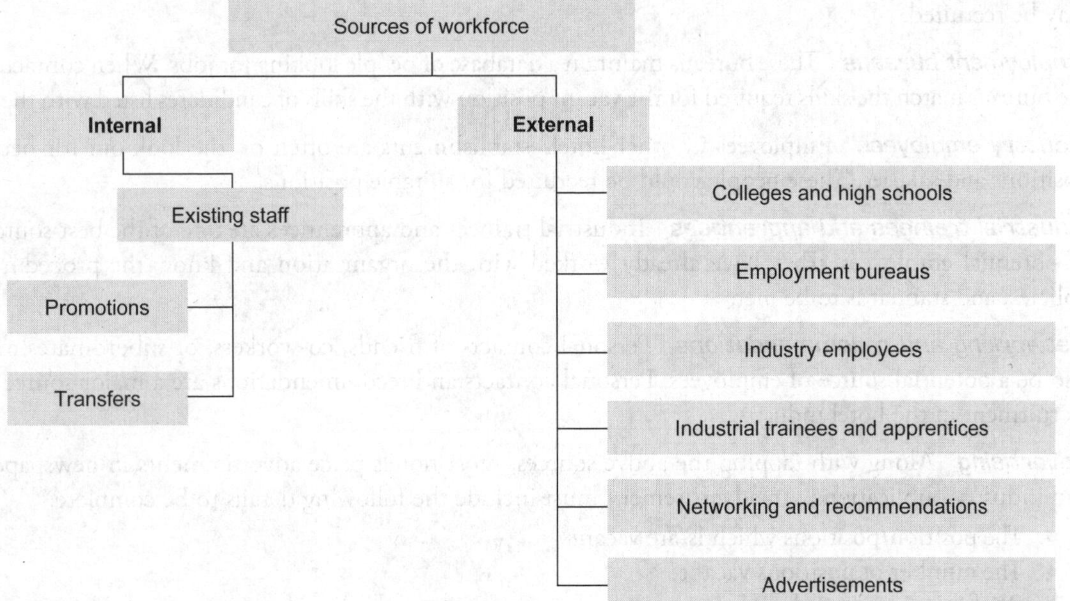

Fig. 3.3 Sources of workforce for the purpose of recruitment

Internal sources Opportunities arising from internal sources should be thoroughly examined before scouting for external sources. Internal sourcing encourages growth within the organization and prevents stagnation and discontentment among the staff. Internal sourcing is advantageous to the executive housekeeper also, since the manager gets employees who have already proven themselves and are familiar with the property. Internal sourcing involves promotions and transfers.

Promotions It is essential that the executive housekeeper identifies employees who could be promoted to the next level, training, and grooming them for the promotion. This is referred to as succession planning. Possibilities for promotion enhance the morale and productivity of employees.

Transfers Inter-departmental transfers are an option that makes employees more flexible. Employees can be then accommodated in any department when need arises. Keeping transfers as an option calls for cross-training, so that employees can learn the duties of more than one position.

Advantages of internal sources The advantages of internal sources are as follows:

- Technique of motivation
- Morale of employees can be improved
- Suitability of internal candidate can be judged better
- Loyalty, commitment, and a sense of belongingness can be enhanced
- Cost of selection can be minimized
- Cost of training and orientation can be minimized
- Trade unions can be satisfied

External sources External sourcing is necessary for entry-level jobs and whenever creative inputs from external candidates need to be used at specific positions.

Colleges and high schools Qualified candidates can be recruited through various hotel management colleges across the country. For some lower-rung positions, high-school students looking for job openings may be recruited.

Employment bureaus These bureaus maintain a database of people looking for jobs. When contacted, the bureaus match the skills required for the vacant position with the skills of candidates listed with them.

Industry employees Employees of other hotel establishments are often on the look-out for better positions and salaries. These people could be recruited for suitable positions.

Industrial trainees and apprentices Industrial trainees and apprentices are one of the best sources of potential employees. They have already worked with the organization and know the procedures, policies, and standards to be met.

Networking and recommendations Personal contacts of friends, co-workers, or subordinates may also be a potential source of employees. Personal contacts and recommendations are a major source of recruitment in the hotel industry.

Advertising Along with tapping the above sources, most hotels place advertisements in newspapers and industry publications. An advertisement must include the following details to be complete:

- The position/positions which is/are vacant
- The number of positions vacant
- Brief description of the job
- The type of person required for the job (educational qualifications, experiences, and so on)

- Conditions (such as salary and perks)
- The address to which the application (along with the resumé) is to be sent and the relevant telephone and facsimile number

Advantages of external sources The advantages of external sources are as follows:

- Suitable candidates with skill, talent, knowledge, etc. are generally available
- Cost of employees can be minimized as employees selected from this source are generally placed in minimum pay scale
- Personnel can be balanced with different background, experience, skill, etc.
- Latest knowledge, skill, and creative talent can be brought into the organization

Selecting Employees

The process of selection involves screening application forms and resumés, interviewing, and evaluating. Selection is a process of identifying and hiring people whose probability of success in the job at hand is maximum and who are likely to stay long enough with the organization to add to its development.

Screening applications and resumés

The following criteria should be looked into while screening candidates:

- Age, qualifications, and experience
- Compatibility with job requirements
- Social skills
- Family background
- Health status
- Special interests
- Mental make-up—self-confidence, presence of mind, and initiative
- Ethical values

Resumés should be checked thoroughly to see that the candidate conforms to the job requirement. Resumés that do not meet the requirements should be weeded out. Check the following while screening resumés:

- Neatness, layout, language, and spellings
- Gaps in work history
- Omission of any information
- Reasons for leaving previous jobs
- Whether the signature matches the handwriting in the application

Avoid candidates who have worked in various jobs for very short periods (also referred to as 'boomers') and seem overqualified. After the screening of applications, notify the candidates regarding tests and interviews they must subsequently appear for.

Interview

Once the screening of applications is over, candidates may be given objective tests involving written and practical work. This is followed by individual interviews with qualifying candidates. Individual interviews are usually conducted by a panel of four to five interviewers. The following are some guidelines for preparing, conducting, and concluding an interview smoothly.

Preparing for the interview

- Select the interview panel members.
- Choose the date, time, and venue.

- Notify the candidate.
- Jot down specific points or questions on resumés.
- Read the job description, job specification, and resumés thoroughly before the interview.

Beginning the interview

- Greet the applicant.
- Observe his/her physical appearance and body language.
- Break the ice by putting the candidate at ease.

Conducting the interview

- Ask relevant questions to gather the required information.
- Determine the applicant's values, work standards, expectations, and outlook on other people.
- Use open-ended questions so that the applicant does 80% of the talking.
- Record important decisions.

Closing the interview

- Allow the candidate to ask a few questions.
- If the candidate is suitable, sell the company and the job.
- Let the candidate know when the outcome of the interview would be intimated to him/her.
- Thank the applicant for applying and for coming.

Types of Interviews

We will discuss some different types of interviews in this section.

Traditional one-to-one interview An interview of a candidate is conducted by an individual interviewer.

Panel interview A panel interview is conducted by two or more interviewers and is designed to reduce individual interviewer bias and to field questions from various perspectives.

Group interview In a group interview the interviewee is pitched against other candidates during the interview. The candidate is given a chance to demonstrate leadership potential, communication, and coordination skills.

Informational interview An informational interview gives a chance to the interested individuals to meet with a professional to gather industry and career information and advice to help determine if the career is worth pursuing.

Screening interview Screening interview is the initial round of interview generally done by the human resource department to weed out unsuitable candidates before the suitable ones can meet the actual interviewer. This type of interview is also done by job agencies to select candidates to be furthered for hiring in an organization.

Behavioural interview A behavioural interview is aimed at gauging a candidate's previous behaviour to indicate his or her future performance. Questions such as 'describe a past work experience where you had to use problem-solving, adaptability, or leadership' feature in these interviews. The interviewers look for detailed information on how the candidate has dealt with situations in the past.

Stress interview A stress interview allows interviewers to see how well the candidate will be working under pressure. These types of interviews may include a variety of odd behaviour, including being held in the waiting room for long periods of time, posing offensive questions, being met with long silence or cold looks and so on.

Mealtime interview A mealtime interview, as the name implies, is an interview set over the course of a meal, usually lunch. These interviews are conducted in situations where the position requires a high level of interpersonal skills. A mealtime setting allows the interviewers to observe how the interviewee acts in a social setting and his or her dining etiquette.

Pitfalls in Interviewing

The interview panel members should be aware of the various pitfalls that may occur during interviewing despite the best intentions. Some common pitfalls are listed here.

Devil's horns effect (also called the 'negative halo effect') The interviewer may get overly affected by a negative quality in the applicant. As a result, the interviewer becomes blind to the positive qualities that the applicant might possess and selectively perceives everything about the applicant as negative.

Halo effect The interviewer may get similarly affected by a positive quality in the applicant. As a result, the interviewer becomes blind to the negative qualities that the applicant might possess and perceives everything about the applicant as good.

Contrast error Most interviewers tend to compare one applicant with the other and this causes the contrast error. The interviewer must compare the applicant with the requirements of the job.

First impression error The interviewer is affected positively or negatively by the first impression the applicant creates.

Recency effect The interviewer is affected positively or negatively by the last impression the applicant creates.

Given below are some guidelines for becoming an ideal interviewer:

- Be a good communicator.
- Be a good listener.
- Be a role model and appear enthusiastic about the job.
- Be a good judge of people.
- Understand and accept differences among people.

Evaluating

The process of evaluation takes place partially during the interview itself and is concluded, ideally, soon after the interview is over. For the purpose of evaluation, the interview process is recalled, details are discussed among panel members, and a final evaluation of the candidate is arrived at. To avoid procrastination and confusion, a decision—negative or positive—should be made about each candidate.

Hiring Employees

Once suitable candidates are identified and the references checked, the human resource department extends the job offer to them at the earliest. Medical examinations must be undergone by the selected candidates. Finally, identification cards, time-in swipe cards, and relevant forms need to be collected by the new employees. The executive housekeeper must also inform other employees about the identity and position of the new employee and prepare them to extend their cooperation to the team member.

Orienting Employees

With the hiring process over, the new employees are now on the payroll of the establishment. The newcomers need to be introduced to people and be familiarized with the environment in which they are to work. This is done through an orientation or induction programme. Orientation is the guided adjustment of a new employee to the organization, his/her work environment, and the job. The following should form part of the orientation programme:

- The history of the organization
- General policies and practices of the organization
- Departments; their location and functions
- Staff benefits: location of staff toilets, locker rooms, restrooms, staff mess, and so on
- Safety regulations and other procedures
- Organizational hierarchy, defining the employee's position and reporting relationships

The orientation may take place through formal methods—using film slides, demonstrations, and lectures—or informal methods. Most hotels have a training department, which takes care of the orientation programme in general.

Executive housekeeper's role in orientation

The executive housekeeper needs to chalk out a departmental orientation programme for new employees. Most executive housekeepers do not conduct the entire orientation programme themselves; they delegate it to a supervisor. The following should be covered in a departmental orientation:

- An overview of:
  - the job, duties, and responsibilities,
  - the goals to be met by the employee, and
  - the immediate tasks to be accomplished.
- Guest relations and security.
- Work schedules—the number of hours and types of shifts.
- The pay-cheque procedure.
- The grooming standards set by the hotel.
- The work standards expected.

Exhibit 3.8 shows a checklist for orienting new employees.

Training Employees

Training is the overall enhancement of human ability by developing knowledge, skills, attitude, and behaviour in order to achieve individual goals. Training relates not only to new employees, but is an ongoing process for the entire team. Training is effective only when the knowledge gained is applied at work and tested for usefulness. The steps in planning a training programme are presented in

Exhibit 3.8 Checklist for orienting a new employee into housekeeping

1. *The welcome:*
    - Greet the employee.
    - Introduce yourself and make the employee feel at ease.
2. *Offer an overview:*
    - Show the employee where he/she fits into the organizational hierarchy.
    - Inform the employee of his/her duties and responsibilities.
3. *Lay down the work standards:*
    - State the number of rooms to be checked (in case of a supervisor) or cleaned (in case of a GRA).
    - State the time ideally taken to check or clean a room.
    - Hand over a procedure manual containing the SOPs.
    - Point out where the duty roster is displayed.
    - Discuss leave procedures.
    - Discuss procedures for swiping in and reporting for work.

Figure 3.4. The first step in training is to assess the need for training in the department. The second step is to identify areas in which training is required and list them according to priority. The third step is to determine what type of training is needed in each area. The fourth step is to plan the training programmes and set time periods for implementing them. The fifth step is to evaluate the programme.

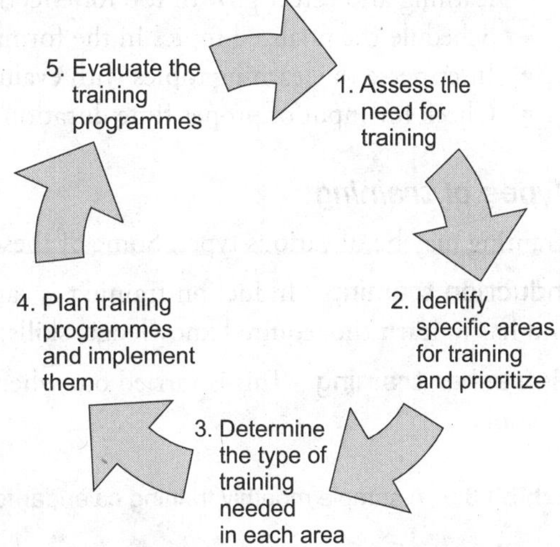

Fig. 3.4 Steps in planning a training programme

Benefits of training

The benefits of training are as follows:

- New employees learn in a comfortable atmosphere.
- New employees understand the importance of the job and the expectations to be met.
- Existing employees improve their work performance.
- Flexibility is incorporated due to cross-training.
- The incidence of accidents is reduced and safety is enhanced.
- Reduced expenditure on maintenance of machines results.
- Employees are motivated and their job satisfaction improves.
- Employees' and overall productivity improves.
- Employee turnover is reduced.
- The executive housekeeper gets more time for management activities.
- Standards and quality of work improve.
- Supervision improves.
- More profits flow in due to better business.

Making a Training Calendar

The first step in training employees is to analyse training needs and then chalk out a departmental training calendar. The topics to be scheduled in the calendar would depend on the needs analysed. It is advisable to schedule training of short durations on daily basis and make a monthly calendar. The monthly calendar is to be ratified by the L&D manager or HR head. A sample training calendar for employees is presented in Exhibit 3.9.

- Prepare the format of the monthly training calendar as shown in the Exhibit.
- List down topics arrived at after carrying out training needs analysis.
- Ensure that 'essential and mandatory' topics are covered, for instance, fire safety training, chemical safety training, first aid ad so on.
- Ascertain that 'essential technical' topics are included. These would include on the job training on departmental SOPs of bedmaking, floor polishing, linen specification and handling, carpet shampoo and so on.
- Ensure that 'employee development' topics are included that address employees' need for new learning and career growth too for effective employee engagement in training.
- Schedule the finalized topics in the format of the monthly training calendar.
- Intersperse the learning topics with evaluation and ice breaker sessions on periodic intervals.
- Check for input of proper time duration for each topic.

Types of training

Training may be of various types. Some of these are described in this section.

Induction training Induction training is carried out when an employee is new to the organization and has to learn the required knowledge, skills, and attitude for his new position.

Refresher training This is carried out when an old employee has to be re-trained to refresh his/her memory.

Exhibit 3.9 A sample monthly training calendar for housekeeping department

Hotel Spring Leaves International

HOUSEKEEPING TRAINING CALENDAR – JANUARY 2022

Saturday	Sunday	Monday	Tuesday	Wednesday	Thursday	Friday
1.1.22	2.1.22	3.1.22	4.1.22	5.1.22	6.1.22	7.1.22
20 minutes	30 minutes	20 minutes	20 minutes	20 minutes	20 minutes	20 minutes
Standards of personal hygiene & grooming	Role play activity	Bed making as per SOP	Bathroom cleaning as per SOP	Glass cleaning as per SOP	Carpet shampoo as per SOP	Setting up GRA cart as per SOP

Remedial training This is carried out for old employees when there is a change in the present working style, which may be related to a competitive environment, technological changes, or guest expectations.

Cross-training This training enables employees to work in departments other than their speciality in periods of staff shortage.

On-the-job training This type of training takes place while a trainee is working on a daily schedule. The trainee in this case is under the guidance of a trainer or a 'buddy'. As part of on-the-job training in housekeeping, the new employee may be instructed in topics such as

- the use and care of equipment,
- the use and storage of cleaning agents,
- setting up of the room attendant's cart, and
- linen, laundry, and uniform-handling procedures.

Simulation training In simulation training for housekeeping, an un-rented model room may be set up and used to train several employees. The advantage of simulation training over on-the-job training is that the training process may be stopped in between, discussed again, and repeated if required for reinforcement. The trainee here does not have to prepare the room for guest occupancy.

Off-the-job training Off-the-job training takes place away from work, in a classroom, by means of workshops, demonstrations, lectures, discussions, seminars, audio-visual presentations, case studies, and role-playing. Some topics for instruction may be:

- Controlling expenses
- Ways to meet standards
- Demonstration of new equipment
- Stress management

Methods/Techniques used commonly in hospitality training

Role play Participants enact roles on the basis of a written script or an oral description of a particular situation. For instance, a session on communication - 'phrases to use with guests' can be effectively delivered through role play. Common phrases to be used by housekeeping employees with guests are presented in Exhibit 3.10.

Exhibit 3.10 Common phrases that may be used by housekeeping employees in guest communication

Common phrases in guest communication

Face-to-face communication phrases:

- "Namaste, welcome to our hotel."
- "It's good to see you again, Mr./Ms. ...."
- "How are you doing today, Mr. ...."
- "May I help you?"/"How may I assist you?"/"Could I be of any assistance?"
- "My name is .... Do call me for service at your convenient time."
- "Sorry to have kept you waiting, Sir/Madam."
- "The lady/gentleman with you......". (And not "Your wife/husband.......")
- "Hope you enjoyed your stay with us."
- "Please"/"Pardon me"/"Kindly excuse me"/"Thank you" (to be used where appropriate)

Demonstration The tasks such as bed making are performed and explained to the trainee. The trainee is then supervised while he practises the task.

Case study Analysis is done on problem identification, causes, and remedy.

Management games The game is built around a model of a business situation and trainees are divided into teams representing the management of competing teams.

In-basket exercise A variety of situations that an executive has to deal with on a day-to-day basis in his work are presented. It helps in acquainting employees about their job where a number of problems are kept in the 'in basket' (usually kept on the desk of the employee). The worker has to look at the problems which could also be complaints from different employees and simultaneously deal with those problems. As the employee solves these problems, he/she transfers them to the 'out-basket'.

Lectures These are delivered by an instructor to a group of trainees with the use of instructional aids and training devices.

Video presentation Instructional videos on such tasks as bathroom cleaning and flower arrangement are presented and the trainees are asked to practise them.

Self-study Carefully planned instructional material can be used to train and develop employees.

The four-step training method

Prepare, present, practise, and follow up—these are the four steps for effective training programmes.

Prepare to train Training should not be haphazard, but sequentially planned according to the needs of the staff. Therefore, preparation is required in chalking out a training programme. This involves analysing the job and the staff's training needs.

Job analysis Job analysis plays a significant role. The trainee will benefit from the training only when the trainer knows exactly what is expected of the employee at work. Job analysis is the process of determining what knowledge each employee needs, what tasks each employee needs to perform, and the standards to which the employee must perform the tasks. The three components of a job analysis are job knowledge, a job list, and job breakdowns. *Job knowledge* identifies what an employee needs to know to perform the tasks to the expected standards. A *job list* enumerates in simple terms the various tasks to be accomplished. A *job breakdown* is the complete know how required to perform a particular task while meeting the required standards.

Analysing the staff's training needs This is a must in order to prioritize training activities. The training needs of new employees and existing staff should be assessed separately. A new employee's training needs can be chalked out on the basis of job lists. The tasks mentioned in the job list should be prioritised according to simplicity and importance. The training sessions should be started with simple tasks. A sample training module for Hotel Operations Trainee (HOT) programme in housekeeping is presented in Exhibit 3.11.

To assess a current employee's training needs, their work performance needs to be observed for 2–3 days. Their performance on these tasks should then be rated on a scale of 1 to 5. On tasks in which they score less than 3, the staff need training.

The three basic areas in which employees should be trained are skills, attitude, and knowledge.

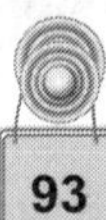

Exhibit 3.11 A sample training module for HOT programme in housekeeping

Hotel Spring Leaves International

HOT PROGRAMME MODULE – HOUSEKEEPING

Programme duration: 12 months

S. No.	Training zone	No. of weeks	Training elements with operational procedures	Evaluation
1.	Induction	0.5	Orientation and mentor allocation	Quiz & review by mentor
		0.5	Property rounds, joining formalities and medicals	
		0.5	Cross exposure	
2.	Theory	0.5	Theory sessions & handover of key learning observations	

Skills training Skills include the practical and technical aspects of the job that an employee has to perform. Skills training is essential for an employee to meet the standards set by the organization. Some important skills that a trainee GRA needs to learn are:

- Arranging the room attendant's cart
- Bed-making
- Dusting (damp and dry)
- Vacuuming
- Floor and carpet cleaning
- Cleaning of hard surfaces
- Window and mirror cleaning
- Bathroom cleaning
- Performing the turndown service
- Using equipment
- Safety and security procedures

Attitude training Though it is imperative that employees with a positive attitude are selected during recruitment, a new employee's attitude may need to be shaped to a certain extent. Housekeeping trainees need to be guided into thinking that no task is menial, and that all tasks are important in rendering service to a guest. The development of interpersonal skills also comes under the head of attitude training.

Attitude training may be required in the following areas:

- Rendering service to the guests
- Dealing with superiors and subordinates
- Cleaning public areas and bathrooms
- Management
- Personal hygiene and grooming

Knowledge training A new employee needs to gain knowledge regarding the organization, its procedures, policies, and rules, and his/her co-workers. Some of the areas in which new employees require knowledge are:

- The layout of the entire hotel
- Hotel managers and HODs
- Co-workers with whom he/she is to coordinate

- Employee rights and benefits
- Grievance procedures
- Emergency procedures
- Telephone courtesy
- The housekeeping department's common procedures (for example, handling keys and ensuring maintenance)
- Room status codes

Present the training programme Start the training session with an introduction. While planning how to introduce a topic, keep the following points in mind:

I = Interest—Create interest about the topic.
N = Need—Explain the importance of the session.
T = Title—Emphasize the title.
R = Range—Discuss the range of the topic to be covered.
O = Objective—Enumerate the objectives to be achieved at the end of the session.

The content is the main part of the training session. It should evince clarity of thought. Attention research studies have shown that multi-sensory delivery helps a person to concentrate attention and integrate all the relevant information. Certain statistics regarding retention of information are presented in Exhibit 3.12. The exhibit shows the percentage of information retained through the five senses—vision, hearing, feeling, smelling, and tasting. These studies make it evident that training sessions must include discussions, demonstrations, audio-visual aids, and exercises, apart from lectures. This goes on to justify an old Chinese proverb, which says: I hear—I forget, I see—I remember, I do—I understand.

Exhibit 3.12 Retention of information

Sense	Information retained
Seeing	75%
Hearing	13%
Feeling	6%
Smelling	3%
Tasting	3%

Teaching skills to trainees When teaching skills to trainees, they need to be told as well as shown how to perform tasks. Job breakdowns act as guides to accomplishing this step in training. The new employee should be given written job breakdowns a day in advance, so that they can participate in the training session readily. Some recommendations for teaching new skills to a trainee are listed here:

- Demonstrate the skill at a normal speed.
- Break down the presentation of large amounts of information into sessions for easier assimilation.
- Repeat the demonstration at a slower pace, asking the trainees to perform along with you.
- Encourage the trainees; once they are confident, allow them to practise on their own.
- Follow up to see how the trainee is performing.

Summarizing and concluding the session This includes:

- recapitulation of the main points,
- inviting further clarification and discussion, and
- an assessment of the trainees' learning.

Practise After the training session, give the trainees ample opportunity and time to practise on their own, because when they do, they understand better. Encourage them during the practice and appreciate correct performance. Do not allow short cuts at this stage, or else they will become a habit later.

Follow-up Follow-up is important to make the employees good workers and comfortable in their jobs. Follow-up includes continuing on-the-job training, appraising performance, giving feedback, and evaluating progress.

Scheduling

The foremost step in scheduling is to determine fixed and variable staff positions. 'Fixed' staff positions are the ones that must be filled regardless of the occupancy level and volume of business. Managerial and administrative staff come under this head—for example, the executive housekeeper, assistant housekeepers, and supervisors. 'Variable' staff positions are the ones that vary in relation to changes in the hotel occupancy—for example, room attendants, and housemen.

Parameters to Consider

The executive housekeeper schedules employees by first checking the occupancy levels forecasted by the front office and then referring to the staffing guide table (see Exhibit 3.7). The employees need to be scheduled into various shifts.

Shift types

Most hotels operate 24 hours a day and these hours are covered in three shifts. Each shift's duration is 9 hours and these shifts are normally scheduled to overlap by an hour with the next shift to facilitate handovers and takeovers.

Straight shift This type of shift extends for a period of 9 hours with a break of 1 hour. For example, the morning shift and evening shift (also called afternoon shift) are both straight shifts.

Night shift/graveyard shift A standard night shift is actually a type of straight shift that normally starts from 10 p.m. and concludes at 7 a.m.

Break shift/split shift This type of shift is split into two sessions that add up to a regular shift of 9–10 hours. This includes a break of approximately 3–6 hours.

Rotating shift An employee may be given a particular shift for a week or two, and then changed over to the next shift. This rotation is done to ensure that all employees get a fair share of all the shifts.

Other scheduling concerns

While scheduling, the implications of a change of shifts must be considered. For example, changing over from a morning shift to an afternoon shift or from an afternoon shift to a night shift is acceptable, whereas changing from a night shift to a morning shift without a break is not.

Other scheduling considerations are as discussed below.

Overtime Employees may be asked to work overtime when there is a shortage of staff. This entitles the employee for double and/or compensatory off. Overtime must be avoided as it decreases productivity and increases employee cost.

Alternative scheduling techniques Getting the right staff for various job positions is challenging and it is sometimes wise to consider alternative scheduling techniques to accommodate and retain good staff. Alternative schedules vary from the typical 9–5 work hours. These schedules may attract the right kind of people out of those who find it difficult to fit into a 9–5 job. The alternate scheduling options are discussed in this section.

Part-time Part-time employees (PTE) do not work 9 hours a day like full-time employees. They may work only 4–5 hours per day. In the housekeeping department, the ideal example of a part-time position is that of a florist. The candidate for this position could be, say, a homemaker trained in flower arranging and willing to work 4–5 hours a day.

Flexi-time In this kind of scheduling, an employee can start and end his/her shift-time according to convenience and is paid accordingly.

Compressed work schedules An employee working 9 hours a day and 6 days a week puts in 54 employee hours per week. If the employee wishes, these 54 hours can be compressed within 5 days a week, that is, the employee would be required to work nearly 11 hours a day and get 2 days off to compensate.

Job sharing A full-time job may be shared between two part-time employees. The part-time employees involved usually work in different shifts. Job sharing is advantageous in cases where one partner resigns from the job and leaves. At such a time, the other employee stays and trains the new partner.

Legal Aspects of Scheduling

The executive housekeeper should be aware of certain legal aspects—The Shops and Establishments Act and the state employment rules—while drawing up schedules for employees. Some important issues are as follows.

Work hours Hours of work for employees should not exceed 9 hours per day.

Break for rest The break for rest is usually half an hour. Continuous work should not exceed 5 hours without a break.

Holidays and days off The employer should prepare a list of closed days at the beginning of each year and the same should be displayed in a conspicuous notice.

Work spreadover The work spreadover of an employee must not exceed 11–14 hours in a day and not more than two breaks should be given.

Child labour No child should work in any establishment.

Work environment Employees should be given clean, safe, and favourable conditions to work in.

Maternity leave Women should be entitled to maternity leave. Nursing women should be given an extra break for feeding their infants if the establishment is running a crèche.

The sample of a leave application form is given in Exhibit 3.13.

Work Schedules

A work schedule is a document that lists the actual tasks to be carried out by an employee in a particular shift and the time frame in which to undertake each task. The document includes the following:

- The position of the employee
- The area of operation
- The time at which the employee has to perform the allotted task
- Timings of meals, breaks, and any special job
- Time for tidying equipment and closing up

Work schedules must be written in simple language and have a concise form. Since the amount of work in a day may take longer than the length of one shift, several work schedules need to be compiled for use in one day. The number of schedules made for a given area is thus an indication

Exhibit 3.13 Sample of a leave application form

Hotel Cloud 9

Leave Application Form

Employee name .... Date of joining ....
Department .... Weekly off ....
Designation and grade .... Date of application ....

Sir/Madam,
I, ..., wish to avail, casual ☐/ sick ☐/ earned ☐, leave
of .... days, from the date .... to ....

Purpose: ....
....

Signature of employee ....
Signature of HOD: Approved/Refused ....
Signature of HR Manager ....

of the number of staff required to clean that area on the particular day. The schedules should be handed over to the employees when they report for work. A sample work schedule for a houseperson is given in Exhibit 3.14.

Planning Duty Rosters

Duty rosters specify the allotment of jobs, hours of duty, and days off for each member of the staff. To make for an even share of duties, the roster should be rotated every five weeks. Duty rosters must be simple in format, easy to interpret, clearly written, and displayed on the staff notice board at least a week in advance. A sample duty roster for GRAs is presented in Exhibit 3.15(a) and for managers and supervisors and housekeeping associates at a 100-room property in Exhibit 3.15(b). Duty rosters for other positions may be drawn up on the same lines.

Exhibit 3.14 Sample work schedule

Position: Houseman Area: Lobby

Time	Activity	
7.00 a.m.	Report to work; collect equipment and supplies.	
7.10 a.m.	• Clean glass doors. • Dry-mop floor at the entrance. • Damp-mop the entrance, including steps. • Sweep porch area.	• Damp-dust lounge area. • Damp-mop the lobby floor. • Disinfect house telephones. • Discard old flower arrangements.

Exhibit 3.15(a) Sample duty roster for GRAs in the housekeeping department

	Week 1						
GRA ↓	**Mon**	**Tue**	**Wed**	**Thu**	**Fri**	**Sat**	**Sun**
Jacob	8–5	8–5	8–5	8–2 5–9	8–5	Day off (R)	8–5
Mary	Day off (R)	8–5	8–5	8–5	8–5	8–2 5–9	8–5
Rosie	8–5	8–5	8–2 5–9	8–5	Day off (R)	8–5	8–5
Thomas	8–5	8–2 5–9	8–5	8–5	8–5	8–5	Day off (R)
Mini	8–2 5–9	8–5	Day off (R)	8–5	8–5	8–5	8–5
Paul	8–5	8–5	8–5	Day off (R)	8–2 5–9	8–5	8–5
Joseph— Reliever (R)	8–5	Day off	8–5	8–5	8–5	8–5	8–5

Exhibit 3.15(b) Sample duty roster for a 100-room property (Refer Exhibit 3.4 for guidelines)

Hotel XYZ

DUTY ROSTER
(100 room hotel with 10,000 sq. ft. public area)

Department: Housekeeping **Month:** January

MANAGERS AND SUPERVISORS

Sl No.	Name	Designation	Area	Shift	Weekly off	Reliever
1.	Mr. A	Executive housekeeper	All areas	9.00 a.m. – 6.00 p.m.	Sunday	–
2.	Ms. B	Assistant housekeeper	All areas	1.00 p.m. – 10.00 p.m.	Monday	–
			Morning Shift			
3.	Mr. C	Housekeeping supervisor	Floors	7.00 a.m. – 4.00 p.m.	Monday	R 1
4.	Ms. D	Housekeeping supervisor	Floors	7.00 a.m. – 4.00 p.m.	Tuesday	R 1
5.	Mr. E	Housekeeping supervisor	Public area	7.00 a.m. – 4.00 p.m.	Wednesday	R 1
6.	Ms. F	Linen room supervisor	Linen room	7.00 a.m. – 5.00 p.m.	Sunday	–
7.	Mr. G	Uniform room supervisor	Uniform room	7.00 a.m. – 5.00 p.m.	Sunday	–
8.	Ms. H	Desk supervisor	Control desk	7.00 a.m. – 5.00 p.m.	Thursday	R 1

Advantages of a duty roster

Planning a duty roster in advance helps to ensure:

- The exact number of staff required to be on duty at any given occupancy.
- That staff working hours are as per their employment contract.
- That regular off-days are availed for enhancing productivity.
- Knowledge of which employees are present on the premises in instances of emergencies.
- Accuracy in attendance and payroll reports.

Steps in making a roster

The steps in making up a duty roster are as follows:

Step 1 Ascertain occupancy levels and events expected in the hotel. This information is provided by the sales and marketing department at the beginning of the financial year. On a daily and a weekly basis, more specific reports of occupancy are available through coordination with the front office department. The overall forecasts of occupancy must be considered before scheduling the employees' annual leave. These forecasts also help the executive housekeeper to follow the staffing guide to ensure sufficient staff at peak periods and avoid excess employee during slack periods.

Step 2 Ascertain the spread of duty hours to be scheduled in the duty roster, whether 12 hours, 16 hours, or 24 hours. Decide whether the positions will work for 5 or 7 days per week.

Step 3 Ascertain the type of shift—straight shift, break shift, rotating shift, or any other alternative scheduling—to be used.

Step 4 Ascertain the number of full-time and part-time staff on the payroll.

Step 5 Ascertain the number of work hours per day and per week required for various positions.

Step 6 Incorporate coffee breaks and mealtime allowances in the roster.

Step 7 Ascertain that each employee gets a weekly off day after 6 working days. Provide for compensatory offs. Schedule one reliever per 6 employees.

Step 8 Ascertain closed days and restricted holidays, and any contingency planning that may be needed.

Managing Workplace Diversity

Workplace diversity refers to differences in the various defining personal traits of an organisation's employees in aspects of religion, culture, ethnicity and race, age, gender, physical abilities, socio-economic status, education, marital status, work experience, and career paths. These traits not only reflect the identity of employees but also the way they are perceived by their colleagues.

Diversity-oriented organisations fare much better in terms of productivity, innovation, performance and profitability. For instance, as per McKinsey Diversity Database, companies with racially and ethnically diverse workforces financially outperformed non-diverse teams by as much as 35% and those with gender diversity by 15%. Hospitality leaders across the world realize the significance of a diverse workforce and have been very proactive to ensure they create diversity-based teams in their organisations.

Dimensions of Workplace Diversity

Primary aspects: age, race, gender
Secondary aspects: religion, culture, education, physical abilities, socio-economic status
Workplace aspects: work experience, job position, and career paths
Style aspects: communication style, leadership style, work habits

Advantages of having a Diverse Workplace

- Diverse workforces bring in new perspectives and fresh ideas to the table as the hired employees are from a larger talent pool.
- Diverse teams encourage healthier workplace cultures. Both employees and customers get a clear message that efficiency and hard work is rewarded in the organization irrespective of an employee's race, religion, age, physical abilities, or gender.
- A diverse workforce understands the needs of diverse clients in hospitality industry in a better way leading to greater guest satisfaction.
- A diverse workplace gives insights to hospitality managers as to the demographics of the target markets.
- Multilinguistic workforce from varying religious and ethnic backgrounds can be of great assistance for hospitality chains having operations spread out in national and international markets.

Managing a Diverse Workforce

Housekeeping employees come from varied backgrounds and a housekeeping manager must be adept at handling diversity at workplace. There should be a culture of tolerance, transparency in operations, open communication channels, and effective conflict management interventions. The following strategies assist in managing a diverse workforce:

- Set standard rules and regulations for all employees so that all are treated at par and it is easier to maintain discipline.
- Create teams with diverse employees to encourage their understanding of varied cultures and overcome prejudices.
- Treat each employee as an individual, understanding their strengths and weaknesses and avoid making assumptions based on their background.
- Keep channels of communication open. There should be regular communication of policies, procedures, rules and regulations using methods and means to break communication barriers such as language.
- Carry out sensitivity training to disseminate awareness amongst employees on how to coexist harmoniously with colleagues from varied backgrounds. It is vital that specific sensitivity training be conducted at managerial level also.
- Communicate the code of conduct outlining the organisation's policy towards diversity. Other important documents highlighting diversity to be communicated are zero-tolerance policy, non-discrimination policy, grievance policy, compensation and benefits, employment conditions and termination grounds.

Motivating Employees

Motivating refers to the stimulating of an employee's interest in his job so that he is challenged into being attentive, observant, concerned, dedicated, and committed. Motivation is the result of satisfying the basic needs of the employee—physiological and monetary requirements; security and safety; acceptance; recognition; and self-development. Different factors motivate individual employees, and managers must use this knowledge effectively.

Methods of Motivating Employees

Employees can be motivated in a number of ways, ranging from providing cash incentives to delegating responsibilities in order to make them feel capable. Some such methods are discussed in this section.

Financial incentives Incentives may include payments of bonuses according to the profits achieved by the organization and ensuring an equal distribution of service charges. Salary and wages must also be competitive. Perks such as accommodation and transport are also financial incentives that motivate employees. However, it is important to understand that money per se is not the sole motivating factor for many employees.

Recognition Recognize and appreciate a job well done. It is not only complaints that have to be communicated, but also positive remarks from guests and managers. Awards such as 'Best Employee of the Year' or 'Employee of the Month' or 'Best Trainee' can act as a tremendous boost to employee performance. Other incentive programmes can be chalked out to motivate employees as well.

Participation Involve the employee in solving problems and facing setbacks. More fresh ideas come forth in this way, and at the same time, employees feel they are an important part of the team.

Communication In an organization where the channels of communication are open, the employees are well-informed and aware of the happenings in the department. They feel a sense of belongingness. An organizational newsletter acts as a sounding board and a mode of passing information along. Departmental notice boards should also convey and invite messages and information.

Delegating responsibilities Giving extra responsibility enriches an employee's routine job. It makes employees feel more capable and enhances their personal and career growth.

Training and cross-training Training improves the productivity of employees and makes them feel as if there is constantly something to learn in the job. Cross-training makes employees more flexible. They thus have more scope to grow in the organization.

Performance appraisal Appraisals help in evaluating the employees' performance. Challenging objectives can be very effective motivators if set by managers in consultation with the employees themselves and their supervisors. When employees know that their performance is being evaluated, they tend to be more productive.

Discipline Managers must always be just and fair while dealing with employees. Nothing is worse than not taking disciplinary action when called for. Leaving disciplinary issues unattended can demotivate other employees. Managers must themselves be role models, being unbiased and good at their work to win the respect of their subordinates.

Employee welfare Managers must set the interests of their subordinates before their own interests. They must have a genuine liking for people, understand them, and empathize with them.

Gestures such as greeting them every day, wishing them on their birthdays, and showing concern about their problems create a positive work environment for both subordinates and managers.

 Performance Appraisal

Performance appraisal refers to the process of evaluating an employee's job performance against set standards, providing feedback on his/her performance, and taking corrective action if the performance is not up to the mark. Employee performance appraisal is one of the most important aspects of managing personnel in which the executive housekeeper is involved.

Performance appraisal should be an ongoing process. Systematic, formal appraisal of employees should be done at periodic intervals throughout the individual's employment. The rule of thumb is to evaluate employees as often as necessary to let them know how they are doing and what they need to do to improve. For many employees, an annual performance appraisal may not be enough. Managers may need to informally appraise their employees periodically in addition to the annual, more formal performance appraisal. The first regular appraisal should occur at the end of a probationary period of employment, which may be of 3–6 months' duration, or sometimes more. After successfully completing their period of probation, the employee should be told when to expect the next appraisal.

Performance appraisals must contain the following information:

- A statement of observed strengths.
- An indication of whether assigned objectives have been met.
- A statement of observed weaknesses.
- A statement of counselled action—what the employee should do to improve their performance and what the employer will do to assist.
- An estimate of when the employee should be ready for promotion.

Functions of Performance Appraisal

Performance appraisals fulfil many different needs of the organization. Most of these needs fall into one of two categories: (i) improving work performance, and (ii) taking work-related decisions.

Performance feedback The basic use of a performance appraisal is to provide performance feedback. This feedback is intended to reinforce or help improve employees' performance. Employees normally want to know how well they are doing. Regular, scheduled appraisals enable managers to keep employees informed about their performance.

Employee training and development Appraisals can help to identify the employees or managers who are ready to move on. Appraisals can also be used to schedule training programmes by need on a departmental basis. For instance, a houseman may need additional training on new floor-cleaning equipment. Managers can determine the need for this training by conducting a training-oriented performance appraisal. In addition, appraisals can be useful aids in establishing career goals or long-term plans in conjunction with an employee's record over previous performance appraisals. Managers can provide effective employee guidance and career counselling keeping these in mind.

Aid to decision-making When used as an administrative tool, performance appraisals provide an effective way to link rewards and discipline to performance. Employees who are performing well may receive favourable evaluations that can lead to merit pay, promotions, career development assignments,

or beneficial transfers. Those who consistently receive poor evaluations can be legitimately identified for disciplining, demotion, or termination. Performance appraisals can provide some background in cases of disciplining, discharge, or grievance.

Evaluation of training policies and programmes Evaluating personnel before and after training measures the effectiveness of a training programme. Performance appraisals can be used to do this. The close contact during an evaluation provides an opportunity for managers and subordinates to discuss the goals and problems associated with specific policies or programmes. During an evaluation, managers may learn from employees that certain policies or programmes do not work as they were designed or intended to. Thus, evaluation can serve as a post-implementation test for new policies.

Validation of the selection process The goal of selection is to predict which candidates will perform best and which candidates will fit best in the organization. These predictions should be tested to determine whether the selection system works effectively. Performance appraisals provide an excellent opportunity to do this. For instance, when performance appraisals identify that recently hired employees are not performing well, managers may have evidence that the system of selection does not work well. On the other hand, appraisals may indicate that the system of selection works, by showing that many recently hired employees are meeting the organization's standards. Performance appraisals can also justify selection decisions.

Principal Appraisal Rating Systems

When developing an appraisal system, managers must first determine the type of behaviour they will rate. The three principal types of ratings used are:

- trait-based rating,
- behaviour-based rating, and
- results-based rating.

Trait-based rating This type of appraisal is used primarily to assess the personal characteristics of employees. These ratings weigh factors such as company loyalty, communication skills, attitude towards supervision, ability to work as part of a team, and decision-making ability.

Behaviour-based rating These assess employees in terms of their behaviour rather than their personal characteristics. For instance, such appraisals may rate employees on their friendliness towards guests, their helpfulness, how often they thank guests for their patronage, and so on. Hospitality operations often emphasize an employee's behaviour towards guests and other employees as much as that employee's actual ability to perform specific tasks.

Results-based rating These are based on the results achieved by the employee.

Methods of Appraising Performance

There are a number of performance appraisal methods; these can be classified as traditional and modern methods. The choice of any one method or a combination of some of these methods depends upon the purpose as well as the capability of the system. A sample performance appraisal form using the method of grading is presented in Exhibit 3.16. Figure 3.5 enumerates the various types of performance appraisals in terms of methodology.

Exhibit 3.16 Sample half-yearly appraisal form for non-supervisory staff

Employee name:				Designation:			Date of joining:	
Sl. No.	**Criteria**	**Initial date—Ratings**	**Final date—Ratings**	**5—Excellent**	**4—Good**	**3—Above average**	**2—Average**	**1—Below average**
1.	Technical Knowledge	5 4 3 2 1	5 4 3 2 1	Excellent knowledge of job and related work	Good knowledge of job, seldom needs help	Good knowledge but needs guidance and help at times	Acceptable knowledge, needs constant guidance	Poor knowledge
2.	Job effectiveness	5 4 3 2 1	5 4 3 2 1	Highly effective, manages job and time well. Role model for others	Effective. Can perform better using full potential	Effective but at times needs guidance	Is effective when guided but slips back again	Not effective
3.	Quality of work	5 4 3 2 1	5 4 3 2 1	Highest degree of quality, neatness, and accuracy	Good work but scope for improvement in neatness and accuracy	Good work but lacks consistency in neatness and accuracy	Average work, neatness and accuracy; needs constant guidance	Poor quality of work
4.	Extent of supervision required	5 4 3 2 1	5 4 3 2 1	No supervision is required, capable of performing independently	No supervision is required but at times makes mistakes in taking decisions	Needs occasional supervision but normally does the job well	Needs constant supervision to meet the standards	Poor worker, does not measure up to standards even after constant supervision
5.	Initiative	5 4 3 2 1	5 4 3 2 1	Shows keen sense of enthusiasm. Takes on additional responsibility	Good interest in work and asks for more duties	Enthusiastic but very selective about additional responsibility	No initiative but takes additional responsibilities when told	No initiative. Not interested in taking additional responsibility

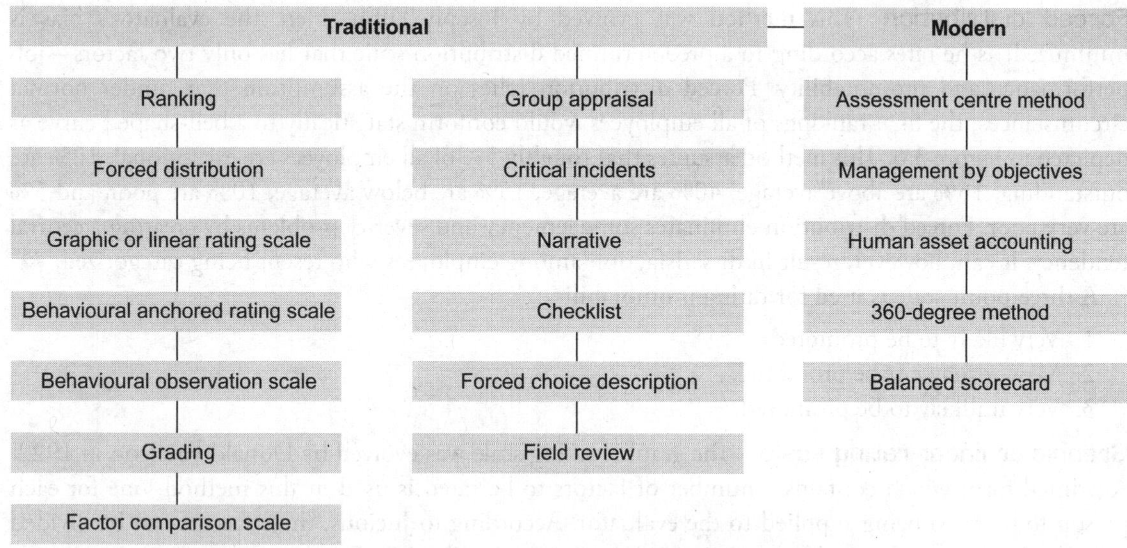

Fig. 3.5 Methods of performance appraisal

Traditional methods

There are many of these, having been developed over the last several decades.

Ranking Two ranking methods are commonly used. Each method eventually results in ranking employees from best to worst or first to last.

Straight ranking/simple ranking This is the oldest method of performance appraisal. In this method, the employee and his performance are considered an entity by the evaluator. Here, the ranking of an employee in a work group is done against others in the group. Persons are tested and placed in a simple grouping. There are certain limitations to this method. In practice, it is difficult to compare a single individual with a group of other human beings having different behavioural traits. The task of ranking is especially difficult when a large number of people are ranked. Simple ranking does not provide a systematic procedure for determining relative rank, hence there may be snap judgements.

Paired comparison Each employee is compared with all the others in a group, but taking them one at a time, as depicted in the example discussed in this section. The number of times each individual is compared with another is tallied on a piece of paper. These numbers yield the rank order of the entire group. The number of decisions is determined by the formula:

$$N(N-1)/2$$

where N is the number of persons to be compared.

An example Let us consider the paired comparison of Lizzy, Mary, Jacob, and Raj. Now, consider that:

- Mary is better than Jacob.
- Raj is better than Mary.
- Lizzy is better than Jacob.
- Lizzy is better than Raj.
- Raj is better than Jacob.

Here, Lizzy is ranked first, Raj is ranked second, Mary is ranked third, and Jacob is ranked fourth.

Forced distribution This method was evolved by Joseph Tiffin. Here the evaluator's bias is minimized, as he rates according to a predetermined distribution scale that has only two factors—job performance and promotability. Forced distribution relies on the assumption that, under normal circumstances, the final rankings of all employees would conform statistically to a bell-shaped curve as depicted in Figure 3.6. This method assumes that roughly 5% of all employees are exceptional, 10% are outstanding, 15% are above average, 40% are average, 15% are below average, 10% are poor, and 5% are very poor. Forced distribution eliminates some leniency and severity problems by creating a central tendency. It can, however, result in dissatisfaction among employees who resent being categorized.

A three-point scale is used for rating promotability:

1. Very likely to be promoted.
2. May or may not be promoted.
3. Very unlikely to be promoted.

Graphic or linear rating scale The graphic rating scale was evolved by Donald Paterson in 1922. A printed form which contains a number of factors to be rated is used in this method, one for each person to be rated being supplied to the evaluator. According to Jucious, these factors can be divided into two groups: employee characteristics and employee contribution. Employee characteristics include qualities such as initiative, leadership, attitude, decisiveness, enthusiasm, loyalty, coordination, and so on. Employee contributions include quality and quantity of work, goals achieved, leadership offered, responsibility assumed, attitude towards superiors and associates, and so on.

Sometimes a discontinuous graphic scale or multiple-type scale is used, where one factor is distributed along a scale consisting of appropriate boxes. The continuous graphic rating scale permits a statistical tabulation of scores, which indicates the worth of every individual. This method was introduced by Walter D. Scott. The evaluator can here make as fine a discrimination of merit as he chooses.

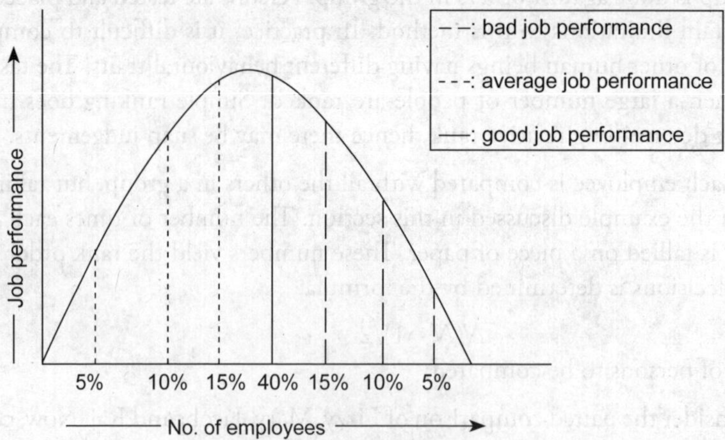

5%—Exceptional; 5%—Very poor; 10%—Outstanding; 10%—Poor; 15%—Above average; 15%—Below average; 40%—Average.

Fig. 3.6 Bell-shaped curve for the forced distribution method

Behaviourally anchored rating scale (BARS) BARS requires appraisers to rate employees along a continuum. Appraisers rate the specific actions or dimensions of an employee's work based on critical incidents. The critical incidents written out on a BARS appraisal form provide specific examples of what are considered to be good and bad behaviours.

Critical incidents are work-related events that managers observe and record to form an accurate picture of a job's requirements. Normally, the critical incidents used on a BARS form are developed by a committee of subordinates and managers. Since employees participate in determining the criteria for ranking, the BARS method is often more accepted by the employees than other methods of performance appraisal. BARS often provides more accurate ratings of overall performance. The major weakness of the BARS method is the amount of time and the expense required to develop a viable system. Each job requires a totally different appraisal form, since critical incidences are different for each. The format for a BARS form is presented in Exhibit 3.17.

Behavioural observation scale (BOS) The BOS was developed in response to criticism of the BARS method. Since the BARS method allows only one measure of each employee on a specific scale, some researchers thought that it would not provide a fair assessment of employees who only sometimes performed poorly. Instead of using critical incidents as the measurements, the BOS method establishes the critical incidents as the behaviour to be observed and asks appraisers to evaluate how often employees behave in this way. A sample BOS format is presented in Exhibit 3.18.

Grading The evaluator considers certain features and marks them according to a scale. The selected features may be analytical ability, cooperativeness, dependability, self-expression, job knowledge, leadership, or similar. An example of a grading scale is presented in Exhibit 3.19.

Factor comparison scale or man-to-mass comparison method In this method, certain factors are selected for the purpose of analysis, such as (say) leadership, dependability, and initiative. A scale is designed by the evaluator for each factor. A scale is also created for each selected factor instead of comparing to key men, in respect of one factor at a time.

Group appraisal method Here, employees are rated by an appraisal group consisting of their immediate supervisor and three or four other supervisors who have knowledge of that job. They discuss the standards of performance and the actual performance, and offer suggestions for future improvements.

Exhibit 3.17 BARS format

Position: Guest room attendant (GRA)		
Excellent	10 points	Description of critical incidents
	9 points	Description of critical incidents
Good	8 points	Description of critical incidents
	7 points	Description of critical incidents
Average	6 points	Description of critical incidents
	5 points	Description of critical incidents
Below average	4 points	Description of critical incidents
	3 points	Description of critical incidents
Poor	2 points	Description of critical incidents
	1 point	Description of critical incidents

Exhibit 3.18 Behavioural observation scale

1. Efficient bed-making	1	2	3	4	5
	Almost never				Almost always
2. Efficient cleaning	1	2	3	4	5
	Almost never				Almost always
3. Coordination with co-workers	1	2	3	4	5
	Almost never				Almost always

Exhibit 3.19 Example of grading scale

1. Dependability	1	2	3	4	5
2. Job knowledge	1	2	3	4	5
3. Cooperativeness	1	2	3	4	5

1 – Exceptional; 2 – Above average; 3 – Average; 4 – Below average; 5 – Poor.

The advantages of this method are that it is very simple and it is devoid of any bias as it involves multiple judges. The disadvantage of the method is that it is time consuming.

Critical incidents This method attempts to measure a worker's performance in terms of certain events or episodes that occur in the performance of the job, referred to as critical incidents. The basis here is the principle that there are certain significant acts in each employee's behaviour and performance, which make all the difference between success and failure on the job. The incidents are then ranked in the order of frequency and importance. The advantage of this method is that it provides information that is readily useful in performance appraisal. The critical incidents method also creates symbolic goals or stories that depict behaviours to emulate. The disadvantage of this method is that managers must keep careful logs of each critical incident they observe.

Narrative method Evaluators using the narrative method simply write an essay that describes the employees they are rating. Ideally, evaluators should take the time to write essays that present an accurate picture of employee performance. When carefully written, these essays are very useful in filling up gaps left by more quantitative methods. Narrative essays should provide written suggestions on how employees can improve. Managers typically do not take the time to write careful essays that describe the performance of their employees, though.

Checklist The evaluator does not evaluate employee performance in this method, but supplies reports about it. He/she answers a series of questions concerning an employee and his behaviour in positive and negative terms. This method suffers from bias on the part of the evaluator and it is difficult to weigh a number of statements about employee characteristics and contributions. A sample checklist is presented in Exhibit 3.20.

Exhibit 3.20 Sample checklist

1. Is the employee really interested in his job?	Yes/No
2. Is he regular in his job?	Yes/No
3. Is he respected by his subordinates?	Yes/No
4. Does he show uniform behaviour to all?	Yes/No
5. Does he give recognition and praise to employees for work well done?	Yes/No

Forced choice description In this method, the rating elements are several sets of adjectives relating to job proficiency or personal qualifications. The appraiser selects from these pairs the statement that he feels best describes the employee. This method is objective, as the evaluator cannot be biased and he is forced to choose at least one statement and yet the options are limited. The disadvantage is that the method is very detailed and the evaluator finds it difficult to rate a person as he does not know how the items are scored. An example of this method is presented in Exhibit 3.21.

Field review This method is used for a large organization. Here ratings are obtained by largely using a simple three-way categorization—outstanding, satisfactory, or unsatisfactory. Thus, no appraisal forms need to be filled out. The personnel department interviews line supervisors to evaluate their respective subordinates. The supervisor is required to give his opinion about the progress, level of performance, and weaknesses of his subordinates verbally, which are made into notes and placed in respective personnel files. The success of this method depends upon the competence of the interviews. This evaluation keeps the supervisor on his toes and minimizes bias.

Modern methods

The assessment centre method, management by objectives, and human asset accounting are referred to as the modern methods of performance appraisal.

Assessment centre method In this method, many evaluators join together to judge an employee's performance in several situations to determine the employee's potential for promotion. This involves a paper-and-pencil test, interviews, and situational exercises. The method is also used to select employees

Exhibit 3.21 Forced choice description method

Employee name: ------------------------------

Designation: ------------------------------

Please tick one from each pair of the following:

1. (a) Makes little effort at individual instruction.	(b) Makes maximum effort at individual instruction.
2. (a) Organizes his work well.	(b) Disorganized in his work.
3. (a) Makes people feel at ease.	(b) Lacks the ability to make people feel at ease.
4. (a) Has a cool and even temperament.	(b) Is very rash and temperamental.
5. (a) Is very punctual and disciplined.	(b) Is rarely punctual and disciplined.

for lower-level positions. The merit of this system is that it is a better method for identifying managerial potential.

Management by objectives The management by objectives (MBO) method was evolved by Peter Drucker in 1954. The MBO method involves meetings between subordinates and managers or between managers and their supervisors in which joint goals are established. Specific plans for achieving each goal are also established, as are the means for measuring progress towards the achievement of these goals. An MBO system requires regular meetings to assess progress made towards the goals established. Ultimately employees are rated on their achievement of the goals. The steps in establishing an MBO programme are as follows:

1. Employee proposes goals for upcoming evaluation period.
2. Employee and managers discuss goals, modify as necessary, and reach an agreement on specific goals, which are established and agreed to upon in writing.
3. Employee and managers agree on specific action plan to attain goals.
4. Managers encourage goal attainment informally during evaluation period.
5. At the end of the period, employee and managers meet again to discuss accomplishments and agree on the extent to which goals were attained.
6. Process is repeated.

Human asset accounting This refers to activity devoted to attaching money estimates to the value of a firm's internal human organization and its external customer.

360° feedback This has been described as an appraisal technique designed to produce a rounded picture of the individual in *A Dictionary of Human Resource Management*. It is based on the principle that the individual must receive feedback from all angles, not just his/her line manager. So, in addition, feedback comes from subordinates, peers, work colleagues from other departments, customers/clients, etc. These various appraisers describe the person's competences and behaviours, typically using an anonymous, questionnaire-based feedback form.

Balanced scorecard (BSC) As a model of performance appraisal, the BSC articulates the links between leading inputs (human and physical), processes, and lagging outcomes, and focuses on the importance of managing these components to achieve the organization's strategic goals. The BSC works by choosing measures and targets. It also gives light to the company's vision and mission. These two elements must always be referred to, when preparing a BSC.

The four steps required to design a BSC included in Kaplan & Norton's writing on the subject in the late 1990s are as follows:

1. Translating the vision into operational goals
2. Communicating the vision and link it to individual performance
3. Business planning; index setting
4. Feedback and learning, and adjusting the strategy accordingly

To aid the identification of measures, the writers proposed the following four perspectives:

Financial perspective It encourages the identification of a few relevant high-level financial measures. Designers of appraisals were encouraged to choose measures that helped inform the answer to the question 'How do we look to shareholders?'

Customer perspective It encourages the identification of measures that answer the question 'How do customers see us?'

Internal business processes perspective It encourages the identification of measures that answer the question 'What must we excel at?'

Learning and growth It encourages the identification of measures that answer the question 'How can we continue to improve, create value, and innovate?'

These are depicted in Figure 3.7.

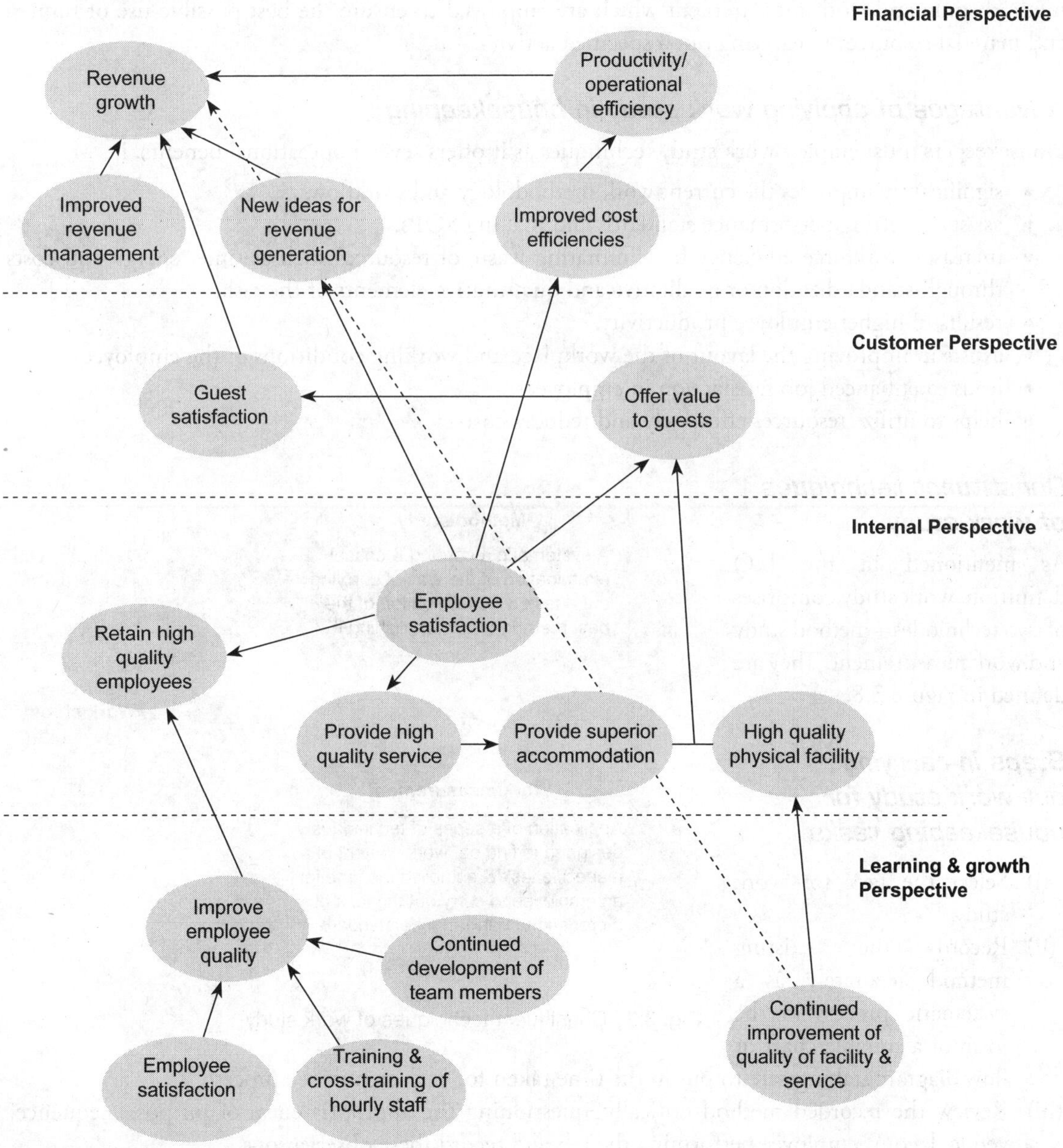

Financial Perspective
Revenue growth
Productivity/ operational efficiency
Improved revenue management
New ideas for revenue generation
Improved cost efficiencies
Customer Perspective
Guest satisfaction
Offer value to guests
Internal Perspective
Employee satisfaction
Retain high quality employees
Provide high quality service
Provide superior accommodation
High quality physical facility
Learning & growth Perspective
Improve employee quality
Continued development of team members
Continued improvement of quality of facility & service
Employee satisfaction
Training & cross-training of hourly staff

Fig. 3.7 The four perspectives in balanced scorecard

Source: Doran, M., K. Haddad,and C. Chow (2002),'Maximising the Success of Balanced Scorecard Implementation in the Hospitality Industry', *International Journal of Hospitality and Tourism Administration*, 3(3), pp. 33–58, http://www.informaworld.com. Used with the permission of Taylor and Francis Ltd.

Work Study, Time and Motion Studies and Job Analysis

Work Study

The International Labour Organization defines work study as a term that embraces the techniques of method study and work measurement which are employed to ensure the best possible use of human and material resources in carrying out a specified activity.

Advantages of applying work study in housekeeping

Housekeepers must employ work study techniques as it offers several operational benefits; it,

- significantly improves the current work methodology and workflow.
- assists in setting performance standards and making SOPs.
- increases workforce efficiency by eliminating waste of resources such as time, energy and costs through standardization of qualitative and quantitative elements of the task.
- results in higher employee productivity.
- assists in improving the layout of the workplace and working conditions of the employees.
- leads to enhanced job satisfaction in employees.
- helps to utilize resources effectively and reduces costs.

Constituent techniques of work study

As mentioned in the ILO definition, work study comprises of two techniques – method study and work measurement. They are defined in Figure 3.8.

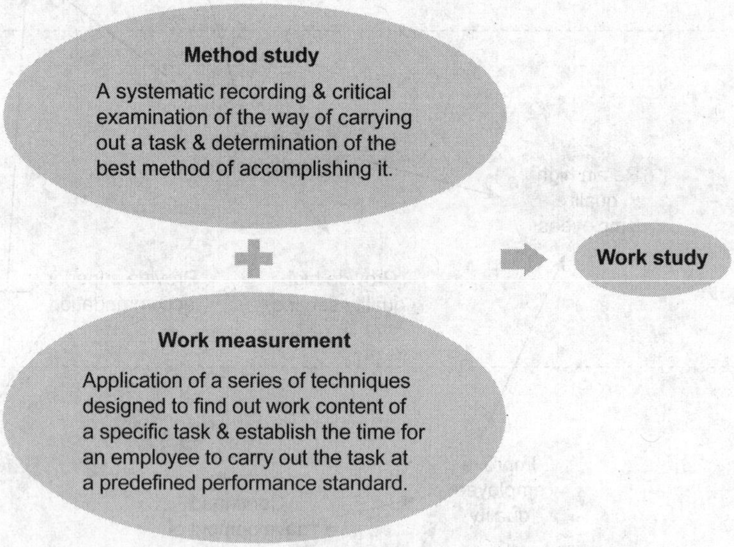

Method study
A systematic recording & critical examination of the way of carrying out a task & determination of the best method of accomplishing it.

+

Work measurement
Application of a series of techniques designed to find out work content of a specific task & establish the time for an employee to carry out the task at a predefined performance standard.

→ **Work study**

Fig. 3.8 Constituent techniques of work study

Steps in carrying out work study for housekeeping tasks

(i) Select the task for work study.
(ii) Record the existing method accurately as a systematic process in the form of a suitable chart or flow diagram, taking care to put in the time taken for each step in the process.
(iii) Review the recorded method critically, questioning the appropriateness of purpose, sequence, venue, layout, employee performing the job and record these observations.

(iv) Discuss the procedure step by step with the employee performing the task daily, if there is a way of further simplifying the methods involved in the task or doing it more efficiently & economically.

(v) Compute the average standard time and work content using time and motion study.

(vi) Define and create an SOP with the new method and time, making it the standard of performance.

Time and Motion Study

Extensive research in the form of time and motion studies to analyse work methods has helped the industry to find better and easier ways to carry out tasks and save time and energy, and the same is true for the housekeeping tasks as well.

Time and motion studies combine the *Time Study* work of Frederick Winslow Taylor with the *Motion Study* work of Frank and Lillian Gilbreth.

Time study

Time study is mostly observing and recording the time required for performing each detailed task of an operation. It involves the following steps:

1. Dividing the work into various parts or components.
2. Recording the time taken by different employees in completing the task.
3. Selecting the average worker.
4. Recording the time taken by the average worker to perform similar work under normal conditions.
5. Setting up the standard time. Every worker is required to complete the work within the standard time.

Motion study

Motion study is the sequence of eliminating wastefulness resulting from using unwanted steps. The aim of motion study is to identify the scheme of work or the best suited method of doing a given work. The steps involved in a motion study are as follows:

1. Selecting an efficient worker.
2. Analysing the movement involved.
3. Recording the best motion involving the minimum time and effort.
4. Selecting the most efficient working system.

These work measurement techniques help in determining the best method of doing a work and the standard time allowed for it. It is on these rules that the standard is set.

The time and motion studies for a task calculate how long it takes, on an average, to perform a certain task. The sample format given in Exhibit 3.22 may be used for the purpose. This helps in calculating staffing levels.

To do a time and motion study, several staff members perform the same task (say, bed-making), one by one. Their movements are studied and clocked. The results are compared and an analysis is done as to how long it takes on an average to perform the task. The best practices derived from this study are then used by everyone, so that the resulting performance will be more standardized.

Exhibit 3.22 Time and motion study format

Area:			**Starting time: ....**	
Task:			**Completion time: ....**	
Employee names:			**Duration:.................**	
Time	**Name of employee A**	**Name of employee B**	**Name of employee C**	**Remarks**

Advantages of time and motion study

The advantages of the time and motion study are as follows:

1. It improves the methods and procedures of performing various jobs.
2. It helps in improving the layout of the hotel facility.
3. It improves the utilization of resources.
4. It reduces human effort by proper designing of processes.
5. It helps to develop suitable working conditions.

Techniques involved in time and motion studies

Time and motion studies may be carried out using any of the techniques discussed in this section.

Pathway chart This technique involves the study of the path covered by the worker in the undertaking and completion of a task. A floor plan of the work area is drawn to scale and fixed to a board on the wall. A long thread is pinned down at the starting point on the plan. The line of motion is marked using this thread—whenever the worker turns, that point is marked with a pin and the thread wound around it. The length of the thread gives an idea of the distance traversed in the completion of the task. The time taken is also noted down. Various pathways are tried out to find the simplest and smallest route to finishing the task successfully. This is done to achieve the least exertion and minimal loss of energy and time. This technique helps pinpoint all movements that can be reduced or eliminated.

Process chart All tasks, in order to be completed, require a specific process or activity. In this technique, a close study of the process adopted is carried out and the flow of activity closely studied. A record of the time taken to finish the task is kept. All unnecessary movements and steps are then listed down, so as to be avoided in the final process adopted.

Operation chart This technique helps one track down all wasteful expenditure of time and energy in all activities. The technique requires a detailed study of all the smaller activities making up a work process. The movements of the two hands are studied in great detail and a fine analysis shows where in the job delays are occurring.

Micro-motion film analysis Using a timing device, every activity is filmed. Then a detailed study, especially of the finer movements of the hands and other parts of the body, helps analyse the areas where changes need to be or can be made to carry out the task with the least expenditure of time and energy.

Cyclography This is also a technique that uses filming. Here, a bulb is attached to the worker's body (may be the hand, the legs, or the back). As the body or the body part so highlighted moves during the activity, the path taken is lighted by the electric bulb and hence easily captured by slow photography. The analysis of the complete film or the record of movements helps reveal how smooth and rhythmic the movements of the activity are. Thus, the worker can be guided to make the necessary changes.

Chronocyclography In this technique, a film of the activity is made with small lights attached to the middle finger. The pattern or movement is filmed and finally analysed to find out which movements were unnecessary or arrhythmic and can be eliminated or improved upon.

Job Analysis

Job analysis is the process of examining a job in order to identify its component parts and the circumstances in which it is performed. It is a way of determining what knowledge an employee must have, what tasks each employee needs to perform, and the standards to which he or she must perform them. Job analysis involves an examination of the following:

- *Job knowledge* (or identifying the purpose of the job)—what it exists for and what key results are expected from it.
- The *setting* of the job—the physical, organizational, and social conditions of the job.
- The *task list*—the main tasks that have to be performed in order to achieve the requisite results.
- A *job breakdown*—one must be developed for each task performed by each employee position.
- The *resources or facilities* available to the employee—what people, equipment, services, and so on the employee can call upon.

Job analysis is the foundation for training employees well and preventing performance problems.

Teamwork and Leadership

The current trend in housekeeping operations is to form teams to accomplish tasks rather than scheduling employees on an individual basis. The three important determinants of teamwork are leadership, the building of the right kind of groups or teams for better productivity, and membership (which reflects the individual contributions people will make towards team goals).

A housekeeping team may consist of one supervisor, several (2–5) GRAs, and one houseman. This team under the supervisor becomes totally responsible for a particular section of guestrooms in the hotel. Cleaning performance, say, is then measured on a team basis rather than on individual basis.

Team Cleaning—An Example of Teamwork

In team cleaning, two or more GRAs together clean one guestroom at a time. Usually teams of two GRAs each are assigned to 30–35 rooms. Team members rotate duties of bedroom and bathroom cleaning. Team cleaning is successful when ideas come from the employees themselves and they are given a free hand in their implementation. Team cleaning works in hotels that are willing to make a change to meet new challenges.

Promoting teamwork within each team requires special effort. A teamwork checklist, such as the one shown below, should be followed by the executive housekeeper to make it a success.

- Reward teamwork by praising the team and giving them choice assignments, raises, and promotions—just as you would individual performers.
- Include teamwork as a criterion during the employee's performance appraisals.
- Rotate special assignments, allowing everyone an opportunity to shine as an individual occasionally.
- Consider ideas generated jointly by the team as well as individual ideas.
- Share information and give the team a say in decision-making.
- Give credit to the team for jobs well done.
- Set an example of cooperation with others yourself.

Advantages of teamwork

There are many advantages of teamwork. Some of these are as follows.

- A principal advantage to the manager is in being able to schedule a group of people as though they were one entity.
- Cooperation and workers' morale will be higher when they are part of a small unit rather than solitary individuals in a large group of people.
- Team spirit will cause the entire group to excel in operations. GRAs who excel in room cleaning help the poorer performers on the team to improve.
- Absenteeism and tardiness get better resolved at the team level because one member being absent or late could have a negative effect on the entire team's reputation.
- With increasing concern for safety and security, assigning two or more GRAs to clean a room could save expenses on liabilities and lawsuits.
- Mundane cleaning tasks may become fun when performed as a team.
- Fewer tools are needed—for example, one room attendant's cart, one vacuum cleaner, and one hand caddy can equip a team of two.
- Some heavier cleaning tasks are accomplished more easily and faster with two people—for example, moving beds, turning over heavy mattresses, making up a double bed, and so on.
- Bringing new employees up to the required standards becomes easier since they have buddies to coach them along the way.
- There is saving on costs since team workers complete work faster, have better attendance, meet with fewer accidents, and develop greater interest in improving the processes.

Some guidelines for team cleaning

When planning for team cleaning, the executive housekeeper must address the following considerations:

- Have linen and cleaning inventories equally distributed so that teams do not fight over supplies.
- If a team must stop because it is faced with some hurdle, the work output of 2–3 people is stopped, as opposed to only one in the traditional method of guestroom cleaning. Hence, the executive housekeeper should make sure that adequate supplies are available and teams are given an accurate list of room assignments.
- Scheduling may require special effort to accommodate team members getting the same days off.

Leadership

For teamwork in housekeeping to be successful, the department leader, that is, the executive housekeeper, needs to be an inspiring role model as a team player as well as an effective leader. The leader of any group can help to build its members into a well-knit team by sharing visions, goals, and strategies with them.

Leadership is the capacity to frame plans that will succeed and the faculty to persuade others to carry them out in the face of difficulties. Leadership quality in a manager makes people look up to him/her for advice, feel motivated to work for and respect the manager, and be loyal to the manager. An executive housekeeper who can mobilize the trust and support of the staff achieves great heights. Some executive housekeepers who are good planners and organizers fail to achieve results because they are not effective as leaders. An executive housekeeper who is a good leader will ensure the following activities:

- Draft a compelling vision
- Communicate passionately
- Get cooperation from others
- Inspire and pull employees towards goals
- Provide direction and momentum
- Be assertive if necessary
- Learn from other leaders
- Make decisions in line with the vision
- Get feedback
- Command and not demand respect and loyalty
- Do some self-evaluation as well

Different leadership styles, as presented in Table 3.1, may be used by executive housekeepers. Some distinctly make people work by order or force; others join the group and initiate activity; still others use persuasion; while some, by their pleasant and endearing manner, generate the enthusiasm for work and achieve goals in the best possible manner. An executive housekeeper who is an effective leader uses all these styles to different extents, according to the nature of the decisions to be made and as the situations demand.

Table 3.1 Styles of leadership

Leadership style	Characteristics
Autocratic	Imposes own decision with/without explanation to subordinates
Participative	Decision made after prior consultation with subordinates
Democratic	Joint decision arrived at
Laissez faire	Decisions taken by delegation

Most often, executive housekeepers tend to use the participative style and depend more on communication, adopting a supportive attitude and sharing needs, values, goals, and expectations with their staff. When employees, regardless of their level of education, are involved in decision-making, they become highly contributive to successful decisions of major consequence. They are then not only committed to the outcome of these decisions, but are also involved in the success or failure of such decisions and are thereby motivated to continue their participation and personal growth.

A self-assessment needs to be carried out by executive housekeepers to find out which style of leadership they adopt as their principal one in actuality. The questions listed below need to be addressed for such self-assessment.

Do I tend to...

- think 'I' or 'we'?
- be concerned with things or with people?
- drive employees or coach them?

- say 'go' or 'let's go'?
- take credit or give credit?
- instil fear or enthusiasm?
- see today or look at tomorrow?
- let the employee know how the job is to be done or show them how to do the job?
- depend on authority or goodwill?
- work hard to produce results myself or work hard to help employees produce results?
- let employees know where I stand or where they stand?
- fix blame for breakdowns or show how to fix the breakdown?
- 'use' employees or to 'develop' them?

Employee Welfare and Discipline

Two of the most important functions or duties of a good team leader is ensuring the welfare of subordinates and maintaining discipline.

Employee Welfare

Good employees are hard to come by. Once found, it is up to the executive housekeeper to be concerned with their welfare in order that they stay. Each employee should be recognized as an individual and not just as another pair of hands. The executive housekeeper should know all employees by name and also know something of their lives beyond their work, as this knowledge will enable her to understand, sympathize, and make allowances for individual performance, when necessary. Welfare should also cover the families of the workers, especially in India, where because of strong family ties, the well-being of workers is closely affected by their family's welfare.

The executive housekeeper should aim at gaining maximum at minimum cost through a loyal and cooperative workforce. There are certain needs of employees that need to be addressed in order to achieve this aim. These are often referred to as 'staff welfare provisions'. These welfare services may fall under either the statutory requirements guided by various acts formulated by the Government of India or those over and above the legal minimum requirements. The latter are referred to as 'fringe benefits' or 'perks', and employers are not legally bound to provide them. Staff welfare provisions address various needs, falling under these heads:

- Physical needs
- Physiological needs
- Psycho-social needs

Physical needs This refers to the need for comfort at work, for which welfare activities are directed towards provision of:

- Proper lighting for good visibility
- Optimum temperature and humidity control for comfort
- Fresh air free from bad odours, toxic gases, and so on, ensured through good ventilation systems
- Low noise levels
- A clean, sanitary environment
- Safety procedures and safety devices
- Well-designed equipment and furniture
- Clean uniforms

Physiological needs Satisfying these optimally calls for the provision of the following:

- Safe drinking water
- Mess facilities
- Rest periods and rooms/areas designated for the purpose
- Clean toilets
- Medical facilities
- Recreational facilities

Psycho-social needs These include the following:

- Adequate wage payments
- Pension, provident fund, insurance, and loan facilities
- Accommodation
- Transport facilities
- Infant crèches for working mothers
- Working hours when the person is working with other people rather than alone
- Leisure and holidays
- Counselling services to address and obviate stress
- Training and development opportunities
- Paid holidays, sick leave, and medical reimbursements
- Maternity and paternity leave, the latter being a recent trend in India and given only by a few corporate companies yet

Discipline

At some point, most managers are faced with the unpleasant but necessary task of disciplining an employee. In some instances, problems may be corrected without a formal disciplinary process. When a manager fails to address improper behaviour, the behaviour is reinforced and encouraged. Overlooking these problems may set the stage for accusations of favouritism, discrimination, and unfair practices. Every well-run company must have rules and regulations governing the conduct of its employees in order to achieve the company's objectives.

In the housekeeping department, the executive housekeeper should not make more rules for her staff than are necessary, but those that she makes must be enforced. The executive housekeeper must at all times act as an example to her staff, keep a cool head, and ensure that discipline is maintained at a reasonable level, consistent with management policy.

Discipline should be imposed in case of problems in the following issues/areas:

- Attendance
- Working hours
- Uniforms
- Smoking
- Care and use of hotel property
- Safety procedures
- Following instructions
- Standards of cleanliness
- Working areas
- Restroom usage
- Alcohol and drugs
- Security procedures
- Hotel facilities
- Standards of appearance
- Telephone usage
- Lost-and-found items
- Deadly weapons

Employees must adhere to the rules and regulations governing these issues.

Disciplinary action

There may be recourse to one of the following courses of action in disciplining, as and when necessary.

Informal counselling Before setting out to take disciplinary action, get to know the reason behind the concerned employee's behaviour, especially if the person has never had a negative record before. If the problem is understood, some accepted alternative could be worked out without affecting others or the course of work. Many a times, an informal counselling session is enough to set things right.

Progressive formal discipline If after counselling, the employee still does not change the culpable behaviour, start with the progressive formal disciplinary process. This constitutes the following actions, executed one level at a time for each repetition of the offending behaviour:

(a) Spoken warning
(b) Written warning
(c) Suspension
(d) Termination

To be consistently fair in the application of rules and deliver equitable treatment to all employees, a system of issuing written warnings must be developed, such as to offer constructive criticism and provide the employee with an opportunity to improve or correct a disciplinary problem. A written warning is issued for any violation of rules or for sub-standard work and is signed by the manager as well as the employee concerned. If the employee is not in the probationary period of employment and has been confirmed on the payroll of the company, as a disciplinary action, he may be discharged from duties if he has been given three written warnings for the same or different offences over a single year.

Certain recommended behaviours on the part of a leader when taking disciplinary action are listed here. Do…

- conduct a thorough investigation of the incident.
- document the action taken.
- be firm, fair, and consistent.
- stick to the decision.
- be mindful of the unwritten rules of the organization.
- support the employee, though not the behaviour.

Conducting a disciplinary conference

These are the steps to be taken when meeting with an employee over disciplinary concerns:

1. Review the personnel file of the employee being disciplined.
2. Greet the employee; create a warm, receptive atmosphere. Explain the purpose of the conference.
3. Review the problem in a specific and objective manner.
4. Give the employee a chance to explain the problem from his perspective. Listen.
5. Ask the employee to develop a plan of action to correct the undesirable behaviour.
6. Summarize commitments agreed to clearly. Establish a follow-up date.
7. Explain the need for written documentation. Allow the employee to read and sign the disciplinary report.
8. Explain what the next course of action will be if the undesirable behaviour persists.
9. Concluding the conference is a critical part. The employee may be upset. This is a good time to express confidence in the employee and to reassure him/her that you will be available to help in any way possible.
10. The written documentation signed by both parties must be forwarded to the personnel department and filed in the employee's personnel file.

Quality Management

Quality management is a continued effort and highly significant for ensuring guest satisfaction and trust. ISO 9000:2015 defines quality as 'the degree to which a set of inherent characteristics of an object (product, service, process, person, organisation, system or resource) fulfils requirements.' Quality implies many factors such as freedom from defects, fitness for purpose and use, degree of excellence and conformity to set standards.

Quality management refers to a disciplined approach of integrating the application of qualitative, quantitative and management techniques to continuously improve the processes within an organisation in an endeavour to meet and exceed customer expectations.

Benefits of Quality Management

Quality management is essentially an integrated effort of the stakeholders of the organisation - the management, employees and vendors to meet and exceed guest expectations. The benefits of quality management to an organisation are immense; it,

- ensures improvement in work culture, systems and processes leading to superior quality of services and products.
- leads to customer satisfaction and eventually a loyal customer.
- results in higher productivity of the organisation's departments.
- ensures close coordination and inculcates teamwork in employees.
- helps organisations to reduce waste of inventory and resources.
- ensures increased revenues.

Guest's Perception of Quality

In the hospitality industry, service and product quality is essentially guest-oriented, i.e., it is dependent on guests' needs and expectations. Service quality is not easy to measure, therefore, hospitality managers rely on guest's quality perception and expectations to arrive at desired results. Guest's perceptions are being made during the service delivery process and while using or consuming the product and then again after accomplishing these.

For a hospitality business it is crucial to analyse the factors that drive consumer behaviour as perceptions vary for different guests. Knowing how guests perceive product and service quality and measurement of the same is highly advantageous to hotels to maintain the required quality standards which make for a repeat customer. Whether guest perception fails to match guest expectation, or matches and exceeds the same, it finds a way on social networking platforms through e-WOM or electronic word of mouth. This in turn invariably shapes perceptions of other potential customers.

Management of product and service quality primarily emphasises on managing gaps between guest expectations and perceptions. Guest perceptions can be gauged through online reviews, surveys and feedbacks that are valuable mechanisms through which hotels can procure specific data to manage quality.

Tools in Quality Management

Adoption of quality management tools ensures improvement in systems and processes leading to superior quality of services and products.

Six-Sigma Six-Sigma focuses on improving quality by minimising and subsequently eliminating inefficiency and defects from processes and systems to improve a business. It entails measuring a process' or system's capability using statistical analysis and hence it is implemented by specially trained employees of an organisation, who are certified as 'Green Belts' or Black Belts', based on their expertise. The key principles of Six-Sigma are outlined in Figure 3.9.

The term Six-Sigma is derived from the statistical 'Bell curve', where one Sigma (1σ) represents one standard deviation away from the mean. The defect rate is considered extremely low if the process exhibits six Sigma's (6σ), three of them being above the mean and three below. Six-Sigma process is customer-centric and based on customer feedbacks.

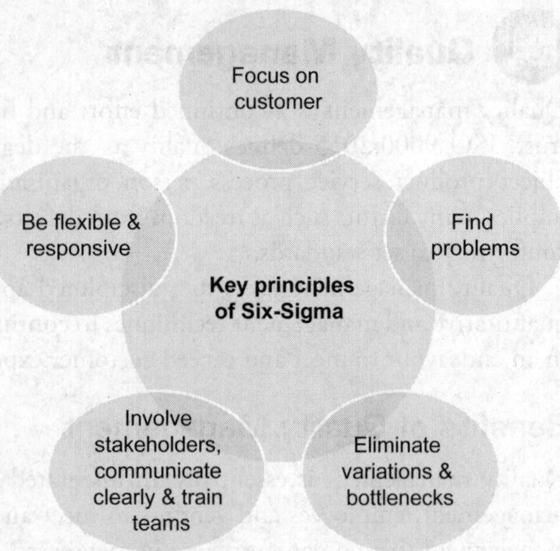

Fig. 3.9 Key principles of Six-Sigma

The two Six-Sigma methodologies are DMAIC and DMADV and their definitions are presented in Figure 3.10. Where DMAIC focuses on improving processes and systems in the existing business practices, DMADV channelises efforts towards creating new products, services, processes, strategies and policies.

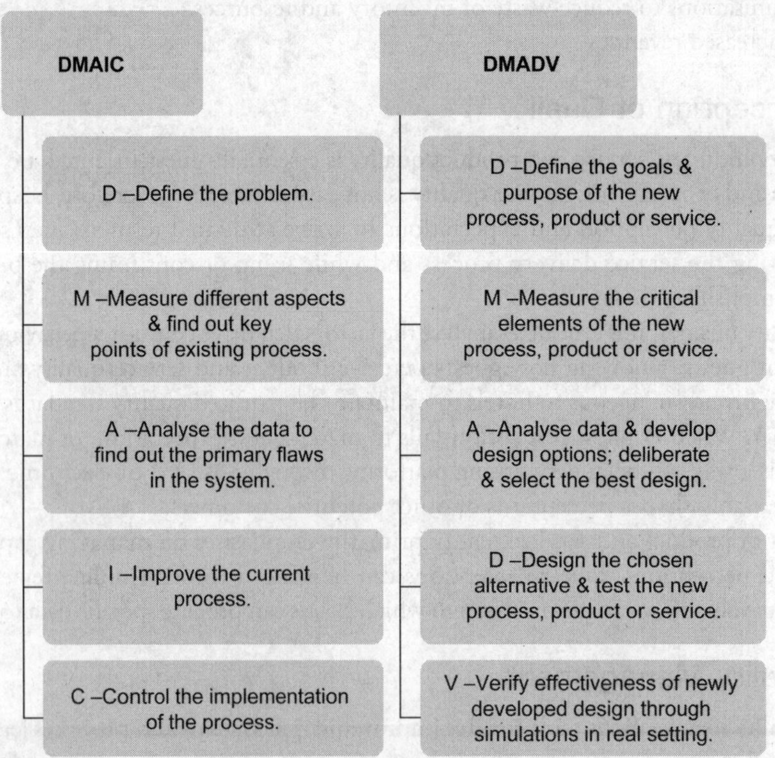

Fig. 3.10 The two methodologies of Six-Sigma

Kaizen A Japanese word, Kaizen can be broken down to 'Kai', meaning 'change' and Zen, meaning 'for the better'. In a workplace, Kaizen refers to a systematic approach to continuous improvement by each and every employee, from the topmost executive to the lowest rung staff member. The five elements of Kaizen are presented in Figure 3.11 and the six steps in its implementation are presented in Figure 3.12.

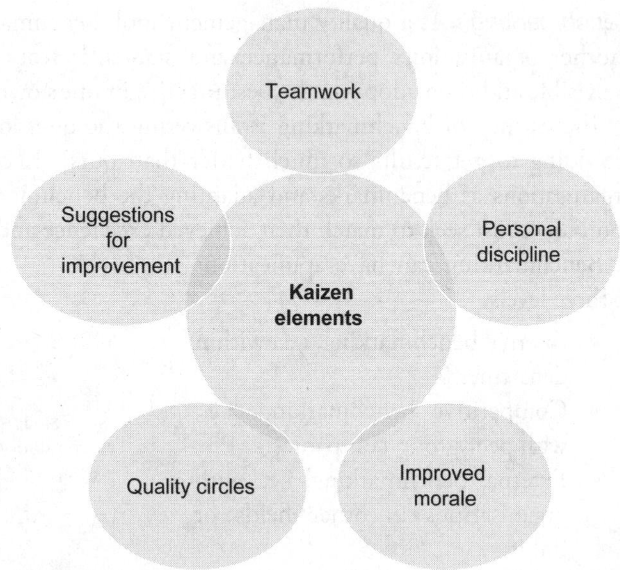

Fig. 3.11 Elements of Kaizen

5-S While Kaizen is beneficial in introducing changes in processes, 5-S works to improve processes through workspace organisation. 5-S creates an environment where continuous improvement (Kaizen) can thrive. Implementation of 5-S is essential in quality management as it ensures an organised workplace to maintain effective and standard work conditions. 5-S is the acronym for five Japanese words – Seiri, Seiton, Seiso, Seiketsu and Shitsuke. Table 3.2 outlines the meaning and elements of 5-S.

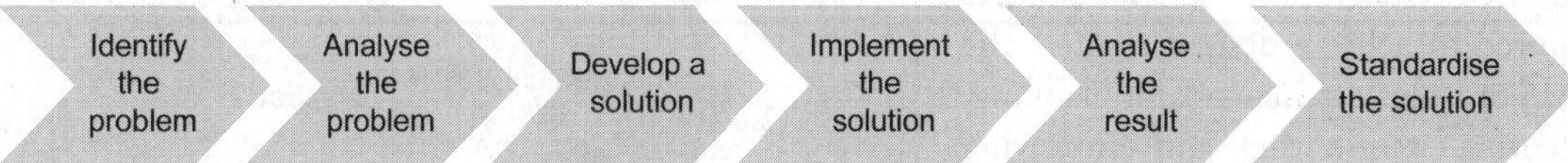

Fig. 3.12 The six steps in implementation of Kaizen process

Table 3.2 Meaning and elements of 5-S

Step	Meaning	Action to implement
Seiri	Sort	Segregate necessary and unnecessary items and get rid of the latter. Items not used in more than a year may be discarded. Frequently used items should be kept close to the work station.
Seiton	Set in order	Ensure a well-organised workplace, there should be 'a place for everything and everything in its place'. Arrange and label items in their place so that they are easy to find and place back.
Seiso	Shine	Maintain a clean workplace and make efforts to keep it clean. This includes all aspects of cleaning such as cleaning schedules and frequency, cleaning equipment and agents, hazards and their mitigation and so on.
Seiketsu	Standardize	Ensure compliance to the above 3-S's as a standard, constant routine by all in the organisation. The work culture should encourage adherence to best practices so that they turn into habits.
Shitsuke	Sustain	The management must be committed in ensuring conformity to 5-S as an element of discipline. This includes creating awareness about 5-S, structured implementation, formulating guidelines of evaluation of implementation, provide supporting resources and leadership, conduct of inspections and audits and recognizing best performers.

Benchmarking As a quality management tool, benchmarking refers to going backstage and observe another organisation's performance and standards from the wings, where the tricks of the trade are visible and then adopting the best practice in one's own organisation.

The essence of benchmarking is answering the question, 'What is it that the other organizations are doing to get results so much better than ours?' Keeping the best practices of the best-in-class organisations as benchmarks and adapting the benchmarks to best fit its own culture and needs, a company must seek to match their achieved excellence and make efforts to surpass it.

Benchmarking can have applications at three levels,

- Internal benchmarking, i.e., within departments
- Competitive benchmarking, i.e., with peer group companies
- External benchmarking, i.e., with organisations in other fields or industry

ISO Quality Management System ISO Quality Management System (QMS), ISO 9000:2015, comprises activities by which the organization identifies its objectives and determines the processes and resources required to achieve desired results. The QMS provides a framework for planning, executing, monitoring and improving the performance of quality management activities. The seven principles of QMS are outlined in Figure 3.13.

Fig. 3.13 The seven principles of ISO – QMS

SUMMARY

The importance of managing personnel over and above any other resource may be understood by the detail and length of this chapter alone. Managing a large workforce, as is found in most housekeeping departments in hotels, is a big challenge for the executive housekeeper.

The chapter begins by discussions of the various documental tools that an efficient housekeeper must use to manage personnel effectively. Job descriptions are the most important of all the tools since they convey to the employee all the relevant details of reporting relationships, working conditions, duties and responsibilities, and any other additional responsibilities he/she must be aware of. Job descriptions help employees to develop a clear focus towards their job and achieve the goals set for them. Further, the position description is discussed as a tool used in dealing with managerial-level staff. The other documental tools discussed in the chapter are: job specifications, job lists, job assignments, job breakdowns, job procedures, and procedure manuals. All the important documents are explained with examples for clear understanding. It needs to be stressed here that executive housekeepers need to be professional themselves if they expect some degree of professionalism from their employees. Systems and procedures developed for managing personnel will help not only the executive housekeeper, but also the entire crew of employees.

Using these helps to make sure that employees take pride in their work assignments and have a clear understanding of the job at hand.

The chapter goes on to deal with the calculation of staff strength. Developing a departmental staffing guide has been given a lot of attention here as, especially in India, this useful method of zero-base scheduling is not being followed by most hotels. A sample staffing guide has been worked out for easy comprehension of the concept of zero-base scheduling. Sample calculations for arriving at number of GRAs needed at different occupancies have been given.

The next section deals with the functions of recruiting, selecting, hiring, orienting, and training employees. It is important that each organization identifies the potential sources of workforce for their housekeeping department. Internal and external sources that could be tapped are discussed in this section. The entire process of interviewing has been discussed and a word of caution about the pitfalls during interviewing that the interviewer may face has been included. The process of orientation and the executive housekeeper's role in the same is essential. A checklist for orienting new employees into the housekeeping department has been provided to help formulate an orientation programme. Training, which is essential for overall human growth and to achieve individual goals, has been dealt with in detail. Training remains a limited field in many hotels. The benefits of training are listed and the training process is explained step by step. A sample HOT training module and a sample monthly training calendar is provided. After being trained, a new employee has to be scheduled for day-to-day jobs in housekeeping. Scheduling is essential for the variable positions (for example, GRAs and housemen) in the department especially. The various shifts commonly followed in India have been outlined. The alternative scheduling techniques that may be considered in housekeeping departments at Indian hotels have been mentioned. The legal rules and regulations to be followed while scheduling employees have been outlined. A sample duty roster has been drawn up.

A word needs to be added here on the scheduling scenario in Indian hotels. The rules and regulations about working hours, break times, and off days are difficult to follow strictly in India. The reasons for this are the round-the-clock operation of hotels and the flexible employment laws in India. Unqualified workers are given preference over qualified staff, especially in the lower rungs, as they may be hired on lower wages. As far as staff welfare is concerned, many hotels are lagging far behind their foreign counterparts, though some are trying to catch up with the global trends in the hotel industry. All the aforementioned factors are collectively responsible for a huge staff turnover in the Indian hotel industry. Also presented is the concept and management of workplace diversity, the knowledge of which is essential for a manager to handle today's diverse workforce.

The section on motivating employees will prove useful to managers in the housekeeping department. A good amount of attention has been given to appraising an employee's performance. In today's scenario, performance appraisal is no longer a prerogative of only the human resource department. The individual department head's participation is crucial in the process. Various methods of appraising performance have been discussed with examples. Individual properties need to draw up their own formats. A sample performance appraisal has also been presented.

The next section is on work study, time and motion studies and job analysis. Work study, time and motion studies help to figure out better and easier ways to carry out tasks and to save time and energy. Job analysis is the foundation for training employees and helps prevent performance problems. The next section discusses teamwork and leadership in housekeeping. Teamwork is now a trend in housekeeping as many executive housekeepers have realized its benefits. Teamwork is successful under good leadership. The leader of any group can build its members into a well-knit team by sharing visions, goals, and strategies with them. An executive housekeeper who can mobilize the trust and support of staff achieves great heights. The participative style of leadership has been stressed here. The section on employee welfare will help managers to get the best out of their employees. Employees are satisfied in an organization if their basic needs from a workplace are met. It is easy to select and hire employees, but very important and difficult to retain them, especially the good ones. Managers need to constantly address the issue of motivation and employee welfare. The concluding section deals with an important topic—employee discipline. All kinds of improper behaviour, however minor, must be addressed and dealt with. In the housekeeping department, the executive housekeeper must not make more rules for his/her staff than are necessary, but those that he/she makes must be enforced. Further, the course of a formal disciplinary action is discussed in detail. Further, quality management, its importance and techniques are discussed in depth.

The executive housekeeper must remember to be a role model in all respects if she is to expect optimal performance and behaviour from the employees of her department.

KEY TERMS

5-S A process originating in Japan; it is essential in quality management to ensure an organized workplace to maintain effective and standard work conditions. 5-S is acronym for five Japanese words – Seiri, Seiton, Seiso, Seiketsu and Shitsuke.

Amenities Services or items offered to guests or placed in the guestrooms for convenience and comfort at no extra cost.

Apprentice A worker who enters into an agreement with an employer to learn a skilled trade through a special training programme, combining practical training with related off-the-job technical instruction. Apprenticeship is sometimes regulated by statute or legal agreement.

Balanced scorecard or BSC A model of performance appraisal that articulates the links between leading inputs (human and physical) processes, and lagging outcomes, and focuses on the importance of managing these components to achieve the organization's strategic goals.

BARS Behaviourally anchored rating scale. This performance appraisal method requires appraisers to rate employees on a scale continuum. Appraisers rate the specific actions or dimensions of an employee's work based on critical incidents.

Benchmarking Refers to going backstage and observing another organisation's performance and standards from the wings, where the tricks of the trade are visible and then adopting the best practice in one's own organization.

BOS Behavioural observation scale. The BOS method establishes critical incidents as the behaviour to be observed and asks appraisers to evaluate how often employees behave in this way.

Buddy In the buddy system of scheduling, a new GRA is paired with another experienced GRA in servicing a guestroom. This experienced GRA is referred to as a 'buddy'.

Chamois leather Chamois leather is used mainly in cleaning and polishing. Originally, skins of chamois goat antelope were used, but now they are usually skivers, that is, split skins of sheep or simulated leather. Chamois leather is used wet for cleaning windows and mirrors. It is also used dry as a polishing 'cloth' for silver.

Cleaning supplies Cleaning agents and small cleaning equipment that are used in cleaning the guestrooms and public areas in a hotel.

Contingency plan Planning done for uncertain events.

Critical incidents A measure of a worker's performance in terms of certain events or episodes that occur in the performance of the job.

Cross-training Cross-training involves training employees to work in departments other than their speciality in periods of staff shortage.

Fringe benefits These are benefits given to staff, supplementing their salaries. The management of an organization is not legally bound to give these. They are also referred to as perks. Examples are medical allowance and leave travel allowance.

FTE Full-time employees.

GRA Guestroom attendant.

Graveyard shift Night shift.

Guest supplies These are items placed in the guestroom free of cost for the use and comfort of guests.

Hand caddy A portable container for storing and transporting cleaning supplies, carried on a room maid's cart.

Horticulturist Horticulturists lead a team of gardeners to maintain the landscaped areas and gardens of a hotel.

HOT Acronym for Hotel Operations Trainee.

House telephone A telephone kept in the lobby for visitors to call up guests in hotel rooms.

Induction See Orientation.

Internal customer Refers to employees in organizations which prioritize employee satisfaction and welfare.

Job analysis Process of determining what knowledge each employee needs, what tasks each position needs to perform, and the standards to which the employee must perform the tasks.

Job assignment Job assignment is a list of tasks to be performed by an individual guestroom attendant in a specific area or section of rooms on a specific day as an individual assignment.

Job breakdown A form that details how the technical duties of a job should be performed.

Job description A job description is a detailed document identifying all the likely duties of a job position as well as reporting relationships, additional responsibilities, working conditions, and any know-how necessary about equipment and materials.

Job knowledge Information that employees must have and understand in order to perform their tasks.

Job list/task list A list identifying all the key duties of a job in the order of their importance.

Job procedures Also referred to as standard operating procedures (SOPs) or 'work cards', these specify the way in which a task is to be performed.

Job specification A job specification is a document detailing the minimum qualities or traits required by an individual to perform a particular job.

Kaizen Originating in Japan, Kaizen refers to a systematic approach to continuous improvement by each and every employee, from the topmost executive to the lowest rung staff member in an organization.

Laissez faire A style of leadership where a leader believes in delegating assignments and important tasks to others in the team.

Lobby Area provided near the reception as a common meeting point for all guests.

Lounge A place in a hotel where guests can sit back and relax. It is a public area, suitably furnished for relaxation.

MBO Management by objectives. A method of performance appraisal evolved by Peter Drucker, MBO involves meetings between employees and managers or between managers and their supervisors, in which joint goals are established. Specific plans for achieving each goal are also established, as are the means for measuring progress towards achievement of goals.

Occupancy The number of rooms actually in use/ occupied.

OPL On-premises laundry. An in-house area in the hotel where linen and uniforms are washed, dry-cleaned, and pressed.

Organization chart A schematic representation of the relationships between positions within an organization, showing where each position fits into the overall organization and illustrating the divisions of responsibility and lines of authority.

Orientation Orientation or induction is the guided adjustment of a new employee to the organization, the work environment, and the job. The process communicates the organization's basic philosophy, policies, rules, and procedures.

Performance appraisal The process by which an employee is periodically evaluated by his or her manager to assess job performance and to discuss steps the employee can take to improve job skills and performance.

Performance standard A required level of performance to meet quality standards set by the organization.

Porch A covered approach to the entrance of a building.

Position description Position descriptions are written for employees with management prerogatives and give their basic function, scope, and specific responsibilities.

Procedure manual A procedure manual is a document developed for employees working in an organization, which gives information about standard procedures to be followed for various activities being carried out in the organization or the department.

Productivity standard An acceptable amount of work that must be done within a specific time frame according to an established level of performance.

PTE Part-time employees.

Quality management Refers to a disciplined approach of integrating the application of qualitative, quantitative and management techniques to continuously improve the processes within an organisation in an endeavour to meet and exceed customer expectations.

Room attendant's cart A lightweight wheeled vehicle used by room attendants for transporting cleaning supplies, guest amenities, linen, and equipment needed to complete a block of cleaning assignments.

Sani-bin These are small metal or plastic containers with lids, kept in toilets for the collection of soiled sanitary towels.

Six-Sigma A statistical analysis-based method of quality management, Six-Sigma focuses on improving quality by minimising and subsequently eliminating inefficiency and defects from processes and systems to improve a business.

Staffing guide The staffing guide is a scheduling and control tool that enables the executive housekeeper to determine the total employee hours and the number of employees required to operate the housekeeping department at specific occupancy levels of the hotel.

SOP (standard operating procedure) A document of a standing nature that specifies a certain method of operating or a specific procedure for the accomplishment of a task. SOPs can be developed for all important housekeeping activities and tasks.

Vanity area A unit comprising a wash basin and mirror, surrounded by a flat area where soap, dental kits, shaving kits, and tooth glasses are kept.

Window squeegee Small, manual cleaning equipment with a handle, rod, and rubber blade. It acts just as a windshield wiper in clearing away excess water from windows while washing.

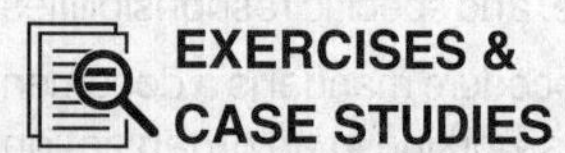

Work emphasis This is a statement mentioned in the position description, relating how a manager should allot his/her time and efforts. For example, a manager may have his/her work emphasis chalked out as 50% administrative work, 30% operations, inspections, and training tasks, and 20% coordination and follow-up.

Workplace diversity Refers to differences in the various defining personal traits of an organisation's employees in aspects of religion, culture, ethnicity and race, age, gender, physical abilities, socio-economic status, education, marital status, work experience and career paths.

Work schedules Work schedules list the actual work to be undertaken by particular employees during particular periods of the day.

Work study As per ILO, a term that embraces the techniques of method study and work measurement which are employed to ensure the best possible use of human and material resources in carrying out a specified activity.

Zero-base scheduling Zero-base scheduling refers to hiring employees while taking into account the actual occupancy for a specified period of time.

4

Contracts and Outsourcing

Learning Objectives

After reading this chapter, you should be able to
- understand the significance of contracts and outsourcing
- appreciate the fact that much deliberation goes into considering the contracting out of a particular function in housekeeping
- elaborate on the types of contracts and the services offered on contract basis in housekeeping
- look at some guidelines for hiring contractors and drawing up contract specifications
- understand the ways of pricing contracts
- chalk out the advantages and disadvantages of using contract services

Introduction

Hotels are increasingly opting for contract services and outsourcing to sustain cost-effective housekeeping operations and to ensure that the resources and assets of the property are utilized to the maximum. A research carried out on star category hotels in India, '*Outsourcing – A study on benefits to housekeeping department in hotels*' in 2015, by Tyagi and Zagade found that 96% hotels outsourced some or the other housekeeping functions; the most outsourced services being pest control (94%), public area janitorial services (80%), public area cleaning (76%) and flower decorations (78%). Out of the surveyed hotels, 94% agreed that outsourcing saved time and costs for the company. All hotels agreed that outsourcing helped overcome skills and specialised equipment shortages.

The number of companies offering outsourcing services and the types of outsourcing services available are growing rapidly and India is not lagging far behind. Major hotels and corporate companies are relying more and more on outsourced professional housekeeping service providers to cater to their needs.

Defining Outsourcing and Contracts

Outsourcing is a 'conscious business decision to move internal work to an external provider'. A *contract* can be defined as 'an agreement between two parties negotiating a business deal'.

Both these terms are now being used interchangeably. However, while all outsourcing involves a contract, all contracts are not necessarily related to outsourcing. For instance, you can have internal staff (that is, employees) on contract as well.

Some of the first processes to be outsourced in hotels include janitorial, security, and catering services.

When are Outsourced Services Considered?

When choosing between outsourced and in-house services, their costs, the quality of the services, and the convenience are important points to consider. A contractor must be 20–30% more productive than direct workforce (or in-house staff) in order to provide an equal service at an equal cost and still get a fair profit. The decision as to whether the initial investment in in-house operations is possible and worth the monthly savings is one that belongs to the hotel's management and owners. There are always pros and cons to consider when assessing the need for outsourced services. A few questions to ask before considering outsourcing are as follows:

- What are the costs involved? Would a contractor be more economical?
- Is there a time, resource, or expertise constraint?
- Are there tasks that are too risky or specialized for in-house personnel?
- Would an outsider have more credibility?
- Is the activity part of the core business?
- Can the contract be managed effectively?

Outsourcing contracts will not work unless they are properly managed. Steps for determining and implementing such contracts include evaluating costs, setting objectives, and appraising results. The goal of such contracts is to develop a trusting partner relationship in which both parties are winners. To hire a contractor, the HR department in coordination with purchase department, initiates a bidding process with at least three contract providers. The submitted bids are evaluated on the basis of price, the vendor's experience, references, and previous assignments of the vendor with the hotel, if any. A cost-benefit analysis is carried out to find out if the contractor will be more economical than having the task done in-house.

Contract Services in Housekeeping

Hotels may go in for the following types of outsourcing contracts:

- *Complete cleaning programmes*, with all the work and responsibility undertaken by the service provider.
- *Regular, selected cleaning* within an establishment to assist the existing housekeeping staff, for example, the cleaning of public areas at night.
- *Periodic services* to assist existing housekeeping operations such as window cleaning, cleaning of walls and ceilings, and cleaning of carpets.
- *Hiring contracts* with various rental firms for linen, equipment, conference utilities, etc.
- *Leasing contracts* for equipment, furniture, and furnishings, which are drawn up for a given number of years. For furniture and upholstery, these are usually written for a 5–7-year lease period; for soft furnishings, the lease is generally for 3 years.
- *The entire housekeeping operations* of the property put out on contract by a hotel, with the whole gamut of housekeeping activities becoming the responsibility of the contractor.
- *Consultancy services*, where a housekeeping expert visits the hotel and guides the existing staff on achieving professional standards.

The following are some areas of housekeeping where services may be offered on contract basis:

- Cleaning—deep cleaning, public area cleaning, cleaning of hard to reach areas, polishing of different surfaces, carpet, and floor cleaning, or full cleaning services
- Linen hire—entire hotel linen or specialized linen like banqueting items
- Equipment and furniture hire
- Laundry—complete or part
- Flower arrangements and decorations
- Pest control
- Horticulture and landscaping
- Eco-friendly garbage disposal
- Other services such as shoe-polishing machines, guest amenities such as hangers, etc.

Hiring Contract Providers

These are the steps the management should follow once they have decided to outsource a particular service for the hotel:

- Put out tenders to at least three contractors and compare quotes.
- Check out their existing market credibility by contacting previous/current clients. It is very important to get reliable referrals from other hotels, members of professional organizations, or business associates.
- Check references thoroughly and visit other job sites.
- Check whether the contractor is registered and licensed under The Contract Labour Act 1970 of the Government of India.
- Preferably select a contract provider with a local office.
- Check on the type and amount of training provided to workers.
- Check on the degree to which the contract provider undertakes supervision of the work.
- Prepare detailed contract specifications, indicating the exact number of working hours, areas of operations and responsibility, processes to be used, frequency of service, time-table, and any special projects.
- Consider the effect on existing workforce with regard to possible redundancy and redeployment.

Some guidelines a hotel can follow to make its outsourcing contracts a success are provided here.

- Greet the contracted workers when they arrive and review the job parameters.
- Visit the job site shortly after work has begun to ensure that the hotel's expectations are being met.
- Give the project a spot-check and a rundown at completion to review the contractor's work and to ensure that specifications are being met.
- Make sure you are properly insured.
- Keep equipment and supplies belonging to the hotel and those belonging to the contractor separate.
- Consider not paying in advance.

Contract Specification

It is essential that the executive housekeeper provides the service provider with a clearly defined and detailed specification of the work to be done, how it is to be done, and so on. It is from this that the service provider draws up the contract. Contract specifications should be carefully worded and should necessarily cover the following points:

- The period or duration of the contract, date of signing the contract, and a provision for regular review of the specifications.
- The schedule of areas to be serviced and the frequency with which a job is to be done. This is important, as the level of cleanliness depends on the time lapse between successive cleaning processes. For example, horizontal surfaces may need daily dusting and vertical can do with weekly.
- A description of the method, equipment, and materials required, as well as the hotel's quality expectations, including appropriate penalty and cancellation clauses.
- A list of the security requirements. Sometimes, all contract staff are vetted and specified rooms have to be kept locked.
- A provision for adequate supervision, listing the hotel's requirements specifically.
- A provision for storage areas, lockers, and perhaps accommodation for the contracted staff.
- The time expectations for the job, covering sickness and annual leave.
- A verification of the insurance coverage for workers, guests, hotel employees, and assets.
- Specified frequencies of inspection agreed upon with the service provider.
- The remuneration for the job, the terms and conditions of payment, and a termination procedure.

Both parties should sign these contract specifications. A sample of contract specification is presented in Exhibit 4.1.

Service-level agreement in contracts A service-level agreement (SLA) is part of a service contract where a service is formally defined. An SLA formalizes arrangements between an organization and a supplier to deliver specific services, at specific levels, and at an agreed upon price. A contract may include one or more service level agreement(s). If the level of service does not adhere to the agreement and the SLA metrics are often missed, the organization may be entitled to some form of compensation such as a payment or a credit. Setting, tracking, and managing SLAs are important aspects of managing contracts.

Exhibit 4.1 A contract specification sample

Hotel XYZ

Date –..............
Ref No. – ....
To,
....

SUB: PROJECT FACADE CLEANING (IN & OUT)

Please find below the details and rate for façade cleaning of glass & louver at the premises.

Scope of work

1. Area not reachable from ground floor
2. All glasses & louvers inside & outside

 Pricing of Contracts

The basis of payment for outsourced services may include one or more of the following:

- A management fee for consultancy services.
- A unit rate agreement.
- A fixed period cost.
- A cost for the job plus a percentage of fees.
- A cost for the job plus a fixed fee.
- Time plus materials cost.

Management consultancy fees In this type of contract, there is a transfer of knowledge and skills. The hotel provides the workforce, equipment, material, and other tangible items for the work. This is more common where a hotel is making losses and it hires the services of a consultant who could bring a turn around in the loss making unit. Once profits are made, the consultant is given a one time payment as per agreed terms.

Unit rate agreement Most contracts are agreed on a unit-rate basis. The executive housekeeper provides details of the area to be covered and the frequency of the job, and asks the service provider for the costs. The contractor measures the area and calculates the cost thus

$$\text{Man-hours} = \text{areas} \times \text{time} \times \text{frequency}$$

For example, if a contracted firm has to clean five different areas, taking two hours each, twice a week, then man-hours will be calculated as:

$$\begin{aligned}\text{Man-hours} &= 5 \times 2 \times 2\,\text{hours}\\ &= 20\,\text{hours/week}\end{aligned}$$

To the cost of wages (for workers and supervisors), the firm adds costs of equipment, agents, and supplies, plus overheads and profits, and then quotes a price.

Fixed price/Fixed period cost Under this type, contract work is done for fixed or set price based on the competitive bidding with the type of the contract. There is a prior knowledge of the cost and the contract can be given at the specific rate. Here, either the amount can be given in lump sum payment or in three or four installments. The main disadvantage of this type of contract pricing is that there is no control over the material used by the contractor.

Cost plus percentage of fees The contractor is paid for the work performed, plus he is given a percentage of the cost as his service charge. The main disadvantage here is that it induces the contractor to increase the cost, for then, his service charge would increase.

Cost plus fixed fee Better than the mode of pricing discussed before is one in which the contractor is paid for the costs of the job and given a fixed fee. In this case, there is no point in the contractor's cutting costs, as he has a guaranteed profit margin.

With the costs-plus-fixed fee type of contract, the executive housekeeper specifies the staff, equipment, and so on, to be employed. The specifications should be the same as for in-house workforce and the housekeeper should compare the contractor's bid with her own in-house cleaning costs.

A sample costing of a contract using man-hours is shown in Exhibit 4.2. The same calculation could be worked out using area instead of work hours, as shown in Exhibit 4.3.

Time plus materials cost The contractor is given the cost of all the materials and the workers used in the job. A set time frame is made within which he has to complete the job. If he is not able to deliver in time, his service charges can be reduced.

Exhibit 4.2 Sample calculation for costing of contract services using man-hours

300 hours per year @ ₹ x per hour = ₹300 x per year

Supervision = ₹*y* per year

Small equipments and supplies = ₹*z* per year

Capital equipment (written off over 5 years)

5 vacuum cleaners = ₹*a*

1 floor polisher = ₹*b*

1 scrubber = ₹*c*

2 carpet shampoo machines = ₹*d*

₹*a* + ₹*b* + ₹*c* + ₹*d* = ₹*m*

Capital investment over 5 years = ₹*m*/5

Cleaning agents = ₹*n* per year

Total cleaning cost/year = ₹300*x* + *y* + *z* + *m*/5 + *n*

Exhibit 4.3 Sample calculation for costing of contract services using area

Total area to be cleaned = 60 ft. × 50 ft.

60 ft. × 50 ft. @ ₹ *x*/sq. ft. twice monthly = ₹3,000 × 2(*x*)

= ₹12 [3,000 × 2(*x*)] per year

Supervision = ₹*y* per year

Small equipments and supplies = ₹*z* per year

Capital equipment (written off over 5 years)

5 vacuum cleaners = ₹*a*

1 floor polisher = ₹*b*

1 scrubber = ₹*c*

2 carpet shampoo machines = ₹*d*

₹*a* + ₹*b* + ₹*c* + ₹*d* = ₹*m*

Capital investment over 5 years = ₹*m*/5

Cleaning agents = ₹*n* per year

Total cleaning cost/year = ₹3,000 × 2(*x*) + *y* + *z* + *m*/5 + *n*

Advantages and Disadvantages of Outsourcing

The decision to avail of outsourcing requires a lot of groundwork. There are many pros and cons that need to be considered. Different properties may have different needs in terms of the services to be given out on contract. The same kind of service may not be suitable for two different hotels. Ultimately the management and the owners need to brainstorm over whether outsourcing is essential for their particular property or whether the idea is just the result of a trend.

Advantages

The following are some possible advantages of outsourcing:

- There is no capital outlay for equipment, so that money is available for investment in other purposes. (In most cases, the contractor provides all supplies and equipment.)
- There is no equipment lying idle (particularly specialized gadgets).
- Contracts alleviate the necessity of buying or hiring specialized equipment.
- The difficulty of finding, training, organizing, and supervising staff is passed on to the service provider.
- Good contract firms provide skilled workers, well trained in their area of expertise. This is because they may be able to offer higher salaries than hotels employing workers directly and can therefore attract more highly qualified and competent staff.
- Extra work may be carried out at certain times without increasing the basic staff.
- Accurate budgeting can be done for a fixed period.
- Contractors provide uniformed workers and take responsibility for all their wages and benefits.
- The contractors are accountable for the results. Their workers stay on the job until it is done.
- The hotel receives the benefits of the service provider's up-to-date know-how in their area of expertise and of the latest equipment and technology.
- Knowledgeable experts can provide sound advice and help reduce costs and legal risks. In addition, independent contractors are required to carry their own liability and workers' compensation insurance.
- Contract services alleviate many of the problems between the management and workers' unions.
- Contract services can generally be terminated faster and more easily than the services of regular employees, while reducing the likelihood of employment claims and lawsuits.

Disadvantages

The following are some possible disadvantages of outsourcing:

- Contracting weakens the authority of the management over the quality and loyalty of the staff.
- Workers brought in by the contract providers are not representatives of the hotel and may not have the requisite skills for guest interactions, or the same pride in their work or job satisfaction.
- There is loss of flexibility in effecting changes, as the housekeeper no longer controls the entire operations.

- There is a natural tendency among contractors to use cheaper products, which may be of poor quality and may damage the building and its contents in the long term.
- There may be poor supervision, with the standard of work falling below par as a result.
- Workers may not show up within the designated time frame.
- There may be problems regarding security.
- There may be problems regarding liaison and cooperation between departments.
- Contract cleaners may not meet the hotel's standards of quality. One of the reasons for this is the sudden growth of contract cleaning firms, resulting in cut-price tenders being offered and accepted (clients usually accept the lowest priced tender), which do not enable the contractors to employ a sufficient number of employees of the right calibre to do the job properly.

SUMMARY

This chapter starts with an insight into the way contract services and outsourcing have become recent trends in housekeeping operations. The terms 'contract' and 'outsourcing' both have been defined here in their correct sense, though they are now often used interchangeably. A lot of deliberation is required on the part of clients when choosing between outsourcing and direct (in-house) workforce. The common considerations have been enumerated. The various types of contracts and the various services on offer have been noted. (This list is by no means exhaustive, since many novel areas and functions may now be an option for outsourcing.) Guidelines as to how to zero down upon an ideal service provider have been given. Once a third-party firm is decided on, certain tricks of the trade to maximise the advantage to the client have been listed. The most important aspect of contracts is the drawing up of the contract specifications, which has been discussed at length. Different functions and areas to be contracted need to have contract specifications worded differently. Many hotels may have their own team of lawyers involved in the activity of chalking out the contract specifications, since there are many legal aspects involved. Finally, the ways of pricing a contract are presented, along with sample costing calculations to help reach a clearer understanding.

KEY TERMS

Contract A contract is an agreement between two parties negotiating a business deal.

Contract specification This is a document giving clear and precise instructions about the task—frequency, expected performance, and other relevant details of the services required from the service provider.

Deep cleaning Intensive or specialized cleaning undertaken in guestrooms or public areas.

Horticulture The science of growing plants or gardening.

Janitorial services This refers to the cleaning of bathrooms and toilets, primarily.

Outsourcing A conscious business decision to move internal work to an external provider.

SLA An SLA or service-level agreement formalizes arrangements between an organization and a supplier to deliver specific services, at specific levels, and at an agreed upon price.

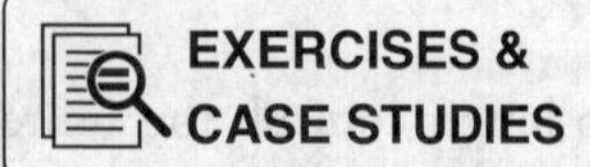

5 Planning Housekeeping Operations

Learning Objectives

After reading this chapter, you should be able to

- appreciate the importance of planning housekeeping operations and understand the role of each planning document
- understand the steps involved in the planning process and plan the work of a housekeeping department on paper, using the various planning documents

Introduction

Housekeeping is a 24/7 operation. It is imperative that the executive housekeeper plans and organizes the work of the department for smooth and efficient functioning. Planning is the executive housekeeper's most important management function, providing direction and focus to all activities.

When this planning is done methodically, half the battle is won. If the executive housekeeper plans out the work well, he/she and the staff are clear about the responsibilities of the department as well as their individual tasks. Planning the work of the housekeeping department requires a step-by-step, systematic approach to ensure that the work is not only done, but also done correctly, efficiently, on time, and with the least cost to the department. Systematic planning makes the enormous task of housekeeping seem easier. On the other hand, haphazard planning or no planning at all will lead to crisis situations on a day-to-day basis; increasing stress levels for many, escalating departmental expenses, and sometimes dissatisfaction among guests (and consequently, the management).

The scope of the planning to be undertaken by the executive housekeeper is vast, and only the basic planning activities are discussed in this chapter. Advanced planning activities such as budgeting, controlling expenses, and so on, are discussed in later chapters.

The Planning Process

The step-by-step planning process may differ slightly from one hotel's housekeeping department to another's and different terminology may be in use across companies, but essentially the sub-processes and tasks are the same. The planning process is depicted in Figure 5.1. Housekeeping planning should be done on paper and needs to be properly documented. The questions that arise at the

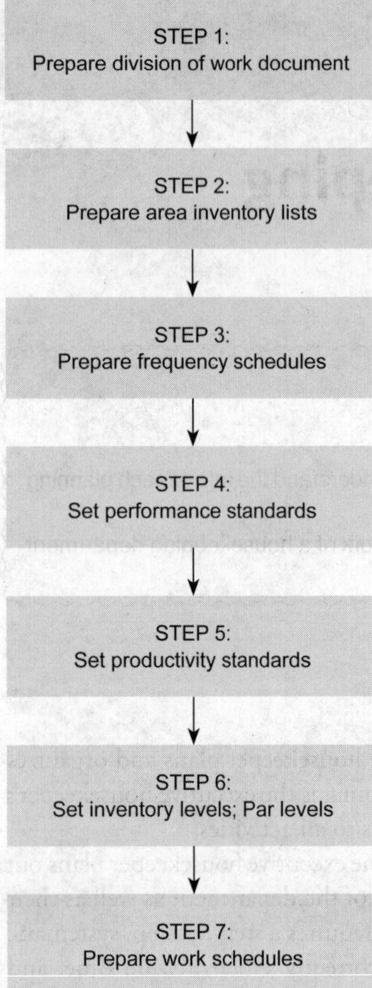

Fig. 5.1 The planning process for housekeeping operations

beginning of the planning process lead to the formation of the basic planning documents. These questions and documents are listed in Table 5.1.

The answers to the initial questions, we have seen, lead to the subsequent steps of drawing up the planning documents that the executive housekeeper must follow. These documents are discussed, step by step, in this chapter.

Step 1: Division of Work Document

In the first step of planning, the executive housekeeper identifies the areas that will come under the purview of housekeeping department for maintenance and upkeep. This is especially important in a newly opened property. Most housekeeping departments in luxury hotels are involved with cleaning guestrooms and the related public areas. The other 'back of the house' areas are taken care of by the stewarding assistants. However, in mid-scale properties, the housekeeping department may also be responsible for such areas as dining and banquet rooms, meeting rooms, recreation rooms, employee areas, and management offices.

The executive housekeeper should make a list of all the guest and employee areas of the property in a division-of-work document and put down on paper who would be responsible for cleaning and maintaining each area. To ensure all possible areas to be cleaned have been covered, the executive housekeeper must make regular tours of the property. It also helps to mark the areas on a blue print of the property plan. Different coloured markings may be used for the different departments that are responsible for the maintenance and care of the various areas.

This division-of-work document should be presented to the executive committee for review and approval.

Table 5.1 Basic planning documents

Initial planning questions	Resultant planning documents
1. What work has to be done?	• Division of work document • Area inventory lists
2. When and how often does the work have to be done?	• Frequency schedules
3. How and to what standards must the work be done?	• Performance standards
4. How long will it take to accomplish the work in accordance with the standards set?	• Productivity standards
5. What amounts of equipment and supplies should be provided to the staff to meet the performance and productivity standards set?	• Inventory levels
6. Who will do the work?	• Work schedules

Step 2: Area Inventory Lists

Once the division of work document is finalized, the executive housekeeper needs to concentrate on the areas that are her/his department's responsibility. The next important planning task is to prepare a list of all items and surfaces within a particular area that require the attention of housekeeping personnel. The more detailed the list, the more efficient the cleaning and maintenance of the areas will be, in all probability. Area inventory lists also aid in supervision. Separate area inventory lists need to be made for all areas that the department is responsible for. A sample of a guestroom area inventory list is given in Exhibit 5.1.

Step 3: Frequency Schedules

Frequency schedules show how often the items listed in an area inventory list are to be cleaned or maintained. The frequency of cleaning is directly related to the type and amount of soiling expected in the area or on the item to be cleaned.

The following factors are to be borne in mind while planning frequency schedules.

- Degree of soiling
- Type of soiling
- Usage of area
- Amount and frequency of footfalls/traffic
- Location
- Type of surface
- Accessibility
- Cost
- Standard of cleaning
- Company policy

Frequency schedules divide the cleaning and maintenance tasks into daily, weekly, monthly, or periodic tasks. These are discussed in further detail in Chapter 11, under frequency of cleaning. Many tasks in the public areas are scheduled for the night. The higher the standards of cleanliness and hygiene sought, the more frequent the cleaning needed. It should be remembered, though, that some tasks should not be done too often, as excessive cleaning of certain surfaces can damage them. These periodic tasks done at longer intervals are designated as deep cleaning tasks or special projects.

Exhibit 5.1 Sample guestroom area inventory list

Bedroom		Bathroom	
• Doors, locks, chains, stops	• Spreads, bedding, mattress	• Bathroom doors	• Vanitory unit
• Lights, switches	• Dressers, nightstands	• Lights, switches	• Fixtures, faucets
• Ceiling	• Lamp shades, lamps, bulbs	• Walls	• Toilet—flush handle, cistern, seat
• Walls	• Chairs, sofa	• Floor tiles	• Tissue holder
• Floor tiles	• Ashtrays and waste-paper basket	• Ceiling	• Sani-bin
• Woodwork	• Carpet	• Mirrors	• Exhaust vent
• Drapes and hardware	• Pictures and mirrors	• Tub, grab bars	• Amenities
• Windows	• Closet and safe	• Shower head	
• Heater/air conditioner settings	• Mini bar		
• Telephone	• Amenities		
• Television and radio			
• Headboards			

Deep cleaning and special projects should be scheduled for periods of low occupancy, and many such tasks take place during the night shift. A sample frequency schedule for cleaning a guestroom is presented in Exhibit 5.2.

Exhibit 5.2 Sample frequency schedule for cleaning in the guestroom

Bedroom		Bathroom	
Cleaning tasks	**Frequency**	**Cleaning tasks**	**Frequency**
• Clean doors, locks, chains, stops	1/D	• Damp-dust bathroom doors	1/D
• Clean lights, switches	1/W	• Clean lights, switches	1/W
Check lights, switches	1/D	Check lights, switches	1/D
• Clean ceiling	1/M	• Clean ceiling	1/M
• Dust walls	1/W	• Dust walls	1/W
Wash walls	1/6M	Wash walls	1/6M
• Vacuum clean/mop floor tiles	1/D	• Mop floor tiles	1/D
Buff floor tiles	1/M	Buff floor tiles	1/M
Polish floor tiles	1/6M	• Damp-dust mirrors	2/D

Step 4: Performance Standards

Performance standards describe how and to what standards the work is to be done. In other words, performance standards lay down the required quality levels for employees' performance. The best-developed performance standards are the ones that are prepared in consultation with the staff who actually perform the tasks. Performance standards are achieved when:

- Cleaning methods are correctly selected and systematically followed.
- The ideal cleaning agents are used on the various surfaces involved.
- The correct pieces of equipment are used on the various surfaces involved.
- Cleaning tasks are carried out at required frequencies.
- All the employees carry out their cleaning tasks in a consistent manner.
- Time-and-motion studies are periodically carried out in the department to obtain best practices in housekeeping.

Once performance standards are set, the executive housekeeper should ensure that these are communicated through training to each and every employee and that there is 100% conformity to the standards. Supervision, inspection, and evaluation are key processes in ensuring conformity to standards. It is easier for both employees and manager if the standards are compiled in a manual. The executive housekeeper must be constantly on the alert for new, more efficient, and more cost-effective methods. The performance standards should be reviewed and revised at least once a year. A sample of the standard operating procedure used as the performance standard for cleaning a vanity unit is given in Chapter 12.

Step 5: Productivity Standards

Productivity standards communicate the quantity of work expected to be completed by each employee of the department. Housekeeping managers must know how long it should take an employee to perform the main tasks in the area inventory lists, as this knowledge helps in determining staffing requirements. Efficient housekeeping is achieving a balance between performance standards and productivity standards. Standard time rates have been calculated for specific tasks under standard conditions of equipment, agents, and method. Practically speaking, though, every hotel must develop their own productivity standards, as there are several factors that influence these standards, which vary from one property to the other. Some of these factors may be:

- The type and age of the property.
- The accessibility of the work area from the service areas.
- The amount of traffic in the work areas.
- The function of the work area.
- The expected standards of cleaning.
- The types of surfaces involved.
- The degrees and types of soiling.
- The frequency of cleaning.
- The types of cleaning supplies and equipment available.
- The quality of supervision and inspection.
- The quality of employees.

A sample productivity standard calculation for GRAs is worked out in Exhibit 5.3.

Exhibit 5.3 Productivity standard calculation for GRAs

Step 1	**Time taken to service one guestroom by GRAs** (in accordance with the performance standards set using time and motion studies)	**30 minutes**
Step 2	**Total shift time of a GRA**	9 hours = 9 × 60 minutes = **540 minutes**
Step 3	**Total time available for guestroom servicing**	
	Total shift time	540 minutes
	Less: Beginning of shift duties	–10 minutes
	Less: Coffee break	–15 minutes
	Less: Lunch break	–45 minutes
	Less: End of shift duties	–10 minutes
		= 460 minutes
Step 4	**Number of rooms to be cleaned by the GRAs in 1 day shift** is obtained by dividing the time available for servicing guestrooms by the time required to service one guestroom.	460 ÷ 30 = 15.33 = **16 rooms**
	Therefore the productivity standard for GRAs is	**16 rooms per 9 hour shift**
	The productivity standard may also be expressed as	30 minutes per room **= 0.5 hours per room per 9 hour shift**

Step 6: Equipment and Operating Supply Inventory Level

Once all standards are set and the staff members have been trained to follow them, the executive housekeeper must ensure that the employees have the necessary material resources to carry out their tasks. These material resources are the necessary equipment and operating supplies, which should be adequate in quality and quantity to meet the performance and productivity standards. The term 'inventory' here means the stocks of purchased operating supplies, equipment, and other items held for future use in housekeeping operations. The executive housekeeper is responsible for two types of inventories:

Recycled inventories These are items that have relatively limited useful lives, but are used over and over again in housekeeping operations. Recycled inventory items include linen, uniforms, most machinery and large pieces of equipment, and guest loan items such as hot-water bottles, heating pads, irons, ironing boards, and so on.

Non-recycled inventories These, on the other hand, are items that are used up repeatedly during the course of routine housekeeping operations. Items of non-recycled inventory include most guest amenities, cleaning supplies, and smaller pieces of equipment such as brooms, mops, cleaning cloths, and so on.

The executive housekeeper must establish reasonable levels for both recycled and non-recycled inventories. Overstocking should be avoided, as it ties up cash and calls for a larger storage area. There should be an effective purchasing system to consistently maintain the inventory levels set by the executive housekeeper. To maintain the inventory levels, the executive housekeeper needs to determine the par level for each inventory item.

Determining the Par Levels

'Par' here refers to the standard quantity (or numbers) of each inventoried item that must be on hand to support daily, routine housekeeping operations. Par levels are determined differently for the two types of inventories. Inventory levels for recycled items are measured in terms of a par number. The par number is a multiple of the standard quantity of a particular inventory item that must be on hand to support day-to-day housekeeping functions. In the case of non-recycled inventory items, the par number is the range between two figures: a *minimum inventory quantity* and a *maximum inventory quantity*. The minimum inventory quantity refers to the lowest number of purchase units (items per case) that must be in stock at any given point of time. The on-hand quantity for a non-recycled inventory should never fall below this figure. The minimum quantity figures are established based on the rate of consumption of a particular inventory item over a certain period. The following formula may be used:

$$\text{Minimum quantity} = \text{Lead-time quantity} + \text{Safety stock level}$$

where the lead-time quantity is the number of purchase units that are used up between the time that a supply order is placed and the time that the order is received in hand, and safety stock level is the number of purchase units that must always be on hand in case of emergencies, damages, delays in delivery, and so on, so that the daily operations and functioning of the department are smooth even in emergencies.

The maximum inventory quantity, on the other hand, refers to the greatest number of purchased units that should be in stock at any given point of time. Storage space, the cost of the item, and its shelf life ('best before' date) are certain factors that must be kept in mind when establishing the maximum inventory level for a non-recycled inventory item. A sample inventory format for non-recycled items is presented in Exhibit 5.4.

Step 7: Work Schedules

Once the executive housekeeper is through with planning the work and resources, the employees can start on their work schedules. As explained earlier in Chapter 3, the work schedule is a document that

Exhibit 5.4 Sample inventory format for non-recycled items

Item	Supplier	Purchase unit	Cost per purchase unit	Opening inventory	Items received in this period	No. of Items used	Items in stock	Lead-time quantity	Minimum inventory quantity	Maximum inventory quantity	Par level

lists the actual tasks to be carried out by an employee in a particular shift and the time frame in which to undertake each task. The number of schedules made for a given area is thus an indication of the number of staff required to clean that area on the particular day. For guestroom cleaning, the executive housekeeper should schedule GRAs by giving each of them room sections of 15–16 guestrooms reasonably contiguous to each other. In case of team staffing, 30–35 guestrooms contiguous to each other can be assigned. To plan out guestroom cleaning, it is recommended that a pictorial representation (in the form of a line drawing) of the location of all guestrooms within the hotel be developed. The housekeeper can then plan out the room sections to be cleaned by GRAs individually or as a team with greater ease. The work schedules should be handed over to the employees as they start their shift. (For a sample work schedule, refer Chapter 3, Exhibit 3.14; it gives more details on scheduling).

SUMMARY

Planning the work of the housekeeping department is an especially challenging task if the property is newly opened. Planning activities for a new hotel are discussed in Chapter 33. For a hotel that has been operating for some time, many systems and procedures for day-to-day operations would already have been developed. Whether the hotel is new or a long-operational one, planning is necessary and one of the major management tasks, an executive housekeeper is responsible for. The chapter begins with the importance of planning in housekeeping operations and goes on to discuss the basic planning activities. The questions (where, what, how, and who) that arise when planning begins lead to the creation of the planning documents. Each of these documents—the division of work document, area inventory lists, frequency schedules, performance standards, productivity standards, equipment and supply inventory levels, and work schedules—have been discussed with examples where appropriate. The scheduling process too needs to be planned by the housekeeper. This topic has been covered in Chapter 3: Managing Housekeeping Personnel.

The division of work needs to be drawn up at the onset of operations so that the housekeeping department's areas of responsibility for cleaning and maintenance are clearly identified. Further, specific sub-areas, items, and surfaces need to be enlisted in an area inventory list. The more detailed and thorough this list, the better the cleaning operations and supervision in these areas. Frequency schedules, determining how often the cleaning tasks need to be carried out, are a must. Once frequency schedules are planned, they must be adhered to. Else however efficient the planning looks on paper, the results will be below standard. Performance standards must exist in all hotels so that attendants as well as supervisors understand what quality of work is expected from them. Productivity standards should be planned as well, as they help in framing the staffing guide. Individual properties should set their own productivity standards. A fine balance between performance and productivity standards is the key to good house-keeping management. When a housekeeping department is understaffed, performance standards are difficult to achieve. On the other hand, if the department is overstaffed, manpower costs are high and profits are less.

This chapter further discusses how inventory levels for equipment and supplies are maintained

for efficient and smooth running of the operations. The all-important concept of par is explained. The number of par stock to be kept on hand again is an individual property's decision. The concluding section deals with planning schedules briefly. Scheduling is discussed in detail in Chapter 3.

Each executive housekeeper has a different style of functioning and many like to introduce and experiment with new concepts and ideas. This is a welcome trait and will yield positive results if all these concepts are worked out on paper and planned in advance.

KEY TERMS

Amenities Services or items offered to guests or placed in the guestrooms for convenience and comfort at no extra cost.

Area inventory list A list of all items and surfaces within a particular area that require the attention of the housekeeping personnel.

Bedding A collective term for all articles on a bed; but normally refers to launderables.

Buff To smoothen the floor with a low-speed floor polishing machine.

Cleaning supplies Cleaning agents and small pieces of cleaning equipment that are used in cleaning the guestrooms and public areas in a hotel.

Damp-dust A method of cleaning where the item to be cleaned is wiped with a damp cloth.

Deep cleaning Intensive cleaning undertaken in guestrooms and public areas, usually carried out according to a special schedule.

Division of work document A document that lists all the guest and employee areas of the hotel property and delegates responsibility for the cleaning and maintaining of each area.

Exhaust vent An opening for ventilation, sometimes fixed with an exhaust fan to facilitate influx of fresh air.

Faucets Taps.

Fixtures Hardware items present in guestrooms that cannot be moved or are difficult to move as a whole since they are fixed in position. For example, wash basins, baths, and lighting fixtures.

Frequency schedule A schedule that indicates how often the items listed in area inventory lists are to be cleaned or maintained.

GRA Guestroom attendant.

Guest loan items Guest supplies not normally found in a guestroom, but available upon request—for example, hair-dryers and ironing boards.

Inventory (noun) The stocks of purchased operating supplies, equipment, and other items held for future use in housekeeping operations.

Lead-time quantity The number of purchase units of items that are used up between the time that a supply order is placed and the time that the order is received in hand.

Maximum inventory quantity The greatest number of purchase units that should be in stock at any given point of time.

Minimum inventory quantity The lowest number of purchase units (items per case) that must be in stock at any given point of time.

Nightstand A small stand or cabinet designed to stand beside a bed or elsewhere in a bedroom, as a place to put anything likely to be required during the night; also called night table.

Non-recycled inventory items Items that are used up during the course of routine housekeeping operations. Non-recycled items include most guest amenities, cleaning supplies, and smaller pieces of equipment.

Operating supplies The items essential to carry out day-to-day housekeeping operations. These include guest supplies and cleaning supplies.

Par The standard number of each inventoried item that must be in hand to support daily, routine housekeeping operations.

Par number A multiple of the standard quantity of a particular inventory item that must be on hand to support day-to-day housekeeping functions.

Performance standards The required quality level of employee performance.

Periodic tasks Tasks that have a frequency schedule of more than one month.

Planning The specification of goals and the means to accomplish those goals (these are to be defined by the housekeeper).

Productivity standards Productivity standards are the expected quantity of work to be done by each employee of the department.

Recycled inventory items Items that have relatively limited useful lives, but are used over and over again in housekeeping operations. Recycled items include linen, uniforms, most machinery, larger pieces of equipment, and guest loan items.

Room sections A group of 15–16 guestrooms reasonably contiguous to each other.

Safety stock level The number of purchase units that must always be on hand in case of emergencies, damages, delays in delivery, and so on.

Sani-bin Small metal or plastic containers with lids, kept in toilets for the collection of soiled sanitary towels.

Special projects A method of scheduling less frequent cleaning. Deep cleaning tasks are often scheduled as special projects.

Stewarding assistants Staff responsible for the upkeep and cleanliness of the 'back of the house' areas.

Time-and-motion studies The time-and-motion study for a task calculates how long it takes on an average to perform a certain task. Time-and-motion studies help to find better and easier ways to carry out tasks and to save on time and energy.

Toilet tissue Toilet paper, almost always in the form of a roll, placed for the use of guests in bathrooms.

Tooth glass A glass placed on the vanity unit as a guest supply and used for gargling or to keep the guest's toothbrush, dentures, or other similar items in.

Vanity unit A unit comprising a wash basin and mirror surrounded by a flat area where soap, a dental kit, a shaving kit, and tooth glasses are kept.

Work schedules A document that lists the actual tasks to be carried out by an employee in a particular shift and the time frame within which to complete each task.

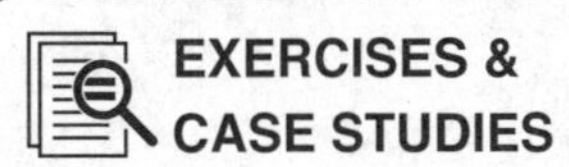

6 Daily Routines and Systems

Learning Objectives

After reading this chapter, you should be able to

- understand the activities, operational procedures, and shifts in the 'housekeeping day'
- identify the forms, reports, and formats used to accomplish the daily routine
- list the order of servicing guestrooms
- get insights into the work carried out in various shifts in the housekeeping department

Introduction

Planning is vital for the housekeeping department. The success of this planning is reflected in the daily routine followed in the housekeeping department. The executive housekeeper guides his/her team in carrying out the daily routine, which he/she would have established and improved upon since the inception of the hotel. The entire planning process, however efficient on paper, will result in an inefficient housekeeping set-up if not transcribed into good daily routine activities.

The Housekeeping Day

In a hotel that has been functioning for some years, housekeeping operations follow a set daily routine, with the required systems in place. A key concept in this daily functioning is the 'housekeeping day' (Fig. 6.1).

The 'housekeeping day' refers to that part of the 24 hours in a day when housekeeping operations are in full swing. For systematic management of the daily routine of the housekeeping department, the 'housekeeping day' is divided into three shifts, as is the case operationally too. Needless to say, more staff are scheduled in the morning shift than the other shifts, since the workload peaks during this shift. The three shifts are usually as follows:

- Morning shift: 7.00 a.m. to 4.00 p.m.
- Afternoon shift: 2.00 p.m. to 11.00 p.m.
- Night shift: 11.00 p.m. to 8.00 a.m.

The daily routine may differ slightly from one hotel to the other and shift timings may vary considerably, depending on their location and target clientele.

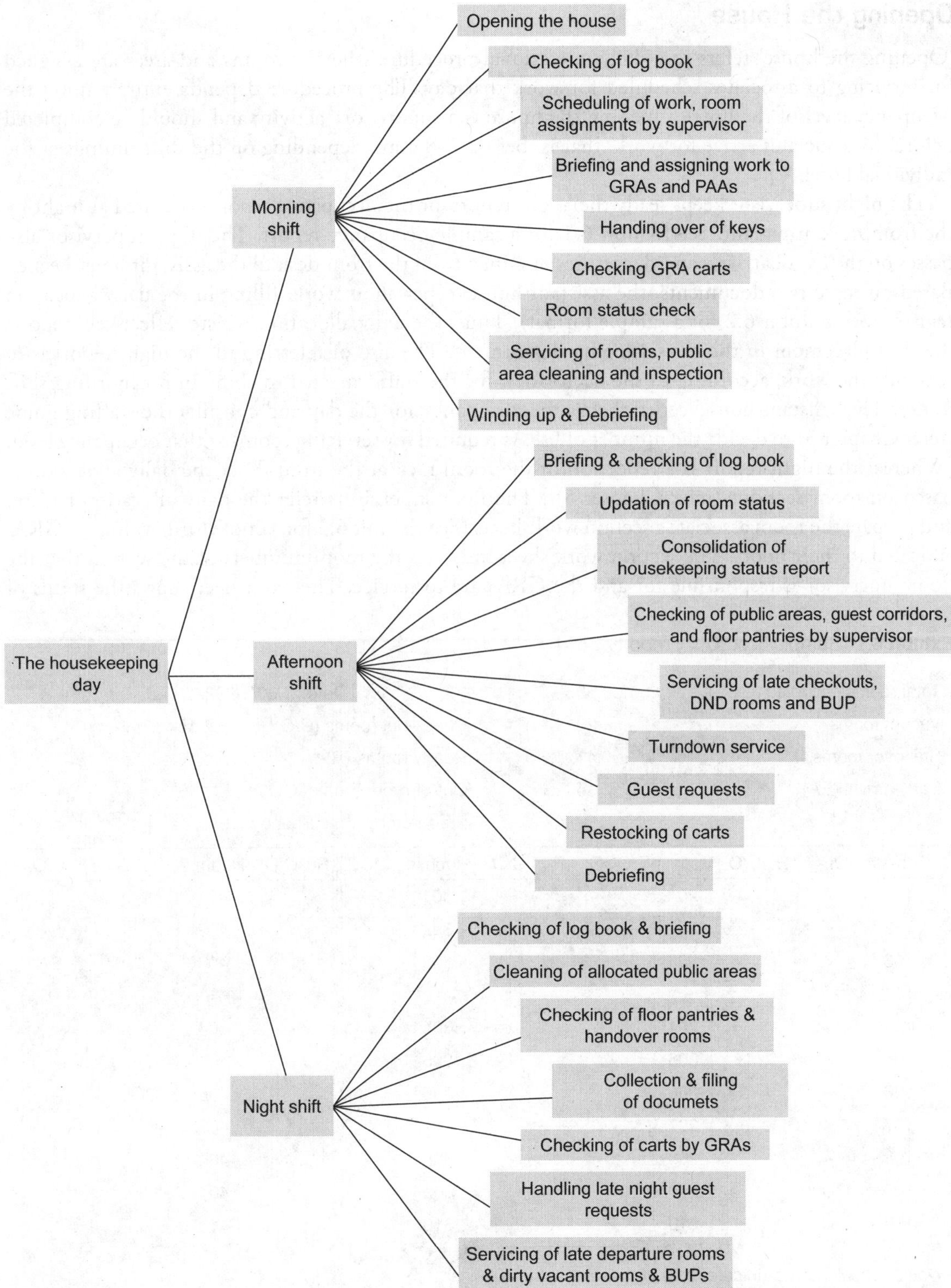

Fig. 6.1 The housekeeping day

Opening the House

'Opening the house' refers to a daily operational procedure whereby rooms and areas are assigned for servicing to associates scheduled for work that day. The procedure depends entirely upon the occupancy level of the hotel. Opening the house is a supervisory activity and should be completed before the associates arrive for work, that is, before 7–8 a.m., depending on the shift timings at the individual hotel.

The night supervisor keeps ready the 'night report' or the occupancy report generated at night by the front desk attendant. See Exhibit 6.1 for a sample occupancy report. The night supervisor also passes on the list of arrivals and departures obtained from the front desk to the assistant housekeeper. Based on these two documents, the assistant housekeeper allots work, filling in the daily allocation register (See Exhibit 6.2 for a sample format). Thus, the daily allocation register effectively reports the staff placement in the housekeeping department. The aim of referring to the night report is to schedule the work, according to the occupancy, for the staff expected to come in for morning shift duties. The assistant housekeeper checks the occupancy for the day and consults the staffing guide (refer Chapter 3) to decide the number of GRAs required for servicing rooms at that occupancy level. [Whereas the night report is a reflection of the room rack at the front desk, the daily allocation is based on room sections (refer Chapter 5).] The floor supervisors refer the daily allocation register and prepare the room associate's section worksheets (See Exhibit 6.3 for sample format) for the GRAs allocated to their floors. The section work sheet indicates the room numbers of the section that the floor supervisor is responsible for and the GRAs are to service. The worksheet shows the status of

Exhibit 6.1 Sample occupancy report

Total rooms occupied (OCC)	.......58.....	Date: ...30/1/2022.......	
Vacant rooms	.......20.....	Check-out rooms (C/O)	....15.....
Stayover rooms	.......41.....	Ready rooms (R)	......0.....
Early arrival (EA)	.........4.....	Out-of-order rooms (OOO)	......3.....
		Prepared by ..... L Shenoy	

Room #	OCC	R	C/O	Room #	OCC	R	C/O	Room #	OCC	R	C/O	Room #	OCC	R	C/O
101	✓			201	✓			301	✓			401	✓		
102	✓			202				302	✓			402			✓
103	✓			203				303	✓			403			EA ✓
104	OOO			204				304	✓			404			
105	✓			205	✓			305			✓	405	V		
106	✓			206	✓			306				406	OOO		
107	✓			207	✓			307				407	✓		
108	✓			208			✓	308				408	✓		
109	OOO			209				309			✓	409	✓		
110				210	✓			310	✓			410	✓		

Notes: Check marks indicate rooms to be serviced.

Exhibit 6.2 Sample format of daily allocation register

HOTEL XYZ

DAILY ALLOCATION REGISTER

Date: .... Day: ....

Occupancy: .... Room count: .... House count: .... Arr.: .... Dep: ....
SPATT: .... MOD: ....

MORNING SHIFT

Floor	Section		Associate name & sign	HK area/ Public area	Associate name & sign	Public area	Associate name & sign
1st	A	B		Desk control		Banquet – 2	
2nd	A	B		Linen room		Business centre	
3rd	A	B		Uniform room		Spa	
4th	A	B		Sewing room		Gym	
5th	A	B		Laundry		Pool side	
6th	A	B		Lobby		Parking	
7th	A	B		Mediterranean restaurant		Garden	
8th	A	B		Pan-Asian restaurant		Female locker	
9th	A	B		Banquet -1		Male locker	

rooms (as per FO) in the entire section. This is then clipped onto the room associates' carts. The associates fill in the timings of each task accomplished and other necessary details such as the status as per housekeeping, no. of pax., lost & found articles, missing/broken items, reportable matters, guest messages and so on. Once each room has been cleaned and inspected, the floor supervisor puts a check mark against that room number on the worksheet.

As part of their opening duties, the supervisors take over from the previous shift staff and check the keys. They peruse the log book (see Chapter 16 for format), which is used to convey information from one shift to the other. Another document consulted by the supervisors is the banquet function prospectus (BFP). This gives them prior intimation of the various conferences and parties to be held in the hotel and lists the expected responsibilities of all the support departments, including housekeeping, for the same. The housekeeping responsibilities for a banquet may include providing table and decoration linen, decorative artefacts, flower arrangements, and special accessories; cleaning the hall prior to and after the event; and so on. The BFP is sent well in advance to the housekeeping department to allow planning for these tasks.

Morning Shift

The morning shift employees punch in their cards and proceed to the locker room to change into their uniforms. Normally, the soiled uniforms would have been exchanged on a one-for-one basis the

Exhibit 6.3 Sample room associate's section worksheet

HOTEL XYZ

ROOM ASSOCIATE'S SECTION WORKSHEET

Date: .... **Floor:** .... **Associate's name:** ....
Shift: .... **Section:** .... **Supervisor's name:** ....

Rm. No.	Status-FO	Status-HK	Time in	Time out	No. of pax	FT	HT	BT	BM	BR	Lost & found	Extra items	Missing or broken items	Room opened for			Remarks
														Lndry.	Mntn.	Pest cntrl.	
Pick-up Rm.																	

Task of the day: ....

Messages/feedback: ....

Corridors cleaned: .... **Caddy cleaned:** .... **Trolley set-up:** ....
Garbage cleared: .... **Equipment cleaned:** .... **Pantry set-up:** ....
Fire exit & service landings cleaned: .... **Linen/Amenity shortage:** ....

Reportable matters (unusual occurrences): ....

Associate's signature: .... **Supervisor's signature:** ....

Room status codes: OCC: Occupied; Ex. Arr.: Expected Arrival; Ex. Dep.: Expected Departure; EA: Early Arrival, EM: Early make up, VIP; VIP Exp; HWC: Handle with care; SO: Sleep Out; OOO: Out of Order; OOS: Out of Service; V/R: Vacant and ready; V/D: Vacant and Dirty; SB: Scanty Baggage; ONL: Occupied but No Luggage; SL: Single Lady; GRS: Guest Refused Service; DND: Do not disturb, LSG: Long stay guest; SPATT: Special attention guest

previous evening. The uniformed employees then report to the control desk or housekeeping central at the allotted time for the morning shift, which may vary between 7.00 a.m. to 8.00 a.m., depending on the individual hotel. The activities carried out by the employees in the morning shift are described in this section.

Briefing The deputy housekeeper or the executive housekeeper, being the managerial staff, will hold the briefing session for all employees at the beginning of a work shift. This process facilitates a two-way communication between the management and the staff. Usually this is the time at which grooming standards are checked, before allocating jobs to the staff. A sample SOP detailing what is to be communicated in the course of a 10 minute briefing session is presented in Exhibit 6.4.

Exhibit 6.4 A sample SOP for daily briefing

SOP Name:	**Departmental Briefing**		
Effective Date:	**23.12.2019**	**SOP Author:**	**Shefali Shyam**
SOP No. :	**103**	**SOP Approver:**	**Vijay Dewan**
For Job title:	**All HK staff**	**SOP Owner:**	**Hotel Sundown, Coorg**

Objective: To ensure two-way communication within the department for dissemination of information regarding hotel activities, discussion of new ideas and review of daily performance in not more than 10 minutes.

Procedure	Standard
1. Assemble and mark attendance	• Morning and night shift employees to be present punctually for briefing at 7.00 a.m. at HK control desk. Attendance of incoming staff to be marked in attendance register.
2. Check grooming	• Ensure grooming and personal hygiene as per company standards.
3. Inform about the day's tasks and events.	• Inform about the following: - Mention the current house position, arrivals and cross check and announce job allocation for each area. - Any VIPs in the house, the rooms blocked for them, VIP name, profile and preferences. - Long staying guests, their names and room numbers. - OOO rooms and preventive maintenance rooms. - Training for the day.

Room assignments After briefing, the floor supervisors hand over the room associate's section worksheets to the GRAs. These blank worksheets are prepared in triplicate so that they can be used for updating the room status in the afternoon and evening. Each worksheet indicates the rooms that the concerned GRA has to service, giving their status as per front office as indicated in the daily allocation register. It also lists any 'pick-up' rooms the GRA has to service apart from rooms in his/her section. The GRAs clip these sheets onto their carts before proceeding for work. The section worksheets help the GRAs to prioritize the servicing of rooms. For example, rooms with a check-out status are usually serviced first, but if a room needs early make-up, it is given first priority even over these. A sample room associate's section worksheet is presented in Exhibit 6.3. The first two columns in this example have been filled up by the floor supervisor and the next two are filled up by the GRA.

Handover of keys Once the GRAs have received their section worksheets, they are handed the floor master keys for their particular floors by the deputy housekeeper. The keys in the housekeeping department are usually hung in a key cabinet mounted on the wall next to the control desk. The key cabinet should be kept locked at all times. Each GRA has to sign for the keys received in a key control sheet. Refer Chapter 16, Exhibit 16.3 for the format of the same.

Readying the cart The GRAs, armed with the master keys, then proceed to the floor pantries on their individual floors, where they make additions and alterations to their room attendant's cart according to the room occupancy. It is to be noted that the carts are kept ready for servicing guestrooms by the staff from the previous shift, in this case, the night shift staff. Setting up of GRA's cart is discussed in Chapter 7 and a diagram is presented in Figure 7.11.

Room status check At this stage, one of the most important morning shift activities to be undertaken by the housekeeping staff is the physical checking of the room status. The various room status codes and their definitions are presented in Chapter 9, Table 9.2. Hotels have varying procedures regarding who carries out this activity. The two most common procedures are explained here:

All-rooms check The GRAs carry out a physical check of the room status and enter it in their section worksheets. In many properties, the GRAs, after carrying out a physical check of the room status, relate the same to the control desk supervisor over the phone. Along with the room status, the GRA also indicates how many guests occupy a particular room. If there is any discrepancy between the room status received from the front desk and the actual physical status of the room, the GRA should immediately inform the floor supervisor, so that it can be cleared up with the front desk. A consolidated report is then generated from the information received at the control desk by the control desk supervisor. This is called the housekeeping room status report.

Vacant-only check In many properties, to avoid disturbing guests just to check the status of the room, a discrepancy report is generated by the inspection of only 'on change' and 'vacant and ready' rooms. In fact under this system, to save time, the GRAs do not approach any guestrooms in the morning till they are ready to clean that room. The discrepancy check can be left to the floor supervisor, who may inspect 'vacant and ready' and 'on change' rooms to be assured of their status. Any discrepancy can be marked in the section worksheet clipped onto the room attendant's cart. All floor supervisors, after completing the physical checking of the room status in their section, convey any discrepancy to the control desk executive, who then prepares a discrepancy report (See Exhibit 6.5 for format). Discrepancy check is carried out twice a day, once in morning shift and next in the evening shift. The control desk supervisor consolidates the information received and generates the housekeeping room status report. The format of a completed housekeeping status report is given in Exhibit 6.6.

Exhibit 6.5 Format of a Discrepancy report

HOTEL XYZ

DISCREPANCY REPORT

Date: .... **Shift:** .... **Room No.** ....

Room Status	Status as per HK (✓)	Status as per FO (✓)	Remarks
Occupied			
Vacant			
Do Not Disturb			
Sleep Out			
Scanty Baggage			
Occupied, No Luggage			
Double Locked			
Out of Station			
Out of Order			

Name & sign of HK manager: .... **Name & sign of FO manager:** ....

Name & signature of Security officer: ....

Exhibit 6.6 Format for housekeeping room status report

Room No.	Room status code	No. of pax.	Room No.	Room status code	No. of pax.	Room No.	Room status code	No. of pax.
101	OCC	2	201	V/R	–	301	OCC	4
102	OCC	2	202	V/R	–	302	OCC	2
103	OCC	1	203	OOO	–	303	V/R	–
104	V/R	–	204	OCC	1	304	OC	–
105	OCC	2	205	OC	–	305	OC	–
106	OCC	3	206	OC	–	306	OCC	2

Note: V/R: Vacant and ready, V/D: Vacant and dirty, OCC: Occupied, OC: On change, SB: Scanty baggage, ONL: Occupied - No luggage, SO: Sleep out, UR: Under repair, SL: Single lady, DND: Do not disturb, GRS: Guest refused service, LSG: Long stay guest

Room service and inspection Having collected their carts and supplies, the GRAs now proceed to service the guestrooms. The procedure of servicing/cleaning guestrooms is discussed in detail in Chapter 12. As on-change rooms, normally the first priority, are cleaned by the GRAs, the floor supervisors inspect the rooms and inform the control desk supervisor to release these rooms to the front office for sale. In case a room requires some maintenance work, the floor supervisor updates the status to 'OOO' and informs the front desk; a maintenance work order is generated; and, in coordination with the maintenance department, all efforts are made to post the room status back again to 'vacant and ready'.

The order of cleaning guestrooms is as follows:

1. Guest requests for early make-up (EM).
2. VIP rooms (before 11.00 a.m.).
3. 'Check-out' status rooms 'blocked' for new arrivals.
4. 'Check-out' rooms.
5. Occupied rooms with 'please make my room' signs posted.
6. Stayovers.
7. Rooms that had a DND card displayed earlier in the morning.
8. Rooms where guest had refused service (GRS), to be serviced at guest's convenient time mentioned.
9. Rooms due to move to 'check-out' status much later in the day.

Public area assignments Majority of the public area cleaning already gets accomplished during the previous night.

Early during the morning shift, while room cleaning and inspection continues, the public area supervisor inspects the public areas, such as the entrance, lobby, guest corridors, elevators, and staircases to determine whether any emergency attention is required due to any untoward incidents at night. In case such emergency cleaning activities are necessary, the public area supervisor schedules public area associates to accomplish the job. Otherwise, the associates work on their routine cleaning schedules for public areas. Public area cleaning is discussed in detail in Chapter 13.

DND procedure Most rooms would have been serviced by afternoon except the ones that displayed a DND card through the morning. Usually these DND cards would have been taken off by this time of day and the GRAs can knock, enter, and service the rooms.

All hotels have a DND policy to ensure guest privacy and safety.

- The associate assigned to the floor should make a note in the section worksheet, of all rooms with Privacy indicator on/DND card hung outside the door twice during the morning shift.
- If the guest is staying for more than a day, check when the last service was provided and inform the duty manager. The guest relations executive (GRE) or duty manager contacts the guest on telephone and checks for his well- being and asks for service to be provided. If the guest agrees for service to be given, housekeeping desk control is informed; if not, the guest is asked the convenient time for room to be serviced.
- If the guest has arrived early in the morning and placed the DND card outside the room, morning service is not given and the information is entered in the log book for the second shift.
- In the afternoon shift by 3.00 p.m., if the room is still on DND, the GRE places a call to the guest to enquire if the room may be serviced. If the guest refuses service, the executive should convey regret for disturbance and end the call. In case the guest asks for the room to be cleaned, enquire the convenient time of service and accordingly inform the housekeeping control desk. In case, the guest does not pick the call, the floor supervisor inserts a DND slip under the door. A sample format of the DND slip is presented in Exhibit 6.7.
- In the scenario of the guest not responding within 12 hours of room being DND, the front desk and security should be informed. A team comprising housekeeping floor supervisor, front office executive and security officer should approach the room and knock as per the hotel policy. If there is no response from the guest, the room is opened using the grand master key with HoD's approval. In case, it is observed that the guest is sound asleep, the team should exit the room quietly. In case the guest wakes up, a team member should introduce himself/herself and explain the purpose of getting inside the room even when the Privacy sign was on. In case it is observed that the guest is in distress, appropriate action is taken. Under no circumstances any occupied room should be on DND for more than 12 hours without a check.

Once the GRAs are through with the servicing of all rooms including DND and GRS (rooms in which guests had refused service), usually by late afternoon, they undertake a physical check of the room status, fill in the information on the blank duplicate of their section worksheet, and hand it over to the

Exhibit 6.7 Sample format of a DND slip

HOTEL XYZ

Dear Mr./Ms. ....

Your room has a 'Do Not Disturb' sign displayed at the door and hence not been serviced to respect your privacy. Kindly call Housekeeping at Extn. .... for service. If you need extra towels or guest supplies, we will be happy to deliver them to your room.

Executive Housekeeper

Room No.: ....

Date: ....

floor supervisor. The floor supervisor submits this to the control desk supervisor. The worksheets from all the GRAs are consolidated by 3.30 p.m. to generate the second housekeeping status report for the day and this is passed on to the front desk.

Winding-up tasks, reporting, and handover The GRAs now send all the soiled linen (collected in the soiled linen bags on their room attendants' carts) down the linen chute. Or, as on many properties in India, the housemen take the soiled linen to the laundry on a linen trolley.

Around 3.30 p.m., the GRAs re-stock the carts for evening guestroom servicing. They wash the used tooth glasses collected during the day, dispose the trash, mix the correct dilution of cleaning agents, re-stock the hand caddies with cleaning supplies, re-stock linen, and leave the floor pantry neat and clean. The floor supervisors collect and file away all forms and reports and they submit their worksheets at the control desk. The supervisors make relevant entries in the log book. This is the time when the afternoon shift crew is reporting for work. There should be a shift overlap of at least an hour to facilitate handover and takeover of duties. The morning shift staff hand over keys at the control desk, sign the key control sheet, daily allocation register and assemble for their debriefing.

Debriefing and going off duty This session, similar and complementary to the briefing at the start of a shift, may include the following:

- Discussing problems faced by any staff member.
- Sharing experiences and inviting ideas or practical solutions to tackle any particular common problem.
- Handover of any incomplete work to the staff on the next shift.
- Checking the next day's duty roster.

After the debriefing, the morning shift employees proceed to the uniform exchange counter to exchange their soiled uniforms for fresh ones for the next day's work. If the morning shift began at 8.00 a.m., the employees should then be free to punch their cards on their way out at 5.00 p.m. in a typical 9-hour straight shift scenario.

Afternoon/Evening Shift

As with the morning shift, the afternoon shift too starts with a briefing.

The afternoon shift (also called evening shift in some properties) GRAs update the room status again by undertaking a physical check of guestrooms by 4.30 p.m. The third blank section worksheets prepared earlier are filled in with the updated status. Updating the room status again at this time is important, since many changes may have taken place due to guest check-ins and check-outs after 3.00 p.m. The 'check-out' rooms will now be ready rooms. The final housekeeping status report based on this check is consolidated at the control desk, tallied with the front desk, reviewed by the executive housekeeper, and then a copy is sent to the financial controller.

Around 4.30 p.m., a supervisor checks all guest corridors and service areas to ensure that no equipment, soiled linen, or trash is left behind and that the floor pantries are tidy. They also read the day's entries in the log book. The afternoon GRAs now clean the 'late service request' rooms and 'brush up' (BUP)/ Touch up rooms that had been serviced earlier in the day when they were occupied, but are now vacated. Only a very light servicing is required in these rooms, hence the term 'brush up'.

The GRAs then provide the turndown service in all the occupied rooms, and expected arrival rooms from 4.30 p.m onwards. This is usually the time when guests are expected to be out on business, for dinner, or other engagements. (Refer to Chapter 12 for the procedure for the turndown service).

Any 'late check-out' room also needs to be serviced for late-arriving guests or walk-in guests. Any guest request specifically made in the evening hours is also noted down on the room assignment sheet and transferred to the guest log book. Finally, guest requests and requests for guest loan items required in the evening are met.

By 6.00 p.m., the front office resolves all discrepancies, some through a simple phone call and others by physically re-checking. The evening GRAs re-stock the room attendants' carts in the floor pantries for the next day's work and go off duty.

Night Shift

Quite a few staff are scheduled in the night shift as many public area cleaning tasks are performed easily at this time, when footfalls are least. A night supervisor is in-charge of all such activities.

Role of the Night Supervisor

The night supervisor takes over from the supervisors of the previous shift. He checks the log book for any instructions entered by the previous shift staff. He then takes a briefing of the night staff regarding the work to be accomplished. The night supervisor is responsible for looking over the cleaning activities scheduled in the public areas at night. He takes his first round of the areas scheduled for cleaning at the beginning of his shift. The second round of the public areas is taken later in the night when the scheduled work is completed. A check of all the floor pantries is also the responsibility of the night supervisor. He also checks any fumigated rooms and other handover rooms which were under maintenance. The night supervisor is responsible for filing the following documents:

- Night report to housekeeping department
- Originals and copies of all the daily work reports
- All the section worksheets
- Copies of the housekeeping status report
- Completed key control sheet
- Night supervisor's report on evening activities
- A consolidated guest history sheet to understand and record the preferences of repeat guests

Early in the morning, the night supervisor collects the night report and the arrivals/departures list from the front desk to open the house.

Role of the Night GRA

The night GRA sets up the floor pantries, checks the room attendants' carts, washes the drinking glasses, and keeps them ready for the morning crew to place on the cart. A major responsibility includes handling late-night guest requests. There are days when there are many guest requests at late hours, which keep the GRA on his toes. Equally important is the servicing of late departure rooms and dirty vacant rooms, which are given high priority so as to keep them ready for sale by morning. Ready rooms are also brushed up (BUP) for early morning arrivals.

Role of Night Public Area Associates

The public area associates scheduled in the night shift take up the following cleaning activities:

Porch and entrance

- Scrubbing of floors and steps, water wash

Lobby

- Dry and wet mopping, dusting and glass cleaning, water wash of the lobby at least thrice a week
- Periodic marble polishing
- Glass and surfaces cleaning
- Thorough cleaning of bell desk, lobby manager's desk, travel desk and reception
- Floor scrubbing and WC cleaning of gents' and ladies' cloak rooms
- Thorough cleaning of guest elevators

Restaurants

- Thorough cleaning of all restaurants including high level dusting, A/C grill cleaning, floor scrubbing, furniture dusting and cleaning, glass cleaning and wood polishing
- Thorough cleaning of cloak rooms attached to the restaurants

Banquets

- Thorough cleaning of all banquet halls including carpet vacuuming, high level dusting, skirting cleaning, floor scrubbing, A/C grill cleaning and follow up with maintenance for AHU servicing and cleaning of fixtures
- Set up of banquet halls for the next day's function

Leisure areas

- Thorough cleaning of gymnasium
- Cleaning of swimming pool, cabanas and cloak rooms

Back Area

- Cleaning of administrative offices
- Cleaning of all back offices
- Cleaning of entire back area and all fire exit staircases
- Cleaning of housekeeping department
- Cleaning of service lifts and service lift landing areas

SUMMARY

This chapter discusses the basic daily routine of the housekeeping department in a hotel in a sequential manner. As is evident, the scheduling of the whole 'housekeeping day' is done with the help of various forms and reports. The day starts early with the night report and the arrivals/departures list being passed on from the front desk to the housekeeping department. Through these reports, the occupancy of the hotel for the day is estimated and the required number of staff scheduled, with reference to the staffing guide. The forms generated from this activity are the daily allocation report and the section work sheet. These activities are part of the procedure of opening the house.

These activities need to be accomplished before the arrival of the workers for the morning shift. The activities from here on are divided into segments according to the three shifts—morning, afternoon/evening, and night.

Morning activities start with the briefing process, after which the supervisors hand the GRAs their section worksheets. This sheet helps the GRAs to prioritize guestrooms for cleaning. The relevant keys are handed over to the workforce at the control desk. The employees sign the key control sheet and then proceed to the floor pantry to organize their room attendants' carts to start the servicing of rooms.

Some properties encourage GRAs to confirm and update the room status themselves, whereas others prefer the floor supervisors to carry out the physical check. Whatever the method adopted, it should be kept in mind that the guests should not be disturbed just to physically check and update the status of rooms. A consolidated housekeeping room status report is generated at the control desk based on the physical check. The GRAs then begin servicing the guestrooms according to priority and the floor supervisor inspects the rooms in order. The rooms are then passed as 'ready rooms' to the front office for sale. In case the GRA reports that any maintenance work is to be carried out in the guestroom, a work order form is generated by the control desk supervisor. Meanwhile, the public area supervisor directs the workforce of housemen according to the schedule of cleaning for the public areas. Any room status discrepancy between the front office and the housekeeping department is resolved by a physical check.

In the early afternoon, the rooms that displayed a DND card in the morning are serviced. Requests for a late service were earlier made a note of and these rooms may also be serviced now. The ideal way to deal with the situation if a DND card has been hung up for an overly long time has also been discussed in detail.

During the afternoon/evening shift, a room status check is called for again. The reports from the GRAs are re-consolidated and, after the approval of the executive housekeeper, sent to the front desk by 3.30 p.m. The evening shift GRAs undertake a physical check again at around 4.30 p.m. to update the room status. A final consolidated housekeeping status report is sent to the front desk and a copy is forwarded to the financial controller. Other evening activities include the turndown service, 'brush ups', attending to guest requests, and preparing the room attendants' carts for the next day's work.

The night supervisor's crucial role in opening the house early in the morning is outlined. Many public area cleaning tasks are scheduled in the night.

KEY TERMS

Banquet function prospectus (BFP) This document gives prior intimation of various conferences and parties to be held in the hotel and chalks out the responsibilities all support departments, including housekeeping, are expected to take on for the same.

Briefing A briefing session is held for all the employees at the beginning of a work shift, usually presided over by the HOD to facilitate two-way communication between the management and the staff.

BUP 'Brush up'—very light servicing given to a room that has been given a full service earlier in the day, when it was occupied, but which is now vacated. Also referred to as Touch up.

Check-in Arrival and registration of a guest at the hotel.

Check-out room A room from which the guest has left is coded as C/O.

Crib Cot for babies, provided to guests on request.

Daily routine The series of administrative and work-related events that occur between 6.30 a.m. and midnight form the routine for a housekeeping department in the guestroom area and public areas of a hotel.

Daily allocation A document prepared by the deputy housekeeper, assigning work in various areas to supervisors and associates based on the occupancy of the hotel.

Debriefing A debriefing session or meeting is held at the end of a shift by managerial staff to discuss problems, share ideas, and evolve solutions.

DND card A 'do not disturb' card, which may be hung outside the guestroom by the guest to inform staff and visitors that the occupant does not wish to be disturbed.

Emergency key A key that can open all the guestrooms of the hotel even if they are double-locked.

Financial controller The financial controller is the head of the controls department and is responsible for ratifying all the inventory items of the operational departments. He is responsible for revenue analysis and all the control procedures.

Floor master keys Floor master keys open all guestrooms on a particular floor that are not double-locked. A GRA is given this key to service rooms on a particular floor.

Floor pantry A service room provided on each floor for GRAs to store cleaning agents, equipment, guest supplies, guestroom linen, and room attendants' carts.

Gate pass An authorization given to an employee to take guest or hotel property out of the hotel.

GRA Guestroom attendant.

GRS A room status meaning Guest refused service.

Guest loan items These are guest supplies not normally found in a guestroom, but available upon request—for example, hair-dryers and ironing boards.

Hand caddy A portable container for storing and transporting cleaning supplies, carried on a room attendant's cart.

Housekeeping control desk The nerve centre of the entire housekeeping department for the dissemination of information and communication to and from the department. Sometimes referred to as housekeeping central.

Housekeeping day The housekeeping day refers to that part of the 24 hours in a day during which housekeeping operations are in full swing.

Housekeeping room status report A report generated by the housekeeping department that indicates the current housekeeping status of each guestroom, based on a physical check.

Linen chute A passage in the form of a tunnel for sending soiled linen from the floor pantries of all floors to a central place near the laundry, from where it can be collected by the laundry staff.

Log book An important register in the housekeeping department, it is here that instructions and messages for staff on the next shift are written down by employees working on the previous shift.

Room attendant's cart A lightweight wheeled vehicle used by room attendants for transporting cleaning supplies, guest amenities, linen, and equipment needed to complete a block of cleaning assignments.

Make-up Servicing of the room while a guest is registered in the room.

Night report See occupancy report.

Occupancy report Also called a night report, this document is prepared each night by the front desk attendant and indicates the rooms occupied that night and ones that are to become 'check-outs' the following day.

Occupied room A room registered to a guest and/or his/her luggage.

'On change' room A room in need of housekeeping services before it can be registered to an arriving guest.

OOO 'Out of order', the status of a guestroom not rentable because it is being repaired or redecorated.

Opening the house Refers to a daily operational procedure whereby rooms are assigned for servicing to GRAs scheduled for work that day.

Open section A group of rooms that is not part of a room section for cleaning purposes.

Pick-up rooms Rooms from the open section assigned to different GRAs to balance out the workload.

Room associate section worksheet This worksheet indicates the room numbers of the section that the floor supervisor is responsible for and the GRAs are to service. The worksheet shows the status of rooms (as per FO) in the entire section. The associates fill in the timings of each task accomplished and other necessary details such as the status as per housekeeping, no. of pax, lost & found articles, missing/broken items, reportable matters, guest messages and so on.

Room rack An array of metal file pockets designed to hold room-rack slips arranged by room number. The room rack summarizes the current status of all rooms in the hotel.

Room section A group of 13–20 guestrooms, as close together as possible, that is allotted for cleaning and servicing to one GRA on an eight-hour shift.

Room status discrepancy A situation in which the housekeeping department's description of a room's status differs from the room status information at the front desk.

Scanty baggage A room status indicating a room that is occupied by a guest with small, light luggage that could be carried away in his/her hand without obviously indicating a guest departure, should the guest walk out with it.

SPATT Special attention guest.

Staffing guide A document that serves as a scheduling and control tool, enabling the executive housekeeper to determine the total work hours and the number of employees required to operate the housekeeping department at specific occupancy levels in the hotel.

'Stayover' room A room occupied by a guest who is not checking out today and will remain at least one more night.

Tooth glass A glass placed on the vanity unit as a guest supply and used for gargling or to hold the guest's tooth brush, dentures, and so on.

Turndown service A special service provided by the housekeeping department in which a room attendant enters the guestroom early in the evening to re-stock supplies, tidy the room, and turn down the covers on the bed in preparation for the night.

Walk-in A guest who appears at the hotel in person and requests a room without holding a prior reservation.

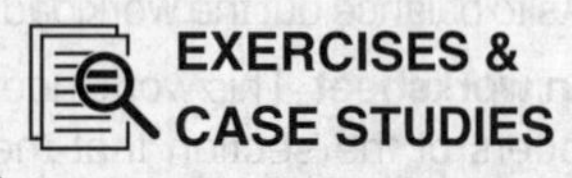

Work order form A work order form is made out by the housekeeping department when any scheduled maintenance work is to be carried out in guestrooms or public areas. This form is sent to the maintenance department to request them to undertake the repair as soon as possible.

7

Housekeeping Inventories

Learning Objectives

After reading this chapter, you should be able to

- draw up a classification of housekeeping inventories
- discuss the types, use, maintenance, storage, and selection of diverse cleaning equipment
- review the types, use, storage, and selection of cleaning agents used by housekeeping staff
- appreciate the importance of systems and procedures in the issuing and control of cleaning equipment and agents
- describe the various types of linen handled by housekeeping staff
- enumerate the types of uniforms used in hotels and describe their significance

Introduction

Housekeeping inventories refer to the stocks of purchased operating supplies, equipment, and other items held for future use in housekeeping operations. As discussed in Chapter 5, the executive housekeeper is responsible for two kinds of inventories, those of recycled and non-recycled items. Recycled inventories are for those items and pieces of equipment that have relatively limited useful lives, but are used over and over again in housekeeping operations. Non-recycled inventories include items that are used up during the course of routine housekeeping operations. Inventory control and stock-taking are discussed in Chapter 17. The important housekeeping inventories are listed in Figure 7.1.

Cleaning Equipment

Efficient cleaning and maintenance are dependent upon high-quality cleaning equipment, correctly used. Though only 5 to 10% of the overall cost incurred on cleaning is accounted for by cleaning equipment and agents, selecting the ideal equipment plays a major role in the cleaning process. There will often be several ways of carrying out any particular cleaning task and different types of equipment that can be employed for it. It is the executive housekeeper's responsibility to select the most appropriate piece of equipment, according to the hotel's requirement. Most types of cleaning equipment fall under the category of recycled items, but a few large pieces of equipment may be considered fixed assets. The correct choice of quality cleaning equipment could save costs due to breakdowns, reduce fatigue, and also ensure overall efficiency in operations.

Equipment used in the cleaning of surfaces, furniture, and fittings in a hotel building include both manual and mechanical equipment (see Figure 7.2). The care and cleaning of manual and mechanical equipment are discussed in Table 7.1.

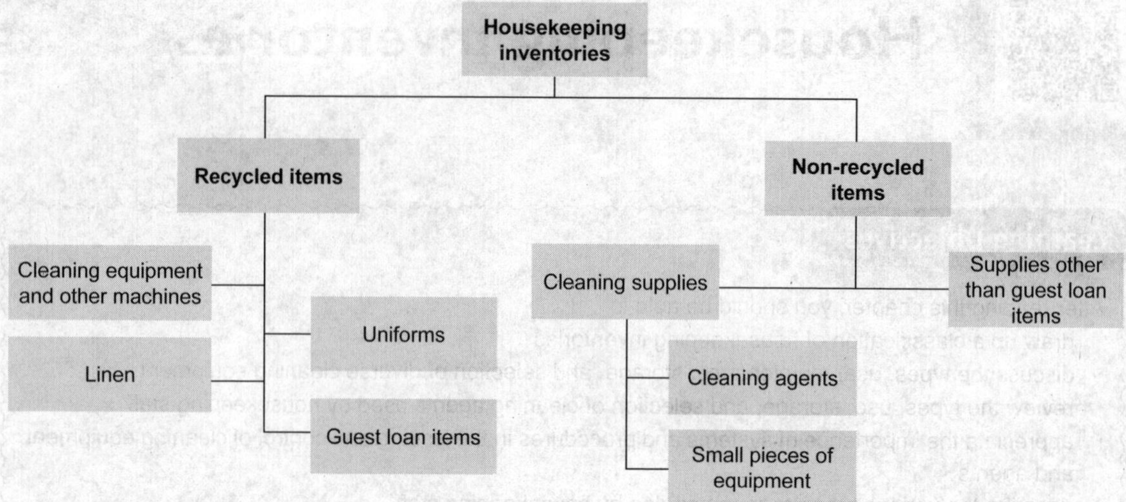

Fig. 7.1 Various housekeeping inventories

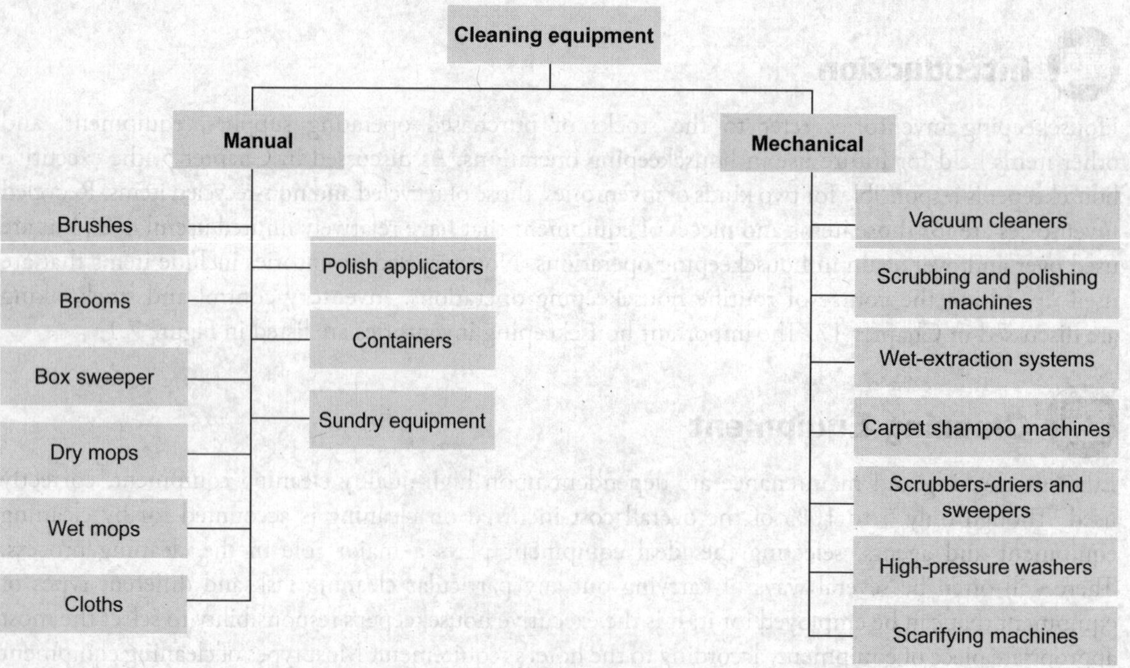

Fig. 7.2 Classification of cleaning equipment

Table 7.1 Care and cleaning of manual and mechanical equipment

Manual equipment	Care and cleaning
Brushes	• Brushes should be gently tapped on a hard surface to loosen dust and debris after the cleaning process. • Frequent washing with water is avoidable since the brushes may lose some of their stiffness in this way. If they must be washed frequently, the final rinse should be in cold saline water to help the brushes regain their stiffness. • Brushes should be cleaned of all fluff and threads before washing. They may be washed in warm, mild soapy water. A disinfectant should be added to the rinsing water for toilet brushes. • If brushes with natural bristles (vegetable or animal origin) have been used for wax polishing, washing soda (1 tbsp to 2 litres of water) should be added to remove grease thoroughly. • Brushes should be washed by beating the head up and down, with the bristles facing downwards, so that water splashes up between the tufts. They should be rinsed well in the same way in cold water. After shaking off excess water, the brushes should be left to dry in such a way that the remaining water may drip off the side of the brush or the top of the head stock. • Brushes should never be left resting on their bristles, else they will splay out; if left resting on their stock, water will rot the stock in time. The best way would be to hang the brushes bristle downward. When possible, brushes should be dried in the sun or open air. • To extend the life of a brush, lacquer should be applied to the stock and handle with an oil can and allowed to harden.
Brooms	• Brooms should be shaken free of dust and fluff. They should never be stored standing on their bristle, or the bristles will bend out of shape, resulting in inefficient cleaning. • Brooms should be stored either lying horizontally or hanging bristles downward. • Soft brooms should never be used on wet surfaces. • Stiff brooms such as the coconut fibre brooms can be used on wet surfaces, but must afterwards be cleaned thoroughly in saline water and dried in the sun before storing.
Box sweepers	• The friction brush should be kept clean, else the efficiency of the equipment will be seriously impaired. • After the cleaning process, the dustpans should be emptied of all the collected dust.

Manual Equipment

Manual equipment can include all types of equipment that clean or aid in the cleaning process by directly using maneuver, operation, and energy of employees. Figure 7.3 shows some common manual equipment used in housekeeping operations.

Brushes

These may be designed to remove dry or wet and/or ingrained dust and dirt from hard or soft surfaces. Figure 7.4 shows some brushes used in housekeeping.

Basic parts of a brush The basic parts of a brush are as follows:

Bristles These may be of animal, vegetable, or man-made origin. Horsehair, nylon, and polypropylene are commonly used to make bristles for cleaning brushes. In general, the finer, softer bristles are best for smooth and hard surfaces. The harder the bristles, the softer the surface on which the brush should be

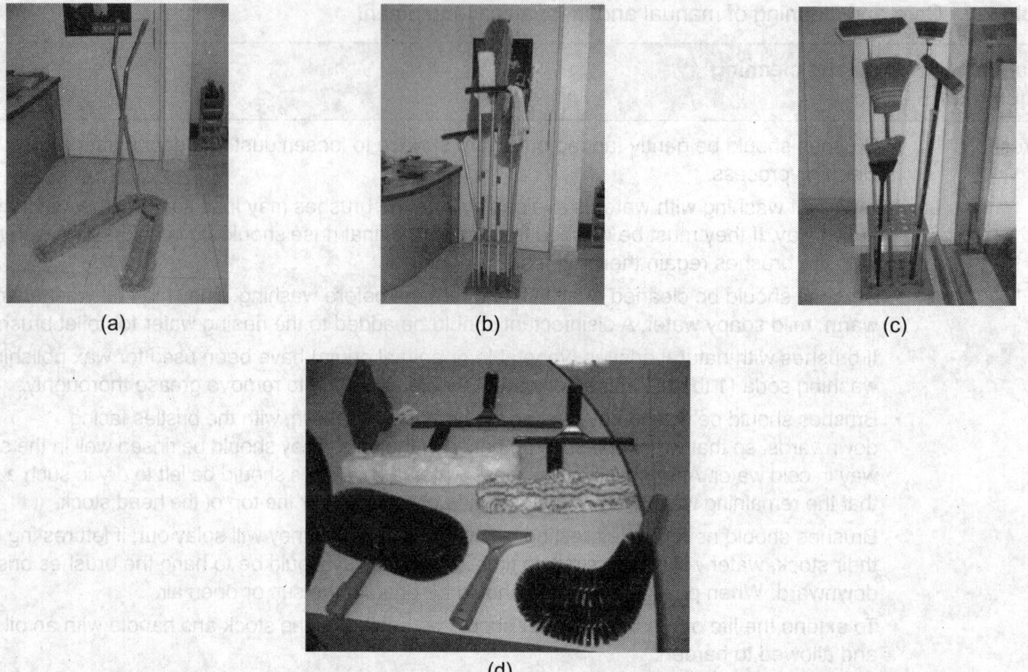

Fig. 7.3 Common manual equipment used in housekeeping: (a) A V-sweeper; (b) Types of mops; (c) Brooms with plastic bristles; (d) Brushes with window squeegees.

Source: Roots Multiclean Limited

used, exception being toilet brushes and brushes found on all-purpose floor machines. Bristles, if not maintained properly, have a tendency to bend, splay, or fall out of the stock. Bristles should be closely set in tufts and the stock well covered with tufts.

Head stock This is the part of the brush into which the bristles are inserted. The stock may be made of wood, metal, or plastic. A good brush is one that has a sturdy stock.

Handle Brush handles may be detachable or non-detachable. Detachable handles must be fixed firmly in place on the stock when the brush is in use.

Types of brushes Three main types of brushes are used for cleaning surfaces.

Hard brushes Hard brushes have bristles that are fairly stiff and well spaced out. They are most suitable for the removal of heavy soil and litter from carpets and for cleaning rough surfaces.

Soft brushes Soft brushes have bristles that are fairly flexible and set close together. These help to remove loose soil and litter on hard, smooth surfaces. Such brushes may be designed to dust carpets and furniture, too, especially those made of cane, wicker, or bamboo.

Scrubbing brushes Scrubbing brushes have short, coarse bristles designed for use on surfaces that have become stained and heavily ingrained with dirt. These brushes should only be used to remove stubborn, heavy soiling from small areas that are difficult for a scrubbing machine to access. Long-handled scrubbing brushes, called deck scrubbers or T-scrubbers, are useful for cleaning larger areas as well as corners.

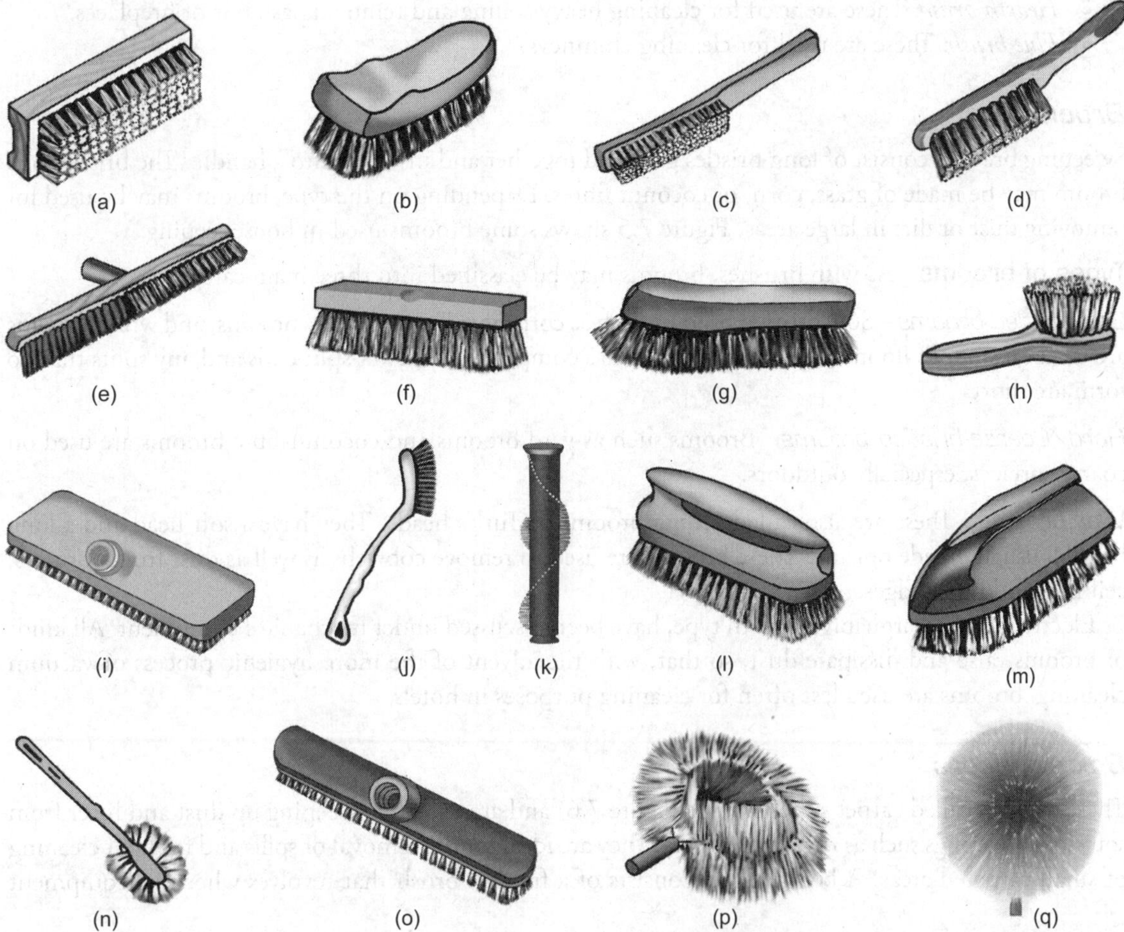

Fig. 7.4 Brushes used in housekeeping: (a) Spot removal hard brush; (b) Upholstery brush; (c) Long handled curtain and pleats brush; (d) Soft metallic bristle brush; (e) Nylon fibre carpet brush; (f) Natural fibre carpet brush for rugs; (g) Horsehair bristle carpet brush; (h) Leather cleaning brush; (i) Short bristle scrubbing brush; (j) Grout cleaning brush; (k) Carpet brush roller; (l) Oval shaped hard brush; (m) Iron shaped hard brush; (n) WC brush; (o) Nylon bristle deck scrubbing brush; (p) Oval wall dusting brush; (q) Nylon bristle wall dusting brush

Brushes are also classified on the basis of their functions:

- *Toilet brushes*: These are WC brushes, radiator brushes, and Johnny mops.
- *Bottle brushes*: These are used for cleaning overflow vents in wash basins and tubs.
- *Cloth scrubbers*: These are used for scrubbing clothes.
- *Deck scrubbers*: These are used for cleaning large areas.
- *Carpet brushes*: Carpet brushes are used for brushing carpets.
- *Upholstery brushes*: These are used to loosen out dust embedded between the fabric fibres in upholstered chairs and sofas.
- *Feather brushes*: These are brushes with feathers, for light dusting.

- *Hearth brush*: These are used for cleaning heavy soiling and removing ash out of fireplaces.
- *Flue brush*: These are used for cleaning chimneys.

Brooms

Sweeping brooms consist of long bristles gathered together and inserted into a handle. The bristles of a broom may be made of grass, corn, or coconut fibres. Depending on the type, brooms may be used for removing dust or dirt in large areas. Figure 7.5 shows some brooms used in housekeeping.

Types of brooms As with brushes, brooms may be classified into three main categories:

Soft-bristled brooms Soft-bristled brooms such as corn-fibre brooms, grass brooms, and whisk brooms are used on smooth floors. A good soft broom has comparatively fewer split ends and any splits that do form are short.

Hard/Coarse-bristled brooms Brooms such as yard brooms and coconut-fibre brooms are used on coarse surfaces, especially outdoors.

Wall brooms These are also called ceiling brooms or Turk's heads. They have a soft head and a long handle, usually made of cane. These brooms are used to remove cobwebs as well as dust from cornices, ceilings, and high ledges.

Electric brooms, arguably a fourth type, have been discussed under mechanical equipment. All kinds of brooms raise and dissipate dust, so that, with the advent of the more hygienic process of vacuum cleaning, brooms are used less often for cleaning purposes in hotels.

Box sweepers

These are also called carpet sweepers (see Figure 7.6) and are used for sweeping up dust and litter from soft floor coverings such as rugs and carpets. They are ideal for the removal of spills and for light cleaning of small carpeted areas. A box sweeper consists of a friction brush that revolves when the equipment

Fig. 7.5 Brooms used in housekeeping: (a) Natural fibre broom; (b, c) Nylon bristle brooms; (d, e) Nylon bristled street brooms; (f) Coconut fibre yard broom; (g) Natural fibre broom; (h) Long handled triangular grass broom

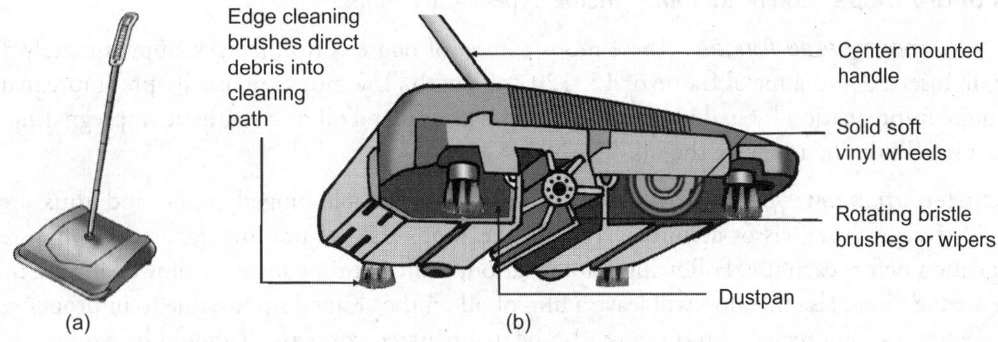

Fig. 7.6 Carpet sweeper: (a) Carpet sweeper; (b) Parts of a carpet sweeper

is pushed manually over the carpet or floor. The dust gets thrown up into built-in dustpans, which are hinged at the bottom to facilitate emptying after use. Choose sweepers with a wide base that is low enough to be pushed under furniture and that will clean close to a wall. In sweepers meant to clean hard floors as well as soft floor coverings, the brush can be lowered to the floor to sweep.

Dry mops

Also called dust control mops, these are designed to remove soil and debris from floors, walls, and ceilings without raising and dissipating dust. These mops (see Figure 7.7) generally consist of a handle to which a metal frame is attached. The mop head is either inserted into the frame or stretched over it, according to the type.

Fig. 7.7 Mops: (a) Dry mop; (b) Impregnated dry mop; (c) Dry and wet microfibre mop; (d) Disposable dry mop head; (e) static duster; (f) Do-all mops; (g) Kentucky mop with looped end; (h) Foss mop; (i) Sponge mop; (j) Squeegee heads

Types of dry mops There are four principle types of dry mops.

Mops with impregnated fringes These mops consist of dense cotton fringes, approximately 15 cm in length, inserted into a metal frame of 15–120 cm length. The mops are usually pre-impregnated or will require impregnation by soaking in or spraying with mineral oil or a synthetic impregnating fluid. The dust is held on the mops by the oil.

Impregnated mop sweepers These mops consist of a double-hinged frame and thus are also called 'V sweepers' or 'scissor-action sweepers'. The mops can be pre-impregnated or may require impregnation before each use. Following impregnation, sufficient time must be allowed for the mineral oil to cure the fibres, else the mop will leave a film of oil on the cleaned surface due to improper curing. To be effective, an impregnated mop must also be manoeuvred correctly. It should be worked in long, even strokes in a continual movement, keeping the mop head in contact with the surface all the time. This way, maximum dust collection and minimum dust dissipation is ensured.

Dry and wet microfibre mops These lightweight mops are very convenient as they have dual function of dry and wet cleaning. The mop head made of microfibres is attached with velcro on a flat base with a long handle. The microfibres traps dirt effectively while dry cleaning. For wet cleaning, the mop head is made wet with an appropriately diluted cleaning solution and used in the similar way as a wet mop.

Static mops These mops consist of acrylic, nylon, or polyester strands fixed to a backing stretched over a metal frame. When in use, the fringes splay out to form a large surface area, holding dust by means of a static charge that builds up on the fringe. Static mops are more easily maintained than impregnated mops.

Disposable mops These mops consist of a handle with a soft pad at the end, onto which cheap cotton or a synthetic material is affixed. The material has properties enabling it to attract and hold dust. The fabric is held in place by clips or a special tape and is usually purchased in large rolls, from which the desired amount can be cut. The fabric is disposed of after each use and replaced immediately. Although very expensive due to the constant replacement of the head, they are extremely hygienic and are particularly suitable when infection control is required.

Wet/damp mops

These mops (see Figure 7.7) are used in conjunction with buckets for the removal of dirt adhering to a surface. The mop heads can be made of cotton, sponge, or any other fibre capable of absorbing moisture well.

Types of damp mops There are four types of damp mops available.

Do-all mops These mops consist of strands of twisted cotton fixed to a circular metal plate, which in turn is fixed to a stock.

Kentucky mops These mops consist of cotton strands fixed to a length of cotton fabric, which is in turn inserted into a flat metal stock. They are available in weights ranging from 330 g to 670 g. The strands may be stitched together or unstitched. The former are less likely to tangle, can be laundered more easily, and are likely to last longer than unstitched mops.

Foss mops These consist of a dense cotton fringe inserted into a heavy metal stock. They are available in a wide range of weights.

Sponge mops These consist of a cellulose sponge fixed to a replaceable, lever-controlled head, hinged for wringing out and attached to a long handle. Using a sponge mop is one of the easiest ways to wash a hard floor. Short-handled sponge mops are also available, for cleaning windows.

Squeegee A squeegee consists of a long metallic handle and a wooden or rubber blade to remove excess water from a surface being cleaned. It is effective when followed by mopping with a damp mop. A smaller version called the window squeegee is used for wiping away water from windows after washing.

Cloths

Various cloths are used extensively in wet and dry cleaning by housekeeping staff. For efficient and correct usage, cloths may be colour-coded and the staff well trained in their use.

Types of cloths A variety of cloths are available for specific purposes (see Figure 7.8).

Dusters and cloth mittens (mitts) These are meant for dusting and buffing. Soft, absorbent, plain, or checked cotton material, or flannelette of upto 15 sq. cm are ideal for dusters. When used for damp dusting, they must be sprayed with a fine mist of water or dusting solution. Cloth mitts may be impregnated with a mineral oil instead. Dusters must be folded several times into a hand-sized pad before use so as to provide a number of clean surfaces and avoid spreading dirt again to a clean surface instead.

Swabs and wipes These are all-purpose cloths made of soft, absorbent material. They are used for wet cleaning and damp dusting of all surfaces above floor level. They are also used for cleaning sanitary fittings such as bathtubs and wash basins. Wipes include loosely woven or knitted cotton cloths and non-woven cloths. Synthetic sponges may also be grouped under this category. They are available in various sizes and shapes. Sponges are better than other cloths for washing walls, glass, woodwork, and upholstery.

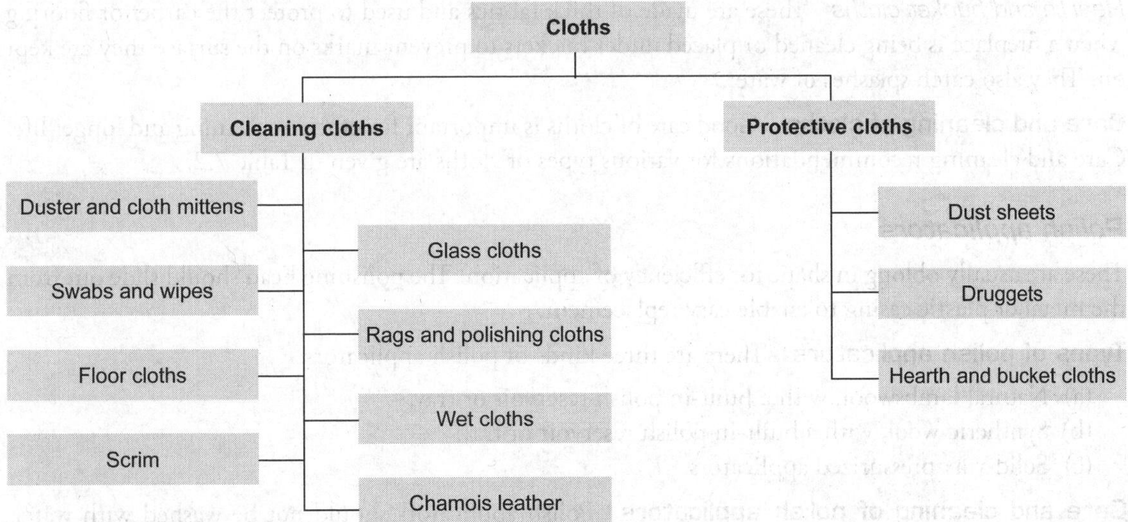

Fig. 7.8 Types of cloths used in housekeeping

Floor cloths Floor cloths are bigger, thicker, and made of coarser cotton material than all-purpose swabs. They are used to wipe WC pedestals and remove spills from floors.

Scrim This is a loosely woven linen material resembling fine sackcloth. Scrim, because of its high absorbency and lint-free nature, is often used instead of chamois leather for cleaning mirrors and windows.

Glass cloths Glass cloths are made up of linen tow yarns and do not leave behind lint. They can therefore be used for wiping mirrors and drinking glasses. These should not be confused with fabrics made from glass fibres (glasscloth)!

Rags and polishing cloths Rags are disposable cloths usually obtained from the sewing room or bought by the sack from tailors. They are used for applying polish or strong cleaning agents and are disposed of when dirty. Polishing cloths need to have a fleecy, napped surface, and pieces of flannel are ideal.

Wet cloths Wet cloths need to be very absorbent and of a manageable size, so that they can be wrung out by hand easily during cleaning. They are used for mopping large floor areas.

Chamois leather Real chamois leather is the skin of the chamois goat antelope, but now various cheaper imitations are available. These simulated chamois leathers are usually skivers, that is, split sheepskin. Chamois leather can be used wet for cleaning windows and mirrors; when dry, it is used as a polishing cloth for silver and other metals. It is also ideal for wiping squeegee blades.

Dust sheets Dust sheets are made of any thin cotton material, being about the size of a single sheet. Discarded bed sheets or curtains from the linen room are ideal for use as dust sheets. They are used to cover floors, furniture, and other articles during spring-cleaning or decorating.

Druggets These are made up of coarse linen, fine canvas, or clear plastic. They may be of the size of a carpet square or a runner. They are placed on the floor in doorways to prevent excessive dirt being trekked in or out during bad weather and during redecorating projects. They are sometimes placed in the passage between the kitchen and dining area as well to catch spills and debris.

Hearth and bucket cloths These are made of thick fabrics and used to protect the carpet or flooring when a fireplace is being cleaned or placed under buckets to prevent marks on the surface they are kept on. They also catch splashes of water.

Care and cleaning of cloths Good care of cloths is important for efficient cleaning and longer life. Care and cleaning recommendations for various types of cloths are given in Table 7.2.

Polish applicators

These are usually oblong in shape for efficiency of application. The polishing head should slide out from the metal or plastic casing to enable easy replacement.

Types of polish applicators There are three kinds of polish applicators.

(a) Natural lambswool, with a built-in polish reservoir or tray.
(b) Synthetic wool, with a built-in polish reservoir or tray.
(c) Solid-wax pressurized applicators.

Care and cleaning of polish applicators Polish applicators should not be washed with water. Wiping away excess polish with newspaper or rags before it dries should suffice. It is important to label the applicators with the type of polish for which they are to be used so that each applicator is used with just one kind of polish to avoid mixing different products.

Table 7.2 Care and cleaning of cloths

Cloth	Care and cleaning
Dusters and cloth mittens	Wash, rinse, and dry thoroughly after use. If cloth mittens are impregnated with mineral oil after washing, keep them covered or they will attract dust.
Swabs and wipes	Wash in hot detergent water, rinse, and dry thoroughly after use. Those used on WCs should be disinfected after washing.
Floor cloths	Wash in hot detergent water, rinse, disinfect (as floors may harbour many germs), and dry thoroughly.
Scrim	Wash, rinse, and dry after use.
Glass cloths	Wash, rinse, and dry after use.
Rags and polishing cloths	Rags should be disposed of after use. Polishes with a strong odour may contain flammable chemicals and storing rags and polishing cloths used in their application may prove a fire hazard.
Wet cloths	Wash in hot detergent water, rinse, and dry thoroughly. Disinfect periodically to prevent them from becoming unhygienic.
Chamois leather	If not maintained properly, leather gets cracked and is damaged easily. Remove excess dirt from it with newspaper. Wash only when necessary, in plain cold water. Rinse and either store damp or dry flat. When dry, rub to soften the leather again.
Dust sheets	Shake well outdoors after use. Wash, rinse, and dry when necessary. Fold neatly and store when not in use.
Druggets	Shake well by tapping on the ground outdoors if made of plastic. Use a hard brush to clean away stubborn dirt from cloth. Wash, rinse, and dry canvas and linen ones frequently. Plastic ones can be damp wiped instead.
Hearth and bucket cloths	Shake well after use. Wash, rinse, and dry thoroughly after use. Use a hard brush to clean away stubborn soiling.

Containers

Work becomes much easier and efficient if the staff are given appropriate containers in which to carry, transport, collect, and store supplies and other items.

Types of containers The various types of containers (Figure 7.9) used are as follows.

Buckets These may be made of plastic or galvanized iron. Plastic buckets are more popular these days as they are lighter in weight, quieter in use, and easier to clean. Buckets to be used with mops may have one or two sections, and may have a wringer device that can be detached for easy cleaning. Twin buckets on a low trolley enable the brush to be rinsed more effectively each time. Larger buckets should have castor wheels, which must be kept free of hair, fluff, and dust. Buckets should be thoroughly washed, inside and out, every time they are used and then allowed to dry before being stored.

Basins and bowls These are used to carry small amounts of water, cleaning solutions, and powders for cleaning small areas.

Dustpans These (see Figure 7.10) are used in conjunction with a broom or brush for gathering dust. They may be made of plastic or metal, plastic ones being the usual choice these days. Dustpans with

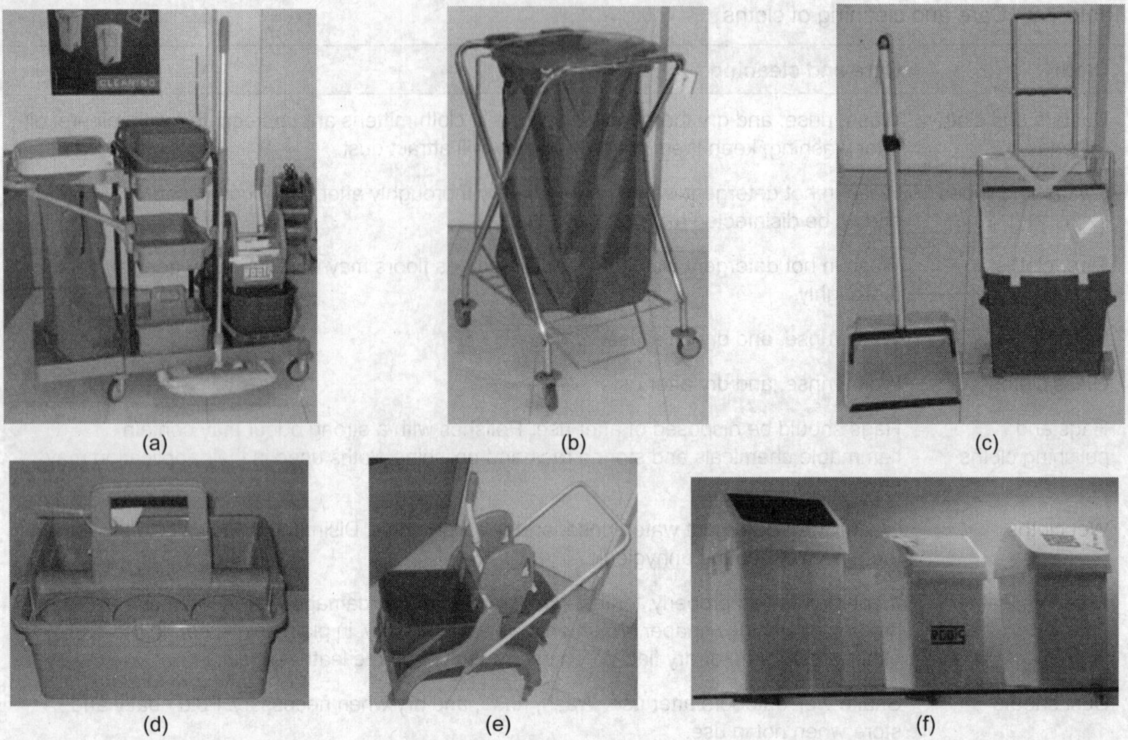

(a) (b) (c)

(d) (e) (f)

Fig. 7.9 Various containers used in housekeeping: (a) Room associate's cart; (b) Laundry sack on trolley; (c) Types of dustpans; (d) Hand caddy; (e) Buckets with wringer attachment; (f) Sani-bins

Source: Roots Multiclean Limited

long handles that eliminate stooping are ideal. In order that dustpans be effective, the edge in contact with the floor must be thin, sharp, and flat. They should always be emptied after use and occasionally washed. They should never be stored resting on their flat edge, as it will wear out and warp so that the pan becomes inefficient. Store dustpans suspended from a hook or lying horizontally, sideways.

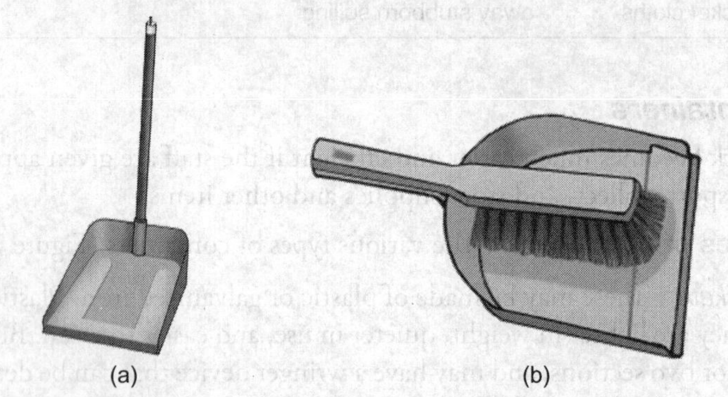

Fig. 7.10 Dustpans: (a) Long handled dustpan; (b) Dustpan with brush

Dustbins The housekeeping department is concerned with dustbins in four areas:

In guestrooms These bins may be made of plastic or wood. Some properties also use jute or wicker bins. Individual dustbins in guestrooms may be lined with a disposable inner lining made of recycled paper or plastic. These bins must be emptied and wiped daily. They should be washed once a week.

In the service rooms These are used to collect waste from guestrooms, brought in by the room attendants' carts. The carts contain a sack called the trash bag for guestroom trash. There should be two types of bins in the service room, a metal bin for disposing of ash from guestroom ashtrays and colour-coded plastic or thick paper bins for other types of trash. The latter can be incinerated directly if required.

In public areas such as guest corridors and lobbies These bins may have a creative design since they are constantly on view. They should be emptied daily.

In waste-collection areas These are usually located outside the main building and are hidden from view. These bins should be kept covered and emptied at least every alternate day.

Sani-bins These are metal or plastic bins with lids. They are found in toilets for the collection of soiled sanitary towels. They should be lined with plastic or paper bags for easy cleaning. The bins must be emptied and wiped daily for reasons of hygiene. Disposable paper bags (sani-bags) should be provided in the guest toilets for wrapping sanitary towels before discarding in the sani-bin.

Spray bottles These are lightweight containers that deliver a fine mist of water or cleaning solution through a fine nozzle, particularly used for spray cleaning. It is essential that the nozzle is properly adjusted and free from any blockage. The nozzle must be maintained clean by spraying clean, pure water through it after use.

Polish applicator trays These are used in conjunction with a polish applicator mop for polishing floors with a liquid polish. They should be labelled with the type of polish that they hold. Cleaning them after use is difficult. Pour any excess polish back into the polish container. Soak the tray in a small amount of a solvent used to remove that particular type of polish. Wipe with rags and store.

Hand caddies Also called 'cleaning caddies' or 'cleaners' boxes', these were originally made of wood or metal but are nowadays usually made of plastic. They consist of a box with a handle and a compartmentalized, fitted tray. They are used by room attendants for carrying cleaning supplies from room to room on the GRAs cart for guestroom cleaning. After each shift, they must be cleaned and topped up with replacement supplies for use in the next shift. The procedure for stocking a cleaning caddy is given in Table 7.3.

Carts and trolleys These are more useful than hand caddies when a large amount of supplies and items are to be carted or replaced. They are ideal for the efficient removal and carriage of smaller pieces of cleaning equipment, cleaning agents, linen, and rubbish. They eliminate the time wasted in assembling equipment at the work location or moving them from one place to another. The various kinds of carts and trolleys that may be used in the housekeeping department are discussed here.

Room associate's cart Also called a room attendant's trolley, this is perhaps the most significant piece of equipment in the housekeeping department. It is like a giant tool box, stocked with everything necessary to service a guestroom effectively. Most such carts available now are made of metal, but sometimes wooden carts may be in use. The cart should be spacious enough to carry all the supplies needed for a GRA to complete half a day's room assignments. Since the cart is large and may be heavily loaded, it must be easily manoeuvrable as well. The ideal cart would have fixed wheels at one end and castor-wheels at the other. The cart should be well organized so that the GRAs do not have to waste time in searching for supplies or make frequent trips back to the supply room. Also, if the cart is not stacked neatly, it will look very unsightly when in guests' view. There is usually one such cart for each

Table 7.3 Procedure for stocking a caddy for cleaning guestrooms

SOP Name:	**Procedure for stocking the cleaning caddy for servicing rooms**		
Effective Date:	**23.12.2019**	**SOP Author:**	**Shefali Shyam**
SOP No. :	**139**	**SOP Approver:**	**Vijay Dewan**
For Job title:	**Housekeeping associates**	**SOP Owner:**	**Hotel Sundown, Coorg**
Objective: To stock an efficiently organised cleaning caddy to carry on the GRAs cart for cleaning guestrooms.			
Equipment & tools needed:	Cleaning caddy, GRAs cart	**Supplies needed:**	Cleaning supplies and tools, cleaning agents
Procedure	**How-to do**		**Additional information**
1. Clean the caddy.	Damp-wipe an empty caddy with a duster cloth.		Cleaning caddies are usually stocked or replenished with supplies in the floor pantry.
2. Fill or replenish the cleaning agents.	From the dispensers in the pantry, fill/replenish the following cleaning agents in their respective spray bottles and place in the caddy. • All-purpose surface cleaner • Glass cleaner • Disinfectant • Room freshener • Chrome fixture polish • Furniture polish • Bathroom deodorizer • WC cleaner		The spray bottles should be labelled clearly. Ensure spray mechanisms on the bottles are functioning properly. Handle all chemicals as per instructions in MSDS.

room section and it is stored in the floor pantry along with other housekeeping supplies. Figure 7.11 shows an organized room attendant's cart.

Most of these carts have three deep shelves—the lower two for linen and the top, partitioned shelf for small supplies. The carts also have a sack for soiled linen, detachable trash bags, and storage space for a vacuum cleaner and a hand caddy. Many carts also contain a locked box in which to store guestroom keys, in case a floor master key is not being used.

While arranging the linen on the cart, it should be kept in mind that the heavier linen must be placed on the lowermost shelf and the smaller, lighter ones on the top shelf. Housekeeping supplies that are usually placed in the room attendant's cart are listed in Table 7.4. See the video of organizing a GRA's cart by scanning the QR Code.

Janitor's trolley This (see Figure 7.12a) is used for carting and storing cleaning supplies. It is used during the cleaning of public areas or any special cleaning projects scheduled for guestrooms. It includes a detachable trash bag and a place for storing cleaning agents and small pieces of cleaning equipment.

Mop-wringer trolley This (see Figure 7.12b) piece of equipment consists of a mop and one or twin buckets with an attached wringer, all mounted on a trolley with castor-wheels. It may have provisions for holding cleaning agents as well as a trash bag.

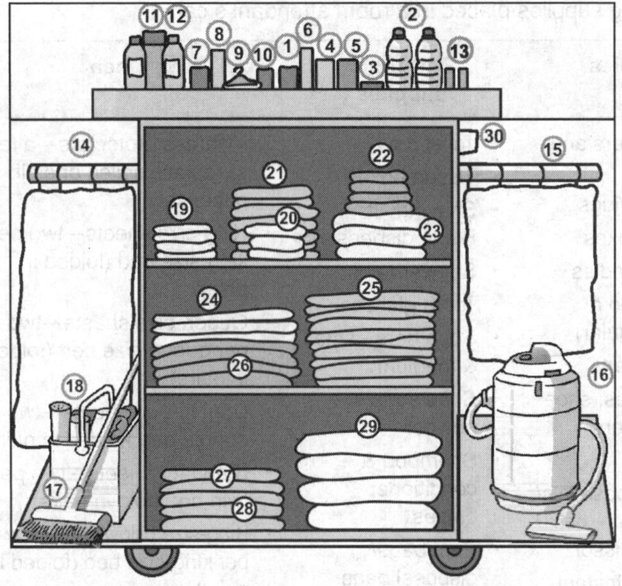

1. Water tumblers, coasters and trays
2. Drinking water bottles/jugs
3. Ashtrays and matchboxes
4. Sewing kits, Bible/Gita, shoe mitts, shoe shines, shoe horns, shoe basket liners
5. Hospitality tray items
6. Room compendium items, stationery kits, scribbling pads
7. DND cards, guest house rules, service directory, breakfast knob cards, 'polish my shoe' cards, IRD menu, tent cards, 'clean my room' cards, conservation cards
8. Laundry forms, laundry bags
9. Cloth hangers
10. Light bulbs
11. Toilet rolls, tissue boxes, blade dispensers, shower caps, tooth glasses
12. Shampoo & conditioner bottles, soap bars, soap suds, shower gel, foam bath, body lotion, body talc, loofah pads, cotton wool, dental kit, grooming kit, cologne, after shave
13. Toilet strips, sanitary pads, disposal bags
14. Soiled linen bag
15. Trash bag
16. Vacuum cleaner
17. Broom
18. Hand caddy: all purpose cleaner, window cleaner, bowl brush, cloths and sponges, rubber gloves, disinfectants, naphthalene balls, room freshener, deodouriser, Brasso, wax polish, scrubber, waste bin & sanibin liners
19. Face towels–2/room
20. Hand towels–2/room
21. King pillowcases–2/bed(fold in pairs)
22. Standard pillowcases–2/bed(fold in pairs)
23. Bath towels–2/bathroom & bath sheets - 2/ VIP room
24. Standard sheets–2/twin bed(fold in pairs)
25. Double sheets–2/double bed(fold in pairs)
26. King sheets–2/king bed(fold in pairs)
27. Mattress protectors
28. Bath mats
29. Bedspreads (a few a to replace if necessary)
30. Guest key box

Fig. 7.11 An organized room associate's cart

Linen trolley These are used for the transfer of clean linen from the laundry to the linen room or from the linen room to the floor pantries, and so on. Linen trolleys may be made of aluminium or steel.

Laundry sacks These, in fact, may or may not be mobile (and hence may not necessarily be trolleys). They may be made of wicker, fibreglass, or plastic. A very popular choice is the one made of tough cotton, with drawstrings, as it can be washed frequently.

All carts and trolleys need to be kept clean, wiped daily, and stored in a locked, dry, well-ventilated area when not in use. A thorough cleaning may be done once a week. The wheels may be oiled during

Table 7.4 Housekeeping supplies placed in a room attendant's cart

Guestroom supplies	Bathroom supplies	Linen	In the hand caddy
• Water tumblers, coasters and tray • Drinking water bottles/jugs • Ashtrays and matchboxes • Candle stands and candles • Sewing kits (also called a 'Dutch wife' in the singular) • Bibles or Gitas or Qurans • Shoe mitts, shoe shines, shoe horns, shoe basket liners • Service directories • Grooming kits/ All purpose kits/ For your care kits- comb, nail file, ear buds, small scissor • Hospitality tray items [Instant coffee sachet, tea sachets (regular, earl grey, green, chamomile), sugar sachets, demerara sugar sachets, sugar substitute sachets, milk creamer pods, condiments packet containing salt and pepper powder] • Room compendium items - writing sheets with hotel logo, envelopes, book marks, picture post cards; business kits/ stationery kits - paper clips, all pins, sharpeners, erasers, staples, cello tape, rubber bands, ballpoint pens and pencils; scribbling pads • Cloth hangers; light bulbs • Copies of the house rules • Breakfast knob cards; DND cards; 'Polish my shoe' cards; IRD menu; tent cards;'make my room' cards; 'collect my laundry' cards; conservation cards • Disposable slippers • Laundry bags; laundry lists	• Toilet rolls • Tissue boxes • Shaving kit, Blade dispensers • Shower caps • Tooth glasses • Soap bars - small & medium • Soap suds or powder • Shampoo & conditioner bottles • Sani-bags/ disposal bags • Bottles of bath foam, shower gel • Loofah pads • Packets of cotton wool • Dental kit (tubes of tooth paste & tooth brushes) • Bottles of cologne, after shave lotion • Bottles of body lotion, body talc • Toilet strips (disinfected paper strips to 'seal' the toilet seat) • Sanitary pads	• Mattress protectors—a few, to replace soiled ones if necessary • King-size sheets—two per king-size bed (folded in pairs) • Queen-size sheets—two per queen-size bed (folded in pairs) • Double-bed sheets—two per double bed (folded in pairs) • Standard sheets—two per twin bed (fold in pairs) • King-size pillow cases—two per king-size bed (folded in pairs) • Standard pillow cases—two per bed (folded in pairs) • Bath towels/Bath sheets—two per bathroom (folded individually, with hotel logo facing outwards) • Hand towels—two per room (folded individually, with hotel logo facing outwards) • Face towels—two per room (folded individually, with hotel logo facing outwards) • Bath mats—one per bathroom • Bed spreads—a few to replace soiled ones if necessary	• All-purpose cleaner (in spray bottle) • WC cleaner • Window/Glass cleaner (in spray bottle) • WC brush • Window/glass squeegee • Johnny mop • Dusters and sponges • Rubber gloves • Disinfectant • Naphthalene balls • Room fresheners • Deodorizers • Brass polish • Wax polish • Scrubber pads • Broom • Waste bin liners • Dust pan

this cleaning. Carts or trolleys should never become general dumping grounds when not in use.

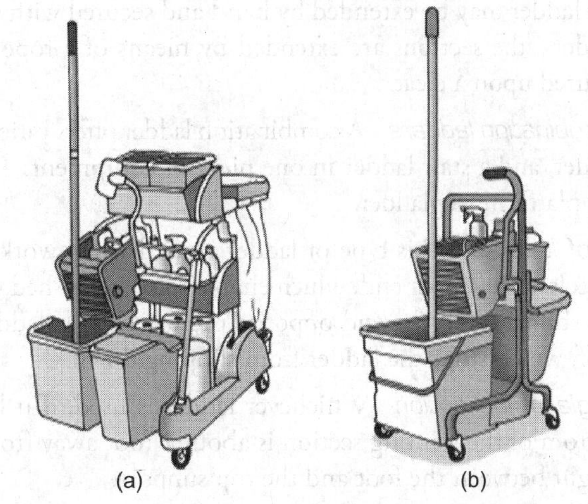
Fig. 7.12 (a) Janitor's trolley and (b) Mop-wringer's trolley

Sundry equipment

This includes other miscellaneous pieces of equipment used in the housekeeping department—ladders, carpet beaters, abrasive pads, rubber gloves, airing racks, flit pumps, and choke removers.

Ladders Ladders are generally made of wood or metals such as aluminium. These days, fibreglass ladders are also available. The different parts of a ladder are the rungs (treads), stiles (side rails), spreaders (the hinge-and-brace arrangements), and footpads. When buying a ladder, one should primarily consider the following points:

- What kind is needed for the work it is going to be used for—for occasional work, it may be cheaper to hire a ladder rather than purchase one.
- The weight that the ladder must bear.
- The condition of the ladder.
- The physical work environment it will be used in.

There are five main types of ladders used on hotel properties.

Single-section standing ladders or stair ladders This is the simplest, old-fashioned ladder, with two straight stiles and rungs fixed across them at a minimum of 254 mm intervals. The ideal ones are those with both stiles curved at the apex for safety.

Stepladders Various types of stepladders are available. A *basic stepladder* has two rectangular stiles fitted with treads that are a minimum of 76 mm in width. The treads should lie horizontal, parrallel to the ground when the ladder is placed at an angle of 75 degrees. A *platform stepladder* gives a more stable work position with a high, level platform for holding tools and materials in use. It is available in various heights, with or without a high-level handrail. The platform must not be more than 3.85 m above the ground. The *A-type platform ladder* opens up like a pair of scissors to make a free-standing set of steps with a small platform at the top, thus leaving the worker's hands free and eliminating the need to keep getting off to get tools and materials. It is very stable and, if fitted with a handrail above the platform, extra safe. The steps may be folded together for easy storage of the ladder. A *swing-back stepladder* is self-supporting. Locking stays are fitted to brace the steps. When opened up, the treads of the ladder lie horizontal.

Extension ladders Extension ladders are used for working at greater heights. These consist of two or three parts that can be slid along each other to add the required height. They are available with two or three extensions and in various 'closed' lengths of 2.5 to 3.5 metres. A *double extension ladder*, which can give a length of upto about 8 metres, should be sufficient for most two-storey properties. Longer, 3-section ladders can give lengths of upto about 10 metres. In the case of smaller extension ladders,

the ladder may be extended by hand and secured with stay locks that rest on a selected rung. On larger ladders, the sections are extended by means of a rope loop running down the side of the ladder and secured upon a cleat.

Combination ladders A combination ladder offers various arrangements to give a stepladder, an extension ladder, and a stair ladder in one piece of equipment. The sections fold down to about the same size as the platform stepladder.

Roof ladders This type of ladder is used when working on a pitched roof. The roof ladder has two wheels at the upper end, which enables it to be pushed up along the slope of the roof without damaging the shingles. On the end opposite the wheels, the ladder forms a hook to fit over the top ridge of the roof, which stops the ladder from slipping down.

Angle of inclination Whichever ladder is used, if it leans at an angle, it should be ensured that the bottom of the slanting section is about 1 foot away from the vertical support for every 4 feet of ladder height between the foot and the top support.

Maintenance and storage Ladders should be stored in a sheltered area, away from the sun and rain. Wooden ladders especially are adversely affected by exposure to heat combined with dampness. They need a dry, well-ventilated storage area. Wooden ladders used outdoors should be treated with shellac, varnished, or given two coats of linseed oil as a protective treatment. A wooden ladder should never be painted, as this can hide any defects that arise, making the ladder potentially unsafe. Straight (stair) and extension ladders should be stored horizontally on racks or hooks, with support points at the top, middle, and bottom of the ladder to prevent sagging and warping. All ladders should be kept scrupulously free of oil, grease, wet paint, and other slip hazards. Periodically tighten the reinforcing rods under the steps of a stepladder, spreader hinges, and other joints. Despite all these precautions, ladders should nevertheless be carefully inspected for wear and damage before each use. In case of any damage, it is always best to discard it.

Carpet beaters Beating of carpets, though not recommended, sometimes becomes a necessity. Wire beaters should be avoided as they may damage the rug. Instead, rattan beaters should be used. While beating, it is best to place carpets and rugs with their naps down on the grass. They should never be hung up and beaten.

Abrasive pads These are available in the form of non-woven, nylon netting pads suitable for the removal of localized, heavily impacted soiling by abrasion. Pads with different abrasive properties are produced. Wire-wool and steel wool pads should be used with caution as they may damage certain surfaces.

Mechanical Equipment

The various pieces of mechanical equipment (Figure 7.13) used in the housekeeping department are usually powered by electricity or gas. The staff should be well trained in the operation of these equipment since incorrect usage will not only lead to inefficient cleaning, but may also become a safety hazard. The popular brands of mechanical equipment used in hotels are Karcher, Taski, Eureka Forbes, and Roots. Please refer to the scan code for pictures of cleaning equipment.

Vacuum cleaners/suction cleaners

Vacuum cleaners remove debris, soil, and/or water from a surface by suction. All vacuum cleaners work on the same operating principle. In all types, a motor drives an impeller, which sucks in air through an

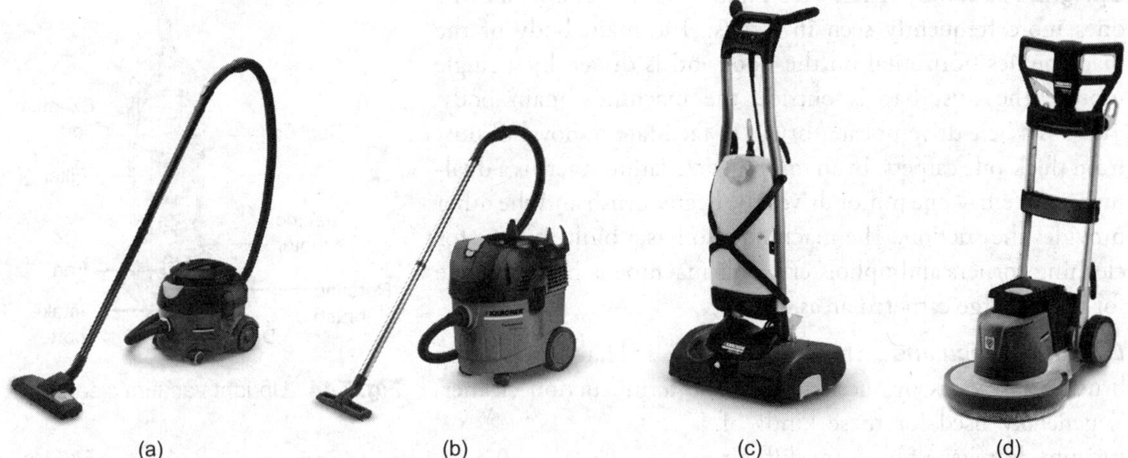

(a) (b) (c) (d)

Fig. 7.13 Mechanical equipment used in housekeeping: (a) Dry vacuum cleaner; (b) Wet and dry vacuum cleaner; (c) Carpet cleaner (upright); (d) Floor scrubber.

Courtesy: Karcher Cleaning Systems Pvt. Ltd.

inlet, creating a difference in pressure between the air within and that outside the machine. Air drawn in from the inlet passes through and out of the machine. Usually the air is sucked in together with soil, debris, or water. The dust is collected into a container provided, which may be enclosed within the body of the machine (as in cylindrical and canister models) or on the outside in the form of a bag (upright models). The dust-collecting apparatus in the heavy-duty models used in hotel properties usually consists of two types of dust bags. The inner bag is made of disposable paper and the outer one is made of fabric.

Types of vacuum cleaners Various types of vacuum cleaners are available:

Dry vacuum cleaners These are used for removing dust and small pieces of debris from floors, upholstery, furnishings, walls, and ceilings. Those using a flexible hose come with attachments such as a floor-cleaning head, a power head, a crevice-cleaning head, an upholstery-cleaning head, a dusting head, and extension tubes. Many variations of the dry vacuum cleaner are in use:

Electric brooms These are very lightweight vacuums without a motor-driven beater brush. They are used only for light vacuuming and for touch-ups on carpets and hard floors. In other words, they come in handy when a full vacuuming is not required.

Dustettes These are small, lightweight vacuum cleaners used for cleaning curtains, upholstery, carpet edges, mattresses, computers, and music systems. They clean by brushing and suction, and are very easy to handle. They may be carried in the hand or be strapped to the back of the operator.

Backpack vacuums These are very efficient for cleaning high, hard-to-reach areas. The vacuum unit in these machines can be easily strapped to the back of the operator. The machines have hand-held wands that come with various attachments for flexibility in cleaning. They are ideal for use on curtains, drapes, and ceiling corners. They are very handy for cleaning staircases too. These vacuums are also referred to as *piggyback vacuums*.

Upright vacuums These (see Figure 7.14) vacuums are the ones more frequently seen in hotels. The main body of the machine lies horizontal on the floor and is driven by a single motor. The dust bag is outside the machine's main body. There is a belt-driven beater brush to facilitate removal of dust from thick-pile carpets. In an improved variation, there is a dual-motor system—one motor drives the beater brush and the other provides the suction. The machine also has a built-in hose for cleaning corners and upholstery. This machine is most suitable for use on large carpeted areas.

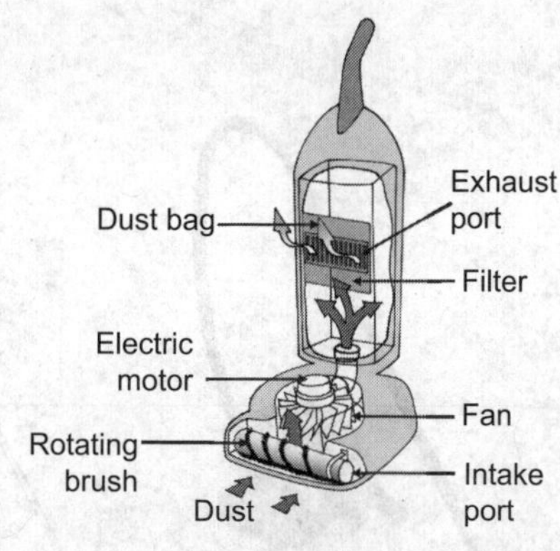

Fig. 7.14 Upright vacuum cleaner

Cylindrical vacuums These (see Figure 7.15) have no rotating brushes and work by suction only. The term 'suction cleaner' is generally used for these kinds of vacuum cleaners. A filter-cum-diffuser is fitted at the outlet, which removes fine dust and microorganisms from the flow of air passing through the outlet. The filter-cum-diffuser also reduces air disturbance and noise. The dust bag is inside the cylindrical body of the vacuum cleaner. A flexible hose along with different attachments is used to clean a variety of surfaces. These are the type commonly used by GRAs in guestroom cleaning.

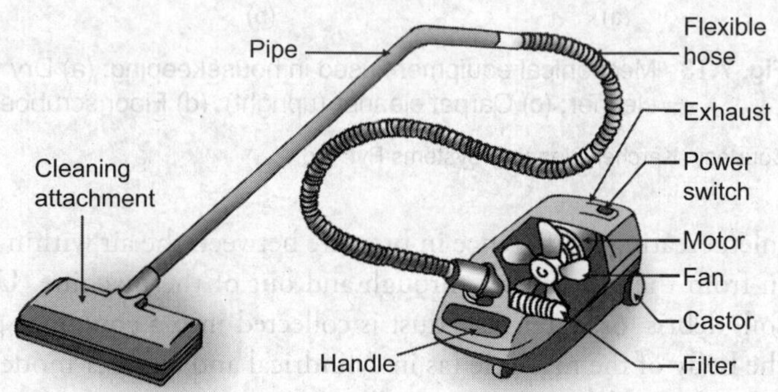

Fig. 7.15 Cylindrical vacuum cleaner

Robotic vacuums These (See Figure 7.16) work on chargeable battery and have side brushes and a brush roller to loosen the dirt and then vacuum it into the dust collector. They have smart automatic versatility in cleaning different surfaces such as smooth floors or carpets. With their 360° internal mapping system, the robot vacuum intelligently scans and maps out and then navigates using a calculated, systematic cleaning path and pattern. Most of them are enabled with dirt detect sensors and in case the robot runs out of charge in its stipulated time, it goes automatically to its port, recharges itself and resumes the cleaning work. The robots have in-built infrared sensors for circumventing obstacles and drop-sensing technology to evade falls. Some of the robot vacuums even take voice commands. They are also wi-fi enabled so that housekeepers can program the cleaning schedule to no-traffic hours.

Robot mops These are robot vacuums designed to both sweep and mop hard floors, but not carpets. The professional-grade robot has water tank attachment and uses precision jet spray and a vibrating cleaning head attached with a disposable cleaning pad to gently scrub dirt and stains and power suction that takes up the waste water.

Pile-lifter vacuums These vacuum cleaners are used to groom long-pile carpets. They lift up the carpet pile that has become packed down and restore their vertical orientation. It is especially useful before shampooing the carpet, more so if the soiling is heavy.

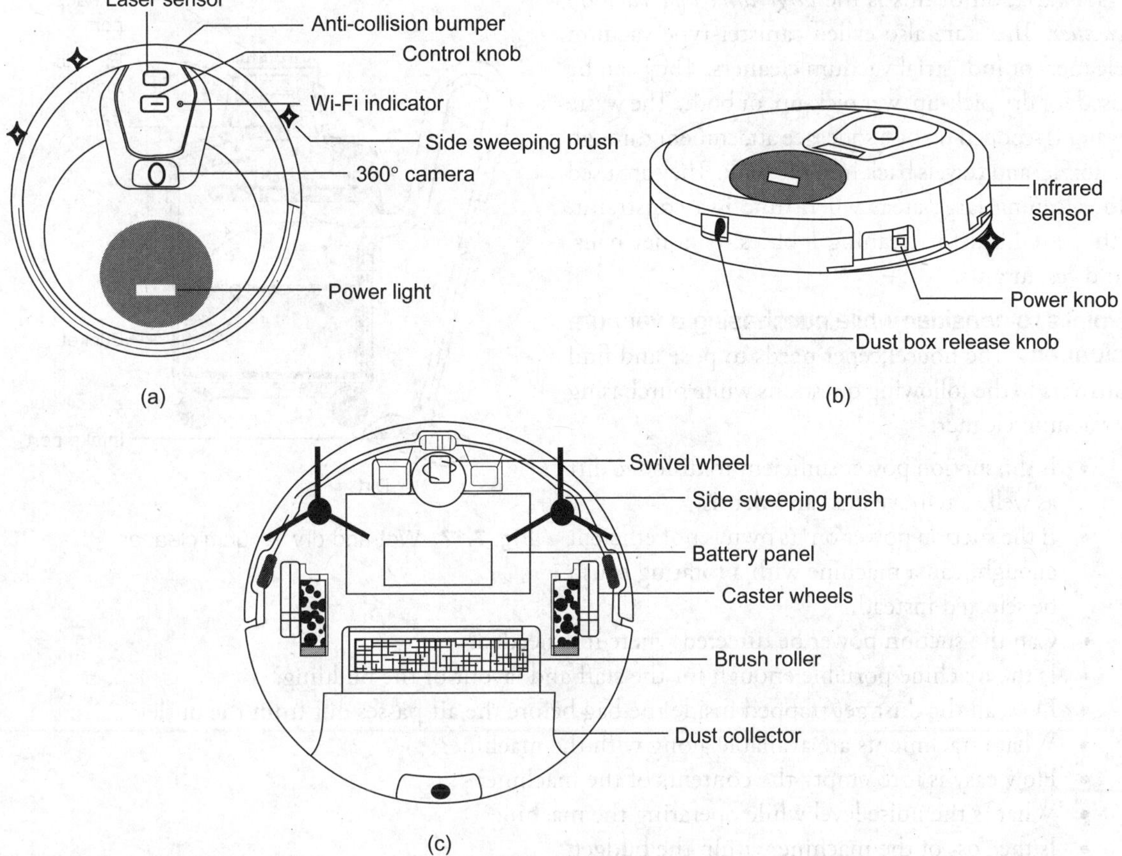

Fig. 7.16 Robot vacuum (a) Top view; (b) Side view; (c) Bottom view

Centralized vacuum In this type of unit, suction is generated at one point in a building. Meanwhile, soiling can be removed at vacuum points elsewhere in the building by suitable nozzles linked to detachable flexible hoses. The collected dirt is then conveyed by a network of pipes to a central container. This unit is expensive to install and is generally done at the building construction stage. The advantages of this kind of system are:

- It is extremely hygienic, since all the dust is carried away from the point of cleaning.
- Maintenance costs are usually lower.
- Operative fatigue is lower.
- There are no frayed flexes to repair and no individual machines to go wrong.

Wet-and-dry vacuum cleaners These (see Figure 7.17) are extremely useful in hotel housekeeping operations. They can pick up spills and excess wash water when on the wet mode. When on the dry mode, they help in removal of dust and debris. In hotels, these machines are usually used in their wet mode to pick up spills. They are also required when large areas of floors are being stripped of polish and cleaned. They have a flexible hose with attachments such as a squeegee head. The waste water collects in a tank that needs to be emptied after use.

A variation of this is the *large tank-type vacuum cleaner*. These are also called canister-type vacuum cleaners or industrial vacuum cleaners. They can be used for dry pick-up, wet pick-up, or both. The waste water is scooped up by a squeegee attachment through a nozzle, and travels back into the tank. They are used for cleaning large areas when time is a constraint. They are ideal for cleaning lobbies, banquet halls, and restaurants.

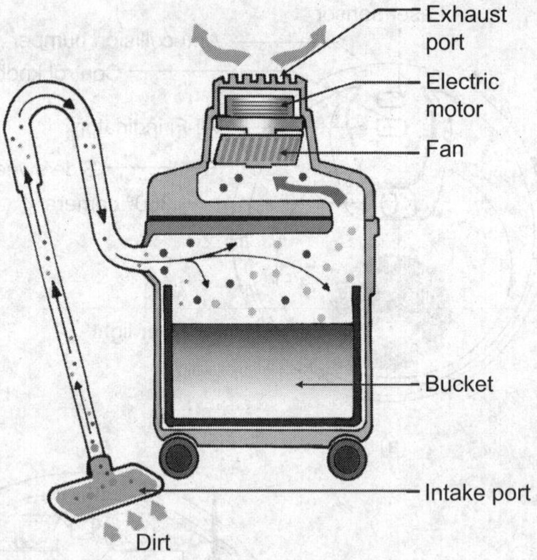

Fig. 7.17 Wet-and-dry vacuum cleaner

Points to consider while purchasing a vacuum cleaner The housekeeper needs to pose and find answers to the following questions while purchasing a vacuum cleaner:

- Is the suction power sufficient to dislodge dirt as well as remove dust and debris?
- If the suction power on its own is not efficient enough, can a machine with a rotating brush be selected instead?
- Can the suction power be directed where it is needed?
- Is the machine portable enough for the staff and layout of the building?
- Does all the dust get trapped inside the bag before the air passes out from the outlet?
- What attachments are available along with the machine?
- How easy is it to empty the contents of the machine?
- What is the noise level while operating the machine?
- Is the cost of the machine within the budget?

General-purpose floor machines (scrubbing and polishing machines)

These are designed for scrubbing, buffing, burnishing, scarifying, and spray maintenance. Figure 7.18 shows a scrubbing machine.

Scrubbing The bristle tips of a brush or the surface of a pad abrade and cut the soilage to remove it.

Buffing The bristle tips of a brush or the surface of a pad create a high-gloss finish on the floor surface. In case of a surface on which a polish has been applied, it will involve the generation of local heat to harden waxes and resins.

Burnishing The tips of a brush or the surface of a pad abrade and cut the floor surface to create a smooth surface with a glossy finish. In case of a polished surface, it will involve the removal of a surface layer of polish.

Scarifying The bristle tips or the edge of a cutting tool cut into impacted soilage, removing it by means of a chisel-like action.

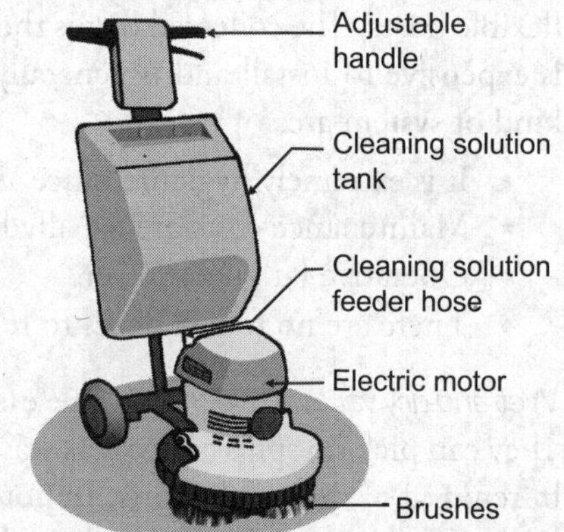

Fig. 7.18 Scrubbing machine

Spray cleaning The bristle tips of a brush or the surface of a pad abrade and cut the soilage from a surface. It differs from scrubbing in that only a fine mist of the cleaning solution is applied to the floor and a thin film with a glossy finish is formed on the floor surface. It can be used to maintain an unpolished floor or a floor protected by a hard polish.

Spray burnishing This is similar to spray cleaning, but the term is applied to the maintenance of floors where a buffable or semi-buffable polish has been applied and the bristle tips of a brush or the surface of a pad remove both soilage and a surface layer of polish to leave a smooth, glossy surface. Resins and waxes in the maintenance product form part of the restored finish.

These machines consist of one large or several small brushes that revolve and scrub the floor. Water and detergent are released from a tank attached to the machine. These machines can be used for shampooing carpets, polishing floors, and spray maintenance. Such general-purpose machines are preferred in many establishments as the machine can be put to greater use because of its versatility. In some machines, coloured, abrasive nylon pads replace the scrubbing brushes. For normal-speed machines,

- beige pads are used for buffing;
- green pads are used for scrubbing; and
- black pads are used for stripping.

The lighter the colour of the pad, the lesser abrasive the action. These machines may come with or without the suction capacity to pick up water. If the machine is one without a suction action, then a wet vacuum will have to be used in conjunction with it while scrubbing. The usual attachments for these machines are brushes, drive discs, coloured nylon pads, a water tank, a shampoo tank, and a sprayer.

Wet-extraction systems

These machines are used to restore the surface appearance of carpets, upholstery, and curtains. They remove the more deeply embedded soilage not easily removed by suction cleaning. They are also useful in the application of soil-retardant finishes on carpets.

Types of wet-extraction systems There may be various types of wet extraction systems.

Hot-water extraction machines These (see Figure 7.19) are machines with no rotary action. They carry a tank for hot water and detergent, which are used for deep-cleaning carpets. The hot water and

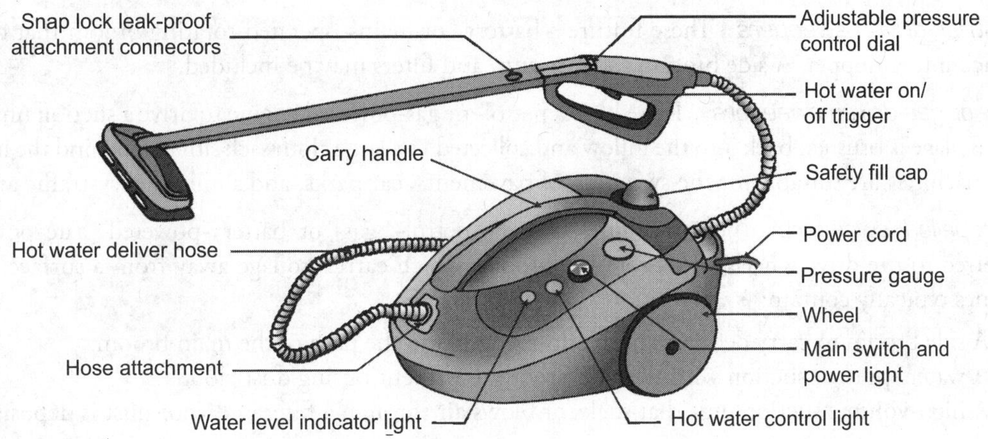

Fig. 7.19 Hot-water extraction machine

detergent are shot into the carpet from high-pressure spray nozzles. The dirt is thus flushed to the surface and this, along with the soiled water, is removed by suction into a container in the machine.

Solvent extraction machines These machines are primarily used for cleaning upholstery and curtains and to a lesser extent for carpets.

Carpet shampoo machines

These machines, as indicated by the name, are designed for the deep cleaning of carpets that are heavily soiled.

Types of carpet shampoo machines There are four broad groups of carpet shampoo machines:

Steam extraction machines Though these machines are universally called steam extraction machines, there is in fact no generation of steam and the cleaning agents are simply hot water and detergent. Hot water containing the detergent is injected at a prescribed rate and subsequently extracted by a wet vacuum system built into the machine.

Cylindrical-brush dry-foam machines This system has a cylindrical brush that scrubs and picks up in one pass the foam generated by the machine.

Rotary-brush wet-shampoo machines A rotary brush cleaner in conjunction with a wet shampoo is employed for the cleaning of carpets here. The machine comes with a range of accessories, including vacuum and drying equipment.

Small rotary-brushes wet-shampoo machines This is also a rotary-brush cleaner, but employs two brushes instead of one and is somewhat smaller than the rotary-brush wet-shampoo machine.

Scrubber-driers and sweepers

These machines remove debris, soilage, and/or water. They are suitable for large areas where mechanical sweeping, scrubbing, and drying are required.

Types of scrubber-driers and sweepers The various types available are as follows:

Power sweepers These are self-propelled or manually propelled machines designed to remove debris and loosen soilage from roads, pavements, carpets, and large areas of hard flooring.

Pedestrian-driven sweepers These feature a battery- or mains-operated rotating broom that carries dirt back into a hopper. A side broom, suction unit, and filters may be included.

Petrol- or gas-driven sweepers These have a petrol- or gas-powered engine to drive a suction unit and brush. Soilage is brushed back into the inflow and collected in a large cloth sack situated behind the motor. These machines are suitable for the sweeping of pavements, car parks, and similar heavy-traffic areas.

Self-propelled sweepers These machines may be petrol-, gas- or battery-powered. The power is transferred to the drive wheels and a rotating broom, which carries soilage away from a surface. Such machines typically contain:

- A side broom to carry debris from the floor edges into the path of the main broom.
- A water spray or suction with the side broom to prevent raising dust clouds.
- A high-volume suction unit that sucks or blows air through a filter as dirt or dust is deposited in the hopper.
- A filter shaker or air-flow reverser to prevent blockages.

High-pressure washers

This type of equipment is designed to remove soilage by subjecting the surface to water, steam, and/or sand under pressure. Water under pressure physically dislodges the dirt. The process can be assisted by the use of hot water, steam, or sand.

Scarifying machines

Scarifying is the process by which heavy grease, mud, wet sawdust, and thick deposits are removed from the surface of floors. The process is employed when simple scrubbing has been ineffective. Here the dirt deposits are broken up by the chisel-like action of a wire-brush cutting tool.

Types available Two kinds of scarifiers are available:

Heavy-duty scrubber-polishers These single- to three-brush machines can have a brush weight of 65 kilograms or more. They are used in conjunction with a scarifying assembly. Dislodged dirt is removed by a second operation involving sweeping.

Self-propelled scarifiers These consist of a revolving tool, a hopper into which the dirt is thrown up by the tool, and a suction-unit filter to remove finer particles.

Storage, Distribution, and Control of Cleaning Equipment

Proper storage and regular maintenance of equipment goes a long way in enhancing their durability. Important factors in equipment storage are outlined below:

- The equipment store should be under lock and key to prevent misuse.
- The store room should be maintained well-ventilated and dry at all times as dampness accelerates rusting and encourages mildew growth, leading to degeneration of equipment.
- The store should not be congested and provide easy access to shelves to facilitate cleaning.
- Sufficient hanging rails, racks and cupboards with proper labelling should be provided.
- Equipment accessories should be stored in labelled shelves in cupboards.
- Sensitive and expensive equipment must be covered with dust sheets during storage.
- All equipment should be cleaned before storing. Equipment used wet, such as buckets and pails, wet and dry vacuum cleaner must be thoroughly dried.
- Mops should be, disinfected, wrung out and dried thoroughly before storage.
- Brooms and brushes should not be stored resting on their bristles.
- The EHK should inspect the store periodically.

When issuing equipment for use, proper records must be maintained with information regarding:

- the items issued
- the attachments given along with them
- to whom they were issued
- the date and time of issue
- the area where they are to be used
- by whom they were issued
- the date and time of return

The signature of the personnel involved must be obtained on the document during both issue and return.

A card-index system is a useful method of collecting all the relevant information about each piece of equipment being used in a particular establishment. A sample card index is presented in Exhibit 7.1. This system is of great value to the manager and the supervisor for the following reasons:

Exhibit 7.1 Sample card for equipment indexing

Equipment History Index-Card

Equipment:	Index No. ....
Make:	No. of attachments: ....
Model No.:	Name of attachments: ....
Capacity:	....
Date of purchase:	Date first used: ....
Cost of equipment:	Attachments cost : ....
Period of guarantee:	Life expectancy: ....
Specific user (if any):	Other users (if any): ....
Areas where used:	Other areas (if any): ....
Supplier details:	Local service centre rep. details: ....
....	....

Complaint	Cause	Spares replaced	Service person	Signature

- It gives up-to-date information concerning the equipment.
- It indicates the location of the equipment.
- It indicates who usually operates the equipment.
- It contains a record of what servicing has been carried out, costs, new accessories supplied, and so on.
- When purchase of new equipment is being considered, this information can be used as a reference to check on reliability.

Selection of Cleaning Equipment

It is the responsibility of the executive housekeeper to procure the ideal, most efficient equipment for her staff to ensure maximum productivity. The choice of equipment to be purchased is made after considering the following factors:

Safety in operation.

Suitability to the type of area, surface, work, amount of obstruction, and cleaning frequency.

Versatility to undertake various types of cleaning.

Work performance and quality in terms of capacity of machine and consumer reports on performance.

Ease of handling in terms of size, weight, and height of the machine and ease of manoeuvering and operating.

Portability in terms of ease of transfer between floors and provision of wheels and detachable parts.

Durability as judged by sturdiness, robustness of construction, and consumer reports on life expectancy.

Noise level which is a more important consideration for hospitals than hotels.

Availability of spare parts and accessories, easy servicing conditions, and lead time after booking of equipment.

Protective design which may feature a protective edging to prevent damage to walls, furniture, and fittings and no sharp edges.

Ease of maintenance uncomplicated minor maintenance, reliable AMC and servicing conditions and warranties.

Ease of storage in terms of ease of dismantling detachable parts and storage space required (compactness).

Cost as a sum of initial costs, operating costs, maintenance, and depreciation, as well as hiring considerations as opposed to purchasing.

Other Machines

The other machines used in the housekeeping department include the various types of laundry and pressing equipment, which are discussed in Chapter 19.

Cleaning Agents

Cleaning is primarily the removal of dust and dirt. Dust, being composed of loose particles, is removed comparatively easily by the use of various types of equipment. Dirt however, owing to its adherence to surfaces by means of grease or moisture, requires the use of cleaning agents in conjunction with the right equipment if it is to be removed efficiently. Refer to Chapter 11 for details on the chemistry of effective cleaning agents.

Cleaning agents in general can be defined as natural or synthetic substances that are used to assist the cleaning process—that is, the removal of dirt and grit and the maintenance of a clean appearance on the surface. The various kinds of cleaning agents used by the housekeeping department staff are depicted in Figure 7.20. The popularly used cleaning agents in hotels under the brand names ECOLAB and TASKI from Diversey are depicted in Table 7.15 (a) and (b), respectively.

Water

Referred to as the universal solvent, this is the prime agent in the cleaning process. However, though an excellent solvent, water alone is not a sufficiently effective cleanser to meet the standards most hotels require. Indeed, it does not even wet a surface properly, as its surface tension prevents it from spreading easily. For water to be effective in cleaning, it must be used in conjunction with other cleaning agents such as detergents, soaps, and so on. From the perspective of cleaning, there are two types of water—hard and soft. Soft water is ideal for cleaning purposes and also to make up the proper dilutions of other cleaning agents.

Sources of water

Water is available in abundance in some parts of the country, but is scarce in others. Sources of water may be surface, sub-soil, or deep-soil.

Fig. 7.20 Various types of cleaning agents

Surface water Obtained from streams, rivers, and lakes, it may contain both organic and inorganic impurities in large amounts.

Sub-soil water Coming from shallow wells and springs, it is not likely to be contaminated with suspended matter and organic impurities. However, some gases and mineral matter are generally dissolved in it.

Deep-soil water Deep-soil water, pumped up from deep wells, has percolated through much soil and rock to reach its resting depth. Therefore, it has a very high content of minerals such as calcium, magnesium, iron, sulphur, phosphates, and silica as well as dissolved gases such as nitrogen, carbon dioxide, and oxygen. The mineral salts dissolved in this water result in its hardness and render it unsuitable for cleaning purposes.

These days most cities, towns, and some villages have running water supplied by the public works department (PWD). This water is filtered and chlorinated before being piped.

Hard water and soft water

Water that contains more than 60 ppm (parts per million) of calcium and/or magnesium is called *hard water*. When the mineral content is in the range of 61–120 ppm, the water is said to be *moderately hard* and if it exceeds 180 ppm, the water is considered *very hard*. When the level of dissolved calcium and/or magnesium is below 60 ppm, it is said to be *soft water*. However, water from all sources contains varying amounts of calcium and magnesium, usually in the form of bicarbonates, sulphates, and chlorides. It is their relative proportions that determine how 'hard' the water is and in what way.

Temporary hardness This is caused by bicarbonates of calcium and magnesium being dissolved in water. Temporary hardness is so called because it can be removed by simply heating the water to a temperature above 72°C.

Permanent hardness This is caused by sulphates and chlorides of calcium and magnesium dissolved in water. It cannot be removed by boiling and requires chemical treatment to render the water 'soft'.

Effects of hard water

Calcium and magnesium salts dissolved in water inhibit lather formation from soaps and detergents, so that much more detergent will have to be added to precipitate out the calcium and magnesium before cleaning can occur. This process causes a lot of scum to be formed, which may further soil the surface. When hard water is used for laundering, for instance, it causes premature ageing of fabrics due to constant friction with the deposits from hard water. The fabrics also become coarse and uncomfortable to wear. Hard water also causes scale and fur to be deposited in boilers, pipes, and various appliances. Iron and sulphur salts can cause discolouration. Sulphur also causes a rotten-egg odour. Dissolved phosphates, on the other hand, can actually enhance the cleaning power of some detergents!

Methods of softening water

Water which has a hardness greater than 50 ppm needs to be softened. Temporary hardness can be removed by boiling the water (or heating above 72°C). In the reaction that takes place at these temperatures, dissolved bicarbonates decompose with the liberation of carbon dioxide and the carbonates precipitate out as scum or fur. These should be removed by filtration before using the water for cleaning.

$$Ca\,(HCO_3)_2 \rightarrow CaCO_3 \downarrow + CO_2 \uparrow + H_2O$$

In the case of magnesium bicarbonates, the resultant carbonate further decomposes into magnesium hydroxide.

$$Mg\,(HCO_3)_2 \rightarrow MgCO_3 + CO_2 \uparrow + H_2O$$

$$MgCO_3 + H_2O \rightarrow Mg(OH)_2 \downarrow + CO_2 \uparrow$$

The most practical way of removing hardness, however, is to treat it chemically. This is done in one of the following ways:

Alkali method The alkali calcium hydroxide is used to remove the hardness from water in this method.

Lime soda method In this method, sodium carbonate and calcium hydroxide are both used to remove the hardness.

Addition of sequestering/chelating agents Sequestering agents are organic or inorganic compounds that react with metallic ions and form a complex. These metallic ions will still be present in the water, but will be unable to react with soaps or detergents as they are held in the complex formation. Thus, the water is rendered soft. The most commonly used sequestering agents are EDTA (ethylene diamine tetraacetic acid), NTA (nitrilo triacetic acid), and sodium hexametaphosphate.

Ion-exchange method or zeolite process Zeolites are hydrated silicates of sodium and aluminium. Hard water is made to percolate through the zeolite. In the chemical ion-exchange reaction that takes place, any hardness is almost totally removed. Ion-exchange units are available as attachments that can be fitted into the plumbing system at the point where the water supply enters the hotel.

Organic base-exchange method Organic-base exchangers are synthetic resins containing the sulphonic and carboxylic acid groups. When hard water is passed through these resins, the acids react with the calcium and magnesium salts to produce products which are non-reactive.

When the last two methods are used in succession, they yield very soft, pure water.

Detergents

These are cleaning agents that, when used in conjunction with water, loosen and remove dirt and then hold it in suspension so that the dirt is not re-deposited on the cleaned surface. They can be of two types—*soapy detergents* and *synthetic detergents* (non-soapy). The three basic properties of a good detergent are:

- Good wetting power—to lower the surface tension of water and enable the surface of the article to be thoroughly wet.
- Good emulsifying power—to break up the grease and enable the dirt to be loosened.
- Good suspending power—to suspend the dirt in solution, thus preventing its re-deposition.

Composition and action of detergents

All detergents are primarily composed of three parts.

Active ingredients In soapy detergents, the active ingredient is obtained from natural oils and fats. These are composed of long fatty-acid chains. The fatty acids commonly found in nature are the palmitic, stearic, oleic, and linoleic acids. These fatty acids occur in nature as triglycerides. The active ingredients in synthetic detergents are the surface-active agents or surfactants obtained from petrochemicals. Surfactants are of four types. They are summarized in Table 7.5.

Builders These give bulk to the detergent. A builder is a compound that has no surface-active properties but increases the efficiency of the detergent. They are added to facilitate better handling and dilution. In case of liquid detergents, the diluent can be water; in the case of powders, sodium sulphate is used. Builders can be inorganic or organic. The various types of builders are summarized in Table 7.6.

Additives Added to the detergent, these may be bleaching agents, blueing agents, fluorescent brighteners, enzymes, and so on. *Optical brighteners* or *fluorescent whiteners* help to counteract the yellowing

Table 7.5 Types and properties of surfactants

Anionic	Cationic	Amphoteric	Non-ionic
Ionize in water, carrying a negative charge on the hydrophobic part of the molecule.	Ionize in water, carrying a positive charge on the hydrophobic part of the molecule.	Contain both positively and negatively charged groups in the molecule.	Do not ionize in water.
Good wetting power.	Very weak cleansing power, so never used alone. Used to impart softness and counteract anionic detergents in combination.	Used to impart softness and as dye fixers.	Have good emulsifying powers.

Table 7.6 Various builders used in detergents

Inorganic builders	Purpose	Organic builders	Purpose
Sodium sulphate	• Acts as an inert filler, making an expensive powder cheaper. • Gives the powder free-flowing properties. • Improves foam formation.	CMC (carboxymethyl cellulose)	• Mainly helps in improving the suspending power of detergents. • Acts as a thickening agent. • SCMC (sodium carboxymethyl cellulose) is especially effective on cotton. • Ethyl hydromethyl cellulose is effective on synthesis.
Phosphates (e.g., di- and trisodium phosphates)	• Soften water. • Act as sequestering agents. • Chloridated trisodium phosphate has bleaching and sterilizing properties.	PVP (polyvinyl pyrrolidone)	• Prevents re-deposition of dirt and grime.
Silicates (e.g., sodium sesquisilicate)	• Enhance the detergency of the detergent by softening water, acting as buffers emulsifying grease, and helping in the suspending action. • Sodium silicate prevents corrosion of aluminium in the body of washing machines and solution tanks.	• Tetra acetyl ethylene diamine (TAED)	• Used as a new bleaching agent because of the need for high temperatures for other agents.

of fabrics that occurs with age. They are compounds that absorb ultraviolet light and reflect it back as blue light, creating an illusion of whiteness. *Photo-activated bleaches*, on the other hand, have an action that is chemical and not physical: They convert oxygen to the nascent form when activated by sunlight. *Chelating agents* are compounds capable of binding the mineral salts that make water hard. EDTA (ethylene diamine tetra acetic acid) and NTA (nitrilo tri acetic acid) are chelating agents used in small amounts in detergents. They chelate calcium and magnesium salts. DTPA (diethylene triamine penta acetic acid) is used to chelate iron salts. Zeolites are also being used in some detergents. Hydrothropes help when, due to the presence of inorganic salts, the solubility of the liquid detergent decreases. *Hydrothropes* help to keep all the materials in solution. *Enzymes* such as proteases, lipases, and amylases are incorporated into detergents to attack stains of different kinds. Advanced research has lead to the development of enzymes that are stable upto temperatures of 60°C and a pH of 10.5–11. Their action is very slow and therefore they require a soaking time of 30 minutes or so. *Perfumes* are added to cover up the unpleasant smell of some synthetic detergents. *Dyes*, usually blue and green, are used to colour powdered detergents and make the product more attractive. *Ground pumice* is added to detergents to create a coarse texture so that stubborn dirt may be removed due to friction.

How detergents work

It is the surface-active agents or surfactants in the detergent that are responsible for the three basic properties of detergents. Each molecule of the surfactant has a hydrophilic ('water-loving') head and a hydrophobic ('water-hating'), oleophilic ('grease-loving') tail. In other words, the hydrophilic head is attracted to water, whereas the hydrophobic tail is attracted by grease and repelled by water. When the detergent is added to water, the following actions take place:

Wetting action The detergent lowers the surface tension of the water. The surfactant molecules tend to arrange themselves at the water–air interface. The hydrophobic tails of the surfactant molecules are repelled by water, creating a pull in the opposite direction to that of the inward pull of the water molecules.

Emulsifying action The hydrophobic tails of the surfactant molecules are also oleophilic in nature, that is, they are attracted to grease. The tails, thus, penetrate the grease and lift it off the fabric surface. The dirt also gets lifted away as it is entrapped in the grease.

Suspending action Since the grease molecules are entrapped by the surfactant molecules, their contact with other surfaces is prevented. The grease (with the embedded dirt) is thus held in a stable emulsion in the water. This is also partly due to the fact that the hydrophilic heads at the other end from the grease molecules are attracted to water. Most of the surfactants now carry a mild charge, that is, they ionize and repel each other. This also aids in the suspending power of the detergent.

Figure 7.21 shows the role of surfactants in removing dirt from a surface.

Types of detergents

Various types of detergents are available for use in different areas and on different surfaces. Figure 7.22 summarizes these various types of detergents.

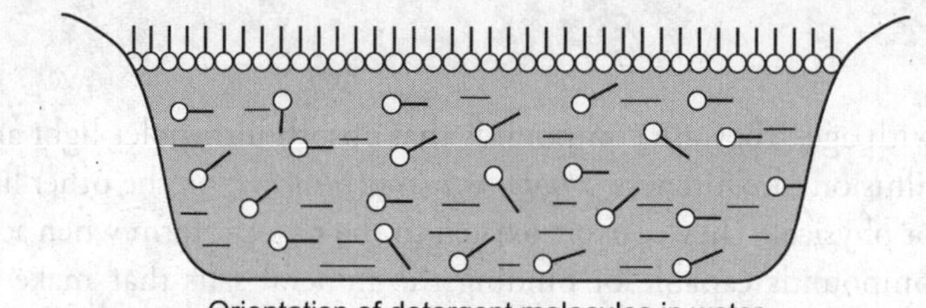

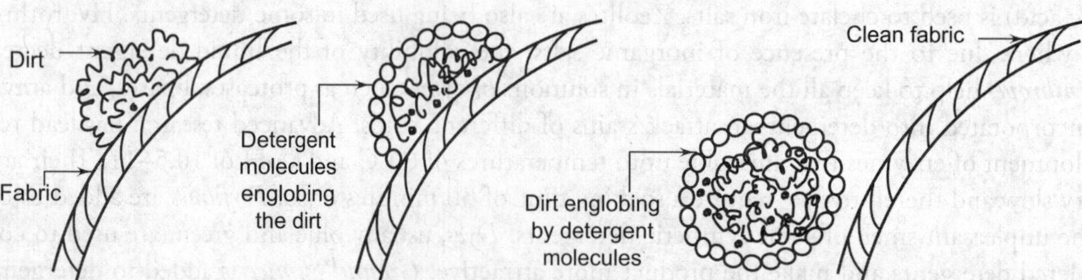

Fig. 7.21 Action of detergent molecules on dirt

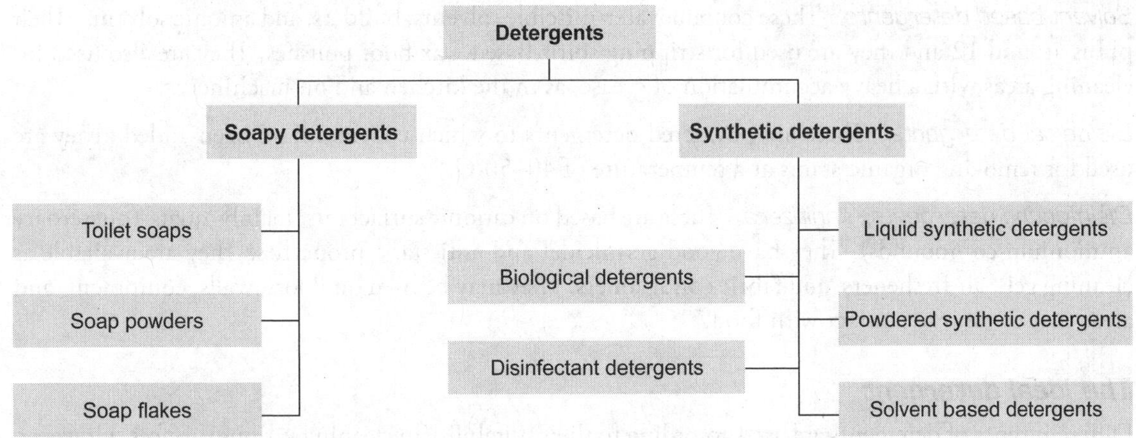

Fig. 7.22 Types of detergents

Soapy detergents/soaps These are obtained when fat/oil is treated with an alkali. The process is called saponification. Soaps are relatively inexpensive. Soaps are effective only in soft water; in hard water they form a scum that is difficult to rinse away. Detergents from this category used in housekeeping are:

Toilet soaps They are used in different kinds of packaging for guestrooms and cloakrooms. They contain perfume, dyestuffs, and antioxidants such as vitamin E. They do not contain any builders.

Soap powders They dissolve rapidly in water and lather well, and comprise upto 40% of builders.

Soap flakes The simplest of all detergents, they dissolve easily and are used for delicate fabrics washed at lower temperatures.

Synthetic detergents These are soap-free and have replaced the use of soaps in many cleaning processes. They are not affected by hard water and have good suspending powers. Based on their chemical nature, they may be neutral detergents (anionic, non-ionic, cationic, or amphoteric) or alkaline detergents as we have discussed earlier. Alkaline detergents are widely used in the housekeeping department, as they are very strong detergents, ideal for removing grease. They have a pH of 9–12.5. Though they do not foam much, they require thorough rinsing because of their slippery nature in solution. They will also patch the cleaned surface if not rinsed well. They are used on heavily soiled surfaces and for removing water-based floor polishes. Since they have such a high pH, they are harmful to the skin and, therefore, the staff must take special precautions while using them. However, the various categories of synthetic detergents in common use in housekeeping are:

Liquid synthetic detergents These are light-duty detergents for hard surfaces and lightly soiled fabrics. They contain 20% anionic surfactants and 6–12% non-ionic surfactants. They are neutral in reaction with pH 7.0.

Powdered synthetic detergents These are heavy-duty detergents suitable for heavily soiled surfaces and fabrics. They contain 20% anionic surfactants, 2% non-ionic surfactants, about 33% alkaline builders, 9% bleach, 20% fillers, SCMC (sodium carboxymethyl cellulose), brighteners, and 15% water.

Solvent-based detergents These contain water-miscible solvents, builders, and anionic solvents. Their pH is around 12 and they are used for stripping spirit-based wax floor polishes. They are also used for cleaning areas with a heavy accumulation of grease, as in the kitchen and on machinery.

Biological detergents These are powdered detergents to which enzymes have been added. They are used for removing organic stains at a temperature of 40–50°C.

Disinfecting detergents/sanitizers These are based on cationic surfactants, mainly 'quats' (quaternary ammonium compounds). They have good germicidal and anti-static properties. They are available as cleaning gels, air fresheners, and fabric conditioners. They may be used on floors, walls, equipment, and areas that come into contact with food.

The ideal detergent

Different types of detergents are used according to their suitability in cleaning various surfaces. However, the selection of detergents should be based on certain criteria to ensure that the optimal detergent is bought and the housekeeper gets value for money. An ideal detergent should

- have good wetting, emulsifying, and suspending powers;
- readily dissolve in water;
- cleanse quickly with minimum agitation;
- be effective in all ranges of hard water, without producing scum;
- be effective over a wide range of temperatures;
- be harmless to the skin and the surface to be cleaned;
- be easy to rinse away; and
- be biodegradable.

Various 'all-purpose detergents' are now available that combine most of the aforesaid qualities. However, buying the very best detergent will be of no use if the staff are not trained to use them in the correct way. Certain points to consider when using detergents are listed here:

Do…

- dilute as per the manufacturer's recommendations, using the measuring scoops and dispensers provided.
- use the right detergent for the surface to be cleaned.
- use protective gloves when using strong detergents.
- dissolve the detergent thoroughly before use.
- rinse away all traces of detergent from the surface and any cleaning equipment employed.
- label detergent containers neatly.
- store detergent containers in a dry, well-ventilated storage area.
- wipe up any spilled detergent, as it may be a safety hazard.

Abrasives

These are substances or chemicals that depend on their rubbing or scratching action to clean dirt and grit from hard surfaces. They are used to remove very stubborn stains on various surfaces.

Types of abrasives

Based on the scale of hardness for various substances shown in Figure 7.23, abrasives are classified as:

Fine abrasives These include precipitated whiting (filtered chalk) and jeweller's rouge (a pink oxide of iron) used for shining silver. They are also constituents of commercial silver polishes.

Medium abrasives These include rotten stone, salt, scouring powder, and scouring paste. Scouring powders are made up of fine particles of pumice mixed with a soap/detergent, an alkali, and a little bleach.

Hard/coarse abrasives These include bath bricks, sandpaper, pumice, steel wool, and emery paper.

Glasspaper (6–7), calcite (3), sandpaper (6–7), fine ash, emery powder and paper (7–9), jeweller's rouge (a pink oxide of iron) (6.5), powdered pumice (6), precipitated whiting (filtered chalk), feldspar (6), ground limestone, sand, carborundum (9), steel wool (4), and nylon scourers are some commonly used abrasives. The numbers in brackets denote the range and level of hardness on the scale.

Abrasives are usually not used alone in cleaning agents. For example, a cream or paste meant for cleaning utensils contains about 80% of finely ground limestone, along with other substances such as bleaches, anionic surfactants, alkaline builders, and perfumes. The use of various abrasive agents for cleaning different surfaces is summarized in Table 7.7.

Reagents

These bring about cleaning by a chemical reaction requiring a distinctly low or high pH. They thus include acids and alkalis that aid in the cleaning process. To understand the action of acids and alkalis

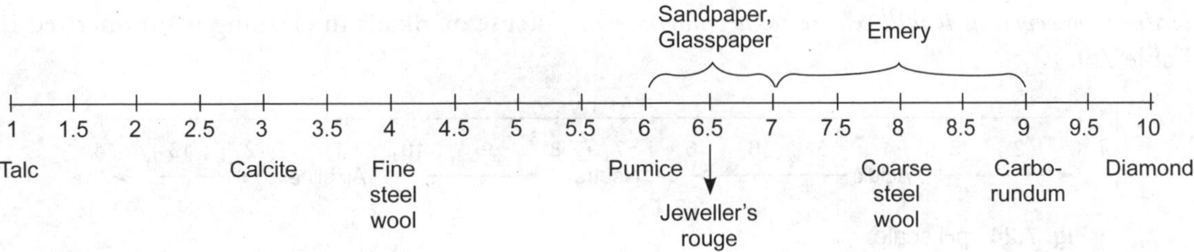

Fig. 7.23 Scale of hardness

Table 7.7 Use of abrasives in cleaning different surfaces

Surface	Abrasive	Surface	Abrasive
Brass	Abrade with emery.	Leather	De-grease with care and abrade with glass paper.
Ceramics	Abrade with carborundum and water.	Silver	Abrade with fine emery
Copper	Abrade with emery.	Steel, iron	Abrade with emery.
Glass	Abrade with carborundum.	Stone	Abrade with wire brush.
Gold	Abrade with fine emery.	Wood	Abrade with glass paper or fine steel wool.
Lead, tin	Abrade with fine emery.		

one must have knowledge of the term pH. pH is a measurement of the level of acid or alkali in a solution or substance. In the pH range of 0 to 14, a reading below 7 shows an acid and one above 7 shows an alkali. A pH scale is shown in Figure 7.24.

Types of reagents

Reagents may be acids or alkalis.

Acids Acids used as cleaning agents may vary from mild acids (such as acetic acid) with a pH of 3 to strong acids (such as dilute or concentrated hydrochloric acid) with a pH of 1. Mildly acidic substances used commonly in cleaning include lime, vinegar, tamarind, and buttermilk. Acids may be used in solution alone or may be part of some special formulations, as in toilet cleaners. *Housekeeping staff need to be trained in the safe handling of strong acids, as they are highly corrosive.* They literally 'eat away' dirt. Rubber gloves should always be used while handling them. They should be used in very small quantities as they emit toxic fumes as well. *Strong acids should be thoroughly rinsed away after the cleaning process.* Table 7.8 summarizes the use of different acids in cleaning.

Alkalis These are used as cleaning agents in the form of liquids and powders. They are particularly useful in the laundry. *Very strong alkalis should be used with the utmost caution as they are corrosive and toxic.* These are called caustic alkalis. Many alkalis act as bleaches. Caustic soda-based cleaning agents are used to clear blocked drains and to clean ovens and other industrial equipment. *Ammonia is a strong grease emulsifier and should also be carefully used as it emits strong fumes.* It is also added to abrasive formulations. Toilet cleaners to which bleach has been added are very effective. *It should be kept in mind that sodium chlorite bleach should never be used with an acidic toilet cleaner, however, as it will release toxic chlorine gas.* The use of alkalis in cleaning is summarized in Table 7.9.

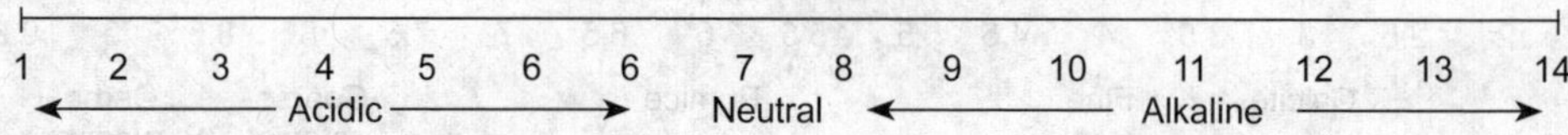

Fig. 7.24 pH scale

Table 7.8 Acids and their use in cleaning

Acid	pH	Uses
Concentrated HCl (once referred to as 'spirits of salt')	1	Removing stubborn hard-water deposits.
Dilute HCl	1	Removing stubborn scales and deposits from sanitaryware. Removing excess cement from newly cemented tiled areas.
Oxalic acid	2	Removing stubborn hard-water deposits.
Acetic acid	3	Removing tarnish and stains from metals such as copper and brass (the acid must be washed off quickly). Neutralizing alkalis used in cleaning. Preventing colours from running during washing.
Sodium acid sulphate	5	Removing hard-water deposits and scales from toilets.

Table 7.9 Alkalis and their use in cleaning

Alkali	pH	Uses
Sodium hydroxide (caustic soda)	14	Removing stubborn grease from ovens and equipment. Clearing blocked drains.
Ammonia	11	Removing stubborn grease.
Sodium carbonate (washing soda)	10	Used as an alkaline builder in synthetic and soapy detergents. Clearing blocked drains
Sodium perborate	10	Removing stains and whitening due to bleaching action at higher temperatures (above 40°C).
Sodium hypochlorite	9	Removing stains and whitening due to bleaching action on various types of surfaces. Acts as disinfectant.
Sodium bicarbonate (baking soda)	8	Removing stubborn grease from smooth, delicate surfaces. Removing stains such as tea, coffee, and fruit juice.
Sodium pyroborate (borax)	8	Same as above.
Sodium thiosulphite	7	Removing iodine stains.

Organic Solvents

Grease is soluble in organic solvents such as carbon tetrachloride, acetone, turpentine, and methylated spirit. Thus, these organic solvents are used extensively in the removal of grease, dry-cleaning of fabrics, and stain removal. Solvents are also useful in cleaning surfaces that may be harmed by water. Organic solvents evaporate rapidly from a surface and are therefore, ideal for cleaning glass surfaces such as mirrors and windows. *Organic solvents should be handled with care as they are harmful to the skin, flammable, and poisonous.*

Disinfectants and Bleaches

Disinfectants aid in the cleaning process by bringing about varying ranges of microbial control (see Table 7.10). The term 'disinfectant' is now used as a general term that covers all kinds of agents that bring about germ control. Most disinfectants have a strong smell and therefore should be used only in recommended amounts in areas where germ control is required.

Table 7.10 Varying ranges of microbial control

Microbial control	Action
Disinfection	Killing most microbes, but not their spores.
Bactericidal	Killing most bacteria, but not their spores.
Bacteriostatic	Making the environment non-conducive for the growth and reproduction of bacteria.
Antiseptic	Making the environment non-conducive for the growth and reproduction of disease-causing (pathogenic) microbes.
Sanitation	Reducing the microbial count to an acceptable level.
Sterilization	Killing all kinds of microbes as well as their spores.

Type of disinfectants

Disinfectants can be categorized in terms of their chemical action and composition:

Phenols These are hydroxyl derivatives of the aromatic hydrocarbon benzene. They are used in dilute or high concentrations to disinfect surfaces in hospitals especially. In hotels, diluted phenols are used with their sharp smell masked by other additives.

Halogens The elements chlorine and iodine may be used as disinfectants. Chlorine is used both as a bleach and as a disinfectant on many surfaces. Iodine is not often used to disinfect surfaces because it tends to leave brown stains.

Quaternary ammonium compounds ('quats') These are cationic surfactants useful as bacteriocides.

Natural pine oils Pine oils are obtained from pine trees. They are germicidal to some extent, but are mainly added to cleaning formulations for their pleasant smell.

Guidelines for using disinfectants

Certain points to consider while using disinfectants are given in this section.

- Clean the surface first with detergent and rinse with soft water only.
- Rinse away the detergent solution thoroughly before using a disinfectant on the surface.
- Use the correct disinfectant for the range of disinfection required. See Table 7.10.
- Use the disinfectant at the correct dilution for it to be effective. Different surfaces may require different dilutions of the same disinfectant.
- Allow the recommended time for the disinfectant to act.

Bleaches used in cleaning of hard surfaces are stabilized alkaline solutions with a high pH. The alkali sodium hypochlorite acts as a powerful bleach and is used on WCs and sinks for the removal of stains. Fabric bleaches are discussed in detail in Chapter 19.

Glass Cleaners

These are composed of an organic, water-miscible solvent such as isopropyl alcohol and an alkaline detergent. Some glass cleaners also contain a fine, mild abrasive. Most glass cleaners are available as sprays or liquids. They are sprayed directly onto windows, mirrors, and other glass surfaces or applied on with a soft cloth and rubbed off using a soft, lint-free duster. A glass cloth is ideal for the purpose. Soft water to which some methylated spirit or vinegar is added is an inexpensive glass cleaner that can be readily made in the housekeeping department.

Deodorizers

Deodorizers aid in the cleaning process by counteracting stale odours and sometimes also introducing a fragrance to mask them. They are used in restrooms, guestrooms, guest bathrooms, cloakrooms, and public areas such as lobbies. Some deodorizers leave no trace of a perfume cover-up. They are usually available as aerosol sprays, liquids, powders, and crystalline blocks. The crystalline blocks are effervescent and manufactured using the principle of time-released aromatic chemicals. Naphthalene balls also serve as effective deodorizers. If thorough cleaning and good ventilation are provided, money need not be spent on expensive deodorants.

Laundry Aids

Laundry aids are discussed in detail in Chapter 19.

Toilet Cleaners

These are strong, concentrated cleaning agents designed to clean and disinfect WCs and urinals. They are available in liquid, powder, and crystalline forms. They are acidic in nature as their main function is to remove stubborn stains and limescale. They all contain some form of disinfectant.

Liquid toilet cleaners These contain dilute hydrochloric acid, a bleach, and pine oil. *Adequate protective gear should be worn by the user while using such a toilet cleaner.*

Crystalline toilet cleaners These contain sodium acid sulphate, anionic surfactant, and pine oil.

Powdered toilet cleaners These cleaners contain a soluble acidic powder, chlorinated bleach, a fine abrasive, and an effervescing agent to help the active ingredient spread in water.

Whatever the form of toilet cleaner used, they should never be mixed with other cleaning agents since harmful gases may be produced in the resulting reaction.

Polishes

These chemicals produce a shine by providing a smooth surface from which light is reflected evenly. Polishes are primarily applied to a surface to form a hard, protective layer and thus guard against finger marks, stains, and scratches. They also create an attractive sheen on the hard surface.

Classification of polishes

Polishes are used on metal, furniture, and flooring and are classified according to the type of surface they are used on (see Figure 7.25). On metals, they also smooth out any unevenness on the surface of the article and in case of flooring and furniture, they provide a smooth protective layer.

Metal polishes These remove the superficial tarnish that forms on metal surfaces due to the attack of certain compounds in the air and some foodstuffs. These polishes also eliminate any scratches on the metal. They consist mainly of a very fine, mild abrasive, generally either precipitated whiting or jeweller's rouge. Most polishes also contain a fatty acid, a solvent, and water. On buffing, they remove tarnish and produce a shine. In hotels, hard surfaces where metal polishes are used include door-plates and handles, foot rails in bars, staircase banisters, ashtrays, bathroom fittings, tableware, and cutlery.

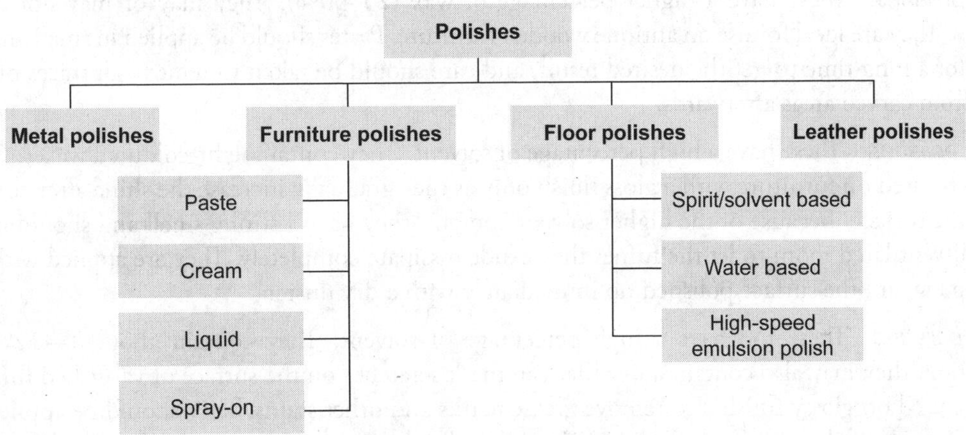

Fig. 7.25 Classification of polishes

In metal polishes such as Brasso and Silvo, the grease solvent or acid mixed with the abrasive powder aids in the removal of tarnish. Long-term polishes contain some ingredients that coat the surface of the metal and retard the process of tarnishing in future. Metal polishes are available in the form of milky or clear liquids and powders. Care should be taken in applying the correct polish as polishes meant for hard metals may damage the surface of soft metals. Because of their solvent content, metal polishes have a strong smell and should be used in a well-ventilated room to let fumes dissipate. The container should be closed immediately after pouring out the polish into the polishing tray. If not, the solvent in the polish will evaporate, rendering it ineffective.

Certain recommendations on the use of metal polishes are given here:

- Cover the surrounding area with newspaper or protective sheets.
- Carry out any polishing work in a well-ventilated room.
- Use an appropriate polish applicator or disposable rags.
- Use a cocktail stick covered with a rag to apply polish in narrow, hard-to-reach nooks and corners.
- Remove polish with cotton or a soft, dry cloth.
- Buff the polish with rags and dusters, preferably with ones with a napped surface.
- Wash any polished cutlery in warm detergent solution before use.
- Leave the area and equipment clean and tidy after polishing work is complete. Dispose of the rags and newspapers used.

Furniture polishes These contain a wax or resin, a solvent, water, and silicone. The wax or resin helps to keep the furniture surface supple. It also protects against abrasion and absorption of stains and spills. The main role of the wax, however, is to provide a smooth surface from which light is reflected evenly, producing an attractive sheen. The types of waxes commonly used are carnauba, beeswax, ozokerite, and paraffin wax. The solvent and water are meant to remove grease stains and water-soluble stains, respectively. Silicone is used to make the polish easier to apply. It also gives an added gloss and improves resistance to moisture, heat, dust, and smears. Silicones thus give a harder and longer-lasting finish. Furniture polish needs to be applied frequently only in the case of untreated, unvarnished wood. Painted and varnished furniture should not be polished too often. Most pieces of furniture manufactured these days are polished with a permanent synthetic resin and thus do not require further application of polish. As a preventive maintenance activity, they can be buffed regularly with a duster during dusting. As seen in Figure 7.25, furniture polishes are available in various forms, differing in their wax content.

Paste polishes These have a higher percentage of wax (25–30%). They may or may not contain silicones. They are ideal for use on antique wooden furniture. Pastes should be applied in small amounts, buffed for a long time to get the desired result, and care should be taken to remove all traces of excess polish from carved areas afterwards.

Cream polishes These have a high percentage of solvent. They contain light-coloured waxes. Creams need to be used on furniture with a gloss finish only as they gradually increase the shine after continual use on the surface. Because of the higher solvent content, they have a strong smell and should be used in a well-ventilated room to let the fumes they exude dissipate completely. They are applied with a dry or damp rag and the surface polished up immediately with a dry duster.

Liquid polishes These too have a high percentage of solvent. They contain about 8—12% wax. In addition, they may also contain a dye that can mask scratches on the surface of varnished furniture. They are used on glossy finishes to remove grease marks and other stains. They should be applied with a dry rag and buffed up with a soft, dry cloth while still moist to produce a good sheen.

Spray-on polishes These contain about 8% wax and a high amount of silicone. Sprays contain aerosols to make their application simpler. These polishes clean as well as polish, and pre-dusting of the surface is not required. They are ideal for use on non-porous surfaces such as glass, chromium, plastic, and varnished or gloss-painted wood. They reduce the static electricity on the surface so that dust is not attracted to it readily. The ideal way to apply spray polish is to first spray it on the duster and then rub this on the surface. This minimizes wastage, an important consideration for these polishes especially, as they are expensive.

Certain points should be kept in mind while working with furniture polishes:

- Apply the polish on a clean surface.
- Use the least quantity required to accomplish a good polishing of the surface, else it may result in stickiness that will attract more dust.
- Use soft, disposable rags for applying polish to the surface, except in the case of a spray-on polish.
- Always keep the polish container closed when not in use, else the solvent will evaporate and the polish will dry out.
- Use polishes undiluted, unless it is specified otherwise by the manufacturer.
- *Be careful while using polishes with a high solvent content since they are flammable.*

Floor polishes These have a two-fold function. They not only lend an attractive sheen to the surface, but also provide a protective coat on it. Floor polishes should not be applied too frequently. They should be used only when simple buffing does not produce the desired sheen on the floor. The main aim in using floor polishes is to deposit a layer of wax on the surface. Therefore, they are also referred to as floor waxes. The right kind of polish should be used along with the right equipment. Polish-applicator mops should be labelled neatly with the kind of polish they are each used for to avoid mixing of products. The wrong polish may easily damage a floor surface and mar its appearance. The two basic types of floor polishes are spirit/solvent-based and water-based floor polishes. A special group of floor polish called high-speed emulsion polish is also discussed in this section.

Spirit/solvent-based polishes This kind of polish may be in the form of a liquid or a paste. They contain a blend of waxes and silicone dispersed in a solvent (a white spirit or Freon). The waxes used may be natural (carnauba or ozokerite) or synthetic (polyethylene). After the polish has been applied to the floor, the solvent evaporates and the wax left behind is buffed up using a polishing machine. The silicone helps in easy application of the polish and gives a more lasting finish. Additives such as perfumes and dyes are also added to solvent-based polishes. Solvent-based polish is used on porous floors such as wood, wood composition, cork, magnesite, and linoleum.

Water-based polishes These are available in the form of a creamy liquid emulsion containing a blend of natural (carnauba and montan) and synthetic waxes suspended in water by means of an emulsifying agent (ammonia or a synthetic detergent). They account for 80–85% of all floor polishes manufactured. After the polish has been applied to the floor, the water evaporates and the wax is deposited on the surface in a hard film. Colloidal silicon is sometimes added to water-based polishes as an anti-slip agent. Plasticizers and either alkali-soluble resins or metal-complexed polymers are also added. Plasticizers aid in the easy application of polish. Alkali-soluble resins are meant to provide weak break points in the water-based polish to facilitate cleaning with alkaline detergent solutions. The metal in the metal-complexed polymers shields the break points against the penetration of detergent solutions. Usually only occasional buffing is required for these polishes. They are therefore, also referred to as dry-bright polishes. Often these polishes are made into liquid sprays by the addition of high amounts of emulsifying agents. The polish is then sprayed on and buffed immediately. Water-based polishes may be fully buffable (containing 45–60% wax and 20–40% polymers), semi-buffable (containing 25–40% wax and 45–60% polymers), or dry-bright (containing 5–15% wax and 50–70% polymers). The amount of wax determines the amount of polishing required to achieve a desirable amount of shine. These polishes are not meant for porous surfaces, as water will damage them. Water-based polishes are used on porous floors only when they have been sealed properly. These polishes are used mainly on semi-porous surfaces such as thermoplastics, PVC, rubber, asphalt, terrazzo, marble, and natural materials such as Cuddapah tiles and so on.

Some guidelines on the use of floor polishes are provided here:

- Use an appropriate sign to warn people walking along that area of the fact that floor polishing is being carried out.
- Ventilate the area well before starting.
- Apply the polish to a clean, dry floor.
- Rinse the floor thoroughly using a neutralizing agent such as diluted vinegar after stripping the old polish.
- Apply several thin coats of polish rather than a few thick coats.
- Work systematically to ensure that all areas are covered.
- Allow sufficient drying time before applying a second coating.
- Buff thoroughly to reduce the slipping hazard.
- Remove any extra build-up of polish with an appropriate abrasive pad.
- Leave all polishing equipment clean and store them properly.

Leather polishes These contain a special blend of waxes, a spirit solvent, and occasionally a dye. They are available in the form of creams and liquids. They help keep the leather supple and impart a sheen to it. They also prevent deterioration of old leather articles.

Some do-it-yourself polishes

Some methods of making do-it-yourself (DIY) polishes are presented in Tables 7.11, 7.12, 7.13, and 7.14. When unsure about applying polish to a surface, first apply it on a small area not in view.

Floor Sealers

These are applied to flooring surfaces as a semi-permanent finish that acts as a protective barrier by preventing the entry of dirt, grit, liquids, grease, stains, and bacteria. They prevent scratching and provide an easily maintainable surface. The right type of seal should be applied to each type of floor for effective protection and an attractive appearance. According to their functions, floor sealers can be finishing, protective, or a combination of both.

They are also grouped as permeable, semi-permeable, and impermeable, according to their penetrability vis-à-vis water. Permeable seals can be used on wood, cork, stone (except slate), and magnesite floors. Impermeable seals should be avoided on these floors as the moisture naturally found within these floors will then get entrapped and may cause disintegration of the flooring. Impermeable seals may be used on PVCs, thermoplastic tiles, and rubber floors.

Sealers may be reinforced by the application of floor waxes. Floor sealing should always be done on a clean and dry surface. Most sealers require a hardening time of 12–16 hours and 2–3 coats are recommended.

Table 7.11 Furniture polish for dark wood

Ingredient	Amount
Turpentine	2 parts
Methylated spirit	1 part
Linseed oil	2 parts
Vinegar	1 part

Method: Combine all ingredients in a bowl and shake well to form an emulsion.

Table 7.13 Furniture polish for light coloured wood

Ingredient	Amount
White wax	1 part
Petrol	2 parts

Method: Break the wax into small bits and put in a lidded can. Add petrol and shake well till it becomes creamy.

Table 7.12 Furniture polish for all types of wood

Ingredients	Amount
Beeswax	25 g
Turpentine	25 ml

Method: Heat the beeswax on a moderate flame till it melts. Remove from flame, add turpentine, and stir well till the mixture is cool.

Table 7.14 Cream polish for leather and wooden furniture

Ingredients	Amount
Soap (shredded)	1 tbsp
Water	1 cup
Beeswax (shredded)	2 tbsp
White wax (shredded)	1 tbsp
Turpentine	1 cup

Method: Place the beeswax and white wax into a bowl. Mix in turpentine so that the waxes are submerged in it. Heat the mixture over a water bath till the waxes dissolve. In another bowl, dissolve the soap in water. Combine the contents of the two bowls. Beat the mixture to a creamy consistency. Store in wide-mouthed bottles.

Types of floor sealers

There are six main types of floor sealers, depending on their composition.

Oleo-resinous sealers These are clear, solvent-based sealers used on wood, wood-composition, cork, and magnesite floors. They consist of oils, resins, solvents, and driers. They not only impart an attractive surface gloss, but also penetrate the floor, darkening the colour and highlighting the grain of wood floors. They are comparatively cheaper than other sealers.

One-pot plastic sealers These are also called one-can sealers. They are made up of synthetic materials. They impart a gloss to the floor surface but do not penetrate it. They are used on wood, wood-composition, cork, and magnesite floors. Polyurethanes can also be used on concrete. The three types of one-pot plastic seals are:

(a) Urea-formaldehyde resin with an acid catalyst
(b) Oil-modified polyurethane
(c) Moisture-cured polyurethane

Two-pot plastic sealers This type of sealer is composed of a base such as urea-formaldehyde or polyurethane and an accelerator or hardener. The two components are kept separate until use, else a chemical reaction occurs between them and the mixture hardens in the can. Because of the separate components, the shelf life of these sealers is longer. The accelerator in itself has a shorter shelf life, however. The two components should be mixed in the recommended proportions, else the sealer will

not harden and will result in a patchy finish. This type of sealer should be used in a well-ventilated room as they smell strongly of solvent fumes. They may be used on wood, wood-composition, cork, and magnesite floors.

Pigmented sealers As the name implies, these sealers contain colour pigments, which, apart from providing colour, also strengthen the sealer. They may be used on concrete, wood, wood-composition, magnesite, asphalt, and stone floors. There are two types available:

(a) One-pot synthetic rubber
(b) Two-pot polyurethane

Water-based sealers These are composed of acrylic polymer resins and a plasticizer. The particles of the resin penetrate the pores on the floor surface to provide a plastic skin. These are less durable sealers and should be reinforced with a water-based floor wax. However, they can easily be touched up, removed, and renewed. They may be used on marble, terrazzo, magnesite, linoleum, rubber, thermoplastic tiles, PVCs, asphalt, concrete, stone, and quarry tiles.

Silicate dressings These consist of a base of sodium silicate dissolved in water. This is not a true sealer. The sodium silicate reacts with the lime in concrete floors to form insoluble calcium silicate. The water acts as a carrier, and after it evaporates, silicate glass is formed. These simply reinforce concrete and stone floors, and prevent the accumulation of dust on their surface. Silicate dressings are much cheaper than sealers.

Selecting the right sealer

Most sealers are expensive. So a lot of thought should be put into buying the ideal seal for the particular flooring to get maximum durability and value for money. The following points need to be kept in mind while selecting floor sealers:

- The type of floor
- The amount of traffic in the area
- The availability of the floor for future sealing
- Good fixing or 'keying', durability, appearance, and anti-slip qualities
- Ease of application, repair, removal, and renewal
- Odour and fumes
- Drying time
- Shelf life
- Cost-effectiveness

Applying floor sealers

Whichever type of floor sealer is chosen, the following recommendations should be followed while applying floor sealers.

- Use appropriate signs to warn passers-by that sealing is being carried out, else it may be a safety hazard.
- Ensure the floor surface is clean, chemically neutral, and dry before applying the sealer. Otherwise the seal will not 'key' to the floor surface.
- Maintain an ideal room temperature of 21°C.
- Keep the room well-ventilated.
- Protect the area from flies and pests until the sealer is dry.
- Keep on hand only the required amount of sealer and store the rest tightly lidded, else the whole bulk may deteriorate.

- Apply several thin coats rather than a few thick ones.
- Allow the recommended drying time between coats.
- Clean and store all equipment, such as sealer applicators, neatly after use.

Floor Strippers

These are used to remove a worn-out floor finish so that a new sealer or polish can be applied. Most are based on alkalis with a high pH. There are two main types available. One is based on ammonia and the other is a non-ammoniated product. Ammonia has an intense odour and therefore the area treated should be well-ventilated for many days to get rid of the smell. Alkaline detergents with a high pH are also used as floor strippers. It should be kept in mind that any residual stripper solution needs to be rinsed away thoroughly with a mildly acidic rinse. The ideal way is to add vinegar to the last rinse of water.

Carpet Cleaners

These are composed of neutral water-soluble solvents, emulsifiers, de-foamers, soil repellants, sanitizers (occasionally), optical brighteners, and deodorizers. They are available as sprays, powders, foams, and liquid shampoos. Whichever type is selected, it is essential that they be used in the correct dilutions.

Some Common Cleaning Agents

Some common cleaning agents used in professional housekeeping are as follows:

Ammonia Liquid ammonia is a solution of ammonia gas in water, held as ammonium hydroxide. It is a strong alkali used for softening water, cleaning window panes, and emulsifying grease.

Bath brick This is a reddish-brown powder, also obtained in brick form. It is used for scouring and polishing metals such as brass and copper. In powdered form, it is used for cleaning earthenware.

Benzene Obtained from the distillation of coal tar, benzene is used as a grease solvent and for removing paint and tar stains.

Borax Chemically sodium borate, this white crystalline powder is used to soften hard water and to remove coffee and tea stains.

Bran The husk of the wheat grain, it is used in dry-cleaning as a grease absorbent.

Fuller's earth This is an ash-white clay that readily absorbs grease. It is used on coloured wood surfaces.

Hydrochloric acid This is a corrosive and poisonous mineral acid, used diluted for removing stains in bathrooms.

Jeweller's rouge Chemically this is ferric tetroxide, a pinkish powder used for polishing silver. It is a constituent of commercial silver polishes too.

Lemon Lemon is used for removing ink stains from wooden surfaces.

Linseed oil This is obtained from the crushed seeds of the flax plant. It is a constituent of furniture polishes and paints. It darkens unpainted wood slightly.

Magnesia Chemically magnesium carbonate, this fine white powder is used for dry-cleaning felt, fur, and woollen articles.

Methylated spirit This is used for cleaning window panes and mirrors to a shine. It is a constituent of varnishes and lacquers.

Oxalic acid This is an organic acid used for the removal of stains from fabrics and bath fittings. It is also used for cleaning porcelain.

Paraffin oil Not to be confused with paraffin wax, this liquid is a product of distillation of crude petroleum and is used for cleaning greasy iron and steel articles. It also cleans greasy earthenware when used in combination with bath bricks.

Petrol This too is obtained from petroleum distillation. It is highly inflammable and is used for dry-cleaning and for removing grease stains.

Pumice This is a light, porous rock of volcanic origin. It is used as an abrasive for hard metals, earthenware, and enamel.

Rottenstone This is a decomposed siliceous limestone and is used for cleaning copper, brass, and earthenware.

Common salt Chemically sodium chloride, this is used as a medium-grade abrasive. It is used for stiffening the bristles of brushes and stiff brooms. Salt is also added as a mordant while washing coloured clothes. (A mordant is a substance that prevents undue loss of colour while washing clothes.)

Sand This hard compound of silica is used as a hard abrasive on stone floors and hard, coarse wood.

Sawdust It acts as an abrasive and a grease absorber.

Shikakai Sometimes called soap-nut or soapberry, but more accurately soap-pod (to distinguish from the fruit of reetha). This is used for non-abrasive cleaning of tarnished metals.

Soda It emulsifies grease and aids in the cleaning of dirty pans.

Steel wool This is steel manufactured into long filaments, in varying grades of fineness. It is used for scouring hard metals and dirty pans.

Turpentine This is a constituent of paints. It is also a diluent for paints and removes tar stains.

Vaseline This is obtained as a residue in petroleum distillation. It prevents rust formation on metals, acts as a lubricant, and may be applied on leather to make it soft and supple.

Vinegar Chemically this is 4% acetic acid. It is used to remove stains and tarnish from metals such as copper. It is also effective in removing streaks from glass surfaces such as window panes and mirrors.

Whiting/precipitated whiting Chemically this is calcium carbonate in pure form. It is used as a mild abrasive on soft metals and in cleaning white-painted articles.

There are also branded cleaning agents such as those from Ecolab and Taski from Diversey used in hotels [Tables 7.15 (a) and 7.15 (b)].

Selection of Cleaning Agents

The use of cleaning agents is meant to save time, effort, and money. If selected well, all the three objectives may be fulfilled. The following points need to be considered when selecting cleaning agents:

- The type of soilage
- The type of surface
- Composition of the cleaning agent
- Ease of use, saving of effort and time
- Toxicity or side-effects
- Odour
- Range of action or versatility
- Shelf life
- Packaging volumes and quantities
- Cost-effectiveness

Table 7.15(a) Ecolab chemicals

Cleaning product	Use & Description
Room care products	
Oasis Pro™ 20 Neutral Disinfectant Cleaner	A multi-purpose, neutral pH, germicidal detergent and deodorant that can be used on multiple surfaces, including finished floors and metals
Glass Cleaner	A plant derived surfactant, effectively removes tough soils including smoke and grease films. Streak-free, fast-drying performance on windows, mirrors, glass, plastic, acrylics and painted surfaces. Green Seal Certified
Oasis Pro™ 66 Heavy Duty Alkaline Bathroom Cleaner and Disinfectant	Daily maintenance alkaline bathroom cleaner, sanitizer/ disinfectant; lemon-scented, used for removal of hard water marks (pH 10.7); concentrate
Peroxide Multi-Surface Cleaner	A plant-based surfactant, cleans multiple surfaces; offers excellent cleaning and leaves a streak-free shine. Green Seal Certified
Oasis Island Wave Room Refresher	A fresh ocean breeze heavy duty air freshener carrying notes of juicy melon with a hint of soothing coconut
Toilet Bowl Cleaner	WC cleaner; cleans hard stains
Specialty chemicals	
Helios Brillant	Ceramic hob and stainless steel cleaner; cleans and maintains all metal surfaces such as stainless steel, chrome, nickel and brass
Lemoneze	For removal of heavy hard water marks, grease and lime scale deposits on stainless steel, chrome & tiles; ready to use product
Chromol	Maintains and protects stainless steel surfaces and leaves a glossy protective film that prevents re-soiling
Mikro-Quat	Multi-use formula for cleaning, disinfection and deodourizing in one operation in hospitals and kitchens
Lime-A-Way	Effectively removes hard water deposits and lime scale from dish machines and surrounding stainless steel
Floor Care Range	
Sigla	Polish maintenance for marble, granite and wooden floor; neutral pH
Wash 'N Walk No Rinse Floor Cleaner	A no-rinse, daily floor cleaner for degreasing quarry tile or other floors without finishes or waxes
StoneMedic® MPC Marble Polishing Compound	A user-friendly, highly effective, ready mixed paste used to polish, restore and maintain worn marble, travertine, limestone, agglomerates, and other calcium containing materials
Easy Glow Daily Floor Maintainer	Cleans lightly soiled floor finishes and maintains and improves the shine in one, easy labour-saving step
Carpet care products	
Floordress T500	Foaming carpet shampoo used with rotary or mist-foam carpet shampoo machines
Revitalize™ Rug and Room Deodorizer	A pleasantly scented rug and room freshener for use with any vacuum cleaner to freshen both the carpet and room in one easy step
Revitalize™ Miracle Spotter	A multi-purpose spotter ideal for both common and the 'unknown' spots and stains

Source: ECOLAB. Used with permission.

Table 7.15(b) Taski cleaning agents

Cleaning product	Description	Area/Surfaces on which used	Use/Dilution
TASKI R1 Super	Bathroom cleaner + Sanitizer concentrate	• All surfaces in the bathroom, i.e sink, tub, tiles, floors and fittings • Safe for use on marble and granite	• Normal soiling: 20 ml in 1 litre water • Heavy soiling: 50 ml in 1 litre water
TASKI R2	Hygienic hard surface cleaner concentrate	• All hard surfaces such as TV cabinets, telephones, picture frames, glass mirrors and shiny floors like polished marble, granite, etc.	• Hard surfaces: 20–50 ml in 1 litre water • Glass: 10–20 ml in 1 litre water
TASKI R3	Glass cleaner concentrate	• All types of glass, windows, mirrors and glass display cases	• 20–50 ml in 1 litre water
TASKI R4 Shine-up	Furniture maintainer	• All wooden surfaces such as tables, chairs and bedside tables • Can be used to maintain polished metal surfaces	• Ready to use product
TASKI R5	Air freshener	• Freshens and deodorises guestrooms, banquet halls and office rooms	• Ready to use product
TASKI R6	Toilet bowl cleaner	• Removes lime scale deposits and stubborn stains in toilet bowls and urinals	• Ready to use product
TASKI R7	Floor cleaner concentrate	• Used for both wet mopping as well as scrubbing with a machine on all kinds of surfaces	• Normal soiling: 20 ml in 1 litre of water • Heavy soiling: 50 ml in 1 litre water
TASKI R9	Bathroom cleaner concentrate (specially for hard water stains)	• All fittings and walls in bathrooms • Do not use in acid sensitive area	• 50–100 ml in 1 litre water
TASKI SPIRAL	Floor cleaner concentrate	• Used for both wet mopping as well as scrubbing with a machine on floor • Designed for cleaning oil and grease from the surface.	• Normal soiling: 20 ml in 1 litre of water • Heavy soiling: 50 ml in 1 litre water

Source: Diversey. Used with permission.

Note: See chapter on Linen and Laundry Operations for Clax range of cleaning chemicals from Diversey.

Storage of Cleaning Agents

Cleaning agents with a longer shelf life are usually bought in bulk because of the reduced costs that accrue from the economies of scale. Other agents are bought and replenished periodically. Storage of cleaning agents is crucial and the various points to be kept in mind are mentioned in this section.

- Ensure that the storage racks are sturdy. Heavier containers must be kept on the bottom shelf.
- The store should be kept clean and well-ventilated at all times.
- Label all containers neatly with a waterproof marker.
- Ensure that the lids are tightly secured.

- When dispensing cleaning agents, use appropriate dispensers and measuring apparatus.
- Ensure that no residual deposits of cleaning agent are left around the rims of the containers.
- Avoid spillage; if a spill occurs, clean it up immediately.
- Follow a systematic procedure for rotating stocks.
- Organic solvents, strong reagents, polishes, and aerosol-based agents should be kept away from heat sources.
- Check stocks regularly. The format of a stores stock sheet is shown in Exhibit 7.2.
- The store should be kept locked when not in use.

Issuing of Cleaning Agents

The housekeeper should implement proper systems for the methodical issuing of cleaning agents from the housekeeping stores. Supplies may be issued in the following ways:

Requisitioning This system of issuing is followed in large hotels. The floor supervisor maintains a requisition book with requisition slips in triplicate (Refer Exhibit 2.33, Chapter 2). A requisition slip is filled out by a GRA whenever supplies are diminishing. This is signed by the floor supervisor and the book is then sent to the housekeeping stores. The storekeeper collects the requisitioned items and signs the triplicate copies of the requisition slip. The storekeeper then issues the requisitioned items, which are collected by a porter and transported to the floor in question with one signed copy of the requisition slip. The second copy is sent to the executive housekeeper and the third copy remains in the requisition book, which too is returned with the fresh supplies.

Full for empty This system of issuing is followed in smaller hotels. Empty containers of used-up cleaning supplies are taken to the housekeeping stores by individual GRAs. The store assistant then replaces the empty containers with full ones. The disadvantages in this system are that it works well only when the housekeeping stores are open round the clock and that constant supervision is required. The topping-up method is an improvement on this system of issuing.

Exhibit 7.2 Format of a stores stock sheet

Hotel Snowflakes

STORES STOCK SHEET

Date: ....

S. no	Name of Item	Unit	Stock in hand	Stock received	Total stock	Less issues	Book stock	Actual stock	Difference in stock
1.	All purpose detergent	500 ml bottles							
2.	Mansion polish	1 litre tins							
3.	Floor cleaner-soap oil	5 litre cans							
4.	Air freshener	20 blocks per carton							

Signature of Housekeeper: .... Signature of Storekeeper: ....

Topping-up The difference between this method and the earlier one is that here the GRAs approach the housekeeping stores only at a fixed time each week for getting their supplies topped up. An even better system is having the GRAs deposit their hand caddies in the housekeeping stores at the end of the shift, so that the store assistant may replenish or top up the cleaning agents and keep them ready for the staff on the next shift.

Guest Supplies

Guest supplies include all items that are conducive to the guest's material comfort and convenience. These may be grouped under guest amenities, guest expendables, guest essentials, and guest loan items.

Guest amenities all the luxury items that a hotel provides to its guests at no extra cost.

Guest expendables those guest supplies that are expected to be used up or taken away by the guest on leaving the property.

Guest essentials items that are essential to the guestroom but are not used up or expected to be taken away by guests.

Guest loan items supplies that are not normally found in the guestroom, but are available to the guest on request.

The different types of guest supplies are listed in Table 7.16.

Table 7.16 Categories of guest supplies

Guest amenities	Guest expendables	Guest essentials	Guest loan items
• Coffee maker • Docking station • Universal power adapter • Spike guard • Quality pens • Chocolates • Biscuit platter • Bathrobe • Small indoor plant or flowers in vase • Shoe basket with liner • Beverages in minibar • Snacks • Hair dryer • Ironing board and iron box • Weighing scale	• Laundry bags and laundry forms • Match box • Room compendium - envelopes, postcards, writing sheets with logo, book marks; stationery kit/business kit - all pins, paper clips, staples, eraser, sharpener, cello tape, rubber bands; scribbling pad pen, pencil • Magazines • Utility bag • Sewing kit/Dutch wife - small skeins of white and black threads, a sewing needle, a pair safety pin, a pair each of white and black buttons, a pair of snap buttons • Shoe mits shoe shine, shoe horn • Disposable slippers	• Cloth hangers • Drinking glasses & coasters • Hospitality tray with cups, saucers and spoons • Water jugs/water bottles • Ashtrays • Waste baskets with liners • DND card • Breakfast knob card • Room service menu card • Polish my shoes card • Make my room card • Conservation card • Collect my laundry card • Tent cards	• Medical aids - hot water bottles, ice pack, nebuliser, steam inhaler, thermometer • Feeding bottle steriliser • Baby diapers & baby wipes • Electric shaver • Alarm clock • Bed board • Crib • Roll away bed • Nail clipper & nail polish remover • Sanitary pads • PPE - gloves, face mask • Bottle of disinfectant and sanitizer

(Contd.)

Table 7.16 *Contd.*

Guest amenities	Guest expendables	Guest essentials	Guest loan items
Bathroom amenities • Bath gel, bath salts, bubble bath • Body lotion, body talc, body oil, deodorant, tanning lotion • Shower cap • Shampoo, hair conditioner • Grooming kit/For your care kit/All purpose kit—nail file, ear buds, comb, small scissors • Loofah pad	• Hospitality tray items - Instant coffee sachet, tea sachets (regular, earl grey, green, chamomile), sugar sachets, demerara sugar sachets, sugar substitute sachets, milk creamer pods, condiments packet containing salt and pepper powder • Candy/mints **Bathroom expendable supplies** • WC strip (to seal the WC after cleaning & disinfection) • Tissue box • Toilet roll • Face tissues • Soap bars—bath, hand • Soap suds/flakes • Sani-bags • Cotton wool swabs • Face wash • Shaving kit—after shave, shaving cream, razors, cologne • Dental kit—toothbrush, toothpaste, mouthwash	• Service directory • Guest house rules • The Bible or Gita or Quran • Linen—bed and bath linen **Bathroom guest essentials** • Blade dispenser • Tooth glasses	• Mosquito repellent cream and spray • Pillows from pillow menu • Yoga mat • Ice bucket • Bottle opener & corkscrew • Phone charger • Books • Children's toys & games • Cloth drying rack

Linen

The word 'linen' or 'house linen' is used collectively to describe all launderable items maintained, stored, and issued for guest use by the housekeeping department. The linen maintained by the housekeeping department is classified in Figure 7.26.

Guestroom Linen

Guestroom linen consists of bed and bath linen. Many hotels have their name and logo embroidered into the linen for identification and standardization. This is called monogramming. The most usual types and sizes of bed and bath linen are given in Tables 7.17 and 7.18 respectively. The quality of linen is discussed in detail in Chapter 19.

Bed linen

This category includes all the launderable articles on the bed. Bed 'linen' may be made from linen, cotton, or synthetic fibres. Blends are becoming more popular now. Bed linen includes sheets, pillowcases, blankets, bedspreads, duvet covers, and mattress protectors.

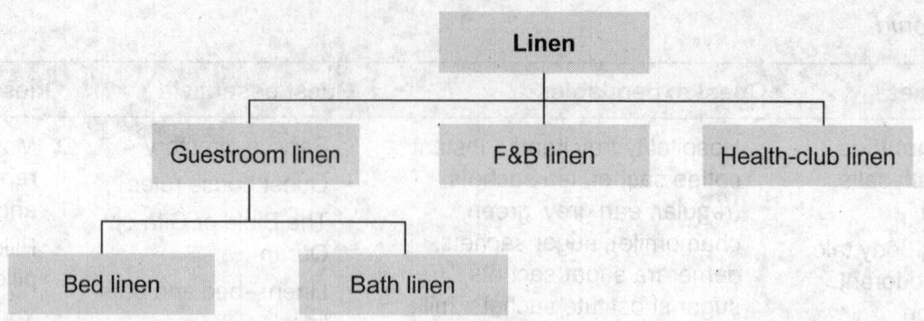

Fig. 7.26 Linen used in hotels

Table 7.17 Types and sizes of bed linen

Bed linen	Types	Size in inches	Size in cm
Sheets	Small single	72 × 108	180 × 270
	Standard single	80 × 117	203 × 295
	Double	90 × 108	225 × 270
	Queen-size	108 × 117	270 × 295
	King-size	117 × 126	295 × 315
Crinkle sheets	Single	72 × 108	180 × 270
	Double	90 × 108	225 × 270
Pillowcases	Standard	20 × 30	50 × 75
	King-size	20 × 36	50 × 90
Blankets	Single	70 × 100	175 × 250
	Double	90 × 100	225 × 250
	Queen-size	100 × 117	250 × 295
Duvet covers	Single	55 × 80	135 × 200
	Double	70 × 75	175 × 190
Bedspreads	May be fitted spreads or throw-over spreads	Varies with bed sizes; should just touch the floor	
Mattress protectors	Single or double, according to bed	Slightly shorter than the sheets	

Note: A wide variation is often found in sizes, since products differ in American, British, and Indian markets. Following the conventions with manufacturers, width of the linen is mentioned first.

Sheets Pure cotton sheets are available, but these days many hotels prefer a polyester-cotton blend. Sheets come in various sizes and should be long enough to be tucked in well. The appropriate measure would be:

Size of the mattress + thickness of the mattress on both sides + thickness of mattress protector + 6 in. on each side for tuck + 3 in. for shrinkage

They are available in a wide range of pastel colours but white is the most preferred. Earlier, sheets were made with a wider hem at the top than the bottom, but now top and bottom hems of equal width

Table 7.18 Types and sizes of bath linen

Bath linen	Size in inches	Size in cm
Bath sheets	40 × 70	100 × 175
Bath towels	30 × 54	75 × 135
Face towels	12 × 12	30 × 30
Hand towels	15 × 24	38 × 60
Wash cloth	12 × 12	30 × 30
Bath mats	24 × 36	60 × 90
Pool towel	36 × 80	91 × 203

Note: A wide variation is often found in sizes, since products differ across American, British, and Indian markets. Following the manufacturers' convention, the width of the linen is mentioned first.

are preferred. This is because in the latter case, the sheets can be turned around periodically so that the wear of the sheet will not be concentrated in the same place and they will not require extra handling time in ensuring that the top of the sheet is at the head of the bed.

In the standard method of bed-making, two plain sheets and one crinkle sheet are required per bed. Crinkle sheets are also called night spreads, snooze sheets, or third sheets. They are typically made in a seersucker weave and some may have light patterns too. They are both decorative and protective.

Pillowcases These are usually made of the same material as the corresponding sheets. Pillowcases should be of a size that can fit easily over the pillow. An appropriate measure would be:

Size of the pillow + 1 in. lengthwise and widthwise

Frills and laces should be avoided as their maintenance is cumbersome. Pillowcases that match the fabric and pattern used in the bedspreads rather than the sheets are sometimes called shams (though this is in fact simply the American word for a pillowcase). These are used in very formal settings.

Blankets These should be lightweight for comfort but at the same time act as a thermal insulator. They are generally a little shorter than the sheets as they do not require much tucking. The choice of blanket colour varies from hotel to hotel. Some prefer to use light colours so that the guests may be impressed by the hotel's standards of cleanliness. Others use dark colours so that maintenance is easier. Usually blankets have a trim of satin at the top and bottom edges.

Duvet covers These are like large sacks made of cotton or a blended fabric. They should be of a comfortable size for the duvets to fit in. An appropriate measure would be:

Size of the duvet + 2 in. (lengthwise) & 4 in. (widthwise) for shrinkage

They are often patterned. Many hotels use duvets with a decorative duvet cover instead of both blankets and bedspreads. They are sometimes referred to as comforters.

Mattress protectors These are also called mattress pads or mattress covers. They may be in the form of quilted, felt, vinyl, or rubber pads. They have a two-fold function—they protect the mattress from stains and spills and provide a padded layer between the guest and the mattress for greater comfort.

Bedspreads These are also called counterpanes. They usually have attractive patterns. There are two main types of bedspreads—fitted spreads and larger throw-over spreads. Fitted spreads fit snugly at the corners of the bed, whereas throw-over spreads are allowed to drape in folds and cascades over the foot and corners of the bed. Throw-over spreads can be held in place under the pillows and then carried over them to the head of the bed to be tucked. However, many properties now place decorative pillows over the bedspread rather than beneath. Bedspreads should be of a width to just touch the floor. If they are used with dust ruffles, they may be coverlets instead, just the size of the mattress.

Dust ruffles A dust ruffle is a pleated or gathered decorative fabric skirting that extends around the sides and foot of a bed, covering the mattress and the frame of the bed. They are often made of satin or an attractively patterned material with a good drape. The ruffles, pleats, or gathers of this material may be sewn onto a muslin sheet placed between the mattress and the box springs, thus holding the dust ruffle securely in place.

Bath Linen

This category includes all kinds of towels found in a guest bathroom, wash cloths, and bath mats. The preferred colour at most properties is white, though they are available in many other hues, both pastel and dark. Towels are almost always made of cotton terry cloth or Turkish towelling with uncut pile for high absorbency.

Bath sheets These are extra-large bath towels provided in VIP rooms in luxury hotels providing world-class service.

Bath towels There is a lot of variation in bath-towel sizes. White ones are preferred since dyed ones may fade in time or the dye may run in case of dark colours.

Face towels These were earlier made of linen woven in a fancy huckaback weave, but now they are almost exclusively made of terry cloth or Turkish towelling.

Hand towels These, like face towels, are now made of Turkish towelling rather than the older huckaback and waffle weaves. They are provided both in guest bathrooms and cloakrooms.

Wash cloths These are made of soft terry cloth and used by guests for scrubbing their face and body clean while taking a bath.

Bath mats These are also made of Turkish towelling but the material tends to be much heavier. They are highly absorbent and are kept in guest bathrooms for guests to dry their feet after coming out of a bath and to catch drips or splashes so that chances of slipping on bathroom floor tiles are reduced. Earlier, *tub mats* with either rubber or cork backing were used instead, but they could not be laundered frequently and thus were unhygienic. They have therefore been completely replaced by Turkish towelling bath mats, which can be laundered frequently.

F&B Linen

These are linen used in restaurants and banquet halls. F&B linen are table cloths, napkins, slip cloths, underlays (all constituting table linen), frills, runners, tray mats, and waiters' cloths.

Table linen Linen used on the table are referred to as table linen or napery. Table linen includes table cloths, napkins, slip cloths, and underlays.

Table cloths and napkins Good-quality table cloths and napkins are made exclusively of damask. Damask is a self-patterned twill-weave fabric of linen, cotton, or a cotton-polyester blend. Table cloths are usually squares made in varying sizes, according to the seating capacity of the table. Oblong table cloths are made for rectangular tables. Napkins are also called 'serviettes' and are basically square in shape.

The usual sizes for table cloths and napkins are presented in Table 7.19.

Table 7.19 Table linen sizes

Table linen	Specifications	Size in inches
Table cloth (square)	2-seater table	36 × 36
	4-seater table	54 × 54
	6-seater table	63 × 63
	8-seater table	72 × 72
Table cloth (oblong)	6-seater table	52 × 72
	8-seater table	90 × 72
Napkins/serviettes		18 × 18
		24 × 24

Slip cloths These are also called 'overlays', 'throwovers', or 'naperon'. The square slip cloth is laid over the table cloth, usually diagonally, to protect it from spills and stains. It also renders an attractive formal appearance, often contrasting in colour with the table cloth. The standard size is 40 × 40 inches.

Baize cloths These are also called 'underlays' or 'silence cloth'. It is usually made of felt. Baize cloth is laid under the table cloth to render it non-slip and cover the sharp edges of the table. It also absorbs the sound of cutlery.

Frills These are also called 'skirts'. These are made of satin and enhance the appearance of buffet tables and such. They may be pleated or unpleated.

Runners These act as display aids and may also be used to visually unite two smaller tables set against each other in lieu of a long table.

Tray and salver mats These are placed on trays and salvers to prevent cutlery from slipping around. They also absorb any moisture from the bottoms of plates and other crockery being carried on the tray. Tray mats are oblong in shape, whereas salver mats are usually circular.

Waiter's cloths These are used by waiters during service. They are usually made of cotton casement fabric.

Health-club Linen

This category includes a few limited types of linen. In a luxury hotel, the health-club linen may include some bath towels, a few bath sheets, and some hand and/or face towels, along with a few sheets for the massage tables.

Uniforms

Uniforms are garments of a specified material, colour, and design, usually provided by the establishment, for staff. In most hotels, the housekeeping department is the custodian of uniforms for all hotel employees. Uniforms are exchanged at the uniform exchange counter on a one-for-one basis or clean for soiled. In some properties, however, uniforms are purchased and handed over to the staff for them to maintain their individual sets. A reasonable uniform programme should allow the issue of two uniforms to each employee upon employment and a third set on confirmation.

Uniforms are issued for the following purposes:

- Ensuring a well-groomed appearance at all times for all employees on duty.
- Identifying hotel staff and differentiating them from the guests at a glance.
- Differentiating staff from different departments and of different grades.
- Ensuring work comfort (this is a function of uniform design).
- Encouraging a feeling of belonging in the employees of the organization.

Uniforms should fit well and allow for comfort in movement, since much reaching and bending is involved in the work of hotel employees. Half-length sleeves are better for employees who do hands-on work. Pockets are handy and always helpful. Uniforms are discussed in more detail in Chapter 20.

Uniforms used by different departments of a hotel must usually be in sync with the theme of the hotel while being distinctive from each other. Many Indian hotels use elements of traditional or regional dress as uniforms to lend authenticity to the environment. Departmental uniforms must also be designed keeping in mind practical ease, comfort, appearance, protection, and various other factors. Some standard types of uniform used in various departments in Indian hotels are listed in Table 7.20.

Table 7.20 Standard types of uniform in Indian hotels

Uniform article	Meant for		Departments/Positions for which used	Purpose	
	Male	Female		Appearance and practicality	Protective
Apron	✓	✓	FP, KS		✓
Belt	✓	✓	All departments	✓	
Blouse		✓	HK, FO, FS, SL	✓	
Bow tie	✓	✓	FS	✓	
Cap	✓	✓	KS, SC	✓	✓
Chef's cap	✓	✓	FP	✓	
Chef's coat	✓	✓	FP	✓	✓
Chef's trousers	✓	✓	FP		✓
Coat	✓	✓	FS, FO, HK, SL, Managers	✓	
Dungarees	✓		EG		✓
Gloves—cloth	✓	✓	FS	✓	
Gloves—rubber	✓	✓	EG, HK		✓
Gumboots	✓		EG, KS, HK		✓
Jacket	✓	✓	FO, FS	✓	
Kurta	✓		HK, FO	✓	
Lab coat	✓	✓	HK		✓
Midi		✓	FO, HK, FS	✓	

Personal Protective Equipment (PPE)

Housekeeping department has requirement of another set of inventory items more than any other department except for maintenance and these are personal protective equipment or PPE. PPE are equipment or items worn to minimise exposure to workplace hazards that may cause injuries or illnesses. The hazards may be physical, mechanical, chemical, electrical, or radiological in nature. PPE include gloves, face masks and respirators, safety goggles, face shield or visor, hair covers, ear plugs or muffs, knee pads, shoe covers, slush boots, hard hats, safety harnesses, lanyards and body belts, coverall suits, gowns, vests, and waterproof aprons. Figure 7.27 shows some important PPE used in housekeeping tasks.

(a) (b) (c) (d) (e)

(f) (g) (h) (i) (j)

(k) (l)

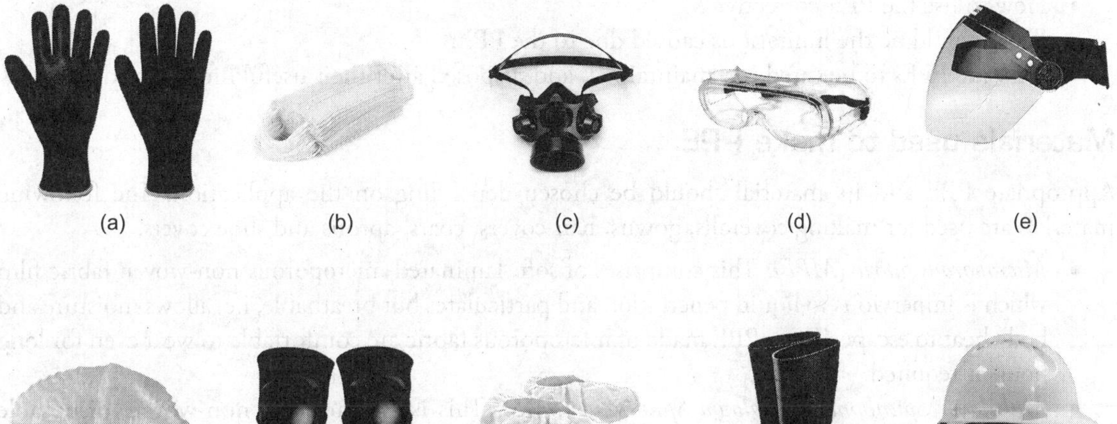

Fig. 7.27 PPE used in housekeeping tasks (a) Gloves; (b) Face masks; (c) Respirator; (d) Safety goggles; (e) Face shield; (f) Hair cover; (g) Knee pads; (h) Shoe covers; (i) Slush boots; (j) Hard hat; (k) Safety harness, lanyards and body belts; (l) Coverall suit

The managers and supervisors must refer MSDS to check which PPE are required to handle chemicals. The PPE must conform to BIS standards and must be:

- of safe design and construction
- stored in hygienic environment
- comfortable and of proper fit to encourage use by employee
- available whenever their use is called for
- used as per prescribed standards
- purchased in a sterile packaging

Housekeepers must train the employees in correct PPE usage. The following aspects should be covered:

- When is PPE required to be worn?
- What kind of PPE is necessary for the task at hand?
- How to correctly don (put on), adjust and doff (take off) PPE?
- How to use the PPE correctly?
- What would be the limitations caused due to the PPE?
- How are PPEs to be cared for, maintained, and disposed after their useful life is served?

Materials used to make PPE

Appropriate PPE and its material should be chosen depending on the application. The following materials are used for making coveralls, gowns, hair covers, coats, aprons and shoe covers.

- *Microporous fabric (MPF):* This comprises of soft, laminated microporous non-woven fabric film which is impervious to liquid penetration and particulates but breathable, i.e, allows moisture and body heat to escape. Thus, PPE made of microporous fabric are comfortable to wear even for long hours if required.
- *Multilayer Spunbond Meltblown Spunbond (SMS):* This is a trilaminate non-woven, disposable fabric, its three layers being top layer consisting of spunbond polypropylene (PP), middle layer made of meltdown PP, and bottom layer again consisting of spunbond PP. Its various layers make the fabric durable and provide protection against particulates and liquid splashes.
- *Spunbond Meltblown Meltblown Spunbond (SMMS):* This material is similar to SMS, but contains an additional middle layer of meltdown PP. It is mainly used in making gowns for healthcare set up.
- *Polypropylene (PP):* PP is lightweight, breathable, tear-resistant non-woven fabric that provides resistance to dust, dirt and light liquid splashes and sprays. It finds applications in industries such as food processing, cleaning, healthcare and others.
- *Polyethylene (PE):* This material is a durable, single layer, thin plastic film which offers chemical resistance. It acts as a barrier to dust, dirt, liquid splashes and sprays but has a main drawback in that the fabric is non-breathable. It is used in industries such as cleaning, food processing, oil and gas and construction.
- *Chlorinated Polyethylene (CPE):* Chlorine content added to Polyethylene makes it more comfortable and durable than PE, rendering it breathable, waterproof, chemical resistant, flame-resistant and an effective microbial barrier. It also offers oil resistance to the material. It can be worn for longer hours and provides heavy duty protection. It finds application in industries such as healthcare, cleaning, construction and so on.
- *Polyethylene coated (PE coated):* This is a multilayer fabric in which PE is coated on either side of a fabric to provide an impervious coating to reinforce protection against chemicals, body fluids and liquids.

PPE used by Housekeepers

Various PPE used in carrying out hazardous housekeeping tasks are discussed here:

Gloves Gloves are required to be worn when handling hazardous chemicals and sharp objects, dealing with potentially contaminated surfaces, performing disinfection activities. Gloves are made of a variety of materials such as cotton, padded cotton, terry cloth, wool, metal mesh, reinforced heavy leather, latex, nitrile rubber, butyl rubber, neoprene, polyvinyl chloride (PVC) etc. and should be selected based on the task involved, as shown in Table 7.21. While working with chemicals, the chosen gloves should be impervious to liquids and the material safety data sheet (MSDS) must be checked for information on the suitable PPE. Length of the gloves should be sufficient to provide proper protection to the hands, those reaching mid forearm are ideal. Rubber latex gloves may cause allergic reactions in some people.

Face masks Face masks are needed to cover the nose while working in an infectious environment or dealing with chemicals. 3-ply pleated masks providing more than 90% microbe filtration efficiency are preferred in environments with potential biohazards. Masks must be of breathable material, have a soft, snug fit for comfort. They must have secure elastics on both sides, expandable ear loops and a pliant nose clip for adjustable fit on nose bridge.

Respirators When employees are dealing with dangerous chemicals or pesticides and working in environments with highly infectious airborne pathogens, they must wear respirators with filtering and breathing apparatus. Respirators must custom-fit securely over the face and be leak proof. Employees must be checked for medical fitness before donning respirators.

Safety goggles These are worn as eye coverings to offer protection against accidental or potential chemical sprays, smoke and hazardous airborne splinters or particulates. Safety goggles must be made of impact resistant, lightweight material such as polycarbonate and coated with anti-scratch finish. The lens must be transparent and zero power. The safety frame must be strong and heat resistant and the goggles must have a elastic band outer edge cover. The safety goggles must cover the eye from eyebrow to cheekbone and across the nose to the bone area on the sides of the face. Well-fitting goggles with adjustable band must be selected which provide unobstructed view in front and sides.

Table 7.21 Selection of gloves based on usage

Type of glove	Usage
Cotton, terry cloth	General duty tasks, aesthetic value
Nitrile rubber, butyl rubber, rubber latex, neoprene, PVC	Handling hazardous chemicals (Select based on concentration of chemical, duration of contact and MSDS)
Nitrile rubber, butyl rubber	Dealing with potentially contaminated products and wastes
Metal mesh, reinforced heavy leather	Dealing with sharp objects and edges
Reinforced heavy leather, reinforced heavy rubber	Abrasion hazard
Heat-resistant leather with lining, padded cotton	In medium heat hazard
Leather, wool, insulated plastic, insulated rubber	In cold temperature hazard

Face shield/Visor Face shields are required to be worn when the tasks involve flying splinters or dust hazard due to chipping, drilling, polishing, sawing, welding, and so on. It is also indicated in hazards such as sparks, chemical splashes, radiation or electric arc splash. They may provide some level of barrier protection against airborne biological infectious agents. A good quality face shield is lightweight, covers the entire face and is made of impact resistant material such as polycarbonate with anti-fog and scratch resistant finish.

Hair covers Hair covers act as particulate and microbial barrier and prevent hair from contaminating a work environment or vice versa. Hair covers should be made of breathable, stretchable fabric and not shed lint. It should be lightweight and have securely fitting elastic edges. Disposable hair covers are preferred, in case non-disposable ones are used, they should be washable and sterilisable.

Knee pads Knee pads are to be worn for reducing the impact on knees whenever housekeeping tasks require kneeling on hard surfaces for extended periods. While selecting knee pads assess how they protect, support and provide comfort while kneeling. It is also important that the knee pad material is breathable, else it may result in itching. The padding should have high density foam cushion supported by a PVC outer shell and adjustable straps.

Shoe covers These disposable covers are worn over uniform shoes to provide protection against infectious spills, microbes and chemicals. Good quality shoe covers are made of durable, breathable, non-slip fabric, fit securely over shoes with elastic bands around the ankles. They should be easy to don and doff.

Slush boots Housekeeping staff need foot protection with slush boots when the tasks pose hazards which are electrical, falling objects, corrosive substances, burns, potential microbial dumps, and crushing, puncture or penetrating actions. Good quality slush boots are washable, sterilisable, slip-resistant, chemical resistant, impervious to liquids, impact resistant and should cover the feet till appropriate length.

Safety harnesses, lanyards and body belts These are fall protection equipment to be worn if the employee is working at a level of 3 meters or more. The equipment must be inspected before use and replaced if defective. While inspecting, pay attention to the buckles, ropes, hardware, and entire surface of webbing. Written record of inspection must be maintained. The manufacturer's instructions must be followed in proper application, use, fitting and adjusting these equipment.

Coverall suits and gowns These provide protection against hazardous chemical sprays, liquid splashes and potentially infectious body fluids. While selecting coverall suits, it should be ensured that the material meets regulatory standards, is durable, abrasion resistant, impervious to fluids, breathable and light coloured. 90 gsm non-woven material is recommended where potential biohazards are present. The design should be such that they provide protection to the front and back of the body. Zippers should not be preferred in front. Ultrasonically welded seams should be preferred over stitched ones.

SUMMARY

In this chapter, we have discussed the recycled and non-recycled inventory items in the housekeeping department. Recycled-item inventories include cleaning equipment, linen, uniforms, and guest loan items. Non-recycled-item inventories include cleaning supplies and guest supplies other than guest loan items. The larger pieces of equipment discussed in this chapter are not precisely part of the housekeeping inventories and it would be more apt to classify them under fixed assets. They have, however, been included in this chapter since these pieces of equipment are part of the responsibilities of the housekeeping department in terms of daily maintenance, care, and storage, just like other housekeeping inventories. Though an establishment may spend only 5–10% of the overall cost of cleaning on equipment and agents, the role they play in maintaining a hygienic and aesthetic environment is tremendous.

The cleaning equipment have been discussed under the broad categories of manual and mechanical equipment. The types, use, care, and storage of various categories of equipment have been dealt with in detail since correct use and correct maintenance increases the life expectancy of any piece of equipment, whether manual or mechanical. To avoid repetition, laundry equipment have not been discussed at length here; refer to Chapter 19 for the same.

Many new and different types of equipment are available these days. However, they all fall under one of the categories described in this chapter. Many types of equipment manufactured nowadays are meant to combine two or three different cleaning operations.

A housekeeper should select equipment for the department keeping certain factors in mind to get the maximum functional life out of it. These factors are listed in the text.

Different types of cleaning agents have been discussed in detail. In some places, some basic knowledge of chemistry is expected on the reader's part. Even so, all efforts have been made to explain the terms and concepts clearly, either in the text or as part of the list of key terms below.

Some cleaning agents are toxic, some corrosive, and some may cause dangerous reactions if not judiciously used. Wherever applicable, a word of caution has been put in. An interesting section on do-it-yourself polishes may not only help save expenditure for the housekeeping department, but can also be implemented to generate a sense of creativity in the housekeeping staff. The rule of thumb is: when unsure about applying polish to a surface, try applying it in a small area not in view. The factors to consider when selecting cleaning agents have been listed. The storage and requisition of cleaning agents has been given particular importance, as they are crucial daily/routine tasks.

Guest supplies have been listed under the four categories of amenities, expendables, essentials, and loan items. The term 'linen' as used in hotels has been defined. Linen has been classified into the categories of guestroom linen (bed and bath linens), F&B linen, and health-club linen. The common sizes of different types of linen, which differ slightly in different texts and sources because of manufacturers' variations, have been listed and the varying requirements of hotels explained.

A wide variety of uniforms may be found in hotels across India. Many hotels now prefer their employees to retain the feel of the locality and to showcase the culture and tradition of the place. Thus ethnic uniforms are in, especially at three- and four-star properties. The uniform garments that can be commonly seen in Indian hotels are listed.

All these inventory items need assessment on a regular basis to ascertain whether the items are suitable and continue to meet the hotel's requirements.

KEY TERMS

Abrasives Substances or chemicals that depend on their rubbing or scratching action to clean dirt and grit from hard surfaces—for example, sandpaper, steel wool, powdered pumice, and so on.

Aerosols Particles dispersed in gas packed under pressure, with a device for releasing it as a fine spray.

Antiseptic An agent that makes the environment non-conducive to the growth and reproduction of disease-causing (pathogenic) microbes.

Bactericidal An agent that kills most bacteria, but not their spores.

Bacteriostatic An agent that makes the environment non conducive to the growth and reproduction of bacteria.

Baize cloth A coarse-woven cloth laid under the table cloth to make it non-slip and cover the sharp edges of the table. It also absorbs the sound of cutlery. Baize cloth is also called underlay, molleton, or silence cloth.

Bath sheets These are extra-large bath towels provided in VIP rooms in luxury hotels providing world-class service.

Beeswax Beeswax is a glandular secretion from young worker honeybees and is used to build their honeycomb structures. The wax is harvested by removing the honey by centrifuge and melting the remaining comb. The melted wax is then filtered and cast into moulds.

Biodegradable Substances capable of being decomposed by living organisms.

Blade dispenser An apparatus with a cavity for dispensing fresh razor blades and a disposal slot for enabling disposal of used razor blades.

Breakfast knob cards Cards hung by guests on the knobs of guestroom doors to pre-order breakfast at night so that the order reaches the staff on time and the guest is not disturbed for placing the order early in the morning.

Buffing Polishing, say, the floor with a low-speed polishing machine.

Builders A builder is defined as a compound that has no surface-active properties but increases the bulk and the efficiency of a detergent.

Burnishing Polishing the floor with a high-speed floor machine to achieve an extremely high gloss.

Carborundum Silicon carbide, used as an abrasive.

Card index system A card index system is a useful method of collecting all relevant information about each piece of equipment being used in a particular establishment. It gives information regarding the make, date of first operation, location, user, and servicing details of the equipment.

Carnauba Carnauba wax comes from the outer waxy coating of the palm fronds of the Brazilian carnauba palm (*Copernicia cerifera*). Carnauba wax is the hardest natural vegetable wax.

Caustic alkalis Very strong alkalis such as sodium hydroxide (caustic soda).

Chamois Chamois leather is used mainly in cleaning and polishing. Originally the skins of chamois goat antelopes were used, but now they are usually skivers, that is, split sheepskins, or simulated skins. Chamois leather is used wet for cleaning windows and mirrors. It is also used dry as a polishing cloth for silver.

Cleaning agents Substances, natural and synthetic, used to assist the cleaning process.

Cleaning equipment Physical cleaning aids, manual or mechanical.

Cleaning supplies Cleaning agents and small pieces of cleaning equipment that are used in cleaning the guestrooms and public areas in the hotel.

Compendium Another name for guest stationery folder placed at the writing table in guestrooms.

Conservation card Also referred to as Linen reuse card, Eco card or Sustainability card, it indicates a choice to guests to opt for change of linen on alternate days, in line with the hotel's sustainability programme.

Coverlet A bedspread that just covers the top of the dust ruffle but does not reach down to the floor.

Crib A cot for babies, provided to guests on request.

Crinkle sheet A distinctively woven sheet used to cover and protect the blanket. It is also called a third sheet. Other names for a crinkle sheet are snooze sheet and night spread.

Damask Damask is a self-patterned fabric in twill weave. It may be made of linen, cotton, or a cotton-polyester blend.

Disinfected strip A thin strip of paper placed atop and encircling the toilet seat to let guests know that the toilet has been disinfected for their use. It is also called a toilet strip.

Disinfectants Specifically, substances used to destroy pathogenic microorganisms. The term 'disinfectant' is now used as a general term to cover all kinds of agents that bring about germ control.

DND card A 'Do Not Disturb' card, hung outside the guestroom by the guest to inform staff and visitors that the occupant does not wish to be disturbed.

Docking station A device into which a laptop, smartphone, or other mobile devices my be placed for charging or/and providing access to power supply and peripheral devices.

Dustette These are small, lightweight vacuum cleaners used for cleaning curtains, upholstery, carpet edges, mattresses, computers, and music systems. They clean by brushing and suction and are very easy to handle. They may be carried by hand or strapped to the back of the operator.

Dust ruffle A pleated, decorative skirting that extends around the sides and foot of a bed.

Dutch wife Another term for the sewing kit provided as a guest amenity. It contains small skeins of white and black threads, a sewing needle, a pair safety pin, a pair each of white and black buttons, a pair of snap buttons.

Duvets Quilts filled with down feathers or synthetic fibres. Many hotels use duvets with a decorative duvet cover in lieu of both blankets and bedspreads. They are sometimes referred to as comforters.

Fixed assets These are tangible assets of a long-term nature, such as land or large pieces of machinery and equipment.

Flannelette A plain-woven cotton fabric with a brushed or napped surface.

Floor pantry A service room provided on each floor for GRAs to store cleaning agents, equipment, guest supplies, guestroom linen, and room attendants' carts.

Galvanized iron Iron coated with a layer of zinc to discourage corrosion.

GSM Grams per Square Metre.

Guest amenities All the luxury items that a hotel gives away to guests at no extra cost.

Guest essentials Items that are essential to the guestroom and are not expected to be used up or taken away by guests.

Guest expendables Guest supplies that are expected to be used up or taken away by the guest on leaving the property.

Guest loan items These are guest supplies not normally found in a guestroom, but available upon request. For example, hot water bottles, thermometers and so on.

Guest supplies Guest supplies include all items that are conducive to the guest's material comfort and convenience. They are further subdivided as guest amenities, guest essentials, guest expendables, and guest loan items.

Hard water Water that contains more than 60 ppm (parts per million) of calcium and/or magnesium is called hard water.

Hopper A heavyweight container used for carrying away mud and debris.

Hospitality tray A tray usually placed above or near the minibar in guestrooms for guest to stir up their own tea/coffee. On it are placed the coffee maker, cups, saucers, spoons, varieties of tea and coffee sachets, sugar sachets, milk creamer pods and condiments packet containing salt and pepper powder.

House linen The term 'house linen' is used collectively to describe all launderable items maintained, stored, and issued for guest use by the housekeeping department.

House rules Certain special rules of the hotel set down in a document by the hotel's management for guests.

Impregnation In this context, filling mop heads with a permeating substance that attracts dust particles.

Inventories The stocks of purchased operating supplies, equipment, and other items held for future use in housekeeping operations.

Issuing The process of distributing inventory items from the store room to authorized individuals through the use of formal requisitions.

Jeweller's rouge A pink oxide of iron used as a fine abrasive, for polishing silver and so on.

Johnny mop A brush used for cleaning toilets. It can pump water through an inlet-outlet system in its handle and head to swab the toilet.

Lacquer Coloured varnish made of shellac dissolved in alcohol.

Linen Material woven from fibres of the flax plant. The term 'linen' is also used loosely to denote household articles that were originally made of linen and may now be made of other fabrics, such as bed and table linen, and by extension other housekeeping launderables such as bath linen. Actual linen material is less elastic and more absorbent than cotton, which is now preferred for most of these items.

Lint Short fibres that may be loosened and shed from a fabric.

Mini-bar A fixture in modern guestrooms, this is a miniature refrigerator stocked with juices, liquor, and snacks for the convenience of guests.

Montan Crude montan wax is a naturally occurring vegetable wax extracted by solvents from lignite deposits and peat. Refined montan has undergone extra processing to remove any resins and asphalt. The colour ranges from dark brown to light yellow. Montan wax imparts a high gloss and increases water repellence and scuff resistance.

MSDS Materials Safety Data Sheet is a form containing detailed safety information about a chemical.

Naperon A naperon is laid over the table cloth, usually diagonally, to protect it from spills and stains. It also gives the table an attractive formal appearance, usually contrasting with the table cloth in colour. A naperon is also called a slip cloth, overlay, or throw-over cloth.

Napery Table linen—table cloth and napkins.

Non-recycled inventory items Items that are used up during the course of routine housekeeping operations. Non-recycled items include most guest amenities, cleaning supplies, and small pieces of equipment.

Ozokerite/Ozocerite A waxy mineral, a type of paraffin wax, that is a mixture of hydrocarbons and occurs in association with petroleum.

Paraffin wax Paraffin wax is a petroleum wax made from de-oiled slack wax. Paraffin wax is brittle and

highly resistant to moisture. Due to its low cost, paraffin wax is frequently added to other wax blends.

pH scale A scale that indicates the acidity and alkalinity of substances. On a pH range of 0 to 14, a pH of 7 is neutral, acids have pH values less than 7 and alkalis have values of more than 7.

Pile The surface of a carpet consisting of fibres or yarns that form raised loops that may be cut or sheared or may be left intact.

PPE Personal Protective Equipment, clothing or equipment that is worn to provide protection against hazardous substances and environment.

Precipitated whiting Filtered chalk used as a mild abrasive.

Quats Quaternary ammonium compounds, used as disinfectants.

Recycled inventory items Items that have relatively limited useful lives but are used over and over again in housekeeping operations. These include linen, uniforms, most pieces of machinery and larger pieces of equipment, and guest loan items.

Rotten stone Decomposed siliceous limestone used as a polishing powder.

Safety lanyards Safety lanyards refer to the PPEs in the form of ropes and cords that connect a harness to an anchor point to secure workers working at heights, preventing them from a fall. Lanyards also secure working tools and light equipment to the worker's body.

Sanitation Reducing microbial counts to an acceptable level.

Saponification A reaction in which fat/oil reacts with alkali to form soap.

Shams The American term for pillowcases. In the Indian hotel industry, 'shams' is used for pillowcases that match the fabric and pattern used in bedspreads rather than the sheets. These are used in very formal settings.

Shellac Shellac is lac melted into thin flakes, refined, and used for making varnish by mixing with alcohol. Lac is a sticky, resinous substance secreted on trees by insects.

Shoe mitts Flannel mitts kept in hotel rooms as guest supplies for cleaning shoes. Nowadays, instead of flannel fabric, rice-paper tissue is used to make these. Some establishments may simply provide a square of this fabric or tissue instead.

Soap flakes or powder or suds Fabric detergents in one of these forms provided in guest bathrooms for guests to wash their own garments with.

Soft water Water in which the level of dissolved calcium and/or magnesium is below 60 ppm.

Spike guard An appliance consisting of multiple sockets (4–6) for electric and electronic devices, an extension cord and a couple of fuses.

Spirit of salt Concentrated hydrochloric acid.

Spores Microorganisms in their restive, protective state when environmental conditions are unfavourable. When the conditions become favourable again, the spores develop into reproductive microorganisms.

Squeegee A manual cleaning equipment with a sharp-edged rubber, plastic or metal blade and a long handle, used for removing excess moisture from hard surfaces such as floors and window panes.

Sterilization Killing all kinds of microbes as well as their spores.

Surfactants Surface-active compounds that impart a good wetting power, emulsifying power, and suspending power to detergents.

Tent cards Hotel publicity cards in the shape of tents placed in guestrooms.

Terrazzo Flooring which consists of marble, granite, and other decorative chips set in cement.

Tow yarns Yarn produced from short linen fibres is known as tow yarn. Tow yarn produces a softer, more absorbent fabric than the yarn made from longer linen fibres.

Upholstery Textiles used for furniture décor.

Vanity unit A unit comprising a wash basin and mirror surrounded by a flat area where soaps, a dental kit, a shaving kit, and tooth glasses may be kept.

WC Water closet; a toilet bowl and flush.

White wax A wax produced by bleaching beeswax.

Wicker Wicker is derived from the shoots (osiers) of willow plants. It is used for making woven items such as bread baskets, flower baskets, mats, trays, stools, sofas, chairs, and tables.

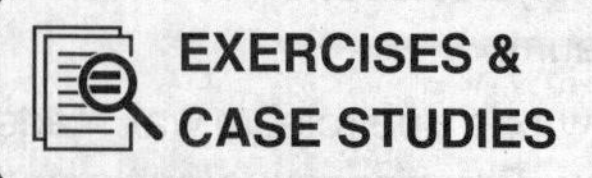

8 Composition, Care, and Cleaning of Different Surfaces

Learning Objectives

After reading this chapter, you should be able to

- appreciate the importance of maintaining different surfaces, such as metals, glass, plastics, etc.
- understand the importance and methods of protecting hard surfaces from wear and tear, tarnishing, and so on
- discuss the methods of cleaning and maintaining different surfaces

Introduction

Hard surfaces are found in various forms, in different areas, in all hospitality establishments. To keep the hotel property looking as fresh as it did the day it first opened, housekeeping employees involved in the care and maintenance of these hard surfaces must know the composition of these surfaces, the specific type or variant, and the optimal cleaning and maintenance procedures. Adequate training should be imparted to the staff on the care and maintenance of the surfaces, because once spoilt, these surfaces usually cannot be revived to achieve their original appeal or function. The types of hard surfaces commonly used in hotels include metals, glass, plastics, ceramics, wood, stone, etc. In addition to these, housekeeping staff are also responsible for the care and cleaning of surfaces such as leather, rubber, etc.

Metals

Metals form the whole or a part of many fixtures, fittings, and items of furniture. The most commonly used metals are silver, steel, copper, brass, bronze, aluminium, and iron. These metals may be used in door and window fittings, wall panels, light fittings, sanitaryware, restaurant cutlery, cooking utensils, guestroom accessories (such as ashtrays, vases, and picture frames), and furniture (such as beds, chairs, and tables). Most metal surfaces get tarnished, scratched, or rusted unless treated or protected.

Protective Finishes on Metals

In this section, we shall discuss the various types of protective finishes on metals, which protect them from damage.

Painting Paint may be applied to steel and wrought iron to make them look decorative. Paint also prevents exposure of the metal surface to air containing oxygen and moisture. Before painting, the metal must be cleaned to remove surface dust and any trace of rust. The paint should be applied evenly, in several coats. Any damage to the paintwork should be repaired immediately.

Electroplating This is done using the process of electrolysis. In this process, protective or decorative metals such as chromium, zinc, tin, silver, or gold are deposited on brass, steel, or copper. It is a very durable finish.

Galvanizing In this process, the base metal—usually steel or iron—is coated with a layer of zinc to avoid corrosion. This is not used as a decorative finish. Rather, galvanizing makes the article more durable. It is a treatment extensively used for buckets, dustbins, and sinks.

Enamelling In this process, molten glass is applied to metal surfaces such as steel and iron, which later sets to form a transparent, tough, smooth, and easily cleaned surface. The enamel may 'craze' (crack on the surface) on wear, however.

Lacquering In this process, shellac—dissolved in alcohol—is coated over brass or copper to reduce tarnishing.

Anodizing This is another electrolytic treatment by which aluminium is protected from corrosion. It also acts as a decorative finish by enhancing the appearance of aluminium. Anodized aluminium is now extensively used for door and window fittings.

Tin-plating In this process, steel or copper is dipped into molten tin to render it corrosion resistant.

Plastic-coating Plastics can be coated over steel and iron for colour coding (as in pipes) or for decorative purposes.

Commonly used Metals and Alloys

The uses as well as the cleaning procedures for commonly used metals and their alloys have been discussed in this section.

Silver

This soft, malleable, and ductile metal has a brilliant sheen when well polished. Small amounts of the metal in elemental form occur naturally in the earth, but most of the silver we use is extracted from silver ores. Silver is chemically unaffected by pure water, pure air, and a majority of foodstuffs, but gets scratched easily if pure. Silver is used as the plating in electroplated nickel silver, for making cutlery, utensils, vases, and decorative artefacts.

Types of silver The two forms in which silver is most commonly used are sterling silver and silver plating. Sterling silver is an alloy containing 92.5% silver, and the rest is mainly copper. Copper is added to harden the silver and at the same time does not affect the other properties of the metal. Sterling silver is more expensive than silver-plated alloy and for this reason is seldom used in hotels. Table silver or 'silverware' is usually made of silver-plated alloy, by plating 'blanks' of nickel silver alloy. 'Nickel silver' does not contain any silver at all; it is a term for alloys that look like silver (being white metal) and made of nickel, copper, and often (but not always) brass, along with a few other metals for added strength and shine. The 'blanks' are simply pieces of cutlery made of this alloy. Indeed, that is what most so-called 'silverware' is made of, with no actual silver being involved in the cheaper grades. However, the better quality of tableware is then plated with silver. The 'blanks' are immersed in a complex solution of silver salts and, by the process of electrolysis, silver is transferred to their surface. This results in electroplated nickel silver (EPNS).

Maintenance problems The discussion here applies to both sterling silver and plated articles, which have pure silver on the surface.

Silver pits These are small pits that form on the surface of the article. Silver, especially cutlery, gets 'pitted' when left in contact with salt for too long. To prevent pitting, silver cruets should always be fitted with glass liners and silver spoons should not be kept in salt for long.

Tarnishing of silver This is due to the action of compounds of sulphur, present in industrial atmospheres and in certain food stuff such as egg yolk, fish, onion, certain juices, green vegetables, and pickles. If soap is not rinsed off completely after washing silver, it gets tarnished rapidly. Chemically, the tarnish is silver sulphide, which varies in colour from yellow through brown to blue-black, depending on its thickness. Tarnish cannot be removed by simple washing operations and requires specific removal procedures.

Cleaning procedures Silver needs to be cleaned and polished on a regular basis. When it gets tarnished, more complex cleaning methods have to be employed.

Regular cleaning Wash the article in a hot solution of synthetic detergent, scrubbing with a piece of cotton cloth. Then rinse in clean boiling water in an enamelled tray. A sheet of aluminium and some soda can be placed in the tray. Once the articles are clean, drain the water away and wipe dry whilst still warm, rubbing hard with a lint-free linen cloth or chamois leather. Another way to get rid of tarnish is to soak the article for two hours in water leftover from boiling potatoes and then clean. Polish till a good sheen is achieved or use the polishing methods discussed in this section. Store silver that is not in use wrapped in tissue paper (the acid-free variety), place in air-tight containers in a dry place.

Silver dip A silver dip solution is used when tarnished silver is to be cleaned. It is usually a pink-coloured liquid based on an acid solution of a thiourea compound into which the articles are immersed completely (friction is not required) for removal of tarnish. The silver should remain in the liquid for a very short time. The articles should be lifted out, washed with warm water, and dried. While working with silver dip, stainless-steel containers should not be used since the dip attacks steel. Enamel or plastic containers must be used instead. Silver dip should not be used too frequently on the silver, either, since it is harder on the silver because of a chemical reaction between the silver and the liquid that can corrode the metal. However, many establishments use silver dip frequently since it is faster than other methods.

Polivit or aluminium-soda method In this method, silver articles are immersed in a hot soda solution containing a plate or a sheet of perforated aluminium for 10 minutes. The aluminium sheet or plate is commercially available for this purpose under the tradename Polivit®. It is best to place it in an enamelled or galvanized iron bowl. It should be ensured that at least one silver article is in direct contact with the aluminium foil, and each article with either the foil or another article. A chemical exchange then takes place to remove the tarnish, transferring the sulphur to the aluminium. The articles are then removed, rinsed with boiling water, and dried with a lint-free linen cloth.

Polishing procedures After cleaning and removing any tarnish, the silverware should be polished to restore its original shine. Silver may be polished using one of the following aids:

Proprietary preparations These preparations are usually based on precipitated whiting and jeweller's rouge. The polish is rubbed on the article, allowed to dry, and removed by buffing. Some preparations

Table 8.1 Preparation of liquid silver polish

Ingredient	Quantity
Shredded soap	1 tbsp
Boiling water	1 cup
Precipitated whiting	3 tbsp
Ammonia	1 tbsp
Spirit	2 tbsp

Method of preparation: Put all the dry ingredients except soap into a bottle. Dissolve the soap in boiling water and pour over the dry ingredients in the bottle. Add ammonia and spirit into the bottle. Keep the bottle tightly capped. Shake the mixture well before using. The method of use is the same as for similar commercial preparations.

Table 8.2 Preparation of plate powder

Ingredient	Quantity
Precipitated whiting	8 parts
Jeweller's rouge	1 part

Method of preparation: Mix together both the powders and store in a tin. This powder can be mixed with methylated spirit and applied on silver when polishing is required. The method of polishing is as discussed for commercial plate powder.

require rinsing and drying after polishing. Silvo is an example of silver polish available in the Indian market. However, an effective liquid silver polish can be readily made in the housekeeping department. The ingredients and method are given in Table 8.1.

Plate powder This pink powder should be mixed with just enough methylated spirit to make a smooth paste. Alternatively, water may be used; but methylated spirit is preferred since it evaporates faster and the silverware is then available for polishing much more quickly. The smooth paste is rubbed thoroughly onto the silver article with a clean rag and left to dry. It is then rubbed off with rags. The article should now be rinsed well in boiling water and buffed with a clean cloth. Though this method is somewhat time-consuming, it gives good results. Plate powder too can be prepared in the department using the method given in Table 8.2.

Long-term silver polish A long-term silver polish forms a very thin, colourless, transparent, and impervious film that is chemically bonded to the silver. The film does not have any odour, taste, or other detectable properties. This thin film can get removed by abrasion, however, so aftercare is essential.

Burnishing machine A burnishing machine consists of a revolving drum with a safety shield. In this revolving drum, highly polished steel balls are immersed in a detergent solution with the silver articles. The machine rotates and the friction from the steel balls polishes the silver. These articles are then rinsed in hot water and dried. The burnishing machine is used for polishing large quantities of silver articles. Care should be taken to keep the ball bearings covered with water when not in use, since they rust rapidly otherwise.

Steel

Steel is an alloy of iron. The alloy contains mainly iron and carbon; other materials are found in small quantities. It is used in the form of pressed chrome steel for the manufacture of baths, sinks, and so on; stainless steel is used in making cutlery, protective panelling, sanitaryware, furniture, trays, and cooking utensils. Steel is sometimes galvanized or enamelled to prevent corrosion. If an enamelled steel surface gets stained, it can be washed with a mild liquid abrasive.

Types of steel commonly used These are the forms most likely to be encountered in a hotel property.

Chrome steel Steel is coated with chromium for manufacturing taps, bath handles, shower fittings, and so on. These can become spotted with water marks or get greased, but they do not tarnish. Water spots and grease can be easily cleaned away.

Stainless steel This is steel to which 8–25% of chromium has been added, making it corrosion-resistant. Stainless steel is tough, durable, and can take a mirror-polished finish.

It is used in making cutlery, sinks, WCs, and so on. For spoons and forks, steel containing 18 per cent chromium and 8% nickel is generally used. However, even stainless steel can be harmed by silver-dip solutions, acidic solutions, alkaline bleaches, salt-vinegar mixtures, and excessive heat. An important source of possible corrosion for wet stainless steel is contact with galvanized articles or aluminium ones. In this process, a zinc or aluminium corrosion product is deposited on the steel by electro-chemical action.

Galvanized steel Steel may be coated with zinc (galvanized) to prevent tarnishing. This kind of steel is used for making buckets.

Steel may also be nylon- or plastic-coated for furniture legs or painted in different colours for identification purposes. Anodized, tin-plated, and lacquered steels are also used as they do not corrode.

Cleaning and polishing procedures Stainless steel is washed in a hot solution of synthetic detergent using a soft nylon scrubber, rinsed with clean water, and immediately dried thoroughly with a linen cloth. The use of harsh abrasives should be avoided as they may scratch the surface.

Chrome steel and galvanized steel are wiped or washed with synthetic detergent solution, stains removed with soft steel-wool, the articles rinsed with clean water, and buffed with a linen cloth.

For cleaning greasy stains, sodium bicarbonate can be used on all types of steel. Steel occasionally needs polishing to remove scratches and stubborn water spots. A proprietary polish for hard metals or a spray polish may be used for the purpose.

Copper

This metal with an orange-brown tinge has a light sheen of its own. It is used for wall panelling and counter tops in bars and restaurants; bowls, vases, and urns in lobbies and guestrooms; and utensils in the kitchen. Copper is even used in cutlery and serving dishes in some ethnic Indian restaurants. Copper cookware should be lined with tin or nickel for protection, as the copper may react adversely with some foods. Such utensils should be re-lined or discarded as soon as signs of wear are seen in the inner lining. Copper may also be lacquered to avoid tarnishing.

Cleaning and polishing procedures Copper is washed in warm water and then rubbed with a mixture of salt, fine sand, and vinegar, using rags, to clean. It is then rinsed in warm water and dried with a flannel cloth. A thin coat of vegetable oil is applied to the surface to retard further tarnish. In case of heavily tarnished copper, a weak ammonia solution will remove the greenish deposits on the surface. If the lacquer has come off at certain places, the rest may be removed with acetone before reapplication. Copper can also be polished with a proprietary polish. Unlacquered copper requires frequent polishing to avoid the greenish deposit of tarnish forming on the surface. A long-term hard-metal polish can be used for this purpose.

Brass

This is a golden-brown alloy of copper and zinc. It is used in making door and window fittings, stair rods and railings, foot rails in bars, taps, ashtrays, and ornaments. Brass tarnishes and scratches easily. To avoid this, brass fixtures are usually lacquered.

Cleaning and polishing procedures To clean brass articles, remove surface dirt with a duster and rub the articles with a paste made of white flour, salt, and vinegar in equal parts. This will remove mild tarnish. Make sure to rub away all the mixture. Alternatively, a mixture of 30 ml oxalic acid and 300 ml soda solution will also remove tarnish. Corroded brass should be treated with spirit of salt (hydrochloric acid) and then rinsed thoroughly. In very bad cases, if possible, soak the brass article for 12 hours in washing soda solution (approximately 30 g), then rinse and polish. Never use a tamarind-salt mixture to clean brass (although many consider it 'traditional') as the surface may become damaged. Polish with Brasso or Kiwi Brass Polish, using damp rags or cotton. A long-term hard-metal polish can also be used on brass.

Bronze

This is a brown alloy of copper and tin. It is used primarily in making works of art and medals. It does not tarnish easily.

Cleaning procedure To clean a bronze article, wash well with water and then apply a mixture of one part muriatic acid and two parts water with a piece of flannel. Allow the solution to dry and then polish the bronze well with vegetable oil.

Aluminium

This silvery, lightweight metal is highly malleable and ductile. It is used to make light fittings, insulation wires, window frames, venetian blinds, furniture items, door and window fittings, saucepans, and other utensils. Aluminium is not tarnished by air. It is, however, damaged by soda and other alkalis as well as stained by acids. Aluminium may therefore, be anodized to prevent damage to the surface. It also scratches and bends easily.

Cleaning procedure To clean aluminium, wash in a hot solution of synthetic detergent, using soft steel wool to scrub. Use mild abrasives only in the case of difficult stains. Discolouration in saucepans can be removed by boiling a solution of water and lemon juice in them, rinsing, and then drying. Alternatively, add 15 ml borax to 500 ml of the washing solution. In case of aluminium showpieces, some liquid wax polish may be applied to maintain the gloss.

Iron

This silver-white metal of great strength is used in making furniture, buckets, dustbins, and cookware. Iron can be forged or cast. Wrought iron is iron that has been forged, that is, it has been shaped by heating in fire and then hammering while hot. Cast iron is a hard alloy of iron, carbon, and silicon that has been cast in a mould. Non-enamelled cast iron is flame- and oven-proof.

Maintenance problems Utensils made of cast iron need to be seasoned before first use to prevent rusting. Before seasoning, the article has to be washed in mild soap and water, then thoroughly dried. Seasoning is done by rubbing the inside surface with vegetable oil and heating in a slow oven for about two hours. Enamelled cast-iron utensils do not need seasoning and are easier to clean. If handled carelessly, however, the enamel may chip away. If the utensils are put under cold water immediately after use, while still hot, the enamel may again flake off. Therefore, before cleaning, allow the utensil to cool gradually.

Cleaning procedure Unprotected iron should be washed only when necessary and then thoroughly dried. Galvanized iron needs regular washing and thorough drying. Rust can be removed from galvanized items with fine steel wool dampened with oxalic acid. Do not store iron in damp areas. Before long-term storage, coat with oil or black lead (graphite).

Pewter

This is a grey alloy of tin with lead or other metals. It was used in making old-fashioned tankards and goblets. It tarnishes easily and should be cleaned frequently as the tarnish is difficult to remove. Pewter is often lacquered to protect it from tarnishing.

Cleaning procedure To clean, wash pewter in a warm solution of synthetic detergent and rub well while drying. Any grease on the surface may be removed by wiping with methylated spirit before washing. Polish pewter with a proprietary metal polish.

Glass

Glass is a transparent, lustrous, and brittle material made from silica or sand. A mixture of pure, fine sand, soda or potash, and other ingredients is carefully measured out. This is called 'batch'. The batch is fed into a furnace and heated to an extremely high temperature, above 1300ºC, where it fuses into molten glass. From the furnace, the molten glass is led away for shaping. After shaping, the glass is cooled by a process called 'annealing', in which the glass travels on a conveyer belt through an annealing oven. In the annealing oven, after the initial re-heating, the glass gradually cools as it passes through. Glass is used in making doors, windows, furniture, vases, lighting fixtures, mirrors, partitions, tableware, kitchenware, and bottles.

Classification of Glass

Glass can be classified in various ways according to its constitution, specific properties, use, and form.

On the basis of constitution and properties

The exact materials from which a type of glass is manufactured can alter its properties, and hence the uses it may be put to. Some of these commonly seen in a hotel property are described in Table 8.3.

In addition to the types of glass mentioned in Table 8.3, silvered glass for mirrors is made by coating one side of a glass panel with silver, or sometimes copper, followed by a coat of paint and a layer of enamel. This backing should not be damaged while cleaning. Silvered glass may be used as large tiles or smaller mosaic pieces or as reflective sheets. Silvered glass should not be soaked in water to clean, but wiped with a damp cloth or a cloth soaked in methylated spirits, which evaporate quickly, before they can damage the backing.

Table 8.3 Types of glass, as per constitution and specific properties

	Soda-lime glass	Lead crystal or lead glass	Borosilicate glass
Ingredients	Sand, soda ash, and limestone	Sand, lead oxide, and potash	Sand and borax
Properties	Inexpensive, ordinary glass	An attractive glass, with fine lustre (due to the lead oxide added) and brilliance; softer than soda-lime glass, and can be cut easily	Hard, heat-resistant (since borax cuts down the rate of expansion when glass is heated)
Use	For inexpensive, flat or hollow glassware—tumblers, plates, cups, saucers, ashtrays, bottles, shelves, windows, pictures, and mirrors	For expensive hollow glassware—bowls, drinking glasses, and vases	For ovenware, flameproof glass cookware

On the basis of use and form

Another way to classify some of the commonly used types of glass is according to form and function, which depend on the way the glass is made. These are listed in Figure 8.1.

Flat glass Flat glass is usually soda-lime glass and is used in making windows, tabletops, and shelves. Flat glass does not allow ultraviolet rays to pass through. Flat glass can be of two types.

Sheet or plate glass Sheet glass is drawn continuously from the molten mass and passed through an annealing tower, after which it can be cut to the desired lengths. The faster the sheet is drawn, the thinner the glass will be. Sometimes there are flaws in the sheet, so that a certain amount of distortion occurs. This type of glass needs to be polished after annealing. Thus, it is used as ordinary window and picture glass.

Float glass This type of glass does not require polishing after annealing. It provides clear, undistorted transparency and is used in shop windows, mirrors, and protective covering for furniture.

Fibreglass Glass can be manufactured as a textile fibre, which may be used for making curtains and fire blankets. Fibreglass may also be manufactured as rigid sheets of plastic or other material with glass filaments embedded for strength. These sheets can be moulded and are used for sanitaryware, furniture, and wall panels. Fiberglass is fire-proof, impermeable, and resistant to damage by pests, sunlight, or air.

Obscured glass This is a type actually derived from sheet or float glass. It is textured on one side, so that some light passes through and some is blocked or distorted, so that the material is not entirely transparent. The pattern is produced when molten glass is made to flow from the furnace between embossed rollers. Obscured glass is used in making bathroom windows and for screening areas where privacy or diffused light is desired.

Hollow glassware This is produced by blowing, moulding, and pressing molten glass into the desired shapes. Casts or moulds of wood or iron are often used for shaping the glass. The moulds may be patterned, giving an imitation 'cut-glass' effect, which is very even and smooth-edged, unlike the real thing. Blown glass shapes may be less regular and call for more skill in the person using a pipe to literally 'blow' the glass bubble into shape before it solidifies.

Safety glass This is another kind of glass that is made from sheet or float glass in various ways.

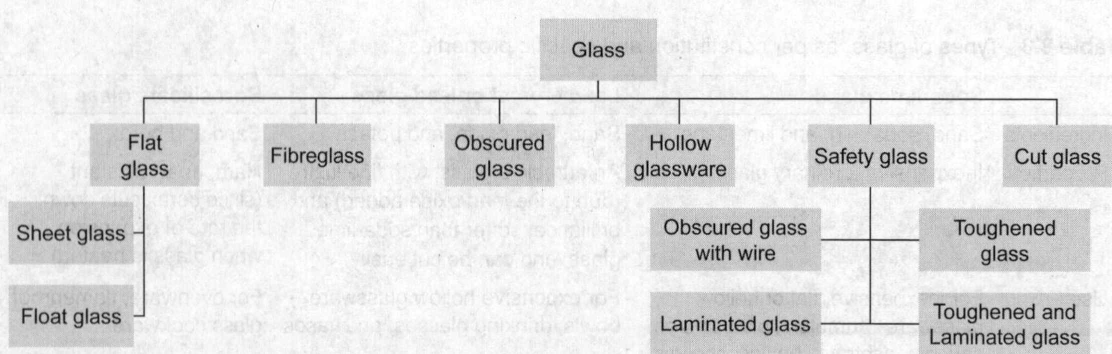

Fig. 8.1 Types of glass, classified according to use and form

Obscured glass with wire Wire is incorporated in obscured glass during the rolling process. If broken, the glass pieces will be held in place by the wire until knocked out of the 'frame' for repair.

Laminated glass This consists of two thin sheets of glass with transparent plastic sandwiched between them. If a laminated glass sheet breaks, the glass pieces will adhere to the plastic layer.

Toughened glass This is made by heating the glass sheet to a temperature just below softening point and then cooling the surface rapidly. As a result, a skin is formed, which, if the glass breaks, will cause the pieces to shatter into tiny, harmless fragments that will be less likely to fall out of its frame as their weight is easily supported.

Toughened and laminated glass This safety glass is made by the combination of the aforementioned two methods of laminating and toughening. This combination creates a glass five times tougher than other safety glasses.

Cut glass This is produced by hand-cutting shaped glass articles using abrasive copper wheels that rotate at a very high speed. The 'cuts' have a matt surface in the beginning from being ground, but become highly reflective when polished. Cut glass is polished by treating the entire article with acid. Hand-cut lead crystal glass has prismatic grooves that emit rainbow-coloured reflections. This glass is expensive and used for chandeliers, decanters, vases, and quality table glassware. Glass can also be decorated by the somewhat similar process of etching. In this process, the article is coated with a protective wax and a pattern is cut into the wax with a steel needle. On immersing the article in an acid bath, the acid eats into the unprotected patterned areas.

Cleaning Procedures for Glass

The discussion that follows takes into account most of the glass objects you are likely to find on a hotel property.

Flat glass Even slight marks and smudges show prominently on glass surfaces. Therefore, glass surfaces, especially flat sheets, require frequent cleaning. Dusting should be done daily with a lint-free cloth. Damp dusting needs to be done whenever necessary. Light soiling and greasy fingerprints should be wiped away with a solution of vinegar and water (1:1) or a solution of 9 ml liquid ammonia in approximately 1 litre of warm water. Glass cleaners applied with a sponge also clean glass effectively. For cleaning larger surfaces, a small window squeegee may be used. Stubborn marks on mirrors—such as toothpaste deposits, hair-spray, and make-up—should be removed by wiping with a cloth moistened with methylated spirit. Newsprint contains an effective solvent, therefore, newspaper can be used to remove marks from windows too. Use a lint-free cloth to dry the glass surface afterwards.

Hollow glassware and other glass articles Textured or engraved glassware should be cleaned whenever necessary, using a soft nylon brush. Abrasives should be avoided. Discoloured or stained bottles and vases can be cleaned using a mixture of crushed eggshells, synthetic detergent, and warm water. For jars and bottles, a mixture of construction sand and water can also be used to remove discolouration. Alternatively, clean by filling them one-fourth full with a mixture of vinegar and water (1:1) and add a few potato pieces, gently shaking till the marks disappear. To remove lime deposits from hard water in water jugs, vases, and tumblers, soak the items in distilled water for an hour, scrub with a nylon scrubber and synthetic detergent solution, and rinse with water. Dry the articles with a lint-free cloth.

Chandeliers Cut-glass chandeliers are delicate, expensive, and therefore used mainly in lobbies, banquet halls, and VIP suites. Cleaning chandeliers is a time-consuming, laborious process; but it should be done with utmost care since parts from a chandelier, once broken, may not be easy to replace. For cleaning purposes, chandeliers are taken down, dismantled piece by piece, and dipped into a warm solution of synthetic detergent. Each piece is then gently cleaned with a nylon scrubber and rinsed in clean warm water. A second rinsing is done in a mixture of one teaspoon liquid ammonia in 2½ litres of water. This results in a brilliant sparkle. Alternatively, surgical spirit can also be used for the final wipe.

Another method, which is more efficient, uses an upholstery shampooing machine. The machine sprays a detergent solution through a fine nozzle with enough pressure to clean each prism. The dripping wash water is collected in a catch basin installed below the chandelier.

Polishing Procedures for Glass

Application of glass polish or spray-on furniture polish for polishing glass is effective but expensive. Polishing glass with damp chamois leather or simulated skins also gives good results, and is cheaper. The daily polishing after a cleaning may be done with just a lint-free cloth, however.

Plastic

Plastics are resinous synthetic polymers that have the following qualities, advantageous and disadvantageous:

- They are light in weight.
- They are quiet in use.
- They are resistant to most chemicals.
- They are non-conductors of electricity.
- They are easy to clean.
- They are largely non-absorbent, except thermoplastics, which absorb grease.
- They are resistant to moths and other pests.
- They are available in attractive colours.
- They are on the whole reasonably priced.
- They can be scratched if harsh abrasives are used on them.
- They have a tendency to discolour and crack.
- They produce toxic fumes on burning.
- They attract dust due to static electricity.
- They are non-biodegradable.

Plastics have become one of the most widely used groups of surfaces in homes and commercial establishments—including hotels—today. In the hospitality industry alone, they are used in making furniture, wall coverings, floor coverings, cleaning equipment, protective coatings, and utensils.

Types of Plastics

Plastics may be of two types according to their properties—thermosetting plastics and thermoplastics.

Thermosetting plastics

These are hard plastics that are moulded by heat and pressure and do not usually soften when they are reheated. Examples of thermosetting plastics are melamine, phenolics, and laminates.

Melamine This group of plastics is used in making tableware, trays, laminated worktops, wall panels, and shelves.

Phenolics These are used in making buckets, trays, telephones, door handles, electrical fittings, and laminates. Phenolic plastics are not affected even by boiling in water, so that they are suitable for making kitchenware.

Laminates Melamine, phenolics, and other plastic resins are together used to produce plastic laminates. Laminates are manufactured by subjecting layers of paper impregnated with plastic resins, such as phenolics or melamine, to high temperature and great pressure. A texture may also be introduced in laminates. Plastic laminates may be stuck directly to wall surfaces, to plywood, or to other supporting material. They may also be used for making wall panels, countertops, and furniture.

Thermoplastics

These are soft plastics that soften when exposed to heat and harden again when cool. Most of the plastic materials used in hotels fall under this group. Some thermoplastics are extremely heat-sensitive while others may withstand higher temperatures. Thermo-plastics include acrylics, acetal resins, cellulose acetate and nitrate (as nitrocellulose esters), polyamides, polyesters, polyethylenes, polypropylenes, polystyrenes, polyurethane foams, polytetrafluoro ethylene (PTFE, otherwise known by the trademark Teflon®), polyvinyl chloride (PVC) derivatives, acrylonitriles, and some other plastics produced as synthetic fibres. Properties and uses of several common thermoplastics are given in Table 8.4.

Cleaning and Maintenance Procedures

Plastic surfaces are easy to clean and maintain. Daily damp-dusting should be done since plastic attracts dust due to static electricity. Light soilage can be removed by wiping with a warm solution of synthetic detergent, followed by rinsing and air-drying. Never rub plastics with a dry cloth, as this increases their static electricity and makes them attract more dust. Textured surfaces need mild scrubbing with a soft brush. Stains should be removed by rubbing with a cloth soaked in methylated spirit. Small soiled items may occasionally be soaked in a mild solution of hypochlorite bleach. Where plastics come into contact with food, such as in refrigerators, a solution of 9 ml sodium bicarbonate to 300 ml water (and not synthetic detergents) should be used for cleaning. The surface should then be rinsed thoroughly with clean warm water. Synthetic detergents are avoidable since foods may absorb their odour.

Given below are some precautions that will help in the maintenance of plastics:

- Do not expose to direct heat, such as from cigarette butts, hot plates, and so on.
- Do not use harsh abrasives.
- Do not buff with a dry cloth.
- Do not apply strong acids or alkalis.
- Do not drag heavy objects over plastic surfaces.
- Do not allow them to suffer heavy impacts, as this can damage some plastics.

Table 8.4 Common thermoplastics

Name/Group	Properties	Uses
Acrylics	Lightweight; strong; scratch easily; damaged by very hot liquids	Sanitaryware, trays, telephones, furniture, and protective panels
Acetal resins	Resist boiling, chipping, and scratching	Knife handles
Cellulose acetate and nitrates	Pliable	Brush handles, door handles, light fittings, and lamp shades
Polyamides	Withstand sterilization temperatures (especially nylon)	Kitchenware, knife handles, bristles of brushes, curtain fittings, and abrasive pads
Polyesters	Lightweight, water resistant, and resist colour change	Trays, lampshades, and, when reinforced with glass fibres, sinks, furniture, and seamless floorings
Polyethylenes	Can be manufactured as pliable or rigid; rigid form withstands boiling	Rigid form used in manufacture of sanitaryware, kitchenware, trays, and lamp shades

Ceramics

Ceramics are made from sand and clay. Different proportions and types of clay are mixed with other ingredients to produce various kinds of ceramics (see Figure 8.2). After mixing the ingredients and shaping, the clay is fired at a high temperature to render it hard. The article is then glazed and fired for a second time. If a glaze or sealer is not applied, these articles remain highly porous. Ceramics are used for making sanitary fittings, drain pipes, vases, floor tiles, wall tiles and finishes, cooking utensils, and crockery. Ceramics should be handled with care since they are prone to cracking and chipping. Ceramic plates used in hotels usually have rolled edges to avoid the problem of chipping at the rim. Sanitas handles (where the entire article, with its handle, is moulded together as one piece rather than being attached just before firing, which can result in cracks) are preferred for jugs and cups in hotels since these are not as easily broken.

Common Types of Ceramics

As Figure 8.2 shows, there can be quite a lot of variation in the ceramic's final qualities, depending on the proportion of ingredients and the manufacturing process.

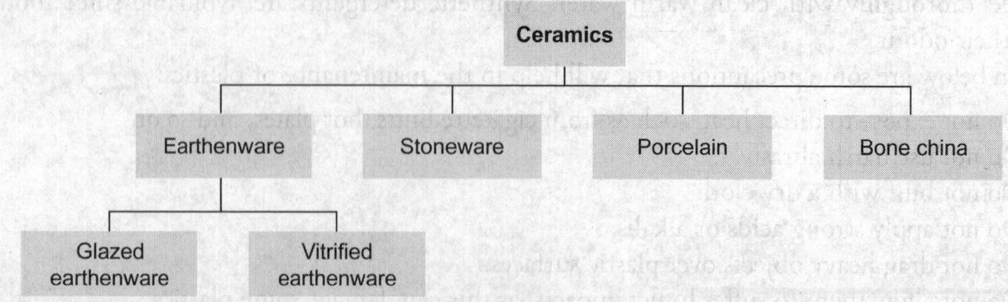

Fig. 8.2 Various types of ceramics

Earthenware This thick, heavy, and highly porous material is moulded out of clay and baked. It is used in making jugs, bowls, vases, and ashtrays. Earthenware should be handled with care, as it chips and breaks easily. This type of ceramic may also be glazed or vitrified.

Glazed earthenware These contain a large amount of a fine white clay called ball clay. This makes them thick and opaque. A glaze is applied on the surface as this clay structure is highly porous.

Vitrified earthenware This is also known as vitreous china. It is very hard and heavy because of its higher flint content. Compared to other earthenware, this is fired at a higher temperature, so that consistent and complete fusion takes place. Vitrified articles are thus stronger, heavier, less easily chipped, and more expensive than other kinds of earthenware.

Terracotta Made from fine clay baked, this type of earthenware is usually left unglazed. Terracotta articles are naturally brownish red in colour. The material is used for pottery, ashtrays, vases, and ornamental building materials.

Stoneware This is similar to earthenware but has a higher stone content. It is also fired at a higher temperature than earthenware, resulting in a stronger material. Since the material is impervious, glazing is not required. Many stoneware articles are flame- and oven-proof.

Porcelain This is made from kaolin (china clay) and china stone or feldspar. Unlike bone china, however, it does not contain calcinated bone. Porcelain has a translucent body and a transparent glaze. It is an extremely hard and strong ceramic. Since it is extremely expensive, it is not in much used in hotel establishments. Porcelain can, however, be used to make cups, saucers, and other types of crockery.

Bone china This is different from porcelain in that it contains bone ash. It also has less feldspar and more china clay than porcelain. The addition of bone makes the clay easier to work and gives it strength. Bone china is fired at very high temperatures, making it very thin but strong and impervious because of the complete fusion that takes place. Harsh abrasives should be avoided as designs are often applied to the outer surface of this material. Bone china is used to make fine cups, saucers, and other types of crockery.

Cleaning Procedures

Ceramics should be handled with care during cleaning since they are easily cracked and chipped. Extremely hot or too cold water should be avoided. A warm, neutral synthetic detergent solution should be used for cleaning ceramics. The articles must be rinsed thoroughly and dried with a lint-free duster. Stains may be removed by rubbing with a damp cloth to which sodium bicarbonate has been applied.

Wood

Wood is hard, compact, fibrous, and porous. Good wood makes for a rich, warm, and beautiful surface. It is an extremely versatile surface material, with its varied colours and different grain patterns, and is used throughout hotel establishments. Being a porous material, wood absorbs water as well as dust. It is also prone to fungal attacks and pest infestations.

Classification of Wood

This categorization is based on the origin as well as the treatment that wood has undergone before use. Wood is used in hotels in various forms, listed in Figure 8.3.

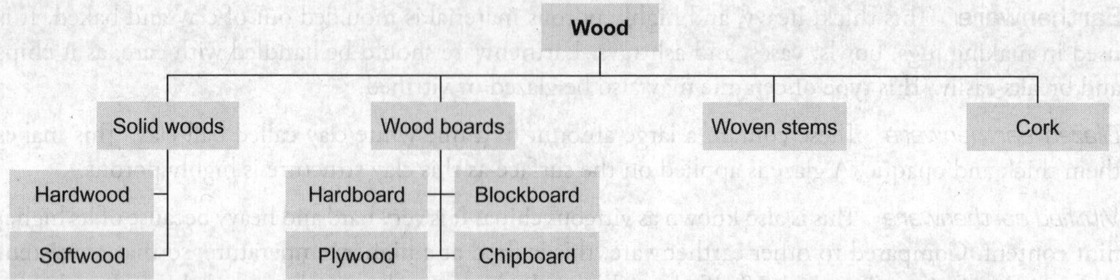

Fig. 8.3 Various forms of wood in common use

Solid woods

Depending on its strength and resilience, it may be hard or soft wood. Irrespective of the kind of wood, it is important to keep in mind that all of them are absorbent and will require different surface protection treatments, depending on their use.

Hardwood These are obtained from broad-leaved, deciduous trees. The most popular hardwoods are teak, oak, ash, beech, birch, walnut, and rosewood. They are very strong and heavy, and thus can stand a good amount of wear and tear. Hardwoods have a more refined grain and shorter fibres than softwoods. Because of these properties, hardwoods do not dent or splinter easily and are preferred in the construction of floors, walls, furniture, and furnishings. Hardwoods are expensive, however, and are nowadays more often used as a veneer on other wood products.

Softwood These are obtained from coniferous trees. Commonly used softwoods are pine, fir, cedar, and rubberwood. Compared to hardwoods, softwoods are lighter in weight, cheaper, more prone to wear and tear, indentations, grooves, and splintering. The colours of softwoods vary with individual tree species, but in general they are lighter in colour than most hardwoods. Softwoods do not have much visual appeal and are therefore in out-of-view areas as far as possible in most traditional places. They are also used in the construction of sub-floors, ceilings, joists, and furniture.

Wood boards

A variety of wood boards are available at significantly cheaper rates than solid wood planks. These are much lighter than solid wood and most have undergone treatments such as termite-proofing and waterproofing.

Hardboard This is a type of thin, flexible board made of compressed and processed wood-pulp fibre. It is smooth on one side and has a mesh-like texture on the reverse. Hardboard is used to make door panels, picture backings, cupboard and wardrobe backings, bases of drawers, and as a base for floor tiles.

Plywood This type of board is manufactured by gluing together many thin sheets of hardwood, which are termed 'plies'. The bonding is done in such a way that the grain of each ply is perpendicular to the grain of the sheets adjacent to it. Plywood is very strong, yet can be shaped during manufacture. Since it does not have good visual appeal compared to solid wood, it is often veneered with hardwood or laminate. Plywood is used to make tables, desks, shelves, countertops, and cupboards.

Blockboard Each blockboard is made up of plywood veneers laid over a core of wood strips. The inner strips of wood may be upto 3 cm in thickness, making the board strong and durable. Blockboard is used for making worktops, tabletops, and shelves.

Chipboard This type of board is manufactured from compressed wood chips and synthetic resin. It is strong and heavy. Like plywood, this too is often veneered or laminated. Chipboard is used for making closets, cabinets, drawers, wardrobes, and worktops.

Woven stems

Cane and wicker are included in this class. Cane is derived from the hollow, jointed stems of giant reeds and grasses (such as bamboo) or the solid stems of slender palms (such as rattan). Wicker is typically derived from the shoots (osiers) of willow plants. Both materials are used in making woven items such as bread-baskets, flower-baskets, mats, trays, stools, sofas, chairs, tables, and beds. Cane and wicker products are usually cheaper than solid wood.

Cork

This is a material obtained from the outer, light-brown bark of the cork oak. The bark is ground into large granules, mixed with synthetic resin, pressed into sheets at high temperature and pressure, and then cut into tiles or strips of varying widths. It is possible to achieve colour variations by the application of different pressures and temperatures. Cork has a warm and restful appearance. It also has excellent acoustic properties. The disadvantages of cork are that it is extremely porous; it easily dents, burns, and stains; and granules may come loose. Because of the high porosity of natural cork, it is now marketed with various types of coatings. The different varieties are waxed cork, resin-reinforced waxed cork, and vinyl-coated cork. Cork is used to make bathmats (though these are not typically used in hotels as they cannot be cleaned often), noticeboards, floor coverings, and wall coverings.

Protective Treatments for Wood

Wood surfaces often require extra protection since they are mostly porous and absorb moisture. They also tend to get stained and scratched. The most common treatments are listed in this section, followed by a section on the maintenance and cleaning requirements for various types of wood, regardless of protection.

Beeswax This is the comb material secreted by bees. It is applied to solid wood furniture and floors. To be effective as a protective finish, several coats of it need to be applied. It should be allowed to dry and rubbed in well to get a good gloss.

Varnish This is a clear, pale solution of a resinous substance such as amber, copal, or shellac dissolved in oil, turpentine, or alcohol. Either natural or synthetic resins may be used to make varnish. On drying, varnish forms a hard and transparent film on the wood surface. The finish may be glossy or matt. Varnish is most commonly applied on wooden floors, furniture, and doors.

Lacquer Shellac or cellulose lacquer is a durable finish applied to solid wood furniture. The finish may be glossy or matt. It is damaged by water, heat, and solvents.

Oil Tung oil or linseed oil.

Polyurethane finish Polyurethane may be applied as a matt or glossy finish to wood. Two to three coats are usually needed, rubbing with fine glasspaper before each coat. After applying polyurethane, the wood should be polished with beeswax to smooth down the polyurethane finish. In case of new wood, polyurethane should be applied after the application of shellac or a cellulose sealer.

French polish This is a solution of shellac and methylated spirit. It is applied on small furniture items made of solid wood. However, this finish is easily damaged by water, heat, and solvents.

Paint Essentially, paint is made up of a pigment dissolved in an organic binder. The function of paint may be to provide protection or decoration or both. The unique property of paint is that it also lends colour along with protection to the wood surface. Paints are available for various effects, such as glossy, matt, silk, and pearl. This finish, however, is damaged by abrasives and heat.

Maintenance of Wood

While all the finishes above render varying degrees of protection to a wood surface, regular cleaning and care are still needed to ensure optimum performance and long life. This includes taking into account certain maintenance issues with wood, which may require small repairs. That said, wood remains a very versatile and fairly resilient surface for its aesthetic appeal and price.

Care and cleaning procedures for wooden surfaces Wood, being porous, deteriorates in contact with an excess of water. Therefore, the least possible amount of water should be used for cleaning wood. Always dry-dust the surface first with an impregnated mop, or vacuum-clean. Then remove excess soiling by damp-dusting in case of small articles and light damp-mopping for larger surfaces. Wooden floor surfaces need to be buffed with a floor polisher two times a week. Spills and stains should be removed immediately from wood surfaces so that they are not absorbed into the surface (see Table 8.5). Cork should only be dusted or vacuumed daily.

Cane and wicker also need to be vacuumed daily as dust may get entrapped and deposited in the nooks of the weave. They should then be wiped once a week with a solution of warm water and baking soda or borax, followed by a wiping with cold saline solution (1 tablespoon salt in 1 litre water). The last wipe with saline stiffens, bleaches, and removes stains from the strands. The items should then be left to dry in open air.

Wood laminates such as Formica and Sunmica need to be cleaned with a microfibre dust mop daily. Once in a month, the surface needs to be damp mopped with a microfibre mop with the cleaning solution sprayed on it. Stains must be dealt with immediately.

Table 8.5 Surface repairs on wood

Problem	Repair
Watermarks	To remove white rings and spots caused by water, wipe the marks with a soft cloth impregnated with a little methylated spirit. If this method is not successful, mix equal quantities of methylated spirit, pure turpentine, and linseed oil; shake the mixture well; and rub it over the marks very gently with fine wire-wool.
Ink stains	Apply domestic bleach with fine wire-wool and immediately wipe with a clean cloth. If this fails, apply a little vinegar with fine wire-wool, rubbing in the direction of the grain; leave for an hour; wipe with methylated spirit to remove all traces of the acid; and leave the surface to dry.
Alcohol	Wipe immediately. Rub with olive oil. If the stain persists, mix ash in the olive oil and rub lightly in a circular motion.
Heat marks	Rub with equal quantities of raw linseed oil and pure turpentine.
Cigarette burns	On unpolished wood, a slight burn may be removed by sanding with fine glasspaper. For wax finishes, rub the mark hard with turpentine, following the direction of the grain.
Scratches	Surface scratches may be removed by applying a mixture of equal quantities of methylated spirit, pure turpentine, and linseed oil. The mixture should be shaken well and applied with a soft cloth.

Faux Wood

Faux wood is made from a combination of several components such as synthetic polymers (poly vinyl chloride or polypropylene), veneers, and adhesives. Exposure to ultraviolet radiation is damaging to most plastics, hence many exterior faux wood products incorporate chemical compounds that help to prolong the life of the material. The products are moulded or extruded and given the texture and colour of genuine wood. Faux wood siding is made from fibre cement, which is a mixture of sand, cement, and cellulose fibres that are textured and coloured to mimic real wood. Faux wood effectively imitates the look of wood while being very low priced. It also stands up to harsh environmental conditions such as exposure to sunlight and coastal climates, better than real wood. It is commonly used to make blinds, furniture, flooring, decorative home beams, and various types of sidings.

Care and Cleaning of Faux Wood

The procedure for cleaning faux wood is different than cleaning real wood. Faux wood items should be dusted with a static duster and then damp wiped. Faux wood flooring should be swept daily with a dry mop and damp mopped to remove dirt and dust. A neutral detergent may be added to the mop water. It is important to avoid harsh chemicals that may discolour faux wood.

Stone

A variety of natural stones are used as hard surfaces in hotel establishments. The popular ones are marble, sandstone, granite, quartzite, and slate. Stones are used mainly as floor finishes and external wall surfaces. Other areas where they may be found are tabletops, countertops and tops of vanity units, furniture, decorative idols, and ashtrays. Stones such as marble are often used as flooring and on walls in luxury bathrooms and foyers. The properties and uses of stone, as flooring material, is discussed in detail in Chapter 27.

Natural Stones in Use

Some natural stones commonly used in hotels are as follows.

Marble This is metamorphosed and crystallized limestone. It is available in many colours and patterns—white, black, grey, green, brown, and pink. It can be given a glossy or a matt finish.

Sandstone This sedimentary rock is composed of compressed sand.

Granite This is a granular, crystalline stone composed of quartz, feldspar, and mica.

Quartzite This is a compact granular stone made up of silica.

Slate This is a grey or blue-grey stone formed when layers of mud and silt build up and solidify over millions of years. These layers allow slate to be easily made into slabs.

Maintenance and Cleaning

While the maintenance and care of stones will also be dealt with in greater detail in Chapter 27, here are the basics on cleaning stone surfaces and objects.

Stone surfaces may be cleaned using synthetic detergent and hot water. Stains may be removed using fine abrasives. For large areas, a wet-pickup vacuum cleaner may be used. Use of acids and strong alkalis should be avoided, as they may cause pits on the surface.

Faux Stone

No other material conveys the feel of tradition and solidity in hotels better than stone. But stone is expensive and hence the popularity of faux stones for walls and flooring. Faux stone is available in the form of manufactured stone and faux stone veneers. Manufactured stone is made from cement, aggregates, iron oxides and other pigments, and is moulded, textured, and finished to look like genuine stone, whereas imitation stones are made up of a very high-density polymer. Manufactured stone comes in individual mounds that fit together with mortar, whereas faux stone veneers come in thin panels for easy installation. Manufactured stones are about 30% lighter than the real stone, whereas faux stone veneers are only a few pounds per panel.

Care and Cleaning of Faux Stone

Before cleaning the surface, first one should confirm the material with which the surface is made. Second, the cleaning procedure and the cleaning agent should be tried out in a smaller area for any adverse effect. Manufactured stone is cleaned by scrubbing gently with a brush dipped in neutral detergent and then wiping with a damp mop. For faux stone veneer, damp wiping with a mild detergent followed by damp wiping with water should take care of most residues. Harsh chemicals should never be used else the surface may lose colour and finish.

Leather and Leatherette

Leather is made from the skins of various animals—including sheep, goats, pigs, and cattle—by tanning or a similar process. It is one of the most durable and versatile of all natural materials. The skins are treated in various ways to give different varieties of leather, ranging from the soft, flexible types such as suede and kid to the tougher types such as hide and sturdy varieties of pigskin (see Table 8.6). Leather can be

Table 8.6 Various types of leathers in common use

Leather	Uses	Cleaning
Buckskin	Shoes and belts	If heavily soiled, sponge with soap and water, then apply a proprietary white cleaner.
Calf and similar shiny-surfaced leathers	Shoes and handbags	Good quality wax polish cream may be used, but do not apply too lavishly.
Chamois ('wash' leather) and simulated sheepskins	Gloves, cleaning windows and glassware, and silver polishing	If heavily soiled, rinse in warm water and then knead in warm soapy water. When clean, immerse in fresh soapy water, squeeze gently, pull into shape, and hang up without rinsing. The leather should be rumpled between the hands when still slightly wet to soften it. Never squeeze if it is dry and stiff, or it may crack.
Crocodile, alligator, lizard, and snakeskin	Shoes and handbags	Remove dust with a soft brush and apply neutral shoe cream.

dyed in a variety of colours and is used for belts, shoes, gloves, purses, wallets, luggage, upholstery, desk tops, and book bindings.

Leather is expensive and should be kept supple to prevent cracking. Leather also picks up oil and grease readily. General cleaning of leather involves daily dusting or suction cleaning. In case of soiling, wipe the leather with a soft cloth wrung out of warm water and mild synthetic detergent. Follow with damp-dusting with clean water and then dry thoroughly. Occasionally, leather may be polished with a good furniture polish cream to keep it supple. Solvents should not be used on leather as they will stiffen it.

Leatherette is faux leather or artificial leather usually made by covering a natural or synthetic fabric with vinyl and is thus considerably lower in cost than original leather. It is mainly used in making upholstery covers and classic book bindings. It tends to get sticky in hot weather as it is primarily plastic. Being non porous, synthetic leather is easier to clean, needing just a damp wipe.

Rubber

Rubber is a group of natural or synthetic substances characterized by elasticity, water repellence, and electrical resistance.

How Rubber is Made

Natural rubber is obtained from the milky white fluid called latex found in many plants. In the manufacture of rubber articles, the crude rubber is treated with compounding ingredients in several mixing machines. The mixture is then applied mechanically to a base or is shaped. The coated or shaped mixture is placed in moulds and vulcanized.

Types of Rubber

Not all rubber is vulcanized (or 'cured'), however. Vulcanization is not a necessary step in rubber processing or manufacture, but is often used to impart strength to the final product. Also, there are other processes of making synthetic rubber or treating rubber for a different finish. Depending on the process of manufacture, rubber can be of the following types.

Crude rubber Uncured rubber is used to make crepe rubber, which is used in insulating blankets and so on.

Vulcanized rubber Rubber products are vulcanized at high temperatures and pressures in the presence of vulcanizing agents such as sulphur, selenium, and tellurium. The proportion of sulphur varies from 1:40 in soft-rubber goods to as much as 1:1 in hard rubber. Cold vulcanization is used for soft, thin rubber goods such as gloves, mattress protectors, and other sheets. Vulcanized rubber is also used in making conveyor belts, rollers for mop-wringers, rainwear, shower curtains, and diving gear.

Foam rubber This is manufactured directly from latex by using emulsified compounding ingredients. The mix is then whipped mechanically in a frothing machine to make up a foam containing millions of air bubbles. This foam is poured into moulds and vulcanized by high heat to make such articles as mattresses and seat cushions.

Synthetic rubber This is produced from unsaturated hydrocarbons by the process of polymerization. Of relevance to the housekeeping department are the synthetic foam rubbers used mainly for upholstery, mattresses, and pillows.

Maintenance of Rubber Products

Rubber, especially the vulcanized variety is a fairly sturdy material. However, given here are also a few precautions to be taken while cleaning and using rubber articles.

Cleaning Procedures for Rubber

Clean rubber with a neutral detergent solution and rinse with water. Rubber is a hygienic material and is not prone to mould growth or pest infestations. However, it is sensitive to grease, strong alkalis, and excessive heat. Hot water should not be used in cleaning since the rubber will soften.

SUMMARY

Housekeeping staff must have an insight into the types, composition, care, and maintenance of all hard surfaces they are responsible for cleaning. They must possess a thorough knowledge of the chemical agents that can or cannot be used on these surfaces. This chapter deals with the types, composition, and cleaning of hard surfaces such as metals, their alloys, glass, plastics, ceramics, wood, stone, leather, leatherette, and rubber. Where applicable, ways of protecting the surfaces by application of different finishes is also discussed. Different sources and authors give other, alternative methods of cleaning the surfaces mentioned. However, one must use methods that are tried, tested, and approved by experts. Many hard surfaces are expensive and, in most cases, once damaged, they are not easily restored to their original appearance and function. It would not be fair to clean them by trial-and-error methods. If a new method is to be tried, do it on a very small area of the surface, which is not in use or view. As technology advances, specific cleaners have become available for cleaning each of the various hard surfaces found in a hotel. The executive housekeeper must balance the cost of these cleaning agents and the degree of cleanliness they provide as against other, more traditional cleaning agents. It should, however, be kept in mind that there should be no compromise in maintaining the standards of cleanliness at any cost.

KEY TERMS

Abrasive Substances or chemicals that depend on their rubbing or scratching action to clean dirt and grit from hard surfaces. For example, sandpaper, steel wool, powdered pumice, and so on.

Acoustics The properties of materials, usually those used on ceilings, walls, and floors, that determine how well they absorb sounds.

Alloy A mixture composed of two or more metals. For example, brass is an alloy of copper and zinc.

Black lead Graphite.

Chamois Chamois is a kind of leather used mainly in cleaning and polishing. Originally, skins of the chamois antelope were used, but now they are usually skivers, that is, split sheepskin or simulated skins. Chamois is used wet for cleaning windows and mirrors. It is also used dry as a polishing cloth for silver.

Ductile Having a property that allows certain metals to be drawn into wires.

EPNS Electroplated nickel silver, which is made by electroplating nickel silver blanks dipped in a solution of silver salts. On electrolysis, silver coats the blanks.

Feldspar A white or flesh-red mineral ore containing aluminium and silicates in various proportions.

Flannel A plain-weave cotton fabric with a brushed or napped surface.

Glasspaper A thick paper covered with glass dust and used for polishing.

Glaze As applied on clay articles, this is basically composed of glass-forming minerals (silica or boron) combined with stiffeners (such as clay) and melting agents (such as lead or soda).

Jeweller's rouge A pink oxide of iron used as a fine abrasive for polishing silver and so on.

Kaolin (also called China clay) A fine white clay produced through the decomposition of feldspar.

Laminate Material manufactured by fixing together layer upon layer of plastic to get a rigid or flexible material.

Leatherette Artificial or faux leather.

Lint-free Refers to fabrics that do not shed small fibres as a result of abrasion and wear.

Malleable (of metals) Having a property that allows them to be pressed into sheets.

Precipitated whiting Filtered chalk, used as a mild abrasive.

Sanitas handles Cup and jug handles that are moulded onto the clay bodies. They are not as easily broken as those stuck on just before firing and are, therefore, preferred for use in hotels.

Shellac Shellac is lac melted into thin flakes, refined, and used for making varnish by mixing with alcohol. Lac is a sticky, resinous substance secreted on trees by lac insects.

Spirits of salt Concentrated hydrochloric acid.

Tanning A process by which raw hide is converted into leather by soaking in a liquid containing tannic acid or by the use of certain mineral salts.

Tarnish A discolouration caused by a chemical reaction between a metal and substances found in water, air, and food. Different metals undergo different types of tarnishing. For example, silver darkens; iron gets a brownish-red rust; and copper gets a green tarnish.

Veneer A thin outer coating of finer wood on another wooden surface.

Window squeegee Small, manual cleaning equipment with a rod handle and rubber blade. It acts like a windshield wiper in clearing away excess water from windows while washing.

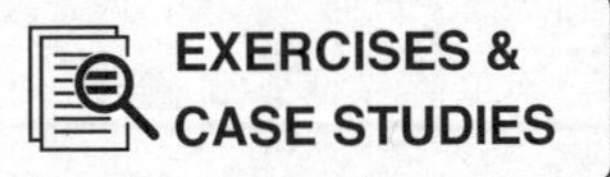

9 Hotel Guestrooms

Learning Objectives

After reading this chapter, you should be able to
- appreciate the importance of the guestroom for a guest
- identify, describe, and draw layouts of different types of guestrooms
- define the guestroom status codes
- perceive the significance of rules and reportables on guest floors
- understand the layout of a guestroom corridor and its importance

Introduction

The guestroom is the main product of a hotel, as it contributes to more than 65% of the total sales, making the profit percentage from room sales very high. The 'sale' of a room means leasing the room for occupation for 24 hours at a pre-determined cost. Thus, a room sold on a particular day earns revenue for that day, and then it can be sold again, and again. Rooms are sometimes referred to as 'highly perishable commodities' as rooms not sold for the day lose out on the revenue for that day. In addition to earning revenues, guestrooms also have a role in the image-building of the hotel.

Guests may stay in a hotel for pleasure, convenience, or from necessity. Whatever the reason for the stay, they will always expect a certain standard of service and comfort. It is hence essential for each and every hotel employee to understand the importance of a guestroom for a guest. The housekeeping staff, in particular, have the responsibility of making the guestroom 'a home away from home' for the guest.

Importance of the Guestroom to a Guest

It is extremely important to understand the expectations of a guest when he/she pays to stay in a room. Providing a guest a *clean and comfortable bed and bath experience* is the essence of hospitality service. People nowadays travel a lot, more than they did earlier, and the expectations from hotels are constantly on the rise. In such a scenario, continuous analysis of guest expectations becomes necessary. Although a hotel is often referred to as 'a home away from home', there would be similarities between

a guest's expectations from a hotel and that from his/her home. These similarities would dictate that the guestrooms be neat, hygienic, comfortable, private, and above all safe. The most important consideration here is that the hotel staff need to understand and respect the guest's expectations from the guestroom and them.

Clean and hygienic room Primarily, a neat room is the basic minimum expectation of any guest, and the staff need to ensure this by laying out fresh linen and presenting a clean room on a daily basis.

Comfortable room A plush bed and a luxurious bath lead to the element of comfort in guestrooms. Hotels usually have wooden or carpeted flooring to add to the comfort. The ambient temperature should be maintained in the guestroom and the guest should be given a choice to modify this temperature.

Safe and private room Safety is a key factor with regard to guestrooms—guests would want the guestroom location to be safe and not accessible to one and all. The doors should have a double locking system operable from inside, along with strict control measures in the hotel with regard to the handling of guestroom keys and master keys. Fire-exit layout maps being placed in the rooms is a necessity as well. There should be minimal staff interaction inside guestrooms as guests consider the guestroom their private haven.

Convenient and functional room If the guest can have things organized at the click of a button, be it food, laundry, or any other service or information, it makes up for convenient, hassle-free stay. Basic necessities in terms of amenities should be well-placed. Internet and Wi-fi connectivity, LED interactive television, and channel music have also become basic necessities to today's traveller. Many hotels provide mood lighting facility, self-operated by the guest by clicking a button. The guest would also expect to be able to get in touch with ancillary departments providing services to guests from the room itself. The various services such as room service, restaurants, housekeeping, valet, and so on should be clearly indicated with explanation and intercom numbers in the literature on the house rules and in the information kits placed in each guestroom. It is increasingly becoming a common practice in upscale hotels, for all types of guest request calls to be handled by a common central services unit.

Well-furnished and decorated room Ergonomically designed and furnished beds and furniture, soothing flooring, and dressed windows add to the comfort and luxurious look of the guestroom. The décor should be calming and help to relax the guest. At the same time the interiors should be decorated in a way to spell luxury since the guests pay a lot and expect it.

Easy access to guest service areas Irrespective of its location, a guestroom should offer easy access to other guest service areas, such as restaurants, gymnasiums, swimming pools, and so on, with clear directions to and from the room or elevator being posted in corridors.

Types of Guestrooms

It used to be customary in many hotels to have rooms of more or less the same standard throughout a property, but that trend is changing now. Guests are now being offered a choice of more expensive rooms with upgraded facilities, as well as the establishment's standard options. Hotels now offer a wide variety of rooms catering to the needs of different types of travellers. These are outlined in Table 9.1.

Sample layouts of the most commonly found types of rooms are presented in Figures 9.1, 9.2, 9.3, 9.4, 9.5, and 9.6. Planning of guestrooms is discussed in detail in Chapter 28 on Facilities Planning and Facilities Management.

Table 9.1 Types of guestrooms

Guestroom type	Description
Single room	A room assigned to one person, having one bed
Twin room	A room with two twin beds meant for one person each
Hollywood twin room	A room with two twin beds but a common headboard, meant for two people. If so desired, the beds can be bridged together to make it appear a single bed
Double room	A room with a double bed for two persons
Triple room	A room assigned to three people, which may have two or more beds
Quad room	A room assigned to four people, which may have two or more beds
Queen room	A room with a queen-size bed
King room	A room with a king-size bed
Double double room/ twin double family room	A room with two double beds, meant for four people
Studio room/extension room	A room with a studio bed
Sico room	A room which has a Murphy or Sico bed or similar (a pull-out or convertible or fold-away bed)
Mini suite/junior suite	A single large room with a bed and a sitting area
Suite room	A combination of one or more bedrooms and a parlour. It may also contain a bar, a small kitchenette, and other facilities
Inter connecting rooms	Rooms with individual entrance doors from the outside and a connecting door between, so that guests can move between rooms without going through the hallway
Adjoining rooms	Room with a common wall but no connecting door
Adjacent rooms	Rooms close to each other, but not necessarily adjoining—perhaps across the hall or corridor from each other
Cabana	A room adjacent to the pool area, with or without sleeping facilities, but with provision for relaxing in a sofa. These are mainly used for changing
Duplex/bi-level suite	A two-storey suite, with parlour and bedrooms connected by a stairway
Efficiency room	A room containing some kitchen facilities
Hospitality suite	A parlour with a connecting bedroom, to be used by guests to entertain his own guests or for companies offering cocktails during conventions, entertaining, and trade shows. A hospitality room usually contains a bar and occasional tables as well. This type of room is let out and charged on an hourly basis
Lanai	A room overlooking a landscaped area, a scenic view, a waterbody, or a garden. It may have a balcony, a patio, or both. This type of room is commonly found in resorts

(Contd.)

Table 9.1 *Contd.*

Guestroom type	Description
Smoking rooms	Rooms in a separated section or floor, well away from non-smoking areas, let-out to guests who opt for smoking in room. The doors of such rooms display a signage of the same. Ashtrays and matches are typical amenities. Smoking rooms are well-ventilated, not connected to the centralised HVAC and feature windows that may be opened and easily cleaned window treatments such as blinds or shutters or heavy cotton curtains. Carpets, rugs and heavy upholstery materials are avoided. Walls are treated with stain and odour blocking primer which helps to eliminate 90% of the smell. Wallpaper is not used since the paper as well as the glue allow smoke to permeate. Porous materials such as wood board are avoided in furniture and surfaces.
Parlour/saloon	A living or sitting room; a room not used as a bedroom
Sample room	A display room that is used for showing merchandise. It may or may not be provided with sleeping facilities
Family room	A room with two double beds, meant for two, three, or four persons
Penthouse	A room that opens onto the roof and may be accompanied by a swimming pool, patio, a tennis court, and other facilities and amenities
Executive room	A room that has a large bedroom with a sitting area, provided with chairs and usually a sofa and coffee table. This type of room typically has a workstation/lounge near the window. This is really a combination bedroom-cum-sitting room

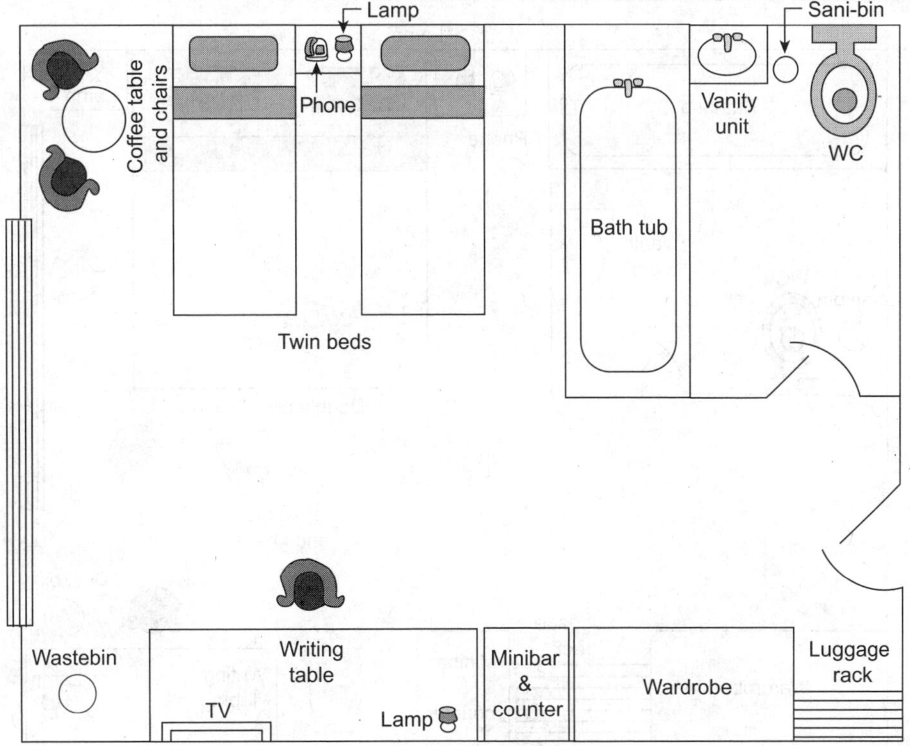

Fig. 9.1 Sample layout of a twin room (not to scale)

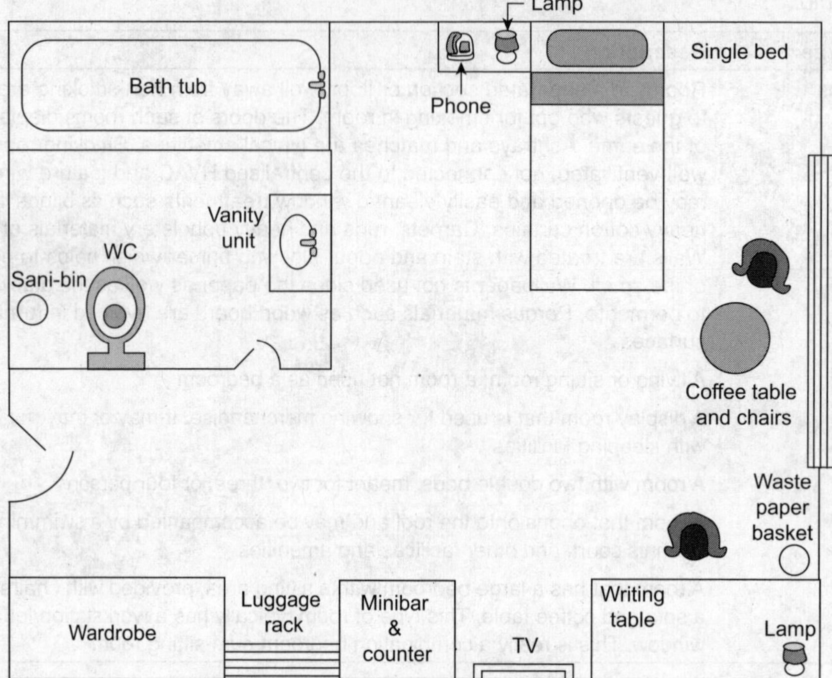

Fig. 9.2 Sample layout of a single room (not to scale)

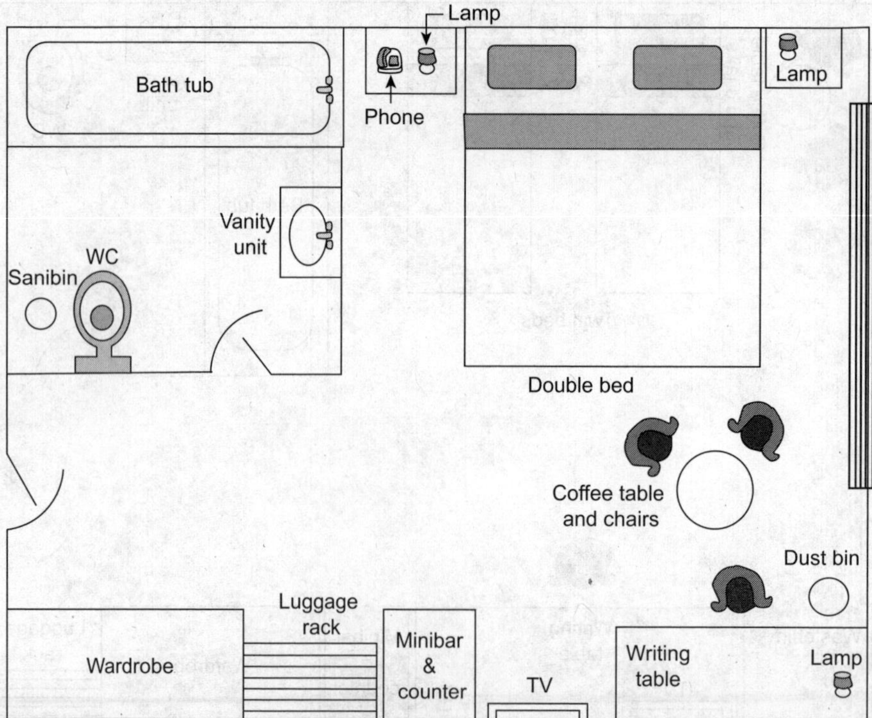

Fig. 9.3 Sample layout of a double room (not to scale)

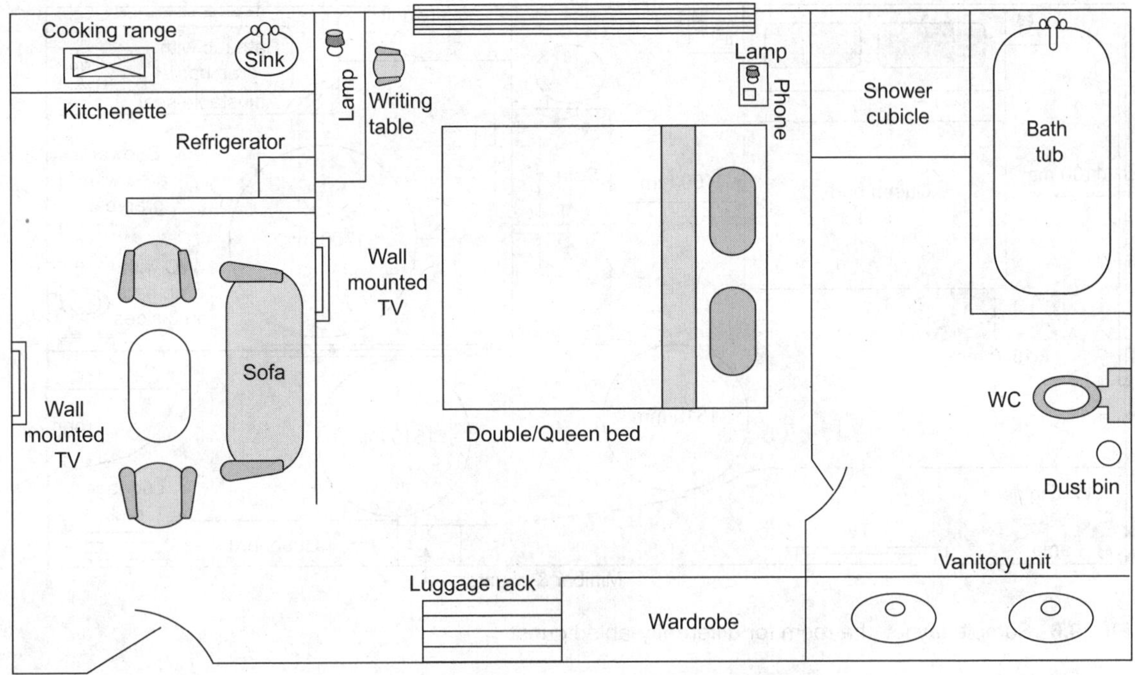

Fig. 9.4 Sample layout of a suite (not to scale)

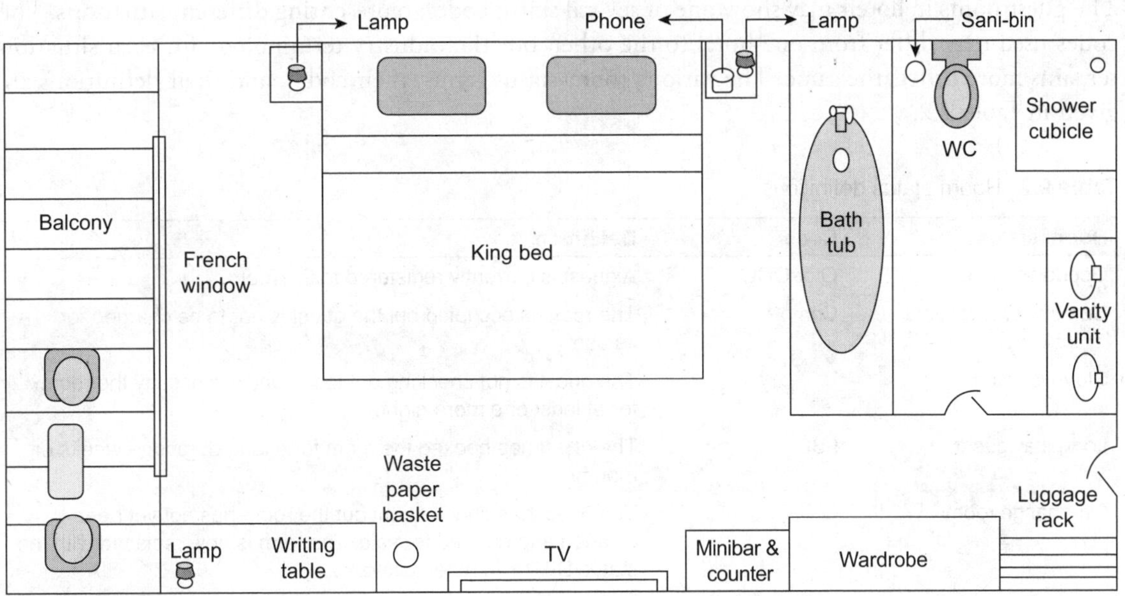

Fig. 9.5 Sample layout of a king room with balcony

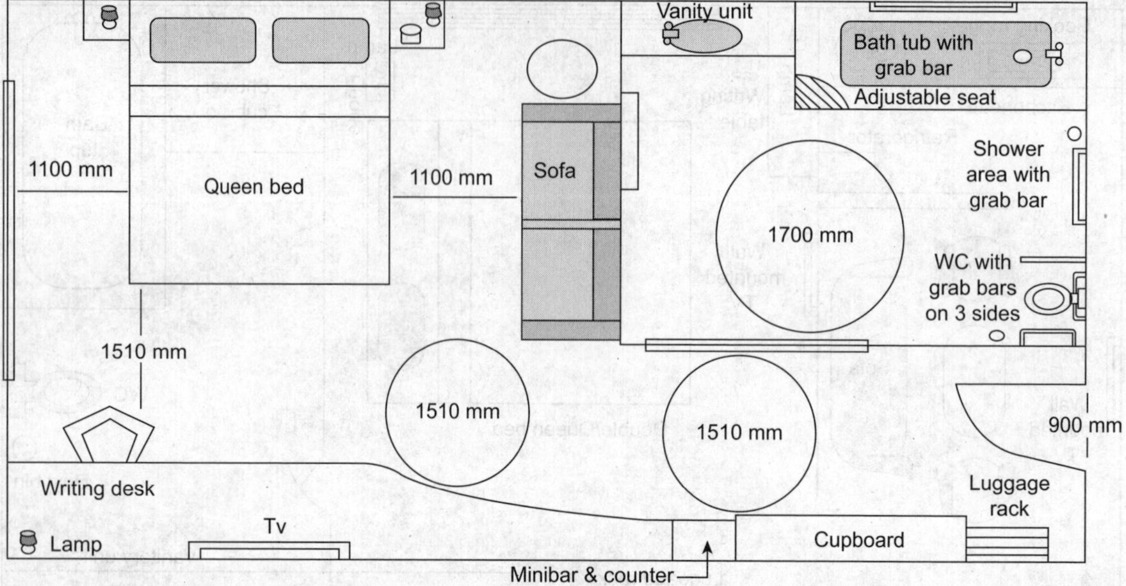

Fig. 9.6 Sample layout of a room for differently-abled guest

Guestroom Status

The guestrooms in hotels may show one of several status codes, representing different situations. The codes used may differ from one hotel to the other, but the industry terminology for each situation remains more or less the same. The various room-status terms, their codes, and their definitions are given in Table 9.2.

Table 9.2 Room status definitions

Room status	Code	Definition
Occupied room	O or OCC	A guest is currently registered to the room.
Complimentary room	Comp.	The room is occupied but the guest is not to be charged for its use.
Stayover room		The guest is not checking out today and will occupy the room for at least one more night.
Long stay guest	LSG	The guest has booked the room for a long duration - weeks or month/s.
On-change room	O/C	The guest has checked out but the room has not yet been cleaned and readied for sale. The term is now replaced with the status DIRTY in hotel software.
Do not disturb	DND/PRIVACY	The guest has requested not to be disturbed.
Sleep-out room	SO	A guest is registered to the room, but the bed has not been used.

(Contd.)

Table 9.2 *Contd.*

Room status	Code	Definition
Skipper		The guest has left the hotel without making arrangements to settle his/her account.
Scanty baggage	SB	The guest has very light luggage that could be carried away in his/her hand without indicating an obvious departure, should he/she walk out with it.
Sleeper/not cleared	NC	The guest has settled his/her account and left the hotel, but the front office staff have failed to properly update the room status.
Vacant-and-ready/vacant-and-cleaned/checked-and-ready room	V/C or CR	The room has been cleaned, inspected, and is ready for an arriving guest.
Out-of-order room	OOO	The room cannot be assigned to a guest. It may need maintenance work to be done, refurbishing, or extensive cleaning.
Lockout room		The room has been locked so that the guest cannot re-enter until he/she has been given clearance by a hotel official.
Did not check out	DNCO	The guest made arrangements to settle his/her account but has left without informing the front office.
Due-out room		The room is expected to become vacant after the following day's check-out time.
Check-out/vacated/departure room	CO or C/O	The guest has settled his/her account, returned the room keys, and left the hotel.
Late check-out		The guest has requested and is being allowed to check out later than the hotel's standard check-out time.
Guest refused service/Service refused	GRS/SR	The guest has declined service of guestroom by the room associate at the stipulated time.
Late service	LS	The guest has asked for service of guestroom later than the specified time.
Early make up	EM	The guest has requested for early servicing of the guestroom than the usual time.
Vacant room	V	A room in which no guest has slept the previous night and which is not yet occupied.
Luggage in	L	The guest's luggage is in the room but the bed has not been slept in.
Under-repair/Out of service room	UR/OOS	The guestroom is not to be assigned to any guest as repair work is being carried out.
No luggage/Occupied but no luggage/no baggage	NL/ONL or NB	The guest is staying in the room but is without luggage.
Double-lock room	DL	A room which has been double-locked. No other key can open this room door except the grandmaster key or the emergency key.
Single lady	SL	A room assigned to a single lady.

Guest Floor Rules

The importance of a guestroom to the guest must be understood and appreciated by all housekeeping staff. There are certain rules to be followed by housekeeping staff as they go about their work on the guest floors. The hotel's management sets these rules and they are communicated to the staff through employee manuals and briefings. The most essential and usual are:

- The staff should be friendly and polite to guests, greeting them according to the time of the day.
- A GRA should not knock on the door or try to access a guestroom when the 'do not disturb' card is displayed on the door knob. If the card has been displayed for a long time, the matter should be referred to the supervisor. (Refer to Chapter 6 for details of how to deal with a DND room status).
- GRAs should follow the standard procedure for entering a guestroom. The same is outlined in Chapter 12, under 'Cleaning an occupied room'.
- GRAs should keep the guestroom door wide open when cleaning it.
- GRAs should keep their carts parked in such a way that the guest corridors are free for movement. Ideally, carts should be parked along the corridor wall, 3 inches away from it. The room-service tray should not be kept in the guest corridor.
- The staff should not leave any kind of notes for guests.
- If a guest acts in a strange manner or one that makes a GRA uncomfortable, the GRA should make an excuse to leave and contact the supervisor.
- GRAs should not throw away any paper or item found in check-out rooms. All items found should be reported to the supervisor and handed over at the lost-and-found counter.
- The staff should communicate with each other in low tones on the guest floors, and only when necessary. Unnecessary speech, especially gossip, is to be avoided.
- The staff should always remain calm in front of guests—running about in haste or due to panic must be avoided.
- The staff should keep an eye open for any suspicious and untoward activity being indulged in by a guest on the guest floor. They should remain alert at all times and display presence of mind.
- Staff should readily offer assistance and relevant information to guests. However, when they do not have the requisite knowledge, they should consult their supervisor.
- The staff should not accept tips. When accepting gifts from guests, they should also request a letter stating this gift and explaining the guest's action.
- The staff should at no time argue with a guest, however unreasonable he/she may be. They should refer the problem to a supervisor when such a situation presents itself.

Guest-floor Reportables

The housekeeping staff, especially the GRAs, are rightly referred to as the 'eyes and ears of the establishment'. There are two reasons for this. Firstly, GRAs have the most frequent access to guestrooms, and secondly, they are expected to have (as a personal attribute) an eye for detail. There are certain reportable matters that must be brought to the notice of a supervisor or manager by the GRAs.

Room status information Certain categories of room status information should be conveyed to the managers. These are rooms that turn out to be NB/NL, SB, or DND.

NB/NL No baggage/no luggage refers to a room in which a guest with no luggage is registered. The GRA should note this down on the room assignment sheet when servicing the room. This is important, as such a guest may 'skip' easily without paying the bill. Alternatively, the room may have such a status due to unauthorized occupation.

SB Scanty baggage refers to a room that has a guest with very light luggage. Such a guest, if he/she is a 'premeditator', can skip easily without settling his/her account with the hotel. 'Premeditators' are guests who arrive with a small piece of luggage and stay in a hotel with the prior intention of skipping without paying the bill.

DND GRAs also need to inform supervisors about DND rooms that have displayed the same status for a long time. This could be due to the fact that the guest inside is ill or maybe up to some illegal activity behind closed doors. In some instances, guests have even been found dead in a DND room.

Change in number of persons ('pax') GRAs can easily gauge the number of people occupying the room by the number of beds that have been slept in and the amount of bath linen used. This information is crucial in cases where guests may have an extra person staying with them without paying for that person. For example, a twin room supposed to be a single occupancy room according to the front office may be found to have double occupancy by the GRA. Sometimes, though, the situation may be due to a guest request to the management.

Damaged or missing hotel property When a GRA enters the guestroom to service it, he/she should cast a keen eye around to check whether there is any damage to any guestroom fixture or fitting, or if any standard items are missing. In case anything is missing or damaged, it needs to be reported immediately to the front office, so that the guest may be charged according to the management policy. Usually, the hotel's management ensures that a clause is mentioned about missing and damaged articles in the 'guest house rules'.

Pets Hotels do not allow pets to be kept in guestrooms. When guests bring along pets, they are politely asked to put them in the custody of staff appointed to take care of pets, keeping them in special kennels. However, some guests may carry in pets without an authorization. If GRAs observe this kind of situation, they should immediately report the matter to the supervisor.

Illegal items Some guests may take undue advantage of the privacy of the hotel guestroom and indulge in certain illegal activities. They may be in possession of illegal drugs, arms and ammunition, and so on. If anything suspicious is observed, GRAs should report the matter to the supervisor as soon as possible.

Sickness GRAs should inform the housekeeper if they notice a guest is in ill health, as they may require medical aid. The housekeeper may then confirm that a doctor is on call, in case the necessity should arise. It may also happen that the guest may have to be given some first aid immediately.

Guest Corridors

Guest corridors should not be treated just as mere passageways leading to guestrooms. A lot of planning goes into the layout of the corridor and its fixtures. Guest corridors act as connectors for all the rooms and lead to service elevators, guest elevators, staircases, and fire exits. While planning guest corridors, the designer keeps in mind that room doors should not open directly facing each other. The corridors must have good ventilation and sufficient lighting at all times. A sample layout for a guest corridor is depicted in Figure 9.7.

In a hotel, corridors are the places where most of the fire-fighting equipment may be strategically located. These may include fire extinguishers, buckets of sand, sprinkler systems, and so on. The length of a guest corridor is limited by the stipulated distance to a protected fire-escape staircase. For corridors with sprinkler

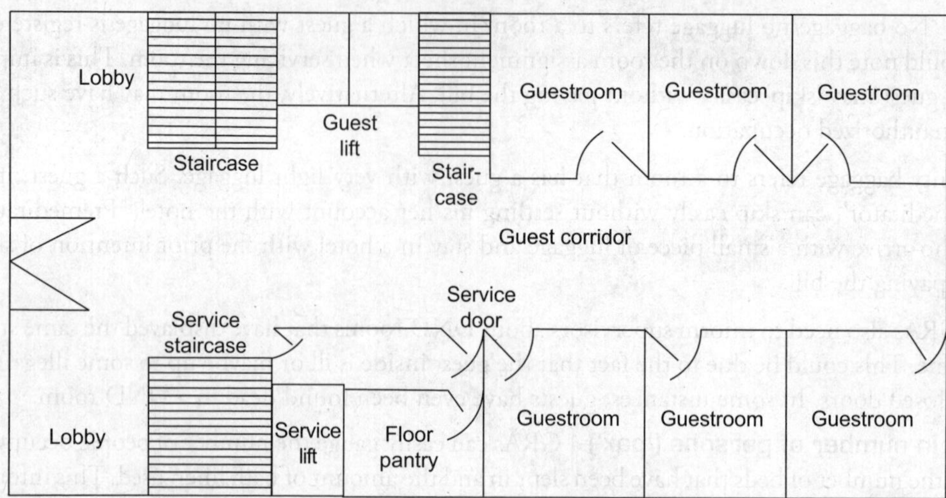

Fig. 9.7 Sample layout of a guest corridor

systems and fire exits at/near opposite ends, allowing two directions of escape, maximum distances usually range from 45 to 60 metres. Dead-end corridors with one exit are limited to a length of 7.6 metres.

Corridors on the guestroom floors may be either *double-loaded central corridors* or *single-loaded side corridors*. Central corridors have guestrooms on both sides of the corridor, whereas side corridors have guestrooms on only one side of the corridor. As a rule, emergency stairs must be sited near the ends of each corridor.

Guest lifts are best located off the main lobby, within control of the front desk. These should open into a small guest lobby leading to the guest corridors on each floor. Guest and service lifts, normally in the ratio 2:1, 3:2, or 4:3, are often situated back to back for economy, with the service lifts arising from 'back of the house' areas and opening into a separate service lobby on each floor.

SUMMARY

This chapter deals specifically with the guestroom—the main product that the hotel sells to earn profits. A hotel is referred to as 'a home away from home' because of the security, safety, comfort, cleanliness, hygiene, and privacy provided by the guestroom. The guestroom is the primary work area for the GRAs. All efforts by the housekeeping department are directed towards providing a homely experience to guests.

The chapter begins with a discussion of the importance of a guestroom for a guest. In other words, the guest's expectations from a guestroom and the staff servicing the guestroom have been discussed.

Further, the types of guestrooms have been listed, with their descriptions. We have attempted to cover all types of rooms in this chapter, but there may be individual variations existing in some properties. For instance, two hotels in south India offer a room termed a 'pool villa'. In one hotel, it refers to a room that has a private mini swimming pool as part of the guestroom area, whereas in the other hotel, the same term refers to guestrooms with a view of an artificial pool.

The layouts depicted are not to scale and are meant to be samples for better comprehension of the types of rooms. Guestroom status codes are discussed as used in most Indian hotels. One property may not be using all the codes and some properties may be using slightly different terminology for a similar status or situation.

General rules and reportable matters for a guest floor have been outlined. Individual properties may have some additional rules to be followed.

Lastly, the importance and layout of guest corridors have been discussed, as they are closely associated with the hotel guestrooms.

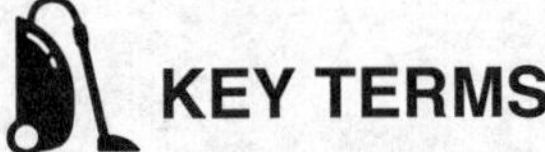

KEY TERMS

Cabana A room adjacent to the pool area, with or without sleeping facilities, but with provision for relaxing on a sofa. It is mainly used for changing.

Disinfected strip A thin strip placed atop and encircling the toilet seat to let guests know that the toilet has been disinfected for their use. It is also called a 'toilet strip'.

DNCO This room status means that the guest made arrangements to settle his/her account but has left without informing the front office.

Double-locked An occupied room in which the deadbolt has been turned to prohibit entry from the corridor. Only a grandmaster key or an emergency key can open it.

Duplex A two-storey suite with parlour and bedrooms connected by a stairway.

Emergency key A key that can open all guestrooms of the hotel, even if they are double-locked.

Grandmaster key The grandmaster key opens every hotel room and, often, all housekeeping storage rooms.

Guest house rules Certain special rules set by the hotel's management for the guests to observe while on the property.

Guestroom key A key that opens a single guestroom door if it is not double-locked.

Hollywood twin room A room with two twin beds but a common headboard, which is meant for two people. If the need arises, the beds can be bridged together to make it appear a single bed.

King-size bed A king-size bed is the largest size of bed available, with a dimension of 6 ft. × 6 ft. 6 in. (Eastern king) and 6 ft. × 6 ft. 10 in. (California king).

Lanai A room overlooking a landscaped area, a scenic view, a water body, or a garden. It may have a balcony, a patio, or both.

Master keys Master keys open guestroom doors that are not double-locked.

Murphy bed This refers to a bed that folds up into the walls and looks like a bookshelf or cupboard when folded away, being named for a leading manufacturer of such beds. It may also be called a Sico bed (after another leading manufacturer of foldaway or 'wall beds').

Parlour A sitting room, usually one having a concealed bed.

Premeditator A guest with a small piece of luggage who stays in a hotel with the prior intention of skipping without paying the bill.

Queen-size bed A queen-size bed has the dimensions 5 ft. 6 in. × 6 ft. 6 in.

Scanty baggage A room status indicating the guest has only small, light luggage that could be carried away in his/her hand without indicating an obvious departure, should a guest walk out with it.

Sico bed See Murphy bed.

Skipper A room status that indicates the guest has left the hotel without making arrangements to settle his/her account.

Sleeper This room status means that the guest has settled his/her account and left the hotel, but the front office staff have failed to update the room status.

Stayover The status of a room occupied by a guest who is not checking out today and will remain at least one more night.

Studio bed This is a dual-purpose bed that is used as a divan in the daytime and converts into a bed in the night after the removal of bolsters and covers.

Vacant The status of a room in which no guest has slept the previous night and which is not yet occupied.

Vacated The room status depicting that the room's guest has settled his/her account, returned the room keys, and left the hotel.

Wi-fi Wireless fidelity. This is an amenity provided nowadays by world-class hotels. Wi-fi enables guests to access a wide range of information, applications, and computing resources without connectivity problems.

10 Standard Contents of a Guestroom

Learning Objectives

After reading this chapter, you should be able to

- list the standard contents of a guestroom
- discuss guestroom furniture with regard to their classification, types, selection, and materials commonly used
- understand the sequential method of furniture arrangement in guestrooms
- identify the various guestroom fixtures and fittings, and discuss their care and maintenance
- enumerate the various kinds of beds, mattresses, and bedding, and discuss their maintenance and cleaning
- recognize the various types of soft furnishings used in hotel guestrooms, and discuss their maintenance
- appreciate the importance of accessories in guestrooms
- outline the ideal placement of various guest supplies in the guestroom

Introduction

The contents of a guestroom vary depending on a hotel's target clientele and room categories. A luxury hotel is expected to offer world-class facilities and amenities. On the other hand, a budget or economy-class hotel will offer only the basic facilities and amenities for a budget-conscious traveller.

However, the contents of any hotel guestroom can be categorized as furniture, fixtures and fittings, soft furnishings, accessories, and guest supplies. Guestroom furniture, fixtures and fittings, soft furnishings, and accessories are discussed in detail in this chapter. Guest supplies have already been discussed in Chapter 7; the placement of these supplies in the guestroom will be outlined in this chapter. Guestroom furnishings include carpets too, but many hotels are doing away with the provision of carpets in individual guestrooms, as it is a maintenance challenge. Therefore, carpets will be discussed separately in Chapter 27.

Guestroom Furniture

Furniture may be defined as the movable articles that make a room suitable for living or working in, though with the advent of built-in furniture, the term 'movable' may no longer be strictly applied to the definition. The types and designs of furniture encompass such a wide range that it is easy to achieve almost any style. The characteristics of good furniture are that in addition to being designed for a specific purpose, it is carefully related to the user's comfort and complements the interior architecture. In simple words, the furniture must be both functional and attractive. It is important to choose the right type of furniture, keeping in mind the kind of use it has to undergo.

Selection of Furniture

Some factors that need to be kept in mind while selecting furniture for guestrooms are discussed in this section.

Comfort and ergonomics The shape and size of the piece of furniture in relation to the human body is a paramount consideration for comfort, and this science is called ergonomics. For instance, in a well-designed and soundly constructed chair, the height and width of the seat and the back rest, the height of the arm rests, and the angle of its various parts provide the maximum of comfort for the average person to work or relax in. A well-designed chair should offer more than one comfortable sitting position. The height of a table and a chair in relation to each other, the height and depth of a wardrobe—all these should be ergonomically viable.

Practicality in design and size Practical design features not only save money and space, but make the piece of furniture easy to use. As such, dimensions of furniture meant for a room must be in coordination.

Serviceability The service aspect depends mainly on the design of the furniture with relation to its use. For instance, shelves are more serviceable than drawers in the bedroom, and built-in furniture can save on space, labour, and wall coverings.

Durability Hotel furniture must be sturdy enough to withstand considerable wear and tear, as it will be handled by a large number of guests. The durability of furniture depends directly on its construction, the materials used, and the amount of wear it is subject to.

Construction The executive housekeeper should ensure that all furniture is constructed with corner blocks to withstand hard and abusive use (see the section on types of furniture joints). They should also be well finished and be possible to re-finish as and when required. Furniture should not have rough, unfinished edges. Drawers should slide in and out smoothly, doors should have efficient hinges and locks, and handles should be sturdy and conveniently placed.

Ease of maintenance This factor is especially pertinent when there is a quick turnaround of rooms. The design of the furniture should be as simple as possible for ease of cleaning. Carvings, crevices, ledges, and so on, can be dust traps, and need to be cleaned regularly. Each piece of furniture should have a 25 cm gap from the floor to its base for ease of cleaning. Sofas with removable, washable covers should be preferred. Shelves are easier to maintain than drawers, and the use of self-shine protective coatings can further ease cleaning and maintenance.

Mobility and flexibility Housekeeping work becomes much easier when furniture items may be easily moved from room to room as required. For this reason, castors are fitted on heavier pieces of furniture. Mobility and flexibility in furniture enable rooms to be put to different uses as well.

Versatility A piece of furniture should be versatile, that is, it should suit more than one purpose. For instance, a fitted wardrobe that combines hanging space and shelf space can provide adequate space and is a neater piece of furniture than a separate wardrobe with only hanging rails plus a chest of drawers.

Style and aesthetics The atmosphere to be achieved depends on the design and style of the furniture to a great extent. The choice could be a modern or an old world style, depending on the theme of the room. For instance, a chair for the dressing table or the writing table should be chosen with the particular dressing or writing table in mind. Any chair in the guestroom of a budget hotel may not be necessarily suitable for a luxury hotel, and vice versa.

Cost The cost of the furniture is an important consideration. However, quality need not be compromised for low cost. Quality furniture may also be found at a reasonable price, if the housekeeper is aware of the sources and conducts a good survey before making the decision to buy.

Some guidelines for selecting furniture

Certain points that need to be checked before finalizing the purchase of a piece of furniture are outlined here. Check whether the furniture

- is free from coarse, unfinished edges.
- is sturdy and stands firm on the floor.
- is free from surplus adhesive.
- is reinforced with suitable, well-fitted joints.
- is well balanced, whether empty or full (especially crucial for case goods).
- has drawers or sliding doors that move smoothly along the tracks.
- has efficient hinges, bolts, latches, locks, and handles.
- has smooth, conveniently placed handles.
- has furniture glides in case a carpet is in use.
- has castor wheels that manoeuvre well and have no sharp edges.

Types of Furniture

There are primarily four types of furniture found in hotel guestrooms, based on the way they are placed. Furniture may be free-standing, cantilevered, built-in, or fitted.

Free-standing This type of furniture can be rearranged whenever necessary, but the disadvantage is that they accumulate dust behind, above, and beneath them. Examples of free-standing furniture are traditional chairs and beds.

Cantilevered Cantilevered furniture are fixed on brackets fitted to the wall and hence, there are no legs to get in the way of cleaning.

Built-in These pieces of furniture are fitted and fixed into architectural spaces set aside for them in the construction of the building. Usually their cost is incorporated into the building costs. If required, they can be installed later, but in that case may work out to be more expensive. Since built-in furniture has no gaps behind, above, or below, cleaning is minimized. However, the disadvantage is that once built in, the particular piece of furniture cannot be moved, thus reducing its flexibility. Wardrobes and cabinets in guestrooms are often of the built-in type.

Fitted Though the terms 'built-in' and 'fitted' are often used interchangeably, there is a slight difference. Fitted furniture is made to fit into existing alcoves and niches, thereby saving space, but is essentially a standalone item with its own sides, base and top apart from the room walls, ceiling, or floor. The room appears more spacious and streamlined when fitted furniture is used. However, they have the advantage of being movable if necessary, though they are not as easy to move as free-standing furniture.

Based on their other characteristics, furniture may also be categorized as one or more of the following types:

Upholstered Good upholstered furniture consist of a webbed base, coiled springs, two layers of filling material, hessian, webbing, calico covering, and a decorative outer covering of fabric. Leather may be an alternative to a fabric covering. Leather, if maintained well, is durable and may last four times as long as a fabric covering. Sofas and chairs used in hotels are generally upholstered.

Modular A manufacturer of modular furniture works to a standard basic measurement or module, so that different pieces can be joined together in a variety of ways to suit individual requirements. Modular furniture is usually built against a wall, and thus makes the most economical use of space within a room and simplifies floor cleaning.

Antiques Actual antique furniture will belong to a period before the year 1840, though nowadays any piece of furniture that is more than 100 years old is considered an antique. Good antiques are valuable and expensive. These may be available from a known collector or from antique shops run by professionals.

Types of Furniture Joints

Furniture parts can be put together or assembled in five ways: using staples, nails, screws, glue, or joints. Most pieces of furniture use more than one method. Joints are the places where one component in a piece of furniture fits into another. In good furniture, the joints are often reinforced by synthetic glue. Where joints are impractical, screws are the best fasteners—they should be secure and screwed in all the way. Staples are used on cheaper furniture and should not be used for joining pieces that bear weight or undergo stress. Nails are stronger than staples, but not as strong as other joining methods. A good joint can make all the difference to the life span of a piece of furniture.

Dovetail These joints are often found at drawer corners. Dovetails should fit together smoothly. Desks, luggage racks, chests of drawers, and pieces that provide storage (called case goods) are primarily constructed using dovetail joints. Furniture pieces in which the dovetail joints are too small or cracked should not be purchased.

Double dowel These joints use two dowels to peg the joint together. They are sturdy joints used to create the frame for case goods or to attach legs to the side rails of chairs.

Butt These are joints in which two pieces are simply joined together end to end. They are weak joints and should not be used in places subject to stress or weight.

Mitre These are used at the corner of tables where two angled surfaces meet to make up a right angle, and are reinforced with dowels, nails, screws, or a splint.

Tongue and groove These joints are used to join two boards together, side by side, as in a table top, such that they slide into each other and hold together.

Mortise and tenon These joints are the strongest of all when joining pieces of wood at right angles. The end of one piece of wood is shaped to fit into a hole in the other. This type of joint construction distributes stress over a wide area.

Corner block These are used at corner joints as screwed reinforcement, to provide extra support, in quality furniture.

Figure 10.1 shows the various types of joints used in furniture making.

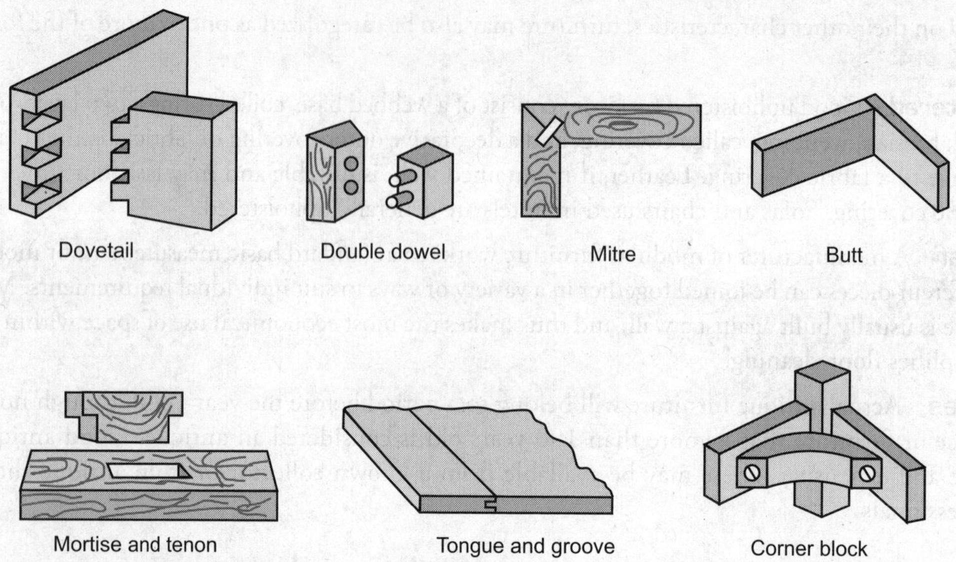

Fig. 10.1 Types of joints

Materials used for Making Furniture

The material used for the construction of furniture affects the durability, appearance, and cost of the finished article.

Wood

Historically, the most common material for making furniture is wood, but other materials such as metal and stone were also used. The designs in wooden furniture reflect the style of every era from ancient times to up-to-the-minute contemporary. Whereas in most earlier periods a single style dominated, a diversity of old and new styles influence present-day design. In many hotels, the most valuable pieces of furniture are antiques, dating back 100–300 years or more. Wooden furniture that dates back to a period before the year 1840 is considered an antique. The oldest surviving example of wood furniture dates back to 2680 BC, and is from Old Kingdom Egypt.

Types of wood used in furniture making Let us now discuss the various types of woods that are used in furniture making.

Solid wood The types of solid wood used in India for making furniture are discussed in this section, together with their properties.

Maple The scientific name of this genus, *Acer*, is derived from the Latin word for hard. The colour of maple woods ranges from cream to light reddish-brown. They are usually straight-grained, though sometimes found with a highly figured bird's-eye or burl grain. The wood is heavy, hard, strong, tough, stiff, close-grained, and possesses a uniform texture. Maple shows excellent resistance to abrasion, indentation, and shock. This wood is extensively used in making furniture and cabinets.

Walnut This is one of the finest hardwoods. Walnut mixes well with other woods and natural materials to provide a friendly atmosphere in otherwise austere interiors. The wood develops a rich patina that

grows more lustrous with age. Its colour ranges from light gray-brown to dark purplish-brown, with plain to highly figured grains. This species produces a greater variety of figure types than any other. The wood is moderately heavy, very strong, and exceptionally stable.

Mahogany This wood has an interlocked or straight grain, often with a ribbon figure, and a moderately coarse texture. It has a creamy-white sapwood and reddish brown heartwood, often with a purple cast. It is moderately heavy and hard, with medium bending and crushing strength, low stiffness and shock resistance, moderate decay resistance, and good stability in use. It is fairly easy to work with, although interlocked, woolly grain can be troublesome. It glues, nails, and screws satisfactorily. It takes stains well and polishes to an excellent finish.

Ebony This is a category of hardwood. It has a straight to irregular grain with a fine, even texture and an almost metallic lustre. The heartwood colour varies from medium brown to jet black to grey, depending on the species. The sapwood is light grey. This wood is very heavy, hard, strong, and stiff, with high resistance to shock and decay. Though the wood steam-bends reasonably well, it is brittle. It is also difficult to work due to its hardness. Its heartwood in particular has a severe blunting effect on cutting edges. This wood requires pre-drilling in order that nails or screws may be inserted. It glues satisfactorily and takes an excellent finish. It is used in making luxury furniture, carved pieces, and decorative veneers.

Rosewood This wood is also known as East Indian rosewood, Bombay rosewood, Bombay blackwood, *sheesham*, *sitsal*, Malabar wood, *biti*, *ervadi*, and *kalaruk*. It grows mainly in southern India. The wood commonly has an interlocked grain with a uniform, moderately coarse texture. It has a purple-brown heartwood with attractive dark streaks and a yellowish white sapwood, often with a purple tinge. The wood is heavy, hard, dense, amenable to steam bending, with high bending and crushing strength, medium shock resistance, and good stability. The heartwood in particular is very durable. The wood holds screws and nails well and glues satisfactorily. It finishes nicely, although a filling is usually recommended.

Teak This is also known as Burma teak, Rangoon teak, Moulmein teak, *jati sak*, *rosawa*, and by many other local names. The wood is generally straight-grained, with a coarse, uneven texture, medium lustre, and an oily feel. It has a yellow-brown to dark golden-brown heartwood and greyish or white sapwood. It is moderately hard and heavy, with low stiffness and shock resistance, moderate bending strength, moderate amenability to steam bending, and excellent decay resistance and dimensional stability. It stains and finishes well, although its natural oils can cause adhesion difficulties. It is used in making indoor and outdoor furniture, panelling, plywood, decorative veneers, and carved furniture.

Willow The willow species used for furniture making include black willow, white willow, crack willow, and close-bark willow. The wood is typically straight-grained, sometimes interlocked, with a fine, uniform texture. The wood has a pale reddish-brown to greyish-brown heartwood and a whitish sapwood. It is light, soft, and weak, with low shock resistance, decay resistance, and good steam-bending properties. It glues, screws, nails, and finishes satisfactorily. It is used for making Venetian blinds, veneers, and inexpensive items of furniture.

Rubberwood This is primarily a hardwood, creamy white to light brown in colour. This wood is being used nowadays for making furniture with an elegant contemporary look. The wood shows attractive darker stripes. However, it needs to be re-finished frequently.

Plywood This is made by bonding together an odd number of wood veneers or plies of wood, 1–2 mm thick, under pressure. Alternating veneers are arranged at right angles to each other to give maximum strength. Plywood is equally strong along both axes, whereas solid wood is strongest along the grain. Plywood (7-ply or 9-ply) is frequently used for table tops, where stability is essential. Carved and shaped parts of furniture can be pre-formed, thus eliminating much nailing and gluing. Both plywood and solid wood may have decorative veneers on the surface.

Veneers These are cut out from the barks of trees by thinly slicing a continuous piece from the bark. The veneer is usually stuck to plywood by gluing to give the appearance of solid wood. Various other kinds of veneered material include batten board, laminated board, chipboard, and blockboard.

Wicker and cane

These types of furniture have become popular in hotels for their light weight and ethnic character. Cane and wicker have been discussed in Chapter 8. What needs to be added here is that when choosing cane furniture, one must check that there are no splits around the rings or the furniture will ultimately splinter and be difficult to repair. Also, cane, wicker, and rush furniture should be examined for unravelling or flaking at the time of purchase and at regular intervals during use.

Iron and steel

Iron and its alloy steel are now being increasingly used in hotel furniture. Painted cast-iron is used for outdoor furniture such as chairs and tables. Molten cast iron is poured into a mould to make garden benches, chairs, and tables, usually in an antique style. Wrought iron is made by welding bent rods of steel together. Wrought iron is cheaper for its weight and the furniture made from it comes in both contemporary and traditional styles. Wrought-iron furniture lasts longer and when it does show signs of wear, it may be repainted to renew its appeal. Wrought iron weathers with age and resembles antique furniture when it does, a property that is preferred in hotels. However, wrought iron should not be used in locations where it will be exposed to salty sea air, since this will result in rusting.

Aluminium

The advantage of aluminium furniture is that it is low in cost, lightweight, and does not rust. However, aluminium is not used much in making furniture for hotels. Where used, it is often coated with plastic.

Plastic

Plastic, like aluminium, is cheap and lightweight. It is a low-maintenance material and is now often used for outdoor furniture. These can easily be stacked and stored. Plastic is adversely affected by prolonged exposure to strong sunlight, however. To overcome this disadvantage, ultraviolet-ray inhibitors are now added to plastic furniture during manufacture. Very cold temperatures may also make plastics brittle.

Common Furniture Items in Guestrooms

The usual furniture in guestrooms include beds, luggage racks, bureaus, nightstands, coffee tables, chairs, a writing table, a wardrobe, (in some rooms) a dresser/drawers, a curio, a credenza, and an ottoman.

Table 10.1 outlines the specifications for some basic furniture items of guestrooms in hotels. Individual properties may give their own specifications, depending on the size and theme of the room.

Table 10.1 Specifications for hotel furniture

Furniture item	Specifications
Chairs, upholstered chairs, and sofas	• Seats should be long and wide enough to relax buttocks, thighs, and knees. • The minimum width of an *armchair* should be 48 cm. A *wing chair* should have a minimum width of 56 cm between the wings. • The depth of the seat should be approximately double the height of the *armchair*. For instance, 33–38 cm high seats should have 60–70 cm depth. • The depth of the seat may be equivalent to the height of the *upright chair*. For instance, 42–45 cm high seats may have a depth of 42–50 cm. • The arms on chairs should not protrude more than 25 mm beyond the front edge of the chair seat. • Chairs meant for convention rooms and conferences must be easily stackable. • Chairs for use with tables should allow at least 30 cm gap between the table and the chair for ease of sitting. • Upholstery material should be easily detachable for ease of cleaning.
Tables	• Tables should be made to suit the primary use—working, dining, or occasional. • Table tops should have an easily maintained finish, preferably heat- and stain-resistant. • Round tables are for informal occasions, whereas an oblong table suits a formal setting. • The height of the *writing table* from the chair seat should be at least 30 cm to allow for free knee movement. The total height of the table may be approximately 76–84 cm. • A *coffee table* should be 35–50 cm high.
Wardrobe	• These should be made in accordance with the type of guests and their length of stay. • If free-standing, furniture glides must be fixed to the legs to protect the carpet. • In a *single wardrobe*, the minimum width of the hanging space for clothes should be 60 cm; in a *double wardrobe*, it should be 90 cm. • The depth may be 56–60 cm. • The height to accommodate full-length dresses should be 175 cm. The full height of the wardrobe should not exceed 200 cm, else its top will be difficult to reach. • The hanging rail should not be too close to the top and should be firmly fixed.
Luggage rack	• The ideal ones are those made of solid wood. • The dimensions should be about 120 cm in width and 53 cm in depth for a 46-cm high rack.
Nightstand (bedside table)	• These should ideally have a drawer that is 10 cm in height. • The dimensions of a nightstand should be about 56 cm in width, 46 cm in depth, and 60 cm in height.

 Furniture Arrangement

The foremost rule in furniture arrangement is that the furniture should be bought keeping in mind the size and shape of the guestroom in which it will be used. It is highly recommended that the housekeeper gets a floor plan of the rooms and plots them on a graph according to a suitable scale. The floor plan should also indicate where doors and windows are let into the walls. Then scaled cut-outs (using the same scale as the floor plan), called templates, of the furniture owned by the hotel (or being considered for purchase) should be made (see Fig. 10.2). The furniture measurements should be taken with a metal coiled-spring tape and

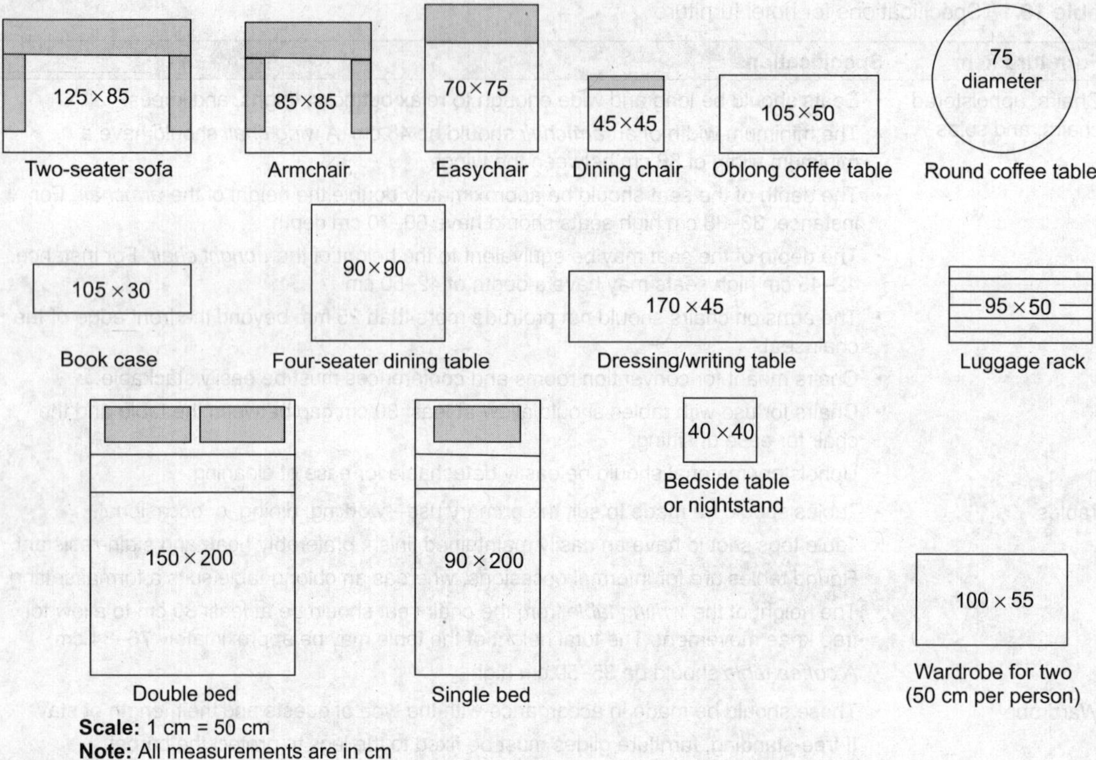

Fig. 10.2 Standard furniture templates used in planning furniture arrangement

not a tailor's measuring tape. Thick coloured paper should be used to make the cut-outs (templates) so that they stand out from the graph paper. These should then be arranged on the floor plan according to the requirements of the living space. A sample furniture arrangement for a suite is shown in Fig. 10.3.

The next step is to create a centre of interest around which to group the furniture. Some guestrooms have a natural focal point, such as a fireplace or a window with a picturesque view. In guestrooms that do not have such architectural features, a focal point of interest can be created and the furniture grouped around it. One of the most practical solutions is to create a picture wall, where pictures or paintings can be hung in a symmetrical or asymmetrical arrangement. Another way is to hang a single striking painting or a decorative mirror on the wall.

Consider convenience as well as aesthetics in furniture arrangement. For instance, furniture meant for social spaces should be arranged in conversational groupings so that people can talk comfortably without having to shout to be heard. Whenever possible, the furniture planning in a room should accommodate more than one use. For instance, in a large guestroom, an undisturbed area can be arranged conveniently for quiet reading.

Making allowances for traffic patterns is also crucial to furniture arrangement. This can be easily achieved by studying the floor plan. Determine the traffic paths that cross it, that is, the ways in which people are apt to enter and leave the room. These paths should not cross any conversational grouping or any area set aside for undisturbed activities or relaxation.

While placing furniture, arrange the larger pieces first and then distribute the smaller ones in stages. Do not place any piece of furniture in such a way as to touch the wall, else it may leave lines of dirt

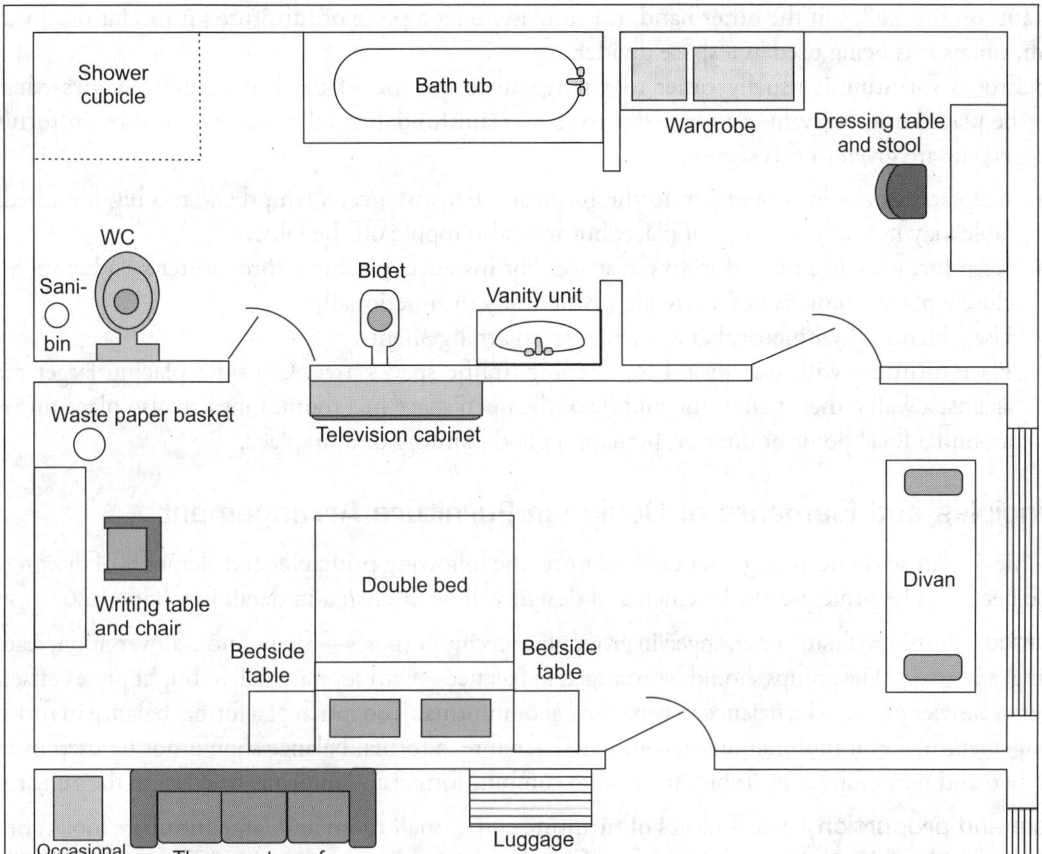

Note: Not according to scale

Fig. 10.3 Sample furniture arrangement in a suite

or stains on the wall. On the other hand, it is unwise to let a piece of furniture jut too far out into the room, unless it is being used as a space divider.

Bedroom furniture is usually easier to arrange since the size of the bed usually dictates where it must be placed and everything must defer to it. Certain fundamental points to consider in furniture arrangement are given in this section.

- Keep accessories in proportion to the furniture. For instance, a lampshade too big for a bedside table may not only look out of place, but may also topple off the table.
- Keep furniture in proportion to the space. For instance, placing a three-seater sofa between two closely placed doors is not advisable aesthetically or functionally.
- Use a blend of symmetrical and asymmetrical arrangements.
- Place furniture with due regard for keeping 'traffic spaces' free. Consider placing larger pieces against a wall rather than in the middle of the open space in a room. One can also place furniture around a focal point of interest, perhaps a good painting or a fireplace.

Principles and Elements of Design in Furniture Arrangement

In achieving an aesthetic arrangement of furniture, the following principles and elements of design need to be heeded. The principles and elements of design will be discussed in detail in Chapter 26.

Balance Furniture should be arranged in groups for specific purposes—for instance, conversation, reading, dining, and so on. The groups should be arranged in balance—with several small or bright pieces offsetting larger or heavier pieces. The balance may be formal or informal. Too much of a formal balance in furniture arrangement makes it monotonous and stilted. Therefore, a formal balance should not be used in more than two or three groups in the room. It is best to combine formal and informal balances in the same room.

Scale and proportion Small pieces of furniture suit a small room and large furniture looks apt in a large room. Massive and too-small furniture, if mixed in one group, tend to clash. The pieces of furniture as a unit should be in proportion to the wall space. Certain proportions are inherently pleasing. Good proportions of furniture space to wall space are 2:3, 3:5, and 4:5. These proportions may be used in arranging any group of furniture with regard to height, width, or overall visual mass.

Line The lines of furniture may be straight, curved, parallel, vertical, horizontal, or diagonal. They may be delicate or strong, soothing or harsh. All lines have certain individual characteristics; but in furniture arrangement, they should harmonize gracefully. Too many different kinds of lines used in one group of furniture lead to an air of confusion.

Colour The colour schemes for the furniture should be planned keeping in mind their size, shape, and use; other furnishings; and the colour scheme of the room as a whole. Colour schemes will be discussed in greater detail in Chapter 27.

Texture The roughness or smoothness of the materials from which the furniture is made gives a character and feel to the room. Textures should be graduated when mingled.

Rhythm In furniture arrangement, rhythm is the result when the observer's eye moves from one piece of furniture to the other in a group and from the furniture of one area to the other in a pleasing and ordered way. Room rhythm in a furniture arrangement may be achieved by repetition of an accent or the use of colours and design so that the eye is carried from one point to another. One way to achieve rhythm is for the eye to be carried from a colourful window to chairs, pictures, and accessories, each repeating in correct proportion the main colour scheme of the room.

Furniture Arrangement in Guestroom Areas

Some points relating to the placement of furniture are given here, area by area.

Entrance or verandah This area should have a furniture arrangement that expresses warmth, cheer, and pleasantness. The furniture here may include a chair or two and a low table. Attention should be paid to the kind of material used, as not all materials will be suitable for verandahs and entrances. These are ideal places to use cane, wicker, or painted wrought-iron furniture. These types of furniture have a lightweight feel in visual terms.

Living room The living room in larger guestrooms usually contains upholstered furniture to seat the maximum number of people who may occupy the room and one or two more to accommodate guests. Each large chair should be within easy reach of a table on which an ashtray or refreshments may be placed, and should, if possible, face the door so that those entering the room can be seen and welcomed. Tables and chairs should harmonize in weight, size, and style. Tall pieces of furniture should be placed parallel to a wall. Seating should be placed in accordance to the wall, either parallel or at right angles. Small chairs may be placed diagonally. Other furniture to be placed in this area are a television cabinet and sometimes a chest of drawers.

Dining area Most guestrooms do not have a separate dining area. In these rooms, a large coffee table and a few chairs suffice for any meal served in the guestroom. The table and chairs should be set so as not to interfere with traffic. Hotels can experiment with furniture of bright cheerful colours for this grouping, but the colours chosen should harmonize with the colour scheme of the room as a whole.

Bedroom The usual set of furniture in a guest bedroom is a bed, two bedside tables, a dressing table, a chest of drawers, a coffee table, chairs, a luggage rack, and a writing table. Most economy guestrooms are primarily bedrooms with regard to their function. Traffic lanes around the bed should be clearly defined. Unless the room is very large, all furniture except the coffee table with its chairs and perhaps the bed are best placed against the wall.

Kitchen Some hotel guestrooms have a small kitchen, where usually modular cabinets are utilized as furniture. It is mainly storage furniture that is found in the kitchen, in the form of cabinets and basket drawers.

Guestroom Fixtures and Fittings

Fixtures and fittings are the hardware items present in guestrooms that cannot be moved or are difficult to move since they are fixed in position—for example, mirrors, lighting fixtures, and the wash basin and other sanitary fittings.

Types of Fixtures and Fittings

The main categories of fittings and fixtures found in the guestroom are listed in this section.

Doors, windows, and locks

Guestroom doors are usually made of solid wood and fitted with a cylinder lock with the provision of double locking. A six-levered cylindrical lock with a deadlock latch is recommended. The best security is provided by a mortise deadlock set in the woodwork of the door. In this locking system, when the key is turned, a thick, square-edged bolt slots deeply into the door frame. Doors may also have peep holes with a one-way optical lens. Some guestroom doors also have a brass door-knocker. The door handles too are usually made of brass. Hinged windows with standard latches are reasonably secure. All ground-floor windows, however small, should be lockable. These may be in the form of lockable handles or locking stays. Windows will be discussed in greater detail in Chapter 27.

Telephone

This piece of equipment serves many purposes in guestrooms now. It is not only a means of communication for the guest, but also serves as a room control system. In many properties, guestroom telephones are linked to the property management system software, allowing GRAs to inform and update the guestroom status over the phone. The guestroom telephone also gives the guest access to other services of the hotel, such as room service, and permits him to make STD and ISD calls. Usually a telephone extension is provided in the guest bathroom too.

Guestroom safe

This fixture has gained popularity in recent times. Most deluxe hotels now provide safes in the guestrooms for guests to keep their important documents and money in. Many different models are available, with a variety of features. Guestroom safes may be electronic or manual; wall-mounted, floor-mounted, or built into wardrobes or nightstands.

Minibar

This is also a novel fixture found in almost all deluxe guestrooms these days. It is like a mini refrigerator in which mineral water, juices, liquor, soda, and some snacks are stocked. Minibars may use a manual system for checking consumption of items, or they may be fully automated. Usually hotels have minibars with the manual system. In this system, the housekeeping staff need to keep a physical inventory of items consumed and to be charged to the guest's account. In an automated bar, the removal of an item is automatically logged in a software inventory. Minibar management is discussed in depth in Chapter 12.

Television

The usual size of television provided in guestrooms is 36–42 inches with the minimum being 19 inches, with remote. A television in today's guestroom is not only an in-room entertainment system but also an interactive information and control system. The wall-mounted smart OLED and LED HDTV systems are customizable and connected to high bandwidth Wi-Fi. The entertainment system comes loaded with apps and OTT providing streaming services, shows, and movies apart from broadband TV services and external device connections. As control systems, TVs, through Internet of Things (IoT), can manage voice-activated in-room temperature, lighting, drapery and locks, in-room dining orders and bookings of restaurants, spa, and such hotel services. As interactive information systems, TV can display personalised, welcome messages, hotel events and services, tariffs and menus, electronic programme guide, flight and weather information through apps; and guests can access their social media.

Radio

Channel music modules may be installed, with the tuner in the nightstand or attached to the television set.

Air conditioner

Individual guestrooms usually receive centrally filtered air at controlled temperature and relative humidity. This air is circulated through the air-conditioning plants on the property and then enters the guestrooms through inlets in the form of metal or wood grilles. The guestroom thermostat temperature is usually set at 24°C in hotels now.

Heating equipment

In India, these are used in hotels located at hill stations, mostly. Most of these establishments use some form of central heating, controlled by a thermostat. There are three kinds of central heating systems.

Full central heating This system provides for a pre-set temperature in all living areas.

Background central heating This system supplies heat to all living areas, but at temperatures lower than that of partial central heating.

Partial central heating This system provides some but not all living areas with full heat.

The heat circulation medium may be hot water, steam, or warm air, produced by burning a solid fuel, oil, coal, or gas or by the use of electricity. In many heat-control systems, radiators and grilles are required. Radiators are usually enclosed behind a grille, which should be placed as inconspicuously as possible in the guestroom. Where the building is not centrally heated, individual heat-control systems are provided in the form of electric fires and convector gas fires. Some hotels may even have fireplaces with coal fires.

Lighting fixtures

A myriad of lighting fixtures are available for both walls and ceilings. Lighting fixtures should be decorative as well as utilitarian. They will be discussed in greater detail in Chapter 27.

Internet and Wi-Fi fixtures

All guestrooms in upscale hotels are Wi-Fi (wireless fidelity) enabled nowadays as guests are now travelling with their own technology. A guestroom should provide multiple sockets for charging and operating various technology gadgets. Hotels usually have a high-range router installed in corridors of all floors to cater to Wi-Fi access in all rooms. These in turn are connected to the main router in the server room.

Sanitary fittings

Available in different kinds of material such as ceramic, metals, and plastic, sanitary fittings should have surfaces that are smooth, easy to maintain, non-porous, and not easily damaged by strong chemicals. Sanitary fittings used for collecting and disposing of waste are connected to a drainage system. Those associated with toilets, urinals, and sluices are called 'soil' fittings and baths, bidets, sinks, and showers are called 'waste' fittings. See the QR code for the images of various sanitary fittings.

Types of sanitary fittings The most usual types of sanitary fittings are listed in this section.

Wash basins and vanity units Vanity units are also referred to as 'vanitory units'. Vanity units and wash basins may be made of ceramic, marble, granite, or a synthetic polymer such as acrylic. A new entrant for wash basins is glass, which is available in many colours. Though wash basins are available in many colours, it should be remembered that the darker the colour, the less the light reflected on the face from the overhead light. The usual size of wash basins in guest bathrooms is 56 cm × 40 cm. There may be larger ones in more luxurious settings. Basins may be cantilevered or may stand on a pedestal and should include smooth-edged soap wells. Vanity units and wash basins are usually coordinated with a wall-mounted mirror and an accessible shaving mirror. Faucets and handles may be made of nickel, chrome, or brass. The maximum recommended temperature of water for a washbasin is 41°C.

Bath tubs These are frequently made of enamelled cast iron, enamelled steel, or acrylic. Acrylic bathtubs are often reinforced with fibreglass. They come in various colours, with soap dishes and grip handles incorporated in them. The most functional size required for a bath tub is a minimum of 80 cm wide and 170 cm long. The tub should hold a minimum of 128 litres of water. The faucets attached could have separate controls for hot and cold water or a single-lever control. A luxury bath tub also has a hand shower with several settings for different pressures. The maximum recommended temperature of water for a bathtub is 44°C.

Shower stall or cabinet These are found in deluxe hotels and almost always have glass walls and doors. The minimum size should be 1 sq. metre. The placement of the shower head should be ergonomic with reference to its location and accessibility for adjustment, and the floor should be non-slip. The maximum recommended temperature of water for a shower is 41°C.

WC and urinals These are usually made of vitreous china. The toilet seat and the lid are usually of plastic. The WC may be cantilevered or may stand on a pedestal. The recommended height is approximately 35–40 cm and a depth of 60 cm. The WC cisterns may be built-in (one piece), separate, or concealed, or be substituted by a pressure-flush valve. The WC flush can be of single-syphon, double-syphon, or wash-down type, but most star-rated hotels use a quiet double-symphon flush system, with a one-piece WC (with built-in cistern). For better water conservation, 7.5–9 litre single-flush cisterns are preferred. In case of double-flush cisterns, the ones with a half flush option are preferred. The standard colour for WCs is enamelled white. A toilet paper holder should be affixed close by.

Hygiene faucets Alternately called health faucets, or jet sprays, these are handheld sanitary devices found attached to the walls next to WCs and bidets. They are primarily meant for delivering a continuous spray of water through a lever-triggered, perforated nozzle for cleaning.

Bidets These are more usual in the Middle East and Europe. The recommended width and height are 38 cm either way, with a length of 60 cm. The ones with spout faucets having a water-temperature control are preferred. The maximum recommended temperature of water for a bidet is 38°C.

Towel rails These are usually of steel, chrome, or brass. They should stand sufficiently away from the wall after fitting so that there is enough space to hang the thickest of folded towels.

Care and cleaning of sanitary fittings Daily cleaning of sanitary fittings is extremely important as they may harbour disease-causing bacteria. In cleaning sanitary fittings, begin with the least dirty ones, moving on to the dirtier, so as to prevent the spread of bacteria. A neutral detergent should be used for the regular daily cleaning of all sanitary fittings. The use of disinfectant is beneficial, but it should be used only after thorough daily cleaning, to kill any remaining germs. Once a week, an alkaline detergent may be used on sanitary fittings for the removal of dirt and obliteration of most bacteria. An alkaline detergent is more effective on greasy dirt than a neutral detergent and removes greasy marks in the bath. However, this type of detergent should not be used too frequently as it may damage surfaces and irritate the skin on contact. An acidic cleaner is very strong and therefore, should only be used for urinals and WCs. It removes water marks and urine or faecal stains. Depending upon the degree of soiling, an acidic cleaner may be used once a week or once in two weeks. While cleaning, accessories such as taps, plugs, chains, pipes, overflows, the underparts, and the surrounding walls should be given due attention. Adequate protective gear by way of rubber gloves and plastic aprons should be used and hands should be washed thoroughly after cleaning. Cleaning agents used in the sanitary areas must never be mixed with each other. For instance, if an acidic toilet cleaner has been applied to the WC and left to do its work, and then a bleach is added, toxic, asphyxiating gases may be produced.

Beds, Mattresses, and Bedding

Beds, mattresses, and bedding are an essential part of hotel accommodation. Beds and mattresses are of great importance for sleeping in comfort. However, the beds must not only be comfortable, but also look inviting. This is accomplished by the use of suitable items of bedding. Bedding includes all the articles placed on the bed by way of bedclothes, including bed linen as well as covers, quilts, and pillows.

Guestroom Beds

Good beds are an investment in comfort and health. An ideal bed cradles the body while its underlying firmness maintains correct posture. The types of bed generally used in hotels include conventional guestroom beds and extra beds such as cribs, sofa beds, murphy or sico beds, and zed beds or rollaways.

Understanding the construction of beds

Most beds consist of the following parts:

- a *frame* on which the springs and mattresses rest—this is usually a rectangular, metal or wooden framework, some having a raised edge all around so that the mattress fits in and is held in place (but in hotels, these frames make bed-making difficult).
- a *base*, which may be made of open coiled springs, wire mesh, or laminated wood strips to provide resilience and support.
- a *mattress*, which lies on top of the springs and provides extra padding.
- a *headboard*, made of painted or varnished wood or an upholstered type. In most hotels, headboards are not part of the beds. They are typically mounted on the walls behind the beds and not on the frames. Headboards in suite rooms are often designed to match other pieces of furniture.
- a *footboard*, usually made of wood or metal and lower in height than the headboard.

Bed frame There are basically two types of bed frames—platform and metal.

Platform frames/box frames These are usually made from wood. They provide the bed springs and mattresses with a platform or box on which to rest. While platform frames are raised off the floor by feet, box frames lie tight to the floor.

Metal frame These consist of four lengths of angle iron with a metal leg attached to each corner. Larger beds also have two cross bars added for extra support. The metal legs may have castors or furniture glides attached to them.

Bed base A bed consists primarily of a mattress supported by a base. The base may be made of open coil springs, wire mesh, solid wood or plywood, or slatted wood.

Base springs Springs add resiliency and durability to the bed. They are made by joining wire springs or coils together and covering them with padding. The wooden framework of the bed may either surround approximately half the height of the coiled springs, giving a 'sprung edge', or the whole height to give a 'firm edge'. A firm edge helps prevent the springs from sagging when the bed is sat on. There are primarily four types of spring constructions:

Box springs The coils for these are made of heavygauge steel. Box springs are mounted on a wood frame and covered with a pad. A sturdy fabric called ticking covers the springs and pad. Box springs act as shock absorbers, cushioning the weight and movements of the sleeper.

Metal-coil springs These may be arranged in two layers. The springs on the bottom are tightly coiled for good support. The top springs are loosely coiled for resilience. Metal-coil springs also come in a single layer with metal bands criss-crossing the surface or with extra wire at the top of the springs to form a semi-closed surface on which the padding or the upholstered base lies.

Flat bedsprings These are strips of metal attached lengthwise to a frame with helical hooks. These hooks are small coils with hooks at both ends. Flat bedsprings are most frequently found on rollaway beds.

Stretched springs These are in the form of highly coiled springs attached to the frame on one side and resilient thick metal wires on the other side. The wires criss-cross each other and cover the middle of the frame, with the springs lying on the sides.

Headboard Most hotels now prefer headboards to be wall-mounted. The main objective of the headboard is to protect the wall from developing greasy stains from a guest's head. To fulfil this purpose, the headboard must rise upto 30–45 cm above the top of the mattress. Headboards may be made in different shapes, using different materials, but should be easy to clean and maintain.

Footboard Footboards are usually of the same material and colour as the headboard of the bed. Most hotel beds have footboards that are at the same level or at a level slightly higher than that of the mattress.

Posters These are generally affixed to four corners of old-fashioned beds in form of decorative vertical columns made of solid wood. Typically seen in heritage hotel guestrooms, such beds are called four-poster beds.

Extra beds

These may not always resemble the conventional guestroom bed in construction.

Cribs These are available as guest loan items in hotels and are usually collapsible to save storage space. They should have adequate locking mechanisms to ensure that they do not collapse when an infant or a child is put to sleep in them.

Rollaway zed beds Zed beds get their name from their three-part folded frame resembling the letter 'Z'. These can be rollaway beds on rollers or castors. They generally have a thin latex-foam mattress that rests on a base of stretched springs attached to a rectangular folding frame. There are better-quality ones available that have interior-sprung mattresses.

Sofa beds These provide extra seating by day and a bed by night. The better ones have a slatted wooden base with an interior-sprung mattress. The wire-mesh ones may be cheaper but tend to sag in time.

Murphy or sico beds These beds fold up into the wall, giving the impression of a book shelf, a wardrobe, or a cabinet. The fitting of the unit is the main consideration. These beds come in handy when rooms are let more than once in 24 hours, for meetings by day and a bedroom at night. This way the staff need not undertake the heavy task of converting the room for one purpose to the other.

Bed boards These are not extra beds, but they may help in enlarging a smaller bed if necessary. They are pieces of wood (generally plywood) as wide as the bed and almost as long, and may be placed between twin beds.

Selection of beds

In hotels, the most oft-recommended beds are those with box springs or metal-coil springs. With box springs, it is best to use interior-sprung mattresses to bring the bed to a standard height. With metal-coil springs, any kind of mattress may be used. Though flat bedsprings are the least expensive, they are also the least durable. Flat bedsprings are, however, commonly used in rollaways, since these beds are used infrequently. The better flat bedsprings have helical hooks connecting the metal strips to each other.

Care and cleaning of beds

To clean open-spring beds, dust and brush the open springs periodically and wipe with an oily rag. Use an underlay cloth made of felt on open-spring bed bases. The dust ruffles should be laundered as and when necessary. Check for loose headboards and footboards regularly. Remove the dust from the base of the bed using a soft brush or a vacuum cleaner with an upholstery attachment. Remove any stain, dirt, or grease mark from the headboard, footboard, base, and legs of the bed as well. Periodically polish the wood or metal areas, excepting the springs. Remove fluff and dust from the castor wheels, applying a little oil when they seem to squeak or feel stiff.

Mattresses

These may be medium-firm, extra firm, or super firm. An ideal mattress should give support and at the same time conform to the body contours. When choosing mattresses, it should be borne in mind that they ought to be at least 6 inches longer than the average sleeper's height.

Types of mattresses

There are primarily five types of mattresses.

Interior-sprung mattresses These mattresses have an inner layer of springs between layers of insulation and padding. Interior-sprung mattresses are of three types.

Open-spring mattresses These have hourglass-shaped wire coils sandwiched between wire frames.

Pocketed-spring mattresses The springs in these are cylindrical, and each is enclosed in a fabric or foam pocket.

Continuous-spring mattresses In these, the springs are made from wire that is linked and intertwined in a mesh-like pattern. Continuous-spring mattresses are ideal for double beds because they compress to the shape of the body. Thus, they are also referred to as 'posture-springing mattresses'.

The springs may be tied together with wire or helical hooks. Usually they are well padded with layers of cotton, coiled hair, rubber, or plastic foam, and the whole unit is then tightly covered with a strong ticking. Interior-sprung mattresses should have a reinforced edge for added strength. They vary in depth from 12–22 cm approximately. Their quality and price depends upon the number and gauge of the springs, the type of padding, and the quality of the ticking.

Latex or foam-rubber mattresses These mattresses are made from synthetic rubber that is whipped into foam with a chemical setting agent while in a semi-liquid state and poured into heated moulds. In the moulds, the foam gets shaped, set, and vulcanized without losing any of its tiny air cells. A good foam mattress may be about 10 cm deep (minimum) and have layers of foam, with the firmest layer at the bottom and the softest at the top. They normally have a right and a wrong side. These mattresses are extremely resilient—they regain their original shape rapidly after being lain on, and therefore, require no turning. They are not prone to attack by moths and other pests, either. The latex ones are more durable than the synthetic foam mattresses.

Solid-stuffed mattresses These mattresses are made by filling a ticking with padding. The padding may be in the form of animal hair, cotton, kapok, wool, coir, or flock. All stuffed mattresses are prone to attack by moths and other pests. They are also absorbent and require frequent turning when in use. They may also require frequent re-making as they tend to sag easily. For these reasons, hotels offering quality service do not opt for these mattresses.

Plastic mattresses These are made from polyethylene and vinyl foam. They are non-absorbent and resistant to attack by moths and other pests. For use in hotels, they should be treated with a fire-retardant finish since they produce toxic fumes on catching fire.

Water mattresses These resemble interior-sprung mattresses in appearance. Well-designed ones have water-filled cells in the centre of the mattress. These cells are covered with vinyl-covered urethane foam and the perimeter of the mattress has a row of inner spring coils that are meant to provide support to a person sitting on the edge of the bed. The ticking can be removed—there is a zipper along the top of the mattress—so that the cells can be serviced as necessary.

Sizes of mattresses

Standard mattress sizes have been given in Table 10.2.

Table 10.2 Standard mattress sizes

Mattresses	Size in feet and inches	Size in cm
Single	3 ft. × 6 ft. 3 in.	90 × 190
Single XL	3 ft. 3 in. × 6 ft. 6 in.	100 × 200
Double	4 ft. 6 in. × 6 ft. 3 in.	135 × 190
Queen	5 ft. 6 in. × 6 ft. 6 in.	165 × 200
King	6 ft. × 6 ft. 6 in.	180 × 200
California king	6 ft. × 6 ft. 10 in.	180 × 210
Crib	2 ft. 4 in. × 3 ft. 3 in.	70 × 100

Selection of mattresses

The following attributes must be checked when selecting a mattress.

Firmness Test the mattress to make sure it feels comfortable. Also make sure that the firmness is consistent across all parts of the mattress. Do a rest test to appraise the firmness, comfort, and support provided by the mattress. The housekeeper should insist on a sample mattress for a rest test before finalizing the purchase.

Construction Find out how the mattress is made. More expensive mattresses typically have a damask ticking, thicker padding, higher coil counts, and a cushion sewn into the mattress. Coil count and configuration seem to have little effect on durability, however. Sagging in mattresses is caused by the padding, not the coils. Therefore, when comparing mattresses, look for thicker, higher-quality padding. Different levels of durability and performance can be determined by different construction techniques (primarily by the type and thickness of the padding).

Size There are various sizes available according to the standard sizes of beds. Choose a larger size for a bigger room. Choose a smaller-sized bed if the room is not large enough to accommodate a large bed. Also remember, however, that a healthy sleeper moves anywhere from 40 to 60 times per night. It is important to choose a size that will allow sufficient freedom of motion while the guest sleeps and that will help the guest to relax while going to sleep (that is, he/she should not have to be in fear of falling off).

Softness Make sure that the mattress is soft at contact points; if not, the body will begin to ache, causing one to toss and turn and not sleep well.

Support The mattress should be firm enough to keep the body well aligned during sleep. If too soft, the spine and neck will not be supported and the occupant will get a sore neck and back.

Appearance Examine the colour, fabric, and stitch pattern to assess quality. However, remember that the mattress will be covered with sheets 99.9% of the time.

Ticking This is the mattress' outermost layer. Most are made of a cotton-polyester blend, polyester, or vinyl. Vinyl is used on cheaper mattresses. The blanket ticking should be sturdy, with a weight of at least 170 grams per square inch. The seams around the edges of the mattress should be rolled or reinforced.

Quilting and top padding Most mattresses have a few layers of padding attached to the ticking. These are generally made of foam.

Middle padding This padding often starts with 'egg-carton' foam and may also include thick wads of cotton called 'garnetted cotton'.

Insulated padding This padding lies directly on top of the springs to prevent them from being felt. Common materials include matted fabric, plastic fibres, and coco padding (made of fibre from coconut husks).

Coil count There should be more than 300 coils with a minimum of 13-gauge wire in the full-size version of the model you are considering. Likewise, there should be a minimum of 375 coils of 13-gauge wire in a queen-size mattress, and 450 coils of 13-gauge wire in a king-size. A high coil-count alone does not necessarily indicate a better product. The wire gauge is important—the lower the number, the more durable the wire (that is, a 13-gauge wire is thicker than a 15-gauge). Also, the number of turns in a coil and the type of technology will make a difference. The total weight of the spring is what you are trying to determine when evaluating the number of coils, the gauge of wire, and the number of turns. The heavier the spring, the better the support and durability provided.

Coil configurations The organization of the coils in, for example, hourglass formation or individual pockets.

Handles Most mattresses include handles to use when positioning the mattress. They are not meant for carrying the full weight, however.

Box spring (foundation) Box spring foundations provide extra softness and comfort. They can be simply a wooden frame covered with boards, a wooden frame with springs, or a metal frame with springs. Mattresses and box springs should be bought as a set because they are engineered to work together.

Care and cleaning of mattresses

Alternately rotating and flipping the mattress on a periodic basis can help minimize body impressions. While a mattress is brand new, slight body impressions may form, especially on extra-plush mattress surfaces. A body impression is the natural nesting and conforming that occurs as the cushioning materials contour to the sleeper's body. Turn spring mattresses over weekly for the first six weeks, and every three months after that. Reverse the mattress from head to foot as well. Turning mattresses regularly may increase their life span by 50%. A system of labelling mattresses at the corners to indicate the months

of rotation and turning, as shown in Exhibit 10.1, helps GRAs to follow a periodic mattress-turning schedule. Foam mattresses do not need turning; however, the single-layer ones may be turned. The mattress and base should be cleaned with a soft brush every month.

Do not use a vacuum cleaner on a daily basis as this may pull the upholstery out of shape. Check for tears, distorted springs, or any other damage periodically; check screws and nuts on the legs or castors of the bed frame and box spring at the same time, and tighten if necessary.

While making the bed, allow the mattress to breathe for at least 15 minutes—other guestroom cleaning tasks may be accomplished during this time. It is important to air the mattress in this way to dry out the moisture absorbed from the body during the night. Every bed should be covered with a moisture-proof mattress protector. The ideal ones are made of vinyl and are stain-resistant, non-allergenic, and flame-retardant.

See Table 10.3 for some additional tips on mattress care.

Exhibit 10.1 Mattress labelling for periodic turning schedule

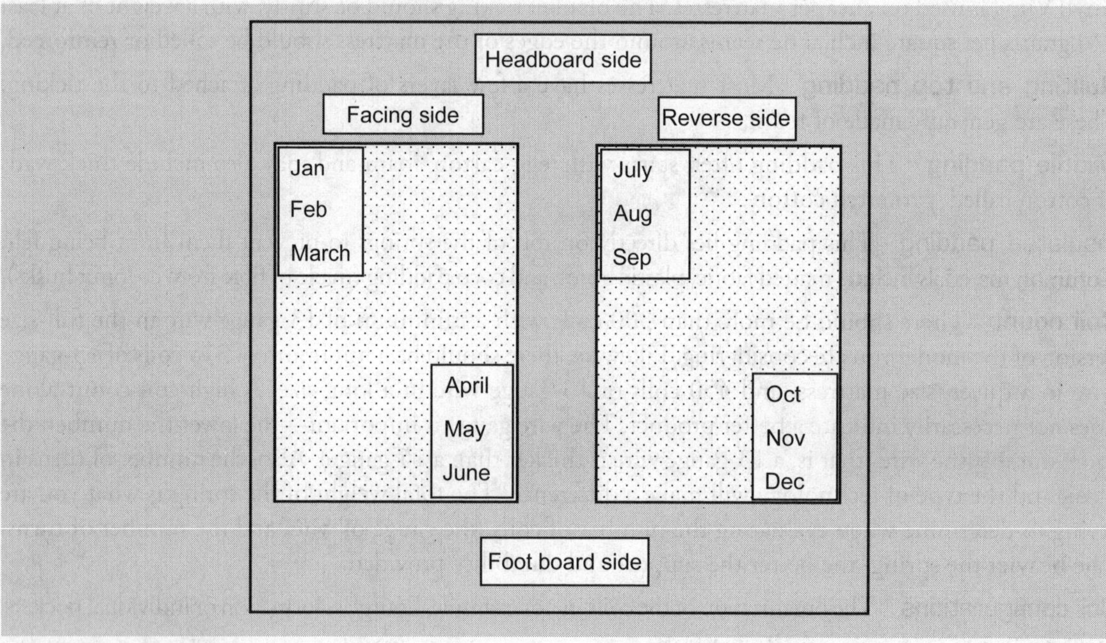

Table 10.3 Mattress care

Do	Don't
• Let the mattress breathe.	• Dry clean or wet the mattress. Vacuuming is the only recommended method.
• Use a protective, washable mattress pad.	• Remove the tag giving product information—it may be required during warranty claim.
• Purchase a sleep set (box spring plus the mattress) for satisfactory mattress performance and to increase mattress life.	• Bend, fold, drag, or drop the mattress
• Use a sturdy bed frame.	• Allow the mattress to be jumped upon.
• Rotate and flip the mattress regularly, as recommended by the manufacturer.	

Bedding

The term 'bedding' may be applied to all the bedclothes placed on the bed, such as mattress protectors, duvets or blankets, quilts, eiderdowns, pillows, and all other bed linen, such as sheets and bedspreads. The launderable bedding articles, collectively called 'bed linen', have already been discussed at length in Chapters 7 and 19. In this chapter, we shall discuss blankets, quilts, eiderdowns, and pillows.

Mattress protectors

The main function of a mattress protector is to protect the mattress from spills and stains. They also provide a padded layer between the guests and the mattress. Good quality mattress protectors are made of a quilted fabric, in which the filling may be of cotton or synthetic fibres. Cheaper mattress protectors are made of vinyl that has been felted.

Pillows, shams and bolsters

The best and most expensive pillows are filled with down. Others have a mixture of down and feathers, and some are filled with man-made fibres. Foam pillows are suitable for people allergic to dust and feathers. The life of a pillow varies according to the filling. A good down pillow, used constantly, may last upto 10 years. Feather pillows do not last as long. Foam pillows may also last about 10 years. Kapok, the cotton-like fibre from the seeds of the silk-cotton tree, was earlier used as a filling for pillows; but it is not used for pillows in hotels now since kapok-filled pillows cannot be laundered or dry-cleaned.

An ideal pillow should be neither too soft nor too hard. While selecting pillows, the housekeeper must first test their comfort using sample pillows supplied by the manufacturers. The second factor to be considered should be longevity. The use of protective pillow covers can double the life of the pillow for a fraction of the cost of buying a new pillow.

The fabric that encloses the filling is called the 'tick' or 'ticking' and is usually made of 100% cotton or polycot. For pillows with natural filling, a 100% cotton ticking with a minimum thread count of 180 is recommended. Ticking for synthetic-filled pillows can be blends ranging from 50/50 to 80/20 polycot. Hotel pillows usually have white ticking, often with a white-on-white pattern.

Finishes may be applied to pillows to make them hypo-allergenic, mildew-proof, moth-proof, flame-retardant, and fluid-proof.

Shams are usually placed along with standard pillows. They are in the form of cushions that typically match the fabric and pattern used in bedspreads or foot throws, also called foot runners. They add bright spots to a pristine white hotel bed.

Bolsters are elongated pillows used on settees, divans, and beds. In the past, they sometimes formed an under-pillow; but they are not used on the bed any more. Bolsters need not be as resilient, as the guest's head does not lie on them. They mainly act as a support for the arms.

Care and cleaning of pillows and bolsters Dust and shake the pillows lightly before making the bed. Any damage to the ticking should be repaired immediately. If the pillows have a synthetic filling, they may be washed individually on a regular basis. Pillows with natural fillings should be dry-cleaned when necessary. Latex and foam pillows can be wiped clean.

Pillow menu Many luxury hotels are now offering a pillow menu for guests to choose from eight to ten varieties of pillows such as orthocare, supersoft, silk cotton (hypoallergenic), cotton, buckwheat hull, aircare, relaxed support, slim rest, memory foam, bath support, and so on. The pillow menu card is placed on the bedside table and the guests can indicate their preference by a checkmark. The request pillow is delivered and presented with an embroidered pillow band around it, along with a card describing the features of the pillow. However, it is a challenge for the linen room to store each kind separately and handover the right pillow on request. To overcome this, each type of pillow (except the bath support pillow) may be lined with a different coloured cloth piping and stored.

Blankets

These are available in different sizes to fit all standard beds. Wool blankets are soft, warm, and wear well. They should be treated with moth-resistant finishes. Acrylic blankets are not as warm as wool, but they dry quickly and are moth-proof. A wool-and-rayon mix gives warmth and good wear at a lower price. Cotton blankets give less warmth, but are easy to wash and ideal for children's cots. Lightweight cellular blankets are made up of a series of pockets or cells that hold warm air. Sometimes an underblanket is also provided in hotels—this is also called a 'bed pad'. Blankets are generally a little shorter than the sheets as they do not require tucking in at the top.

A blanket should be lightweight for comfort, but at the same time must act as a thermal insulator. The choice of blanket colour varies from one hotel to the other. Some prefer to use light colours so that the guests may be impressed by the hotel's standards of cleanliness. Others use brown or another dark colour so that maintenance is easier. Usually blankets have a trim made of satin at the top and bottom edges.

Construction of blankets There are four basic methods of blanket construction:

Single-needle punched This construction is used for low-priced blankets as it produces blankets of low durability.

Fibre-woven This process involves a double-needle procedure that not only pushes the fibre through the blanket, but pulls it back for a firmer bonding weave. This results in a blanket more durable than one with a single-needle construction. This type of blanket is, however, still less expensive than a loom-woven blanket.

Loom-woven This method of construction gives the most durable product and is used for all premium blankets.

Moulded This type of blanket is constructed of nylon flocking moulded onto polyurethane foam.

Two different types of weaves are used in making blankets. Blankets with an open-weave construction are used in warm climates or during the summer months because the open-weave construction allows more body heat to escape. For other purposes, conventional woven blankets are used since they are more durable.

Finishes A blanket edge may be finished in one of two ways, being self-stitched or bound. Typically, either satin or nylon is used for the edge bindings, usually pieces about 3–7 inches wide. In hotels, it is simpler if different sizes of blankets are of different colours. For instance, all twin blankets may be beige and all double blankets may be navy blue. Other factors to consider are washability; resistance to moths, mould, and mildew; hypo- or non-allergenic materials; touchability; and flame-retardancy.

Electric blankets There are primarily three types of electric blankets: the overblanket, the preheat underblanket, and the low-voltage underblanket.

Overblanket The all-night overblanket is used above the top sheet and should have a light covering above it to prevent loss of warmth. A special device prevents it from overheating, and it can be safely left on all night. A thermostat adjusts to keep the warmth constant, whatever the temperature of the room.

Preheat underblanket This is laid between the mattress and the bottom sheet. It should be tied to the bed with tapes or tucked in with flaps attached to the border. It is used to preheat the bed and must be switched off before going to bed.

Low-voltage underblanket An all-night low-voltage underblanket draws power from the mains, but has a transformer that reduces the risk of a shock even if the blanket gets wet.

Care and cleaning of blankets Any damage should be repaired as soon as it is detected. Conventional blankets should be laundered or dry-cleaned when necessary. Stains and grease marks should be removed by spot-cleaning or dry-cleaning. On a daily basis, while making the bed, gently shake out the blankets.

After use, the plug of the electric blanket should be removed from the socket to disconnect the electric supply. These blankets should be kept as straight as possible and not crumpled or bent. They should never be allowed to get wet. Frayed flexes and other defects should be repaired by sending them for servicing to the manufacturer. The staff should not attempt to undertake any repair on electric blankets thermselves.

Duvets, eiderdowns, and quilts

Duvets or continental quilts give warmth without excessive weight or the restricting, tucked-in feeling of ordinary bed linen. A duvet is made of light but bulky material sewn between two layers of cloth. Down and feather fillings are the warmest. Synthetic fibres may be less warm, but are ideal for people allergic to natural fillings. Many hotels use a duvet with its cover as a bedspread, in which case a bottom sheet, a pillow, and a duvet with cover are all that are needed to make the bed. Duvets are three times lighter than the combined weight of all the linen that covers a guest in conventional bed-making, but they are just as warm. The warmth of a duvet is rated in 'togs', the average duvet having a rating of 10.5 togs and the warmer ones having a higher tog.

Eiderdowns, as the name suggests, are exclusive quilts filled with down feathers from the eider duck, which makes them very expensive. Cheaper imitations made with synthetic fibres are now available, which should not be really termed 'eiderdowns'.

Quilts are generally placed under the fold of the top sheet to keep them clean and avoid stains. They provide a warm but lightweight covering. The term 'quilts' is now generally used to cover eiderdowns, duvets, and all types of coverings with different fillings.

Care and cleaning of duvets and quilts Mend any tear and damage as soon as possible. Remove stains and grease marks immediately by dry-cleaning. Follow the manufacturer's instructions for regular cleaning of duvets and quilts. Always use duvets and quilts with easily launderable covers, so that these can be removed and washed separately. The cover of a duvet should be 2—4 inches larger than the duvet on each side to give it room to expand. Smooth out duvets and quilts with a light hand while making the bed. When storing feather-filled quilts and duvets, use moth-repellent chemicals.

Soft Furnishings

These articles serve various functions. Some may be simply decorative, providing colour, pattern, and texture to the room; some are protective; and others may provide warmth and comfort. Bedspreads and blankets have already been discussed in Chapter 7 and earlier in this chapter.

Types of Soft Furnishings

The soft furnishings in a guestroom include cushions, loose covers, curtains, blinds, bedspreads, and quilts.

Cushions

These can soften the stark lines of modern furniture and transform stools, chairs, and sofas into comfortable seating. They are the ideal type of furnishings to introduce colour, pattern, and texture into an otherwise plainly furnished room. They can be used in numerous ways to bring cheer to the room. They may be used in the form of scatter cushions; some may be used as back-rests in chairs; as shams on the bed; others may be shaped to fit sofas and chair seats. Indeed, they may be made in a wide range of sizes and shapes. Also, cushions may be covered in any of a variety of fabrics.

Cushion fillings The choice of filling depends upon the intended use of the cushion. Cheap fillings are adequate for decorative cushions, such as small scatter cushions that do not see much wear. Box cushions for chair tops, stools, or window seats need to be precisely shaped and able to withstand harder wear. They should ideally be filled with firm foam. The various types of fillings used are outlined in this section.

Feather mixtures These are used as filling for the best-quality readymade cushions. Feathers retain their resilience almost indefinitely. The various mixtures used are:

- Goose and duck down is the most expensive type of cushion filling. It is also the softest, most resilient, and as it is bulky for its weight, makes the lightest cushion.
- A feather-down mixture is less expensive, but heavier than pure down. A cushion with this filling is not as soft as an all-down cushion.
- Goose or duck feathers do not have as much bulk as down and therefore, more feathers are needed to fill a cushion, resulting in a heavier cushion.
- Chicken feathers are the cheapest type of feather filling. They are usually curled to increase their bulk and resilience.

Kapok Obtained from the silk-cotton tree, kapok is cheap, soft, and resilient. Its disadvantage is that it tends to become lumpy in time. It should only be used for decorative cushions and not for hard wear, since it deteriorates on washing or dry-cleaning.

Fibre filling Terylene, a polyester fibre, is often used for cushion fillings as it is light, resilient, non-allergenic, non-absorbent, and completely washable.

Polystyrene beads These are mainly used for large cushions. They are packed fairly loosely in the cushion, but compress under weight and so make a filling firm enough to sit on and comfortable enough to lie on.

Foam crumbs and chips These make the cheapest commercial filling and are easily laundered. However, they give a very lumpy finish to the cushion.

Whole foam This is widely used in cushions because it is comfortable, easy to use, inexpensive, non-allergenic, and long-lasting. It weighs less in relation to its bulk and stands up to constant use without distortion. Foam can be made into many shapes and can be moulded according to the furniture as well. The two types of foam used are *latex foam*, made from natural and synthetic rubber, and *polyurethane foam*, made from plastic. Latex foam is the more expensive of the two and more resilient. Latex foams may be plain or pin-core foams. In the latter, there are small holes on both sides of the foam sheet. Both latex and polyurethane foam deteriorate and eventually break down if exposed to sunlight. Hence, they should always be kept covered with fabric.

Care and cleaning of cushions Cushions should be shaken daily and patted lightly into shape. They should be repaired as soon as they develop tears. They should be dusted and suction-cleaned regularly with an upholstery attachment. Cushion covers should be removed and laundered regularly.

Loose covers

These may protect new furniture, enhance the appearance of a worn sofa or chair, or harmonize a piece of furniture with a new colour scheme. The best fabrics to use for making loose covers are closely woven cotton-and-linen blends. The material used should be easily launderable or possible to dry-clean. A closely woven fabric is advisable, as it does not allow dust to penetrate, is abrasion-resistant, and holds its shape. The fastening used may be velcro, hooks and eyes, or zippers. To protect upholstered furniture from soiling at the arms and back, decorative and protective shields called antimacassars are used. They may be of the same colour as the loose covers, but are generally off-white or cream linen. They should be fastened firmly to the surface. Decorative foot throws or runners on the bed too may be considered as loose covers. These are made of silk brocade or shiny rayon damask.

Care and cleaning Loose covers should be dusted daily. Suction-cleaning may be done occasionally. They should be detached and laundered or dry-cleaned when necessary. Attend to stains and grease marks immediately. Mend any tear as soon as possible.

Curtains

These often contribute more to the atmosphere of a room than any other item of furnishing. Plain, heavy curtains draping to the floor are used to create a formal setting. Short curtains made of light, brightly patterned fabrics are used to create an informal, relaxed atmosphere. Apart from creating the desired atmosphere, curtains give flexible control of privacy, heat, light, and to some extent noise. The material chosen for curtains should not soil easily or collect dust. It should also be washable and resistant to fading from sunlight or repeated laundering. The fabric's drape, dimensional stability, and flame-retardancy are also important factors. Besides, curtains must provide privacy without blocking sunlight during daytime. Net, sheer, or lace curtains provide enough privacy during the day while allowing sunlight to filter in. At night, however, this is not sufficient, hence heavy curtains are needed both for privacy and for keeping streetlights and such out.

The various fabrics used for making curtains are cotton, linen, rayon, glass fibres, acrylics, and silk for luxurious settings. Curtains are subject to abrasion from being drawn together and apart, being brushed against, and rubbing against the floor and the window frames and sills. The abrasion resistance of the curtain depends upon its component fibres. Synthetic fibres such as polyester and nylon have excellent abrasion resistance.

Silk is an expensive fabric and silk curtains are used to create a luxurious ambience in world-class hotels.

Fabrics made of glass fibre, wool, and acrylic are fire-retardant and suitable for use as curtains.

Sheer curtains are normally made of cotton or polyester, the latter being far superior as regards durability, appearance, and maintenance.

Care should be taken to minimize their exposure to sunlight and airborne dirt as these reduce the curtains' functional life. Good curtains are usually lined and heavy curtains are interlined. The lining helps the curtains to drape well, as well as protecting from sunlight and airborne dust. Curtains should be hung to reach half an inch above the floor.

Types of curtains Glass curtains, sash curtains, draw curtains, and draperies are the most commonly used curtains in hotel guestrooms. These have been discussed in detail in Chapter 27.

Care and cleaning of curtains Bring down and launder or dry-clean curtains occasionally, since dust and grime lead to deterioration of the fabric. Heavy curtains may be washed only once a year unless

they are highly stained and require immediate attention. Before sending them for wash, the blackouts and velcro, if used, must be removed. Sheer curtains should be washed whenever the room is taken on preventive maintenance. If stained, they should immediately be sent for washing. While hung up, they should be vacuum-cleaned frequently using an appropriate attachment. Solvent extraction machines are ideal for cleaning heavy curtains. Mend any damage to the curtain and the lining immediately. A record detailing the frequency of cleaning curtains must be maintained.

Valances and swags

Valances are gathered or pleated fabrics draped across the top of a window or covering a shaped form placed above it. They conceal the curtain tops and the rods from which the curtains hang. Swags are decorative drapes meant to hide the curtain headings and usually taper to a cascade (also called a 'tail').

Valances and swags should be vacuum-cleaned regularly. Valances and swags are discussed in greater detail in Chapter 27, under window treatments.

Blinds, shades, shutters, and screens

There are many types of coverings apart from curtains that are used on windows to ensure privacy and to block out light.

Blinds These can be of several designs and mechanisms. Roller blinds, Roman blinds, Venetian blinds, vertical louvre blinds, pinoleum blinds, balastore blinds, pleatex blinds, and Austrian blinds are some of the most commonly used blinds. For a detailed discussion on the different types of blinds, refer to Chapter 27.

Shades These come in two main variants—bamboo shades and fabric roller shades. For a detailed discussion on shades, refer to Chapter 27.

Shutters and screens These usually consist of moveable wood slats arranged on a framework. Moving in sections, they can provide varying degrees of privacy and light control. They may also act as a layer of indoor insulation over the windows. Screens are often in the form of hardboard panels with cut-out panels or fabric stretched on a frame. They are attached to the window frame and so do not allow flexibility in the control of light. There are now tracks that allow a screen to be moved to one side when an unrestricted view is desired. Shutters and screens have been discussed in greater detail in Chapter 27.

Care and cleaning of blinds, shades, shutters, and screens Dust them thoroughly on a daily basis. They should be damp-wiped occasionally. Get any damages repaired as soon as possible. Get specialized contractors in for periodic cleaning.

Guestroom Accessories

Accessories are elements that bring charm, individuality, and vitality to a room. The right accessories help to stress the decorative theme of the room. They can be the ultimate expression of the style of furnishing that is employed. 'Accessories' is a term that refers to most of the additional furnishings needed to make a room viable in all senses. Accessories include the small objects that are both useful and decorative. Variety is a source of pleasure in accessories. Accessories differ in size, height, texture, colour, period,

cost, and origin. Furnishings depend upon accessories for charming effects to such an extent that it is possible for the very same furniture to appear uninteresting in a furniture store and yet become the focal point of a room properly furnished.

Common accessories in hotel guestrooms include pictures on the walls; decorative, ceramic, or terracotta vases and lamps; brass articles and artefacts; stone sculptures; crystal artefacts; candlesticks; wall hangings; ornamental mirrors; and so on. Accessories and their classification are discussed in greater detail in Chapter 27 on Interior Decoration.

Placement of Guest Supplies

Guest supplies include all the items that are conducive to the guest's material comfort and convenience. They are subdivided into guest amenities, essentials, expendables, and loan items as outlined in Chapter 7, Table 7.16. Many hotels follow a common pattern in placement of guest supplies in their guestrooms.

In the Bedroom

The guest supplies placed in various areas of the guest bedroom are discussed in this section.

Behind the door The following are placed here:

- A DND card, the reverse of which may be the 'please make up my room' card, on the door knob on the inside of the door
- A detailed map of fire exits is ideally affixed behind the door
- A notice reminding guests of the safe-deposit facilities at the cashier's desk

At the writing table These are the usual supplies on and around the guestroom desk:

- A guest stationery folder (also referred to as a room compendium) with monogrammed note papers, envelopes, post cards with the hotel's pictures, and guest comment forms are placed on the table. A note pad, pen, pencil and stationery kit are also placed alongside
- The spa menu outlining the services of the spa with their pricing is placed
- Tent cards (publicity cards folded in the shape of a tent) giving information about special events and shows in the hotel are also placed on the desk or on the nightstand
- Room tariff card for the different kinds of rooms offered, in a frame or holder
- An ashtray (in smoking rooms only)
- A candle, a candle holder, and a matchbox
- The hotel brochure
- A docking station for charging multiple devices
- A spike guard with multiple power sockets
- A universal power adapter in the drawer of the desk
- A lined wastepaper basket next to the writing table, on the floor
- A chair with backrest is placed in front of the writing table

On the bedside table Any of a variety of supplies may be found on or in the nightstand:

- The telephone and the service directory are placed on the bedside table
- A note pad and a pencil are placed beside the phone

- An ashtray and a matchbox. In twin rooms two ashtrays with matchboxes are kept on the two bedside tables. This is done in smoking rooms only.
- A breakfast knob card is usually kept on the first shelf or in the drawer of the bedside table. This card is placed on the pillow during evening service in many hotels
- A pillow menu card with details of various types of pillows offered by the hotel is displayed on the bedside table
- A conservation card, Sustainability card, You care -Linen reuse card or Eco card placed as a tent card. A sample of the card is presented in Chapter 32, Exhibit 32.1
- In the lowermost shelf of the bedside table, a Bible, Gita, or Quran is placed. In Buddhist countries, *The Life and Thoughts of Lord Buddha* may be placed
- A channel music panel may be affixed to the bedside table
- A bedside lamp is placed on the bedside table. If there are two tables, there may be two bedside lamps
- A Good Night kit, containing two small vials of certain essential oil blends, ear plugs, eye pad, and a couple of mints, is placed in the upper drawer of the bedside table
- Two 500 ml mineral water bottles are kept on coasters or a small tray on the bedside table

On the coffee table These are the usual supplies here:

- An ashtray and a matchbox are placed on the coffee table in smoking rooms only
- The house magazine or a tourist magazine, a business magazine and a newspaper are also neatly arranged on the coffee table
- The room service menu is placed on the coffee table or on the minibar counter
- A letter of greeting signed by the general manager, wishing guests on special holidays or feasts, may be placed on the coffee table

In the drawer and cupboard These are usually found in the wardrobe or chest of drawers, or else sometimes in a nightstand drawer.

- A sewing or mending kit (a 'Dutch wife') is placed in a drawer. It comprises of two small skeins of black and white threads, two buttons, two snap buttons, a needle and a safety pin
- Laundry bags and two laundry lists specifying laundry facilities, charges and terms and conditions.
- A Yoga kit containing a Yoga mat, aroma oil diffusers and oil vials, Yoga attire, and a Yogasana book
- A couple of canvas/jute utility bags may also be placed in the wardrobe for guests to keep their shoes or wet swimming suits in, or to use for other purposes
- A hair dryer in the cupboard drawer or in a receptacle in the bathroom
- Clothes hangers (6 coat hangers and 2 clip hangers), all facing one direction, are hung on hooks or a hanging rod inside the cupboard
- A fragrance sachet hanger
- The guestroom safe is usually affixed inside the cupboard. It is lined with an underlay and may have a jewellery tray
- An iron box and a light-weight ironing board are placed in the vertical compartment of the cupboard
- Two extra pillows are placed on top shelf of the cupboard
- An umbrella is placed on the cupboard shelf

Below the luggage rack The luggage rack usually has a lower shelf for guests to keep their shoes on. The shoe mitt, shoe horn and a shoe shine kit is also be placed on this shelf. A shoe basket with a shoe liner is placed next to the luggage rack.

At the dressing table These supplies may be on or near the dressing table where there is one. Else they may be part of the vanity unit in the bathroom:

- An upholstered stool is placed under the dressing table and it can be pulled out when required
- A mirror is mounted on the wall with appropriate lighting facility
- Combs and brushes are placed in the dressing-table drawer
- For your care kit/Grooming kit comprising of cotton swabs, ear buds, nail filers, tooth pick, and a small nail clipper is placed on the dressing table or in the dresser drawer or on bathroom vanity counter

On the bed Ideally, there would be nothing on the bed except the linen listed here, but sometimes a small gift or box of chocolates may be placed on the pillow as part of the turndown service.

- A mattress, with a mattress protector on it
- Bed sheets, night spread, pillows with pillowcases, a duvet with cover or a blanket, few shams, a foot throw and a bed spread in some hotels

In the television cabinet This, of course, is fairly obvious—this is where you would find the television, usually one equipped with a satellite network, and the remote control. A channel list is placed on the TV counter.

In the minibar All, some, or none of these may be included, depending on the type of hotel and the type of guestroom, as well as sometimes the profile of the guest.

- Mineral water bottles
- Beverages such as liquor and soft drinks
- Ice trays
- Lemon wedges
- Some chocolates

On the minibar counter These supplies may be on a small side table near the guestroom entrance, or on the counter atop the minibar.

- Hospitality tray with a variety of tea bags and sachets of coffee powder, demerara sugar, white sugar, zero-calorie sweetener, milk creamer pods and a condiment packet containing salt and pepper powder
- On the same tray, a 1 litre bottle of RO water, a couple of cups, saucers, underliners, spoons, few paper napkins, a couple of highball glasses and coasters
- A kettle and/or coffee maker
- Some savoury snacks in packets
- An ice bucket and ice tongs on a tray
- Minibar price list

In the Sitting Area

The following items are usually found in the sitting area:

- A sofa and two easy chairs
- An occasional table and a pot pourri on it
- A lampshade

In the Bathroom

A bathroom usually has the following fixtures and guest supplies:

- A full length mirror at the entrance
- A bath robe hung on a hook behind the bathroom door
- A bath tub and a bath mat
- A water closet
- A tissue holder with a tissue roll, and a hygiene faucet affixed on the wall near the WC
- A pot pourri, that is, dried flower petals with added fragrance, in a bowl
- A small/ miniature indoor plant

On or near the vanity unit Supplies near the vanity unit are as follows:

- Vanity tray with monogrammed soaps, loofah pads, 40–50 ml bottles of shampoo, conditioner, body lotion, cologne, aftershave lotion, and bath gels
- Shower caps, gargle/tooth glasses with coasters, tissue box, sani-bag, razor blades, dental kit, and shaving kit
- A digital weighing scale on a shelf under the vanity counter
- A vanity mirror and a magnifying shaving mirror mounted on the wall with appropriate lighting facility
- A sani-bin beside the WC or under the vanity counter

On the towel rack The towel rack consists of the following supplies:

- Bath towels and bath sheets on the towel rack
- Hand towels and face towels (these may also be near or on the vanity unit)
- Wash cloths

In the Balcony

In the balcony are placed the following:

- Two chairs with cushions
- A balcony table
- A retractable clothes line

SUMMARY

In this chapter, we have discussed the standard contents of a hotel guestroom. Due to the stiff competition in the industry and the advent of foreign hotel chains in India, many innovative trends, contents, and supplies are being introduced in hotels. Students, therefore, need to keep abreast of the latest developments with regard to the contents of a guestroom.

In terms of content, furniture occupies a large expanse of area in the guestroom. Hotels spend a considerable amount on these as a long-term investment. Indeed, if carefully selected, a piece of furniture can have a long functional life. Factors to be considered in selecting furniture have been outlined. The options available in terms of types of furniture and materials used in their construction have been discussed. Specifications based on the ergonomics for guestroom furniture are outlined. Furniture arrangement has been given considerable attention, as it is a vital aspect functionally as well as aesthetically. Further, important guestroom fixtures and fittings have been enumerated.

The main piece of furniture in the guestroom is the bed. A good bed means a good night's sleep—the basic requirement of a traveller. Hence, beds, mattresses, and bedding have been dealt with in much detail in this chapter. The selection of beds and mattresses is vital in achieving the objective of a good night's sleep, as is their care and cleaning. Certain items of bedding have been discussed in this chapter. The reader may refer to Chapter 7 for other bedding articles. Items of soft furnishing, which includes cushions, curtains, loose covers, and blinds, have also been discussed.

Accessories are often left out in discussions on the contents of a guestroom. However, their importance should be emphasized and they should be used to full advantage to bring out various moods and themes in guestrooms. The accessories commonly used in guestrooms have been discussed in this chapter.

The chapter concludes with the common pattern of placement of guest supplies in hotel guestrooms. The exact placement may differ from hotel to hotel.

KEY TERMS

Antimacassars These are decorative pieces of cloth used as shields for the arms and backs of upholstered furniture to protect them from soiling.

Antiques Antique furniture belongs to the period before the year 1840, though nowadays any piece of furniture that is more than 100 years old is considered an antique.

Armchair Large, comfortable chair with padded arms and cushion.

Bath sheets These are extra-large bath towels provided in VIP rooms in luxury hotels providing world-class service.

Bed boards These are pieces of wood (generally plywood) as wide as the bed and almost as long, placed between the bed base and the mattress.

Bedding A collective term for all articles on a bed.

Bidet These are sanitary fixtures meant for the thorough washing of the genitals and anus; but these are now increasingly being used as footbaths.

Breakfast knob card Cards hung by guests on the guestroom door knobs to pre-order breakfast at night so that the order reaches the staff on time, and the guest need not be disturbed to obtain the order early in the morning.

Burl grain Knotted grain in wood.

Calico Plain white, unprinted cotton cloth (British usage; in America, it refers to printed cotton fabric.).

Cantilevered Fixed on brackets or fitted to the wall, so that there are no legs to get in the way of cleaning.

Case goods Furniture made of wood with a top and sides, such as desks, luggage racks, chests of drawers, and pieces that provide storage.

Castors These are wheels fixed at the base or to the legs of furniture and equipment to make them mobile.

Compendium Another name for the guest stationery folder kept on the writing table in guestrooms.

Conservation card Also referred to as You care -linen reuse card, Eco card or Sustainability card, it indicates a choice to guests to opt for change of linen once in 2–3 days, in line with the hotel's sustainability programme.

Credenza A piece of furniture used as a sideboard, characterized by a long top and storage space below.

Cribs Cots for babies provided to guests on request.

Curio Primarily a glass display cabinet with a mirror on the back and metal or wood frame, used to display objects of some common theme.

DND cards 'Do not disturb' card, hung outside the guestroom by the guest to inform staff and visitors that the occupant does not wish to be disturbed.

Docking station A device into which a laptop, smartphone, or other mobile devices my be placed for charging or/and providing access to power supply and peripheral devices.

Down Soft, fluffy feathers found underneath the contour feathers of adult birds, especially that of ducks and swans and used for stuffing pillows, cushions, and quilts.

Dutch wife Another term for the sewing kit provided as a guest amenity.

Duvets Quilts filled with down feathers or synthetic fibres. Many hotels use duvets with a decorative duvet cover to replace both blankets and bedspreads. They are sometimes referred to as comforters.

Eiderdown The soft, fluffy feathers beneath the contour feathers of adult eider ducks, used for stuffing pillows, cushions, or quilts; also the name given to quilts made from these feathers.

Ergonomics The study of people in relation to their working environment.

Fixtures Hardware items present in guestrooms that cannot be moved or are difficult to move since they are fixed in position. For example, wash basins and WCs.

Foot throw or foot runner A decorative cloth panel made of silk brocade or shiny rayon damask laid across the duvet on the foot end side of a hotel bed. It matches the shams placed against the pillows.

Furnishings These include soft furnishings, carpets, fittings, and furniture.

Furniture glides Small disks or squares affixed to the base of furniture legs to protect carpet pile.

Good Night kit A kit containing two small vials of certain essential oil blends for relaxation, pillow mist, ear plugs, eye pad, and a couple of mints; it is usually placed in the upper drawer of the bedside table.

Grille Metal lattice work or screen of metal wires or bars.

Guest amenities All the luxury items that a hotel gives away at no extra cost to guests.

Guest essentials Items that are essential to the guestroom and are not used up or expected to be taken away by guests.

Guest expendables Those guest supplies that guests are expected to use up or take away when leaving the property.

Guest loan items These are guest supplies not normally found in a guestroom, but available upon request. For example, hot water bottles, ice packs.

Guest supplies All items that are conducive to the guest's increased material comfort and convenience. They are further subdivided as guest amenities, guest essentials, guest expendables, and guest loan items.

Hygiene faucets Handheld sanitary devices found attached to the walls next to WCs and bidets, primarily meant for delivering a continuous spray of water through a lever-triggered, perforated nozzle for cleaning. Also called health faucets or jet sprays.

Heartwood The dense inner part of a tree trunk, yielding the hardest timber.

Helical hooks Small coils with hooks at both ends, used in construction of beds and mattresses.

Hessian Strong coarse cloth of hemp or jute.

Hospitality tray A tray usually placed above or near the minibar in guestrooms for guests to stir up their own tea/coffee. On it are placed the coffee maker, cups, saucers, spoons, varieties of tea and coffee sachets, sugar sachets, milk creamer pods and a condiment packet containing salt and pepper powder.

Inlay The setting of wood, metal, ivory, or other pieces into a surface for decorative effect.

Kapok It is the smooth, light, and lustrous fibre obtained from the seeds of the silk-cotton tree. It is used as a filling for cushions, pillows, and quilts.

Laquer Coloured varnish made of shellac dissolved in alcohol.

Louvres Angled slats of plastic, wood, or glass inset into windows or shutters to control entry of air and light.

Luggage rack A furniture item provided in guestrooms for placing the guest's luggage on.

Minibar A fixture in modern guestrooms, it is a miniature refrigerator stocked with juices, liquor, and snacks for the convenience of guests.

Monogram Letters of identification, woven or printed on articles in a distinctive or decorative pattern.

Mortise A space cut in a piece of wood to receive a projecting piece of similar shape.

Murphy bed This kind of bed folds up into the walls and looks like a bookshelf or cupboard when folded away. It is also called a sico bed. Both names derive from manufacturers of such furniture.

Night spread A distinctly woven sheet used to cover and protect the blanket. It is now more often called a 'third sheet'. Other names for the night spread are 'crinkle sheet' and 'snooze sheet'.

Nightstand A small table or cabinet designed to stand beside a bed or elsewhere in a bedroom, as a place to put anything likely to be required during the night; also called a 'night table'.

Ottoman A piece of furniture consisting of an upholstered seat, without a back or arms, often used as a footstool at the foot end of beds in guestrooms. Most ottomans are hollow and may be used for storage as well.

Patina The smooth texture and colour changes of a wood or metal surface produced by age and wear.

Pillow menu A list of various types of pillows provided by a hotel to guests, usually free of charge. It allows guests to make an alternative pillow choice.

Some common pillow alternatives are orthocare, hypoallergenic, memory foam, buckwheat hull, and so on.

Pot pourri A blend of dried, naturally or artificially scented plant material such as petals, tiny florets and twigs used to impart a gentle fragrance in rooms. It is placed in a decorative bowl or a diffusing sachet.

Sani-bin These are small metal or plastic containers with lids, kept in toilets for the collection of soiled sanitary towels.

Sapwood Soft outer layers of recently formed wood between the heartwood and the bark of the tree.

Service directory This is a booklet in which the services offered to guests by the hotel are listed, along with the intercom numbers to reach the relevant department.

Shams The American term for pillowcases. In the Indian hotel industry, 'shams' is used for pillowcases that match the fabric and pattern used in bedspreads rather than the sheets. These are used in very formal settings.

Shoe mitt Flannel cloths, usually in the shape of a mitten, kept in hotel rooms as guest supplies for cleaning shoes. Nowadays instead of flannel, rice-paper tissues are used.

Sico beds See Murphy bed.

Soft furnishings These include curtains, cushions, loose covers, bedspreads, and quilts, but not carpets.

Spike guard An appliance consisting of multiple sockets (4–6) for electric and electronic devices, an extension cord and a couple of fuses.

Spline Flexible wood strip.

Swag A piece of drapery hung to hide the curtain heading and very often completed with a cascade (sometimes termed a 'tail').

Tenon The tongue or projecting part of wood that is fitted into the space called the mortise.

Tent cards Hotel publicity cards in the shape of tents, placed in guestrooms.

Ticking A strong, sturdy cloth used to cover mattresses, pillows, and upholstery; a cover made of this.

Universal power adapter A plug-in device that can plug into multiple types of sockets making it convenient to adapt to plug variations in different countries.

Upholstery Textiles used for furniture décor.

Valance This is a decorative heading made of frilled or pleated material that hangs from a valance rail, fixed over the top of the curtain to hide the hardware and to add to the decor of the room.

Vanity units A unit comprising a wash basin and mirror, surrounded by a flat counter where soaps, a dental kit, a shaving kit, and tooth glasses are kept.

Veneer A thin outer coating, often of finer wood on another wooden surface.

Webbing Strong, closely woven fabric used to support upholstery.

WHB The term WHB refers to wash basins.

Wicker Shoots (osiers) of willow plants, used for making woven items such as bread baskets, flower baskets, mats, trays, stools, sofas, chairs, and tables.

Wing chair A comfortable upholstered chair with a high back and extending sides, or 'wings'.

Zed bed Fold-away beds with a slatted wood frame that folds into a double-hinged shape of three sections; named after the letter 'z' which it resembles because of its three jointed parts.

Cleaning Principles Procedures and Organization

Learning Objectives

After reading this chapter, you should be able to
- understand the nature and types of soil on various surfaces and the ways in which soiling presents itself
- lay down the standards for cleaning
- understand the scientific terminology that appertains to cleaning
- list the principles of cleaning and describe the various procedures of cleaning
- outline the safety and hygiene factors in cleaning
- categorize cleaning tasks with regard to their frequency and explain how cleaning may be organized in various ways in hotels
- understand the importance of SOPs in cleaning

Introduction

Cleaning is the removal of dust, dirt, foreign matter, tarnish, and stains from various surfaces with the aid of certain cleaning agents and equipment. Dust, dirt, and foreign matter deposited on a surface are referred to as soil. This may include substances such as sand, mud, pollutants, smoke, and fumes brought into the building from outside. Some types of soil, such as sewage, hair, dead skin cells, and fibres shed from the clothing are generated by the occupants of a building.

Cleaning is carried out for the following reasons:

Aesthetic appeal The environment is made visually attractive and appealing.

Hygiene Effective, frequent cleaning controls the growth and reproduction of pathogenic bacteria and other germs.

Maintenance Surfaces and articles, however good in quality, will have a long, functional life only when they are cleaned on a regular basis.

Safety Cleaning is done for safety against health hazards, fire hazards, and slip hazards.

Types of Soil

As explained earlier in the chapter, soil is the collective term for deposits of dust, dirt, foreign matter, tarnish, and stains.

Dust This is composed of loose particles deposited from the air. It contains both organic (human and animal hair, dead skin cells, particles of excreta, pollen from plants, and so on) and inorganic (sand, dry earth) matter. Although dust is light, it is heavier than air and thus settles readily on any surface, horizontal as well as vertical.

Dirt This implies dust held together firmly by moisture or grease on rough surfaces.

Tarnish This is a discolouring or deposition on a metal or alloy surface caused by chemical reaction with certain substances found in air, water, and foodstuffs. Each metal gets a different type of tarnish when exposed for too long to these substances. For instance, iron gets a reddish-brown rust, copper gets a greenish deposit of verdigris, and silver gets blackened. There are different methods for the removal of tarnish from different metals.

Stain This is a discoloration caused on a hard or soft surface by a substance containing dyes, proteins, acids, or alkalis. Stains are difficult to remove by routine cleaning processes. Any stain must be removed as soon as possible by using powders to absorb it, solvents to dissolve it, or an acidic or alkaline cleaner to neutralize it.

Foreign matters These may be dead flowers, contents of wastepaper baskets and ashtrays, as well as stains from the deposition of foreign substances (as opposed to the result of a chemical reaction).

Nature of Soil

All the above types of soil may be categorised under at least one of the following heads, depending on the nature of the substance responsible.

Inorganic or mineral A homogeneous chemical element or compound, solid, liquid, or gaseous substance, having a chemical composition resulting from the inorganic processes of nature.

Organic A substance that has a plant or animal origin. Organic compounds are basically hydrocarbons, that is, they essentially contain the elements—carbon, hydrogen, and oxygen.

Osmological These are substances containing either organic or inorganic matter that emit an unpleasant odour.

Bacterial Some soils may contain live bacteria or their spores, which may cause diseases or infections.

Entomological These soils harbour insects, especially those that are carriers of disease and infection.

Standards of Cleaning

Depending on the purpose of the area and surfaces to be cleaned, various standards of cleaning may be imposed. Once a standard has been established, there should be strict adherence to the cleaning methods required, and efficient training and supervision is called for. There may be different standards of cleaning for different surfaces and areas, as follows:

Physically or aesthetically clean When this standard is set, the area or surface is supposed to be free from apparent dust and dirt, as when wiped by hand.

Chemically clean This standard means that the area should be free from harmful chemicals on the surfaces and in the surrounding air.

Bacteriologically clean To meet this standard, the surfaces should be cleaned so as to be free from any harmful bacteria that may cause disease or infection. This is referred to as 'clinical standard' as most hospitals follow this standard for their general wards.

Entomologically clean This means that the area should be free from harmful insects or pests.

Osmologically clean This cleaning standard demands that the surfaces and areas should be free from any organic or inorganic matter that may emit an odour.

Clinically or terminally clean This refers to the standard of cleaning usual in operation theatres and intensive care units in hospitals, where surfaces need to be constantly sanitized against all kinds of pathogenic microbes.

The Science of Cleaning

To understand the process of cleaning using various agents, one needs to know the terminology associated with cleaning agents, cleaning processes, and the surfaces being cleaned.

Terminology of Cleaning

These are certain basic terms from chemistry and biology, knowledge of which is required for a better understanding of all that the cleaning processes entail. The list given in Exhibit 11.1, which organizes them alphabetically, and it is recommended that the reader go through the entire list to understand all the terms.

Exhibit 11.1 Some common terminology in cleaning

Terminology used in cleaning	
Acids: Substances made up of hydrogen ions combined with anions. *See Anions.* *Aerobic:* Refers to the presence of oxygen in a reaction. *Aerosols:* Particles dispersed in gas and packed under pressure with a device for releasing them as a fine spray. *Alcohols:* Organic compounds containing the OH^- ion as the reactive group. They are commonly called 'spirits'. *Algae:* These are mainly aquatic, eukaryotic, single-celled or multicellular plants without true roots, leaves, and flowers. They are typically autotrophic, photosynthetic, and contain chlorophyll. They may also attach to underwater structures, rocks, or other submerged surfaces. *Alkali:* An inorganic compound made up of hydroxyl ions (OH^-) combined with cations. *See Cations.* *Anaerobic:* Refers to the absence of oxygen in a reaction. *Anion:* A negatively charged ion. *See also ion.*	*Antiseptic:* An agent that makes the environment non-conducive to the growth and reproduction of disease-causing (pathogenic) microbes. *Asepsis:* Rendering a surface free of microbes and infection. *Atom:* The smallest particle of an element that displays the properties of that element. *Autoclave:* Equipment used to sterilize articles using steam under pressure. *Bacteria:* Single-celled micro-organisms that can exist either independently or as parasites. *Bactericide:* An agent that kills most bacteria, but not their spores. *Bacteriostat:* An agent that makes the environment non-conducive to the growth and reproduction of bacteria. *Biodegradable:* Substances that can be decomposed by the action of living organisms. *Cations:* A positively charged ion. *See also ion.*

(Contd.)

Exhibit 11.1 *Contd.*

Terminology used in cleaning	
Caustic alkalis: Very strong alkalis such as sodium hydroxide (caustic soda). *Cells:* All living organisms are made up of basic units called cells. *CFCs:* Chlorofluorocarbons—organic compounds containing carbon, chlorine, and fluorine. These are substances used in air-conditioning and refrigeration systems. When these substances break down on exposure to ultraviolet rays, the resultant products react with the protective ozone layer of the earth and damage it. *Chemical compounds:* Substances whose molecules are composed of atoms of at least two different elements. For instance, sodium carbonate (Na_2CO_3). *Chemical reaction:* A process that leads to a chemical change. The substances that take part in the reaction are called reactants, while the substances produced in the reaction are called products. *Chlorine:* An element of the halogen group used as a sanitizer and a bleach. *Corrosion:* The wasting away of metals layer by layer due to the formation of metal compounds on the surface is called corrosion. Corrosion in the case of iron takes the form of rusting. *Detergents:* Cleaning agents that, when used in conjunction with water, can loosen and remove dirt, and then hold it in suspension so that the dirt is not re-deposited on the clean surface. They can be of two types—soapy detergents and synthetic detergents (non-soap). *Dilution:* The process of reducing the strength of a cleaning agent by adding other solvents, usually water. *Disinfectants:* Substances used to destroy pathogenic micro-organisms. The term 'disinfectant' is now used as a general term that covers all kinds of agents that bring about germ control. *Elements:* These are substances, metals or non-metals, that cannot be further divided into two or more substances. *Germs:* A common term used for microbes, especially bacteria. *Halogens:* A group of reactive elements belonging to the seventh group in the periodic table. The important elements in this group are chlorine, bromine, iodine, and fluorine.	*Health:* A state of complete physical, mental, social, and spiritual well-being, and not just the absence of disease/infirmity. *Hydrocarbons:* Compounds containing carbon and hydrogen. *Hydrogen:* The lightest element, existing in gaseous form at standard temperature and pressure. It is a component of water, acids, and many other compounds. *Hygiene:* The science that deals with the preservation of health by maintaining high standards of cleanliness. *Inorganic compounds:* Compounds that consist of chemical combinations of two or more elements that are not carbon. *Iodine:* A deep brown halogen, used as a disinfectant because of its highly reactive nature. *Ions:* An atom is composed of a positively charged nucleus and negatively charged electrons moving around it. An atom is electrically neutral, but if another electron is added to it or removed from it, the substance acquires an electrical charge and becomes an ion. If one or more electrons are added, the charge of the atom becomes negative and it is called an *anion*. On the other hand, if one or more electrons are removed from the neutral atom, it becomes positively charged and is called a *cation*. *Micro-organisms:* Very minute living organisms that are impossible to see through the naked eye and may only be viewed through a microscope. They include bacteria, fungi, protozoa, algae, and viruses. *Molecules:* The smallest particle of an element or a compound that has independent existence. A molecule of an element displays the chemical properties of that element and a molecule of a compound displays the chemical properties of that compound. *Nitrogen:* The most abundant gas in the earth's atmosphere (78%). It is used in the production of ammonia and nitric acid. *Neutralization:* An acid and a base, when mixed in the appropriate proportions, form a neutral solution. Such a reaction is called a neutralization reaction. *Organic compounds:* Compounds containing carbon, hydrogen, and oxygen. *Oxygen:* An element that occurs as molecules of O_2, a colourless and odourless gas that forms 21% of the air. It is also a component of ozone (O_3) and water (H_2O).

(Contd.)

Exhibit 11.1 *Contd.*

Terminology used in cleaning

Pathogenic: Disease-causing (used for particular kinds of bacteria or other micro-organisms).

Pests: Insects and other small creatures that are harmful or cause damage.

Pesticides: Agents, usually artificial, used to destroy pests.

pH scale: A scale that indicates the degree of acidity or alkalinity of a substance. According to the scale, a pH of 7 is neutral, acids have pH values less than 7, and alkalis have values more than 7.

Phenol: It is an organic, alcoholic compound derived from benzene and used in the manufacture of disinfectants. The old name for phenol is 'carbolic acid'. Phenol is toxic, hence skin contact must be avoided when handling it.

Pollution: The presence of harmful and undesirable constituents in the environment resulting from human activities. Pollution may be of air, water, soil, and sound.

Quats: Quaternary ammonium compounds, used as disinfectants.

Radicals: In many chemical reactions, a cluster of atoms acts as a unit. These clusters are called radicals. For instance, sulphate (SO_4^{2-}), carbonate (CO_3^{2-}), bicarbonate (HCO_3^-), and so on are radical groupings.

Reagents: Chemical solutions, such as acids, alkalis, or alcohols, that are used in various reactions.

Saline: (of a solution) Containing salt.

Salts: Neutral substances formed when acids react with alkalis. The term 'common salt' refers to NaCl as formed naturally.

Sanitizer: An agent used for reducing the microbial count to an acceptable level.

Spores: Micro-organisms in their restive, protective state when environmental conditions are unfavourable. When the conditions become favourable again, the spores develop into reproductive micro-organisms.

Sterilization: The process of killing all kinds of microbes as well as their spores.

Surfactants: Compounds that impart good wetting power, emulsifying power, and suspending power to detergents.

Valency: An atom of each element has a definite combining capacity, called its valency. It is measured with reference to hydrogen. For instance, the valency of hydrogen itself is 1 and that of carbon is 4, which means that an atom of hydrogen can combine with or displace a single atom of hydrogen while an atom of carbon can displace or combine with four atoms of hydrogen. The formula of a compound depends on the valency of the combining elements.

Waste: A collective term for that which is unwanted, useless, unused, or discarded. The terms 'trash', 'rubbish', 'refuse', 'garbage', 'residue', 'ashes', 'biologic waste', 'liquid by-product waste', and 'solid by-product waste' all imply waste materials as referred to in various cultures or when in various forms.

Water: This is the universal solvent H_2O, and the most basic cleaning agent.

Principles of Cleaning

These are the basic rules to follow in any kind of cleaning activity, whatever the nature of the surface or the soil.

- All soil should be removed.
- Soil should be removed without harming the surface being cleaned or the surrounding surfaces.
- The surface should be restored to its original state after the cleaning process.
- The cleaning process should be efficient, using a minimum of equipment, cleaning agents, effort, and time.
- The simplest method should be tried first, using the mildest cleaning agent.
- The cleaning methods least harmful for the surface should be used.

- Cleaning should proceed from high to low wherever possible.
- When cleaning an area, start with the cleaner surfaces and articles and then go on to clean the more heavily soiled ones, so as to prevent the spread of soil from dirty to cleaner surfaces.
- While wet-cleaning or polishing the floor, the cleaner should walk backwards while cleaning in front of him.
- Suction cleaning should be preferred over sweeping wherever possible.
- Sweeping should be done before dusting, and dusting before suction cleaning.
- Noise levels while cleaning should be kept as low as possible.
- Stains should be removed as soon as they occur.
- The cleaner should take all safety precautions while cleaning. In particular, cleaning agents and equipment should be stacked neatly to one side.
- The cleaner should start cleaning from the farthest end of an area, working towards the exit.
- After the cleaning process is over, all equipment should be washed or wiped as applicable, dried, and stored properly; cleaning agents should be replenished and stored; waste discarded; and the area left neat and tidy.

Safety and Hygiene Factors in Cleaning

Cleaning may pose certain hazards and the associates must be made aware of them through training. They must be trained to work safely and follow all hygiene standards set by the hotel. The safety and hygiene factors to be borne in mind while cleaning are outlined below.

Safety factors

- The associates must wear protective gear or personal protective equipment (PPE) as required by the task at hand. For instance, if cleaning acid or a hazardous chemical is being used, thick rubber gloves, mask, safety goggles, and rubber boots must be worn.
- Cleaning chemicals must be handled with utmost precautions as per MSDS while handling and transporting, especially dispensing and refilling.
- All chemical containers and dispensers must be labelled properly. Any special precaution must be clearly mentioned on the label.
- The place where dispensing and dilution takes place must be well-ventilated.
- Caution signs must be displayed when working on wet floors.
- Broken glass must be shoved on to a dust pan without touching by hands.
- Liquid spillages must be mopped up as soon as they occur to avoid slipping accidents.
- It must be ensured that cigarette butts from smoking rooms are extinguished before being disposed into trash bags.
- Polishing rags with solvents must be disposed responsibly as they are a potential fire hazard.
- First aid kits must be kept updated and placed in appropriate areas.
- Mops must have flexible swivel heads so as to avoid inappropriate postures.
- Defective equipment, for instance, ones with loose wires or frayed cords, must not be used and reported immediately to the supervisor.
- Long flexes in equipment being operated must be handled carefully; the flexes must be stretched along a wall and not across the floor.
- Ladder safety precautions must be taken whenever a task employs their use in high reach areas.

- Ergonomic principles must be followed in lifting, bending, pushing, and stretching. Seek assistance in case the weight to be lifted is too heavy for one person. These are discussed in detail in Chapter 23.
- Supervisors and managers must also be cautious against repetitive motion injuries (RMI) and stress injuries, especially to lower back, elbows, and neck while working on computers at their work stations.
- Personal belongings or keys must never be stored on the room associate's cart.

Hygiene factors

Safety and hygiene factors complement each other and ensure a safe work environment for workers. Hygiene factors in cleaning are outlined below.

- Personal hygiene standards are a must to follow by all employees and this includes proper grooming and appropriate uniform.
- The workplaces such as pantries and stores must be kept cleaned at all times.
- Cleaning solutions must be diluted and dispensed fresh.
- Mops with wringer mechanisms must be opted for to avoid wringing by hand.
- Mop water should be changed frequently to ensure dirt and germs are not spread.
- Vacuuming should be preferred over brooming.
- Colour coded dusters must be used and employees must be trained to use them appropriately. For instance, WC dusters are typically coded red, and should be stored separately in the hand caddy on room associate's cart.
- Disinfect high touchpoints such as door handles and telephones.
- Sani bins, and not open waste bins, must be used in guest bathrooms and public restrooms.
- It is as important to close down cleaning as to carry out cleaning. All tools and equipment must be washed and dried before storing in their appropriate places.
- Masks, gloves, and slush boots should be worn while handling garbage.

Cleaning Procedures

Cleaning processes may be either manual or mechanical. They may involve washing (using water as a cleaning and rinsing agent), friction (as in using an abrasive), static electricity (as in using a static mop), suction (as in using a vacuum cleaner), or force (as in using pressurized water). The various types of cleaning processes are summarized in this section.

Manual methods

These do not call for mechanized or electronic equipment.

Sweeping This is done to collect dust when the floor surface is too rough for a dust mop. Push brooms are used for large areas and corn brooms are best for corners and tight spaces. A broom with a long handle is most suitable ergonomically. Use short, smooth strokes and sweep directly into a long-handled dustpan without dissipating the dust. Keep the head of the broom flat on the floor at all times. When using a long-handled broom, use smooth strokes to sweep away from yourself. It is important in sweeping to develop a rhythm and 'bounce' the push broom to avoid rolling the bristles under.

Sweeping is not the most efficient, hygienic, or advanced way of removing dust, as so much of it becomes airborne. Sweeping has in many cases been replaced by the use of suction cleaners now. Sweeping with a dry mop is called 'mop-sweeping'.

Equipment required Broom, dustpan, dust bin for collection of dust.

Dusting This task requires a systematic and orderly approach for efficiency and ease. Room attendants should start dusting articles at the door and work clockwise around the room. This minimizes the chances of overlooking a spot. Fold the duster three times and then thrice again. This gives you 18 clean folds, making the duster more effective. No corners of the duster should be left hanging.

A soft, lint-free cloth should be used as a duster. Avoid using old rags, which leave behind their own dust and lint. Microfibre dusters are highly effective and efficient in removing dust and dirt. For organised, hygienic cleaning, colour coding of dusters is recommended as presented in Table 11.1.

In all cases, begin dusting from the highest surfaces so that dust does not fall on items already cleaned. In case you are using a dusting solution, spray a small amount onto the cloth. Never spray dusting solution directly onto the surface being cleaned as it can stain or cause stickiness. The duster should not be unfolded in the room after dusting, nor be shaken outside the window. Carry the duster away carefully to such a place where it can be washed and dried.

Equipment and agents required Cloth duster, microfiber duster, feather duster, and dusting solution if necessary.

Damp-dusting This is the most preferred way of cleaning in hotels as surfaces can be wiped as well as dusted, removing any sticky or dirty mark at the same time. A suitable lint-free cloth at the correct level of dampness should be used so as to avoid leaving any smears.

Equipment and agents required Cloth duster, water, plastic bowl, and a neutral detergent if necessary.

Dust-mopping/dry mopping/mop sweeping This is the preferred way to remove dust, sand, or grit from a floor. If these substances are not removed from the floor on a daily basis, they will continually scratch the surface finish, diminishing its lustre, and will eventually penetrate down to the floor itself. Dust-mopping is done with a dust-control mop that may or may not be impregnated with a cleaning solution. Using such a solution stops the dust from rising. While dust-mopping, use figure-of-eight strokes and keep the mop head on the floor at all times. Do not drag the mop straight backwards. On finishing each figure of eight, swivel the mop around and on the return, pass and overlap the areas that have been wiped by about 8 inches. When sweeping in open spaces, clean in long straight lanes, covering the whole area by moving up and down. Use a dustpan to sweep up

Table 11.1 Colour coding of dusters for cleaning tasks in hotels

Duster Colour code	Area of use
Red	Surfaces with higher risk of cross-contamination and spread of infection in restrooms – WCs, bidets, and urinals
Yellow	Surfaces with lower risk of contamination in restrooms – vanitory units, bath tubs, cabinets, and tiles
Green	Surfaces where food and beverages are prepared and served – kitchens, bars, and cafeteria
Blue	General purpose cleaning on various surfaces, glass and mirror with low risk of contamination – lobby areas, corridors, admin offices, and so on

accumulated trash. Always carry the mop head upwards very carefully after you are done, and then shake into a bag to clean. Dust-mopping removes gross soil but also redistributes and/or leaves behind large amounts of fine particulates.

Equipment required Dust-control mop, dustpan, dust-collection bag, and dust bin.

Spot mopping Spot mopping is essential to the preservation of a floor surface. Liquids and solids that are spilled on the floor, if left for any length of time, may penetrate the finish and stain the floor. Even acids from fruit juices may wreak havoc on a floor if they are not immediately cleaned up. Clean, cold water should be used so that the finish on the floor is not softened. Detergents should be avoided unless necessary—that is, unless the substance has been allowed to dry on the floor.

Equipment and agents required Mop and bucket or a mop-wringer trolley, cold water, and a very dilute solution of neutral detergent if necessary.

Wet-mopping/damp mopping A damp mop is used to remove spills and adhered soil that were not removed during the dry removal process. Wet-mopping will remove light to heavy soil from the floor surface, which could otherwise become embedded in the surface or encapsulated in the seal or finish. Before the floor can be wet-mopped, it must first be dust-mopped. Add neutral or mildly alkaline detergent to the mop water for wet-mopping. The detergent used must be of the variety that needs no rinsing, or else spray diluted detergent from a spray bottle and mop with a damp mop. If using mop water, immerse the mop in the bucket and wring it out until it is only damp.

First finish mopping near the baseboards in smooth strokes. Then mop the entire area with figure-eight strokes. The water in the bucket should be changed when it becomes dirty. A brush may be used for stubborn spots and a squeegee should be used to help speed the drying of the floor.

Equipment and agents required Wet mop and bucket or mop-wringer trolley, squeegee, and detergent solution.

Manual scrubbing For modern surfaces, very little hand-scrubbing is required. Scrub gently in straight lines away from yourself, working backwards. Rinse well in order to remove any detergent from the surface. Use a squeegee to clear away excess rinse water. Follow up with mopping.

Equipment and agents required Long-handled scrubbing brush, mild detergent, bucket, squeegee, water, and mop.

Manual polishing Apply the polish sparingly. Use cotton rags to apply polish and a cloth for buffing. Use a soft brush for carved articles to get the polish into crevices. Use the polish appropriate for a particular surface. For instance, proprietary polishes for metals—Brasso, Silvo, and so on—should be used on these surfaces.

Equipment required Proprietary polish and cotton rags.

Spot cleaning This refers to the removal of stains from various kinds of hard and soft surfaces. To remove a localized stain, the whole surface need not be treated with stain-removal agents. Just the area where the stain discolours the surface is treated and cleaned in the process of spot cleaning. Spot cleaning may be used as a cleaning method on walls, fabrics, carpets, or flooring.

Mechanized methods

These utilize equipment powered by electricity as well as mechanical gadgets.

Suction cleaning This is the basic and preparatory step to all other mechanized procedures and should be performed regularly. Very often it must also be repeated at the end of these processes. The goal is to remove as much dry soil as possible so that it does not spread, scratch the finish, or damage the surface. Vacuuming with high-filtration machines is the most complete method of dry-soil removal as it picks up, packages, and removes soil without spreading it around.

Wet-vacuum cleaners are now available, which help to mop up water from floors as well. These are usually dual-function machines that can be used for both wet and dry work. Extraction machines for cleaning carpets also work on the principle of suction.

Equipment and agents required Wet/dry vacuum cleaner with attachments and a mild detergent for wet-cleaning if necessary.

Spray buffing This process uses a 175- or 300-rpm (revolutions per minute) floor machine and a soft pad or brush. The operator sprays a light mist of a commercial cleaning preparation or detergent and a finishing solution in front of the machine. As the machine goes over the area, soil, scuffs, light scratches, and marks are removed and the shine is restored to the surface. Vacuuming or dust-mopping is a follow-up step to remove loosened dirt.

Equipment and agents required 175- or 300-rpm buffing machine with beige pad, spray bottle, detergent, and finishing solution.

Polishing This process uses a 175–1500-rpm floor machine and a soft pad or brush to remove some soil and put the shine back in the finish. Vacuuming or dust-mopping should be carried out as a follow-up step to remove loosened dirt.

Equipment required 175–1500-rpm floor machine and soft pad or brush.

Burnishing This process uses an ultra high-speed floor machine (1500–2500 rpm) to restore a deep gloss to the floor finish. Since the finish is 'tempered' by the friction and heat produced by the burnishing machine, the floor looks better for a longer time, which reduces costs by extending the time between the scrubbing-and-stripping cycles. Vacuuming or dust-mopping and damp-mopping are preparatory steps, and should also be used as follow-up procedures to remove loosened dirt.

The method of burnishing described earlier is carried out on flooring and should not be confused with the burnishing of silver articles in a burnishing machine. For burnishing of silver, refer to Chapter 8.

Equipment required 1500–2500 rpm floor machine.

Scrubbing This process removes embedded dirt, marks, deeper scuffs, and scratches from the floor along with some of the finish. The type of pad or brush, the type of detergent, the water temperature, and the weight and speed of the machine all determine whether the process is considered light or heavy scrubbing. For instance, aggressive pads, higher-pH detergent solutions, and fast, heavy machines perform the deepest scrubbing. Light scrubbing removes just one or two coats of finish. Heavy scrubbing removes all or most of the finish, down to the protective sealing coat.

Equipment required Floor maintenance machines with a green pad (refer to Chapter 7 for a discussion on the types of abrasive pads used in floor maintenance machines).

Stripping This is a very aggressive process that can and should remove all of the floor finish and sealer, leaving a bare floor ready for re-finishing. A strong stripping agent, a coarse pad or brush, hot water, and intensive work make stripping a costly, time-consuming, and sometimes even hazardous process, which should be used only when no other process will achieve the desired results. Diligent use of other maintenance procedures delays the need for stripping.

Equipment required Floor-maintenance machine with a black pad.

Laundering This is the cleaning method used for washable fabrics. It is a process in which soil and stains are removed from textiles in an aqueous medium. It involves the sub-routines of washing, bleaching, drying, and pressing, all carried out using specialized laundry equipment and cleaning agents, called 'laundry aids'. Other sub-processes such as spot-cleaning, starching, and softening may also be involved. Refer to Chapter 19 for further details on laundering.

Dry-cleaning This is the method in which soil and stains are removed from textiles in a non-aqueous medium.

Frequency of Cleaning

Cleaning tasks may be divided according to the frequency of their scheduling, which depends upon the level of soiling, the type of surface, the amount of traffic, the type of hotel, and the cleaning standards set. Employees should be given the procedures and frequencies for carrying out various tasks outlined in a handbook or manual. The information may also be displayed on a noticeboard in the floor pantries.

Daily tasks These are the routine operations carried out on a day-to-day basis by the staff of the housekeeping department. These include the regular servicing of guestrooms, cleaning of bathrooms and toilets, suction-cleaning of floors, and floor coverings, and so on.

Weekly tasks These, as the term implies, are routine tasks carried out on a weekly basis. These may include the polishing of metal surfaces, dusting of hard-to-reach areas, and so on. To accomplish weekly cleaning tasks in a systematic way, housekeepers organise it as 'Cleaning of the day', carried out as an extension of the usual servicing of the guestroom. Under this, small tasks which would take about 5-8 minutes additionally in the guestroom, are scheduled once on a particular day of the week as these areas do not get soiled heavily. A sample of 'Cleaning of the Day' tasks is presented in Table 11.2.

Table 11.2 Sample 'Cleaning of the Day' tasks

Day of the week	Cleaning task scheduled
Monday	Cleaning behind picture frames
Tuesday	Cleaning of wardrobe doors
Wednesday	Vacuuming under the bed
Thursday	Cleaning behind television and console
Friday	Cleaning of tile grouting
Saturday	Cleaning of minibar gasket
Sunday	Cleaning behind the WC

Periodic tasks These are carried out on a monthly, quarterly (every three months), half-yearly, or annual basis (spring cleaning). Some of the usual periodic tasks in a hotel include the shampooing of carpets, washing of walls, cleaning of chandeliers, and stripping and polishing of floors.

Organization of Cleaning

For cleaning to be efficient, it must be well organized. Different ways of organizing the cleaning of various areas are outlined in this section.

Orthodox/conventional/traditional cleaning In this way of cleaning, a GRA completes all the tasks in one guestroom before going on to the next room in the section allotted to him/her. On an average, a GRA may be required to clean 12–20 rooms in an 8-hour workday, not including break times.

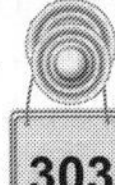

Block cleaning In this way of cleaning, the GRA moves from room to room and completes the same task in every room, before returning to begin the cycle again for the net task on the list. This involves 'blocking' several rooms at a time to form a 'room section', and usually more than one GRA will be at work in the section. For instance, one GRA might make all the beds in that particular room section, while another GRA cleans the toilets, and a third GRA dusts and cleans the area, replenishing supplies that are low.

Team cleaning In this method, two or more people work together in the same area, either on the same task or on different tasks. To organize the team cleaning of guestrooms, two GRAs may be scheduled to clean 30–35 guestrooms a day.

Deep cleaning and special projects Deep cleaning refers to the intensive cleaning schedule in which periodic cleaning tasks are scheduled for monthly, quarterly, half-yearly, or annual frequencies. Deep cleaning is essential at periodic intervals since regular daily or weekly cleaning, however efficient, is too superficial to present an attractive, fresh-looking environment to guests over the long term. Deep cleaning involves some tasks that require the housekeeping department to work in coordination with the maintenance department. A sample deep cleaning SOP is presented in Table 11.3.

SOPs for cleaning pillows, lamp shades, upholstery and minibar are given in Table 11.4 a, b, c, and d respectively. Many tasks involved in deep cleaning are complicated and time-consuming ones, requiring special equipment, techniques, expertise, and group effort. These tasks are usually scheduled as special projects. A sample guestroom special cleaning record is given in Table 11.5.

Table 11.3 Sample guestroom deep cleaning SOP

SOP Name:	**Procedure for deep cleaning of guestroom**		
Effective Date:	**23.12.2019**	**SOP Author:**	**Shefali Shyam**
SOP No. :	**128**	**SOP Approver:**	**Vijay Dewan**
For Job title:	**Housekeeping associates, Housemen**	**SOP Owner:**	**Hotel Sundown, Coorg**
Objective: To ensure in-depth, thorough cleaning of a guestroom			
Equipment & tools needed:	Vacuum cleaner, general purpose floor machine, carpet shampoo machine, dusters, scrubbing pads, chamois, sponge wiper, step ladder, mattress protector, bed linen	**Supplies needed:**	All-purpose cleaner, glass cleaner, WC cleaner, carpet shampoo (1:8 dilution ratio), water

Procedure	How-to do	Additional information
1. Clear away all amenities from room.	Take out all amenities from the room and place them in trolley.	Stack the items presentably as the trolley is parked in guest corridor.
2. Keep away electrical and electronic equipment.	Unplug table lamps and telephones and place in wardrobe. Keep adapters, docking stations, spike guards and other electronic equipment in wardrobe shelf. After cleaning replace electric and electronic equipment and check for proper working.	Line shelves with newspaper beforehand to ensure wardrobe surfaces are not scratched while placing items.

Table 11.4 (a) SOP for cleaning pillows

SOP Name:	**Procedure for cleaning pillows**		
Effective Date:	**23.12.2019**	**SOP Author:**	**Shefali Shyam**
SOP No. :	**129**	**SOP Approver:**	**Vijay Dewan**
For Job title:	**Housekeeping associates, Housemen**	**SOP Owner:**	**Hotel Sundown, Coorg**
Objective: To clean pillows in the guestroom			
Equipment & tools needed:	Vacuum cleaner, clean garbage bag, sponge for spotting	**Supplies needed:**	Solvent for spotting
Procedure	**How-to do**		**Additional information**
1. Spot clean stains.	Remove any stain by spotting with a solvent.		
2. Clean the pillow.	Place pillow in a clean garbage bag. Insert the nozzle of the vacuum cleaner into the bag, to touch the pillow. Gather the open end of the bag close on the nozzle and turn the vacuum on. When the pillow is deflated to the maximum because of sucking action switch off the vacuum and take the nozzle out. Remove the garbage bag. Fluff up the pillow.		Ensure that the vacuum is set on suction mode. During deep cleaning, send the pillows to the linen room for replacing the ticking and re-stuffing.

Table 11.4 (b) SOP for cleaning fabric lamp shades

SOP Name:	**Procedure for cleaning fabric lamp shades**		
Effective Date:	**23.12.2019**	**SOP Author:**	**Shefali Shyam**
SOP No. :	**130**	**SOP Approver:**	**Vijay Dewan**
For Job title:	**Housekeeping associates, Housemen**	**SOP Owner:**	**Hotel Sundown, Coorg**
Objective: To clean lamp shades made of fabrics			
Equipment & tools needed:	Soft brush, towel duster, clean discarded towel	**Supplies needed:**	Neutral soap solution (1:10 dilution ratio)
Procedure	**How-to do**		**Additional information**
1. Remove accessories.	Remove lamp shade tassels before washing.		To keep lamp shades looking fresh and bright, wash them periodically.
2. Clean the fabric lamp shade.	Brush the shade gently with a soft brush. Wet the shade completely with a mild soap solution. Dip a towel duster in soap solution and clean the shade with gentle pressure. Wash the shade thoroughly with clean flowing water to remove all soap deposits. Dry the shade over a clean discard towel. Damp wipe the ribs of the frame.		The strokes should be from top to base and never sideways or breadth-wise, else the cloth will lose firmness. Ensure complete removal of soap deposits, else cloth will stain.
3. Replace accessories.	Refasten the tassels on the shade after it is dried. Reattach the shade on the lamp and check for proper operation.		

Table 11.4 (c) SOP for cleaning upholstery

SOP Name:	**Procedure for cleaning upholstery**		
Effective Date:	**23.12.2019**	**SOP Author:**	**Shefali Shyam**
SOP No.:	**131**	**SOP Approver:**	**Vijay Dewan**
For Job title:	**Housekeeping associates, Housemen**	**SOP Owner:**	**Hotel Sundown, Coorg**
Objective: To ensure thorough cleaning of upholstery			
Equipment & tools needed:	Wet pick-up vacuum cleaner with upholstery attachment, sponge, white rags, dust sheets	**Supplies needed:**	Cleaning solvent, vinegar, upholstery shampoo
Procedure	**How-to do**		**Additional information**
1. Protect the floor.	Cover the floor under and around the upholstered furniture with dust sheets.		
2. Remove dust from upholstery.	Vacuum the upholstery.		
3. Perform pre-spotting test for colour fastness.	Wet a white rag with solvent. Press hard against an area that is out of view. If the colour comes off, dilute the solvent with vinegar. Repeat the test. If the colour still comes off, dry clean the upholstery instead of shampooing.		
4. Spot stains.	If the colour does not come off, spot any stains.		

Table 11.4 (d) SOP for cleaning minibar

SOP Name:	**Procedure for cleaning minibar**		
Effective Date:	**23.12.2019**	**SOP Author:**	**Shefali Shyam**
SOP No. :	**132**	**SOP Approver:**	**Vijay Dewan**
For Job title:	**Housekeeping associates, Housemen**	**SOP Owner:**	**Hotel Sundown, Coorg**
Objective: To clean minibar in the room			
Equipment & tools needed:	Dusters	**Supplies needed:**	Detergent solution
Procedure	**How-to do**		**Additional information**
1. Take minibar off service.	Turn off the power and empty the mini bar.		Turning off power will also defrost the minibar.
2. Clean the minibar.	Clean the inside of the refrigerator using a detergent solution and wet duster. Damp wipe shelves and trays. Clean inside the door panel. Thoroughly dry all surfaces with duster. Damp wipe external surfaces, top, sides, back and front.		Leave the door open for air drying.
3. Replace contents.	Replace all contents and switch the power on.		Check for proper operation of minibar.

Spring-cleaning This is a term used for a periodic annual clean and general maintenance of the hotel guestrooms and other areas, carried out in off-season periods (not necessarily spring, which was the traditional time for a thorough house-cleaning once). The term is often used interchangeably with deep cleaning. Spring-cleaning may involve a complete overhaul of the rooms and is, therefore, scheduled for the off season or very low-occupancy periods. Spring-cleaning involves many tasks on which the housekeeping department works in close coordination with the maintenance department.

Table 11.5 Sample Guestroom Special Cleaning Record

Guestroom Special Cleaning Record														
Room nos. →	**201**	**202**	**203**	**204**	**205**	**206**	**207**	**208**	**209**	**210**	**211**	**212**	**213**	**214**
Particulars ↓	**(Recording of dates)**													
Bed cover														
Mattress protector														
Bed skirting														
Head board & footboard														
Mattress														
Heavy curtains														
Sheer curtains														
Sofa upholstery														

Intensive cleaning tasks may have to be carried out, for which an entire floor of rooms will have to be taken off sale at a time, for a day or two. Spring-cleaning tasks in the guestrooms may include the following:

- Removal of all guest supplies, soft furnishings, and carpets from the rooms.
- Sending launderable articles to the laundry.
- Polishing wooden furniture, shampooing upholstery, and covering them with dust sheets.
- Shampooing carpets.
- Stripping and polishing floors.
- Cleaning accessories such as lamps, lamp shades, and picture frames.
- Stripping any wall covering such as paint or wallpaper and re-painting the walls.
- Washing ceilings and walls.
- Thoroughly cleaning lighting fixtures, air-conditioning vents, and windows.
- Cleaning the minibar.
- Thoroughly cleaning bathrooms, including walls, floor tiles, fixtures and fittings, and shower curtains.
- Removing limescale from surfaces, fixtures and fittings.
- Vacuum-cleaning the mattresses.
- Changing the mattress protector.
- Rotation of scatter cushions.
- Airing the room.
- Restocking guest supplies.
- Restoring soft furnishings and carpets.
- Clearing the rooms to the front desk for sale at the end of a thorough clean.
- Oiling rollaway beds.
- Oiling door hinges.
- Heavy pest control

Spring clean tasks in public areas may also include the following apart from the above similar tasks:

- Dome cleaning.
- Honing marble floors.
- Regrouting tiles.
- Replacing mirrors and glass surfaces or resilvering mirrors.
- Cleaning chandeliers
- Replacing sanitary fixtures
- Repainting walls.
- Servicing of equipments as per AMC.

Features that Ease Cleaning

Smooth textures; straight, neat, and smooth lines; and medium-toned colours are some of the design features in a surface that make for easier cleaning. Surfaces with these features collect less dust compared

to surfaces with rough textures, intricate raised patterns, and grooves. Medium-toned colours show less dirt than surfaces of darker or lighter shades.

Corridor walls get soiled easily with smear and scuff marks. Hence, the lower accessible part of the wall should be covered with a dado. Moulded, coved ceilings-wall edges that discourage dust accumulation and lend themselves easily to cleaning should be preferred over sharp edges.

Furniture should be so designed that cleaning under and behind them is easy. Furniture on castor wheels and glides are easily movable, making cleaning under and behind them easier. Bed frames should not have a raised edge. Though raised edges help to keep the mattress sunk in place, they may graze the hands of GRAs badly during bed-making.

With regard to carpets, the shorter the carpet pile, the easier the cleaning. Upholstery too should have the minimum of decorative features such as buttons, gathers, and ruffles.

Surfaces such as solid wood are now being substituted by laminates wherever possible. While solid wood requires regular buffing and polishing, laminates are low-maintenance surfaces. A regular damp-dusting is usually sufficient for laminates. The drawback of laminates is that they lack the richness and elegance of solid wood. Wood-polishes that are stain-resistant and long-lasting are a boon to housekeepers as wooden surfaces become fairly easy to maintain with the use of these polishes.

Another high-maintenance surface that requires constant polishing is brass. Brass becomes easily tarnished, and more so in coastal climates. Laminated brass surfaces are easier to maintain as they do not require regular polishing, and should be preferred in hotels.

INSIGHT: KAYAKALP – A GOVERNMENT OF INDIA INITIATIVE

'Kayakalp', literally meaning 'turnaround', is an initiative to promote cleanliness and hygiene in public healthcare facilities, launched by the Ministry of Health & Family Welfare, Government of India, on 15th May 2015. The aim of this initiative is to appreciate and recognise the efforts of health care facilities to create a healthy environment. The guidelines for this initiative were also issued to enable health facilities maintain certain standards and enhance the quality of healthcare.

The objectives of the 'Kayakalp' Scheme are:

- to promote cleanliness, hygiene and infection control practices in public healthcare facilities, through incentivising and recognising such public healthcare facilities that show exemplary performance in adhering to standard protocols of cleanliness and infection control;
- to inculcate a culture of ongoing assessment and peer review of performance related to hygiene, cleanliness, and sanitation;
- to create and share sustainable practices related to improved cleanliness in public health facilities linked to positive health outcomes.

The guidelines are divided into six thematic areas:

- Hospital upkeep
- Sanitation and hygiene
- Waste management
- Infection control
- Hospital support services
- Hygiene promotion

SUMMARY

It is said that cleanliness is next to godliness. The guests who come to stay at a hotel expect it to be as clean as their homes, and sometimes even cleaner, since they are paying a price for it. Time and again, it is proved through surveys that guests coming to stay repeatedly in a preferred hotel do so because of the high cleanliness standards of the hotel. It is up to the executive housekeeper to set the standards for cleanliness and maintain them. The whole crew of the housekeeping department should be made to understand the importance of efficient cleaning and know the implications of an unhygienic environment.

This chapter begins with an explanation of the importance of cleaning. When we say that a surface is soiled, it means that there is dust, dirt, and foreign matter on it. The ways in which soil can present itself are numerous, and each of these may require a specific cleaning method or a blend of two or three methods of cleaning, described later in the chapter. Understanding the nature of the soiling is important so as to select the appropriate equipment and cleaning agents.

Cleaning standards can be varied. It depends on the type of establishment in question as well as the functions and use of the specific area or surface. Cleaning has been presented as a science, as it has its base in chemistry and to some extent in biology, including microbiology.

Efficient cleaning results when certain principles are followed. These principles have been listed. Cleaning procedures have been grouped as manual and mechanized methods. To clean a surface, usually a combination of two or more procedures is used. Safety and hygiene factors in cleaning have been outlined. Cleaning, however efficient, will not show results unless the optimal frequency for various cleaning tasks is maintained. Thus, cleaning tasks may be scheduled as daily, weekly, and periodic tasks, according to their frequency.

An efficient housekeeper organizes her staff to clean in an organized way. Various ways of organizing cleaning tasks have been presented in this chapter. Hotels often follow more than one method for different room sections. Traditional cleaning was the most widely used routine earlier, but housekeepers today have come to realize the benefits of team cleaning. It is very important that before commencing cleaning, the GRA prepares for the cleaning tasks ahead, else a large portion of time may be wasted in making frequent trips to the floor pantry and the store.

KEY TERMS

Alloy A mixture of two or more metals.

AMC Annual Maintenance Contract

Ashes A type of waste that is a residue from fire or burning.

Autotrophic Organisms that manufacture their food on their own.

Bidets Sanitary fittings meant for the thorough washing of the genitals and anal area. These are increasingly being used as foot baths these days.

Biological waste These are wastes resulting directly from human and animal bodies, a majority of the waste produced in hospitals, for instance.

Block cleaning When cleaning is organized in this way, the GRA moves from room to room and completes the same task in every room, before moving back to the first room with a new task to begin the cycle again. This involves 'blocking' several rooms at a time as a 'room section'. Usually, more than one GRA will be at work in each section.

Cleaning The removal of dust, dirt, foreign matter, tarnish, and stains from various surfaces with the aid of certain cleaning agents and equipment.

Cleaning agents Substances, natural and synthetic, used to assist the cleaning process.

Cornices These are 4–7 inches deep, box-like shapes used at the top, horizontal portion of the drapery treatment on a window to hide the poles and other hardware.

Dado A stronger, more easily cleaned material used to surface the lower part of a wall, approximately upto 150 cm height from the floor. A dado is essential to prevent damage caused by banging of trolleys, luggage, and rubbing and scratching that may be caused by people in hotels. Also referred to as wainscoting.

Deep cleaning Intensive cleaning undertaken in guestrooms and public areas according to a special schedule.

Dilution/Dilution ratio The ratio of the solute (the substance to be diluted) to the solvent (the substance in which to be diluted, e.g. water). For cleaning chemicals, it is represented as

solute ratio : solvent ratio

Ergonomics The study of people's efficiency in relation to their working environment.

Eukaryotic Refers to a cell that has a nucleus.

Grommets Metal rings in the upper hem of curtains to reinforce the material so that it may be hung on the rods with hooks without danger of tearing.

Grouting A term used to describe the areas or binding material between raised or filling elements of flooring or wall treatments (such as tiles).

Laundry aids Materials used to improve laundering results (such as soaps, detergents, bleaches, bluing agents, and fluorescent brighteners), or those that accomplish specific functions or effects in laundering (such as stain removers, softeners, and stiffeners).

Liquid by-product waste This is waste that is liquid in nature and usually hazardous. It should ideally be treated first with disinfectants prior to disposal in the sewage system.

Microfiber duster It is made of ultra-fine polyester and polyamide blended fibres, which have extremely minute strands that attract, capture, and hold dust, dirt, and microbes effectively. The positively charges microfibres attract dust and dirt particles that tend to have a negative charge.

MSDS Materials Safety Data Sheet is a form containing detailed safety information about a chemical.

Orthodox cleaning This is the traditional way of organizing cleaning activities in a hotel, where a GRA completes all the tasks in one guestroom before going on to the next room in the section allotted to him/her.

PPE Personal Protective Equipment, clothing or equipment that is worn to provide protection against hazardous substances and environment.

RMI Repetitive Motion Injuries

Soil Dust, dirt, and foreign matter deposited on a surface are together referred to as soil.

Solid by-product waste These are hazardous wastes that are solid in nature, which should ideally be sterilized, packaged, and then thrown away as trash.

Spring-cleaning A term used for a periodic/annual cleaning of the hotel guestrooms or other areas, usually carried out in the off season (not necessarily in spring, though the traditional annual cleaning of houses after winter in temperate climates gives us the term). The term is often used interchangeably with 'deep cleaning'.

Stain A discolouration caused on hard and soft surfaces by products containing dyes, proteins, acids, and alkalis, which is difficult to remove by routine cleaning processes.

Squeegee A piece of manual cleaning equipment with a rubber or metal blade and a long handle, used for removing excess moisture from wet surfaces.

Tarnish A discolouration caused by a chemical reaction between a metal surface and substances found in water, air, and food. Different metals undergo different types of tarnishing. For example, silver darkens, iron gets a brownish-red rust, and copper gets a green tarnish.

Team cleaning In team cleaning, two or more people work together in an area, either on the same task or on different tasks.

Traditional cleaning See 'Orthodox cleaning'.

Wainscoting See dado.

12

Servicing Guestrooms

Learning Objectives

After reading this chapter, you should be able to

- get insights into the tasks involved in servicing of guestrooms
- describe the procedure of bed-making and discuss the daily cleaning of guestrooms
- outline the procedures for the turndown service and second service
- understand how in-room minibars are managed
- appreciate the importance of 'closing down' after cleaning and give an account of the procedure to be followed

Introduction

Servicing of guestrooms involves all tasks that provide a clean, comfortable, safe and aesthetically appealing environment to guest staying in the rooms. The major tasks include cleaning and replenishing amenities and supplies, maintenance, minibar management, turn down service and second service.

Guestroom Servicing Procedures

Preparing to Service Guestrooms

Efficient servicing of guestrooms needs to be planned for, not only by the managers, but also by the GRAs. The GRAs need to plan the order of guestroom cleaning, for instance, which in turn can be chalked out with the help of their section work sheets clipped onto their carts. The GRAs would, on reaching the floors later, take a quick walk down the guest corridor to ascertain if any rooms have 'Please clean my room' tag hung on the knob, because these early make up requests would be given attention first. Refer to Chapter 6 for the order of cleaning guestrooms and for room associate's section worksheets.

After collecting the keys and their section worksheets, the GRAs proceed to the floor pantries, where they need to assemble the cleaning and guest supplies, linen and required equipment on the room attendants' carts and cleaning caddies. If the carts and caddies are well organized, with all the supplies and equipment in their rightful places, the GRAs' work becomes more efficient. The stocking of the cart has been discussed in detail in Chapter 7. Once the cart is organized, a GRA is set to service the guestrooms. Before discussing the daily servicing of guestrooms showing various status codes, one should understand the method of bed-making, an integral part of servicing guestrooms.

Bed-making procedure

A neatly made up bed adds greatly to the appeal of a guestroom for the guest. The aim of a GRA should be to make a neat bed efficiently, saving both time and energy as far as possible. A GRA who is adept at making beds should be able to finish making a single bed in a maximum of 3 minutes and a double bed in a maximum of 7 minutes. The linen required to make a bed are stacked in the room attendants' cart.

Bed-making involves making the bed with the bed linen already on the bed. Changing or re-sheeting the bed involves stripping the bed of all soiled linen and making the bed with fresh linen. Luxury hotels change bed linen once a day, but many also leave the the option to the guest to choose bed linen change once in two days as part of their water conservation programme. When a guest chooses this, the room associates, while servicing the room re-make the bed using the existing sheets. The procedure of remaking the bed with existing linen is outlined in Table 12.1.

Earlier, most hotels used to follow one standard method of bed-making, but nowadays there are different styles being used by different properties. The common methods of bed-making followed in hotels are outlined in this section.

Traditional method using a blanket In this method, the bed is made up with all the sheets and the blanket is tucked in on both sides. The procedure is presented in Table 12.2 and a diagrammatic representation of the same is shown in Figures 12.1 – 12.12.

Table 12.1 Sample procedure for making the bed reusing the linen

SOP Name:	**Procedure for making the bed reusing linen on the bed**		
Effective Date:	**23.12.2019**	**SOP Author:**	**Shefali Shyam**
SOP No. :	**134**	**SOP Approver:**	**Vijay Dewan**
For Job Title:	**Housekeeping associates**	**SOP Owner:**	**Hotel Sundown, Coorg**
Objective: To make a neat, comfortable bed reusing linen already on the bed while servicing an occupied room.			
Equipment & tools needed:	Well-stocked GRAs' cart	**Supplies needed:**	Linen water, fresh linen (in case existing one is stained or damaged)
Procedure	**How-to do**	**Additional information**	
1. Strip the bed of pillows and duvet.	Remove the pillows and duvet, inspect the covers for stains and place them on a clean surface.	Replace with a fresh pillow or duvet cover from the cart if any stains are found.	
2. Place the bedsheet on the bed.	Straighten the mattress protector if required. Straighten the bottom sheet, inspect for stains or damage. Spray a fine mist of linen water to ease out the wrinkles, re-tuck at headboard and footboard side, mitre the four corners and re-tuck tightly on the sides.	Place any personal items such as magazines, reading glasses or books carefully on the nightstand. Replace the sheet if stained or damaged. To make linen water, add two drops of the signature essential oil fragrance of the hotel to 500 ml soft water in a clean spray bottle.	
3. Place the duvet on the bed.	Place the duvet on the bed, starting 1 ft. away from the headboard. Spray a fine mist of linen water on the duvet cover to ease out the wrinkles.		

Table 12.2 Procedure of traditional method of bed-making with fresh linen and a blanket

SOP Name:	**Procedure for making the bed with fresh linen and a blanket**		
Effective Date:	**23.12.2019**	**SOP Author:**	**Shefali Shyam**
SOP No. :	**135**	**SOP Approver:**	**Vijay Dewan**
For Job Title:	**Housekeeping associates**	**SOP Owner:**	**Hotel Sundown, Coorg**
Objective: To make a neat, comfortable bed with fresh linen and blanket.			
Equipment & tools needed:	A well-stocked GRAs' cart **Supplies needed:**		Fresh linen – bed sheet – 2, night spread – 1, blanket – 1, pillow cases – 2 or 4 as per standard
Procedure	**How-to do**		**Additional information**
1. Strip the bed.	Remove the pillow cases from the pillows and leave the cases on the bed. Place the uncovered pillows on a chair close at hand. Ease out the bed sheets from their tucks, remove the blanket and place it on the chair. Remove the soiled bed sheets by bringing together the corners towards the centre, enclosing the soiled pillow cases to make a closed bundle. Place the soiled linen on a chair.		In an occupied or stayover room, place any personal items left on the bed such as magazines, reading glasses, jewellery or books, carefully on the nightstand. Guest clothing left on bed to be folded neatly and placed in the same position after bedmaking. In a departure room, if any personal belongings of guest are found on the bed, they are treated as lost and found. The soiled linen should be placed in the soiled linen bag on the GRAs cart after bedmaking is done.
2. Straighten the mattress protector.	Straighten and smooth down the mattress protector with a light hand.		Check the mattress protector for stains or damage. Change if necessary.

Modern method, using a duvet The current trend in hotels is bed-making with duvet. This involves use of only one bed sheet along with the duvet and the duvet cover is changed along with the sheet when beds are made during cleaning of rooms. The sides of the duvet may be left open or tucked in depending on the standard followed in the hotel. The procedure is described in Table 12.3. Please refer to the QR code for more pictures and video.

Many housekeepers insist on working on only one side of the bed at a time, and moving on to work on the other side only when finished with the previous one. Whatever the method adopted, the GRA should not move around the bed using unnecessary steps that could slow down the procedure.

Daily Servicing of Guestrooms

A GRA may have to service anywhere between 13 and 18 guestrooms in a day, the standard being 14. Hence, a GRA adept at his/her work will take not more than 30 minutes to accomplish the servicing of one room. After the GRA finishes servicing one room, he/she informs the floor supervisor that the prepared guestroom can be inspected.

In this section, we shall discuss the daily cleaning of occupied and stayover rooms, check-out or departure rooms, vacant rooms, rooms 'under repair', and VIP rooms. The procedure for entering the guestroom for servicing is detailed in Figure 12.13. The cleaning process in the guestroom has been summarized briefly in Figure 12.14.

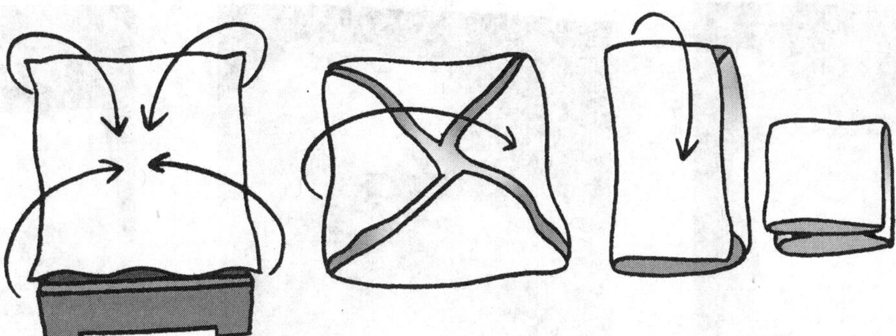

Fig. 12.1 Stripping the Bed

Fig. 12.2 Straightening the mattress protector

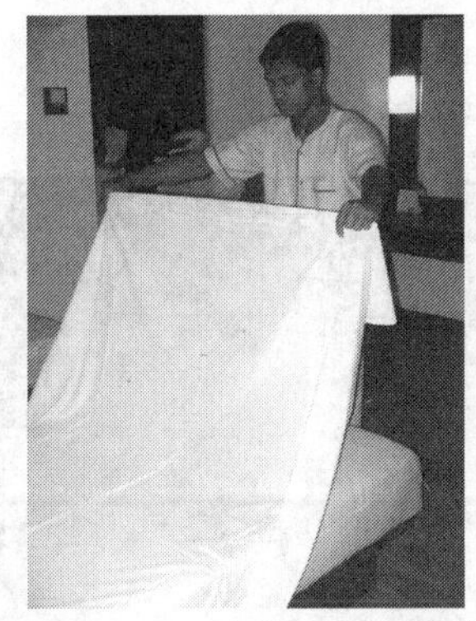

Fig. 12.3 Placing the bottom sheet

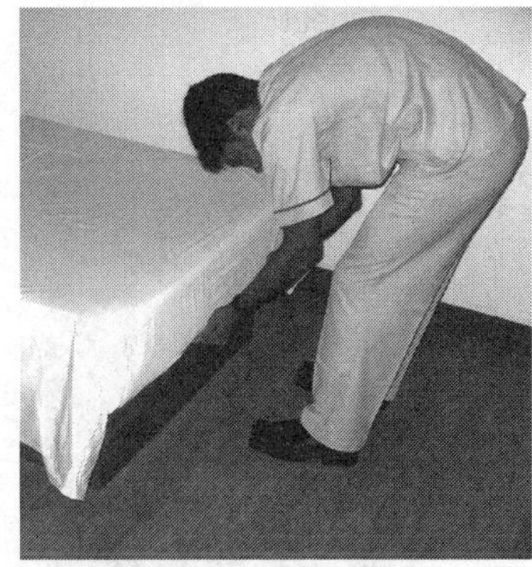

Fig. 12.4(a) Tucking the sheet at the foot of the bed

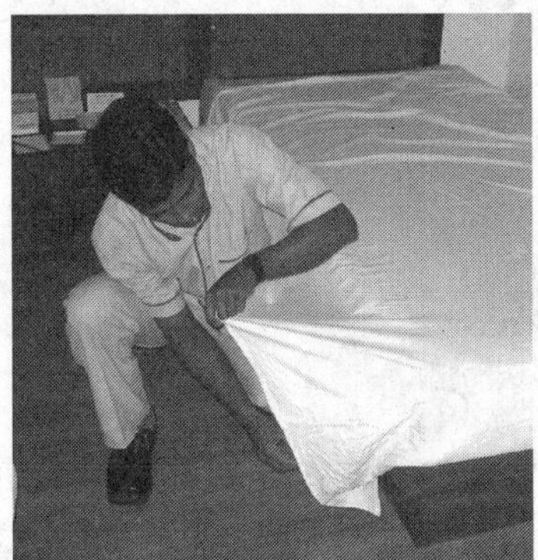

Fig. 12.4(b) Lifting a flap of the sheet (appx 30 cm from corner)

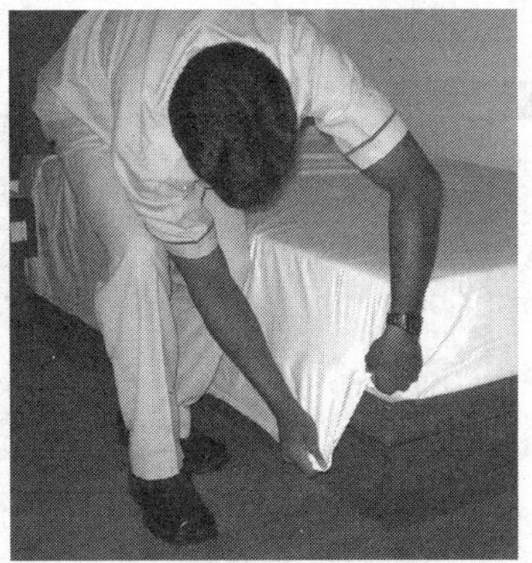

Fig. 12.4(c) Dropping the flap after tucking the remaining portion of the sheet

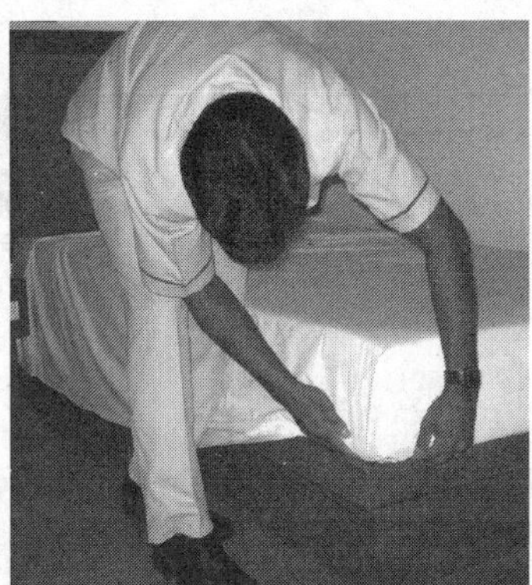

Fig. 12.4(d) Tucking in the Flap to get a mitred corner

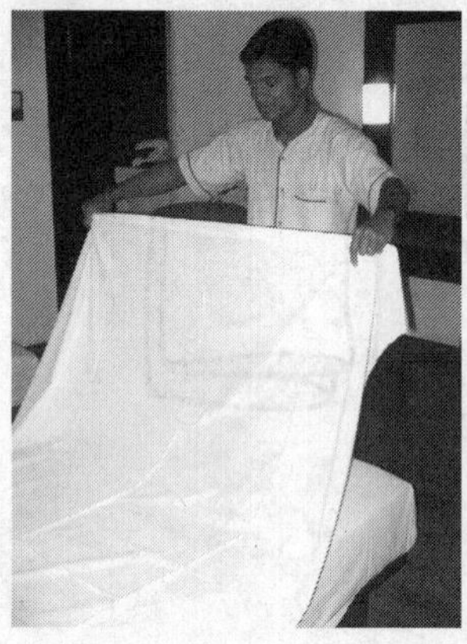

Fig. 12.5 Placing the top sheet

Fig. 12.6 Placing the blanket

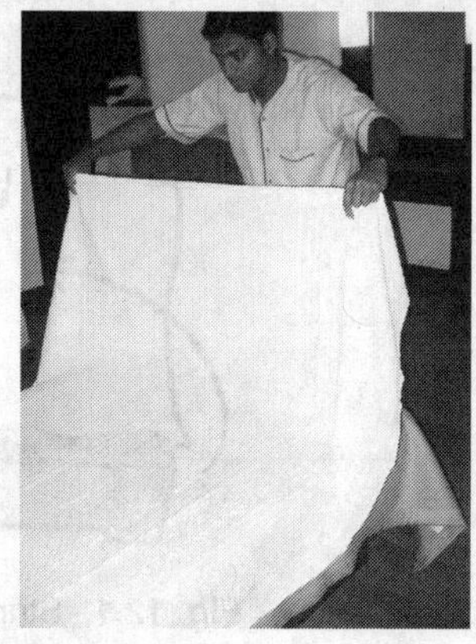

Fig. 12.7 Placing the crinkle sheet

Fig. 12.8 Folding the top sheet and crinkle sheet back over the blanket

Fig. 12.9 A bed with the three sheets and blanket tucked in

Fig. 12.10 Placing the pillow

Fig. 12.11 Placing the bedspread

Fig. 12.12 Covering the pillow with the bedspread

Table 12.3 Procedure of modern method of bed-making with fresh linen and a duvet

SOP Name:	**Procedure for making the bed with fresh linen and a duvet**		
Effective Date:	**23.12.2019**	**SOP Author:**	**Shefali Shyam**
SOP No. :	**136**	**SOP Approver:**	**Vijay Dewan**
For Job Title:	**Housekeeping associates**	**SOP Owner:**	**Hotel Sundown, Coorg**
Objective: To make a neat, comfortable bed with fresh linen and duvet.			
Equipment & tools needed:	A well-stocked GRAs' cart	**Supplies needed:**	Fresh linen – bed sheet – 1, duvet cover – 1, pillow cases – 2 or 4 as per standard
Procedure	**How-to do**		**Additional information**
1. Strip the bed.	Remove the pillow cases and duvet cover from the pillows and the duvet respectively and place the covers on the bed. Place the uncovered pillows and duvet on a chair close at hand. Remove the soiled bed sheet by bringing together the corners towards the centre, enclosing the soiled pillow cases and duvet cover to make a closed bundle. Place the soiled linen on a chair.		In an occupied or stayover room place any personal items left on the bed such as magazines, reading glasses, jewellery or books carefully on the night-stand. Guest clothing left on bed to be folded neatly and placed in the same position after bedmaking. In a departure room, if any personal belongings of guest are found on the bed, they are treated as lost and found. The soiled linen should be placed in the soiled linen bag on the GRAs cart after bedmaking is done.
2. Straighten the mattress protector.	Straighten and smooth down the mattress protector with a light hand.		Check the mattress protector for stains or damage. Change if necessary.
3. Place the bed sheet on the bed.	Unfold a fresh sheet. Place it on the bed, right side up. Tuck in at the headboard and footboard side, mitre the four corners and tuck tightly on both the sides.		

Servicing of an occupied room (stayover)

When an assigned associate proceeds to service an occupied room, the guest may or may not be inside the room at the particular time. Follow the procedure for entering the guestroom as outlined in Figure 12.13. The servicing of an occupied room is subdivided into several steps that are detailed in the SOP given in Table 12.4.

Servicing a vacated room (departure/on-change/check-out)

A vacated room is one from which the guest has left, settling his/her account, returning the room keys, and departing the hotel. This guestroom would have been occupied in the night. The cleaning of a vacated room must be a little more thorough than cleaning an occupied room. Refer to the scan code to see the video for 'Servicing a vacated room'. There are also no guest belongings scattered around the room to be tidied in a vacated room. Needless to say, the procedure of 'entering the guestroom' explained for an occupied room does not apply to a vacated room. That the room has been vacated can be ascertained from the room assignment sheet. But if you are in doubt at any time, do follow the procedure given in Fig. 12.13 for entering an occupied guestroom.

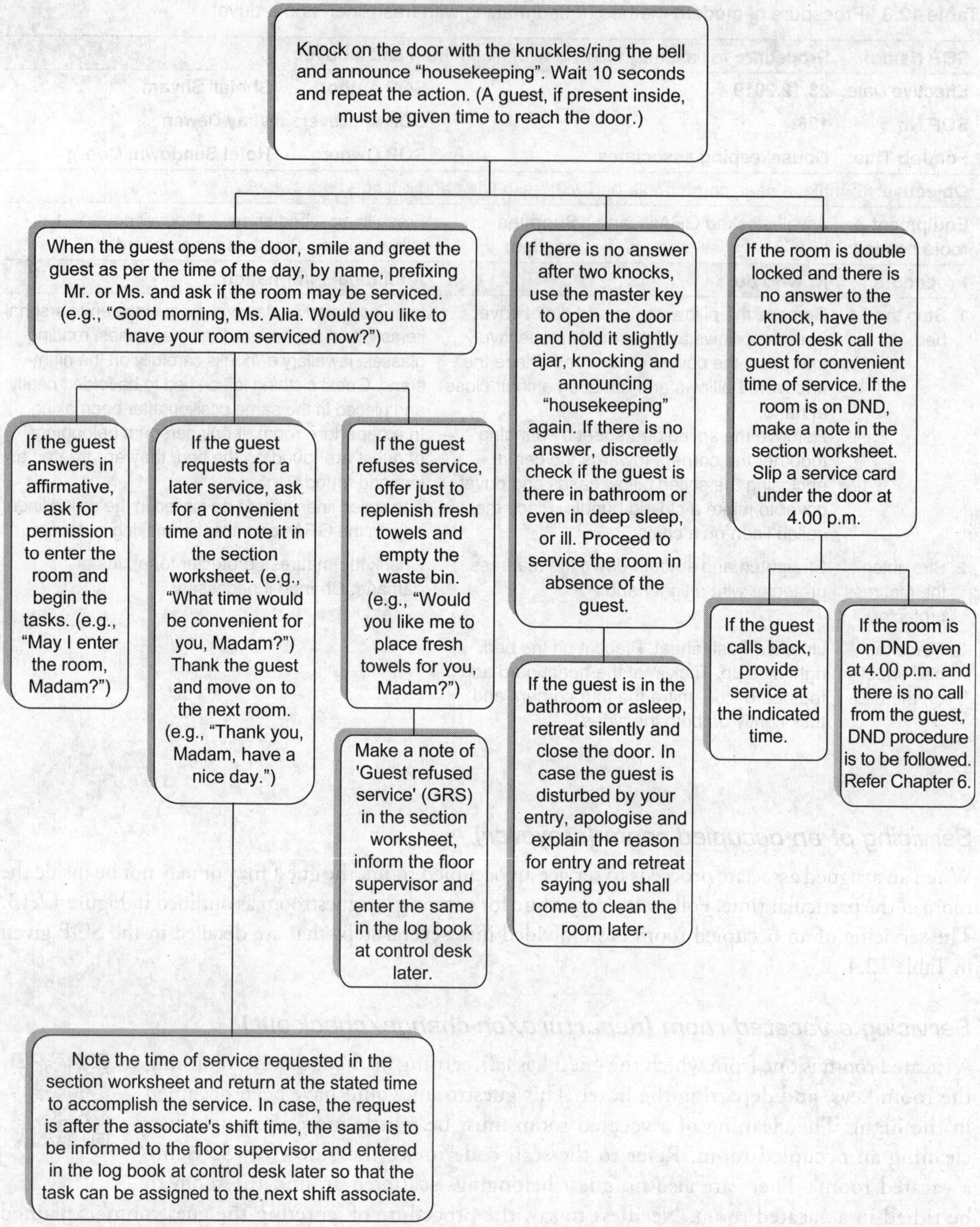

Knock on the door with the knuckles/ring the bell and announce "housekeeping". Wait 10 seconds and repeat the action. (A guest, if present inside, must be given time to reach the door.)

When the guest opens the door, smile and greet the guest as per the time of the day, by name, prefixing Mr. or Ms. and ask if the room may be serviced. (e.g., "Good morning, Ms. Alia. Would you like to have your room serviced now?")

If the guest answers in affirmative, ask for permission to enter the room and begin the tasks. (e.g., "May I enter the room, Madam?")

If the guest requests for a later service, ask for a convenient time and note it in the section worksheet. (e.g., "What time would be convenient for you, Madam?") Thank the guest and move on to the next room. (e.g., "Thank you, Madam, have a nice day.")

If the guest refuses service, offer just to replenish fresh towels and empty the waste bin. (e.g., "Would you like me to place fresh towels for you, Madam?")

Make a note of 'Guest refused service' (GRS) in the section worksheet, inform the floor supervisor and enter the same in the log book at control desk later.

Note the time of service requested in the section worksheet and return at the stated time to accomplish the service. In case, the request is after the associate's shift time, the same is to be informed to the floor supervisor and entered in the log book at control desk later so that the task can be assigned to the next shift associate.

If there is no answer after two knocks, use the master key to open the door and hold it slightly ajar, knocking and announcing "housekeeping" again. If there is no answer, discreetly check if the guest is there in bathroom or even in deep sleep, or ill. Proceed to service the room in absence of the guest.

If the guest is in the bathroom or asleep, retreat silently and close the door. In case the guest is disturbed by your entry, apologise and explain the reason for entry and retreat saying you shall come to clean the room later.

If the room is double locked and there is no answer to the knock, have the control desk call the guest for convenient time of service. If the room is on DND, make a note in the section worksheet. Slip a service card under the door at 4.00 p.m.

If the guest calls back, provide service at the indicated time.

If the room is on DND even at 4.00 p.m. and there is no call from the guest, DND procedure is to be followed. Refer Chapter 6.

Fig. 12.13 Procedure for entering the guestroom

Enter the guestroom
- For occupied rooms, knock on the door and announce 'housekeeping'. On entering the room, keep the door wide open and position the cart in front of the door.
- In case the room is on DND, make a note in assignment sheet and proceed to the next room.

Prepare to clean the room
- Ventillate the room and check the curtain hardware. Remove any used room service trays.
- Switch on all electrical appliances to check and then switch them off. Empty waste and sani-bins.
- While cleaning a vacated room, check for any item left behind by the guests.

Clean the guestroom
- Damp dust all the surfaces.
- Vacuum the carpet.
- Vacuum the soft furnishings.
- Vacuum and mop the floor.
- Clean and disinfect the telephone. Refer Table 12.5 for the SOP.

Replenish guestroom supplies
- Place all the supplies as per hotel policy.

Make the bed
- Strip the bed. Deposit all the bed and bath-soiled linen in the soiled linen bag on the cart.
- Make the bed with fresh sheets.

Clean the bathroom
- Apply the WC bowl cleaner.
- Damp-dust all surfaces.
- Disinfect the wall phone.
- Clean the bath tub, shower area, vanitory unit, and surrounding tiles. Dry and polish the surfaces with a clean duster. Refer Tables 12.6, 12.7, and 12.8 for SOPs to clean vanitory unit, bath tub and shower cubicle respectively.
- Clean shower curtain.
- Replenish toiletries, clean the WC, and disinfect the seat. Refer Table 12.9 for SOP to clean WC.
- Check all electrical appliances.
- Mop the floor.

Conclude work in the guestroom
- In an occupied room tidy the guest belongings.
- Inform the floor supervisor to inspect the cleaned room.

Fig. 12.14 The cleaning process in a guestroom

Table 12.4 Procedure for servicing an occupied room

SOP Name:	Procedure for servicing an occupied room (stayover)		
Effective Date:	23.12.2019	SOP Author:	Shefali Shyam
SOP No. :	137	SOP Approver:	Vijay Dewan
For Job Title:	Housekeeping associates	SOP Owner:	Hotel Sundown, Coorg
Objective: To service an occupied room with maximum efficiency and as per company standards.			
Equipment & tools needed:	A well-stocked GRAs' cart	**Supplies needed:**	Guest supplies and amenities, fresh linen, cleaning supplies and equipment
Procedure	**How-to do**		**Additional information**
1. Enter the guestroom.	Follow the SOP for entering the room. Park the cart in front of the room blocking the open door and carry in the cleaning caddy and vacuum cleaner.		The SOP for entering the room is outlined in Fig. 12.13.
2. Beginning tasks to service the guestroom.	Ventilate the room by drawing back the drapes and opening the windows and patio or balcony doors. Remove room-service trays and used tea trays. Switch on all electrical appliances such as lights, fans, air-conditioners, television, and so on, to check that they are in working order. Switch them off after the check. Empty ashtrays and wastepaper baskets from the room, and the sani-bin from the bathroom into the trash bag on the cart.		While drawing back the curtains, check the curtain rings and tracks. Coordinate with IRD for clearance of used trays. Any maintenance defect in the guest-room should be immediately informed to the floor supervisor or the control desk so that they can coordinate with maintenance department for repairs.

Table 12.5 Procedure to clean the telephone

SOP Name:	Procedure for cleaning telephones		
Effective Date:	23.12.2019	SOP Author:	Shefali Shyam
SOP No. :	138	SOP Approver:	Vijay Dewan
For Job Title:	GRA	SOP Owner:	Hotel Sundown, Coorg
Objective: To clean and disinfect the telephone in the guestroom.			
Equipment & tools needed:	Duster, toothbrush, cotton swab	**Supplies needed:**	All-purpose cleaner, disinfectant solution
Procedure	**How-to do**		**Additional information**
1. Check the telephone for functioning.	Take the telephone off the hook and inspect its working condition.		Report any malfunction to maintenance.
2. Clean the telephone.	Spray all-purpose cleaning solution on a duster and wipe the entire surface of the telephone – base, hand-set, cradle and cords.		Do not spray the cleaning solution directly on the phone. Check for exposed wires.
3. Clean the ear and mouthpiece.	Clean thoroughly the ear and mouthpiece removing any greasy build-up of hair oil or cosmetics. Gently scrub the grooves and vents with a toothbrush. Apply a disinfectant with a cotton swab.		The room number label on the face plate of the telephone should be clear, the face plate should not be damaged.
4. Close down cleaning.	Replace the cradle back on the telephone and ensure that the cord hangs without entangled loops. Check again for dial tone. Give a final wipe to remove any finger smudge marks.		

Table 12.6 Procedure for cleaning vanitory units

SOP Name:	**Procedure for cleaning vanitory units**		
Effective Date:	**23.12.2019**	**SOP Author:**	**Shefali Shyam**
SOP No. :	**140**	**SOP Approver:**	**Vijay Dewan**
For Job Title:	**GRA**	**SOP Owner:**	**Hotel Sundown, Coorg**
Objective: To clean the vanitory unit as per company standards.			
Equipment & tools needed:	A well-stocked cleaning caddy – micro-fiber duster, glass cloth, sponge, tooth-brush, small squeegee, PPE – gloves	**Supplies needed:**	Hygienic surface cleaner, glass cleaner, guest amenities, fresh face towels
Procedure	**How-to do**		**Additional information**
1. Clear the vanitory counter before cleaning.	Wear the gloves. Keep aside toiletries and supplies from the vanitory counter.		Do not touch any jewellery items or cases.
2. Clean the vanitory counter.	Spray the hygienic surface cleaner on a microfibre duster and clean the sink and the faucets. Remove any soap residue or scum. Remove any hair, lint or debris from the drain perforations. Scrub the vanity drain and drain rim with a toothbrush. Leave the sink drain-stopper in open position. Dry the surfaces with a dry duster. Polish the chrome fixtures and remove any stains or smudges. Wipe down the hardware beneath the vanity area.		Make sure faucets are closing properly and there is no dripping. In occupied room, if any personal toiletries are left by guest on vanitory counter, clean under them and place back neatly. Wipe down pipes under sink in checkout rooms.

Table 12.7 Procedure for cleaning bath tub

SOP Name:	**Procedure for cleaning the bath tub**		
Effective Date:	**23.12.2019**	**SOP Author:**	**Shefali Shyam**
SOP No. :	**142**	**SOP Approver:**	**Vijay Dewan**
For Job Title:	**GRA**	**SOP Owner:**	**Hotel Sundown, Coorg**
Objective: To clean the bath tub as per standards set by the company.			
Equipment & tools needed:	A well-stocked cleaning caddy - sponge, toothbrush, dusters, PPE – gloves	**Supplies needed:**	All-purpose cleaner, hygienic surface cleaner, floor cleaner, fresh bath linen
Procedure	**How-to do**		**Additional information**
1. Remove soiled bath linen.	Wear the gloves. Remove soiled bathmat and towels.		
2. Clean the retractable clothesline above the bath tub.	Wipe the retractable clothesline with all-purpose cleaner sprayed on a duster.		Check for proper retraction and extension of clothesline.

Table 12.8 Procedure for cleaning shower cubicle

SOP Name:	**Procedure for cleaning shower cubicle**		
Effective Date:	**23.12.2019**	**SOP Author:**	**Shefali Shyam**
SOP No. :	**143**	**SOP Approver:**	**Vijay Dewan**
For Job Title:	**GRA**	**SOP Owner:**	**Hotel Sundown, Coorg**
Objective: To clean the shower cubicle as per company standards.			
Equipment & tools needed:	A well-stocked cleaning caddy - sponge, toothbrush, dusters, PPE – gloves	**Supplies needed:**	Glass cleaner, hygienic surface cleaner, floor cleaner, fresh bath linen
Procedure	**How-to do**		**Additional information**
1. Remove soiled bath linen.	Remove soiled bathmat and towels.		
2. Clean the shower cubicle walls.	Spray glass cleaner on the shower wall surface. Using a sponge, begin cleaning the shower wall from inside, working from high to low. Buff thoroughly to remove the accumulated stubborn water marks and soap scum stains. Wipe clean the exterior wall surface and dry.		Report any damage, chipping, scratches, mould/mildew on the shower cubicle walls to supervisor.

Table 12.9 Procedure for cleaning WC

SOP Name:	**Procedure for cleaning WC**		
Effective Date:	**23.12.2019**	**SOP Author:**	**Shefali Shyam**
SOP No. :	**141**	**SOP Approver:**	**Vijay Dewan**
For Job Title:	**GRA**	**SOP Owner:**	**Hotel Sundown, Coorg**
Objective: To clean the WC as per company standards.			
Equipment & tools needed:	WC brush, sponge, red colour dusters, PPE – gloves	**Supplies needed:**	All-purpose cleaner, WC cleaner, disinfectant solution, 'sanitised for your care' strip, tissue roll to replace
Procedure	**How-to do**		**Additional information**
1. Apply the WC cleaner.	Wear the gloves. Apply WC cleaner through the nozzle in the toilet bowl all around, under the interior rim and let the cleaning chemical work for 10 minutes.		Be careful not to splash the cleaner on the skin or eyes. Till the 10 minutes pass, clean the vanitory unit.
2. Scrub clean the WC.	Begin scrubbing under the rim with the WC brush, scrub the inside of the toilet from top to bottom and ensure it is stain-free. Flush until water in bowl is clean. Rinse the WC brush in the incoming flow of flush water.		The WC cleaner should be used to clean only the interior surface of the WC. Check for proper functioning of the flush.

All the cleaning tasks for an occupied room apply to the cleaning of a vacated room too. Additional tasks may be:

- Check for any items left behind by the guests who have departed. On finding such articles, follow the procedure for dealing with lost-and-found articles explained in Chapter 22.
- Remove any cobwebs or dust from the ceilings.
- Wipe out drawers and closets from inside. Check coat hangers and replenish supplies if necessary.
- Suction-clean the carpet.
- Suction-clean all soft furnishings.
- Check whether any maintenance work is needed.

  Before leaving, take one last critical look around the room, keeping in mind that your last look will be the guest's first look at the room.

Servicing a vacant room

The term 'vacant' room implies a different situation from a 'vacated' room. A vacant room is one in which no guest has slept the previous night and which is not yet occupied. This room would have already been serviced earlier when the last guest to have stayed in it departed from it. Thus a vacant room needs only a light dusting and a check of all electrical appliances. In the bathroom, the WC should be flushed. In the event of a vacant room having been unoccupied for a long time, however, it may need to be cleaned in the manner of a vacated room. A GRA should also look for signs of illegal occupation in the night by checking if the bed has been slept in, the bathroom supplies used, and so on.

Servicing VIP rooms

Very important person (VIP) rooms are always given priority for service. The front desk should give advance information to housekeeping about the arrival of any VIP. The cleaning of rooms meant to be occupied by a VIP must be as thorough as that for a vacated room. What differs is the extra complementary amenities and giveaways that are kept in the VIP room (see Table 12.10). These amenities may differ from hotel to hotel. VIP rooms may also require some extra time during cleaning due to the thoroughness expected and the added amenities to be placed. The inspection of a VIP room should also be more thorough.

VIPs are categorized into four different groups, according to the degree of their importance: VIP 1, VIP 2, VIP 3, and VIP 4. The more important ones are termed 'VVIP', including such personages as the President of India.

VIP 1 These are heads of state, ministers, high-ranked government officials and celebrities.

VIP 2 These are presidents, MDs and CEOs of large companies, the management and directors of the hotel itself, well-known personalities, and other high-ranking officials such as auditors and convention coordinators.

VIP 3 These are regular repeat guests of the hotel and people known personally to the management or directors of the hotel. Also included in this category are hotel headquarter representatives.

VIP 4 These may be the 'handle with care' guests and certain groups of people known to the hotel managers. These also include reporters, media and press officials.

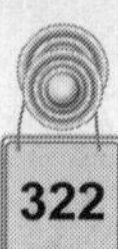

Table 12.10 Guestroom amenities for VIPs

VIP 1	VIP 2	VIP 3	VIP 4
Full bar: This includes whisky, gin, vodka, beer, soft drinks, cocktails, and mixers (soda lime, cordial, and water).	**Partial bar:** Beer, soft drinks, and water	**Partial bar:** Beer, soft drinks, and water	**Partial bar:** Beer, soft drinks, and water
Snacks: Assorted nuts and cookies	**Snacks:** Assorted nuts and cookies	**Snacks:** Assorted biscuits	--------
Petit fours	Petit fours	-------	--------
Assorted chocolates	Assorted chocolates	--------	--------
Large flower arrangement	Medium sized flower arrangement	Small sized flower arrangement	Small sized flower arrangement
Large fruit basket	Medium fruit basket	Small fruit basket	Small fruit basket
Personalised guest stationery	Personalised guest stationery	--------	--------
Personalised bath robes	Personalised bath robes	--------	--------
Soft slippers	Soft slippers	Soft slippers	--------
Combs and hair brushes	Combs and hair brushes	Comb and hair brushes	--------
Upgraded, coloured bath sheets and towels	Upgraded, coloured bath sheets and towels	--------	--------
Bath foam, assorted soaps, and eau-de-cologne	Bath foam, assorted soaps, and eau-de-cologne	Bath foam and eau-de-cologne	--------
Terry bath mat	Terry bath mat	Terry bath mat	--------

Dealing with 'under repair' rooms

It is the housekeeping department's responsibility to have guestrooms prepared for repair work by the maintenance department. The housekeeping department can take a room out of service, declaring it as OOO, when major repair work is required in the particular room. On an annual or half-yearly basis, some rooms may be declared 'under repair' when the maintenance department carries out preventive and scheduled maintenance in the guestrooms. The housekeeping responsibilities here include:

- Taking the room out of service, informing the front office of an OOO guestroom status, and hanging the OOO sign on the door knob.
- Removing all guest supplies from the bedroom and bathroom and having them stored in the floor pantry.
- Removing all the soft furnishings from the room and storing these in the linen room; sending launderable articles to the laundry.
- Covering the mattress and the bed with dust sheets large enough to enclose the headboard too.
- Disconnecting the telephone, wrapping in a cover, labelling it, and storing it on a closet shelf.
- Sending all easily movable furniture, all accessories, and loose articles and accessories to the floor pantry or store for storage, ensuring that all the items leaving the room have a label stuck on them indicating the number of the room they were transferred from.
- Covering the larger pieces of furniture left in the room with dust sheets.

- Disconnecting the television and radio and covering them with large transparent polythene sheets.
- Sending the carpets for shampooing.
- Removing any flower arrangement or indoor plant, the latter being handed over to the horticulturist.
- Sealing all taps and sinks other than a single source of water supply.
- Closing all the doors and windows to avoid any noise from disturbing other guests; opening the windows to ventilate the room after the repairs are completed.

Turndown Service

The turndown service is provided by the housekeeping department in the evening at deluxe hotels, as a special service to guests. It is, therefore, also referred to as 'evening service' or sometimes 'night service'. 'Turndown' refers to making the bed ready for sleeping in by removing any bedspread or duvet and turning down the covers between 5.00 to 7.00 pm. Along with this function, a few other tasks are carried out in the evening to make the guestroom environment conducive to and comfortable for a good night's sleep. To provide the turndown service, a GRA enters the guestroom early in the evening to replenish supplies, generally tidy the room, and turn down the beds. The procedure is given in Table 12.11.

Second Service

Second service is provided on the special request of a guest after the guestroom has already been serviced earlier in the day. The guest may ask for this chargeable service after he has had visitors in the room for a party or meeting, as a result of which the room may have become dirty or disorganized. Second service may involve the following tasks:

- Removing room-service trays and used plates, dishes, glasses, and bottles.
- Emptying and damp-dusting ashtrays; emptying the waste basket.
- Damp-dusting surfaces in the guestroom that are likely to have been used by visitors and guests.
- Mopping the floor in the sitting area.
- Making the bed if required.
- Replacing glasses and refilling water jugs.
- Cleaning the bathroom thoroughly, including the toilet bowl and placing the disinfected toilet strip.
- Replacing soiled linen with fresh.
- Spraying an air-freshener if the room has any residual odour of food or cigarette smoke.
- Exiting and locking the door if the guest is out.
- Recording the service provided appropriately so that it may be added to the guest's bill.

Minibar Management

Minibars are set up at least two hours prior to the guests' arrival. Beverages and cold items are set up in the mini-refrigerator and the other items on the minibar counter. Minibars are revenue generating in-room features and at the same time a convenience for guests who are willing to pay for it.

Table 12.11 Procedure of providing turndown service in an occupied room

SOP Name:	**Procedure for providing turndown service in an occupied room**		
Effective Date:	**23.12.2019**	**SOP Author:**	**Shefali Shyam**
SOP No. :	**144**	**SOP Approver:**	**Vijay Dewan**
For Job Title:	**Housekeeping associates**	**SOP Owner:**	**Hotel Sundown, Coorg**
Objective: To provide efficient turndown service in an occupied room in the evening.			
Equipment & tools needed:	GRAs' cart stocked for turndown	**Supplies needed:**	Fresh towels, bathroom amenities, flower buds, mint candies, 'Good night' message card, cleaning supplies
Procedure	**How-to do**		**Additional information**
1. Enter the guestroom.	Follow the procedure of entering the guestroom as per SOP in Fig. 12.13.		
2. Clear waste from the room.	Empty and damp-dust the ashtray (in smoking rooms), replace matchboxes, and generally tidy the room and re-arrange amenities. Empty the wastepaper basket and sani-bin. Remove any service trays.		Coordinate with IRD for clearance of service trays.
3. Place away guest belongings and bed accessories.	Hang any scattered-about clothes left by the guest in the cupboard or fold neatly and place on a chair. Fold the foot throw, remove the sham and place both in the top shelf of cupboard or in the ottoman. If bedspread is used: Remove the bedspread gently by folding it neatly in a three-way fold and put it away in the ottoman or the cupboard. To make a three-way fold: • Bring the top edge of the bedspread towards the bottom of the bed approximately three-fourths of the way down. • Bring the bottom edge up towards the head of the bed, approximately three-fourths of the way up. • Fold the right-side edge to the centre and then the left side. • Double over once to hold folds in place and put away.		This depends on hotel policy.
4. Turn down the bed for sleep.	*For bed made with duvet:* Ease out the duvet panel near the headboard, on the side the guest is most likely to use and turn back to make a neat triangle fold. *For bed made with blanket and crinkle sheet:* Turn back the top sheet, the blanket, and the crinkle sheet on one side in one operation to make a neat triangle fold, as shown in Figure 12.15. Turn down the sheets on the side the guest is most likely to use.		In a single-occupancy twin room, turn down the bed nearer to the bathroom. In a double-occupancy twin room, turn down the duvet of each bed on the side facing the night lamp. On a double bed being shared by two people, turn down the duvet on both sides.
5. Arrange the pillows.	Provide pillows as specified by guest in the pillow menu. Fluff up the pillows and place them flat on the bed. Figure 12.16 shows a turned down bed with an optional decorative panel and pillow.		

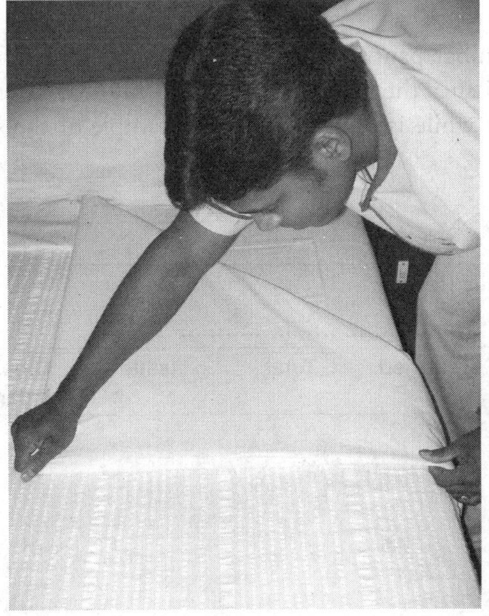

Fig. 12.15 Turning down for evening service

Fig. 12.16 A turned down bed with decorative panel and pillow

Minibar contents

The minibar menu in standard rooms in business hotels typically include savoury snacks, cookies, crackers, chocolates and soft beverages whereas in luxury hotels alcoholic beverages also feature on the minibar menu. A sample of minibar menu is presented in Exhibit 12.1. Also placed on the minibar counter are napkins, coasters, stirrers, and a bottle opener.

Exhibit 12.1 A sample minibar menu

Hotel Sun Down

MINIBAR MENU

Code	Minibar Item	Quantity	Cost
Snacks			
1	Assorted roasted salted nuts	1	₹250
2	Banana Chips	1	₹100
3	Potato wafers	2	₹75
4	Digestive crackers	1	₹150
5	Assorted berries	1	₹225
6	Chocolate	1	₹275
7	Cookies	1	₹75

Issuing of minibar items

Minibar items are stored and issued from the minibar pantry or the housekeeping store. The store keeper maintains an inventory of the items and issues them on requisition to minibar attendants. A minibar daily report is filled by the storekeeper while issuing the items. A sample of the same is shown in Exhibit 12.2.

Exhibit 12.2 Minibar daily report

Minibar Daily Report

Date: .... Time: ....

Item Code	Particulars	Opening balance	Returned	Total	Issue	Closing balance
1	Assorted roasted salted nuts					
2	Banana Chips					
3	Potato wafers					
4	Digestive crackers					
5	Assorted berries					

Stocktaking of minibar items

A weekly inventory of minibar items is conducted by the Assistant Housekeeper and discrepancies are cleared. A sample format for stocktaking or inventory is presented in Exhibit 12.3. Indent is placed once safety stock level is reached in the minibar pantry. A particular date in a month is designated for checking expiry dates on minibar items. Expired items are handed over to F&B.

Exhibit 12.3 A sample format of minibar stocktaking report

Hotel Sun Down

MINIBAR STOCKTAKING REPORT

Date: .... Shift: .... Time: ....

Code	Minibar Item	Areas			Total
Snacks		Rooms (Time:............)	Pantry (Time:............)	Store (Time:............)	
1	Assorted roasted salted nuts				
2	Banana Chips				
3	Potato wafers				
4	Digestive crackers				
5	Assorted berries				
6	Chocolate				
7	Cookies				

Replenishment procedure for minibar

Minibars are checked and replenished daily by a minibar attendant whose responsibility is to maintain stocks of minibar items, replenish minibars and report consumption by guest to the front desk so that the same can be posted in the guest folio. In many hotels, the responsibility lies with the guestroom associates while they are servicing the rooms. While replenishing items, coasters, napkins, stirrers and clean glasses are also checked and replaced. Vacant and clean rooms are cleared only when the minibar is replenished and stocked as per the set standards.

Minibars may be managed in two ways:

Manual system In a manual minibar management system, a minibar attendant checks consumption in occupied rooms and those due for checkout and confirms the same with the guest. A minibar consumption report, as shown in Exhibit 12.4 is filled by the attendant as a checklist. In some hotels, the guest is encouraged to fill up consumption and the same is tallied by a physical check by room associate. The format of minibar slip used in such a case is presented in Exhibit 12.5. The consumption report is filed at the control desk. The control desk executive feeds the consumed item codes in the PMS and the same is posted in the guest's folio by the front desk executive. In some hotels, the minibar charges can also be posted by the supervisor via programmed codes in the room telephone which is linked to the PMS. The consumed items are replenished by the minibar attendant.

Automated system In an automated minibar management system, the minibar has shelves with either infrared or RFID sensors, where each minibar item is tagged by a particular code. When a minibar

Exhibit 12.4 A sample format of minibar consumption report

Hotel Sun Down

FLOOR MINIBAR CONSUMPTION REPORT

Floor No. .... Date: .... Shift: .... Time: ....
Name of associate: .... Signature of associate: ....

Room No. →		01	02	03	04	05	06	07	08	09	10	11	12	13	14
Time in															
Time out															
Minibar Item ↓	**Quantity ↓**														
Snacks															
Assorted roasted salted nuts	1														
Banana Chips	1														
Potato wafers	2														
Digestive crackers	1														
Assorted berries	1														
Chocolate	1														
Cookies	1														

Exhibit 12.5 A sample minibar slip

Hotel Sun Down

MINIBAR SLIP

Name of Guest: .... Room No: ....

Dear Guest,
This minibar is stocked with a selection of snacks and beverages for your convenience. During your stay, it will be replenished once a day and items consumed will be charged to your room account. Please call IRD at 113 should you wish to personalise your minibar. Kindly fill in your record of consumption and place it on the table.

Code	Minibar item	Quantity	Cost	Consumption	Amount
Snacks					
1	Assorted roasted salted nuts	1	₹250		
2	Banana Chips	1	₹100		
3	Potato wafers	2	₹75		
4	Digestive crackers	1	₹150		
5	Assorted berries	1	₹225		
6	Chocolate	1	₹275		
7	Cookies	1	₹75		

item is taken out by the guest and is not returned back to the shelf in 60 seconds, the price amount automatically gets posted in the guest's account. The automated system not only tracks consumption but also inventory levels, expiry dates and generates daily replenishment reports. Complaints abound about the automated system that guests are charged even if they have not consumed the items but taken them out just to check the label. Hence, it is recommended that before settling the guest account, the automated minibar be checked physically by the room associate to confirm consumption. The advantages of an automated system are:

- Elimination of manual error
- Enhanced associate productivity
- Efficient expiry date management
- Organized inventory management

Closing Down after Cleaning

Closing down after cleaning is as important as preparing to clean. The equipment, agents, and other supplies, should be stored away properly and the work area left neat and tidy for the staff coming in for the next shift. Cleaning equipment and agents lying helter-skelter may become a safety hazard, as would spills and debris. Moreover, mechanized equipment not stored properly may result in damage; manual equipment not washed and dried may deteriorate, resulting in inefficient cleaning; and cleaning agents left carelessly may deteriorate, increasing cleaning costs. Dirty cloths and equipment can harbour and spread harmful bacteria. Trash not disposed appropriately may be an attraction for pests. This is why step-by-step closing down is essential. The tasklist is presented in Table 12.12.

Table 12.12 Closing-down tasks

For	Tasks
Cleaning agents	• Leave the containers neatly labelled and tightly capped on shelves meant for cleaning agents in the floor pantry.
Linen	• Any fresh linen remaining in the cart should be put back, with the fold side facing out, on the appropriate shelves in the floor pantry. • Any fresh linen received should also be placed neatly, with the fold side facing out, on the shelves. • Send the soiled linen from the room attendant's cart down the linen chute or place in the linen trolley for transport to the laundry.
Guest supplies	• Refill the toiletries from bulk containers, where applicable. Arrange neatly on appropriate shelves in the floor pantry.
Room attendant's cart	• Empty the trash and soiled-linen bags into appropriate receptacles. • Empty the trolley shelves and damp-dust. Remove any fluff from castor wheels and wipe them down. • Re-stock as required.
Brooms and brushes	• Refer to the section on the care and cleaning of brooms and brushes in Chapter 7.

System for Recycling Used Guest Supplies

A standard system should be set for dealing with used in-room guest supplies. Guest supplies once used and left behind in the room after the guest has checked out, are recycled to the maximum. The used items are brought down on daily basis from the guest floors to the housekeeping department and recycled. A system for recycling used guest supplies is outlined in Exhibit 12.6.

Exhibit 12.6 Procedure of recycling used guest supplies

Recycling used guest supplies	
Used supplies	**Recycling procedure**
Scribbling pads	The unused pages in the scribbling pads are removed carefully and handed over to stores from where it is sent to the printers for binding into new scribbling pads.
Soaps	These are placed in discarded laundry bags and handed over to a soap recycling vendor.
Shampoo bottles	Shampoo from the bottles is refilled in dispensers and used in staff lockers.
Sewing kits	The unused items such as buttons, threads, needles and safety pins from the opened sewing kits are collected in separate boxes and sent periodically to the sewing room for use of hotel tailors.
Shower caps	These are washed and sent to the uniform room from where they are issued to maintenance department for use by masons and painters when requirement arises.
Toilet rolls	Toilet rolls consumed more than half are used in the locker rooms.
Laundry bags	Those meant for discarding are mended and used for packaging lost and found articles. Ones which are beyond repair, are cut down to make drying cloths.

SUMMARY

Cleanliness and hygiene of their hotel room is the foremost attribute that brings the guests back to the hotel as repeat client and this has been substantiated through various global surveys.

Guestroom servicing has been discussed in considerable detail in this chapter, as the guestroom is the primary commodity that a hotel has to sell. Nowdays, the term 'cleaning' is being replaced by 'servicing' with regard to guestrooms, since the prescribed procedure usually involves many other activities other than the cleaning. The different styles of bed-making have been listed and the most prevalent method of making the bed has been explained at length with the help of diagrams. The daily cleaning of guestrooms of different status has been explained.

Minibar management has been outlined in detail with various forms and formats. The turndown service, which is provided in all deluxe hotels and especially in VIP rooms, has been explained. The 'second service', a chargeable service that may be requested by the guest, is explained and the tasks listed. The chapter concludes with a discussion of the process of closing down after cleaning, and its importance and also how used guest supplies are reused or recycled.

KEY TERMS

AMC Annual Maintenance Contract

Breakfast knob card Cards hung by guests on the knobs of guestroom doors to pre-order breakfast at night so that the order reaches the staff on time, without the guest having to be disturbed for taking the order early in the morning.

Check-out room A room from which the guest has left; it is coded as C/O.

Cleaning The removal of dust, dirt, foreign matter, tarnish, and stains from various surfaces with the aid of certain cleaning agents and equipment.

Cleaning agents Substances, natural and synthetic, used to assist the cleaning process.

Coverlet A bedspread that just covers the top of the dust ruffle. It does not reach down to the floor.

Crinkle sheet A distinctively woven sheet used to cover and protect the blanket. It is now called a third sheet. Other names for the crinkle sheet are 'snooze sheet' and 'night spread'.

Departure room A room from which the guest has checked out or is going to check out shortly. Its cleaning procedure is the same as for a vacated room.

Disinfected strip A thin strip placed atop and encircling the toilet seat to let guests know that the toilet has been disinfected for their use. It is also simply called a 'toilet strip'. Often the displayed words printed on it—'Sanitised for your use'—make this clear.

Dust ruffle A pleated, decorative, floor-length skirting of fabric that extends around the sides and foot of the bed.

Duvet Quilts filled with down, feathers, or synthetic fibres. Many hotels use duvets with a decorative duvet cover to replace both blankets and bedspreads. They are sometimes referred to as 'comforters'.

Floor pantry A service room provided on each floor for GRAs to store cleaning agents, equipment, guest supplies, guestroom linen, and their carts.

Foot fold A pocket-like pleat created at the foot of the bed using the extra length of top sheet, so as to allow guests to tuck in their feet while allowing comfortable wiggle-room for movement.

Foot throw or foot runner A decorative cloth panel made of silk brocade or shiny rayon damask laid across the duvet on the foot end side of a hotel bed. It matches the shams placed against the pillows.

Good night kit A kit containing two small vials of certain essential oil blends for relaxation, pillow mist, ear plugs, eye pad, and a couple of mints; it is usually placed in the upper drawer of the bedside table.

IRD In Room Dining.

Linen chute A passage in the form of a tunnel for sending soiled linen down from the floor pantries on all floors to a central place near the laundry, from where it can be collected by the laundry staff.

Mitring Mitring is done for folding sheets or blankets at the corners during bed-making to make them fit the contour of the mattress neatly, without any creases. Mitring is also referred to as the making of 'square corners', 'hospital corners', or 'envelope folds'.

Occupied room A room in which a guest is registered.

On-change room A room in need of housekeeping services before it can be registered to an arriving guest.

OOO 'Out of order'—the status of a guestroom not rentable because it is being repaired or redecorated.

Re-sheeting Re-sheeting the bed involves stripping the bed of all soiled linen and making the bed up with fresh linen.

Room assignment sheet This document indicates the rooms that the GRA has to service and their status, as given in the daily work report. The sheet also lists any pick-up room that the GRA has to service apart from rooms in his/her designated section.

Sani-bin A small metal or plastic container with a lid, kept in the toilet for the collection of soiled sanitary towels and tissues.

Second service A chargeable servicing/cleaning of the room provided on the special request of a guest after the guestroom has already been serviced as per the day's schedule.

Shams The American term for pillowcases. In the Indian hotel industry, 'shams' is used for pillowcases that match the fabric and pattern used in bedspreads rather than the sheets. These are used in very formal settings.

Stayover room A room occupied by a guest who is not checking out today and will remain at least one more night.

Turndown service A special service provided by the housekeeping department in which a room attendant enters the guestroom early in the evening to re-stock supplies, tidy the room, and turn down the covers on the bed.

Vacant room A room in which no guest has slept the previous night and which is not yet occupied.

Vacated The room status signifying that the guest has settled his/her account, returned the room keys, and left the hotel.

Vanity unit A unit comprising a wash basin and mirror surrounded by a flat surface where soaps, a dental kit, a shaving kit, and tooth glasses are kept.

WC Water closet.

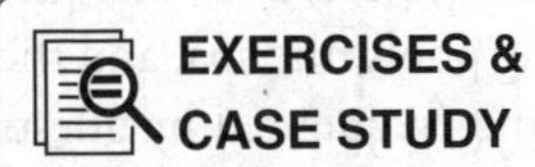

13 Cleaning Public Areas

Learning Objectives

After reading this chapter, you should be able to
- understand the meaning of the term 'public areas' and list the public areas in a hotel
- appreciate the importance of cleaning and maintaining the public areas
- list the daily, weekly, and periodic cleaning tasks for public areas
- discuss the cleaning processes for the various public areas

Introduction

The public areas in a hotel comprise the 'front of the house' areas such as entrances, lobbies, lounges, the front desk, guest corridors, elevators, and restrooms; functional areas such as restaurants, banquet halls, bar, and waiting rooms; and leisure and recreation areas such as swimming pools, the spa, and the health club. In other words, the areas of the hotel that are in constant view and frequented by guests are referred to as public areas.

A neat and clean public area is reflective of the cleanliness standards throughout the hotel property, because guests see these areas first and form an overall impression of the hotel based upon these. The housekeeping department is responsible for the cleanliness and maintenance of these public areas in the hotel. It is impractical to take public areas 'out of service' for the purpose of cleaning, hence, all cleaning and maintenance activities for these areas are scheduled for low-traffic hours and for the night. A sample list of cleaning tasks scheduled in the night shift in public areas is given in Table 13.1.

The cleaning of public areas involves cleaning hard-to-reach areas and may involve the use of ladders. While using ladders, the housemen should take all safety precautions. Ladder safety has been dealt with in Chapters 7 and 22.

Many hotels get their public areas cleaned by contractors. Like cleaning in other areas of the hotel, the cleaning routine for public areas can be divided into daily, weekly, monthly, and periodic tasks. These tasks are summarised in Table 13.2.

A systematic way to accomplish the cleaning of public areas consistently is to plan *area inventory lists* and *frequency schedules* for all tasks in the public areas. A sample weekly cleaning schedule for public areas is given in Table 13.3. Refer to Chapter 5 for more information on area inventory lists and frequency schedules. As and when associates complete their cleaning tasks, the public area supervisor inspects them with assistance of a detailed checklist. Refer Chapter 15 for sample public area checklists.

Table 13.1 Public area cleaning tasks scheduled at night

Area	Cleaning tasks
Entrance & main porch	High dusting of pillars and ceilings Steps and floor scrubbing, water wash
Lobby	Dusting, dry & wet mopping, glass cleaning, vacuuming of carpets Thorough cleaning of bell desk, concierge's desk, duty manager's desk, travel desk and reception Cleaning and disinfection of all telephones Thorough cleaning of back office Polishing of furniture Polishing of brassware fixture and artifacts Periodic floor polishing as per schedule Periodic deep cleaning of carpets and curtains, lighting fixtures as per schedule

Table 13.2 Frequency of cleaning tasks in public areas

Cleaning tasks in public areas based on frequency			
Daily tasks	**Weekly tasks**	**Monthly tasks**	**Periodic tasks**
• Dusting & damp-wiping surfaces	• Scrubbing floors	• Spray cleaning & buffing floors	• Washing walls
• Emptying ashtrays and bins	• Dusting walls	• Polishing of furniture & woodwork	• Stripping & repolishing or resealing floors
• Suction cleaning upholstery	• Dusting and wiping lighting fixtures	• Cleaning hard to reach areas	• Shampooing carpets
• Mopping hard floors	• Cleaning & polishing hard surfaces		• Washing windows
• Cleaning glass surfaces	• Vacuuming carpets		
• Arranging flowers			
• Cleaning washroom areas			

Table 13.3 Sample 'Cleaning of the Day' – weekly cleaning schedule for public areas

Day of the week	Cleaning scheduled	Cleaning tasks
Monday	AC grills and cobweb cleaning	AC grills and cobweb cleaning of restaurant, banquet halls, business centre, meeting rooms and board room
Tuesday	Dusting of artifacts	Dusting of artifacts in restaurants and lobby
Wednesday	Vanitory unit and WC cleaning	Thorough cleaning of all public area restroom vanitory units and WCs
Thursday	Upholstery cleaning	Thorough vacuuming of all upholstered furniture in lobby in non-peak hours, in banquets and restaurants in closed hours, in meeting rooms in non-occupied hours; upholstery shampooing to be carried out if required, followed by drying in shade
Friday	Telephone cleaning	Thorough cleaning and disinfection of all telephones in public areas
Saturday	Window cleaning	Cleaning of lobby windows during non-peak hours; cleaning of windows in the restaurants, banquet halls and meeting rooms and board room
Sunday	Carpet cleaning	Thorough inside-out vacuuming and fluffing up of all carpets and rugs in public areas

Entrances

The guests get their first impression of the hotel from the entrance and the lobby. For this reason, some hotels may have elaborate or dramatic design features at the entrances, cleaning of which may be a difficult proposition for the housekeeping department. Entrances, if not cleaned and maintained daily, can easily acquire a neglected look due to the heavy traffic and exposure, which can be very unappealing for an arriving guest.

The preventive maintenance of floors at the entrance is important, since this is the inlet point for dust and dirt trekked in by all the guests' shoes. If the dirt and grit are not prevented from entering the establishment at this stage, they will eventually become embedded in the floor and deteriorate the surface.

Sidewalks and Driveways

Hotel sidewalks and driveways help create a brand image of the property and it is essential to keep them clean at all times. Cleaning these areas pose challenges due to constant usage and exposure to weather elements and pollution. The procedure for cleaning sidewalks and driveways is given in Table 13.4.

Façade Cleaning

The impressive look of the façade of a hotel helps the hotel to leverage a favourable impression on the guests who enter its portals. Façade of the hotel refers to the external front face view of the hotel

Table 13.4 Procedure for cleaning driveways and sidewalks

SOP Name:	**Procedure for cleaning driveways and sidewalks**		
Effective Date:	**23.12.2019**	**SOP Author:**	**Shefali Shyam**
SOP No.:	**145**	**SOP Approver:**	**Vijay Dewan**
For Job Title:	**Housemen**	**SOP Owner:**	**Hotel Sundown, Coorg**
Objective: To efficiently clean driveways and sidewalks to set cleaning standards.			
Equipment & tools needed:	Power sweeper machine, jet spray machine, steam cleaning machine, scraper, large wastebin with liner, hard broom, long handled scrubbing brush, squeegee, long handled dustpan, PPE (slush boots, thick apron, gloves), 'Cleaning in progress' signage stands	**Supplies needed:**	Grease-cutting, emulsifying detergent
Procedure	**How-to do**	**Additional information**	
1. Remove debris.	Remove any visible trash, fallen leaves and twigs and debris from the driveway and sidewalks.	Clean half the driveway first, leaving the other half open to traffic. Place 'Cleaning in progress' signage stand. Use a hard broom and long handled dustpan and dump the debris in waste bin.	
2. Scrape off sticky matter.	Use a scraper to remove any gum or sticky matter.	Use gloves as PPE.	

building as it looks to a visitor about to enter the hotel. Façade materials may be a combination of the following:

- Stone cladding
- Masonry walls
- Glass walls and windows
- Galvanized metal veneers
- Coated metals such as chromium and copper coated steel
- Wood panels and shingles
- Asphalt and fibreglass shingles

Periodic cleaning and maintenance of façade is essential to maintain its aesthetics and for long term conservation of the structure. Most hotel façades are imposing structures featuring high walls and windows, ornate structures, tall pillars and/or elevated glass panels which invariably are exposed to the elements of the weather, dust and pollutants. These pose cleaning challenges of safety and require special skills and equipment and housekeepers prefer to outsource façade cleaning for the same reason. The contractual firms have specialised equipment and trained personnel to handle the risky cleaning. The following must be borne in mind:

- The contract specification should specify procedures, frequency, equipment and cleaning agents and safety standards to be followed by the contractor. Refer Chapter 4 for details on contract specification.
- The façade cleaning schedule must be verified with the EHK a day in advance and communicated with maintenance, security and front office departments for coordination.
- The terrace area must be inspected by deputy housekeeper and security and work permit to be issued post checking only, for commencement of work.
- The contract firm supervisor and the deputy housekeeper must inspect the safety gear and PPE before the cleaning commences.
- A public area supervisor should be present to monitor the work from the hotel's side; work must not commence without his presence.
- Façade cleaning work must be carried out in good natural light, between 7.30 am and 4.30 pm.
- Parts of façade in and above or affecting guest areas should be cleaned post 10 am only after a clearance from floor supervisor for non-disturbance to DND rooms, single lady rooms and honeymoon suite.
- A physical assessment for fitness condition of the employee undertaking the task must be carried out.
- Façade cleaning must not be carried out in inclement weather conditions.

The procedure for façade cleaning is given in Table 13.5.

Flooring and Mats

Key features here are the doormats and runners that act as the reservoirs for dust and dirt, rubbed away from the shoes. One doormat or runner should be placed just outside the entrance, to prevent most of the dirt and soil being brought in with the guest's shoes. Another doormat or runner must be placed just inside the entrance, to remove any remnants of dust from the shoes so that they do not leave any footprint on the floor.

Other cleaning and maintenance tasks for this area are listed in this section.

- The doormats and runners must be vacuum-cleaned daily to remove dust and grit.
- In the rainy season and during times of heavy traffic (such as in the high season), cleaning the mats twice a day or even more often may be called for.
- The floor at the entrance has to be mopped frequently throughout the day.
- Plants at the entrances should be watered when required.

Table 13.5 Procedure for façade cleaning

SOP Name:	**Procedure for cleaning the façade of the hotel**		
Effective Date:	23.12.2019	**SOP Author:**	**Shefali Shyam**
SOP No.:	146	**SOP Approver:**	**Vijay Dewan**
For Job Title:	**Public area supervisor, Housemen, contract supervisor & workers**	**SOP Owner:**	**Hotel Sundown, Coorg**
Objective: To efficiently clean the façade of the hotel to set cleaning standards following all safety precautions.			
Equipment & tools needed:	Cleaner's trolley stocked with cleaning agents and equipment, cobweb brush, hard bristle brush, sponge mop, dust bins, dust pans, PPE - safety harness, belts and lanyards, ropes, hard helmets, climbing shoes, dust masks, safety goggles	**Supplies needed:**	Glass cleaner, all-purpose surface cleaner, stain remover, touch up paints, silicone conservator
Procedure	**How-to do**		**Additional information**
1. Assemble supplies and equipment.	Assemble and check safety equipment, toolbox and PPE. Assemble the cleaning equipment and replenish cleaning agents in spray bottles.		Check rigging, pulley mechanism and anchors for work at heights. Ascertain the fitness of the workers before commencement of work. Hotel work permit to be filled and signed. Fill the safety checklist before commencement of work.
2. Set up work area.	Setup work area. Barricade top and bottom. Put signage of 'Cleaning in progress'.		

Doors

Many entrances are arches without doors. But very often, the main entrance to the property may have glass or wooden doors. Glass doors may be of the push/pull, sliding, or revolving type. Glass doors easily develop streaks as guests place their fingers on the surface. Hence, doors and door tracks are usually cleaned thoroughly early in the morning, when the entrance lobby is relatively free of traffic. This and the cleaning tasks for a few other fixtures are listed here.

- Glass doors should be cleaned twice a day, and where public traffic is high, the frequency of cleaning may have to be even three or four times daily. A proprietary glass-cleaner may be used for the cleaning or a vinegar-and-water solution may be used for glass that is not too soiled.
- Dirt, grease, and scuff marks (from shoes knocking against the threshold) on the door frames should be damp-dusted with an alkaline detergent and water, and re-wiped with clean water to remove all traces of the detergent.
- Wooden doors should be damp-dusted once daily. A neutral detergent should be used with water for damp-dusting once a week to avoid the build-up of layers of dust.
- Brass knobs and handles should be polished weekly, and in case of lacquered brass, only damp-dusting is sufficient.
- Lights and lighting fixtures should be checked daily and cleaned weekly.

Lobbies

These are areas provided as a common meeting point for guests near the reception. Many lobbies are carpeted, while others have hard flooring. Cleaning processes for the two kinds of flooring will be different. Floors in the lobbies need to be cleaned frequently since these are spaces where guests interact, relax, and check in. Like entrances, these are also heavy-traffic areas. Hence, cleaning should be scheduled for the night or early morning, when there are fewer people around. Lobbies may have high ceilings, elaborate chandeliers, and other features that are difficult to clean. In many hotels, these features are cleaned and maintained by contractors. It is important to note that hotel lobbies and lounges are cleaned in the same way.

Daily Cleaning

The daily tasks should be scheduled in such a way that the lobby may be cleaned with the least inconvenience to guests. The procedure for daily cleaning of the lobby is presented in Table 13.6.

Periodic Cleaning

Some cleaning tasks need not be carried out daily. These should be scheduled on a periodic basis, for once in a week, once in a month, once in six months, or once in a year. These tasks are summarised in Table 13.7.

Table 13.6 Procedure for daily cleaning of lobby

SOP Name:	**Procedure for cleaning the lobby**		
Effective Date:	**23.12.2019**	**SOP Author:**	**Shefali Shyam**
SOP No. :	**147**	**SOP Approver:**	**Vijay Dewan**
For Job Title:	**Public area associates**	**SOP Owner:**	**Hotel Sundown, Coorg**
Objective: To efficiently clean the hotel lobby to set cleaning standards.			
Equipment & tools needed:	Cleaner's trolley stocked with cleaning agents and equipment, vacuum cleaner, cobweb brush, dust control mop, wet microfibre mop, small squeegee, dusters, glass cloth, dust bins, dust pan, 'Cleaning in progress' sign-stand, bin liners	**Supplies needed:**	Glass cleaner, all-purpose surface cleaner, floor cleaner, dis-infectant solution
Procedure	**How-to do**	**Additional information**	
1. Perform high dusting tasks and spot clean walls.	Check for and remove any cobwebs from ceilings and wall corners using a cobweb brush. Spot clean stains and marks from the walls.	Check the lights and lighting fixtures for proper functioning.	
2. Clear away trash.	Empty ashtrays and sand urns and damp-dust them. Empty the dustbins kept behind reception counter, bell desk, concierge counter, travel desk, duty manager's desk, and guest relations desk. Re-line them with fresh liners.	Before clearing the ashtray, ensure that all cigarette butts are put out.	

Table 13.7 Periodic cleaning tasks in the lobby

Periodic cleaning tasks in the lobby				
Weekly tasks	**Monthly tasks**	**Quarterly tasks**	**Bi-annual tasks**	**Annual tasks**
• High-level dusting - ceilings, hard-to-reach areas such as tops of fans and cornices	• Dusting very high ceilings	• Scrubbing hard floors	• Bringing down and cleaning elaborate chandeliers	• Lobby floor polishing
• Vacuuming upholstered furniture thoroughly with upholstery attachment	• Jet pressure cleaning of lobby porch	• Carpet shampooing	• Upholstery shampooing	• Changing upholstery
• Vacuum clean blinds and curtains.	• Thorough cleaning of AC vents		• Cleaning lampshades	• Re-laquering brassware and chandeliers
• Polishing wooden furniture			• Cleaning leather chairs	

Front Desk

The front desk is the hub of activity in the 'front of the house' part of the property, since all arriving guests are registered to their rooms from here and many enquiries are made here. Hence, the cleaning should be done at non-peak hours so as not to interrupt the flow of business. When guests approach the front desk during the cleaning process, cleaning should be stopped momentarily and the employee doing the task should step aside. Cleaning tasks should in no way hamper the flow of work at the front desk. Front desks may be elaborately designed or be simply practical in design—in the latter case, they will be easier to clean. The front desk in most hotels is a part of the entrance lobby, so that all cleaning tasks for the lobby apply to the front desk as well.

Specific Cleaning Tasks

The front desk calls for some exclusive cleaning tasks as well.

- Empty wastepaper baskets as and when required in the day.
- Damp-dust the desk, taking care to wipe under the telephone wires and computer cables. The front panel of the desk should be damp-dusted and a neutral detergent should be used to remove scuff marks from guests' shoes.
- All the railings and fixtures should be damp-dusted. If made of brass, they should be polished according to a schedule.
- Damp-dust all the telephones with a disinfectant solution and wipe with a dry duster twice daily.
- Damp-dust the computer components and fax machines and then wipe with a dry duster daily. Any smear on the computer screen may be wiped with a proprietary glass-cleaner. It should be ensured while cleaning the computers that the machines are switched off.
- Suction-clean the carpet under the desk. If the floor is uncarpeted, mop the hard floor.
- Damp-wipe the furniture. Upholstered furniture should be suction-cleaned with an upholstery attachment.

Elevators

These too must be cleaned at night time when they are least used. They should always be taken out of service for cleaning. The necessary signboards indicating that cleaning is being carried out must be displayed prominently. Elevator doors are usually made of steel and sometimes they may be covered with wooden panels. Steel doors show grease marks from fingers easily. Elevators should be cleaned daily and a more thorough cleaning may be done on a periodic basis. The procedure for cleaning elevators is outlined in Table 13.8.

Table 13.8 Procedure for cleaning the elevator

SOP Name:	**Procedure for cleaning the elevator**		
Effective Date:	**23.12.2019**	**SOP Author:**	**Shefali Shyam**
SOP No. :	**148**	**SOP Approver:**	**Vijay Dewan**
For Job Title:	**Public area associate**	**SOP Owner:**	**Hotel Sundown, Coorg**
Objective: To efficiently clean the elevators of the hotel to set cleaning standards following all safety precautions.			
Equipment & tools needed:	Cleaner's trolley stocked with cleaning agents and equipment - vacuum cleaner, cobweb brush, dust control mop, wet microfibre mop, small squeegee, dusters, glass cloth, cotton swab, dust bin, dust pan, 'Cleaning in progress' sign-stand	**Supplies needed:**	Glass cleaner, neutral detergent, floor cleaner, disinfectant solution
Procedure	**How-to do**	**Additional information**	
1. Take the elevator out of service.	Bring the elevator to a specified floor and take it out of service. Place the 'Cleaning in progress' sign-stand outside the elevator.	This is as per hotel policy.	
2. Clean the elevator.	Lightly damp-dust the ceiling and light fixtures. Clean the air-conditioning or ventilation duct using a suction cleaner. Damp-wipe the steel doors, inside and out, using a neutral detergent solution and then wipe clean using water. Dry and buff with a clean duster to shine.	Vacuum clean the ceiling and the elevator fan once a week. Lighting fixtures must be thoroughly cleaned weekly.	

Staircases

Like any other public area, staircases should be cleaned when there is least traffic and hence, night time cleaning is ideal. The appropriate way to clean staircases is to divide them into half lengthways and clean one half at a time. This is required not only to prevent dirty footprints on a wet floor, but also as a safety precaution so that there are no accidents due to slipping on wet steps. Here, too, the various cleaning tasks may be carried out at different periodicities—daily, weekly, or less often. While cleaning staircases, care should be taken that dirt and debris do not fall downwards through the gaps in banisters and railings. Any kind of sweeping should be directed towards the wall.

The specific tasks are the following:

- Carpets should be suction-cleaned daily and any stain should be attended to immediately. Due to practical reasons, a backpack type of vacuum cleaner is best for suction-cleaning staircases.

- Hard-floored staircases should be suction-cleaned and then damp-mopped. They can be scrubbed weekly with a deck scrubber, using a neutral detergent. If a floor sealer has been applied, however, scrubbing should be avoided. Use of excess water should be avoided on wooden stairs.
- While cleaning the floor, the vertical risers of each step should be cleaned as well as the treads.
- Damp-dust the wall skirtings weekly.
- Damp-dust the banisters and handrails daily. If they are ornately carved, a vacuum cleaner with a crevice-cleaning attachment should be used.

 Guest Corridors

A long corridor should be divided into sections for cleaning. As for staircases, the corridor should be divided into half lengths so that the other half is open for use while one half is being cleaned. Appropriate cautionary signs should be used to indicate that cleaning is in progress. Many hotel corridors are fully carpeted. These carpets should not only be attractive, but also sturdy and durable to withstand everyday wear and tear.

The cleaning procedure for guest corridors and lift landing foyers are given in Table 13.9.

Table 13.9 Procedure for cleaning guest corridors, lift landing foyer

SOP Name:	**Procedure for cleaning guest corridors, lift landing foyers**		
Effective Date:	**23.12.2019**	**SOP Author:**	**Shefali Shyam**
SOP No. :	**149**	**SOP Approver:**	**Vijay Dewan**
For Job Title:	**Public area associate**	**SOP Owner:**	**Hotel Sundown, Coorg**
Objective: To clean the guest corridors, lift landing foyers on guest floors to set cleaning standards.			
Equipment & tools needed:	Cleaner's trolley stocked with cleaning agents and equipment - vacuum cleaner, cobweb brush, dusters, microfibre dusters, sponge, glass cloth, 'Cleaning in progress' sign-stand, step ladder	**Supplies needed:**	Glass cleaner, surface cleaner, air freshener, brass polish
Procedure	**How-to do**		**Additional information**
1. Prepare to clean guest corridor and foyer.	Place 'Cleaning in progress' sign and always leave one half of the corridor passage free for guests to walk.		Start at one end and work in one direction to clean the corridor walls. Inform maintenance for any paint touch ups. Thorough cleaning of walls may be done weekly.
2. Do the high dusting tasks and clean the walls and fixtures.	Remove any cobwebs from ceilings and wall corners. Clean the walls in the corridors and foyer with a sponge sprayed with surface cleaner. Spot-clean any finger mark or smudge on the walls. Clean the wall skirtings or baseboards all along the corridor and foyer with damp microfibre duster.		Inform maintenance if lighting fixture or AC repairs are needed. Ensure paintings are hung parallel to corridor and foyer wall lines. Inform maintenance if repairs are needed.

Public Restrooms

This refers to the washrooms and toilets in the hotel meant for use by guests in general, and not restricted to guests registered at the hotel. Washrooms may have elaborate mirrors, other ornate fixtures, and some pieces of upholstered furniture. The sanitary fittings commonly found in washrooms are WCs, urinals, sluices, bidets, and vanity units or pedestal-type wash basins. Public restrooms need to be cleaned thoroughly twice a day at the minimum; when guest traffic is more, the frequency will have to be higher. In lower traffic periods, frequent but light tidying may be required.

Refer to Chapter 10 for the general cleaning of sanitary fittings. Some of the primary areas of concern are enumerated here.

Cleaning vanity units or wash basins Refer to Chapter 12 for the daily cleaning procedure for vanity units.

Cleaning WCs, bidets, shower cabinets, and baths The daily cleaning processes for these are the same as followed in a guest bathroom. These have been discussed in Chapter 12. The weekly cleaning of WCs involves the use of an alkaline detergent. In case of heavily soiled and stained WCs with a limescale problem, acid cleaners need to be used.

Cleaning urinals These may require the use of an acid cleaner more frequently. Toilet cleaner should be applied to all the inner surfaces of the urinal and allowed to stand for 10 minutes. Any debris from the drainage channel should be removed. While the cleaner is left to sit, clean the surrounding surfaces, walls, and the outer part of the urinal. Then, using a toilet brush, scrub the urinal bowl thoroughly and flush to rinse away the cleaner.

Cleaning activities scheduled at night in public restrooms

- General cleaning tasks carried out in morning shift such as damp mopping of floors, vacuuming of floor mats, dusting, cleaning, and polishing of sanitary fixtures and so on is repeated.
- Cleaning of vanity mirrors is carried out.
- Scrubbing of WCs with acidic cleaners to remove stains is done.
- Cleaning of lighting fixtures is carried out.
- Soap solutions are replenished in dispensers.
- Hand driers are checked and cleaned.

Banquet Halls

These may be used for dinners, conferences, conventions, exhibitions, and so on. For conventions and conferences, hotels provide audio-visual aids that may include liquid crystal displays (LCDs), digital laser projectors (DLPs), and other presentation devices, as well as appropriately arranged tables and chairs. When banquet halls have bookings for several functions on the same day, cleaning them becomes more of a challenge. A larger workforce and good organization will be required on such days. The cleaning process includes daily cleaning tasks and weekly cleaning tasks and is outlined in Table 13.10.

Table 13.10 Procedure for cleaning of banquet halls

SOP Name:	**Procedure for cleaning of banquet halls**		
Effective Date:	**23.12.2019**	**SOP Author:**	**Shefali Shyam**
SOP No.:	**150**	**SOP Approver:**	**Vijay Dewan**
For Job Title:	**Public area associate**	**SOP Owner:**	**Hotel Sundown, Coorg**
Objective: To clean the banquet to set cleaning standards.			
Equipment & tools needed:	Cleaner's trolley stocked with cleaning agents and equipment - vacuum cleaner, dust control mop, wet mop, cobweb brush, dusters, microfibre dusters, glass cloth, dust bin, dust pan, 'Cleaning in progress' sign-stand, step ladder	**Supplies needed:**	Glass cleaner, surface cleaner, air freshener, fresh table cloths, frills, chair covers and bows if needed, mineral water bottles, glasses, coasters, mints and candies in bowls, table centrepiece arrangements, notepads, pencils
Procedure	**How-to do**		**Additional information**
1. Prepare to clean banquet hall.	Place 'Cleaning in progress' sign outside the banquet hall.		
2. Remove cobwebs and clean walls.	Remove cobwebs from ceiling and wall corners. Spot-clean walls for stains. Clean the wall skirtings. Clean walls periodically. Check lighting fixtures. Clean them weekly. Bring down and clean chandeliers once in six months. Clean any glass surfaces with glass cleaner.		Coordinate with maintenance if lighting fixture repairs are needed.

Restaurants and Dining Areas

These need to have visual appeal as well as meet sanitation standards. In many properties, housekeeping may be responsible for maintaining the dining areas in conjunction with the service staff of the dining room. In such properties, the housekeeping department takes on the tasks of the thorough weekly cleaning, whereas the service staff are responsible for the daily cleaning and maintenance. Housekeeping is also responsible for the supply of clean table linen and for the collection of dirty linen.

The cleaning tasks here include:

- Vacuuming the carpeted areas, moving out the dining chairs to clean under the tables; spot-cleaning any stain.
- Damp-dusting the furniture daily; polishing wooden furniture once a month; vacuuming upholstered furniture.
- Wiping all glass surfaces with a proprietary glass-cleaner.
- Spot-cleaning the walls.
- Checking and cleaning the lighting fixtures.
- Following the regular schedule of pest control.

Cleaning activities scheduled at night in banquet halls/dining halls/restaurants

- Periodic carpet shampooing, AC grill cleaning, cleaning of fans, and lighting fixtures is carried out.
- High dusting is done.
- Upholstered furniture is vacuumed.
- All furniture is damp-wiped.

- Damp mopping of floor is carried out.
- Surfaces and counters are damp-wiped.
- Water in the floral vases is changed.
- Periodic polishing of brass fixtures and articles is carried out.
- Planters are cleaned.
- Telephone is cleaned and disinfected.

Leisure and Recreation Areas

Leisure areas in hotels include the health club, saunas and solariums, swimming pool, spas, and changing areas, discotheques and nightclubs. These are areas meant for the recreation and relaxation of guests.

Health Club or Fitness Centre

All hotels have an exclusive area for guests to exercise and work out in, perhaps using exercise equipment. Many airline crews and other groups sign contracts with hotels for their employees' stays only if they have some gym facilities with trained staff. The equipment found in health clubs include treadmills, bench presses, rowing machines, cycling machines, dumbbells, and so on. The flooring in health clubs should be non-slippery and should not be polished to a very high shine, or else it will not provide good friction for anti-skid properties. The walls will usually have several mirrored panels. Health clubs also have shower cubicles and lockers. The cleanliness of the whole area, including the equipment, is the housekeeping department's responsibility. The tasks involved are:

- Damp-dusting equipment, after first making sure that they are switched off.
- Damp-dusting all furniture. Wooden furniture should be polished monthly.
- Damp wiping the top and side surfaces of lockers.
- Damp wiping the inside of lockers with disinfectant solution.
- Cleaning all glass surfaces, including windows and mirrors.
- Removing any stain from the walls by spot-cleaning as soon as noticed.
- Checking and damp-dusting all lighting fixtures.
- Sweeping and mopping (or suction-cleaning) a hard floor. A disinfectant cleaner should be added to mop water.
- Cleaning the shower cubicles and replenishing toiletries.
- Removing soiled linen such as bath towels, hand towels, and so on, and replacing with fresh ones.

Saunas and Solariums

Saunas are steam-bath cubicles made of wood or glass. Solariums are enclosed glass areas for the enjoyment or therapeutic use of sunrays.

Cleaning saunas

The insides of saunas are prone to mould, as they are warm and moist over long periods. Moss may collect outside too, where there is a lot of moisture. To clean saunas, a bleach should be added as a cleaning agent to the water and a nylon scrubber needs to be used. A concentrated solution of bleach should be used in the most badly affected areas. After cleaning with the bleach, the sauna should be rinsed thoroughly with cold water to remove all residual bleach. The sauna should then be left open to dry so that the fumes from the bleach dissipate. A deodorizer may be used to counteract the smell of the bleach too.

Cleaning solariums

This primarily involves cleaning the glass panels. A proprietary glass-cleaner or a solution of vinegar in water may be used for the purpose. Refer to Chapter 8 for more on the cleaning of glass surfaces.

Swimming Pools, Spas, and Changing Rooms

Regular cleaning and disinfecting of swimming pools is important from the point of view of hygiene. If not cleaned to a regular schedule, swimming pools may become carriers of waterborne infections. Swimming pool water becomes contaminated with body fats and oils, sweat, saliva, urine, cosmetics, and airborne dust particles. However, ideally the pool should contain as few bacteria as drinking water.

Any repair and maintenance work needed in the swimming pools is done by the engineering and maintenance department. The daily cleaning of the swimming pool usually comes under the purview of the housekeeping department.

The primary concerns in cleaning swimming pools are water clarity and water chemistry control. *Water clarity* results from effective filtration to remove all particulate matter. When filters are not effective, they may need cleaning by a backwash cycle, in which a reversed water flow is created through the valves. This forces the discharge of debris into the sewer system. Water chemistry control implies the chemical safety of the water for swimming and involves the maintenance of a neutral pH to control the growth of harmful bacteria in the pool water. If the water is too alkaline, the sides and bottom of the pool will become slippery and prone to black algae. If the water is too acidic, it may deteriorate the pool finish and damage the pump. Chlorine or bromine were earlier used for this purpose, but now are discouraged because of certain health hazards such as eye irritation, hair loss, and skin rashes resulting from exposure to these. Nowadays, ozone is increasingly being used instead for the treatment of pool water.

Ozone is injected into the water supply at the point where it enters the pool. Ozone treatment also makes the pool water clear, sparkling, and attractive. It does not affect the neutral pH of water. Moreover, ozone is odourless—unlike chlorine—and does not pose any health hazard to swimmers.

Spa baths are small pools of warm water with the temperature maintained at a maximum of 39°C. Jacuzzis are small pools in which alternate jets of warm water bring about a therapeutic effect. They are cleaned in the same way as swimming pools.

The daily cleaning tasks of the housekeeping department with regard to swimming pools, spas, and changing rooms also involve:

- Skimming the surface of the pool water for floating debris, using a skimmer net attached to a long pole.
- Sweeping and mopping floor surfaces.
- Suction-cleaning any carpeted area.
- Spot-cleaning the walls.
- Checking and cleaning lighting fixtures.
- Cleaning any glass surface.
- Emptying wastepaper baskets.
- Damp-dusting any furniture.
- Removing soiled linen and replacing with fresh ones.
- Replenishing toiletries.

Discotheques, Pubs and Nightclubs

Many hotels have discotheques, pubs or nightclubs in their premises, located away from guestroom areas so as not to cause disturbance to in-house guests. Walk-in and in-house guests gather in nightclubs to socialise with drinks, food, and dance during the evening, stretching on till late night. Stains caused due to food and drinks spillage, chewing gum, vomit, tobacco and cigarette ash are challenges to deal with for housekeeping staff. Thorough cleaning of nightclubs is essential to achieve a hygienic environment before they open for the next day. The procedure to clean nightclubs is outlined in Table 13.11.

Table 13.11 Procedure to clean nightclubs, pubs, or discotheques

SOP Name:	**Procedure for cleaning nightclubs, pubs or discotheques**		
Effective Date:	**23.12.2019**	**SOP Author:**	**Shefali Shyam**
SOP No. :	**151**	**SOP Approver:**	**Vijay Dewan**
For Job Title:	**Public area associate**	**SOP Owner:**	**Hotel Sundown, Coorg**
Objective: To clean the nightclub, pub or discotheque to set cleaning standards.			
Equipment & tools needed:	Cleaner's trolley stocked with cleaning agents and equipment - vacuum cleaner, ozonator, hard-bristled broom, long-handled scrubbing brush, squeegee, wet mop, cobweb brush, dusters, microfibre dusters, glass cloth, blunt knife, 'Cleaning in progress' sign-stand, step ladder, dust bins, dust pan, PPE – gloves, safety boots	**Supplies needed:**	Glass cleaner, floor cleaner, ice, air freshener, wooden floor polish, drain cleaning product, disinfectant solution
Procedure	**How-to do**		**Additional information**
1. Prepare to clean the nightclub.	Place 'Cleaning in progress' sign outside the nightclub. Empty ashtrays and waste bins. Operate the ozonator in the closed nightclub for about 1-2 hours to refresh the stale air. Ventilate the facility by opening all doors and windows to remove residual ozone gas and to refresh the internal air. Wear heavy duty gloves and safety boots and enter to clean the nightclub after 4 hours of ventilation.		Make sure no cigarette butts are burning when emptying ashtrays. No one should enter the facility while the ozonator is operational, till 4 hours of room ventilation is done thereafter.
2. Remove cobwebs and clean walls.	Remove any broken glass carefully using a hard bristled broom and dustpan. Remove cobwebs from ceiling and wall corners. Spot-clean walls for stains.		Coordinate with maintenance if lighting fixture or AC repairs are needed.

Lawns and Gardens

Many hotels are known for their beautifully maintained lawns and gardens. The landscaped areas may include lawns, gardens, rocky cascades, ornamental grasses, climbers on trellis, flower beds, flagged pathways, flowering trees, hedges, and so on. The hotels have horticulturists/gardeners who are part of housekeeping department, to maintain such landscaped areas. The cleaning and maintenance tasks in lawns and gardens include,

1. Removing and composting biodegradable plant wastes.
2. Mowing the lawn grass.
3. Pruning outgrowing hedges and composting the cut plant components.
4. Disposing of any plant material that shows signs of disease.
5. Conserving seeds from dead flowers.
6. Weeding

7. Pruning certain woody shrubs such as rose bushes,which bloom only on new branches. This also encourages new growth to set in.
8. If ornamental grasses have stagnated, they may be cut to within a few inches of the ground.
9. Adding compost to soil.
10. Staking of plants which have thin stems. It is always better to use natural materials for staking.
11. Mulching the garden as it conserves water, feeds the soil, cools plant roots, and smothers the weeds.
12. Cleaning planters.
13. Cleaning benches or sit out area.
14. Sweeping pathways.

SUMMARY

Public areas serve to showcase a hotel. Guests form their first impression of the hotel, its cleanliness and maintenance standards, from the condition of the hotel's public areas. This chapter deals with the importance and cleanliness of the various public areas of a hotel. Like cleaning in all other parts of the hotel, public areas also are cleaned on a daily, weekly, and periodic schedule. Area inventory lists and frequency schedules play a vital role in the cleaning of public areas. Driveways and sidewalks have to be maintained clean at all times of the day. Façade of the hotel is cleaned on a periodic schedule as it poses many cleaning challenges. Entrances, lobbies, and the front desk may have to be attended to by housekeeping staff several times a day, depending on the inflow of guests and the occupancy level of the hotel. These areas need to be cleaned at non-peak hours of the day, when traffic is low, since taking them out of service is impractical.

Elevators, however, do need to be taken out of service while cleaning and therefore should be cleaned at night or early in the morning. While cleaning all public areas, appropriate signs should be displayed indicating that cleaning is in progress. Guest corridors and staircases need to be divided in two lengthwise while cleaning, so that there is space available for passage while the other half is being cleaned.

In public restrooms, various sanitary fittings need cleaning and disinfecting.

Banquets and convention halls may require a large carpeted area to be cleaned, as well as furniture to be arranged according to special layouts. Ornate lighting fixtures here also need to be regularly cleaned.

In restaurants and dining areas, housekeeping assists in cleaning on a weekly or periodic basis for the removal of stains from carpets and walls, polishing of furniture, and pest control.

Leisure and recreation areas include swimming pools, spas, health clubs, saunas, solariums, and the associated changing areas, discotheques and nightclubs, and lawns and gardens. In the health club, health equipment, floors, and mirror panels on the walls need to be cleaned regularly. Maintenance and cleaning of swimming pools primarily entails the maintenance of water clarity and water chemistry control. Many hotels hire contractors for cleaning the public areas, since many specialized cleaning tasks are involved.

KEY TERMS

Area inventory lists A list of all items and surfaces within a particular area, that require the attention of housekeeping personnel.

Bidets Sanitary fixtures meant for the thorough washing of the genitals and anal area. These are increasingly being used as foot baths these days.

Buffing Polishing the floor with a low-speed polishing machine.

Convention A formal assembly of representatives sharing a common field of interest to air their views.

Damp-dusting A method of cleaning where the item to be cleaned is wiped with a damp cloth.

Façade Refers to the external front face view of the hotel building as it looks to a visitor about to enter the hotel.

Frequency schedule A schedule that indicates how often the items listed in the area inventory list are to be cleaned or maintenance tasks carried out.

Jacuzzis Whirlpools; small pools in which alternate jets of warm water bring about therapeutic effects.

Lobbies These are the areas provided near the reception as common meeting points for all guests.

Lounge A place in a hotel where guests can sit back and relax. It is a public area, suitably furnished for relaxation.

Mulching Applying a layer of, usually but not exclusively, organic material to the surface of an area of soil to conserve soil moisture, improve soil fertility, retard the growth of weeds, and enhance the visual appeal of the area. Common organic mulches are varied mixtures of wood chips, grass clippings, leaves, bark chips, and straw.

Ozonator Ozone generating machines that help remove odours and freshen the air.

Preventive maintenance A systematic approach to maintenance in which situations are identified and corrected on a regular basis to control costs and keep larger problems from occurring.

Public areas The areas of the hotel that are in constant view of guests and that are frequented by guests.

Public restrooms The washrooms and toilets in a hotel meant for use by guests in general, and not restricted to the guests registered in the hotel's guestrooms.

Runners In this context, lengths of matting made of synthetic or natural fibres, placed at entrances to prevent dirt and dust from entering the building. (Another use of the term 'runner' in housekeeping is for a person who is charged with the duty of picking up and delivering guest laundry from and to guest floors respectively.)

Sauna Steam-bath cubicle made of wood or glass.

Solarium Area or room enclosed by glass panels, meant for the enjoyment or therapeutic use of sunrays.

Spa baths Small pools of warm water with the temperature maintained at a maximum of 39°C, used for therapeutic purposes.

Staking The practice of providing a means of support to delicately stemmed plants using thin bamboo sticks, cane, well-branched stems, wires, etc.

Suction-clean Vacuum-clean.

Therapeutic Having a healing effect.

Trellis Metal grilles or cane or bamboo frameworks used in the garden to train climber plants or to hang pots from.

Upholstery Textiles used for furniture décor.

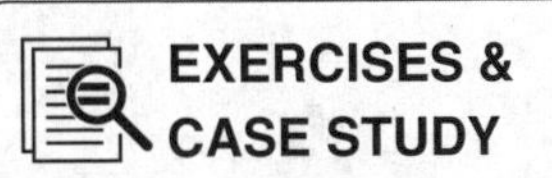

Please scan QR code to access All Exhibit & Tables

14 Infection Prevention and Control Protocols for Hospitality Accommodation Facilities (with Special Reference to Covid-19)

Learning Objectives

After reading this chapter, you should be able to

- understand the nature of infections and their mode of spread, especially with reference to COVID-19
- realize the importance of following guidelines and regulations to prevent and control infections
- list the standard components and protocols of an infection prevention programme at an accommodation facility
- summarize cleaning practices adapted to clinically clean standards with focus on high touchpoints, disinfection, and enhanced cleaning frequencies
- understand the way housekeepers rework budgets with increased cleaning costs
- list out the technological advancements that facilitate operations of rooms division during infection prevention and control
- outline modifications in infrastructure design and facilities, both temporary and anticipated in future projects

Introduction

The year 2020 mandated all industries and institutions to lay down infection prevention and control protocols in the event of outbreak of Coronavirus Disease or COVID-19, after the World Health Organization (WHO) declared it a global pandemic on March 11, 2020. Guidelines for the 'new normal' were laid down by regulatory bodies and as regards the hospitality industry, regulations issued by the WHO, Ministry of Health and Family Welfare (MoHFW), Ministry of Tourism (MoT), FHRAI and FSSAI were to be stringently followed. It became imperative for the management and staff of hospitality properties to understand the Novel Coronavirus or SARS CoV-2 in depth in order to tackle the wave of widespread infection and to get the trust of its stakeholders back, the stakeholders being guests, staff, business partners, and vendors. Well-known hospitality brands refreshed their brand standards to conform to the 'new normal'. Many hospitality brands coordinated with hygiene partners such as Diversey and Ecolab and inspection and certifying agencies such as Bureau Veritas to get assistance in conforming to the modified standards.

Understanding Infections and COVID-19

An infection is caused by a pathogen entering and multiplying in the human body. It may be a bacterium, virus, fungi, or a protozoan. For a full-blown infection to occur with symptoms, the microbes need to multiply, and this occurs in their incubation period. The incubation period is the time period between the entry of the microbe into a human body and the occurrence of the first symptom. To tackle any infection, it is imperative that the chain of infection is understood.

The Chain of Infection

The chain of infection is a model to describe how a pathogen moves from person to person, resulting in an infection. This chain needs to be broken or controlled with relevant means. Figure 14.1 presents the chain of infection of a pathogen.

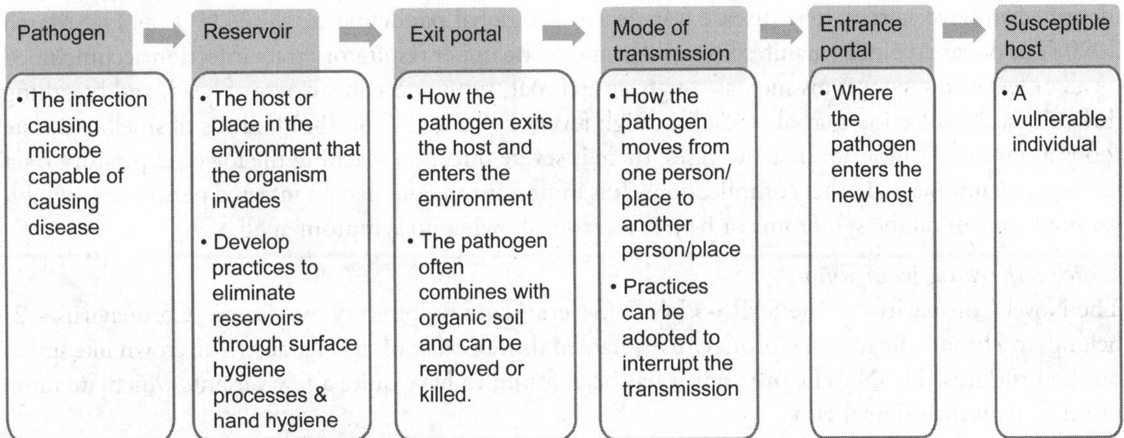

Fig. 14.1 Chain of infection of a pathogen

Mode of Transmission of an Infection

There are three main ways an infection is transmitted, and a pathogen may employ one or more modes of transmission mentioned below:

- **Airborne transmission** occurs when an infected person sneezes, coughs, is not following the guidelines of respiratory hygiene, or vomits, releasing small infection droplets into the air, which are capable of travelling more than a metre. A vulnerable individual may get infected with these if they enter the nose, mouth, or eyes.
- **Droplet transmission** occurs when an infected person sneezes, coughs, is not following the guidelines of respiratory hygiene, or vomits, spreading large infection droplets into the air, which are capable of travelling up to one metre. A vulnerable individual may get infected with these if they enter the nose, mouth, or eyes.
- **Contact transmission** may occur through direct transmission or indirect transmission.
  – *Direct transmission* occurs due to skin to skin contact between an infected and a vulnerable person.

– *Indirect transmission* occurs due to body to surface and body to body contact. The infected person contaminates an object or a surface and a vulnerable person comes in contact with it, contracting the infection indirectly.

The precautions to be taken in containing infection spread through the three modes of transmission are outlined in Figure 14.2.

Other than the above three modes of transmission, two additional modes may be operative:

- **Vector transmission** occurs when a person is bitten or exposed to the fluids of an insect or animal, which is a carrier of the pathogen.
- **Vehicle transmission** occurs due to the consumption of contaminated water or food.

A better way to understand an infectious disease is through answering the interrogative pronouns regarding the disease and here we undertake an analysis of COVID-19 as a relevant example.

What is the disease and what symptoms does it present?

The novel Coronavirus causes COVID-19, that is Coronavirus Disease, 19 referring to the year it was identified to have started. The disease was declared a global pandemic by the WHO on 11th March 2020. The disease typically manifests as mild to moderate upper respiratory tract infection accompanied by all or few of the symptoms such as cough, sore throat, runny nose, heaviness of head, and breathing difficulties; the infection may also result in high fever of over 101°F or 38.3°C. Loss of smell and taste too is a common symptom. In acute cases, there is severe infection reaching the lower respiratory tract causing pneumonia and other complications. It is important to note that an infected person may exhibit varyingly one or all the symptoms or be just a carrier showing no symptom at all.

Which is the causative organism?

The Novel Coronavirus or the SARS- CoV-2 (Severe Acute Respiratory Syndrome- Coronavirus – 2) belongs to a broad category of Coronaviruses, named thus because of the characteristic crown like spikes on their surfaces. The Novel Coronavirus has been found to have quite a few variants which are more infective than the original virus.

When does an infected person show symptoms?

The incubation period is found to be 1–14 days but can be longer in rare cases. This implies that a person infected is likely to show symptoms anytime between 1–14 days. It has also been observed that people with a robust immune system can even go asymptomatic, being carriers, but not showing a single symptom.

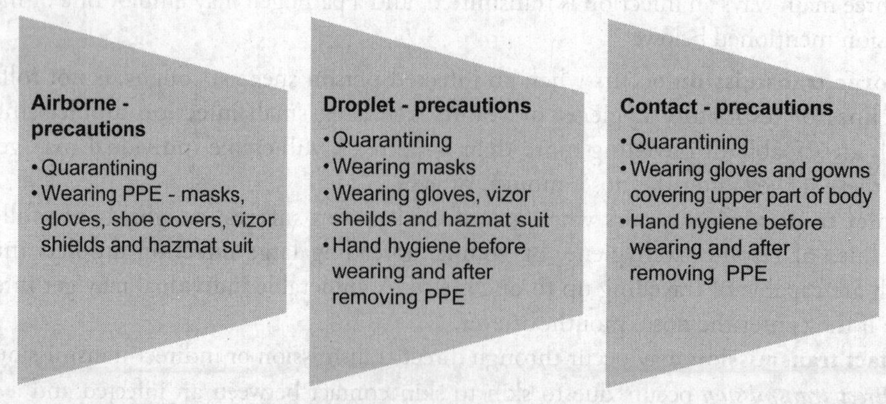

Fig. 14.2 Precautions to contain infection spread through the three modes of transmission

How does it spread and who is a carrier?

Coronavirus infection spreads amongst humans by:

Direct contact transmission brought about when people come in close proximity, shake hands with infected persons, or come in contact with parts of their body or their fluids or excretions

Indirect contact transmission resulting from touching objects and surfaces contaminated by infectious persons

Airborne and droplets transmission resulting from infectious droplets created in the air when infected persons cough, sneeze, talk, or vomit

People are most contagious when showing symptoms, i.e., when they are symptomatic, but it is important to remember that asymptomatic persons too spread the infection. Enclosed areas promote infections and interactions with physical distancing in open areas are least likely to spread infections.

How can infections be prevented and controlled? What precautions need to be taken?

Infections can be prevented or controlled by focusing efforts on reducing the chances of its transmission. It is a good practice to begin by assuming that everyone is a potential carrier of the infection and thus inculcating a routine to follow standard protocol procedures for infection prevention and control/ standard precautions at all times.

- Physical distancing with no touch policy
- Hand hygiene practices
- Respiratory hygiene practices
- Personal hygiene practices
- Personal protective equipment usage
- Cleaning and disinfection at clinically clean standards
- Safe fabric handling

Why are protocols necessary to be followed?

It is vital to keep in mind that prevention is better than cure and all facilities must take necessary precautions instead of trying to handle an outbreak, which would incur high cost to the business and also lead to loss of trust in stakeholders. Hospitality facilities have higher needs and concerns for infection prevention because of the:

Nature of hospitality guests Hospitality guests arrive at the property from varied geographic areas, domestic or international. Thus, the risk of pathogens entering the property are higher; in fact, in a few countries, outbreaks of some hazardous infections started and spread from hotels in the past.

Time spent inside the facility Hospitality guests spend a considerable number of hours per day, and several days at the facility, in the guestroom, F&B outlets, recreational areas and so on, ranging on an average from 10–12 hours, thus the probability of spread of a potential pathogen is higher.

High frequency of contact with high touchpoints Doorknobs, door handles, elevator buttons, handrails, light switches, television, and AC remotes, and all such high touchpoints receive multiple touches from hospitality guests, every day of their stay at the facility, increasing the chances of spread of pathogens.

Creating a Road Map for the Hospitality Property for Infection Prevention and Control

A road map or action plan for infection prevention and control must be drawn in consultation and compliance with the local and national health/ industry authority. FHRAI, FSSAI and such associations have recommended action plans for hospitality properties in response to COVID-19 pandemic.

The road map outlined by Federation of Hotel and Restaurant Association of India (FHRAI) is traced in Figure 14.3.

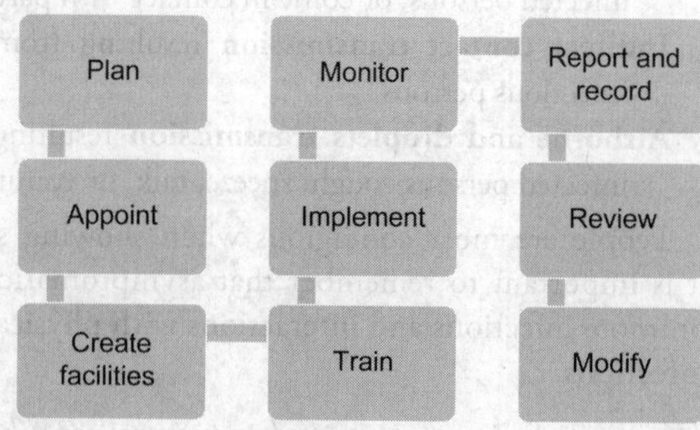

Fig. 14.3 Road map for infection prevention and control

Standard Components of an Infection Prevention Programme for Hospitality Accommodation Facilities

Contingency Assessment and Planning

Contingency planning for a potential infection spread must be in place before the crisis is on head. A Rapid Action Team or Emergency Response Team or Task Force comprising of representatives from all the departments at the property and headed by an official from the higher management or a specially appointed consultant must be constituted, and they should identify potential gaps posing risk of spread of infections after assessment. Recommendations for hygiene and safety modifications may be in the form of:

- Modifying infrastructure such as installing hand hygiene stations and PPE stations
- Procuring materials specific to infection prevention and control such as disinfectant cleaners, PPE and so on
- Modifying SOPs to tackle potential spread of infection
- Modifying par stock levels for higher stock of supplies essential in infection prevention such as disinfectants, sanitizers, liquid soaps, paper towels, trash bags and bins and so on
- Allocating space of storing the supplies meant for tackling potential spread of infection
- Stringent documentation of methods, materials, incidents, audits and such records
- Enhanced training relevant to infection prevention and control

This team is also responsible for effectively preventing spread of infections and managing cases of infection, and mitigating any safety risks for guests, staff, and other stakeholders. The team must also keep abreast of any new guidelines and regulations issued by local and central authorities. This team shall also be accountable to document and record all relevant measures and incidents for future reference. It is also a best practice to appoint a dedicated Hygiene Manager/ COVID-19 Coordinator/Special Officer who is competent in planning, developing, and implementing property-specific infection prevention and control protocols with reference to COVID-19, in line with local and central government guidelines.

Communication Resources

Appropriate communication resources in the form of posters, in-room material, tent cards, signages and door hangers regarding ideal behaviour to fight the spread of infections, and dos and don'ts have been released by certain regulatory authorities and should be made available by the management to communicate messages regarding precautions and guidelines to guests and staff. The property must display vivid communication regarding the following mandatorily.

- COVID Awareness poster – at lobby/reception
- Physical distancing of 6 feet – at reception and strategic places
- Hand hygiene procedure – at reception and in-room
- Respiratory hygiene – at reception and in-room
- Emergency helpline numbers – at reception

Most hospitality brands have displayed on their websites and booking platforms, detailed initiatives taken at their properties to keep the guests and staff safe from the spread of infections. The external communication of enhanced operating procedures for cleaning and disinfection goes a long way in winning the trust of the clients back.

Physical Distancing with No Touch/Contactless Policy

A safe physical distance of 2 m (6 feet) must be maintained between guests and staff at all points, especially at the reception. No direct touch policy must be in place, even in terms of handing over objects such as debit cards, pens, etc. For staff too, biometric attendance shall be suspended, scanning codes are recommended for the same.

Hand Hygiene

Hand hygiene is the most effective way to prevent and control the spread of infections. It should be ensured at the hospitality facility that strategically placed, sensor-based or foot-pedal operated hand hygiene stations are made available for staff especially at employee areas such as time office, staff lockers, uniform room, cafeteria, service elevator landings, corridors, washrooms, and for guests at various high-risk points in public areas. Staff need to be trained in the method and frequency of performing hand hygiene. Nails must be clipped short. The property can develop the frequency on the lines of WHO model '5 Moments of Hand Hygiene' followed in healthcare facilities. Hand hygiene should be performed by staff when they:

- Sneeze or cough in their hands
- Have used washrooms or toilet
- Begin to wear and after removing PPE
- Begin and complete a routine activity which involves touching surfaces, e.g., cleaning of guestrooms, receiving purchased items, disposal of garbage and so on
- Begin to prepare food
- Observe that their hands are visibly dirty

Correct handwashing procedure

Proper steps of handwashing must be followed for effective hand hygiene in infection prevention and control. The recommended handwashing time by WHO is 20–30 seconds and all the mentioned steps must be completed thoroughly.

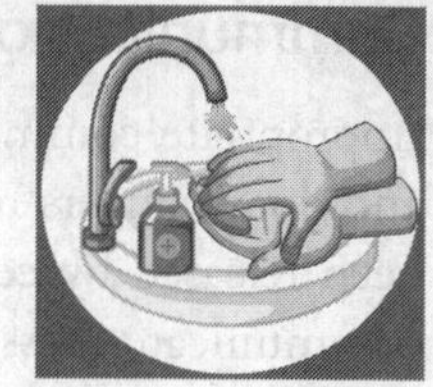

Step 1 Wet hands with water and apply sufficient liquid soap from a dispenser to cover the hand surfaces, creating good amount of lather by rubbing the palms. It is ideal to have the water at a temperature of about 35°C to 45°C.

Step 2 Rub the palms together in circular motion, rotating clockwise and anticlockwise.

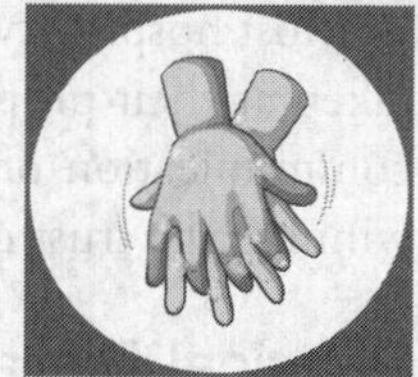

Step 3 Interlace the fingers of both hands, one above the other, using the right palm to rub the back of left hand and vice versa.

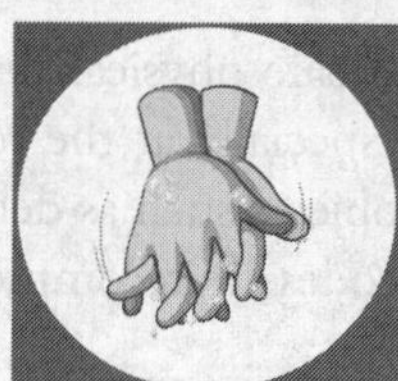

Step 4 Link the fingers of both hands clasped together, palms facing and rub the palms and fingers together.

Step 5 Clasp the fingers together, clutching the upper part, with the right and over the left and rub the backs of the fingers against the palms and vice versa.

Step 6 Rub the left thumb clasped in right palm using rotational motion and vice versa.

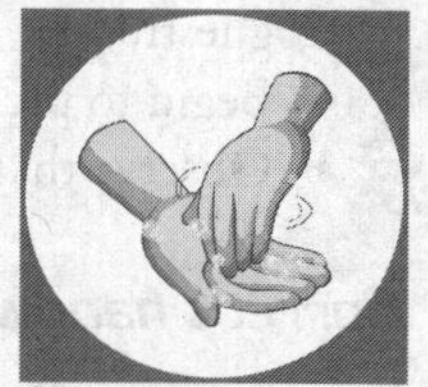

Step 7 Rub the fingers of right hand in circular motion in the left palm and vice versa.

Step 8 Rinse hands thoroughly in warm running water.

Step 9 Dry hands thoroughly with a single use tissue towel or an air hand dryer.

Correct hand sanitizing/hand rubbing procedure

Proper steps of hand sanitizing or hand rubbing must be followed for effective hand hygiene in infection prevention and control. The recommended hand sanitizing time by WHO is 30 seconds and all the mentioned steps must be completed thoroughly.

Step 1 Dispense sufficient hand sanitizer (about 3 ml) through, ideally, a sensor-based or foot pedal operated dispenser.

Step 2 Cover the hands evenly with the liquid sanitizer.

Step 3 Rub the fingers of right hand on the left palm and vice versa.

Step 4 Rub the palms together.

Step 5 Rub the back of left hand with the right hand, fingers interlaced and vice versa.

Step 6 Rub the palms together, interlacing the fingers.

Step 7 Clasp the fingers together, clutching the upper part, with the right and over the left and rub the backs of the fingers against the palms and vice versa.

Step 8 Rub the left thumb clasped in right palm using rotational motion and vice versa.

Step 9 Allow the hands to air dry. Do not rinse or rub the hands dry.

As per WHO recommendations, hands must not be washed with soap and water immediately before or after using an alcohol-based hand sanitizer.

Respiratory Hygiene Practices

Training and communication posters should be employed to get the message of respiratory hygiene across to stakeholders. Use of masks while coughing or sneezing is strictly advisable for possible carriers of infection. As such, all should be trained to sneeze into their elbows instead of their hands. Covering mouths with tissue towels while sneezing or coughing must be advised to all staff. It must also be emphasized that the tissue towels must be disposed of responsibly and hand hygiene be performed. Staff should be advised to keep hands away from the mouth, nose, and eyes.

Personal Hygiene Practices

Personal hygiene as such is a tenet in hospitality industry inculcated in each and every staff even in normal circumstances of operations. But it takes even more importance during an infection prevention and control programme. Personal hygiene elements such as daily baths, clean hair and nails, clean and sanitized uniforms, hand hygiene, respiratory hygiene, and hygienic behaviours must be reinforced through training.

Personal Protective Equipment (PPE)

PPEs of proper quality, when used correctly, provide sufficient barrier to prevent exposure to infections. Appropriate 3 ply masks, vizor/face shields, gloves, shoe covers, hazmat suits, upper body gowns, or apron shields need to be provided to employees depending on the extent of their contact with guests at the property. Heavy duty gloves are required for high-risk areas. It is important that staff be trained in the use of PPE, including the correct method to don/wear and doff/remove them and performing hand hygiene before and after using them. On request, some of the PPEs may need to be provided to guests too. It is a good practice to install PPE stations for guests with supplies of masks, gloves, and tissues near the front desk. Disposable PPE must be discarded responsibly in a colour coded plastic bag, labelled as hazardous waste.

Use of gloves by associates

Associates must be trained to use gloves the right way.

1. They must perform hand hygiene before putting on the gloves.
2. They must change the gloves any time hands need to be washed.
   - After using the toilet
   - After touching parts of the body
   - After handling dirty tools and equipment
   - After eating or drinking
   - After handling raw food
   - After any activity that may have contaminated or soiled the gloves
3. They must perform hand hygiene after removing the gloves.

Safe doffing/removal of PPE after use

The Centres for Disease Control and Prevention (CDC) gives clear guidelines for doffing of PPE and the associates must be trained in the procedure and follow the same every time.

Gloves

The outer surfaces of gloves may be contaminated. In case hands get contaminated during glove removal, immediately perform hand hygiene. For glove removal, follow the steps outlined below.

- With a gloved hand, grasp the palm area of the other glove and peel off the first glove without much agitation.
- Hold the removed glove in the gloved hand.
- Slide fingers of un-gloved hand under the worn glove at wrist and peel off the second glove over the first glove.
- Discard the removed gloves in a biohazard waste disposal bag.
- Perform hand hygiene.

Masks

The outer surfaces of the masks may be contaminated and contact with such surfaces must be avoided. In case hands get contaminated during mask removal, immediately perform hand hygiene. For mask removal, follow the steps outlined below.

- Unfasten the bottom ties or elastic of the mask and then the ones on the top and remove without touching the front outer surface.
- Discard the removed mask in a biohazard waste disposal bag.
- Perform hand hygiene.

Gowns/suits

The outer surfaces of the gown/suit may be contaminated, especially the sleeves and the front. In case hands get contaminated during gown removal, immediately perform hand hygiene. For gown removal, follow the steps outlined below.

- Unfasten the gown ties at the back; ensure that sleeves do not come in contact with body surfaces while doing so.
- Touching only the inner surfaces of the gown, gently pull the gown away from neck and shoulders without much agitation.

- Turn the gown inside out.
- Fold the gown or roll into a bundle without much agitation and discard in a biohazard waste disposal bag.
- Perform hand hygiene.

Clinically Clean Standards and Practices for Environmental Hygiene

Hygienically clean standards must be upgraded to clinically clean ones to prevent and control infections. This would involve modifications in products, processes and tools, i.e., cleaning and disinfection of surfaces using Environmental Protection Agency (EPA) approved disinfectant cleaners and equipment, employing specified procedures at relevant frequencies. Managers must ensure sufficient supply of recommended disinfectant cleaners, cleaning tools such as microfibre dusters, spray bottles and so on, and also train staff on modified SOPs devised as per infection prevention and control regulations. The main factors in cleaning must be kept in mind and these are presented in Figure 14.4.

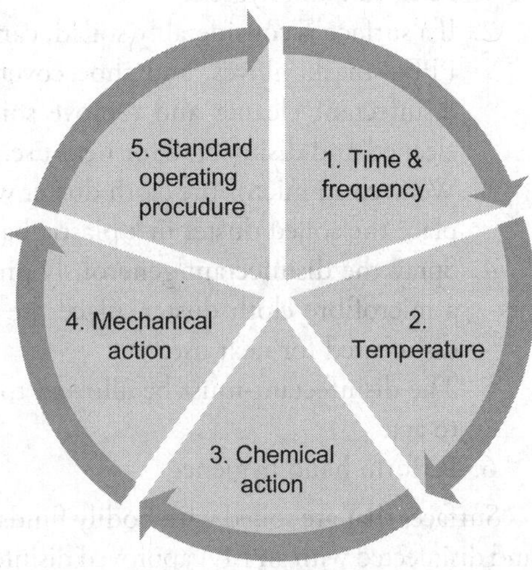

Fig. 14.4 Primary factors in cleaning

While developing the clinically clean standards for infection prevention and control, specify the following and develop a comprehensive checklist to ensure compliance.

- Specify the surface/area to be cleaned.
- Specify the materials required—chemicals, equipment, tools, and PPE.
- Specify the time taken to carry out the cleaning effectively.
- Specify the amount of mechanical action that is required for effective cleaning.
- If applicable, specify the temperature at which the water must be for cleaning.
- Specify the modified cleaning frequencies.
- Detail the step by step modified process; ensure to include
  - Instructions to perform hand hygiene before and after cleaning
  - Instructions regarding usage of PPE for safety from chemicals and pathogens
  - Specify proper flow in the room/area so as not to re-contaminate disinfected surfaces
  - Specify cleaning process to proceed from
    - cleanest to dirtiest, to lower the risk of re-contamination
    - high to low
    - dry to wet

Determining Frequency of Cleaning and Disinfection

The frequency of cleaning and disinfection is directly proportional to the following environmental variables. The higher the quantum of primary environmental variables, the more the frequency of cleaning and disinfection. The secondary environmental variables affect the frequency depending upon their types and composition.

Primary environmental variables

- Soil load
- Foot falls
- Risk of spread of infection

Secondary environmental variables

- Type of soil
- Composition of cleaning product
- Type of surface

Disinfecting Hard Surfaces to Clinically Clean Standards

1. Perform hand hygiene.
2. If a surface is considerably soiled, carry out this step, else begin at the next one. Wear appropriate PPE—mask, gloves, and shoe cover. Wet a clean microfibre cloth duster with EPA approved disinfectant cleaner and remove soil, place the soiled duster in a plastic bag with seal, to be cleaned and disinfected for next use. For high-risk areas use red colour microfibre duster.
3. Wet a clean microfibre cloth duster with EPA approved disinfectant cleaner and wipe the surface, place the soiled duster in a plastic bag with seal, to be cleaned and disinfected for next use.
4. Spray the disinfectant generously on the surface and spread it on the entire surface evenly with a microfibre cloth duster, place the soiled duster in a plastic bag with seal, to be cleaned and disinfected for next use.
5. The disinfectant must be allowed to air dry on the surface, giving necessary contact time for it to act.
6. Perform hand hygiene.

Surfaces that are soiled with bodily fluids or respiratory secretions of ill guests or staff must be cleaned and disinfected with an EPA approved disinfectant cleaner containing 1% sodium hypochlorite, equivalent to 1000 ppm of available chlorine, allowing for a contact time of 10 minutes. The surface must be then rinsed or wipe-rinsed with clean water. In case recommended branded disinfectant cleaning products are used, follow the guidelines provided on the label by the manufacturer.

On high risk, high touchpoint surfaces such as doorknobs and handles, elevator buttons, electric switches, remote controls and telephones, where use of sodium hypochlorite bleach is not suitable, 70% alcohol should be used. Apply alcohol on the clean surface and let it air dry.

In infected areas, prefer to use disposable, single use cloths and mopheads in case of absorbent cleaning materials and discard them as biohazard waste. Non-porous cleaning tools must be effectively disinfected with 0.5% sodium hypochlorite solution, allowing contact time of 10 minutes. For branded disinfectant cleaning products, follow the guidelines provided on the label by the manufacturer.

High Risk Areas and High Touchpoints

High risk areas in the facility are those which receive high footfalls, gather large groups, liable to frequent bodily spills and where levels of hygiene are likely to be slackened. Such areas pose potential risks for spread of pathogens and need to be cleaned and disinfected with increased frequency regularly. Appropriate hand hygiene stations must be available at such areas so that staff and guests are visibly prompted to perform hand hygiene.

High touchpoints are those surfaces in the facility that are frequently touched by staff and guests. The common high touchpoints identified in hotels are listed in Table 14.1, but each property must assess their own.

Table 14.1 High touchpoints in various areas of the hotel

Public areas	Guestrooms	Employee/Heart of the house areas
• Doorknobs, push plates and handles	• Doorknobs, push plates and handles	• Doorknobs and handles
• Reception, concierge, and bell desk counters	• Safety latches	• Electric switches
• Elevator buttons, call buttons and handrails	• Electric switches	• Cupboard and drawer knobs and handles
• Railings	• Minibar handles	• Furniture armrests
• Luggage trolleys	• Cupboard handles	• Public phones and intercoms
• Hand sanitising station surfaces	• Furniture armrests	• Furniture armrests
• PPE station surfaces	• Remote control	• Table tops
• Electric switches	• Telephone	• Refrigerator handle
• House phones and intercoms	• Room amenities – electric kettle, spoons and cups, hairdryer	• Microwave handle
• Public computers and accessories, printers, and scanners	• Food contact surfaces & tabletops	• Faucets
• Point of sale (POS) machines	• Washroom door handle	• Dispenser head pump or actuator
• Key cards	• Flush handle and buttons	
• Drawer knobs and handles	• Toilet seat	
• Furniture armrests	• Shower panel controls	
• Tables tops	• Faucets	
• Beverage dispensing machines	• Dispenser head pump or actuator	
• Gym equipment		
• Public washroom faucets		
• Counters and seats in public washrooms		
• Flush handles and buttons in public washrooms		

Usage of Disinfectants

Clinically clean standards require usage of recommended disinfectants during the cleaning process as per SOP developed by the property. Adequate quantities of disinfectant should be available at the facility to facilitate infection prevention and control. While using disinfectants, a few considerations must be kept in mind.

Use recommended products: The regulatory agencies and health authorities in each country recommend products that may be used for disinfection purposes. The accommodation facility must ensure that recommended products are used for disinfection as they have maximum efficacy. It is a best practice to use EPA approved cleaning products if guidelines are not clear.

Abide by safety considerations: Before using the disinfectant cleaner product, it is vital to peruse the Material Safety Data Sheet (MSDS), accompanying the product for information about potential risks associated with the use of the product, the guidelines on the various precautions the user must take, and the PPE to be donned while using the product.

Follow the directions on label: The label on a disinfectant cleaner packaging gives information regarding directions for dilution, method of application, and contact time-period for efficacy. The disinfectant will be effective only if the labels are followed stringently in use of the product.

Follow correct dilution: Some disinfectant cleaners are ready to use products, but others require dilution. Correct dilution ratio, as per the guidelines on the label, must be followed. If the product is highly diluted, it will be ineffective as a disinfectant and pose a health safety risk. If the product is too concentrated, it may harm the surface and increase cleaning costs.

Allow contact time for disinfection: A disinfectant product is effective only when it wets the surface for recommended contact time-period, mentioned on the label. Therefore, it is crucial to leave the product to airdry after application, and not wipe it away. If wiped away, prior to its action time, the chemical will not effectively kill the pathogens against which the infection prevention and control programme is being run.

Know the type of disinfectant cleaner: Two types of disinfectant cleaners are being used, one step disinfectant cleaners and two-step disinfectant cleaners. The usage and effectiveness on surfaces for both must be understood clearly before use. One step disinfectant cleaners take care of removal of organic soil, dust and dirt along with pathogens. Two step disinfectant cleaners need to be applied twice, once to remove organic soil and second time, to carry out the disinfection function.

Commonly used Disinfectants, Branded Products and Disinfecting Strategies in Hospitality Facilities

- 1% sodium hypochlorite
- Accelerated Hydrogen Peroxide (AHP)
- Diversey Oxivir Concentrate
- Diversey Virex II 256
- Ecolab Peroxide multi surface cleaner
- Diversey Taski R1 Super
- High bar pressure dry steam cleaning
- UV – C- Wands and Arc
- Electrostatic sprayers with EPA approved hospital-grade disinfectant

Cleaning Practices for Health Safety

The following section details modified cleaning practices for health safety. Table 14.2 outlines the modified cleaning practices for health safety in various areas of the hotel pertaining to accommodation operations.

Safe Fabric Handling and Laundering

To prevent and control the spread of pathogens, it is essential that linen be handled responsibly so that potential pathogens are not dispersed in the environment or a staff handling the soiled linen does not get infected. Linen and laundry handling protocols are discussed in detail later in the chapter.

Ensuring Resources and Supplies

A preliminary assesment of resources and supplies requirement to tackle a potential infection must be made keeping in mind the lead time. Sufficient linen, PPE, disinfectant cleaners, microfibre dusters, hand hygiene products, colour coded garbage bags, single kit amenities must be available for staff to perform their routine activities being mindful of hand hygiene and other precautions. Compulsory provision of supplies and PPEs mandated as 'must have' by regulatory authorities are hand sanitizers, 3 ply masks, gloves, garbage bags, deep cleaning chemicals, and thermal guns. 'Good to have' are other PPEs such as gowns, aprons and so on.

Table 14.2 Modified cleaning practices and frequency for health safety

Area	Modified practice	Frequency
Staff entrance	Body temperature check with thermal gun for all staff	At all shifts
Entrance, Porte cochère	Disinfection of high touchpoints	Every 4 hours at daytime
Entrance, Porte cochère	Body temperature check with thermal gun for all guests	For all arrivals
Front desk	Placement of alcohol-based sanitizer/hand rub near front desk, preferably on shoe operated dispenser	At all times
Front desk	Front desk disinfection, especially hand contact surfaces	Every 4 hours at daytime
Front desk	Staff wear masks	At all times
Front desk	Hand hygiene performed by staff	Every hour or assisting a guest
Front desk	Hand hygiene performed by guests	Request made after every staff assistance received

Sustained Training

Training all categories of staff on regular basis on the importance of following the modified SOPs laid down for infection prevention and control is essential for the programme to be effective. Training requirements include usage of PPE, demonstration of SOPs, methods of disinfectant usage, dilution ratio of disinfectants, motivation sessions and so on. Multi-tasking takes on centre stage now as all brands are emphasizing on it with associates from front office, housekeeping, and F&B required to come out of their department silos. Training priorities include:

- Department-based training on SOPs specific to the infectious disease, such as COVID-19
- Training on physical distancing and no touch policy
- Training on hand hygiene, respiratory hygiene, and personal hygiene
- Training on PPE and uniform handling
- Training on proper dilution and use of disinfectant cleaners for efficacy
- Training on monitoring, reporting, and documentation
- Cross-training
- Training on staff motivation and engagement

Compliance Monitoring and Auditing

Regular monitoring of compliance towards hand hygiene, correct usage of PPE, cleaning and disinfection process through stringent internal and external auditing is essential. Effective infection prevention and control can be carried out only if each and every staff follows SOPs all the time.

Vaccination

Effective vaccination of staff against the pathogen, as per the country's government regulations, goes a long way in prevention and control of infections. This will ensure that guests would not spread infections to staff and vice versa.

Guidelines and Protocols for Rooms Division and Relevant Ancillary Departments for Infection Prevention and Control with Reference to COVID-19

General Guidelines and Protocols

- Establishing a Rapid Response Team
- Appointing a dedicated Hygiene Manager
- Symptomatic persons not allowed entry into premises
- Thermal screening at security, persons with temperature above 98.6°F not allowed into the premises
- Security personnel must be well-informed and trained in screening guests
- Staff in quarantine shall not come to work
- Arogya Setu app recommended to be installed by all stakeholders
- CCTV cameras to be properly functional at all times
- Contact details of local health and municipal authorities and assistance centres, government and private hospitals must be available as a ready reckoner at the reception in case a guest or staff takes ill
- Contact numbers of Duty Manager, Resident Manager and Reception Executive to be made available in all rooms
- Create one isolation room for every 50 rooms in the property
- Employees at high risk (pregnant, elderly above 65 years or persons having co-morbidity—hypertension, diabetes and certain underlying diseases) not to be exposed to front line work
- Replace biometric attendance system at employee entrance, use of scan codes are recommended for the same
- Physical distancing-based staffing to be followed in all departments, admin staff may work from home
- Follow zero-contact policy in interactions between staff–guest, staff–staff and guest–guest
- Stagger the usage timings of staff canteen, lockers, and changing rooms
- Hand hygiene stations, preferably sensor-based or foot-pedal operated, are to be installed
- Alcohol-based (70%) sanitizers must be placed at strategic critical touchpoints
- Not more than one person shall be allowed in the elevator at a time, unless the guests are from the same room. Elevator floors shall have floor markings on the way of standing
- Disinfect the staff shuttle, especially the high touchpoints
- Driver of the staff shuttle must wear masks and gloves and the staff shall wear masks too
- Physical distancing to be maintained in the staff shuttle
- Orientation on new roles, additional duties, and schedules must be undertaken
- Treated fresh air (TFA) units shall always be on in employee areas or heart of the house areas
- Air Conditioning, if operated must be maintained at 24°C – 30°C
- Relative humidity must be maintained at 40–70% through effective HVAC systems

- All staff become their own housekeepers. Associates and managers are to disinfect their own workstations every 45 minutes
- All staff must be provided sanitized uniforms and the required PPE as per the SOPs of the tasks allocated

Human Resource Department Protocols to Prevent and Control Infections

- Symptomatic persons not allowed entry into premises
- Thermal screening at security, persons with temperature above 98.6°F not allowed into the premises
- Staff in quarantine shall not come to work
- A list of dos and don'ts to be provided to the staff
- Arogya Setu app recommended to be installed by all stakeholders
- Employees at high risk (pregnant, elderly above 65 years or persons having co-morbidities–hypertension, diabetes and certain underlying diseases) not to be exposed to front line work
- Replace biometric attendance system at employee entrance; use of scan codes are recommended for the same
- Physical distancing-based staffing to be followed in all departments; admin staff may work from home
- Follow zero-contact policy in interactions between staff–guest, staff–staff, and guest–guest
- Stagger the usage timings of staff canteen, lockers, and changing rooms
- A best practice at some hotels is to have a pleasant alarm sounding every 45 minutes to remind associates to perform hand hygiene
- Any staff developing symptoms of infection during work hours must be immediately isolated and provided medical assistance
- HR department shall maintain a register for monitoring health indicators of staff. The health indicators would include fever, sore throat, cough, running nose, and shortness of breath.
- Staff not complying with guidelines issued shall be warned and moved out of work
- Orientation on new roles, additional duties, and schedules must be undertaken
- All staff must be provided sanitized uniforms daily and the required PPE as per the SOPs of the tasks allocated

Protocols for staff transport

- Disinfect the staff shuttle, especially the high touchpoints
- Driver of the staff shuttle must wear masks and gloves
- The staff boarding the shuttle shall wear masks
- Arrange to carry out thermal scanning and symptom checks before staff board the shuttle
- Sanitizer dispenser must be available at the shuttle entrance and staff must perform hand hygiene while boarding
- There must be provision of sufficient tissues and masks in the shuttle
- Physical distancing to be maintained in the staff shuttle
- Encourage staff to use their own transport rather than depending on public transport

Dos and don'ts for staff

- Follow restricted movement around guestrooms.
- Maintain 6 feet distance with other staff and guests at all times.
- Perform hand hygiene regularly.
- Adhere to zero-touch policy.
- Wear masks at all times.
- Communication with in-room guests must be strictly via intercom or mobile phones.
- Use sanitized trays and trolleys to deliver requested items in guestrooms.

Protocols for Material Handling

Many pathogens spread via inanimate objects too, for instance, the novel coronavirus. Keeping this in mind, the following recommendations are to be followed while handling materials coming into the property.

- Secondary packaging must not be allowed into the property.
- Pre-sanitization of receiving area must be carried out.
- Ensure only one supplier/vendor at a time near the receiving area.
- Minimum physical distance of 1 m shall be maintained between persons during the receiving function.
- All materials must be handled with gloved or sanitized hands only.
- All materials must either be sanitized or quarantined as per requirement and nature of material.

Protocols for Maintenance and Repair

Maintenance crew must wear appropriate PPE and carry out thorough inspection, as per SOP, of a vacated room disinfected by the housekeeping staff. The inspection must assess all maintenance and repair requirements. In case of occupied rooms, maintenance managers and crew must, as much as possible, resolve minor issues such as AC or television remotes not working, via video call to guests for them to carry out minor interventions on their own. The crew must enter the room, with complete PPE compliance, only if a complaint is not resolved this way, and the guest must be requested to stay out in the floor lounge or lobby, till the repair is carried out.

Protocols for Front Office

The front office with its gamut of functions such as uniformed services and reception has a crucial role to play in promoting and enhancing the sense of trust in guests when they arrive at the property.

Protocols for guest transport

- Sanitize guest transport vehicle by fogging interior and exterior surfaces and disinfect high touchpoints prior to every pick-up and drop.
- Chauffer of guest transport must be in full uniform with face mask and hand gloves.
- Chauffer of the guest transport must maintain physical distancing with the guests in the vehicle.
- Masks, sanitizers, sealed wet wipes, and mineral water bottles shall be available and offered to guests in vehicles.
- Valet parking is not encouraged.

Protocols for security at porch and bell desk

- Security associates shall spray the wheels of the guests' vehicles with disinfectant cleaner.
- Greet the guests with a traditional 'namaste' or by placing the right hand on the heart.
- Security check shall be carried out only through the door frame metal detector. Hand-held metal detector shall not be used.
- Guest luggage must be disinfected with disinfectant spray prior to scanning.

Protocols for reception

- Masks and gloves must be worn by reception staff at all times.
- Encourage guests to use the hand hygiene station installed near the reception.
- Area cleaning checklists must be displayed near the reception.
- Display and communicate dos and don'ts to the guests.
- Maintain physical distance of minimum 1 m with guests at the reception desk.
- Maintain zero contact policy with guests and minimize interaction.
- Provide facility to maintain physical distance of 2 m (6 feet) between guests at reception.
- Communication between the guest and in-house associates must be through intercom or mobile phone.

Front office check-in protocols

- Greet the guests with a traditional 'namaste' or by placing the right hand on the heart.
- Carry out contactless check-in process. Prefer to accept e-ID proofs and e-payments and send receipts via e-mail.
- Use an effective PMS form to solicit additional guest information so as make traceability of the guest easy after departure.
- Keep the Arrival-Departure register updated with thorough information.
- Facilitate filling up of self-declaration forms by International guests and maintain the same in a specified file. The self-declaration forms include the travel history and medical condition details about the guest.
- Sanitize card machines and use trays to accept and offer debit/credit cards back.
- Brief guests about dos and don'ts as per hotel policy.
- Guests who are at high risk, such as elderly above 65 years, pregnant, or having co-morbidities such as hypertension, diabetes shall be advised to take extra precautions.
- Inform guests about the facilitation of daily thermal screening and oximeter readings.
- Promote usage of Arogya Setu app to survey all guests except foreign nationals.
- Allow only single room occupancy unless the guests are a family unit.

Front office check-in protocols for guests showing symptoms of infection

- Check-in must not be denied to guests with symptoms.
- Direct the guest to perform hand hygiene at the hand hygiene station installed near the reception.
- Physical distancing of 6 feet must be maintained from the guest.
- Offer medical assistance to the guest and direct him/her to quarantine in the room.
- Deep clean and disinfect the reception and elevator.
- Follow up on the guest's health condition, enquiring about his well-being daily on the intercom.

If the guest's illness persists,

- Call the helpline number provided by the local health authorities.
- Facilitate shifting of the guest to the health facility.
- Facilitate testing for the staff who came in contact with the guest.
- Seal and quarantine the room for minimum 72 hours.
- Post quarantining, the room must be fumigated, deep cleaned, and disinfected.
- The reception, public areas, and the entire floor must be fumigated and deep cleaned.
- Soiled linen from the room must be processed chemo-thermally.
- In case a guest with potential infection skips, the police must be informed and assisted in investigation.

In case of outbreak/a positive case

As far as possible, an outbreak of an infectious disease at an accommodation facility must be prevented at all costs because it gravely dents the brand's value and reputation and incurs high cost to the business. The outbreak must be reported to the local health authorities after taking quarantine precautions.

- When there is even a slight concern or indication of a potential infection, isolate and quarantine the guest or staff immediately.
- Empathize with the guest and provide support maintaining isolation norms.
- Inform the local health/municipal authority and the nearest medical facility.
- Organize testing for guest or staff and in case positive, continue the quarantine. Affected staff must be excused from work and asked to quarantine at home for appropriate period of recovery, till they are at a position where they shall not spread an infection, depending upon the pathogen.
- Cleaning of quarantine room should be avoided till absolutely necessary and if to be done, should be carried out with appropriate disposable of PPE such as masks, vizors, gloves, shoe covers, hazmat suits, with all precautions, including hand hygiene.
- Increase the frequency and thoroughness of cleaning and disinfection, disinfecting high risk areas hourly.
- Rooms vacated by ill/recovered guests must be left as such for at least 72 hours and then aired, disinfected thoroughly, and deep cleaned.
- All disposables from the room must be transferred and disposed in red coloured garbage bags with hazard indication.
- Staff must dispose PPE as per procedure and perform hand hygiene.

Dos and don'ts for guests

Guests must be advised by the reception staff on the following dos and don'ts to be followed strictly while on the premises. The list of dos and don'ts for guests must also be prominently displayed near the reception, in the guestroom, and sent to guests via social media platforms.

- Avoid stepping out of the guestroom unnecessarily.
- Keep the guestroom door closed at all times.
- Avoid interaction with guests occupying other guestrooms.
- Avoid visiting containment zones, high risk areas, and crowded places in the city.

- Wear a mask whenever outside the guestroom or in presence of staff.
- No visitors shall be allowed in the guestroom.
- Peruse the awareness and emergency information placed in guestrooms.
- Keep a distance of 6 feet with staff and other guests at the property.
- Perform hand hygiene frequently.
- Place all disposable cups, plates, bottles, etc. in garbage bag after use.
- If balcony is shared between two guestrooms, the guests of these rooms shall not come in contact with each other.

Front office check-out protocols

- Guests must inform the reception via intercom or mobile phone at least an hour before check-out.
- Guests must check-out only after confirmation from the reception.
- Payments must be done in advance via digital mode. Scan codes must be provided at prominent areas for facilitating the payment. Bank details must be provided to the guests or displayed prominently in case payment is being made by the guest via internet banking.
- Solicit filling up of guest feedback via e-survey and utilize the same to enhance standards of service.

Protocols for Housekeeping

Housekeeping operations planning for infection prevention and control revolve around the aspects presented in Figure 14.5.

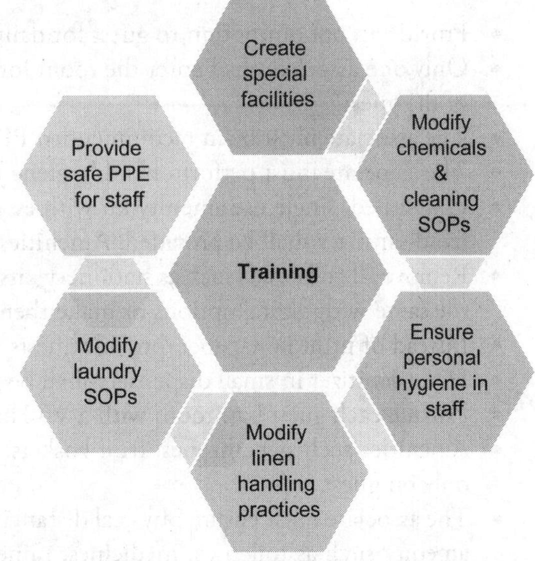

Fig. 14.5 Aspects in infection prevention and control protocols for housekeeping

Public area cleaning protocols

In use public areas such as lobby, elevators, restaurants, meeting rooms, and corridors must be cleaned and disinfected 4 times a day, ensuring high touchpoints are disinfected. It is recommended that public areas such as spa, health club and gym, and pool areas remain closed as chances of spread of infection are higher in such areas due to bodily spills. Public area cleaning practices with their frequency is presented in Table 14.3.

Guestroom cleaning protocols

- Only one associate, with PPE as per the SOP, shall be allocated to service a guestroom.
- Ventilate all unoccupied guestrooms and public areas on daily basis.
- Deep clean all non-occupied guestrooms and washrooms regularly on rotation schedule.
- A best practice is that once a vacated guestroom is cleaned and disinfected, it must be sealed, till a guest is allocated to the room so that the guest is assured that no one has entered the room after it has been sanitized.

Table 14.3 Public area cleaning practices with frequency

Area/surface	Modified cleaning practice	Frequency
Main gate & security cabin	Clean using disinfectant cleaner. Disinfect high touchpoints and countertops.	Twice in a shift
Entrance, Porte cochère/porch area	Spray disinfectant on surfaces.	Twice a day
Entrance, Porte cochère/porch area	Disinfection of high touchpoints including countertops/ intercom/announcement mikes/other equipment	Every hour/after each use
Entrance, Porte cochère/porch area	Spray disinfectant on mats.	Twice in a shift
Garden benches	Spray disinfectant on benches.	Beginning of each shift/after every guest use
Lobby	Floors to be dry mopped and damp mopped with disinfectant cleaner	Twice in a shift
Lobby	Front door contact surfaces disinfection	Every hour during daytime
Lobby	Disinfect Table tops, countertops, intercoms and high touchpoints	Every half an hour

- Provide an opt out option to guest for daily cleaning of room and change of linen.
- Only one associate shall enter the room for servicing; the cleaning must proceed only in absence of the guest.
- The associate must be in recommended PPE as per the SOP.
- The associate must perform hand hygiene before and after servicing the room.
- One sealed, single use amenity kit with essential bath amenities, gargle glasses and alcohol-based hand sanitizer shall be provided. Amenities shall not be reused after guest check-out.
- Remove all collaterals such as stationery kits, guest directory, pen, notepad and paper. Supplement the same with digital options or make them 'on-request'.
- Instead of print newspaper, provide guests access to digital news and e-newspapers.
- Hand sanitizer in small dispensers shall be provided in rooms.
- Provide each guest bathroom with a WC brush cleaning kit.
- Amenities such as bathrobes, fruit baskets, snacks and non-essential amenities shall be provided only on guest request.
- The associate must ensure physical distancing of 1 m with guests while delivering any on-request amenity such as toiletries, medicines, mineral water bottles or bath linen, the amenity must be delivered on a sanitized tray.
- Linen in occupied rooms shall be changed only on guest request.
- The associate must clean and disinfect all hard surfaces and soft furnishings as per the SOP.
- High touchpoints must be disinfected.
- It is a best practice to rest a departure room for 72 hours, if occupancy levels permit, and then cleaning and disinfecting before checking for maintenance issues.
- The associate must carry out steam cleaning of sofas, curtains, pillows, and cushions in departure rooms.
- Pillows and mattresses may be covered with Teflon covers in occupied rooms.

- In-room carpets shall preferably be removed, else disinfected after every departure.
- Linen change in departure rooms must be mandatorily done as per SOP.

Guestroom cleaning practices with their frequency is presented in Table 14.4.

Planning for offering guests opt-out housekeeping service

Many guests have begun preferring not to receive housekeeping services during their stay. This way, associates do not enter rooms and safety of both guests and associates is ensured. Crucial points in implementing opt-out housekeeping services are as follows:

- Calculate the number of nights and the number of guests to determine the number of towels, sheets, and sealed amenities such as bottled water, coffee, tea sachets, essential toiletries that shall be needed.
- The guest must be informed in advance about what opt-out housekeeping service would entail. Some properties solicit guest preferences even before arrival, via email, so that the room may be prepared as per their request.
- A best practice would be for the rooms division manager to enquire the following from the guest prior to arrival.
  - Have you reviewed our hotel's health, hygiene, and safety policies?
  - How many people shall be staying in the room with you?
  - What essential amenities and toiletries would you like placed in the room?
  - Are you agreeable to our hotel's associate entering your room for cleaning and sanitizing?
  - Would you like to opt-out of the regular housekeeping services, considering the current situation?

Table 14.4 Guestroom cleaning practices with frequency

Modified cleaning practice	Frequency
Deep clean unoccupied guestrooms and keep them sealed till allocation to guest	On rotation
Deep clean and disinfect occupied guestrooms. Disinfect high touchpoints	After 72 hours of every guest departure
'Room sanitized for your safety' card to be hung on the door	After room cleaning and disinfection
Clean and disinfect guestrooms, disinfect high touchpoints, in absence of guests	Daily for occupied rooms with option of guest to opt out
Linen change carried out by designated staff with PPE, with minimum agitation, soiled linen bagged in room and bags sealed	After every guest departure and for occupied rooms only on guest request
Comforters and pillows quarantined after each guest stay in low occupancy	After each guest stay
Heavy curtains, sheer curtains, blinds, rugs, dust ruffles, upholstered furniture and headboards to be sprayed with disinfectant cleaner/ steam cleaned	After each guest stay
Bathroom disinfection, disinfect high touchpoints	After every guest departure and daily for occupied rooms with option of guest to opt out
Guest laundry bagged by guests themselves in launderable/ disposable bags and collected by a designated staff	Once a day
Glassware and crockery to be sent for dishwashing at 80°C	After every guest departure and daily for occupied rooms with option of guest to opt out
All individual disposable amenities to be disposed of.	After every guest departure

- Check on daily basis with the guest on phone about any requirements.
- In the event that a few items or amenities are needed, the same are placed outside the guestroom door on sanitized trays and the guest informed on intercom.

Linen handling protocols

- Collection of soiled linen from floors and various outlets must be handled by designated valets with proper PPE such as 3 ply masks, gloves, and aprons.
- The soiled linen should be collected with minimum agitation so as to prevent any potential aerosolization of pathogen or infected fluids becoming airborne.
- Individual counting of linen on floors must be discontinued.
- Collection must take place in colour coded bins that can be closed. Use of linen chutes is not encouraged during implementation of infection prevention and control programme.
- Linen carts, trolleys, and bags must clearly be labelled for soiled linen or clean linen and they should not be used interchangeably.
- Hand hygiene station must be installed at the linen and uniform room.
- Staff must wear appropriate PPE when handling linen and perform hand hygiene before touching clean linen.
- Counting shall be carried out while removing from bins or bags only in the linen room or laundry, avoid individual re-counting.
- Linen must not be placed on floors or dirty surfaces.
- Deliver and receive any requested bath linen or guest laundry through trays and trolleys only.
- Linen must be issued using First In- First Out (FIFO) policy of storage.

Laundry protocols

- The staff in the laundry must wear PPE such as 3 ply masks, gloves, and apron shields.
- Maintain a one-way operation in the laundry, i.e., dirty in and clean out, to avoid cross-contamination. At no point should any soiled linen come in contact with clean ones. Surfaces handling these linen should strictly not be used interchangeably.
- Receive soiled linen and uniforms in a sanitized area in the laundry.
- Linen sorting and segregation must be done with recommended PPE as per SOP.
- Discard linen with deep stains of blood or bodily fluids.
- The high touchpoints on laundry machines and equipment must be sanitized after each use.
- Laundering processes for infection prevention and control must take care of disinfection of linen and uniforms. There are three ways disinfection may be brought about in the laundry procedure—thermal, chemical, and chemo-thermal. In COVID-19 infection prevention and control, thermal and chemo-thermal procedures are employed. The important aspect is to keep in mind two essential factors in disinfection, contact-time and temperature of water. WHO thermal disinfection guidelines specify wash process to be set at 71°C (160°F) for 25 minutes. In severe cases, such as COVID-19 infection prevention and control, RAL-GZ 992/3 guidelines of Robert Koch Institutes, Germany (RKI) of 85°C (185°F) for 15 minutes or 90°C (194°F) for 10 minutes may be carried out. The following thermal disinfection formula is used by laundry managers to verify the time and temperature being employed.

Time in minutes × (Temperature in °C – 55°C) ≥ 250

Chemo-thermal disinfection utilizes a temperature range of 40°C – 60°C along with approved laundry disinfectant chemicals.

- Machines must be loaded as per recommendation. Overloading will not allow proper disinfection.
- Ensure water quality and hardness is as per standard recommendation, else disinfection chemicals may be ineffective.
- Discontinue the use of starch in linen.
- Maintain ironing temperature between 105°C – 110°C on linen.
- Ensure that linen is completely dried and aired before being sent into circulation.
- In case of infected linen, as per the Ministry of Health and Family Welfare, India guidelines, sodium hypochlorite solution with 525 – 615 ppm of available chlorine should be used for pre-treatment of the infected linen by pre-soaking with 20 minutes of chemical contact time followed by freshwater rinse.
- Washable PPE, as per the WHO guidelines, must be cleaned with soap and water and decontaminated with 0.5% sodium hypochlorite solution after each use.
- Wash guest laundry separately if they are from different guestrooms. Use thermal wash if type of fabric permits, else use chemo-thermal wash.

Waste management protocols

Solid waste and garbage should be collected at source in bins keeping segregation in mind with appropriate PPE and then disposed of hygienically, as per rules and regulations of the local municipal authority.

- Staff handling waste must be donned in appropriate PPE as per SOP.
- Waste segregation and disposal shall be as dry, wet, glass, biodegradable and hazardous medical waste in colour coded bins and bags.
- Single use PPEs must be segregated and disposed as 'biohazard waste' in proper colour coded bags with hazard indication.
- Wastes such as masks and tissues from a potentially infected guest's room must be sealed in a red coloured 'biohazard disposal waste bag' with hazard indication.
- The waste disposal bags must be tied tightly after they are three-fourths full.
- Hand hygiene must be performed after handling waste.
- Ensure timely removal of wastes from the premises by the appointed vendor.

Managing Housekeeping Budget in COVID Times

The devastating impact that the global COVID pandemic has had on the hospitality industry, many hotels across the country are struggling to stay in business, not even able to break even and pay back debts. Preparing budgets in this scenario is a challenging task for housekeepers with the cleaning costs going significantly high as expected. The budgets would incur costs of sanitization, PPE, specialized cleaning supplies and so on. The housekeeper can no longer base the budget on historical data and occupancy forecasts, because the demand now is unpredictable. The key is to begin on a blank state, think out of the box and flexibly, work on controlling costs, bringing in operational discipline and focus efforts on creative ways to generate revenues. A point of contention is also that where the cost of disinfection and PPE are reflected in the housekeeping expense in the budget, these materials are being used by all departments. Thus, Finance Officers need to bear in mind that when housekeeping buys materials for the 'new normal', it is used by everyone. The following strategies are recommended in planning housekeeping budget in times of a pandemic.

- Zero based budgeting is recommended which resets the budgets at the start of each new period instead of increasing the budget by a fixed percentage. This will require evaluation of each expense and revenue projection irrespective of past performance.
- It would also be a best practice to budget in advance for two situations, 35% occupancy and 65% occupancy, so that the housekeeper can implement one of the two plans based on the occupancy.
- Focus on a shorter planning cycle of month over month since demand is unpredictable. The housekeeper can then react to changing dynamics more rapidly than staying with an annual plan. This shall result in shorter lead times and careful planning is crucial.
- Estimate the new budget and communicate the modifications throughout management lines as early as possible.
- Micromanage all expenses by continually checking inventory levels. Frequency of certain outsourced services not required as much during low occupancy must be decreased. Evaluate all expenses and initiatives and control costs as much as possible.
- Cut down on costs temporarily, go in for clutter-free rooms, cutting down frill amenities, providing only very-essential ones and putting others on 'only on request' list. Accessories such as decorative pillows and foot throws may be done away with.
- Reduce contractual employees while retaining essential manpower in proportion to the occupancy, till the situation becomes favourable.
- Perform time and motion studies with 'new normal' SOPs to derive real time requirements of time for room cleaning and public area cleaning and number of associates required for housekeeping operations. This will help streamline staff schedule planning, relook at staff ratio to rooms actually occupied, staff ratio per guest and staff ratio per square feet.
- Allocate resources towards direct or indirect revenue generating items and eliminate all other frill inventories.
- Devote a portion of the budget to required innovation and technology to tackle infection spread.
- Various floors and wings may have to be shut to ensure cost efficiency.
- Take advantage of technology such as online checklists, location-based room assignments, accurately predicted room cleaning times and automated reporting to reduce costs.
- Take advantage of lower occupancy which will mean less frequent restocking and decreased wear and tear of existing inventory due to lowered usage.

The Cost of Cleaning

According to information gleaned from a survey of Indian housekeepers by the authors, before the pandemic, a standard leisure room took about of 35–45 minutes to clean at a cost of ₹750–1,000 per room at single or double occupancy. Incorporating the new cleaning protocols shall push the cleaning time for a standard leisure room up to 45–60 minutes at a cost of ₹1,000–1,200 per room.

As per a study carried out by a hotel operations platform, Optii Solutions, on 'cost of post-pandemic housekeeping', before the pandemic, a standard leisure room took an average of 39.3 minutes to clean and $9.42 per room in terms of staff time for cleaning a single or double occupancy room. Incorporating the new cleaning protocols shall push the cleaning time for a standard leisure room up to 42.3 minutes at a cost of $10.12 per room. The time and cost would increase to 45.2 minutes and $10.80 per room respectively, when children too stay in the room. In case of business travellers, the metrics would work out to be lesser, being 31.8 minutes at a cost of $7.60 per room.

As per the authors' survey, the cleaning frequency of public areas and employee or heart of the house areas has increased and thus the cost has escalated 4–10% depending on occupancy levels at various properties. The implementation of COVID-19 safety guidelines and regulations have increased housekeeping operational costs (OPEX) by 10–20%. The CAPEX too goes up by 15–30% when investing in new cleaning technologies and disinfection equipment which is the need of the hour. These infection prevention and control costs include procurement of disinfectant cleaners, sanitizers, dispensers, and PPE kits in high numbers, colour coded microfibre dusters in high numbers, garbage bags, hand hygiene kits and stations for guests and staff, thermal scanners, pulse oximeters, communication materials, fumigation machines, UV-C machines, electrostatic sprayers, steam cleaners and so on. Many housekeepers wisely suggest that infection-prevention related costs must not be shown under housekeeping costs.

Use of Technology to Facilitate Infection Prevention and Control

Hospitality brands are investing in technology integration such as Internet of Things (IoT), Artificial Intelligence (AI) and Machine Learning (ML), Virtual Reality (VR), and Robotics, into their operations to reduce human intervention, thus facilitating infection prevention and control at their properties. Automation is being brought in, in various operational activities to adhere to contactless experience and operations by avoiding touch with potentially infected surfaces. Some of the new age technology interventions being adopted by accommodation facilities to raise the bar of hospitality experience for guests are:

- Motion detected sliding doors/revolving doors for main entrance
- Automated keyless entry systems
- One-card identification systems
- Passport and ID scanners
- Mobile phone-based automated check-in and check-out
- Facial recognition check-in
- Biometric scanner verification integrated check-in
- Self-check-in kiosks
- Contactless mobile based remote payment platforms
- Tap-on mobile phone payments
- Contactless payment readers in POS terminals
- Television based remote check-out
- Digital concierge services
- AI bots or Chatbots as virtual travel assistant
- Robots as concierge
- In-room tablets connecting guest to hotel facilities
- Sensor-based automated lighting systems
- Two-way opening doors
- Hands-free, sensor-based electric switches
- Voice-activated elevators
- Mobile phone-controlled guestroom entry system
- Sensor-based faucets and fixtures
- Gesture controlled flushing system in public washrooms
- Cobots – collaborative robots in housekeeping cleaning
- Pulsed xenon-based intense germicidal light emitting robots for decontamination
- Cloud based IoT Housekeeping software for systems and compliance
- Digital checklists for SOPs
- Digital inspection templates
- QR code scanning technology for checkpoints
- AI based compliance monitoring for standards
- AI based customer data analysis and collection
- Self-disinfecting rooms
- Electrostatic sprayers with disinfecting liquids
- Use of nanotechnology in cleaning – stay clean films with nano particles

Modifying Infrastructure Design and Facilities to Facilitate Infection Prevention and Control

The COVID-19 pandemic has changed the way the hotels are conceptualized and built. The future of hospitality design will now be seen by designers through the lens of health and well-being. Hospitality designers and architects are engaged in research for bringing in innovative designs to facilitate infection prevention and control through facility design. It is important to bear in mind for hoteliers that for existing hotels, their focus must be on implementing temporary measures rather than a considerable design revamp. For instance, instead of erecting a plain giant screen wall, it will be more effective and aesthetic to place a bookshelf in the lobby.

Implementing Temporary Measures

- Create new required signages in the lobby and public area spaces, matching with the brand design, colour, fonts, and graphics.
- Design aesthetic floor marks at the reception and in the elevators to encourage guests to keep the 6 feet physical distance.
- De-clutter spaces and surfaces so as to make cleaning and disinfection easier, allow unobstructed natural light and air circulation so that chances of microbes adhering to contactable surfaces is minimized.
- Demarcate and set up spaces for sanitization zones, isolation zones, and special buffer zones to accommodate for physical distancing during each guest and staff activity and quarantining.
- Foot pull and push mechanisms may be attached to existing doors so that door handles are not used.
- Introduce step or arm pull mechanisms on doors and sanitary fixtures such as faucets in guestrooms and washrooms.
- Prefer disposable components such as single-use tissue linen bedsheets and pillow covers for guestrooms.
- Allow guests to request portable gym equipment such as dumbbells and weights, yoga mats, training bicycles, resistance bands, pilates loops, and so on into their rooms. The property can encash on provision of virtual instruction sessions in the use of gym equipment and physical training.

Rethinking Hospitality Design in Future Projects in lieu of Infection Prevention

- Elements and spaces will be designed in a manner that involves contactless experiences and zero-touch interactions for the guests and incorporate elements to provide enjoyment of spaces through visible sense via artificial intelligence. Hands free designs will be brought in to ensure zero-touch on surfaces such as doors and sanitary fittings.
- As hospitality industry imbibes the 'new normal', disinfection of spaces shall be a constant feature and the design of entrances of accommodation facilities shall be modified to accommodate and blend such measures aesthetically into the design, for instance inbuilt hand hygiene stations and PPE stations.
- The designers shall focus on designs that enable physical distancing and sensor-based systems. Consequent modifications shall be brought about in lobbies, meeting spaces, conference rooms

and F&B spaces. Lobbies, lounges, and other common areas will have larger space allocations to make them multi-purpose, adaptable and allow flexibility in usage. An apparent trend on these lines would be outdoor spaces used for restaurant seating in hospitality properties. Lobby restaurants with physical distancing norms may become a trend in spacious lobbies in some properties which may do away with space-demanding restaurants, thus combining functions of a lobby and F&B. Also foreseen are conference and meeting room designs that can open to connect with outdoors. Event halls would be designed to incorporate French windows opening to outdoor spaces and terraces. Flexibility will be a major factor in design of meeting and conference rooms with spaces broken down into smaller more manageable clusters with facility for private dining too, which when later required and permitted can be combined to cater to larger number of clients. Such spaces will offer themselves to be booked by clients in a variety of ways.

- Business centres and event halls in hospitality properties will be focusing on adding green screens, webcams, and high-end webcasting and broadcasting equipment to cater to the shift towards virtual rooms and workplace instead of live events.
- Designers shall work on providing design innovations incorporating automation and user-centric design that enables flexibility and control.
- Designers shall be working towards creating buildings that are minimum maintenance with sustainable, energy-efficient building systems also incorporating technology-based systems and artificial intelligence for cleaning and disinfection.
- Designers will rethink on the selection of building materials, finished surfaces and their designs, choosing those that are resilient and lend themselves effectively and efficiently to maintenance of clinically clean standards and do not promote microbial growth. Furniture design will see modifications as contact surfaces on them shall be minimized, as in armrests for chairs will be eliminated in new designing.
- As guests become increasingly mindful of their health and well-being, designers shall focus on incorporating more open spaces with fresh air inside the property, enhancing green spaces and environment that prioritizes rejuvenation, relaxation, and quality of sleep.
- Designers shall be working on bringing in aesthetic solutions to provide clearly displayed, visual evidence to guests that their health is in safe hands at the property. For instance, apparatus employing UV light disinfection must be on clear display aesthetically instead of concealing it away out of guest sight. The cleaning and disinfecting crew must be in forefront now and cleaning should be carried out evidently in guests' eyes, contrary to the traditional thought that cleaning must happen away from guests' eyes.
- Antimicrobial rugs will be in and normal carpets and rugs will not be used anymore.
- It will become imperative that infection transmission be curbed by controlling the quality of internal air. Accommodation facilities shall now invest in high-calibre air filtration systems as a new luxury to promote health and well-being. Internal air conditioning systems will incorporate High Efficiency Particulate Air (HEPA) filters to enhance efficiency and effective exchange of fresh air. These filters are designed to trap 85–99.97% of particles that are 0.3 microns and greater and take them out of circulation through sieving, diffusion, direct impaction or interception. These filters thus filter out dust, mould, bacteria, pollen and other airborne particles of size 0.3 micron and greater, as this size is the Most Penetrating Particle Size (MPPS). HVAC systems will be better designed to limit the amount of shared air in a room. The Indian Society of Heating, Refrigerating & Air Conditioning Engineers (ISHRAE) and International Facility Management Association (IFMA) task force in their COVID-19 guidance

document recommend maintaining a relative humidity of 40–70% and setting temperatures between 24–30°C. It also mandates the provision of a minimum fresh air volume of 3 cubic meter/hour per person. It also advises minimum air changes of around 10-15 ACHP (Air Changes Per Hour) for good ventilation. The task force document suggests the mechanical exhaust air be 70–80% of the fresh air quantity.

- As the hospitality industry goes into cost effective mode, the design ethos shall be moving away from luxury to 'simple and healthy'. Hospitality projects are foreseen to see a reduction in design budgets by 30%. The ornamental layer that provides the look of luxury will give way to raw, rustic yet aesthetic forms of designing, using indigenous, sustainable, low-maintenance, local materials. The rough aesthetics shall give way to smooth surfaces such as tiles and stones that lend themselves more efficiently to disinfection.
- Designers will pay more attention to strategic architectural planning, incorporating passive and active design strategies to reduce operational costs incurred. Passive design strategies would include aspects such as optimal building orientation, using awnings, sunshades, façade screens and shaded green open spaces, using stepped circular balconies with flora to break up the heat effect of the building and incorporating open courtyards to block heat radiation from the South and West and to bring in the healing benefits of sunlight. Active design strategies include aspects such as incorporating green building concepts and theory of biophilia, use of natural ventilation, maximizing natural light, interspersing water bodies in interior design, and use of energy star rated appliances, e-windows, use of efficient HVAC systems with HEPA filters and harnessing energy from clean renewable energy resources.
- Guestroom designs shall be modified to include visible perception cleanliness instead of displaying clinically clean look.
- Guestrooms may be designed now with private dining options and mini gym equipment as fitness spaces shall be diminishing and shifting into the privacy of guestrooms.
- Designers will be going in for more of hard surfaces and fewer porous surfaces to facilitate low-maintenance and ease of cleaning.

SUMMARY

Just as security protocols became an integral part of hospitality industry SOPs post 9/11, the COVID-19 scenario has had a sweeping impact on the way hospitality operations are carried out. On a lighter note, it is presumed that the COVID-19 pandemic shall segregate the timelines as BC and AC, instead of BC and AD, where BC would stand for 'Before Corona' and AC for 'After Corona'. The industry has adopted the 'new normal' guidelines laid down by the regulatory agencies. The chapter outlines the nature of infections and their mode of transmission, especially with reference to COVID-19. The importance of following guidelines and regulations to prevent and control infections has been discussed. The standard components of an infection prevention programme at an accommodation facility are explained in depth. The chapter lists down the infection prevention and control protocols laid down in accommodation facilities with relation to rooms division and related departments. It also summarizes cleaning practices adapted to clinically clean standards with focus on high touchpoints, disinfection, and enhanced cleaning frequencies. A brief is given on the way housekeepers rework budgets with increased cleaning costs during COVID times. Also listed are the various technological advancements that facilitate operations of rooms division during infection prevention and control. The chapter concludes with an outline of modifications in infrastructure design and facilities, both temporary and anticipated in future projects.

KEY TERMS

3 Ply masks 3 ply masks recommended for hospitality staff are made of three layers of fabric. The inner layer is of an absorbent material such as cotton, middle layer is of non-woven, non-absorbent material such as polypropylene, and the outer layer of non-absorbent material such as polyester or polyester blend.

AHP Accelerated Hydrogen Peroxide is a synergistic blend of hydrogen peroxide, surfactants and such ingredients that bring about effective cleaning and disinfection.

Air Changes Per Hour (ACPH) Air Changes Per Hour is a metric that indicates how many times an HVAC system can fill up the full volume of a room with fresh air.

Artificial Intelligence (AI) Artificial Intelligence refers to the ability of a computer system to imitate the abilities of the human mind, grasping from examples, experiences, identifying objects, figuring out solutions to problems, comprehending and responding to languages, making decisions, and combining such capabilities to execute functions like a human.

Biometric attendance The concept of using devices to verify the identity of a person for attendance purposes at a workplace. The system could be based on identifying fingerprints, face recognition, voice patterns, and iris scans.

CAPEX Capital expenses.

Chatbots A chatbot or a chatterbot is a machine that uses an artificial intelligence software that can simulate a conversation with a user in natural language through text or voice interactions.

Clinically clean standards Standards of cleanliness that facilitate cleaning and disinfection, eliminating pathogens. It is followed routinely in healthcare facilities.

Cobots Cobots or collaborative robots operate in responsive coordination with humans, interacting with them in a shared workspace to perform their tasks. They synergistically enhance human capabilities with their robust strength and flexibility, precision, and data capabilities.

Containment zones Specific geographic areas where COVID-19 or such infective positive cases are found in large numbers, created to map and prevent local transmission of infection.

COVID-19 Coronavirus Disease, 19 referring to the year it was identified to have originated. Caused by the novel coronavirus, the disease was declared a global pandemic by the World Health Organization on 11th March 2020.

Cross training Cross training involves training employees to work in departments other than their speciality in periods of staff shortage or to enhance employee skills.

Dilution ratio The ratio of the solute (here the chemical substance to be diluted) to the solvent, usually water, for instance 1 part chemical to 10 parts water.

Electrostatic sprayers These sprayers operate on the principle of electrostatically charging disinfectant liquids as the chemical leaves the nozzle spray. This causes the chemical droplets to cling to virtually any surface, providing consistent surface coverage to make the disinfection process effective.

Fogging A technique to facilitate disinfection, pest control and odour management through an equipment (fogger) using a fine spray to apply a chemical solution.

Hand hygiene Primary measures to maintain one's hands with processes that reduce potential pathogens on its surface to reduce the risk of transmitting pathogens. Hand hygiene includes use of hand rubs and hand washing procedure in specified ways.

HEPA filters High Efficiency Particulate Air filters enhance the efficiency and effective exchange of fresh air in HVAC systems. These filters are designed to trap 85–99.97% of particles that are 0.3 microns and greater and take them out of circulation through sieving, diffusion, direct impaction or interception. These filters thus filter out dust, mould, bacteria, pollen and other airborne particles of size 0.3 micron and greater, as this size is the Most Penetrating Particle Size (MPPS).

High touchpoints High touchpoints are those surfaces in the facility that are frequently touched by persons present in the facility, thus increasing the risk of transmission of pathogens via indirect contact.

HVAC Heating Ventilation and Air Conditioning systems are mechanical systems that provide temperature and humidity related comfort to occupants, supplemented with maintenance of indoor air quality.

Incubation period The incubation period is the time period between the entry of the microbe into a human body and the occurrence of the first symptom.

Internet of Things (IoT) Refers to the connection of computer-based devices within everyday objects via the internet, enabling them to share data.

Machine Learning (ML) A field of Artificial Intelligence, with the concept that a computer programme can learn and adapt to new data from experience without human intervention.

Microfibre duster It is made of ultra-fine polyester and polyamide blended microfibres, which have extremely minute strands that attract, capture, and hold dust, dirt, and microbes effectively. The positively charged microfibres attract dust and dirt particles that tend to have a negative charge.

MSDS Material Safety Data Sheet is a form containing detailed safety information about a chemical.

Nanotechnology A field of research, innovation and subsequent application concerned with creating materials on the scale of atoms and molecules (nanoparticles). A nanometre is one-billionth of a metre. The technology is especially useful in developing self-cleaning coatings.

New normal A previously unfamiliar or atypical situation that has now become standard, usual, or expected. Here, the new guidelines and protocols of functioning in the hospitality industry because of COVID-19 scenario.

OPEX Operating expenses.

Pathogen Refers to a disease-causing microorganism.

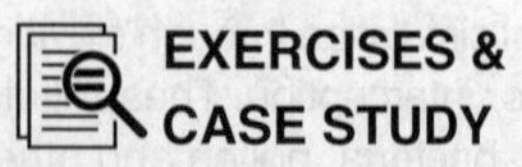

Porte cochère A covered entrance of the hospitality facility, large enough for vehicles to halt for alighting of guests and then pass through.

PPE doffing Refers to the act of removing Personal Protective Equipment such as gloves, masks, and gowns.

PPE donning Refers to the act of wearing Personal Protective Equipment such as gloves, masks, and gowns.

PPE Personal Protective Equipment; clothing or equipment that is worn to provide protection against hazardous substances and environment.

ppm Parts per million; a unit of measurement commonly used to trace amounts of substances.

Pulsed xenon Describes broad range of light wavelengths generated by xenon (an inert gas) flashlamps used for sterilization applications.

Quarantine The period for which a person is kept in isolation to prevent the spread of an infectious disease.

TFA Treated Fresh Air is the recirculated fresh air in an enclosed space by circulating treated outdoor air using air filters and conditioning it using cooling systems.

Virtual Reality (VR) Refers to images and sounds created to simulate a three-dimensional world by a computer that seems almost real to the user, the users can interact with the platform using sensors.

Zero-based budgeting It is an approach to making a budget from zero-base. The budget is not based on historical data, starts at scratch and relooks at each and every item of expense and computes their operation costs.

15 Supervision in Housekeeping

Learning Objectives

After reading this chapter, you should be able to

- appreciate the crucial role of a supervisor
- understand the purpose and the systematic method of guestroom supervision
- develop inspection checklists for use in guestrooms and public areas
- discuss the art of checking VIP guestrooms
- list the commonly neglected areas with regard to guestroom cleaning
- handle guest complaints

Introduction

In the day-to-day running of the housekeeping department, the executive housekeeper relies to a great extent on her supervisory team to train and monitor the semi-skilled and unskilled workforce. Good supervision leads to efficient work using the correct cleaning agents, equipment, and procedures. Good supervisors will themselves have thorough, up-to-date, and practical knowledge of cleaning agents, equipment, and methods, so that junior staff members respect them and their abilities. The supervisory-level staff in the housekeeping department include the assistant housekeeper, floor housekeeper, linen room supervisor, public area supervisor, and so on.

Role of a Supervisor

The supervisor's role is much more than just overseeing the work of semi-skilled and unskilled staff. Supervisors carry the responsibility of directly managing the human resources, the most important resource of the housekeeping department. Though an executive housekeeper may call meetings or meet all the staff during briefings, the actual link between the managerial level and the lower-rung staff are the supervisors. The supervisors keep the managers apprised of the standard of performance of their workforce. They have the whole and sole responsibility of not only getting the work done, but getting it done efficiently and within the time period set as a standard by the hotel.

Another resource that the executive housekeeper has is money. It is with the availability of this resource in mind that she prepares the budget. The enormous task of implementing the budget by operating within the forecasted costs falls on the supervisors' shoulders. The supervisors make sure that the correct cleaning agents are used in the proper dilution and only on the surfaces they are meant for. They oversee the use of the cleaning equipment suited for a particular cleaning procedure. They train the junior staff to meet the standards of cleanliness expected by the hotel and this is an ongoing on-the-job training. The physical control of cleaning standards is also the responsibility of the supervisory staff. The supervisors pass on information from the housekeeping managers to the workers, and vice versa. They also maintain the records of the housekeeping department and ensure that the staff under their supervision follow the codes of conduct and discipline set down by the management. And it is the supervisors who are directly responsible for any deterioration in or failure to meet the standards set by the executive housekeeper.

In their supervisory role, supervisors automatically become representatives of the teams working under them. An effective supervisor recognizes all the employees on the team individually as unique human beings, empathizes with them, helps them increase their productivity while always considering their safety, and motivates them to perform collectively towards achieving the set goals. An efficient supervisor delegates responsibility to attendants by assigning them cleaning areas or room sections, welcomes their ideas and opinions, and implements their ideas after ratification. The supervisor, apart from offering skills training to team members, also trains up the members in basic etiquette, formal speech, and in case there is a language barrier, a working knowledge of English, thus helping them to interact with guests.

On the other hand, a supervisor also needs to anticipate the guest's needs, looking at things from the guest's perspective so that proactive service can be provided. Proactive guest service is possible only when the supervisors keep their staff highly motivated. A motivated employee is professional, takes pride in his/her work, and provides quality service consistently.

Supervisory Posts

The housekeeping department usually has the following supervisory positions:

- Floor supervisor
- Public area supervisor
- Night supervisor
- Control desk supervisor
- Linen room supervisor
- Uniform room supervisor
- Laundry supervisor

Each supervisor is responsible for certain functions and leads a team of attendants to accomplish them. The specific duties and responsibilities of all the supervisors have been listed in Chapter 2. The assistant housekeeper, though, is not strictly a supervisor as per the designation, but many of the duties for this position are supervisory.

General Duties of a Supervisor

The general duties and responsibilities of supervisors are as follows.

- To ensure that staff are aware of their hours of work and that they adhere to the planned duty roster.
- To make any adjustment necessary in their off-days in consultation with the concerned employees.
- To instruct the staff in cleaning routines and schedules.
- To regularly fill up the cleaning and maintenance checklists and inventories after a complete physical check.
- To liaise with the maintenance department for any maintenance work required in guestrooms or public areas and to initiate work-order forms.
- To inspect and record room status regularly and liaise with the reception desk.
- To issue the relevant keys, keep track of them, and get them safely back.

- To be responsible for following the correct procedure in dealing with lost-and-found articles when employees hand these in.
- To check the stocks regularly, take delivery of stocks, and issue supplies to attendants.
- To supervise the staff involved in the cleaning and setting up of banquet halls, meeting rooms, and other event venues.
- To coordinate with contract service providers for functions such as pest control, carpet maintenance and so on.
- To check and record the amount and condition of the house linen during collection, dispatch, storage, repair, and use.
- To arrange for the induction and training of staff.
- To assist the EHK in preparing monthly income-expenditure report, a sample format of which is presented in Exhibit 15.1.
- To regularly apprise managers of individual staff performance.
- To inform the employees of staff welfare schemes and other facilities.
- To liaise with staff from other departments in a way that shows respect for their skills and abilities.

Exhibit 15.1 Format of monthly housekeeping income-expenditure report

Hotel Spring Leaves International

MONTHLY HOUSEKEEPING INCOME-EXPENDITURE REPORT

Month: .... **Date of submission: ....**

Expenditure heads	Annual amount sanctioned	Expenditure previous month	Expenditure current month	Variance	Year to date
Cleaning supplies					
Guest supplies					
Flowers					
Minibar cost					
Stationery					
Linen purchases					
Uniforms					
Upholstery					
Horticulture					
Furnishings					
Laundry					
Guest laundry cost					
Pest control					
Miscellaneous expenses					

Income heads	Budgeted	Income previous month	Income current month	Variance	Year to date
Minibar sales					
Guest laundry sales					

Signature of EHK: ....

Specific Functions of Supervisors

We shall now discuss some of the most important functions that supervisors in the housekeeping department are responsible for.

Public Area Inspection

Public areas are cleaned by associates and housemen during non-peak hours and inspected systematically by public area supervisors. The supervisors not only plan and implement daily cleaning tasks in public areas but also schedule periodic cleaning and maintenance tasks so as to keep the front of the house areas looking as fresh and impressive as they did when the hotel first opened for business. Many activities in the public areas, such as façade cleaning, floor maintenance, carpet shampooing, landscaping, etc. are outsourced. The supervision of these contractors' work also comes under the purview of public area supervisors.

Guestroom Inspection

This is a planned, systematic process in which guestrooms are checked for cleanliness and maintenance and accordingly approved for occupancy (or not) by supervisors. The supervisors inspect guestrooms keeping in mind that their last look will be the guest's first look at the room. The inherent trait of 'an eye for detail' is the most important aid to supervisors inspecting guestrooms. The supervisors inspect for anything that is not upto the establishment's standards before the guest finds them amiss. Room inspections also recognize the need for deep cleaning and other maintenance activities.

A systematic method should be followed while inspecting guestrooms so that the process is thorough, leaving no room for neglect. The executive housekeeper should develop an efficient checklist to help supervisors in this aspect of their work. The inspection of bedrooms and bathrooms may be carried out in a clockwise or anti-clockwise direction, moving from high to low levels, first checking every article on the wall or against the wall. The supervisors then need to check all the free-standing items, again working in the same particular direction. The floor and ceiling should be checked after this. Then, a final look around the room is important to place things in perspective.

Checklists, reports and records

Inspection of the cleaned areas forms a major part of a supervisor's work. In this regard, inspection checklists are vital tools for a supervisor. Checklists should be developed for all the areas that the housekeeping department is responsible for cleaning and maintaining. The ideal checklist itemizes all surfaces and articles, lays down the standards of cleanliness to be achieved, and allows space for supervisors to indicate checks and record any observation. The more detailed the checklists, the more thorough is the inspection, and the more in conformance to set standards is the cleaning. Whatever anomalies the inspection brings to light should be rectified promptly, else the purpose of inspection is defeated. Samples of public area inspection checklists are presented in Exhibits 15.2 and 15.3. A sample of a guestroom inspection checklist is given in Exhibit 15.4. Floor supervisors keep a tab on the frequency with which cleaning tasks are being accomplished using frequency records, a sample of which is given in Exhibit 15.5. Floor supervisors also fill in supervisor's report for the floors they are responsible for. A sample of a floor supervisor's report is presented in Exhibit 15.6. Checklists, as work organisation tools, are used not only by supervisors but also the departmental head as she/he supervises the work of the supervisors and the entire department. A sample checklist that may be followed by executive housekeepers is given in Exhibit 15.7.

Exhibit 15.2 Sample public area daily cleaning inspection checklist – Main porch & lobby

Hotel Spring Leaves International

SUPERVISOR'S INSPECTION CHECKLIST FOR PUBLIC AREA – MAIN PORCH & LOBBY

Date .... **Time:** .... **Shift:** ....

Time: → **Task:** ↓	**7am – 9am**	**9am – 11am**	**11am – 1pm**	**1pm – 3pm**	**3pm – 5pm**	**5pm – 7pm**	**7pm – 9pm**	**9pm – 11pm**	**11pm – 1am**	**1am – 3am**	**3am – 5am**	**5am – 7am**
1. Cleaning of entrance ramp and staircase												
2. Damp wiping of ramp and staircase handrails												
3. Damp wiping of walk-through metal detector booth												
4. Cold fogging and damp wiping of scanning machine with disinfectant solution												

Exhibit 15.3 Sample public area daily cleaning inspection checklist – Lobby washroom

Hotel Spring Leaves International

SUPERVISOR'S INSPECTION CHECKLIST FOR PUBLIC AREA – LOBBY WASHROOM

Date: .... **Time:** .... **Shift:** ....

Date:........../ Day:............ **Task:** ↓	**7am – 9am**	**9am – 11am**	**11am – 1pm**	**1pm – 3pm**	**3pm – 5pm**	**5pm – 7pm**	**7pm – 9pm**	**9pm – 11pm**	**11pm – 1am**	**1am – 3am**	**3am – 5am**	**5am – 7am**
1. Cobweb cleaning												
2. Cleaning of wall skirtings												
3. Damp wiping of door and its hardware. Wiping of door handles with disinfectant solution.												
4. Spot cleaning of walls												

Exhibit 15.4 Sample supervisor's inspection checklist for guestroom

Hotel XYZ

SUPERVISOR'S INSPECTION CHECKLIST FOR TWIN GUESTROOM

Date: .... **Area:** .... **Time:** .... **Shift:** ....

Supervisor's name & signature: ....

Sl No.	Room Nos → PARTICULARS ↓	101	102	103	104	105	REMARKS
	Entrance & Vestibule Area						
1.	Main door (including frame)						
2.	Door lock/knob						
3.	Double lock						
4.	Number plate						
5.	Door stopper/ closer						
6.	Door hinges						
7.	Safety latch						
8.	Peep hole						
9.	Door bell						
10.	Knob cards (behind the door)						
a.	DND						
b.	Please Clean My Room						
c.	Collect My Laundry						
d.	Polish My Shoe						
e.	Breakfast knob card						
11.	Fire exit map (behind the door)						
12.	Switchboard						

Exhibit 15.5 Floor supervisor's guestroom tasks frequency record

Floor supervisor's guestroom tasks frequency record

Room No. → Particulars ↓	101	102	103	104	105	106	107	108	109	110	111	112	113	114
Window cleaning	2/5 12/5 22/5	3/5 13/5 23/5	2/5 12/5 22/5	3/5 13/5 23/5	2/5 12/5 22/5	3/5 13/5 23/5	2/5 12/5 22/5	3/5 13/5 23/5	2/5 12/5 22/5	3/5 13/5 23/5	2/5 12/5 22/5	3/5 13/5 23/5	2/5 12/5 22/5	3/5 13/5 23/5
Coffee kettle cleaning	4/5 11/5 18/5 25/5	5/5 12/5 19/5 26/5	4/5 11/5 18/5 25/5	5/5 12/5 19/5 26/5	4/5 11/5 18/5 25/5	5/5 12/5 19/5 26/5	4/5 11/5 18/5 25/5	5/5 12/5 19/5 26/5	4/5 11/5 18/5 25/5	5/5 12/5 19/5 26/5	4/5 11/5 18/5 25/5	5/5 12/5 19/5 26/5	4/5 11/5 18/5 25/5	5/5 12/5 19/5 26/5
Brassoing	10/5 24/5	11/5 25/5	10/5 24/5	11/5 25/5	10/5 24/5	11/5 25/5	10/5 24/5	11/5 25/5	10/5 24/5	11/5 25/5	10/5 24/5	11/5 25/5	10/5 24/5	11/5 25/5

Signature of Floor Supervisor: ....

Exhibit 15.6 Floor supervisor's report – Front & back

Hotel Spring Leaves International

FLOOR SUPERVISOR'S REPORT (FRONT)

Floor: .... **Date:** .... **Day:** .... **Time:**........................

Room No.	Status	Pax	Time in	Time out	Remarks	Room No.	Status	Pax	Time in	Time out	Remarks
1						15					
2						16					
3						17					
4						18					
5						19					
6						20					
7						21					
8						22					
9						23					
10						24					
11						25					
12						26					
13						27					
14						28					

VIP rooms inspection

Flowers placement in rooms

Fruit basket placement in rooms

Carpet spotting check

Exhibit 15.7 Executive housekeeper's checklist – Front and back

Hotel Spring Leaves International

EHK'S CHECKLIST (FRONT)

Date: .... **Day:** .... **Time:**................................

Sl. No.	Particulars	Indicate ✓/ Fill details
1.	Log book	
2.	Guest feedback	
3.	Guest complaint	

(Contd.)

Exhibit 15.7 *Contd.*

4. Staff feedback
5. Rooms inspection
6. Linen reuse rooms
7. VIP rooms inspection
8. Public areas inspection
9. General maintenance – Rooms **Today** **Till date** **Monthly target**
10. General maintenance – Public area **Today** **Till date** **Monthly target**

Inspection of VIP rooms

This is in fact not a typical supervisor's responsibility, though a supervisory task. VIP rooms are checked personally by the assistant housekeeper or the executive housekeeper. The guestroom is opened and looked over to gauge how it will be seen by the VIP guest when he/she enters the room. Then a more thorough checking is done. See Exhibit 15.4 for the items and surfaces mentioned in the checklist. The room should smell fresh, with no bad odours or dampness. White-ragging is carried out on random surfaces—this means checking the cleanliness of any area by wiping a white rag across it to see the degree of soiling. All the neglected areas mentioned in the next section ('Inspection modules for neglected areas') should also be checked. The toilet bowl should be checked by running a damp cotton swab under the rim. Finally, the housekeeper should check that all the VIP amenities are in place. Details of VIP room amenities have been given in Chapter 12, in Table 12.10.

Inspection modules for commonly neglected areas

Various inspection modules are used for the thorough inspection of guestrooms, so that certain areas and aspects that tend to be neglected while cleaning and inspection are particularly checked by supervisors. Some hotels develop these as separate lists and some incorporate these neglected areas in their routine inspection checklists. These modules often have easy-to-remember names such as the Quick Six Inspection or the Dirty Dozen.

In general, the most commonly neglected areas in guestrooms include:

- The area between the bed and the nightstand, where food particles, dirt, and debris may accumulate since this area is usually hidden by the bedspread.
- The interiors of drawers and wardrobes, where dust may accumulate in crevices.
- Surface below the lamps and other accessories kept on tables, where dust accumulates because they tend to be overlooked.
- The tops of picture frames hung on walls, which tend to gather dust as they are not easily visible to the eye.
- The top edges and backs of doors, which if not cleaned on a regular basis may collect a lot of dust.
- The diffuser grilles of radiators or air-conditioners, which can collect stubborn dirt.
- Ceilings, which may show cobwebs if not attended to daily.

- The carpet area behind free-standing furniture that is near but not against the wall, such as a credenza standing to one side.
- Pillows and pillowcases, which should be free of wrinkles or stray hairs and which should have a fresh smell.
- The general odour of the room, which is often overlooked. The room should have a fresh smell.
- The tiled area next to the shower, which collects grime and shows water marks if not attended to daily.
- The area behind the toilet bowl, including pipes, cisterns, and the toilet-roll receptacle, which all provide surfaces and nooks where dirt settles.
- The area under the vanity unit and towel racks, which are hard to reach and may accumulate a lot of dust and debris. The tiles behind the vanitory unit also get water marks and soap marks easily.
- The faucet filters, which may be stained brown due to dirt collecting in them.
- The air vents in the toilet, which are hard to reach and which, if neglected during routine cleaning, may collect stubborn grime and dust.
- The baseboards in the guest bedroom as well as the bathroom, which too accumulate dust.

Handling Guest Complaints

Guests often express their displeasure when certain situations or services at the hotel are not to their satisfaction. Many guests curb their tendency to complain when they are not pleased with one or two of the hotel's services, but when the displeasure builds up through a series of problems, the guest does complain. It may be that for every guest who complains there are five or six who keep quiet. Then again, hotels also have guests who complain just for the sake of complaining and like to find fault with everything. In hotel jargon, these guests are called 'handle with care' (HWC) guests. It is extremely vital for the executive housekeeper to take cognisance of each and every complaint, take corrective action and follow up. A guest complaint stratification report is updated whenever complaints arise and it is submitted to the general manager monthly. The format of the same is presented in Exhibit 15.8.

Exhibit 15.8 Format of monthly guest complaints stratification

Hotel Spring Leaves International

MONTHLY GUEST COMPLAINTS STRATIFICATION

Month: .... **Date of submission:** ....

S. No.	Feedback date	Room no.	Name of guest	Check-in date	Check-out date	Problem description	Employee concerned	Root cause analysis	Corrective action taken	Remarks

Signature of EHK: ....

Types of guest complaints

There are primarily four types of guest complaints that employees in a hotel come across:

- Technical/mechanical
- Service related
- Attitudinal
- Unusual

Technical/mechanical complaints These complaints relate to the malfunctioning of hotel equipment or a set of guest supplies provided by the hotel. These may be due to problems with the air-conditioning, guestroom safes, room furnishings, door keys, plumbing, television sets, or elevators. Efficient and alert housekeeping attendants help minimize mechanical complaints. Effective use of the log book and of maintenance work orders is essential. At times, the technical problem in itself is not the cause of complaint, but rather the delay in rectifying the problem.

Service-related complaints These complaints arise when guests feel they are not receiving value for money in terms of the services provided by the hotel. For instance, a guest may complain about a delay in procuring a guest loan item, problems in phone services, carpets that are not clean, a stale odour in the room, linen not having been changed, and so on.

Attitudinal complaints These complaints are a result of tactless or rude behaviour towards guests on the part of hotel employees. Sometimes these complaints may also result from employees using guests as a sounding board for their problems at work or from guests overhearing conversations between employees.

Unusual complaints As the name suggests, these are odd complaints that often have no foundation and their solutions are usually not in the hands of the hotel staff. These complaints are the results of the whims and fancies of guests. For instance, guests complaining about the size of the suite, the absence of a swimming pool, plane timings, bad weather, and so on.

Dealing with complaints

Here are some guidelines a supervisor should follow when confronted with a plaintive guest.

- Listen with concern and empathy.
- Offer an apology for a genuine complaint.
- Isolate the guest, if possible, so that other guests may not overhear the conversation.
- Stay calm. Avoid responding with hostility or defensiveness.
- Be cautious of injuring the guest's sense of self-esteem; rather, try to pander to it subtly. Show that you take a personal interest in the problem. Use the guest's name frequently in the conversation. Take the complaint seriously. Give the guest your undivided attention. Concentrate on the problem, not on apportioning blame. Certainly do not insult the guest.
- Take notes. Writing down the facts saves time if someone else must get involved. Also, guests will tend to slow down if they are speaking faster so that you can write, which helps them calm down too. More importantly, the fact that a staff member is concerned enough to write down what they are saying is reassuring to the guests.
- Tell the guest what can be done. Offer choices. However, do not promise the impossible, nor exceed your authority.
- Set an approximate time for the completion of corrective action. Be specific, but do not underestimate the amount of time it will take to resolve the problem.
- Monitor the progress of corrective action.

- Follow up. Even if the complaint was resolved by someone else, contact the guest personally to ensure that the problem was resolved to his/her satisfaction. Report the entire event, the actions taken, and the conclusion of the incident.

Wowing the Guests

The aim of all hotel experience creators is to earn a significant position in guests' minds, ensure they don't have the chance to forget the brand's hospitality and stimulate their emotions in order to cultivate their loyalty to the hospitality brand. Such experiences exceed customer satisfaction and expectation and in general hoteliering terms are referred to as 'WOW' moments. A 'WOW' may be considered as that moment of achieving exceeded customer satisfaction that comes about when an employee does something they don't necessarily have to do as part of their usual job, that which the guest is not expecting to be done and which elicits a response of 'Wow' from the guest when it is done. Each and every employee can be a Wow creator as they go about their daily business of hoteliering. At times, there may be instances of guest complaints due to product, people or process failure, but these must be salvaged through timely and appropriate service recovery and be converted into an opportunity to create Wow moments. Creating Wow moments needs relentless efforts, constant product upkeep and customization, consistent process review and continuous training interventions. In this section, how housekeepers may create WOW moments is outlined.

- *Remembering the guests' names:* A repeat guest is wowed if his/her name is remembered and used by the associates. A first- time guest may be wowed by having their name fed in system such that whenever they call, they are addressed by their name along with the standard hotel greeting.
- *Making guest history work:* Apart from remembering the guests' names, it works in favour to remember small details about them, little clues being left by them, which can be recorded and kept in mind, such as where they like their slippers left, which daily newspaper they prefer to read, the kind of pillow they prefer and so on. A tailored in-room experience keeping in mind guest preferences is not just and exercise in meeting guest expectations, it anticipates and fulfils needs, a sure shot way of driving home the concept of 'a home away from home'. To a keenly observant associate, the opportunity to make the clues work towards a WOW moment may be limitless.
- *Offering unique experiences and amenities:* A thoughtful itinerary of out of the box experiences and unique amenities goes a long way in generating wow moments, resulting in creating repeat guests and positive word of mouth publicity. Refer to the Case study section of this Chapter for instances of such experiences and for details of innovative amenities refer the Case study presented in Chapter 10.
- *Penning personalised notes:* Many housekeepers employ personalised notes as a tool to convey that conscientious care has been taken to make the guests' stay as comfortable as possible. For instance, an associate who is aware that a guest likes to drink warm water as soon as he comes in from work, keeps the kettle on, at stipulated time and leaves a handwritten note with the guest's name, conveying the same to the guest. Refer to the Case study section of this Chapter for a case on handwritten notes.
- *Voicing heartfelt responses:* Varied ways of phrasing usual responses, instead of rote-learned phrases add a refreshing change and cuts down on rigid formality and puts the guest at ease. For instance, for a business guest who, the employee knows is heading for a meeting shortly, the associate or supervisor could say, "I hope you have a successful meeting, Ms. Kurien." or while leaving a room, say, "Is there anything else I can help you with, Ms. Kurien?"

- *Regaling interested guest with local tales:* Leisure travel guests from foreign lands get the feel of the place when employees regale them with titbits of local tales and history of the land.
- *Engaging children:* As more and more guests travel with families, it serves as a great initiative on part of the hotel to help keep the young ones entertained. Simple, thoughtful gestures such as placing age-related toys and bedtime books, small edibles, or such treats are ways to engage children and earn appreciation from their parents.
- *Delivering a WOW service:* Over and above the points mentioned, half the battle in creating Wow moments is won when housekeeping staff meet all expectations of the guests by providing proactive and seamless service throughout the guest's stay at the hotel.

SUMMARY

This chapter deals with the important role of supervision in housekeeping. Supervision is a role usually delegated to the supervisors by the executive housekeeper. There are many resources—manpower, material, and financial—that the executive housekeeper has to manage. She plans how best to utilize these resources. The next step is the implementation of her plans, and the supervisors of the housekeeping department are her supports in this process. The executive housekeeper delegates the resources and responsibilities to her supervisors. Effective supervision leads to consistent excellence in the performance of attendants and other workers. The supervisor is the leader of a team of attendants and responsible for the team's performance in accordance with the standards set by the executive housekeeper. This chapter outlines the role of supervisors in the housekeeping department. Their general duties and responsibilities are listed.

A major part of a supervisor's work involves inspection of jobs done. The trait of 'an eye for detail' comes to the aid of supervisors in this function. Inspections are carried out by supervisors in public areas and guestrooms. In this chapter, we have focused on guestroom inspection. The all-important tool of a supervisor—the inspection checklist—has been presented. Checklists come in many formats and the one given in this chapter is just a sample. Some checklists enumerate the areas or surfaces and require the supervisor to rate them on a scale of 1 to 5 (or a descriptive scale) with regard to their cleanliness or function.

The inspection of a VIP room is a process much more thorough than for any other guestroom. This is usually undertaken personally by the executive housekeeper.

Certain commonly neglected areas that the GRAs tend to overlook while cleaning guestrooms have been given. In all hotels, supervisors should develop their own list of neglected areas. A supervisor who ensures that his/her team maintains cleanliness in these areas too is sure to meet high cleaning standards consistently.

An important part of a supervisor's work is to handle any guest complaint on behalf of the housekeeping team. This requires a lot of tact, diplomacy, and maturity on the part of the supervisor. The types of guest complaints that supervisors may have to deal with are explained and certain tips for handling guest complaints are listed.

Supervisors and managers lead their team in achieving and exceeding guest satisfaction. A section on wowing the guests is included, outlining how housekeepers may work at creating 'WOW' moments.

KEY TERMS

Amenities Services or items offered to guests or placed in guestrooms for their convenience and comfort at no extra cost.

Baseboards A decorative, sometimes functional, horizontal band of usually the flooring material at the base of a wall.

Credenza Sideboard.

Dirty dozen A checklist of 12 areas identified in guestrooms that elude the GRAs' attention and tend to accumulate dust. These are mostly hard-to-reach areas and are hidden from the guest's eye.

The state of cleanliness in these areas reflects the standard of cleanliness in the hotel.

DND card 'Do not disturb' card, to be hung outside the guestroom by the guest to inform staff and visitors that the occupant does not wish to be disturbed.

Faucets Taps.

Fixtures Hardware items present in the guestrooms that cannot be moved or are difficult to move since they are fixed in position. For example, wall-mounted lamps and wash basins.

Guestroom inspection A planned, systematic process in which guestrooms are checked for cleanliness and maintenance needs and then okayed for occupancy by supervisors.

'Handle with care' (HWC) guests Guests who may have had some unpleasant experiences in the hotel or had some complaints, genuine or otherwise, are labelled as 'handle with care' guests by that hotel for the remainder of their stay or a future sojourn.

Inspection checklists Documents that list item by item all the surfaces and articles in guestrooms or public areas and the standards of cleanliness laid out for them, with space for supervisors to indicate approval or record their observations.

Log book An important register in the housekeeping department, it is here that instructions and messages for the staff of the next shift are written by the employees on the current shift.

Nightstand A small table or cabinet designed to stand near a bed as a place to hold anything likely to be required during the night. It is also called a 'night table' or 'bedside table'.

Room sections A group of 15–16 guestrooms reasonably contiguous to each other.

Service directory A booklet placed in hotel guestrooms in which the services offered by the hotel are listed along with their intercom numbers.

Vanity unit A unit comprising a wash basin and mirror surrounded by a flat counter where soap, a dental kit, a shaving kit, and tooth glasses may be kept.

Vestibule A small entrance hall or passage way between the outer door and the interior of a house or building.

VIP Very important person.

White-ragging A method followed in guestroom inspection in which a white rag is rubbed on a recently cleaned surface to check the degree of soil, thus indicating the standard of cleanliness.

Work order form A work order form is made out by the housekeeping department when any scheduled maintenance work is to be carried out in guestrooms or public areas. This form is sent to the maintenance department for them to undertake the repair as soon as possible.

WOW moment The moment of achieving exceeded customer satisfaction that comes about when an employee does something they don't necessarily have to do as part of their usual job, that which the guest is not expecting to be done and which elicits a response of 'Wow' from the guest when it is done.

16 Housekeeping Control Desk

Learning Objectives

After reading this chapter, you should be able to
- appreciate the importance and role of the housekeeping control desk
- list the forms, formats, and registers maintained at the housekeeping control desk
- explain the role of the control desk in coordination with the front office and maintenance departments
- understand the procedures for handling telephone calls
- explain the procedure for dealing with lost-and-found items
- understand the importance of a gate pass
- discuss the handling of difficult situations in the housekeeping department
- explain the procedure for handling guest transfers
- outline the role of computers and housekeeping software at control desk

Introduction

The housekeeping control desk is the central hub of the housekeeping department. This is the area in the department where all information is received and from where messages are dissipated to housekeeping and other staff present in various parts of the hotel. Thus, the control desk may be considered the nerve centre for to-and-fro communication and coordination in the housekeeping department.

In most hotels, this is the area where housekeeping employees report for work; collect the respective keys, sign for them; peruse the log book; get their briefing; and at the end of their shift, report back to. It is here that all departmental reports, records, and registers pertaining to housekeeping operations are maintained, updated and kept available for reference.

The main physical feature visible in most control desk areas is the key cabinet on the wall, where all floor master keys and store keys are kept under lock and key. Another common feature here is a large noticeboard displaying notices, general information, duty rosters, cleaning schedules, VIP lists, list of crews and groups in the house, and so on.

Needless to say, the control desk is manned round the clock for efficiency and smooth communication in the department at all times. The job description of a control desk supervisor is detailed in Chapter 2.

Role of Housekeeping Control Desk

The housekeeping control desk or the housekeeping central as it is referred to in some hotels, acts as the control and coordination hub, being the point of communication between the housekeeping employees, guests, and other departments of the hotel. Thus, the efficiency of the control desk determines the productiveness and smooth operations at the department. The essential functions of the control desk are enlisted below.

- ensuring smooth communication and coordination between housekeeping and other departments such as maintenance, front office, food and beverages, security, sales and marketing, and so on.
- receiving calls, messages and special requests from in-house guests over the telephone and passing on to assigned staff for action.
- maintaining various important records, registers, forms, and formats so that they are available and easily accessible for updation and reference to associates, supervisors and managers.
- keeping the PMS pertaining to housekeeping operations updated.
- serving as the centre where employees are assigned duties as per allocation and duty roster.
- being the centre where housekeeping staff report for work during their shift, attend briefing and report back again after their shift is over for debriefing.
- controlling all the keys pertaining to the department and its work.
- being the central point of indenting of items from stores.
- receiving and disseminating information on room status from front office to floor housekeepers such as VIP rooms, crew in the house and group stays and vice versa.
- receiving information from floors regarding inspected and ready rooms, updating the same in the room status on PMS so that it is conveyed to the front office.
- conveying minibar consumption to the front office to post in guest account.
- passing on information to front office on laundry utilization by guest to be charged to guest account.
- issuing gate pass for items to be taken off premises.
- organising found items to be stored and dealt with as lost and found.

Forms, Formats, Records, and Registers

Many important forms, formats, records, and registers are maintained at the control desk. Some of the common ones are outlined in this section.

Attendance register All housekeeping staff sign an attendance register kept at the control desk as a departmental level record, when they report for their shift. The leaves are marked in the register as per the duty roster by the control desk supervisor. The format of the attendance register is given in Exhibit 16.1.

Daily allocation register The daily allocation register filled by the executive or deputy housekeeper is kept at the control desk for all housekeeping employees to refer and follow as it outlines the work assigned to supervisors and GRAs based on the occupancy of the hotel. This register is a ready reckoner of staff placement in the housekeeping department. A sample format of this register is given in Chapter 6, Exhibit 6.2.

Exhibit 16.1 Format of the attendance register

Hotel Spring Leaves International

REGISTER OF ATTENDANCE

Department: .... **Month:** ....

S. No.	ID No.	Employee name	1	2	3	4	5	6	7	8	9	10	11	12	13	14	15	16	17	18	19	20	21	22	23	24	25	26	27	28	29	30	31	Days P & A

Duty roster file Duty roster prepared by housekeeping supervisors, giving details of staff scheduling for a month, are displayed on the noticeboard at the control desk and a copy is filed in the duty roster file for reference. Thus, this file has a record of previous rosters for reference. A sample duty roster has been presented in Chapter 3, Exhibit 3.15 (b).

Leave application form Leave application form books are kept at the control desk for easy access to staff. All filled leave applications too are filed at control desk. The format of a leave application form is given in Chapter 3, Exhibit 3.13.

Daily pre-briefing record A daily pre-briefing record prepared by assistant housekeeper prior to the briefing for a shift is maintained at the control desk. The manager taking the briefing refers to the details from this document during briefing. A sample format of a daily pre-briefing record is presented in Exhibit 16.2.

Exhibit 16.2 Sample format of daily pre-briefing record

Hotel Spring Leaves International

DAILY PRE-BRIEFING RECORD - HOUSEKEEPING

Date: .... **Day:** ....

Attendance	Grooming	Reports	Keys handover	Motivational thought
....	....	....	....	....

Occupancy previous night .... **Occupancy tonight** ....

Arrivals	Check outs	%	OOS rooms	OOO rooms

VIP/HWC guests (in-house & expected)

Guest name	Room no.	Arrival	Departure	Remarks

Key control register This is one of the most important registers maintained at the housekeeping control desk and is updated at the beginning and end of each shift. It is a part of the key-security system to be followed by the housekeeping department. Each employee who is handed over a key, any key, from the key cabinet is supposed to sign for it in a key control sheet in this register. At the end of each shift the control desk supervisor checks the register to ensure all keys are returned. The format of a key control sheet is given in Exhibit 16.3.

Exhibit 16.3 Format of a sheet in the key control register

Key control sheet

Date: ....

Key name & code	Name of key holder	Time out	Signature	Issued by	Time in	Signature	Received (indicate ✓)/ Remarks

Log book Another important register kept for reference at the housekeeping control desk is the log book. The log book is used to record all messages that staff from an earlier shift want to convey to the employees on the next shift. All managers, supervisors and associates reporting for work should peruse the log book for any important message left for them by the staff of the previous shift. The format of the log book is given in Exhibit 16.4.

Exhibit 16.4 Format of a page in the housekeeping log book

Hotel Spring Leaves International

HOUSEKEEPING LOG BOOK

Date: .... Day: ....

Shift	Time	Occurrences/ Follow ups	Remarks

Key history register This carries the records of all keys lost in the housekeeping department and those for which new keys or duplicates are being used. Ideally, though, for any key lost, a new lock-and-key unit should be installed rather than using a duplicate. This is done in the interests of security.

Maintenance register This register is used for recording all the maintenance work required in rooms. Based on the information contained in the register, the control desk attendant fills out the work order form (refer Chapter 2 for format) to be sent to the maintenance department. The format of the maintenance register is given in Exhibit 16.5.

Memo book This contains records of all the pending maintenance work for which the housekeeping department initiated work orders. The format is as shown in Exhibit 16.6.

SOPs book A book containing all the standard operating procedures (SOPs) to be followed in the housekeeping department is usually available for reference at the control desk. An example of a standard operating procedure document has been given in Chapter 12, Table 12.4.

Departure register This register is maintained at the control desk to record departures from guestrooms. The format of a sheet in the departure register is given in Exhibit 16.7.

Exhibit 16.5 Format of a page in the maintenance register

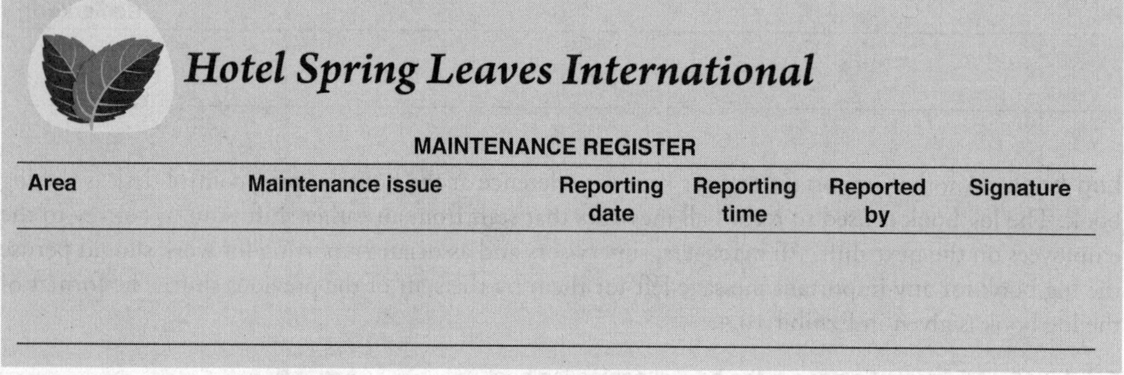
Hotel Spring Leaves International

MAINTENANCE REGISTER

Area	Maintenance issue	Reporting date	Reporting time	Reported by	Signature

Exhibit 16.6 Format of a sheet in the memo book

Memo book

Work order no.	Date	Description of maintenance work	Location/ room no.	Reported by	Job completed on	Signature of supervisor

Exhibit 16.7 Format of a sheet in the departure register

Departure register

Date: ....

Room nos.	Name of the guest	Time of departure	Given by	Cleared by	Time	Signature of the desk attendant

Guest messages register The housekeeping control desk also acts as a point of contact for in-house guests who require any housekeeping-related service. The housekeeping control desk is responsible for taking these guest messages and passing them on to the concerned staff. The message could be about the provision of certain guest loan items, a request for a second service, or a complaint and so on. A guest message register is maintained for this purpose at the control desk. The format of a sheet in the guest message register is given in Exhibit 16.8.

Exhibit 16.8 Format of a page in the guest message register

Hotel Spring Leaves International

GUEST MESSAGE REGISTER

Date: .... Day: .... Shift:.................... Control desk supervisor: ....

S. no.	Room no.	Name of guest	Message	Time received	Message conveyed to	Action taken	Time	Remarks

Guest history updated: .... Signature of EHK: ....

Housekeeping control desk register This register gives consolidated information on various aspects such as clearance of rooms to front office, housekeeping follow ups, details of room transfers and guest loan items given in rooms. The format of housekeeping control desk register is given in Exhibit 16.9.

Exhibit 16.9 Housekeeping control desk register

Hotel Spring Leaves International

HOUSEKEEPING CONTROL DESK REGISTER

Date: .... Day: ....

<table>
<tr><th colspan="8">Departure</th><th colspan="6">Follow ups</th></tr>
<tr><th rowspan="2">Room No.</th><th colspan="3">2nd & 3rd Floor</th><th rowspan="2">Room No.</th><th colspan="3">4th and 5th Floor</th><th>Room No.</th><th colspan="5">Follow up points</th></tr>
<tr><th>Time recd.</th><th>Cleared to FO</th><th>Time cleared</th><th>Time recd.</th><th>Cleared to FO</th><th>Time cleared</th><td></td><td colspan="5"></td></tr>
<tr><td></td><td></td><td></td><td></td><td></td><td></td><td></td><td></td><th colspan="6">Under repair rooms</th></tr>
<tr><td></td><td></td><td></td><td></td><td></td><td></td><td></td><td></td><th>Room No.</th><th>Reasons</th><th>Date</th><th>Time taken</th><th>Date clrd. to FO</th><th>Time</th></tr>
<tr><td></td><td></td><td></td><td></td><td></td><td></td><td></td><td></td><td></td><td></td><td></td><td></td><td></td><td></td></tr>
</table>

Carpet shampoo register This records the carpet-cleaning schedule that has been followed, recording each such project as it is completed. The format is given in Exhibit 16.10.

Babysitting register Babysitting is provided as a service by most hotels' housekeeping departments for guests who have small children. The guests requiring the service contact the housekeeping control desk and the desk attendant enters the request in the babysitting register. The format of a babysitting register is given in Exhibit 16.11.

Register for missing guest items This register is of great importance as the missing items may be found later and there should be a record giving the details of the item. Also, sometimes there may be a pattern in the articles missing from guestrooms and the name of a single employee may be found involved in each case. A format for the same is given in Exhibit 16.12.

Purchase requisition form All items to be bought for the department through the centralised purchase department are filled in this format and submitted to the purchase department in advance, after approval from the financial controller. A sample of the purchase requisition form is presented in Chapter 2, Exhibit 2.34.

Exhibit 16.10 Format of a sheet in the carpet shampoo register

Carpet shampoo register						
Date and time	Location/ room no.	Name of attendant	Date of last cleaning	Type of carpet and remarks	Signature of attendant	Signature of supervisor

Exhibit 16.11 Format of a page in a babysitting register

Babysitting register						
Date and time	Room no.	Name of the guest, number and age of children	Time of babysitting		Name and signature of housekeeping staff delegated	Remarks
			From	To		

Exhibit 16.12 Format of a page in the register for missing guest items

Missing property						
S.no.	Date	Description of the missing item	Name of the guest	Room no./ location	Reported by	Names of the GRA and supervisor who serviced the room

Stores indent book The stores indent book is kept at the control desk so that the supervisors may indent for housekeeping supplies that are required by the GRAs. The supervisors fill up the indent sheet in the book and the desk supervisor forwards it to stores after approval for the issue of supplies. The format of an indent sheet is given in Exhibit 16.13.

Consumption reports Reports detailing consumption of housekeeping supplies and amenities are maintained at the control desk to aid in preparing budgets, find out cost per occupied room for the given head of expenses and also to keep a check on expenses. A sample format for a consumption report for guest supplies is given in Exhibit 16.14. Similar reports are maintained on consumption data of cleaning supplies, laundry and so on.

Exhibit 16.13 Format of an indent sheet in the stores indent book

Hotel Spring Leaves International

STORES INDENT BOOK

S. no.	Indented items	Unit	Quantity indented	Quantity issued	Remarks

Prepared by: ....

Issued by: ....

Authorised by: ....

Received by: ....

Exhibit 16.14 A sample format of consumption report for guest supplies

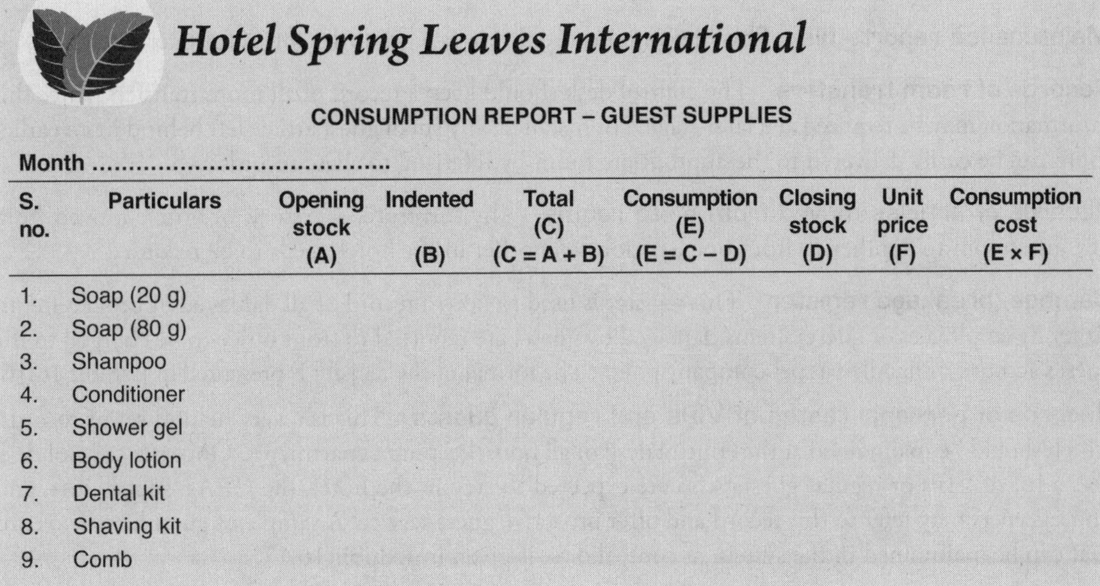

Hotel Spring Leaves International

CONSUMPTION REPORT – GUEST SUPPLIES

Month ....

S. no.	Particulars	Opening stock (A)	Indented (B)	Total (C) (C = A + B)	Consumption (E) (E = C – D)	Closing stock (D)	Unit price (F)	Consumption cost (E × F)
1.	Soap (20 g)							
2.	Soap (80 g)							
3.	Shampoo							
4.	Conditioner							
5.	Shower gel							
6.	Body lotion							
7.	Dental kit							
8.	Shaving kit							
9.	Comb							

Accident report book This records all the accidents of any sort that employees or guests have met with at the hotel. The format may be as shown in Exhibit 16.15.

Exhibit 16.15 Format of an accident report book

S.no.	Date of accident	Name of staff/guest	Nature of accident	Action taken	Supervisor in charge

Accident report form An accident report form is filled up when any employee or guest meets with an accident on the hotel premises. The format of an accident report form is given in Chapter 22. The information from these is then entered in the accident book.

Room status reports file This contains the previous housekeeping room status reports filed in order for reference. These reports are especially useful to the executive housekeeper in evaluating the levels of workload under different conditions. A sample housekeeping room status report may be referred to in Exhibit 6.6 of Chapter 6.

Discrepancy report file This contains reports of all discrepancies cleared with front office. A discrepancy, as explained in earlier chapters, is a situation in which the housekeeping department's description of a room's status differs from the room status information being used by the front office to assign guestrooms. The format of a discrepancy report is presented in Chapter 6, Exhibit 6.5.

Room inspection checklists file All room inspection checklists are filed in the room inspection checklists file kept at the control desk. These reports may be referred to in case there are guest complaints on cleaning. The executive housekeeper will be able to find the supervisor in charge of inspecting the particular guestroom in this file and confirm whether he/she checked the particular surface in question. A sample checklist is presented in Exhibit 15.4 in Chapter 15.

Maintenance reports file This file contains the previous work order forms for later reference.

Records of room transfers The control desk should keep a record of all room transfers, since this information may be required at a later stage. For instance, any small guest article left behind in an earlier room can be easily delivered to the appropriate room by referring to these records.

Records of articles moved from or to rooms Any furniture, accessory, or article moved from one guestroom to another or from one location to another in the hotel needs to be recorded.

Damage/breakage register This register is used to keep a record of all damaged or broken items, either by employees or guests. Items damaged by guests are reported to front office to be charged to the guest's account or handled as per company policy. The format of the register is presented in Exhibit 16.16.

Records of personal tastes of VIPs and regular guests This is a very helpful set of records, which should be maintained at the control desk of all housekeeping departments. Once the control desk gets a list of VIPs or regular guests who are expected to stay in the hotel, the GRAs, supervisors, and housekeepers may refer to this record and offer proactive guest service. A sample of guest history record that can be maintained in the system at control desk is given in Exhibit 16.17.

Exhibit 16.16 Format of damage/breakage register

Hotel Spring Leaves International

DAMAGE/BREAKAGE REGISTER

S. no.	Date	Time	Damaged item & description	Room no./Area	Name of guest/ employee	Found by	Remarks

Prepared by: .... Authorised by: ....
Issued by: .... Received by: ....

Exhibit 16.17 Format of guest history record

Hotel Spring Leaves International

GUEST HISTORY RECORD

Guest ref. no.: ....
Name of guest: .... Guest's address: ....
Designation: ....
Company: ....
Guest's birthday: .... Phone no.: ....
Guest's marriage anniversary date: .... Email Id: ....

Visit no.	Date of arrival	Room no.	Date of departure	Special instruction (VIP level – 1,2,3,4; Repeat; HWC; SL; Blacklisted)	Guest preferences (if not blacklisted)	Remarks

Lost and found register This register is filled in by the control desk supervisor when any article found in hotel's public area or guest room is deposited at the control desk. Lost and found function is discussed later in the chapter and the format of the register is given in Exhibit 16.20.

Leave application forms Leave application forms are stocked at the control desk so that they are easily accessible to employees who wish to take leave. A sample of leave application form is given in Chapter 3, Exhibit 3.13.

Work order forms Work order forms are used by the control desk to initiate scheduled maintenance in guestrooms and public areas. A sample work order form has been given in Exhibit 2.32 of Chapter 2.

Coordination with Other Departments

The control desk acts as the nerve centre for coordination with the other departments in the hotel. The coordination of the housekeeping department as a whole with various other hotel departments has been discussed in Chapter 2. The control desk primarily coordinates with the front office department and the maintenance department.

Coordination with Front Office

The control desk attendant receives the night report, the arrivals and departures list, the VIP list, and the list of crews and groups in the house from the front office. Based on these documents, the housekeeping department schedules the workers for cleaning, maintenance, and servicing of guestrooms and related areas.

Night report This report, prepared each night by the front desk attendant, indicates the rooms occupied that night and ones that are to become check-outs the following day. Based on this report, the executive or assistant housekeeper schedules employees for servicing these rooms. Once the rooms have been cleaned and made ready, the floor supervisor calls the control desk or the front desk directly, releasing the room for sale.

Arrivals and departures list The front office sends the arrivals and departures list to the control desk for the supervisors' reference, so that they can ensure that 'departure rooms' are ready on time for arriving guests.

VIP list The list of VIPs coming to stay at the hotel is passed on from the front office to the control desk. On receiving this information, the executive or the assistant housekeeper personally supervises the servicing of the VIP rooms. The housekeeping department also needs to make arrangements for flowers in the VIP guests' rooms, for which advance notice is required.

Groups in the house It is vital that the control desk be informed about the groups being registered in the hotel, as servicing their rooms requires a special schedule since the members of the group move together in terms of arrivals, sightseeing trips, and departures.

Crew in the house Airline crew members are registered in contiguous rooms in the hotel. They often have odd sleeping hours because of international time differences. These crews are given some special amenities, such as complementary biscuit platters and so on, as per the hotel's agreement with the airline. All these factors require that the housekeeping department be given advance notice of crew arrivals for special scheduling of GRAs cleaning these rooms.

Coordination with Engineering Department

All maintenance requirements needed on floors are entered in the maintenance register kept at the control desk. The control desk attendant notes down the room number, the maintenance work required, and the name of the GRA or the supervisor who called attention to the problem. From here on, the role of the control desk in initiating the scheduled maintenance is crucial. The moment any housekeeping personnel detects a problem that requires attention from maintenance, he/she calls the housekeeping control desk, stating the nature of the repair needed, the kind of assistance required, and the location in which it is required. The control desk then fills out a work order form (Refer Exhibit 2.32 in Chapter 2) in triplicate, each copy being of a different colour. One copy is sent to the

executive housekeeper and two copies to maintenance. The chief engineer keeps one of these copies and gives the other to the tradesperson assigned to do the repair. When the job is completed, a copy of the tradesperson's completed work order is sent to the executive housekeeper for acknowledgement of work completed satisfactorily. If this copy is not sent to the executive housekeeper within an appropriate amount of time, housekeeping issues another work order, which signals maintenance to provide a status report on the requested repair.

Lost-and-found Articles

All unclaimed articles found on the hotel premises should be handed over to the housekeeping control desk. Notices should be put up regarding the handing over of any personal property found so that all staff members are aware of where such property should be handed over.

What is a Lost-and-found Article?

Any article left behind by the guest in a checkout room or public area is referred to as lost-and-found article. The categories of lost-and-found articles are listed in Figure 16.1.

Fig. 16.1 Categories of lost-and-found articles

Lost-and-found Procedure

All lost-and-found articles should be stored in the lost-and-found cupboard, which is always kept locked. The lost and found room should be accessible only to the executive housekeeper and the control desk supervisor. A flowchart explaining the procedure for dealing with lost-and-found articles is shown in Figure 16.2.

Records by way of lost-and-found forms (see Exhibit 16.18) are maintained regarding the date of finding, time of finding, place of finding, name of the finder, description of the article, signature of the receiver, and signature of the finder. Efforts should be made to find the rightful owner of the article. If the owner of the article is known, that guest's address can be acquired from the front office or the travel agent and a letter informing the guest about the lost property may be written in the format shown in Exhibit 16.19.

The details should be recorded in a lost-and-found register, the format of which is outlined in Exhibit 16.20.

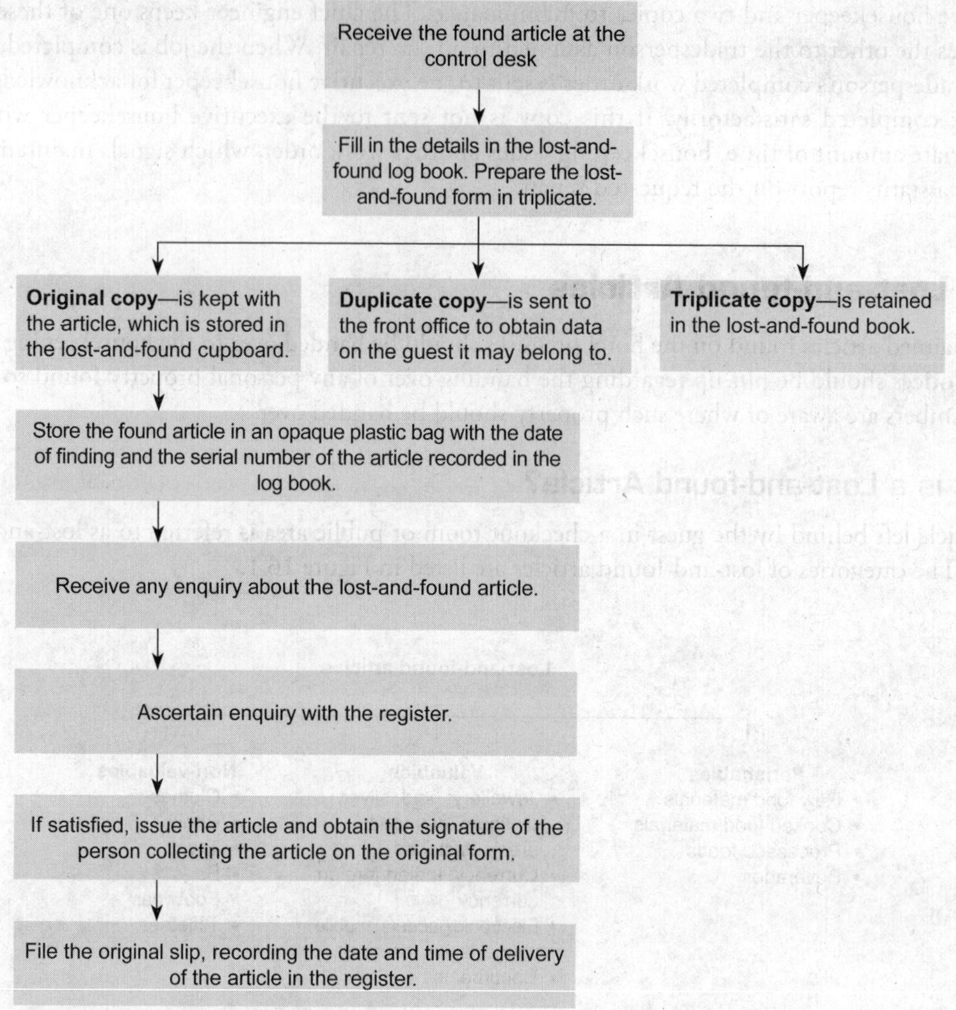

Fig. 16.2 Flowchart depicting the lost-and-found procedure

Exhibit 16.18 Sample lost-and-found form

Lost and found form

Date: .... **Time:** ....

Place: .... **Finder's name:** ....

Article/s found	**Description of article/s**	**Guest's address and contact number**

Signature of the control desk supervisor: ....

Exhibit 16.19 Format of letter to inform guest

Respected Sir/Madam,

We would like to inform you that the .... found by .... on .... date at .... time is lying with us and has not been claimed by any one so far. Therefore, Sir/Madam, if it belongs to you, kindly intimate us the details of the article so that we can arrange for sending it to your address. We, as our policy, keep an unclaimed article for a period of 6 months. If there is no response from your side before this period, we are not liable for any claims made later.

Thanking you,

Exhibit 16.20 Sample format of a lost-and-found register

Lost and found register								
Sl no.	**Date**	**Type of article**	**Place or room no. where found**	**Finder's name**	**Finder's signature**	**Name of the claimant**	**Claimant's signature**	**Remarks**

Lost-and-found Enquiries

All enquiries about items missing or lost articles are referred to the housekeeping control desk. Upon receiving an enquiry from the guest, the control desk supervisor first checks in the lost-and-found log book to see whether such an item is recorded. If found recorded in the log, the article is then taken out of the cupboard and the guest is informed that he or she may come to claim the article. If the guest is in the hotel, he or she is guided to the housekeeping control desk. On arrival at the desk, the guest is asked to describe the article in detail. If the description is a satisfactory match, he or she is asked to sign the lost-and-found log book, giving name, address, and telephone number. The date and time are also recorded. The article is then handed over to the guest. The finder of the article is informed of the same via a formal letter as shown in Exhibit 16.21.

Exhibit 16.21 Sample letter for informing the finder of the article

To the finder

....

....

Dear Sir/Madam,

I would like to inform you that the .... found by you in the .... and handed over to the house-keeping control desk, has been claimed by .... The article was handed over on .... against his/her signature recorded in the lost and found log book kept at the control desk.

Your name and address as the finder of the article have been supplied to the claimant.

Thank you for your action in handling the article.

When a lost article has been positively identified by an enquirer no longer in residence at the hotel and it is to be mailed to the enquirer, the article is packaged for mailing by a member of the housekeeping staff assigned with the task. The person taking the package for mailing signs the lost-and-found log book, assuming temporary custody of the article. The guest is informed over the phone that he or she will be receiving the article shortly and should acknowledge receipt of the same. The hotel usually charges the guest for mailing expenses.

Disposal of Articles not Claimed

Lost-and-found articles may be stored for 3–6 months by a hotel, depending on the hotel's policy. If at the end of this period the article has not been properly claimed by its rightful owner, it will be offered to the finder as his or her personal property. The format of the letter for this is given in Exhibit 16.22.

If the finder desires the article, he or she will be issued a gate pass by the housekeeping department, authorizing the removal of the article from the hotel. The finder is asked to submit a letter of indemnity while taking possession of the article. The format of the letter is given in Exhibit 16.23.

Should the person not desire the article, it may be auctioned or given to a charitable organization. How the article is disposed of is also noted down in the lost-and-found log.

Exhibit 16.22 Sample letter informing finder of unclaimed property

To the finder

....

....

Dear Sir/Madam,

The .... found by you and handed over to the housekeeping desk control has not been claimed yet. You may now apply for its possession and should call at the desk to sign in the lost and found log book, when the article in question will be handed over to you. If you do not wish to claim the article, please return it to the undersigned.

Exhibit 16.23 Sample format for letter of indemnity

To

....

....

I the undersigned hereby acknowledge having received the .... found by me on .... and undertake to indemnify against any claim or any demand which may be made against the company in respect of this property.

Signed ....

Witness ....

Gate Pass Procedure

A gate pass is a document of validity that is made and given to any employee or contractor who is legally taking out of hotel premises any of the following:

- Any property belonging to the housekeeping department, for repair or cleaning (returnable articles).
- Items discarded by the housekeeping department (non-returnable articles).
- Articles auctioned off by the housekeeping department (non-returnable articles).
- Any gift given to the employee by guests as a token of appreciation (non-returnable article).

In all these cases, the employee needs a gate pass issued by the executive housekeeper and approved by the security department. When an employee accepts a gift from the guest, he/she should also request the guest for a letter acknowledging that the item is a gift. A gate pass is issued to the employee only after perusing this letter. It must be noted, however, that most properties discourage employees from accepting gifts from guests in any case.

Different gate passes are made out for returnable and non-returnable articles. For returnable articles, the gate pass is made out in triplicate—one copy to be retained by the executive housekeeper, the second copy for the employee's own records, and the third copy for security approval. The security department should keep track of all the articles that have to be brought back by employees/contractors taking them out on a gate pass. In the case of non-returnables, only two copies of the gate pass need to be made, one copy for security and the other for the employee. A sample each of returnable and non-returnable gate passes are presented in Exhibit 16.24a and b respectively.

Exhibit 16.24 (a) Format of returnable gate pass

Hotel Spring Leaves International

RETURNABLE GATE PASS

To .... **Date:** .... **Gate pass no.** ....

We are forwarding the material listed below. Please sign and return the acknowledgement copy immediately. The materials listed below are returnable by:

Date: .... **Responsibility:** ....

S. no.	Description of item	Type/part no.	Unit	Total quantity	Remarks

Note: Please bring this copy along with the materials failing which material entry shall be prohibited.

Vehicle no. .... **Time out:** .... **Time in:** .... **Date:** ....

Receiver's name and signature: .... **Prepared by:** ....

Authorised signatory: .... **Signature of security officer:** .... **Seal**

Exhibit 16.24 (b) Format of non-returnable gate pass

Hotel Spring Leaves International

NON-RETURNABLE GATE PASS

S. no.	Description of item & purpose of taking out	Quantity	Remarks

Time out: .... Date: .... Receiver's name and signature: ....

Prepared by: .... Authorised signatory: ....

Signature of security officer: .... Seal

Handling Telephone Calls

The control desk manages intra- and inter-departmental communication, and handling telephone calls is the major function in the process. In general, too, it may be required of all employees to answer telephones when the need arises and, therefore, they must be trained well in telephone skills. It is always advantageous when the hotels have a telephone policy in place so that the procedures of answering, transferring, and making telephone calls can be strictly adhered to.

Answering calls Certain must-dos in answering telephone calls are listed in this section.

- Answer all calls promptly, at the most before the third ring.
- Answer politely, with a smile on your face, as it can be 'heard' by the person at the other end.
- Start with a greeting apt for the time of the day.
- Introduce yourself by name.
- Identify your department.
- Ask how you may be of assistance.
- Listen to the caller attentively and let him/her finish speaking before replying.
- Request any other information required for you to clarify what precisely the caller needs. Understand his/her needs completely.
- Ascertain the caller's name and identity. Use the caller's name when speaking.
- Assure the caller of your assistance, outlining the course of action you propose to take.
- Take the proposed action and get back to the caller to inform him/her of what has been done. Check that all is now to their satisfaction.

In case the assistance required is not in your hands or the kind of assistance required is some other employee's responsibility, transfer the call to the concerned person after informing the caller of the same.

Transferring calls When you have understood the caller's needs but you are not able to provide assistance, transfer the call to a member of the staff who you know will be able to fulfil the need. Before transferring the call, inform the caller of the name and department of the person he/she is being connected to. When the concerned person comes on line, explain briefly about the caller's requirements and then make the connection. In case you find that the extension is busy, inform the caller of this and ask whether he/she would like to be called back later or wants to hold the line for some minutes. In the former case, take the caller's contact number and ask for an ideal time to call back.

Holding calls When a caller is holding the line to be connected to the concerned person, he/she may feel the wait has been too long even though it may be just a few seconds' delay. This is a natural reaction while holding a call. Therefore, you should check frequently whether the caller still wishes to remain on hold or wants to be called back. While the caller is on hold, you can put on the 'on-hold music'. Avoid leaving the caller unattended for too long. Before finally connecting the line, inform the caller that you are connecting him/her now.

Taking messages There are situations when you have to take messages on some other employee's or guest's behalf. Write the message down on a message pad with a pencil. Take the message accurately, in a neat handwriting. Ensure that you fill in the date, the time, the name of the person for whom the message is intended, the name of the caller, the contact number of the caller, and a brief description of the message. Inform the caller that you will definitely pass on the message as soon as possible. After disconnecting, ensure that the concerned person receives the message as soon as possible.

Making calls Before making a call, ascertain whether and why it is needed. Decide on what you are going to convey. If required, make notes to help you put forth the points you mean to. Dial the number or the extension of the person you want and ask for him/her. Convey the information you have to deliver or ask for information you need clearly. Thank the person on the line.

Whether making or receiving calls, you should follow some golden rules of telephone etiquette. These are listed in this section.

- Answer promptly.
- Smile and be polite.
- Speak slowly, clearly, in a pleasing tone.
- Listen attentively to the other person without interruption.
- Ascertain and use the other person's name frequently.
- Ascertain the caller's need and be helpful, offering the relevant information if you can provide it.
- Be friendly but do not get too familiar.
- Note down important points from the exchange if required.

Handling Difficult Situations

Aside from these routine tasks, there may be some unexpected difficulties that the housekeeping department may have to deal with. The control desk plays a major role in handling such situations. The situation may be an emergency such as a fire, a worker or a guest meeting with an accident, the aftermath of a guest complaint, or a security problem. Alertness and presence of mind are helpful traits in dealing with difficult situations, and should be cultivated in individual employees. In a hotel, ideally all kinds of difficult situations should be catalogued and policies should be set forth for dealing with such situations. Moreover, employees should be trained in handling difficult situations through role-play, demonstrations, and drills. Two difficult situations are presented in this section and the possible ways to handle them have been described.

Situation 1 A guest calls the housekeeping control desk and says he is attempting suicide.

Dealing with the situation This situation implies that the guest is in a state of mental depression and needs counselling. The desk attendant should not panic; he/she must display presence of mind by ideally keeping the guest engaged on the phone by constantly talking and making him/her talk back. In the meanwhile, the desk attendant should get another member of staff to alert the security department so that they can access the room and take custody of the guest.

Situation 2 A guest calls up the control desk to say that she had given a shawl for dry-cleaning, mentioning the same on the laundry list. The shawl has been returned to her considerably shrunk.

Dealing with the situation The desk attendant should apologize to and try to pacify the irate guest. Then the desk attendant should inform the laundry supervisor about the situation, so that he/she can in turn apologize in person to the guest. The hotel must replace the shawl with a new one.

In this case, the problem probably arose because the laundry attendants did not pay heed to the 'special instructions' column in the laundry form, in which the guest had stated that the shawl needed only dry-cleaning. The laundry staff must have given the shawl a normal wash. The laundry supervisor should thus ensure that the staff pay heed to the 'special instructions' column in the laundry form in future.

Handling Room Transfers

Many a time, the control desk has to coordinate a 'room transfer' for a guest who may wish to be transferred to a room other than the one he/she has been registered in. The guest may request this change due to many reasons—the small size of the room currently allotted, acoustic reasons (for instance, the room being next to the elevator), the view from the room not being scenic, the room costing more than the guest's budget, and so on.

Once the front desk gives the clearance for the room transfer and provides an alternative room number to the housekeeping control desk, a supervisor and an attendant are assigned to help the guest with the transfers. All hotels have guidelines and policies laid out for handling room transfers. All the housekeeping employees concerned need to know these policies. The GRA may be required to pack the guest belongings, though this is very rare. The supervisor should personally supervise the attendant at all times. The GRA may, in case of light luggage, be required to carry the guest's belongings safely to the newly assigned room. In most hotels, the supervisor may call on the bell desk staff to aid in transferring heavy guest luggage. The GRA then places the guest items in the room as appropriate, making sure that the guest clothes are not creased in the process. The vacated room should be re-checked to ensure that no guest articles are left behind. The guest transfer should be recorded at the housekeeping control desk.

Role of Computers at Housekeeping Control Desk

A major portion of management of housekeeping operations is done through computers. PMS or MIS software such as Opera, Fidelio and IDS are a boon to housekeeping managers in managing the day to day operations of the department. The user-friendly housekeeping software modules have considerably reduced the burden of administrative work being done manually by housekeepers earlier. The main functions a housekeeping software provides at the control desk are:

Occupancy forecasts The PMS used by the hotel conveys the occupancy forecasts to housekeepers who then use this information for manpower planning and scheduling and also determine par stock of supplies, amenities and linen.

Rooms management Updated records such as occupancy report, arrival and departure reports and housekeeping status report are available in the system so that there is two way information flow between housekeeping and front office, making coordination efficient and smooth. The status of each room and whether it is dirty or cleaned and inspected, or OOO, etc. is always accessible. Moreover, information on VIPs, groups and crew in the house, room transfers, etc. is also available through the software.

Guest history management Guest history can be created and stored for future reference in the system. The housekeeping software keeps track of guest history, and can fetch the details of guest preferences and special instructions at any given time. Housekeepers can easily access the information and provide proactive service to repeat guests.

Guest feedback and requests Guest feedback, appreciation and complaints, special requests, etc. can be maintained and tracked through the system.

Customise inspection modules and checklists Customised inspection modules and checklists can be generated through the software to assist the supervisors as a handy tool.

Coordination with maintenance Periodic and scheduled maintenance tasks are coordinated with the maintenance department through the system. Repairs are notified instantly, rectified and the rectification communicated rapidly so that rooms are released for sale on time. Maintenance schedules are tracked by the software.

Chalking out cleaning schedules The housekeeping software helps devise cleaning schedules and keeps track of them, thus making the task easier for housekeepers.

Work allocation and scheduling of employees Automated room and public area assignments are generated based on the occupancy reports and housekeepers allocate work accordingly. The system generates data on the number of employees required in each shift for assignments in rooms and public areas based on the occupancy level of the hotel.

Productivity tracking The system can track productivity of associates as they service rooms and punch in the time of releasing the room for inspection by the supervisor. In the same way, the productivity of supervisors too is mapped.

Scheduling training The housekeeping software assists in designing the training calendar and implement training programmes on schedule.

Events communication Information about banquet functions and special events are notified through the system so that housekeepers can plan tasks and schedule employees accordingly.

Managing lost and found articles Detailed records of lost and found articles can be maintained in the system.

Inventory management and par stock calculations The software has material management function which generates par stock calculations, tracks inventory levels, and notifies when reorder levels are being reached. Cleaning supplies, guest supplies, linen and other inventory items are thus efficiently managed by housekeepers.

Expenditure and budget calculations The software can be used by housekeepers to prepare budgets and keep track of consumption and expenditure. Consumption and expenditure reports are generated easily for submission.

Generation of records and reports Most of the records and reports of the housekeeping department are maintained and generated through the housekeeping software. All forms and formats presented earlier in the chapter are maintained in the system.

Guest laundry reports The control desk associate updates guest laundry utilization details in the software and the details are retrieved by the front office and posted to the guest folio.

Minibar reports Minibar consumption is posted in the software by the control desk associate and this feed is accessed by the front office to update the minibar account in the guest folio.

Linen and laundry management Modules are available in the software to manage linen inventory and circulation. Laundry manpower scheduling, equipment AMC details, HLP reports, chemicals stock, wash formula details, guest laundry handling etc. can be efficiently managed through the software.

INSIGHT: HOUSEKEEPING SOFTWARE AND MOBILE APPS – A CASE OF OPERA

Opera Cloud Housekeeping Features

The primary housekeeping features of the Opera Cloud PMS used in many hotels and resorts globally are outlined in this section. The Rooms Management function allows housekeepers to schedule daily room cleaning, maintenance, and housekeeping staff activities. It provides information on room status, out of order/out of service rooms, and forecasting. Housekeepers can assign daily housekeeping duties, collect and view room status, view room forecasts based on reservations, view room floor plans and photographs or drawings of the property, resolve room occupancy discrepancies, and resolve room maintenance requests.

Housekeeping Board The software provides an area referred to as housekeeping board to manage status of all rooms. The housekeeping room statuses featured are: Inspected, Clean, Pickup, Dirty, Out of Order and Out of Service. The board displays room information such as room numbers and status, reservation status, day and evening room sections, room assignment status, guest service request status, location, and turndown status. Guest service status selections are DND or Make up Room.

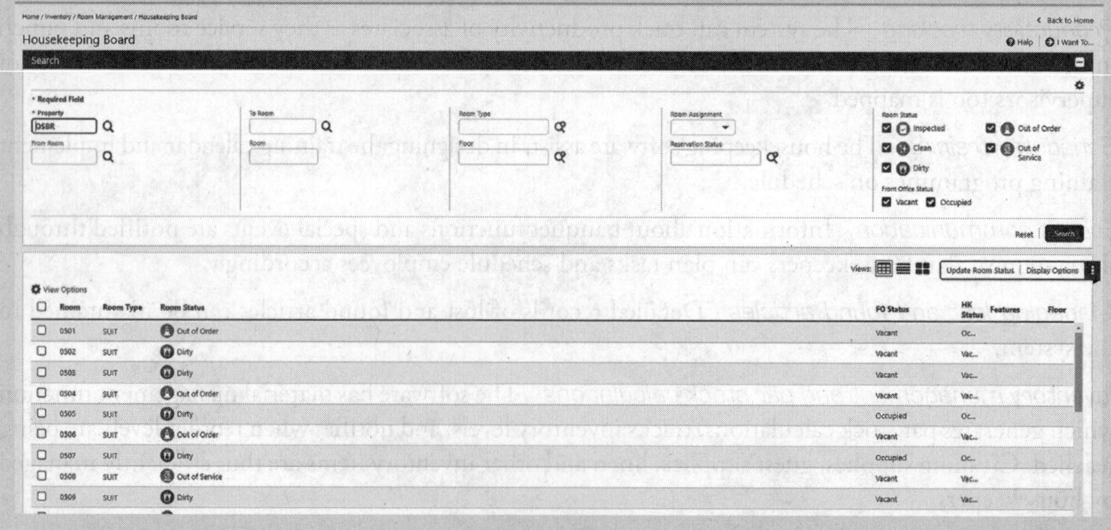

(Contd.)

INSIGHT *Contd.*

Manage Task Sheets Task Sheets are daily work assignments created for housekeeping attendants. On Task Sheet Companion, daily task sheets for each attendant can be created, edited and generated manually or automatically and the EHK can manage and reassign rooms to attendants as required. It also provides a task timer, break-time recorder and next room tracking.

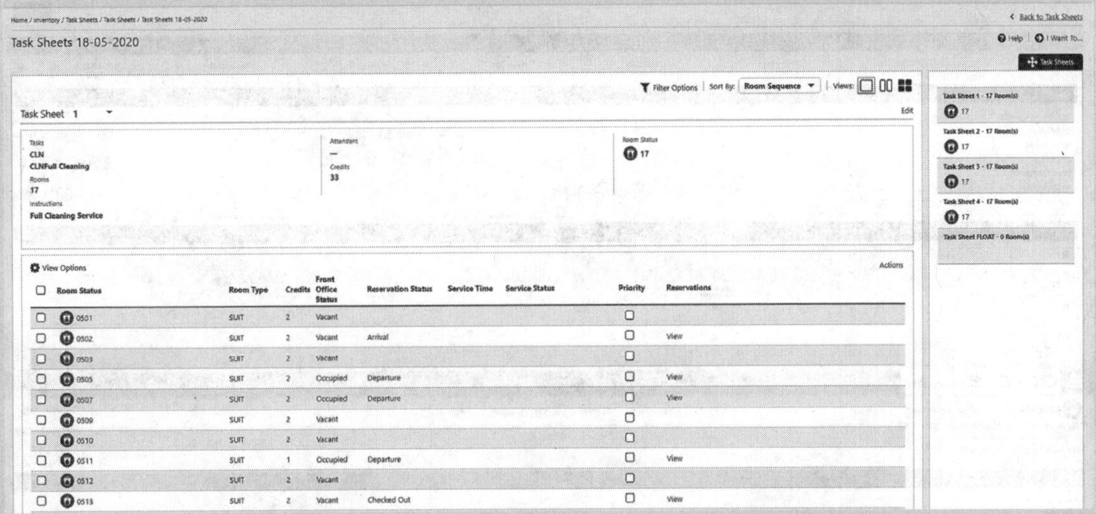

Home / Inventory / Task Sheets / Task Sheets / Task Sheets 18-05-2020

Back to Task Sheets

Task Sheets 18-05-2020

Help | I Want To...

Task Sheets

Filter Options | Sort By: Room Sequence | Views:

Task Sheet 1

Edit

Tasks
CLN
CLNFull Cleaning
Rooms
17
Instructions
Full Cleaning Service

Attendant
—
Credits
33

Room Status
17

Task Sheet 1 - 17 Room(s) 17
Task Sheet 2 - 17 Room(s) 17
Task Sheet 3 - 17 Room(s) 17
Task Sheet 4 - 17 Room(s) 17
Task Sheet FLOAT - 0 Room(s)

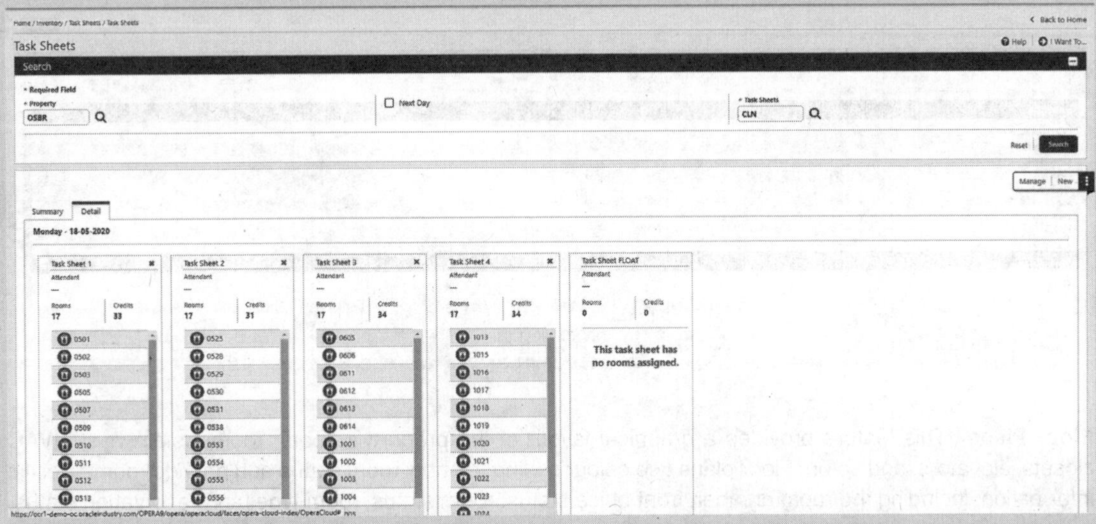

View Options

Actions

Room Status	Room Type	Credits	Front Office Status	Reservation Status	Service Time	Service Status	Priority	Reservations
0501	SUIT	2	Vacant					
0502	SUIT	2	Vacant	Arrival				View
0503	SUIT	2	Vacant					
0505	SUIT	2	Occupied	Departure				View
0507	SUIT	2	Occupied	Departure				View
0509	SUIT	2	Vacant					
0510	SUIT	2	Vacant					
0511	SUIT	1	Occupied	Departure				View
0512	SUIT	2	Vacant					
0513	SUIT	2	Vacant	Checked Out				View

Home / Inventory / Task Sheets / Task Sheets

Back to Home

Task Sheets

Help | I Want To...

Search

* Required Field
* Property
OSBR

Next Day

* Task Sheets
CLN

Reset | Search

Manage | New

Summary | Detail

Monday - 18-05-2020

Task Sheet 1	Task Sheet 2	Task Sheet 3	Task Sheet 4	Task Sheet FLOAT
Attendant —	Attendant —	Attendant —	Attendant —	Attendant —
Rooms 17, Credits 33	Rooms 17, Credits 31	Rooms 17, Credits 34	Rooms 17, Credits 34	Rooms 0, Credits 0
0501	0525	0605	1013	This task sheet has no rooms assigned.
0502	0528	0606	1015	
0503	0529	0611	1016	
0505	0530	0612	1017	
0507	0531	0613	1018	
0509	0538	0614	1019	
0510	0553	1001	1020	
0511	0554	1002	1021	
0512	0555	1003	1022	
0513	0556	1004	1023	
			1024	

https://ocr1-demo-oc.oracleindustry.com/OPERA9/opera/operacloud/faces/opera-cloud-index/OperaCloud#

HK Forecast This feature provides a summary forecast of the different housekeeping tasks to occur each day; for long-stay operations each room type can be setup with a task cycle, thus ensuring a daily quick clean and a weekly full service. Task supplies such as towels, bed linen, soaps etc. can also be forecasted. Forecast rostering feature is also provided to assist in designing duty rosters.

In the Housekeeping panel, the housekeeper can use the calendar to see the tasks that are scheduled for the reservation each day. One can also edit the calendar and add or remove a task from the reservation.

(Contd.)

INSIGHT *Contd.*

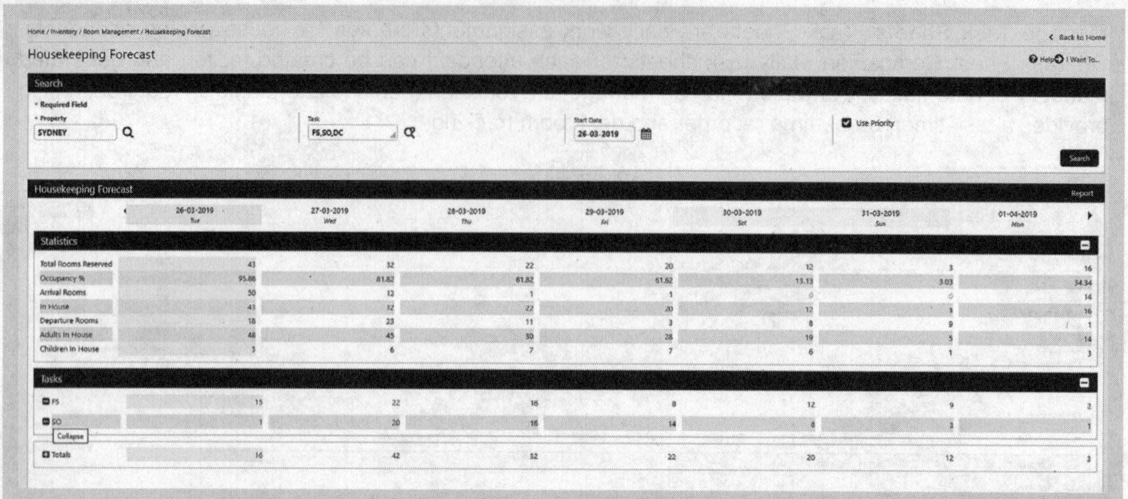

Home / Inventory / Room Management / Housekeeping Forecast

< Back to Home

Housekeeping Forecast

Help I Want To...

Search

* Required Field

* Property: SYDNEY

Task: FS,SO,DC

Start Date: 26-03-2019

Use Priority

Search

Housekeeping Forecast — Report

	26-03-2019 Tue	27-03-2019 Wed	28-03-2019 Thu	29-03-2019 Fri	30-03-2019 Sat	31-03-2019 Sun	01-04-2019 Mon
Statistics							
Total Rooms Reserved	43	32	22	20	12	3	16
Occupancy %	95.88	81.82	81.82	61.62	13.13	3.03	34.34
Arrival Rooms	50	12	1	1	0	0	14
In House	43	32	22	20	12	3	16
Departure Rooms	18	23	11	3	8	9	1
Adults In House	48	45	30	28	19	5	14
Children In House	3	6	7	7	6	1	3
Tasks							
FS	15	22	16	8	12	9	2
SO	1	20	16	14	8	3	1
Totals	16	42	32	22	20	12	3

Collapse

ORACLE Hospitality — Thursday, 23 Dec, 2021

OPERA Cloud — Client Relations — Bookings — Front Desk — Inventory — Financials — Channel — Miscellaneous — Reports

Home / Inventory / Room Management / Housekeeping Forecast

< Back to Home

Housekeeping Forecast

Help I Want To...

Search

* Required Field

* Property: ROSIE

Task:

Start Date: 23-12-2021

Use Priority

Search

Housekeeping Forecast — Report

	23-12-2021 Thu	24-12-2021 Fri	25-12-2021 Sat	26-12-2021 Sun	27-12-2021 Mon	28-12-2021 Tue	29-12-2021 Wed
Statistics							
Total Rooms Reserved	26	24	19	10	8	7	7
Occupancy %	2.39	2.52	2.07	1.48	1.33	1.26	1.26
Arrival Rooms	12	2	1	0	0	0	0
In House	14	17	18	10	8	7	7
Departure Rooms	8	4	6	9	2	1	0
Adults In House	28	26	18	10	8	7	7
Children In House	6	6	2	0	0	0	0
Turndown	6	6	4	4	4	3	3
Tasks							
DEEP	7	4	6	4	2	0	0
FS	5	4	5	2	1	0	0
KSHEET	8	6	4	4	2	0	0
TOIL	14	11	12	6	3	0	0
QSHEET	5	4	5	2	1	0	0
SANITIZA	4	3	2	2	1	0	0
LIGHT	2	3	1	1	1	0	0

Floor Plans This feature provides a graphical layout of the property's floors, rooms, stairways, HVAC closets, elevators, and so on. Floor plans use colour coding to show room status and provide room-specific information, including the room number, front office status, room status, room type, and reservation status.

Room Maintenance This feature helps the housekeeper to record, view, report and resolve maintenance requests such as repairing a faulty lock or air conditioning unit, a leaky faucet, and so on for configured rooms.

Attendant Console Through this feature the EHK is appraised of the progress details of each room attendant or the task sheet. Housekeepers can evaluate the time it takes to clean a room, completion percentage of tasks, total and completed number of credits, and relative location of a housekeeping attendant. The information is gathered from the Task Sheet Companion, which attendants use to keep track of their task sheets and room cleaning statuses.

(Contd.)

INSIGHT *Contd.*

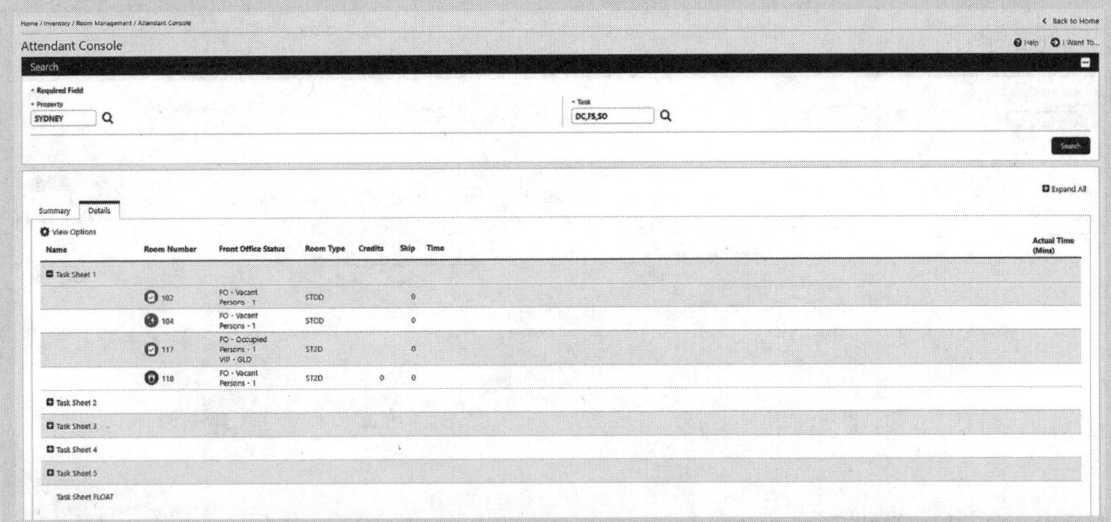

Service Request This feature provides the ability to define, track and report guest service requests on a room, reservation, profile or a combination of these. Service requests go through a pre-set flow - creating the request, completing it and then following up on the resolution with the guest.

Room Discrepancy This feature allows the housekeeper to view room discrepancies and manage sleep and skip discrepant rooms.

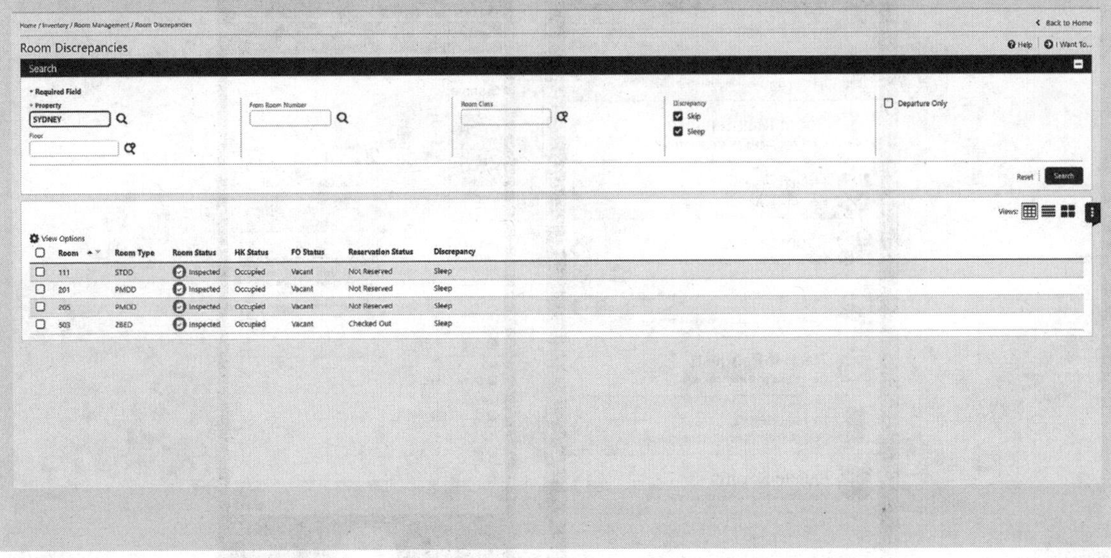

(Contd.)

INSIGHT *Contd.*

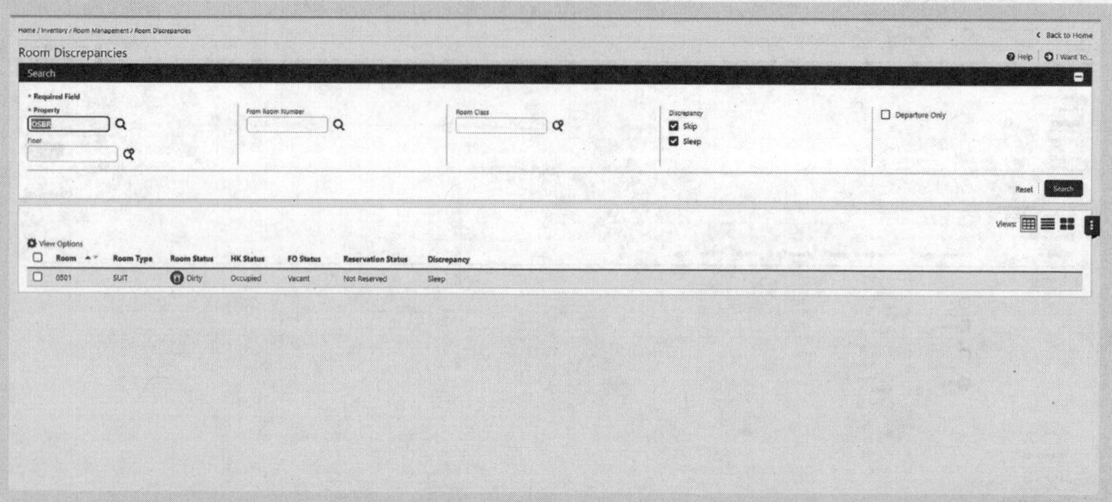

Mobile and Tablet Task Companion This feature is available on tablet or mobile for room attendants to view their assigned task sheet and manage the rooms assigned to the task sheet. The interactive feature allows them to update room status; create, view and resolve housekeeping traces/requests (actionable to-do), profile housekeeping notes and much more.

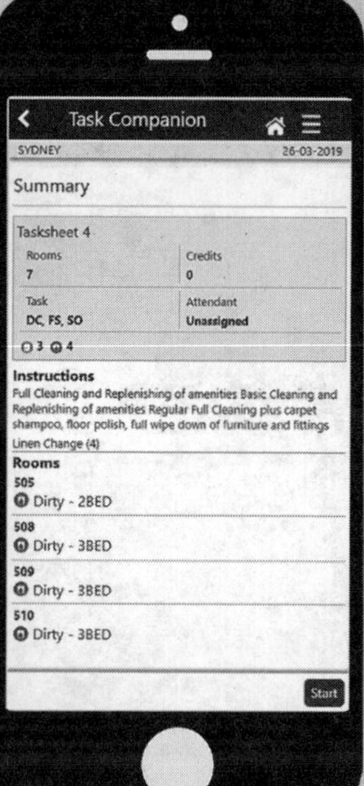

(Contd.)

INSIGHT *Contd.*

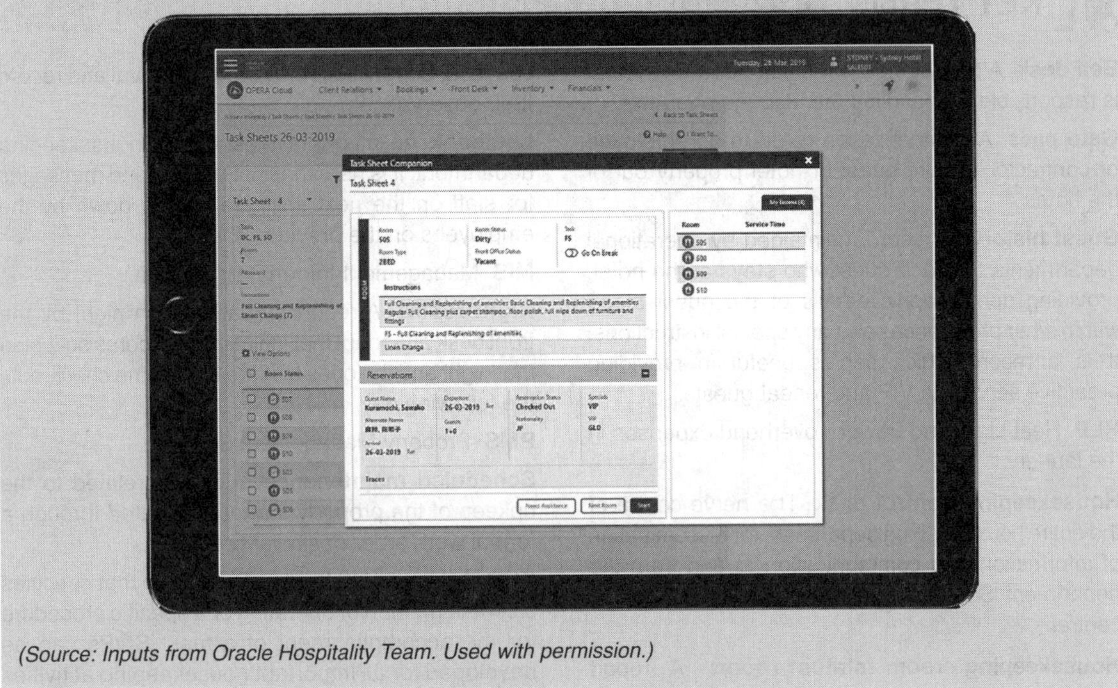

(Source: Inputs from Oracle Hospitality Team. Used with permission.)

SUMMARY

This chapter describes the importance and functions of the housekeeping control desk. The housekeeping control desk is the nerve centre of all communication from and to the housekeeping department. The housekeeping control desk is sometimes also called 'housekeeping central' because of its key role in the housekeeping department.

The documentation and files maintained at control desk are discussed in detail, with sample formats for a clear understanding of the kind of work the control desk is responsible for. The housekeeping department coordinates with other hotel departments to give the best possible service to the guests. The control desk coordinates directly with the front office and the maintenance departments.

The chapter also has a discussion on the procedure for handling lost-and-found articles, which in almost all hotel properties is the responsibility of the housekeeping department. The procedure of issuing gate pass is also explained.

Handling telephone calls is one of the major tasks of the control desk attendant. This function is dealt with in detail as it is the most important channel of passing communication in hotels. As a part of his/her daily routine, the desk attendant has to answer phone calls, take messages, pass on messages, and transfer calls. All these functions are explained in the section on handling telephone calls.

Many a times, certain difficult situations present themselves at the control desk. Each situation has to be dealt with in a different way, but certain hotel policies must be followed while dealing with the situations. Two such instances have been presented with possible solutions.

Room transfer is another function that the control desk needs to coordinate. The methodology for the same has been given. The chapter concludes with a discussion on the significant role of computers at the control desk and an insight on Opera Cloud software features is presented.

KEY TERMS

Bell desk A part of the front office department that is responsible for handling the luggage of guests.

Gate pass An authorization given to an employee or contractor to take guest or hotel property out of the hotel.

Guest history A record maintained by operational departments for each guest who stays at the hotel, providing demographic details of the guest along with his/her preferences and any special instructions. It is a record which serves useful in providing proactive service to VIP and repeat guests.

HLP Heat Light and Power - overhead expenses in the laundry.

Housekeeping control desk The nerve centre of the entire housekeeping department for dissemination of information and communication to and from the department. Sometimes referred to as housekeeping central.

Housekeeping room status report A report generated by the housekeeping department that indicates the current housekeeping status of each guestroom, based on a physical check.

Housekeeping supplies Cleaning supplies and guest supplies.

Inspection checklists Documents that itemize all the surfaces and articles in guestrooms or public areas and lay down standards of cleanliness for them, with space for supervisors to indicate approval and record their observations.

Log book An important register in the housekeeping department, it is here that instructions and messages for staff on the next shift are written down by the employees on the previous shift.

MIS Management Information System.

Night report A report prepared each night by the front desk attendant that indicates the rooms occupied that night and the ones that are to become check-outs the following day.

PMS Property Management System.

Scheduled maintenance Activities related to the upkeep of the property that are indicated through a formal work order or similar document.

SOP A document of a standing nature that specifies a certain method of operating or a specific procedure for the accomplishment of a task. SOPs can be developed for all important housekeeping activities and tasks.

VIP Very important person.

Work order form A work order form is made out by the housekeeping department when any scheduled maintenance work is to be carried out in guestrooms or public areas. This form is sent to the maintenance department to undertake the repair as soon as possible.

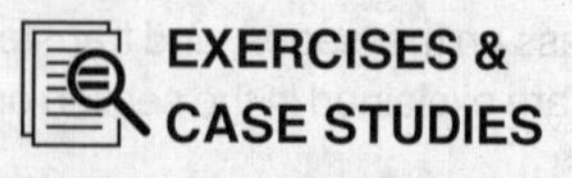

17 Budgeting for Housekeeping Expenses

Learning Objectives

After reading this chapter, you should be able to

- understand the concept of a budget and the advantages of preparing a budget
- plan and describe the types of budgets made in the housekeeping department
- outline the various housekeeping expenses
- explain the budget-planning process in the housekeeping department
- understand the income statement of the rooms division
- explain the importance and procedures of inventory control, stock-taking, and controlling expenses
- understand the concept of par stock or par level
- discuss the types of purchasing and explain the purchasing procedures for various inventory items in the housekeeping department

Introduction

Budgeting is one of the main planning activities of an executive housekeeper. It is the process by which, based on the actual performance of establishments in the past, estimates of expenditure and receipts are made and adjusted for forecasting future outcomes. Budgets can be defined in many ways:

'A budget is a plan by which resources required to generate revenues are allocated.'

'A budget is a plan which projects both the revenues the hotel anticipates during the period covered by the budget and the expenses required to generate the anticipated revenues.'

Advantages of Preparing a Budget

There are several advantages in preparing a budget. It provides an opportunity for taking a critical look at the costs of the department, reviewing past planning and present accomplishments, and then taking appropriate steps to accomplish more in the coming financial years. The executive housekeeper's responsibility in the budgetary process is two-fold. First, the executive housekeeper is involved in the planning process that leads to the formulation of the budget. This entails informing the rooms division manager and general manager what expenses the housekeeping department will incur in the light of forecasted room sales. Second, since the budget represents an operational plan for the year, the executive housekeeper ensures that the department's actual expenses are in line with the budgeted costs and with the actual occupancy levels.

The budget thus acts as a guide that provides the managers with the standards by which they can measure the success of operations. By comparing actual expenses with allocated amounts, the executive housekeeper can track the efficiency of housekeeping operations and monitor the department's ability to keep its expenses within the prescribed limits. Budgets provide a financial framework within which the housekeeping department operates. Thus, budgets should be carefully prepared and used to govern the department's spending.

The budget also acts as a guide as to which things need repair or replacement. It helps to determine what valuable pieces of equipment may be purchased and to pinpoint the areas where emphasis will be placed for the coming year. It can be said that the budget is an instrument used by the management for controlling and directing activities, especially purchasing activities.

Types of Budgets

Budgets may be of different kinds, based on the types of expenses involved, the departments, and the flexibility of expenses, as shown in Figure 17.1.

Categorized by Types of Expenditure

Based on the types of expenses and assets involved, budgets may be categorized into capital, operating, and pre-opening budgets.

Capital budgets Capital expenditure budgets or CAPEX budgets allocate the use of capital assets that have a life span considerably in excess of one year—these are assets that are not normally used up in day-to-day operations. Furniture, fixtures, and equipment (FFE) are typical examples of capital expenditures. Capital expenditures in the housekeeping department may include room attendant's carts,

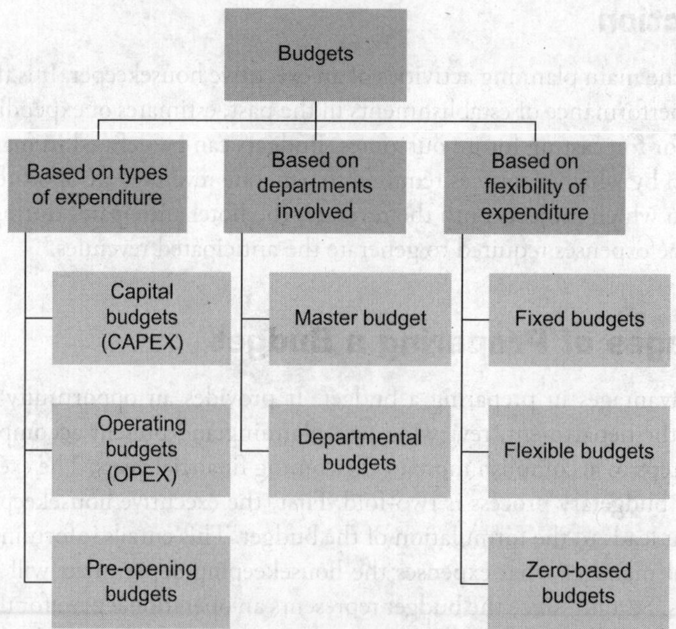

Fig. 17.1 Types of budgets

vacuum cleaners, general floor machines, carpet shampoo machines, sewing machines, and laundry equipment. The hotel building itself is also a capital asset.

Operating budgets Operating expenditure budgets or OPEX budgets forecast expenses and revenues associated with the routine operations of the hotel during a certain period. Operating expenditures are those costs the hotel incurs in order to generate revenue in the normal course of doing business. In the housekeeping department, the most expensive operational cost is of salaries and wages. The cost of all non-recycled inventory items, such as cleaning and guest supplies, are also operational costs.

Pre-opening budgets These force the planning necessary for the smooth opening of a new hotel. These budgets allocate resources for opening parties, advertising, generation of initial goodwill, liaisons, and PR. Pre-opening budgets also include the initial cost of employee salaries and wages, as well as supplies, crockery, cutlery, and other items.

Categorized by Departments Involved

Based on the department involved, budgets may be categorized into master budgets or department budgets.

Master budget These represent the forecasted targets set for the whole organization and incorporate all incomes and expenditures estimated for the organization.

Department budget Each department of the hotel forwards a budget for its estimated expenses and revenues to the financial controller. For instance, there would be a housekeeping budget, an F&B budget, a maintenance budget, and so on. In fact, the rooms division budget is in this case the combined budget of the front office and the housekeeping department.

Categorized by Flexibility of Expenditure

Budgets may also be classified on the basis of the flexibility of expenditure:

Fixed budgets These budgets remain unchanged over a period of time and are not related to the level of revenues. Such budgets include budgets for advertising, administration and contracts.

Flexible budgets These budgets predetermine expenditure based on the revenue expected and differ with different volumes of sale.

Zero based budgets These budgets are developed from level zero, i.e., commencing right at the beginning of the budget process, where all accounts have a value of zero, unlike the usual process where accounts start with the previous year's balance. This leads to a budget process which ensures optimal allocation of resources and erases out unnecessary expenses as it involves justification of resources allocation and business volume on part of managers. It entails that the managers justify the need and details of every expenditure. With aid of softwares and forecasting tools at their disposal, zero based budgeting is preferred by many management heads as it results in detailed evaluation of the cost effectiveness of departmental operations.

Housekeeping Expenses

Expenses that need to be budgeted for by the housekeeping department may be operating expenses or capital expenditures. These are outlined in Table 17.1.

Table 17.1 Housekeeping expenses

Operating expenses		Capital expenses
• Salaries and wages	• Uniforms	• Equipment and machines
• Employee benefits	• Laundry and dry-cleaning	• Furniture
• Contract services	• Pest control	• Fixtures
• Operating supplies	• Flowers and horticultural expenses	
• Linen	• Miscellaneous expenses	

Operating Expenses (OPEX)

Operating expenses include the following types of costs:

Salaries and wages This is the largest expense category in the housekeeping department, as the department easily has the largest workforce of all departments in the hotel. This category of expenses includes regular employee pay, overtime pay, incentives, leave encashments, and bonuses.

Employee benefits This category of expenses includes insurances on pay, employee pensions, payroll taxes, employee medical expenses, employee meals costs, employee provident funds, staff parties, and social events. In many organizations, the salaries and wages and the employees' benefits are calculated as one expense category, referred to as 'SWB' (salaries, wages, and benefits).

Contract services Expenses incurred on any contract service employed by the housekeeping department for special cleaning processes are included in this category.

Operating supplies These expenses include the costs of non-recycled items inventoried by the housekeeping department, such as guest supplies and cleaning supplies.

Linen New linen needs to be bought throughout the year as replacements and the cost of these is budgeted for under this expense category. These expenses also include all linen hire costs.

Uniforms This category includes the expenditure forecasted for purchasing material for uniforms, tailoring costs, or costs of renting uniforms.

Pest control This function may be contracted or carried out by the housekeeping department employees, and has to be budgeted for accordingly.

Flowers and horticultural expenses These include costs of flower arrangements in public areas and guestrooms and also garlands for guests where applicable.

Miscellaneous expenses This category includes costs of office stationery items such as log books, registers, forms, formats, writing material, and so on, as well as telephone, lighting, water consumption, and other such establishment expenses.

Capital Expenses (CAPEX)

Capital expenses include the cost of equipment and machines, furniture and fixtures, etc.

Equipment and machines This category of expenses involves the equipment and machines used by the housekeeping department (such as floor-cleaning machines, vacuum cleaners, and so on) and those provided in the guestrooms for guests' use (such as minibars, safes, and so on).

Furniture and fixtures The budget for guestroom furniture and fixtures is under the purview of the housekeeping department since it is responsible for their cleaning and maintenance.

Budget-Planning Process

The rooms division's budget-planning process depends on two main factors:

1. Forecasted room sales or occupancy levels
2. Cost per occupied room

Forecasted Room Sales

The room sales for the year are forecasted by the front office manager. The monthly break-ups are also outlined in this forecast. This information is given to the heads of departments far in advance for the preparation of departmental budgets.

Cost per Occupied Room

The executive housekeeper works out the cost per occupied room based on historical data, a sample of which is shown in Exhibit 17.1.

Exhibit 17.1 Sample historical data of operating expenses

Year →	2014–15	2015–16	2016–17	2017–18	2018–19
(A) Room sales (no.)	50,000	49,000	52,000	53,000	30,000
(B) Operating cost (₹)	180,00000	191,10000	208,00000	217,30000	12900000
(C) Cost/occupied room (no.)	360	390	400	410	430

Note: C = B ÷ A

Operating costs

These can be variable, semi-variable, or fixed.

Variable operating expenses These fluctuate with the occupancy level. These expenses include guest supplies, laundry, and such costs that increase or decrease in proportion to occupancy levels.

Semi-variable operating expenses These fluctuate partly according to the occupancy levels. For instance, employees in the housekeeping department cannot be hired or fired according to daily occupancy fluctuations. A minimum number of employees have to be on the rolls, no matter how low the occupancy may be. However, the executive housekeeper should work out annual leave and weekly off-day schedules based on occupancy forecasts to schedule manpower efficiently. Other semi-variable costs are cleaning supplies, flowers, linen, and uniforms.

Fixed operating expenses When pest control is on contract, this expense is deducted on a monthly basis and does not depend on occupancy.

Since the housekeeping expenses fluctuate based on the occupancy, the executive housekeeper uses only cost per occupied room as the guiding factor in planning the budget. Every operating expense needs to be planned individually for better control. Once the executive housekeeper knows the predicted occupancy levels, the expected expenses for salaries and wages, cleaning supplies, guest supplies, laundry, and other areas can be determined on the basis of the formula mentioned in Exhibit 17.1 that expresses cost in terms of 'cost per ocupied room'.

A history-based budget calculation is shown in Exhibit 17.2.

$$\text{Cost/occupied room} = \frac{\text{Operating expenses}}{\text{Room sales}}$$

Exhibit 17.2 Sample history-based budgeting calculation

A hotel had the following consumption of amenities and supplies for the months of October, November, and December 2021. Let us calculate

(a) the total cost of amenities and supplies for the month of October, November, and December 2021.

(b) the budgetary allocation for guest amenities for the housekeeping department for the last quarter of 2022 (i.e., October, November, and December 2022) based on the following data, at a forecasted occupancy of 75%.

Sl no.	Item	Unit Price (in ₹)	October 2021 Occupancy 90%		November 2021 Occupancy 86%		December 2021 Occupancy 79%		Revised Unit Price (in ₹)
			Total Consumption (A)	Total Cost	Total Consumption (B)	Total Cost	Total Consumption (C)	Total Cost	
1.	Shampoo	5.00	4,200		3,900		3,200		6.00
2.	Moisturizing lotion	7.00	1,700		1,600		1,500		8.00
3.	Shower gel	4.00	2,300		2,200		1,900		5.00
4.	Soap	5.00	4,500		4,100		3,700		6.00
5.	Shower cap	2.00	1,400		1,300		1,200		2.50
6.	Dental kit	10.00	4,500		4,200		3,700		12.00

Calculating individual operating expenses

Given in this section is an outline of the considerations in each category.

Salaries and wages To calculate this expense, the salaries and wages paid to all job positions—such as the executive housekeeper, assistant housekeeper, supervisors, GRAs, linen room attendants, housemen, and so on—have to be taken into account. The executive housekeeper first works out the number of employees required at various positions. If the occupancy levels are fluctuating considerably, the executive housekeeper should employ only the minimum staff required on the payroll and the rest of the staff should be hired on a daily-wages basis if workers are easily available. Duty rotas need to be planned effectively so that annual leaves and weekly off-days can be given on days of low occupancy. The most important tool in planning this expense is the staffing guide explained in Chapter 3. Once the number of work hours for each job position is determined as per the level of occupancy by consulting the staffing guide, the number of hours can be multiplied by the position's average per-hour wage to calculate the expected cost for that job position. The sum of the calculations (number of work hours × wage per hour) for all positions gives the total salaries-and-wages expense for the budget. The format used for calculation may be as shown in Exhibit 17.3.

Employee benefits These calculations depend on the number of work hours expected to be scheduled, the job positions involved, and the hotel's policies regarding employee benefits. In most properties, employee benefits include the cost of on-duty meals, payroll taxes, provident funds, medical expenses for the employees and their immediate family or insurance, pensions, staff parties, and social events. For calculation, the format given in Exhibit 17.4 may be used.

Exhibit 17.3 Calculating expenses for salaries and wages

Sl no.	Position	Wage/hour	Work hours	No. of employees	Wage expenses
1.	Executive housekeeper				
2.	Assistant housekeeper				
3.	Supervisors				
4.	...				
				Total no.	Total expenses

Exhibit 17.4 Calculating employee benefits expenses

Sl no.	Job positions	No. of employees	Expense of 2 meals per employee	Medical expenses	Expense of staff parties	Other perks	Employee benefits expenses
1.	Executive housekeeper						
2.	Assistant housekeeper						
3.	Supervisors						
4.	...						
Total expenses							

Contract services The cost of all contract services is averaged throughout the budget period of one year. Considering the historical data of contract services already used will lend an insight into the expense level to budget for.

Operating supplies The major types of operating supplies include guest supplies and cleaning supplies.

Guest supplies These are non-recycled inventory items and variable in cost. This expense category will depend on the 'cost per occupied room'. The executive housekeeper finds out the consumption factor of each item based on historical data. For instance, if the consumption factor arrived on for soap is 0.8; the budgeted room sales is 4,000 for a month; and the cost of a bar of soap with the hotel's monogram is ₹2.00, the budgeted expense for soap will be

$$\text{Consumption factor} \times \text{Budgeted room sales} \times \text{Cost of one unit}$$

$$= 0.8 \times 4{,}000 \times 2$$

$$= 6{,}400$$

In case two soap bars are to be placed in one guestroom, the amount obtained is multiplied by 2. In all cases, the amount needs to be further multiplied with the par number to be maintained for each guest supply. The monthly expenditure may be calculated using the format in Exhibit 17.5.

Cleaning supplies These are non-recycled inventory items that are semi-variable in cost. The higher the occupancy, the higher the volume of cleaning supplies used. It also needs to be remembered that the executive housekeeper schedules deep cleaning tasks during slack periods. Thus, 'cost per occupied room'

Exhibit 17.5 Monthly expenses on guest supplies

Forecasted monthly room sales = ...					
Sl no.	**Guest supply item**	**Consumption factor**	**Rate per item (₹)**	**Par number to maintain**	**Guest supply expense**
1.	Soap (80 g)				
2.	Soap (20 g)				
3.	Shampoo				
4.	Shaving kit				
5.	....				
Total expenses					

cannot be relied upon here. To calculate the expense for cleaning supplies, the executive housekeeper must refer to historical data and add provisions for any new products. The cleaning supplies expenses may be calculated using the format given in Exhibit 17.6.

Linen For budgeting linen expenses, the executive housekeeper needs to calculate the cost of linen per occupied room based on historical data. The higher the occupancy, the more the frequency of washing the linen. Historical data gives some guidelines in calculating linen expenses. A sample format for calculating linen expenses is given in Exhibit 17.7.

Exhibit 17.6 Calculating cleaning supplies expenses

Sl no.	**Cleaning supply item**	**Quantity used/month (based on historical data)**	**Rate per unit (₹)**	**Cleaning supply expenses**
1.	Soap oil			
2.	All-purpose detergent			
3.	Glass cleaner			
4.	....			
Total expenses				

Exhibit 17.7 Format for calculation of linen expenses

S.no.	**Linen type**	**No. of rooms (A)**	**No. of items/room (B)**	**Par (C)**	**Discard % (D)**	**Unit rate (E)**	**Amount [(A x B x C + D) x E]**
1.	Single bedsheets						
2.	Double bedsheets						
3.	Duvet covers						
4.	Pillow cases						
5.	....						
							Total:

Uniforms This expense includes the cost of uniform materials, stitching costs, accessories, and footwear. Each department is debited for its employees' uniform expenses. The executive housekeeper thus, needs to budget for uniforms for all housekeeping employees. To calculate uniform costs:

- Calculate the number of uniformed employees in all positions of all departments, keeping in mind the male–female ratio.
- List all types of uniforms.
- Decide how many pars are required and how often uniforms are to be exchanged.
- Consider turnover of employees.
- Provide for daily-wage employees, trainees, and so on.
- Include the costs of repairing uniforms.
- The total cost incurred at one time is divided equally between 12 months.

A sample format to calculate uniform budget is given in Exhibit 17.8.

Laundry The laundry expenses are primarily variable, except for uniforms. The executive housekeeper can refer to the historical data for calculation of laundry expenses as shown in the sample in Exhibit 17.9. To calculate the laundry expenses, the cost per occupied room needs to be known. Laundry expenses include:

- Chemical cost
- HLP (Heat Light and Power)
- Employee cost

Exhibit 17.8 A sample format for uniform budget calculation

S.no.	Type of uniform	No. of employees	No. of sets per employee	Rate per unit	Amount
1.	Saree – red, silk				
2.	Blouse – dark indigo				
3.	Coat – Black				
4.	Trousers – Black				
5.	Shirt – white				
6.	Shirt – Light blue				
7.	Chef coat				
8.	Chef cap				
9.	....				
				Total:	

Exhibit 17.9 Sample calculation of laundering expenses based on historical data

Year →	2015–16	2016–17	2017–18	2018–19
Room sales	52,000	53,000	30,000	42,000
Room linen (nos.)	3,00,507	3,20,000	1,68,000	2,35,200
Pieces per occupied room	5.8	6.00	5.6	5.6
Total cost	12,62,130	14,40,000	8,40,000	12,23,040
Cost per piece	4.20	4.50	5.00	5.20

The cost of laundering is expressed as follows.

$$\text{Cost per piece of weight unit} = \frac{\text{Total cost incurred in a month}}{\text{Total number of pieces or total weight of linen}}$$

Flowers The costs are primarily variable according to occupancy, but arrangements displayed in the public area do not depend on the occupancy. Historical data are a reliable tool in budgeting for this expense.

Budgeting Capital Expenses

Capital expenditure

The decision to incur capital expenditure in housekeeping arises from

- renovation of rooms or public areas
- addition of rooms or public areas
- replacement of equipment, furnishings, carpets, etc.
- introduction of automation in the department

Having received a decision from management on capital expenditure, the housekeeper should observe the following steps. A sample format for capital budget is given in Exhibit 17.10.

Supplier identification It is the executive housekeeper who does the field work in identifying suppliers. Considerations to be kept in mind are

- reliability of supplier's operation
- quality of product
- cost factors of product, transportation, and handling charges
- whether suppliers meet time parameters of supply
- whether suppliers meet the special specifications

Receiving competitive quotations Several suppliers should be identified because the hotel can then have the advantage of competitive prices. Quotations should be called for after informing the exact quality and quantity requirements of the hotel to the suppliers.

Selection of a supplier Usually a supplier with the lowest quotation is the apparent choice, but the decision should be a joint one with the involvement of the GM.

Making the budget This involves putting down the cost of the product, freight and transport, and handling charges.

Exhibit 17.10 Sample format for capital budget

Sl no.	Item	Item lifespan	Quantity	Unit price	Cost	Specification	Justification	Remarks

Signature of EHK: .... **Approved by:** ....

Income Statement of the Rooms Division

The income statement—or the annual profit and loss statement (P&L statement)—is reviewed by the rooms division manager with all the department heads, including the executive housekeeper, at the beginning of the budgeting process. This statement lists all sources of income that can be called 'revenue' and all the debited items that are paid out or are actual losses. Debits are then subtracted from the income. If the income is higher than the debits, the hotel posts a profit. If the debits are higher than the income, the hotel reports a loss, called a 'deficit'. Revenues and deficits are reported as gross totals, before any adjustment. Sales taxes are figured in or reported as net. The result of the income statement gives the management a baseline from which to start planning the next budget. A sample of an income statement is given in Exhibit 17.11.

Exhibit 17.11 Sample rooms division income statement 2019–20

Sl no.	Particulars	Budgeted	%	Actual	%	Variance	%
1.	Rooms sold	4,500	100	3,800	100	700	15.5
2.	Room revenue	1,35,00,000	100	95,00,000	100	40,00000	29.6
3.	ARR	3,000		2,500		500	
4 a.	Front office	4,05,000	3	3,80,000	4	25,000	6
4 b.	Housekeeping	8,10,000	6	7,30,000	7.7	80,000	9.8
5.	SWB total	12,15,000	9	11,10,000	11.7	1,05,000	8.6
6.	Linen	1,35,000	1	71,250	0.75	63,750	47
7.	Laundry	2,70,000	2	1,71,000	1.8	99,000	36.6
8.	Uniforms	2,70,000	2	2,00,563	2.1	69,437	25.7

Controlling Expenses

An operating budget is a valuable tool for controlling expenses and monitoring the course of operations during a specific period. Each month, the hotel's accounts department produces statements reporting the actual costs in each of the expense categories in the budget. These income statements or profit and loss statements are nearly identical to the operating budget. The actual costs are listed alongside the budgeted costs. Such reports enable the executive housekeeper to monitor how well the housekeeping department is doing in comparison with the budgeted goals and constraints. A monthly housekeeping income-expenditure statement, as shown in Chapter 15, Exhibit 15.1, is prepared by the EHK for submission to the general manager.

Controlling expenses in the housekeeping department means comparing actual costs with the budgeted amounts and assessing the variances, as shown in Table 17.2.

Table 17.2 Budgetary variances

	Favourable variance	Unfavourable variance
Revenue	Actuals exceed budget	Budget exceeds actuals
Expenses	Budget exceeds actuals	Actuals exceed budget

While comparing actual and budgeted expenses, the executive housekeeper should first determine whether the forecasted occupancy levels were actually achieved. If the number of rooms sold is lower than anticipated, a corresponding decrease in the department's actual expenses should be expected. Similarly, if the occupancy levels are higher than forecasted, the executive housekeeper can expect a corresponding increase in the housekeeping expenses. In either case, the decrease or increase in expenses should be proportional to the variation in occupancy levels. The executive housekeeper's ability to control housekeeping expenses will be evaluated in terms of his/her ability to maintain the cost per occupied room that is expected for each category. A sample cost analysis of HK expenditure (for guest supplies) is presented in Exhibit 17.12.

Exhibit 17.12 Sample cost analysis of housekeeping expenditure (only guest supplies depicted)

Category	Item	Unit price (A)	Quantity (B)	Amount (A × B)	Cost Per Room (CPR)
Guest Supplies	Soap (35 g)	8.99	800	7192.00	9.62
	Shampoo	10.12	200	2024.00	2.71
	Conditioner	10.04	200	2008.00	2.69
	Shower gel	10.16	300	3048.00	4.08
	Body lotion	10.11	200	2022.00	2.70
	Dental kit	9.00	500	4500.00	6.02
	Shaving kit	16.61	200	3322.00	4.44
	Comb	4.26	100	426.00	0.57
	Loofah	6.00	100	600.00	0.80
	For your care kit	5.93	100	593.00	0.79

Minor deviations between actual and budgeted expenses can be expected and are not a cause for alarm. Serious deviations from the budgeted plan, however, require investigation and explanation. If the actual costs far exceed the budgeted amounts while the predicted occupancy level remains the same, the executive housekeeper needs to identify the source of the deviation. In addition to discovering why the department is 'behind budget', the executive housekeeper needs to formulate a plan to correct the deviation and get the department back 'on budget'. For example, re-examination of staff-scheduling procedures or closer supervision of standard practices and procedures may be necessary. Other steps might include evaluating the efficiency and cost of products being used by the housekeeping department and exploring alternatives.

Constant control is required on the part of the executive housekeeper to ensure that the actual expenses tally with the budgeted expenses. To control expenses, the capital budget should be prepared with care as it involves a large sum of money to be spent on a small number of items. Asset tracking records must be maintained for guestrooms and public areas. A sample format for tracking assets is shown in Exhibit 17.13.

Controlling Operating Expenses

As far as controlling operating expenses is concerned, the executive housekeeper must ensure the following:

Effective documentation All inventories should be documented to monitor their usage rates and costs. Consumption reports must be updated and referred for this. A sample format of consumption report for guest supplies is given in Chapter 16, Exhibit 16.14.

Exhibit 17.13 A sample format for asset tracking

Asset tracking record – Guestrooms

Room No. ....

S.no.	Item	Description	Purchase date	Age track	Type of repairs	Date of repair	Date of replacement if any	Remarks
1.	Double bed							
2.	Mattress							
3.	Carpet							
4.	Lamp							
5.	Upholstery							
6.	Drapes							
7.	Curtains							
8.	Curtain hardware							
9.	....							

Zero-base scheduling This refers to hiring employees by taking into account the actual occupancy for a specified period of time. Following the staffing guide (as shown in Chapter 3) helps in controlling the largest housekeeping expense—that of salaries and wages for employees.

Right purchasing The executive housekeeper coordinates with the purchase department to purchase for the housekeeping department. The onus of controlling expenses on purchasing is entirely on the executive housekeeper, as he/she decides the right quality, right quantity, right price, right source of supply, and right time for purchasing.

Efficient training and supervision Training for new employees as well as training on new methods for older employees is a tool for controlling expenses. Efficient training ensures that the productivity and performance standards are met by all employees consistently. Lower productivity and performance standards may considerably increase housekeeping expenses. Efficient training and supervision also tend to bring down the expenses on cleaning supplies, as employees are then careful about usage rates and wastage. Thus, the cost of cleaning supplies per occupied room is kept under control.

Cost Control in Specific Areas

Some specific methods of controlling expenses in various areas in the housekeeping department's purview are outlined in this section.

Guestrooms and public areas In order to control expenses in guestrooms and public areas, the following measures can be taken:

- Staff must be trained to use cleaning supplies and equipment efficiently and economically. Supervisors must control and monitor their use. Wastage can often be reduced by physical observation and analysis of stock records.
- Appointing multi-skilled staff and giving them proper training to retain them controls expenses. This also enables the department to grow well, as experienced staff know the likes and dislikes of guests.

- The use of a key-tag or electronic-lock system helps conserve power by ensuring that the lights are switched off automatically as soon as the guest walks out of the room and the key tag is removed. This proves very cost-effective.
- A lacquer finish helps brass items last longer and show less wear, which reduces the use of proprietary polishes such as Brasso and indirectly saves labour, time, and money.
- Air-conditioners in currently vacant but occupied rooms should be kept on a low-power (energy saver) setting to save electricity while still preventing a musty smell.
- To clean and scrub 'back of the house' areas, soap oil, or floor cleaner may be substituted by half-used soaps and shampoos. This not only saves expense on floor cleaners but also is a method to use up discards.
- In VIP rooms, replace only those flowers that are shedding petals instead of changing the entire arrangement. Use long-lasting flower species, such that they may be slightly more expensive to source but their longevity compensates for the cost of a repeat purchase.
- In guest bathrooms, use plants such as the money plant, which look attractive and require fresh water only once in a while, thus avoiding the use of flowers in a bud vase that have to be continually replaced.
- Amenities such as dental kits, shaving kits, and combs should be placed in guestrooms only after getting confirmation of their occupancy from the front office, so as to avoid the misuse of these items by staff.
- Restrooms and toilets in public areas can have motion sensors to control power consumption.

Linen room The following practices can be adopted for cost control in this area:

- Old, condemned white sheets may be cut up and used in banquet halls as tablecloths for exhibitions and such.
- Old shower curtains can be cut up and stitched into aprons for the butchery department instead of purchasing traditional aprons.
- Condemned towels can be turned into dusters and mop cloths for cleaning surfaces.
- Ensure consistent stock-taking to help reduce the cost of equipment and materials.

Stores For controlling expenses in stores, effective stock-taking and control must be ensured as it significantly reduces the expenses involved in the provision of cleaning and other services.

Horticulture For cost control in horticulture, the practices listed here can be followed:

- A sprinkler system should be installed for watering the lawns instead of using hosepipes.
- Dead plants, leaves, and kitchen garbage can be composted in a compost pit built in a vacant part of the premises away from the accommodation areas. This saves on fertilizer costs as well as making efficient use of waste.

Inventory Control and Stock-Taking

The term 'inventory' refers to the stocks of purchased operating supplies, equipment, and other items held for future use in housekeeping operations. The executive housekeeper is responsible for two types of inventories. Recycled inventory items have relatively limited useful lives, but are used over and over again in housekeeping operations. These include linen, uniforms, most machinery and large pieces of equipment, guest loan items such as hot water bottles, heating pads, irons, and ironing boards, and so on. On the other hand, non-recycled inventory items are used up during the course of routine housekeeping operations. These include most guest amenities, cleaning supplies, and small equipment such as brooms, mops, cleaning cloths, and so on.

The executive housekeeper must establish reasonable inventory levels for both recycled and non-recycled inventories. Over-stocking should be avoided as it ties up cash and calls for a large storage area. There should also be an effective purchasing system to consistently maintain the inventory levels set by the executive housekeeper.

Stock-taking

This is the physical verification of inventory by counting up stocks of all items at periodic intervals. Stock-taking is also termed 'conducting inventory'. The frequencies for stock-taking of recycled and non-recycled inventory items are mentioned in Table 17.3 and Table 17.4, respectively.

To maintain the inventory levels, the executive housekeeper needs to determine the par level for each inventory item. Refer the section on 'Determining the Par Levels' in Chapter 5 where the process is discussed in detail.

Table 17.3 Stock-taking frequency for recycled inventory items

Linen	Monthly/bi-monthly/quarterly
Uniforms	Annually
Machinery and equipment	Quarterly/annually
Furniture	Annually

Table 17.4 Stock-taking frequency for non-recycled inventory items

Guest supplies	Weekly/fortnightly
Cleaning agents and materials	Weekly/fortnightly
Stationery	Weekly/fortnightly

Purchasing

As explained earlier, the expenses for housekeeping purchases are planned mainly in the form of a capital budget or an operating expense budget. The purchases can be of local or imported items. Indents for the purchase of stock items are usually generated from the main stores on the basis of re-ordering levels. On the other hand, the housekeeping department generates the indents of non-stock items. Stock items are the regular operating supplies such as soaps, shampoos, letterheads, and cleaning supplies. Non-stock items are non-consumable items such as crystal vases for flower arrangements, wooden hangers, and so on.

Efficient purchasing practices can make a significant contribution to the executive housekeeper's role in controlling expenses. The housekeeping department coordinates with the purchase department for all its purchases. Though the main aspect of the purchasing function is to procure a certain material or item, the material has to be the best buy at the right price. This calls for regular market surveys on the part of the housekeeping and purchase departments. Salespeople and vendors are regularly met for updates on the latest developments in other hotels and the industry as a whole. Each year, all products purchased for the housekeeping department are re-evaluated in terms of performance, durability, and sustainability to determine whether there is something new and better in the market. Product information is exchanged with other departments to assess the quality and price of the same or similar supplies. In case of a new product, detailed description and exact specifications, including size, colour, material, function, and approximate price need to be listed to save time for the purchase department as well as the supplier.

If the executive housekeeper is convinced that a particular supplier does a better job than other competitors, it is customary to name the company in the specifications that go to the purchase department. Although different properties have different procedures for processing and approving purchases, the evaluation of what is needed for the housekeeping department, when, how much, and from whom are the responsibility of the executive housekeeper.

Principles of Purchasing

There are five primary principles of purchasing that need to be upheld by the housekeeping and purchase departments: right quality, right quantity, right price, right time, and right source of supply.

Right quality The housekeeping department is responsible for providing guests with a clean, comfortable, safe, attractive, and luxurious environment. To meet and exceed the guests' expectations in this regard, the department needs to buy the best products. Value for money is a factor in each of the products supplied to the guestrooms and public areas. The entire range of items has to meet the standards and specifications determined by the department and the hotel's management.

Right quantity Placing a purchase order of the right quantity is of utmost importance for any organization. A supplier's lure of huge discounts for large quantities should not influence the department's decision. The following factors should be kept in mind when ordering the right quantity of material:

- The cost of the order being placed.
- The cost of storage and carrying charges for holding stocks.
- Quantity discounts.
- Stock levels and order points.
- Buffer stocks.
- Budgetary controls.

Right price One of the major concerns for both the housekeeping and the purchase departments is to get the material at the right price. An in-depth knowledge of the market is vital to make sure that the right price is being paid, that is, the payment corresponds to the exact value of the material purchased. While calculating the right price of ex-showroom, the station of dispatch, discounts, packaging, duties, taxes, and so on should all be considered to arrive at the gross price of the item. The terms of payments should also be attended to.

Right time The material should be made available at the right time. 'Lead time', which is the period between the indent originating from the consumer department to the instant when the material is ready for use, should be minimal. The total lead time, which includes the suppliers' lead time plus internal processing, clearance, receipt, and inspection time, should be as low as possible to work on lower inventory levels. The time should also be right as regards ensuring immediate availability of a particular product in the market.

Right source of supply The right source of supply is critical to the execution of the other principles of purchasing. If the source is right, the right quality and quantity at the right price and at the right time and place are a natural consequence. The selection of the ideal supplier is crucial for both the housekeeping and the purchase departments, in which they are aided by:

- Knowledge and experience
- Catalogues
- The Internet
- Hotel suppliers' directories
- Salespersons
- Trade associations and associated companies
- Libraries
- Counterparts

Stages in Purchasing

There are two stages in purchasing: the pre-order stage and the post-order stage.

Pre-order stage The following steps are involved in the pre-order stage of purchasing.

Receipt of purchase indent The indents should be checked for specifications, quantity required, the last supplier, and that supplier's rates. If any clarification is required, it should be referred to the indenting entity at once. If the item indented is not part of the planned budget, it needs the approval of the unit head before the indent is processed.

Floating of enquiries Where there is only one manufacturer of a particular product, it is better to contact that manufacturer straightaway instead of approaching commissioned agents or traders. The enquiry should contain complete information.

Procurement of samples for approval The concerned people in the organization must approve of the samples before an order is finalized.

Quotation and ordering The order should be placed with the right supplier, who must be identified on the basis of the right quotation for the right quality.

Post-order stage The following steps are involved in the post-order stage:

Issue of purchase order The purchase order should be issued once the pre-order stage is complete and the right supplier has been identified. Since it is a legal contract between the buyer and the supplier, the purchase order should include all details of the transaction. It should have the date of issue, purchase order number, expected date of delivery, product specifications, quantity (expressed in the appropriate units), brand, batch number, date of manufacture, and so on. Also, delivery instructions should be clearly mentioned, including packaging and mode of transport, time of delivery, and charges. Discounts, if any, must be mentioned in the purchase order as well. Terms of payment, taxes, and insurance should be clearly spelt out and the order should bear the purchase manager's signature, verifying the contents and the terms and conditions. In most organizations, the purchase order has to be approved by the financial controller and the general manager.

Confirmation of receipt of purchase order The supplier should confirm receipt of the purchase order in writing. A duplicate copy of the order should be signed, acknowledging, and accepting all the terms and conditions of purchase.

Follow-up There should be a regular follow-up to ensure that the items requested will be delivered on time.

Dispatch advice A dispatch advice note should be sought from the supplier to expedite the process of receipt.

Receipt note When the items are received in good condition and found to meet the desired standards after inspection, the receiving department should make out a goods receipt note (GRN) before transferring them to the main store. If the items do not match the standards prescribed on the purchase order, the purchase manager and the supplier are intimated immediately and the goods are rejected. If the items are deemed suitable for receipt, they are accepted and a GRN is sent to the department concerned to apprise it of the arrival of the goods.

Payment After the goods have been received and transferred to the department concerned via the main stores, the purchase department has the important function of following up on payments.

Types of Purchasing

Various types of purchasing methods are used in hotels. A single purchasing activity may also be a combination of several types.

Formal buying/competitive-bid buying Formal quotations are invited from sellers against written specifications for each item to be purchased. These requests for bids may be made through newspapers or other publications that are widely distributed, or they may be posted to interested sellers who can be contacted on the telephone. Along with specifications, the buyers also include in their requests such conditions as the last date for accepting quotations, approximate time allowable between order and delivery, mode of delivery, terms of payment, discounts, and so on. The quotations received remain sealed until the date of opening, which is also indicated in the buyer's request. They are then opened by the purchase manager in the presence of the bidders and representatives from the department for which the purchase is intended, as well as accounts and administrative staff, who are witness to the quotation accepted. The usual practice is to accept the quotations of the lowest bidder, unless the products clearly fail to meet the specifications.

Wholesale buying In this method of purchasing, a contract is signed with a wholesaler for the purchase of items at a specific price for a future period, along with the quantities required and when. The agreement specifies the intervals between deliveries for the contract period.

Negotiated buying This method involves negotiations between the buyer and the seller regarding prices and quantities. The method is generally used for items that are in limited supply, where both buyer and seller are keen that the product be picked up quickly. The buyers contact the sellers directly, negotiate for the price and quantity, and request that bids be submitted as soon as possible. Two types of contracts may be signed between the buyer and the seller. In a 'firm at opening price' (FAOP) type of contract, the buyer agrees to take the supplies at a price to be established in the future when the availability of the items is known. In a 'subject to approval price' (SAP) type of contract, the buyer has the option of rejecting the order if the price fixed in the future is not considered acceptable by him/her.

Contract purchasing/systems contract This method of purchasing assists the buyer and the seller to improve the re-ordering of items that are repeatedly called for with minimal administrative expenses. The method is similar to blanket-order purchasing as described later, except that the agreement is a long-term one and suppliers are, therefore, not changed frequently. Also, far more formal methods are used to select a supplier in order to eliminate personal considerations. The supplier selected is usually a specialist in the supply of the quantities demanded and offers the buyer discounts on the total contract. The rate of usage and frequency of re-ordering over the contract period need to be known. Under the systems contract, the buyer receives only those brands produced or sold by the contractor. This method of purchasing is commonly used for the purchase of housekeeping supplies.

Blanket-order purchasing A blanket order is an agreement to provide a specific quantity of listed items for a period of time at an agreed price. If the price is not settled at the time of placing the order, a method of determining it is included in the contract. Another type of blanket-order agreement is to furnish all the requirements for particular items for a specific period. In this case, the quantity is not re-evaluated until the fixed time period has elapsed. The blanket-order method

is best for items that are required in small quantities but more frequently and whose usage rate cannot be accurately forecast. A blanket order is usually contracted for one year, but variations exist across establishments.

Stockless purchasing In this case, the buyer does not keep the stocks of goods ordered; the supplier warehouses them for the buyer instead. The inventory is thus owned by the supplier. Sometimes the consignment may be kept with the buyer; however, it still belongs to the supplier. In such cases, the term 'consignment buying' is used.

Purchase by paid reserve In this method, money is paid in advance for a commodity to ensure continuity of supply throughout the year.

Total-supply purchasing In this type of purchasing, all required items are supplied by a single supplier. This helps in reducing the paperwork and negotiations need to be done with only one person.

Cost-plus purchasing In this method of purchasing, a supplier buys all the commodities and provides them to the housekeeping department. The supplier is given a small commission for this.

Centralized purchasing This type of purchasing is mainly practised by chain hotels. They purchase items for all their main properties together. This method helps them to source the items at cheaper prices as the quantity of the order is more, resulting in an economy of volumes.

Standing order In this method, daily suppliers are fixed for perishable items such as flowers or groceries.

Purchasing from van sales This method is rarely used for purchasing in the housekeeping department. In this method, purchasing is done from mobile shops that move from one place to the other.

Cash-and-carry method In this method of purchasing, the items are purchased from supermarkets such that prices are competitive and there are no minimum order levels. The disadvantages may be non-availability of certain items and non-availability of delivery services.

Weekly/fortnightly purchasing In this type, purchasing is done only weekly/fortnightly. This ensures regular availability of the items and makes the suppliers' prices more competitive.

Daily market purchasing/petty-cash system In this method of purchasing, item quantities in the store are checked on a daily basis and only items falling short are purchased. This method operates on a petty-cash system. 'Petty cash' is the sum of money set aside to meet minor expenses. It is effective for purchasing small orders from the local market in exchange for a bill so that a cash payment is made. The disadvantages are the possible non-availability of items in an emergency and the possibility of fluctuating prices.

Cash-on-delivery buying This ordering system involves payment on acceptance of a delivery. The order may be placed over the telephone or through the Internet.

Cheque-payment ordering/paperless purchasing This is a purchase order-and-draft system. It is a combination of the order and a blank cheque for payment. Besides the product specification, the order also contains delivery instructions, bank account number, unit price, quantity, taxes, discounts, and terms of payment. The supplier completes the pre-signed blank cheque, which states the maximum limit of the payment. A duplicate copy of the completed cheque is returned to the buyer for their records.

Auction buying This method of purchasing is useful for furniture and equipment that are not obsolete. Sometimes, certain export shipments that were rejected by the originally intended buyer are also auctioned to other buyers.

Annual Purchases of Guestroom Supplies, Cleaning Supplies, and Linen

These items may be divided into recycled and non-recycled inventory items. Let us first discuss the purchase of non-recycled inventory items.

Purchasing non-recycled inventory items

Worksheets are developed by the executive housekeeper to monitor usage rates and costs for the different types of non-recycled inventory items. For each product, the monthly use report identifies the vendor, the product name, and its intended use. Each month, physical inventories provide the executive housekeeper with information concerning how many purchase units of each item have been used. A sample worksheet for guest supplies is given in Exhibit 17.14.

Every week or fortnight, the floor supervisors take an inventory of these items. These are compiled with the par stocks to be maintained before ordering new supplies. A sample floor consumption order report is given in Exhibit 17.15.

All the items to be ordered are compiled from the floor consumption order reports and entered in the stores indent/requisition form, a sample of which is given in Exhibit 2.33, Chapter 2. The original copy of the stores indent is presented to stores, which in turn provides the items. On receipt of the items, the housekeeping department checks the quality and quantity of the items before accepting them. The received items are then disbursed from the housekeeping store to the various floor pantries, based on the floor consumption report.

Exhibit 17.14 Sample worksheet for gauging consumption of non-recycled items

Sl no.	Items	Units used	Cost per unit	Total cost	Cost per occupied room	Usage per occupied room
1.	Air freshener					
2.	Bath soap (20 g)					
3.	Shampoo					

Exhibit 17.15 Sample of a floor consumption order report

Floor Consumption Order Report					
Sl no.	**Items**	**Min. level**	**Max. level**	**Actual level**	**To order**
1.	Air freshener				
2.	Bath soap (20 g)				

Signature: ....

Purchasing recycled inventory items

For the purchase of recycled inventory items, the executive housekeeper raises a purchase requisition/ indent form and forwards it to the financial controller and general manager for approval. For a sample purchase requisition form, refer to Exhibit 2.34, Chapter 2.

Once the requisition is approved, it is directed to the purchase manager. The purchase manager then makes out a purchase order, which is sent to the supplier. The purchase order is similar to the purchase requisition, but also has the terms and conditions printed at the back. Once the items are received, the executive housekeeper checks the quality and specifications of the items before approving the consignment. Once approved by the executive housekeeper, the items are sent to the housekeeping stores with two copies of the GRN. The original GRN is retained in the department and the duplicate is signed by the executive housekeeper and sent back to the purchase department. The purchase department forwards the approved GRN with the bill (*challan*) to the accounts department for payment. The purchase cycle for recycled inventory items is outlined in Figure 17.2.

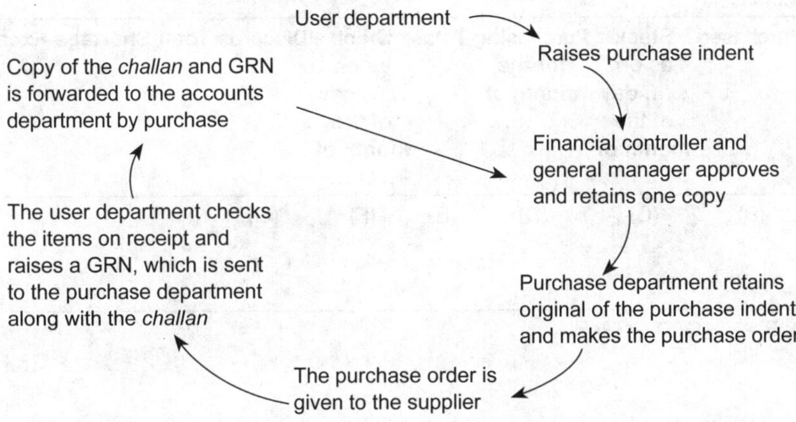

Fig. 17.2 Purchase cycle for recycled inventory items

Annual linen purchases Linen is the most important recycled inventory item in the housekeeping department. It is also the biggest expense, next to the salaries and wages of the housekeeping staff. Linen articles may require replacement due to wear and tear of initial linen purchases or items getting lost in the course of use. Linen articles that may need to be frequently replaced include bed linen and bath linen. The inventory records for linen (see Exhibit 17.16 for a sample) are a tool to help establish how long the existing stocks will last. To ensure that the purchased linen is worth the money spent, the executive housekeeper should consider:

- The suitability of the products for their intended use
- The expected useful lifespan of the linen
- The purchase price
- The costs of laundering

The cost of maintaining linen over its useful life is usually much greater and more important than its initial purchase price. Thus, the cost per use should be calculated in order to evaluate linen purchases, using the following formula:

$$\text{Cost per use} = \frac{\text{Purchase cost} + \text{Lifespan laundering costs}}{\text{Number of lifespan launderings}}$$

where, Lifespan laundering cost = Item weight × Laundering cost per kg × Number of launderings withstood by item

The quantity of each item of linen to be purchased annually is decided by assessing the hotel's quarterly requirements in order that the ideal par stock of linen is maintained. The inventory records are used to calculate an annual consumption rate that determines how much linen is used up and cannot be considered in the linen par. The annual linen purchases are made using the following formula:

Annual order = (Par stock level − Linen on hand) + Expected annual consumption

where, Consumption = Discards + Discrepancies

Exhibit 17.16 Sample inventory records for linen

Monthly room linen inventory

Month: ....

Sl no.	Item	Size	Purchased	Stock as on ...... day of the month of	Purchasing for the month of	Total	Stock as on ...... day of the month of	Discards	Total	Shortage	Exceed	To purchase
			(B)	(C)	(D)	(E)	(F)	(G)	(H)			

Note: B + C = D; E + F = G; D − G = H.

 Vendor Management

Vendor management refers to the planning and processes involved in managing suppliers or vendors by organisations. It includes activities such as selection of vendors, responsible procurement, contract negotiations and risk management. Vendors in hotels vary from sole proprietors to large branded companies. It is a wise strategy not to rely too heavily on a particular vendor and have options open.

Importance and Advantages

Standardised vendor management is crucial to handling and engaging with vendors effectively and brings in many advantages to the hotel company. It results in evaluation and selection of an ideal vendor through a smooth process within a short time frame. A standardised process will reduce risk of supply chain disruption, enable timely procurement, ensure the materials meet brand standards, lead to better negotiations, provide opportunities for cost saving, and offer the benefit of a shorter vendor onboarding process. An effective vendor management process leads to a productive relationship with vendors ensuring fulfilment for requests such as customised products, better deals and shorter lead times.

Vendor Management Process

Vendor management process involves many activities outlined below.

Evaluation and selection of vendors This calls for considerable research on the part of housekeeper and the purchase team of the hotel. The evaluation criteria generally used in organisations are appropriate quality, value for money, sustainability commitment, handling and packaging capability, on-time delivery, flexibility, reliability, experience, market reputation, performance history, specialised personnel, staff training,

financial stability, service capability, usage of specialised equipment, adoption of technology, certifications and licenses.

Scrutiny of vendor documents and licenses Documents and licenses such as business registration, trade license, service tax registration, VAT registration, ISO certification and ecomark or equivalent certification.

Negotiation of contracts Chalking out contracts specifying all crucial agreements between both parties is important. Details of chalking out contract specifications is discussed in-depth in Chapter 4.

Onboarding of vendors This stage entails approval of the proposed vendor after relevant documentation such as tax forms, licenses, insurance details and registration with the company contact and payment account details supplied by the vendor to the hotel company to set up the vendor as a ratified supplier.

Monitoring of vendor performance It is vital to keep the vendor on probation period to observe performance for a few months and this should be part of the contract. During this time the vendor's performance is monitored and evaluated against set key performance indicators or KPI, some of which may be conformance to quality and standards, adherence to delivery date and so on.

Engaging with vendors Housekeepers must engage with and guide their suppliers for a mutually beneficial partnership, service and product innovations, and performance. They should set realistic KPI to evaluate the suppliers. The vendors progress should be evaluated on these KPI, communicated to them in advance, and they should be informed whether expectations are being met. A probation period clause in the contract helps the vendors to address issues and implement corrective actions. Regular site visits to the key vendors help ensure compliance with code of conduct and standards, and check whether procedures laid out are implemented in reality. Face to face meetings with the vendors must be conducted to customise products and services, and help vendors to reach sustainability goals. Vendor recognition and reward programmes are an effective way to engage with vendors. Special events may be organised to showcase their contribution to the hotel company. Offer long-term contracts to the best vendor performers. Acknowledge vendor partners who have shown considerable improvement in their services and products since they onboarded the hotel company.

Monitoring and managing risks This involves continuous monitoring of the vendor in terms of risks such as contract breaches, non-adherence to compliances, non-delivery of goods or services, and unlawful practices or lawsuits that may impact the operations of hotel company. There should be clear and structured action for non-compliance or breach of contract.

Timely bill settlement of vendors Vendors must be paid timely as per the terms of the contract agreement.

Updation of vendor management software Most hotels use vendor management softwares which offer features to manage vendors effectively and the vendor data is consolidated in one place.

Responsible Procurement

Procurement decisions in hospitality industry can have a significant impact on the environment as significant number of products are imported from far-off countries to cater to guest demands, thus increasing the carbon footprint. Hotels are now increasingly moving towards responsible procurement in tandem with their sustainability commitment. Responsible procurement looks beyond the traditional parameters of price, quality, functionality and availability, and involves choosing products and services that have a reduced effect on the environment and society when compared to similar items that serve the same purpose.

Principles of responsible procurement

Hotel companies adopting the principles of responsible procurement stand to reap many benefits such as saving on costs, product innovation, improvement in sustainability goals, enhanced goodwill and reputation, loyal clientele, financial incentives and tax benefits, social benefits, for instance, of local job creation, local sourcing, community engagement, and so on. The principles of responsible procurement are:

- Researching and going in for green alternatives to products where possible
- Considering life cycle costing of the product
- Sourcing sustainable products with eco certifications
- Opting for energy efficient products
- Going in for the highest quality the budget permits
- Sourcing locally produced products
- Choosing natural, biodegradable products
- Opting for recyclable and recycled or reclaimed products
- Choosing fair trade products
- Avoiding disposable products that add to the landfill
- Engaging suppliers for mutual sustainability goal improvement
- Avoiding false claims of sustainability commitment or 'green washing'.

At the core of responsible procurement is the principle of life cycle costing or LCC, a technique of costing that establishes the total costs of purchasing a product or service from 'cradle to grave' by posing questions related to each stage of its life cycle. It considers questions such as the origin of the product, what it is made of and under what conditions, it's carbon footprint, how far it has been transported- in other words encouraging local sourcing, the components of its packaging and ways of disposal, the end use of the product, how it will be disposed after its intended use ultimately and so on. A checklist that may be followed for evaluation of vendors for responsible procurement is given in Exhibit 17.17.

Exhibit 17.17 Checklist for vendor evaluation for responsible procurement

Hotel Spring Leaves International

VENDOR EVALUATION CHECKLIST FOR RESPONSIBLE PROCUREMENT

Date: ....

Vendor company name: .... **Contact no.** ....
Name of representative: .... **email ID:** ....
Address: ....
....

(Contd.)

Exhibit 17.17 *Contd.*

S. no.	Particulars	Indicate ✓/×	Remarks
	Raw material		
1.	Locally sourced		
2.	No negative environmental impact		
3.	No harm to local environment on extraction		
4.	Least energy input during extraction		
5.	Recycled material		
6.	Exploitation-free practices (no child labour, no human rights violation etc.)		
	Manufacturing		
7.	Environmental policy and programme in place		
8.	Legal compliances met		
9.	Monitoring and assessment of environmental impacts		
10.	Successful action taken to offset effects of carbon footprint		

SUMMARY

The executive housekeeper prepares a house-keeping budget annually to allocate the resources required to generate revenues. While preparing the budget, the executive housekeeper reviews past planning and present accomplishments. The executive housekeeper must then ensure that the housekeeping department's actual expenses are in line with the planned budget. The budget is thus a useful tool that can track the efficiency of housekeeping operations. Budgets should be considered the financial framework within which the department operates, thus controlling expenses.

The various types of budgets are described in the chapter and the operating budget is discussed in detail as housekeeping is an operational department. The planning of a budget by taking into account the individual housekeeping expenses has been explained. The housekeeping budget may be regarded as a subset of the rooms division department's budget. This budget is calculated based on forecasted room sales by the front office and the cost per occupied room forecasted by the executive housekeeper. Maintaining the correct records in the housekeeping department is essential, as these are valuable documents of reference for obtaining historical data on expenditures, costs per occupied room, room sales, consumption of supplies, and so on.

The annual profit and loss statement is discussed in detail as this is the first document of reference at the beginning of the budget process. This statement determines the baseline from which to start planning the next budget. Expenses in the department need to be monitored and controlled for efficient management of the department. Controlling expenses in the house-keeping department means comparing actual costs with the budgeted amounts and assessing variances. Effective documentation, efficient training and supervision, right purchasing, and zero-base scheduling are the four aspects to be ensured for controlling expenses.

The consumption and use of inventory items needs to be documented consistently, as it is valuable in inventory control. Stock-taking is an important subroutine in inventory control. Establishing par levels is crucial to budgeting for housekeeping expenses. Calculation of par levels for both recycled and non-recycled inventories has been explained. The function of purchasing has been described in detail, as optimal purchasing is one means of controlling expenses. Purchasing procedures for both types of inventory items and in particular for the annual purchasing of linen have been described. Vendor management and responsible procurement functions have been discussed in depth.

KEY TERMS

ARR Average room rate.

Budget A budget is a plan that projects both the revenues that the hotel anticipates during the period covered by the budget and the expenses required to generate the anticipated revenues.

CAPEX budget Capital expenditure budget.

Capital budgets These allocate the use of capital assets that have a lifespan considerably in excess of one year—these are assets that are not normally used up in day-to-day operations.

Carbon footprint The amount of carbon dioxide, a major green house gas emission by an individual or an organisation through their activities.

CPR Cost Per Room. Also referred to as CPOR, Cost Per Occupied Room.

Deep cleaning Intensive cleaning undertaken in guest-rooms and public areas according to a special schedule.

FFE Furniture, fixtures and equipment.

GRN 'Goods received' note.

Inventories The stocks of purchased operating supplies, equipment, and other items held for future use in housekeeping operations.

LCC Life cycle costing, a technique of costing in responsible procurement that establishes the total costs of purchasing a product or service from 'cradle to grave' by posing questions related to each stage of its life cycle.

Lead time The period between the indent originating from the department in which it will be used and the the goods indented becoming ready or available for use.

Logistics Refers to the entire process of organising the way resources are acquired, stored, and transported to their final destination.

Non-recycled inventory items Items that are used up during the course of routine housekeeping operations. These include most guest amenities, cleaning supplies, and smaller pieces of equipment.

Operating budgets These forecast the expenses and revenues for the routine operations of the hotel during a certain period.

Operating expenses Those costs that the hotel incurs in order to generate revenue in the normal course of doing business.

Operating supplies The items essential to day-to-day housekeeping operations, including guest supplies and cleaning supplies.

OPEX budget Operating expenditure budget.

Par level The standard number of each inventoried item that must be in hand to support daily, routine housekeeping operations.

Performance standards The quality levels that employees' performance is required to meet.

Pre-opening budgets These budgets allocate resources for opening parties, advertising, initial generation of goodwill, liaisons, and PR. Pre-opening budgets also include the initial costs of employees' salaries and wages, supplies, crockery, cutlery, and other such items.

Productivity standards The quantity of work expected to be completed by each department employee.

Recycled inventory items Items that have relatively limited useful lives but are used over and over again in housekeeping operations. These include linen, uniforms, most machinery, larger pieces of equipment, and guest loan items.

Staffing guide A scheduling and control tool that enables the executive housekeeper to determine the total work hours and the number of employees required to operate the housekeeping department at specific occupancy levels of the hotel.

Stock-taking The physical verification of inventory items by counting up stocks of all items at periodic intervals. Stock-taking is also termed 'conducting inventory'.

SWB Salaries, wages, and benefits.

Zero based budgets Zero based budgets are developed from level zero, i.e., commencing right at the beginning of the budget process, where all accounts have a value of zero, unlike the usual process where accounts start with the previous year's balance.

Zero-base scheduling The hiring of employees for a specified period of time by taking into account the occupancy expected during that time.

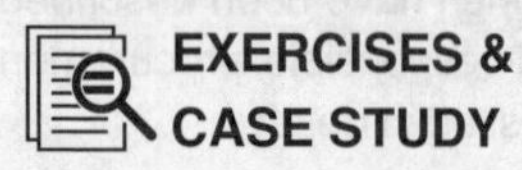

18 Textiles

Learning Objectives

After reading this chapter, you should be able to

- use textile terminology correctly
- classify different types of fibres and provide examples of each category
- identify different types of fibres, yarns, and fabrics by their characteristics
- predict fabric performance based on your recently acquired knowledge of fibres, yarns, fabric construction and finishes, and informative labelling
- make wise selections of textile products for specific uses
- suggest technical specifications for linen commonly used in hotels
- list and explain the various finishing processes
- care for textile products in a satisfactory manner
- appreciate the ethnic textiles of India

Introduction

The housekeeping department constantly deals with various types of bed linen, bath linen, table linen, uniforms, guest laundry, and soft furnishings. All fabric products are collectively called 'linen' in hospitality jargon, even though the fabrics may be made of fibres other than linen. Pure linen fabrics are generally used only for napery nowadays. Other hotel linen are made from blends of cotton with other fibres. Every housekeeper should, therefore, have a good knowledge of the various textile fibres and the fabrics made from them, since he/she is responsible for the care and maintenance of all the aforementioned textile items.

Textile Terminology

The term 'textile' is derived from the Latin word *textilis*, in turn from the verb *texere*, which means 'to weave'. Today, the term refers to and includes all fabrics, made of all kinds of yarns and fibres, and not just the woven kind. 'Cloth' is a general term used for a fabric or textile. A *fibre* is the basic unit from which any fabric is made. Fibres may be classified as staple or filament. *Staple* fibres are short-length fibres. *Filament* fibres are long and often continuous for a length of yarn. The physical and chemical properties of the fibres contribute to the nature of the fabric woven from it. *Yarns* are threads or thread-like structures made by twisting together several staple fibres or filament fibres. It is yarn which is used for weaving or knitting textiles. The process of making a yarn from fibre is called *spinning*.

A fabric is typically made by the interlacing of yarns or fibres. The most common process of such interlacing is weaving. Different types of weaves are used to make fabrics with varying characteristics. (After weaving, knitting is the most usual method of fabric construction.) Weaves influence the texture, durability, elasticity, absorbency, lustre, and appearance of fabrics. Generally, firm, closely woven fabrics with an equal number of yarns running lengthwise and crosswise are strong and durable. The yarns running lengthwise through a fabric are called *warp* yarns or 'ends' and the crosswise yarns in a fabric are called *weft yarns*, filling yarns, or 'picks'. The term *thread count* is used to indicate the number of warp ends and weft picks per unit of measure of a fabric. The longitudinal, visibly distinct edge of a fabric, closed by loops of weft yarn, is called the *selvedge*. The selvedge is usually denser and, hence, stronger than the rest of the fabric. It prevents the fabric from unravelling.

A fabric may be made from more than one type of fibre. Different fibres can be blended together to form a single yarn, or different types of yarn can be mixed in the fabric. Each type of fibre has its own advantages and limitations. Textile scientists have worked out two ways to overcome the most common limitations of fabrics: blending of fibres and application of finishes on fabrics.

Blended fabrics are made of yarn in which two or more fibres are mixed while the yarn is spun. Another class of blends is union fabric. In *union fabrics*, each yarn is of a single type of fibre. For example, the warp yarns may be made of cotton and the weft yarns made of wool. In other words, in most blends, fibres are mixed before spinning, while in union fabrics, fibres are mixed during weaving or plying of yarns.

A *finish* is a treatment imparted to a fabric to improve its qualities (such as appearance, hand, and drape) or introduce certain characteristics, such as water repellence, fire retardant qualities, and so on.

Other relevant textile terms are explained where they appear in the text of this chapter.

Classification and Identification of Textile Fibres

From ancient times to just a century ago, all the fibres used in making fabrics was obtained from natural sources, mostly plants. Nowadays, many man-made fibres have been created. Fibres are classified according to their source, length, and content. The classification of fibres is depicted in Figures 18.1, 18.2, and 18.3.

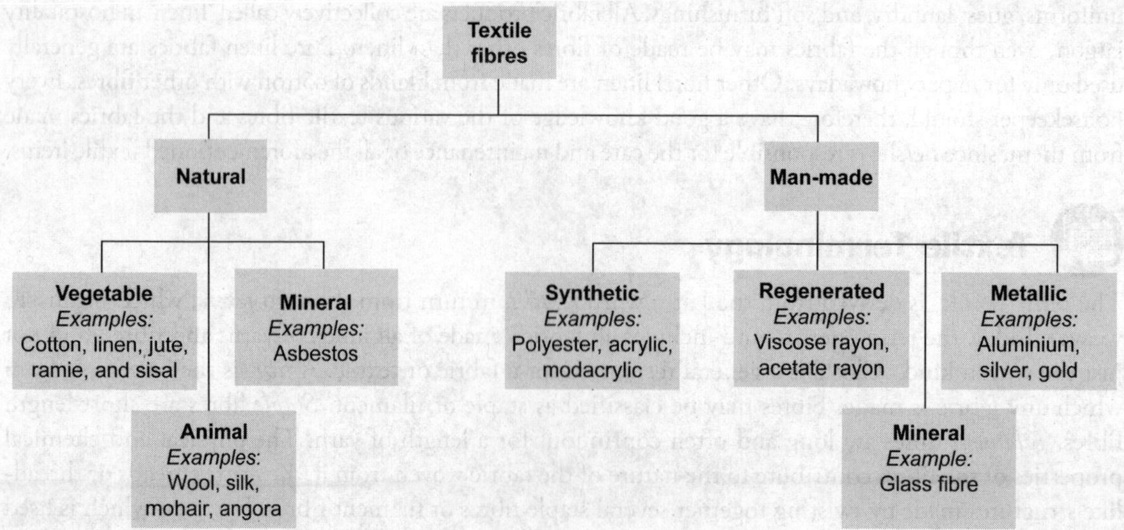

Fig. 18.1 Classification of fibres based on source

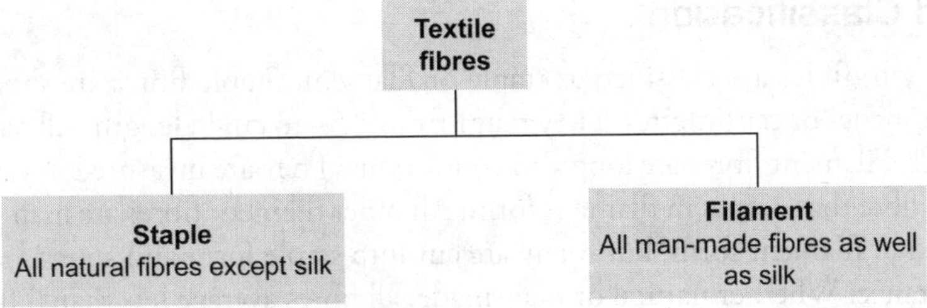

Fig. 18.2 Classification of fibres based on length

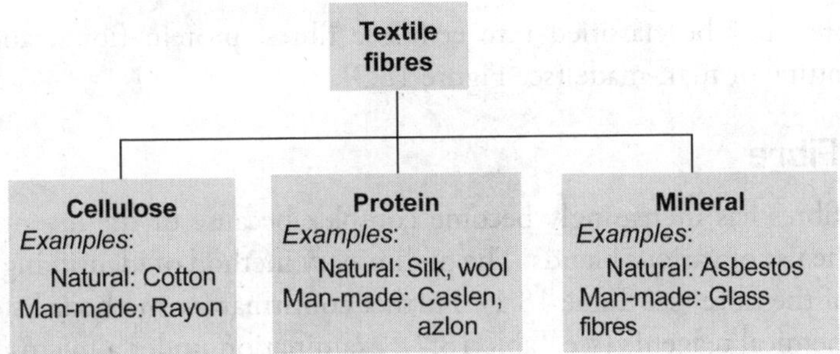

Fig. 18.3 Classification of fibres based on content

Source-based Classification

Based on source, fibres may be classified into two categories—natural and man-made.

Natural fibres

Natural fibres—that is, those obtained from nature—are classified as vegetable, animal, and mineral fibres. Vegetable fibres found in the cell walls of plants are cellulosic; whereas animal fibres derived from both insects and mammals are proteins. The mineral fibre asbestos is mined from certain types of rocks.

Man-made fibres

These are manufactured in various ways. Man-made fibres can be synthetic, regenerated, metallic, and mineral fibres.

Synthetic fibres These are manufactured from petrochemicals. Here, the raw material is completely different from the end product. For example, polyester is made from the raw materials ethylene glycol and terephthalic acid.

Regenerated fibres Unlike synthetic fibres, these are made from substances retrieved from natural sources, which are then converted into fibre form. For example, wood pulp (chemically a cellulose) is converted into cellulose fibres such as viscose rayon. Man has also processed proteins from corn and soyabean to make a fibre (azlon). Milk has been processed chemically and converted into protein fibres (caslen). These products, however, were not commercially successful.

Metallic fibres These are produced from metals such as gold, silver, and aluminium, obtained by mining and refining.

Mineral fibres These man-made fibres are made from substances such as glass or graphite.

Length-based Classification

Based on their length, fibres are classified as staple or filament. Staple fibres are shorter in length and measured in either inches or centimetres. They range from 1.5–46 cm in length. All natural fibres except silk are staple fibres. Filament fibres are long and continuous. They are measured in yards or metres. Silk is the only natural fibre that occurs in filament form. All other filament fibres are man-made. Man-made fibres are produced in filament form, but many are cut into staple form and spun into yarn to vary the texture and appearance. Whether natural or man-made, all fibres average less than 0.05 cm in diameter.

Content-based Classification

Based on content, fibres may be classified into cellulose fibres, protein fibres, and mineral fibres. These may either be natural or man-made (see Figure 18.3).

Identification of Fibre

The identification of fibres has increasingly become complex because of the invention of numerous varieties of fibres and the use of various blends. The preliminary method of identifying fibres is by visual examination and feel of the fibre (see Table 18.1). Further confirmatory methods listed in this section are carried out using chemical reagents (see Table 18.2), examination under a microscope, or by doing the burning test (Table 18.3).

Table 18.1 Visual and tactile characteristics of fibres

Fibre	Length	Lustre	Texture
Cotton	Staple	Medium	Smooth
Wool	Staple	Low/medium	Rough
Silk	Filament	High	Smooth and soft
Rayon	Filament	High	Smooth and soft
Nylon	Filament	Low to high	Smooth and soft
Dacron	Filament	Low to high	Smooth and soft

Table 18.2 Solubility of fibres

Fibre	Chemical reagent	Reaction
Cotton and linen	Cuprammonium	Dissolves
Cotton and linen	Iodine	Blue colour
Silk and wool	Picric acid	Permanent yellow colour
Silk	Hot concentrated hydrochloric acid	Completely dissolves
Wool	5% caustic soda Colourless lead acetate vapour	Completely dissolves Vapours turn it brown
Rayon	Cuprammonium hydroxide	Turns slimy and then completely dissolves
Acetate	Acetone	Completely dissolves
Nylon	90% phenol	Completely dissolves
Dacron	Metacresol	Completely dissolves

Table 18.3 Characteristics of fibres when burnt

Fibre	Approaching flame	In flame	Removed from flame	Odour	Ash
Cotton	Scorches; ignites readily	Burns quickly, with a bright yellow flame	Continues to burn rapidly; has a yellow afterglow	Smell of burning paper	Light, feathery, greyish (mercerized cotton gives a black ash)
Linen	Scorches; ignites easily	Burns slower than cotton if yarn is heavier; yellow flame	Continues to burn	Smell of burning paper	Feathery grey ash
Wool	Smoulders slowly without a flame	Burns with a small, slow, flickering flame, sizzles, and curls	Ceases to burn	Smell of burning hair or feather	Crisp, dark ash, irregular in shape; crumbles easily
Silk	Smoulders	Burns, then melts slowly and sputters	Ceases to burn	Smell of burning hair but less noticeable than wool	Round, crisp, shiny black bead; easily crushed
Polyester	Fuses and shrinks away from flame	Burns slowly with melting	Burns with difficulty	Slightly sweetish	Hard, round, brittle, black bead
Rayon	Ignites quickly	Burns quickly with yellow flame	Continues to burn but no afterglow	Smell of burning paper	Light grey, feathery ash
Nylon	Fuses and shrinks away from flame	Burns slowly and melts	Flame tends to dim and go out	Pungent	Hard, round, grey, uncrushable beads
Dacron	Fuses and shrinks away from flame	Burns slowly and melts	Burns with difficulty	Slightly sweet	Hard, round, brittle black beads

Tactile and Visual Examination

The first step in identification of a fibre is always the inspection of its appearance and feel. Grasp the edge of the cloth between the thumb and the index finger, with the thumb on top. Rub the thumb and the forefinger across the cloth lengthwise and then in a circle. Feel for pliability, elasticity, warmth, softness, smoothness, body, and hand. Visual examination should be combined with the sense of touch to observe the lustre or sheen, fuzziness, flatness, and coarseness of a fabric.

Vegetable fibres are usually cooler to the touch than animal or synthetic fibres. A 100% cotton fabric without a finish is without a hand. Linen is cool and pliable. Silk is very soft, lustrous, smooth, and slippery. Wool is warm and resilient. Rayon is cooler to the touch than acetate. However, it is very difficult to identify each fibre by mere touch because the types of yarn used, the finish, and the construction can often change the feel of the fabric.

Procedure

Unravel a small length of yarn each from the warp and the weft. Keep them separate. Observe the following characteristics and tabulate the results as shown in Table 18.1.

Length of the fibre Hold the yarn up against light or use a magnifying lens to observe whether its surface is fuzzy or smooth. This indicates whether it is made up of staple or filament fibres. To confirm the answer thus obtained, untwist the yarn and check the length of the individual fibres. (*Note:* Almost all natural fibres with the exception of silk are staple fibres.)

Lustre See whether the yarn has high, medium, or low lustre. (*Note:* Most man-made fibres have good lustre, but the degree may vary depending on the process of manufacture. Almost all natural fibres, with the exception of silk, possess a medium to low lustre).

Texture Observe how the warp and filling yarns feel between your fingers. Whether soft or hard, rough or smooth, warm or cool, stiff or flexible. Textile fibres can vary from one another in texture. (*Note:* Generally, man-made fibres are smooth, though not very soft unless specially finished. All natural fibres are of a soft texture, though the degree of this may vary.)

Microscopic Analysis

This is one of the most reliable methods for identification of textile fibres. When fabrics are woven out of a mixture of fibres, it is difficult to get clear results from the other methods.

Procedure

For microscopic analysis of fibres, observe the following procedure:

1. Clean the microscope lens, slide, and cover glass thoroughly.
2. Place a drop of distilled water or glycerine on the slide.
3. Untwist a length of yarn and separate the fibres. Place a single fibre on the slide.
4. Cover with another slide and press down to eliminate air bubbles. Remove excess moisture if present.
5. Mount the slide on the microscope and then focus at low power first.
6. Then shift to high power and observe the longitudinal structure of the fibre (diameter and surface structure) and record your observations.

Positive identification of most natural fibres can be made by using this test, since they each have their own characteristics. Longitudinal striations in these are always irregular and uneven. Man-made fibres are more difficult to identify because some of them look alike and their appearance may be changed by variations in the manufacturing process. Most man-made fibres appear as smooth, translucent cylinders. Some may be uniform, some may have striations, and some may be plain and transparent. Checking cross-sectional appearance is helpful if more careful examination is desired.

The following are some observations you may make.

Cotton It appears as a hollow tube with a thin cell wall, flattened, ribbon-like, and twisted. The diameter is irregular. Under high power magnification, the complex structure shows a central canal surrounded by a wall made up of many concentric layers of cellulose.

Linen The fibre shows a thick cell wall with a very narrow central canal, which is visible only under high power magnification. This fibre is characterized by peculiar markings known as 'nodes', which resemble the ridges along a length of bamboo.

Wool In a cross section of woollen fibre, two distinct layers are noticed. The outer layer consists of overlapping scales and the inner is a continuous rod containing a fluid. The diameter appears irregular. A longitudinal section of the fibre will show only the overlapping outer scales.

Silk Cultivated and wild silk appear different under the microscope. Cultivated silk just unreeled from the cocoon is called 'raw silk'. After being boiled to remove some of its gum, it is called 'pure white silk'. Under a microscope, raw silk shows double rod-like filaments, covered with lumps of gum that give the fibres a striated or cracked appearance. Pure white silk is cylindrical or rod-like in appearance, without a central canal and with a smooth surface that reflects light. Wild silk fibre, when seen under the microscope, appears broad and flat, uneven in width, and with characteristic markings that run obliquely across the fibre.

Synthetic fibres Viscose rayon shows its fibres to be corrugated and flattened with a little lustre. Nylon fibres appear fine, round, smooth, and translucent. The diameters of these fibres appear uniform.

Chemical Method or Solubility Test

This serves as a confirmatory test along with the microscopic test. This test is used to identify man-made fibres as generic categories and to confirm the identification of natural fibres. Differences in the chemical nature of various fibres cause them to be sensitive to different organic solvents, acids, and bases. These differences make it possible to identify a fibre by this test.

Procedure

The procedure for a solubility test is listed in this section.

1. Take warp and weft yarns separately from the fabric.
2. Untwist the yarns and tease out the fibres to provide a large surface for the solvent to penetrate.
3. Take a watch glass, petri dish, or test tube and place a few fibres in it from either the warp or the weft yarn.
4. Test with the required reagents as given in Table 18.2. The solution should be stirred for 5 minutes and the reactions noted and recorded. For wool, the lead acetate test is done instead. Placing a small mass of woollen fibres in a dry test tube, cover its mouth with a piece of lead acetate paper and heat gently till you get dense fumes from the fibres. If the sample is wool, the colourless lead acetate paper will turn brown in colour.
5. If you have used the warp yarn for the test, repeat with the weft (and vice versa).

Usually, this test is conducted at room temperature. In some cases, the solvent may have to be boiled or heated. (*Note:* Most fibres get completely dissolved when suitable reagents are used, but a few become slimy and are not completely dissolved.)

Precautions The following precautions should be taken for this test:

- The chemicals used in this test can be dangerous, so this test must be conducted in a laboratory.
- Use a proper chemical laboratory, exhaust hoods, gloves, aprons, and goggles.

Burning Test

This test can be used to identify the general chemical composition of fibres—whether cellulose, protein, mineral, or man-made polymers (thermoplastic)—and thus identify the group to which a fibre belongs. Blends cannot be identified by the burning test.

Procedure

Observe the following procedure for the identification of fibres through the burning test:

1. Ravel out the warp and weft yarns separately and untwist them to form a loose mass of fibres.
2. Test one at a time by holding with tweezers in a horizontal position and introducing slowly into the edge of a flame and then withdrawing it. (A candle, match, or spirit lamp can be used.) Repeat this several times to confirm results.
3. Observe the following aspects and record the results; check these against Table 18.3.

When approaching flame Observe the nature of ignition—whether the fibres ignite readily or slowly, or whether they melt rather than burn.

When in flame Observe the nature of the burning and the speed with which it burns—fast, slow, or with difficulty. Observe the nature of the flame—its colour and also the sound—while it is burning.

After removal from flame Observe the flammability after removal from flame.

- Does it continue to burn, or is it self-extinguishing?
- Is there any afterglow?

Odour Observe whether the burning fibre is emitting an odour of paper, hair, chemicals, or is aromatic.

Residue Observe the appearance and colour of the ash. Feel whether it is soft, crisp, or hard and note the crushability of the ash.

Characteristics of Textile Fibres

Of course, each specific type of fibre has unique properties. However, natural fibres as a group share certain characteristics; hence, we shall consider them first, before moving on to man-made fibres.

Natural Fibres

The most commonly used natural fibres in hotels are of vegetable origin—cotton and linen. Silk, an animal fibre, is also used, when a luxurious look is required in hotel interiors. All vegetable fibres are cellulosic in nature and are similar in structure and appearance. All animal fibres are proteins in composition and they can vary widely in appearance and structure. The characteristics of vegetable and animal fibres are outlined in Table 18.4.

Natural fibres are expensive because of the high costs of production; their maintenance cost is high too. Natural fibres, however, have a few distinctly desirable properties and are, therefore, often blended with man-made fibres.

Vegetable fibres

These are natural fibres from plant sources.

Table 18.4 Characteristics of vegetable and animal fibres

Vegetable fibres		Animal fibres	
• Strong, with a crisp feel	• Mothproof	• Soft feel	• Attacked by moths
• Dull in appearance	• Affected by mildew in damp conditions	• Varying of lustre	• Not affected by mildew easily
• Good heat	• Bleached in sunlight, but not adversely affected	• Poor heat	• Damaged by long hours of exposure to sunlight
• Non resilient and crease easily	• Not harmed by alkalis	• Resilient and thus resist crushing	• Damaged by alkalis
• Stronger wet than dry	• Loses strength if brought in contact with acids	• Stronger dry than wet	• Loses strength and gets damaged if exposed to chlorine bleaches
• Absorbent		• Absorbent	

Cotton The cotton bush has been cultivated for more than 5,000 years. Archaeological findings indicate that cotton was used for textiles even in the Indus Valley Civilization. Today, cotton has emerged as the most important textile fibre in the world. It is a fibre obtained from the downy covering of the ripe seed pod of the bushy cotton plant, which grows 1–2 metres tall. The cotton fibre is the shortest of all textile fibres. It is primarily composed of cellulose.

Manufacture of cotton Table 18.5 outlines the processing of cotton fibres required to produce cotton yarn.

Quality of cotton Raw cotton is creamy white in colour. The fibres are flat and ribbon-like. They have natural convolutions, a property that enables the fibres to cohere to one another so that, despite its short length, cotton is one of the most spinnable fibres. The quality of cotton fibre depends on its length, strength, fineness, and maturity. Other factors affecting quality are colour, leaf residue, and the ginning process. There are three groups of commercially important cotton:

Upland cottons The fibres are from 7/8 to ¼ of an inch in length and are derived from cotton plants native to Mexico and Central America.

Long staple cottons The fibres are 15/16 to 1½ inches in length and are derived from Egyptian and South American cotton. These are considered to be of finer quality as they can be made into softer, smoother,

Table 18.5 Processing of cotton fibres to obtain cotton yarn

Operation	Process and purpose
Harvesting	The seed pods, called 'bolls', are harvested when they begin to burst, exposing the fleecy white cotton fibres.
Ginning	The fibres are separated from the dried husks and seeds by the process of ginning in a machine called a 'cotton gin'. The cotton gin has rows of saw-toothed bands that pull the fibres away from the seeds as well as removing other extraneous material.
Baling	The cotton fibres are compressed into large, rectangular bales, which are supplied to those making the yarns.
Picking	To make the yarns, the fibres are first thoroughly cleaned. This process takes place with the help of machines called 'pickers'. Pickers clean the fibres and form them into a 'lap', which is a collection of randomly arranged fibres. These laps resemble the absorbent cotton rolls used for medical purposes.
Carding	The lap passes through a carding machine fitted with 'cards'. A card has a head with many fine wires that separate the fibres and pull them parallel. A thin web of fibres is formed in this machine and, as the web moves along, it passes through a funnel that forms it into a rope-like strand of roughly parallel fibres known as 'carded slivers'.
Combing (optional)	This optional process is carried out for obtaining high-quality yarns that are required to have better evenness, fineness, smoothness, and also more strength. A comb-like device arranges the fibres parallel to each other and separates out the smaller fibres. The material obtained is called a 'combed sliver', which is superior to the carded sliver.
Drawing	Slivers are successively passed through rollers rotating at different speeds to draw out the fibres. (If the yarns are to be blended, the slivers may be of different types of fibres).
Roving	The fibres are reduced in diameter in the roving machine. A roving frame draws out the fibres into thinner slivers and introduces a slight twist into the would-be yarn.
Spinning	The slivers are further reduced in diameter and twisted fully into yarns in the spinning frame. The finished yarns are then wound onto bobbins.
Winding	In this process, the yarns are rewound from the bobbins into spools. The yarn is now ready to be used for making fabric by weaving, knitting, or compressing.

more lustrous fabric. They command a higher price and are produced in smaller quantities than other cottons. They may, therefore, be identified on a label as 'suprema' or as 'long staple' or 'extra long staple'.

Short staple cottons The fibres are less than ¾ of an inch in length and are produced primarily in India and Eastern Asia.

Advantages of cotton There are several advantages in using cotton.

- Cotton is a highly versatile fibre, processed into a wide range of fabrics:
  - Sheer fabrics such as chiffon, organdie, and voile
  - Medium-weight fabrics such as broadcloth, drill, flannel, poplin, terry cloth, and long cloth
  - Heavyweight fabrics such as brocade, corduroy, denim, and velveteen
- Cotton can be mercerized to improve its lustre, absorbency, amenability to taking dye, and strength. (Also see 'Special finishes applied to cotton fabrics'.)
- Textured effects are easily achieved on cotton by:
  - introducing varying yarn structures, such as crimped yarns or high-twist yarns.
  - adapting the fabric construction method, as with seersuckers and crepes.
  - application of special finishes, such as embossing and napping.
- Cotton can be easily dyed or printed with almost all classes of dyes except acid and basic dyes.
- Cotton has good absorbency and is 25% stronger when wet than when dry, so that it is easy to launder.
- Cotton does not build up static electricity like synthetic fibres do.
- Cotton is a good conductor of heat and, therefore, very comfortable to wear.
- Cotton is durable since the fibre is strong.
- Cottons are easily dry-cleaned.
- Cotton can stand very high wash temperatures and is, thus, extensively used in hospitals, where sterilization of fabrics is important.
- Cotton fabrics may be treated with a resin finish to make them crease-resistant.
- Cotton can be given various other treatments, such as fire-retardant, mildew-resistant, and water-repellent finishes.

Disadvantages of cotton Some disadvantages of cotton are discussed in this section:

- Untreated cotton creases easily, since the fibre's resilience is very low. Pile fabrics made of cotton tend to flatten easily.
- Cotton fabrics tend to shrink when washed, especially when strong alkalis such as bleaches are used.
- Cotton fabrics shed lint because of the hairiness of the fibres.
- Cotton fabrics soil more easily than ones made from smoother fibres such as linen.
- If left damp, cotton is susceptible to mildew. Cottons must, therefore, be stored in dry conditions.
- Cotton is flammable.
- Cotton is easily damaged by acids; even the acidic nature of normal perspiration will harm the fibres.
- Cotton fabrics take a long time to dry compared to synthetic ones.
- Cotton weakens and turns yellow after repeated exposure to sunlight.

Special finishes applied to cotton fabrics Cotton has many desirable properties, but we have seen there are a few shortcomings too. To overcome these limitations, certain finishes are applied to cotton.

Care should be taken during cleaning cotton fabrics on which finishes have been applied, since many of the finishes may be unstable.

Mercerizing Mercerized cotton is produced by impregnating the yarn or fabric with caustic soda (sodium hydroxide) under conditions where the fibres are stretched. Mercerization results in smoother, rod-like fibres that have a permanent gloss or sheen. It also gives cotton a greater affinity for dyes and improves its strength and absorbency.

Schreinerizing Cotton is given a temporary lustre by this finishing process. However, this finish is lost after repeated washings.

Beetling This is a mechanical finish by which cotton is given a lustre. After undergoing beetling, cotton looks like linen.

Calendering This finish smoothes out wrinkles, adds sheen, and gives a smooth, even surface to the fabric.

Napping This finish produces a raised effect on the cotton fabric to impart a soft feel to it. Cotton given this 'fuzzy' finish resembles wool. For example, flannelette is produced by napping cotton.

Sizing In this finish, starch and certain other agents are applied on cotton to stiffen and soften the fabric. It also imparts body and weight to the fabric and gives it a smooth finish.

Anti-crease treatment/tebilization The cotton fabric is impregnated with a resin that prevents creases from forming. The process also makes the fabric shrink-proof.

Permanent-press treatment Cotton is treated with resins to produce durably pressed garments, with permanent creases or pleats. Shape retention is also improved.

Shrink-proofing Cotton fabrics with this finish are already pre-shrunk before being sold. The finish may be given by chemical or mechanical means to eliminate or minimize shrinkage.

Sanforizing Cotton fabrics are given this mechanical treatment to ensure they have less than 1% shrinkage.

Flame-proofing Commercial flame-proofing of cotton fabrics is permanent as long as the manufacturer's washing instructions are followed.

Anti-mildew treatment Cotton is given a chemical treatment that helps retard or prevent the growth of mildew and mould in hot, humid climates.

Water-proofing Chemicals and resins are applied to make the fabric water-repellent and resistant to waterborne soils.

Glazing Resins are applied on cotton fabric to give gloss and smoothness.

Stiffening Cotton is treated with gum, glue, starch, or resins to give stiffness, smoothness, and strength.

Embossing This finish produces three-dimensional patterns and designs on the cotton fabric.

Linen This fibre is obtained from the stem of the flax plant through processes similar to the manufacture of cotton. Flax is an annual plant growing to a maximum height of about 40 inches. The stem is slender and straight. The flowers are pale blue in colour. The fibres for linen yarn grow in the 'bast' or woody part of the stem of the flax plant and hence are called 'bast fibres'.

Manufacture of linen Flax plants are grown close together to prevent the stems from branching, for once a branch breaks out from the parent stem, the fibres above that point are of little value. The plants are pulled out by hand or machine. After pulling, the seeds are removed and used for the production of linseed oil. The manufacture of linen is outlined in Table 18.6.

Table 18.6 Manufacture of linen from flax

Operation	Process and purpose
Retting/ steeping	In this process, the fleshy part of the stem is rotted in contact with water. The process is carried out by exposing the stems to the action of running or stagnant water or to the action of dew and sun. Retting is a fermentation process in which certain bacteria, the spores of which already exist in the plant, come to life and digest the gum (pectin) that binds the fibres to the stem. Retting is a week-long process carried out in large retting tanks. After retting, the stems are removed by pressing them between fleeted rollers and beating them with revolving blades. The bundles of stems are then dried in the fields.
Scrutching	In this process, the softened woody outer portions are broken up and removed. Earlier, scrutching was carried out by placing a bunch of fibres in the cleft of a 'scrutching post' and striking it with a flat beater. Nowadays scrutching machines are used, operating on the same principle.
Hackling/ combing	The inner core of the stem that now remains varies in length from 10 inches to several feet. These are separated into long and short linen fibres by passing the cores through a series of combs. The long fibres called the 'line' emerge smooth, fine, glossy, and ready for spinning. The shorter fibres known as 'tow' are left behind and used in the manufacture of inferior linen. The fibres are now ready to be spun into yarn.
Spinning	The long glossy line is spun, either wet to give very fine yarn or dry to form coarser yarn. After the fabric has been woven, it may be bleached. Dressing is also added to the cheaper varieties of fabric, but the effect is lost after washing. The long line fibres are used for better-quality linen fabric. They have the lustre and body so typical of linen. Short tow fibres are used for less expensive linen.
Bleaching	The natural colour of linen varies from dark to yellowish grey. However, linen is sold in different degrees of bleach—full bleach, half bleach, and natural. Bleaching is done naturally by spreading the fabric out on grass in the sun. The more the cloth is bleached, the more it is weakened, so that a piece of full-bleached linen is weaker than one only half-bleached.

Quality of linen Linen fibres are smooth and much longer than cotton, and thus can be made into a finer, stronger yarn, more durable than cotton. Yarn produced from shorter linen fibre is known as *tow yarn*. Tow yarn produces a softer, more absorbent fabric than that produced from the longer fibres known as *line yarn*. Tow yarn is used for making glass cloths, towels, and fabrics that need to drape well. Line yarn produces a stronger material with more resistance to dirt. Line yarn is therefore used for bed and table linens and upholstery. Linen fibres blended with cotton to make a mixed yarn are called 'union yarn'.

Advantages of linen The advantages of using linen are discussed here.

- Linen is two to three times stronger than cotton and, hence, more durable.
- It withstands constant washing, which in fact enhances its softness.
- Linen fibres are longer than cotton and, therefore, less fluffy. Hence, the fabric remains clean for a longer time and any soiling is easily removed.
- Linen is easy to launder as it is very absorbent and stronger when wet. It also has good resistance to most alkalis, including soap.
- It resists moths.
- Linen does not get damaged even on constant exposure to sunlight.
- Linen cloths do not shed lint and so are used for wiping glass and mirrors.
- Linen is a good conductor of heat and thus suitable for making uniforms.
- Linen can withstand high ironing temperatures when damp.

Disadvantages of linen There are some disadvantages in using linen as well. These are discussed in this section.

- Linen fibres are non-resilient and, therefore, the fabric creases and shrinks easily.
- It shows wear along crease lines and seams.
- Linen exhibits poor crease retention after pressing.
- Linen is susceptible to mildew if left damp.
- It does not have a good affinity for dyes.
- Linen fabrics take a long time to dry since the fibres are very absorbent.
- Linen is flammable.
- It is expensive.

Special finishes applied to linen The special finishes applied to lines are as follows.

Beetling Beetling gives linen fabrics an added lustre.

Crease-proofing The linen fabric is impregnated with a type of plastic which prevents creases from forming. The process also makes the fabric shrink proof.

Anti-mildew treatment Linen is given a chemical treatment that helps retard or prevent the growth of mildew and mould in hot, humid climates.

Calendering This finish smoothes out wrinkles, adds sheen, and gives a smooth, even surface to the linen fabric.

Embossing This finish produces three-dimensional patterns and designs on linen fabric.

Tentering This finish straightens out the edges and weaves of linen fabric and makes it even in width. Tentering is done after any dyeing or wet-finishing process.

Table 18.7 illustrates the differences between cotton and linen.

Jute This silk-like, grey-brown fibre is obtained from stems of the jute plant. Jute fabric, however, has not been as successful commercially as cotton or linen, largely because the fibres are not durable and deteriorate when exposed to moisture.

Advantages The advantages of jute are as follows:

- Jute is inexpensive and can be blended with other fibres for economic and aesthetic reasons.
- It can be treated with various finishes to improve its durability and its resistance to water, fire, mildew, and rot.
- Jute has good affinity for all types of dyes.
- Jute can be treated with caustic soda to give it a wool-like appearance.

Limitations The limitations of jute are discussed in this section.

- Jute fibres are weak and non-durable.
- It sheds lint.
- Jute fibres have a coarse feel.
- Jute fibres are difficult to bleach.
- Jute fibres rot easily and are susceptible to microbial decomposition.
- Jute is difficult to launder or dry-clean.

Table 18.7 Differences between cotton and linen

Properties	Cotton	Linen
Strength	Cotton has good strength; when wet, its strength is temporarily increased by 30%.	Linen is 2–3 times stronger than cotton. It is extremely durable. It gains even more strength when wet.
Absorbency	Cotton has good absorbency.	Linen is preferable to cotton in terms of absorbency.
Drying	Cotton does not dry rapidly.	Linen dries more rapidly than cotton and, therefore, is excellent for towelling material as it is more absorbent too.
Drapability	Cotton does not have a good body and suppleness to drape easily.	Linen has more body than cotton and also the fibres are longer. Therefore, it drapes better than cotton.
Cleanliness	Cotton fibres are relatively rough and therefore soil and stain easily. Cotton also does not give up stains easily.	Linen fibre has a very smooth surface and does not soil and stain easily as dirt does not adhere to it. It also gives up stains easily.
Shrinkage	Cotton if not sanforized, shrinks considerably.	Linen does not shrink considerably.
Bleaching	Cotton bleaches easily.	Linen is more difficult to bleach than cotton.
Ironing	Cotton must be moderately damp while ironing.	Linen must be thoroughly damp while ironing because of its stiffness. The ironing temperature should be hotter than that used for cotton.
Use of detergent	Heavy-duty detergent may be used for washing cotton.	Heavy-duty detergent should not be used on linen as it will turn linen yellowish.
Effect of sunlight	Cotton loses strength in sunlight and has a tendency to turn yellow.	Linen is much more resistant to sunlight than cotton.
Affinity for dyes	Cotton has good affinity for dyes. Colourfastness is usually good.	Linen does not have good affinity for dyes.
Cost	Cotton is cheaper than linen.	Linen is expensive and is, therefore, blended with cotton to produce cheaper fabrics.
Crease pressing	Cotton crease is pressed easily.	Linen fibres are very stiff and, therefore, should not have creases pressed firmly into them. Deep repeated fold should be avoided because they cause cracking of fibres at folds.

Ramie, hemp, sisal, and kapok Ramie and hemp are also obtained from the stems of plants.

Ramie is a woody fibre resembling flax. It is also known as rhea or China grass. It is strong, coarse, absorbent, lustrous, and has a good affinity to dyes. In spite of possessing many desirable qualities, ramie is not used much because of low supply. Ramie is used, however, for making rope, twine, sacking, and nets.

Hemp too resembles flax and is used to manufacture rugs and carpets. It is also used to make twine, canvas, and sacking. Its main use, however, is in the making of shipping cordage, as the fibre does not rot in water.

Sisal is obtained from the leaves of a plant resembling cactus. The fibre is used for making twine, rope, and sacking. Sisal is also commonly used for making mats. A drawback is that it rots in water.

Kapok is obtained from the seed of the silk-cotton tree. Kapok fibres are smooth, light, and lustrous. It is much cheaper than cotton and is used for filling of cushions.

Coir and Pina Coir is a coarse brown fibre obtained from coconut husk. It is used in making rope and coarse matting and is also used as stuffing for upholstered furniture. Nowadays coir is being dyed and used for making bags too.

Pina is obtained from the leaves of the pineapple plant. It is used in making mats and bags.

Animal fibres

Most of these are derived from the hair (fur or pelt) of various animals, but silk is a secretion from insect larvae.

Wool This is fibre obtained from the fleece of sheep. The fibres have a natural crimp or wave that give wool its resilience. The fibres are not smooth but have overlapping scales that trap air between the fibres, causing woollen material to impart warmth. Wool is used to manufacture two types of yarn, woollen and worsted. Worsted yarn is smooth, fine-quality yarn that is more expensive than 'woollen yarn'.

Varieties of wool Wool is graded under four classes: fine, medium, long, and carpet wools.

Fine wool The wool of the Merino sheep is an outstanding example of this type. Fine wool fibres may vary in length from 1½ to 5 inches. 'Botany' is another name for Merino wool.

Medium wools These are obtained from the Oxford Shropshire, Hampshire, Suffolk, Dorset, and other breeds of sheep. The fibres are of medium fineness and are from 2½ to 6 inches long. Shetland wool from sheep raised in the Shetland Islands finds special use in imported and domestic woollen items.

Long wools These are obtained from large sheep such as Cotswolds, Lincoln, Leicester, and Romney Marsh. These sheep produce long, strong, and lustrous wool. The fibre length varies from 5–6 inches for a Romney Marsh to 10 or even 15 inches for Cotswolds.

Carpet wools This type of wool is made up of fibres that vary in length from as short as 1 inch to as long as 15 inches. Strength and resilience are its primary qualities. To get uniformity of properties, several grades are usually blended in carpet manufacture. These wools are obtained from various cross-breeds.

Wool production This is today a scientifically controlled process to produce the finest-quality wool for consumers. There are about 200 breeds of sheep that yield wool the world over. Wool may be sheared from healthy living animals or pulled from the hide after the animals have been slaughtered for meat. The sheared wool from live sheep is called 'fleece' or 'clip wool', while the wool recovered from hide is called 'pulled wool' and is often of inferior quality. Preliminary grading of wool fibres is done in the fleece stage as this helps to determine the final cost of the yarn. Domestic wool reaches the mill in losely packed bales. The raw wool or newly sheared fleece is also termed 'grease wool' because it contains the natural oil (lanolin or wool wax) secreted by the sheep. When this wool is washed, it loses 20–80% of its original weight as the lanolin and other extraneous matter are removed. The fibres then need to be graded and segregated according to length, diameter, and quality. Table 18.8 explains the processing of wool fibres into woollen and worsted yarns.

Advantages of wool The advantages of wool are discussed here.

- Woollen fibres have short crimps and folds that trap air. Since air is a poor conductor of heat, fabrics made of these fibres retain warmth.
- Wool has excellent absorbency, which makes it comfortable for the wearer.
- Wool remains cool when made into light-weight fabrics.
- Woollen fibres are very resilient and hence, wool fabrics resist creasing.

Table 18.8 Processing of wool fibres

Operation	Process and purpose
Sorting and grading	Wool sorting is done by skilled workers who are expert at distinguishing the quality of wool fibres by touch and sight. The grading is done on the basis of length, fineness, elasticity, and strength of fibres. As many as 20 separate grades of wool fibres may be obtained. The grade of fibres determines the type of product for which it will be used.
Scouring	Scouring removes the natural grease present in the fleece, as well as the dust and dirt. The raw wool is thoroughly washed in a scouring machine containing warm water, soap, a mild solution of soda ash, and other alkalis. If some impurities are still present, the fibres are put through a carbonizing bath of dilute sulphuric acid or dilute hydrochloric acid to 'burn out' the foreign matter. After partially drying, the wool is treated with a blend of oils to lubricate it.
Carding	It is in this process that the distinction made between woollen and worsted yarn arises. *Carding for 'woollen yarn':* In the manufacture of 'woollen yarn', the purpose of carding is to disentangle the fibres by passing them between rollers covered with thousands of fine wire teeth. In the process, the wool fibres tend to end up lying parallel to each other, which would make the resulting woollen yarn quite smooth if left to happen. This is undesirable, as woollen yarns should be fuzzy for better insulation. Hence, using of an oscillating device, one thin sliver is placed diagonally overlapping another sliver, thus leaving the fibres in each sliver parallel to each other but not to those in the adjacent sliver, so as to retain a fuzzy appearance. After carding, 'woollen' slivers go on directly to the spinning process. *Carding for worsted yarns*: In the manufacture of worsted yarns, the essential purpose of carding is again to disentangle the wool fibres by passing them between rollers covered with fine wire teeth. However, since worsted yarns should be smooth, the fibres are encouraged to lie as parallel as possible. After carding, the carded slivers go through a gilling and combing process before being spun into yarn.
Gilling and combing (these operations are only for the manufacture of worsted yarns)	The gilling process removes shorter staple fibres and straightens the fibres. The combing process removes the shorter fibres (1–4 inches in length), places the longer fibres as parallel as possible, and further cleans the fibres by removing any loose dirt and debris.
Drawing (this operation is only for the manufacture of worsted yarns)	This process doubles and re-doubles the slivers of wool, making them into more compact bundles called 'slubbers'.
Roving (this operation is only for the manufacture of worsted yarns)	A slight twist is introduced in this process to hold the thin slubbers intact.
Spinning	In the spinning process, the wool rove for worsted yarn is drawn out and twisted tightly into yarn. Woollen yarns are made by intermittent spinning where the drawing and twisting takes place in one operation. These yarns are given a slacker twist.
Twisting	For some specific purposes, 2–3 yarns are twisted together with an appropriate twist. Two-ply yarns are generally used for machine knitting and three- or four-ply yarns are used for hand knitting.

- Wool dyes easily into a wide range of colours.
- Wool does not soil easily.
- Wool can be laundered and dry-cleaned.
- Woollen fabrics are water-repellent and flameproof.
- Wool can be given shrink-proof and moth-resistant finishes.

Limitations of wool Wool has certain limitations. These are discussed here:

- Wool is highly absorbent and thus takes a long time to dry. Wool can hold upto 30% of its weight in water without feeling wet.
- Wool is very sensitive to alkaline substances.
- Wool is adversely affected by chlorine bleaches.
- Wool fibres are weak and this weakness increases when the fibres are wet. Wool tends to stretch and lose its shape when wet.
- Wool scorches easily.
- Woollen garments tend to stretch during wear.
- Wool requires special handling in laundering or dry-cleaning to prevent felting, shrinkage, or stretching out of shape.
- Wool is damaged by moth larvae, mildew, and bacteria.
- Wool adsorbs and retains smells from the surroundings.
- Wool yellows with prolonged exposure to sunlight.
- Wool may produce allergic reactions in some people, causing a skin rash or irritation.
- Wool tends to build up static electricity.
- Good quality wool is expensive.

Special finishes applied on wool These include dylanizing, shrink-proofing, moth-resistance treatment, weighting, and napping.

Dylanizing Wool fibres may be coated with a synthetic film to reduce tangling and felting. This treatment also renders the fabric shrink-proof.

Shrink-proofing A mechanical or chemical finish may be given to wool to eliminate or minimize shrinkage.

Moth-resistance treatment A chemical treatment in which a substance toxic to moth maggots is applied to wool, making it resistant to attack by moths and carpet beetles.

Weighting Wool is treated with magnesium chloride, which makes it absorb more moisture, thus increasing its weight.

Napping This finish produces a raised effect on woollen material, making it softer and warmer.

Other hair fibres Various other animal hair are used in making fabrics, but these have not become as successful commercially. Mohair is obtained from Angora goats and is used blended with wool or cotton. Angora itself is derived from either angora goats or long-haired angora rabbits. Cashmere is the soft, fine hair of the Cashmere goats and wild goats of Tibet (though there is also a woollen fabric that imitates this and goes by the same name!). Hair is also shorn from camels, llamas, yaks, and alpacas for weaving.

Silk This natural, continuous protein filament is widely acclaimed as a luxury fibre. Silk is produced by silkworms as they spin their cocoons. The finest quality of raw silk comes from the cocoon of the *Bombyx mori*, a type of silkworm. The protein in silk fibres is called fibroin. Silk is the strongest of all natural fibres. In spite of its high cost, silk has long been one of the most popular fabrics because of its unique properties. Soft, supple, strong, and lighter in weight than any other natural fibre, silk is pursued for its lightness and warmth, its sheerness and its strength and resiliency. It is considered the queen of fabrics. The manufacturing process for silk is outlined in Table 18.9.

Table 18.9 Manufacturing of silk thread

Operation	Process and purpose
Cultivation	Silkworms are bred for the sole purpose of producing raw silk. The farming of silkworm cocoons for their filament is called sericulture. Under natural conditions, silkworms breed only once a year; however, scientific manipulation of their breeding cycle can allow cocoons to hatch upto three times a year. The filament thus produced is in the form of a double strand of fibroid, held together by a gummy substance called serecin or 'silk gum'.
Sorting	The cocoons raised by the silk farmers are delivered to a factory called a 'filature'. Here the silk is unwound from the cocoons so that the strands can be collected into skeins. The cocoons are first sorted according to colour, size, shape, and texture, as all these will affect the final quality of silk.
Softening	After sorting, the cocoons are put through a series of hot and cold immersions to soften the serecin in order to permit the unwinding of the filament as one continuous thread. In this operation, only 1% of the serecin is removed from the fibre, since this gum is an essential protection during the further handling of the delicate filament.
Reeling	The process of unwinding the filament from the cocoon is called reeling. As the filament of a single cocoon is too fine for commercial use, 3–10 strands are usually reeled at a time to produce the desired diameter of raw-silk thread. As the reeling of the filament from each cocoon nears completion, operators attach a new filament to the moving thread. The gummy serecin aids in holding the several filaments together while they are combined to form the single thread. The usable length of the reeled filament is 300–600 metres. The diameter of silk fibre is so fine that an estimated 3,000 cocoons are required to make one metre of silk fabric. The silk filaments are reeled into skeins that are packed in small bundles called 'books' (weighing 2–4.5 kg). These books are then aggregated into bales (weighing about 60 kg each). In this form, the raw silk is shipped to all parts of the world.

Types of silk, based on origin Based on its origin, silk is classified under two main categories: (a) cultivated or mulberry silk is made by the silkworms (*Bombyx mori* of *Bombycidae* family), which are cultivated on mulberry leaves; (b) wild silk is obtained from silk-producing insects that do not feed on mulberry leaves (unlike the ones spoken of earlier). These insects belong to the family *Saturniidae*.

The important types of wild silk are:

Tussar/tussore silk A type of silk produced from a wild species of oak-feeding moth native to India and China. The silk fibres are coarser, with a tan colour.

Muga silk The muga silk moth (*Antherea Assama*) is found in Assam, where it is domesticated for its silk. Muga silk is superior to tasser in gloss and other qualities. Assam is the only place in the world producing the rare golden-yellow 'muga silk', an excellent material for embroidery.

Eri/endi silk This silk comes from the *Eri* or *Aarrindi* moths of Bengal, Bihar, and Assam, which belong to the Saturniidae family. The silkworms feed on castor leaves and are reared indoors. The filament is so exceedingly delicate that it is impractical to wind off the silk; instead it is spun like cotton.

Types of silk, based on fibre type Based on the length, silk is classified as follows:

Filament/nett silk These are made from continuous long filaments.

Spun silk This is made from short lengths of inferior silk filaments or filaments from broken cocoons. It is not as lustrous or durable as reeled silk.

Reeled silk/raw silk The term 'reeled silk' is applied to the raw silk strand that is formed by combining several filaments from separate cocoons.

Dupion silk Silk woven from an uneven, double-thread produced when two cocoons nest together.

Advantages The advantages of silk is discussed in this section.

- Silk fabrics have a natural lustre and a soft feel.
- Silk is the strongest of all natural fibres.
- Silk is absorbent and thus comfortable to wear.
- It dries quite rapidly, even though it is absorbent.
- It has natural shrink resistance.
- Silk is naturally flame-resistant.
- Silk does not soil easily as the fibres are smooth.
- It is a non-conductor of heat and hence is suitable for winter wear.
- Silk fibres are moderately resilient and, therefore, resist creasing to some extent. The creases disappear on hanging.
- Silk fibres can be used to manufacture a wide variety of fabrics:
  - Sheer fabrics such as chiffon, georgette, China silk, and crepe de Chine
  - Heavy and stiff fabrics such as brocade, broadcloth, taffeta, and velvet
- Silk can be easily dyed into brilliant shades.
- It can be laundered and dry-cleaned following the manufacturer's instructions.
- White silk can be bleached using hydrogen peroxide or sodium perborate.

Disadvantages The limitations of silk are as follows:

- Silk is weakened by sunlight.
- Silk fibres become weaker when wet.
- Silk is sensitive to alkalis. Strong alkali soaps should not be used on silk as it yellows the fabric.
- Silk is easily marred by water spots.
- Silk takes up dyes easily, but some dyes tend to bleed and are not fast to washing.
- Silk scorches easily.
- Silk is weakened at high temperatures.
- Silk is sensitive to acids. Even perspiration weakens the fabric.
- Silk is prone to attack by mildew, silverfish, and carpet beetles if not stored properly.
- Silk yellows with age.
- Silk is expensive.

Special finishes applied on silk The special finishes applied on silk are:

Weighting After getting rid of most of the gum serecin during the manufacturing process, silk becomes light and delicate, losing its drapability. Weighting is a chemical treatment given to silk to assist draping. To weight coloured silks, tin chloride is used, followed by treatment with sodium phosphate. Black silks are weighted with metallic mordants such as iron salts and logwood.

Calendering This finish is given to silk for enhancing its lustre.

Cireing This finish gives body and lustre to silk.

Natural mineral fibres

Asbestos, a natural mineral fibre, is obtained from rocks. It is acid-proof, rust-proof, and flame-proof. It can withstand extremely high temperatures and is, therefore, used for making firefighting suits and fire-resistant fabrics. However, manufacture of asbestos is banned in many countries since it is carcinogenic.

Man-made Fibres

These fibres can be synthetic, regenerated, metallic, and mineral fibres. Many man-made fibres are non-cellulosic polymers. These are synthesized by combining carbon, oxygen, hydrogen, and other simple chemical elements into larger, complex molecular combinations called polymers. Another source of man-made fabrics is the protein from such natural products as corn or milk. Man-made fibres created from other sources include mineral fibres, metallic fibres, and rubber fibre.

Synthetic fibres

Polyester This polymeric fibre is composed of the ester obtained by the reaction of a dihydric alcohol with terephthalic acid.

Advantages The advantages of polyester are as follows.

- Polyester fibre is very strong, resulting in durable fabrics.
- Polyester is crease-resistant. It requires little or no ironing.
- Polyester fibres are very smooth and thus, the fabrics resist soiling. Since the fibres are electrostatic, they attract dust that clings to the surface but which is easily removed with frequent washing.
- Polyester can be laundered and dry-cleaned easily.
- Polyester dries rapidly as it has poor absorbency.
- Polyester has good resistance to sunlight.
- Polyester can be heat-set to retain pleats and creases.
- Polyester is a wash-and-wear fabric.
- Polyester can be bleached and dyed with disperse dyes.
- Polyester is resistant to acids and most alkalis.
- Polyester fabrics are moth- and mildew-resistant.
- Polyester can be blended with other fibres to lend them durability and crease resistance, and to impart wash-and-wear properties.

Disadvantages The limitations of polyester is discussed here:

- Fabrics made of polyester staple fibre tend to pill on constant wear. Pills are minute, rough, spherical fibre protrusions that mar the surface appearance and feel of fabrics.
- Polyester fabrics are highly electrostatic and, due to this, cling to the wearer. Build-up of static electricity also causes polyester to attract dust.
- Polyester has low absorbency.
- Polyester has poor affinity for dyes.
- Polyester has an affinity for greasy soils and grease-borne stains.
- Polyester has a low melting point; hence, care is needed in laundering to ensure that washing and ironing temperatures are not too high.
- At high temperatures (including dry heat), polyester—like most synthetic fabrics—melts and may produce highly poisonous fumes.

Special finishes applied to polyester The special finishes applied to polyester are as follows.

Anti-static treatment Polyester may be given a chemical finish to prevent the build-up of static electricity.

Soil-release and spot-resisting treatments Polyester may be given a resin treatment that protects the fabrics from stains and facilitates the removal of oily stains.

Bulking Polyester yarns are heat-set into a crimped state. Fabrics made with these crimped polyester yarns are soft, warm, fairly absorbent, and easily stretched. They can hold more air.

Nylon This is a thermosetting synthetic fibre. It was the first non-cellulosic synthetic fibre ever manufactured. Various types of nylon are being manufactured nowadays, the most commercially viable one being nylon 6. Other types are nylon 6,6, nylon 7, nylon 11, nylon 4, nylon 8, and nylon 10. Essentially, all are polyamides in composition. The numbers refer to the number of carbon atoms in the polyamide. For example, nylon 6 is produced from an amide called caprolactam, each unit of which contains 6 carbon atoms, by ring-opening polymerization (other nylons are polymerized by condensation). Nylon 6,6 is so called because each of the two component chemical compounds (hexamethylene diamine and adipic acid) contain 6 carbon atoms per molecule. The chemicals are obtained from such raw materials as coal, petroleum, or such cereal products as oat hulls or corn cobs.

Advantages The advantages of nylon are as follows.

- Nylon is extremely strong and durable, even in the wet state.
- Nylon fibres are resilient and therefore the resultant fabrics are crease-resistant.
- Nylon is resistant to alkalis and thus bleached easily.
- Nylon fabrics are moth- and mildew-resistant.
- Nylon fabrics resist waterborne stains.
- Nylon fabrics can be heat-set to retain pleats and creases.
- Nylon fibres can be produced to have a bright, semi-dull, or dull lustre.
- Nylon is easy to launder and dry-clean.
- Nylon dries quickly.
- Nylon fabrics need little or no ironing.

Disadvantages The limitation of nylon are:

- Nylon builds up static electricity.
- Nylon fabrics are damaged on prolonged exposure to sunlight.
- Nylon fabrics absorb greasy stains that are difficult to remove.
- Nylon melts in fire, producing toxic fumes.
- Spun nylon fabrics (made from staple nylon fibres) tend to pill.
- Undyed nylon tends to pick up dyes and soil from the water during laundering.
- Nylon requires a low ironing temperature.

Special finishes applied on nylon The special finishes applied on nylon is discussed here.

Anti-static finish This is applied for reducing static build-up.

Bulking Nylon yarns are heat-set into a crimped state. Fabrics made with these crimped nylon yarns are soft, warm, fairly absorbent, and easily stretched. They can hold more air.

Embossing This finish produces three-dimensional patterns and designs on nylon.

Permanent press This finish gives a permanent shape to nylon fabrics. Pleats and creases can be heat-set.

Moireing This finish produces a shimmering, watery-line effect on nylon fabrics.

Nylonizing Nylon fibres are treated with molten nylon 3 for increasing their absorbency.

Water repellency This finish is given to nylon for added protection against water.

Other synthetic fibres Grouped according to their composition, these are as follows:

- Polyacrylonitrite, or acrylics such as Acrilan, Dralon, Courtelle, and Orlon and modacrylics such as Teklan.
- Polyurethane, such as Spandex.
- Polyvinyl, such as Saran.
- Polyethylene, such as Courlene.
- Polypropylene, such as Spunstron.

Regenerated fibres

These are made from a substance retrieved from natural sources, most commonly cellulose, which is converted into fibre form. An example of regenerated cellulosic fibre is viscose rayon. Other forms of rayon are acetate rayon, triacetate rayon, cuprammonium rayon, and polynosic rayon. Regenerated protein fibres have also been experimented with. These fibres are extracted from the proteins of such natural products as milk (caslen from the milk protein casein), soyabeans, and corn (azlon).

Viscose rayon This regenerated cellulosic fibre is obtained from wood pulp.

Advantages The advantages of rayon are as follows.

- Viscose rayon can be made into a wide range of fabrics—both lightweight and heavy, durable ones.
- Viscose rayon is lustrous and soft, with a good drape.
- Viscose rayon can be blended easily with other fibres to give blends.
- It is very absorbent.
- Viscose rayon can be bleached.
- It has a good affinity for dyes.
- Viscose rayon can be given a variety of finishes to overcome its limitations.

Disadvantages The limitations of rayon is discussed here.

- Viscose rayon is weak and its strength decreases further by a 50–70% when it is wet.
- Viscose rayon is non-resilient and hence creases badly.
- It shrinks progressively with repeated washes. It is too weak to withstand repeated washing.
- Viscose rayon is very absorbent and hence does not dry quickly.
- Viscose rayon is damaged by weak acids.
- It is prone to mildew.
- Viscose rayon fabrics require a low ironing temperature.

Special finishes used on rayon fabrics The special finishes used on rayon are as follows.

Anti-crease treatment Applied in the same way as to cotton.

Shrink-proofing Applied in the same way as to cotton.

Flame-proofing Applied in the same way as to cotton.

Moireing This finish produces a shimmering watery-line effect.

Permanent press Pleats and creases can be heat-set on rayon fabrics.

Trubenizing In this finish, two sheets of rayon fabric are fused together with the application of heat. This gives stiffness to the fabric and the trubenized rayon thus produced is used in making cuffs and collars of uniforms in the hotel industry. This finishing process is possible because rayon is thermoplastic.

Anti-mildew treatment A chemical finish is given to rayon that helps retard the growth of mildew and mould in hot, humid climates.

Mineral fibres

Glass fibre is a kind of mineral fibre that is commonly used.

Glass fibre It is produced by combining silica, sand, limestone, and certain other minerals. These fibres are non-absorbent, easily laundered, highly resistant to chemicals and strong sunlight, and are inherently fireproof.

Yarn

To be made into fabric, most textile fibres must first be made into yarn. The ways in which the fibres are brought together creates the variety of yarns available for use in fabric construction. The term 'yarn' can be defined as 'a continuous strand made of textile filaments or materials, in a form suitable for weaving, knitting, and other methods of fabric construction'.

Types of Yarn

Based on the method of construction, yarns are classified as simple yarns, complex yarns, and textured yarns.

Simple yarns

These are the yarns where the number of twists is equally distributed along the length of the yarn. They are smooth and uniform in diameter. Simple yarns can be described as spun or filament yarns based on the length of the fibres used to make them. Spun yarns are composed of short staple fibres that are twisted together, resulting in fuzzy yarns with protruding fibre ends. They are suitable for fabrics in which absorbency, warmth, and a cotton-like texture are required. Filament yarns are composed of long filament fibres, tightly twisted or grouped together. Filament yarns may be smooth or uniformly wavy. There are two types of filament yarns—mono-filament and multi-filament. A mono-filament yarn, as the name suggests, is made up of a single filament, whereas a multi-filament yarn is composed of several filaments.

Simple yarns are further classified as follows:

Single strand yarn This yarn has only one strand, made up of fibres twisted together. It is the product of the first twisting operation that is performed by the spinning machine. This type of yarn is used in home furnishing fabrics.

Ply yarns This is made by the second twisting operation, carried out by a machine called the twister, which combines two or more single yarns. When two single-strand yarns are used to make a ply yarn, it is known as a 'two-ply yarn'; when three single-strand yarns are used, it is called a 'three-ply yarn'. Two- and three-ply yarns are found in embroidery threads, sewing threads, and strings used for packaging.

Cord yarns These are made by a third twisting operation, twisting together two or more ply yarns. Cord yarn is used for making sewing threads and ropes as well as for the manufacture of certain fabrics for industrial purposes.

Complex yarns

These yarns have non-uniform parts and are irregular at regular intervals. The irregularities are in the size and twist. These yarns are also called 'fancy yarns' or 'novelty yarns' because of their appearance and effects they produce in the fabric. Various types of complex yarns are ratine, spiral yarn, knot yarn (variously called knob, knub, or spot yarn), snarl or spike yarn, curl or loop yarn, and flake yarn.

Textured yarns

These are filament or spun yarns that have been given a greater apparent volume than a conventional yarn. Mechanical, chemical, heat-treatment processes, or a combination of these may be used to get the apparent increase in volume. The different types of textured yarns are stretch yarns, high-bulk yarns, and loop-bulk yarns.

Yarn Characteristics

The quality and characteristics of any yarn are determined by—apart from the type and quality of fibres—the yarn twist and the yarn count.

Yarn twist

This is the spiral arrangement of the fibres around the axis of the yarn. The twists bind the fibres together and give strength. They also help in varying the appearance of the fabric.

Fine yarns require more twists than coarse yarns.

Degree of twist The amount of twist given is expressed as TPI (twists per inch). The higher the TPI number, the stronger the yarn (up to a certain point). The optimum ranges are 3–6 TPI for filament and 10–20 TPI for staple fibres. The number of twists also affects the price of the yarn because the higher the number of twists, the smaller the quantity produced from a given amount of fibre and so the higher the price.

Staple yarns have more twists than the filament yarns. In a woven fabric, the warp yarns typically have more twists than the weft yarns. Based on the TPI, yarns are classified in the following way:

Low-twist (0–3 TPI) These are also referred to as 'soft-twist'. This level of twist produces yarns with a soft and lustrous surface. They are used in satins and as weft yarns of fabrics that are to be napped. Yarns with this degree of twist are not very strong.

Medium-twist (3–7 TPI) These are also called 'ordinary-twist yarns'. This level of twist is applied mainly to yarns made of staple fibres. It results in firm, compact, and stronger yarn. This is the degree of twist given to most warp yarns.

High-twist (7–12 TPI) This type of yarn is also referred to as 'hard-twist'.This level of twist is used to produce very strong and compact yarns. The crepe effect in chiffons and georgettes is achieved by using yarns with a high twist. Sewing threads also employ yarns with a high twist.

The three types of twists are illustrated in Figure 18.4.

Direction of twist The direction of the twisting is another characteristic that determines the properties of yarn. Yarn may be twisted clockwise or anti-clockwise.

The S twist In this type, the arrangement of fibres in the yarn corresponds to the slope of the letter S, that is, the yarn is twisted in the clockwise direction.

Fig. 18.4 Types of yarn based on TPI

The Z twist In this type, the fibres are arranged in such a way as to correspond to the slope of the letter Z, that is, the yarn is twisted anti-clockwise.

The durability of yarns can be further increased by efficient plying of the S and Z twists. Also, various effects in the appearance of the fabric can be obtained by a combination of yarns of different twists.

Yarn count

In the spinning process, there is always a relationship between the original quantity of fibre and the length of the yarn produced from that amount of fibre. This relationship determines the fineness of the yarn. The fineness is designated by a number called the 'yarn count' or 'yarn number'. It is determined by the drawing process in case of yarns made of natural fibres. For filament yarns, the count depends on the size of the perforations in the spinerette, the rate at which the solution is pumped through the spinnerette, and the rate at which the yarns are drawn. Yarn count is expressed in terms of the weight per unit length, called tex (for natural-fibre yarns) or denier (for filament-fibre yarns).

Fabric Construction

Fabrics can be manufactured in many ways, as depicted in Figure 18.5.

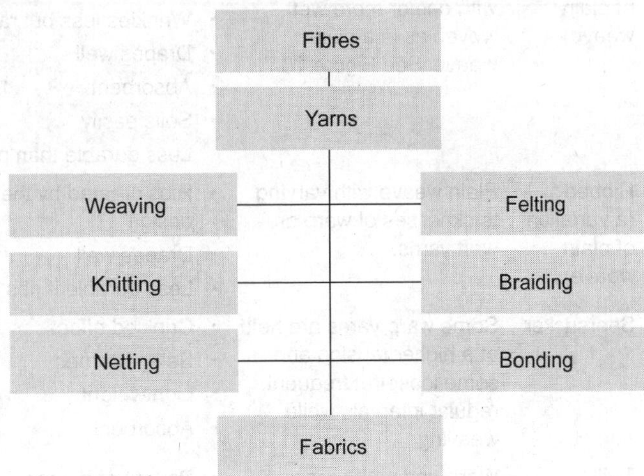

Fig. 18.5 Fibre to fabric

Weaving

This is the most widely used method of fabric construction. Weaving is carried out on a loom where two or more sets of yarns are interlaced at right angles. The lengthwise yarns are called 'warp' and the crosswise yarns are known as 'weft'.

The process of weaving

This consists of the following steps.

Shedding This is the raising of one or more harnesses to separate the warp yarns and form a shed.

Picking This is the passing of the shuttle through the shed to insert the filling or weft yarns.

Beating up/battening This is the process of pushing the weft yarns into place in the cloth with the reed.

Taking up and letting off This is the winding of finished cloth onto the cloth beam and releasing of excess warp from the warp beam.

Woven fabrics from the loom have a distinct selvedge, running lengthwise along the margins of the fabric. Woven fabrics vary in their interlace (pattern) and balance (ratio of warp yarns to weft yarns). The various weaves are discussed here.

Weaves

A 'weave' can be defined as the system of interlacing warp and weft threads in order to produce a textile fabric. The appearance and characteristics of fabrics depend not only on the types of fibre and yarn used, but also on the type of weave. The characteristics of some basic weaves used in the construction of woven fabrics are outlined in Table 18.10.

Table 18.10 Basic weaves and their characteristics

Name of weave	Interlacing pattern	Characteristics	Typical fabrics
Plain	Each weft thread passes alternately over and under each warp thread to form a pattern of squares. See Figure 18.6.	• Flat appearance • Highest number of interlacings per square inch • No distinct design unless yarns have contrasting colours or thickness • Wrinkles and ravels most • Less absorbent	voile; gingham; percale; flannel; and cheesecloth
Basket (a variation of plain weave)	Two or more warps are simultaneously interlaced with one or more weft, woven as in a plain weave. See Figure 18.7.	• Looks balanced and flat • Fewer interlacings than plain weave • Wrinkles less but ravels more • Drapes well • Absorbent • Soils easily • Less durable than plain weave	Oxford; monk's cloth; and aida fabric
Ribbed (a variation of plain weave)	Plain weave with varying thicknesses of warp or weft yarns.	• Ribs created by the weave provide texture and design • Drapes well • Less durable if ribs are thicker	Broadcloth; poplin; repp; and taffeta
Seersucker	Some warp yarns are held at a higher tension and some looser at frequent, regular intervals while weaving	• Crinkled effect • Self-patterned • Lightweight • Absorbent	Seersucker fabric (such as crinkled sheets)
Twill	Warp and weft yarns float over two or more yarns from the opposite direction (respective perpendicular yarns) in a regular progression to the right or left. See Figure 18.8.	• Pattern of diagonal lines • Strong, with firm texture • Fewer interlacings than plain weave but can have higher count • More pliable than plain weave • Wrinkles less but ravels more	Denim; gabardine; drill; flannel; and tweed

(Contd.)

Table 18.10 *Contd.*

Name of weave	Interlacing pattern	Characteristics	Typical fabrics
Satin	Warp yarns float over four or more yarns from the opposite direction in a progression of two to the right or left. See Figure 18.9.	• Flat, smooth, and lustrous surface • Fewer interlacings than plain weave, but can have high thread count • Excellent drapability • Floats prone to snagging	Satin fabric
Sateen (variation of satin weave)	Weft yarns float over the warp yarns. See Figure 18.10	• Flat, lustrous surface • Fewer interlacings than plain weave • May be of staple yarns and schreinerized • Can have high thread count • Prone to snagging	Sateen fabric
Dobby	Special loom attachment allows upto 32 different interlacings. See Figure 18.11.	• Decorative • Small geometric designs composed of short floats • May have a textured surface	Huckaback and pique
Jacquard	Each warp yarn is controlled individually and an infinite number of interlacings are possible. See Figure 18.12.	• Decorative • Wide range of intricate designs possible • Multi-colour effects possible • Drapes well	Brocade; damask; and tapestry
Crepe or momie	Combination of plain and satin or sateen weave.	• Irregular, indistinct pattern with pebbly-textured surface • Has good strength and resilience • Drapes well	Moss crepe; sand crepe; and wool crepe
Pile	Extra sets of warps or wefts, called 'pile', are woven perpendicularly into ground yarns of plain or twill weave to form loops.	• Three-dimensional effect • Soft, warm, and resilient • Absorbent	Cut and uncut pile give variety of textile products, ranging from towelling to rugs
Cut pile	Pile loops are cut.	• Soft brush-like surface • Soils easily but does not show soil readily	Corduroy; velvet; velveteen; and carpeting material
Uncut pile	Pile loops are left uncut.	• Soft, though rougher than cut pile • Loops may be present on both sides of the fabric • Absorbent	Terrycloth (Turkish towelling)
Cellular weave	Warps and wefts are loosely woven to create 'cells' in the fabric.	• Retains warmth as the cells hold air	Cellular cloth (for blankets)
Leno/gauze	Pairs of warps are twisted over each other with each passing of weft.	• Open mesh structure • Sheer but durable • Lightweight	Grenadine and lace
Double cloth	Two fabrics of independent weaves woven together with extra set of yarns	• Two different surfaces; may be reversible • Strong and heavy • Thick and warm	Blanket cloth and upholstery

Fig. 18.6 Plain weave

Fig. 18.7 Basket weave (2/1)

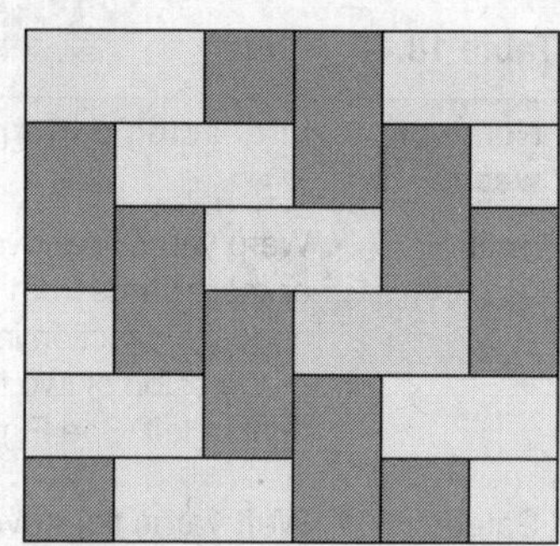

Fig. 18.8 Twill weave

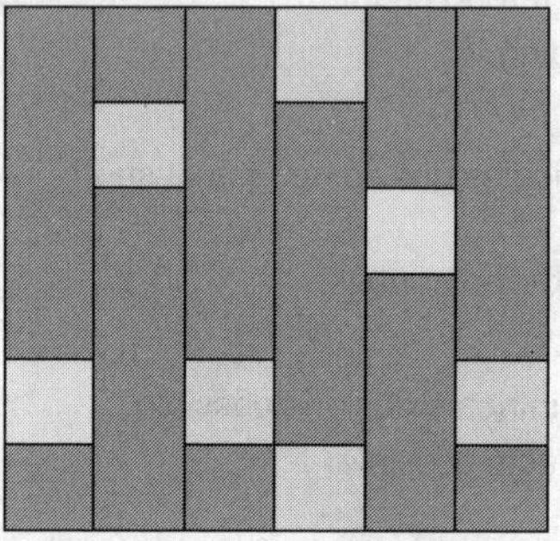

Fig. 18.9 Satin weave

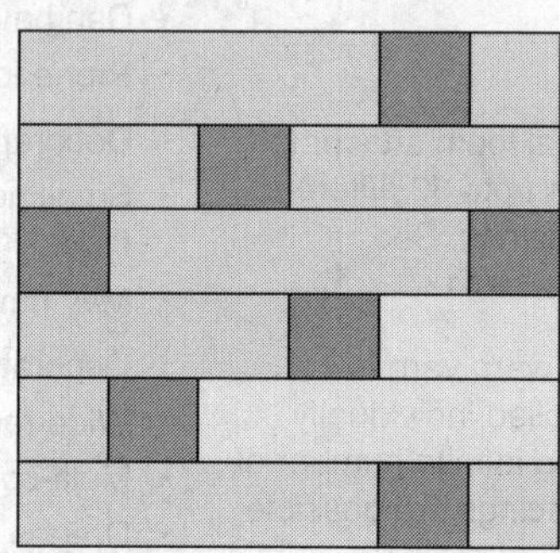

Fig. 18.10 Sateen weave

Fig. 18.11 Dobby weave

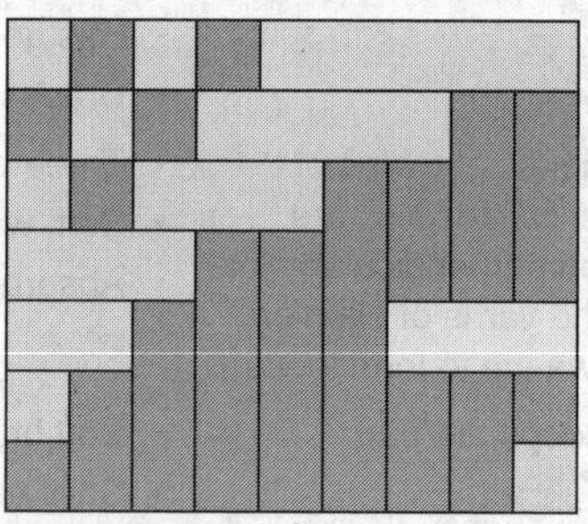

Fig. 18.12 Jacquard weave (damask fabric)

Other Methods of Fabric Construction

Knitting In this method of fabric construction, one or more yarns are formed into a series of interlocking loops with the help of needles. Most often, one thread is used to form a series or row of loops, which in turn is held by another row, and in this way a stocking stitch or another pattern of stitches is formed, the pattern depending on the shapes of the loops, the way the thread is carried from loop to loop, and the way the loops interlock. This results in stretchy fabrics that are porous and resilient. These fabrics pull out of shape easily if washed incorrectly and may also ladder.

Netting Openwork fabrics such as lace are manufactured by this method. The yarns are interlaced, interlooped, twisted, and knotted to form openwork fabrics, usually forming a pattern.

Felting In this method, fibres are directly converted into fabric without being spun into yarn. Originally, only wool fibres were used for felting since they have a natural tendency to mat due to the presence of scales along the hairs. To felt them, wool fibres are carded, combed, and laid down in a thick layer; they are then sprayed with water and run through hot agitating plates under pressure, which causes the fibres to become entangled and matted together into a sheet. Nowadays, felt is also made from fibres that do not mat easily. In this process, a series of barbed needles is punched repeatedly into a web of fibres, which entangles and mats them. This is called *needle felting*. Felted fabrics do not unravel easily, but will pull apart and flatten easily. These fabrics lack strength, but are used where their other properties—they absorb sound and are cheap—set off this disadvantage.

Braiding Narrow, stretchy fabrics are formed by this method of fabric construction, in which yarns are interlaced diagonally and lengthwise.

Bonding Bonded fabrics are produced from man-made and natural fibres by mechanical, chemical, thermal, or solvent processes, or combinations of these. For instance, when a web of fibres is bonded together using adhesives, the process is called *adhesive bonding*. Thermoplastic fibres with a low melting point are bonded by means of heat in a process known as *thermoplastic bonding*. In *laminated bonding*, two types of fabrics are bonded by adhesives. Bonded fabrics are cheaper than woven or knitted fabrics and are widely used for disposable products.

Tufting Tufted fabrics are produced by inserting threads into the surface of the fabrics. These threads may be cut or left intact.

Blends and Unions

All mixed-fibre fabrics are blends in layman's terms. Technically, though, one must understand the difference between a 'blend' and a 'union' fabric. *Blends* are fabrics made of yarns in which two or more fibres are mixed while the yarn is being spun. These yarns may be used either in the warp or the weft or in both directions. In a *union fabric* (also called a 'mixture'), each yarn is of a single type of fibre—that is, warp yarns are of a particular type of fibre and the weft of another fibre. There may also be two or more kinds of yarns in each direction. In other words, in a blend, fibres are mixed before spinning; in union fabrics, fibres are mixed during weaving or plying of two or more yarns.

In both blends and unions, the desirable properties of individual fibres balance their undesirable characteristics. For instance, a blended fabric may stand up to more than five hundred washes; a 100% cotton fabric can last for only 150–200 washes. Today, some bath linen are being manufactured using a small percentage of polyester fibres in the base fabric with an all-cotton pile on the surface, yielding a product with the superior absorbency of cotton and the strength of the synthetic fibre polyester. Such fabric has an added advantage over 100% cotton in that it does not shrink as much.

Another case is that of terrycot, a polyester-cotton blend. This fabric combines the high absorbency of cotton with the excellent wrinkle resistance of polyester. It is important to establish a critical blend ratio to ensure the best qualities of each of the constituent fibres are present in the final fabric. For example, a blend of 67/33 polyester/cotton exhibits good absorbency and good wrinkle resistance.

Blends are also preferred for improved aesthetics, lustre, drape, texture, colour, and cost reduction. Characteristics of some blends are shown in Table 18.11.

Table 18.11 Characteristics of blends

Blends	Percentage of component fibres	Characteristics	Uses
Polyester/cotton	67/33	• Most popular blend • As strong as polyester • Wrinkle-resistant • Wash-and-wear • Absorbent	Apparel
Polyester/cotton	80/20	• Lightweight • As strong as polyester • Absorbency lower than the 67/33 blend	Upholstery, drapery, and rainwear
Polyester/cotton (percale—it is made of combed fibres)	50/50	• Greater absorbency than the above blends • Faster drying time than cotton • Slight lustre • Softer hand • 20% weaker than polyester	Apparel and bed linen
Polyester/wool	60/40	• Excellent wrinkle resistance and crease retention • Good shape retention and drape • Durability • Good resilience • Resistance to pilling	Suiting and dresses
Polyester/wool	50/50	• Greater warmth than above blends	Suiting and dresses
Polyester/rayon	65/35	• Strong and durable • Good drape • Good hand • Absorbent	Dresses and curtain material
Acrylic/cotton	80/20	• Comfortable to wear • Durable • Wash-and-wear • Absorbent • Lower cost	Sportswear
Jute/polypropylene /cotton	25/50/25	• Increased strength of jute	Carpet backings and bags
Jute/cotton	25/75	• Low cost • Ethnic look	Drapery and apparel

Textile Finishes

'Textile finish' is an all-inclusive term for a number of treatments that can be applied to a freshly woven fabric to enhance its properties or to overcome its limitations. Finishes may be applied to the fabric to improve its appearance, produce variety, improve its suitability and utility for certain purposes, increase its weight and stiffness, or to produce imitations of other fabrics or effects. Various types of finishes are outlined in Figure 18.13.

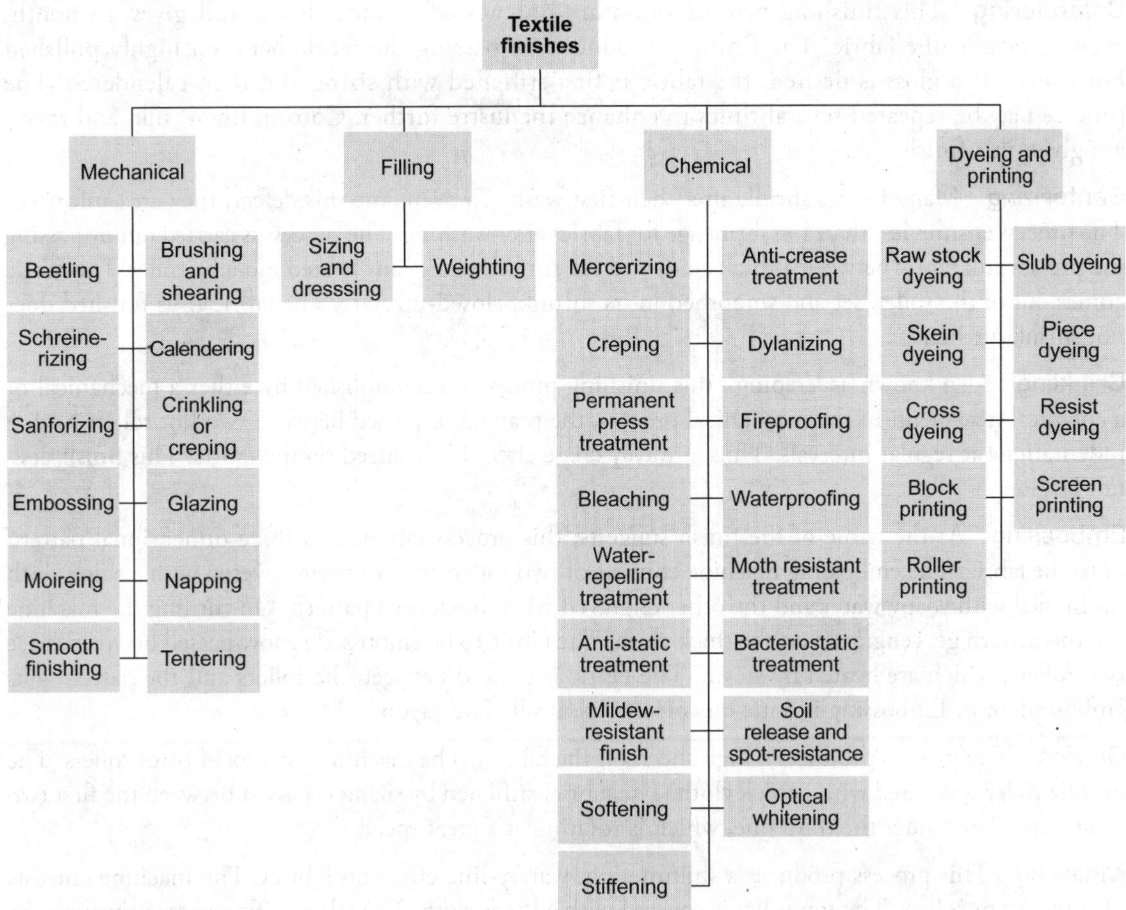

Fig. 18.13 Various types of finishes

Mechanical Finishes

These are the physical finishing processes carried out on fabrics:

Beetling This process renders the fabric lustrous and soft as well as giving it a firm, leathery feel. Beetling was originally carried out by beating the fabric surface with wooden mallets, but now a machine with a number of steel hammers is used. The fibres are flattened by the impact, the weave is closed up, and thus the desired lustrous effect is produced. This finish is typically given to cotton and linen. After beetling, cottons look like linen.

Brushing and shearing This process clips any short end of fibres or yarns sticking out of the fabric. The fabric is passed through two roller brushes and both sides of the material are cleaned at the same time.

Schreinerizing This is a finish that gives strength and lustre to cotton. Steam rollers with thousands of ingrained diagonal lines press down on the fabric as it is rolled between them. The reflection of light from the ridges of the diagonal lines on the fabric gives a lustrous effect. This is not a permanent finish as the lines disappear with repeated washing.

Calendering This finishing process smoothes out wrinkles, adds sheen, and gives a smooth, even surface to the fabric. The finish is produced by passing the fabric between highly polished hot rollers. If a gloss is desired, the fabric is first stiffened with sizing and then calendered. The process may be repeated several times to enhance the lustre further. Cotton, linen, silk, and rayon are given this finish.

Sanforizing Many fabrics shrink after their first wash. To overcome this defect, they are sanforized. The process ensures less than 1% shrinkage for fabrics after washing. The process is carried out by passing the pre-shrunk fabric between a thick cloth and the surface of a steam-heated metallic roller. The fabric comes out of the roller, set and smoothed in its shrunk, closed-up state. The fabric thus finished does not shrink further.

Crinkling Also known as 'creping', this finishing process is accomplished by either a mechanical or a chemical treatment. In the mechanical process, the material is passed between two hot rollers having indentations at regular intervals. Thus, a wavey crepe effect is produced on the fabric. This finish does not last long.

Embossing As the name of the finish suggests, this process embosses a three-dimensional pattern onto the fabric. The embossing machine consists of two rollers, one of them covered with a thick cloth moistened with soapy water and the other engraved with the desired pattern. On turning the machine on, the pattern gets engraved on the thick cloth. The fabric to be embossed is now passed between these two rollers, which are heated by steam. The fabric is pressed between the rollers and the pattern gets embossed on it. Embossing is done on cotton, linen, silk, and rayon.

Glazing The process produces a high sheen on the fabrics. The machine consists of three rollers. The middle roller is covered with a thick cloth. The fabric, stiffened by sizing is passed between the first two rollers and then under the third one, which is rotating at a great speed.

Moireing This process produces a shimmering, watery-line effect on fabrics. The machine consists of three steam rollers. The top roller is covered with a thick cloth. The fabric is first passed through the two rollers below and then under the top, cloth-covered roller. The top roller rotates at a greater speed, pressing down on the fabric heavily and producing the desired effect.

Napping This produces a raised effect on the fabric and renders it soft and warm. The fabric is first passed over a revolving cylinder covered with teasels (short bent wires). The teasels scratch the fibres up to form a nap on the fabric surface. The nap thus formed is then clipped to a uniform height by passing it through a shearing machine. Cotton and wool are given this finish. Napped cotton fabrics such as flannelette resemble wool.

Smooth finishing In this finish, the loose fibres projecting from either the yarn or the fabric are singed off by passing the fabric or skeins of yarn through a gas flame or even an electric plate at a rapid speed. The fabric is then calendered.

Tentering This finish is given to fabrics when their edges become uneven due to the processes of dyeing or wet-finishing. The tentering process straightens out the edges and the weaves of the fabrics, making it even in width. The machine has a frame through which the fabric is passed. A chain on either side of the frame catches the selvedges of the fabric and controls the pulling process for straightening out the material. Steam coils arranged underneath the frame dry the material during the process of stretching. Silk, wool, cotton, linen, and rayon may all be tentered.

Filling Finishes

Different types of filling finishes are discussed in this section.

Sizing and dressing In this finish, used on cotton, filling agents such as starch, China clay, magnesium sulphate, or magnesium chloride are applied on cotton. The process consists of passing the fabric between two steam-heated rollers. The sizing solution is poured in a regulated stream over one of the rollers. Addition of paraffin, glycerine, or oil to the sizing solution produces softness in the fabric. A wax may be added as well to give lustre to the fabric. The sizing wears off after repeated laundering. Linen is not sized unless it is of a poor quality.

Weighting This filling finish is given to silk and wool. The filling agents used are metallic salts. Silk is weighted using the metallic salts tin chloride and tin tannate, either in the yarn stage or as a woven fabric. It may also be weighted during the dyeing process, where the metallic salts are added to the dye. In the weighting process, the silk fibres absorb the metallic salts and swell. These salts are not removed even after repeated laundering. However, heavily weighted silk wears poorly—it cracks at the folds and rots if left in contact with perspiration.

In the weighting of wool, the metallic salt used is magnesium chloride. This makes the wool fibres absorb more moisture, thus increasing the fabric's weight.

Chemical Finishes

The different types of chemical finishes are as follows.

Mercerizing

Cottons are given a high degree of lustre through the chemical action of caustic soda (sodium hydroxide). The process consists of impregnating the fabric with a cold solution of caustic soda applied under tension to reduce shrinkage. Mercerized cotton also takes up dyes more readily.

Anti-crease treatment

This finish is also known as crease-proofing, tebilizing, or wash-and-wear finish. The process is used mostly for cotton, which wrinkles badly. The finish is produced by impregnating the fabric with a solution of synthetic resins such as phenol formaldehyde, urea formaldehyde, and acrylic resins. The fabric is then dried at a high temperature in a moist atmosphere. A clear insoluble resin is thus formed in the fabric, which improves its resilience. For white fabrics, urea formaldehyde is used since it is colourless. Phenol formaldehyde is dark in colour and, hence, suitable for use only on dark-coloured fabrics.

Creping

The crepe finish achieved by the chemical process is obtained by the treatment of fabric with caustic soda. Soda paste is applied on the fabrics in a definite design of stripes or figures. Parts to which the paste is applied shrink, leaving the other parts unshrunken. Thus, a crepe effect is produced on the fabric. The chemical process of creping is more long-lasting than the mechanical one.

Dylanizing

This finish is a chemical treatment given to wool to control felting and shrinkage.

Permanent press treatment

This finish is also called the 'crease-retentive finish' or 'durable press'. In this process, a resin treatment is given to a fabric, which is then stitched into a garment. The garment is then given a heat treatment at 150–160°C for 3 minutes. The pleats or creases set into the garment and become permanent. The garments require only light pressing henceforth and the creases stand up to the usual laundry processes.

Fireproofing

This chemical finish is also known as the 'flame-retardant finish'. Certain chemicals such as THPC (tetrakis-hydroxymethyl phosphonium chloride), THPOH (tetrakis-hydroxymethyl phosphonium hydroxide) and several boron-phosphorus, halogen-phosphorus, nitrogen-phosphorus, and antimony compounds confer flame-retardant properties to fabrics. A simple do-it-yourself method for making fabrics flame-retardant is to immerse the fabric, as a last rinse after washing, in a solution of 7 parts of borax and 3 parts boric acid dissolved in 90 parts of water.

Bleaching

This is necessary if any staining or discolouration have occurred during prior manufacturing processes. Bleaching results in a pure white material. When fabrics have been bleached for finishing, they are referred to as 'bleached goods'. Bleaching can be carried out by oxidizing or reducing agents. The chief oxidizing bleaches are ozone, hydrogen peroxide, hypochlorites such as sodium hypochlorite, sodium chlorate, sodium chlorite, potassium persulphate, and sodium perborate. The main reducing bleaches are stannous chloride, titanous chloride, zinc dust, sodium sulphite, sodium bisulphite, sodium sulphide, and glucose.

Waterproofing

In this finishing process, the interstices of the fabric as well as the surface of the fibres are covered with a thin skin or film, so that the fabric not only sheds water, but also becomes impermeable to air and moisture. This is accomplished by any one of the following methods:

Rubberizing the fabric To do this, the fabrics are treated with a rubber solution.

Application of latex To do this, the fabrics are treated with rubber latex.

Oiling of fabrics In this process, fabrics are treated with layers of linseed oil and metallic salts. The resultant fabrics are called 'oilskins'.

Water-repelling treatment

In this finishing process, the fibres are made water repellent by coating with hydrophobic substances or by a chemical reaction. The difference between a water-repellent finish and a waterproof finish is that with the former, the fabric remains porous to air—in other words, these are fabrics that breathe. The hydrophobic substances used in this process may be aluminium acetate, anionic paraffin wax, casein, glue, gelatin, or silicones.

Hydrophilic finish

This is a fibre or fabric coating process that modifies the surface properties of fibres with low moisture affinity such as polyester and nylon to render them moisture absorbent. A hydrophilic or water affinity agent such as a partial ester or polyhydric alcohol is applied in the process. This finish also confers anti-static and anti-soiling properties to the fabrics.

Anti-moth treatment

This finish is especially important for wool. Wool is treated with chemicals such as fluorine compounds, chlorinated sulphonamides, and quaternary phosphonium compounds to make it mothproof. The finish wears off after a few washes, but is fast to dry-cleaning.

Anti-static treatment

The static electricity that develops in synthetic fabrics causes problems such as clinging of the garment to the wearer, attraction of dirt, and sparking. Such fabrics are given a chemical treatment that enables the fabric to attract and retain water molecules, thus helping to dissipate the electric charge from the fabric surface.

Bacterio-static treatment

This is also called 'anti-bacterial finish'. A chemical treatment makes the fabrics resistant to bacterial growth, as it does not allow microbes to thrive when they come into contact with it. This finish is given to linens used in hospitals.

Anti-mildew treatment

Cellulosic and wool-blended fabrics are prone to mildew in humid climates if left moist in the dark. This chemical finish resists the growth of mildew or mould on the fabric surface. Many other finishes, such as the crease-resistant finish, fireproof finish, and water-repellent finish, also confer mildew resistance on the fabric.

Soil release and spot-resisting treatment

Some finishes make the fabric resistant to waterborne stains while others make them resistant to oil-borne stains. There are also finishes that render fabrics resistant to both types of stains. Repeated laundering, however, reduces the effectiveness of the finish. A soil-release finish can be accomplished by the treatment of fabric with any one of the following chemicals:

- Polymers containing carboxylic groups.
- Compounds containing oxyethylene or hydroxyl groups.
- Fluorocarbons containing hydrophilic groups.
- Chemically reactive compounds.

Softening

Fabrics tend to start feeling harsh after repeated laundering. This is due to the build-up of salts (present in hard water) on the fibres during the last rinse of the washing process. Softness can be imparted to these fabrics using chemical softeners in the laundry process. Softeners coat the fibres of the fabric and make them softer and fluffier. Treatment with softeners also prolongs the life of the fabric, cuts down static build-up, and improves the performance of any wash-and-wear finish. Softeners also act as bacteriostats. Too much softener, however, decreases absorbency.

Softeners are surface-active agents with a long hydrophobic ('water-hating') chain and a short hydrophilic ('water-loving') group. The hydrophobic part determines the softening character of the softener. The type of ionic charge (positive or negative) on the softening agent influences its orientation on the textile. Anionic softeners are not preferred since they are required in high concentrations and do not give as good

a surface feel as cationic softeners. Soaps of sodium and potassium stearate with glycerol monostearate are anionic softeners used on cotton and rayon fabrics. Cationic softeners are much more effective and are absorbed by the fibres in the final rinse. The cationic compounds used in this process are quaternary ammonium salts (such as distearyl-dimethyl ammonium chloride), alkylolamides, and imidazolium salts.

Softeners are available in various concentrations—5%, 10%, 15%, or more, the most common being the 5% strength. Since most softeners are cationic in nature, they should not be added along with soaps, anionic washing powders, or liquid detergents. The softeners should ideally be dispersed in water meant for the last rinse. The clothes should then be thoroughly agitated for 2–3 minutes in this water to ensure even absorption of the softeners by the fabric. The fabric is then dried.

Optical whitening

White fabrics tend to yellow after repeated use and laundering. This yellowish tinge can be masked by using optical whiteners during the laundry process. It is important to understand that bleaching is not an optical whitening process, since it whitens the fabrics by destroying the colouring matter; optical whiteners only mask the yellowish tinge. The two types of optical brighteners are laundry blues and fluorescent brightening agents.

Laundry blues These are actually blue dyes, soluble in water. They are added to white fabrics in the final rinse. Their blue cast masks the yellowness of the fabric and makes it appear whiter. The blues get leached out in subsequent washes. The three dyes that have been used as laundry blue are: (1) Ultramarine blue; (2) Prussian blue; and (3) Aniline blue.

Of the three dyes, ultramarine monopolizes the market today and is available in both powder and liquid form. The powder form contains another additive as an extender. The extender may be sodium bicarbonate, sodium carbonate, dextrin, glucose, glycerine, glucose, or corn syrup. A small amount of aniline is also added sometimes. Ultramarine blue may be man-made or obtained from natural sources. Most of the ultramarine blue in the market is man-made and is manufactured from kaolin, sodium carbonate, sodium sulphate, and sulphur. These substances are thoroughly mixed together and coal is used to reduce the sulphate to sulphite. The final product is a double silicate of sodium and aluminium together with sodium sulphate. Ultramarine blue is sensitive to even weak acids, and acid-resistant ultramarine blues are now being manufactured. Ultramarine blue is not adversely affected by alkalis except lime.

Let us now discuss the action of blueing. White light is made up of seven colours—violet, indigo, blue, green, yellow, orange, and red. A coloured object has a particular colour because it reflects only that colour of the spectrum. For example, a red fabric reflects only the red colour of the spectrum. An object appears white when it reflects all the seven colours of the spectrum, whereas an object appears black when it absorbs all the colours of the spectrum. When a blueing agent is used on white clothes, additional blue colour is reflected.

Fluorescent brightening agents Fluorescent brightening agents (FBAs) are colourless chemical compounds that have a strong tendency to absorb light of shorter wavelengths, that is, in the ultra violet region—and re-emit light of longer wavelengths—that is in the visible range. These chemicals are also called 'white dyes' and 'fluorescers'. When present on fabric, a fluorescer does not absorb light in the visible region and hence, reflects the entire visible radiation incident on it.

However, it absorbs some ultraviolet rays from sunlight and emits this. The emitted rays are of a longer wavelength. Fluorescent light, which has a preponderance of blue light, adds on to the reflected light, which is deficient in blue light, thus restoring the balance of different colours and producing a brilliant white effect.

Stiffening

A certain amount of crispness in fabrics gives them a fresh look. This crisp appearance is obtained by using stiffeners. Commonly the term 'starching' is used for the process, even though the stiffening agent may be something other than starch. Stiffening is carried out for the following purposes:

- To impart crispness to the fabric to give a neat appearance.
- To help keep clothes clean for a longer time by holding down the surface fibres that catch dust and dirt.
- To facilitate stain and soil removal since, after stiffening, stains and dirt remain on the surface and do not penetrate into the fabric.

Stiffening agents are classified as shown in Table 18.12. The methods of use of these stiffeners is summarized in Table 18.13.

Table 18.12 Classification of stiffening agents

Category	Type	Name
Natural	Starches	Maize, wheat, rice, sago, potato, tapioca, arrowroot
	Gums	Arabic, tragacanth, locust beans, guar, agar
	Glues	Gelatin, albumin, casein
	Gluesx	Pre-gelatinized acid-modified, oxidized, chlorinated dextrin
Modified natural	Cellulose derivatives	Carboxymethyl cellulose (CMC), hydroxymethyl cellulose, methyl cellulose, hydroxypropyl cellulose
	Gums	Meyprogum, Indalca
	Glues	Soyabean
Synthetic	Vinyl	Polyvinyl pyrolidone, polyvinyl alcohols, polyvinyl ethers
	Acrylic	Polyacrylic acid and its derivatives, polyacrilamides

Table 18.13 Methods of using stiffeners

Stiffener	Preparation and use	Fabrics on which used
Hot-water starches	Make a paste in a little cold water and pour into boiling water. Cook till the solution is translucent. Prepare to whatever consistency is required for light, medium, or heavy starching.	Cotton, linen, and rayon Cotton, linen, and rayon
Cold-water starches	Pre-cooked starches dissolve in cold water. Mix to obtain light, medium, or heavy starching. Follow directions on the package.	Silk
Gelatin	Add 30 g of gelatine to 2 cups of cold water and heat until it dissolves. Dilute 1 part of this solution in 8–15 parts of hot water for use.	
Gum Arabic	Add 30 g gum Arabic to 2 cups of cold water and heat until it dissolves. Dilute 5–10 times in hot water.	Silk, wool
Gum tragacanth	Mix 20 g of tragacanth in 2 cups of cold water and heat until it dissolves. Dilute 8–12 times in hot water.	Wool, silk, and dark cottons
Glue	Dissolve 1 g glue in 1 cup of water by boiling. Keep the quantity to 1 cup, by adding hot water as needed.	Wool
Synthetic sizings	Dilute to required consistency and use.	Wool, cotton laces

Note: A small amount of borax may be added when preparing the starch solution to help preserve it. Addition of 2% boric acid acts as an antiseptic. It helps to prevent mildew formation on the starched fabric.

Dyeing and Printing

Not strictly speaking 'finishes', these processes are used to enhance the appearance of fabric by adding colour and pattern.

Raw stock dyeing The fibres of wool, cotton, linen, and silk are dyed by this method. The stock of fibres is rotated in the dye bath, then removed and dried.

Slub dyeing This method is used in dyeing wool fibres after these have been combed. The skeins of wool slivers are hung on rods. The rods are then placed on top of the dye bath. The rods are made to rotate, so that the slubs keep constantly moving through the dye bath. They are then rinsed and dried.

Skein dyeing/yarn dyeing Yarn of almost all types of fibre may be dyed by this method. Cotton and linen are generally dyed at the yarn stage, as the penetration of colour in skein dyeing is much better. Skeins of yarn are hung on rods, which are placed in a dye bath. These rods rotate, causing the skeins to circulate through the dye bath.

Piece dyeing This may be used on fabrics made from any fibre. The penetration of colour in this type of dyeing is not as thorough as in the aforementioned forms of dyeing, however. The pieces (unit lengths of fabric) are wrapped around rollers, which are placed in the dye bath and left there until the pieces are saturated with the colour.

Cross dyeing Fabrics woven with mixed yarns such as cotton or wool with acetate rayon or viscose rayon are dyed by this method. The affinity of the dyestuffs to the yarns differs according to the two kinds of yarns mixed in weaving. Therefore, the fabrics are dyed in two successive dye baths. In one dye bath, the dye suitable for one kind of yarn is used and another dye suitable for the other yarn is used in the next dye bath.

Resist dyeing This is a simple dyeing method by which many intricate designs can be produced in the fabric. Various methods are in use.

Tie-dyeing In the tie-and-dye method, the parts of the fabric or the yarn that are to resist the dye are tied with string or narrow strips of cloth, which have been waxed to increase dye resistance and get better results. The skeins of yarn or the fabric are then dipped into the dye bath. The material is then rinsed and dried. When the ties are removed, a pattern of undyed portions is left.

Batik This is another form of resist dyeing in which hot melted wax is used as the resist material.

Block printing In this method of printing, blocks made of wood are carved with designs and cut to a thickness of 1/4 inch. The paste of dye is poured into trays lined with cloth. The fabric to be printed is spread on a padded table and held taut and smooth. Then the block is dipped into the tray so that it is smeared with paste of one colour and stamped on the material, which is then allowed to dry. Another block smeared with a paste of a different colour is then stamped over it to form multi-coloured patterns. The process is repeated over the entire fabric surface to be printed.

Screen printing In this method, a silk bolting cloth or wire cloth is stretched over a wooden frame to absorb the excess colour paste. Over this, a line drawing of the design for a single colour is made. The areas of the screen thus demarcated, portions of it that the colour is not to spread over are filled in with waterproof varnish. The fabric to be printed is stretched on a table padded and covered with oilcloth. The wooden frame with the screen is placed on the material and the paste of colour is brushed over its surface and then lightly pressed down. The colour is then allowed to dry. Then another frame

carrying a different colour and different pattern outline is used in the same way to build up the pattern. The process continues till the design is complete. A separate screen is required for the application of each colour in the design.

Roller printing This is done by printing machines consisting of several engraved copper cylinders or rollers. The roller is as wide as the cloth. The number of rollers required depends on the number of colours used in the design as one roller can print only one colour.

Ethnic Textiles of India

A housekeeper must have knowledge of the various indigenous textiles of the country they work in as traditional textiles are part of showcasing the culture of the region in hotels. Housekeepers are often involved in selecting such textiles and the care of these too is under their purview. India has a rich heritage of textiles and almost every state produces some or the other unique ethnic textile it is famous for. Many of the textiles described in this section have GI tags. Please scan the QR code to access all ethnic fabrics images described in this section.

Handwoven Fabrics

Khadi (See Figure 18.14). No other fabric represents India better than Khadi. The term itself is derived from 'khaddar' meaning handspun fabric. Originally made from handspun cotton yarns and handwoven, it is now also made in silk and wool. The fabric has a rugged texture and a unique feature in that it keeps the wearer warm in winters and cool in summers. Khadi is used in making ethnic garments, furnishings and accessories.

Brocades The highly ornamental brocade fabrics are woven in such a way that the intricate designs look embossed due to the extra warp or weft woven in gold and silver threads or rich silk threads on the background fabric. Banarasi brocades and saris from the holy city of Banaras have a GI tag and are world famous. Apart from saris, they are used in furnishings and other accessories. Kinkhab (See Figure 18.15) is the best-known Banarasi brocade, in the form of heavy silk brocaded with silver and gold. Baluchari fabrics (See Figure 18.16.) from Murshidabad in West Bengal are unique in that they are woven with only silk on silk and not gold or silver zari. Baluchari saris from Murshidabad have a GI tag.

Fig. 18.14 Khadi

Fig. 18.15 Kinkhab Banarasi brocade

Fig. 18.16 Baluchari fabric

Fig. 18.17 Kancheepuram silk

Kancheepuram silk (See Figure 18.17) One of the most expensive fabrics, Kancheepuram or Kanjeevaram silk originates from Kancheepuram in Tamilnadu, and has a GI tag. It is used in making saris for festive occasions. These handloom woven fabrics are made from pure mulberry silk and gold zari. The motifs are drawn from the temple architecture and natural surroundings and comprise of peacock, parrot, bird's eye, terracotta pot and so on. Scenes from religious epics too are common.

Pashmina (See Figure 18.18 via scan code) Derived from the fleece or *pashm* of the Changthangi goat reared in Ladhakh by the Changpa tribe, Pashmina is handspun and handwoven by Kashmiri weavers in twill tapestry technique. The resulting fabric has a gloss and is fluffy and soft. The fabric is then embroidered by hand using silk threads and is used in making shawls, coats, stoles and scarves. Pashmina is highly expensive due to the laborious processes involved in all the stages of its crafting. Kashmir pashmina has a GI tag.

Paithani (See Figure 18.19 via scan code) These rich handloom silk fabrics originate from the villages of Paithan and Yeola in Maharashtra and are mainly used in making saris for festive occasions. The intricate motifs are woven in interlocking twill tapestry technique and look the same on both sides of the cloth. Silk threads in bright jewel hues such as ruby red, emerald green, vibrant yellow, and midnight blue are used for weaving. The motifs are geometrical patterns of flowers such as lotus, parrots, peacock, and paisley. A broad band of zari and bright threads in the sari veil is another feature of Paithani. Paithani saris and fabrics have GI tag from Maharashtra.

Apatani fabrics (See Figure 18.20 via scan code) These are woven by Apatani tribe of Ziro, Arunachal Pradesh. The woven fabric is known for angular and zig zag geometric patterns and finds use in daily wear of the tribe. The fabrics are woven for rituals and festive occasions.

Kulvi patti (See Figure 18.21 via scan code) These intricately woven distinct border motif designs from the Kullu Valley of Himachal Pradesh are part of the traditional caps and Kullu shawls worn by the locals in the hills. The shawls which have GI tag from Himachal Pradesh typically have three lines of kulvi pattis. The brilliantly coloured pattis are woven into the plain background fabric of angora or pashmina wool.

Muga silk fabrics (See Figure 18.22 via scan code) With a GI tag for being endemic to Assam, produced traditionally by the Garo community, muga silk is known for its fine texture and durable natural yellow gold tint, the lustre increasing with every wash. Muga silk is used to make traditional garments of Assamese women, the *Mekhala Chador*.

Eri silk fabrics (See Figure 18.23 via scan code) From the state of Meghalaya comes the eri silk fabric, also known as 'peace silk' as the silk fibres are extracted from the cocoon using 'non-violent' methods. The moths are reared in baskets in households and mature ones are placed on cocooning mountages. The cocoons are then sundried, degummed, and then hand-spun with a traditional spindle. The yarns are dyed with natural dyes obtained from plants and minerals; traditionally only three colours, lac red, turmeric yellow and mineral black are used. Khneng embroidery embellishes the borders of the fabric with motifs inspired from a local centipede.

Panja durries (See Figure 18.24 via scan code) Produced in the town of Panipat in Haryana, Panja is a rich, thick woven handloom fabric used in making durries and rugs. The name derives from the claw-like metal tool which forms a part of the loom implements. In Rajasthan, Panja durries were traditionally woven from coarse goat and camel hair, but these have been replaced with thick cotton yarns.

Wraps of North East Phanek tribal weave (See Figure 18.25 via scan code) forms the traditional Manipuri costume, the black striped or block coloured wrap handwoven in cotton and silk threads with a heavily woven or embroidered border at the lower end. The border motifs vary from tribe to tribe, often portraying a legend. The weave is now also used in scarves, stoles and waistcoats. Puan cloth (See Figure 18.26 via scan code) is the traditional wrap of Mizoram, portraying few colours and predominantly white and black. The type of puan worn by the wearer divulges the status of the native. The motifs include ginger flower, roses and stars. All five Mizo puan cloths have GI tags. Chakhesang textiles (See Figure 18.27 via scan code) of the tribe from Nagaland of the same name, is woven from yarns extracted from the stinging nettle plant. These fabrics are used in weaving shawls, bedsheets and wrapping cloth for babies. Chakhesang Naga shawls have Gi tag.

Kasavu (See Figure 18.28 via scan code) Originating from the state of Kerala is the Kasavu, a soft, off-white, unbleached, handwoven cotton with gold threaded borders. The cloth is used to make saris, and mundu-veshti sets. Kasavu cloth garments are an integral part of all celebrations and festive and religious occasions. Kasavu has a GI tag from three clusters in Kerala.

Handprinted Handwoven Fabrics

Kalamkari (See Figure 18.29 via scan code) This naturally dyed fabric comes mainly from Machilipatnam and Srikalahasti in Andhra Pradesh, where it is still made with ancient techniques and has GI tags. *Kalam* refers to pen and *kari* means craftsmanship, and the artisans draw intricate designs on the milk and cow dung prepared fabric with bamboo reed pen and then natural dyes are applied with thicker pens in various steps. Originally practised on pure cotton, now it is also done on silk. The fabrics are used in making wall hangings and panels, saris, dress materials, bags and accessories.

Ikat Ikats are yarn resist dyed fabrics and may be in the form of single ikat or double ikat. In single ikat, either the warp or weft yarn is resist dyed as per the design and then woven in intricate designs. The famous GI tagged ikats of India include Pochampally ikat (See Figure 18.30 via scan code) and Telia Rumal (See Figure 18.31 via scan code) from Telangana, Sambalpuri Ikat (See Figure 18.32 via scan code) from Odisha, and Patola from Gujarat. Patola (See Figure 18.33 via scan code) is an ikat fabric GI tagged from Patan, Gujarat. Once favoured and affordable only by the royalty, the painstakingly intricate, time-consuming dyeing and weaving technique makes the silk patola one of the most expensive woven fabrics. Each warp or weft silk yarn is tied in accordance with the intricate designs using cotton threads and dyed using natural colours extracted from onion skin, madder root, marigold, pomegranate rind, lac, cochineal, indigo, henna and so on. The tie and dye process is repeated depending on the number of colours in the design. The motifs are characterised by geometric patterns of flowers, birds and animals.

Bandhani or Bandhej & Lahariya Traditionally created by the Khatri community of Gujarat, Bandhani (See Figure 18.34 via scan code) is a cloth resist dyeing technique which produces white dots wherever the dye resists penetrating tied cloth. It is mainly done on finer varieties of cotton and silk fabrics with the tie-dyed dots in motifs of flowers, plants, human and animal figures. Jamanagari bandhani has a GI tag.

The same technique of cloth resist dyeing from Rajasthan is called Bandhej (See Figure 18.35 via scan code). Apart from white resist dots, patterns of flowers and geometric designs are also created by tiny squares. Another tie-dyeing technique from Rajasthan is the Lahariya (See Figure 18.36 via scan code) in which diagonal white lines are created by tightly rolling the fabric and tying resist threads at regular intervals. It is traditionally used to make headgear of menfolk of the region.

Embroidered Fabrics

Kashida (See Figure 18.37 via scan code) A delicate embroidery style from Kashmir, Kashida showcases intricate needlework on cotton, wool or silk fabrics with embroidery threads in silk, or wool. The motifs are inspired from natural surroundings of the Kashmir valley and comprise of birds such as kingfisher, parakeet and magpie, butterflies, chinar leaves, cherries, grapes, plums and almonds. The main stitches used in the embroidery are chain stitch, darning stitch, fly stitch, stem stitch and satin stitch.

Phulkari (See Figure 18.38 via scan code) Phulkari, literally meaning 'flower work' has its origin in Punjab and is accomplished on handspun and handwoven, dyed khaddar cloth. For the embroidery, untwisted, soft silk threads in bright colours are used and inspiration for motifs range from nature such as flowers, birds, flora and fauna to daily-use items such as sword, rolling pin and vegetables, executed in geometrical and stylized designs. One motif is typically left unembroidered or embroidered in an unusual colour, depicting the concept of warding off the evil eye. Phulkari is traditionally done on the bridal veil and also on the canopy cloth used in religious occasions. Phulkari has a GI tag from Punjab, Haryana and Rajasthan.

Chamba rumal (See Figure 18.39 via scan code) These fabrics of either delicate muslin or coarse, handwoven khaddar, showcase the ethnic embroidery style of Chamba in Himachal Pradesh. The embroidery is executed in double satin stitch with untwisted, silk threads dyed in bright colours. The reversible motifs are nature-inspired, comprising flora and fauna of the region, particularly willow and cypress trees, shrubs, flowers, goat, deer, peacock, parrot, horse, tiger and so on. Also portrayed are common musical instruments. Earlier done exclusively on square pieces of cloth used on religious occasions, the Chamba embroidery has found its way into fabrics for caps, cushion covers, silk wall hangings, blouses and slippers. Chamba rumal has a GI tag from Himachal Pradesh.

Chikankari (See Figure 18.40 via scan code) The popular embroidered fabric of Lucknow in Uttar Pradesh, is traditionally done on fine white cotton cloth with untwisted white cotton or silk thread. Nowdays it is also done on chiffons, georgettes and crepe silks. Three types of stiches are used, flat stitches of stem and herringbone, raised stitches of French knots and bullion, and pulled stitches or jaali work. The motifs are nature-inspired flowers and creepers in lacy patterns. Shadow work carried out in herringbone stitches is a unique feature of this embroidery. Chikankari fabrics in varied pastel colours are used in making kurtas, saris, and summer wear garments. Lucknow chikan craft has a GI tag from Uttar Pradesh.

Zardozi (See Figure 18.41 via scan code) A rich embroidery traditionally done in gold and silver threads, Zardozi is practiced in cities of Lucknow, Bareilly, Bhopal, Benaras and Agra in Uttar Pradesh,

Delhi and Chennai. Lucknow zardozi has a GI tag. The embroidery is stitched on luxury fabrics such as velvet, silk and satin using various kinds of decorative metal wires, sequins, beads and pearl. The main stitches employed are satin, chain and stem stitch. The fabric to be embroidered is stretched and fastened on a wooden frame and the embroidery is worked with a hook, the motifs being floral and geometrical patterns. It was traditionally done on wall hangings, palanquin covers, cushion covers, jackets and shoes but now finds its use in dress materials too.

Kasuti (See Figure 18.42 via scan code) The traditional embroidery of Karnataka and having a GI tag from here, Kasuti is done on handwoven cloth of dark colour with cotton threads. The four basic stitches used are simple running stitch (Negi), double running stitch (Gavanti), zig-zag running stitch in stepwise manner (Murgi), and cross stitch (Menthi). The motifs are geometrical representations of flora and fauna, and those inspired from architecture and religion of the region. The kasuti embroidered fabrics are used in saris, cushion covers, curtains, bed covers, handbags, belts and so on.

Kantha (See Figure 18.43 via scan code) This unique running-stitch embroidered fabric hails from West Bengal and Odisha. The embroidery is traditionally stitched with mercerised cotton threads on layers of old silk and cotton saris and dhotis meant for reuse, cotton quilts, blankets, and bedsheets. The motifs consist of flora and fauna, birds, human figures, pots, musical instruments and geometrical patterns. Nakshi Kantha or the kantha embroidered quilt has a GI tag from West Bengal.

Shisha work fabrics (See Figure 18.44 via scan code) Mirror work embroidery of the tribes from the Kutch and Kathiawar region of Gujarat is very popular in fabrics used to make bags, pouches, ghagra cholis, and doorway and wall hangings etc. The unique features of the embroidery are the use of lightweight mirrors or mica bound with stitches in multicoloured threads of silk or cotton. The main stitches used are buttonhole, chain, herringbone, satin, interlace, and darning stitches. The motifs are derived from the flora and fauna of the region such as creepers, flowers, trees, elephants, parrots, peacocks, human figures and also geometrical designs. The tribes have many styles of mirror work such as Abhla Bharat, Mochi Bharat, Soof Bharat, Moti Bharat and Kachcho Bharat. Kutch embroidery has a GI tag from Gujarat.

Use of Textiles in Hotels

Cotton is the most diversely used fabric. However, 'pure' or 100% cotton fabrics are not much in demand in hotels because of certain undesirable properties, such as their tendency to crease easily, soil easily, and shed lint, their high rate of shrinkage, their susceptibility to mildew, and their longer drying time. At the same time, cotton blends with other fibres are extremely popular. Sheeting made from cotton-polyester blends have replaced pure cotton in many hotels. Cotton-polyester blends are also used for making upholstery, drapery material and F&B linen. Satin band material, which is cotton woven in satin weave, is widely used as table linen in fine dine restaurants and speciality F&B outlets in luxury hotels. Cotton blends also make good materials for staff uniforms.

Linen materials have been traditionally used for table and bed linens, although now mostly replaced by cotton in this use. Inferior grades of linen are made into drying cloths for use in kitchens and bathrooms and also to make up the inner lining of curtains. Linen is also used for making newspaper bags, mail bags, and hosepipe covers. Linen thread may be used to stitch upholstery and carpets. The fibre is also made into canvas, double and single damask, and slubbed dress linen. Linen may also be used as a material for uniforms.

Jute is primarily used for making hessian, sacking, dhurries, and cheap pile fabrics. Jute is also used in the manufacture of twine, rope, and carpets, especially carpet backing. Bleached jute is sometimes used as a filling weft to cotton warp in 'linen' towelling.

Ramie, a vegetable fibre, has been found suitable for weaving into fine table linen such as tray cloths, table cloths, and napkins as the material stiffens easily when ironed damp. Ramie is more absorbent than cotton. It also dries more rapidly than cotton and linen.

In case of wool, Merino is used for high-quality worsted and hand-knit woollens, blankets, and speciality fabrics. Certain types of tweeds are made from carpet wools. Carpet wools are used for making carpets and mattress fillings. The heavy-duty wool used for uniforms and coat lengths are serge, gabardine, whipcord, and twill.

Indian tussar silk is used as tapestry and upholstery material. Upholstery materials may use mixtures of spun silk and other fibres. Many hotels use silk as a curtain material for a luxurious look in restaurants and lobbies. Some deluxe hotels use silk saris as uniforms for the female front office staff.

The regenerated fibre rayon is used in the form of drapery satin, taffeta, brocades, jacquards, and table damask woven out of rayon yarn. Rayon yarn may be used in upholstery fabrics to add richness to the base fabric of cotton or wool. The use of rayon also increases the fabric's resistance to deterioration by sunlight.

Acetate fabrics are used for making baby blankets, curtains, and upholstery material. Glass fabrics are used for products such as shower curtains, table cloths, bedspreads, awnings, lampshades, window dressings, and upholstery.

SUMMARY

From the ancient days, India has been famous for its beautiful fabrics. Mention of spinning and weaving is found in the Puranas and the Vedas. The *Arthashastra* makes mention of wool, cotton, hemp, and flax fibres used for spinning in ancient times. Textile fabrics are now used not only for clothing, but also as soft furnishings in a big way.

Over the past few decades, new fabrics have emerged, modern methods of manufacture have come to be used, new finishes have evolved, and textile technology has become a science in itself.

A student of housekeeping management and operations should have a fundamental knowledge of textile fibres, weaves, finishes, and so on since, in hotels, the housekeeping department is responsible for handling the hotel's fabrics in terms of selection, cleaning, and maintenance—be it bed linen, bath linen, soft furnishings, uniforms, or guests' clothing.

The chapter begins with a description of the basic textile terms. The classification of fibres and their identification using different methods has been explained in detail as this helps housekeepers in selection of fabrics for hotel linens and uniforms. Further, important fibres have been individually discussed in depth so that their characteristics, advantages, and limitations are understood.

Before the fabric construction process, the fibres are usually made into yarn. The types of yarn and the yarn characteristics of component fibres in a fabric determine the fabric's properties to a great extent. The methods of fabric construction have been discussed briefly. A visit to a textile mill is highly recommended to gain an insight into these processes. Different kinds of weaves and their characteristics have been explained with illustrations for better comprehension. The type of weave a fabric is constructed of drastically changes the fabric's properties.

Most hotels are increasingly preferring blends and union fabrics for their superior performance in terms of aesthetics, lustre, drape, texture, colour, and cost reduction. These have been discussed in the section on blends. Textile finishes have been dealt with in detail, though special finishes applied to individual fibres/fabric are also mentioned while discussing the fibres.

The next section covers ethnic textiles of India as many hotels showcase them and use furnishings and uniforms made of heritage textiles.

The use of textiles in hotels is varied and one may find fabrics on the walls, floors, and furniture as soft furnishings, apart from being used as staff uniforms. A brief discussion on the use of textiles in hotels is presented as a conclusion to the chapter.

KEY TERMS

Awnings Decorative sheets of canvas or other thicker fabric used for shade against the sun or rain. In hotels, these are seen outside windows and over banquet tables.

Balance Here, the ratio of warp to weft yarns.

Bast fibres Fibres obtained from the 'bast' or woody part of the stem of a plant.

Beetling A finishing process for cotton and linen in which the fibres are flattened and the weave is closed up, producing the desired lustrous effect.

Blends Blended fabrics are made of yarn in which two or more fibres are mixed while the yarn is spun.

Calendering This is a finishing process that smoothes out wrinkles, adds sheen, and gives a smooth, even surface to the fabric. The finish is produced by passing the fabric between highly polished, hot rollers.

Carcinogenic Cancer-causing.

Cultivated silk This is made by silkworms (*Bombyx mori*) of the Bombycidae family, which feed on mulberry leaves.

Damask A glossy fabric with intricate, jacquard-woven designs made from cotton, silk, viscose rayon, or mixtures. It is the preferred fabric for table linen.

Denier The yarn count for filament fibres is expressed in terms of weight per unit length, each unit being called a 'denier'.

Dupion silk Silk woven from an uneven double thread produced when two cocoons nest together.

Dylanizing This finish is a chemical treatment given to wool to control felting and shrinkage.

Ends See Warp yarns.

FBAs Fluorescent brightening agents. These are colourless chemical compounds that have a strong tendency to absorb light of shorter wavelengths (that is, in the ultraviolet part of the spectrum) and then emit light of longer wavelengths (that is, in the visible range). This makes the fabric on which they are applied appear a brilliant white.

Fibre A fibre is the basic unit from which a fabric is made. Fibres may be classified as staple or filament.

Fibroin The protein of silk fibres.

Filament fibres These fibres are long and continuous in length. They are measured in yards or metres. Silk is the only natural fibre found in filament form. All other filament fibres are man-made.

Filling yarns Weft yarns.

Finish A treatment given to a fabric to improve its qualities—such as appearance, hand, or drape—or to introduce certain characteristics such as making it water-repellant or fire-retardant.

Flannelette A cotton fabric in plain weave with a brushed or napped surface.

Flax A plant whose bast fibres are used in the manufacture of linen.

Hydrophobic Water-hating.

Jacquard A decorative weave resulting in intricate, often multi-coloured designs, woven on Jacquard loom, invented by Joseph Marie Jacquard.

Line yarn The yarn produced from longer linen fibres. Line yarn produces a strong material with high resistance to dirt and is used for bed and table linens and upholstery materials.

Linen Material woven from fibres of the flax plant; household articles (such as bedclothes or napery) that were originally made from this material, though now cotton and other material is often preferred; the term is also loosely used to denote all launderable articles in the linen room. Actual linen material is less elastic and more absorbent than cotton.

Mercerization A finishing process in which cottons are given a high degree of lustre through the chemical action of caustic soda (sodium hydroxide).

Mixture Same as union fabrics.

Moireing This finishing process produces a shimmering watery-line effect on fabrics.

Napery Table linen—table cloth and napkins.

Napping A finishing process that produces a raised effect on the fabric and renders it soft and warm. Cotton and wool are given this finish. Napped cotton fabrics such as flannelette resemble wool.

Optical whiteners Substances that mask the yellowish tinge developed in white fabrics after repeated laundering.

Percale A blended fabric made from combed fibres of polyester and cotton (50:50). Percale has a slight lustre and a softer hand than cotton. It is the preferred fabric for sheeting.

Picks See Weft yarns.

Pile weave A weave in which extra sets of warps or wefts, called 'pile', are woven perpendicularly into the ground fabric of plain or twill weave to form loops. The loops may be cut or left uncut.

Pills Minute rough, spherical fibre protrusions that mar the surface appearance of fabrics.

Ramie A woody fibre resembling flax. It is also known as rhea or China grass. It is strong, coarse, absorbent, lustrous, and has a good affinity to dyes.

Raw silk Cultivated silk just unreeled from the cocoons. The term also refers to the fabric or yarn processed from this untreated silk.

Regenerated fibres Fibres are made from substances retrieved from natural sources, which are then converted into fibre form. For example, wood pulp (chemically cellulose) is converted into cellulose fibres such as viscose rayon.

Sanforizing A process that ensures less than 1% shrinkage of fabrics after washing. The process is carried out by passing the pre-shrunk fabric between a thick cloth and the surface of a steam-heated metallic roller. The fabric comes out of the roller set and smoothed in its shrunk, closed-up state.

Schreinerizing A finish given for imparting strength and lustre to cotton in which steam rollers with thousands of ingrained diagonal lines press down on the fabric as it is rolled between them. Reflection of light from the ridges of the diagonal lines on the fabric gives a lustrous effect.

Seersucker A weave in which some warp yarns are held at tension and some loose at regular, frequent intervals while weaving. This produces a fabric with a crinkled effect. Crinkle sheets used as bed linen are often made in this weave.

Selvedge The longitudinal, visibly distinct edge along the length of a fabric on either side, closed by loops of weft yarn. The selvedge is usually more compact and stronger than the rest of the fabric.

Serecin The natural gum present in silk filaments that binds them together.

Sericulture The science dealing with the cultivation of silkworms for the production of silk.

Softeners Substances that coat the fibres of a fabric and make them softer and fluffier.

Spinnerette A device with a nozzle for forming filaments of synthetic fibres.

Spinning The process of making yarn from fibres.

Spun silk Silk is made from short lengths of inferior silk filaments or using filaments from broken cocoons. It is not as lustrous or durable as reeled silk.

Staple fibres Fibres that are shorter in length and measured in inches or centimetres. They range from 1.5 to 46 cm in length. All natural fibres except silk are staple fibres.

Tebilization A finish produced by impregnating cotton fabric with a solution of synthetic resins to make the fabric crease-resistant.

Tentering This finish is given to fabrics when their edges become uneven due to the processes of dyeing or wet finishing. The tentering process straightens out the edges and the weaves of the fabric, making it even in width.

Tex The yarn count for natural fibres is expressed in terms of weight per unit length, each unit of which is called a tex.

Textiles The term literally means that which has been or may be woven, but is now used to refer to and cover all fibres, yarns, and fabrics.

Thread count Indicates the number of warp ends and weft picks per unit of measure of a fabric.

Tow yarns Yarn produced from shorter linen fibres. Tow yarn produces a softer, more absorbent fabric than that produced from the longer fibres. Tow yarns are used for making glass cloths, towels, and fabrics that need to drape well.

TPI Twists per inch. The amount of twist given to a yarn is expressed as TPI.

Trubenizing In this finish, two pieces of rayon fabrics are fused together by the application of heat. This brings stiffness to the fabric and the trubenized rayon thus produced is used in making cuffs and collars of hotel uniforms.

Union fabrics A class of blended fabrics in which each yarn is of a single type of fibre.

Upholstery Textiles used for furniture décor.

Warp yarns The yarns running lengthwise in a fabric are called warp yarns or ends.

Weave The system of interlacing threads of warp and weft according to definite rules in order to produce the whole or part of a textile fabric.

Weaving The process of interlacing yarns or fibres to make a fabric.

Weft yarns The crosswise yarns in a fabric are called weft yarns, filling yarns, or picks.

Weighting This filling finish is given to silk and wool to increase the fabric's weight. The filling agents used are metallic salts. Silk is weighted using the metallic salts tin chloride and tin tannate.

Wild silk This silk is obtained from silk-producing insects that do not feed on mulberry leaves. The insects belong to the family Saturniidae. Some varieties of wild silk are tussar and muga.

Yarn count In the spinning process, there is always a relationship between the amount of original quantity of the fibre and the length of yarn produced from that amount of fibre. This relationship gives the fineness of the yarn. The fineness is designated by a number called the yarn count or yarn number.

Yarns Thread-like structures made by twisting together several staple fibres or filament fibres and used for weaving or knitting.

Yarn twist The spiral arrangement of fibres around the axis of the yarn. The twists bind the fibres together and give strength. They also help in varying the appearance of the fabric.

19

Linen and Laundry Operations

Learning Objectives

After reading this chapter, you should be able to

- list the activities carried out in the linen and uniform room and understand its planning and layout
- describe the linen exchange procedure for guestrooms and F&B areas
- establish the par stock of linen for a given hotel operation
- explain the importance and various aspects of linen control
- select linen according to its quality and lifespan
- be aware of the option of linen hire for housekeepers
- understand the types of laundries and the planning and layout of an on-premises laundry
- list the essential laundry equipment, aids, and materials and discuss the laundry process
- discuss the various aspects of stain removal, dry-cleaning, and handling of guest laundry
- appreciate the need to use care labels on garments and interpret some common ones

Introduction

Linen is the housekeeping department's second largest expense featuring after salaries, wages and benefits of housekeeping workforce. Linen is expensive to replace, and if it is well maintained, correctly laundered, and properly stored, its life can be extended. Soiled, worn, or creased linen leave a bad impression of the cleaning standards in a hotel. Guests dissatisfied by this may be lost forever. Efficient linen and laundry management ensures that large volumes of soiled linen are washed and treated so as to look neat, smell fresh, and feel crisp and that they are disbursed at the right time and to the right place. Linen may be cleaned either on or off the hotel premises. Hotels whose laundry output is sufficiently high and which have adequate space available opt for on-premises laundry (OPL). Chapter 2 gives detailed descriptions of the duties of various laundry personnel.

The Linen and Uniform Room

The linen and uniform room is a central depot for all hotel linen and this is the place from where clean articles of linen are distributed throughout the establishment. The uniform room almost always exists in close association with the linen room. The bulk of clean linen and uniforms awaiting reuse are stored here.

Linen Room Organization

There are primarily two types of linen rooms—centralized and decentralized.

Centralized linen room In this system, linen from all floors are collected and sorted in one central area. The linen room supervisor has complete control over the linen room. All linen issues and receipts go out from here.

Decentralized linen room In this system, each floor maintains its own par stock of linen. As and when necessary, these are replenished from the main linen room. The linen par is stored in floor pantries, and the floor supervisors are responsible for maintaining the par level. This system works well in hotels that have a large number of floors. The system is also used in resorts, where rooms are spread out across a large expanse of area.

Activities in the Linen and Uniform Room

The following activities are carried out in a linen room:

- Collection of soiled linen
- Counting and sorting of soiled linen
- Packing of soiled linen for the laundry
- Dispatch of soiled linen to the laundry
- Receipt of fresh linen from the laundry
- Checking and sorting of fresh linen
- Storage of fresh linen
- Distribution of fresh linen to the floors and other areas
- Stock-taking for linen and maintenance of records
- Stitching, repairing, and monogramming of all hotel linen and uniforms
- Uniform selection
- Uniform storage and issue
- Discarding of unusable linen

Planning the Linen and Uniform Room

The planning considerations for an efficient linen room are discussed in this section.

Location The linen room must be such as to facilitate the easy flow of linen to and from the laundry. In case a commercial laundry is being used, the linen room should be accessible for receipt and dispatch of linen from the back entrance of the hotel. The linen room's location must also facilitate easy issue and receipt of linen from the guest floors and other departments. Therefore, it should be situated near the service elevator. Another consideration for the linen room's location is easy access from the executive housekeeper's office. The linen room should also be a good distance away from the food production area, as linen absorbs odours easily. Also, the location should be such that it allows for proper ventilation of the linen room.

Space The total space allocated for the linen room will depend on the size of the hotel and the activities to be carried out in the linen room. The minimum space requirement for a linen room is 6 sq. ft., which may suffice for a small hotel. Space is required for linen storage areas and a linen exchange counter. Space is also allocated for the storage of uniforms and for a uniform exchange counter. Set apart from these should be a soiled linen collection area. Adequate space is also needed for the inspection tables, the linen room supervisor's desk, the guest laundry area, and the sewing room.

Entrance A common entrance-cum-exit point is ideal for security reasons. It should be at least 4 feet wide and without a threshold so as to ensure easy movement of trolleys. A stable-type door is recommended so that unauthorized persons are deterred from entering the room. This barrier itself can serve as the linen exchange counter.

Floor and walls The floor must be sturdy enough to bear the load of heavy trolleys moving across it. Tiles should be avoided as they tend to chip. Walls should be of a material that can be easily cleaned at frequent intervals. Tiled walls are ideal.

Lighting and ventilation Though most of the linen room is meant for storage, adequate ventilation is important to prevent growth of mildew, even though natural light may be less. Shadowless lighting in the form of fluorescent lamps is required. The air must be free of humidity and maintained at a temperature of 20°C.

Storage Linen storage shelves should be designed for maximum utilization of space. The shelves also need to be sturdy and firmly fixed as the weight they bear may be considerable. They may reach up to the ceiling provided that there is ample ventilation and that equipment is available for safe access. There should be a clearance of 6 inches below the lowermost shelf. All shelves must be slatted for thorough ventilation of stored linen. The depth of the shelves should be about 18–20 inches if they are against the wall. In case the shelves are to be accessible from both sides, the depth may be 36–40 inches. Linen articles meant to be stored for longer periods of time should be stored on shelves with slatted sliding doors or curtains to prevent dust settling. Storage shelves should also be allocated for condemned linen or discards.

Soiled linen area This area should be close to the entrance and must be large enough to accommodate all the soiled linen. There should be enough space to sort and count the linen and to move and park the trolleys. The floor and storage units in this area should consist of surfaces that do not stain damp linen.

Linen exchange counter This is usually a window without any grilles, wide enough to pass bundles of linen through. The window normally opens downward, with the shutter forming a counter. The area below this counter may be used to park trolleys to collect the soiled linen. When not in use, this counter should be taken up and kept bolted as a window shutter. As mentioned earlier, the stable-type door at the entrance of the linen room may also function as an exchange counter.

Inspection area This area consists mainly of the inspection table, which should be large enough to accommodate the freshly washed linen that needs to be inspected. A 100-room property may require a table of about 10 ft. × 6 ft. size. A folding table or one that may be dismantled is ideal. The colour of the tabletop should contrast with the colour of the linen. If a one-piece or non-folding table is used, the space below the table may be utilized for storage.

Uniform storage area Uniforms are normally hung on hangers, numerically segregated according to designation and department. A mobile uniform stand may also be used. Standard-sized uniforms are segregated according to size and stacked in racks. An exchange counter should be located close to the storage area.

Guest laundry area In hotels where the OPL does not directly accept the guest laundry, space must be allocated for storing, marking, and recording soiled guest articles before they are sent to the laundry. Fresh guest laundry on receipt from the laundry must be stored according to room numbers or hung on hangers for delivery. A table, a mobile rail for hanging clothes, and racks designed to hold the laundry as per room numbers may be designed for the purpose. A sink and an ironing table are also necessary for a hotel with no OPL.

Linen room supervisor's desk The desk should be located in such a way that the supervisor has a good view of the entire room, especially the transaction points. The desk, cupboards, and drawers should be designed to accommodate the files and records maintained in the linen room. It also accommodates the telephone.

Layout of the Linen and Uniform Room

Sample layouts of the linen room are given in Figures 19.1 and 19.2.

Storage of Linen

While in storage, linen must be kept free from dust. It is inevitable that where linen is handled, dust and fluff will be present. Therefore, all fresh linen should be stored under cover. Linen may be covered by curtains drawn across the shelves or they may be stored in cupboards with slatted sliding doors. Articles that are not in frequent use, such as mattress protectors, curtains, and blankets, may be stored covered with dust-sheets. Details on linen storage space and shelves are discussed earlier in the section on 'Planning the Linen and Uniform Room'. The linen stock should be rotated in order on 'first-in, first-out' basis. While placing fresh linen on shelves, especially the heavier ones, it should be ensured

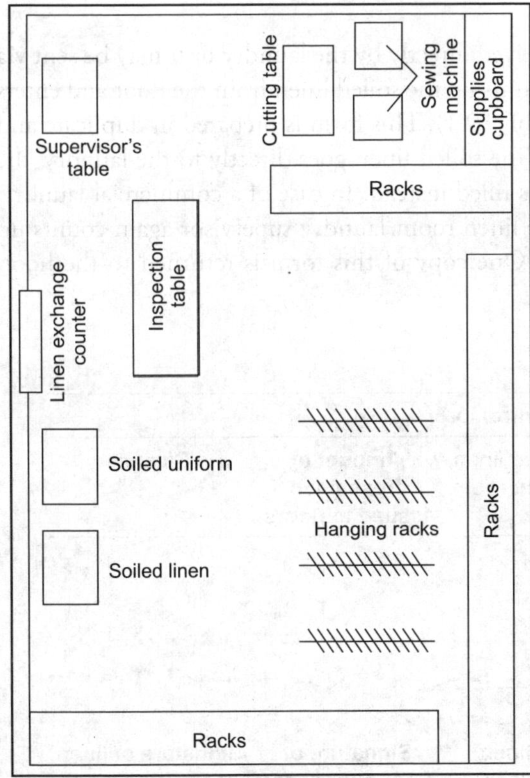

Fig. 19.1 Sample layout of a linen room in a 100-room hotel

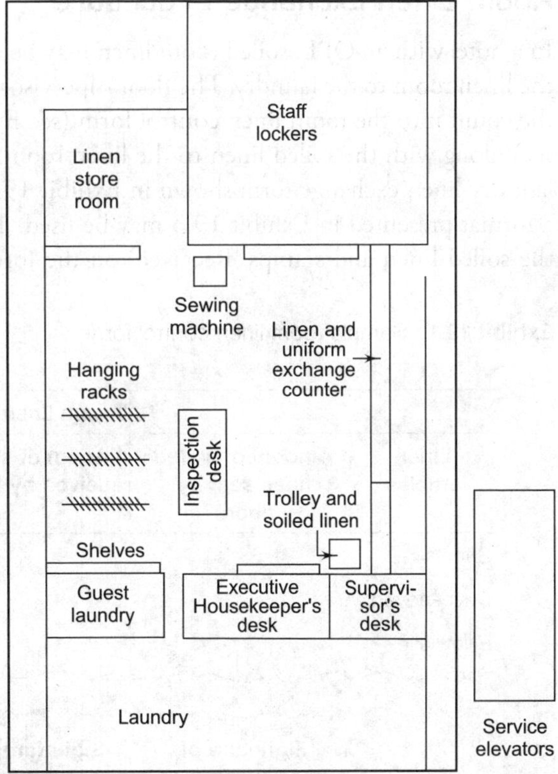

Fig. 19.2 Sample layout of a linen room in a large hotel

that the folds face outwards. Also, heavier linen should be placed on lower shelves. Smaller articles such as face towels and serviettes are placed in bundles of 10.

 Linen Exchange

Linen is provided for rooms and F&B areas following one of these four procedures:

Fresh-for-soiled/one-for-one This is a simple method of linen exchange. Fresh linen is provided only if an equivalent soiled article is given back. The advantage in this method is that there need be no record format. Usually uniforms are exchanged according to this method. Even though fresh-for-soiled or one-for-one is the simplest exchange, in case of large numbers of linen, it will take more time on account of the counting of both fresh and soiled and the fetching of the requisite amount of fresh articles.

Set amount In this system, a set amount of linen is provided on a daily basis.

Topping up This is the bringing up of the stock to the optimum level at periodic intervals or whenever it falls short of the predetermined optimum.

Requisition This method of linen exchange is mostly used for banquet linen, where the requirements may vary from day to day. A requisition slip is filled in, on the basis of which linen is provided.

Room Linen Exchange Procedure

In a hotel with an OPL, soiled room linen may be received directly by the laundry or it may be sent via the linen room to the laundry. The floor supervisor counts up the soiled linen from the floor and enters the count into the room linen control form (see Exhibit 19.1). This form is prepared in duplicate and sent along with the soiled linen to the linen room. If the soiled linen goes directly to the laundry, the laundry linen exchange form shown in Exhibit 19.2 is filled instead. In case of a commercial laundry, a format presented in Exhibit 19.3 may be used. The linen room/laundry supervisor again counts up the soiled linen and stamps 'Received' on the form. One copy of this form is returned to the floor,

Exhibit 19.1 Sample room linen control form

Room linen control form				
Linen articles	**Amount of soiled linen sent by floors**	**Amount of soiled linen received by linen room**	**Amount of fresh linen issued to floors**	**Balance**
Sheets				
Duvet covers				
Pillow slips				
	Signature of floor supervisor	**Signature of linen room supervisor**	**Signature of floor supervisor**	**Signature of linen room supervisor** ....

Exhibit 19.2 Sample laundry linen exchange form

Laundry linen exchange form

Linen items	Balance brought forward	Soiled linen	Total	Fresh linen	Re-washed linen	Balance carried forward

Signature of floor supervisor .... Signature of laundry supervisor ....

Exhibit 19.3 Format for room linen form for contract laundry

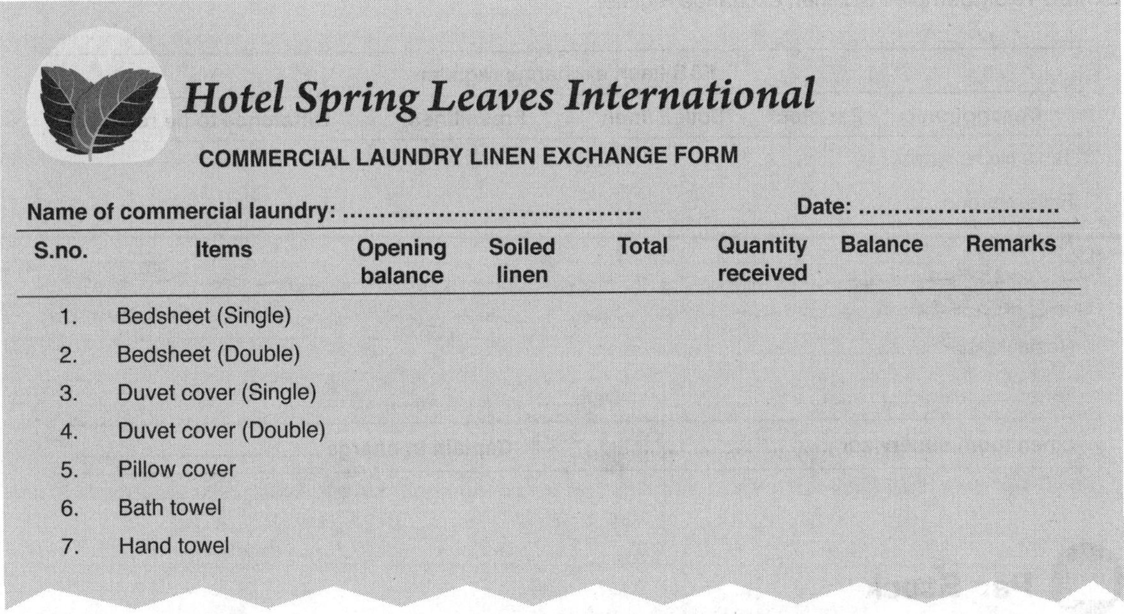

Hotel Spring Leaves International

COMMERCIAL LAUNDRY LINEN EXCHANGE FORM

Name of commercial laundry: .... **Date:** ....

S.no.	Items	Opening balance	Soiled linen	Total	Quantity received	Balance	Remarks
1.	Bedsheet (Single)						
2.	Bedsheet (Double)						
3.	Duvet cover (Single)						
4.	Duvet cover (Double)						
5.	Pillow cover						
6.	Bath towel						
7.	Hand towel						

the second and the third copy are filed at the linen room and the laundry respectively. The linen room supervisor issues fresh linen on a one-for-one basis, filling out the linen exchange form (see Exhibit 19.4) and signs it. If the linen room is short of linen, the supervisor enters the balance amount and issues them with the next lot. The form is countersigned by the floor supervisor and maintained in the linen room.

Restaurant Linen Exchange Procedure

Articles of restaurant linen are exchanged at stipulated timings. An F&B employee brings the soiled linen to the linen room. The linen room staff check the soiled linen received for damages. All items are counted and verified with the count in the F&B linen exchange form. The count is entered in the linen exchange register for F&B (see Exhibit 19.5). The fresh linen is issued and the details are also entered in the linen exchange register.

Exhibit 19.4 Sample room linen exchange form

Room linen exchange form

Floor .... **Date** .... **Time** ....

Linen item	Soiled linen received	Fresh linen issued	Balance	Remarks
Sheets				
Duvet covers				

Signature of floor supervisor .... **Signature of linen room supervisor** ....

Exhibit 19.5 Sample F&B linen exchange register

F&B linen exchange register

Description	Par stock	Soiled linen	Fresh linen	Difference to be rectified
Table cloths white				
Frills–maroon				
Napkins				

Restaurant ....

Time .... Date ....

Linen room supervisor .... **Captain in-charge** ....

Par Stock

This refers to the amount of each type of linen required to make up all the guestrooms of the hotel at a given time, and so is the minimum quantity of clean linen that must be on hand at any time. The par-stock quantity of linen is also referred to as 'house set-up'.

Importance of Par Stock

Maintaining the quantity of inventory items as per par stock is necessary and confers many benefits to the hotel and housekeeping operations. Maintaining par stock ensures that operations do not run out of supplies at any given time, even if there is a sudden peak in occupancy. Par stock ensures that optimum amount of supplies such as linen are available without overstocking which would not only incur high costs but also lead to misuse or thefts and call for extra storage space which comes at a cost in hotels. Keeping supplies as per par stock calculations enables the housekeeper to plan materials budget and then conform to the set budget. Par stock thus gives a clear representation to the hotel's management as to the optimum amount to be invested in supplies for running smooth operations. When inventory is maintained as per par stock, inventory management and stock taking becomes easier for auditors as inventory quantities are already set. Par stock thus helps in managing and controlling inventory.

A number of factors, outlined in this section, go into the setting up of the par stock for linen.

The laundry cycle Does the hotel have its own laundry? If yes, the number of sets can be reduced as the linen is washed the same day. If a contract laundry handles the linen, the delivery period has to be taken into account and extra stocks kept on hand for the interim period.

Occupancy level and usage How busy is the hotel? What are the peak periods? The summer season and humid climates necessitate more frequent changes of towels. Whether lowering the par would lead to overuse of each linen article, leading to rapid deterioration and condemnation, is also to be taken into account.

Replacement The general rule of thumb is to store one full par-stock quantity of new linen on an annual basis as replacement for worn-out, damaged, lost, or stolen linen articles.

Emergency A power failure or equipment damage may shut down the hotel's laundry operations and interrupt the movement of linen through the laundry cycle. One par stock of linen is kept on hand for such emergency situations.

Thus, a par number has to be set up to maintain the par stock of linen. The 'par number' is a multiple of the 'one par' or set-up quantity required to support daily housekeeping functions. Thus two pars of linen comprise the total number of each type of linen needed to outfit all guestrooms twice. In the same way, three pars of linen is the total number of each type of linen needed to outfit all guestrooms three times, and so on. In most deluxe hotels, the par number is kept at 4–5 times the set-up. For instance, in a 100-bed property with an OPL, there may be 500 pairs of sheets so that:

- 100 pairs, the first par, would be in circulation 'today'.
- 100 pairs, the second par, by way of 'yesterday's' linen, would be in the on-premises laundry.
- 100 pairs, the third par, comprise the linen to be stripped from the guestroom beds 'today' and meant for laundering 'tomorrow'.
- 100 pairs, the fourth par, being the emergency linen in the linen room.
- 100 pairs, the fifth par, of replacement linen stored in the linen room.

In hotels where the soiled linen is washed on the same day they are stripped away, 3½ pars of linen may be maintained. Where contract laundries handle the linen, 6 pars of linen may have to be maintained. Linen par stock estimation format for bed, bath and F&B linen is presented in Exhibit 19.6.

Linen Control

This is carried out in five phases:

- Routine checking of linen for appearance and hygiene standards.
- Quantity control of the daily flow of linen stock/linen exchange procedure.
- Monitoring linen usage and maintenance.
- Stock-taking or physical inventory of linen.
- Proper documentation of linen through the master linen inventory control sheet.

Exhibit 19.6 Format for estimation of par stock

Par stock estimation for linen					
Room Linen (Specification: par no. set at 4, bedmaking with duvet)					
Type of room	**Linen item**	**No. of rooms (A)**	**Std. no. of linen per room (B)**	**Par no. (C)**	**Par stock calculation**
Twin room	Single bed sheet		2	4	(A × B × C)
	Single duvet cover		2	4	(A × B × C)
	Single duvet		2	+ 20% of rooms	(A × B) + 20% of rooms
	Single mattress protector		2	+ 20% of rooms	(A × B) + 20% of rooms
	Pillow		2	+ 20% of rooms	(A × B) + 20% of rooms
	Pillow cover		2	4	(A × B × C)
	Bath towel		2	4	(A × B × C)
	Face towel		2	4	(A × B × C)
	Hand towel		2	4	(A × B × C)
	Bath mat		1	4	(A × B × C)

Routine checking of linen for appearance and hygiene standards

The executive housekeeper must emphasize the inspection of fresh and soiled linen not only by the linen room staff but also other staff handling linen. Stringent checking should be carried out by the linen room staff. In an OPL, the function of inspecting linen may be carried out by the laundry staff. However, where the laundry is contracted out, the onus falls on the linen room staff. Spot checking of linen should be carried out by supervisors in areas where linen may be left behind, such as service rooms, staff changing rooms, and so on. If inspections of all articles are carried out thoroughly, a high standard of linen quality is maintained and the chance of a guest finding a torn or stained article is minimal.

Quantity control of the daily flow of linen stock/linen exchange procedure

This is the quantity control of linen sent from the floors and departments to the linen room for despatch to the laundry. To maintain an initial record of the par stock of linen in each department and on each floor and also of any subsequent increase in the quantity of linen, an indent (see Exhibit 19.7) is made by the floor supervisor and the department in charge. The original copy of the indent is given to the linen room while the duplicate remains on the floor or with the concerned department. If the extra linen items issued to the floor or department as per the indent are returned, the signature of the linen room supervisor is obtained on the duplicate copy. This ensures that extra linen items that are not required daily on the floor or in the department are returned and are no longer the responsibility of the floor or department in question.

Exhibit 19.7 Sample linen indent form

Linen indent

Floor/department .... **Sl. No.** ....

Purpose of indent .... **Date** ....

Linen article	Amount	Remarks

Signature of floor/department in-charge ....

Proper linen exchange procedures are essential in the control of linen (refer to 'linen exchange' in the previous section).

The control of linen in the linen room is carried out by

- the daily supervision of the work done by the linen room attendants, and
- by the use of the linen room entry book.

The linen room entry book (see Exhibit 19.8) contains daily records of the soiled linen brought to the linen room from the various floors and departments as well as the amount of soiled linen sent to the laundry. There is no duplicate for this record, as it is for the reference of the linen room staff only. It is signed and maintained by the linen room supervisor and it helps him/her to keep track of the day-to-day movement of the linen handled by the staff. It also indicates why the total amount of soiled linen received in a day is not equal to the amount despatched to the laundry.

Monitoring linen usage and maintenance

Standards must be set and followed for usage and maintenance of each type of linen whether it is bed, bath, spa, health club or F&B linen. These include standards on laundering of linen, type, and amount of cleaning agents used in the wash process, storage, and exchange of linen and so on. This ensures that linen is maintained well, not misused and the right linen is used for the specific purpose. Staff should be trained on linen usage and maintenance and any misuse found should entail disciplinary action.

Exhibit 19.8 Sample page from a linen room entry book

Linen room entry book

Linen article	1st floor	2nd floor	3rd floor	Bar	Coffee shop	Restaurant A	Restaurant B	Kitchen	Staff	Total soiled linen received	Total soiled linen delivered	Remarks

Signature of the linen room supervisor ....

Stock-taking or physical inventory of linen

Stock-taking of linen is a physical verification, by counting, of the stocks of all linen items at all points in the cycle. It is carried out at periodic intervals or at the time of the 'closing of books' for evaluation purposes. Accurate recording of entries is important during stock-taking so that the overages and shortages can be determined from the difference between the physical count of balances and the balance appearing in the accounts inventory ledger.

The physical counting is done after every 3 months and is known as a 'quarterly inventory'. First, all items—including discards—are segregated and grouped. Then items in circulation and items kept in store are counted up separately and the totals are added together. The discards are stamped 'condemned' and set aside. Now the counted total should tally with the last inventory figure plus the issued items received after that. The inventory must be conducted in the presence of the housekeeper, with stock-taking for uniforms, room linen, and restaurant linen being done on separate days.

Samples of the room linen inventory form and linen inventory statements are given in Exhibits 19.9 and 19.10.

Exhibit 19.9 Sample room linen inventory form

Room linen inventory form

Floor .... Date ....

Floor supervisor ....

Room no.	B/S		P/S	D/C		M/P		B/T	H/T	F/T
	Single	Double		Single	Double	Single	Double			
101										
102										

Total stock on floor .... Grand total ....

Note: B/S = Bedsheet P/S = Pillowslip D/C = Duvet cover M/P = Mattress protector
B/T = Bath towel H/T = Hand towel F/T = Face towel

Exhibit 19.10 Sample linen inventory statement

Linen Inventory Statement

Linen item	Rate	Actual requirement	Un-issued linen in hand	Previous month's stock in hand	Present stock in hand	No. of condemned pieces	No. of missing pieces	Remarks

Signature of executive housekeeper ....

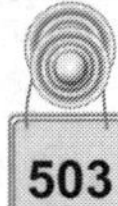

Proper documentation of linen

The master inventory control sheet (see Exhibit 19.11) helps the executive housekeeper analyse the results of the physical inventory. By subtracting the counted total for each linen article (item 15 in Exhibit 19.11) from the expected quantity corresponding (item 6), the executive housekeeper can accurately determine the number lost. This figure is recorded (item 16). Linen loss is the difference from the total obtained during the previous inventory. While physical inventories reveal the losses for linen items, they do not show why these losses occur. If the difference between the expected and actual quantities is high, further investigation is needed.

After each physical inventory, the executive housekeeper should make sure that the par levels are brought back to the level originally established for each linen item. The par numbers for each linen type are recorded (item 17). These figures represent the standard numbers for each linen type that should always be maintained in inventory. By subtracting the actual quantities for each linen type on hand (item 15) from the corresponding par levels (item 17), the executive housekeeper can determine the quantities of each linen type that are needed to bring inventories back to par. These amounts are recorded (item 18).

By subtracting the quantities of linen that are 'on order' but not yet received (item 19), the executive housekeeper knows precisely how many of each linen type still needs to be ordered to replenish the par stock. This figure is recorded (item 20). As a result of the physical inventory, the executive housekeeper can determine the amount of linen needed to replace lost stock and maintain the established par levels.

Exhibit 19.11 Sample master inventory control sheet

Master inventory control sheet

Location name .... Inventory date .... Inventory prepared by ....

Signature of executive housekeeper ....

Signature of general manager ....

Part 1

1. Linen item →								
2. Last inventory data								
3. New received								
4. Subtotal (2 + 3)								
5. Recorded discard								
6. Total (4 – 5)								

Part 2

7. Storage room								
8. Storage room								
9. Storage room								
10. Linen room								

The completed master inventory control sheet should be submitted along with the linen discard record (see Exhibit 19.12(a) and (b)) to the general manager. The general manager will then verify and initial the report before transferring it to the accounts department. The accounts department will provide the executive housekeeper with valuable cost information related to usage, loss, and expense per occupied room. This information is useful in determining and monitoring the housekeeping department's budget.

Physical inventories of table linen used by the F&B department should be handled much in the same way as room linen. The same general rules and procedures should be followed and the same general form used. Inventory lists should be prepared for each F&B outlet, including banquet facilities, that itemize all types, sizes, and colours of table linen that the hotel uses. The inventory should be taken when the movement of table linen to and from the laundry can be halted and each F&B outlet is fully stocked to its established par levels. By following the same procedure as used for room linen, the total inventory of table linen can be calculated and the executive housekeeper can determine the need for replacement stock.

Exhibit 19.12(a) Sample linen discard record, front page

Linen discard record

Signature of executive housekeeper ....

Signature of general manager .... **Period ending** ....

Date	Bath towel	Hand towel	Face towel	Bath mat	Double sheet	Single sheet	Remarks

Exhibit 19.12(b) Sample linen discard record, reverse

Linen discard record (Reverse)

Items	How discarded	Items	How discarded

Remarks ....

....

Signature of executive housekeeper ....

Linen Quality and Lifespan

Linen is the highest annual cost inventory in the housekeeping department, hence getting good value for the money spent should be an important priority for an executive housekeeper. Therefore, the housekeeper must have thorough knowledge of the composition, construction, and properties of various types of fibres and fabrics.

General Selection Criteria for Fabrics

The fabrics chosen must not only retain their appearance throughout their useful life, but must also be serviceable, easy to maintain, and long-lasting. The general criteria for the selection of fabrics for bed linen, bath linen, soft furnishings, F&B linen, and health-club linen are outlined here.

Strength The strength of the fabric depends upon the type of fibre used. Synthetic fibres (such as polyester and acrylic) have more strength than natural ones (such as cotton and wool). The type of weave and the closeness of the weave also affect the fabric strength. The strength of the selvedge too should be checked by tugging at it.

Laundering Linen and laundering costs come right after employee costs on the list of highest expenditures. Synthetics require lower temperatures and shorter cycles while laundering than cottons. No-iron blends do not require pressing.

Comfort This depends on the feel, texture, softness, and weight of the cloth. Any fabric that comes into contact with the skin must be absorbent. Cottons have very high absorbency compared to synthetics.

Shrinkage Synthetics do not shrink, whereas natural fibres shrink by about 6–8% unless they have been sanforized. Wool loses its shape if not carefully laundered.

Colour Pattern, texture, and colour, in fabrics can impart character to a room. At the same time, one should not forget the need for ease of maintenance. Most hotels prefer white linen as they can be safely laundered without fear of their colour fading. Coloured fabric should be checked for dye stability. Fabrics dyed at the yarn stage (vat-dyed) are definitely more colour-fast than ones dyed at the fabric stage. Dyed natural fibres will fade after several washes. Dark-coloured fabrics show dust and lighter marks, whereas light-coloured ones show dirt and stain easily; these will be less apparent in a medium-toned fabric. The colours chosen must also be easily available when replacements are required.

Pattern and texture A patterned fabric can hide marks. Abstract patterns will not hide marks as much as mottled patterns. Large patterns can make a large area look filled and vice versa. As for texture, a more open texture collects more dust and dirt.

Flame-retardancy Flame-retardant fabrics should be used for drapery, upholstery, and carpets. Wool is naturally flame-retardant and most suitable as carpeting material in blended form. Housekeepers must ensure that fabrics for bedding materials, draperies, curtains and upholstery are given a flame retardant finish by manufacturers.

Thermal insulation The warmth of a fabric used for coverlets and such is determined by its thermal insulation properties, measured in units called 'togs'. This must be checked for blankets. Drapery should also help to maintain the temperature of a room to some extent.

Décor of the room The colour, texture and pattern of fabrics chosen for draperies, curtains, upholstery and soft furnishings should coordinate with the colour scheme and theme of the room.

Budget The housekeeper must choose the best quality fabrics the budget at hand allows for. Not only the initial costs, but the costs incurred in maintaining the fabrics also are important considerations.

Bed Linen

Launderable bed linen includes sheets and pillow cases, duvet covers and bedspreads.

Sheets, pillowcases and duvet covers

Good bed sheets, pillowcases and duvet covers should have a pleasant feel and good appearance and should wear well.

Materials The fabrics recommended for sheets, pillow covers and duvet covers are cotton and polycot. Polycot sheets combine the advantages of cotton and polyester. However, many hotels use monogrammed Egyptian cotton sheets since Egyptian cotton is durable, has a crisp appearance, and is comfortable. The average lifespan of cotton sheets is about 200 washes, whereas polycot sheets may last more than 500 washes. After 100 launderings, cotton loses 35–40% of its tensile strength, whereas cotton-polyester blends lose only 3–7% of their tensile strength. Thus, cotton-polyester blends are more durable than straight cotton. Blends also do not shrink as much as cotton. If cotton is tumble-dried, it will shrink by 5–8%, whereas a blend shrinks by only 0–3%. The cotton-polyester blends are preferred by hotels because of the price factor too. The blends are more economical to launder as they retain 15–50% less water than a full-cotton sheet after extraction. The blends are also more resistant to abrasion. Blends of 65% polyester and 35% cotton or of 50% polyester and 50% cotton prove to be the best.

Linen too is often used as sheeting material as it has many advantages over cotton.

Construction When the cotton fibres in a blend are carded before spinning, the resultant fabric is rough and looks dull. These make muslin sheets. When cotton fibres are combed before spinning, the resultant fabric is smooth and has a greater tensile strength. Percale sheets are made in this manner and are preferred for use in hotels. The most common weave used for sheeting is the plain weave. The night spread or crinkle sheet, however, is typically made in the seersucker weave (refer Chapter 18 for details on carding, combing, and seersucker weave).

Fabrics for sheeting are graded by their thread count and tensile strength. A sheet that has a thread count of at least 180 is the standard for hotels. This means that there are 180 threads in every 1-inch sq. area of the sheet. Ideally, there should be 94 threads in the warp and 86 in the weft. The warps and wefts should both lie fairly close together.

The tensile strength is determined by the amount of weight it takes to tear a 1 inch × 3 inch piece of fabric.

Finish Fabrics that come straight from the loom without receiving any finishing are called 'grey goods'. Various finishing treatments—such as bleaching, mercerizing, and sanforizing—may be given to the grey goods, depending on the properties required. Cotton-polyester sheets are normally chemically modified during manufacturing to provide a 'permanent press' or 'no-iron effect'. A fabric treated thus remains fairly smooth after laundering and while in use too.

Colour and size White is the most preferred colour for sheets used in hotels. Sheets may come in either a 'torn sheet' size (or 'cut sheet' size) or as a 'finished sheet'. The torn-sheet size is the size of the sheet before hemming. The finished sheet has a top and a bottom hem. Hems should be firmly stitched and the thread ends tied and stitched in neatly. The top hem should be 2 inches deep and the bottom ½ inch. However, nowadays many hotels have the same width of hem at the top and the bottom, so that both ends may be used interchangeably, thus avoiding excessive wear on one area of the sheet. Sheets should be of the minimum standard sizes so that they are easier to tuck in securely. Pillowcases should be 2–4 inches wider than the pillow to allow for shrinkage and ease. Pillowcases of the tuck-in tab-type are preferable as they eliminate the need for tapes and buttons for fastening. Duvet covers should fit the duvet snugly, so purchase size of duvet covers should be 2 inches more on length and 4 inches more on breadth than the duvet to allow for shrinkage. The preferred duvet opening is envelope style which features an internal flap that encloses the duvet and hold it in place.

Quality Sheets that have minor imperfections are available as 'seconds' and usually have the manufacturers' tags cut off. Most hotels accept seconds. A linen case marked '1F/12S–81 × 104 in', for instance, means it contains 1-dozen first-quality and 12-dozen second-quality double sheets.

Bedspreads

Good quality bedspreads are purchased keeping in mind the following guidelines:

- The readymade sizes are seldom satisfactory, hence bedspreads should be made to order.
- The appearance, colour, and print should match the décor.
- The durability and wearing quality of the fabric and the effect of laundering on the weave and colour need to be considered.

Materials The bedspread should complement the colours and other design elements in the guestroom, but the fabric should be durable and easy to maintain. Synthetic fabrics are dominating the bedspreads in hotels. Most hotels prefer to have a washable bedspread fabric that is guaranteed to maintain its shape through repeated washings.

Finishes Bedspreads are often sat on or folded and stacked away for later use. Hence the material should be crease-proof. The fabric should also be fire-retardant. Dust ruffles to complement the spreads are usually cotton-polyester blends.

Cushion covers These should not soil easily or collect dust. They should not slip about and should be washable.

Upholstery covers The fabric used for upholstery covers should be strong, resistant to soiling, closely woven with a non-fluffy surface, resistant to snagging, and should not cling to guests' clothes or skin due to static.

Bath Linen

Bath linen comprise towels, bathmats, shower curtains, etc. The types of materials available for bath linen are discussed here.

Towels and bathmats

The foremost requirement of towelling material is that it should be absorbent. The fabric should also be durable and soft.

Materials A cotton and linen blend is ideal, as pure linen is very expensive and pure cotton is not as strong or absorbent. Some properties use 100% cotton towelling. The huckaback weave is most suitable for face towels whereas Turkish towels with an uncut pile are more suitable for bath towels, hand towels, and bathmats. The uncut pile provides a larger surface area for the absorption of moisture.

Bathmats also need to be made of a heavier material. Heavier towels are more absorbent.

Also, the longer the pile, the greater the absorbency of the towel, but the durability may be adversely affected, as long pile tends to get pulled while in use and during laundering. The recommended pile height is 1/8 inch. The pile should be close for greater absorbency. Uncut pile is more absorbent but cut pile has a much softer feel. White towels are more absorbent as coloured towels have already absorbed dye; they are also more durable as the dyes do affect the strength of the fibres somewhat.

Finish and pattern The selvedge for towelling should be firmly woven and ¼ inch wide. The hems should be firmly stitched. Selvedges along the length are more durable than hems. A logo may be woven into the fabric.

Shower curtains

The most common materials used for shower curtains in hotels are waterproof. These include nylon, vinyl, fibreglass, or PVC-coated materials.

Whether white or coloured, the folds of plastic curtains tend to stick together when hanging wet. Nylon curtains have a better finish and can be obtained in pastel colours or white, with or without patterns. They last better with a plastic lining. Fibreglass curtains are very brittle but are soil-resistant and resilient to fire, acid, rot, moisture, absorption, shrinkage, stretching, and attack by insects. However, they should never be wrung, as the fibres may then break, and these curtains may also grey with age.

Table Linen

These have both practical and aesthetic uses, so napery must be clean, fresh, and crisp.

Table cloth Fabrics for table cloths should be able to resist stains and to retain their colour and shape even after frequent laundering.

Materials Tablecloths made of linen, polycot, or linen-cotton union damask are preferred. Linen is expensive. Damask gives a good appearance. Single damask has an equal number of wefts and warps in a satin weave and has a thread count of 175; in double damask, the weft threads are at least 1½ times more than in a sateen weave, the yarn is finer, and it has a thread count of 200 to 300. Double damask looks better than single damask, but is not as durable.

Size The tablecloth must be sufficiently large to hang 9 inches below the table edge. A 5% allowance for shrinkage along the length must be provided.

Napkins These are usually made of 100% cotton or linen as they need to be absorbent. Also, it should be possible to starch them so as to allow them to be folded into fancy shapes.

Slip cloths These are placed over the tablecloth to achieve a contrasting effect and hence are normally coloured.

Underlays Baize or any other felted material is suitable for these. Molton is a cheaper alternative.

Skirts, frills, and runners Drapability is an important requirement in these fabrics. Satins made of synthetic fibres are used as they are durable and colour-fast.

Waiters' cloths A 100% cotton casement is the preferred fabric for the waiter's cloth.

Linen Lifespan

The lifespan of linen is measured in terms of how many times it can be laundered before becoming too worn to be suitable for guestroom use and discarded. Expected lifespan of linen is shown in Exhibit 19.13. This depends on the quality of the fabric used. Thus, it is vital to record when the linen item was put into circulation and how many washes it has since undergone. It can then be ascertained how long they last. This also enables the housekeeper to judge the quality of the fabric as compared to the previous lot. The quantity and quality of chemicals used and the processes in the laundry could also be monitored on the basis of such information. Marking and tagging of linen, thus is an important procedure, especially for room linen.

Marking or tagging of linen

Each piece of linen is marked or tagged according to a standard coding system before being put into circulation. A tag with the hotel logo printed on it is stitched on the inside hemming, near the corner of each piece of linen. Before putting the linen into circulation, the date, month and year of taking the piece into circulation is stamped on the inside hemming, alternatively, a tag with the marked date is attached. Generally, fresh bed linen is put into circulation every quarter depending on wear and tear and rate of discard, which is kept at a minimum. Hence, room linen is put into circulation in April, June, September and December. Accordingly, they need to be labelled for the date/month/year of being put into circulation as, for instance, 12–04–22 for 12th April 2022, 12–6–22 for 12th June 2022 and so on.

Durability, laundry considerations, and purchase price are the main criteria that an executive housekeeper has to bear in mind while selecting linen.

Exhibit 19.13 Expected lifespan of guestroom linen, F&B linen and staff uniforms

Guestroom linen lifespan					
S. No.	**Linen item**	**TC/GSM**	**Lifespan**	**Discard on reflectance**	**Par stock**
1.	Bedsheets	300 TC	125–150 washes	80–85%	3 + 1
2.	Duvet covers	300 TC	125–150 washes	80–85%	3 + 1
3.	Pillow covers	300 TC	100–125 washes	80–85%	5 + 1
4.	Bath towel	550 GSM	125–150 washes	80–85%	3 + 1
5.	Hand towel	550 GSM	85–100 washes	80–85%	4 + 1
6.	Face towel	550 GSM	75–90 washes	80–85%	5 + 1
7.	Bath mat	550 GSM	75–100 washes	80–85%	3 + 1
8.	Bath robe	550 GSM	100 washes	80–85%	2 + 1

F&B linen lifespan			
S. No.	**Linen item**	**Lifespan**	**Discard on reflectance**
1.	Damask napkins – white	75–100 washes	85%
2.	Napkins – coloured	75 washes	NA

The housekeeper needs to calculate the cost per use in order to evaluate alternative linen purchases using the following formula:

$$\text{Cost per use} = \frac{\text{Purchase cost + Lifespan laundering costs}}{\text{Number of lifespan launderings}}$$

where,

Lifespan laundering cost = Item weight × Laundering cost per kg × Number of launderings withstood

The expected useful life of the linen is often more important than the purchase price in determining whether alternative products are economical or not. The cost of laundering linen over their useful life is usually much greater, and therefore, more important than their initial price.

 Discards and their Reuse

Discarded or condemned linen are items that are no longer useful in their present condition due to some irreversible damage such as a permanent stain or simply wear and tear. 'Cutting down' refers to the using of any discarded materials for some other purpose, such as bed sheets being used as dust sheets or being made into pillow covers and buffet sheets. Turning discards into rags is one of the simplest and most common ways of recycling. Discarded pillow cases are cut down to wiping cloths and pillow liners. Large discarded sheets can be cut down for use as crib sheets, aprons, and other such articles. Worn out towels are cut down, restitched and converted into towel dusters, wipes and kitchen towels. Napkins discarded due to low reflectance may be reused as waiter's cloth. Discarded upholstery material may be stitched into laundry bags and newspaper bags. At some properties, discarded linen are sold to hotel staff at reasonable prices. Some properties also donate used linen to charities. Whatever the norm, all discards should be accounted for and properly recorded (presented in Exhibit 19.12(a) and (b) earlier). In fact, linen meant to be treated as discards are first ratified and stamped as 'discard' by a designated personnel from the accounts department in presence of the EHK.

 Linen Hire

Good quality linen is expensive to buy and to maintain. Hotels now have an option of hiring linen from linen hire firms, which not only takes care of their linen supply but also the laundering.

Commercial linen hire firms rent room and F&B linen in various quality ranges for hotels to choose from and strive to offer value for money. Many hotels prefer to hire linen as it saves on a recurring investment. The hotel company enters into a contract with the hire firm to periodically deliver an agreed amount of the chosen quality of linen to the hotel. Before entering into a contract, the housekeeper must check referrals and find out about the performance of the company. The advantages of hiring linen from a firm are many:

- The hotel saves on the capital outlay for all types of linen.
- Linen hire works out cheaper for the hotels.
- There are extensive savings on the laundry costs and the need for an in-house laundry is eliminated.
- There is considerable saving on storage space as extra par stock need not be maintained.
- Since less staff is to be scheduled to take care of linen in the linen room or the laundry, worker costs are cut down.
- The hire firm ensures that the linen supplied is always of good quality and as per the hotel's standards, so there is no worry of replacing worn out linen.

- Linen firms also extend assistance to hotels when linen is required on short notice.
- Budgeting of linen expenses become easier for the housekeeper as the contract expenditure is fixed.
- Hire firms can offer modified types of linen in case a hotel goes in for refurbishment or renovation.

There may be a few disadvantages too:

- Unexpected occupancy fluctuations may lead to the hotel falling short of linen.
- There is no scope for customising the linen and many times choices too are limited.
- There is a minimum usage level agreed upon with the hire firm and if occupancies go low and the linen is not put to use, the minimum charges still apply.
- Extra cost may be incurred if there are damages or loss of linen.
- There are no discards available which may be put to use as rags or dust sheets.

The Laundry

The 'laundry' can be defined as a place where the washing and finishing of clothes and other washable articles are carried out.

Types of Laundries

A hotel may operate its laundry services through the following types of laundries:

Commercial/off-site/contracted laundries

These cater to hotels on a contract basis. The contract specifies the rate for laundering different articles of linen, the time taken for laundering, and so on. Usually the soiled linen are laundered and delivered back to the hotel within 24–48 hours. The laundries may, however, hold back 3–5% of the soiled linen for stain removal and other special treatments. Contract laundries are a good option if the hotel does not want to make a heavy investment in setting up its own laundry or has space constraints.

Advantages to the hotel The advantages of contract laundries are as follows:

- No capital outlay.
- Little technical expertise required.
- Employee costs are saved.

Disadvantages The following are the disadvantages of contract laundries.

- Less control over standards.
- Delivery and collection delays.
- Higher stocks required as it takes a longer time for the whole process to complete a single laundry cycle, including transportation.
- Loss of articles may increase.
- Extra costs for special treatments.

On-premises/on-site/in-house laundry

An on-premises laundry (OPL) is the hotel's own laundry, situated on its premises. It may be run by the management or managed on a contract. Many hotels make this heavy investment to provide quality service to guests. More care is taken while laundering in-house since it is the direct responsibility of the hotel. Services are faster (a maximum of 8 hours to return laundered articles), hence par stocks are reduced.

There is better supervision, better control, and hence a longer life for linen. There are fewer chances of pilferage since the linen do not leave the premises. However, a contingency plan must be made, to be implemented in case of equipment failure.

Advantages to the hotel The advantages of OPLs are as follows:

- No losses or 'shortfalls' of missing articles are likely to occur.
- Less stock required as the cycle is quicker.
- Can cover emergency requirements.
- Is a capital asset.

Disadvantages The following are the disadvantages of OPLs.

- The initial capital investment is high.
- Higher employee costs.
- Technical expertise or special management is required.
- High cost of maintenance, repairs, and overheads.

Laundromats

These are self-service laundries usually found in motels. Laundromats may be utilized by using coin slots to pay by the load or by making a fixed monthly payment. In some resorts, long-stay guests too can use the equipment.

Planning an OPL

The decision of whether to include a laundry on the premises should ideally be made during the initial planning stages for the facility. If this is not done, considerable costs may be incurred to change the plumbing and electrical systems later. Hot water, cold water, steam, gas, large sewer drains, and water lines are essential plumbing considerations. Hot water of temperatures between 160°C to 180°C should be available for sanitizing the machines. Both 110 volts (for equipment manufactured in Europe) and 220 volts (for equipment manufactured in India) grounded electric outlets should be provided in strategic locations for the operation of laundry equipment.

Location The location of the laundry must be strategic enough to obviate transportation problems and because of the noisy and humid nature of the area. The laundry should, if at all possible, be easily accessible from the linen room so that heavy bundles of laundry can easily be transported from one location to another. It should be located away from guest areas, however, because of acoustic reasons, vibration, and humidity problems anticipated in a laundry. It should preferably be along the outside wall of the building to provide adequate venting. Moreover, the laundry should be located so that it can be operated and/or used by both men and women.

Size The rule of thumb for hotel laundries is 7 sq. ft. per room (not including soil storage). For soil storage, 1 cubic foot for every 3.6 kg (upto a height of 4 feet) is usually allotted, though it is difficult to state an optimum size because of individual institutions' needs.

Ventilation This is essential to exhaust moisture-laden air from the dryers out of the laundry room. Laundry rooms also require adequate ventilation through regular doors or windows to take in a supply of fresh air equal to the amount of air removed from the room through exhaust fans or similar. Without ample intake through regular doors or windows, or at least a separate forced dry-air supply, dryers will not operate at their specified efficiencies.

Equipment selection Laundry equipment must be considered in relation to initial cost, life expectancy, maintenance, and depreciation. Overhead costs of utilities such as electricity, water, and gas need to be considered. Generally it is wise to install two washers instead of one because:

- It takes less time to accumulate a full load for a smaller machine.
- There will be some back-up if one machine needs servicing.
- Small, odd lots can be handled more efficiently.
- It will be possible to wash two different kinds of goods concurrently, for example, heavily soiled uniforms and lightly soiled sheets.
- Small machines impose less of a shock load on the hot-water and electrical systems.

Wet laundry must be moved from the washer-cum-extractor to the dryer, while dry laundry must be moved to storage shelves and thence to shower areas and 'equipment issue' areas. To facilitate these transfers, utility baskets, hampers, and carts must be provided. A worktable (4 ft. × 6 ft.) with castor wheels on the legs is very convenient for folding towels and other laundry. It can readily be moved about the room as needed too. There should be cupboards or bins as well, for the storage of detergents, soaps, bleaches, and other cleaning agents.

Workforce The rule of thumb for a small institutional laundry is that one person should be able to handle a weight of about 36 kg an hour.

Other costs Costs of laundry aids such as soap, bleach, detergents, and other chemicals should be estimated and consideration should be given as to how bulk quantities of these supplies will be stored. Decisions have to be made as to who will maintain and supervise the laundry and what workforce will be utilized.

Layout of an OPL

The layout of the laundry in terms of positioning machines should be such that there is an easy flow of traffic. Pay close attention to entries, exits, columns, drainage locations, exhaust areas, ventilation, and machinery access. Separate the soiled- and clean-laundry handling areas as much as possible to prevent recontamination of clean articles. A sample layout of a laundry is presented in Figure 19.3.

Doors These need to be large enough to initially get the equipment into the room as well as to effectively enter and exit with utility carts and/or laundry baskets. Swing doors are good for cart movement. They should have windows for safety and bumpers or guards to protect their appearance. The thresholds should be flush with the floor.

Ceilings They should be impervious to moisture and have good sound-absorption properties (acoustics). An 8–10 feet high ceiling is adequate.

Floors These are very important in a laundry. They should be level concrete slabs capable of supporting the heavy cleaning machines. The floor around the machines should be sloped and there should not be any low spots in the floor where water can pool. Concrete is the most suitable floor material and can be covered by one of the synthetic resinous materials available with a smooth yet non-slip surface.

Walls These should be constructed of a material that is durable, moisture-resistant, and insulating. Windows should be avoided so that the wall space can be used for storage shelves and bins; however, if they are required, care should be given as to their placement in order to eliminate glare. Windows should be constructed with wire glass and be located high on the wall.

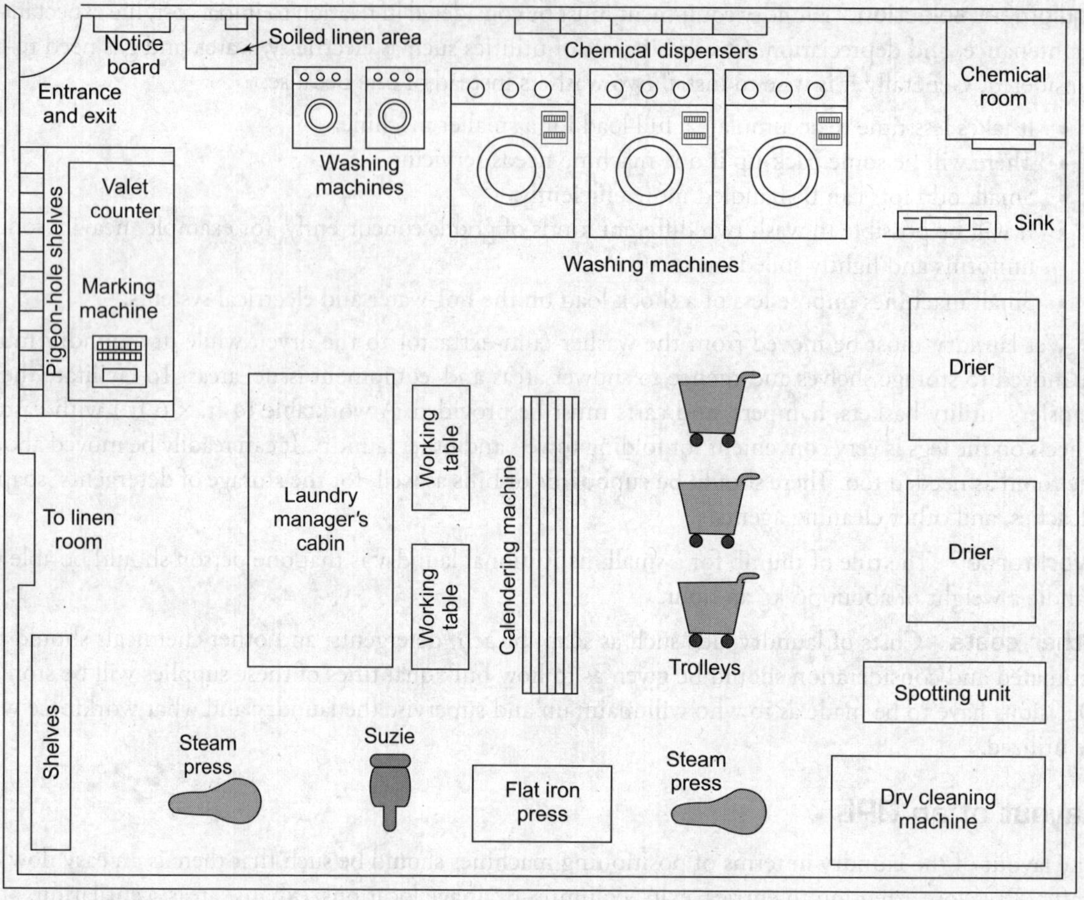

Fig. 19.3 Sample layout of a laundry

Machinery and work areas Allow at least 18 inches between any two machines (the same applies to a piece of equipment and a wall). Dryers can usually be placed side-by-side (allow about an inch between them), however. Provide at least a 2-feet space between the back of a machine and the wall. If space is tight, try locating machines in front of a large door to a hall or to the outside. The door can be opened for servicing the machines.

Try to locate the dryers next to an outside wall. They must be vented. Soiled storage and sorting should take place near the washers. Dryers should be at a minimal distance from the washers, but they should not interfere with their loading and unloading (or sorting).

The folding table and area should be located so that finished work can smoothly move towards its final storage area in preparation for distribution. The spotting unit should be located in a well-ventilated area.

Laundry Equipment

Sophisticated machinery is needed in laundries to cope with the various types of fabrics and other items to be laundered, dried, and pressed, given the huge amount of laundry to be completed in a given time period.

The type and amount of equipment should be chosen keeping in mind the amount of linen to be processed by the laundry. Laundry equipment include washing machines, washer-cum-centrifuge and extractors, hydro-extractors, and dryers.

Please refer to the scan code for pictures of various laundry equipment.

Washing machines Those used in hotel laundries are typically of the tumbler type. Their capacities typically vary from 7 to 200 kg. The wash barrels of those used in hotels are usually of stainless steel. Machines with a capacity of 100 kg or more generally have a drum that has two or three compartments. These are also referred to as 'tunnel washing machines'. The unit may be end-loading (Figure 19.4) or front-loading. These machines may work on steam or electricity.

Washing machines consist of a motor, inside and outside shells, and a casing. The outside shell is stationary and holds the wash water. The inside shell holds the laundry and is perforated to allow water for various cycles to flow in and out. The machine's motor rotates either the perforated inner shell (on wash-wheel washers) or an agitator (agitator washers). The rotating shell or agitator helps the detergent to break up soil on fabrics in the wash cycle and remove detergents and other chemicals during the rinse cycles. Washing machines with microprocessors are computer-controlled.

Most automatic washing machines have detergent- and solution-dispensing capabilities. In other machines, an operator adds detergent and solutions manually through hoppers or ports. Washing machines should have at least five ports—two for detergents and one each for bleach, sour, and softener.

While buying a washing machine for the hotel laundry, it is best to select strong industrial equipment from a reliable supplier. A thorough market survey of known brands and models must be undertaken to decide what is suitable for the hotel's laundry operation. A heavier machine is generally more durable. Once a machine is bought, the executive housekeeper should ensure that all maintenance procedures are followed and the machine is used as per instructions.

Washer-cum-centrifuge and extractors These machines range in capacity from 7 to 300 kg. They may operate on steam or electricity or even a combination of the two. These washers have extraction capabilities as well. The motor spins the inside shell rapidly to remove most of the excess water after washing is completed. Such washers eliminate the need for a hydro-extractor.

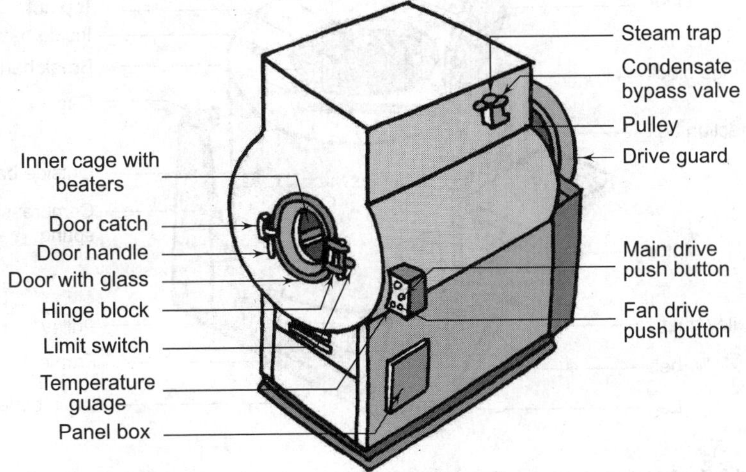

Fig. 19.4 End-loading washing machine

Hydro-extractors These are large centrifuges, ranging in capacity from 7 to 70 kg. A typical hydro-extractor is illustrated in Figure 19.5. The basket is made of stainless steel. They are electrically operated. Clothes from the washer are put into a hydro-extractor to remove about 50–75% of the excess water. The water is extracted from the washed linen by means of centrifugal force or by the application of pressure. After extraction, the linen are left damp but not wet. They are then ready for pressing.

Dryers These are units of tumbler-type equipment meant to remove moisture from damp, tightly packed linen (that have come out of hydro-extractors) by tumbling them in a rotating cylinder through which heated air passes. They are generally used for no-iron articles and towels as these linen do not require pressing.

Loading is generally done from one end. The heated air may be produced by electricity, gas, or steam. To ensure the dryer's energy efficiency, air flow must be continuous. Most dryers have an internal lint-removal mechanism. Preventive maintenance should be carried out for dryers regularly. Dirt or lint clogging the air-supply vents should be cleaned out twice daily. The ducts should be checked regularly for leaks and the lint containers should be emptied regularly.

Pressing Equipment

Many types of pressing equipment are available for ironing different articles, such as calenders for sheets, curtains, and tablecloths; sleeve presses; flat-bed presses; and so on.

Flat-bed presses These are available in various sizes and can be heated by electricity or steam. A foot control helps in operating the press (see Figure 19.6). Some are available as twin presses and rotate from front to back horizontally. An article of linen is put under one press and then this is sent behind while another article is put under the press. This is sent behind in its turn as the first one comes forward. The first garment, which has now been pressed, is removed while the second is being pressed, and a third is inserted in its place. In this way, there is no waste of time or space; else the operator would have to handle two machines simultaneously and keep moving between the two.

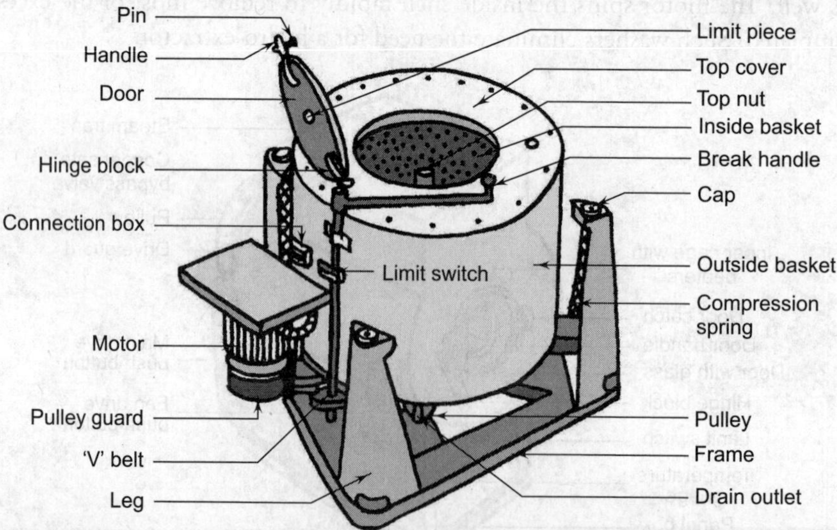

Fig. 19.5 A typical hydro-extractor

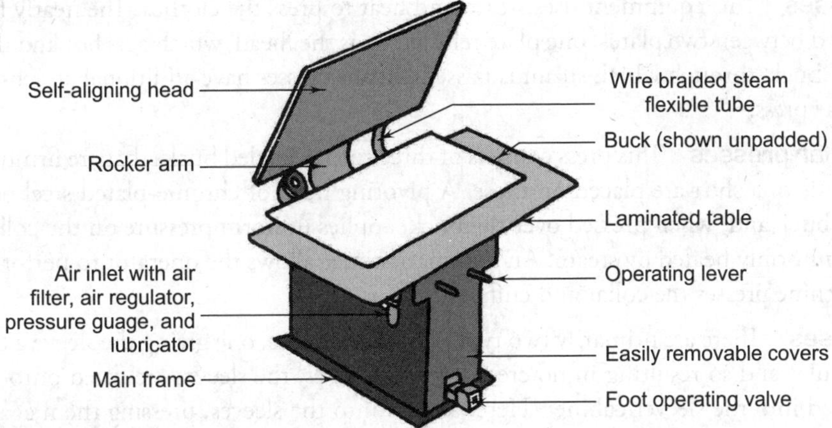

Fig. 19.6 A flat-bed press

Flatwork ironers These are similar to flat-bed presses except that the ironers roll over the material while presses flatten the whole of it at once. Also, the articles to be ironed are fed gradually into the ironer, whereas on a flat-bed press, they need to be placed on the surface manually. Some ironers also fold the article automatically.

Calenders These are large presses meant primarily for bed sheets, bedcovers, table-cloths, and similar articles. They consist of a series of rollers (see Figure 19.7) in pairs, connected by a number of narrow conveyor belts. The speed of the rollers is adjustable. The sheet is fed in manually. The lifting of the article is done either manually or pneumatically. The sheets can also be folded automatically in some calenders, which are fitted with an additional gadget for the purpose.

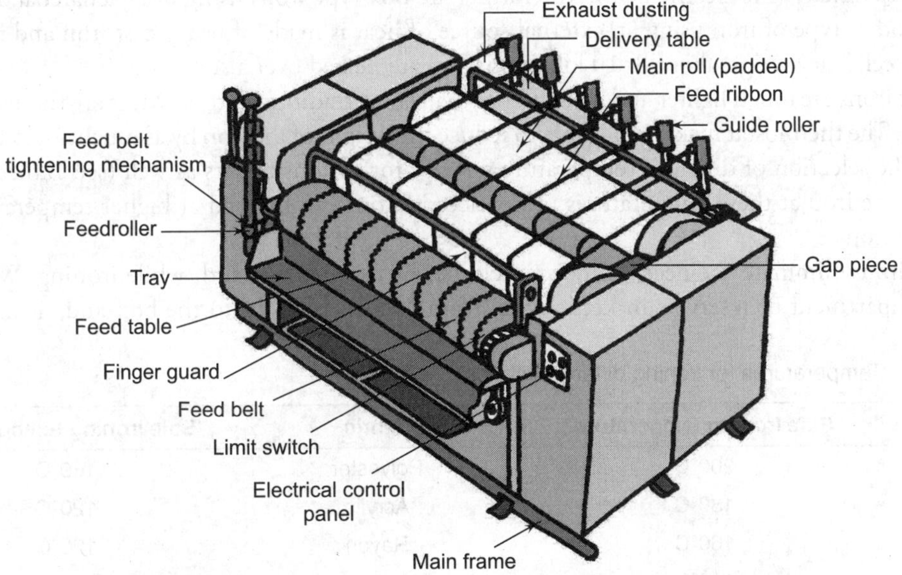

Fig. 19.7 A calendering machine

Steam presses This equipment uses steam and heat to press the clothes. The neatly folded clothes are sandwiched between two plates, one plate referred to as the 'head' which gets hot and the other plate referred to as 'buck' through which steam is passed. Steam presses have additional attachments like the cuff-and-collar press.

Cuff-and-collar presses This press consists of three spring-loaded bucks that are firmly padded. The collars and cuffs of a shirt are placed on these. A pivoting head of chrome-plated steel bears the same shapes as the buck and, when pressed over the buck, applies uniform pressure on the collars and cuffs. The head is uniformly heated by steam. An automatic timer allows the operator to perform other tasks while the machine presses the collar and cuffs.

Sleeve presses There are primarily two types of sleeve presses, one giving the sleeve a top crease and the other circular and so resulting in no crease. In both cases, the sleeves are fitted onto the buck and are then moved into the sleever cabinet. Here, air fills into the sleeves, pressing them against the head and removing all the wrinkles.

Steam cabinets These are boxes in which linen such as curtains, bedspreads, and blankets are hung so that steam may be passed through them. The steam effectively removes the wrinkles from these articles. However, operating steam cabinets is time-consuming and a worker is required to hang individual articles in the box. Therefore the use of these machines is viable in terms of cost only in large hotels.

Steam-air garment finishers/suzies/genies This consists of an open-mesh nylon air form bag that shapes garments such as dresses and jackets with a gentle cushion of steam and hot air to restore them to an as-good-as-new appearance. The garment is draped on the form, then the steam and air timers are preset. A foot switch starts the steam cycle. Penetrating steam softens and relaxes the garment fibres. Just before the steam cycle ends, the blower automatically starts and the air bag expands gradually to gently shape, dry, and set the finish of the garment.

Hand/flat irons Hand irons fall into two categories—those using an external heat source and those heated by electricity (the electric iron). The former are box-type irons using heavy charcoal or coconut shells. Another type of iron using an external source of heat is made of heavy cast iron and faced with polished steel. They weigh about 8–10 kilograms and are heated over a stove.

Electric irons are much lighter and easier to use than these traditional irons. Most are thermostatically controlled. The thermostat makes it possible to reduce the weight of the iron by as much as 1.5 kilograms. It allows the selection of different temperature settings for various fabrics as well (see Table 19.1) and maintains the iron at these temperatures. Thus electric irons can be used at higher temperatures than traditional irons.

Steam irons eliminate the need to moisten clothes or use a damp cloth while ironing. Water filled into a compartment or reservoir in kettle-type steam irons is brought to the boil and, at the press of

Table 19.1 Temperatures for ironing different fabrics

Fabric	Safe ironing temperature	Fabric	Safe ironing temperature
Linen	200°C	Polyester	160°C
Cotton	180°C	Acrylic	120°C
Wool	160°C	Rayon	120°C
Silk	160°C	Modacrylic	No ironing
Nylon	160°C		

a button on the handle, a shot of steam emerges from perforations and grooves in the sole plate. The flash-boiler type of steam irons make instantaneous steam when individual drops of water come into contact with a heated chamber.

Ironing board To be used with hand-held irons, the ironing board should be well padded and smooth. It should be covered with a firm, white, woven cover stretched firmly and fastened well. It should stand firm and be of the correct height—75 cm from the ground is generally comfortable. It typically has a tray of asbestos on the right-hand side, on which a hot iron can be safely rested.

Folding Machines

Folding machines do not fold the linen as such, but aid the worker in doing so. The machines hold down one end of the linen to be folded so that the worker can fold it more easily.

Spotting Units

These consist of a spotting board, a spotting gun, and a steam attachment. A spotting board is a table that is partly solid and partly perforated. This surface is hard, smooth, and made of marble, masonite, stainless steel, or some other material that is resistant to acids, alkalis, and other spot-cleaning agents used. Dabbing and brushing of stains is done on the solid area of the table. Doing this on the perforated area could damage the fabric.

The spotting unit has three treadles: one for air, one for steam, and the third one for vacuum. During operation, the spotting gun is held vertically above the stain and at least 10 centimetres away. Steam is shot through the stain and the spot-cleaning agent used gets flushed out from the fabric. Figure 19.8 illustrates a spotting unit used in hotel laundries.

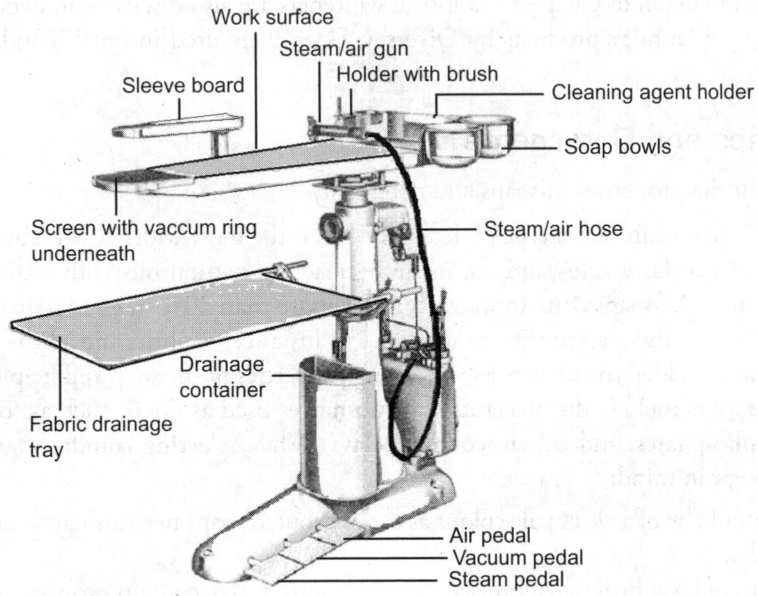

Fig. 19.8 Spotting unit

Dry-cleaning Equipment

These are similar to washing machines of the tumbler type. They are available in a wide range of capacities. They are steam-powered or electrically operated. They carry out washing, extraction, drying, and deodourizing in a continuous process. Solvent filtration and distillation are carried out in a closed system.

The *hot-head offset dry-cleaning press* is a press designed for additional versatility in finishing silks, especially long gowns and dresses. It is also convenient for pressing silk saris. It has a polished chrome-plated hot head, which gets uniformly heated by steam. The 'buck', which is the ironing board, is wide so that draping and removal are easily done.

Carts, Trolleys, and Sacks

These are used for the transfer of clean linen from the laundry to the linen room and from the linen room to the floor pantries, and so on. Linen carts and trolleys may be made of aluminium or steel.

Laundry sacks may or may not be mobile. They may be made of wicker, fibreglass, or plastic. A very popular choice is the one made of tough cotton, with drawstrings, which can be washed frequently.

Laundry Agents or Aids

Laundry 'aids' are the materials used to improve laundering results (bleaches, optical whiteners) or to accomplish specific functions or effects (soaks, stain removers, softeners, stiffeners).

The important laundry agents or aids are water, laundry soaps and detergents, stiffening agents, bleaches, alkaline agents, acid agents, organic solvents, and absorbents. Water as a general cleaning agent has been discussed in detail in Chapter 7. Optical whiteners are also discussed in detail in Chapter 18.

The Clax range of laundry products by Diversey, extensively used in hotel laundries, are given in Table 19.2.

Laundry Soaps and Detergents

Let us now look at the properties of soaps and detergents.

Soaps 'Soap' is technically also a type of detergent and is the most widely used fabric cleaner. 'Soaps' are the sodium salts of fatty acids and are made by reacting natural oils with sodium hydroxide or another caustic alkali. All soaps contain water, but not more than 30% in good soaps. Other additives are also included to give the soap specific properties. For instance, naphtha and a little mineral oil, such as paraffin oil, may be added to enhance the cleansing properties of the soap and help in the removal of grease. Other additives include disinfectants and substances used as fillers, such as sodium carbonate, sodium silicate, phosphates, and certain colloidal clays. While selecting laundry soaps, the following criteria must be kept in mind:

- The soap should be of a clear, pale colour as dark-coloured soaps may contain impurities that aren't easily visible.
- The soap should feel firm when pressed. If it feels soft, it may contain excessive amounts of water and will be wasteful in use.

Table 19.2 Clax range of laundry products

Product	Description	Use
Clax 100 L Crystal	Superior Performance Detergent	• Advanced laundry detergent with built-in alkali booster for light and heavy soils • Suitable for most of the fabrics processed in OPL and commercial laundry, i.e, cottons, polyesters and cotton-polyester blends
Clax Rinse	Neutralising Agent	• Mildly acidic powder which has the properties of neutralising both alkalis and chlorine. • Its addition in the last rinse completely neutralises any excess alkalinity as well as bleach.
Clax 200 Color Safe	Surfactant Booster	• Super concentrated liquid emulsifier specially formulated for effective cleaning of fabrics regularly exposed to mineral oils and grease stains such as chefs' uniforms, mechanics' overalls etc. • It increases effectiveness of normal laundry detergents.
Clax Ultra	Fabric Washing Powder	• Clax Ultra is a main wash detergent specially formulated for use in commercial and on premise laundries. • The product has been developed for automatic and manual dosing and can be applied at soft to medium hard water.
Clax Sept	Fabric Sanitizer	• Specially formulated for use in commercial and on premise laundries.
Clax Hypo	Chlorine Bleach	• Stabilised chlorine bleach. • The product finds applications in laundries as well as kitchens.
Clax Sonril	Liquid Destainer for use at high temperatures (80°C+)	• Liquid laundry bleach based on stabilised hydrogen peroxide • This oxygen bleach is formulated for bleaching during the main wash, at temperatures at and above 80°C.
Clax Suspend Extra	Water Conditioner	• Formulated for water conditioning in all laundries. • It is effective in the sequestration of iron and water hardness salts (calcium and magnesium).
Clax XtraSoft	Fabric Softener	• Concentrated fabric softening liquid specially formulated for use in commercial and on-premise laundries • It is suitable for application on most types of fabric and can be manually or auto-dosed.

Source: Diversey

- Many hard soaps, especially cheap brands, on the other hand, contain an excess of fillers such as sodium silicate to disguise the low percentage of soap.
- A good laundry soap dries to form a firm, unspeckled surface. Soaps that develop white crystals on the surface should not be used, as this shows an excess of harmful alkalis.
- A rough-and-ready test of a good oil-based soap is to break a bar across and examine the fracture; the fracture should be granular, not striated.

Detergents Soap-free detergents have properties similar to soap—such as foaming, wetting, and cleaning—but they are able to make soluble salts out of the calcium, magnesium, and other metal salts that make water 'hard' and render ordinary soap insoluble. Detergents and soaps act by lowering the surface tension of water. The presence of surfactants helps to lower the surface tension, which in turn helps the detergent solution to penetrate grease and dirt deposits on the fabric. Many additives are added to detergents to make them heavy-duty performers (see Chapter 7).

Fabric Stiffeners and Softeners

Fabric stiffeners and softeners have been discussed earlier in Chapter 18. Fabric softeners are added with sours in the final wash cycle. Softeners make fabrics more supple and easier to finish.

Bleaches

These are chemicals capable of whitening fabrics and removing stains by destroying pigmented matter. They also disinfect and deodorize. Their action of combating yellowing and discolouring is due to a chemical reaction—it is generally oxidation, but may sometimes be reduction. Various types of bleaches, their nature, and the fabrics on which they can be safely used are indicated in Table 19.3.

Types of bleach

Bleaches can be classified into the following categories:

Oxidizing bleaches These bleaches release oxygen, which combines with the stains to form a colourless compound. The bleach should be left in contact with the fabric only until the stain is removed, or else the fabric will be weakened.

Open air and sunlight This is the world's oldest and cheapest method of bleaching. Hanging clothes out in the sun to dry keeps white clothes sparkling. Sunlight bleaching can also be used for stain removal for bleached cotton and linen fabrics. When an article is laid out on grass or spread over a bush, some additional bleaching may take place due to the chlorophyll in the leaves.

Sodium hypochlorite (Javelle water) This is made using the following ingredients: 277 g washing soda; 57 g chloride of lime; ½ litre boiling water; and 1 litre cold water.

To make Javelle water, dissolve the washing soda in boiling water. Mix the chloride of lime with cold water, allow to settle, and strain off the clear liquid without stirring. Mix this filtrate with the washing-soda solution. Allow the precipitate of calcium carbonate that is formed to settle. Again strain off the clear liquid and store the residue in dark-coloured bottles as it is unstable to light. This compound readily gives off nascent oxygen, a powerful bleaching agent. It should only be used to bleach white cottons and

Table 19.3 Types of bleaches and their uses

Name of the bleach	Formula	Nature	Fabrics on which used
Bleaching powder	$CaOCl$	Oxidizing	Cotton
Sodium chlorate	$NaClO_3$	Oxidizing	Cotton
Sodium chlorite	$NaClO_2$	Oxidizing	Cotton
Sodium hypochlorite	$NaOCl$	Oxidizing	Cellulosic
Sodium perborate	$NaBO_2{\cdot}H_2O_2{\cdot}3H_2O$	Oxidizing	All
Sodium percarbonate	$2Na_2CO_3{\cdot}3H_2O_2$	Oxidizing	Cellulosic
Sodium peroxide	Na_2O_2	Oxidizing	Cellulosic
Hydrogen peroxide	H_2O_2	Oxidizing	All
Potassium permanganate	$KMnO_4$	Oxidizing	Cotton
Sodium hydrosulphite	$Na_2S_2O_4$	Reducing	Proteinic
Sulphurous acid	HSO_3	Reducing	Proteinic
Oxalic acid	$H_2C_2O_4$	Oxidizing/reducing	Cellulosic and proteinic

linen, and never on any other fabric. In particular, Javelle water should not be used on silk or wool as these fabrics are dissolved in it.

Dilute the Javelle water with an equal amount of hot water and dip the stain into the bleach till it is removed. Do not allow the article to soak for more than 20 minutes. To speed up the action, a few drops of vinegar may be added. Rinse very thoroughly, never allowing any bleach to dry on the fabric. A small amount of ammonia in the rinse water will help remove the smell of bleach from the fabric.

Sodium chlorite This is suitable for cellulosic and synthetic fibres. It is a finely divided crystalline powder obtained when chlorine peroxide reacts with sodium peroxide. Sodium chlorite is used in its anhydrous form for bleaching. The bleach is not hygroscopic and is extremely stable. Cold aqueous solutions have only a mild oxidizing power. On heating or acidification, they develop a strong oxidizing power.

Hydrogen peroxide This is an effective bleach, yet not harmful to most fabrics. It can be used in various concentrations, depending upon the degree of bleaching required. A pint to a gallon of water is the average dilution. A teaspoon of concentrated ammonia solution or of sodium perborate may be added to each gallon of the diluted solution to make the action stronger. After bleaching, the garment should be rinsed thoroughly.

Sodium perborate This is made from borax, caustic soda, and hydrogen peroxide. It is used in many 'oxygen' washing powders. It dissolves in water to make an alkaline bleaching solution that contains hydrogen peroxide. To prepare the bleach, sodium perborate is dissolved in water. If animal-fibre fabrics are to be treated, the solution is first neutralized with acetic acid and then made slightly alkaline with a little ammonia. Sodium perborate is especially effective when the action is started at a low temperature and the heat gradually increased. Its repeated use can tenderize cotton and linen.

Potassium permanganate This has a high content of oxygen, which enables it to combine with and remove obstinate stains such as perspiration and mildew. It can be used on animal as well as vegetable fibres. For use with animal fibres, the bleach is dissolved in warm water. For use with cotton and linen, the bleach is dissolved in hot water. During bleaching, the articles will be stained a characteristic brown due to the formation of manganese dioxide. This is removed by dipping the fabric in one of the following solutions:

- Sodium hypochlorite
- Oxalic acid (diluted)
- Two volumes of hydrogen peroxide acidified with a teaspoon of vinegar (acetic acid) to one volume of bleach

The brown stain disappears almost at once. The fabric is then thoroughly rinsed.

Bleaching powder This has been the traditional bleach for cotton fabrics. It has now been superseded by sodium chloride and other bleaches. It is still widely used in commercial laundries, however. Bleaching powder is a white, amorphous hypochlorite of calcium, having the smell of chlorine. It decomposes on contact with air and hence has to be stored in airtight containers. A good bleaching powder contains 38% available chlorine. Bleaching powder solutions are alkaline in nature due to the presence of free lime. During the reactions occurring in bleaching, calcium carbonate is formed and gets deposited either on the fabric being bleached or on the equipment used. Bleaching powder also attacks metals, forming oxides and hydroxides that deteriorate cellulose. For these reasons, bleaching powder should ideally not be used on fabrics.

Reducing bleaches Reducing bleaches work by removing oxygen from the colouring matter of the stain.

Sodium hydrosulphite This is a valuable agent for bleaching all fibres, particularly wool and silk, which cannot be treated with sodium hypochlorite. It acts by taking oxygen out of the stain, especially when dissolved in hot water, and becoming sodium metabisulphite. When the latter is exposed to air, it is split up into sodium sulphate and sulphur dioxide, which is itself a reducing agent. Sodium hydrosulphite should be stored in an airtight container in a moisture-free place away from heat as it can decompose by absorbing oxygen and evolving sulphur dioxide gas. It can be used in its concentrated form to remove spots caused by grass, faecal matter, leather polish, mildew, ink, potassium permanganate, and dye stains. If the bleach inadvertently runs into a coloured part of the fabric, the bleached colour can be restored by dipping the affected area immediately in an alkaline solution, scrubbing with soap, or sponging with vinegar. When using this bleach, only vessels of wood or earthenware should be used, as in contact with metals it leaves a black stain on all fabrics.

Sodium bisulphite This is a mild reducing agent produced by the partial neutralization of sulphurous acid by caustic soda. Like sodium hydrosulphite, its bleaching action is due to the formation of sulphur dioxide, which takes oxygen out of the stain. Neutralization or thorough rinsing must follow the bleaching process, otherwise sulphuric acid will appear in the fabric through the action of oxygen.

Sodium thiosulphate This is a bleach for cottons. It is made by mixing 7 g sodium thiosulphate, 3.5 kg of 36% acetic acid, and 8 cups of water.

Overbleaching

The overbleaching of cotton and linen during laundering is one of the main causes of general weakening of the fabrics. The fibres then become brittle and harsh, emitting a distinct 'crackle' when rubbed together. To guard against overbleaching, always use a bleach of known strength. Keep the temperature below 60°C (140°F) and add measured quantities of dilute bleach gradually. Chlorine bleach especially should not be used at temperatures above 71°C (160°F).

The right way to bleach

It is important to use bleach in the right way.

Never use bleach directly on fabric Never pour bleach, whether liquid or powder, directly onto the fabric. It must first be diluted in a small container and then added to the water in the tub before the fabrics are immersed. Some bleaches may be used in the wash cycle during laundering. Some manufacturers recommend that the bleach be used together with the detergent. Others recommend pre-soaking the fabric in bleach for 10–15 minutes. Hot water and agitation help to dissolve the bleach and hasten its action.

Use the right amount of bleach Bleach should be used according to the manufacturer's directions or as per the guidelines given above. All measurements should be precise.

Wash off thoroughly Washing the fabrics thoroughly after bleaching is important because if the bleach remains in the fibres, the fabric will weaken and degenerate.

Antichlors

These are used during the after-wash/bleach rinse to ensure that all the chlorine in the bleach has been removed. Polyester fibres especially tend to retain chlorine and are typically treated with antichlors when chlorine bleach is used.

Alkaline Agents/Alkaline Builders

Some alkaline agents/builders used in laundering are discussed in this section.

Washing soda (sodium carbonate, $Na_2CO_3.10H_2O$) This is the most commonly used additive in detergents. It is usually purchased in the form of soda crystals that readily dissolve in boiling water. It is used along with soap to improve the cleaning power of soap, particularly on the boil. Washing soda also softens water and emulsifies grease stains. It is used for removing vegetable stains and scorch marks in particular. However, washing soda should be used with care. If used in excess, the wash solution becomes alkaline, injuring fabrics. Washing soda also tends to make white clothes yellowish and fades prints. It is hard on the skin too.

Borax (sodium tetraborate, $Na_2B_4O_7.10H_2O$) This compound occurs naturally and is sold as a white powder. It is a mildly alkaline substance, readily soluble in cold water, and can be used safely on any fibre. The alkalinity is useful in removing acid stains. The addition of borax to starch solution (in 1:16 ratio) prevents its scorching or browning at the high temperature used in finishing collars. Too much borax, however, will make the collars too stiff and cause them to crack. Borax also has a bleaching action. Cotton and linen fabrics yellowed by age are whitened by boiling in a solution of borax.

Ammonium hydroxide (NH_4OH) This is sometimes purchased as a concentrated solution. It must be used with care as its pungent vapours may cause coughing and choking. Ammonia (NH_3) is also used. Ammonia is a strong alkali, capable of yellowing silk and wool, making colours bleed, and in time tenderizing the fabric. A 10% solution of ammonium hydroxide may be safely used on coloured fabrics, however. It is used to treat grease and mild scorch stains on animal fabrics. It also removes acid stains and to remove the smell left after using Javelle water.

Acid Agents

These are useful for neutralizing alkalis and for stain removal. Mild acids used to neutralize any residual alkalinity in fabrics after washing and rinsing are called 'sours'.

Oxalic acid This is a poison and should be kept in a jar labelled as such. It is sold in the form of white crystals. Its uses include the removal of obstinate fruit stains, bleaching of brown stains left after the use of potassium permanganate, and removal of the tannin base of ink stains together with hydrogen peroxide. It may be used as a cleanser for white straw hats as well.

Oxalic acid has a strong action and should be neutralized by borax or ammonia after the required result is achieved to prevent damage to fabrics. It should never be used on wool or silk as it causes brown stains that cannot be removed. Care must also be taken not to treat fabrics with oxalic acid at temperatures above 60°C (140°F).

Salt of lemon This is a compound of potassium oxalate and oxalic acid, referred to as potassium binoxalate. It is also called 'salt of sorrel'. It is used in the same way and in the same proportions as oxalic acid. It too is a poison. Salt of lemon should always be used with a wooden spoon.

Acetic acid This is one of the most important acids in use in the laundry. Acetic acid is sold in several strengths, glacial acetic acid being the strongest and purest. It should not be stored in metal vessels, but only in glass, enamelware, or earthenware vessels. A weak solution of vinegar is used as a steeping bath to remove excessive bluing agents and as a neutralizing agent. Treatment with a weak solution of acetic acid during the final rinse will not only fix colours, but in many cases also gives added brightness to the colours.

Oleic acid This is a straight-chained fatty acid. It produces soap when mixed with an alkali. It is used for the spot-removal of machine grease and oil stains. Oleic acid is used on cotton and linen. It is unsuitable for coloured fabrics. It must be rinsed away thoroughly from garments or a rancid odour will remain.

Solvents

Solvents are applied to the most delicate fabrics either to remove stains or to dry-clean them. They do not injure the fibres or the colour of the fabrics. They are used as spot-cleaning agents.

Cleaning benzene (C_6H_6) or petrol This is obtained from the distillation of shale oil or petroleum. It is highly inflammable and should not be kept or used indoors in large quantities; of course, it must never be used, even in small quantities, near an open fire either. It is valuable for removing stains containing grease.

Carbon tetrachloride (CCl_4) This is more expensive than cleaning benzene, but is similar in action and has the advantage of being non-flammable. It is, however, very toxic and should be used only near an open window or in well-ventilated rooms as it is extremely volatile and evaporates quickly. It is a good solvent for paint and can be used on all fabrics.

Acetone This is a useful solvent for many stains. Acetone is an effective spot-cleaning agent for stains caused by cosmetics, nail polish, lipstick, paint, varnish, and shoe polish. Acetone is highly inflammable. Also, it should not be used on acetate fabrics as it readily dissolves them.

Methylated spirit This is ethyl alcohol (C_2H_5OH) mixed with methyl alcohol (CH_3OH), which makes it poisonous. It is sold coloured with a violet dye to draw attention to this fact. Although not a very good solvent, it can be used to remove sealing wax, silver nitrate, and other silver stains. It dissolves acetate fabrics, but is safe for use on others.

Paraffin This is a mixture of hydrocarbons. It is a white, waxy solid obtained as a residue from the distillation of petroleum and shale. It is used for removing grease and paint stains on the rubber fittings in laundry appliances.

Turpentine ($C_{10}H_{16}$) This solvent is more expensive than paraffin. It has a distinctive smell and is both inflammable and volatile. It acts as a solvent for grease, varnish, paint, and printer's ink. It is also useful for cleaning rubber rollers. Its one disadvantage is its odour, which may be removed by dry-cleaning again. The advantage with turpentine is that it is safe on acetate.

Absorbents

These are substances suitable for removing grease spots from all fabrics and for the general cleaning of light-coloured fabrics that are evenly soiled. Some examples of absorbents are common salt, bran, fuller's earth, powdered magnesia, and French chalk.

The Laundry Process

The laundry process may be divided into the following main stages:

1. Pre-washing
2. Washing
3. Rinsing

4. Hydro-extraction
5. Finishing

A diagrammatic representation of the entire laundry/linen cycle is presented in Figure 19.9 and a detailed discussion follows.

Fig. 19.9 The laundry/linen cycle

Pre-washing

The following steps are undertaken at the pre-washing stage.

Collecting and sorting soiled linen The GRAs strip the linen from beds and bath areas and put them directly into the soiled-linen bag on the room attendant's cart. Linen should never be piled on the floor where they may get walked on and soiled further or damaged. F&B linen are also placed in hampers for delivery to the laundry. Stained linen should be knotted in one corner to help in sorting. Soiled linen should be sent as soon as possible to the laundry so that stains do not set in. In many hotels, soiled linen are sent to the linen room for sorting, counting, and recording before being sent to the laundry. In case an off-site laundry service is used, the soiled linen are marked in the linen room before being transported.

Transporting soiled linen to the laundry Large hotels have a linen chute that runs down the entire height of the building to the laundry's soil and sort area. In other hotels, soiled linen is usually transported to the laundry on linen carts or in laundry sacks. Linen carts should be free of protrusions that could snag or tear items.

Sorting The soil and sort area in the laundry should be large enough to store a day's worth of laundry without slowing down other activities in the laundry. The articles are sorted out according to the following parameters:

- Degree of soiling is the first check. The soiled linen is separated into categories of stained, unstained, heavily soiled, medium-soiled, and lightly soiled articles.
- The articles are further sorted by colour and fastness of dye.
- They are then further sorted by fibre type.
- Linen that need repair are separated and sent to the tailor for mending before washing. In case the article to be mended is heavily soiled, it is first washed and then mended.
- Monogramming of new linen must be carried out before washing in order to control pilferage and help in identification.
- Condemned or discarded linen are sorted out and cut down before washing.
- 'Light linen' are separated. These are linen that have, after continuous use, lost their lustre and become worn out. They can no longer be offered to VIPs. However, being still in good condition and in one piece (not torn), they may be used for houseguests or for staff members staying in the hotel. These are stocked and washed separately. These differ from condemned linen in that they are not torn; however, they are no longer in 'standard' condition.
- All fancy accessories and attachments such as buttons, buckles, rings, and so on are removed from linen to be washed. False collars in curtains must be removed as well.
- All pockets are emptied and all folds checked.

Weighing and loading The articles, once sorted, are weighed while dry. This is necessary as each washing machine has specific loading instructions that have to be followed. Weighing is also useful for measuring the productivity of the laundry workers.

A modular system of loading is the simplest. Each type of linen article has a known weight, so these are counted into piles until the appropriate total weight is reached. For instance, if a bed sheet is known to weigh 500 g and the capacity of each compartment of the washing machine is 25 kg, then 50 sheets are counted out for each compartment. Alternatively, bundles of linen can be physically weighed before putting them into the compartments.

Washing

Whatever the type of machine used, for maximum efficiency, it must be operated according to the manufacturer's instructions. Temperatures, washing times, and processing chemicals vary according to the types of fabrics being laundered. A sample wash programme is given in Exhibit 19.14.

Determine the right wash programme

Laundries and chemical companies primarily use the principle of 'WATCH' to determine wash programme or formula for different types of linen. The abbreviation stands for water, agitation, time, chemicals and heat. The proper wash programme is indicated by the following parameters:

Duration Heavily soiled linen requires more time than lightly soiled linen. The rate at which soil is removed is not constant either, and must be taken into account. It is the highest at the commencement of the wash and gradually becomes less as time passes.

Temperature Generally, the laundry workers should choose the lowest possible temperature to do the job effectively so as to save energy. However, some detergents and chemicals work properly only in hot water and some types of soils require higher temperatures. Optimal washing temperatures for certain linen articles are given in Table 19.4. Where thermal disinfection is involved, specific temperature and time are applied. Refer Chapter 14 for details on thermal disinfection of linen under laundry protocols.

Exhibit 19.14 Sample wash programmes for sheets, pillow cases and towelling materials

Wash programmes for sheets, pillow cases and towelling materials			
Process	**Instruction**	**Specifications for sheets and pillow cases**	**Specifications for towels, bathmats & bathrobes**
Loading	Do not overload machine	As per machine specification	As per machine specification
Washing	Add detergent		
	Clax 100	4–6 g/Kg of linen	4–5 g/Kg of linen
	Clax Boost (Alkali)	3–4 g/Kg of linen	4–5 g/Kg of linen
	Clax 200 S (for removal of oil-based stains)	1–2 g/Kg of linen	–
	Water level	Low	Low
	Temperature	150°F	160°F
	Time	11 minutes after attaining 150°F	20–25 minutes after attaining 160°F
Bleaching	Add bleach	50 ppm/available chlorine	50–60 ppm; 12% chlorine
	Water level	High	High
	Temperature	30–40°C	150°F
	Time	7 minutes	7 minutes
	pH	9.5+	9.5

Table 19.4 Washing temperatures for linen articles

Article	Washing temperature	Article	Washing temperature
Sheets and pillowcases	95°C	Kitchen uniforms and other heavily soiled uniforms, dusters, and cleaning cloths	95°C
Bath linen	60°C	Silk, nylon, and polyester	30°C
Table linen	60°C	Shirts and jeans	40°C
Blankets and bedspreads	30°C		
Curtains	30°C		

Agitation This is the scrubbing action of the machine. Too little agitation, which is frequently caused by overloading washers, leads to inadequate washing. Overloading also causes unnecessary wear and tear on equipment. Too much agitation, on the other hand, can damage fabric.

Chemicals What chemicals will do the best job on particular types of soils and fabric will have to be decided.

Hardness of water Hard water contains salts that mix with soap and some synthetic detergents to form a sticky substance called 'soap curd', which is deposited on the laundry and makes articles stiff. It is the usual process in most hotels for the maintenance department to check for hardness in water two to three times a month. A simple water testing kit is used; ideally water hardness should be below 50 ppm.

Number of wash cycles Several shorter washes are better than one long one. More soil can be removed with freshly made up suds and clean water than with one solution in which the soil remains in suspension and has a chance to re-soil the linen during a long wash.

Wash cycle

The typical wash cycle consists of nine steps:

Flush (1½–3 minutes) This dissolves and dilutes water-soluble salts to reduce the soil load for the upcoming suds steps. Items are generally flushed at medium temperature at high water levels.

Break (4–10 minutes) A high alkaline 'break' (soil-removal) product is added, which may be followed by additional flushes. The break cycle is usually carried out at a medium temperature and low water levels.

Suds (5–8 minutes) This is the actual 'wash' cycle in which detergent is added. The articles are now agitated in hot water at low water levels.

Intermediate rinse/Carryover suds (2–5 minutes) This rinse cycle removes soils and alkalinity to help the bleach work more effectively later. It rinses linen at the same temperature as the suds cycle.

Bleach (5–8 minutes) Bleach, if used, is added to hot water at a low water level. Bleach kills bacteria, whitens fabrics, and removes stains.

Rinse (1½–3 minutes) Two or more rinses at medium temperature and high water levels are used to remove detergent and soils from the linen.

Intermediate extract (1½–2 minutes) This high-speed spin removes leftover detergent and soil from the linen, usually after the first rinse step. This cycle should not be used immediately after a suds step because it could drive soils back into the fabrics. It should also not be used on no-iron linen.

Sour/Softener/Starch/Sizing (3–5 minutes) Softeners and sours are added to condition fabrics. This cycle is run at a medium temperature and at low water levels. Starches are added to stiffen cotton fabrics. Sizing may also replace the sour/softener step.

Final extract (2–12 minutes) A high-speed spin removes most of the moisture from the linen. The length of the spin depends on the fabric type, extractor capacity, and extractor speed.

Rinsing

This is done using hot and cold water, which are usually recovered and recycled from earlier steps during the last rinse in order to save water.

Hydro-extraction

Extraction removes at least 50% of the water used in the rinsing process and thereby reduces the weight of the laundry load to a minimum and prevents pronounced creases from setting into the fabrics. It also reduces the drying time.

Finishing

This stage in the laundry cycle consists of the following processes:

Drying Items that are dried after hydro-extraction generally include towels, washcloths, and some no-iron linen. Drying items and temperatures vary considerably for different types of linen. In every laundry cycle, however, drying should be followed by a cool-down period to prevent the hot linen being damaged or wrinkled by rapid cooling and handling. After drying, linen should be immediately removed for folding. If folding is delayed, wrinkles will set in.

Ironing Sheets, pillowcases, tablecloths, and napkins go directly into flatwork irons. Towels do not need ironing. They should emerge from the tumble-dryer in a soft and fluffy state, whereupon they may be folded by hand or machine. Guest clothing and uniforms are finished on various steam presses.

Folding This can be done by hand or by machine. Whatever the case, washing and drying items faster than they can be folded leads to unnecessary wrinkling and to re-sorting being required. Folding personnel must also inspect the linen, putting aside those that are to be laundered again and rejecting stained, torn, and otherwise unsuitable items. Folding should be done well away from the stored linen area to avoid re-sorting clean laundry. This step should also be considered a quality-control step.

Storing After folding, the items are post-sorted and stacked. Post-sorting separates any odd linen types and sizes in the batch that were missed in the pre-sorting step. There should be enough storage room for at least one par of linen. Finished items should be allowed to 'rest' on shelves for 24 hours after laundering because many types of linen get damaged more easily after washing. Once the linen are on the shelves, yellowing and fading can be spotted easily.

Transferring Fresh, laundered linen are usually transferred to their areas of use by carts.

Stain Removal

A stain is a spot or localized discolouration left on fabric by reaction with or absorption of a foreign substance. Stain removal or spot-cleaning is a skill that demands special attention, specific techniques, and long experience. The two main factors to be borne in mind while attempting to remove a stain are:

- The composition and colour of the fabric.
- The nature and age of the stain.

General Procedure for Stain Removal

Follow the steps given here for removing stains from fabric:

1. Identify the stain.
2. Classify the stain.
3. Select the reagents to be used.
4. Select the procedure to be used.
5. Proceed step by step to remove the stain.

Identification of Stains

For removal of known stains, the first step is to identify the stain. This helps in selecting the reagents and procedures to be adopted for their removal. Different stains show different characteristics. Stains may be identified based on their colour, texture, or odour.

Colour The colour of the stain generally gives a strong clue as to what the stain is. For instance, a red stain may be due to ink, tomato, lipstick, rouge, nail polish, blood, or some medicine. A yellow stain may be caused by turmeric, a medicine, gravy, or mangoes. Blue or black marks may be ink stains.

Texture By touching the surface of the stain, a clue may be obtained. For instance, if the stain is hard to the touch, it may be egg. A soft stain could be oil, ghee, lipstick, or any grease-based stain. Sticky stains may be glue or gum, stiffness may be caused by egg or some other albuminous stain, and paint stains usually have a smooth feel. The visual texture or appearance of the stain also gives some clue to the kind of stain. Wax and paint stains build up on the surface of the fabric. Oils and fats cause translucent stains.

Odour If the surface of the stain is rubbed with the fingers and then the finger and the stain are smelt, it might be helpful in identifying the stain. For instance, egg, perspiration, medicine, food, perfume, and so on have characteristic odours.

Location The area where the stain is located too in some cases gives an indication about the stain. For instance, in shirts and blouses, the stains around the armpit area are invariably perspiration marks.

Classification of Stains

Stains may be classified into different groups and a single stain may fall into more than one class.

Animal stains These are caused by animal products such as blood, eggs, milk, meat, perspiration, urine, and so on. The major content of these stains, except perspiration and urine, is protein. Therefore, warm water should never be used on them as it coagulates the proteins and sets the stain.

Vegetable stains These stains are caused by plant products such as tea, coffee, juices, fruit, grass, tomato, gravy, wine, and so on. Major components of many of these stains are cellulose and plant pigments.

Grease These stains are from grease or some pigmented matter with a grease base. This class includes stains such as butter, curry, oil, paint, varnish, tar, paraffin, car grease, ghee, and so on. A grease solvent or absorbent is required to remove these stains.

Mineral stains These stains are caused by writing ink, medicines, dye stuffs, rust, and so on.

Metalloid stains An example of this class of stains is iodine tincture.

Acidic stains These include stains such as perspiration, urine (fresh), vinegar, and medicines containing nitric acid, picric acid, and so on.

Basic/alkaline stains This class includes stains of perspiration and urine (old).

Natural dyes and pigments This class includes stains caused by henna, betel leaf, tobacco, chocolate, coffee, tea, and so on.

Synthetic dyes and pigments This class includes stains from hair dyes, markers, typewriter ribbons, watercolours, and so on.

Sugar solutions with colouring matter These stains are caused by jams, jellies, soft drinks, syrups, and puddings.

Miscellaneous This class includes stains such as mud, mildew, and scorching that do not fall into any of the aforementioned classes.

Stains are also classified based on their texture on the fabric.

Absorbed stains These are soft textured stains resulting from absorption of fluids which seep easily into a porous fabric material. Examples of such stains are those caused by oil, alcohol, tea, coffee, and so on.

Built-up stains These stains leave a tactile top residue on the surface of the fabric material and are caused by such dense liquids as wax, glue, paint, and tar that do not seep into the fabric entirely.

Compound stains These are stiff-textured stains that get absorbed into the fabric while also forming a top residue on the surface of the fabric. Examples of such stains are those caused by blood and some medicines.

Classification of Stain Removers

There are many classes of stain removers. Their classification is given in Table 19.5.

Principles of Stain Removal

These are outlined in Table 19.6.

General instructions and precautions

These are some things to keep in mind for stain removal.

- All stains should as far as possible be removed while still fresh. If immediate treatment of the stain is not possible, it must be removed before the garment is washed.
- Known stains should be treated with specific reagents meant for their removal. If the nature of the stain is unknown, it should be treated first by the least harmful method, passing on from one process to the next more active until an effective reagent is reached. The sequence mentioned here may be followed:

Table 19.5 Classification of stain removers

Class	Subgroup	Examples
Solvents	Hydrocarbons	Benzene, toluene
	Chlorinated hydrocarbons	Carbon tetrachloride, trichloroethylene, perchloroethylene
	Petroleum-based	Petroleum ether, solvent naphtha, kerosene, turpentine
	Alcohols, ethers, and ketones	Ethyl alcohol, amyl alcohol, amyl acetate, acetone, glycerine
Bleaches	Oxidizing agents	Hydrogen peroxide, sodium perborate, sodium hypochlorite, potassium permanganate, oxalic acid
	Reducing agents	Sodium hydrosulphite, sodium thiosulphate, sodium bisulphate
Oils/fats	Fatty acids	Coconut oil, olein, oleic acid
Emulsifiers	Anionic	Soaps, alkyl aryl sulphonates, fatty acid alcohol sulphonates
	Non-ionic	Fatty alcohol and alkyl phenol condensates, fatty acid condensates, fatty amine oxides
Acids	Organic	1% oxalic acid, 30% formic acid, 1% acetic acid, white vinegar, lime, curds, sour milk
	Inorganic	Dilute hydrochloric acid
Alkalis	....	Ammonium hydroxide (10% liquid ammonia), and 1% sodium bicarbonate
Enzymes	Protease, amylase, lipase	Enzyme soaps
Absorbents	....	Talc, cornstarch, French chalk, fuller's earth

Table 19.6 Principles of stain removal

Nature of the stain	Principle of removal
Acidic	Neutrailization with alkali followed by leaching out
Basic	Neutralization with acid followed by leaching out
Protein	Digestion with enzyme protease
Mineral	Oxidation or reduction (bleaching) followed by washing
Metalloid	Reduction with sodium thiosulphate followed by washing
Fats and oils	Any one of the following processes: • Saponification • Absorption by absorbent powder • Dissolution in solvent
Grease	Any one of the following processes: • Absorption by an absorbent powder • Dissolution in a solvent • Emulsification
Natural dyes and pigments	Oxidation (bleaching)
Synthetic dyes and pigments	Any one of the following processes: • Reduction followed by oxidation • Oxidation followed by reduction • Acidification followed by reduction • Oxidation in acidic medium
Sugar solution with colouring matter	Solubilization of sugar and reduction of colour
Miscellaneous	Each of these stains requires a special treatment

1. Soak in cold water.
2. Soak in warm water.
3. Try to bleach in the open air if time permits.
4. Treat with a cold alkaline solution.
5. Treat with a hot alkaline solution.
6. Treat with a cold acidic solution.
7. Treat with a hot acidic solution.
8. Treat with an oxidizing bleach.
9. Treat with a reducing bleach.
10. In the event of the stain still persisting, which is unlikely, repeat steps (4) and (7).

- Old stains are difficult to remove and may be soaked in glycerine to soften.
- The nature and texture of the fabric should be borne in mind while selecting the reagent for stain removal.
- The reagent and the fabric should stay in contact with each other for the minimum time required for effective stain removal.
- The reagent bottle should be tightly capped after each use.
- The room should have good ventilation.
- After stain removal, the reagent must be neutralized. An acidic solution is neutralized with an alkaline one and vice versa. A thorough rinsing with clean water is essential after each treatment.
- Shortcuts should be avoided.

Classification of stain removal procedures

Stain removal procedures may be classified in the following ways:

By mode of action Stain-removal procedures fall into five categories according to the mode of action of the stain-removal agent:

Solvent action Here water or an organic solvent are able to dissolve out the stain.

Mechanical and emulsifying action This dislodges the stain without dissolving it.

Chemical action Where oxidation or reduction reactions render an insoluble stain colourless and soluble, they can then be washed out of the fabric.

Digestion Here enzyme-containing products are used as pre-soaks or in detergents to break down the stain into soluble substances that can be leached out.

Absorption Certain powders such as fuller's earth are able to adsorb or absorb grease and oils.

By method of application According to the method of application of the stain-removal agent, the process may be classified as follows:

Drop method The stained part of the fabric is stretched over a basin and small drops of the stain-removal agent are poured on it with a glass rod or dropper.

Dip method The stained area of the fabric is immersed in the stain-remover solution. This is the ideal method when the stain is large or if there are many spots spread across the fabric.

Steam method Stains on wool, silk, or any coloured fabric can be removed by steaming. The stained area is saturated with steam by spreading the cloth over a basin half-filled with hot water into which a small amount of the appropriate removal agent has been placed.

Sponge method The stain-removal agent is applied on the stained area of the fabric with a sponge. This is the most frequently used method of stain removal.

Absorption method In the absorption method, the soiled part of the fabric is placed on a sheet of blotting paper. The absorbent powder is spread on the soiled area, rubbed in lightly, and allowed to adsorb or absorb the grease. This method can also be carried out by applying a paste of the absorbent powder, letting it sit, and then scraping off the paste.

Removal of common stains

Removal of stains from cellulosic-fibre fabrics and protein-fibre fabrics differs.

Removal of stains from cellulosic-fibre fabrics Removal procedures of few common stains are discussed in Table 19.7. and a sample stain removal 'how-to' card for use in teaching laboratories is presented in Exhibit 19.15.

Removal of stains from protein-fibre fabrics The common stains and their treatments are as follows.

- Fresh betel-leaf and blood stains are easily removed from wool and silk with water. If the stain has remained on the fabric for sometime, it will need to be treated with a synthetic detergent.
- Lipstick, shoepolish, mascara, and tar stains on protein fabrics are treated as mentioned for cellulosic fabrics.
- Cocoa stains are more easily removed from wool or silk than from cellulosic fibres. Washing with a synthetic detergent is sufficient in the case of protein fibres. Treatment with methylated spirit or a dry-cleaning solvent may also be used instead of washing.

Table 19.7 Removal of common stains from cellulosic fabrics

Stain	Method of removal
Ballpoint ink	Rub lightly with cotton swab soaked in denatured spirit or methylated spirit. An old ballpoint-ink stain may be soaked in glycerine to soften it and then treated.
Betel leaf (paan)	Bleach with 1% potassium permanganate (the fabric turns brown). Then soak in 1% oxalic acid or 1% sodium bisulphite (till brown colour disappears). Launder.
Blood	Soak in cold water for about an hour. Then transfer to lukewarm water containing an enzyme detergent. Soak for 30 minutes. Launder. or Soak the stain in acetic acid for about 2 hours. Rub gently. Neutralize with ammonia solution.
Candle wax	Scrape off surface wax with a blunt knife. Place the stain between two sheets of tissue paper or blotting paper and press with warm iron.
Catechu (kattha)	Apply a dilute solution of potassium permanganate on the stain. Apply sodium bisulphate and treat with solvent soap.
Chewing gum	Remove surface gum with a blunt knife. Apply ice to the stain. Allow to soak in ice-cold water for a few minutes. Launder.
Chocolate, cocoa	Treat as for blood.
Coffee, tea	Pour boiling water over the stain. Apply borax solution and allow to dry. Pour boiling water over it. Launder.
Curry (turmeric and oil)	Apply soap and then bleach in sunlight. When dry, if the stain has not disappeared, wet it and put it back in sunlight again. or Wash with soap and water. Put in the sun to bleach. Apply borax. Soak in potassium permanganate. Bleach with Javelle water.

Exhibit 19.15 Stain removal 'how-to' cards for teaching laboratories

Stain removal 'how-to' cards				
S. no.	**Stain**	**Cleaning agents needed**	**Materials needed**	**Procedure**
1.	Ball point ink stain	1. Isopropyl alcohol 2. Liquid detergent 3. Cold water 4. Hot water 5. Detergent soap	1. Tissue towels 2. Cotton swab 3. Basin/bowl	1. Place the cloth on the tissue towel. 2. Cover the stain with Isopropyl alcohol. 3. Apply liquid detergent over the area dampened with alcohol. 4. Rinse in cold water. 5. Launder with hot water. 6. Dry if the stain has gone. 7. Repeat the process till stain is removed and dry the fabric.
2.	Candle wax stain	1. Ice cubes 2. Boiling hot water	1. Spatula 2. Bowl 3. Rubber band	1. Rub ice cube over the spot to freeze the wax. 2. Chip away as much wax as possible using spatula. 3. Stretch the affected fabric area over a bowl and tie with rubber band. 4. Carefully pour boiling hot water from a foot above. 5. Dry the fabric.

Spotting

Laundries may employ specialists known as 'spotters' who are responsible for stain removal. Spotters have in-depth knowledge of fabrics and dyestuffs. They know about the action of various chemicals on stains, fabrics, and dyes. They also have the skills and techniques required to handle various chemicals and remove stains from different types of fabrics without damaging the material.

Dry-Cleaning

This is the cleaning of fabrics in a substantially non-aqueous liquid medium. Dry-cleaning removes oils as well as many water-soluble and some insoluble materials with the help of detergents and various other agents. The term 'dry-cleaning' is misleading. It suggests that the cleaning is done using dry materials only, whereas the fact is that in addition to dry powders, liquids such as petrol, benzene, and so on are also used. Unlike laundering, dry-cleaning does not cause swelling of the fibres and so does not lead to shrinkage, wrinkles, and bleeding of colours. Dry-cleaning is thus a safe method for cleaning delicate textiles. It was earlier known as 'French cleaning' or 'chemical cleaning' and is based on the principle that most of the dirt or soiling matter is held to the fabric by grease. When this grease is removed, the dirt is removed along with it.

Advantages and Limitations of Dry-cleaning

Let us now discuss the advantages and limitations of dry-cleaning.

Advantages

- Dry-cleaning cleans clothes for which laundering is not suitable.
- It causes no shrinkage (which is often seen in laundering).
- Dry-cleaning does not flatten the pile of fabrics such as velvet.
- Finishes such as moireing are retained even after dry-cleaning.
- Colours do not bleed on dry-cleaning.
- Stains are more readily removed by dry-cleaning.

Disadvantages

- Dry-cleaning is expensive compared to laundering.
- Many dry-cleaning solvents are harmful to health if inhaled for long durations.
- After cleaning with solvents, a certain unpleasant smell tends to be retained by the articles.

The Process of Dry-cleaning

The process of dry-cleaning is discussed in detail in this section.

Marking When soiled garments are delivered for dry-cleaning, they are first sent to the marking area. Here, a piece of white fabric with a number or some other code stamped on it with indelible marking ink is securely attached to the garment. Every article is marked individually to facilitate identification.

Sorting The garments then pass on to the sorting area. At this point, if there are any tears or any seams that have ripped open, the garment is sent to the seamstress for mending. Different types of garments are sorted into different hampers so that each hamper contains only one class of garments and can hold a load of about 45 kg. There are six major groups into which the clothes are sorted:

- White and light-coloured clothes.
- Dark-coloured woollens.
- Dark-coloured clothes.
- Drapery and furniture covers.
- White and light-coloured woollens.
- Raincoats.

At this stage, pockets are checked, parts of the garment showing an excess of dust or dirt are brushed, and fancy buttons, buckles, and so on are removed.

Application of absorbents Absorbents are applied to remove grease spots from all kinds of materials; for cleaning light-coloured fabrics such as white lace, white furs, white shawls, and white felts that are evenly soiled; and for articles such as fur and dark-coloured fabrics that cannot be cleaned by solvents alone. The common absorbents used are starch, powdered magnesia (magnesium carbonate), French chalk, fuller's earth, bran, moong powder, and commercial powders sold in perforated-top tins.

Pre-spotting Heavily soiled areas of the garment are treated with solvents. Volatile dry solvents such as amyl acetate are applied to remove oil-borne stains, while non-volatile solvents are used on paint and varnish stains. Water-soluble stains such as perspiration are spotted with emulsifying agents (water and solvent mixed together). Some pre-spotters are digestive agents. They are mixtures of enzymes capable of digesting food stains. Pre-spotters are applied using a spotting gun, which uses compressed air to help spray the solvent onto the stain or a heavily soiled area. Special spotting tables equipped with steam guns, compressed air, and spot-removal chemicals are used. All chemicals used are removed from the fabric.

Cleaning A load of approximately 45 kg is transferred to the dry-cleaning cylinder. Very delicate clothes are placed in a net bag first. An appropriate solvent is circulated through the clothes. The contact time of the clothes with the solvent and the rinse time vary according to the rate of flow of the solvent and according to the type and size of the workload. This can vary from 5 to 45 minutes depending on fabric composition and degree of soiling. The dry-cleaning machine is constructed in such a way as to mechanically agitate the load. The horizontal drum has ribs built in to help lift up the garments as the drum rotates. These garments then drop back into the solvent. Thus immersion and agitation of the garments in the solvent takes place, loosening the soil and dissolving it out. The drum is also perforated to allow the solvent to flow through.

Extraction Excess solvent is removed from the garments by centrifugal action in a revolving perforated cylinder contained in a tumbler. Modern dry-cleaning machines perform the cleaning and the extraction in the same cylinder. Thus, the operators are not exposed to the solvent vapours during the process. In the older dry-cleaning drums, using petroleum, a separate extractor was used.

Drying After extraction of excess solvent, the garments are dried in a dryer that has a perforated drum enclosed in a tumbler. Hot air is passed through the clothes and is sucked out by an exhaust fan. The temperature is controlled and kept to around 70°C. Garments that might be damaged by tumble-drying are dried in a drying cabinet in which there is a fan.

Filtering and distillation of the solvent Solvents are expensive and therefore filtered out, distilled, and reused; they are not allowed to evaporate after use. This also reduces fire hazards and health hazards to workers in the laundry.

Inspection Dried garments are inspected to check that they are perfectly clean. If necessary, they are spot-cleaned a second time. Wet-cleaning may sometimes be carried out at this stage. In this operation, each article is inspected individually. If any spots or stains are seen, the garment is sent back for re-spotting.

Finishing In this process, the garment is restored as nearly as possible to its original size, shape, feel, and appearance. The clean garments are then pressed. Pressing is the most expensive operation in dry-cleaning.

Packing Buttons and buckles that had been removed are stitched back on. Finally, the garments are packed in paper or suspended from clothes hangers covered with polythene bags. They are now ready for delivery.

Dry-cleaning Materials

Let us now look at the materials used for dry-cleaning.

Dry-cleaning detergents These are not products formulated as laundry detergents. They are primarily surfactants or a mixture of surfactants with a concentration of active ingredients ranging from 40 to 90%.

Absorbents These are powders such as fuller's earth, French chalk, talc, bran, salt, and powdered sulphur, which absorb grease from the fabric.

Solvents An ideal dry-cleaning solvent must be an effective solvent for fats and oils, sufficiently volatile to permit easy drying, easily purified, and of low toxicity. It should not weaken, dissolve, or shrink the textile fibres or cause bleeding of dyes. It must be non-corrosive to metals commonly used in the machinery and be non-flammable as well. The solvents most often used are:

Petroleum solvents/Stoddard solvent These must be clear, water-white, and free of rancid or otherwise objectionable odours. They are generally of a fast-drying type and include the petroleum fractions. High-flashpoint hydrocarbons are the preferred solvents nowdays for dry cleaning. Stringent precautions for fire safety need to be taken when these are used in dry cleaning units.

Halogenated hydrocarbons Primarily, chlorinated hydrocarbons are used. The main advantage of these over petroleum is their non-flammability. The use of perchloroethylene (PERC) gave excellent results and it was the most widely used dry-cleaning solvent, but there are concerns due to its carcinogenicity. Hence it is now increasingly being replaced by hydrocarbons and pressurised liquid carbon dioxide. Trichloroethylene is also less toxic and more stable than carbon tetrachloride. Its major disadvantage is that it causes bleeding of many acetate dyes.

Pressurised liquified carbon dioxide This is considered a more eco-friendly solvent than all other dry cleaning solvents. After each cleaning process, the gaseous CO_2 is recovered, repressurised and liquified for recycling in the dry cleaning unit.

Handling Guest Laundry

Dealing with guest laundry is one of the major responsibilities of the housekeeping department. Guest laundry must be picked up on time, laundered, and delivered back to the guests on time without any mix-ups. Usually guests' clothes collected in the morning are given back the same evening. The flowchart for handling guest laundry is depicted in Figure 19.10.

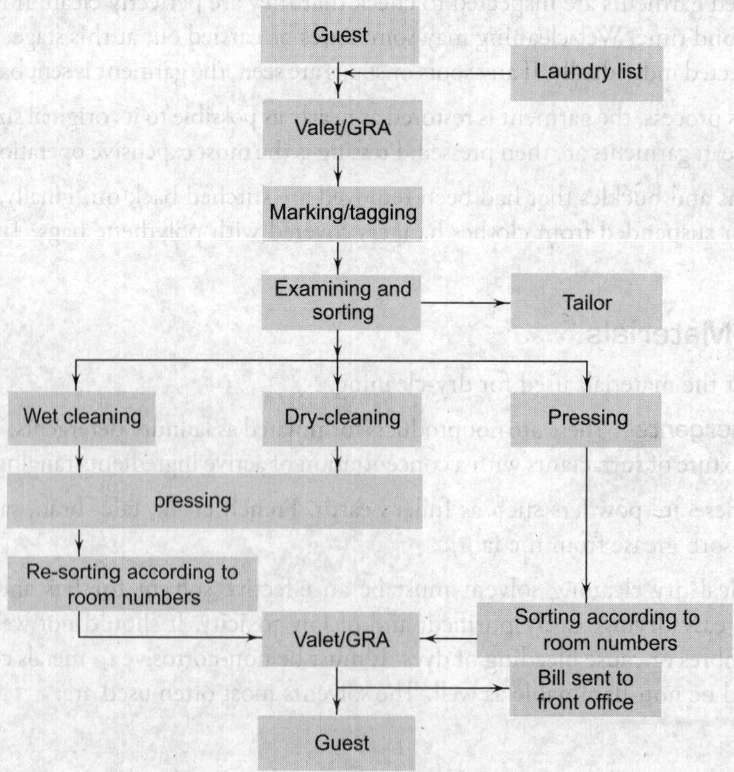

Fig. 19.10 Flowchart depicting handling of guest laundry

Laundry lists

Every guestroom is provided with laundry bags and laundry lists (see Exhibit 19.16). The guest is expected to place the soiled clothes in the laundry bag, fill out the laundry form with the necessary details, and place a call to the housekeeping department to get the laundry collected. Even if the guest does not make a call, the valets should approach the room for guest laundry.

The valet checks the clothes against the list and takes them down to the linen room or in some hotels to the laundry, where the clothes are checked for repairs needed and stray items left in the pockets, they are marked or tagged, and details are recorded in the guest laundry register to avoid misplacement. A sample format of the register is given in Exhibit 19.17. The clothes are washed, dry-cleaned, or ironed according to the guests' requests.

Marking or tagging guest laundry

Guest laundry is marked or tagged according to the room number on a marking machine, see Figure 19.11. The machine seals on the garment a marked thermo-patch which can withstand laundry and dry cleaning processes and then be easily peeled off before the processed laundry is delivered to guests. The following procedure is followed:

Exhibit 19.16 A sample hotel laundry list

Hotel Spring Leaves International

Laundry list

Name of the guest: .... **Service: Normal** ☐ **Express** ☐

Room no.: .... **Date:** .... **Finished garment to be delivered:**

Special instructions: .... **Folded** ☐ **On hanger** ☐

....

Article of clothing	Washing (W)/Dry cleaning (D) & Pressing				Pressing only		
	W/D	Rate in ₹.	Guest count	Hotel count	Rate in ₹.	Guest count	Hotel count
Coat/Blazer		285			150		
Trousers		205			115		
Two-piece suit/Safari suit		490			195		
Shirt/Kurta/Jacket		155			95		
Tie		110			65		
Pyjamas		110			90		
Pyjama suit		240			150		
Dhoti		155			95		
Salwar kameez		285			155		

Exhibit 19.17 A sample format for guest laundry register

Guest laundry register													
Date:				Day:							Shift:		
S. no.	Room no.	Pick-up time	Valet	Items with description	L	P	D	Delivery time	No. of baskets	No. of hangers	Total no. of items	Valet	Remarks
L: Laundry; P: Pressing; D: Dry cleaning													

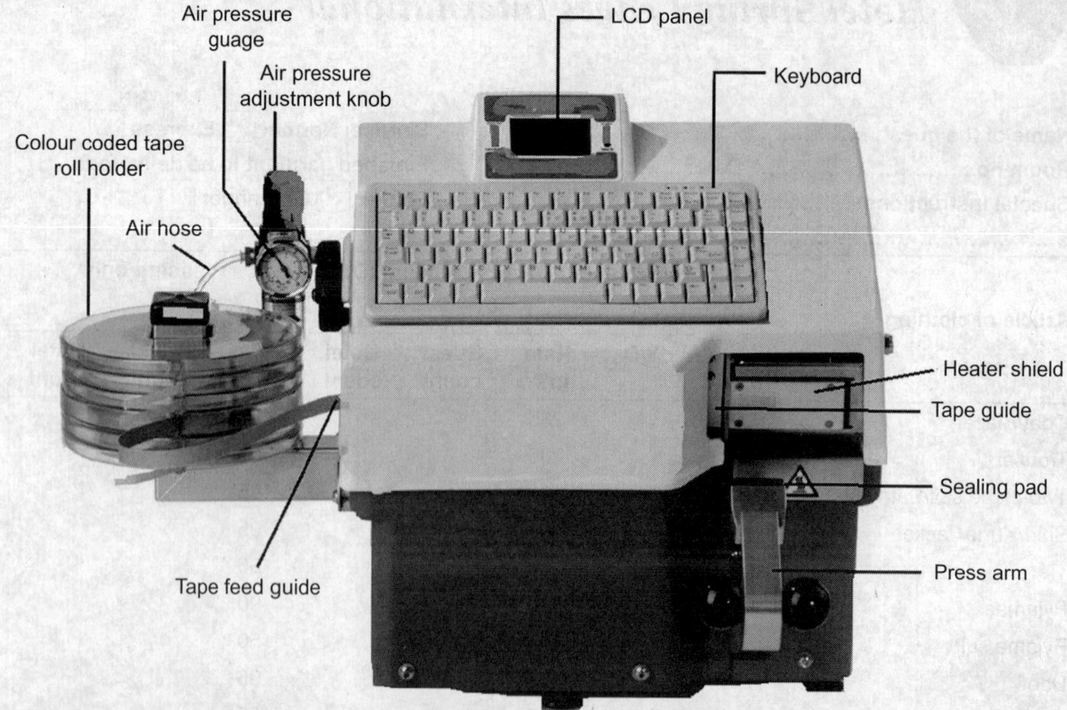

Fig. 19.11 Laundry marking/tagging machine

- Handle only one bag per room at a time to avoid any mix-up.
- Empty the laundry bag, ensure there is no piece of clothing left inside.
- Take out the laundry list and check for the room number, time of delivery, special instructions, whether required on hanger or folded.
- Tally the garments physically with the list. In case the guest has left it unfilled, fill the laundry list.
- Sort out the garments for laundry (L), dry cleaning (D) or pressing (P), as indicated in the laundry list.
- Check the temperature on the tagging machine.
- Directly tag the date and room number on the garments where the labels are located, marking items to be delivered folded or hung on hangers with separate colour tags for the pressman's consideration. Alternately, if colour tags are not available, marking codes may be used, for instance, PO for pressing only, H for garment on hanger, F for garment to be folded and so on.
- Small articles of clothing such as socks and undergarments are usually not tagged separately. They are bunched in a netted bag, which is tagged and all such bags are washed together.
- For delicate garments and nylon and silk, take special care. Tag a separate tag-flag and tie it to the garment.
- In case a special instruction for starching is given by guest for a particular garment, again different coloured tags are to be used.
- Note down the marking number given to each garment in the laundry list filled by the guest for easier identification after processing.
- When moving on to the laundry bag from another room, remember to change the room number on the marking machine.

Re-sorting guest laundry after processing

After pressing, the finished garments are brought to the valet counter to re-sort according to room numbers. A standard process is followed as outlined below:

- All the laundry lists are arranged according to the floors and room numbers in the series of pigeon hole cabinets behind the valet counter.
- The tags on the pressed garments are checked and the garments sorted according to the room numbers on the tags.
- The valet places the sorted garments on the laundry list of the corresponding room number after verifying.
- Working with contents of one pigeon hole at a time, the tags on the garments are peeled off.

Valet service

Most hotels provide valet service for the to-and-fro transfer of guest laundry. Valets collect the soiled guest laundry placed by the guest in the laundry bag along with the laundry list. They verify the contents of the laundry bag against the laundry list. If they do not match, the guest is requested by the valet to rectify the mistake. Valets are also responsible for returning the laundry back to the guests according to the guests' requests.

The usual laundry service for in-house guests is referred to as 'normal service' and entails laundry being collected from guests before 10 a.m. and being returned by evening. On weekdays, there are no additional charges for this service apart from the rates specified on the laundry list. On Sundays and holidays, the normal service is charged at 25% extra. Hotels also have a provision for an express service, which takes about 2–3 hours. Guests are usually charged 50% extra or double the list rates for express service.

Packing and delivering guest laundry

The pressed guest clothing are rechecked for missing buttons or unremoved tags and packed as per the instruction on the laundry list. Suits, coats, trousers and ladies' dresses and sarees are sent on hangers with covers. Only one garment is to be hung per hanger. Good quality plastic hangers are used. Shirts are folded only on guest request and a shirt card and paper bow are used.

The folded articles of clothing are placed in a delivery basket lined with white organza. Care should be taken not to stuff the garments in the basket so as to overflow. Garments are arranged in the sequence they are worn. In case an unremovable stain is still present on a garment, the special laundry treatment card should accompany the garment. The format of the card is presented in Exhibit 19.18.

The baskets and hangers with packed clothing are arranged on the trolley floor-wise, room numbers in sequence, ready for delivery to the guestrooms with the counterfoil of the laundry list. The valet enters the guestroom following the standard operating procedure of entry into an occupied room. The hangers with clothing are hung in the wardrobe, following some sequence such as lighter to darker shades, larger to smaller checks and so on, with enough space between consecutive hangers. The basket with guest clothing is placed neatly towards the foot of the bed. Items found in pockets are delivered back to the guests along with the laundry. A valet card, as shown in Exhibit 19.19. is filled up with details of the guest laundry. If, for reasons such as a room on DND, the valet is unable to deliver the laundry at the scheduled time, the same must be recorded on the valet card and the guest laundry register and the laundry delivered later. In case of express laundry or pressing service, the laundry is delivered as specified by the guest.

Exhibit 19.18 Special laundry treatment card

Hotel Spring Leaves International

Special laundry treatment

Date: ....

Dear Guest,

We would like to inform you that this garment has received special treatment at our laundry but the remaining stains cannot be removed without causing damage to the colour or fabric.

Please be assured that we have done the best we could to deal with the stains.

Thank you for your cooperation,

Laundry Manager

Exhibit 19.19 A sample valet card/Laundry delivery slip

Hotel Spring Leaves International

Valet card

Date: .... Shift: ....

S. no.	Room no.	Laundry pick-up time	Valet	Laundry delivery time	No. of baskets	No. of hangers	Total no. of items	Valet	Remarks

Care Labels

All quality fabrics carry labels indicating how they have to be cared for and what precautions need to be taken in their care to avoid damage to the fabric. In many countries, care labels on fabrics are mandatory by law. Such labelling has not yet been made mandatory in India but exporters of garments and other fabrics are required by the importing countries to stitch care labels on fabrics being exported.

Systems of Labelling and Basic Symbols

There are three main systems followed in labelling. These are the British, the Canadian, and the Dutch systems. All the three systems have the same basic symbols, shown in Table 19.8.

The way in which these symbols are used in the three systems, however, differs. In the Canadian and the Dutch systems, three colours are used:

- Red signifies 'do not carry out the process'.
- Amber indicates that caution is required in carrying out the process.
- Green means that no special precaution is needed.

Table 19.8 Symbols used on care labels

Symbol	Represents	Instructions for
[washtub symbol]	Washtub	Washing
[triangle symbol]	Bleach	Bleaching
[square symbol]	Dryer	Drying
[hand iron symbol]	Hand iron	Ironing
[circle symbol]	Dry-cleaning cylinder	Dry-cleaning

Washing Instructions

The washing instructions for the Canadian, Dutch, and British systems are outlined in Tables 19.9, 19.10, and 19.11, respectively.

Table 19.9 Washing instructions in the Canadian system

Symbol	Colour	Instruction
160°F	Green	Machine-wash using hot water.
120°F	Amber	Machine-wash using warm water.
100°F	Amber	Machine-wash using lukewarm water.
	Amber	Hand-wash using lukewarm water.
	Red	Do not wash.

Table 19.10 Washing instructions in the Dutch system

Symbol	Colour	Instruction
95°C	Green	Wash in hot water.
60°C	Green	Wash in moderately hot water.
40°C	Amber	Wash in lukewarm water.

Bleaching Instructions

The plain triangle indicates that bleaching can be safely carried out. When the symbol 'C1' is included within the triangle, it indicates that chlorine bleaches can be safely used. When the triangle is crossed (×), bleaching has to be avoided. Symbols for bleaching instructions in the Canadian and Dutch systems are listed in Table 19.12.

The British system uses the same symbols in black, indicating whether chlorine bleach may or may not be used and whether bleaching has to be avoided.

Drying Instructions

The drying instructions in the British and Canadian systems are outlined in Table 19.13.

Table 19.11 Washing instructions in the British system

Symbol	Colour	Instruction
1	Black	Machine-wash in very hot (85°C) to boiling water. Hand wash in hand-hot (48°C) water. Maximum agitation may be used.Normal rinse may be used. Spinning or wringing are acceptable.
2	Black	Machine-wash in hot (60°C) water at maximum wash. Hand-wash in hand-hot (48°C) water with maximum agitation. Normal rinse may be used. Spinning or wringing are acceptable.
3	Black	Machine-wash in hot (60°C) at medium wash. Hand-wash in hand-hot (48°C) water at medium agitation. Cold rinse only. Use a short spin cycle to dry or drip dry.

Table 19.12 Bleaching instructions in the Canadian and Dutch systems

Symbol	Colour	Instruction
C1	Amber	Use chlorine bleach as directed on the container label.
C1	Red	Do not use chlorine bleach.
C1	Green	Bleaching with hypochlorite (chlorine bleach) if necessary is permitted.
	Red	Do not bleach.

Table 19.13 Drying instructions in the British and Canadian systems

Symbol	Colour		Instruction
	Canadian	British	
(square with circle)	Green	Black	Dry in a tumble-dryer (in the Canadian system) at a medium to high setting. The British system only indicates that the item may be tumble-dried; the setting is not specified.
(square with circle)	Amber	----	Dry in a tumble-dryer at a low setting.
(square with circle, crossed out)	Red	Black	Do not tumble-dry.

Ironing Instructions

The symbol for ironing is appropriate and clear, but details of temperature vary in each system. In the Canadian system, besides the colour, the temperature is indicated as degrees fahrenheit inscribed on the iron. The Dutch system only indicates temperature through the colours. The British system has one, two, or three dots showing the different temperature ranges to be used. When the fabric is not to be ironed, the iron is crossed out (×). The symbols for ironing instructions in the three systems are outlined in Table 19.14.

Dry-cleaning Instructions

In the Dutch and British systems, a letter is inscribed in the circle. This letter indicates the solvent to be used. The Canadian system does not specify the solvent to be used. Table 19.15 gives the symbols for dry-cleaning instructions.

Certain internationally accepted dry-cleaning codes are given in Table 19.16.

Other Care Labels

Some retailers may have their own care labelling on the fabrics. These may consist of a simple letter code that identifies the five basic cleaning methods:

- MH: Machine-wash hot; tumble-dry.
- MW: Machine-wash warm; tumble-dry.
- MG: Machine-wash gently; tumble-dry on low heat.
- HW: Hand-wash warm; line-dry.
- DC: Dry-clean only.

Table 19.14 Ironing instructions

Symbol	Colour	Instruction
		Canadian system
400°F	Green	A high setting suitable for cotton and linen of upto 400°F may be used.
300°F	Amber	A medium setting of upto 300°F should be used.
225°F	Amber	A low setting of upto 225°F should be used.
	Red	Do not iron.
		Dutch system
	Green	Use a hot iron.
	Amber	Do not use a hot iron.
	Red	Do not iron.

Table 19.15 Dry-cleaning instructions

Symbol	Colour	Instruction
		Canadian system
	Green	May be dry-cleaned.
	Amber	It may be dry-cleaned, but tumble-drying should be done at a low temperature.
	Red	Do not dry-clean.
		Dutch system
A	Green	Use any solvent.

(*Contd.*)

Table 19.15 *Contd.*

Symbol	Colour	Instruction
		Dutch system
P (in circle)	Amber	Use only perchloroethylene or petroleum solvent.
F (in circle)	Amber	Use only petroleum solvent.

Table 19.16 Internationally accepted dry-cleaning codes

Symbol	Process
A (in circle)	Article may be normally dry-cleaned in all solvents usually used for dry-cleaning.
P (in circle)	Articles may be normally dry-cleaned in tetrachloroethylene, trichlorofluoromethane (solvent 11), hydrocarbons (white spirit), or trichlorotrifluoroethane (solvent 113) using the normal dry-cleaning process without restriction.
P (in circle, underlined)	Articles dry-cleanable in solvents given in the above row, but which are sensitive to some dry-cleaning processes and for which there is a strict limitation on the addition of water during cleaning and/or certain restrictions concerning mechanical action and/or drying temperature.
F (in circle)	Articles may be normally dry-cleaned in hydrocarbons (white spirit) and trichlorotrifluoroethane (solvent 113) using the normal dry-cleaning procedures without restrictions.
F (in circle, underlined)	Articles may be dry-cleaned in solvents given under the above category, but are sensitive to some dry-cleaning procedures and hence, there is a strict limitation on the addition of water during cleaning and/or certain restrictions concerning mechanical action and/or drying temperatures.
Crossed circle	Do not dry-clean.

Preparation of Hot and Cold Face Towels

In many hotels, the housekeeping department may be responsible for preparing hot or cold face towels. Hot face towels are offered to guests on arrival at a hotel or restaurant to wipe the face in cold climates. Cold towels are offered for the same purpose in hot and humid climates. In some hotels, the preparation of hot and cold face towels are the responsibility of the F&B department.

Procedure for preparing a cold towel

The following are the steps for preparing a cold towel.

1. Take a fresh face towel.
2. Pour chilled water into a bowl.

3. Add a few drops of aromatic oil (usually the hotel's signature fragrance) to the chilled water.
4. Dip the folded towel into the cold water with a pair of tongs.
5. Take the towel out of the water and squeeze out most of the water.
6. Roll up the face towel and place it on ice cubes in an ice-box or in a refrigerator. (Not in freezer)
7. Present the towel to the guest from a tray/salver when required, using a pair of tongs to proffer it.

Procedure for preparing a hot towel

The following are the steps for preparing a hot towel.

1. Take a fresh face towel.
2. Take hot water in a bowl.
3. Add a few drops of an aromatic oil (usually the hotel's signature fragrance) to the hot water.
4. Dip the folded towel into the hot water with a pair of tongs.
5. Take the towel out of the water and squeeze out most of the water.
6. Roll up the face towel and place it on steam-heated warming equipment.
7. Present the towel to the guest on a tray/salver when required, proffering it with a pair of tongs.

SUMMARY

Linen and laundry operations are important aspects of housekeeping. The planning and layout of the linen and uniform room has been discussed in this chapter. Depending on whether the hotel has an OPL or a contracted laundry, the activities carried out in the linen and uniform room differ. The linen exchange procedure for the guestrooms and for F&B linen has been described, along with the relevant forms and formats.

The successful management of linen depends to a large extent on the par stock of linen maintained by the housekeeping department. How the linen par stock is maintained has been explained in this chapter. Another aspect of linen management is linen control. Maintenance of the quality and quantity of linen, stock-taking, and proper documentation are vital to the control of linen. The quality of linen purchased in the beginning will affect the quantity to be purchased later in the course of housekeeping operations to maintain the par stock. General selection criteria for fabrics meant for bed, bath, F&B, and health-club linen as well as some soft furnishings have been listed. Individual quality requirements for all the above linen types have been discussed. The durability of linen is measured on the basis of its lifespan, that is, how many times the article can be laundered before being categorized as 'light linen' (too worn to be suitable for guestroom use). The expected useful life of an article of linen is often more important than the purchase price in determining whether alternative products are economical or not. The cost of laundering linen over their useful life is usually much greater and more important than their initial price.

Marking or tagging of linen helps keep a tab on when the linen was put into circulation. After the lifespan of a given article is spent, the discarded or condemned linen should be recycled in a usable form. This has been discussed in brief. The correct documentation of discards should be emphasized to control loss of linen.

Linen hire is discussed next as a feasible option available to housekeepers to procure rental linen on reasonable prices. Its advantages and disadvantages are outlined.

The planning and layout of an OPL for hotels is discussed in the next section. The various types of laundry equipment have been described with relevant diagrams. Many laundry aids have already been dealt with in Chapters 7 and 18. The reader should refer to the same where mentioned.

The laundry process is divided into stages and each stage has been discussed, with subheads for clear understanding.

Stain removal or spotting is an important function in the laundry. The section on stain removal is exhaustive, as this is a specialized skill. A trial-and-error method does not work here and there can be no shortcuts for stain removal.

The dry-cleaning process has been outlined briefly, with its advantages and disadvantages. It should be understood that the term 'dry-cleaning' is a misnomer. The actual process does use liquids, apart from the dry powders and agents; but these liquids are non-aqueous.

Dealing with guest laundry is another important responsibility of the housekeeping department. The guest laundry needs to be collected by valets at a stipulated time and needs to be returned by normal or express service as desired by the guest.

Whether it is guest laundry or linen or uniforms being used in the hotel, the linen room and laundry personnel need to interpret certain symbols on the care labels. A detailed section on care labels has been included since following them is essential for the durability and proper maintenance of fabrics.

A brief for the preparation of hot and cold face towels has been given, since in many hotels, this may be the responsibility of the housekeeping department.

KEY TERMS

Acoustics Sound absorption quality of certain materials, usually those used on ceilings, walls, and floors.

Antichlors These reagents are used in rinsing to ensure that all chlorine from bleaching has been removed.

Calender A machine with rollers for the ironing of cloth. It is used in institutional and commercial laundries for ironing bed sheets and other flat articles.

Contingency plan Planning done for uncertain events.

Cutting down This refers to using any discarded materials for some other purpose, such as bed sheets being used as dust sheets or being made into pillow covers.

Damask A glossy fabric with intricate, jacquard-woven designs, made from cotton, silk, viscose rayon, or mixtures. It is the preferred fabric for table linen.

Discarded or condemned linen Hotel linen that is officially declared unfit for use.

Dry-cleaning The cleaning of fabrics in a substantially non-aqueous liquid medium.

Floor pantry A service room provided on each floor for GRAs to store cleaning agents, equipment, guest supplies, guestroom linen, and the room attendant's cart.

Grey goods Fabrics that have come straight from the loom without having received any finishing.

Laundromats These are self-service laundries usually found in motels. Laundromats may be utilized by using coin slots to pay by the load or by making a fixed monthly payment.

Laundry A place where the washing and finishing of clothes and other washable articles can be done.

Laundry aids Substances used to improve the results of laundering (soaps, detergents, bleaches, optical whiteners) or to accomplish specific functions or other effects (pre-soaks, stain removers, softeners, stiffeners).

Light linen This is linen that has, after continuous use, lost its lustre and has become worn out. It can no longer be used for VIPs. However, being still in good condition and in one piece (not torn), it may be offered for the use of houseguests or for staff members staying in the hotel.

Linen Material woven from the fibres of the flax plant; articles made from this material; household articles that were traditionally made from linen material but may now be made of cotton or cotton blends; the term 'linen' is also used loosely to denote all launderable articles in the linen room. Actual linen material is less elastic and more absorbent than cotton.

Linen chute A sloping channel or slide for conveying soiled linen from the upper floors to the laundry, usually situated on the ground floor or in the basement.

Linen hire Procurement of linen on rent by a hotel company by entering into a contract with a hire firm to periodically deliver an agreed amount of the chosen quality of linen to the hotel.

Linen lifespan Refers to the number of times an article of linen can be laundered before becoming too worn to be suitable for guest's use.

Linen par A par stock of linen refers to the amount of each type of linen required to make up all the guestrooms of the hotel at a given time. One par of linen is also referred to as the 'house set-up' quantity.

Marking A process by which a tag with the hotel logo and date of putting into circulation printed on it is stitched on the inside hemming, near the corner of each piece of hotel linen before bringing it into circulation. Also called tagging of linen. Guest laundry is also tagged according to room number.

Methylated spirit Ethyl alcohol to which a little methyl alcohol (a toxic substance) has been added to render the alcohol poisonous, making it unfit for consumption. Some amount of violet dye is also added for identification. This is also called 'denatured spirit'.

Muslin sheets These are sheets made of blends in which cotton fibres are carded before spinning. The resultant fabric is rough and looks dull.

OPL On-premises laundry—an in-house area in the hotel where linen and uniforms are washed, dry-cleaned, and pressed.

Optical whiteners These substances mask the yellowish tinge developed in white fabrics after repeated laundering.

Par number A multiple of the 'one par' set-up quantity of stock required to support daily housekeeping functions. For instance, two par of linen is the total number of each type of linen needed to outfit all guestrooms twice over.

Percale sheets Sheets made of blends in which cotton fibres are combed before spinning. The resultant fabric is smooth and has a greater tensile strength. Percale sheets are preferred for use in hotels.

Tagging See marking.

Salt of lemon This is a compound of potassium oxalate and oxalic acid. It is also called 'salt of sorrel'. It is used for neutralizing strong alkalis.

Salt of sorrel Same as Salt of lemon.

Saponification Reaction in which fat/oil reacts with alkali to form soap.

Seconds Sheets that have minor imperfections are called 'seconds' and usually have the manufacturer's tags cut off.

Seersucker A weave in which some warp yarns are held at tension and some loose at frequent intervals while weaving. This produces a fabric with a crinkled effect. Crinkle sheets used in bed-making are made in this weave.

Selvedge The longitudinal, visibly distinct self-border along the length of a fabric, which is closed by loops of weft yarns. The selvedge is usually more compact and stronger than the rest of the fabric.

Sizing A general term for compounds that coat yarns and fabrics to impart stiffness, smoothness, strength, or weight. It includes starches and synthetic stiffeners.

Soap curd Also called 'soap film' or 'lime soap'. This is a water-insoluble material that forms when soap combines with hardness-causing salts of calcium, magnesium, and so on in hard water.

Soft furnishings These include curtains, cushions, loose covers, bedspreads, and quilts, but not carpets.

Soiled linen Dirty and stained linen that require laundering.

Sorting The process of separating soiled linen into different categories: those requiring dry-cleaning and those that should be laundered under different conditions, such as whites and coloureds. In other words, sorting is governed by colour-fastness, fabric composition, garment construction, and the amount and kind of soil.

Sours Mild acids used to neutralize any residual alkalinity in fabrics after washing and rinsing.

Spotting The specialized function of stain removal carried out by skilled personnel called spotters, using appropriate equipment and stain-removal agents.

Stain A spot or discoloration left on fabrics from contact with and absorption of foreign substances.

Stock-taking (of linen) The physical verification by counting of stocks of all linen items anywhere in the linen cycle, taking place at periodic intervals or at the time of the closing of books, for evaluation purposes.

Suds The foam formed on the surface of a soap or synthetic-detergent solution as a result of agitation. The wash water containing a detergent is sometimes also referred to as 'suds'.

Surfactants Compounds that impart good wetting power, emulsifying power, and suspending power to detergents.

Tensile strength (of a fabric) Strength as determined by the amount of weight it takes to tear a 1 inch × 3 inches piece of fabric.

Thread count Indicates the number of warp ends and weft picks per unit measure of a fabric.

Togs Unit of measure for the thermal insulation properties or 'warmth' of fabrics (especially for blankets).

Torn-sheet size The size of a sheet before hemming.

WATCH Refers to factors that determine a wash programme in the laundry; expands to water, agitation, time, chemicals and heat.

Weave A system of interlacing the warp and weft threads according to definite rules in order to produce the whole or part of a textile fabric.

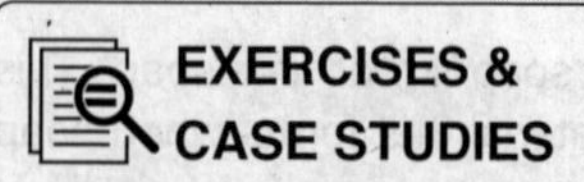

20 Uniforms

Learning Objectives

After reading this chapter, you should be able to

- discuss the designing of uniforms for hotel staff
- establish par levels for staff uniforms in a given property
- understand the procedure for issuing and exchanging of uniforms
- outline the advantages of providing staff uniforms

Introduction

Uniforms are outfits of a specified material, colour, and design, usually provided by the establishment, for certain staff such that all employees in an equivalent or similar position wear identical outfits.

Uniforms are issued to most people who work in the hospitality industry, especially the salaried employees. Employees in the 'back of the house' areas normally wear functional yet pleasing uniforms. Uniforms for the restaurant and front office staff must not only be functional but must also go with the ambience of the area they work in. For example, a poolside restaurant in a resort property can have stewards dressed in Bermudas and a floral shirt with accessories such as a straw hat and sandals. Many hotels now prefer their employees to retain the feel of the region in which the hotel is situated, and to showcase the culture and tradition of the place. A hotel which is very 'Indian' can have a doorman dressed up like a royal Punjabi guard with appropriate accessories. Managers, executives, and senior staff have uniforms to enhance their image. In most hotels, the housekeeping department is the custodian of uniforms for all hotel employees. A reasonable uniform programme should allow the issue of two uniforms to each employee upon employment and a third set on confirmation.

Please refer to the scan code for various type of uniforms used in the hotel industry.

Advantages of Providing Staff Uniforms

- Uniforms ensure a well-groomed appearance.
- They confer prestige on the wearer and promote a distinct brand image.
- They help to create an atmosphere or set the scene; for instance, uniforms may be worn either to match the décor or the theme.
- They are considered by management to make people perform on equal platform.

- They help remove the social differences in staff.
- They aid in identification of the hotel staff and their position to the guest for providing assistance.
- They help differentiate between staff and guests.
- If made in the right design for work, uniforms provide comfort to the staff.
- They instil a sense of belongingness and loyalty to the establishment.
- Uniforms enhance the spirit of teamwork.
- They save money on working clothes and cost of laundering.
- It is easier for staff to take up messy jobs since they know that their own clothes are not involved.
- Some uniforms may have a protective role, such as chef's uniform.

Selection and Design of Uniforms

Terrycots are the most popular choice for uniforms as they have the advantages of both natural and synthetic fibres. Suiting materials are used for trousers and skirts. Drill (cotton) is the popular choice for cooks' coats and aprons as it is cool, durable, and easy to maintain. Gaberdine or any white suiting material may be used for chefs' coats, as they keep up appearances.

Points to be Considered while Designing Uniforms

The following points should be kept in mind while designing uniforms.

General profile of the employees The cultural background, age, and so on of the hotel's employees need to be kept in mind along with the hotel's ethos and the employees' work profiles. Some hotels even involve the staff concerned while designing their uniforms.

Image and identity of the property If the hotel wants to create a desirable, eye-catching, smart, efficient, and professional image, the uniforms should be chosen to reflect, and indeed create, this impression. Emblems, badges, and embroidery can customize the uniforms so as to identify the hotel, the department, and the employee. The uniform can also match the décor and theme of the hotel, thereby reinforcing the image of the property.

Comfort in wear This depends on the right fabric being used, and even more important, on a good fit. Hotel staff have to be active and hardworking, and the uniform should complement this. They may need to reach, bend, stretch, or squat. The fit of the uniform should be such that it does not bind or restrict movement.

Purpose of work Designing for the purpose of the work is of paramount importance. Pockets are an important part of designing. A pair of dungarees or overalls must have several deep pockets for the maintenance employee to keep tools handy. A steward must have pockets that are not very conspicuous to keep a pen, lighter, and so on. Shoes chosen for the cooks must be skid-proof. Short sleeves are more practical for GRAs. Some uniform accessories, such as the headwear of kitchen staff (toque), also fulfil an important hygiene function in addition to making their work easier.

Appearance and style While keeping in mind the environment of the establishment, a uniform should be designed in such a way that it will look equally good on the stout and thin, the tall and short. Well-made garments use fabrics that are designed for heavy wear, and their workmanship must support that. That way, they will stay bright and looking new through countless launderings.

Climatic conditions of the place These must be considered especially if the hotel is not centrally air-conditioned. A full-sleeved terylene shirt with a tie can be stifling for a steward in a humid area. Generally cooks and maintenance crew use 100% drill uniforms.

Budget and value for money In the selection of fabric for uniforms, one should keep in mind the allocated budget, and seek value for money. Laundering and maintaining uniforms is a challenge. Uniforms that look good, are comfortable, and maintain their appearance through a number of laundry cycles are more economical than cheap fabrics that do not perform or last. Blends are easier and cheaper to maintain; however, blends are not recommended for employees working in greasy areas (cooks, maintenance staff) as synthetics and blends do not let go of grease and perspiration stains easily. Also, the fewer the accessories, the less the headache of keeping tab of them, and usually, the lower the expense.

Fabric Fabric selection is also a critical factor to consider when purchasing material for uniforms. Cotton outfits are preferred as uniforms because they are porous and more absorbent than polyester and cotton blends. However, blends with cotton are increasing in popularity because they have better soil-release qualities in general and at the same time retain some coolness.

Ease of availability of materials The fabric and accessories chosen for the uniforms must be readily available whenever new uniforms are required.

Staff turnover This is another challenge. Free-size uniforms can be used in high-turnover areas to address this. Trousers or skirts can have elasticised waistbands to accommodate different sizes.

Uniform Specifications

Whether the housekeepers design the uniforms in-house or work with a specialised uniform vendor, it is imperative to have uniform specifications at hand so that work is clear cut. Based on the specifications given by housekeepers, the vendor prepares the uniform design brief and presents it to the hotel for approval before stitching the uniforms. Uniform specifications are also briefed to all employees when they join the organisation. A sample of uniform specification for front office is presented in Exhibit 20.1.

Exhibit 20.1 Sample uniform specification for front office

Hotel Spring Leaves International

UNIFORM SPECIFICATION

Front office

Designation	Gender	Uniform item	Specifications
Managers	Female	Saree	*Material:* Crepe silk, wash & wear, iron-free *Colour:* Olive green shades *Design:* Paisely print body with solid olive green border
		Blouse	*Material:* Polycot, inner cotton lining *Colour:* Olive green *Design:* Shirt style with spread collar, low waist length, 3/4th sleeve
		Shoes	Black, square toe bellies with 1" block heels
	Male	Suit jacket	*Material:* Polywool, inner polyester lining *Colour:* Charcoal-grey *Design:* Classic fit, single-breasted, two button fastening, narrow notched lapel, single welt pocket- upper left, lower two flap pockets, four inside pockets, double back vent

(Contd.)

Exhibit 20.1 *Contd.*

Designation	Gender	Uniform item	Specifications
		Shirt	*Material:* Polycot (60% cotton, 40% polyester), wrinkle-free Oxford *Colour:* Pale, light lime green *Design:* Traditional fit, long sleeve, button down collar, left chest pocket
		Tie	*Material:* Silk *Colour:* Dark Olive green *Design:* Traditional, 3.5" width, Windsor knot
		Trousers	*Material:* Polywool (54% polyester, 44% wool, 2% spandex) *Colour:* Charcoal grey *Design:* Tailored fit, single pleat, two front pockets, two back welt pockets, belt loops
		Belt	Matte black, solid leather, single prong zinc alloy buckle
		Shoes	Black, Classic Oxford leather shoes, lace up

Uniform Management in Hotels

Efficient management of uniforms in hotels needs the following procedures to be followed.

Establishment of par levels for uniforms Hotels generally maintain 3-par for uniforms.

Preparation of a budget for uniforms The Executive Housekeeper (EHK) with the help of the Uniform Room Supervisor makes the budget for the uniforms for the entire hotel staff. Before budgeting, a detailed survey of the market and current trends needs to be done since the expenditure involved is high.

Developing and implementing an effective uniform control system It is essential that the housekeeping department develops a system of controlling uniform distribution and usage, monitored by the EHK. The system should include recording the following:

- Name of the person receiving a uniform
- Date of issue
- Number of pieces issued
- A record of misplaced or stolen items
- A record of any uniforms that are out on temporary loan

Designing new uniforms The housekeeper has to undertake this task keeping in mind changing trends. The following process is followed:

- After the budget is sanctioned, sample uniforms are made by the EHK for all departments. The points to be considered while designing uniforms have been discussed earlier in the chapter.
- The samples are then sent to the laundry for checks on colour-fastness and durability.
- After approval of samples, a purchase requisition is made and given to the purchase department for the purchase of the fabrics.
- Uniforms are stitched by the tailors at the hotel's sewing room or a uniform contractor.
- Trials are carried out for all the staff members and the required alterations are done.
- The new uniforms received are sent to the uniform room for tagging with codes for each staff member.

Alternatively, housekeepers may work with uniform vendors to design and supply uniforms for their staff. Most hotels prefer to work with specialised uniform vendors and the housekeeping department has the onus of maintaining and issuing the supplied uniforms.

Outfitting new personnel A new employee joining any department has to have a Uniform Request Form (see Exhibit 20.2) signed by the Personnel Manager as well as the HoD. If the employee is a part-timer or trainee, old uniforms in good condition and fit can be issued.

Exhibit 20.2 Uniform request form

Uniform request form

Date: ....

To the uniform in-charge

Kindly issue the following uniform to ....

Department ....

Section ....

Type of employment ....

No. of sets ....

Signature of HoD .... Signature of the Personnel Manager ....

Uniform exchange procedure The following procedure is followed:

- A clean set is issued in exchange for a soiled set.
- The uniform room attendant checks the condition of the uniform for any damage or repair.
- The uniforms are then sorted based on the fabric and sent to the laundry for washing.
- The number and type of soiled uniforms sent to the laundry and fresh ones received are entered in the 'uniform account register'.

Storing uniforms The following steps are followed:

- On return from laundry, the uniforms are sorted out department wise.
- The uniforms received are then tallied with the uniform account register.
- The uniforms are then hung on hangers and stored in the uniform room.
- In many properties autovalet systems are installed. These consist of a computerized system with single or multi-distribution conveyers where the uniforms are hung and delivered from. Now a days in many hotels, heat and waterproof RFID tags are sewn on the uniform labels and registered in the computer database with the garment's information. An RFID reader recognises the code on the returned soiled uniform and the conveyor automatically brings forth the corresponding fresh uniform on hanger to the front for delivery.

Maintenance and upkeep of uniforms The uniform room attendant keeps a check on the condition of the uniforms for any damage or repair. Such repairs should be carried out immediately by the tailors.

Replacement of uniforms If any uniform has to be replaced due to misplacement, theft, or damage, the request has to come from the HoD and be authorized by the EHK. In case of damage caused beyond repair to the uniform due to deliberate damage or gross negligence on part of the employee, the cost of the uniform is recovered from the employee. As such, all replacements of uniforms are carried out prior to them acquiring a worn-out appearance. A standard durability time-frame should be set for all types of uniforms in order to monitor, control and prevent misuse. A sample of standard uniform durability chart is presented in Exhibit 20.3.

Exhibit 20.3 A sample of standard uniform durability chart

Standard uniform durability period chart		
Uniform content/type	**Uniform par/person**	**Minimum durability period**
Cotton	4	12 months
Terry/Poly blend	3	15 months
Silk	3	15 months
Shoes - PVC/rubber	1 pair	9 months
Shoes – Leather	1 pair	12 months

Recovering uniforms from staff who have resigned or been terminated The housekeeping and the personnel department should be informed by the concerned departments about employees who have resigned or have been terminated, so that their uniforms may be taken back. In case the uniforms returned are not in good condition or unjustifiably damaged, the employee may be charged.

Disposal of old uniforms Old and much used uniforms are condemned and sent to charitable institutions. Old uniforms in good condition are used for trainees in various departments.

 Establishing Par Levels for Uniforms

When drawing up a budget for uniforms, consideration should be given to the staff turnover, life expectancy of the garments, seasonal requirements, anticipated changes in décor, and laundry requirements. As a general rule, staff should be supplied with at least 2–3 sets of outfits. Kitchen staff require at least 4 sets of whites, and more if they enter the restaurant.

Number of Sets

When deciding the number of sets of uniforms needed by staff, the following factors are to be considered:

Uniform material The life expectancy of a uniform is between 12–18 months and the material chosen should last for the expected lifespan. Uniforms made of cotton—for example, a chef's coat and trousers or utility workers' uniforms—will need to be changed daily. Terrycot and polyester may need to be changed after every 2 days, whereas for silk it may be 3 days.

Nature of job Some jobs in hotels are strenuous in nature. These jobs include those of GRAs, housemen, utility workers, the maintenance crew, and so on. These workers may require a change of uniform more often. Similarly, staff coming into contact with food as well as those in the 'front of the house' areas would require a change more often than the others. Uniforms for executives are dry-cleaned only periodically.

Frequency of laundering Depending on how often uniforms are sent to the laundry and whether the laundry is in-house or a contracted service would also influence the number of sets required.

Calculating Par Stock Quantity for Uniforms

If uniforms are normally changed every alternate day, the number of pars required is three—on any given day, one is with the employee (in use), one is in the linen and uniform room, and one is in the laundry.

If uniforms are changed every day, as for cooks, five sets are required. More sets may be required if laundering takes more than 24 hours. The following information is required if stocks are to be established:

- Total number of uniformed employees in the hotel, their departments, and their designations
- Man–woman ratio
- Staff turnover patterns
- Frequency of laundering
- Time taken for laundering

Storage of Uniforms

Fresh uniforms received from the laundry by the uniform room are stored according to department and designation of the staff. Each uniform should bear the department's name, the employee's designation, and a serial number on the collar of the shirt or equivalent garment. The uniform room storage area should be properly aired. The humidity of the room should be less than 20%. A sample layout of a uniform room in a large hotel is given in Figure 20.1. In many hotels, staff members are not allowed to take their uniforms outside the hotel. Instead, the employees are provided with lockers to keep their uniforms at the end of the shift. Refer the earlier discussion on 'storing uniforms' too in this chapter.

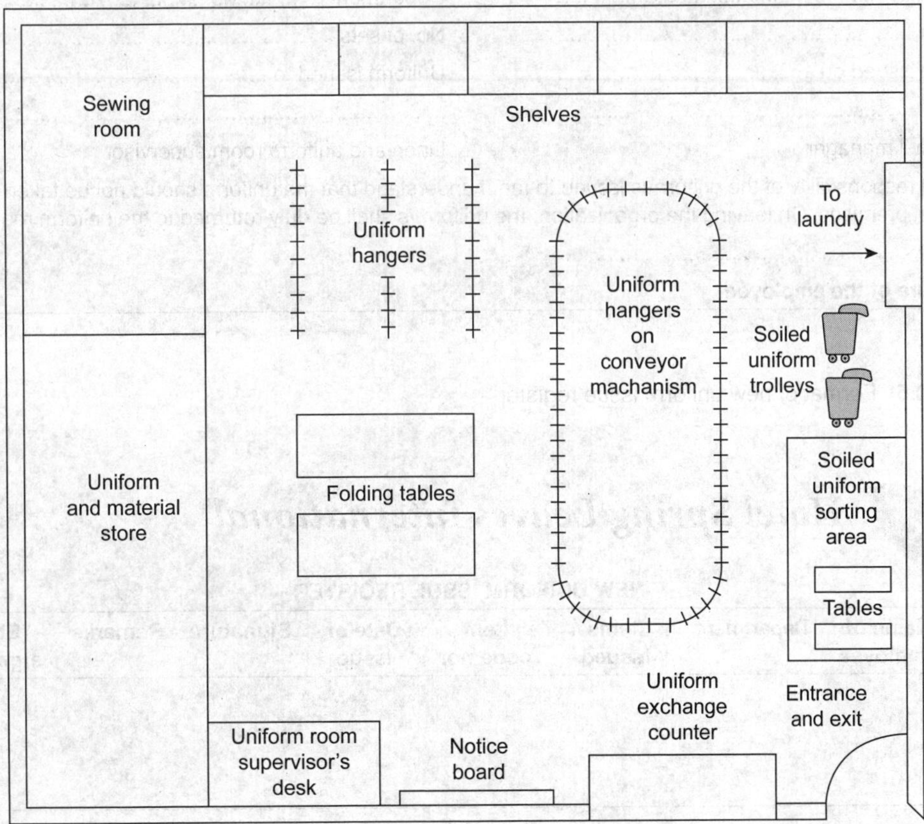

Fig. 20.1 Sample layout of a uniform room layout in a large hotel

 Issuing and Exchanging of Uniforms

In this section, we shall discuss the process of issuing and exchanging of uniforms for employees.

Issuing Uniforms to New Employees

In case of new employees, uniforms are issued against a specific authorization letter received from the personnel department. The employee is required to sign for his or her particular uniform. A uniform issue slip (see Exhibit 20.4) is also provided to the employee by the personnel department to let him/her prove that he/she is a new employee and is part of the organization. The uniform is then issued from the linen room, where the name of the department and the items issued along with the item code are entered in the register and the signature of the employee is taken. The format of new uniform issue register is given in Exhibit 20.5.

Exhibit 20.4 Sample uniform issue slip

Uniform issue slip

Name of employee	Date ....
Token Number	Date of joining ....
Designation	Department ....
Uniform	No. of sets ....
Uniform issued on	Uniform issued to ....
....	....
Personnel manager	Linen and uniform room supervisor

I accept responsibility of the uniform/s issued to me. I understand that the uniform should not be taken out of the hotel premises. On leaving the organization, the uniform/s shall be duly returned to the uniform room.

....

Signature of the employee

Exhibit 20.5 Format of new uniform issue register

Hotel Spring Leaves International

NEW UNIFORM ISSUE REGISTER

S. no.	Name of employee	Department	Items issued	Item code no.	Date of issue	Signature	Remarks	EHKs signature

Issuing Uniforms to Regular Employees

Uniforms are usually given to employees on a one-for-one basis, that is, one fresh uniform for a soiled one.

On leaving the organization, an employee has to get a signature for 'uniform clearance' from the linen room supervisor, failing which the last pay cheque is withheld.

Uniform Exchange Procedure

A uniform register (see Exhibit 20.6) in which the movement of uniforms is recorded is maintained by the linen and uniform room supervisor. The procedure is as follows:

- For regular employees, ensure that they have arrived for uniform exchange at the stipulated time.
- Check the uniform being returned for any damage.
- Issue a fresh uniform strictly on a one-for-one basis, ensuring that it is of the correct size and name (if the uniform is specially tailored for a person).
- Make the uniform exchange slip (see Exhibit 20.7) in duplicate only when the employee deposits a soiled uniform and takes the clean one on the following day. In order to put forth his/her claim, the employee has to produce the uniform slip, authorizing his/her entitlement to the uniforms. The original uniform slip is given to the employee and the duplicate retained in the uniform exchange slip book.
- If the soiled uniform is found to be damaged such that it can be mended, warn the employee. If the uniform cannot be mended, report the matter to the supervisor.
- Soiled uniforms are sent to the laundry for washing and pressing and fresh ones received from the laundry. The laundry uniform exchange form is filled for this exchange and the format is presented in Exhibit 20.8.

Exhibit 20.6 Sample page from uniform register

Uniform register

Date	Laundry no.	Time received at counter	Time cleared from counter	Remarks if any

Linen and uniform room supervisor: ....

Exhibit 20.7 Sample uniform exchange slip

Uniform exchange slip

Sl no: .... **Date:** .... **Token no:** ....

• **Coats**	• **Shirts** ....
• **Saris**	• **Caps** ....
• **Pants**	• **Blouses** ....

Linen and uniform room supervisor: .... **Employee:** ....

Exhibit 20.8 Format of uniform account register

Hotel Spring Leaves International

UNIFORM ACCOUNT REGISTER

Date: ....

Uniform item	Balance brought forward	Soiled uniforms received	Total	Fresh issued	Balance	Remarks

Signature of linen room supervisor: .... Signature of laundry supervisor: ....

Trends in Hotel Uniforms

Ideal uniform designs comprise the attributes of functionality, comfort, appearance, and character. Hotel properties now give immense significance to designing of uniforms and take on board fashion designers who consequently have discussions with the hotel's staff and develop trendy, comfortable uniforms. Some of the emerging trends in hotel uniforms are as follows.

Customized uniforms Where in earlier times, most hotels went on with the usual uniform fare in hotels, the trend now is for a designer to customize uniforms post discussion with the hotel's staff.

Vibrant colours A new trend for vibrant colours has replaced the generic designs that once dominated the hospitality sector. These colours appear as splashes of vibrant hues in scarves, embroideries, accent, or trim rather than the base colours of uniforms. Luxury resorts are embracing brighter, livelier colours in uniforms as representative of their environment. Bright shades of blue, citrus, and clear greens are finding their way in splashes on staff uniforms in such properties. The formal suits too are moving away from the traditional black to dynamic shades of charcoal grey.

Monochromatic look Designers suggest that the uniform that are monochromatic top and bottom, build in simplicity and more sophistication. The look is more flattering than a two colour outfit which cuts people into two. Hence, more and more properties now have front desk staff especially, sporting an all-black, all-grey, or all-brown uniform with a splash of colour in accessories.

Contemporary lines A sleek design as seen in fitted shirts and nipped at the waist apparels for ladies is the trend now.

Blending in the casual look Uniforms are increasingly taking on more of a casual look than formal. Hotels are doing away with the conservatively dressed look, blending in a more casual look in the formal uniforms. As hotels move in to engage the guests in all core areas, bringing in a semi-casual flavour gives employees a fresh, approachable, and relaxed look. An example for the same is a streamlined 3/4th sleeve blouse for lady guest service associates. The staff of many properties also sport the casual look on weekends.

Local flair With increasing competition, hotel properties are distinguishing themselves by building a story into their property with their uniform programme reflecting their local culture and geography. Many properties draw in from their rich cultural and historically significant dressing styles and blend in a part of this heritage with their uniforms.

Comfort gets priority Hotels are also breaking away from the stiff tradition of neck and bow ties, going in for open collars, polo necks, Chinese collars, and so on to bring in the element of comfort in an industry that chips in possibly the longest man-hours on work. Flat, soft, comfortable shoes are preferred instead of completely formal, hard box shoes for employees who are on their feet all day.

Flexibility More pants and skirts options are now available for female employees to choose from. Female front desk employees are starting to don day dresses or skirts with jackets instead of traditional suiting. At many resorts, female hostesses and cocktail servers are embracing retail-inspired garments such as maxi dresses, dresses with higher hemlines and slimmer silhouettes made in body-conscious fabrics, and garments of knitwear fabrics.

SUMMARY

Uniforms are outfits of a specified material, colour, and design, usually provided by the establishment, for certain staff such that all employees in an equivalent or similar position wear identical outfits. In most hotels, the housekeeping department is the custodian of uniforms for all hotel employees.

At most properties, uniforms are exchanged at the uniform exchange counter on a one-for-one basis. In others, uniforms are purchased and handed over to the staff, who maintain their individual sets.

A reasonable uniform programme should allow the issue of two uniforms to each employee upon employment and a third set on confirmation.

A wide variety of uniforms may be found in hotels across India. Many hotels now prefer their employees to retain the feel of the region in which the hotel is situated, and to showcase the culture and tradition of the place.

Staff uniforms are maintained by and issued from the linen and uniform room. The layout of the uniform room has not been separately presented in this chapter since in almost all housekeeping departments, the uniform room is a part of the linen room.

KEY TERMS

Drill Hardwearing, smooth cotton fabric, twill- or satin-woven, which is used for shirts, trousers, and uniforms.

Dungarees Coveralls or overalls made of hardwearing denim or calico material, worn by the maintenance crew in hotels. They typically have multiple pockets to keep the tools handy.

Gaberdine A strong fabric in a tight twill weave, it is made from worsted, cotton, man-made fibre, or blends. The fabric is used for suits, dresses, sportswear, and uniforms.

Par level The standard number of each inventoried item that must be on hand to support daily, routine housekeeping operations.

RFID Radio Frequency Identification.

Toque A toque is the traditional headgear for chefs. It is a type of hat with a narrow brim or no brim at all. They were made popular by the 13th century French chefs.

21 Sewing Room

Learning Objectives

After reading this chapter, you should be able to

- understand the activities carried out in the sewing room
- chalk out the job descriptions and job specifications of the seamstress or tailor
- discuss the equipment used in the sewing room
- sew the basic stitches by hand

Introduction

Space should be allotted in the linen or uniform area for a sewing room where linen, uniforms, and guest clothing can be repaired and attended to. The first essential for successful sewing is a good work area. Ideally it should be a small room set apart for the purpose or, in smaller hotels, a well-lit corner kept solely for sewing.

Activities in the Sewing Room

The following activities are carried out in the sewing room:

- Altering of uniforms
- Patching of table linen
- Repairing expensive linens such as curtains, bedcovers, and slipcovers that require a minimum of repair
- Making of pads for the polishing of silver from used mattress pads
- Converting condemned linen into reusable forms
- Making of pillowcases, sheets, and bed spreads
- Monogramming of uniforms and some linen articles
- Repairing hems of sheets
- Mending of guest clothing
- Repairing mats and rugs
- Stitching of upholstery
- Making recommendations for the quantity of material required for upholstery, curtains, and so on

 Job Specification of a Seamstress/Tailor

Seamstresses and tailors are responsible for the activities carried out in the sewing room. Table 21.1 outlines the job specifications of a seamstress or tailor.

Table 21.1 Job specification of a seamstress/tailor

Job title	Seamstress to tailor
Job summary	To perform skilled tasks in the making and repairing of such articles as draperies, curtains, slipcovers, lampshades, and towels.
Purpose of job	• To mend torn articles using methods such as patching and darning. • To receive and issue linen to GRAs if required. • To maintain cost and production records of stitched materials.
Equipment knowledge	Must be proficient in the use of the following: sewing machine, electric iron, button-holing machine, sewing needles and thimble, scissors, and measuring tape.
Relation to other jobs	Promotion possible to posts of: Head seamstress, linen room attendant, and linen room supervisor.
Job breakdown	The duties of this job may be divided between a seamstress of draperies and curtains and a seamstress of fine linen (such as napkins and tablecloths).
Job combination	The duties of this job may be included with those of linen room maid or linen room supervisor.
Working conditions	Hazards: Possible injury to hands from sewing-machine needles.
Safety precautions	Not only are there eye guards and finger guards on the machines, but also proper grounding of electrical connections is ensured.

 Sewing Area and Equipment

The basic sewing room equipment includes a work table, an ironing board, and sewing machines. Heat-patching machines for neat repair of holes in linen are also useful. An overedging machine is used for remaking discards such as towels into waste cloths. It cuts, seams, and overcasts in one operation.

Good lighting in the sewing room is essential. Storage space should be provided for fabrics, patterns, and smaller equipment. A pegboard screen is useful for hanging tools, clothes, and storage bags. The work surface should be large enough—at least 2 × 1 sq. metre—for cutting and pinning, and also firm enough to bear the load of the sewing machine. Small items such as thread, zippers, and trimmings should be stored in a basket, workbox, or shallow drawer. Repairs should be made with 100% polyester threads, which give strength and do not shrink.

Good quality tools make sewing easier and less time-consuming and the results more professional. All the machines should be dusted and oiled regularly by the operators. A regular servicing schedule should also be made with the company providing the machines.

Cutting tools

Fabric shears or scissors should be used only for cutting fabrics, as using them on paper will blunt them. An appropriate size is 10–12 inches. Use small scissors with sharp, pointed ends for buttonholes, embroidery, and cutting the ends of cotton thread. A seam ripper, which has a tiny protected blade, cuts stitching without harming the fabric. Pinking shears give a zigzag, fray-resistant finish to raw edges.

Measuring tools

Choose a fibreglass tape measure—this material does not stretch. It should be marked with metric as well as imperial measurements. A metre stick or metre rule is essential for working on soft furnishings. It is also useful for marking long lines on patterns or checking hem levels. A set square is needed when cutting curtains or upholstery to ensure true right angles at the corners. Perspex rulers and set squares allow one to see the grain of the fabric.

Pins and pincushions

Use fine, sharp pins, preferably 18 mm long. Shorter pins can be used for lightweight fabrics and paper. Glass-headed pins can be used for sheer or lacy fabrics. Longer, 30-mm pins are needed when cutting out loose covers. A pincushion held on the wrist on a band of elastic keeps pins and needles handy while working. It can also be hung on the sewing machine.

Needles and thimble

Needles are graded by number, ranging from No. 1 (longest and thickest) to No. 24 (smallest and finest). Table 21.2 outlines the appropriate needle sizes for different fabrics. Keep a darning needle and darning mushroom in the work basket. Keep needles threaded in a dry place, such as a felt-paged needle book, to protect them.

Thimbles are protective covers worn on the thumb and second finger when sewing. Steel thimbles are the best. They should fit the fingers snugly.

Clips and weights

When cutting a long piece of fabric, fix it to the edge of the table with clips. Weights are also useful for preventing the material from slipping or twisting off-grain.

Table 21.2 Needle sizes for different fabrics

Fabrics	Fibre	Needle sizes	
		Hand	Machine
Fine: Georgette, voile, chiffon, organdie, net, lace	Synthetic or mixtures	9	9–11
	Cotton or linen	9	9–11
	Wool or silk	9	9–11
Lightweight: Poplin, gingham	Synthetic or mixtures	8–9	11–14
	Cotton or linen	8–9	11–14
	Wool or silk	8–9	11–14
Medium-weight: Gaberdine, brocade, tweed, waterproofed	Synthetic or mixtures	8–9	11–14
	Cotton or linen	7–8	11–14
	Wool or silk	7–8	11–14
		7–8	11–14
Heavyweight: Canvas, heavy furnishing fabrics	Synthetic or mixtures	6	16–18
	Cotton	7–8	14–16
	Linen	6–7	14–16
	Wool or silk	7–8	14–16
Velvet	Synthetic or mixtures	8–9	11–14
	Cotton	7–8	11–14
	Silk	7–8	11–14
Leather and PVC		3–8	14–18

Pattern paper

Special pattern paper is available, marked with squares to make pattern drawing easy. But large sheets of lining paper or brown paper can also be used for soft-furnishing patterns. Tissue-paper patterns that are being used a lot should be transferred to heavier paper.

Marking equipment

Tailor's chalk is used for marking alterations. Test fabrics first to make sure that the chalk will not permanently mark them. Coloured carbon paper can be used with a tracing wheel to transfer pattern markings on to the fabric. For delicate fabrics, use a smooth-edged wheel. For everything else, use a spiked wheel.

Sewing machine

The machines should be able to handle various thicknesses of fabric and blind-stitch so that the stitching does not show on the other side. Computerized machines are more expensive but they are easy to operate, very accurate, and do double duty. Zig-zagging machines or attachments can be used for mending, darning, and sewing of buttons.

Basic Hand Stitches

A few basic stitches for manual sewing are discussed in this section. Hand-stitching can be either temporary or permanent.

Temporary Stitches

Stitches such as tacking or basting are used for holding two or more layers of material together before the permanent stitches are made. Usually these stitches are done in a contrasting colour of thread so that they are easy to remove later. Start and end with a knot, or start with a cross-stitch or a straight stitch at right angles to the basting stitches, leaving about one inch of thread from the end of the length. There are several types of basting stitches. Some of them are outlined in this section:

Even basting Here the stitches and spacing between them are equal to each other in length. So make the stitches about 0.5 cm in length and space them 0.5 cm apart. This is used when firm basting is needed. The length of these stitches can vary from 0.5 to 1 cm, depending upon the firmness required. A sample is shown in Figure 21.1.

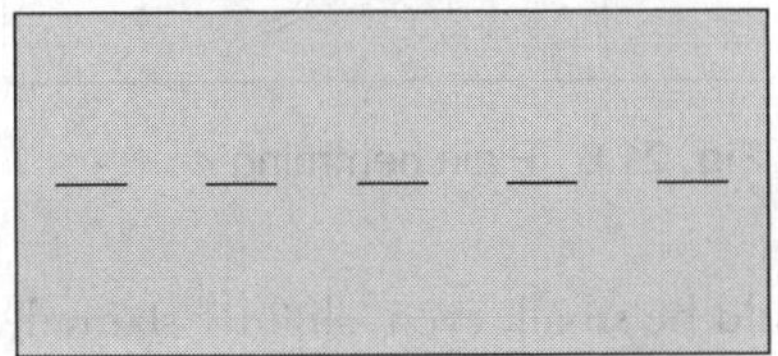

Fig. 21.1 Even basting

Uneven basting Here, the length of the stitches on the upper side is at least twice that on the underside. The size of the stitch on the upper side is usually 1.5 cm. It is used as a guideline or for the seams that do not receive much strain. A sample is shown in Figure 21.2.

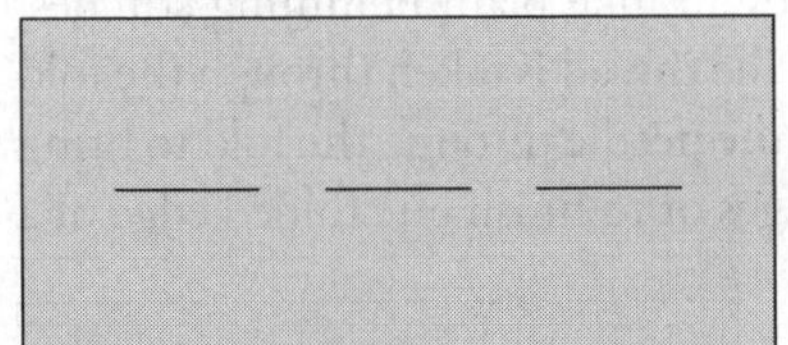

Fig. 21.2 Uneven basting

Extra-firm basting Take a long stitch of about 1.5 cm and then take two or three short stitches for the same length. Continue in the same manner, repeating this pattern. A sample is shown in Figure 21.3. Extra-firm basting is used for seams which receive strain.

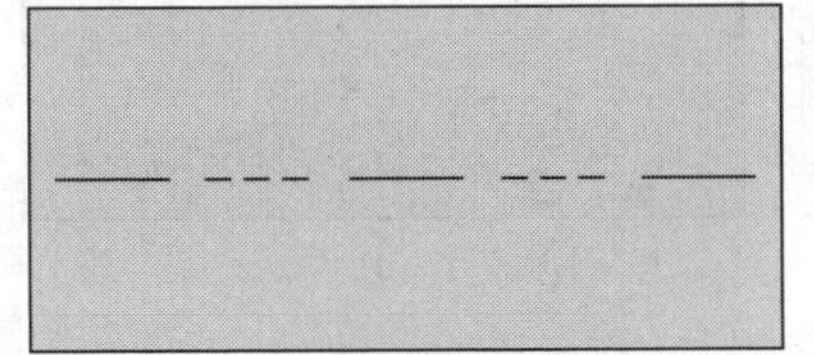

Fig. 21.3 Extra-firm basting

Permanent Stitches

For all permanent stitches, a single strand of thread matching the predominant colour of the fabric is used. Always start and end with a backstitch for permanent stitches. Some important permanent stitches are discussed in this section:

Joining stitches

These are used to sew two pieces of fabric together and make a seam, or to sew together adjacent areas of the same piece of fabric to make pleats, permanent folds, or flounces.

Running stitch This is the simplest form of hand stitching that is used for permanent sewing. Handmade seams, tucks, gathering, shirring, and mending can be done with this stitch. It is similar to even basting, but the stitches are much smaller. The stitches should be straight, fine, evenly spaced, and about 0.1–0.3 cm in length. This is shown in Figure 21.4.

Fig. 21.4 Running stitch

Backstitch The backstitch is strong and is sometimes substituted for machine stitching. Stitches should be about 0.1–0.3 cm long on the upper side of the material. To make the backstitch, push the needle up through the material at a point on the stitching line about 0.1–0.3 cm from its right end. Take a stitch, inserting the needle 0.1–0.3 cm behind the thread emerging at the beginning of the stitching line and bringing it up an equal distance in front of the point of emergence of the thread. Repeat in this way, keeping stitches uniform in size and fairly firm. There are no spaces between backstitches. A sample of the backstitch is shown in Figure 21.5.

Fig. 21.5 Back stitch

Edge-finishing stitches

These are used at the raw edges of unhemmed fabric, sometimes along the inside of seams as well, to prevent fraying. Some are decorative in function as well. At least one (buttonhole stitch) has a dual function.

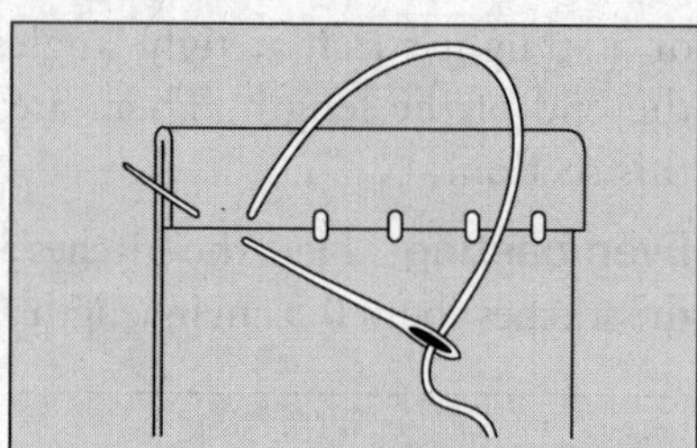

Fig. 21.6 Plain hemming

Plain hemming This is used to secure down a folded edge of the material. Fasten the thread under the fold of the hem. Take a tiny stitch, catching a thread or two of the fabric under the fold and bringing the needle through the edge of the fold. Stitches should be small, even, slightly slanted, and always worked on the wrong side of the fabric from right-hand side to left-hand side. A sample of plain hemming is shown in Figure 21.6.

Blind hemming/invisible hemming/slip stitch These stitches are like plain hemming stitches, except that they are farther apart, the needle is placed on a slant, and the thread is taken through the fold to make it invisible. Take up only one thread of the material and pass the needle through the fold to bring it out at the next point. This stitch can be used to join two folded edges or to finish one folded edge of a single layer of material. A sample of blind hemming is shown in Figure 21.7. Figure 21.7(a) shows how the blind hemming stitch looks on the wrong side of the cloth, and Figure 21.7(b) shows the stitch on the right side.

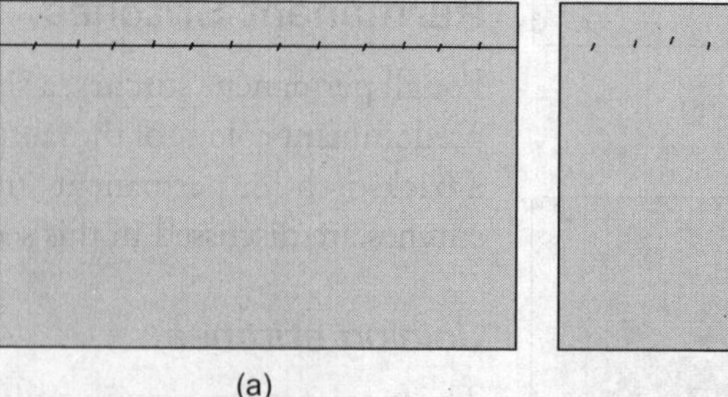

Fig. 21.7 Blind hemming on the (a) wrong side of the cloth; (b) right side of the cloth

Overcasting This is the customary stitch for finishing the raw edges of the fabric to prevent them from unravelling.

Take diagonal stitches over the raw edge (without folding or rolling), spacing them an even distance apart at a uniform depth. A sample of the overcasting stitch is presented in Figure 21.8.

Whipping This is mainly used for joining two edges and for finishing the edge of fine materials. To finish the raw edge of a single material, roll the edge between the thumb and forefinger and hold the roll tightly. To join two edges, hold the edges together. Then take the stitches over the edge with a needle in a slanted position and back again, crossing the first slanting stitch. A sample of whipping is shown in Figure 21.9.

Buttonhole stitch The buttonhole stitch is also known as blanket stitch as it is often used as an edging on blankets.

This stitch is worked from left to right over two imaginary lines. Bring the thread out on the lower line (at point A in Figure 21.10), insert the needle in position in the upper line (at point B in Figure 21.10), making a straight downward motion and then loop the thread under the needle point. Pull the needle through the fabric (at point C in Figure 21.10) to form a loop and repeat this process along the line.

Overcasting, whipping, and buttonhole stitches are used to give a decorative finish to the raw edges of the material. They can also be done with contrasting colour thread.

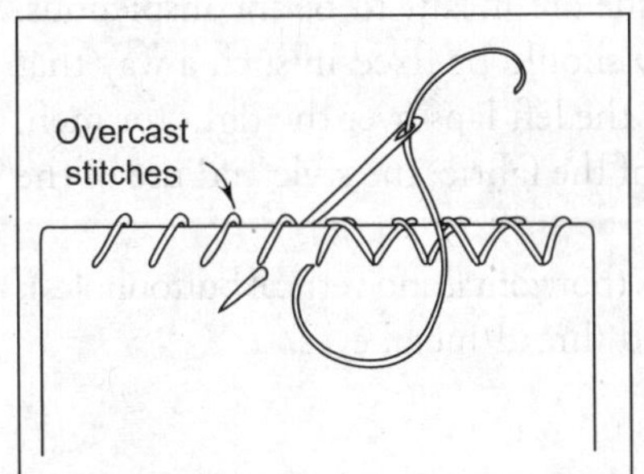

Fig. 21.8 Overcast stitches

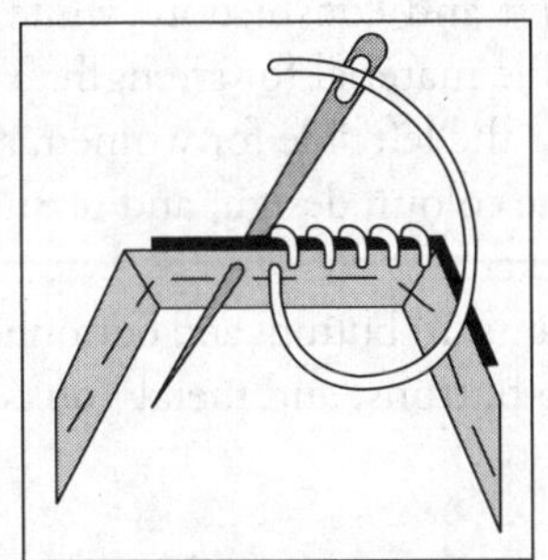

Fig. 21.9 Whipping

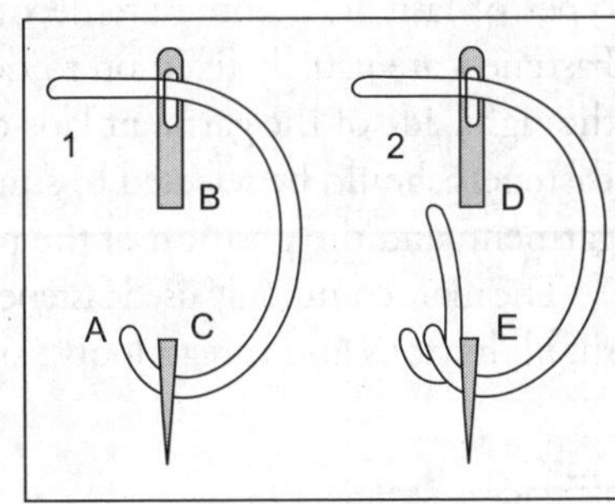

Fig. 21.10 Buttonhole stitch

Mending and Darning

Mending refers to repairing fabrics and clothes which are in need of repair. Such repairs may include taking care of tears, holes, ripped seams, ravelled hems, snapped buttons, stubborn stains or other faults. In hotels, the tailors in the sewing room carry out mending of linen, discards, upholstery, soft furnishings and guest clothes. Mending stiches may be done by hand or machine. Patch work is also an effective way of mending holes or covering stained areas. Discards with tears, holes and stains are repaired and reused in BoH areas or cut down.

Darning is mending of holes in a fabric by filling the hole with interlacing stitches. It should follow, as closely as possible, the way the original fabric was made. Darning too may be done by hand or machine. Invisible darning is done with a matching thread and involves recreating the fabric structure again, i.e., interlacing the warp and weft threads using small running stitches as shown in Figure 21.11. Visible darning has a decorative purpose and hence is done with contrasting, thicker, embroidery threads.

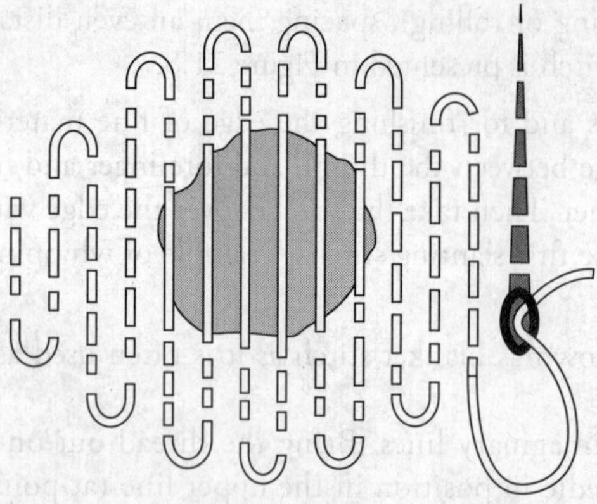
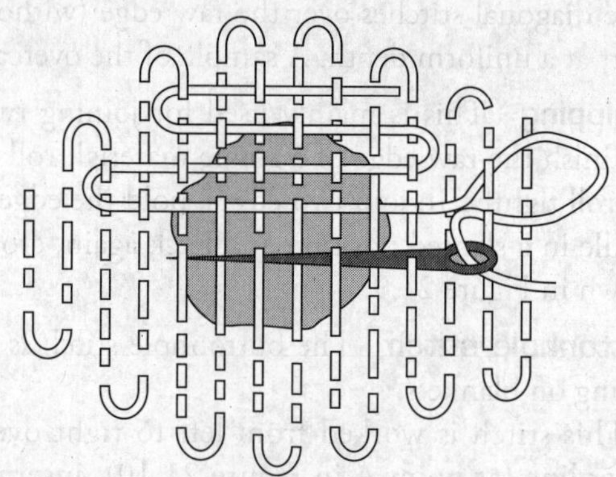

Fig. 21.11 Darning stitches

Fasteners

Fasteners are used on garments and other linen articles mainly to keep plackets closed. There are various types of fasteners. Some are decorative and conspicuous while some are meant to be inconspicuous. Fasteners are usually fixed on to double material for strength. They should be fixed in such a way that the right side of the garment laps over the left side for women, and the left laps over the right for men. Fasteners should be selected to suit the colour, design, and texture of the fabric; the style and use of the garment; and the position of the placket.

The more commonly used fasteners are shirt buttons and buttonholes (horizontal and vertical buttonholes); shank buttons and thread loops; snap buttons; and metal hooks and thread/metal eyes.

SUMMARY

A sewing room is essential in larger hotels, where the turnover of linen is high due to damage. Linens are expensive and should not be discarded because of small tears and holes. They can be recycled as cutdowns, an activity carried out in the sewing room. The sewing room is the domain of the seamstress or the tailor, who is responsible for all the activities carried out there. They suggest the quantity of fabrics needed for soft furnishings, upholstery, and so on, as well as stitching them. In many hotels, they may also be responsible for not only mending but also stitching staff uniforms.

This chapter outlines the activities in a sewing room and the equipment commonly found there. The job specifications of a seamstress or tailor are also given. The basic manual stitches are also shown, along with descriptions of how to work them.

In small hotels, small repairs and mending of linen and uniforms can be carried out in a small well-lit section in the linen room that is set up as a sewing area.

KEY TERMS

BoH Back of the house areas.

Cutdowns 'Cutdowns' refer to the using of any discarded materials for some other purpose, such as bed sheets being used as dust sheets or made into pillow covers.

Darning Mending the holes in a fabric by filling with interlacing stitches.

Monogramming A motif made by creatively overlapping or combining two or more letters or graphics to form a symbol and used by the hotel company as logo. Commonly found machine-embroidered on hotel uniforms and some linen articles.

Seams A seam is a method of joining two or more pieces of materials together by a row of stitching.

Shirring When several parallel rows of gathering (two or more) are used for a decorative finish, these are termed 'shirring'.

Thimbles Protective covers worn on the thumb and second finger when sewing.

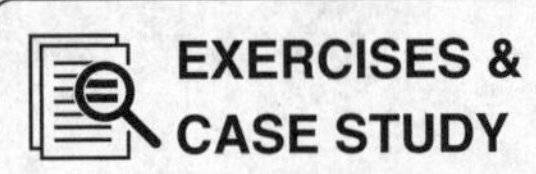

22 Safety and Security

Learning Objectives

After reading this chapter, you should be able to

- understand and differentiate between the terms 'safety' and 'security'
- gauge the importance of work-environment safety and do a job safety analysis
- list the possible hazards for housekeeping employees
- prioritize safety awareness and accident prevention in training
- understand the concept of safeguarding assets
- appreciate the importance of fire prevention and fire-fighting
- practise the basics of first-aid
- deal with emergency situations
- describe the procedures for the control of keys
- plan to prevent guest and employee thefts
- know how to deal with the sickness or death of a guest on the property
- understand how housekeeping staff can protect the premises from terrorist attacks

Introduction

Safety and security are concepts often used interchangeably, and it should be understood that both are means of safeguarding human and physical assets. The term 'safety' is used with reference to such things as disasters, emergencies, fire prevention and protection, and conditions that provide for freedom from injury and prevent damage to property. The term 'security' is used with reference to freedom from fear, anxiety, and doubts concerning humans as well as protection against terrorism and thefts of guest, employee, or hotel property.

Work-Environment Safety and Job Safety Analysis

The management of any place of work are legally bound to provide a hazard-free environment to their employees. The nature of work that the housekeeping staff are involved in, is such that employees may easily become accident-prone if they are careless with equipment, chemicals, or procedures.

Safety Management Programmes

The overall objective of a safety management programme is to eliminate hazards before they cause any serious accidents.

There are 10 steps in the establishment of an effective safety management programme:

1. Review work procedures and inspect work areas for safety hazards.
2. Make departmental heads aware of the nature and variety of hazards.
3. Establish a safety committee.
4. Maintain accurate safety records.
5. Conduct periodic in-house safety inspections.
6. Train staff members to implement safety consciousness.
7. Motivate staff members to be safety conscious.
8. Investigate and analyse all accidents and injuries.
9. Practise safety management and monitor follow-ups.
10. Review the effectiveness of your own safety management programme.

Three Es of Safety

The safety of employees can be ensured by following the three Es of safety: safety education, safety engineering, and safety rules enforcement.

Safety education Safety programmes and policies can only be effective if the staff are trained to think and act safely at work. The best time to start educating employees on safety is during their induction into the establishment, so that they are well versed in safety rules and policies of the establishment before they start their job. Employees should be encouraged to come up with ideas for inculcating safety into the hotel's methods too, and the best ideas should be put into practice and praised or rewarded. The following should be ensured during training:

- Teaching safe methods, with particular emphasis on areas of potential danger and how these can be guarded against.
- Demonstrating the use of safety equipment installed in the establishment, and the location and use of first-aid materials.
- Inculcating in people the ability to recognize the signs of hazards around them.
- Teaching staff the legal implications of non-adherence to safety procedures.

Safety engineering This involves the building in of safety features into the structure of the establishment—in the equipment, furniture, and fittings and in their proper arrangement within the space. Equipment used by the housekeeping employees should be selected to ensure safety in design.

Safety rules enforcement Rules, when not implemented or enforced, are not effective. It is not enough to know about safety themes and procedures, but more important to motivate people to put the knowledge gained into practice. This does not come easily to all employees and, therefore, needs to be enforced by rule and practice.

Occupational Safety and Hazards Standards

Standard universal laws on occupational safety and health (OSH) do not exist because of differences in local values and cultures. Therefore, different countries have developed their own standards on occupational health and safety management systems (OHSMS) according to their needs. India has published, and follows the 'IS 18001:2007 Indian Standards on Occupational Health and Safety Management Systems—Requirements with Guidance for Use', and 'IS 15656:2006 Indian Standards on Hazard Identification and Risk Analysis - Code of Practice' which are adapted to Indian needs.

The main emphasis of the system is on classifying work activities, identifying hazards, determining risks, deciding if a given level of risk is tolerable, preparing risk-control action plans, and reviewing the adequacy of action plans.

Job Safety Analysis

The executive housekeeper needs to develop a 'housekeeping safety manual' for the use of all housekeeping employees. This manual should explain in comprehensive terms the safest methods of performing each task to accomplish a particular job. This has to be done for all the jobs carried out by housekeeping staff. For this purpose, the housekeeper, with the help of the supervisors, needs to carry out a job safety analysis. A *job safety analysis* is a detailed report that lists every job function performed in the housekeeping department and lists potential hazards, safe methods, tips, and 'how-tos' for each task.

Hazard Identification and Risk Assessment (HIRA)

HIRA is a systematic qualitative tool for establishments to identify the potential hazards and assess the risks they pose to human and physical assets of the establishment and the environment. Though the HIRA process may be performed at any stage of a project's life cycle, the earlier it is done, the more manageable are the risks. Unsafe and dangerous conditions are referred to as hazards. Risks are the potentially unfavourable consequences that may result due to the presence of a hazard. The format presented in Exhibit 22.1 may be used in HIRA implementation.

The steps of HIRA

a) Hazard identification
b) Risk assessment
c) Risk elimination or reduction
d) Monitoring of compliance
e) Periodic review

Exhibit 22.1 Qualitative HIRA form

Hotel Spring Leaves International

QUALITATIVE HIRA FORM

S. no.	Identified hazard	Causes	Risks/ Consequences	Safeguards against hazards	Recommendations of HIRA experts

Potential Hazards in Housekeeping Operations

Due to the nature of the work performed by housekeeping staff, they may be exposed to many dangerous and unsafe conditions, or hazards, if they are not careful. To reduce safety risks, all employees should be aware of potential safety hazards. These hazards may include

- faulty equipment;
- damaged flooring or chipped tiles;
- slippery floors and spills not mopped up;
- slippery guest bathrooms;
- cracked or broken glass;
- worn-out electrical insulation or fittings;
- overloaded electrical sockets;
- trailing equipment flexes;
- worn carpets and rugs;
- cleaning equipment left lying around;
- unsafe use of ladders;
- inadequate lighting;
- loose stair treads;
- cleaning agents left uncapped;
- non-adherence to instructions outlined in the material safety data sheets (MSDS) for the use of cleaning chemicals;
- handling corrosive cleaning agents with bare hands;
- mixing certain chemical cleaners, causing undesirable/dangerous reactions;
- cleaning agents kept in unmarked or wrongly marked containers;
- incorrect use of trolleys;
- incorrect methods of bending and lifting;
- unsatisfactory hygiene and sanitation standards; and
- incorrect posture.

Hazardous Materials or HAZMAT

A hazardous material (HAZMAT) is any substance that can cause injury, impairment of health or death to living organisms, or can damage the environment. Various hazardous materials are used in the hotel industry.

Classification of hazardous materials (HAZMAT) Hazardous materials are classified as follows:

Toxic A substance that can cause damage to health, physical or mental impairment, or even death when inhaled, ingested, or absorbed. For example, pesticides and insecticides.

Flammable A substance that can be easily ignited by sparks or flames to cause fire. For example, solvents and fuels.

Explosive A substance that is capable, by chemical reaction within itself, of producing gas at such a temperature, pressure, and speed to cause damage to the surroundings.

Corrosive A material that destroys other materials by chemical reaction. When in contact with human tissue, they may burn and destroy the tissue. At greatest risk are skin, eyes, lungs, and stomach. For example, toilet and oven cleaners and acids.

Infectious A substance that contains viable microorganisms or their toxins and is capable of causing disease. For example, medical waste.

Safety Awareness and Accident Prevention

Safety awareness should be an ongoing programme at all establishments. The management of all establishments should be aware of the laws concerning safe work environments and should be concerned about the safety of their employees. Periodic training should be provided to all staff in order to raise awareness about safety. All employees should be aware of the potential hazards in their respective departments. All heads of departments must ensure that employees follow safe job procedures, correct unsafe conditions immediately, and take adequate time to do the job so that accidents are not caused due to haste. The executive housekeeper should develop a comprehensive list of safety rules to be followed by all housekeeping employees. This can be a part of the 'housekeeping safety manual'. Some safety guidelines for lifting, bending, carrying, and pushing that may be included in the manual are outlined in Table 22.1.

Table 22.1 Safety guidelines for lifting, bending, carrying, and pushing

Lifting from the floor	Reaching down to the floor	Kneeling on the floor	Bending down to a low cupboard	Carrying things on the arm or in hand	Carrying things on the hip	Moving furniture
Wrong way						
Bending over double with arms stretched puts pressure on the spine.	Avoid reaching down to the floor with straight legs and bent back—this causes strain.	Do not kneel with your back arched.	Continuously staying bent over with the legs almost straight may cause back trouble.	Leaning to one side with the arm stretched down is a wrong way to carry a heavy bag or other such weight.	Weight carried below the hips strains one leg and the spine.	Do not push with bent back and outstretched arms.
Right way						
Bend arms, knees and hips to take the strain.	Go down on one knee.	Take the strain on the shoulders and hips with your spine hollowed.	Bend at the knees, with your spine upright, to reach a low cupboard.	Support the bag on your hip with the body upright.	Weight rested on the hip is shifted to both legs.	Keep a straight back, arms bent, and take the strain on your legs.

What is an Accident?

An accident is an unfortunate incident that happens unexpectedly and unintentionally, typically resulting in damage or injury.

Causes of workplace accidents The causes of workplace accidents are many, as follows.

Unsafe work environment A hazardous work environment may result from unsafe physical infrastructure and improper working conditions. Structural hazards such as damaged floorings and cracked or broken glass may lead to accidents. Improper working conditions result from poor ventilation, improper layout of machinery, poor lighting, lack of sanitation, lack of space, high amount of noise pollution, and inadequate fire safety.

Defective equipment Such equipment may pose electrical or mechanical hazards. Their use affects the quality of work as well as puts the user in danger because in such a case operating the equipment requires more concentration and control.

Deficient housekeeping Instances of accident hazards due to poor housekeeping are non-usage of safety signs during cleaning, wet floors, over-polished floors, spills left unattended, improper storage and stacking, and non-disposal of used polishing rags.

Unsuitable uniforms When an employee is not suitably dressed for the job assigned, it becomes an accident hazard. For instance, synthetic materials, flowing sleeves, and high heels should be avoided

in kitchens. Protective aids such as gloves, masks, and goggles should be provided and it should be ensured that they are used by the employees.

Inadequate supervision Accidents may take place due to inadequate supervision.

Inadequate instruction An accident may result in case of no instruction given, instruction not enforced, or wrong or incomplete information given by supervisors.

Unsafe work practices Work practices such as taking short cuts or taking chances, and working in haste are hazards in themselves.

Incapability of employee Many a time, a task assigned to an employee not capable of doing it because of lack of experience or skill leads to an accident.

Lack of discipline A supervisor who does not instil and ensure discipline in employees he trains paves way for accidents happening on floors and public areas.

Unfit employees The following reasons make employees incapable to handle their job safely.

Mentally unfit An accident may happen if the employee is working in a fit of rage or is too tired or excited to concentrate on work.

Physically unfit An employee who is physically incapable or weak or under the influence of alcohol is also prone to accidents.

Lack of concentration An employee not concentrating on the job at hand due to physical or emotional disturbances becomes prone to accidents.

Effects of accidents Accidents have both direct and indirect effect on individuals and the establishment. The direct effects of accidents are as follows.

Injury and stress Accidents result in injury which can cause much pain and absenteeism from work. Accidents also create tension and anxiety for the co-workers.

Expenditure Frequent accidents will result in additional expenditure to the management. Workers must be covered by medical insurance through Employees State Insurance Scheme (ESIS) and disability compensation is required for employees injured on the job.

Indirect effect of accidents There are some indirect effects of accidents, as follows.

Damaged material Accidents very often lead to hotel inventory property being damaged.

Reduced efficiency In case an area is accident prone, the employees, in trying to avoid accidents, work slowly with lesser concentration; other staff being engaged in attending to the injured, cleaning up the mess, doctor's visits and investigations, all of which bring down the efficiency in hotel operations.

Injured employee stayingaway from work Injured employee/s stay/s away from work making the hotel understaffed. The employee needs to be replaced, resulting in time and effort to be spent in training of new employees.

Work schedule hampered Work is completed by co-workers in a hurry and hygiene aspects tend to get overlooked in an attempt to just complete the job.

Accidents lower morale Frequent accidents lower the morale of employees as it indicates that the management is not concerned about customer and employee welfare.

Accidents spoil reputation Serious accidents on hotel properties make for negative publicity of the hotel.

Accidents resulting in fines or imprisonment Under the provisions of Labour Code on Occupational Safety, Health and Working Conditions, 2018 Act, the management of the hotel may face legal action.

Basic Guidelines for the Prevention of Accidents

The following guidelines can be followed for the prevention of accidents:

- Always follow instructions when using any cleaning equipment.
- Replace caps on cleaning chemicals immediately and securely after dispensing.
- Label cleaning agents clearly.
- Keep floors clean and dry.
- Place warning and safety signs around the area while cleaning.
- Always dry hands before touching plugs, sockets, and electrical fittings.
- Mark faulty equipment as 'out of order'.
- Dispose of rubbish carefully.
- Never place cigarette butts or sharp objects in the trash bag on the room attendants' carts.
- Open and shut doors carefully.
- Clean away broken glass carefully.

Procedures to Follow in Case of an Accident

When a guest or employee has met with an accident at the hotel, the procedure followed should be as follows:

1. With the help of another person, check if the victim requires any assistance.
2. Report the matter immediately to the manager concerned.
3. Either administer first-aid (if you are trained to do so) or get help from trained personnel.
4. Shift the victim immediately to a hospital, if required. If the injury is serious, call an ambulance for the same. Follow all necessary first-aid measures until the ambulance arrives.
5. Fill in the accident report form (see Exhibit 22.2) and hand it over to the manager concerned.

Exhibit 22.2 Format of an accident report form for employees

Accident report form (for employees)

Name of the injured person ....
Section ....
Supervisor ....
Date .... Time of report ....
Extent of injury ....
....
Was hospitalization required? ....
Nature of the accident
Time .... Place ....
What happened/cause ....
....
Witness 1 ....
Witness 2 ....
Supervisor's remarks..
....
Supervisor's signature..........................

Role of Housekeeping in Safety

Safety and prevention of accidents is a responsibility to be shared by the executive housekeepers and the employees under them. The executive housekeeper should ensure the following for an accident-free environment.

Periodic training Employees should undergo periodic training and follow instructions when using any cleaning equipment or agent. SOPs should be developed with inbuilt safety precautions.

Effective supervision Supervisors should be aware of the extent of capabilities of the employees under them, make employees aware of hazards, and take responsibility of their employees' safety.

Provide safe equipment It is the responsibility of the housekeeper to provide proper resources for work to be carried out efficiently and safely in the department. Preventive maintenance should be carried out for equipment.

Provide safety gear Hands, feet, and eyes should be protected during work involving hazards such as chemicals. Protective gear includes gloves, goggles, earplugs, boots, aprons, etc. Personal Protective Equipment, PPE have been discussed at length in Chapter 7.

Compliance to MSDS Material safety data sheet (MSDS) is a form containing data regarding physical and chemical properties of a particular substance. It is used as a system for cataloguing information on chemicals. MSDS provides housekeepers with procedures for handling the substance in a safe manner and warns them of its potential hazards. MSDS includes information such as the physical properties—melting point, boiling point, flash point, toxicity, health effects, first-aid instructions, storage disposal, protective equipment to use, and handling procedures. Housekeepers should ensure that the employees working with chemicals are aware of MSDS.

Employee vigilance Managers should keep track of discipline and work habits of employees. The employees should ensure the following to make for an accident-free work environment.

Prevent carelessness 78% of all accidents are caused by employees not noticing an obvious indication of accident hazard due to carelessness.

Take adequate time Jobs should never be done in haste as it becomes unsafe.

Report hazard Housekeeping employees should be responsible and report any hazard. There should be a simple and clear hazard reporting system.

Correct unsafe conditions immediately If it is possible, the employee himself/herself can correct the hazardous condition, else it should be reported to the supervisor. Mark faulty equipment as 'out of order'.

Do the job in the right way Every employee should be responsible and do his/her job in a safe manner according to the SOP, without taking any short cut. For instance, caps should be replaced on cleaning chemicals immediately and securely after dispensing. Warning and safety signs should be placed around the area before staring cleaning. Hands need to be dried before touching plugs, sockets, and electrical fittings.

Use signs and tags Safety signs and tags should be used where possible hazards are present. All devices, structures, and areas where hazards exist should be identified with appropriate signs and warnings. Signs and tags are not intended to be a substitute for safety measures. They are additional safety guidance and increase the employees' and guests' awareness of potential dangers. Tags are temporary means of warning all concerned of the hazardous condition, defective equipment, etc. Three different types of signs and tags are used:

- Danger signs, for immediate hazards
- Caution signs, for potential hazards
- Safety signs, for general instructions

 Concept of Safeguarding Assets

An asset is that which brings in profit or increases the value of the business. Assets can be classified as follows:

- Human assets that include the customers or guests and the hotel employees
- Physical assets that include land, building, infrastructure, facility, equipment, inventory items, and cash.
- Intangible/Intrinsic assets that include the goodwill and the hotel's reputation.

Importance of Safeguarding Assets

The revenue of the hotel is generated from the various services that are rendered by the employees and experienced by the guests. Therefore, personal safety has to be ensured. In all businesses, physical assets need to be safeguarded as they come at high costs. The reputation and goodwill of a hotel is earned over a period of many years and it needs to be maintained and safeguarded.

Therefore, safeguarding of assets is a fundamental requirement for all businesses. The hotel has to ensure that the guests, employees, and the hotel itself are safe. The management should act towards the following:

- Fire prevention and control
- Accident prevention for employees and guests
- Security to guard the assets of a hotel
- Protecting the health of the guests and the employees
- Emergency procedures during disasters

 Fire Prevention and Fire-Fighting

To understand fire prevention and fire-fighting, one must know how fires are classified. A per Indian Standards IS 15683:2018, fires are classified into five groups, based on their source of fuel.

Class A These are fires with trash, wood, paper or other ordinary combustible materials as their fuel source.

Class B These are fires with flammable or combustible liquids such as petrol, diesel, grease, paint and tar, as their fuel source.

Class C These are fires involving flammable gases such as hydrogen and acetylene.

Class D These are fires with certain ignitable metals such as sodium, potassium and magnesium, as the fuel source.

Class F These are kitchen fires caused due to cooking media such as vegetable oils and fats.

Prevention of Fire

Fires may be prevented if fire hazards are identified and eliminated. Some unsafe practices that may lead to fires are as follows:

- Guests smoking in bed
- The hotel not providing sand urns or sufficient and appropriate ashtrays in rooms as well as public areas
- Using high-wattage bulbs in lamps
- Leaving linen chute doors open
- Storing rags and cloths with residues of cleaning polish still on them
- Not unplugging electrical appliances when not in use
- Using faulty electrical equipment or sockets
- Leaving magnifying glasses where the sun can catch them
- Using furnishing materials that are easily combustible

Each establishment must conduct fire drills on a periodic basis and ensure that all staff attend these drills so that they know what is to be done during a fire emergency.

Fire Warning Systems

These may be electrically powered manually operated systems, automatic fire detection systems, or a combination of both. The usual components of such systems are discussed here:

Fire alarms These can be set off by smoke detectors, heat detectors, sprinkler systems, or pull stations. The most common types of fire alarms are the ones operated by pull stations located in corridors, lobbies, and near elevators. The pull alarms are red in colour, with a glass panel that needs to be broken to set off the alarm.

Sprinklers These are found in most hotel establishments, especially in corridors and rooms. They are situated on the ceiling and automatically spray water when the temperature rises above a certain level.

Smoke detectors These are set off by smoke. The two types of smoke detectors available are photoelectric detectors and ionization detectors. Photoelectric detectors are alarms triggered off when smoke blocks a beam of light emanating from the detector. In the ionization type of smoke detectors, the alarm sounds when the detector senses a shift in electrical conductivity between two plates.

What to Do in Case of Fire Emergency

In case a fire breaks out, follow the guidelines given here:

1. Immediately switch on the nearest fire alarm.
2. If possible, try to put out the fire with suitable equipment, remembering to direct the extinguishers at the base of the flames. Do not attempt to fight a fire if there is any danger of personal risk.
3. Close all the windows and switch off all electrical appliances, including fans and lights.
4. Close the door to the affected area and report to your immediate supervisor for instructions.
5. Carry out instructions—for instance, rouse guests in the section and direct them to the nearest fire-escape route. Each guestroom should have the route to the nearest fire escape drawn out and displayed in a place where it is most likely to be seen by the guests.
6. Report to the departmental fire representative for a roll call. The housekeeper on duty should check the list (in the form of the duty rosters) of the staff who are on duty so that all those on duty can be accounted for.

7. Remain at the assembly point until instructed to do otherwise.
8. Do not use the lifts.

Fire-fighting Equipment

Staff should be trained in operating the fire-fighting equipment. Types of fire-fighting equipment vary from simple ones such as buckets of sand and water, fire blankets, and hose reels to more complex fire extinguishers. Water buckets should be constantly checked for adequate water levels and sand buckets should be kept dry. Water should not be used in case of fires involving electricity.

Types of fire extinguishers

Fire extinguishers can be of various types.

Dry powder These are usually meant for multipurpose use with various types of fire. They contain an extinguishing agent and use a compressed, non-flammable gas as a propellant.

Dry chemical foam These are primarily used on flammable liquids, oils, and fats, but may have multipurpose uses.

Halon/vapourizing liquid These contain a gas or volatile liquid that interrupts the chemical reaction that takes place when fuels burn. This type of extinguisher is often used to protect valuable electrical equipment since they leave no residue to clean up. Halon extinguishers have a limited range, usually 4–6 feet. The initial application of halon should be made towards the base of the fire, continuing even after the flames have been extinguished. The BCF (bromochlorodifluoromethane) extinguishers are now banned as chlorofluorocarbons harm the protective ozone layer.

Water-gas or soda-acid extinguishers These extinguishers contain water and compressed gas and should only be used on Class A (wood or paper) fires.

Carbon dioxide These CO^2-based extinguishers are most effective on Class B and C (liquids and electrical) fires. Since the gas disperses quickly, these extinguishers are only effective from a distance of 3–8 feet. The carbon dioxide is stored as a compressed liquid in the extinguisher; as it expands on release, it cools the surrounding air. The cooling will often cause ice to form around the 'horn' out of which the gas is expelled from the extinguisher. Since the fire could re-ignite, continue to apply the agent even after the fire appears to be out.

Fire-extinguisher ratings

Most fire extinguishers available are rated not only according to the type of fire they extinguish but also the size of the fire they can combat. The alphabets in the rating system indicate the class for fire and the numbers preceding the alphabets represent the size of the fire the extinguisher can douse. The ratings appear as 1A, 2A, 3A, 6A, 8B, 13B, 21B, 34B, 55B, and so on. For instance, 1A rating indicates that the extinguisher is to be used on Class A fires and would extinguish fire sizes that may be doused with 1 1/4th gallons of water. The number 1 indicates 1 1/4th gallons of water. Thus, 2A represents an extinguisher for Class A fires that can be doused with 2 1/2 gallons of water. Similarly, 21B indicates extinguisher contents that douse class B fires providing 21 square feet coverage side to side.

In addition, many of today's extinguishers are labelled to indicate that they can be used on different types of fires and will be labelled as such (for example, A-B, B-C, and so on).

 First-Aid

The initial assistance or treatment given to a casualty for any injury or sudden illness before the arrival of an ambulance, doctor, or other qualified person is called 'first-aid'. The notion of 'first' aid itself signifies that the casualty is likely to be in need of 'secondary aid'.

Principles of First-Aid

There are certain important principles involved in first-aid. These are listed as follows.

The first-aid provider must

- act calmly and logically;
- be in control—both of himself/herself and the problem;
- be gentle but firm, and speak to the casualty kindly but purposefully;
- build up trust by talking to the casualty throughout the examination and treatment;
- explain to the casualty what he/she is going to do;
- answer honestly and say so if he/she does not know the answer (that is, avoid giving misleading information);
- never leave the casualty alone but continue to talk to him/her until the ambulance or doctor arrives;
- continuously reassure the casualty;
- never separate a child from its parent or guardian;
- send the casualty to a hospital or doctor by the quickest means of transport;
- always inform the police about serious accidents; and
- inform the relatives of the casualty.

Certain things to avoid in first-aid are listed as follows.

Do not

- touch a wound with your fingers or any instrument.
- put an unclean dressing or cloth over a wound.
- allow bleeding to go unchecked.
- allow a crowd to gather around the casualty.
- move a patient unnecessarily.
- take off clothing unnecessarily.
- allow a patient with a fracture or suspected fracture to be moved until splints have been applied.
- neglect shock.
- risk burning a patient by using an unwrapped hot-water bottle or other heated object.
- fail to give artificial respiration when needed.
- fail to remove false teeth, tobacco, or any other eatables from the mouth of an unconscious person.
- permit air to reach a burned skin surface.
- wash wounds.
- try to reduce dislocations, except of the finger and lower jaw.
- leave a tourniquet on for over 20 minutes without loosening it.
- forget to send for a physician.

The First-aid Box

A first-aid box containing medical supplies for emergency use is usually kept in the housekeeping department. A minimum variety of certain types of supplies should be ensured at all times. A 17½ inch × 10 inch × 6½ inch dirt-proof box is ideal. The first-aid box must at least contain the following items:

- A first-aid book
- Antiseptic cream—useful for cuts and grazes
- Savlon or Dettol antiseptic solution—2 bottles
- Antihistamine lotion—can be rubbed on bites, stings, and sunburn
- Calamine lotion—a medicated liquid containing zinc carbonate, this has a soothing effect on painful sunburn. It can also relieve itching caused by minor insect bites and stings in the absence of an allergy
- Antacid tablets, magnesium trisilicate, or sodium bicarbonate—give relief from mild indigestion and heartburn, a burning sensation caused by stomach acid irritating the gullet
- Anti-diarrhoeal tablets—these are used to relieve diarrhoea by slowing down bowel movements
- Paracetamol—used for relieving pain and lowering a high temperature
- Aspirin—used for relieving pain and lowering a high temperature. Its use should be restricted, however, as it may irritate the stomach lining and has the potential to cause internal bleeding in susceptible people
- Kaolin clay—used to relieve diarrhoea by slowing down bowel movements
- Methyl salicylate ointment—to rub into a strained or bruised muscle. It will also ease spasms and pain
- Chloromycetin eye ointment—2 tubes. This can be used in case of bacterial infections of the eye, such as bacterial conjunctivitis
- Soframycin skin ointment—2 tubes. This is used in bacterial infections of the skin and in burns too
- Travel sickness tablets—these can be taken before a journey or as directed on the label
- Oil of cloves—for an aching tooth, this is used to provide temporary relief
- Clinical thermometer—can be used either orally or under the arm. It should be cleaned with antiseptic after each use, even for the same patient
- Sterilized white absorbent gauze (28 × 8 inches)—1 packet. This dressing can be used dry, with no cream or ointment, to dress a minor wound
- Sterilized dressing (No. 18)—12 packets; for use on fingers
- Sterilized dressing (No. 24)—12 packets; for use on hands and feet
- Large sterilized dressing (No. 20)—12 packets; for use on other body parts
- Sterilized cottonwool (25g)—6 packets; can be used to pad a dressing or to clean an injury with soap and hot water
- Crepe bandage—6 packets; may be needed to bandage a sprained or strained joint such as a wrist or knee
- Adhesive plaster (large)—can be used on minor wounds or to secure a dressing
- Adhesive dressing strip—for cuts and small wounds
- Open-weave bandages—6 packets; to protect wounds from dirt and from friction against clothing
- Roller bandages—various sizes, 18 packets; can be used to secure dressings, to apply pressure to control bleeding, and to give support to sprains or strains

- Unbleached triangular bandage—12 packets; a type of bandage that makes a sling to support an injured wrist or elbow
- Eye pad—for placing on the eye in case of an eye injury
- Tweezers—to remove splinters from the skin. They should be used in good light
- Dressing scissors—to use when cutting away dressings or bandages. The blunt-ended blade should be kept next to the skin
- Safety pins—1 packet of 10; to be used for fixing bandages or slings in place
- Pad and pencil for writing—1 each

First-aid Procedures

The most important techniques to know for first-aid include administering cardio-pulmonary resuscitation (CPR) and the Holger Nielsen method of artificial respiration.

CPR

This procedure is carried out on a person whose respiration has ceased. A constant supply of oxygen is vital for the brain and if breathing stops, blood oxygen levels will be affected as all tissues get oxygen through blood circulation.

The heart maintains this circulation, acting as a pump. If the heart too stops functioning, death will result unless urgent action is taken. The flow of oxygenated blood to the brain is in such case rapidly restored by means of artificial ventilation and chest compression. This dual technique is called CPR.

In case only breathing has stopped, the techniques for chest compression to stimulate or simulate cardiac function can be left out and only artificial respiration is to be concentrated on.

ABC of artificial respiration

The ABCs of artificial respiration are as follows:

- A for *Airway:* Clear airway.
- B for *Breathing:* Restore breathing.
- C for *Circulation:* Restore circulation.

Clearing the airway An unconscious casualty's airway may be blocked, making breathing difficult and noisy. The main reason for this is that muscular control in the throat is lost, which allows the tongue to sag back and block the throat. Follow the steps given below to clear the airway:

1. Remove the obstructing object or substance from the mouth with your fingers, using your first finger as a hook to dislodge it.
2. Extend the neck to open the airway. Place one hand under the nape of the neck, and the other hand on the forehead, and tilt the head back. Lift the chin up gently without closing the mouth.
3. Check if breathing has been restored. If not, start mouth-to-mouth resuscitation.

Restoring breathing This is done by administering mouth-to-mouth respiration. Put your face close to the casualty's mouth and look, listen, and feel for breathing for five seconds, before taking any further action. If the heart is beating, it will generate a pulse in the neck (the carotid pulse) where the main arteries pass up to the head. With the head tilted back, feel the Adam's apple with two fingers. Slide your fingers back along the victim's throat till they sit in the gap between the Adam's apple and the strap muscle; feel for the carotid pulse.

Restore breathing by giving mouth-to-mouth resuscitation. To start mouth-to-mouth artificial respiration:

1. Pinch and compress the nose to close the nostrils.
2. Take a deep breath.
3. Place your mouth around the victim's mouth, making an airtight seal and quickly breathe into the victim's mouth four times.
4. Re-fill your lungs by inhaling deeply after this step. Fill the victim's chest with air once every 5 seconds.
5. Watch the victim's chest movement for rise and fall of chest.
6. Allow the patient to exhale.

If the chest does not rise, check that:

1. The head is tilted sufficiently far back.
2. You have a firm seal around the casualty's mouth.
3. You have closed the nostrils completely.
4. The airway is not obstructed by vomit, blood, or a foreign body.

In case of mouth-to-nose ventilation, where mouth injuries make a good seal impossible or a harmful substance has been ingested through the mouth, the following method is followed:

1. With the casualty's mouth closed, form a tight seal with your lips around the casualty's nose and blow in.
2. Open the mouth to let the breath out.
3. Continue to repeat the procedure mentioned in the first point.

Restoring circulation This is achieved by external cardiac compression. The procedure, also known as external cardiac massage, can be carried out by one individual or two:

1. Place the victim on a hard surface.
2. Kneel at the victim's side.
3. Locate the xiphoid process (see 'Key Terms').
4. Measure 1–2 inches above the xiphoid process. Place the heel of one hand at this point on the sternum. Place the other hand on top of it. Interlock fingers to keep them off the victim's ribs.
5. Keep elbows straight and lean forward, making full use of your body weight to deliver a downward compression upon the breastbone. Apply steady, smooth pressure to depress the victim's sternum by 1½–2 inches.
6. Relax pressure completely, but do not let your hands leave the victim's chest or you may lose the correct hand position.
7. Repeat.

If there are two individuals to perform first-aid, the other person should continue with artificial respiration in the meantime. If there is only one person, perform cardio-pulmonary resuscitation (CPR) for 1 minute as follows:

1. After 15 chest compressions, give 2 quick lung inflations by mouth-to-mouth breathing, and then 2 more inflations if the carotid pulse is still absent.
2. Continue CPR by alternating lung inflations with chest depressions for a minute or until the victim is breathing on his/her own and a pulse is found.

A minute of CPR delivers 60 chest compressions (15 at a time multiplied by 4 times) and 8 lung inflations (2 at a time multiplied by 4 times). To sum up, the main steps of cardio-pulmonary resuscitation are as follows:

1. Clear airway.
2. Breathe into victim's mouth four times quickly.
3. Compress chest 15 times.
4. Give 2 quick lung inflations.
5. Alternate 15 chest compressions with 2 quick lung inflations.
6. In a minute, the victim should revive.

Holger Nielsen method of artificial respiration

In this method of administering artificial respiration, the patient is turned face downwards with the head turned to one side, kneeling at the patient's head and placing both your hands over the shoulder blades. Pressure should be exerted here by slowly rocking forward. For an adult, the pressure weight may be about 13.6 kg. As the pressure is released by rocking backwards, the patient's arms are raised by the elbows to expand the chest. The process is repeated until the doctor or an ambulance arrives. Each phase of expansion and compression should last about 2½ seconds, the complete cycle being repeated 12 times per minute.

The recovery position

Any unconscious casualty should be placed in the recovery position. This position prevents the tongue from blocking the throat and, because the head is slightly lower than the rest of the body, allows fluids to drain from the mouth, thus reducing the risk of the casualty inhaling stomach acids or saliva. The head, neck, and back are kept in a straight line, while the bent limbs keep the body propped in a secure and comfortable position. If you must leave an unconscious casualty unattended, he or she can safely be left in the recovery position while you get help. Before turning a casualty on the side, remove his or her spectacles (if worn) and remove any bulky objects from the pockets.

A person is placed in the recovery position by the following procedure:

1. Kneeling beside the casualty, open the airway by tilting the head back and lifting the chin. Straighten the legs. Draw the arm nearest to you out so that it is at right angles to the body, with the elbow bent and the palm facing up.
2. Bring the arm furthest from you across the chest and hold the hand, palm outwards, against the casualty's nearer cheek.
3. With your other hand, grasp the thigh furthest from you across the chest and pull the knee up, keeping the foot flat on the ground.
4. Tilt the head backward to make sure the airway remains open. Adjust the hand under the cheek, if necessary, so that the head stays in the tilted position.
5. Adjust the upper leg, if necessary, so that both the hip and the knee are bent at right angles.
6. Call for an ambulance. Check breathing and pulse frequently while waiting for the doctor.

Dressings and bandages

A dressing is the primary layer in contact with a covered wound to prevent it from contamination and bleeding. Dressings must be used sterile to deter microbial infection of the wound. Those used in first aid are usually gauze or adhesive dressings.

- *Gauze dressings* These are in the form of thick sterile, loosely woven cotton pads and are used to cover larger wounds. The dressing is held in place with adhesive tape or a bandage.
- *Adhesive dressings* These are in the form of a thin absorbent material held in place with self-adhesive tapes and are meant to cover smaller wounds. They come in varied sizes.

A bandage refers to a length of material used to keep the dressing in place and cover a wound. They serve to retain the dressing in position, cover the wound, apply pressure to control bleeding, restrict movement, prevent or reduce swelling or support a strained muscle or joint. The three main types used in first aid are triangular, roller, and tubular bandages.

- *Triangular bandages* These are usually made of cotton and as the name suggests, triangular in shape. They are used as slings to support and immobilise the upper limbs in case of a sprain, fracture or post-surgery.
- *Tubular bandages* These are in the form of cylindrical tubes of elastic bandages, ideal for areas that are difficult to bandage with roller bandages and also those with lot of movement, such as fingers, toes, elbows, and knees.
- *Roller bandages* These are in the form of long strips of material. There are two types available, crepe roller bandages which are elastic in nature and used to support a strain or sprain and cotton or linen roller bandages which cover a dressed wound. Roller bandaging techniques are presented below.

Techniques of roller bandaging

Based on the area of application various techniques of roller bandaging may be used.

Circular bandaging In this technique, the roller bandage is tied in layers one on top of the other over and over again 3–4 times and held in place with tapes or a knot. The technique is used to hold a dressing in place in such body parts as arms, legs, chest, and abdomen. It also serves as a starting technique for other forms of bandaging.

Spiral bandaging This technique involves tying the bandage in layers, slightly overlapping the preceding turn by $1/3^{rd}$ – $2/3^{rd}$ the width of the bandage. It is used on cylindrical parts of the body with uniform thickness. In case of tapering parts such as thighs, elastic bandages are tied spirally.

Reverse spiral bandaging In this, a spiral bandage is tied but reversed or folded back on itself by 180° on each turn, forming a V as in herringbone pattern. The technique is used when elastic bandages are not available for bandaging tapering parts of the body.

Figure-of-eight bandaging This technique, applied for bandaging moving joints such as wrists and ankles, involves two turns of the roller bandage, crossing each other at the side where the join flexes.

Recurrent bandaging This bandage is for blunt body parts and involves the application of the bandage repeatedly from one side across the top to the other side of the blunt body part. The recurrent bandages are then covered and fixed using circular or spiral technique.

The various types of bandages and tying techniques are depicted in Figures 22.1. a, b, c, d, e, f and g.

First-aid for Common Situations

The procedures for some common accidents and illnesses are discussed here.

Asphyxia/suffocation This may be due to exposure to a poisonous gas or due to something smothering or choking the victim. Try to find the cause of suffocation and remove it. Turn off any leaking gas.

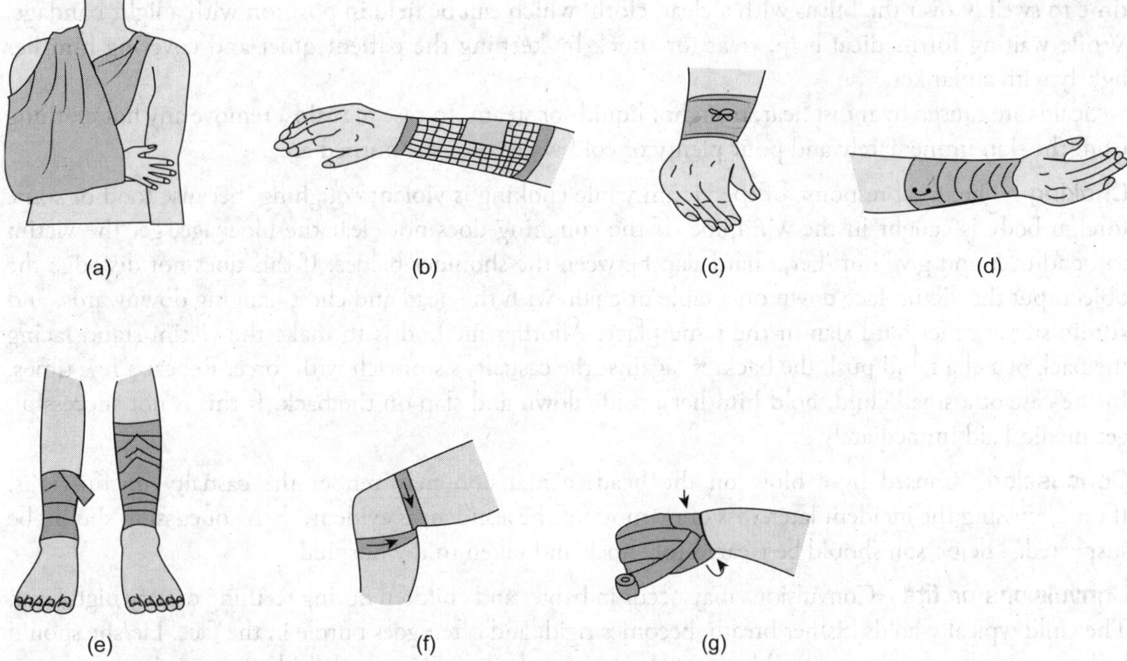

Fig. 22.1 Types of bandages and tying techniques
a) Triangular bandage b) Tubular bandage c) Circular bandaging d) Spiral bandaging
e) Reverse spiral bandaging f) Figure-of-eight bandaging g) Recurrent bandaging

Open the windows or take the victim out into the open. In the case of choking, remove the obstruction from the victim's nose or mouth. In all cases, give artificial respiration if breathing has stopped, using the mouth-to-mouth or 'kiss of life' method (see 'artificial respiration').

Asthma During an attack of asthma, the person has difficulty in breathing and there is a feeling of suffocation. A person who has chronic asthma would have been prescribed the use of an inhaler and other medication during an attack. These medications should be administered to the patient and he/she should be reassured until better.

Burns and scalds Burns may be caused by dry heat or by hot fat or oil. For minor burns on the limbs, immediately hold the injury under cold running water for five minutes. A small burn needs no further treatment. It should simply be left exposed to air. Do not apply any oil or ointment to the burn and do not prick or remove blisters.

Large and deep burns (covering more than 3 sq. inches) need medical attention. If possible, relieve pain by immersing the part in cold water or applying cold, wet cloths. Wrap or cover the injury with a clean cloth and a light bandage. Treat the victim for shock while waiting for medical help. If the victim can be moved, it is best to take him/her to the hospital.

In case of chemical burns on a large part of the body, especially that caused by a strong acid or alkali, put the victim under cold running water, a shower if possible.

In case of fire burns, if the victim's clothing is on fire, smother the flames in a rug or blanket. Then, lay the person flat. Remove any smouldering clothing if it is not adhering to the skin. Otherwise, dampen the smouldering garments with cold water but do not press the wet clothes against the patient's skin. If possible, remove any jewellery, watch, socks or shoes near the burned area before the tissues have time to swell. Cover the burns with a clean cloth, which can be held in position with a light bandage. While waiting for medical help, treat for shock by keeping the patient quiet and covering him/her lightly with a blanket.

Scalds are caused by moist heat, from hot liquids or steam. In case of scalds, remove any hot clothing from the skin immediately and pour plenty of cold water over the burned area.

Choking The usual response of the victim while choking is violent coughing, because food or some foreign body is caught in the windpipe. If the coughing does not clear the blockage, get the victim to bend over and give him/her a hard slap between the shoulder blades. If this does not dislodge the object, put the victim face down on a table or chair, with the head and chest hanging downwards, and administer another hard slap in the same place. Another method is to make the victim stand facing the back of a chair and push the backrest against the casualty's stomach with force. Repeat a few times. In the case of a small child, hold him/her upside down and slap on the back. If this is not successful, get medical aid immediately.

Concussion Caused by a blow on the head, concussion may render the casualty unconscious. If on discussing the incident later, loss of memory of the accident is evident, then concussion should be suspected. The person should be treated for shock and taken to the hospital.

Convulsions or fits Convulsions may occur in babies and children during teething or very high fever. The child typically holds his/her breath, becomes rigid, and often goes purple in the face. He/she should be kept warm by covering with a blanket or being placed into a warm bath with someone in attendance. Meanwhile, a doctor should be called. A person, child or adult, who falls to the ground with the arms and legs shaking violently may be having an epileptic fit; an epileptic fit can also take the shape of a person suddenly becoming 'spaced out'. Move furniture and other obstacles out of the way to reduce the risk of injury if the convulsion is a violent one. Try to slip a knotted handkerchief between the teeth to prevent him/her from biting his/her tongue. Do not force any other object between the person's teeth, never a hard spoon or similar object. In the case of an absence of seizure (becoming 'spaced out'), simply sit with the person until he/she returns to normalcy; do not attempt to shake them awake or similar. On regaining consciousness, the epileptic may be dazed and should be prevented from wandering off in this state.

Cuts and abrasions These may be caused in many ways and may sometimes get infected if not treated properly. The wound should be cleaned with warm water and antiseptic solution and then covered with a clean dressing. In case of bleeding, pressure should be applied on the wound if it is free of foreign particles such as glass or metal. For deep cuts and excessive bleeding, the person should be treated for shock and, if necessary, taken to a hospital.

Dislocation When a joint is dislocated, the casualty is unable to move it in the usual way. There may be a swelling and numbness beyond the point where the dislocation has occurred. Do not attempt to replace the bone in its proper place. Keep the parts as still as possible till medical aid arrives.

Drowning Make sure the casualty's airway is clear by removing any obstructions. Give mouth-to-mouth artificial respiration immediately upon rescue and continue until breathing is restored or medical aid arrives.

Diabetes This is a disorder in which a person's body is not able to regulate the uptake of available sugar, as a result of which excess sugar may appear in the blood and urine. Many diabetics whose sugar levels are difficult to control depend on insulin and a controlled diet. When such a person eats insufficient food, there is an imbalance due to the insulin administered, and the person may become hypoglycaemic. In hypoglycaemia, the patient starts to perspire and becomes nervous or irritable.

If hypoglycaemia is not controlled, the person may go into a diabetic shock, resulting in a coma. At the first sign of hypoglycaemia, the diabetic should be given two lumps of sugar, a piece of chocolate, or a glucose drink. If the patient does not respond, he/she should be taken to the hospital immediately.

Electric shock If the victim is still in contact with the electrical equipment, he/she should not be touched until the electric current has been switched off. It may be necessary to try to drag the appliances away from the victim by pulling the insulating wire leading to it. If this is not possible, separate the victim from the electrical source using a non-conducting object, such as a dry wooden stick. If the casualty's heart does not seem to be beating, give the breastbone in the centre of the chest a sharp thump. If the victim is not breathing, start mouth-to-mouth artificial respiration at once and continue until medical aid arrives. If the victim is breathing but unconscious, place him/her in the recovery position. Treat for burns and shock.

Eye injuries If rapid blinking fails to dislodge a speck of dust fallen into the eye, lift the lid of the affected eye by the lashes and try to remove the object with the corner of a clean handkerchief. However, do not attempt to remove anything from the cornea, which is the transparent, domed front of the eyeball. If the object is embedded in the eyeball or cannot be seen, cover the eye with a gauze pad held lightly in place with a plaster and arrange immediate transport to the hospital.

If any acid or other corrosive agents have come into contact with the eye, they should be washed out immediately. Bathe the eye with cold water—if possible, keeping it under running water for 10–15 minutes to ensure that all the acid is washed out. Take the casualty to the hospital immediately.

Fainting Fainting may be caused by a sudden reduction in blood flow or oxygen to the head. It may be the result of a slowing down of the heartbeat from shock, anxiety, or even hormonal changes in early pregnancy. If someone feels faint, get the person to lie down with the feet raised above the level of the head. Alternatively, sit the person in a chair with the head between the knees. If someone has already fainted, loosen any tight clothing around the neck, chest, and waist. If indoors, open the windows.

Fractures The signs of a bone fracture are pain and tenderness even at a gentle touch, swelling and bruising, or loss of control or deformity of the affected limb. A broken bone needs treatment by a doctor. While waiting for medical help, keep the victim still, try to stop any bleeding, and treat for shock. Do not attempt to move the victim unless absolutely necessary and do not try to straighten the bone. Do not loosen any of the victim's clothing, except around the neck.

Heart attack/stroke A stroke may be caused due to insufficient blood supply to the heart or a clot of blood in the heart or a major blood vessel or in the brain. The symptoms may include chest pain (angina), breathlessness, and feeling faint. The patient should be propped up or allowed to sit forward on a chair and on no account moved until the doctor or ambulance arrives.

Indigestion Stomach discomfort or pain, heartburn, and acidity are often signs of indigestion in the absence of other symptoms. An antacid preparation such as milk of magnesia may provide relief.

Object in the nose Any object stuck in the nose cannot be easily removed. Any attempt to remove it may push it backwards and get stuck deeper, or make it travel down the windpipe, causing more trouble. Ask the victim to breathe through the mouth and take him/her to the doctor at once.

Nose bleed Make the victim sit down with his/her head over a sink or bowl. Pinch the sides of the nose together, apply a cold pad to the bridge of the nose, and wait. Instruct the casualty to breathe through the mouth and not to sniff. If the bleeding has not stopped within 20 minutes, take the person to the hospital immediately.

Poisoning If someone has had a drug overdose or swallowed some harmful substance (such as a toxic substance), a doctor should be called even if there are no ill effects evident. If the victim is not breathing, give mouth-to-mouth artificial respiration. If the poison is still in the mouth, use the mouth-to-nose method of giving artificial respiration. If the victim is unconscious but breathing, place him/her on his/her side with the uppermost arm and leg drawn up and the head tilted back to keep the airway open. Look around for any bottles, tablet casings, berries, and smells of substances such as petrol, paraffin, or cleaning fluid for clues as to what may have been ingested.

Shock After even a minor accident, a victim may experience shock, a condition in which the blood pressure is low and the heartbeat weak. The effect of shock can be lessened by stopping any bleeding, trying to ease any discomfort, and talking reassuringly to the victim. Keep the victim quiet and warm by covering him/her lightly with a blanket. Where possible, have the victim lying down with the head low and the legs raised a little. In the case of a chest or abdominal injury, the victim's shoulder should be raised slightly and supported. Turn the victim's head to one side.

Snake bite Confirmation of a snake bite can be obtained if there are teeth marks on the affected area. Make the person lie down comfortably and allow him/her physical and mental rest; try to reassure them. If the snake is not poisonous, the person should be made to understand that he/she will soon be all right. If the snake is indeed poisonous and has bitten the victim on the hands or legs, tie a rope, handkerchief, or tourniquet near the bitten area so as to avoid the venous blood flow carrying the venom towards the heart. A tourniquet should not be tied so tight that blood flow into that organ is inhibited. Now make an inch-long cut over the bitten area and start sucking and spitting out the venom and blood from the wound; make sure you yourself have no wounds or lesions in the mouth when doing this. In case medical aid is not available immediately, continue the suction for half an hour. Do not give the victim anything to eat or drink.

Sprain The sprained area needs to be bandaged with a crepe bandage immersed in cold water and the casualty should be treated for shock. In case pain and swelling is excessive, the person should be taken to the hospital.

Stroke A stroke is the result of restricted blood supply to some parts of the brain and is also associated with high blood pressure. There may or may not be loss of consciousness, but some degree of paralysis may result. The patient should be treated for shock and taken to a hospital as soon as possible.

Swallowed objects Children may sometimes swallow small objects such as buttons, coins, and so on, which pass out of the body easily. In case a sharp object has been swallowed, however, take the child to a hospital immediately.

Crime Prevention

It is imperative that all properties have a crime prevention committee or a security committee. The committee should consist of key management personnel, including department heads. Supervisors and other selected employees can also be roped in for valuable information and inputs. The committee members should meet on a scheduled basis periodically to review past plans and form new ones. The general responsibilities of this committee should be to

- design a security booklet for all employees;
- develop orientation and training programmes on crime prevention in coordination with the training department;

- analyse and resolve recurring security issues and investigate any security-related incidents;
- conduct spot security checks and inspections of the property;
- liaise with the local police department; and
- monitor the keeping of records and documentation of all security-related incidents.

Dealing with Emergencies

The nature of all emergencies is the same: they are uncontrollable and unforeseen. Thus all properties must be prepared for them and have emergency plans put down in writing. Emergencies may come in any form—earthquakes, floods, tsunamis, bomb threats, and so on. Emergency plans must be a part of the SOPs. These procedures must specify

- *what* procedures are to be followed in case of an emergency;
- *who* will be responsible—the plan should specify employee duties and placement within the facility during an emergency and after the emergency;
- *how* the procedures will be followed; and
- *when* the specified procedures should be followed—for instance, when should the guests be notified of a bomb threat, or when should the evacuation process be initiated?

Planning for an Emergency

A plan clearly defining the actions of all stakeholders, especially management, staff and guests to protect human lives and assets in face of an emergency is crucial. All the people concerned must also be trained to implement the contingency action plan. The plan must cover how the following elements are to be addressed for an emergency.

Emergency response procedures All possible emergency situations must be listed down and response and reporting procedures for these must be outlined. Also mentioned should be the emergency action teams for leading the response action, necessarily consisting of the security officer, telephone operator, maintenance engineer and duty manager. The procedures must also specify how guest and employees would be alerted to an emergency. All employees must be made aware of their responsibilities and action in the face of an emergency.

Employee training Training of all employees in emergency procedures is essential to deal with emergencies.

Emergency checklists Each department head should develop a checklist outlining the actions he/she must take in the event of an emergency.

Evacuation procedures The conditions necessitating evacuation and the evacuation order issuance authority must be specified. Employee teams entrusted with the responsibility of evacuation and rescue must be stated. Evacuation routes and maps specifying the exits and assembly points must be in place and displayed in prominent places and behind guestroom doors for in-house guests. A system of accounting for all employees and guests should be in place.

Emergency resources The names and telephone numbers of internal emergency action teams and outside agencies that may be of help during an emergency need to be listed and kept in a prominent, accessible place.

Drills Fire emergency drills should be conducted periodically and it should be mandatory for all staff to attend these in shifts.

Emergency response kit An emergency response kit containing guest identification tags, a guest identification register, pens, legal note pads, folders, paper clips, and so on should be kept ready and handy.

First-aid training and supplies A thorough training in first-aid procedures, especially cardio-pulmonary resuscitation (CPR), should be given to selected employees. All other employees should be trained in at least the basics of first-aid. A complete first-aid kit should be maintained at all times.

Transportation and housing Forward planning should be done for transportation of guests in case their relocation is required in the event of an emergency. Potential relocation sites should also be identified.

Contingency plan review The contingency plan should be reviewed by people who are responsible for the prevention of losses.

Dealing with Bomb Threats

As an example of dealing with emergencies, the procedure for dealing with a bomb threat is outlined in this section.

Bomb threats may be delivered in writing or orally, in person or over the telephone.

In case of a written threat in the form of a letter, note, or telegram, the message and the envelope should be handled carefully and held only at the corners to preserve fingerprints and other evidence. Protect the document and the envelope, and hand it over to the general manager. Inform the police of the contents of the note.

If the letter is delivered by a messenger, detain the person for questioning by the police, if possible. If the messenger has left the premises, the employee accepting the note should immediately prepare a memorandum listing the circumstances, the time the message was received, any known witnesses, and a detailed description of the messenger.

In case the bomb threat was made orally, as in any employee becoming aware of a bomb threat through a personal contact or by overhearing someone make such a threat, the person should immediately convey the information to the general manager in a discreet manner (so as not to alarm the guests). The police should be informed promptly. The person issuing the threat should be kept under observation, if possible, and the person's physical characteristics noted. These include the person's height, weight, build, colour of hair and eyes, a description of clothes and jewellery, and any other identification feature such as a beard, scar, or limp. If this person leaves the hotel before he or she can be stopped to determine his or her identity, record the mode of transportation and the direction of travel. This may include a bus number, car rental company, the automobile description—including the model, license plate number, and state—and the number of persons in the car. These facts should be furnished to the general manager immediately for communication to security personnel and the police.

The most usual way in which a bomb threat is received is over the telephone. They are usually received by the switchboard operators from a public telephone number. The call is usually brief, so that there is no chance to trace the number. Therefore, switchboard operators should record the information accurately in order to provide the security and police personnel with as much documented information as possible. A sample bomb threat call checklist that may be used by the receiver of the call is presented in Exhibit 22.3.

Housekeeping employees may also be a part of the search team looking for unclaimed, unidentified, or unusual foreign objects that could contain a bomb. All housekeeping employees should be aware of the evacuation plans explained in the safety manual of the property and help in evacuation if necessary. In case of an explosion, the employees should help out in the rescue process and provide first-aid as required.

Exhibit 22.3 A sample bomb threat call checklist

Bomb threat call checklist					
Name of operator			Date of call receipt:		
Caller's identity			Time of call receipt:		
			Duration of call:		
Caller details					
Gender			**Age**		
Male			Adult		
Female			Juvenile		
Not sure			Approx. age		
Background sound					
Clear	....	Dining area	....	Long distance	....
Traffic noise	....	Music	....	Others	....
Train noise	....	Conversation	....		
PA system	....	Deep breathing	....		

Dealing with Terrorism—Steps and Precautions

In the recent past, terrorists have targeted hotels on several occasions, worldwide. Marriott, Islamabad, and then Taj Mahal Palace and The Oberoi Trident, Mumbai were made targets and there were many casualties, both guests and hotel staff. Hotels all over the world are now striving to put anti-terror systems and mechanisms in place.

Good housekeeping not only enhances the ambience of the hotel, it also reduces the opportunity for placing suspicious items or bags and helps to deal with false alarms and hoaxes. The following tips with regards to housekeeping can help reduce the risk of planting dangerous material on hotel properties:

1. Limit the installation and use of litter bins around the hotel and ensure that the few installed are checked and cleared regularly.
2. Procure litter bins which have small openings.
3. Review the location of litter bins. For instance, these should not be placed near support structures.
4. Use of clear bags for waste disposal provides an easier opportunity for the staff to conduct an initial examination for suspicious items.
5. Review the use and security of wheeled bins and metal bins to store rubbish within service areas, goods entrances, and near areas where guest gather.
6. Keep public and communal areas—exit, entrances, reception areas, stairs, halls, washrooms and service corridors—clean and tidy.
7. Keep the furniture in such areas to a minimum, hence ensuring that there is little opportunity to hide devices under sofas and chairs.
8. Lock unoccupied offices, rooms, and storage cupboards.
9. Place tamper proof plastic seals on maintenance hatches.
10. Have in place an agreed procedure for the management of contractors, their vehicles, and waste collection services. The vehicle registration mark of each vehicle and its occupant should be known to security in advance.

11. Ensure stringent checks on the people recruited to the department and those on contract.
12. Set the procedure and train staff to identify and report suspicious activity. Make sure the staff understand that security is part of everyone's responsibilities.
13. Formulate and maintain contingency plans dealing with bomb threats, suspect packages, explosion, structural collapse, and evacuation.
14. Have in place a communications and media strategy which includes handling enquiries from concerned family and friends.
15. Planning should incorporate the seven key instructions applicable to most incidents:
    i) Do not touch suspicious items.
    ii) Move everyone to a safe distance.
    iii) Prevent others from approaching cordoned areas.
    iv) Communicate safely to staff, business visitors, and the public.
    v) Use hand-held radios or mobile phones away from the immediate vicinity of a suspect item, remaining out of line of sight and behind hard cover.
    vi) Notify the police.
    vii) Ensure that whoever found the item or witnessed the incident is available to brief the police.
16. A staff pass system should be followed and a temporary pass system should be adopted for visitors.
17. Screening of hand baggage by appropriate mechanical detectors should be carried out for all guests and employees on entrance to the property.
18. All types of mails and parcels should be screened by detectors.
19. If the risk is from a vehicle bomb, basic principle is to keep all vehicles at a safe place. Non-essential vehicles should ideally be kept atleast 30 meters away from the building.
20. Consider using robust physical barriers to keep all but authorized vehicles at a safe distance.
21. Good quality doors and windows are essential to ensure building security. External doors should be strong, well-lit, and fitted with good quality locks. Doors that are not often used should be internally secured.
22. Use toughened glass with anti-shatter film for windows and doors.
23. Have close-circuit television (CCTV) systems in place. It is important to remember that CCTVs are effective only if they are properly maintained and monitored.
24. Pruning all vegetation and trees, especially near entrances, will assist in surveillance and prevent concealment of any packages.
25. All hotels and restaurants should have an uninterrupted power supply (UPS) available and regularly tested.
26. The owners, management, and workers in the hotel should understand the significance of the level of threat if known, since an attack may come without warning.
27. The security measures deployed at different response levels should not be made public to avoid alerting potential terrorists about what the hotel staff know and what they are doing about it. The three levels of response which broadly equate to threat levels are outlined in Tables 22.2 and 22.3.

Table 22.2 Threat level definitions

Critical	An attack is expected imminently
Severe	An attack is highly likely
Substantial	An attack is a strong possibility
Moderate	An attack is possible not likely
Low	An attack is unlikely

Table 22.3 Response level definitions

Critical	Exceptional	Maximum protective security measures to meet specific threats and to minimize vulnerability and risk.
Severe Substaintial	Heightened	Additional and sustainable protective security measures reflecting the broad nature of the threat combined with specific business and geographical vulnerabilities and judgements on acceptable risk.
Moderate Low	Normal	Routine baseline protective security measures, appropriate to the business and location.

28. Have a proper first-aid facility on premises.
29. Install and maintain sufficient and proper fire-fighting equipment.
30. Vulnerable hotels should provide a booklet for safety to all guests with the following points mentioned:
    i) Do not answer the door in a hotel or motel room without verifying the caller. If a person claims to be an employee, call the front desk and ask if someone from their staff is supposed to have access to your room and for what purpose.
    ii) Keep your room key with you at all times and do not needlessly display it in public. Should you misplace it, please notify the front desk immediately.
    iii) Close the door securely whenever you are in your room and use all of the locking devices provided.
    iv) Check to see that any sliding glass door or window and any connecting room door is locked.
    v) Do not invite strangers to your room.
    vi) Do not draw attention to yourself by displaying large amounts of cash or expensive jewellery.
    vii) Place all valuables in the hotel or motel's safe deposit box.
    viii) When returning to your hotel or motel late in the evening, be aware of your surroundings, stay in well-lit areas, and use the main entrance.
    ix) Take a few moments and locate the nearest exit that may be used in the event of an emergency.
    x) If you see any suspicious activity, notify the hotel operator or a staff member.

Keys and their Control

Individual heads of departments are responsible for all the keys in their areas. The housekeeper is usually responsible for more keys than any other departmental head.

Types of Keys

The housekeeping department is primarily concerned with the following categories of keys:

Emergency key This key opens all the doors in the property, even those that the guests have double-locked. In addition, it also double-locks the room against all other keys. The emergency key, or 'E'-key, overrides the catch or deadbolt put on by the guest for privacy in the room.

Hence, the emergency key should be well-protected. It should be stored in a secure place such as the hotel safe, a safe deposit box, or a metal cabinet that only the general manager or the security officer can access. Some properties may also keep the E-key off the premises. Its use should occur only in emergency situations such as a fire or when a guest or employee is locked in a room and needs immediate assistance. Most housekeeping personnel do not use emergency keys on a day-to-day basis.

Master keys These keys open all guestroom doors that are not double-locked. They are separated into four levels of access:

Grandmaster key This key opens all hotel guestrooms and often all housekeeping storage rooms as well. It can also double-lock a room if access to it has to be denied. This key can be used in emergency situations when it is vital for a manager to enter some or all areas of the hotel. It is itself kept under lock-and-key at the front desk of hotels.

Pass key/master key This key is kept by the deputy or assistant housekeeper and will open any internal door that has not been double-locked.

Sub-master or section master keys These keys open all rooms in one work section of a hotel. A supervisor may be issued more than one key of this type as he or she may be required to inspect the work of more than one GRA.

Floor master key A GRA is given this key to open the rooms he or she is assigned to clean on a floor. The floor key opens all rooms on a particular floor that are not double-locked. If the employee has rooms to clean on more than one floor or area, he or she may need more than one floor key. Floor keys typically open the storeroom for that floor too.

Guestroom keys These are keys issued to guests upon their registration. The guestroom key opens a single guestroom so long as it is not double-locked. Many properties do not list the hotel's name, address, or room number on guestroom keys. That way, if a guestroom key is lost or misplaced, it cannot be traced back easily to the property for criminal use. A code number representing the room number is typically stamped on the key instead. A master code list is maintained at the front desk and is used to recycle by changing the codes. Guests are asked to hand in their keys when they go out and the keys are then put on a key board, which should be kept out of view of passers-by as a security precaution. A guestroom key not hanging on the key board should indicate that the guest is in the hotel.

Supply keys These keys are used within the servicing sector of the hotel by the supervisory-level staff to ensure that stocks and equipment are safely stored away when not in use. Store keys, office keys, and linen room keys are examples of such keys.

Card keys Many hotels nowadays use the card key system. This type of room-locking mechanism uses regular door locks and special plastic cards that act as keys to unlock the doors. The plastic cards look like credit cards with holes punched in them. Some have a magnetic strip instead of the holes. The system uses a computer that codes the cards to lock and unlock the doors. Rather than re-keying the door locks in case of loss of keys, the computer is used to create new room-lock codes for each room. Master keys may be easily created and destroyed through the computerized card system.

Key Control

The control of guestroom keys is one of the cornerstones of hotel security that guests have a right to expect under common law. Key control is the process of reducing guest property theft and other security-related incidents by carefully monitoring and tracking the use of keys in the hospitality operation. If there is no key-card lock system, the following policies should be considered for key control:

Coding

A few precautions to take while coding are as follows:

- Room keys must not have any form of tag that identifies the hotel.
- Keys must not have the room number on them. Keys must be identified by a numeric or alphanumeric code. That code should not, in any way, directly correspond to the building or room numbers.

Issuing keys

Apart from the basic precautions for all keys, there is more stringent security for keys with higher access.

Guestroom keys These are the keys with minimum access, unlocking just the one room. When keys are given to guests upon registration, the guest's room number must not be spoken aloud if there are others within hearing range. Room numbers should be shown to the guests in writing with a reminder that they should note it down if a guest check-in packet is not used. Explain to the guest that the coding system is for their protection.

Guests should be asked by the guest service agents for their room keys upon checkout. Hotel employees, particularly housekeeping and bell staff, who see guests obviously in the process of leaving a room for the final time, taking along their luggage, should ask the guests if they have returned their room key. This is also a good time to thank them for staying with you and make other pleasantries.

GRAs and others who find keys in unoccupied guestrooms or elsewhere should place them in their pockets or in the locked key boxes provided, not on their carts (where they are accessible to others), and turn them in to their supervisor to be returned to the front desk.

Master and sub-master keys All section master keys, room master keys, grand master keys, and emergency master keys (normally kept in a safety box) should be signed out each time they are taken and their return noted in a key control sheet (see Exhibit 16.3 in Chapter 16). All the keys should be stamped 'do not duplicate'.

Custody of keys

These are the precautions to be taken while the key is with a guest or employee after being issued as per the correct procedure.

- Employees should not be allowed to loan the keys assigned to them to one another.
- Employees should hand over keys whenever they leave the property, even for meal breaks.
- Individuals who have been issued master or sub-master keys should be spot-checked from time to time to ensure that they have them on their person.

Changing locks and keys

Whenever a new key is made or a new lock is fitted, certain precautions are necessary.

- A record must be kept of how many keys are made for each room and when they are made. The general manager must review this record on a weekly basis, initialling and dating the key-making log each time he or she reviews it.
- If required as a result of this review, the general manager must instruct the maintenance staff either to re-key a lock or to exchange room locks around within a housekeeping section.
- If new room codes are to be used or locks are being switched, the code on the keys must be adjusted accordingly and overstamped until the old code is illegible, and the new code should be stamped nearby if locks are swapped within a section. As a standard practice, it is recommended that some locks in a section be moved quarterly.
- A log must be kept of all lock swaps and re-keyings.

Loss of keys

This is a time when particular vigilance must be exercised.

- If a section master key is lost under circumstances that may result in a guest being at risk, the entire section should be re-keyed. If a section is being re-keyed, also consider re-keying a new grand master and emergency key so that, in effect, a phased re-keying of the entire hotel is accomplished if it has been some time since this was last done.
- If a master key or emergency key is lost under any circumstances, it must be reported to the owner or the corporate office immediately by the general manager. After the circumstances are discussed, they can decide whether the entire hotel should be re-keyed.
- As an additional step, the general manager or somebody he or she delegates the responsibility to must cross-index all incidents of theft, missing property, damage, and so on as follows:
  a) Room number or location. Watch out for locks that have been moved.
  b) Names of potentially implicated employees (usually more than one). It may be discovered that room thefts never occur when so-and-so is off, or that they occurred, regardless of the room number, when so-and-so was working in maintenance or housekeeping.

Electronic locks

These are a precaution in themselves. Since the introduction of the recordable electronic door lock in the late 1970s, hotel security has been virtually transformed. The focus at the time of its invention was increased guest security. Now there are countries where hotels that do not feature electronic locking mechanisms in guestrooms will be unable to obtain insurance. Even the simplest of key-card locks have been found to reduce break-ins by upto 80%.

Employee key-cards can even be coded to allow access only to their assigned units of responsibility and only during the hours of their shift.

Smart cards/Computerized key cards

Now a days, most modern hotels use smart cards style computerised key cards. 'Smart card' is a generic term for a card the size and thickness of a credit or debit card that is embedded with a microprocessor chip. The chip itself has 'intelligence' by way of computational power similar to that of early personal computers. These powerful computing capabilities make smart cards much more secure than the other types of cards presently in use. They can handle encryption techniques that protect the information stored in the cards. In July 1998, the Hilton New York and Towers became the first hotel to install a locking system fully integrated with true smart-card capacity.

 Scanty Baggage

A guestroom with a guest checking in with very light luggage is coded as 'scanty baggage' (SB). This guest can easily turn 'skipper' by just walking out of the hotel without settling his or her account. Therefore, most managements follow a policy that 'scanty baggage' guests should pay a deposit in advance as a safeguard against skipping out of the hotel. When such a guest checks into the hotel, the front office assistant stamps 'scanty baggage' on the guest's registration card and enters the particulars in the scanty baggage register. The lobby manager or the front office manager has to sign the registration card and the scanty baggage register, and has the discretion to ask for a deposit from the guest. Housekeeping employees must report any suspicious movements of such guests to their manager.

 Guest and Employee Thefts

All hotels face the problem of employee and guest thefts at some time or the other. The management can reduce the volume of soft goods, fixtures, and equipment stolen from the property by reducing the opportunity to steal.

Guest Thefts

There are incidents where guests take away items that are not meant to be taken away by them. These items may be picture frames, bathrobes, towels, and so on. However, some articles are meant to be takeaways. These are small items that prominently display the hotel's monogram. To minimize losses through guest theft, a count of the number of amenities placed in the guestroom if always kept and if the guest asks for extra numbers, then this has to be entered in a log book. The room attendant can check the numbers while cleaning the next day.

Luxury hotels charge a high enough rate to compensate for stolen items. However, these are some measures that may discourage guest thefts.

- Items such as monogrammed towels, bathrobes, etc. may be placed on sale in hotel gift-shops. This may reduce the likelihood of theft since guests have the option of purchasing these items. Having these items on sale also helps set a standard price that can be levied against guests for a missing item.
- Use as few monogrammed items as possible. Most guests take away items as souvenirs and not with the intention of stealing the object per se. The use of fewer items with logos reduces the temptation.
- Always keep the storage rooms closed and locked so that guests do not get a chance to take away items from there. Amenities stored on carts should be stocked in a secure place or in a locked compartment. Guests walking down the hallway or corridor may easily take home a year's supply of shampoo, soap, and so on in a matter of minutes if these are left unattended in the corridor.
- Affix or nail down guestroom items and fixtures to appropriate surfaces. If decorations are not nailed, glued, bolted, or otherwise anchored to the wall and are small enough to fit in a suitcase, they are prime targets for guest theft. The easier an item is to remove, the more likely it is that it will be removed. All pictures, mirrors, and wall decorations should be discreetly affixed to the wall. Lamps should be too large to fit easily into a suitcase or bag. Expensive items such as televisions should be bolted and equipped with an alarm that alerts the front desk or security if an attempt is made to remove the item.

- The closer the room is to the parking area, the easier it is to remove an item from a room. Secure all windows and sliding glass doors so that they cannot be opened all the way. Limit the number of entrances and exits guests may use to get to their room.

Employee Theft

The management should detail explicit regulations concerning employee theft. The employee handbook should spell out the consequences of stealing hotel property. It is important that the management not discriminate against any employee when enforcing these rules:

- While screening applicants for the job, a thorough check of the background, including a check for any criminal convictions, should be carried out. Gaps in the employment history on applications may hide significant information. Reference checks over the telephone are therefore a good practice for managers when they are hiring new employees.
- Colour-coded uniforms and identification badges with the employees' photographs and signatures discourage people bent on thievery from trying to pass themselves off as employees.
- Orientation and training programmes should emphasize the value of honesty.
- Supervisors should closely monitor behaviour and adherence to company policies and procedures during the employee training and probationary period.
- Good inventory control procedures should be followed. Conduct a monthly inventory of all housekeeping supplies, such as toilet paper, amenities, and linen. If the items in storage do not match the usage rate or if too little stock is on the shelves, it may be an indication of employee theft.
- All storeroom doors should be kept locked and these locks should be changed periodically to reduce the opportunity for theft.
- An effective key-control programme, lost-and-found procedure, and gate-pass system should be in place and enforced at all times.
- Regular locker inspections also discourage employees from stealing for lack of a hiding place for articles.
- Employee entrances should have a security staff office that monitors arriving and departing employees.
- Employee parking should be well-lit and sufficiently far from the hotel building.

Sickness and Death

On many occasions, housekeepers find a sick guest on their hands. If the guest is too ill to travel home or it is inconvenient for him or her to do so, as in the case of an overseas traveller, he or she should be seen by the doctor on call at the hotel or by a local doctor. If medical aid is on the way, the housekeeper may have to administer first-aid to the ailing guest. Hotel guests who are ill should be regularly visited by the housekeeping staff. In case of a contagious illness, it is advisable that the local health authorities be informed by the general manager or the doctor.

Sometimes illnesses or accidents lead to death. Staff who encounter such a situation should not touch anything in the room as they might be helpful in establishing the cause of death. The employee should lock the door and inform the executive housekeeper, who in turn conveys the information to the general manager. The police are then informed about the death. The door of the guestroom where a death has occurred should be double-locked and sealed until the police have arrived. The staff should assist in any subsequent investigations being carried out by the authorities.

SUMMARY

All hospitality establishments need to provide a safe and secure environment for both guests as well as employees. Human assets, of course, take priority over the physical assets as regards safety and security.

The executive housekeeper needs to ensure the safety of his or her workers. To ensure employee safety, the housekeeper should organize safety training programmes. Safety training should be given regarding the use of equipment and chemicals, procedures for various jobs, and awareness of potential hazards. The supervisors should be able to plan safety training programmes for employees and new recruits as well. The housekeeper must also ensure that his or her department follows the safety management programme laid down by the hotel.

The department must have a 'housekeeping safety manual' designed specifically for the hotel. The housekeeper and the team need to analyse each task for safety concerns so as to develop a job safety analysis report. Hazards need to be listed and employees should be trained in safe methods of dealing with them. In case an accident happens in spite of taking all precautions, the employees should know the procedure to be followed and the first-aid to be administered.

This chapter discussed fire prevention and fire-fighting in particular. The classification of fires and the types of equipment used to deal with them were described.

First-aid principles were also dealt with in detail. The procedures for administering artificial respiration were explained. It is vital that all employees understand the importance of CPR. It could mean life or death for an unfortunate victim.

Dealing with emergencies in general, bomb threats, as well as steps and precautions against terrorist attacks have been discussed. Another major security concern, keys and their control have been described in much detail.

Guest and employee thefts are common occurrences in many hotels and the managements are always devising policies to tackle these problems. Guest and employee thefts have been discussed and ways to reduce their incidence suggested.

KEY TERMS

Angina Pain in the chest associated with heart disease.

BCF extinguishers A type of halon fire-extinguisher containing BCF (bromochlorodifluoromethane). These extinguishers are now banned.

Contingency plan Planning done for uncertain events.

CPR Cardio-pulmonary resuscitation. By this method of administering artificial respiration, flow of oxygenated blood is rapidly restored to the brain by means of artificial ventilation and chest compression.

E-key or emergency key A highly protected key, this opens all the doors in the property, even those that the guests have double-locked. In addition, it also double-locks the room against all other keys. The emergency key, or E-key, overrides the catch or deadbolt fastened by the guest for privacy.

First-aid This is the initial assistance or treatment given to a casualty for any injury or sudden illness before the arrival of an ambulance, doctor, or other qualified person.

Floor master key The floor key opens all rooms on a particular floor that are not double-locked. Floor keys typically open the storeroom for that floor too.

Gate pass An authorization given to the employee to let him or her take guest or hotel property out of the hotel.

Grandmaster key This key opens all hotel guestrooms and often all housekeeping storage rooms. It can also double-lock a room if access to it has to be denied. This key can be used in emergency situations when it is vital for a manager to enter some or all areas of the hotel. It is itself kept under lock-and-key at the front desk of hotels.

Hazards Sources of danger or unsafe conditions.

HAZMAT A hazardous material is any substance that can cause injury, impairment of health or death to living organisms, or can damage the environment.

Hypoglycaemia Decrease in blood-sugar level, leading to symptoms such as uneasiness, sweating, and giddiness.

Job safety analysis A detailed report that lists every job function performed in the housekeeping department and lists potential hazards, safe methods, tips, and 'how-to's for each task involved in the jobs.

Key control The process of reducing guest and property theft and other security-related incidents by carefully monitoring and tracking the use of keys at a hospitality establishment.

Master keys A class of keys that open all guestroom doors that are not double-locked.

MSDS Materials Safety Data Sheet is a form containing detailed safety information about a chemical.

OHSMS Occupational health and safety management systems.

OSH standards Occupational safety and health standards.

Pass key This key is kept by the deputy or assistant housekeeper and will open any internal door that has not been double-locked.

PPE Personal Protective Equipment.

Safety The term 'safety' is used with reference to such things as disasters, emergencies, fire prevention, and protection and for conditions that provide for freedom from injury and damage to property.

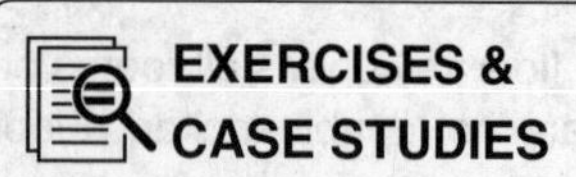

Scanty baggage A room status indicating a room that has been assigned to a guest with small, light luggage that could be carried away by hand without indicating an obvious departure, should a guest walk out with it.

Secondary aid Specific treatment given to a person by a doctor in case of illness, accidents, or other emergencies after first-aid has been given.

Section master key This key opens all rooms in one work section of a hotel. A supervisor may be issued more than one key of this type as he or she may be required to inspect the work of more than one GRA.

Security The term 'security' is used with reference to freedom from fear, anxiety, and doubts concerning humans, as well as protection against thefts of guest, employee, or hotel property.

Skipper A guest who leaves the hotel without making arrangements to settle his or her account.

SOPs Standard operating procedures.

Sub-master key See Section master key.

Supply keys These keys are used within the servicing sector of the hotel by the supervisory-level staff to ensure that stocks and equipment are safely stored away when not in use. Store keys, office keys, and linen room keys are examples of such keys.

Xiphoid process A cartilaginous structure at the lower end of the breastbone or sternum.

23 Ergonomics in Housekeeping

Learning Objectives

After reading this chapter, you should be able to
- understand the meaning and significance of ergonomics at workplace
- discuss the significance of ergonomics in housekeeping operations
- comprehend the risk factor analysis; work simplification and application of ergonomics in housekeeping operations

Introduction

Everyone does some of the work that housekeepers in hotels do. Thus, it is usual to assume that the work of a hotel housekeeper is no more risky than performing these tasks at home. However, contrary to popular perception, housekeeping is a physically demanding and a very tiring job. According to time and motion studies, a guest room attendant (GRA) changes his/her body position every three seconds while cleaning a guestroom. Assuming that the average cleaning time for each room is 25 minutes, it may be estimated that a GRA assumes 8000 different body postures in every eight-hour shift. Apart from the routine guestroom cleaning, which involves making beds, lifting heavy mattresses, changing bed and bathroom linen, cleaning bathrooms, replacing toiletries, etc., GRAs also load cleaning supplies, fresh linen, amenities, etc. on to heavy carts and push them across thickly carpeted floors of hotel corridors. This work profile makes housekeeping an extremely demanding job physically, leading not only to fatigue but a high incidence of musculo-skeletal disorders (MSDs) and musculo-skeletal injuries (MSIs) among hotel housekeepers. In fact, a study in USA covering about 87 hotels found the average rate of injury among housekeepers nearly double than that of non-housekeepers.

Several more studies have found a vast majority of housekeepers suffering from work related physical pain, as a result of the strenuous work that they are subjected to. This is a cause of growing concern among the employers, as well as employees, who find it hard to cope with the pressures of their job.

What is heartening, however, is that most of these disorders and injuries arising out of strenuous, mechanical, and energy sapping work can be mitigated or reduced to a great extent by applying the principles of ergonomics. Ergonomics prevents these types of injuries by fitting the job to the person using proper equipment and work practices. This results in the safest way to work and prevents workplace injuries. Today, more and more hotel organizations are adopting the principles of ergonomics in order to improve working conditions for employees and are finding that it makes good economic sense too. 'Take care of the employees and they will take care of our guests,' J.W. Marriott, the founder of Marriott

International hotel chain is reported to have said. Ergonomics also plays a significant role in achieving the goals of lean thinking in a hotel property by reducing costs and improving productivity through eliminating waste (e.g., unnecessary motions) and reducing mistakes (improving quality). In this chapter we will learn what ergonomics is, and how the application of its principles can make the task of a hotel housekeeper a lot easier and simpler one at that.

Ergonomics

The term 'ergonomics' is derived from two Greek words, '*ergon*', meaning work, and '*nomoi*', meaning natural laws. Ergonomics is the study of how working conditions, equipment, and information can be arranged in an order that people can work with them safely and more efficiently. Ergonomists study human capabilities and limitations in relationship to work demands. They contribute to the design and evaluation of tasks, jobs, products, environments, and systems in order to make them compatible with the needs, abilities, and limitations of people. Improperly designed equipment, furniture, or physical procedures can cause physical strain and fatigue in workers. Such strains can lead to long-term physical disabilities, referred to as musculo-skeletal disorders (MSDs). The prevalence of MSDs, also called Repetitive Stress Injuries (RSIs), is very high among people who are exposed to certain tasks for long periods of time. Two elements—static work and force—are known to contribute to MSDs and RSIs. According to American ergonomist, Holly A. Sweeny, 'static work' refers to the musculo-skeletal effort required to hold a certain position, even a comfortable one. For example, when we sit and work at computers, keeping our head and torso upright requires either small or great amounts of static work depending upon the efficiency of the body positions we choose. 'Force' refers to the amount of tension our muscles generate. For example, tilting your head forward or backward from a neutral, vertical position quadruples the amount of force acting on your lower neck vertebrae. This increase of force is due to the increase in muscular tension necessary to support your head in a tilted position (Sweeny 2005).

Proper ergonomic design helps to prevent injuries that are caused by such repetitive strains.

Many of the occupational risk factors, especially the physical ones (high force, awkward postures, excessive repetition and vibration) can be reduced or eliminated altogether by applying ergonomic principles (especially proper workplace design and appropriate use of assistance devices).

Principles of Ergonomics

Over the years, ergonomists have defined postures which minimize unnecessary static work and reduce the forces acting on the body by applying the following ergonomic principles (Sweeny 2005):

- All work activities should permit the worker to adopt several different, but equally healthy and safe postures.
- Where muscular force has to be exerted, it should be done by the largest appropriate muscle groups available.
- Work activities should be performed with the joints at about mid-point of their range of movement. This applies particularly to the head, trunk, and upper limbs.

These can be achieved by adopting the following practices.

- Avoiding prolonged static postures
- Promoting use of neutral joint postures
- Locating work, parts, tools, and controls at optimal anthropometric locations

- Providing adjustable work surfaces and tool sizes
- Providing comfortable seating, arm rest, back rest, and foot rest
- Utilizing feet and legs, in addition to hands and arms
- Using gravity
- Conserving momentum in body motions
- Providing strategic location (power zone) for lifting, lowering, and releasing loads

The power zone is the lifting region that is considered optimal by ergonomists. This area extends from approximately standing elbow height to standing knuckle height and as close to the body as possible. The power zone optimizes worker strength and durability with the most comfort, by providing the arms and back with maximum leverage. Very often, housekeeping activities such as lifting or lowering occur in locations that are out of the power zone.

Apart from safety and efficiency, the use of ergonomic principles leads to work simplification. Work simplification is defined as the use of equipment, ergonomics, functional planning, and behaviour modification to reduce the physical and psychological stresses caused by activities at home or work. Reducing the physical demands on the body during regularly performed tasks acts to preserve the joints, eliminate fatigue, and reduce the risk of injury or re-injury. Within the workplace simple guidelines can be used regarding task set-up, equipment design, equipment storage, work techniques and routines that can assist in reducing the physical strain in the body. The main aim of work simplification at workplace is to 'work smarter, not harder'.

Ergonomics in Hotel Housekeeping

The very nature of their duties puts hotel housekeepers in high risk category of MSDs and RSIs. Hence, the principles of ergonomics can be applied to mitigate the physical stress level among the housekeeping employees. We shall study the role of ergonomics under the following heads:

- Significance and need of ergonomics in housekeeping
- Analysis of risk factors in housekeeping: ergonomical perspective
- Mitigation of risks in housekeeping by applying ergonomic principles

Significance and Need of Ergonomics in Housekeeping

We have seen thus far, the daily duties of hotel housekeepers make them very vulnerable to contracting physical pains and disorders related to work. A GRA, on an average, cleans 15 or more rooms a day, and does so under the intense time pressure that characterizes hotel work. Table 23.1 enlists the various tasks that GRAs perform in each guestroom. In addition to the in-room tasks, they also load cleaning supplies, fresh linen, and amenities on to heavy carts and push them across thickly carpeted floors of hotel corridors.

The way housekeeping work is organized, i.e., 'room quota' system, it also contributes to pain and high injury incidents among GRAs. According to this system, the GRAs are allotted a certain number of rooms to clean each day. The greater the room quota, the faster the work needs to be done by an individual. If a GRA has a 16 room quota, he/she must clean each room in less than 30 minutes. Housekeepers routinely report that they race through their tasks in order to complete them on time. While rushing through lifting a heavy mattress or cleaning a slippery bathroom floor, GRAs are more likely to get hurt. In addition to static postures, awkward postures are assumed while lifting mattresses, cleaning tiles, and

Table 23.1 Tasks performed by GRAs in guestrooms

Bedroom tasks	Bathroom tasks
• Remove all room service items from guestroom.	• Pick up soiled towels and place on cart.
• Strip bed/s of all sheets, blankets, or duvets.	• Replace soiled towels.
• Place bottom sheet on each bed, mitre 4 times, and tuck in 4–8 times.	• Clean and disinfect WC bowl.
• Place top sheet and blanket on each bed and tuck in 4–8 times.	• Wipe down top and side of WC.
• Spread duvet on each bed.	• Restock toilet roll.
• Remove 4–8 pillow cases per bed and stuff pillows into fresh pillow cases.	• Wipe vanitory unit.
• Dust nightstands and writing desk.	• Clean and dry tooth glasses.
• Restock stationery and other literature.	• Clean sink and polish faucets.
• Dust dresser and TV.	• Replenish toiletries (soaps, shampoos, etc.)
• Clean TV screen.	• Clean mirror.
• Empty trash from room waste bin and ashtrays.	• Scrub bathtub.
• Collect, wash, and dry dirty glasses.	• Clean bath area and walls.
• Dust vents.	• Clean shower curtain.
• Vacuum all floors.	• Empty sanitation bin.
	• Dust vents.
	• Mop floor.

vacuuming in every shift. Further, in order to complete their room quotas, GRAs, many a time, end up skipping meals and breaks that are requisite rest periods. Time pressures are even more intensified when clean linen and towels are under-stocked and supplies are short. Chronic understaffing and increase in number of guest supplies and time consuming amenities have placed housekeepers at a great risk of injury.

In a landmark 1999 study, researchers at the University of California in San Francisco conducted a survey of over 200 housekeeping staff and reported that more than 75% of them experienced work-related pain. In 73% cases, pain was severe enough to necessitate a visit to the doctor. Another study in 2002 surveyed about 1000 housekeeping employees in Las Vegas, and found that 95% of the staff experienced work-related physical pain. Out of these 47% reported severe or very severe work-related physical pain. The latter was most often localized at the lower back (63%), followed by upper back (59%) and neck (43%). A high percentage (83%) complained of constant time pressures.

In 2005, another survey of 600 housekeepers in several cities across North America, including Los Angeles, Boston, and Toronto reported that 91% of them suffered work associated physical pain. Of these, 86% said that their pain started after joining work as hotel housekeepers. In an analysis based on data from 87 unionized hotels operated by Hilton, Hyatt, Intercontinental, Marriott, and Starwood over a seven year period (1999–2005), it was found that the average injury rate of hotel housekeepers was 10.4% as compared to non-housekeepers (other departments) whose average injury rate was 5.6%.

The focus should not be on measuring the number of accidents but on measuring the behaviours and potential causes that may lead to accidents. It is here that the application of ergonomics contributes significantly towards reducing work-related physical stress, which in turn translates into improved productivity and efficiency among employees.

Analysis of Risk Factors in Housekeeping: Ergonomic Perspective

Prevention of injury and accidents is easier if action is taken early through effective analysis of risk factors. An extensive ergonomic risk factor analysis for all housekeeping tasks needs to be carried out by the executive housekeeper who is responsible for all the staff working in the housekeeping department. The ergonomic risk factor analysis involves finding answers to the following questions:

- What kind of work do employees do in the housekeeping department?
- What are the risk factors in each of these tasks?
- How can these risk factors be reduced ?

There are three major risk factors that lead to MSDs:

Awkward posture This refers to postures beyond neutral. The more the joint angle is away from the neutral, the more awkward the posture. Such postures increase the stress on ligaments and joints. This can lead to fatigue and discomfort, and increase the risk of injury. Making beds, cleaning carpets, floors, and bathrooms is hard on the shoulders, back, and knees as shown in Figures 23.1(a), 23.4(a), and 23.5(a).

Excessive repetition In this case the same muscles are used over and over again in repetitive work. Repeated forceful movements, especially in awkward postures, increase the risk of injury.

For example, making beds, changing linen, replenishing toiletries, etc. increase such risk. Refer to Figures 23.2(a) and Fig. 23.6(a).

High force This refers to placing extra pressure and strain on a particular body part. High forces come into play while lifting [Figure 23.3(a)]; lowering, carrying [Figures 23.7(a) and 23.8(a)]; pushing [Figure 23.9(a)], or pulling heavy objects such as carts, especially in awkward postures. High forces are also required to hold a posture, especially for long periods. Muscles produce force to move or hold a posture, thus high forces can result in injury.

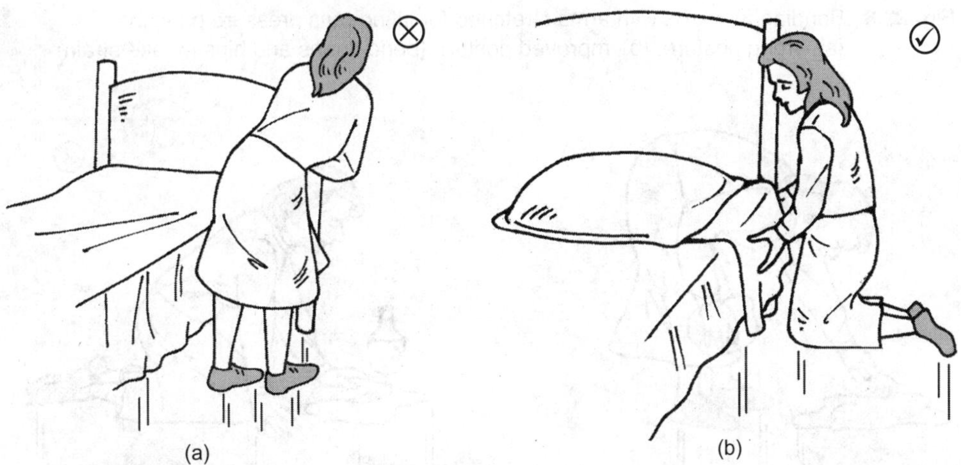

Fig. 23.1 Making beds is hard on back, knees, and shoulders: (a) awkward and strenuous posture; (b) improved and correct posture

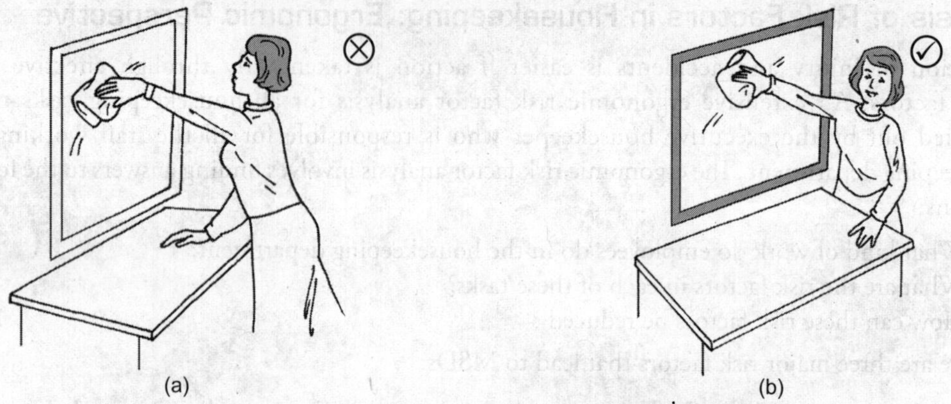

Fig. 23.2 Set-up tasks that avoid twisting of the spine, and bending forwards while cleaning mirrors: (a) awkward shoulder and risk posture; (b) improved or right posture

Fig. 23.3 Bending forwards with arms stretched for lifting puts pressure on spine: (a) wrong posture; (b) improved posture (bend knees and hips to take strain)

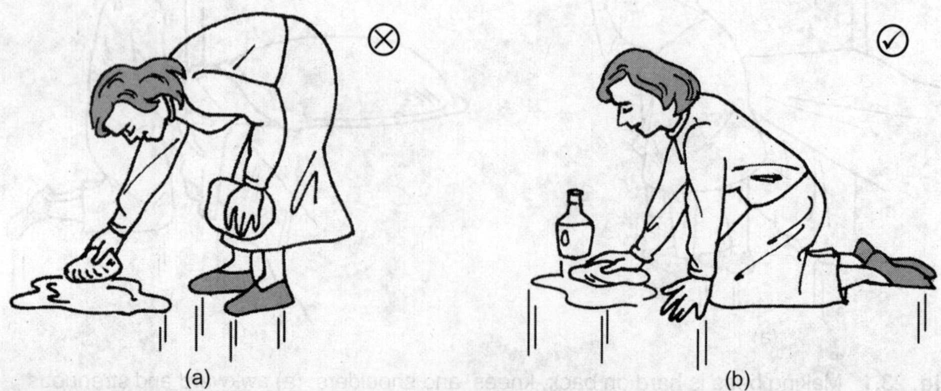

Fig. 23.4 Scrubbing tiles is hard on back and shoulders: (a) avoid reaching the floor with bent back; (b) kneel down to reach the tiles

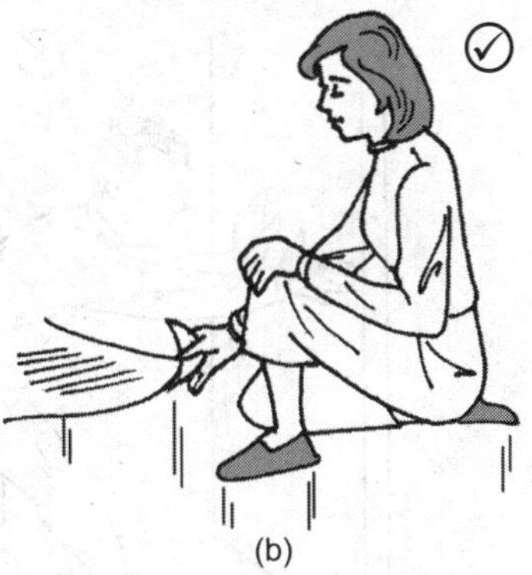

(a) (b)

Fig. 23.5 Dusting carpets is hard on the back and shoulders: (a) do not kneel with back stretched; (b) improve posture by going down on one knee

(a) (b)

Fig. 23.6 Bending down to reach lower shelves of cupboard: (a) do not bend forwards and arch your back; (b) improve posture by bending at knees to reach low shelves

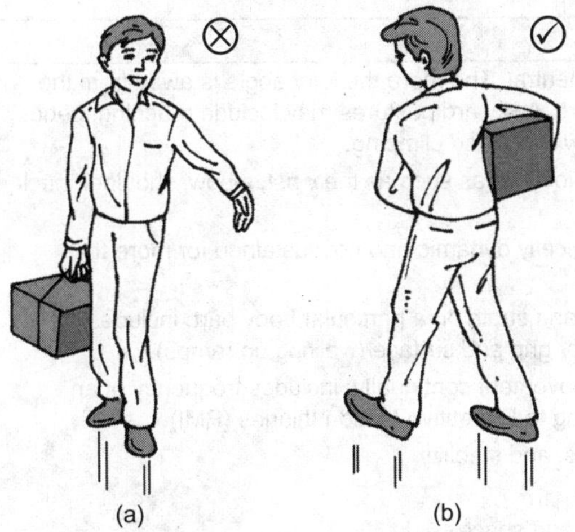

(a) (b)

Fig. 23.7 Keep objects close to body while carrying: (a) leaning to one side with arm stretched down on the other is incorrect; (b) support the object on the hip and use both hands to carry

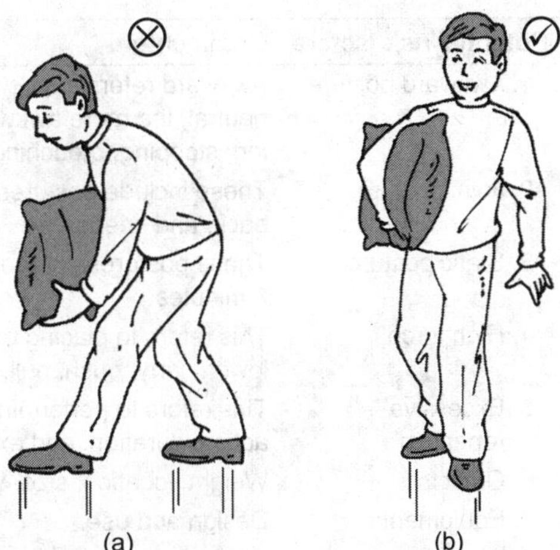

(a) (b)

Fig. 23.8 Carrying objects below hips strains the back: (a) incorrect posture; (b) weight carried on hip shifts to both legs

Fig. 23.9 Moving heavy furniture: (a) do not push with bent back and outstretched arms; (b) keeping the back straight and arms bent, shifts strain on the legs

Other potential risk factors include vibration, cold stress, lack of rest, non-occupational factors (sports, hobbies, home chores, driving, and lack of sleep), personal factors (gender, age, health history, and fitness level), psychological factors (work culture and climate, job attitude and satisfaction, personality traits, personal problems). Table 23.2 lists the risk factors involved in housekeeping tasks.

Exhibit 23.1 presents a sample worksheet of ergonomic risk factor analysis for housekeeping tasks. It is crucial that appropriate controls be put into place in the analysis. A job safety analysis programme (refer Chapter 22) should be coordinated with the ergonomic risk factor analysis. Both these should then be incorporated into the basic training programmes of the hotel property.

Table 23.2 Risk factors in housekeeping tasks

Potential risk factors	Comments
1. Awkward posture	Awkward refers to postures beyond neutral. The more the joint angle is away from the neutral, the more awkward the posture. Awkward postures may include reaching, bending, stooping, crouching, squatting, twisting, and climbing.
2. Joint posture	These include postures affecting the joint areas such as the wrist, elbow, shoulder, neck, back, and knees.
3. Static posture	These postures and positions are typically dynamic and not sustained for more than 2 minutes.
4. High force	This refers to placing extra pressure and strain on a particular body part; includes lift, lower, carry, push, pull, pinch or power grip and surface (walking up ramps).
5. Excessive repetition	This refers to performing the same movement continually; includes frequency of an action, duration, and exposure; leading to Repetitive Motion Injuries (RMI).
6. Objects	Weight, location, size, shape, handles, and stability.
7. Equipments	Design and use.
8. Work area	Work surface height, layout, seating, and space.
9. Environment	Layout, flooring, temperature (cold stress), noise, vibration, chemicals, light, and glare.
10. Work organization	Schedules, workload (lack of rest), and interruptions.

Exhibit 23.1 Sample ergonomic risk factor analysis for housekeeping tasks

Identification		Assesssment		Controls			
Housekeeping tasks/Potential causes	**Risk factors**	**Frequency/ Duration**	**Observations**	**Recommended controls (Samples)**	**Control priority***	**Person responsible****	**Status**
Cleaning rooms and floors	• Awkward posture • Static posture • High force			• Allot a group of GRAs to standardize cleaning of rooms and floors (stress on: minimize twists, using appropriate muscles, focus on working arc, minimizing stress on hands, and so on). • Look out for alternate designs in cleaning tools (such as a toilet brush with a bent handle, mops with wringer mechanism, long handled equipment). • Dry mop in use should have full swivel (360°) at base and is statically charged. • Train staff on using neutral postures and stretching exercises. • Recommend use of appropriate footwear. • Recommend use floor signs to indicate wet areas.			
Cleaning bathrooms/ utility rooms	• High force • Awkward posture			• Recommend use of half filled buckets. • Recommend tipping the bucket to drain, instead of lifting and draining. • Provide mop buckets with wringer mechanism and that empty from bottom. • Provide floor-level sinks and drains. • Use of long handled tools will minimize bending. • Use of angled tools will improve posture.			
Making beds	• Awkward posture • Excessive repetition			• Allot teams to handle bed making for larger beds, instead of individual GRAs. • Provide beds with caster wheels. • Provide knee pads.			

(Contd.)

Exhibit 23.1 *Contd.*

Identification		Assesssment		Controls			
Housekeeping tasks/Potential causes	**Risk factors**	**Frequency/ Duration**	**Observations**	**Recommended controls (Samples)**	**Control priority***	**Person responsible****	**Status**
Moving furniture	• High force • Awkward posture			• Use of lift assist equipments. • Allot additional manpower.			
Equipment design	• Awkward posture • High force			• Following points should guide the purchase decision: Light-weight machines, adjustability features, appropriate wheels for maneuvering, low vibration ratings, low noise emissions, minimal manual handling required, appropriate handle length and design, rubber grips on handles and convenient location of controls. • Trials conducted before purchasing			
Workload Time pressure	• Work organization			• Plan how and when work is conducted. E.g., shorter periods of mopping and buffing are preferred. • Provide for task variety and a change in posture and muscular effort.			
Carrying loads on ramps (e.g., garbage bins)	• High force			• Check with projects/engineering department if ramps can be made longer to decrease the incline.			
Lifting and carrying loads (e.g., soiled linen)	• High force			• Smaller lots to be made with a weight limit. • Provide light-weight carts with appropriate wheels to minimize carrying loads			

Note: Control Priority: 1. recommended for immediate implementation to reduce risk factors.
2. recommended for consideration as a means of reducing risk factors.
3. not for immediate action but for future consideration.

* To be filled in by the housekeeping supervisor

** Organizations will have their own hierarchies in this regard

Mitigation of Risks in Housekeeping by Applying Ergonomic Principles

Housekeeping is a highly challenging task. It can be classified as 'moderately heavy' to 'heavy' work because the energy required is approximately four kilocalories per minute. There is no escaping the work to be carried out by the housekeepers. However, housekeepers can modify their tasks and personal habits in conformity with ergonomic principles to avoid injuries as also reduce their workload. Application of ergonomics to modify housekeeping activities can broadly be studied under the following heads.

- Modifying the workplace layout and equipment
- Modifying loads lifted/way of lifting
- Modifying personal habits
- Controlling the work environment
- Redesigning work practices

Modifying the workplace layout and equipment

Using proper equipment and work practices results in the safest way to work and prevents workplace injuries. Employers must provide user-friendly equipment and establish safe work practices to reduce the risks of MSI. Employers must also instruct workers in these safe work practices, while workers should also abide by employers' instructions to protect themselves. The following are some useful tips in this regard.

- Move the work to a comfortable height to avoid unnecessary stress. Avoid bending over the work, especially so when making beds, scrubbing floors, etc. Refer to Figures 23.1(b), 23.4(b), and 23.6(b) for the right postures for these tasks.
- Maintain a working height at about elbow height (although it is higher for precision work and lower when force is needed).
- Set up work tasks to avoid twisting of the spine, bending forwards, or reaching away from the body, especially while cleaning mirrors, lifting, or dusting carpets. Refer to Figures 23.2(b), 23.3(b), and 23.5(b).
- Store heavier and frequently used items at waist level.
- Keep most-used material within arm's reach.
- Move the work or yourself to avoid reaching.
- If you must reach frequently, check that you reach no more than 30cm to the front of the body (in a seated position) and no more than 50 cm to the front of the body (in a standing position).
- Stand on an appropriate ladder to avoid reaching overhead.
- Use tools or mechanical equipment to reduce the physical force required to complete tasks, for instance, trolleys.
- Lighter vacuum cleaners (preferably the self-propelling type), and lighter service carts with wheels designed for carpeted floors ease the workload of their operators provided this equipment is always kept in good repair.
- Store infrequently used equipment below mid-thigh height or above shoulder height
- Install locking devices on equipment that may be unstable.
- Use lightweight, well maintained equipment with large low-resistive wheels.
- Provide a storage area for handling equipment that is close to the work area.
- Conveniently locate attachments and aids so that staff can easily assist themselves if necessary.

Modifying loads lifted/way of lifting

Lifting loads and pushing carts is among the most injury prone activities in housekeeping. The following tips can greatly help reduce risk of injury while doing heavy work.

- Break large loads into smaller ones to reduce the impact on the body.
- Store frequently lifted material at a level between the waist and shoulders.
- Carry heavy objects close to the body as showed in Figures 23.7(b) and 23.8(b).
- Always push rather than pull loads [Figure 23.9(b)] and use carts with vertical handles to reduce strain.
- Ensure that carts are maintained properly. Tyres should be fully inflated and the wheels should not be bent or misaligned. This will decrease the amount of force required to push the cart.
- Report faulty carts to the supervisor.
- Lift the load with both hands instead of one.
- Alter the handles on loads to make it easier to carry the load.
- Lift the load using a team lift.
- Remember it is more physically demanding to grip smaller items or large items with the hand at full stretch.
- Vary techniques to use different muscles (e.g., alternate arms when scrubbing, vacuuming, and tucking sheets).
- Pad knees (for example, wear knee pads or use a mat or towel) and change position often when kneeling.
- Wear shoes with enough cushioning to relieve the stress on the knees and back when the work involves standing for long periods.

Modifying personal habits

Housekeepers could significantly reduce their risk of injury by making a habit of the following ergonomic principles.

- Always be aware of your posture while working.
- Stand/sit in neutral posture (shoulders back, chin tucked, head upright, elbows as close to the body as possible).
- Avoid twisting and bending motions that exert a strain on the spine.
- Keep alternating tasks.
- Change body position frequently to relieve muscle strain.
- Avoid using your wrists in a hands bent down (flexed), extended (hands up), or twisted position for long periods of time. Maintain a neutral (straight) wrist position when using tools, typing, writing, or reading.
- Warm up before beginning a repetitive or forceful task. Flexibility exercises improve circulation and help compensate for work that must be done in awkward positions.
- Avoid sudden, jerky movements which might 'overload' your muscles during an activity.
- Reduce speed and force. Use the minimum required force and slow down when doing repetitive tasks.
- Use the whole hand and all fingers to grip, grasp, or lift.
- Alternate arms when carrying something heavy.
- Check shoes to make sure they provide comfort, support, and shock absorption.
- Wear the right gear when working in hot, cold, or noisy environments.

Controlling the work environment

At times, the workplace itself adds to the risk of musculo-skeletal injuries if it is found wanting in terms of adequate space, or proper lighting. Some employee-friendly tips on this count include:

- Provide plenty of space so that bending, reaching, and twisting can be eliminated during tasks (sometimes shifting tasks far enough away that the workers have to walk or move their body means they will do the task in a better posture than if they can keep their feet still and twist or reach).
- Provide sufficient lighting so that staff does not have to lean towards an object to view it or strain the eyes.
- Consider the size and type of wheels for trolleys, for instance, larger wheels will make the trolley easier to move.

Redesigning work practices

A change in mindset, reallocation of work, and redesigning some practices keeping in mind the following principles of ergonomics could significantly reduce risk of injury to housekeepers.

- Rotate or distribute the same tasks within the job between different employees, to allow postural change.
- Build stretch breaks into the work routine especially before and after physically demanding tasks.
- It is advisable to plan one's workload and do the heavier tasks at the beginning of the work shift, rather than at the end, when fatigue is at its maximum. When a person is tired, the risk of injuring a muscle is higher.

SUMMARY

Meeting the needs of their guests round the clock make hotels challenging places to work. Most hotels are designed for the comfort of their guests rather than their staff. The quest for perfection and attending to each and every need of clients makes the job of the staff, especially the housekeepers, very demanding and tiring. In order to attract guests and remain competitive, hotel managements pursue a policy that everything should be 'so clean it sparkles'. However, for the demand for spotless cleanliness and hygiene, management often requires their cleaning staff to spend extra time and effort in cleaning by kneeling, leaning, squatting, crouching, slouching, and stretching. These postures, over a period of time contribute to new musculo-skeletal injuries and aggravate old ones. Routine in-room activities of GRAs such as making beds, changing bed sheets and linen, cleaning bathrooms, etc., in addition to pushing heavy carts on carpeted hotel corridors, place them in high risk category of such disorders.

Industry studies have found a high incidence of musculo-skeletal injuries and disorders among the housekeeping staff of hotels as a result of doing heavy mechanical work in awkward postures and due to excessive repetition. The very nature of their job, in the face of chronic understaffing and growing clientele, makes it very difficult to improve working conditions for housekeepers by means of better engineering. However, improvements can be made by selecting more appropriate equipment and modifying body postures.

Nowadays, leading hotel companies are innovating and providing resources to help keep employees healthy and injury-free at the workplace. Ergonomics prevents these types of injuries by fitting the job to the person by using proper equipment and work practices. Ergonomics is the study of how working conditions, machines, and equipment can be arranged in a manner that people can work with them more efficiently. In applying ergonomic principles, training should be provided to employees who are involved with housekeeping activities. It is important that housekeeping staff be informed about hazards in the workplace, including the risk of injuries to the musculo-skeletal system. Therefore, identification of the hazards for such injury at any given hotel is fundamental. Further, individual work practices, including lifting habits, should be shaped by proper training. Training should encourage employers and workers to adopt methods that reduce fatigue. For example, it is advisable to plan one's workload and do the heavier tasks at the beginning of the work shift, than at the end, when fatigue is at its maximum. When a person is tired, the risk of injuring a muscle is higher. Training should explain the health hazards of improper lifting and give recommendations on what a worker can do to improve lifting positions. It should also emphasize the importance of rest periods for the employees' health and explain how active rest can do more for keeping workers healthy than passive rest. The effect of such training can reach far beyond occupational situations because the employees can apply this knowledge in their off-job activities also.

KEY TERMS

Anthropometry The study of human body measurement.

Ergonomics The study of how working conditions, machines, and equipment can be arranged in a manner that people can work with them safely and more efficiently.

Momentum The quantity of motion of a moving body.

Musculo-skeletal disorders (MSDs) Afflictions or conditions arising from injuries to the muscular and skeletal (musculo-skeletal) systems due to prolonged exposure to activities involving high force, awkward postures, and excessive repetition of actions at workplace.

MSI Musculo-skeletal injuries.

Neutral posture This refers to the resting position of each joint, i.e., the position in which there is the least tension or pressure on nerves, tendons, muscles, and bones.

Power zone It is the lifting region in the human body that is considered optimal by ergonomists. This area extends from approximately standing elbow height to standing knuckle height and as close to the body as possible.

RMI Repetitive Motion Injuries.

Room quota system The standard way in which hotels organize housekeeping activities for guestrooms. Based on this system, GRAs are required to service a certain number of rooms in a shift. Usually room quota ranges from 13 to 16 rooms per GRA.

RSI Repetitive Stress Injuries.

Static posture A posture that is held for a long time. A static posture may result in fatigue and even injury over a period of time as a result of 'static force' that muscles have to generate to maintain such a posture.

Work simplification This is defined as the use of equipment, ergonomics, functional planning, and behaviour modification to reduce the physical and psychological stresses on the body of activities at home or work.

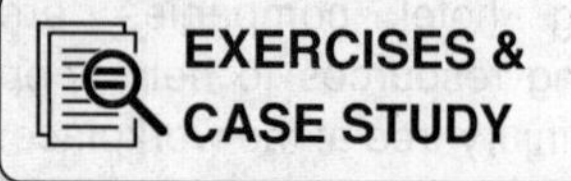

Pest Control and Waste Management

Learning Objectives

After reading this chapter, you should be able to
- identify the living creatures in or in the vicinity of the hotel that are pests
- establish goals for pest control
- explain the characteristics of common pests found in hotels
- practise the basics of integrated pest management using different methods of pest control
- undertake hygienic waste disposal and recycling of wastes

Introduction

Keeping down pests, or 'pest control', is important because pests cause disease and discomfort. Pests are usually such ubiquitous organisms in nature that they may attack the cleanest of establishments. The housekeeping department plays an important role in detecting the presence of pests in or around the establishment and organizing their control or eradication. The pest control function at hotels is usually outsourced to a reputed pest control contractor. The housekeeper, in consultation with the contractor, prepares a pest control frequency schedule and ensures that it is followed. A sample of this schedule is given in Exhibit 24.1. The supervisor in-charge of pest control maintains a pest control log book to record details. The format of same is presented in Exhibit 24.2.

Pest Control

A pest is any organism that

- competes with humans, domestic animals, or desirable plants for food or water;
- injures humans, domestic animals, desirable plants, structures, or possessions;
- transmits diseases to humans, domestic animals, wildlife, or desirable plants; and
- annoys humans or domestic animals.

Types of Pests

The various types of pests include

- insects such as cockroaches, termites, beetles, and fleas;
- arthropods (eight-legged insect-like organisms) such as mites, ticks, and some spiders;

- microbial organisms such as bacteria;
- weeds, that is, any plants growing where they are not wanted;
- molluscs such as snails, slugs, and ship-worms; and
- vertebrates such as mice, and other rodents.

Exhibit 24.1 A sample pest control frequency schedule

Hotel Spring Leaves International

PEST CONTROL FREQUENCY SCHEDULE

Pest control contract company ....

Twice daily	Daily	Bi-weekly	Weekly	Bi-monthly	Monthly	Quarterly
• Garbage room & surrounding areas (especially after removal) • Scrap yard • Kitchen (spraying) • Receiving & storage areas	• F&B areas • Health club & pool areas • Terrace, gardens and compound area (fogging) • Compound wall – inside and outer perimeter (fogging)	• Basement areas • Lobby, other public areas, washrooms, staircases, floor corridors • Cabanas • Service area landings and staircases • Fire exit staircases • Administrative offices	• All rooms on rotation (spraying) • 1st floor rooms – Monday • 2nd floor rooms – Tuesday • 3rd floor rooms – Wednesday • 4th floor rooms – Thursday	• F&b areas (thorough fumigation) • Deep freeze and refrigerator gaskets	• False ceiling and shafts of rooms (spraying) • Manholes and drains (spraying and powder dusting)	• Crash spraying – terrace to basement (within 3 consecutive days) • All rooms (fumigation) • All rooms (Bed bug gel treatment)

Signature of pest control operator .... Signature of Assistant housekeeper ....

Exhibit 24.2 Format of pest control log book

Hotel Spring Leaves International

PEST CONTROL LOG BOOK

Date	Time	Description of pest problem	Location of pest found	Date of pest treatment appointment	Job completed on	Accompanying staff	Signature of area in-charge

Most organisms are not pests. A species may be a pest in some situations and not in others. An organism should not be considered a pest until it is proven to be one. Categories of pests include the following:

- Continuous pests that are nearly always present and require regular control.
- Sporadic, migratory, or cyclical pests which require control occasionally or intermittently.
- Potential pests, that is, pests that do not require control under normal conditions, but may require control in certain circumstances.

It is important to identify the pest before trying to control it. The more one knows about the pest and the factors that influence its development and spread, the easier, more cost-effective, and more successful the pest control will be. To identify and control pests, one needs to know the following details:

- The physical features of the pests likely to be encountered.
- Characteristics of the damage they cause.
- Their development cycle and biology.
- Whether they are continuous, sporadic, or potential pests.
- The goals of the pest management programme.

Pest Control Goals

Whenever you try to control a pest, you should achieve one of these three goals, or some combination of them:

- Prevention: Keeping a pest from becoming a problem.
- Suppression: Reducing pest numbers or damage to an acceptable level.
- Eradication: Destroying an entire pest population.

Prevention This may be a goal when the pest's presence or abundance can be predicted in advance. Continuous pests, by definition, are usually very predictable. Sporadic and potential pests may be predictable if you know the circumstances or conditions that favour their presence as pests.

Suppression This is a common goal in many pest situations. The intent is to reduce the number of pests to a level where the harm they cause is just about acceptable. Once a pest's presence is detected and control is deemed necessary, suppression and prevention are often joint goals. The right combination of control measures can often suppress the pests already present and prevent them from building up again to a level where they are causing unacceptable harm.

Eradication This is a rare goal for outdoor pest situations in particular, because it is difficult to achieve. Usually the goal is prevention and/or suppression. Eradication is occasionally attempted when a foreign pest has been accidentally introduced into a local environment, but is not yet established in an area. Such eradication strategies are often supported by the government.

Eradication is a more common goal indoors. Enclosed environments are usually smaller, less complex, and more easily controlled than outdoor areas. In many enclosed areas, such as dwellings, schools, office buildings, and health care, food-processing, and food-preparation facilities, certain pests cannot be tolerated.

Threshold Levels

Thresholds are the levels of pest populations beyond which you should take pest-control action if you want to prevent the pests in an area from causing unacceptable injury or harm. Threshold levels may be based on aesthetic, health, or economic considerations. These levels, which are also known as 'action thresholds', have been determined for many pests.

A threshold often is set at the level where the economic losses caused by pest damage, if the pest population continued to grow, would be greater than the cost of controlling the pests. These types of action thresholds are called 'economic thresholds'. In some pest-control situations, the threshold level is zero—even a single pest in such a situation is unreasonably harmful. For example, the presence of any rodents in food-processing facilities forces action. In hotels and homes, people generally take action to control some pests, such as rodents or cockroaches, even if only one or a few have been seen.

Common Pests and their Control

Some commonly found pests in hotels and ways of controlling them are discussed as follows:

Bed Bugs

These are tiny parasitic creatures that feed on the blood of humans and other animals. They are more of a nuisance than a danger, although they can cause severe irritation in some people leading to loss of sleep and lack of energy, particularly in children. They are not known to spread disease, however. They cannot fly and must either crawl or be passively transported in clothing or on luggage. By day, they hide in the crevices of beds, furniture, upholstery, wallpaper, and skirting boards, emerging when hungry, usually every few days, to feed. Bed bugs feed at night, sucking blood from exposed surfaces of the skin.

Bed bugs are 4–5 mm long and 3 mm wide with a flat head and flat, oval body. Young bed bugs are yellow to white in colour and as they mature, change in colour towards a light red or brown. After feeding, however, they take on a purple hue. They also give off a very unpleasant odour. Fully fed bed bugs can leave small bloodstains on sheets or walls as they excrete excess fluid before returning to their narrow crevices. Their eggs are laid in these crevices and remain stuck to these surfaces with a cement-like exudate from the body of the bed bug.

To eradicate an infestation, it is necessary to treat the premises thoroughly by fumigation. A professional pest-control officer should do this, as thorough treatment of all bed-bug hiding places requires experience. Pouring boiling water into crevices is a temporary solution to get rid of bed bugs. A thick application of kerosene oil emulsion is also effective against bed bugs.

Beetles

Many types of beetles are involved in causing damage to materials. These include biscuit beetles, carpet beetles, and wood-boring beetles.

Biscuit beetles These are brown with a dense layer of yellow hairs on their body, and adults are 2–3½ mm long. They are not dangerous, but they can be a nuisance when they infest a food cupboard. They are pests that mainly attack cereal products.

Carpet beetles The adult carpet beetle is 2–4 mm long, with a highly convex body. Its colour is variable, often brown or black and mottled with yellow or white scales on its back. These scales sometimes get rubbed off and the beetles then appear dull black in colour. It has greyish yellow scales on its abdomen and prominent antennae. When disturbed, the beetle pulls its legs close beneath its body and remains motionless. It attacks furs, carpets, and all kinds of woollen textiles. The hairy, squat larva is commonly called a 'woolly bear' and grows to approximately 5 mm in length.

Carpet beetles are pests of animal, and occasionally, plant products. They usually target animal wool, leather, and so on and the damage often takes the form of irregular holes in these. However, by the time the larvae are observed, considerable damage has often been done. They have emerged as a major pest to hotel textiles, thriving in the uniform temperatures that result from central heating. Carpet beetles flourish in situations where they can remain undisturbed—for example, beneath carpets, around skirting boards, and in wardrobes.

Frequent and thorough vacuum-cleaning of fluff and dust is essential for control of these pests. In case of an infestation, insecticide powders may be sprayed in the affected areas.

Furniture beetles/woodworm As the name suggests, this beetle makes its home in crevices and cracks of furniture made of unpolished wood. The female lays about 20–60 eggs, which on hatching produce the larvae or 'grub' that are responsible for the actual damage to the furniture, as they are voracious eaters. The larva matures, bores towards the surface of the wood, and changes into a pupa. From the pupa emerges the beetle, which makes an exit hole of about 0.15 cm to free itself. The first sign of infestation is usually small piles of yellowish bore dust found beneath the furniture.

Unpolished wood should be treated with commercial anti-woodworm preservative, polish, varnish, or lacquer to prevent the beetles from laying eggs in the furniture. To kill woodworm, the crevices and exit holes should be sprayed with a proprietary woodworm killer fluid. The best time to apply insecticides to wood is around March to May, when the insects are near the surface of the wood just before they emerge, and so are more susceptible to the insecticide. The life cycle of most wood-boring beetles lasts for more than one year, so that to achieve complete eradication, it is essential to repeat the treatment each year until signs of the attack disappear. It is best to call in experts for treatment of furniture. In case a piece of furniture is badly infested, it is better to burn and destroy it lest other pieces catch the infestation.

Silverfish

These are silvery grey insects that look like minute fish without fins. They are about 1 cm or smaller in length. They are nocturnal insects, primarily found in moist areas, and feed on cellulosic materials such as paper and cellulosic fabrics such as cotton. Keeping moist areas clean and treating them with insecticide will help to get rid of these pests. Pyrethrum and sodium fluoride crystals are effective against silverfish.

Cockroaches

These are several species of nocturnal insects that spend most of the day hiding in cracks, around drains, or in other dark, secluded crevices. Two common species of cockroach are the German and the Oriental. They are both large insects, though the Oriental is the larger of the two by some margin. Adult Oriental cockroaches grow 20–24 mm in length, whilst German cockroaches grow only 10–15 mm in length. The Oriental cockroach is distinguished by its size, and also its colour. It is usually dark brown, whereas the German cockroach is a lighter yellowish brown. The German cockroach, unlike its Oriental counterpart, is able to climb smooth vertical surfaces and generally prefers warmer, humid environments. The Oriental cockroach is more frequently found in cooler, less-humid areas such as basements and drains.

Cockroaches carry food-poisoning bacteria in their bodies and are responsible for the spread of dysentery and gastroenteritis. They will feed on almost anything, from faecal matter to food for human consumption. Contamination occurs when the insect comes into contact with food and work surfaces or alternatively by their faecal contamination of foodstuffs.

Cockroaches are the most difficult pests to eradicate. Proprietary cockroach-killer preparations may be used in the infested areas. However, pest control experts need to be called if the infestation persists.

Fleas

These are a common nuisance. Fleas are picked up in a number of ways. They are usually transferred to dogs from grass when they are walked and to cats from a number of infected sources as they roam. If pets are to stay flea-free, they need to be regularly groomed and treated for flea infestations (especially in summer). Their bedding should also be washed at a high temperature at least once a week, as a pet's bedding can support a flea population of some 8,000 immature and 2,000 adult fleas.

On finding an infestation, the property should be sprayed with an insecticide that will kill adult fleas, their eggs, larvae, and pupae. Pest-control experts should be called in to help with the problem.

Lice

These insect pests are attracted to human hair. They are grey and measure about 3 mm each. The adult lice cling to hair with their hooks and their eggs, called 'nits', stick to hair and clothing, linen, or upholstery fibres. They are easily passed on from one person to the other on close contact. In hotels, they may be left on pillows and upholstery and be easily passed from one guest to the other. Lice cause irritating bites on the scalp and the scratching due to it may even lead to infection.

To prevent head lice, pillowcases and head-rest covers on chairs should be changed and cleaned frequently. Headboards should be wiped daily. In case of an infestation, the person should use specially medicated shampoos for lice and others should not use the infested person's personal belongings such as combs or brushes, towels and clothes.

Moths

Most of the moths that invade human habitations such that we may consider them pests belong to the families Tineidae and Pyralidae. Some species damage clothing, carpets, and other furnishings. Others are common pests that attack stored food products and are often found in houses, hotel kitchens, bakeries, grain stores, and warehouses—anywhere that food is stored, especially dried foodstuffs such as grains, cereals, flour, nuts, and so on. The majority of species are small, rather drab-coloured moths, with little that is distinctive about them. Their larvae (or 'grubs') are likewise quite ordinary-looking and generally pale yellow or whitish in colour. Nearly all the common pest moths have been spread worldwide through commercial trading.

Clothes moths Most clothes moths belong to the family Tineidae. The adult moths are generally small insects with a wingspan of 10–20 mm, more or less brownish in colour but often with a golden or silvery sheen. The head is roughly haired, with the proboscis (or feeding tube) reduced or absent altogether. Hence, the adult insects do not feed and it is their larvae (or caterpillars) that damage our fabrics. Clothes moths in general are nocturnal insects and, although males and spent females sometimes come into the light, they are more likely to scuttle for cover than to fly into the open when disturbed.

The larvae are whitish in colour and feed mainly on dried plant and animal materials. Damage to articles may consist of irregular surface feeding (especially on carpets) or holes eaten completely through the fabric, usually in association with the tell-tale signs of silk webbing produced by the caterpillars. Moths are more likely to attack fabrics soiled by perspiration or urine or stained by the spillage of beverages and food rather than clean fabrics. Furthermore, only natural fabrics are at risk, especially those containing wool or cotton—the larvae will not attack synthetic fibres (nylon, polyester, acrylic, and so on), so that clothing and furnishings made from these materials are relatively safe from moth damage unless they are heavily soiled by sweat, urine, food stains, and such.

From the point of view of damage, the most notorious among moth is the common or webbing clothes moth. Its larvae feed on all keratin-containing materials—hair, wool, silk, feathers, and so on—and will also consume cellulosic matter such as cotton and stored cereal products. Another clothes moth called the case-bearing clothes moth is less troublesome in terms of fabric damage but can still be a serious pest. Its common name stems from the larval habit of constructing a tubular case from silk and fragments of surrounding materials. Larvae of the tapestry moth also damage fabrics, but they prefer coarser material than the previous two types of clothes moth.

Fabrics treated with a mothproof finish are a good option in places prone to moth infestations. A dry atmosphere created by central air-conditioning also reduces infestations and so does the use of insecticides. Vacuum-cleaning will effectively remove larvae that are already present as well as hair, fluff, and other debris that could support future infestations. Take care to vacuum infested areas thoroughly, especially under the edges of carpets, along skirting boards, in corners, underneath furniture, and inside closets, wardrobes, cupboards, and other enclosed, dark, and undisturbed areas where larvae prefer to feed or adult moths may hide. Be sure to dispose of the contents of the vacuum-cleaner bag immediately after you have finished cleaning. A freeze treatment can be used for small items such as ornaments and fur articles by placing them in a home freezer for about a week to kill eggs and larvae, followed by a thorough cleaning of the items.

An insecticide treatment of infested areas is often useful as a supplement to good housekeeping. Sprays may be applied to carpets, especially along and beneath the edges adjacent to skirting, underneath furniture, and other likely areas of infestation where prolonged contact with humans or pet animals is unlikely—clothing and bedding should not be sprayed with insecticides.

Moths attacking foodstuffs The main pest species attacking stored food include the flour or meal moth, the Mediterranean flour moth, and the Indian meal moth. The larvae of these and several other species feed on cereals and cereal products and frequently destroy or damage large quantities of food. They also attack nuts and dried fruit. The larvae of these moths are generally whitish or pale yellowish in colour, with few distinguishing features; but often they can be recognized by their vigorous wriggling when disturbed. They feed on a wide variety of materials, including grain and other stored food products, and many of them live in silken tubes and tunnels. It is always advisable to keep foods such as grains, cereals, flour, nuts, and so on in well-sealed plastic or glass containers—this not only keeps out vagrant moths, but also prevents the spread of insects that might be introduced accidentally (often as eggs and/or larvae) with newly purchased goods, as well as allowing you to spot an infestation early.

The best method of avoiding problems with pests attacking stored products is good sanitation. Be sure that the areas where food is prepared, eaten, and stored are cleaned regularly. Delay in mopping up food spills and leaving food exposed in open packets and containers attracts and harbours these pests. Avoid such practices and, as long as there's also regular cleaning, you will probably never have a problem. The use of insecticides in food-preparation and storage areas is to be avoided completely.

Ants

These insects generally invade in large numbers when they come in search of food, especially sweet substances. They enter through crevices and travel along a definite track in a procession so that when runs are found, the ants can be systematically trapped at the point where they enter an establishment. If the runs cannot be found, the vulnerable areas must be emptied of food, thoroughly cleaned, and borax—which repels them—spread over the shelves until the ants cease to come and eventually go to find food elsewhere. If the nest is located, it can be destroyed by placing 2 tablespoonfuls of carbon bisulphide at the entrance. It must be kept in mind that the vapours of this substance, though they kill the ants, are also highly inflammable—hence it should be used with great care. Boiling water poured over the nest repeatedly also kills ants.

Termites

These are social insects, like ants. They are also called 'white ants' because of their appearance. They have a strict 'caste system' that consists of worker termites, soldiers, and winged reproductive termites (alates), including one or more queen and king termites. The queen termite creates the colony by laying eggs and tending to the colony until enough insects are produced to take care of the colony. The queen can live for more than 10 years and produce hundreds of eggs each year. Colonies can each have several million termites with the help of secondary queens, who also produce eggs. The two most common types of termites are dry-wood and ground termites. Both types of termites eat cellulose found in wood and wood products for nutrition.

Of the two types of termites, ground termites typically do much more damage to structures over a shorter period of time. Ground termites randomly and constantly forage for new food sources and may travel upto 100 yards from their primary nest.

At the surface, ground termites create mud tubes going from the soil to wooden portions of a structure. These tubes provide a protective 'highway' for termites to attack a building. Other less obvious access points may be through

- construction joints;
- retaining wall joints and cracks;
- floor cracks over 1/16 inch wide; and
- plumbing, electrical, and other penetrations of concrete slabs.

Ground termites require three things to survive, food (wood or other cellulose material), a consistent source of moisture, and a moderate to tropical environment. These pests can consume over 15 pounds of wood in a single week. Ground termites can create secondary nests above the ground called 'aerial colonies'. These nests may survive independently of the ground if a source of water is available. Common sources in building interiors include roof leaks, plumbing leaks, leaky showers or tubs, toilet leaks, and so on. Aerial infestations must be located for effective control.

Ground termites die rather quickly from dehydration when exposed to the environment, due to their thin exoskeleton. To maintain the necessary humidity and protect them from predators, they build protective mud tubes and remain unseen most of the time. Ground termites produce chemical substances called 'pheromones', which other termites in the colony can smell and follow to find food and water.

To prevent termite infestations, the soil should be treated before the construction of buildings with an appropriate termite-killer fluid. During construction, wood should not be allowed to come within 6 inches of the ground. Wood impregnated with creosote or sodium arsenate should be used and surrounding areas of the ground be kept in contact with these chemicals.

Dry-wood termites do not need an outside source of moisture and can survive on the small amount of moisture within the wood. The colonies live within the wood and do not require contact with soil. Unlike ground termites, the colonies of dry-wood termite are small, consisting of a few hundred to a thousand-odd termites. Evidence of their activity includes sand-like droppings and exit holes in the walls, ceilings, or wood. However, infestations may continue for around 2 years before evidence of droppings is evident.

To prevent an infestation, use treated lumber during construction and coat any untreated and exposed wood with an appropriate insecticide. Seal all cracks and crevices. In case of an infestation, lightly puncture kick-out holes and inject an appropriate insecticide into the hole. Saturate infested furniture with orthodichlorobenzene. Finally, wax and varnish all wood and coat with linseed oil to cover the pores. Old furniture may be drenched in kerosene before refinishing. To strengthen a damaged piece of furniture, pour molten paraffin over the wood, wipe off excess, and then refinish.

Flies

These filthy insects are dangerous to health as they contaminate food, causing diseases such as typhoid, cholera, dysentery, and so on. They carry the disease germs on their legs and in their saliva. These are transferred to the food on which they sit. To eradicate flies, the first essential step is to destroy all possible breeding grounds early in the year before egg-laying begins. Burn all garbage, keep dustbins covered, and maintain a good standard of cleanliness for the surroundings. A fly poison concocted of 3 teaspoons of formalin in 1 pint of milk or water, with sugar added, should be placed in saucers in susceptible areas to trap and kill flies. Aerosol fly-killer sprays are also effective.

Mosquitoes

These transmit diseases such as malaria, filaria, and yellow fever. As the life cycle of mosquitoes begins in water, do not allow water to stagnate in and around the property. Repair and fill all pits and puddles. Cover drains and pour kerosene oil into these to prevent larvae from thriving there and growing into adult mosquitoes. Fine gauze on windows prevents the entry of mosquitoes.

An effective, eco-friendly method for the control of mosquitoes is to place pots of water around the property for a week or two. During this time, the mosquitoes lay their eggs in the water. Before the eggs can develop, however, this water is discarded, killing the larvae.

Mice and Rats

Both types of rodents share many characteristics. Both are potentially hazardous. However, mice are generally much smaller and are slender enough to squeeze through holes as small as 6 mm in diameter. Physically, mice generally have big ears (in relation to their bodies), brown coats, and grey underbellies. Generally, they also have a thin tail that is equal to the length of their head and body combined.

Rats and mice both carry disease germs (such as plague and typhoid) and may cause food poisoning, infection, jaundice, and so on. As a rule of thumb, there are generally two kinds of mice that can be a nuisance: the house mouse and the field mouse. However, the field mouse is not usually considered a pest until it takes up residence in an inhabited property.

Mice, like rats, can contaminate foodstuffs, worktops, and utensils with their urine, droppings, and fur and are responsible for the spread of many diseases, some of which can be fatal to humans. Unafraid of trying new things, mice can appear quite fickle, gnawing and nibbling at a range of objects before moving on, leaving them partially eaten.

Mice leave quite distinctive droppings. They are black and look like apple pips, but smaller. They also tend to gnaw at everything from electrical appliances to even floorboards. Mice derive most of the water they need from their food and subsequently tend to live in much drier environments than rats. For example, they are almost unknown in sewers. Mice colonies also grow faster than rats due to their ability to reach sexual maturity quicker.

The most effective methods of controlling these pests are poisoning, trapping, fumigating to eliminate their food supply and shelter, and rat-proofing buildings. Proprietary poisons are available to destroy rats and mice as well. In a bad case of infestation, however, it is best to call in the experts.

Fungi

Some fungi, in the form of wet or dry rot, can cause considerable structural damage to a property.

Wet rot This is a generic term for the action of a group of related fungi that attack timber with a moisture content of more than 30%. It is more common than dry rot, though it is usually less serious. Inside the premises, it is more likely to be found in kitchens, bathrooms, and roofs. Outside, it attacks window frames and sills, doors and door frames where water has penetrated the paintwork. Affected timber becomes dark brown to black, spongy when wet and brittle when dry. Yellow or brown streaks or patches are often found in decayed timber. Sometimes decay can be present beneath an apparently sound surface as well.

It is best to call pest-control firms to deal with wet rot. Timber can be treated with water-repellent preservatives to prevent wet rot.

Dry rot Despite its name, this too is caused by a fungus that thrives in damp, still, warm conditions. The fungus spreads by means of strands, some of which transport water to create ideal conditions for it to start up on a new site. The strands look like a mass of white or grey cottonwool. They can climb up from basement to attic, even through two adjoining brick walls. Eventually fruiting bodies form, looking like giant pancakes. These liberate microscopic spores in what looks like a red dust, which can be blown to new areas—again spreading the rot. Areas most likely to be affected are those under floorboards and behind skirtings. The first signs may be a musty, mushroom-like smell. The timber may appear to be warped, paint could flake, and unpainted timber will split across the grain. When touched, decayed timber will crumble into dry powder.

Eradication of dry rot must be thorough and should be handled by experts.

Integrated Pest Management

Integrated pest management is the combination of appropriate pest-control tactics into a single plan to reduce pests and their damage to an acceptable level. Using many different tactics to control a pest problem tends to cause the least disruption to other living organisms and the non-organic surroundings at the treatment site. Relying only on pesticides can cause pests to develop a resistance to pesticides, cause outbreaks of other pests, and harm surfaces or non-targetted organisms. With some pests, using pesticides alone will not achieve adequate control anyway.

To solve pest problems in this integrated fashion, one must

- identify the pest or pests to be dealt with and determine whether control is warranted for each;
- determine the pest control goal(s);
- know what control tactics are available;
- evaluate the benefits and risks of each tactic or combination of tactics;
- choose the strategy that will be most effective and will cause the least harm to both people and the environment;
- use each tactic in the strategy correctly; and
- observe local, state, and union regulations that may apply to the situation.

The strategy to be chosen will depend on the pest identified and the kind and amount of control needed.

Methods of Pest Control

The various methods of pest control are discussed in this section.

Natural controls

Some natural forces act on all organisms, causing their populations to rise and fall. These natural forces act independently of humans and may either help or hinder pest control. You may not be able to alter the action of natural forces on a pest population, but you should be aware of their influence and take advantage of them when possible. Natural forces that affect pest populations include climate, natural enemies, natural barriers, availability of shelter, and food and water supplies.

Climate Weather conditions—especially temperature, day length, and humidity—affect pest activity and their rate of reproduction. Pests may be killed or suppressed by rain, freezing temperatures, drought, or other adverse weather conditions. Climate also affects pests indirectly by influencing the growth and development of their hosts. Unusual weather conditions can change normal patterns so that increased or decreased damage results.

Natural enemies Birds, reptiles, amphibians, fish, and mammals feed on some pests and help control their numbers. Many predatory and parasitic insect and insect-like species feed on other organisms, some of which are pests. Pathogens often suppress pest populations.

Geographic barriers Features such as mountains and large bodies of water restrict the spread of many pests. Other features of the landscape can have similar effects.

Food and water supply Pest populations can thrive only as long as their food and water supply lasts. Once the food source—plant or animal—is exhausted, the pests die or become inactive. The life cycle of many pests depends on the availability of water.

Shelter The availability of shelter can affect some pest populations. Over-wintering sites and places to hide from predators are important to the survival of some pests.

Applied controls

Unfortunately, natural controls often do not control pests quickly or completely enough to prevent unacceptable injury or damage. Then other control measures must be used. These may include the following:

Host resistance Some plants, animals, and structures resist pests better than others. Some varieties of plants, wood, and animals are resistant to certain pests. Use of resistant species, when available, helps keep pest populations below harmful levels by making conditions less favourable for their growth.

Host resistance works in one of three ways:

- Chemicals in the host repel the pest or prevent them from completing their life cycle.
- The host is more vigorous or tolerant than other varieties and thus less likely to be seriously damaged by pest attacks.
- The host has physical characteristics that make it more difficult to attack.

Biological control This involves the introduction of natural enemies—parasites, predators, and pathogens. You can supplement natural control by releasing more of a pest's enemies into the target area or by introducing new enemies that were not in the area before. Biological control usually does not target eradication. The degree of control fluctuates as well. There is often a time lag between the increase of a pest population and the corresponding increase in natural controls. However, under proper conditions, sufficient control can be achieved to eliminate the threat to the plant, animal, or material to be protected.

Biological control also includes methods by which the pest is biologically altered, as in the production and release of large numbers of sterile males and the use of pheromones or juvenile hormones. Pheromones can be useful in monitoring pest populations. Placed in a trap, for example, they can attract the insects in the area so that pest numbers can be estimated. Pheromones can also be a control tool. Sometimes a manufactured copy of the pheromone that a female insect uses to attract males can be used to confuse males and prevent mating, resulting in lower numbers of pests. Applying juvenile hormones to an area can reduce pest numbers by keeping some immature pests from becoming normal, reproducing adults.

Cultural control Cultural practices are sometimes used to reduce the number of pests that are attacking cultivated plants. These practices alter the environment, the condition of the host plant, or the behaviour of the pest to prevent or suppress an infestation. They disrupt the normal relationship between the pest and the host and thus make the pest less likely to survive, grow, or reproduce. Common cultural practices that have this effect include rotating crops, cultivating the soil, varying the time of planting or harvesting, planting trap crops, adjusting row widths, and pruning, thinning, and fertilizing cultivated plants.

Mechanical/physical control Devices, machines, and other mechanical methods used to control pests or alter their environment are called mechanical or physical controls. Traps, screens, barriers, fences, nets, radiation, and electricity can sometimes be used to prevent the spread of pests into an area. Lights, heat, and refrigeration can alter the environment enough to suppress or eradicate some pest populations. Altering the amount of water, including humidity, can control some pests, especially insects and disease agents.

Sanitation Good sanitation practices help to prevent infestations. They can suppress some pests by removing either the pests themselves or their sources of food and shelter. Urban and industrial pests can be reduced by improving cleanliness, eliminating pest harbourage, and increasing the frequency of garbage pick-ups. Another sanitation technique that helps prevent pest spread is decontaminating equipment, materials, and other possible carriers before allowing them to enter a pest-free area or leave an infested area. Proper design of food-handling areas can also reduce access and shelter for many pests.

Chemical control Pesticides are chemicals used to destroy pests, control their activity, or prevent them from causing damage. Pesticides either attract or repel pests. Chemicals that regulate plant growth or remove foliage are also classified as pesticides. Pesticides are generally the fastest way to control pests. In many instances, they are the only tactic available. Application of chemicals may be done through,

Baiting A bait in pest control refers to a palatable substance, usually in gel, paste or block form, laced with fatal, toxic chemicals and placed strategically to invite pests to consume it. It is formulated to be highly palatable to pests and lasts longer than fresh foods. Ideal baits for pests are those that do not have immediate effect but allow the pest to transfer some bait to its nesting population so that the entire population is eradicated. Usually the effects of baits manifest away from the living areas.

Dusting Dust in pest control terms refers to pesticide in powder form. The formulation is available as a potent amount of pesticide blended in a carrier powder to form bulk. The powder is dusted in drains, manholes and crevices where pests may harbour.

Spraying In this method, the pesticide in powder or liquid form is dissolved in a carrier liquid and pressurised in a sprayer mechanism. Spraying ensures the pesticide reaches hard to reach areas as well.

Fumigation This technique uses a gaseous pesticide referred to as fumigant through a machine called the fumigator, to suffocate the pests in the fumigated area. Fumigation is done in a sealed area for the fumes to be effective in even hard to reach areas. After fumigation, it is necessary to de-fumigate the area by running the air handling unit for a few hours continuously.

Fogging This technique utilises ULV foggers to spray the pesticide in the form of an aerosol. Fogging is effective against airborne and flying insects and microbes.

Avoiding the Harmful Effects of Pest Control

Pest control involves more than simply identifying a pest and using a control tactic. The treatment site, whether it is outdoors or indoors, usually contains other living organisms (people, animals, and plants) and non-living things (such as air, water, and man-made and natural structures, objects, and surfaces). All of these could be affected by pest-control measures. Unless you consider the possible effects on the entire system within which the pest exists, your pest-control efforts could cause harm or lead to continued or new pest problems. So you must rely on your good judgement and follow the labels on pesticide containers.

Use of pesticides

All pesticides sold for non-commercial use nowadays are relatively safe. But the following commonsense guidelines on the use of these substances should be followed:

- Read (and follow) the precautions and instructions on the packaging, particularly those relating to handling, storage, and disposal.
- Never exceed the manufacturer's recommended concentration and dose rate. These have been carefully researched to give the safest and best control.
- Always remember to store these chemicals away from young children, pets, food, and so on. Keep children and pets away from recently treated areas, preferably for several days (check the product label for advice about this).
- Always wear rubber or disposable gloves when handling and applying pesticides. Gloves (and anything else) contaminated with chemicals should be thoroughly rinsed in water as soon as possible.
- It is advisable to use a face mask of some sort to prevent inhaling pesticides, particularly when these are applied as fine sprays or dusting powders.
- Use of protective eye wear is also essential while carrying out fumigation.
- Always wash your hands after you have finished using pesticides.
- Never dispose of unused chemicals or their wastes down sinks, drains, or toilets or in water courses or ditches. Take care to protect wildlife and natural habitats from pesticide contamination.

Waste Management

Waste management is the collection, transport, processing, recycling, or disposal of waste materials in a way least harmful to the environment. The term usually relates to waste materials produced by human activity, and is generally undertaken to reduce their effect on health, the environment, or aesthetics. Waste management is also carried out to recover resources from it.

A suitable protocol to manage waste is as follows:

1. Identify and describe the nature and quantity of waste through a waste audit.
2. Modify operational and administrative activity to eliminate, substitute, minimize, or recycle waste.
3. Decide on a disposal route.
4. Store the waste safely.
5. Transfer to the appropriate channel or dispose of via the chosen route.
6. Periodically check that waste controls are effective and comply with current laws.

Segregation of Waste

Before embarking on a waste separation programme, hotels should find out which material can be collected by local waste disposal operators and contractors. In developed countries, where recycling programmes and waste management are relatively well advanced, wastes are separated into many categories such as paper, cardboard, organic waste, plastic, glass, and metals. Waste can be separated by two means, which are as follows.

Source segregation Appropriately sized, colour-coded, and marked containers are placed at all garbage points in hotels and the employees are encouraged to put the different wastes into different lined bags, which can then be disposed of in a proper manner. Commonly in hotels, the garbage bins may be separated into

- paper and plastic for recycling/incineration;
- glass for crushing;
- cans for compacting and recycling;
- organic food wastes for composting; and
- hazardous wastes like batteries.

Contract separation In this method the waste is transported to a facility where they are mechanically or manually sorted out and processed as in the aforementioned cases.

Collection, Segregation, and Disposal of Waste

This section will introduce you to the collection, segregation, and disposal of waste.

Waste collection The wastes are collected from the different areas of the hotel and segregated so that they can be treated appropriately without harming the environment.

Guestrooms The waste from the guestrooms are collected by the housekeeping staff (room attendants), in the maid's cart. They are then segregated in the service pantry. The bins are colour-coded differently so as to facilitate the segregation process. The common colour-coding is as follows:

- Organic waste–Green
- Glass–Yellow
- Paper–White
- Metal–Grey
- Plastic–Blue
- Hazardous wastes–Red

Public areas The same procedure is followed. The waste is collected from the lobby, administration offices, business centres, back office, washrooms, etc. and segregated by the housemen.

Kitchen and back areas The same colour-coding is done in stainless steel bins. Colour-coded stripes or bands on the rims can be used. The waste is collected and segregated by the stewarding staff.

Service area These wastes are collected from banquet halls, restaurants, bars, barbecues, etc. and then segregated.

The collected and segregated waste just mentioned is then transported to the different central garbage areas.

Central garbage areas The central garbage area includes the following:

- *Wet garbage room:* An air conditioned room near the staff entrance
- *Dry garbage room:* Near the staff entrance
- *Newspaper room:* Near receiving area
- *Bottle/Can room:* Near receiving area

Waste disposal The aforementioned waste is then disposed from the premises through different contractors.

- The newspapers and bottles are collected by a contractor arranged by the purchase department for recycling purpose.
- The waste food from kitchen or cafeteria goes to piggery.
- Dry garbage is picked up by a contractor in a van on a daily basis.
- Waste cooking oil is disposed through a separate contractor.
- Batteries, e-waste, and hazardous wastes are disposed through a specialized contractor as these should not get mixed with dry or wet garbage.
- Renovation material or building waste such as cement, steel, stones, bricks, and soil is disposed separately whenever there is some project work in progress.

In many cities, the municipal corporations now handle the disposal of all kinds of segregated wastes.

Recycling

Recycling is the utilization of waste material by changing its form through a definite process. Materials which are recycled are as follows.

Paper Paper collected from various establishments is cleaned, re-pulped, and mixed with varying percentages of virgin pulp and then papers, boxboards, tissues, newsprint, and liner boards are prepared from them.

Food and organic materials Kitchen and yard waste can be composted into a soil conditioner for lawns and gardens. Meat scraps can be made into fertilizer and animal feed.

Plastic Soft drink bottles, and milk and water jugs are converted into resin pellets, then melted and moulded into desired shape such as drainpipes, plastic bags, non-food containers, lids, flower boxes, clothes pegs, automobile bumpers, rope, carpet backing, and certain household appliances. Shredded polyetheylene terepthalate (PET) can be used as fibrefill for quilts, pillows, sleeping bags, and coat linings.

Steel cans or tins The protective tin coating is first de-tinned and then the cans are fed into furnaces where they are made into refrigerator and automobile parts along with old cars, appliances, farm equipment, and industrial scrap.

Glass Bottles and jars are crushed to make 'cullet'. This is mixed with sand, limestone, and soda ash, and then melted and moulded into new containers, fibreglass, and glass beads for reflective paint, etc.

Aluminium Cans and foils are separated by magnets, shredded, de-lacquered, and melted to make new products.

Water Waste water is treated in a sewage treatment plant and this grey water is used for gardening, flushing etc.

The advantages of recycling are as follows:

1. It reduces waste; every kilogram of recycled waste is 1 kg less to the landfill.
2. It reduces collection, hauling, and dumping costs.
3. It saves using natural resources to manufacture a replacement.
4. It uses less energy and creates less pollution during manufacture than products made from virgin sources.
5. Many recycled products have cash value.

Biogas Plants

Biodegradable wet waste from the kitchen and gardens can be processed in a biogas plant. The waste is first segregated carefully to remove any non-biodegradable material or acidic substances (such as too many lemon peels) and then loaded in the biogas plant where it is homogenized to make slurry. The slurry is then processed in a sequential manner first by aerobic and then anaerobic process. The end products of the process are biogas and high-quality manure. Biogas consists of methane and carbon dioxide. The manure has high nitrogen content and acts as an excellent soil conditioner.

Sewage Treatment Plant (STP)

It is now a statutory mandate by state pollution control boards that all hotels set up compact sewage treatment plants on their premises. The STPs work on the principle of aerobic treatment of sewage by aerobic bacteria. The steps involved in the plant are pre-aeration of sewage, bio-reaction in the aeration tank, sedimentation, filtration by sand, and activated charcoal, chlorination, sludge drying, and disposal. The grey water obtained thus may be used in gardening and as flush water in flush tanks.

Effluent Treatment Plant (ETP)

This operation involves physico-chemical treatment (gravity separation, sedimentation, and addition of sequestering chemicals), followed by filtration by sand, adsorption via activated charcoal, chemical oxidation by ozonisation, followed by microfiltration through ultra-filtration and reverse osmosis (RO).

Composting

Many hotels operate back of the house composting programmes. Composting is the aerobic biological decomposition of organic waste such as food waste and grass clippings to turn it into valuable fertilizer as good as humus. The method reduces the amount of solid waste in the hotel's trash and produces good quality, environment-friendly fertilizer. Composting may be done in compost bins lined with some garden soil. It is important to turn the layers of biodegradable material so that the process remains aerobic.

Vermicomposting

Vermicomposting is the term given to the process of conversion of biodegradable matter by earthworms into vermicast that is used as compost. Vermicast is the compact, concentrated mass excreted by earthworms after they consume and process the decaying organic matter from the biodegradable waste. The processing makes the nutrients in the organic matter more bioavailable. Vermicast also contains enzymes that may stimulate plant growth and discourage plant pathogens. Vermicomposting may be done in pits, concrete tanks, or in wooden crates lined with broken bricks or pebbles followed by a layer of coarse sand. This is topped with a moist layer of loamy soil into which locally collected surface and subsurface varieties of earthworms are inoculated. Over this layer are scattered, small lumps of cattle dung and then comes a layer of hay. Water is sprayed on the entire set-up till it is moist but not wet. Old jute bags or palm leaves are then used to cover the set-up. The pH should always be maintained close to neutral. After about a month the palm leaves and jute bags are removed and organic refuse is spread in a 5 cm thick layer. The compost is ready for harvest 45 days later.

INSIGHT 24.1: IT-ENABLED WASTE TO ENERGY AT SMART CITY - JABALPUR

Jabalpur city adopted a Smart IT-enabled Solid Waste Monitoring and Management System to tackle its household and commercial waste. As a part of this Swachha Bharat Mission project, Jabalpur Smart City Limited (JSCL) has built and is successfully operating a waste to energy plant at Kathonda, taking care of municipal solid waste from 79 wards of Jabalpur Municipal Corporation. The collection and transportation of waste is integrated with ICT components such as Radio Frequency Identification (RFID), Geographic Information System (GIS), Global Positioning System (GPS), Bin Level Sensors (BLS), Vehicle Tracking and Monitoring System (VTMS), weight sensors on vehicles, web-based application software, Graphical User Interface (GUI) and so on, and amalgamates the entire process into one monitorable system. The collected garbage at the Kathonda plant is converted into energy utilised in lighting. The innovative characteristics of the project are outlined:

Smart application for SWM resource plan Single point availability of city-wide information on wards, households, schools, offices, government and private establishments, roads etc. mapped on GIS portals with access to any citizen, helps in precise estimations of solid waste generation and optimum allocation of resources through GIS-based analysis.

Sensor enabled smart bins The smart waste approach consists of associating physical waste with digital information. Smart ultrasonic sensors monitor the amount of waste in the bins and transfer this information to the control rooms. Sensors collect the data, evaluate the filling level of the bins and provide the information to the private operator engaged for collection and transportation of waste. Additionally, weight sensors mounted on garbage collection vehicles monitor the weight of the garbage collected by the trucks.

SUMMARY

Pest control is essential for the maintenance of a safe environment. But it must be clearly understood that the pest-control methods should be applied only when pests are identified. This is because pest-control measures may cause undue harm to other living beings too. Apart from this fact, pest-control chemicals may bring about some degree of damage to materials and fabrics in some instances.

It is important to establish a goal for pest control in the case of individual pests, whether the hotel wants prevention, suppression, or eradication of the pests. Guests staying in the hotel may be put off on sighting even one such pest. Therefore in hotels, the threshold pest population is zero for most pests.

The characteristics of and methods of control for some common pests likely to be found in hotels have been discussed in this chapter.

In hotels, pest-control services are often contracted, as it is a highly skilled profession. The housekeeper, however, should insist on an integrated pest management approach from the contractors.

Different methods of pest control have been discussed briefly in the chapter. It should be remembered that for common pests, prevention is better than cure. Maintenance of hygiene and sanitation is the best prevention. This is even more important in today's scenario, where excessive use of chemicals is being discouraged and many hotels are becoming environmentally sensitive.

Finally, waste disposal has been dealt with in brief. Recycling of wastes has been emphasized in this section, keeping in mind contemporary eco-friendly trends. The readers should take up a detailed study of bio-gas and sewage-treatment plants as suggested in the project work section, as this will help in comprehensive understanding of the concept of waste recycling and its various benefits.

KEY TERMS

Bait A bait in pest control refers to a palatable substance, usually in gel, paste or block form, laced with fatal, toxic chemicals and placed strategically to invite pests to consume it.

Biogas An eco-friendly gaseous fuel composed of methane and carbon dioxide. It is produced by anaerobic decomposition of biodegradable wastes.

Composting The aerobic biological decomposition of organic waste to turn it into valuable fertilizer.

Continuous pests Pests that are nearly always present and require regular control.

Crash spraying Pest control spraying treatment from terrace, floors, rooms advancing downwards to kitchen and basement, completed within three consecutive days, specially taking care of eradication of rats.

Eradication Destroying an entire pest population.

ETP It stands for effluent treatment plant.

Fogging A pest control technique that utilises ULV foggers to spray the pesticide in the form of an aerosol.

Fumigation A pest control technique that uses a gaseous pesticide referred to as fumigant through a machine called the fumigator, to suffocate the pests in the fumigated area.

Grubs Larvae of insects are also called grubs.

Lacquer Coloured varnish made of shellac dissolved in alcohol.

Larvae A juvenile stage in the life cycle of insects, starting from after they leave their eggs and lasting until their transformation into pupae.

Moulting (of insects) Shedding of the outer casing or cocoon by insects.

Nymph Immature form of insect that resembles the adult insect; in mites and ticks, the stage between larva and adult.

Organic wastes Wastes that can be broken down through microbial activities of bacteria and fungi, that is, they are biodegradable. These wastes are predominantly composed of carbon, hydrogen, and oxygen containing compounds. Eg., food wastes from kitchens.

Parasite An animal or plant dependent upon another for support and nourishment.

Pathogens Disease-causing organisms.

Pest Any organism that competes with humans, domestic animals, or desirable plants for food or water; or injures humans, domestic animals, desirable plants, structures, or possessions; or spreads disease to humans, domestic animals, wildlife, or desirable plants; or annoys humans or domestic animals.

Pheromones These are substances secreted and released by organisms for detection and response by another of the same species.

Potential pests Creatures that do not require control under normal conditions, but may appear as pests and require control in certain circumstances.

Pupa The third stage in the metamorphosis of an insect, when it is in a cocoon. A pupa is also called a 'chrysalis'.

Recycling Utilization of waste material by changing its form through a definite process.

Sani-bin These are small metal or plastic containers with lids which are kept in toilets for the collection of soiled sanitary towels.

Sporadic pests Creatures that appear as pests (and require control) occasionally or intermittently.

STP Sewage treatment plants that work on the principle of aerobic treatment of sewage by aerobic bacteria.

Threshold levels The levels of pest populations at which you should take pest-control action if you want to prevent the pests in an area from causing unacceptable injury or harm.

ULV Ultra Light Volume.

Vermicast The compact, concentrated mass excreted by earthworms after they consume and process the decaying organic matter from the biodegradable waste. This is used as compost.

Vermicomposting Term given to the process of conversion of biodegradable matter by earthworms into compost.

Waste management The collection, transport, processing, recycling, or disposal of waste materials in a way least harmful to the environment.

White ants Another term for termites.

Woodworm Another name for furniture beetles.

Woolly bears The hairy, squat larvae of carpet beetles.

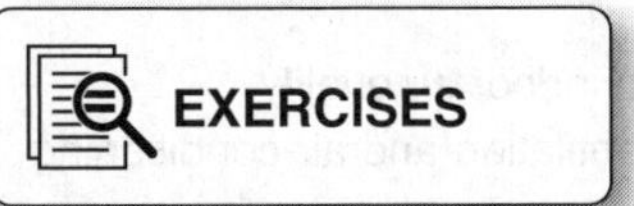

25 Internal Environment

Learning Objectives

After reading this chapter, you should be able to
- understand factors in human comfort and significance of maintaining high indoor air quality
- explain the importance of optimum levels of indoor air quality, heating ventilation and air-conditioning (HVAC), noise control, and lighting
- describe the process of air-conditioning
- understand the measurement of light in a room, or the illumination
- appreciate the importance of the five senses guest experience

Introduction

The managements of all establishments are concerned with providing a safe, secure, and aesthetic environment conducive to work for employees, and to relaxation for guests. The most important considerations in providing an ideal internal environment are maintaining optimum levels of four factors—indoor air quality, HVAC, noise and light. Before discussing these aspects, it is important to understand factors that affect human comfort in an internal environment.

Environmental Factors in Human Comfort

The guest's comfort in a hotel room, to a large extent, is dependent on the following environmental factors – the temperature of the internal air, the radiant temperature, the air velocity, the relative humidity, after humidity and the air quality.

Air temperature This refers to the temperature of air surrounding the human body and is measured in degree Celsius. Too cold or too hot air temperatures in a room lead to discomfort. Air temperature, though the most commonly used indicator of thermal comfort, should be considered in relation to other factors to determine thermal comfort level.

Radiant temperature This refers to the heat being radiated from a heated object, affecting the temperature of the surroundings. Examples include heat from working equipment, light sources, sunrays falling on and heating metal surfaces and so on. Radiant temperature significantly affects how a human body loses or gains heat to the surroundings.

Air velocity Stagnant air makes people uncomfortable. As soon as a room is ventilated, there is visible enhancement in comfort level. Air velocity refers to the average speed of moving air to which the humans are exposed in an enclosed environment.

Relative humidity This is the ratio of the amount of water vapour in the air to the maximum amount of water vapour that the air can hold at the same specific temperature in the room. Ideal relative humidity is 30–65%. High humidity prevents evaporation of perspiration from the skin surface, an effective heat reduction mechanism of human body, and leads to discomfort.

Air quality The maintenance of high indoor air quality is critical as, on an average, humans spend about 90% of their lives indoors. The quality of indoor air is degraded by presence of undesirable gaseous, chemical, biological and particulate elements.

Indoor Air Quality (IAQ)

As per the Environment Protection Agency (EPA), indoor air quality (IAQ) refers to the air quality within and around buildings and structures, especially as it relates to the health and comfort of building occupants. IAQ is measured in terms of the proportion of normal air gases and the concentration of pollutants, and the temperature and humidity conditions present inside a building. In a 2012 survey by Expedia, 60% consumers give better ratings to hotels with higher IAQ. By 2020, IAQ has gained even more prominence, the US Sentiment on IAQ and Covid-19 survey by Carbon Lighthouse found that 91% consumers felt that IAQ is important in the prevention of the spread of viruses and 77% expressed that proof of a hotel's IAQ would impact their decision on where to stay.

Effects of Poor IAQ

The IAQ in a building may be compromised by increased proportion of microbial contamination, especially molds and bacteria, chemicals such as carbon monoxide and carbon dioxide and other allergens that may have negative effects. A building with chronically poor IAQ may is referred to be suffering a 'sick building syndrome'.

The health effects of poor IAQ depends on the concentration of specific pollutants in the indoor air. Minor effects include headaches, eye irritation, respiratory inflammation, mucosal irritation, fatigue and allergic reactions. Acute symptoms include that of asthma, decreased lung function, nausea and asphyxiation. Cancer and heart disease are long term effect of prolonged exposure to poor IAQ.

Indoor Air Pollutants

The pollutants affecting IAQ are those generated from activities and sources within the building and also carried in via the inflowing air from outside the building. Some pollutants which degrade IAQ are,

Volatile organic compounds (VOCs) emanate from paints and varnishes, aerosol sprays, glues and adhesives, cleaning solvents, pesticides, synthetic finishes on furnishings, and carpets, etc. and lead to toxic health effects.

Formaldehyde is a flammable gas that gets released from building materials such as foam and pressed wood products and so on. Its exposure has adverse effects on human health.

Lead is an extremely harmful indoor pollutant especially to children. Activities such as improper scraping or sanding of old lead-based paints, soldering, stained glass making or lead-contaminated soil being tracked indoors cause IAQ to be deteriorated with airborne lead particles.

Tobacco smoke exhaled by smokers of cigarettes, cigars and pipes, gets adsorbed on soft furnishings and is a carcinogen that is detrimental to heart and lungs.

Combustion gases such as carbon monoxide, sulphur dioxide, nitrogen oxides, and hydrocarbons affect human health acutely.

Particulate matter or PM is a complex mixture of solid and liquid particles suspended in air and those of concern are the ones 10 μm or lesser in diameter (PM_{10}) that are easily inhaled and induce adverse health effects. Fine particulate matter of diameter 2.5 μm ($PM_{2.5}$) or lesser remain suspended in the air and cause serious health issues on inhalation.

Biological contaminants those that degrade the IAQ mainly include molds, fungi, mildew, bacteria, spores of microbes, viruses, dust mites, animal dander and pollen. They are allergens and also cause many diseases.

Radon is a carcinogenic, radioactive gas that gets released from the natural breakdown of uranium in the soil, rocks and water and permeates the air in buildings as it seeps through the foundation.

Measuring IAQ

IAQ measurement primarily takes into account three metrices.

Chemicals These include VOCs and other gaseous products such as formaldehyde, carbon dioxide, carbon monoxide and so on.

Biologicals These include living particulates such as molds, fungus, bacteria, pollen and so on.

Comfort This implies measures of air temperature, air velocity, relative humidity, oxygen and carbon dioxide levels and particulate matter.

IAQ is measured with IAQ monitors, aerometers, VOC sensors, and computerised air flow modelling. With the level of pollution going much higher, above acceptable limits in many cities, housekeepers and maintenance crew endeavour to maintain the IAQ within standards inside the hotel buildings. In many upscale hotels, IAQ display boards are placed at lobbies, indicating the real-time IAQ metrics inside the building to guests. QR codes are placed in prominent places in some hotels that invite guests to scan them for visiting their IAQ dashboard for the metrics. Recommended levels of IAQ metrics are presented in Exhibit 25.1. The IAQ metrics usually displayed in hotels are:

- Relative humidity
- Temperature
- Carbon dioxide
- $PM_{2.5}$
- Treated Fresh Air

Exhibit 25.1 Recommended levels of IAQ metrics

IAQ metrics	
Parameter	**Acceptable level**
Carbon dioxide	>1000 ppm
Carbon monoxide	>9 ppm
VOCs	>500 µg/m³
Formaldehyde	>27 ppb
PM_{10}	50 µg/m³
$PM_{2.5}$	15 µg/m³
Humidity	30–60%
Temperature	20–23.6°C in winter 22.8–26°C in summer
Value sources: International Well Building Institute, ASHRAE and EPA	

Improving IAQ

Measures to improve IAQ are,

- Source control by identifying and fixing root causes
- Enhancing ventilation systems
- Use of green cleaning products
- Employing targeted air purifiers
- Effective, well maintained HVAC systems to maintain optimum amount of Treated Fresh Air (TFA)
- Using HEPA filters
- Choosing interior materials with least amount of toxins
- Opting for low VOC products
- Adding IAQ improving biophilic components indoors such as active green walls, vertical gardens and indoor plants
- Timely removal of garbage from premises
- Preventing dust and dirt from entering the building
- Constant monitoring of IAQ metrics

Heating Ventilation and Air-Conditioning (HVAC) Basics

HVAC deals with the conditioning of air within a defined space, usually a residence, public institution or a place of business. Conditioning usually involves heating or cooling, dehumidifying, and filtering or cleaning the air. Typically in a hotel, a central air-conditioner cools and dehumidifies the defined space. Heating is accomplished by an add-on to the system (such as an electric heating strip) or by a separate unit, such as a furnace. Many types of HVAC systems are used as per requirements of a space, as illustrated in Figure 25.1. However, description of each type is out of purview in this basic discussion.

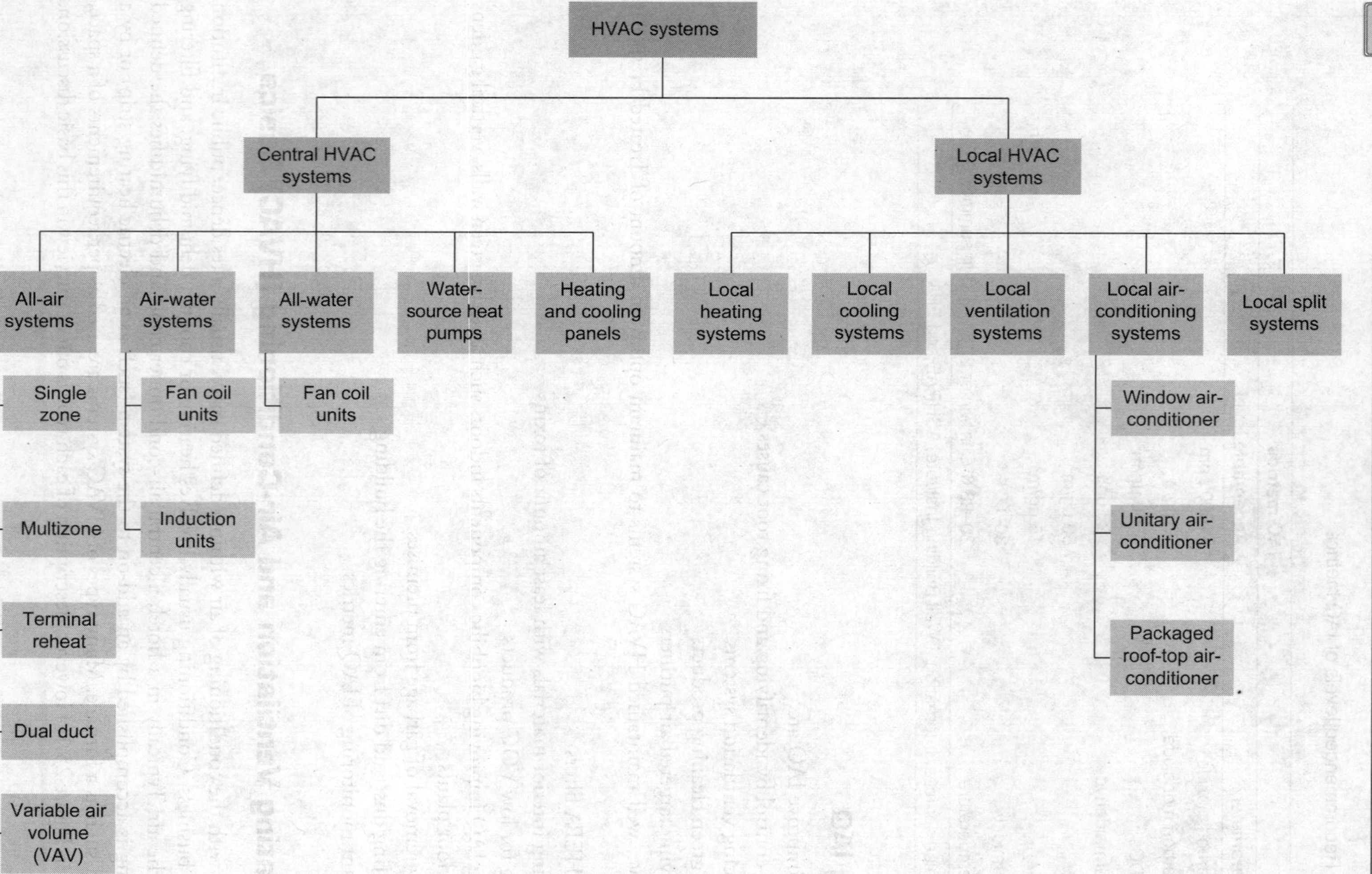

Fig. 25.1 Types of HVAC systems

Source: Adapted from (2018). Types of HVAC Systems. In (Ed.), HVAC System. IntechOpen. https://doi.org/10.5772/intechopen.78942.

How Air-conditioners Cool Air

Central air-conditioners are split systems, having an outdoor unit (the condensing unit) and an indoor unit (the air handling unit or AHU). The function of an air conditioner is to transport heat from one station to another. The vehicle that it uses to carry the heat is called a refrigerant, commonly known as freon.

The compressor in the outdoor unit changes the fluid refrigerant into a high-temperature, high-pressure gas. As that gas flows through the outdoor coils, it loses heat and condenses into a high-temperature, high-pressure liquid. This liquid refrigerant travels through copper tubing into the evaporator coil. There the refrigerant expands. Its sudden expansion returns the refrigerant into a low-temperature, low-pressure gas. This gas then absorbs heat from the air circulating in the duct network. The cooled air is then distributed back to your house or place of business. The cooling cycle continues until the indoor temperature reaches the thermostat setting. Meanwhile, the heat absorbed by the refrigerant is carried back outside through the copper tubing and released into the outside air.

Dirty coils and improper refrigerant levels can cause the system to cool less efficiently than it should. An inefficient system means higher energy bills. It also forces the compressor to work harder than is necessary and can actually shorten the lifespan of the unit. An annual air-conditioning inspection by an experienced technician therefore, includes an inspection of the coils and a checking of the refrigerant charge to ensure that the system is running efficiently.

A zoning system allows the hotel to further control the environment in a personalized and energy-efficient way. The hotel can be divided into two or more zones to do this. Then, through the use of fully modulating dampers, the system can selectively cool or heat certain portions of the building at given periods of the day. With some systems, indoor humidity can likewise be displayed and controlled in zones. A popular alternative to zoning is having two or more units in a larger building. Each unit controls the temperature and humidity in a given portion of the building. Suitable room temperatures for different areas of the hotel are listed in Table 25.1.

How Air-conditioners Dehumidify and Freshen Air

As the warm air circulating through the ducts passes over the evaporator coil, it is quickly cooled and can no longer hold as much moisture as it did at a higher temperature. The excess moisture condenses on the outside of the coils and is carried away through a drain. The process is similar to what happens when moisture condenses on the outside of a glass of ice water on a hot, humid day.

Occasionally, the drain lines may get clogged and the system may not drain properly. This can result in a drain pan overflow, leading to water leaks in the ceiling or walls. The annual air-conditioning inspection by an experienced technician includes an inspection of the drainage system. During the inspection, the technician treats the drainage system with an algaecide to retard the growth of algae, which can clog the system.

Table 25.1 Optimum room temperatures in a hotel

Areas	Temperature	Areas	Temperature
Reception areas, lounge, lobby	18–21°C	Staircases and entrances	20°C
Bedrooms, bathrooms	20–24°C	Administrative offices	18–21°C
Dining areas	18–21°C	Kitchens	18°C
Banquet and convention halls	16°C		

An air-conditioner should be able to maintain a relative humidity of 40–60% and provide approximately 2800 cc of fresh air per person per hour. Relative humidity refers to the amount of moisture in the air. If the humidity is very high, it prevents the evaporation of perspiration, making for a lot of discomfort. On the other hand, if the relative humidity is lower than 30%, it creates a dry atmosphere, causing the skin tissues in the nose and throat to dry out. This in turn leads to sore throats and colds.

Ventilation for the provision of fresh air is necessary to lower the relative humidity. Good ventilation also removes unpleasant odours and smoke, and prevents the internal atmosphere from turning stale or stuffy. Good ventilation is provided by keeping doors and windows open so as to air the internal areas. In case the central air-conditioning system is operational, all forms of natural ventilation should be sealed, since the air-conditioning system controls the amount of filtered air entering a building as well as its temperature and relative humidity.

The fresh air, before entering the building through the system, needs to be treated for external pollutants. Treated Fresh Air (TFA) units cater to air flow through HEPA filters and condition it through appropriate cooling system. High efficiency particulate air (HEPA) filters have filtration efficiency of 99.97% down to 0.3 microns particle size. Air changes per hour (ACPH) are important metrics while deciding ventilation level. For hotel buildings, ASHRAE recommends 1-2 ACPH.

Noise and its Control

In an increasingly polluted world, noise is among the biggest culprits. Noise negatively affects human health and well-being. Problems related to noise include hearing loss, stress, high blood pressure, sleep loss, distraction, loss of productivity, and a general reduction in the quality of life and opportunities for tranquility.

What is 'Noise'?

Sound-control engineers define noise in three ways:

- Unwanted sound
- Any sound not occurring in the natural environment, for example, sounds emanating from aircraft, highways, and other industrial, commercial, and residential sources
- An erratic, intermittent, or statistically random oscillation

Sound intensity is measured in units called 'decibels'. The decibel scale is logarithmic and climbs steeply, so that an increase of about 3 decibels is a doubling of sound volume. In the wilderness, a typical sound level would be about 35 decibels. An average speech reaches upto 65–70 decibels; heavy traffic generates 90 decibels. By 140 decibels, sound becomes painful to the human ear; but ill effects, including hearing loss, set in at much lower levels.

Some of the most undesirable noises are from traffic on the roads, jet planes, garbage trucks, construction equipment, lawn mowers, mechanical and electrical cleaning equipment (such as metal mopping buckets, wet and dry suction cleaners, and laundering equipment), and so on. Noise can create 'acoustic trauma', which is damage to the hearing mechanism caused by a sudden burst of intense noise or by a blast. The term usually implies a single traumatic event, but it can also result in a chronic condition known as 'tinnitus', commonly called ringing of the ears.

The need for noise control stems directly from the overabundance of noise in the environment. The perception of and tolerance to noise is decidedly personal. What annoys one person is of no consequence to another. Thus individuals' 'threshold of pain' in terms of acoustics may be vastly different.

Apart from distressing noise, there is also 'white noise'—it has a technical definition, but most of us would know it if we heard it. Sound engineers define it as 'noise whose energy is uniform over a wide range of frequencies'. It is widely perceived as relatively benign but persistent sound. The hum of a vacuum cleaner, for example, can be considered white noise by those who are not distressed or disturbed by it; some may even find it soothing! A high 'threshold of pain' allows some people to tolerate particular frequencies that others cannot. Pitch and loudness also determine how well an individual can tolerate a particular sound.

Noise Control

The occupational safety and health (OSH) standards stipulate guidelines for noise control in workplaces. Under the OSH regulations in India, no exposure above 115 decibels is permitted, exposure upto 115 decibels is limited to 15 minutes for an 8-hour shift, and average noise levels above 85 decibels are regulated. OSH standards require employers to measure noise levels, to muffle extremely noisy equipment, to provide ear-protection gear if necessary, and to offer regular hearing tests to workers who are regularly exposed to high sound levels.

With new developments in noise control emerging all the time, acoustics is an active field. The variety and range of products available for noise control is impressive. Many of the solutions are portable and can be used for both home and industry. Effective acoustical design can be both functional and attractive, and may be something as simple as a coffered ceiling. Some companies are even designing sound-proofing systems with a do-it-yourself option. The noise-control quality of acoustic materials is measured by a noise reduction coefficient (NRC). For instance, an NRC of 0.65 indicates that the material or surface absorbs 65% of the sound waves that hit it.

In the housekeeping department, noise control can be achieved in the following ways:

- Emphasizing the need for low noise levels while working
- Using plastic buckets instead of metal ones
- Keeping wheels and door hinges well oiled
- Servicing equipment regularly
- Using electrical equipment with silencers. However, a little white noise from equipment should be expected; else the employees will not be able to make out when there is a fault while operating the machines
- Using insulating materials such as rubber, cork, and carpeting on the floors
- Using rubber glides under the legs of noisy furniture
- Scheduling noisy work during low occupancy periods or when guests are not around

Odours and Odour Control

A hotel property, which is maintained, is hygienically clean, and is well ventilated rarely faces odour problems. But achieving both these factors is a great challenge for the housekeeping department. While clearly impractical, if we could leave all windows and doors fully open, all year long, and had fans running indoors to constantly move the air around, our interiors would have no odour problems. This is because nature would control the odours just as it does outdoors. Consider the situation outdoors;

we have the decay of numerous living organisms on earth, plus the daily waste generated by humans and animals, plus the industry and vehicular pollution; and yet nature keeps the air fresh and clean. This is evident in the fact that most people go out for fresh air.

All hotels have faced the problem of unpleasant odours in one or the other location on their property. Housekeepers obviously cannot leave guestrooms and other front of the house areas wide open all year long, so they must eliminate the odour sources where possible and correctly treat indoor air to control the odours in case source cannot be eliminated.

What is Odour?

The term odour means a pleasant or unpleasant smell in the interiors or outdoors. The specific property of odours is that they emanate from a source and the odour molecules disperse into the air in the direction of the air current. We detect odour when the volatile compound responsible for the odour becomes airborne. This airborne compound then stimulates the olfactory glands in the nose and causes a number of complex reactions resulting in the unpleasant smell. With some compounds only a few molecules may be needed to cause this reaction, whilst other compounds create unpleasant odours only when present in high concentrations. This situation can be very dangerous if the compound is a lethal one, such as hydrogen sulphide. Another characteristic property of odour molecules is that they get easily absorbed by materials such as linen, upholstery, and other surfaces.

Odour Control

Odour control in hotels generally refers to the control of unpleasant odours, commonly indoors. Unpleasant odours may be just offensive or sometimes toxic. Odour control is important not only from guest's purview but even for employees, since even low levels in the environment can adversely affect health. To control any odour it is important to identify it or narrow down to its source.

All offensive and toxic odours may be classified into acidic, alkaline, or neutral. Most food related odours arise from organic acids and volatile compounds and are grouped under acidic odour. Alkaline odours are those emanating from faecal matter and ammonia-related products. Neutral odours emanate from neutral compounds found in fish and dairy products.

It is estimated that more than half of hotels world over provide contaminated air to their guests. Odours in hotels originate from multiple sources. Most odours are created from one of two sources, either chemical or biological, albeit some are both.

Chemical odours These generally originate from man-made products. These can include the materials used in construction and the materials used to manufacture furniture and floor coverings, as well as cigarette smoke and small leaks from LP and natural gas pipe fittings. Cleaning products and personal care products are also contributors to the accumulation of chemical odours indoors.

Biological odours These generally originate from leftover food and cooking, insect and rodent infestation, pet cages and cat boxes, gases emitted by humans and pets, sewer gases that leak back into the living spaces, and mould, mildew and bacterial growth occurring in a variety of locations indoors, or within walls or attic spaces.

Since time immemorial, unpleasant odours have been disguised by masking them with a perfumed product. This is a stop gap approach. When faced with an odour problem, the housekeeper should make an effort to locate the source of the unpleasant odour. As far as possible it should be ensured that the source of smell is eliminated where practical. There are four basic methods of odour control:

Odour elimination

Most odours can be eliminated by strategic cleaning and sanitizing and others by correcting building, mechanical, or other conditions that contribute to odours. For instance, many a times carpets are the culprits in odour problems in interiors. After shampooing of carpets it should be ensured that all the moisture and chemical cleaner residue is eliminated preferably by sunning the carpet. The first step in eliminating odours is to discover their points of origin. For instance, removing room service trays promptly will eliminate stale food odour from guestrooms. Simply ventilating guestrooms by keeping a few windows open during daily cleaning will go a long way in eliminating odour. In complex odour problems, case in which the person dealing with the odour is unable to detect it after a while due to the way human olfactory sensors become saturated with odour molecules, it is best to avail an outside person's help in detecting odour sources.

Air purification

To control odours that cannot be altogether eliminated, such as those from cooking, people, or pets, air purification systems can be used. These portable purifiers electronically recreate the missing ingredients to purify indoor air in the same manner that nature purifies the outdoor air. And just as nature never turns off its air purification process, an air purifier must continually operate indoors. Air purification systems reduce the level of harmful airborne contaminants by destroying moulds, particulates, dust mites, pollen, unpleasant odours, smoke, and allergens. This yields cleaner, odour-free air. They are quiet in operation, low in energy consumption, have a galvanized steel construction and are easy to maintain. Air purification systems dealing with smoke use filters loaded with a heavy amount of activated charcoal. The filters need to be replaced every six months in a simple process.

Odour neutralization

Neutralization is the process that nullifies the odour-producing compound, including those persistently produced. During this process, a specially formulated agent is atomized and reacts with the odour-producing compound, neutralizing the compound. An odour neutralizer not only eliminates the unpleasant smell, but also imparts a light and fresh aroma to the location. An odour neutralizer compound should be atomized into the air using hand sprayers indoors or mechanical sprayers outdoors. In fact, eco-friendly biological neutralizers are also available. These are natural products that biodegrade odour producing organic compounds and certain other compounds. Their action is assisted by incorporating in them specially formulated odour-quenching bacteria.

Odour masking

In odour masking, a pleasant smell is introduced in high enough concentrations to mask the unpleasant odour. The nose then only detects the pleasant smell. As mentioned earlier, this is a stop gap approach since the foul smell is not removed but remains in the background and the masking agent may be required repeatedly. The odour masking products are sold in markets as chemical deodorizers. In actual fact, the term deodorizer here is an absolute misnomer. These chemical fragrances, whether evaporated or sprayed, do nothing but cover-up odours by dominating chemicals to the air to deceive the sense of smell. These purported deodorizers become aerosolized by spraying and end up inside the lungs of occupants. Adding chemical masking products into indoor air can actually make matters worse for people with allergies, asthma, or chemical sensitivities.

Light

Light has a functional as well as a decorative role in any establishment, and especially so in hotels. Functionally, light is essential for vision. Different types of tasks demand different amounts of light. Colours can be perceived as distinct from each other only because of the light they reflect. The right amount of light can be very stimulating, relaxing, and may have a very positive emotional effect. Both natural and artificial light should be put to advantageous use for providing lighting in hotels. Light is discussed further as an element of art in Chapter 27.

Measurement of Light or Illumination

A 'lumen' is a measurement of light output from a light source. All lamps are rated in lumens. A measurement of a 100-watt incandescent lamp is about 1750 lumens.

The distribution of light on a horizontal surface is called its illumination. Illumination is measured in foot-candles. A foot-candle is defined as a lumen of light distributed over one square foot area. The amount of illumination required varies according to the difficulty of a visual task. The ideal illumination is the minimum foot-candles necessary to allow one to perform a task comfortably and proficiently without eye strain.

1 foot-candle = 10.76 lux

['Lux' is the measure of illumination level at or on the surface that is being illuminated.]

Table 25.2 lists the lighting requirements of various areas in a hotel.

Another important lighting term is 'efficacy'. This is the ratio of the light output from a lamp to the electrical power it consumes. It is measured in lumens per watt (LPW).

Lighting in Hotels

In the hotel's public areas, such as lobbies and entrances, overhead lighting is most prevalent. Overhead lighting in the form of chandeliers, track lighting, fluorescent lighting with diffuser panels, and wall lights on brackets are the types commonly used. The entrance foyer should have a high level of illumination; hotel lobbies should be well lit; whereas lounges may have softer lights.

Table 25.2 Lighting requirements of various areas in a hotel

Areas	Requirement (in lux)	Areas	Requirement (in lux)
Entrance foyer	300	Bedrooms	50–100
Reception	300	Reading areas	150
Lobbies	150	Dressing tables	150
Lounges	100	Bathrooms	100
Shops and displays	300	Food preparation areas	200–300
Halls	150	Dining rooms and bars	100
Stairs	100	Linen room and store	50
Landings	150	Sewing room	200
Guest corridors	200	General overall lighting	50

Adequate corridor lighting creates a pleasant atmosphere and makes it easier to read room numbers and find keyholes on doors. Ideally, a lighting fixture should be present above each guestroom door in the guest corridors. Well-designed ceiling fixtures, spaced at intervals of twice the ceiling height, usually provide adequate uniform illumination.

Guestroom lighting should provide for general illumination, for writing at a desk, for reading in bed or in an easy chair, for grooming at the dressing table, for visibility in closets and bathrooms, and so on. A variety of light fittings may be used. Lamps with shades are often used on the bedside or on the writing table. The important areas, which should be well lit, are the dressing table, writing desk or work area, and the seating area. The bathrooms usually have overhead lights, most often just inside the door.

Light Switches

Dolly switches that are flicked up and down are the most commonly used switches, but neater, more easily operated rocker switches are becoming more popular. Wall-mounted push-button switches need only a very light touch to operate and are more expensive than dolly or rocker switches. Dimmer switches can vary the amount of light given out by a lamp. They can be used to dim the main room lighting and also may allow it to be used as a nightlight. They can be used to alter the lighting effects according to mood too. Most dimmers can be fitted in place of a normal switch, but because they are more complex, they are more expensive. Since they decrease the power consumed, however, they can save an appreciable amount on the cost of electricity while being energy-efficient. Door switches that turn on the light when the door is opened and off when it is closed can be used for cupboards. Automatic time switches can be used for outside lighting, night circuits, or as security lighting. They can be set to 'turn lights on' or 'turn lights off' at certain hours.

The Five Senses Concept in Guest Experience

More and more properties are designing guests' experiences evoking the five senses, as they impact guests deeply and help create intangible psychological associations with hotel or resort property. Whether it is the smell, sight, touch, taste, or sound, all senses may be used to advantage in enhancing guest experience.

Smell Smell has a more significant impact amongst all other human senses and hotels have been cognisant of this fact. Thus, most of them have a customised signature fragrance which is carried over from the lobbies to the guestrooms to entice guests and creates an imprint in their memory. Housekeepers endeavour to eliminate any bad odours which may impact guests at the property. The cleaning products used have pleasant fragrances too.

Vision Another impacting sense that influences guest preferences is what they see around them. Right from the décor, the repetitive use of hotel colours, the impressive staff uniforms, the view from the rooms, all make a significant impact on guest experience. Colour schemes are cleverly used to create a relaxed ambience in the lobbies, spa, and guestrooms, and alternatively a lively atmosphere at the coffee shops, health club, and bar. Some properties may go for trendy design with modern art elements depending on their target clientele.

Touch The tactile feel or texture is a sense that is perceived through all surfaces guests come in physical contact with. Be it the luxurious feel of the bedsheets, the plushness of the pillows, the warm comfort of the duvet, all add to augment guest experience. This also includes the perception of ambient temperature maintained in guestrooms, lobbies, and other public areas.

Sound Music speaks a universal language and stirs human emotions. Soothing instrumentals playing in the background in the lobby and other guest areas such as restaurants encourage guests to relax. The sounds of water cascading in rippling waterfall in outdoor lounge or dining area too enhances guest experience.

Taste The sense of taste can be used to create a positive guest experience too. A refreshing welcome drink on arrival, titbits of local speciality treats in a welcome platter in the guestroom, speciality teas, signature cocktails or mocktails, all help to enhance guest experience.

It is essential to consider the target market to create the five senses experiences concept since what may be curated for new generation travellers would be different from what would suit a classic luxury property. For a hotel, an ideal way to create five senses guest experience would be to put its accommodation managers in the guest's shoes and take a deliberate walk through the property, taking in the look, feel and smell of the place, critically observe the positive or negative five senses stimulators and document them. Once the concept-suitable senses are identified, further memorable experiences can be created. A five senses guest experience curator format as shown in Exhibit 25.2 can be used for the documentation.

Exhibit 25.2 A format for five senses guest experience curator

Hotel Spring Leaves International

FIVE SENSES GUEST EXPERIENCE CURATOR

Sense	Managers' names	What do we ....?	It evokes feeling of	Does it gel with our concept?	How can we curate it for our concept?
	1				
Smell	2				
	3				
	1				
Vision	2				
	3				
	1				
Touch	2				
	3				
	1				
Sound	2				
	3				
	1				
Taste	2				
	3				

SUMMARY

Optimum indoor air quality, air-conditioning, sound levels and light make for an environment conducive to working in for employees and one conducive to relaxation for guests. Factors in human comfort have been outlined in the chapter. Indoor air quality (IAQ) has been discussed in detail. An important aspect of the internal environment discussed in this chapter is air-conditioning. Most people associate air-conditioning with cooling only. It should be clearly understood from this chapter that air conditioners may also perform the function of heating when the need arises. Apart from cooling or heating the air, the air-conditioners dehumidify (regulate relative humidity) and filter the air (provide ventilation) too. How air-conditioners work has been comprehensively explained in the chapter.

It is important in hotels to maintain optimum temperatures in different areas, which are related mainly to the functions of these areas.

The difference between sound and noise is that noise is largely considered undesirable. Uncontrolled noise in an establishment can not only affect the employees adversely, but also deter guests from repeating their stay at the property. In hotels, the culprits responsible for noise are often housekeeping equipment. The executive housekeeper should take adequate measures to minimize unwanted noise. The employees should be trained in methods of working that create the lowest amount of noise possible. Each employee should realize the importance of maintaining low noise levels.

In many hotels, acoustic materials are used in recreation rooms, convention halls, banquet halls, and audio-visual centres. This chapter discussed ways of noise control in the housekeeping department.

The important aspect of light in the internal environment is discussed in brief. In this chapter, the emphasis is on the measurement and the amount of light in various areas of the hotel. Further information on types, functions, and other decorative aspects of light will be found in Chapter 27. A section describing the five senses guest experience is included.

KEY TERMS

Acoustics Sound absorption, reflection, and conduction qualities of spaces.

ACPH Air Changes Per Hour.

AHU Air Handling Unit.

Air-conditioning The modification of air quality and attributes within a defined space, usually a residence or a place of business. It usually involves heating or cooling, dehumidifying, and filtering or cleaning the air.

Air handler Also known as the 'indoor unit', the air handler is the evaporator section of the air-conditioning system. It circulates and delivers the cooled air.

Algae These are mainly eukaryotic, single-celled or multi-cellular aquatic plants without true stems, roots, or leaves. They are typically autotrophic, photosynthetic, and contain chlorophyll. They may be free-floating or found attached to structures such as rocks or other submerged surfaces.

Compressor The 'engine' which drives the condensing unit of an air-conditioner (or other device). The condensing unit in an air-conditioner serves as a pump that compresses the gas in the high-pressure (condensing) side of the cooling cycle and causes the refrigerant to circulate.

Condensing unit Also known as the 'outdoor unit', the condensing unit of an air-conditioner pumps vapourized refrigerant from the air handler (indoor unit), compresses it, liquefies it, and returns it.

Decibels Units in which sound intensity is measured.

Dimmers Switches that can vary the amount of light given out by a lamp.

Foot-candle A lumen of light distributed over 1 sq. foot of area. It is a unit of illumination.

1 foot-candle = 10.76 lux

HEPA High Efficiency Particulate Air filters.

HVAC Heating Ventilation and Air-Conditioning.

Illumination The distribution of light on a horizontal surface is called its illumination. Illumination is measured in foot-candles.

Lighting efficacy The ratio of light output from a lamp to the electric power it consumes. It is measured in lumens per watt (LPW).

Lumen A measurement of the light output from a light source. All lamps are rated in lumens. The output of a 100-watt incandescent lamp is about 1750 lumens.

Lux The measure of illumination level at or on the surface that is being illuminated.

10.76 lux = 1 foot-candle

NRC Noise reduction coefficient. A scale that indicates the amount of sound waves a material or surface absorbs or reflects.

Refrigerant A substance that absorbs heat to change states (evaporating) from liquid to gas and releases heat by changing states (condensing) from gas back to liquid.

Relative humidity The ratio of the amount of water present in the air to the maximum amount of water that the air could potentially hold in the same conditions. For instance, a relative humidity of 95% indicates that there is 95/100ths as much water in the air as that air is capable of holding at that temperature and pressure.

TFA Treated Fresh Air.

Thermostat A temperature-sensitive switch that controls heating and cooling systems.

Tinnitus A condition characterized by ringing in the ears.

White noise Noise whose energy is uniform over a wide range of frequencies. It is widely perceived as relatively benign but persistent sound. The hum of a vacuum cleaner, for example, may be considered white noise by some.

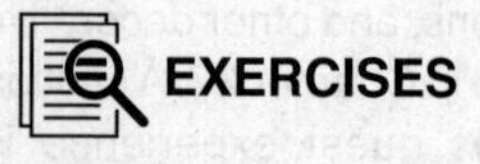

26 Interior Designing

Learning Objectives

After reading this chapter, you should be able to

- realize the importance of successful integration of beauty, expressiveness, and functionalism in interior designing
- apply the elements of art in designing interiors
- utilize the principles of design while coordinating interiors

Introduction

A hotel property's design and decor have a tremendous visual and functional impact on its guests through the image and message it communicates of the brand standards, the ambience it creates and the theme it underlines. The design of the landscaped areas, the façade, lobby, public areas, and rooms play a significant role in achieving guest satisfaction and making for repeat customers. The hotel design process and specifics are covered in further detail in Chapter 28.

Interior design is the orderly arrangement of lines, forms, colours, textures, etc. to create beauty in interiors. A good design shows an orderly arrangement of the materials used and, in addition, creates beauty in the finished product.

Interior decoration can be a highly personal form of self-expression—the sum of one's interests as an individual or as a group—as well as a practical statement created by combining various elements of art using certain design principles. Refer to the scan code of pictures of interior designing.

Objectives of Interior Design

The objective of interior design and decoration is to achieve beauty, expressiveness, and functionalism.

Beauty Whenever one says that something is 'aesthetic', one usually implies that a beautiful piece has been created. Involved in this accomplishment is the organization, selection, and arrangement of materials into an appealing form. Art is the organization of energies and means to gain the kind of response that is termed 'beauty'. Beauty is not the only objective in planning and furnishing accommodation areas; in addition, the areas should express an idea and, most important of all, should function effectively.

Expressiveness An important way to approach the subject of selecting, decorating, and furnishing an area is to express some definite idea or theme in it. These themes could be naturalness, sophistication, formality, royalty, warmth, coolness, freshness, antiquity, and so on. For instance, an atrium lobby profuse with indoor plants, climbers, and creepers, vertical garden gives an instant feel of naturalness.

Functionalism An accommodation product should, most importantly, 'work'. Its spaces and furniture should serve the purpose for which they are intended. For instance, social spaces in the guestroom are for group interaction, so seating should be comfortable, storage convenient, lighting ample, air-conditioning optimal, and appropriate functional and work spaces organized for efficiency. All areas should give the maximum of service, comfort, and pleasure for the minimum of care. Every phase of planning and furnishing should be based on function.

Public areas too are divided according to function, such as places to lounge, socialize, exercise, and garden. Furniture here is arranged in functional groups for study, reading, conversation, writing, eating, and enjoying music.

Other considerations that must be kept in mind while designing are as follows:

- There should be optimum utilization of space available.
- It should be easily maintainable, that is, it should withstand the abuse it receives during operations.
- It should be convenient to the guests.
- It should be practical in cost and within the budget constraints as far as possible.

Basic Types of Design

There are two kinds of designs—structural and decorative.

Structural Design

It denotes the structure or construction of objects. This is comprised of the size, form, colour, and texture of an object, be it the object itself, or the drawing of the object worked out on paper.

Basic requirements The basic requirements of a good structural design are as follows:

- It should be simple.
- It should be well proportioned.
- In addition to being beautiful, it should be suited to its purpose.
- It should be suited to the material from which it is made.

Decorative Design

This is the surface enrichment of structural design. Any lines, colour, or materials that have been applied to structural design for the purpose of adding a richer quality to it constitute its decorative design.

Basic requirements The following are the basic requirements of a good decorative design:

- Decoration should be used in moderation.
- Decoration should be placed at structural points and it should strengthen the shape of the object.
- There should be enough background space to give it an effect of simplicity.
- The background should be suited to the patterns that are to be placed against it.

Structural design is far more important than decorative design since it is essential to every object, while decoration is the luxury of design. A good design is the result of certain elements of art being used according to the principles of design (see Figure 26.1).

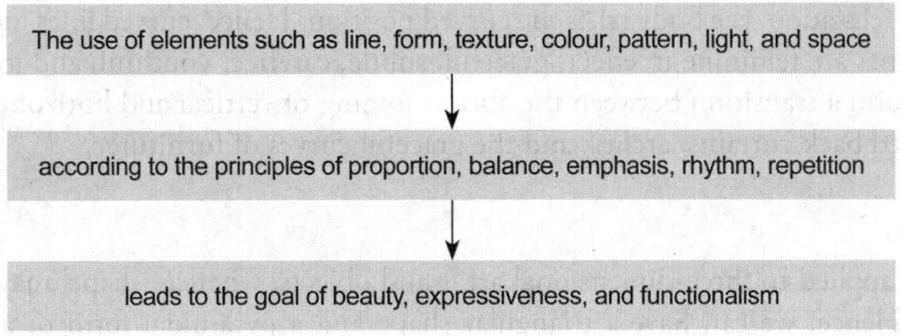

Fig. 26.1 Achieving a good design

Elements of Design

These are primarily the visual components used in creating a design or a composition. The elements that are basic to all visual designs are line, form, colour, and texture. Three additional elements—pattern, light, and space—help to complete it. Each of these basic elements is a well-defined and dissimilar feature of every design. However, the effect of each element is considered only in connection with the other elements and the unit is judged as a whole. These elements, if used according to the principles of design, can ensure a certain degree of beauty in the final product.

Line

This is a very important element in planning and furnishing. It is the most basic design element. Before the artist begins to paint, he or she must establish the directions of the lines of a painting on the canvas or paper. The artist combines horizontal, vertical, diagonal, and curved lines until the effect is pleasing to the eye. Likewise, the architect and the interior decorator must organize and combine lines before they can create beauty in a building or in an interior design. Lines have a positive emotional significance, depending upon their direction and their quality. In any interior, a combination of the four types of lines listed above is generally seen, each having their own influences. Certain associations may be made between man and the lines based on the positions his body takes in different actions.

Vertical lines When standing, a human being is perceived as attentive and ready to act. Hence, vertical lines suggest steadfastness, sturdiness, or an upward aim. These lines are masculine in effect—severe, strong, direct, disciplined, and militaristic. They create a feeling of height. In hotels, the vertical lines of doorways, pillars, columns, draperies, and furniture give the necessary strength and height to rooms.

Horizontal lines When a human being lies down, he or she is perceived as resting or sleeping. Therefore, the horizontal line naturally suggests rest, repose, or steadiness. These lines give solidity and a down-to-earth feeling. They suggest tranquility, serenity, and relaxation. They help to break the effect of the vertical lines carrying one's eyes upward. In hotels, the horizontal lines of tables, sofas, and other furniture complement the severely vertical lines in other parts of an area.

Diagonal lines When running or moving things, the human body is often in a diagonal position and therefore diagonal lines suggest movement and activity. These are lines of action, disturbing the discipline of straight lines and the solidity of horizontal lines. Forward-slanting lines (sloped rightward at the top) suggest 'push' and backward-slanting lines (tops leaning to left) 'pull'. Diagonal lines are also suggestive of sophistication and refinement, and hence arouse interest. In hotels, diagonal lines appear in staircases and sometimes in curtains, draperies, and wallpaper.

Curved lines In relaxation, the body takes the curved position. Hence, curved lines indicate flexibility and grace. These lines are feminine in effect, graceful, subtle, carefree, youthful, and joyous. In hotels, curved lines may form a transition between the abrupt joining of vertical and horizontal lines, such as those formed by tied back curtains, arches, and the graceful curves of furniture.

Form

The term 'form' is applied to three-dimensional areas and objects, whereas 'shape' may refer to a two-dimensional one. Hence, we can have a triangular shape and a pyramidal form or a cuboidal form with a square shape. Without the beauty of form, good texture, colour, or decoration can be of no use. However, a particular chair is not well designed unless it accommodates itself to the human form. The form of an object should thus suit its function.

Texture

The word texture refers to the tactile quality of the surface of any object or area. It refers to the surface quality—how something feels when we touch it and how it behaves when light strikes it. Two basic categories of texture are tactile and visual.

Tactile or actual texture can be felt by hand—be it rough like unglazed brick or smooth like velvet. Visual or 'illusionary' texture may be absolutely smooth to touch, but gives the impression of texture.

Texture plays a very important part in interiors because it affects the quality and quantity of light reflected by the surface. Some terms used to describe textures are listed here:

blistered, bubbly, corrugated, crepe, crinkly, coarse, crystalline, delicate, dull, feathery, filmy, fine, firm, flexible, foamy, frilly, glassy, glossy, granular, grooved, hairy, lacy, leathery, marbled, meshy, metallic, mossy, perforated, pitted, polished, porous, powdery, prickly, reticulated, ribbed, rocky, rough, rubbery, sandy, satiny, scaly, shirred, silky, smooth, solid, spongy, striated, stiff, stratified, thorny, uneven, velvety, wavy, waxy, woody, woolly, etc.

Colour

The appeal of colour is universal. Colour is the impression received by the brain from certain stimulations of the retina in the eye. Its perception occurs because objects reflect or transmit light that enters the eye. Light rays that vary in wavelength and rates of vibration produce different sensations and appear as different colours. Daylight, although it appears as 'white' light, is actually composed of violet, indigo, blue, green, yellow, orange, and red colours of light. Colour is discussed in greater detail in Chapter 27.

Pattern

This refers to any sort of surface enrichment and applies to both two-dimensional and three-dimensional objects. A large room can support more patterns than a small one. Patterns used may be naturalistic, stylized, geometric, or abstract. Generally, pattern should cover just about a quarter of the total surface area. If walls and carpets are plain, then draperies and upholstery may be patterned.

Light

When light strikes an object, it may be reflected, absorbed, or allowed to pass through. Light has a functional as well as an aesthetic effect. Light may be dull or sharp, bright or diffused. Light is discussed in detail in Chapter 27.

The way light is used in interiors has a definite emotional effect on the minds of the occupants of a space.

- Bright light energizes us and has a tendency to foster either hard work or energetic play.
- Subdued light makes us feel relaxed, but if too subdued, may put us to sleep.
- Too brilliant light often causes us to look away in physical and emotional distress.
- A bright, focused light can make one feel 'in the spotlight'.
- Flickering light, as from a fireplace, nearly always draws people towards it.
- Strong contrasts of bright and dark seem dramatic, but if they are too extreme, can be tiring.
- Warm-coloured light seems cheerful and welcoming.
- Cool-coloured light is often more restful.

Space

This is among the most important elements of interior design. The organization of space is basic to architecture and interior decoration. Unless a space is thoughtfully planned, nothing else will seem quite right. Almost any space, if sensitively handled, can be made effective, liveable, and even dramatic. A sense of the beauty of a space makes us want large undecorated walls, and floors can be bound together by other elements without disturbing the effect. The appreciation of good spacing is the reason we may use the minimum amount of furniture and concentrate them in groups so that we can have empty, silent spaces in the rooms. Today, the trend is for spaces to become freer and less obstructed. Indoor spaces can be 'opened up' by means of fewer partitions and large openings between rooms. Indoor spaces can also connect with the limitless outdoor spaces by means of glass walls, large openings, and porches.

Principles of Design

The principles of design help one in determining the quality of a design to assess whether it is artistically good or poor in appearance. While using the basic elements of design or art, we should keep these principles in mind. The principles of design are proportion, balance, emphasis, rhythm, and harmony.

Proportion

The principle of proportion is also called the 'law of relationships'. The principle of proportion underlines all other principles of design. It states that the relations between parts of the same things or between different things of the same group should be aesthetically satisfying. It deals with relationships of size, shape, colour, light, texture, and pattern. In order to achieve designs and arrangements that will hold interest, one must know how to create beautiful relationships within and around a space. Some typically complementary proportions include the following:

The Greek oblong The ancient Greeks, striving for beauty, arrived at the point where they tried to achieve good proportions in nearly everything they created. Among the rules that they evolved was the oblong that they used as the basis of space divisions, called 'the golden oblong' or the 'Greek oblong'. The Greek oblong measures two units on the short side and three on the long side. Its proportions are considered more beautiful than a completely symmetrical shape like a square. The Greek oblong has since been the recognized standard for space relationships through much of Western civilization.

Scale Another important aspect of proportion is scale. A person who must select and arrange things to look good together must develop a sense of scale. In order to judge what sizes must be grouped together successfully, it is necessary to grasp the underlying significance of scale. Pleasing scale requires that

- the sizes of all the elements making up the structure have a consistent, pleasing relationship to the structure and to each other; and that
- the size of the structure be in pleasing proportion to the different objects combined with it.

Balance

Also known as equilibrium, balance is a condition of rest or repose. Through balance, we get a sense of equipoise. This restful effect is obtained by grouping shapes and colours around a centre or pivotal point in such a way that there are equal attractions on each side of that centre.

Balance can be understood well if one understands the principle of the see-saw, as both work on the same principle. Equal weights will balance when they are at the same distance from the centre of a see-saw. If unequal, the heavier weight must be moved towards the centre and the lighter weight away from it for balance to be achieved (by the laws of fulcrums). Balance in design and art is not the same as balance in weight, but is conceived in terms of the amount of attention each element attracts and can be treated in the same way. That is, the more imposing object must be further from the centre than the less imposing, the larger further than the smaller, and so on. The classification of different types of balance is given in Figure 26.2.

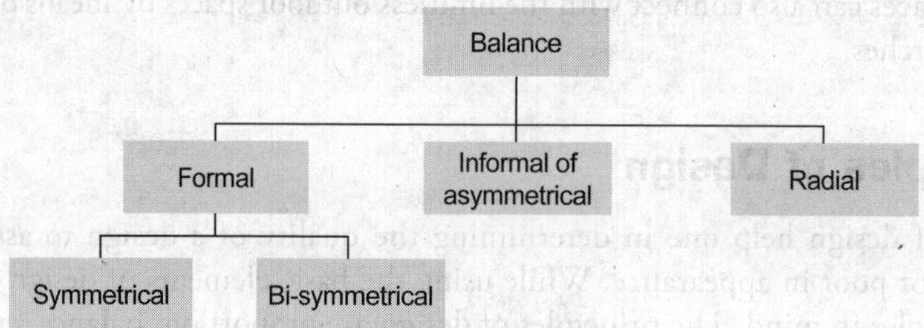

Fig. 26.2 Classification of balance

Formal balance

The 'centre' of the space under consideration is the pivot around which attractions must be adjusted. When objects are alike or are equally forceful in appearance and attraction, they are placed equidistant from the centre. This can be achieved in two ways:

Symmetrical formal balance When objects on either side of the centre are identical or mirror images of each other and are placed at equal distances from the centre, the result is a symmetrical formal balance.

Bi-symmetrical formal balance When objects are not alike but are equal in their power to interest and attract, the result is a bi-symmetrical formal balance.

Informal/asymmetrical balance

This is also referred to as 'active balance' or 'occult balance'. Asymmetry results when the visual weights of two objects do not attract the same amount of attention and so they have to be placed at different distances from the centre. Thus, a 'heavy' weight nearer the centre counterbalances 'lighter' ones further away.

Informal balance is more subtle than formal balance and affords greater opportunity for variety in arrangements. Its success depends upon training the eye to recognize a restful composition.

Radial balance

This is the type of balance that grows out of a central point or axis. It may be observed in the diverging lines that form the pattern of spokes in a wheel, the petals of flowers, and so on. Here, all parts are balanced and repeated around a centre. Its chief characteristic is an impression of circular movement out from, towards, or around a centre.

Emphasis

This is the design principle that directs us to create a point of interest such that the eye is carried first to the most important thing in any arrangement and from that point to every other detail in order of importance. Whenever any object is selected or arranged with reference to its appearance, the principle of emphasis is used, and the success of the result depends upon the knowledge of what to emphasize; how to emphasize; how much to emphasize; and where to place emphasis.

What to emphasize?

A definite plan should be made by classifying the materials and arranging them according to importance, starting from the most important and moving towards the least. The background should of course be less conspicuous than the objects to be emphasized, which are placed against it.

How to emphasize?

There are several means by which one may create emphasis and the most important of these are as follows:

By placing together or grouping The objects grouped together thus must have some common characteristics or similarity so that the group does not create confusion in the mind of the observer.

By use of contrasting colours The eyes are equally attracted by contrasts of light and dark and by contrasting colours. One of the most striking means of calling attention to any object is to place it against a background with which it contrasts. However, note that an arrangement that has equal amounts of light and dark can be very confusing. A good composition would be a dark scheme accented with light or a light scheme made interesting through dark notes.

By having sufficient background Usually plain walls are preferred as the details of the objects placed against them can then be properly observed.

By using unusual elements Emphasis can also be achieved by the use of unusual lines, shapes, colours, or sizes to heighten the effect.

How much to emphasize?

The emphasis should be properly distributed. The designer has to decide the amount of plain and patterned spaces to use and where and how to distribute them. Centre of interest should be limited by directing prominence to one centre and making other centres less prominent.

Where to place the emphasis?

The degree of importance to be given to different parts of the area should be decided. Central positions should be made more conspicuous. It also helps if central areas are placed with less important ones.

Rhythm

This is a major design principle, through which an underlying unity and variety can be achieved. Rhythm is movement. All movement in design is not, however, rhythmic. Sometimes movement is distracting. In designing, rhythm implies an easy connecting path along which the eye may travel. It may also be called 'related movement'. If one observes a plain surface, there is usually no movement in it. The eye remains quiet and stops at any point where it happens to fall. But the moment a picture or an object is placed against it, the eye starts moving in the direction of the lines suggested in the pattern they make together. At that moment, movement is created. Such a movement may either be organized and easy, that is, rhythmic; or it may be restless and distracting, that is, lacking in rhythm. There are three outstanding ways of developing rhythm in interiors.

Repetition of shapes The principle of rhythm as it is gained through repetition is recognized when one is conscious of the swing of a beautifully spaced, regularly repeated pattern in any decorative design. When a shape is regularly repeated at proper intervals, a movement is created that carries the eye from one unit to the next in such a way that one is not conscious of separate units but of a rhythmic advancement, making it easy for the eye to pass along the entire length of the space.

Progression of sizes Progressing sizes create a rapid movement of the eye. Progression can be created by increasing or decreasing one or more of the object's qualities. It is known as an 'ordered' or 'systematic change'. It lays stress not only on movement, but also by channelling movement towards a goal, makes it more lively and dynamic than repetition. It is usually more easily applied to accessories than to large pieces of furniture. Gradations of colour are also used in some fabrics so that the eye will travel from the more dominant one to the more subdued.

Continuous line movement Lines compel the eye to follow the directions they take. This powerful quality may be employed in various ways to control the movement of the eye. The design of a room is usually composed of many different lines, but a predominance of one type will cause the eye to move in that direction. Borders and chair rails are simple ways to introduce continuous lines. Wallpapers, fabrics, and rugs frequently have a dominant line direction that can be employed to create rhythmic movement.

Harmony

This is the fundamental requirement of any piece of work in which appearance as well as use have to be considered. Harmony is the most important of all the principles of design. It is the design principle that produces an expression of unity through the selection and arrangement of discrete objects and ideas. Harmony has five aspects:

Harmony of line and shape This, in turn, can be of three types:

- lines that follow or repeat one another;
- lines that contrast with one another; and
- transitional lines that soften or modify the others.

In producing a harmony of shapes, there should always be an effect of organization. Large objects and large items of furniture should be placed to follow the boundary lines of the enclosing shape and smaller pieces placed at other corners.

Harmony of size When sizes that are too different are used together, they appear inconsistent. The aspect of proportion called 'scale' is allied to harmony. The under-standing and application of the principles of proportion will assure the harmony of sizes.

Harmony of texture Coarse and fine materials used together do not give a harmonious effect and so should be avoided.

Harmony of ideas It is not enough that sizes, shapes, and textures have something in common; there must be harmony in the ideas presented together. Things that may appear appropriate in a royal suite would be distinctly out of place in a cottage setting. Rich period furniture needs a formal setting. It should be understood, however, that it is not necessary to have such an association of ideas in order to have harmony.

Harmony of colours Colour combinations giving the most pleasure are likely to be those possessing harmony or unity. They give the impression that all the colours really belong together; yet, at the same time, there must be sufficient variety to avoid producing a monotonous arrangement.

Units of Design

There are four units of design: naturalistic, stylized, geometric, and abstract. An individual design may be based on any one of the units or may contain a combination of two or more units.

Naturalistic These represent nature—flowers, leaves, fruits, animals, landscapes, and so on. Every effort is made to keep the motifs realistic, so that they appear as exact reproductions. These patterns lend themselves to either formal or informal themes.

Stylized These designs resemble natural objects, but usually the lines are simplified and conventionalized. Sometimes they are distorted. The designer uses various degrees of stylization, depending upon the materials employed and the purpose of the article. These motifs may include outsized patterns, for instance, of flowers and other natural forms in colours that are not natural but are intended to create certain effects (warmth, coolness, brightness).

Geometric These are based on such pure forms as the circle, rectangle, and triangle, although endless variations and combinations of them are used. Geometric motifs include stripes, dots, and checks, as well as many less usual forms.

Abstract Many abstract designs are based on geometric forms. 'Abstract' implies an element of impressionism and a greater freedom than is found in most geometric forms. The shapes and patterns, although derived from the geometric, may be less rigid and formal than the popular conception of a geometrical design. They are also called 'non-representational' because they represent nothing but themselves.

SUMMARY

Successful integration of interior design and decoration leads to achievement of the ultimate goals of beauty, expressiveness, and functionalism in hotel design. Good taste is appreciated by all. At the same time, the created design should 'work', that is, the spaces should fulfil their purpose or function. While designing hotels, architects and designers have continuous discussions with the owners as to what they want to express in the interiors or what theme they want the hotel to portray.

It is important to understand that the structural design is far more important than the decorative design since it is essential to every object, whereas a decoration is the luxury of design. Many a time, this is where designs fall short—the designer has concentrated on decorative design whereas the structural design is not balanced or is poor. Such a design will appear beautiful but will not function to fulfil its purpose. When it is said that the design

should be functional, it also means that cleaning should not be a hassle due to design features. Once a beautiful structure is made, its maintenance is crucial.

The study of the elements and principles of design develops the ability to judge the appearance and function of a design. These elements and principles are basic to all visual arts. They do not provide formulae for creating beauty, but they help determine the proper placement of objects so as to give an impression that everything is in place.

The chapter explains the elements and principles of design in detail. The four units of design are also discussed. An individual design may be based on any one of the units or it may be a combination of two or more units.

KEY TERMS

Atrium A central lobby into which all rooms open or which rooms may overlook.

Decorative design The superficial enrichment of structural design. Any lines, colours, or materials that have been applied to a structure or object to add a quality of richness constitute its decorative design.

Elements of design Primarily the visual components used in creating a design composition. These elements are line, form, colour, texture, pattern, light, and space.

Emphasis The design principle that directs us to create points of interest so that the eye is carried first to the most important thing in any arrangement, and from that point to every other detail in order of its importance.

Harmony The design principle that produces an expression of unity through the selection and arrangement of constant objects and ideas.

Interior decoration Interior decoration is a highly personal expression of the self, the sum of one's interests as an individual or as a group, and a practical statement created by combining various elements of art by using certain principles.

Interior design Interior design is defined as an orderly arrangement of lines, forms, colours, textures, and so on in design so as to create beauty in interiors.

Pattern Pattern refers to any sort of surface enrichment and applies to both two-dimensional and three-dimensional objects.

Proportion The principle of proportion states that the relations between parts of the same thing or between different things of the same group should be satisfying. It deals with relationships in size, shape, colour, light, texture, and pattern.

Rhythm In designing, rhythm means establishing a path along which the eye may easily travel. It may also be called 'related movement'.

Structural design The size, form, colour, and texture of an object.

Texture The tactile quality of a surface—how something feels when we touch it—or the suggestion of tactile qualities when light strikes it.

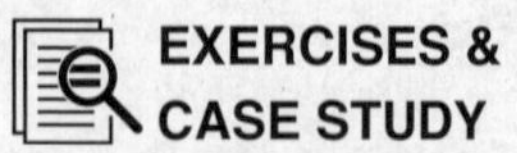

27

Interior Decoration

Learning Objectives

After reading this chapter, you should be able to

- describe the significant role played by colour in interior decoration and plan and implement sample colour schemes for a room
- explain the importance of lighting; classify the various types of light; and discuss the use of lighting fixtures
- discuss the types, selection, and maintenance of floor finishes
- distinguish the various kinds of carpets in terms of construction and design/patterns, and be able to select them and carry out suitable maintenance procedures
- identify the various ceiling and wall coverings
- plan window treatments for various kinds of windows
- get insights into functions, classification, selection and placement of accessories

 Introduction

Interior decoration is a highly personal form of self-expression. It is the sum of one's interests as an individual or a group—a personal statement created by combining various elements of art by using certain principles.

Colour, lighting, floor coverings and finishes, carpets, ceiling and wall coverings, and various window treatments are some important tools used for decorating various areas of a hotel and giving a distinct style to these areas.

 Colour

The study of colours may be approached from any of the five angles: that of physiologists, chemists, physicists, psychologists, or people who work with pigments. Of the many theories of colour (in pigment form), two are in common use. These are generally known as the Prang system and the Munsell system. Of the two, the Prang colour system is more frequently followed in interior decoration. These systems are discussed later in the chapter.

Dimensions of Colour

There are three properties or qualities that may be called the dimensions of colour—these are just as distinct as the length, breadth, and thickness of an object.

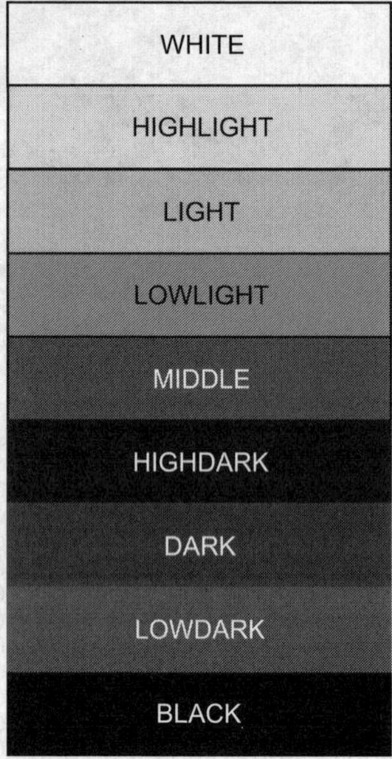

Fig. 27.1 Representation of the value scale

Hue This term indicates the name of the colour such as red, blue, green, etc. The colour of an object is determined by the wavelengths of the light it reflects. An object appears black when all the wavelengths are absorbed and white when all are reflected. Although the words 'colour' and 'hue' are used interchangeably, 'colour' is a general term and 'hue' is a specific term referring to definite identifiable colours.

Value This describes the lightness or darkness of a colour. There are a total of nine values, ranging all the way from white to black. White is the highest value and no hue can be as light as white. Black is the lowest value and no hue can be darker than black. Halfway between black and white come middle values. The value scale is shown in Figure 27.1.

Values can be changed by adding white (or water) to lighten a pigment or by adding more pigment or black to darken them. A value that is lighter than the normal base colour of the pigment is called a tint and one that is darker is called a shade. Lighter values seem to increase the size of an object. Black and dark values seem to decrease the size of an object.

Intensity/chroma This refers to the brightness or dullness of a colour. A very bright colour is said to be of full intensity. Colours at full intensity are very striking and brilliant. If its intensity is so high as to be offensive, it may be considered gaudy, garish, or flashy. A colour that is not bright is said to have been toned down, and if disagreeably so, may be characterized as dull, weak, or drab.

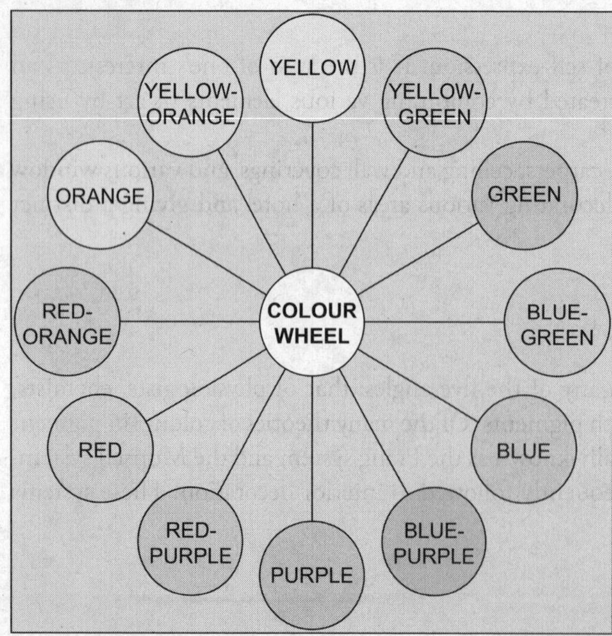

Fig. 27.2 Prang's colour wheel

Warm and Cool Colours

One of the most important factors of colour to be considered in interior decoration is their relative warmth or coolness. Colours that contain greater proportions of yellow or red are considered to be warm; those that contain blue are regarded as cool. Red and orange are thus the warmest of all colours. Blue is the coolest of colours.

The colour wheel (see Figure 27.2) can be divided into two halves. The colours to the left represent the warm colours. The colours to the right represent cool colours. Warm colours tend to excite, cool colours have a tranquilizing effect. Green is one of the most tranquil or restful colours, as it is the colour of fields and trees in nature. Warm colours are often used in rooms that are difficult to heat and they are good in rooms that admit little or no natural light. In rooms exposed

to bright sunlight, a cool atmosphere is desirable. In any colour scheme, either the warm or the cool colours should dominate, equal amounts of each being an unpleasant result.

Advancing and Receding Colours

Warm hues seem to advance and cool ones seem to recede, or go back or further away from you. A cool, light colour on the walls thus helps to make a small room look larger. A warm colour visually draws the walls in, lowers a high ceiling or makes a room that is too large look more compact.

Prang's Colour System

As shown in Figure 27.2, Prang's colour system uses 12 colours represented on a colour wheel.

Colour wheel

The colours in the colour wheel can be classified as primary, secondary, and tertiary colours.

Primary colours These are the basic pigments which form all colours. They cannot be obtained by mixing other hues. Red, yellow, and blue are the fundamental or primary colours, which can be mixed so as to form all the other colours, but which cannot themselves be made by mixing any other colours.

Secondary/binary colours Secondary colours result when two primary colours are mixed in equal amounts. There are three secondary colours.

Red + Blue → Purple

Yellow + Red → Orange

Yellow + Blue → Green

The primary and secondary colours are together called the six standard colours.

Tertiary/intermediate colours When a primary colour and a neighbouring secondary are mixed in equal amounts, an intermediate hue results. In appearance, the intermediate is halfway between its adjacent colours. There are thus six intermediate hues: yellow-green; red-purple; blue-green; red-orange; blue-purple; and yellow-orange.

Munsell Colour System

In this system, the dimensions are shown upon a sphere. Values, in neutral grey, are shown upon a vertical pole, representing the axis of the sphere. The north pole is thus white and the south pole is black. The colours are represented by paths or arms along the radii, running from neutral grey to the circumference or beyond. According to this system, there are five principal hues: red, yellow, green, blue, and purple. The intermediate hues are yellow-red, green-yellow, blue-green, purple-blue, and red-purple.

Instead of the 12-hue circuit of the Prang system, we now have 10 major hues, divided into five principal hues and five intermediate hues.

Colour Schemes and Harmonies

A colour scheme is the combination of colours used for decorating—whether doing up interiors, or for designing a dress, or another purpose. There are two main types of colour schemes—related and contrasting. The classification of colour schemes is outlined in Figure 27.3.

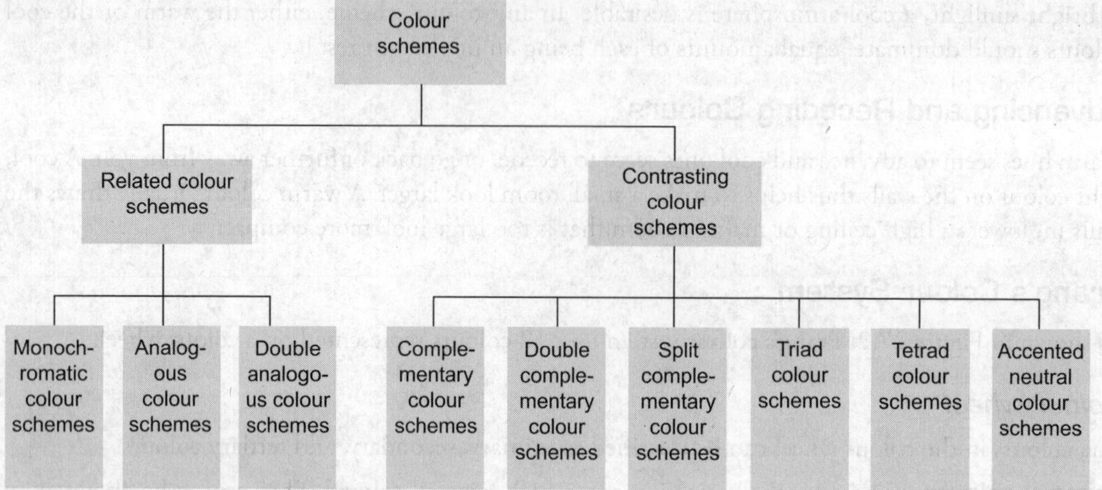

Fig. 27.3 Classification of colour schemes

Related colour schemes

Let us first discuss the related colour schemes.

Monochromatic colour schemes This is also called a one-hue or one-mode harmony. It evolves from a single hue, which can be varied from highlight to low-dark and from full saturation to almost neutral. White, grey, black, and brown add variety, as do applied and natural textures and decorative patterns. Thus, even with one basic hue, the possibilities are many. With this scheme, some degree of success is almost assured because unity and harmony are firmly established. Spaciousness and continuity are emphasized and the effect is quiet and peaceful. A major danger is monotony. This can be avoided by diversifying values and intensities. Such colour schemes are most effective when pale, medium, and dark values of a colour below full intensity are used along with accents of the colour at full intensity.

Analogous colour schemes These are based on hues that lie next to each other on the colour wheel. This scheme can have a minimum of two colours and a maximum of three. The hues should differ in their intensities and values. Analogous colour schemes, although basically harmonious, have more variety and interest than monochromatic schemes. An analogous colour scheme is always either predominantly warm or predominantly cool. When using three colours, one should dominate and other two should be used in smaller areas.

Double analogous colour schemes Any four adjacent hues on the colour wheel make up a double analogous colour scheme. There should be a harmony of hues used in such a scheme, avoiding too many contrasts.

Contrasting colour schemes

The colours chosen in these harmonies lie opposite or nearly opposite to each other on a colour wheel, and hence usually share no similarities.

Complementary colour schemes These are built on any two hues directly opposite each other on the colour wheel. They offer a great range of possibilities. Depending on how the colours are used, such schemes can be most pleasing or least satisfying. When complementary colours are used in a colour scheme, one of the two colours should be used at full intensity and limited to small areas while the larger areas in the opposite colour should be subdued in intensity.

Double complementary colour schemes Two adjacent colours and their complements used together form a double complementary colour scheme. Double complementary schemes combine the harmonious aspects of analogous colours with the contrast found in complementary combinations. In this scheme, the best effect is obtained when there is one outstanding hue used in the largest amount at subdued intensity.

Split complementary colour schemes Another variation of the complementary theme, the split complementary is composed of any hue together with the two hues on either side of its complement (or opposite). One of the three is selected to be the main colour and the other two are used to accentuate it. This makes the contrast less violent than in the simple complementary type of scheme, and adds interest and variety.

Triad colour schemes A triadic or triangular colour scheme is made up of any three colours that are equidistant from each other on the colour wheel. It should be remembered that full intensity hues are seldom used in decorating interiors, and this is particularly true here. Care must be taken to ensure that large areas of colours are subdued and that only small areas of one or two of the three colours are kept at full intensity.

Tetrad colour schemes Any four hues that are equidistant from one another on the colour wheel produce a tetrad colour scheme. Such combinations lead to rich, varied, yet unified and well-balanced compositions.

Accented neutral colour schemes This is the type of scheme in which most of the areas of the room are in expanses of neutral colours, with small areas of a bright colour used for accent.

Planning Colour Schemes

There are certain factors that must be taken into consideration when planning a colour scheme for a room.

Purpose of the room

This is the most important consideration when planning a colour scheme. The colours in a room must suit the purpose of the room and create the mood or atmosphere that needs to be conveyed. At the same time, the colours used must express the interests and personalities of those who will use the room.

In a guestroom, the guest would be invited to relax; therefore, cool, restful colours such as blue and green would be appropriate. It would be just as improper to use pale, dull, or sophisticated colours in the recreation room as to use intensely greyed colours in the bedrooms.

Delicate pastel colours are popular and appropriate in a nursery, but are not suitable for a room occupied by an active adolescent. Also, for a child's room, the décor of the room should be based on the child's own colour preferences as well as reflect the age and interests of the child. As boys and girls grow older, the strong colours they liked as children will often be replaced by more subdued, sophisticated colours.

In the living room, the colours used should induce a feeling of comfort in order to create a welcoming atmosphere for guests. Very bright or very warm colours as well as very cold or depressing ones should especially be avoided. To create an atmosphere of dignity and refinement, sophisticated colours should be used. Sophisticated colours are often toned-down or greyed hues, that may range to the almost-neutral.

A dining room should have appetizing colours. The colours most stimulating to thoughts of food and the enjoyment of eating are peach, pink, and other tints in red and orange. Most unappetizing are tints and shades of yellow-green, blues, and purples. A pale tint of yellow can be appetizing, but darker yellow is often distasteful in this context.

In a kitchen, the colour scheme should be cheerful, light, and bright. Cool colours are thought to counteract the heat of cooking. White or light walls are usually best for visibility. Natural wood is also desirable. The colours used in a kitchen should, however, be stimulating enough to make the cook feel creative. One vital colour, either a primary or secondary, may be used in the interior or woodwork, furniture, and so on. Other colours can be supplied by pots and pans, crockery or plants.

Bathroom walls and fixtures are usually white, for hygiene as well as aesthetic reasons. However, bathrooms are often decorated in colours that are suggestive of water as well, such as green, blue, violet, or grey.

Size and proportions of the room

A small room can be made to appear larger if light, cool colours are used on the walls. A long, narrow room will appear to have better proportions if the smaller end walls are painted a warmer colour, or a darker shade of the same colour is used on the long walls. A square room looks more elongated if two opposite walls are painted a dark colour and the other two a light one. Dark and warm colours make walls move in towards you, light and cool colours make them move out away from you. A ceiling that is too high can be made to appear lower if it is painted darker or warmer than the walls, or if the colour used on the ceiling is extended several inches down the walls.

Sharp colour contrasts also affect the apparent size of rooms. It is usually desirable to make the walls lighter than the floor and the ceiling lighter than the walls; but if the differences are too great, the room will seem to shrink in size. Three or four colours are enough in any room. Black, white, grey, silver, gold, and natural wood are considered neutrals and can be used in addition to these three or four colours in the colour scheme.

Relationship to other rooms

A room should not only be in harmony with itself, but should also harmonize with other rooms in the property. A hallway should harmonize with all the rooms that open onto it and the colours in one room should harmonize with the colours in other rooms that can be seen from it. There should be a feeling of unity or harmony as you pass from one room to another.

Amount of light received by an area

If the area receives a lot of natural light, the colours used should be cool to provide relief from strong daylight and natural heating. An area that receives very little light should be done up in warm colours such as red, orange, and yellow.

Type of surface

A rough surface casts small shadows and so appears darker than a smooth one.

Law of chromatic distribution

This is a general rule to be applied to the various areas in a room. The law states that larger areas in a room must be covered with the most neutral hues in the colour scheme. As the areas reduce in size, chromatic intensity may be proportionately increased. It is usual also to make the walls lighter than the floor and the ceiling lighter than the walls. For this purpose, a room can be subdivided into component areas of colour distribution as follows:

Dominant areas walls, floors, and ceilings.

Medium areas draperies, bed covers, and so on.

Smaller areas sofa sets, small pieces of upholstered furniture, and so on.

Accents ashtrays, paintings, flowers, and so on.

Lighting

Light is a form of energy without which there can be no vision. When light strikes an object, it may be reflected, absorbed, or allowed to pass through.

Importance of Lighting

Light has a definite emotional effect and can be very stimulating. Light is exciting while darkness is depressing. Proper lighting illuminates what we want to see. Light that is too bright exhausts physically and can be tiring. Lighting thus plays both a functional and an aesthetic role in a hotel.

Daylight is an important factor in the appearance of a room, so much so that no décor plans should be made without considering the amount of light that enters a room or is prevented from entering the room by the décor. As much daylight as is desired can be procured by means of glass walls or large windows extending from floor to ceiling. Curtains that can be drawn together or pushed back can also control the amount of light entering a room to suit the time of day and the needs of the occupants.

Artificial light is used to substitute as well as in association with daylight, it can be used to contrast or add emphasis by highlighting specific areas. It can also produce a harmonious effect throughout a room in addition to serving its basic function of producing visibility.

Effective lighting has been a focus for improving the aesthetics of a hotel for quite some time now. Many architects utilize lighting as prime tool in their innovative designs to bring out the ambience and quality of experience in the hotel, especially in its guestrooms. Lights also affect spatial perception. When an architect designs the interiors of a hotel room, he or she must consider whether the effect of lighting used in any design has been enhanced or subdued by various other factors, or whether the required effect or the optimum level of light has been achieved as designed. Even a slight glare from the lighting in a room can cause annoyance or discomfort to guests who stay in it.

The absorptive and reflective characteristics of the materials used within the hotel guestrooms are also important factors affecting the quality of light. All materials, depending on their various colours, textures, and other qualities, have different absorptive and reflective values. A black wall will probably absorb all the light falling on it and reflect nothing, but a yellow wall will reflect back 90% of the light, absorbing a mere 10%. Two similar coloured walls with different textures will also appear different because of the different reflective values of the textures.

While designing the lighting in a room, the architect also has to keep in mind that materials such as mirrored glass, polished aluminium, or stainless steel surfaces used in the decoration of hotel guestrooms can help to provide excellent directional control and also act as efficient reflectors. These materials are most effectively used in creating special decorative effects in the room. On the other hand, materials such as clear glass or plastics have very low absorption and high transmission values. They can be used as protective cover plates for concealed light sources.

Types of Light

Light can be classified in many ways as shown in Figure 27.4. The measurement of illumination/light has been discussed in detail in Chapter 25.

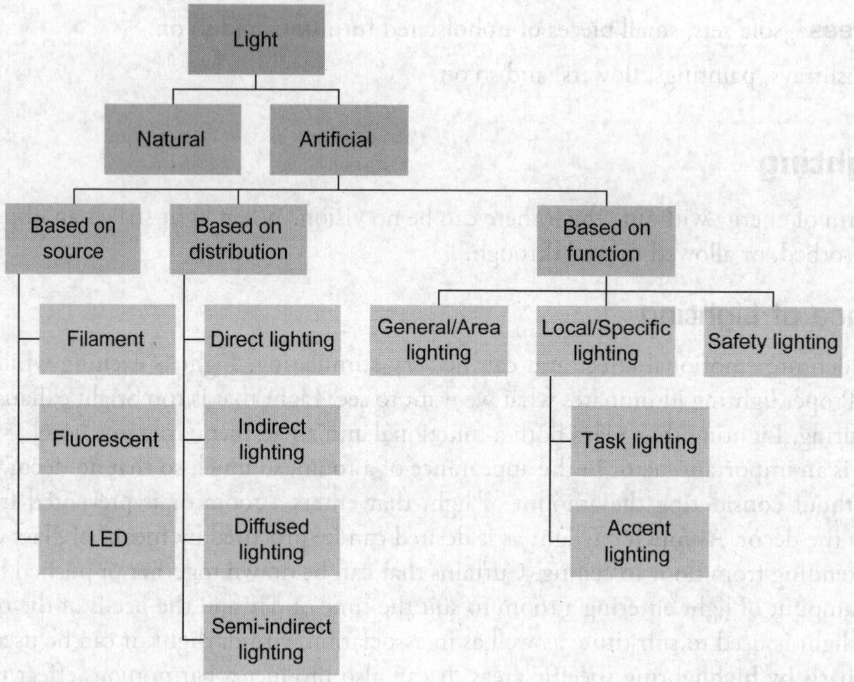

Fig. 27.4 Classification of light

Source-based classification

On the basis of source, light may be classified as natural or artificial light.

Natural light The bright radiant energy of the sun, daylight, is a major determining factor in the design of hotel guestrooms and homes, especially where large wall areas have been decorated with glass.

Artificial light Well-planned artificial illumination helps us to see without strain and helps to prevent accidents. It makes a vital contribution to the attractiveness of homes and hotels. At night, much of a room's character is determined by artificial illumination. This can be accomplished with the different types of lighting fixtures available. Artificial light can be further classified depending upon the way it is produced and the way it is used.

On the basis of the way artificial light is produced, it can be classified into incandescent and fluorescent light.

Incandescent/filament Here, light is produced by heating any material, usually metal, to a temperature at which it glows. Typical incandescent bulbs have a tungsten filament in a sealed glass container. The advantage of this type of lighting is that the fixtures and bulbs cost less than the fixtures and tubes used in the fluorescent or discharge types.

Many gas-filled varieties of incandescent bulbs are now available. Among them are GLS (general lighting service) lamps, which come in a wide variety—such as GLS clear, GLS argents (with a milky coating for glare-free diffused lighting), superlux (silica-coated opalescent bulbs for a silvery light), and special miniature lamps.

Halogen lamps are another source of incandescent light. These are filled with a halogen-mixed gas filling. This prevents the tungsten particles given off by the incandescent filament from condensing on the wall of the bulb. Halogen lamps are mainly used for floor lighting and as a light source in projectors and motor-vehicle headlamps.

Fluorescent/discharge Fluorescent tubes are a luminescent or 'cold' (not produced by heat) source of light. A glass tube with an inside coating of fluorescent powder is filled with vapourized mercury and argon. The ends are then sealed with two cathodes. When the electric current activates the gases in it, invisible UV rays cause the fluorescent coating to produce visible light. Although fluorescent tubes come only in straight or circular shapes, they have considerable diversity in colour. They also consume less energy than incandescent bulbs.

Depending on the pressure inside the tube, they can further be classified into low-pressure and high-pressure lamps.

Low-pressure lamps These are the most widely used tubular fluorescent lamps. They are primarily low-pressure mercury tubes, generally in the form of a long tubular bulb with an electrode sealed into each end and containing mercury vapour at low pressure, with an inert gas for starting the reaction. When a discharge is started, UV rays are produced. The fluorescent powder coating the inner surface of the tube converts these UV rays into visible light.

Conventional fluorescent lamps have a 38 mm diameter and come in ranges of 20W, 40W, and 65W. Slimmer versions with a 26 mm diameter are also available, in ranges of 18W, 36W, and 58W. They save about 10% more energy than incandescent bulbs. Another group of energy-saving fluorescent lamps are the PL and SL series of compact fluorescent lamps. These are available in 5W, 7W, 9W, and 11W ranges.

Low-pressure sodium vapour lamps are the most efficient light sources and are used in yard and street lighting. The light produced by these is yellow in colour.

High-pressure lamps These include high-pressure mercury vapour (HPMV) and high-pressure sodium vapour (HPSV) lamps. HPMV lamps produce a bluish white light, whereas HPSVs produce a golden yellow light.

Light emitting diode (LED) It is the latest trend in the way light is produced. How an LED lamp works is depicted in Figure 27.5. A diode is a type of semi-conductor. In an LED, one half of the lighting element is a semiconductive material with added impurities that contain an abundance of electrons that are negatively charged. This side is called the 'n-type' semiconductor. The other half contains the semiconductive material with added impurities that contain positively charged carriers. This side is called the 'p-type' semiconductor. The boundary between these two is called the 'p-n junction'. As the electric current passes across the p-n junction, the electrons from n-type side fill holes in the p-type side. During this process, the electrons change their state from higher orbit to lower orbit resulting in loss of energy. This loss of energy is in the form of a photon of light.

The characteristics of filament, fluorescent, and LED lamps are outlined in Table 27.1.

Based on the way light is directed on the object/area to be illuminated, artificial light may further be classified into direct, indirect, diffused, and semi-indirect lighting as depicted in Figure 27.6.

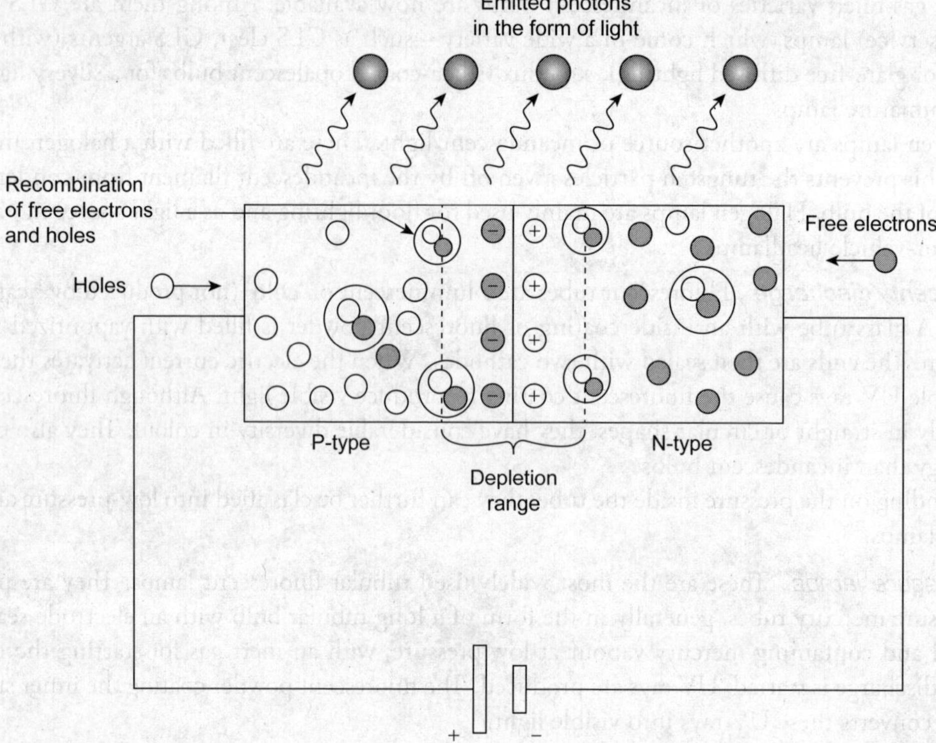

Fig. 27.5 Working principle of LED lamps

Table 27.1 Characteristics of filament, fluorescent, and LED lamps

Filament	Fluorescent	LED
The average life is 1,000–2,000 hours	The average life for a hot-cathode lamp is 5,000 hours and that for a cold-cathode type is 15,000 hours	The average life is 50,000 hours
Low cost	Initial installation cost high	Initial investment is higher than both, but operating cost is much lower than them
Gives direct or diffused light of varying intensity	Gives diffused light with a flat appearance	Various options are available on the colour of white light such as neutral white, warm white, and daylight white
Generates a considerable amount of heat and soils walls	Operating temperature is much lower and does not cause any soils	Heat generated is minimal and energy consumption is very low
Can be used with many different types of shades and fittings	Does not enjoy the same demand, so that fewer shades designed for these shapes are available	A variety of fixtures is available for use of LED
Ideal for pendant lights, spotlights, table and floor lamps	Suitable for cornice lights, obscure corners, and concealed lighting	Extremely versatile, can be used architecturally in lighting

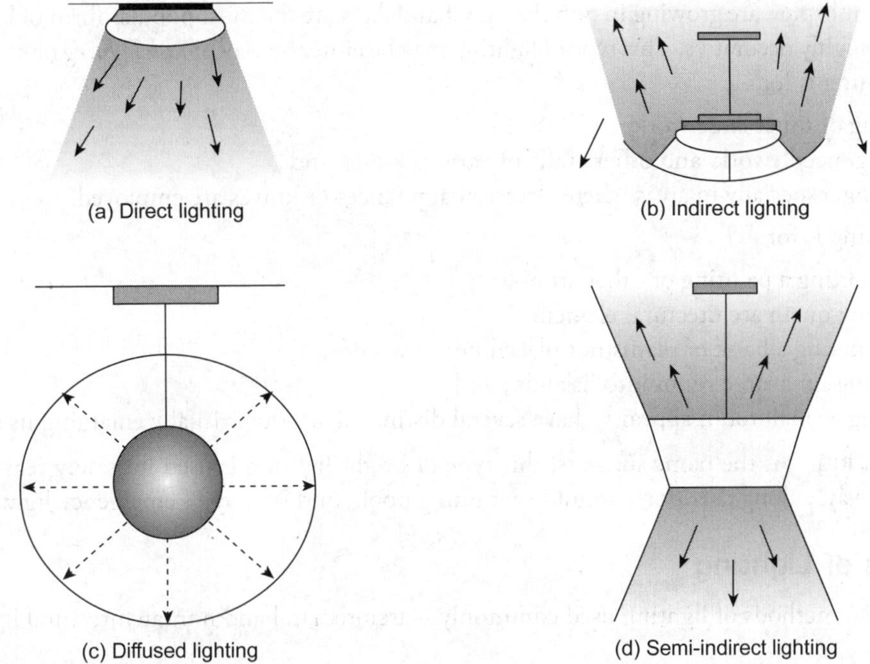

Fig. 27.6 Distribution of light

Direct lighting This kind of light comes from sources such as ceiling fixtures or luminous ceilings that shed light downwards, or from lamps with translucent shades spreading light in all directions.

Indirect lighting This is usually from concealed sources in alcoves, cornices, or valances. It may also come from a lamp with an opaque shade open only at the top—light is then thrown against the ceiling or washes against a wall and is reflected back into the room. It is softer than direct lighting, but often more costly in both installation and operation. When used imaginatively, though, indirect lighting can dramatize a space. Otherwise, it may be monotonous and needs to be combined with local lighting.

Diffused lighting When light fittings are completely enclosed or concealed, as with some globes and ceiling panels, the light is diffused since it passes through the glass or plastic. Diffused lighting is also glare-free and produces a flat appearance.

Semi-indirect lighting It is possible to have some light passing through a diffusing bowl and some reflected off the ceiling where the fixture is open on top. This is called semi-indirect lighting.

Function-based classification

Light may also be classified on the basis of its function.

General or area lighting This illuminates the room more or less uniformly. It brings the design and colours of the whole space to equal attention. It minimizes the bulkiness of furniture, the darkness of shadows, and harsh contrasts.

Local or specific lighting Specific activities at specific locations need specific lighting. Local lighting can be provided by lamps at strategic points. Fixtures attached to walls or the ceiling, under cabinets, alone or in multiples, are growing in popularity. Chandeliers are the most popular form of local lighting and are also highly decorative. This type of lighting may be either by way of *task lighting* or *accent lighting.*

Task lighting is for

- reading or other close work;
- sewing, needlework, and other crafts of various kinds; and
- cooking, especially in areas where electrical appliances or knives are employed.

Accent lighting is for

- highlighting a painting or other art object;
- focusing on an architectural element;
- illuminating a bank of plants not placed near a window;
- breaking up a large room into 'islands'; and
- making a small room appear to have several distinct areas, thus visually enlarging its space.

Safety lighting As the name suggests, this type of bright lighting is used for safety reasons in areas such as stairways, along corridors, around swimming pools, and by way of emergency lighting.

Methods of Lighting

There are two methods of lighting used commonly—architectural and non-architectural lighting.

Architectural and built-in lighting

This method of lighting supplies light that is functional and unobtrusive and is particularly good for contemporary rooms. It may be achieved in the following ways:

Valance lighting A horizontal fluorescent tube is placed behind a valance board, casting light upwards so that it reflects off the ceiling and also downwards to shine on the drapery, thus producing both indirect and direct lighting.

Cornice lighting A cornice is installed under the ceiling, with a fixture hidden beneath so as to direct light downwards only. This can give a dramatic effect on drapery, pictures, and wall coverings.

Cove lighting This consists of placing a continuous series of fluorescent tubes in a groove along one or more walls of a room, about 12 inches from the ceiling. The light reflects off the ceiling and bathes the room in indirect light.

Track lighting Plugmold-type wire-mould strips or track lighting consists of lamps fixed to the ceiling or wall in an array to offer great variety. One strip often holds spotlights, floodlights, and even hanging fixtures that may be turned around to follow furniture placements. The tracks can themselves be movable as well, for still more flexible arrangements.

Soffit lighting This refers to a built-in light source under a panel. It may be fixed to a ceiling or under a cabinet. Soffit lighting is often used over a sink or other work areas.

Non-architectural lighting

These types include various fixtures and lamps.

Ceiling fixtures These have become common nowadays owing to vastly improved designs. Some are inconspicuously recessed into the ceiling or set flush with it. They may soften light with louvres or diffuse it with lenses. Some may be in the form of soft luminous panels that illuminate large areas evenly.

Wall fixtures These remain out of the way and free table and desk surfaces for other things. At the same time, they give direct light where it is needed.

Portable lamps Floor and table lamps can be moved when and where they are needed. They also act as decorative accessories. The placement of such fixtures affects the atmosphere of the room as a whole and the ease with which tasks can be done.

Lighting Fixtures

When buying lighting fixtures to implement a lighting scheme, their appearance as well as the light they produce should be satisfactory.

Shades, globes, and even lamp bases can look quite different when illuminated. They should look good in both their daytime and night-time roles.

Translucent shades contribute a distinct colour cast to their surroundings while opaque shades give localized pools of light rather than all-round illumination. The material chosen for the shade should not be discoloured, faded, or ruined by heat.

Various kinds of lighting fixtures are illustrated in Figure 27.7. Also refer to the scan code for more pictures of lighting fixtures.

Lighting Plans

A variety of lighting is necessary in most rooms and public areas. Provide first for efficiency and safety. Once that prerequisite has been met, you can customize the lighting features to highlight a room's appealing aspects, enhance colours, spark drama and interest, change moods, and cosy up too-large spaces.

Entrance areas and lobbies

The entrance of any establishment should look inviting and the lighting should be in keeping with the character and atmosphere of the place. In a large area, a chandelier, cove lighting, wall brackets or pelmet-type/under-valance fittings can be used to provide general illumination. A false ceiling with mirrors can reflect more light and give the impression of greater height, as well as providing an interesting reflection of the light fittings and the objects and people in a room.

In the lobby, there should be areas of brighter light to attract guests' attention to such key points as the reception desk and to enable them to see clearly to sign the register.

Restaurants and public areas

The atmosphere in a lounge should be one of comfort and restfulness. Sculptures or paintings can be highlighted using spotlights. Concealed uplighters can be used to dramatize foliage and around water features.

Subdued lighting goes well in restaurants and bars. But in cafeterias and coffee shops, in order to encourage a quick turnover, a high degree of illumination, especially at the counters and tables, is necessary.

Chandeliers may look elegant in a banquet hall, but may prove too bright unless tamed by a dimmer switch to soften the mood. Placing a chandelier off-centre or just over the buffet makes the room appear larger. Valance or cove lighting, recessed fixtures or spotlights over the buffet can supplement this general lighting source.

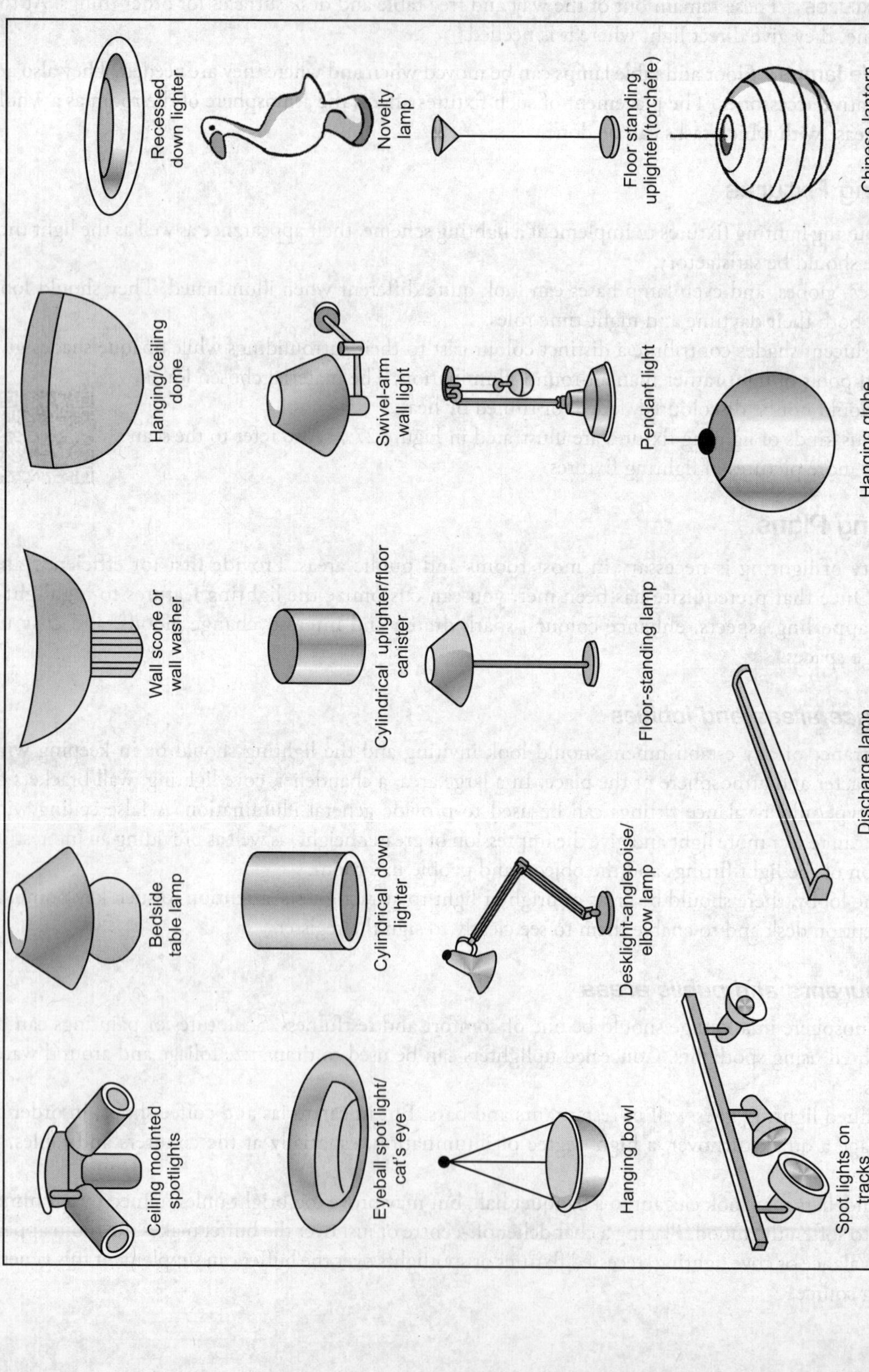

Ceiling mounted spotlights

Bedside table lamp

Wall scone or wall washer

Hanging/ceiling dome

Recessed down lighter

Eyeball spot light/ cat's eye

Cylindrical down lighter

Cylindrical uplighter/floor canister

Swivel-arm wall light

Novelty lamp

Hanging bowl

Desklight-anglepoise/ elbow lamp

Floor-standing lamp

Pendant light

Floor standing uplighter(torchère)

Spot lights on tracks

Discharge lamp

Hanging globe

Chinese lantern

Fig. 27.7 Lighting fixtures

Corridors and staircases

Subdued lighting may be required in the corridors, but gloom should be avoided. Guests must be able to see the room numbers clearly. Light fittings in the corridors should not be spaced further apart than 1½ times their distance from the floor.

Stairs should be well lit to prevent accidents. Lights can be set into the steps themselves or along the walls, just below the handrail. If the lights are overhead, the appropriate switches should be duplicated at each end of each flight of stairs.

For safety reasons, lights for corridors, stairways, and fire exits should be left on during the night as well; also, there should be an emergency lighting system operated from an entirely independent supply.

Guestrooms

Guestrooms do not necessarily require general lighting, but there should be adequate light in the different parts of the room. Switches must be easily accessible, especially near the entrance. Normally an energy-saver control panel, which doubles as a master switch is placed here to be activated by a card key.

Bedside lights are provided beside the beds. To prevent the bedside lamp from tipping off the table, it can be screwed onto the bedside table or wall-mounted swivel-arm lamps can be used instead.

Dressing table lamps should light the face of the person standing before it and not illuminate the mirror itself! Two lamps on either side of the mirror near head height are quite suitable. A light placed above the mirror can cast unattractive shadows under the eyes, nose, and chin.

For reading or writing, there should be good light that is adjustable, preferably from an anglepoise-type desk lamp. A floor lamp can also be placed close to the sofa or armchair for reading purposes. If placed behind the reader, the bottom of the shade should be 47 inches above floor level; if placed beside, 42 inches is desirable.

If there is a painting or a picture in the room, this can be highlighted by using a spotlight.

Wardrobes can be illuminated using lights with no heat gain. The light must shine on the clothes and must be operated automatically using a door switch that turns the light on when the door is opened and shuts it off when the lock clicks into place.

In bathrooms, there should be vapour-proof fittings. The switches should preferably be outside the bathroom. Bare bulbs around the mirror give a clean, shadow-less illumination perfect for make-up. This can be flatteringly softened by hiding the bulbs behind an opaque reflector. Adequate lighting must be provided in the shower area. A plugpoint must be provided for operating shavers and hair dryers as well.

Planning a Lighting System

Designing a lighting system is important for achieving efficiency and aesthetics in lighting. The following factors are involved in planning good lighting systems.

Lighting requirements The amount of light needed for a particular area should be decided and optimized by the lighting plan.

Design To be efficient, the lighting system should be designed according to the function of an area. General lighting is suitable for lighting up bigger areas. Task lighting is suitable for areas meant for work involving minute concentration such as reading and sewing, whereas accent lighting is ideal for highlighting a painting or focusing on an architectural element.

Durability Lighting fixtures come at a high cost; therefore, their durability needs to be assessed before purchase. Highly decorative and delicate fixture designs should be avoided as they are generally not durable. It should be checked if they can be handled easily and whether the ceiling requires any reinforcement due to their installation.

Ease of replacement Many properties have incurred inconvenience when parts in their lighting fixture purchased overseas need replacement. Before purchasing any fixture, ease of replacement of fixtures and bulbs should be checked. The fixtures should be such that replacement can be handled easily by the maintenance department.

Ease of maintenance A significant amount of illumination is lost if lamps and reflectors are not cleaned properly and regularly. Therefore, lighting fixtures and fittings should be such that they are easy to clean and replace.

Energy efficiency Lighting fixtures, designs, and lamps all should contribute to maximum energy efficiency. For instance, a lamp in which the shade does not allow the light to diffuse through is not efficient. An incandescent lamp has an efficiency of 20 lumen/Watt. A fluorescent lamp may have an efficiency of 60 lumen/Watt. This means that three times more energy is required to produce the same amount of light from an incandescent versus a fluorescent lamp.

Heat gains Heat gain refers to the amount of heat energy generated by the source of light which dissipates into the surrounding environment. When artificial lighting is used, especially in indoor areas, the heat gains should be kept in mind. Tungsten lamps generate and dissipate more heat to the surroundings than florescent lamps. Areas such as kitchen and laundry, where heat is already a part of operations, these lamps would add to the discomfort.

Natural light The lighting plan should be such that it fully utilizes the potential of daylight when available.

Indirect effects of elements of designs Colours and textures used in the area greatly influence the type and amount of lighting it needs. Different colours and textures reflect light to varied extents.

Directional controls and reflectors Materials such as mirrored glass, polished aluminium, and stainless steel surfaces used in decoration provide excellent means of directional controls and also act as efficient reflectors.

Cost-effectiveness Fluorescent lamps come at a high initial cost but have a longer life-span. On the other hand, incandescent lamps are low cost, but the average life is much lesser than the fluorescent lamps. LEDs are even cheaper than CFLs.

Floor Coverings and Finishes

Floors are an important aspect of hotel interiors as they are both functional and decorative. The guest's first impression of a hotel is largely determined by the appearance of the flooring in the lobby, the guest corridors, restaurants, guestrooms, and so on.

Floors are subjected to more wear than any other surface in hotels. The type of flooring chosen is thus an important consideration for housekeeping, as it affects the drawing up of cleaning and maintenance schedules. Moreover, approximately 70% of the department's cleaning costs is spent on floor-cleaning in hotels. Floors are also expensive in themselves and are therefore replaced less frequently than other design and architectural elements. The executive housekeeper, in coordination with the architect and interior decorator, should thus select appropriate floor coverings for each area. The executive housekeeper and the supervisors in the housekeeping department should also have some knowledge of the composition of flooring materials and finishes if they are to make decisions about their maintenance.

Selection of Floor Coverings

Various aspects of aesthetics and utility such as the following must be kept in mind while choosing appropriate floor coverings.

Appearance This is usually the first consideration when choosing flooring. As flooring often makes up a wide, uninterrupted surface, it has more visual impact than the furniture set upon it, so choose colours to harmonize with the rest of the room. Colour, pattern, and texture play a large part in the selection of floor coverings. Pale colours, especially blues and greens, as well as shiny surfaces, give a cool, receding appearance. Intense colours such as red and orange and matt surfaces give an impression of warmth.

Closely related to colour is light. A pale or highly polished floor reflects more light than a dark floor. So, the amount of daylight received and the lighting system in a room may affect the choice of flooring too.

The sense of scale in a room or area is influenced by the size of the patterns on the floor. Patterned surfaces tend to make a small room appear smaller. Solid colours make a small room appear larger. Some patterns and colours are more practical than others as they do not show spillage and soiling readily and the flooring retains the appearance of cleanliness longer.

Texture is another aspect of appearance and it is also related to the 'feel' of the flooring. Natural materials have their own texture—soft cork, the rippled surface of slate, smooth terrazzo; synthetic materials may have a texture artificially applied to them.

Comfort This is of paramount importance to both guests and staff. Warmth, quietness, and softness of tread are the factors to consider when assessing the comfort that flooring affords. Soft, resilient surfaces are generally comfortable to walk on, but may prove tiring to people continually walking on them as one must constantly adjust to the 'give' of the floor with each step. Harder floors are noisier and colder, offering less heat and sound insulation. Noisy flooring can cause considerable disturbance and discomfort to the occupants of a room and even to those in adjacent rooms. Also, slipperiness may lead to accidents, though this characteristic is often due to the maintenance treatments given to flooring rather than to the flooring itself. Very shiny flooring often looks slippery even if it actually is not, and this too can affect a person's comfort levels by proving a distraction.

Durability Resistance to wear has to be considered in relation to the kind of use the floor is put to. Due to the wear and tear expected in public areas, the flooring may become 'tired-looking' very quickly. Grit cuts into some floorings more easily than into others. Spillage of water, grease, and food acids is more likely in some places and will harm certain kinds of flooring more than other. Cigarette burns, dragging of heavy furniture, and the use of trolleys occur more frequently in some areas than in others. Areas of more concentrated wear need careful consideration. For instance, the foyer—with its invisible but well-defined traffic lanes to the reception desk, lifts, and cloakrooms—and areas where people hover or turn so that their feet are ground into the flooring, such as near bars, dressing tables, waiter's stations, and such, may show excessive wear. Hard floors, such as quarry tiles, clay tiles, and stone last longer, but durability must also be related to the length of time a floor retains its best appearance. For instance, marble has an indefinite life in terms of durability, but is subject to staining.

Life expectancy As a corollary to the above, the flooring needs to be durable only for the length of life expected of it, and this is not same for all areas. In kitchens and hospital wards, the décor does not change often and so the life expectancy of the flooring may be many years. A guestroom floor surface, however, owing to the frequent changes of décor usual, may not be expected to last more than 7–8 years. A bar floor may not need to last more than 2–3 years, either, especially if it is of a contemporary design.

Safety This is of paramount importance to all occupants of the building. Floor surfaces should have non-slip qualities both when wet and when dry. Over-polishing may cause slipperiness, and this is to be avoided.

Ease of cleaning This is an important factor in the running costs of any establishment. The extra initial cost of flooring that is easier to clean may be recouped over a comparatively short time of maintenance outlay. Flooring that is easy to clean does not necessarily maintain its clean appearance throughout the day, however, and floors cannot usually be constantly cleaned, however easy they may be to clean. So for well-maintained flooring, the flooring material as well as colour and pattern (such as won't unduly show soils) must be carefully selected.

Cost This factor alone may limit the choice of flooring. The true cost of flooring, however, is the initial cost, including laying, plus the estimated maintenance costs.

Sub-floors

When choosing a floor covering, one must also check the type of sub-floor on which it will rest. The two main types of sub-floors are suspended timber and solid concrete.

Suspended timber floors Tongued-and-groove or butted boards are supported by timber joists in this type of base floor. As floorboards move a little when they are walked upon, the choice of floor covering is limited to those types that are not affected by movement or 'give'. This excludes any form of ceramic floor, quarry tiles, clay tiles or bricks, all of which may crack or chip if there is movement in the sub-floor.

A modern development in suspended floor construction is the use of large sheets of materials such as plywood or flooring-grade chipboard in place of wood baseboards. This provides a very flat floor suitable for supporting thin, flexible flooring materials.

Solid concrete floors In this type of base floor, concrete is laid directly onto the hard core and earth at the ground level of all modern buildings. Pre-cast concrete slabs are used for the intermediate floors of multi-storeyed buildings.

Concrete floors are given a cement screed layer on top to smoothe out the roughness and provide a flat surface on which flooring material can be laid. Concrete provides a very stable floor, suitable for use with any form of floor covering.

 Types, Characteristics, and Cleaning of Floor Coverings

Floor coverings and finishes may be classified according to their hardness, porosity, or the material from which they are made. Thus, floor coverings can be hard, semi-hard, or soft. Further, hard floorings may be categorized as either resilient or non-resilient. Some types of flooring are made to serve specific functions. These include non-slip floorings and conductive floorings. The classification of floor coverings is outlined in Figure 27.8.

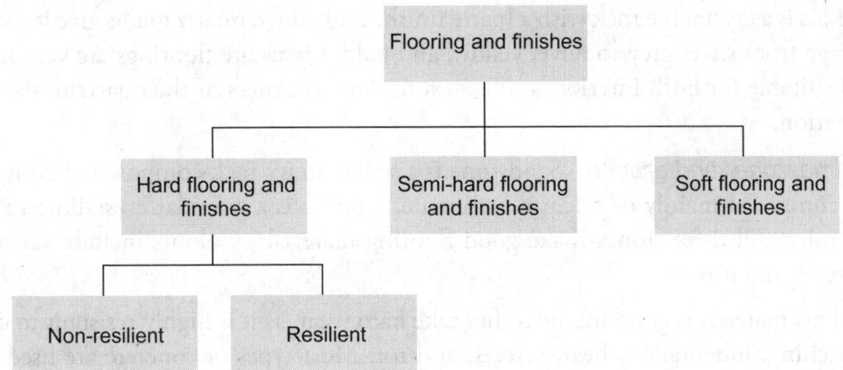

Fig. 27.8 Classification of flooring and finishes

Hard Flooring/Finishes

Hard floorings are durable but noisy, with the exception of some wood floorings. Hard floorings are mostly cold in feel, vermin-proof, impervious to dry rot (except wood), fire-retardant, and easily cleaned as compared to other types of flooring. Hard floorings can further be classified as non-resilient and resilient floorings. The term 'resilient' implies that though the flooring has a certain amount of flexibility and will give or bend beneath the feet, it will come back to its natural shape. The more the dents disappear, the more resilient the flooring. On the other hand, non-resilient floor finishes resist denting because of their hardness.

Non-resilient hard flooring and finishes

Stone, concrete, ceramic, magnesite, and resin floorings fall under this category of hard floorings and finishes.

Stone This is a good choice of flooring for a natural appearance and an almost indefinite life. All types of stone are very heavy and must be laid on a solid concrete sub-floor. Stone floors are resistant to wear, water, indentation, and to most cleaning chemicals. The various types of stone commonly used are:

Marble This is the best known of all stone floorings and is available in a wide range of patterns and colours, including white, grey, pink, green, brown, and black. Marble is primarily crystallized limestone. It may have a banded (serpentine) pattern or may be mottled. Marble is durable, but lighter colours yellow with age. Honed marble is recommended for commercial floors. It gives a satin finish with little or no gloss. Sandblasted or abrasive-finished marble has a matte effect and is suitable for exterior use. Travertine marble is cheaper and is characterized by small cavities on the surface, which offer greater slip resistance; but at the same time, these allow dust to settle. Marble stains easily on coming in contact with ferrous metals and oils. Marble is available in tiles ranging in size from 12 inches upto 18 inches square, but slabs upto 5 × 3 ft. can be obtained on special order.

Slate This is a hard, impervious stone that may be given a polished, sawn, or riven surface. Riven slate is split along its natural layers, so that the natural undulations give it a rippled surface that is less slippery when wet than a smooth surface would be. The natural colours of slate are grey and blue grey. Slate forms when layers of mud and silt build up and solidify over millions of years. For interior use, slate slabs come in standard sizes of 18 × 9 inches, but larger slabs upto 6.5 ft. 6 in. × 3 ft. are also available.

Quartzite This is a crystalline rock with a matte finish. Embedded quartz grains give it a slight sparkle. Its colours range from silver grey to olive, yellow, and gold. Quartzite floorings are very hard-wearing, non-slip, and suitable for both interiors and exteriors. The thickness of the quartzite slab depends on the rock formation.

Sandstone, limestone, and granite Sandstone is a sedimentary rock composed of compressed sand. Limestone is composed mainly of calcium carbonate. Granite is a granular crystalline rock of quartz, feldspar, and mica. All three stones make good flooring materials. Colours include various shades of grey, beige, green, and brown.

Concrete This material is good for areas that take hard wear, as it is highly resistant to chipping and cracking, scratching, indentation, heat, insects, and rot. Most types of concrete are used for exteriors such as patios, but concrete tiles and terrazzo are suitable for indoor use. Concrete floors are often found in utility areas or areas that will receive a great deal of traffic from heavy equipment. Lodging properties often have concrete floors in parking areas, garages, and exhibition areas.

Concrete is a mixture of cement and various fillers such as sand, gravel, crushed stone, and seashells. The elements are mixed in dry form and then combined with water, reacting chemically to form the hard, stone-like material. The curing or 'hardening' of concrete is a hydration process.

All types of concrete flooring are easy to clean, but they should not be polished as this can render them dangerously slippery. The cement in concrete floorings is absorbent and hence cleaning with strong alkalis should be avoided. Concrete may be marked by oil and spillages of such materials as ink and beverages. A solid concrete sub-floor is required for all types of concrete flooring.

Granolithic concrete This is plain concrete structural flooring on which a surface of granite chippings and cement is cast on site. The final surface is hard-wearing and its appearance is improved if the surface is polished to expose the aggregate in the concrete. This heavy-duty flooring is used for basement corridors, storerooms, stairways and laundry areas.

Concrete flags This low-cost flooring is mainly used for terraces and garden paths. A variety of colours, sizes, and shapes is available. Concrete paving stones are available with a finish that imitates the texture of natural stone. They should be laid on sand or a bed of weak-mix concrete, the surface of which is well levelled.

Concrete tiles These are made of coloured cement and hard-wearing aggregate surfaces applied to a concrete backing. They have good wearing properties and are available in sizes from 4 sq. inches to 18 sq. inches.

Terrazzo Terrazzo is a flooring that can be cast on site to form panels of upto 1 sq. metre or can be pressed into tiles off-site. The appearance of terrazzo depends upon the aggregate chippings used. The decorative chippings may be made of pebbles, marbles, or other stones set in a matrix or mortar of cement. Terrazzo flooring is then machine-ground to produce a smooth surface. The matrix is often referred to as grout. Terrazzo may be made in a wide variety of colours and patterns. Terrazzo offers a very hard-wearing surface, but some types can be dangerously slippery when wet, unless special non-slip aggregates are used in the construction. Like most porous surfaces, terrazzo floors must be sealed for durability.

Vitreous/ceramic floorings This refers to flooring materials that have been made of some clay product and fired in a kiln to produce a hard, stone-like quality. 'Ceramic flooring' is the more common name for this type of material. Vitreous materials are primarily composed of silicon materials that flow together and bond during the firing process to form a glass-like ceramic. Combinations of clay, marble, slate, glass, and flint are used to make ceramic tiles. These floorings are known for their imperviousness to water and other soils and for their resistance to abrasion and wear. Ceramics are resistant to chipping, scratching, indentation, heat, acids, water, oils, fats, alkalis, insects, and fungal attack. They offer a long-lasting, hard-wearing floor that is easy to clean. Virtually all ceramic flooring needs a solid concrete sub-floor. An exception is mosaic tiling, which can be laid in a small area on a suspended floor, provided the floor is suitably prepared.

The common types of ceramic flooring are quarry tiles, bricks, glazed tiles, and paver stones. They can be roughly divided into two categories, glazed and unglazed ceramic.

Glazed ceramic tiles/clay floor tiles These are made from refined natural clays fired at high temperatures and glazed. They are available in a variety of sizes, shapes, textures, colours, and patterns. Ceramic tiles with a particularly hard glaze and a wide range of colours are used for more of a decorative finish. Ceramic tiles require a solid sub-floor and can be laid either directly on concrete by bedding them in the cement or may be fixed to the screed with adhesive. They are often used in luxurious bathrooms and patios. Tessellated tiles are small ceramic tiles, often used in mosaics, that give a highly decorative floor. Ceramic tiles are not affected by water, grease, acids or alkalis, but the grouting between them may be. Therefore, the use of strong alkaline cleansers should be avoided. These tiles may also crack or break under heavy weights or impact.

Quarry tiles These are hard-wearing tiles made from blend of unrefined clays hard burnt under pressure to make them durable. Harder tiles are less absorbent, but more slippery. They are available in heather brown, red, and blue colours. Random patterns can be formed by using combinations of whole sizes and half tiles. They can be laid directly on concrete by bedding in cement. Quarry tiles are used in cloakrooms, kitchens, canteens, and other places used for the preparation and storage of food. The standard size is 6 sq. inches of 15 mm thickness. Larger sizes, such as 8 sq. inches, are also made.

Mosaic There are three types of mosaic tiles: clay, glass, and marble. They are made in small squares and other shapes that can be assembled into larger patterns. A wide variety of colours, shapes, and sizes is available. Fully vitrified mosaic tiles are made specially for outdoor use. Ideally, mosaic tiles need a solid sub-floor; but they can be laid on a suspended floor over a small area, such as in a shower enclosure.

Brick These are different from terracotta tiles as discussed later only in thickness and shape; the material is the same. Bricks are usually not glazed and are very porous. They are generally 3 inches × 6 inches in size.

Terracotta tiles These are unglazed, hard-baked tiles made from hand-formed clay. They are available in a range of shapes and sizes, in a wide range of natural colours—from smoky reds through sun-baked oranges. They can be used to create decorative patterns too. Terracotta tiles are porous and therefore need to be sealed with a linseed oil sealant and waxed for added protection. They should not be directly laid on concrete, as migrating salts may appear as a white stain on the tile surface. Over time, terracotta tiles may crack or chip.

Pavers These are tiles that resemble natural quarry tiles. They are produced by compression and are available in a wide range of colours. They are often 12 sq. inches in size and are used either for their appearance or for heavy-duty applications such as in driveways.

Magnesite/Oxychloride Before World War II, these floors were referred to as magnesite. During and after the war, the materials used were perfected into a standardized formula and became known as oxychloride flooring. These floors are poured in much the same way as concrete floors but are composed of magnesium chloride, using magnesium oxide as a binder. They are very durable and more flexible than concrete. These floors are extremely porous and washing them should be avoided as far as possible. Oxychloride floors are also harmed by most chemicals and coarse abrasives. These floors are used in areas where there is little or no risk of water spilling on them, such as in the linen room. This flooring may be sealed or polished to prevent penetration of water and dirt. Various degrees of resilience can be introduced into this otherwise non-resilient flooring by the addition of various fillers, ranging from cork to marble dust. These fillers also change the porosity and durability of the finish.

Resin floorings These are composed of synthetic resins, usually epoxy, polyester, or polyurethane, with appropriate hardeners. Vinyl or marble chips may be included to give a more decorative flooring, resembling terrazzo. Polyurethane floorings are the most common of this type, and give an extremely heavy-duty, hard surface. They are unaffected by spillages of water, food, alcohol, and most chemicals. In spite of the shiny surface, they are non-skid and suitable for use in kitchens, canteens, bathrooms, corridors, and laundries. Epoxy forms a continuous flooring material that has been thus far confined to loading docks, storage areas, and other areas of heavy traffic due to certain disadvantages. Breakthroughs in product formulation have recently seen the development of transparent, low-odour epoxies. When combined with decorative quartz granules or flat multi-coloured chips, they form a seam-free, highly decorative floor. They can provide excellent wear or abrasion resistance, usually 2–3 times that of concrete.

Resilient hard flooring and finishes

Wood, asphalt, and bitumastic finishes can be classified as resilient hard finishes.

Wood This is the oldest material used for resilient floorings. Soft woods such as pine and fir have a high degree of resilience, whereas hardwoods such as oak and maple have low resilience. Hardwood is obtained from broad-leafed trees such as oak, teak, maple, walnut, birch, beech, and so on. Each has its individual colour, grain, and rate of wear. Commonly used soft woods are pine, fir, cedar, and rubberwood. Any type of sub-floor is suitable for wood, except for hardwood blocks, which require a solid sub-floor. In all cases, however, the sub-floor should be level and damp-proof.

The durability of wood flooring depends on good maintenance and on the quality of wood. Hardwoods are resistant to abrasion and indentation, but they should not be used in wet areas. Soft wood boards look good when they have just been sanded and sealed, but do not wear well under heavy use.

Wood floors are warm to the touch and tend to be noisy. They are not slippery unless too much polish is used. The biggest disadvantage of wood floors is their porosity, absorbency, and susceptibility to damage by water. To prevent absorption of spills and dirt, wood flooring should be sealed and/or polished. Strong alkalis cause wood to disintegrate, discolour, and splinter. Wood floorings are poor conductors of heat, and so are good insulators. Wood floors, being resilient, are less tiring to walk on than non-resilient surfaces. Wood is, however, inflammable, susceptible to dry-rot, and scratches and splinters with the dragging of heavy articles across it. Some types of wood finishes are outlined here:

Wood parquet A high-quality hardwood flooring in which decorative hardwoods are cut into blocks and formed into panels, permitting elaborate geometric patterns such as herringbones, basket weaves, and strips. The panels vary from 1 inch to 1¼ inches in thickness; sizes vary from 12 sq. inches to 2 sq. ft. Parquet may be laid over any rigid wooden sub-floor. Parquet is rarely used nowadays because of its high cost and the genuine article should not be confused with plywood 'parquet', which is really just a kind of wooden tile.

Plywood These are made into tiles that can be used to simulate wood parquet, but are generally called 'parquet' these days even when laid simply to resemble a board floor. Various ready-patterned tiles in herringbone, basket-weave, or strip are available. Plywood parquet tiles are not durable in areas of heavy wear. It is supplied in various squares from 9 inches to 3 ft.

Hardwood strip and block These are high-quality wood floorings made of hardwoods. A well-maintained hardwood floor improves with age. Hardwood blocks vary in thickness from ¾ inch to 1¼ inch and the size may be upto 12 × 3 inches. The strips used are upto 4 inches wide, and are carved to have a tongue and groove, which allows concealed nails to fix them together when laying down the floor. Hardwood blocks must be laid out on a dry, solid sub-floor and held in place with cold bituminous adhesives.

Wood mosaic Hardwood 'fingers' arranged in a basket-weave pattern are stuck to a sheet of backing material to form panels 18 inches square and 3/8 inch thick. Wood mosaic has very good wearing characteristics.

Asphalt tiles These are a close relative of linoleum because of the asphalt used in their construction. Generally they are composed of asbestos fibres, pigments, and inert fillers bound with asphalt in the case of the darker varieties and with some other resinous binder in the case of lighter colours.

Bitumastic flooring This is a joint-less, low-cost flooring and consists of a type of asphalt rolled onto a solid sub-floor in a hot plastic state. It is soft in texture, though the appearance is that of a hard floor. However, it is completely impermeable to water. Bitumastic flooring is normally black, red, or brown. It is used in public restrooms, hospital corridors, and other heavy-traffic areas. It is also used as a moisture-proof membrane to protect other floorings against dampness. However, it is damaged by heat and heavy weights and is also harmed by spirits, oils, and acids.

Semi-hard Flooring and Finishes

Semi-hard or smooth floor finishes are durable, but normally less permanent than hard floor finishes. They are all resilient, except thermoplastic tiles. These floorings are resistant to pests as well and are easy to clean.

Linoleum This is made from oxidized linseed oil or a combination of drying oils, wood flour, ground cork, resins, and pigment. This compound is mixed and pressed onto an asphalt-soaked piece of felt or burlap, which is heated to bond the elements. The product is then passed through polishing rollers and allowed to harden. In good quality linoleum, the colour and pattern are inlaid right through the backing, whereas in cheaper quality products, they are superficial and may wear off.

Linoleum is susceptible to strong alkalis that leach the asphalt and cause cracking. Linoleum is also damaged by extreme temperatures—low temperatures cause it to crack and high temperatures soften it. Linoleum is prone to denting and scratching too. Therefore, coarse abrasives should not be used on linoleum. Also, it is absorbent and only the minimum amount of water needed should be used for cleaning.

Sealed and polished linoleum is used in linen rooms, corridors, bathrooms, and canteens.

Cork Obtained from the outer, light-brown bark of cork oak trees, cork is ground into large granules, mixed with synthetic resin, pressed into sheets at high temperature and pressure, and then cut into tiles or strips of varying widths. Colour variations are obtained by the application of different amounts of pressure and temperature.

Cork tiles have a warm and restful appearance. They have excellent acoustic properties. The disadvantage with cork is that it is extremely porous; dents, burns, and stains easily; granules may come loose; and direct sunlight bleaches out the natural colouring of cork. Because of the high porosity of natural cork, however, it is now available with various types of coatings. The different varieties are waxed cork, resin-reinforced waxed cork, and vinyl-coated cork. The tiles are available as follows:

Untreated cork tiles These are formed by compressing the natural granules of cork and baking them to form tiles bonded by its natural resins. They are made mainly in a 12-inch square size, which is 1/8 inch thick. Larger sizes are available, too—upto 18 inches long. Thicker tiles, of upto 3/16-inch thickness, provide greater stability and comfort. The tiles may be waxed or sealed with polyurethane or a special cork seal after laying. Ready-waxed tiles are also available.

Cork tiles with PVC surface A thin PVC skin is bonded to the cork surface to increase its durability. This also seals in any moisture and makes it even more necessary to ensure that the sub-floor is completely dry before laying the cork. PVC-faced cork gives protection against splashes. However, PVC-faced cork is slippery when wet and can be dangerous for flooring in bathrooms and kitchens. They require less maintenance than waxed or untreated cork, though.

Rubber This type of flooring is made chiefly from synthetic rubber. Butadiene styrene in concentrations of at least 20% is commonly used in modern rubber floorings. A filler of clay is often used. It is available in various degrees of flexibility and hardness. Some types are extremely soft and are used as anti-fatigue flooring, while others—such as stair treading—are very hard.

Rubber maintains a good lustre without any finishing treatments, and has a good resistance to chemicals and surface moisture; but it is difficult to scrub clean and is not recommended for installation in areas that have a serious moisture problem. Rubber flooring resists cigarette burns as well. However, rubber is harmed by spirit, grease, sunlight, alkalis, and coarse abrasives.

Rubber flooring is used in entrance halls, canteens, and places where noise should be kept to a minimum. Front-door mats and mats in front of service lifts may be made of rubber too.

Plastic flooring A wide range of colours, designs, textures, and prices makes plastic flooring very versatile. Any sub-floor is suitable for these—except for thermoplastic and vinylized thermoplastic tiles, which need a solid construction.

Those plastic floors which have a high PVC content in the surface, such as flexible PVC tiles and sheets or PVC with various backings, are very hard-wearing. All types are resistant to wear, water, indentation, and to most cleaning chemicals. The various types of plastic flooring are outlined here.

Thermoplastic and vinylized thermoplastic tiles These are made from a variety of asphaltic binders with inert fillers and pigments. They are rigid tiles, set as closely as possible in adhesive. They are laid down in a thermoplastic state, but harden on cooling and may be carried up the wall to form a small coved skirting. These floorings are non-porous. However, they are hard and noisy since they are non-resilient. They also dent from heavy weights, scratch easily, soften with heat, and are damaged by strong alkalis. They are also harmed by grease and spirits. These floorings are typically used in bathrooms, corridors, and offices.

Vinyl asbestos tiles and flooring These use vinyl as a binding agent and asbestos as a filler. Vinyl is practically inert, so it does not combine readily with other chemicals. These floors are thus resilient and easy to maintain. However, this type of flooring is not in demand now because of recent findings that asbestos is carcinogenic.

Vinyl composition tiles These are composed of vinyl resins, plasticizers, colouring pigments, and mineral fillers, some of which may include asbestos. They are recommended for suspended concrete, concrete on-grade, concrete below-grade, suspended double-wood, and plywood suspended floors.

Homogeneous flexible vinyl This has become the most popular of all types of flooring. It is flexible, so it does not crack; it is also very tolerant to most cleaning, stripping, and finishing products in the market. It is available as tiles or sheets, with embossed or textured finishes. Sheets come in widths of 4 ft., 5 ft., and 6 ft. 6 inches. Tiles may be squares of 9 inches, 10 inches, or 12 inches. Larger tiles in a 19½-inch size are also available.

Reverse-printed PVC This type of flooring is produced by a process in which a pattern is printed on the reverse side of a clear PVC sheet, which is in turn bonded to a PVC backing or printed directly onto the backing. This process allows any type of pattern—imitating cork, wood, ceramic floors, or others. However, its durability is only that of the clear PVC layer that protects the pattern.

PVC with various backings In order to increase the comfort of PVC sheet floors, which are often relatively thin and comparatively non-resilient, some softer sheet materials are bonded to the PVC in this type.

Soft Floor Coverings

These are resilient floorings and include all types of carpets, rugs, dhurries, and mats. Soft floorings are quiet, warm, and slip-resistant. They are available in a variety of colours, textures, and patterns.

Carpets These typically consist of a backing or foundation and a surface pile, which may be cut or uncut. The backing may be of jute or cotton; linen and hemp are also used. The pile yarn may be wool, cotton, nylon, or polyester, though wool is the fibre most commonly used in the construction of carpets.

Carpets are used extensively because of their attractive appearance, safety factor, warmth, and sound insulation. They have been discussed in detail in the next section of this chapter.

Mats, rugs and dhurries These may be constructed from textile fibres or harder materials.

Non-slip/Slip-resistant Floorings

These floorings are constructed from flexible PVC with chips of carborundum incorporated into it during manufacture. This renders the surface less slippery. These are used in areas such as shower cubicles, kitchens, ramps, and sloping corridors. Other slip-resistant floorings include ridged quarry tiles and textured rubber floorings. These surfaces should, however, still be kept free of grease, oil, and water spills.

Anti-static/Anti-conductive Floorings

Synthetic flooring materials have a tendency to build up static electricity due to friction from the movement of equipment or human traffic. In such cases, if the atmosphere is charged with a flammable substance, such as a solvent cleaner, the slightest spark could cause a fire or even an explosion. It is, therefore, important to have anti-static floorings in susceptible areas such as computer rooms, maintenance rooms, and so on.

Cleaning of Hard and Semi-hard Floorings and Finishes

This usually involves removal of dust and dirt, polishing, and application of floor seals. All these procedure have been discussed in Chapter 11. However, they have been summarized in Table 27.2 for easy recapitulation.

Table 27.2 Cleaning of hard and semi-hard floor finishes

Floor type	Method
Asphalt composition, bitumastic, thermoplastic	Sweep and damp-mop daily. Occasionally apply self-shine polish. Never use wax polishes, as the spirit in them will damage the surface. Remove marks by rubbing lightly with wire wool; then wipe over with a sponge wrung out in warm water and proceed to polish.
Cement/concrete/clay or quarry tiles, stone and brick	Sweep or dry-mop daily. Periodically wash or scrub with detergent suds. May be sealed to make the floor non-slip and resistant to dust, oil, water, and grease. Polish quarry tiles with liquid tile polish or self-shine tile polish.
Glazed tiles, Terrazzo	Sweep or dry-mop daily; or wipe down with mild detergent solution. Avoid all abrasive cleaners.
Cork	Sweep or damp-mop daily. Wax polish periodically. If sealed, use self-shine polish occasionally.
Linoleum	Sweep or dry-mop daily, or wipe with cloth wrung out in warm water and detergent. Polish with wax or self-shine polish, or use a combination cleaner-cum-polisher.
Marble	Sweep or dry-mop daily. Wash with soft cloth wrung out in warm water and detergent. Rinse well and dry. Remove light stains with a mild abrasive, or marble cleaning solution; rinse off and dry. Marble polishing may be done once a month with polishing powder, buffing it off. Seal marble flooring twice a year after polishing.
Rubber	Sweep and damp-mop daily. Apply self-shine polish weekly until pores are filled and non-absorbent. Wash only when very dirty, and do not over-wet. Avoid oil- or spirit-based sealants and wax polishes.
Vinyl, vinyl asbestos, matt PVC, felt-backed vinyl	Sweep or damp-mop daily. Wash when needed with cloth wrung out in warm soapy water. Polish with self-shine finisher or combination cleaner-cum-polisher. Avoid oil-based sealants, spirit-based cleaners, and solvents. To remove marks, rub gently with wire wool.
Wood, wood blocks, wood mosaic, hardwood strips, plywood parquet	Sweep daily and occasionally mop. If unsealed, apply wax polish periodically and buff with a red pad for a rich finish. If sealed, damp-mop and buff with dry mop. Use self-shine polish periodically.

Carpets

Modern manufacturing processes and the development of man-made fibres have revolutionized the carpet industry, making available carpets in a wide range of materials and textures. The quality of a carpet depends not only on the method of manufacture, but also on how well the carpet is made, the fibres used, the quality of that fibre, and the density of the pile. A good quality carpet should be able to withstand wear from constant footfalls, spillages, cigarette ash, and grit and also have the ability to recover from the effects of heavy or sharp furniture. Its shape and colour should be stable even if deep-cleaned or constantly exposed to sunlight. The pile should be dense and made from strong fibres, held firmly in position.

Composition

Carpets primarily have three components—an underlay, a backing, and a face or pile. The pile is held to the backing with knots (in the case of woven carpets) or with adhesives. An underlay is essential if a woven carpet is to be laid, but many manufacturing techniques provide carpets with backings of sufficient resilience to make an underlay unnecessary. A cross-section of a carpet, revealing its component parts, is shown in Figure 27.9.

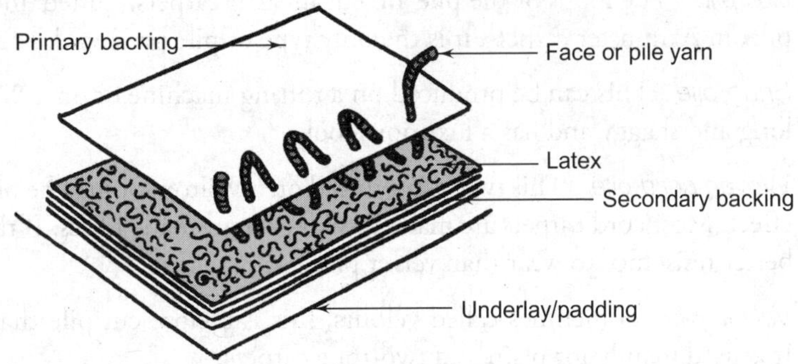

Fig. 27.9 Cross-section of carpet components

Underlay/Padding Underlay or 'under-felt' acts as a shock absorber between the carpet backing and any unevenness in the sub-floor, which could cause the carpet pile to wear unevenly. It tends to make the carpet feel softer and more luxurious as well and helps it to absorb pressure from furniture, provide increased sound and heat insulation, and protect the carpet from rising dust and dirt. Underlays are made of plain needle felt material, impregnated felt-rubber foam, rubber foam with a jute or polyurethane backing, or a combination of needle felt and rubber foam.

An underlay may also be attached beneath the carpet backing, when it is referred to as the secondary backing, or it may be installed separately. Attached underlays make for quicker and easier laying of the carpet, reducing installation costs; but they are easily damaged by moisture. Separate underlays may be more expensive, but they last for many years and can easily be replaced.

Backing The primary backing is the one in which the pile of the carpet is anchored. It may be made of natural materials such as jute, hemp, or cotton; of synthetic materials such as polypropylene, nylon, various resins, or synthetic rubber; or of a combination of natural and synthetic materials. Normally, the primary backing has a back-size, a bonding material that may be of rubber, latex, plastic, or synthetic adhesives, which holds the fibres in place. The back-size is spread in a thin layer over the back of the primary backing and prevents the carpet tufts or loops from shifting or loosening after installation. A secondary backing sometimes laminated to the primary backing provides additional stability, improved shape and resilience, and more secure installation. These are not necessary for woven carpets.

Pile Also called the 'face' of the carpet, this is the part which is seen on the surface and walked on. Hence, it should be strong and resilient. The pile may be made of a blend of fibres or of exclusively synthetic or natural fibres (such as wool and cotton; silk is used in very expensive luxury carpets). The blends used are typically of wool and rayon; wool and cotton; wool, acrylic, and rayon; and so on. The synthetic fibres usually are polypropylene, polyester, and acrylic. The pile fibres' density, height, twist, and weave affect the carpet's resilience and durability.

Carpets can be produced with several different kinds of pile. Variations in texture can be used as effectively as 'colour'. The different types of piles are:

Hard-twist pile This is a cut pile with a heavy twist built into the yarn, giving it a pebbly look. It is used mainly in plain carpets, but it can be combined with other types of pile to give a textured effect. Hard-twist pile does not show shading and tracking like a velvet pile does. (Shading is the twisting of pile, caused by footfalls or the moving of heavy furniture, and shows up as dark patches. Tracking is the smoothing down of the carpet in heavily used areas.)

Looped pile The pile is uncut and is made up of a continuous series of loops. It can give various textures, from a thick and knobbly pile to the closely curled low-loop pile that is like an irregular cord carpet. Looped pile is used in Wilton and tufted carpets.

Cut pile The loops of the pile are cut in such carpets. Tufted and woven carpets are produced in cut pile; in Axminster carpets, it is the only type of pile produced.

Shag pile This can be produced on a tufting machine or on a Wilton or Axminster loom. The pile is long and shaggy and has a luxurious look.

Woven cord pile This type is produced on a Wilton loom. The pile is left uncut, giving a tight, corded effect. Most cord carpets are made of sisal or man-made fibres. If the fibre is of good quality, cord offers better resistance to wear than velvet pile.

Velvet pile Sometimes called velours, this is a close-cut pile that has a smooth, velvety appearance. It is used mainly for plain and two-tone carpets.

Sculptured pile A combination of cut and looped pile gives a carved or sculptured effect. Different lengths of cut pile and of straight and twisted pile can also be combined. These combinations are used mainly in Wilton and tufted carpets.

Types and Characteristics

The various types of carpets are classified in Figure 27.10.

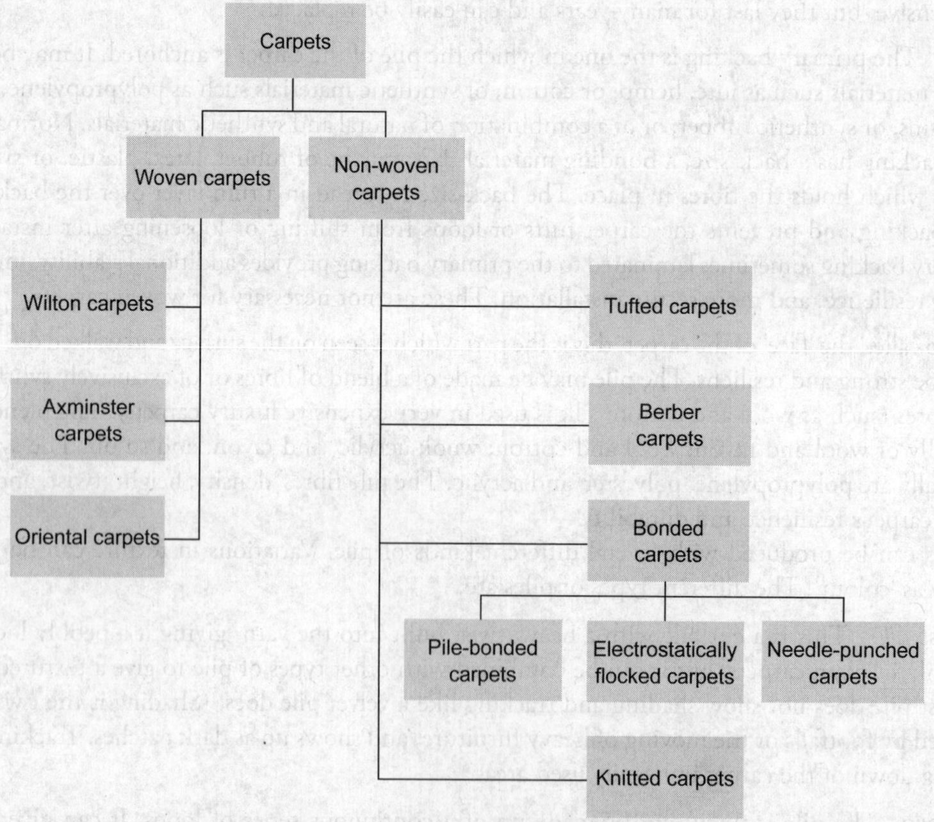

Fig. 27.10 Types of carpets

Woven carpets

Some of the highest-quality carpets are made by the weaving method. The pile and the backing are woven together here so that the pile is locked into position. The weave consists of warp and weft yarns interwoven to form the face pile and backing at the same time. The pile may be either cut or uncut. The uncut or looped woven carpets can take 5–10% more wear. The advantage of woven carpets lies in the slight elasticity of the woven back. When correctly laid, the backing fibres hold the pile tufts erect so that they spring back after they have been walked on. Woven carpets are of three types: Wilton, Axminster, and Oriental. Wilton and Axminster are the names of the looms on which these types of carpets are woven. The main difference is that the Axminster loom allows any number of colours, as the threads are cut off and reintroduced according to the pattern.

Woven carpets are more expensive than non-woven ones, but worth their cost since they are more durable. These carpets are used in reception areas, corridors, dining rooms, and bedrooms.

Wilton carpets These may be produced as patterned, cord, Brussels, or plain.

Patterned Wilton These carpets are woven on a type of loom known as a Jacquard loom. This is an apparatus that produces patterns from coloured yarns. The pattern information is contained on perforated cards. The holes in the cards activate the mechanism that selects the colours to be raised to the pile surface. The Jacquard draws up one coloured thread at a time (corresponding to a set pattern of perforations) to be drawn up to form the pile while the remaining threads are hidden in the backing of the carpet, giving added warmth, resilience, and strength to the carpet. Once the carpet is done, the pile is cut and closed. A textured effect is often created in such carpets by varying the height of the pile. No more than five colours are used, since the incorporation of more colours will result in a very bulky carpet.

Plain Wilton These carpets are made without adding the Jacquard apparatus to the loom. They have extra jute threads called 'stuffers' added to the backing to compensate for the lack of the spare coloured yarns as filling.

Cord These carpets are plain Wilton carpets with an uncut pile.

Brussels These carpets are patterned Wilton carpets that have an uncut pile.

Axminster carpets These carpets are woven in such a way that the pile is almost entirely on the surface. Each pile tuft is individually inserted into the backing, leaving no 'dead' threads to reinforce it. The pile is longer and less close than in Wilton carpets. The backing is very durable and has a distinct ribbed effect. There are three types of Axminster carpets:

Spool Axminster This is the most popular Axminster carpet and a single piece can have an unlimited number of colours in the pattern. The carpet is woven in such a way that the pattern is visible on the reverse side too.

Gripper Axminster This carpet is similar to the spool Axminster carpet, the only difference being the use of a maximum of eight colours, due to its method of creation.

Chenille Axminster In French, *chenille* refers to a 'caterpillar'. The carpet is named thus, since the pile surface is first produced as a long strip and then, during the weaving process, the catcher threads attach the strips of furry pile to the backing. The catcher threads are distinctly visible in the finished carpet, giving the pile a segmented look like a caterpillar. Chenille carpets are soft and thick, and are made in many colours and patterns.

Oriental carpets These hand-woven carpets from the Middle East, Indian subcontinent, and the Far East are available in a variety of sizes, patterns, and colours. Based on the country of origin, they are called Chinese, Indian, Afghan, Persian, Caucasian, or Turkish carpets or rugs. Pakistan and Nepal also produce oriental carpets. With their rich history and colour, oriental carpets are often called the aristocrat of carpets. Carpet-weaving areas can be divided into those using floral designs and those using geometric shapes and patterns.

Floral patterns dominate in Persia and India. Persian carpets use dyes of vegetable origin. Many Persian carpets are made as wall coverings and prayer mats.

Caucasian and Turkoman carpets almost always employ geometric designs and when the rare floral pattern is used in these carpets, the design tends to be stylized and rectilinear.

In Turkey, both floral and geometric designs are used, although the latter are more common.

Chinese carpets are easily recognized by patterns that include dragons, monsters, or exotic birds. All these carpets have a close, silky pile with a well-defined pattern.

Oriental carpets are only made as carpet pieces that are stand-alone rectangles, and not strip or body carpets. They may be used as wall decorations also. The pile is usually of wool, silk, or a blend of these fibres. The weaving process involves stretching the warp threads on a loom and knotting the pile to these threads. When a row of knots is completed, a weft thread is inserted. Once the entire carpet is knotted, the pile is shorn. The precision of the design depends to a large extent on how tightly the carpet has been knotted and how short the pile has been cut. The carpet's density, or number of knots per square inch, is a useful indicator of the fineness and durability of the carpet—the more the number of knots, the better the carpet. A fine oriental carpet will have more than 500—1000 knots per square inch.

Dhurries are popular flat-weave rugs from India. They are usually woven 1/4th inch – 3/8th inch thick and made of cotton, wool, jute or their blends. The colours are vibrant and the designs simple. A unique characteristic of dhurries is that the design is the same on either side. They blend beautifully with both traditional and modern interiors.

Non-woven carpets

These carpets are produced by attaching the surface pile to a pre-fabricated backing.

Tufted carpets These are available plain or patterned and are usually made of synthetic fibre blended with wool. The tufts are needled into a backing—usually made of polypropylene in sheet form, but sometimes made of hessian. The tufts are locked into place with a skim of latex along the back. Then either a foam layer or a secondary backing of woven jute or polypropylene is added. If a foam backing is used, an underlay is not required. The pile is either looped or cut (high or low, or perhaps a mixture of both). Tufted carpets do not fray and may be cut to any shape. To the untrained eye, a tufted carpet may be indistinguishable from a woven carpet, however.

Shag pile carpets are usually single-coloured tufted carpets with a long, luxurious pile. The pile can, however, look tangled and matted if it gets heavy wear. They are hard to maintain too, as the long pile hides a lot of dust.

Berber carpets These carpets have short, nubby tufts. The pile is dense and looped, characteristically made from natural, undyed sheep's wool. They are available in natural neutrals such as white, off-white, fawn, beige, grey, and dark brown.

Bonded carpets These carpets are neither woven nor tufted. The one feature that distinguishes bonded carpets is that the materials used are glued, heat-fused, or in some other way 'bonded' together.

They are all, therefore, typically manufactured from man-made fibres. A well-made bonded carpet is hard-wearing and makes an economical floor covering with good pile. Bonding can produce almost any effect, from completely flat to a corded or velvet pile.

Bonded pile carpets These generally have a pile of nylon or polypropylene, which is stuck to a PVC backing. Bonded pile carpets are also available as tiles. The dense pile has a firm anchorage and the carpets do not fray, seams can be bonded, and the carpets may be stuck to the floor.

Electrostatically flocked carpets Bonding is also used for flocked carpets, which have thousands of small fibres electrostatically bonded to an adhesive-coated backing.

Needle-punched carpets Another method of bonding is the needle punch or needle loom. In these carpets, a mixture of fibres is punched by needles and entangled through a backing fabric. This fabric is then impregnated with an acrylic resin to hold the fibres securely in the backing.

Knitted carpets These carpets are produced by interlacing yarns in a series of connected loops. As in woven carpets, the pile and backing are produced simultaneously. Multiple sets of needles interlace the pile, backing, and stitching yarns together in one operation.

Selection of Carpets

The onus of maintaining carpets is on the housekeeping department, whether it is the daily cleaning or the longer-term carpet-cleaning schedule. It is therefore, imperative that the executive housekeeper knows which types of carpets suit the purpose of various areas in the hotel and is also allowed a say in selecting carpets for the property. Once the types of carpets to be used are decided on, a specification sheet needs to be prepared for the dealer so that the right goods are delivered. The factors that go into the selection of an appropriate carpet are outlined in this section.

Size

Though the available size of the carpet depends upon the weave or type of the carpet, it is essential that the right size is bought for the purpose and the area. For instance, economical wall-to-wall carpeting will be more suited to a banquet hall than carpet squares. Depending on their size, carpets may be categorized as follows.

Body or strip carpeting The narrow width of carpeting is known as a body width, and this is either 27 inches or 36 inches. Such carpeting has no borders so that the pattern can be matched when the strips are joined for laying down close-fitted or wall-to-wall carpeting.

Broadloom carpeting Carpets that are available in a width wider than body/strip width are known as broadloom. The most common widths are 9 ft., 12 ft., and 15 ft. Some broadloom carpets are also available in a width of 18 ft. Tufted broadloom carpets are made in widths of 9 ft. 10½ inches or 13 ft. 10½ inches. Broadloom is a good choice for a fitted carpet if there is a width corresponding closely to one of the measurements of the room, and the room is of a regular shape.

Carpet squares These are loose carpet quadrangles with all their edges neatened. The advantage of carpet squares is that they can be turned round to even out wear. However, carpet 'squares' are not necessarily square. Their size is usually more than 6 ft. 9 inches × 4 ft., and they are often either 12 ft. squares or 9 ft. × 12 ft. rectangles. 'Squares' are also made up from 12 ft. lengths of broadloom with the edges bound.

Carpet tiles These range from 9 inches square to 20 inches square. A popular size is the 12-inch square. These tiles are sold in packs of nine, and can be laid down loose or stuck down. Some have a self-adhesive backing that makes them easy to lay and allows them to be removed if necessary. Some tiles form a pattern when properly oriented against others; others are of plain carpeting.

Stair carpets These usually come in widths of 18 inches and 22½ inches. They may be plain or have a patterned or coloured border.

Rugs and mats These are normally oblong and should be less than 6 ft. 9 inches × 4 ft., with all their edges neatened. Rugs and mats can be placed in areas of heavy use to save wear on the carpet.

Purpose

Manufacturers usually classify their carpets according to the purpose for which they are recommended. The six common categories are:

Light domestic use These are for bedrooms and other rooms that see light use in homes.

Light contract use/medium domestic use These are for medium use in hotels and for home bedrooms exposed to light use.

Medium contract use/general domestic use These are for general use in the home and for hotel bedrooms or public rooms that see medium use.

General contract use/heavy domestic use These are for living rooms, halls, stairs, and other parts of the home where there is heavy use and for banquet halls and public areas in hotels, restaurants, and office buildings.

Heavy contract use These are for public areas that see heavy use, such as shops.

Luxury These are of better quality than category 3, but are not suitable for general use.

The hotel lobby is an area where there is a lot of guest traffic. Hence, a good-quality, hard-wearing carpet is needed if it is to look good and withstand heavy wear for many years. An Axminster made of 80% wool and 20% nylon in dirt-masking colours and patterns would be a good choice. A plain Wilton or tufted carpet would be more suitable for a lounge.

For dining areas, an acrylic-pile carpet is practical, as stains caused by food spills can be easily removed from these. If liquid spills in particular are likely, choose either a polypropylene carpet, which is easily wiped clean, or an inexpensive carpet with a short life.

A staircase needs a carpet that is hard-wearing, with a surface that is safe, and a good-quality pile carpet fulfils both these requirements. Cord, needlefelt, and sisal provide hard wear at low cost. However, Wilton cord is the ideal choice here since it is very resilient and allows the feet a good grip.

Less expensive carpets for light contract use can be used in bedrooms, since they get only light wear. A room used as a study-cum-bedroom or bed-sit will need a high-quality carpet though, similar to that suitable to a living room, or a cheap carpet that can be replaced when the use of the room changes.

Most hotels do not place carpets in bathrooms, except in a few luxury rooms. The main hazard for a bathroom carpet is water. If the floor is likely to become wet, a polypropylene carpet with a polypropylene backing is recommended. In this case, it is unwise to use underlay or have a foam backing, as water may seep down the skirting into the underlay. A low-priced nylon or acrylic carpet would be suitable if the floor does not get too wet.

Construction

The surface pile, the way the pile is anchored to the carpet, and the type of backing are important selection criteria for carpets. Tufted carpets can be produced at a faster rate than woven ones because of the method of fabrication. Where a distinct pattern with several colours is desired, a woven carpet may be preferred instead, however. Needle-punched carpets are used for outdoor installations, whereas flocked carpets are useful in wet areas since they are water-resistant.

Pile density and weight

Any carpet, whatever the making, can be made to resist compression despite traffic, abrasion, soil being ground in, repeated vacuuming, and cleaning if there are sufficient pile yarns in the carpet. How well any carpet performs is mainly a matter of the density of the pile, and this in turn is a function of many characteristics—the gauge, pitch, pile height, stitches per inch, pile weight, yarn size, and so on. *Average pile density* is the weight of pile yarn in a cubic yard of carpet. It is calculated by taking the pile weight, multiplying that by 36, and dividing that product by the pile height (in inches).

$$\text{Average pile density} = \frac{36 \times \text{Face weight}}{\text{Pile height}}$$

In tufted carpets, the number of pile yarns in the warp (ends; across the width) is expressed as the *gauge.* Gauge is given as the number of needles or tufts per width-wise inch expressed in fractions. A medium-weight carpet has a gauge of 1/8 and a heavy-duty carpet has a gauge of 5/64. The numerator indicates the number of inches and the denominator the number of tufts. Thus, 1/8 gauge means that there are 8 tufts across the inch, while 5/64 gauge means that there are 64 tufts in 5 inches, or 12.8 tufts per inch.

In woven goods, the term *pitch* indicates the number of warp yarns in a 27-inch width of carpet. For instance, the standard pitch for a Wilton is 256. To convert gauge to pitch, multiply the number of ends per inch by 27. For instance, a 1/10 gauge is equivalent to 270 pitch, or 10 ends per inch × 27. Similarly, 1/8 gauge is 8 ends of yarn per inch × 27 = 216 pitch.

The number of tufts per lengthwise inch is expressed in *rows* for Axminster and *wires* for Wiltons. This may vary from 4 in an inexpensive carpet to 13 in a densely woven luxury carpet.

Yarn or *face weight* refers to the amount of fibre (per square yard) that is in the face of the carpet (total weight less the weight of the backing). However, this is different from density because tall, less-dense tufts may have the same weight as short, dense tufts. On an average, short, dense tufts will be more resistant to wear and matting. So the greater the weight, the more durable the carpet.

Pile height and style

The length, thickness, and ply of the pile yarn affect the weight of the carpet and ultimately help determine its wear. *Pile height* is the measurement (usually in fractions of an inch) of the pile of a carpet, from the base of the primary backing to the tip of the yarn. On staircases, a longer pile is sometimes better than a low, looped pile, because there is less parting of the yarns on the stair edges. A multi-level, multi-yarn surface available in modern carpets is appealing as well; it also helps to conceal soiling and stains. Earlier, shag piles were considered a luxury feature, but now the popular pile height for hotel rooms is decreasing to 'plush', a moderately long pile that is far denser than most shags. The lower the pile, the denser the weave or tufting should be. Lower pile is much easier to maintain, even though it is considered less glamorous.

Pile fibre

Earlier, wool was the dominant fibre for carpet piles. Wool is soft and resilient, resists abrasion and soiling, has natural flame-retardant properties, feels warm, and retains its appearance well if maintained properly. However, it has some drawbacks.

Wool is expensive and suffers from high static generation. With the advent of various man-made fibres, blends have thus become a popular choice for pile fibres. The blends used are wool and nylon (80/20), polypropylene and acrylic (50/50), and acrylic and rayon (50/50). Characteristics of different pile fibres are given in Table 27.3.

Table 27.3 Characteristics of carpet pile fibres

Fibre	Wear	Soiling	Maintenance
Wool	Can be very hard-wearing if of good quality. It is often blended with nylon to give extra durability. A Woolmark label means the pile is all-wool, and the Woolblend mark means it is 80% wool and 20% nylon.	Best resistance to soiling among all fibres. Good appearance, which is well retained.	Cleans easily and well.
Acrylic	Can be expected to wear well in all areas of the hotel. Resembles wool in handling and appearance. May be given a higher twist, which makes the carpets more resistant to shading and tracking.	Soils and flattens easily. (A densely woven pile will flatten least.)	Cleans easily, releasing dirt readily. Needs good care to retain its appearance.

Resilience

The resilience of a carpet refers to the ability of the pile to recover its original appearance and thickness after being subjected to compressive forces or crushing under traffic. In a hotel guestroom, warmth and comfort are important for guests walking on bare feet or in light slippers. The pile yarn for guestroom carpets should have a more inviting, softer feel than those in busy foyers, lobbies, or corridors.

Dyeing

Colour can be introduced at different stages of manufacture in both tufted and woven carpets of man-made or natural fibres. The various methods of dyeing fibres or yarns for use as carpet pile has been outlined in Chapter 18. If colours must last in strong sunlight or through heavy wear, dope or solution dyeing is ideal. In the process of *dope dyeing*, man-made fibres are spun from a coloured solution. Thus, the filament is completely impregnated with the pigment.

With improved dyes, fading is now not a common problem in carpets. A fade-o-meter is a standard laboratory device for testing a fabric's fastness to sunlight. Other problems related to dyeing in carpets are crocking and bleeding. *Crocking* refers to the colour rubbing off as a result of improper dye penetration or fixation. *Bleeding* is loss of colour when the carpet is wet, due to improper dyeing, use of insufficient mordant, or due to poor quality dyestuffs.

Aesthetics

This refers primarily to the colour, texture, and pattern of the carpet. A spacious lobby or an enormous bathroom should have a carpet with a larger, bold pattern; conversely, a small room should not have a carpet with a big, busy pattern. Remember, however, that intricate patterns can withstand lack of maintenance better than solid colours.

If the purpose is to help people relax and introduce a quiet air, then cool blues and greens are suitable, usually in darker shades. In dining areas, carpets should not have distinct, precise design motifs; rather they should have vague, mottled patterns that will not show stains left from spills. In heavy footfall lanes or near busy elevators or foyers, the hardiest of all carpets should be specified.

Backings

A good carpet should have a firm backing. The secondary backing gives the carpet dimensional stability, so that it resists stretching from foot traffic or from carts being pulled across it. A foam backing of 1/8 to ¼ inch thickness may be added to the primary backing to serve as a self-cushion and to eliminate the need for separate padding.

Underlay/padding

The selection of proper underlay is as complex as choosing the right carpet. In high-traffic areas, carpets are often glued directly to the floor. Installing carpets in this way may help carpets withstand wear upto 25% longer, since friction and air pockets are eliminated. But if comfort and luxury are desired, a resilient underlay is called for. An ideal underlay, properly installed, with a quality carpet and good backing, can prolong the carpet's life by softening the intensity of abrasion. Underlays also provide extra insulation against extremes of cold and heat, and act as an acoustic-dampening layer. It is important to select a moth- and mildew-proof underlay.

Reputation of dealer

Carpets are expensive and their installation needs a lot of skill. It is always wiser to deal with reputed manufacturers, dealers, and installers who have the advantage of guaranteed quality and experience in carpeting. The guarantee of the carpet's quality durability should range from 5–10 years. The supplier should discuss the maintenance needs of the carpeting provided with the housekeeper and, if required, should provide training to the housekeeping employees involved in carpet maintenance.

Installation of Carpet

Housekeepers and housekeeping supervisors should be familiar with the methods of carpet installation, even though the actual installation is best carried out by an experienced installer. The installation methods may be semi-permanent or temporary.

Semi-permanent methods

Some semi-permanent methods of carpet installation are discussed here.

Stretch-in In this type of installation, the carpet is stretched over a separate underlay onto narrow tackless strips or grippers of wood with protruding tacks. The strips have two or three rows of nails, angled up towards the walls, to which the carpet backing is attached during installation. However, such strips can be dangerous when exposed. Stretch-in installation may provide greater cushioning and spring, higher thermal insulation, and superior acoustical advantages (due to a higher noise reduction coefficient), especially when installed with an appropriate underlay. Stretch-in installation should be avoided, however, where the carpet maybe used heavily in terms of movement of furniture or fixtures movement of furniture or fixtures. It also should not be used on ramps or inclines, in places where there is excessive humidity, or where the carpet selected has a special backing designed only for glue-down installation.

Turn-and-tack The edge of the carpet is turned under like a hem and then tacked into position. Unless well fitted, this method can cause unevenness, which traps dust.

Sunken This method may be used where there is a change in floor levels. The carpet is placed into a 'well' and edged with metal or wood strips to even out the floor surface.

Glue-down This is more permanent than the other methods. It is usually used with rubber- or foam-backed carpets and can cause early wear unless the sub-floor is very even. The method employed may be direct glue-down or double glue-down. In the *direct glue-down* method, the carpet is adhered directly to the floor. In the *double glue-down* method, the underlay is adhered to the floor first, and then the carpet is glued to the underlay.

The glue-down method is suitable for most areas, including ramps and heavy-traffic areas. The seams are durable (but more difficult to repair than with the stretch-in method) and there are no restrictions on the size of the area to be carpeted. Special borders or customized design features can be executed with glue-down installation, and the glue-down method is usually less expensive than other semi-permanent methods.

Temporary methods

These usually involve the addition of tape sewn round the edges of the carpet. This tape may contain pegs, hooks, press studs, or velcro strips, which attach themselves to corresponding sockets, loops, or hooks affixed to the floor surface immediately beneath the carpet. Sometimes the carpet is edged with rubber so that it will simply lie firmly in place without any additional anchorage.

Care and Maintenance of Carpets

A regular maintenance programme is a must for carpets, since they are easily soiled or damaged. Good maintenance can increase the life of a carpet considerably.

Most new carpets shed fluff for the first few weeks. During this period, they should be only lightly cleaned with a hand brush or carpet sweeper. Cut off any tufts that stand up noticeably above the surface—do not pull them out.

After the first month, clean with a vacuum cleaner at least once a week, always making the last stroke in the direction of the pile, so that it lies flat. To even out wear on the carpet, move furniture around occasionally so that indented pile can be brushed up. Avoid dragging heavy furniture over carpets, as this damages the fibres. Parts that receive heavier wear, such as in front of a door, can be protected by rugs.

Routine maintenance

This involves the daily removal of dust and dirt from the carpet. The removal of dust may be carried out using a dry-suction vacuum cleaner or a carpet sweeper. Care should be taken to clean the surrounding areas around the carpet too.

Periodic maintenance

This involves deep cleaning of the carpet. The executive housekeeper should prepare a periodic schedule for this. The practice of carrying out a deep cleaning only when the dust and dirt become obviously visible is detrimental to carpets. In many properties, carpet cleaning is contracted out because of the specialized equipment and skills required. Deep cleaning of carpets can be carried out by three different methods: shampooing, hot-water extraction, and dry powdering.

Shampooing Carpet shampoo machines use one of the two types of shampoos: liquid and dry foam. Shampoos are anionic synthetic detergents and should be diluted in the correct measures for optimal performance. Liquid shampoos produce very little foam but tend to leave a residue that traps dirt, making it necessary to shampoo the carpet frequently. Dry-foam shampoos are actually also liquids, but they leave a dry foam on the surface of the carpet after application—hence the name. The foam loosens and lifts out the dirt, holding it on the surface of the carpet pile until it can be removed by dry suction. Dry-foam shampoos contain some solvent in addition to the detergent to assist in the removal of solvent-soluble dirt. Carpets cleaned with a dry-foam shampoo require less drying time as well.

Carpet shampoo machines are used to dispense both types of shampoos. A cylindrical brush works the foam into the pile of the carpet.

Hot-water extraction This is done by a hot-water extraction machine. The machine uses a shampoo solution that does not form foam. It injects the solution under high pressure through the pile to the back of the carpet, where it emulsifies and loosens dirt and grease. Simultaneously, the machine sucks up the solution along with the now-suspended dirt and grease. The use of a wet-suction machine after shampooing greatly accelerates the drying time. The dirty solution is deposited into a tank, from which it is discarded later. After the cleaning process, the carpet is left slightly damp and requires a very short drying time.

Dry powdering In this method, a powder containing absorbents such as sawdust, solvents, and drying agents is sprinkled on the carpet and left for several minutes. The powder absorbs the grease and dirt, and is removed with the help of a dry-suction cleaner. Waterborne dirt is not removed by use of such a powder, therefore this method is not very efficient. The method cannot be strictly considered a deep-cleaning method in fact, and should be used only in conjunction with the other carpet-cleaning methods.

Importance of Floor Maintenance

Hotels and other hospitality venues have unique floor-care needs, and image is a high priority. Floors play a key role in presenting the right appearance, since they are often the first surface a visitor or guest notices when entering an establishment. The reasons why floors should be well maintained are outlined here:

Appearance Clean, shiny floors look good and present a positive first impression to all who enter a building or area. Discoloration in the corners, finishes building up along the edges, dust under furniture, scuffs and black marks, and a dull appearance all indicate inadequate maintenance procedures and/or frequency. In short, floors mirror a facility's cleanliness.

Indoor environment quality (IEQ)/indoor air quality Due to gravity, sooner or later much of what's in the air settles to the floor. Pollutants and contaminants, including microbes riding on soil particles, end up on floors. Floor maintenance procedures can either remove contaminants or redistribute them throughout the building.

Many of the procedures once believed safe are now considered contributors to problems with indoor air quality. This can range from chemical vapours to the dust stirred up by sweeping, dusting, mopping, the use of floor-cleaning machines, and other activities commonly performed as part of daily work routines.

Slip safety Proper floor care prevents accidents and reduces liabilities. Clean, well-maintained floors provide a safer walking surface. Written procedures, adequate and documented frequencies of service, regular training, and the use of 'wet floor' signs are defences against injuries and liabilities for slips, trips, falls, and related accidents.

Pride and satisfaction Properly maintained floors look good and get noticed. Professional cleaners gain recognition from their level of knowledge, skill, and service. It takes dedication and hard work to keep floors looking like new. Cleaning professionals and housekeeping employees should take pride in providing quality floor maintenance, since their work impacts everyone entering the building.

 Ceilings and their Maintenance

Often barely noticed unless a source of problems and sometimes sadly ignored as a design element, ceilings can affect the appearance, space, light, heat, and acoustic properties of a room.

Ceiling Finishes

Ceiling finishes come in the following forms:

Ceiling tiles

These come in panels, with choices of drop ceilings, tiles, and planks.

Drop ceiling panels These rest in a grid system suspended from the ceiling joists. The nature of the grid makes it easy to level any ceiling and offers the added benefit of easy access to pipes and wiring above the false ceiling thus created. Such ceiling panels are available in 2-ft. squares and 4-ft. square panels, in several different textures and styles.

Tiles and planks These are mounted directly on the ceiling and offer a sleeker look than drop ceilings. Since the tiles are mounted directly on the ceiling, less head room is lost than with a drop ceiling too. These tiles come in 12-inch squares as well as planks in three sizes: 6 inches × 48 inches, 6 inches × 80 inches, and 5 inches × 78 inches. They are available in various designs.

Gypsum ceiling boards These are made from crushed gypsum sheathed in paper (smooth on the outward-facing side and natural on the back). This is one of the most common ceiling coverings in use today. Gypsum gives the appearance of plaster without the need for lathed backing strips or the high degree of skill required to apply plaster. Gypsum boards are suitable for painting or for use as a base for popcorn ceilings and most other textured finishes.

Popcorn ceilings These are usually formed as a thick coating applied to the ceiling board with a specialized texturing spray gun. The texture enables one to create the effect of plaster or stucco on ceilings and the coating material is thick enough to hide minor flaws.

Textured paint

This is a particularly thick form of paint, infused with particles to yield a textured or three-dimensional effect. It also enables one to create the effect of plaster or stucco on ceilings. Three types of textured paint are available:

Smooth texture This gives a stucco effect.

Sand texture This gives a slightly rough effect (like sandpaper) because of added sand particles.

Ceiling texture This gives a 'popcorn' effect, much the same as the sprayed-on textured ceilings of that name.

Textured paints are for interior use only. A customised colour can be mixed or a white base can be painted upon after it is dry. An inexpensive applicator (a special texturizing roller cover, a coarse brush, a putty knife, or a trowel) may be used to apply textured paint on the ceiling surface.

Ceiling paper

Embossed papers are usually the best of the many types available for ceilings. All can be emulsion painted when the adhesive has dried. Papering ceilings is more difficult than papering walls, but sometimes it may be the only way to hide a cracked ceiling.

Plank panelling

This is a solid wood product usually milled from a larger stock. Most plank panelling has a tongue milled into one edge and a groove milled into the other. This design makes it possible to nail through the tongue of one board and hide the nails under the groove of the next. Typically, plank panelling comes in widths of 2½ to 8 inches and lengths upto 10 feet. Panelling made from different species of wood help provide just the right nuance for any aesthetic.

Maintenance of Ceilings

Ceilings should be freed of cobwebs and dust regularly. Wall brushes are convenient; but for lower ceilings, a vacuum cleaner with extension pipes and a suitable attachment is very effective. The latter removes the spiders too, so that they cannot produce webs again after a few days! Washing ceilings is usually a part of special projects or deep cleaning.

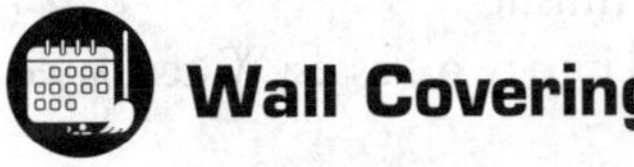

Wall Coverings

Wall coverings may be decorative as well as functional. The primary consideration for wall coverings, though, should be their functional quality, durability, and ease of maintenance.

Practical Considerations

The following points should be kept in mind before applying a wall covering.

Moisture and condensation Check all walls for condensation problems. A slight dampness may be countered by the usage of an anti-condensation paint or by fixing boarding to battens treated with a preservative.

Noise Sound carried through ceilings or walls may be reduced by insulation boards fixed in the same way as for countering condensation. The denser the material, the less the sound that gets through, though loud sounds with vibrations are difficult to deal with.

Types of Walls

The selection of wall covering has a great deal to do with the type of wall being covered:

Brick Make sure that there is no dampness on the wall. If brick walls have been left unpainted, they can be covered with a clear sealant to prevent them from crumbling or becoming dust traps.

Old plaster Plaster is suitable for most wall coverings and paints. However, damp plastering will need stripping and renewing after the moisture problem has been treated at source. If the plaster is uneven or cracked, use wallpaper or other covering materials (rather than a 'finish') or line the wall with lining or ingrain paper before painting or finishing.

New plaster It must be absolutely dry before decorating can begin. If it is to be painted before it is absolutely dry (for decorative effects), emulsion paint is better as it is least likely to blister and allows the wall to breathe. Wallpaper is not to be used until the surface is bone dry. Plasters with lime in it should be treated with an alkaline primer before painting. Plaster boards should also be sealed before papering.

Types of Wall Coverings

Wall coverings may be in the form of paints, wall papers, fabric coverings, wood coverings, tiles, etc.

Paints

These are typically mixtures of four important ingredients: pigments, additives, binders, and solvents. Pigments render colour and opacity. Additives give the paint special properties, such as resistance to rust and fungus. Binders hold the paint together and bind it to the surface for durability. Solvents enable the brushing or rolling of paint across a surface.

Paint offers a wide choice of colours, effects, and degrees of gloss. However, paint used on walls is usually for decoration rather than protection. Paint can be easily applied and cleaned too. While using paint in the interiors, its drying time and lingering odour must be taken into account and sufficient time be allowed for the room to air.

As a wall covering, since the decorative function of paints is foremost, manufacturers categorize paints according to their shine. Paints without a shine are called flat or matt paints while paints with shine may be classified into low-lustre, eggshell, silk or satin, and gloss or high-gloss finishes.

Depending on the binders or vehicles used, paints can be broadly classified into two classes: Water-based paints and solvent-based paints.

Water-based paints In these types, the contents are mixed with clean water only. The various types are:

Lime wash These are colour washes based on lime (that is, calcium hydroxide, $Ca(OH)_2$), inorganic alkalis, fast pigments, and few other additives. Whitewash is a lime wash without pigment. The ingredients of a lime wash are suspended in water prior to application. Glue, casein, salt, alum, drying oil, and tallow

are often used to increase the longevity of a lime wash. It can be applied to both interior and exterior surfaces of a building.

Distemper This is superior to a lime wash and is available in a wide range of colours. It may be defined as a water-based paint consisting of whiting (powdered chalk), some colouring pigment (in case of coloured distemper), and glue mixed in water. It is available in the form of a dry powder or a paste. Depending on the binding material, it may be washable or non-washable. It is economical even in new buildings, which are not fully dried out. Distemper is available as oil-bound or acrylic. Acrylic distemper is superior to oil-bound distemper in terms of finish and durability.

Non-washable distemper should always be removed before painting. Washable distemper can be painted over with a similar distemper after dusting down. Oil-bound distemper is more expensive than non-washable distemper, but it provides a washable paint film which can be repainted over.

Distemper may be applied with a brush or with a spray gun. It is widely used in interiors.

Emulsion paint This type of paint is used as a decorative finish. There are three major types of emulsion paints—polyvinyl acetate, styrene, and acrylic resin. Acrylic emulsions have good adhesive properties, are washable, and are easy to maintain.

Premium emulsions are based on pure acrylic latex and high-opacity pigments. Emulsion paint is thinned with water, easy to apply, and dries rapidly (within 2 hours). It has no odour and is alkali-resistant. It is also durable and washable. It is available in both matt and gloss finishes. However, emulsion paint should not be applied over distemper or a colour wash. It may be applied over oil-bound distemper or oil paint.

Two coats of emulsion paint are necessary for longevity. These two coats should be applied on the same day. They may be applied by brush or spray gun.

Emulsion paints are frequently used in interiors.

Silicate paint This consists of a thin suspension of alkali-resistant inorganic pigments and extenders. It is not damaged by the alkali in cement. It is also porous, hence allowing moisture to escape. It may be directly applied on brick, plaster, and concrete surfaces after wetting; no primer coat is necessary. Two or three coats are normally applied. The painting tools should be cleaned with water immediately after use of silicate paints. Painting with them should be avoided in hot weather. Silicate paints are mostly applied to the interiors and not the exteriors of a building.

Cement paint This type of paint consists of white cement, alkali-fast pigments, accelerators, and other additives. It is available as a dry powder and can be found in several shades. It is economical, water-resistant, and durable even on damp surfaces. However, cement paint should not be used on smooth surfaces, gypsum plaster, or lime wash. It is more durable on rough surfaces. Surfaces finished in cement paint can be repainted with any non oil-based paint later. This is most widely used as an external paint for building exteriors.

Solvent-based paints These are generally made up of six main constituents:

The *base* is generally a metallic oxide in powder form, serving essentially as a pigment and forming the chief ingredient of the paint. The most important purpose of adding this base to the paint is to make an opaque coating to hide the surface to be painted. In addition, it makes the film of paint resistant to abrasion and prevents shrinkage cracks likely to be formed in the film during drying. White lead, red lead, zinc oxide, iron oxide, and titanium whites are the bases commonly used.

Second is an inert *filler or extender*, a cheap pigment added to the paint to reduce its cost. In addition, this substance modifies the weight of the paint and makes it more durable. With good formulations,

the inert filler pigments may be helpful in contributing other useful properties to the paint film as well. The commonly used inert fillers or extenders are barium sulphate, lithopone, silica, silicate of magnesia or alumina, whiting, gypsum, and charcoal.

Third comes the *colouring pigment*, a white or coloured pigment mixed in to get the desired shade of paint.

Fourth is the *vehicle*, a liquid that acts as a binder for the various pigments—bases, extenders, and colouring pigments. The vehicle makes the paint stay in the fluid state and thus helps to spread its ingredients uniformly over the surface to be painted. This forms an elastic, abrasion-resistant, and reasonably impermeable film on drying. Refined linseed oil is a commonly used vehicle in oil paints. Oils from soya beans, fish, sunflower seeds, and tobacco seeds are also being used as vehicles, in various combinations with or without linseed oil.

Fifth is the *solvent or thinner*, a liquid that thins the consistency of the paint in the container and evaporates after the paint film has been applied so that it may solidify. It imparts to the paint film such favourable properties as brushability, smoothness, and easy flow. Turpentine, pure oils, petroleum, spirit, and highly solvent naptha are the commonly used solvents.

Last is the *dryer*, one of a group of materials containing metallic compounds that are used in small amounts for accelerating the drying of the paint film. They act as catalysts for the oxidation and polymerization of the vehicle used in the paint. Lead acetate, manganese dioxide, and cobalt are the dryers commonly used. Not more than 10% (by volume) of dryer should be used in an oil paint. If used in excess, especially in the final coat, they tend to destroy the elasticity of the paint, which finally leads to flaking.

The different types of solvent-based paints available are:

Alkyd paints These paints are based on synthetic resins combined with a vegetable oil, such as linseed oil. These are generally easier to apply and have better durability and wearing properties than the older types of paint. They have good opacity and excellent fastness to light as well. They are available in a wide range of colours.

Aluminium paints These are used for painting wood and metal surfaces. Aluminium powder forms the base in this type of paint. The base is held in suspension and bound by either quick-drying spirit varnish or slow-drying oil varnish, to suit the requirements of the surface to be painted. This paint is well established for its good weather-resisting and waterproofing qualities. It is highly heat-reflective, resistant to the corrosive action of sea-water, and stands up well in an atmosphere contaminated by acid fumes. Because of its brilliant silvery, shining texture, this paint has the advantage of being visible even in darkness. However, it is not used for painting large areas of walls. It is commonly used for painting metal roofs, silos, machinery, oil or gas storage tanks, hot water pipes, and tanks.

Anti-corrosive paints These are generally used as metal-protection paints, for preserving structural steelwork against the adverse effects of fumes, acids, corrosive chemicals, and the ravages of rough weather. Linseed oil is generally used as the vehicle. Sometimes dryers and inert fillers are added to modify the paint to the requirements.

Asbestos paints This type of paint is especially suitable for patching up or stopping leakage in metal roofs. Asbestos or fibrous coatings are sometimes used as moisture-proof covering coats for the outer face of basement walls as well.

Bituminous paints These are alkali-resistant and are chiefly used for painting exterior brickwork and plastered surfaces. They are also used for waterproofing and protecting iron and steel, and are commonly applied on water mains and structural steelwork that is underwater or on fabricated iron and steel products. Such paints usually consist of asphalt, bitumen, or pitch dissolved in mineral spirit or naphtha. When required, drying oils may also be added to the paint to modify its properties. This type of paint is obtained typically in black, but its colour can be modified by incorporating certain pigments such as red oxide. These paints, however, deteriorate when exposed to the direct rays of the sun.

Bronze paints This type of paint is often used for painting interior or exterior metallic surfaces. Aluminium bronze, copper bronze, and copper powder are the pigments commonly used in this type of paint. The vehicle used in these paints is usually nitrocellulose lacquer.

Cellulose paints This type of paint is made from celluloid sheets and amyl acetate substitutes. For making a superior type of paint, nitrocotton is used. It dries very quickly and possesses the additional advantages of hardness, flexibility, and smoothness. It can be cleaned easily and remains unaffected by hot water, smoke, or acidic fumes in the atmosphere, and stands up well to the ravages of rough weather. It is far superior to ordinary house paint and on account of its high cost, its usage is generally restricted to motor cars, airplanes, and so on.

Casein paints The protein casein is extracted from milk curds. It is mixed with a base consisting of white pigment such as whiting, titanium, lithopone, and so on to form this type of paint, which is usually available in powder or paste form. On account of its high opacity, the paint can be applied on new plasterwork without any danger of scaling or alkali burns. The paint can also be tinted any colour desired. It is usually applied on walls, ceiling, wall boards, cement block structures, and so on to enhance the appearance of the surface. When used for exterior surfaces of cement, brick, or stonemasonry, a small quantity of a drying oil or varnish is added to the paint to make it weather well.

Enamel paints This type of paint is made by adding pigments such as white lead or zinc white to a vehicle comprising a varnish. Colouring pigments may also be mixed in to obtain an enamel paint in the desired colour. On drying, it forms a smooth, glossy, relatively hard, and permanent film that is thin but solid. Enamel paints are used both for interiors as well as exterior paintwork. They are not affected by atmospheric pollutants and stand up well to the adverse effects of weather. Enamel paint typically presents a glossy surface; but if desired, an eggshell or flat finish may also be obtained by adding turpentine in smaller or larger quantities. It is commonly used for painting porches, decks, stairs, concrete surfaces, and so on.

Oil paints This type of paint can be used for almost all surfaces, from woodwork and masonry to metal and fabrics. Oil paints basically consist of two main components—a base and a vehicle. Oil paints are manufactured in different shades and grades, and are very commonly used.

Microporous/rubber paints This type of paint has excellent acid-, alkali- and moisture-resistant properties. They can be readily applied on new concrete and lime-plastered surfaces. The paint is made from rubber treated with chlorine gas (chlorinated rubber), which is dissolved in suitable solvents and mixed with other pigments. It is commonly used as a protective coating on cement or concrete floors and both in interior and exterior masonry surfaces.

Textured/'plastic' paints These are usually plaster-based and are intended to give a textured or relief effect to the surface. The texture is obtained by working over the material after application, while it is still wet, using combs, palette knives, strippers, and other tools. Some types are self-coloured; others may require painting over when they are dry.

Characteristics of a good paint The characteristics of a good paint are listed here.

- It should stick to the surface well and should be able to seal the porous substratum.
- Its consistency should provide easy workability.
- The thickness of the paint film should be adequate for good protection and decoration of the surface.
- The paint film should dry rapidly.
- The dried paint film should be able to withstand the effects of adverse weather for a long time, without losing its gloss.
- It should offer resistance to cracking and flaking.
- It should possess good moisture maintenance.
- Its colour should not fade with the passage of time.

Preparation of walls before painting Walls may require preparation before painting, using any of the following treatments:

Primer This can be an oil-based one or an emulsion. Primers are used to seal porous surfaces (especially new surfaces) and are applied before the application of the undercoat or paint.

Undercoat This is used under oil-based paints. Similar to primers, they are designed to provide a non-porous surface in order that the top coat may retain its colour and shine.

(Undercoats and primers should be allowed to dry and then rubbed down, wiped with a clean, dry cloth, and painted over immediately in order to prevent dirt and dust from settling in.)

Paint strippers Ammonia is the simplest of strippers. However, inhalation of ammonia fumes can be dangerous. Proprietary brands of paint strippers are also available, which are safer. Another common method of stripping paint is by burning it off with a butane-gas lamp.

Wallpaper

This type of wall covering evolved as an inexpensive substitute for the tapestries of the wealthy. The choice of wallpaper depends upon the dimensions and uses of the room. Wallpapers have a warmer appearance than paint. They can be stuck back even if they are torn. Smooth finishes do not catch dust, but easily show up marks. The various kinds of wallpaper available are as follows.

Lining paper A preliminary covering of plain paper gives the wall an even porosity, which helps when painting or hanging the final wall covering. On surfaces such as painted walls, this can be essential. There are various grades. It is best to avoid thin papers and use a heavy grade to conceal uneven walls.

Surface-printed papers The cheaper papers are called *pulp*. Higher quality papers, known as *grounded papers*, are given a coating of colour before the design is printed on these. Such wallpapers vary in weight and thickness. Thin papers are cheap, but tear easily when wet. They may also stretch if too much paste is applied. Thicker papers help to hide wall defects.

Washable papers A transparent waterproof film stops moisture, including steam, from damaging the design. These papers are especially suitable for bathrooms and kitchens. They can also be easily cleaned with a damp sponge.

Embossed papers The design is pressed into the paper to make it stand out in relief. This process produces wood-like grain, imitation leather, and textile effects. Duplex-embossed papers have designs with more depth, since two layers of paper are bonded together before the design is impressed. This material is more resistant to stretching.

Anaglypta Two layers of paper and cotton fibre are bonded together and embossed to produce anaglypta. These are available typically in white, but can be decorated with matt or silk-finish emulsion paint. When used as ceiling papers, they are usually left unpainted. Anaglypta can also be used to cover a cracked wall.

Supaglypta This strong, deeply moulded cotton-based paper is good for covering badly cracked walls and ceilings. These surfaces should first be covered with lining paper, then the supaglypta, which looks like plaster, laid on, and finally emulsion-painted.

Ingrained papers These coverings have an oatmeal-like texture, which is useful for concealing a rough wall surface. Small wood chips and sawdust are bonded between two layers of paper during their manufacture. Most of these can be emulsion-painted.

Lincrusta Linseed oil and fillers are bonded to backing paper to make lincrusta. These are supplied in simulated wood effects or with textured designs.

Flock Designs stand out in relief on such papers, which have a velvety pile. This is achieved by gluing nylon, silk, or wool cuttings to the surface during manufacture.

Metallic papers These are made from patterned foil glued to paper backings. However, their reflective surface accentuates any unevenness in the walls, so they should be used only on perfectly flat surfaces.

Hand-printed papers Each roll is prepared separately and therefore costs more than machine printed paper. The designs are outlined more sharply.

Wood-chip papers These have chips of wood inter-layered between sheets of bonded paper and are usually off-white in colour.

Paper-backed hessian Strong, coarse jute or hemp is called hessian. Paper-backed hessian is a type of rough-textured wallpaper available in a number of colours.

Japanese grass cloth This is made of dried grasses sewn close together and glued to a paper backing. They are expensive and not easily cleaned.

Other variations in wallpaper include paper-backed wools, woven grasses, felts, cork, silks, and other textile materials.

Fabric wall coverings

The use of fabrics on walls goes back a long way, to the time when fabrics were the walls of nomadic tents or were hung on stone walls to counteract their coldness. Today, wall fabrics fall into two main categories: fabrics that actually surface a wall in the manner of wallpaper and those that are draped loosely across a wall.

Almost any fabric can be made into a wall covering by tacking it to the wall, but this approach often mars the original surface. A better way is to stretch the fabric on a wooden frame, which can then be attached to the wall at just a few points. The use of double-faced tape or vinyl adhesive allows the fabric to be stripped from the wall without defacing it. Fabric can also be hung in soft folds, as a continuation of window drapery or for its own sake as a supple alternative to patterned wallpaper. This can be useful as a way of hiding an unwanted window or door without actually blocking it. Grass cloth, made of loosely woven grasses and reeds affixed to a paper backing, can be handled like wallpaper as well.

Textiles range from smooth to bold textures, with a number of colours available, but natural or muted tones are most appropriate for large wall surfaces. Carpeting can also be affixed to walls—it provides insulation against both sound and cold, adding a soft, sensuous texture and continuity with upholstery, soft furnishings, and soft floorings.

Textile can also be manipulated to become a wall when it is used as a room divider, separating areas visually by either hanging from the ceiling or while stretched on a frame that can be placed as a screen. Any textile used as a wall covering will bring in softness and act as a moderator between people and architecture.

Plastics

Such wall coverings, owing to their resistance to abrasion, are more hard-wearing and more easily cleaned than most other wall coverings. As they are non-porous, there is a great tendency for the growth of mould, so the adhesive should contain fungicides. The main types are as follows:

Paper- or fabric-backed vinyls These resist steam and water, and can be scrubbed with a soft brush. These may have the appearance of almost any material, such as silk, tweed, hessian, cork, grass paper, wood, stone, or brick. Fabric-backed vinyls are more durable.

Vinyl flock papers These are velvety piles of flock, mostly synthetic, stuck in patterns over the background vinyl wallpaper.

Plastic wall tiles These imitate ceramic tiles.

Plastic laminates These act as a veneer or surface board. Melamine is the resin commonly used during the manufacture of these plastic laminates, which may simulate wood panelling or fabrics. These are particularly appropriate in bathrooms, restrooms, or food-service areas, where the walls may be subject to splashes and spatters.

Expanded polystyrene Available in sheet or tile form, these are used on walls and ceilings to give insulation against heat and sound and to help eliminate condensation. There is a fire risk, however, unless the polystyrene is treated with a fire-retardant finish.

Clear acrylic-plastic sheeting Both the all-purpose and break-resistant types are highly useful on walls inside elevators or in vulnerable spots in corridors where walls are continually being scuffed or marred. This material is combustible, however, and presents a fire hazard.

Wood

The rough texture of wood on walls generates warmth. The woods used for wall panelling are usually hard, well seasoned, and of a decorative appearance. They may cover the wall completely or form a dado. Wood panelling comes in many variations of colour, tone, and texture. It can be both rustic and elegant, and rarely needs heavy-duty cleaning. Wood panelling may be either solid or wood-veneered,

and both last for years with little maintenance, provided certain precautions are taken in respect of dry rot and woodworm; but the initial cost is high.

Wood veneers may be stuck to paper too, giving an effect similar to solid wood at a much lower cost. Veneered plywood panelling is also popular.

Wood panelling may be found in such places as entrance halls and staircases, convention rooms, and restaurants.

Cork

This offers a dramatic and luxurious effect and is easily installed. Its chief virtue is sound control; its main disadvantage is its perishability.

Glass wall coverings

Glass can be used in the form of decorative tiles, and sometimes in the form of mosaics. Coloured, opaque glass sheets or tiles may be used as a wall covering in hotel bedrooms.

Glass wall coverings are also frequently used in the form of mirror tiles, which reflect light and can alter the apparent size of a room or corridor. Sometimes, 'antique' mirror tiles are used, giving a duller surface with less reflection. Large unframed mirrors may also cover part of a wall, for instance over a vanity unit or dressing table, while large framed mirrors are sometimes found along the walls of corridors and lounges.

A glass-less type of mirror is also available now, which has the advantage of not misting up or shattering and is about a fifth of the weight of a conventional mirror of equal size. It consists of a polyester film vacuum-coated with aluminium and mounted on a flat frame.

Fibreglass/spun glass

These wall coverings can be almost indistinguishable from old woodwork or weathered plaster if properly painted. This material can be poured into moulds to duplicate just about any shape or surface.

Metallic wall coverings

Metals may be used on walls for their decorative and hygienic qualities. Metals such as copper and anodized aluminium are decorative and may be used for effect in such areas as bars, where the metal—in combination with rows of bottles and interesting lighting—is most impressive. Other metals, usually stainless steel in the form of tiles, may be used in kitchens, where they present a durable, easily cleaned, hygienic surface in areas where splashing is likely. Metal skirting boards provide coved edges between walls and floor surfaces in such areas.

Metal foil can also be elegant if used sparingly as a wall covering. They are available in a variety of colours. They tend to illuminate a room, but must be used discreetly to avoid creating a gaudy effect. The foils available today are washable and durable.

Tiles

Long relegated to outdoor areas or limited to kitchen and bathroom walls, tiles have finally come into their own again, with ceramic and mosaic patterns that brighten and create a cool, airy feeling in rooms being most popular. Generally easy to clean, the main drawback of tiles is that the grouting may become discoloured or chipped till tiles loosen.

Acrylic (Corian)

A solid acrylic surfacing material, Corian is a well-known brand finding application as kitchen and bathroom wall coverings in hotels and restaurants. Corian, which starts out as a poured acrylic, is sold in solid sheets as well as formed components, and is finding its niche as a material for wall panels, partitions, dividers, façades, wainscoting, valances, countertops, and bath surrounds. The product is non-porous, durable, and stain-resistant, with a smooth surface that eliminates hard-to-clean, dirt-catching crevices. An accidental surface scratch or cut can easily be removed with fine sandpaper without marring the surface, which renders it very durable.

Inorganic wall coatings

These are continuous wall coatings sprayed on with a high-pressure gun that resemble a ceramic glaze. They do not burn, nor deteriorate through oxidation or exposure to moisture. Indeed, they are almost permanent and come in a large range of colours. They typically come with a clear glaze that prevents scratching of the surface. Some types are specifically designed for use in wet areas, such as showers and steam rooms.

Early-warning wall coverings

These wall coverings have the potential to give early warning of a fire in the room in the form of a built-in smoke alarm. Early-warning coverings are available in a range of materials.

Leather

Animal hides are very decorative but extremely expensive. They may be padded and studded with brass studs, and they do not usually cover a complete wall surface. They may be found in luxury establishments in parts of restaurants or bars, but are too expensive to be found in most places. They are also prone to attack by mildew. Nowadays, the effects of leather may be simulated by plastics where required.

Selection of Wall Coverings

The following factors should be borne in mind while selecting wall coverings.

Durability

Certain wall areas in hotels have greater wear and tear than other areas. Walls in areas like corridors tend to be rubbed, stained, and scratched very often due to movement of people, trolleys, luggage, chairs, and so on. In such areas durability of the wall covering material becomes a major concern. A dado is used in such areas. A dado is a stronger and more easily cleaned material for the lower part of the wall, up to 150 cm. Wall skirting upto 10–20 cm is also used to prevent damage to the lower part of the walls.

Acoustics

It refers to the sound absorption quality of a material. The ability of a wall covering material to reduce sound by absorbing it is the foremost selection factor when considering guest comfort in guestrooms, conference rooms, and other public areas. An acoustic rating called the Noise Reduction Coefficient (NRC) should be referred to aid selection of material. Wall covering materials range in NRC from 0.60 to 0.95. For instance, an NRC of 0.95 indicates that the wall covering absorbs 95% of the sound waves that strike it.

Appearance

Wall coverings should be selected to enhance the image of a hotel. Wall coverings have a distinct decorative impact apart from being functional. Colour, pattern, and texture of the material should be considered to suit the purpose, furnishings, and architectural aspects of the room or area.

Fire safety

Certain wall covering materials emit toxic gases when they burn. According to fire regulations, use of such materials is forbidden in guest rooms and public areas in hotels. The wall covering must comply with fire regulations of the country. Many countries have fire codes that specify the use of only class A materials in hotels. Class A materials are those that rate from 0–5 on the Flame Spread Index, which is a scale that measures how quickly flames will spread across a material's exposed, finished surface. These wall coverings may be made of inherently fire-resistant materials or may be treated by the manufacturer with chemical finishes to make them fire retardant.

Ease of maintenance

The wall coverings should be of an easily cleaned and hygienic material.

Maintenance cost

Many a time, even though the initial cost of a wall covering is high, the maintenance cost is negligible. On the other hand, the initial cost may be quite reasonable, but the maintenance cost will be very high. The daily maintenance cost should be considered while selecting wall coverings.

Initial cost

The product and installation cost should be within budgetary guidelines of the hotel.

Maintenance of Walls and Wall Coverings

Periodic cleaning of walls should be scheduled so that obstinate dust and grime do not settle in. Walls are to be maintained by the following cleaning schedules:

Daily cleaning These methods include daily and weekly dusting and vacuuming.

Spot removal This is done whenever the need arises to clean up a stain in specific places on the walls.

Restorative cleaning This involves the use of detergents and solvents on a periodic basis.

Before cleaning the walls, remove any pictures, mirrors, or accessories hung up on them. Push the furniture to the middle of the room and cover them with dust sheets. First wipe down the walls with a cloth-covered brush or a vacuum-cleaner attachment for the purpose. Then remove cobwebs and dust bunnies by dusting from the bottom up.

When washing down painted walls or washable coverings, work from the bottom up. If dirty water runs down a dry area of the painted wall or wall paper, the streaks may be difficult to remove. Wring out a sponge or cloth as dry as possible and clean a small area at a time—about 2-feet square—working in a circular motion. Finally, wipe the washed floor-to-ceiling section dry with a sponge wrung out in clean water, working from the top down. Then move to the area adjoining the area just cleaned.

For both washable and non-washable surfaces, cleaning methods have been summarized in Table 27.4.

Table 27.4 Cleaning washable and non-washable wall coverings

Type	Method of cleaning
Wall carpet, felt, flock (paper-backed), grass, cloth, Hessian and jute, linen, silk	Brush down with a soft, long-handled wall brush or use a vacuum-cleaner with a brush attachment. To remove stains, dust lightly with white talc on cotton wool; leave for a few hours; then brush off. Do not use dry-cleaning reagents or upholstery cleaners, as they may cause discoloration and shrinkage here.
Cork	Brush or vacuum. Then sponge away any marks gently with lukewarm water and mild detergent. Do not over-wet.
Flock (vinyl-backed)	Wipe with sponge wrung out in warm water. Do not rub flock.
Leather	See Table 8.6 for cleaning techniques for different types of leather.
Paint—emulsion	Wipe down with sponge wrung out in mild detergent solution. Then wipe with cold water.
Paint—glossy, silk-finish, vinyl	Wash wall from bottom upwards using a sponge wrung out in mild detergent solution; wipe residue with cold water, working from the top down. If necessary, scrub gloss paint with a soft brush.
Polyurethane varnish	Wipe with a piece of chamois leather wrung out in mild detergent solution. Occasionally spray lightly with furniture polish (from an aerosol can) and rub down with soft cloth.
Tiles—aluminium and ceramic	Wipe down with a sponge wrung out in mild detergent solution; rinse well. Dry with chamois leather. Clean grouting with a soft brush dipped in bleach solution and rinse.
Tiles—mirror	Wipe down with a piece of chamois leather wrung out in vinegar water (1 tablespoon vinegar to 1 pint of lukewarm water)
Wallpaper	Brush or lightly vacuum; then gently sponge away marks with a mild detergent solution. For grease stains, dab on white talc lightly with cotton wool and brush off after a few hours.
Wallpaper—washable vinyls	Wipe down with a sponge wrung out in mild detergent solution.
Wood panelling	Brush or vacuum and rub clean with soft dusters. Periodically apply teak oil or cream. Do not use wax polish.

Windows and Window Treatments

Windows have four practical functions: they admit air, light, vision, and people to varying degrees. How well they perform these functions is a result of their design, placement, and treatment. Their design may be hidden, improved, or accentuated by treatments such as curtains, draperies, shades, and so on.

Assessment of Windows

Any assessment of windows should take into account the following considerations:

View and privacy Is there a view? And if so, should it be an important factor in the interior design scheme? Can it be enjoyed without loss of privacy in the daytime or at night? What are the possibilities for ensuring privacy?

Light Natural light is both cheerful and energy-saving (artificial lighting sources always being more costly than the free sunlight). Window treatments should provide optimal but flexible control of light by means of draperies, shades, and so on.

Ventilation Cross-ventilation in rooms without air-conditioning is a decisive factor for comfort.

Structure of a Window

The component parts of a typical window are shown in Figure 27.11. Windows consist of a wooden frame around the side and top edges, and this fixed part of the window is called a *casement* or *frame*. It is designed to hold the *sash*, which is a wood or metal frame that holds the glass panes and is usually movable. The *sill* forms the base of the window, on which the casement rest. The strip of wood sometimes placed underneath the sill for support is called the *apron*.

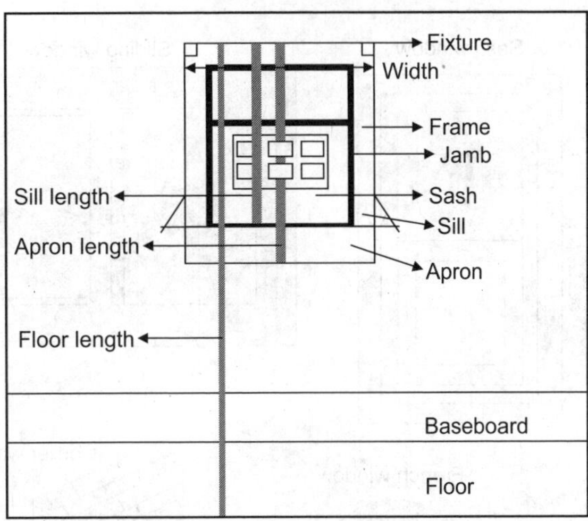

Fig. 27.11 Parts of a window

Types and Designs of Windows

Windows can be classified into two general categories:

Fixed windows These are meant for providing light and a view, essentially.

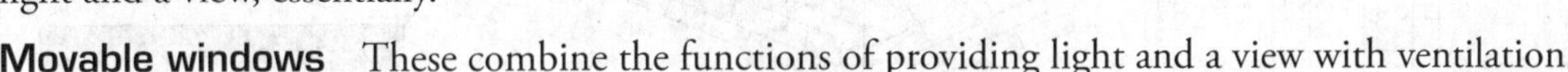

Movable windows These combine the functions of providing light and a view with ventilation.

Today, we often find a combination of the two types in one unit.

The various basic window designs are as follows and refer to Figure 27.12 for the diagrams of types of windows. Also refer to the scan code for pictures of windows.

Single windows A single window is the basic window with a single frame; it opens either inside or outside.

Double-sashed windows This type of window has a sash that can be pushed up and down. Since the part with the glass pane is only half the size of the window frame, half of the window will always be left open. This window must be placed such that robbers do not have easy access to it.

Mullion windows These really consist of a series of windows. Each window can be treated as a separate unit or unified into a single design.

Casement windows These are the most common type of windows. The window panes are in two halves that open outwards from the frame. They are very good for illuminating a room naturally, as they offer least obstruction to light. For inward-swinging casements, the furnishings or drapery chosen should not interfere with the window's operation.

Sliding windows They consist of a pane of standard glass or polymer plastic, bound in vinyl or aluminium frames and built into a track system. They operate horizontally.

Pivot windows They are made up of several glass panes set in a woodwork or metal frame. They are typically used for cross-ventilation purposes. Such a window may have one pane that pivots to the side, or they may all be fixed. They provide very good ventilation and light. The intensity of light let in can be controlled by tilting the panes.

Sash windows These are also called *double-hung windows*. They consist of two glass panes, both of which may be opened independently.

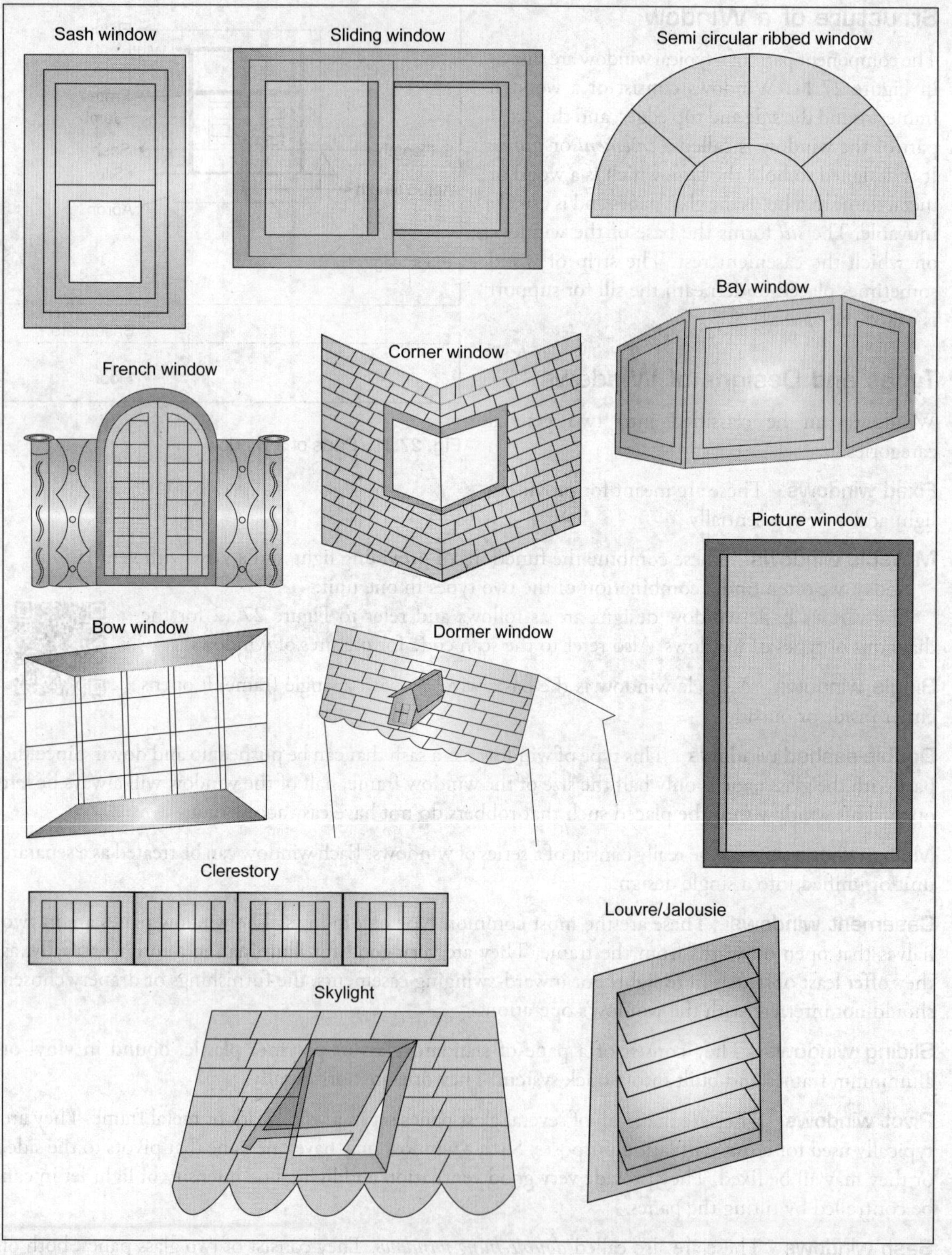

Sash window

Sliding window

Semi circular ribbed window

Bay window

French window

Corner window

Picture window

Bow window

Dormer window

Clerestory

Louvre/Jalousie

Skylight

Fig. 27.12 Various types of windows

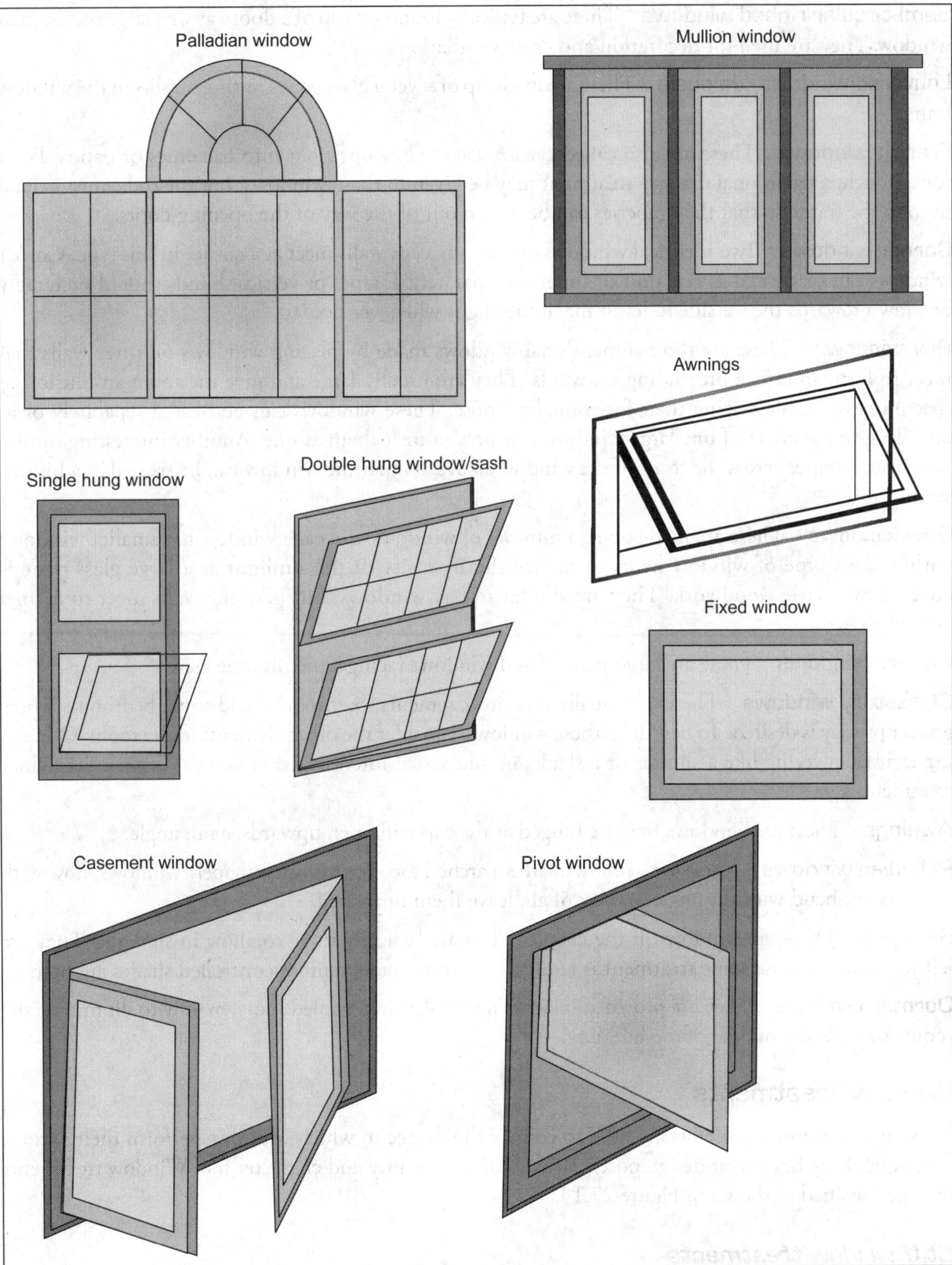

Fig. 27.12 *Contd.*

Semi-circular ribbed windows These are typically found on top of a doorway or a large rectangular window. They are used for decoration and cross-ventilation.

Louvered windows/Jalousie These are made up of several glass panes resting on slits in the window frame.

French windows These are also called *French doors*. They open out into balconies or patios. For a softer touch, a traditional drapery treatment may be given to these windows; but the rods must extend beyond the frame so that the draperies can be drawn out of the way of the opening doors.

Corner windows Two identical windows on two adjacent walls meet at a corner in this type. Corner windows can be treated as one unit or function separately. Drapes or vertical blinds should preferably be drawn towards the outside to let in maximum light whenever needed.

Bay windows These are three-dimensional windows made by placing windows on three walls that meet to form an alcove protruding outwards. They are usually large and give the room an illusion of spaciousness, beside serving their functional purpose. These windows can be treated separately or as one. To give the effect of one large window, it is best to treat them as one. Another interesting option is to install drapes across the front of the window alcove, so that the window can be treated as a hidden seating area.

Bow windows These are made up of a number of windows and each window has smaller windows within. This type of window helps to reduce the intensity of the sunlight as a large glass pane is covered by a little woodwork. They are similar to bay windows, but here the walls meet to form a curved alcove.

Picture windows These are large-paned fixed windows facing a picturesque view.

Clerestory windows These are usually seen in basements, bathrooms, and some bedrooms where greater privacy is desired. To best dress these windows, consider the other elements in the room. One can use a fitted covering like a shutter or a shade, or add visual interest with a vertical down-to-the-floor treatment.

Awnings These are windows that are hinged at the top and open upwards, at an angle.

Palladian windows These are windows with an arched top. To treat such shapely windows, flow with the curve or bend with the angle or, best of all, leave them untreated.

Skylights These are windows in the ceiling. They are basically there to allow in sunlight. They are left untreated. In case some treatment is required, custom-made, remote-controlled shades are best.

Dormer windows They are provided in attics under slanting, gabled roofs, mainly to illuminate the rooms towards the middle of the building.

Window Treatments

In essence, window treatments are used to control the degree to which windows perform their various functions. They have great design potential as sources of beauty and character too. Window treatments may be classified as shown in Figure 27.13.

Stiff window treatments

There are many types of coverings apart from curtains that can be used on windows to ensure privacy and block out light.

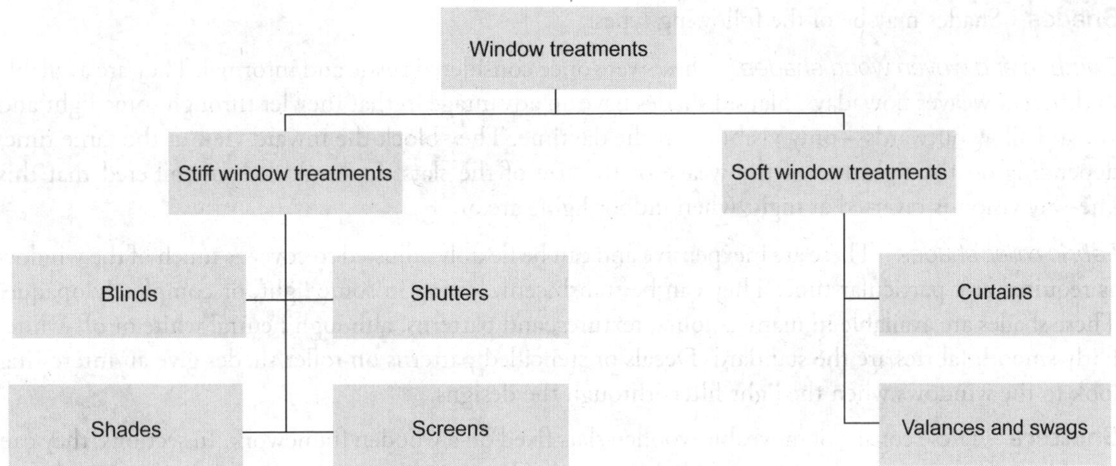

Fig. 27.13 Types of window treatments

Blinds Blinds are of the following types:

Roller blinds These let in plenty of light when drawn up, yet give complete privacy when unrolled and let down. Roller blinds are made of thick fabrics used in conjunction with rollers.

Roman blinds These are made of fabric attached to cords. When the cords are pulled, the blind rises up in accordion pleats to form a pelmet. They are heavier and warmer than roller blinds.

Venetian blinds These actually originated in China, contrary to the name. They are made of parallel slats of wood, metal, or plastic aligned horizontally or vertically. They are popular for their almost complete control of air, light, and view. They are usually low in price and some custom-designed blinds come in different colours and patterns. The versions with very thin slats can have different colours on each side. Their major disadvantage is their affinity for dust and the difficulty in cleaning them really well. The thin-slatted and vertical versions do better in this respect.

Vertical louvre blinds These are most effective on a large floor-to-ceiling window. They work on the same principal as the venetian blinds, except that they close across the window rather than down. The slats are wider than in the Venetian type, but less opaque. They may be made of sheer synthetic fabrics, canvas, silk, or thin wood slats.

Pinoleum blinds These are an inexpensive covering for large windows. They are made from fine strips of wood held together by cotton, and let a pleasant, soft light filter through. They may be mounted on a spring-operated roller or moved up and down by cords.

Balastore blinds These are inexpensive blinds made of strong paper fibre. It is accordion-pleated to act like a folding blind (similar to the Venetian blinds). Balastores are perforated with small holes to let light through without glare.

Pleatex blinds These are made from stronger paper than balastores and have smaller pleats. The paper gives privacy, but lets sunlight through, which is filtered and tinted in the colour of the paper. The four most common colours are orange, green, blue, and parchment (natural).

Austrian blinds These are ruchéd fabrics (trimmed with gathers). They may be used partially raised, and when fully raised, they form a decorative pelmet. They are used in banquet halls and large lobbies for a sumptuous effect.

Shades Shades may be of the following types:

Bamboo and woven wood shades These were once considered rustic and informal. They are available in different weaves nowadays. Slatted shades have an advantage in that they let through some light and air, and allow outwards—only visibility in the daytime. They block the inward view at the same time, depending on the tightness of the weave or the size of the slats. It should be remembered that this one-way vision is reversed at night when indoor lights are on.

Fabric roller shades These are inexpensive and can be flexibly adjusted to cover as much of the window as required at a particular time. They can be translucent, letting in some light, or completely opaque. These shades are available in many colours, textures, and patterns, although neutral white or off-white, fairly smooth fabrics are the standard. Decals or stencilled patterns on roller shades give an interesting look to the windows when the light filters through the designs.

Shutters These consist of moveable wooden slats fixed on a wooden framework. In sections, they can provide varying degrees of privacy and light control. They may also act as a layer of indoor insulation over the glass window panes. *Louvred shutters* are like lightweight doors made of overlapping wooden slats, spaced apart to let light through. For large windows, they are made in hinged sections, which fold flat against one another to reveal the window opening. Although their initial cost is high, shutters last almost indefinitely. They are difficult to dust, but their wood is generally sealed against soils.

Screens These are in the form of hardboard panels with cut-out panels of fabric stretched across the wooden frame. They are attached immovably to the window frame around edges and so do not allow much flexibility in the control of light, unless combined with another type of shutter or pane. There are now tracks that allow screens to be moved to one side when an unrestricted view is desired. The most popular screens in use nowadays are Shoji screens.

Shoji screens are traditional Japanese screens for which modern interiors have a natural affinity. They were originally made of rice paper mounted on a wooden frame coated with black lacquer, but they are now available in translucent plastic materials.

Soft window treatments

Soft window treatments comprise curtains, valances, swags, etc. Let us first discuss the various types of curtains in detail. Valances and swags will be discussed in the section 'curtain headings and accessories' in a latter part of the chapter.

Curtains often contribute more to the atmosphere of a room than any other item of furnishing. Plain, heavy curtains falling down to the floor can be used to create a formal setting. Short curtains made of light, brightly patterned fabrics are used to create an informal, relaxed atmosphere. Apart from creating the desired atmosphere, curtains give flexible control over privacy, heat, light, and to some extent noise.

The various fabrics used for making curtains are cotton, linen, rayon, glass fibres, acrylics, and silk for luxurious settings. Care should be taken to minimize their exposure to sunlight and airborne soils, as these reduce the curtains' functional life.

Good curtains are usually lined and heavy curtains are interlined. The lining helps the curtains to drape well and protect them from sunlight and airborne dust.

Curtains fulfil several important functions:

- They give flexible control over privacy, heat, and light.
- They soak up noise in proportion to the area they cover, the thickness of the fabric, and the depths of the folds.

- They can add colour and pattern to the décor.
- They cover bareness and furnish a room even without furniture.
- They can change the apparent size of a room or conceal architectural flaws.

Types of curtains Curtains may be used to create various window treatments as illustrated in Figure 27.14.

Glass curtains These are also called sheer or net curtains and are usually made of cotton or polyester. They are appealing in light pastel shades.

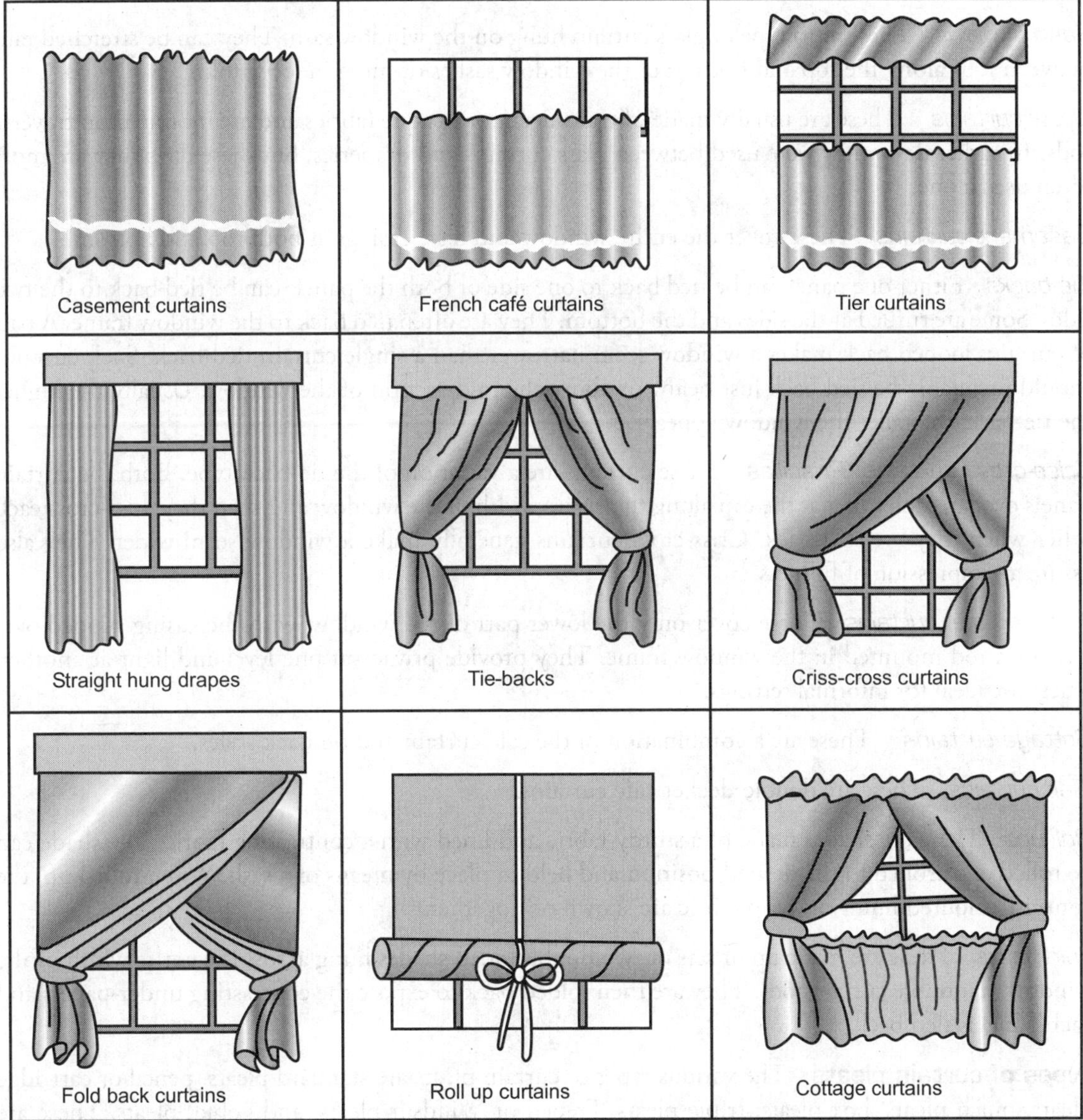

Fig. 27.14 Various window treatment with curtains

Drapes/over-curtains Draperies refer to loosely hung (not taut or stretched) soft furnishings. These are made of heavier fabrics and may be lined. The heading is usually pleated. Draperies can be decorative, as well as providing privacy, darkening a room, and insulating it against the cold. They may be used in the following ways:

- Panel drapes: These cover only the sides of a window area.
- Draw drapes: These span the entire width of the window and can be drawn aside by means of a cord attached to the runners or by remote control.
- Straight-hung drapes: These can be used with a valance or a cornice, but the windows will seem taller without a decorative heading.

Sash curtains These are a type of glass curtain hung on the window sash. They can be stretched taut between rods along the top and bottom of the window sashes or hung in loose folds.

Draw curtains These are usually made of translucent or opaque fabrics and are mounted on traverse rods. In earlier days, they were used between glass curtains and draperies, but these days they are more often used alone.

Casement curtains These cover the entire window and have casings at both top and bottom.

Tie-backs Either one panel can be tied back to one side or both the panels can be tied back to the two sides. Some are ruffled at the sides and the bottom. They are often tied back to the window frame. A pair of curtains looped back makes a window seem narrower than a single curtain tied back. Such curtains should preferably be tied back just below or above the mid-section of the window. Usually the higher the tie-back, the taller the window appears.

Criss-cross curtains/Priscillas These curtains are a variation of the tie-back type. Both the curtain panels overlap each other at the top along the entire width of the window and then they criss-cross each other when they are tied back. Criss-cross curtains generally make a window seem wider. They also assure an impression of fullness.

'French café' curtains These cover only the lower part of the window, with the casing slipped over a tension rod mounted in the window frame. They provide privacy at one level and light at another. These are ideal for informal settings.

Cottage curtains These are a combination of the café curtain and tie-back styles.

Tier curtains These are double-decker café curtains.

Roll-ups These are shades made of a sturdy fabric and lined with a contrasting fabric. The shade can be rolled or unrolled to the desired position and held in place by means of a sash. When rolled up, the contrast-coloured lining and top fabric are shown off together.

Fold-backs These are made up of sets of two double-sided shades hung across the entire width of the window on double curtain rods. They are then folded back to expose the contrasting under-panels and each panel is tied back.

Types of curtain pleats The various types of curtain pleats are standard pleats, pencil or cartridge pleats, pinch pleats, box pleats, triple pleats, French or Windsor pleats, and goblet pleats. These are illustrated in Figure 27.15.

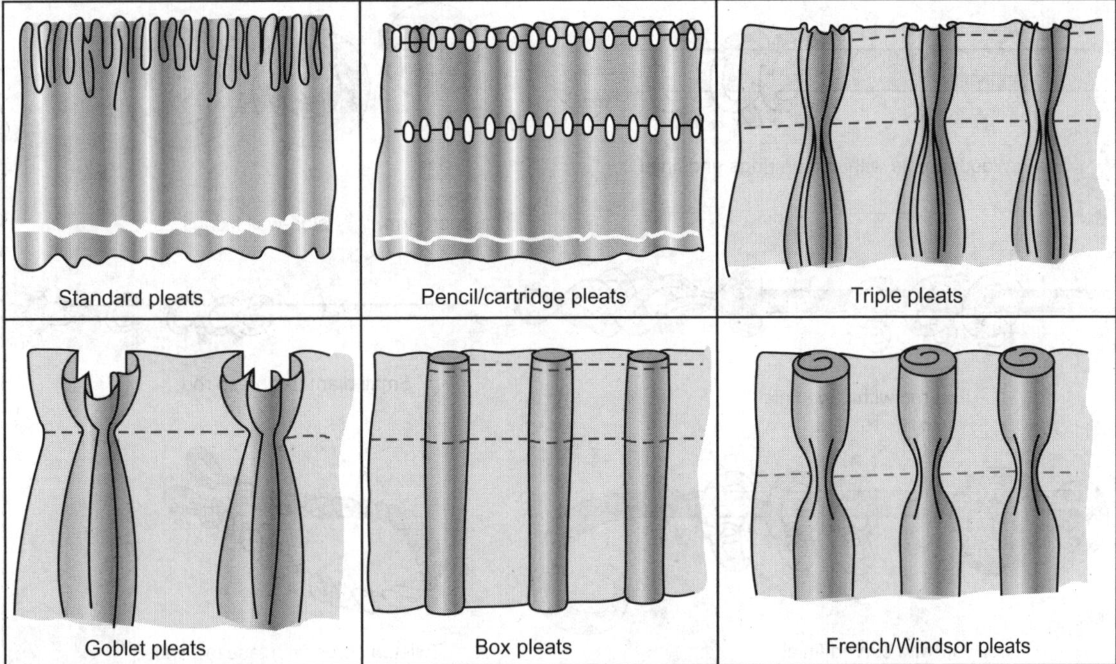

Fig. 27.15 Curtain pleats

Curtain headings and accessories We shall now look at the various headings and accessories used with curtains. The various hardware and accessories used with curtains are illustrated in Figure 27.16.

Pelmets and cornices Cornices are box-like shapes used at the top horizontal portion of the drapery treatment to hide the poles and other hardware. They are generally 4 to 7 inches deep. The width of a cornice should be a little less than one-eighth of the overall length of floor-length drapery. They may be made of wood, plastic, or mirrored glass. Wooden cornices are the most frequently used and a plain wooden board with an interesting moulding at the top and bottom is always in good taste. Wooden cornices may be finished in their natural colour, painted in some other colour, or covered with cloth, cork, or leather. Sometimes the coverings are edged in brass nails. Some popular styles of cornices are illustrated in Figure 27.17.

Valances These are made of fabric that has been pleated, scalloped, or ruffled. They should never exceed one-sixth of the window's height and should be about 8–12 inches in depth. Lambrequins have a backing of buckram, plywood, or masonite, which can be shaped into different designs. These shaped valances may be covered with cloth and edged with fringe. The width of a lambrequin should be about a seventh of the length of floor-length drapery. Some popular types of valances are illustrated in Figure 27.17.

Swags and cascades Swags are decorative, drapery treatments meant to hide the curtain headings and usually taper to a *cascade* (also called a *tail*). These loop and fall luxuriously over a curtain pole, ending in elaborate tails. Headings of this type are appropriate for large, formal rooms with high ceilings. They tend to look too heavy in small or average-sized rooms. The depth of the swag at the centre after it has been draped should be about one-seventh of the drapery length or one-seventh of the distance between the top of the frame and the floor. The width of the cascade at the top should coincide with the width of the drapery when hung.

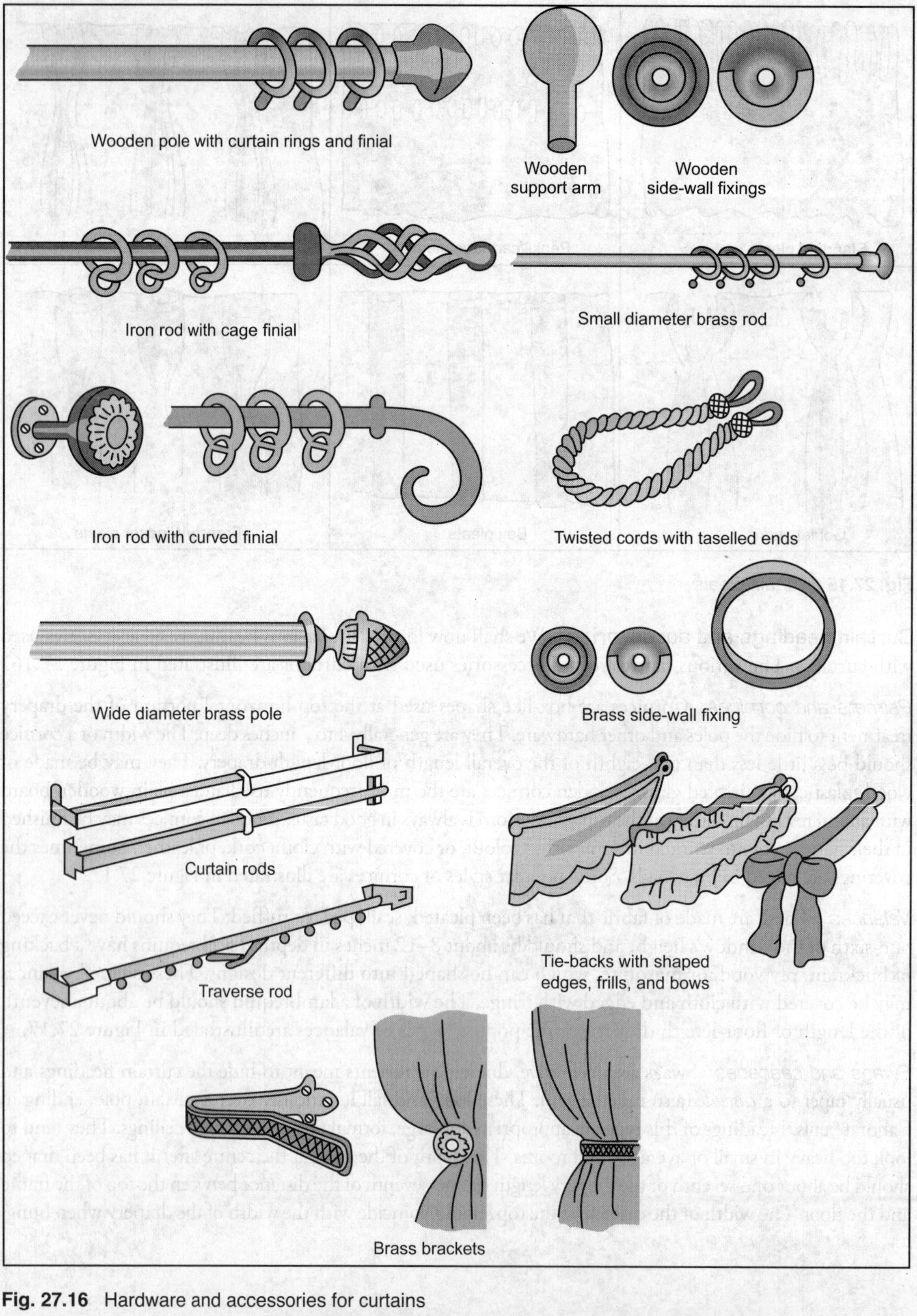

Wooden pole with curtain rings and finial

Wooden support arm

Wooden side-wall fixings

Iron rod with cage finial

Small diameter brass rod

Iron rod with curved finial

Twisted cords with tasselled ends

Wide diameter brass pole

Brass side-wall fixing

Curtain rods

Traverse rod

Tie-backs with shaped edges, frills, and bows

Brass brackets

Fig. 27.16 Hardware and accessories for curtains

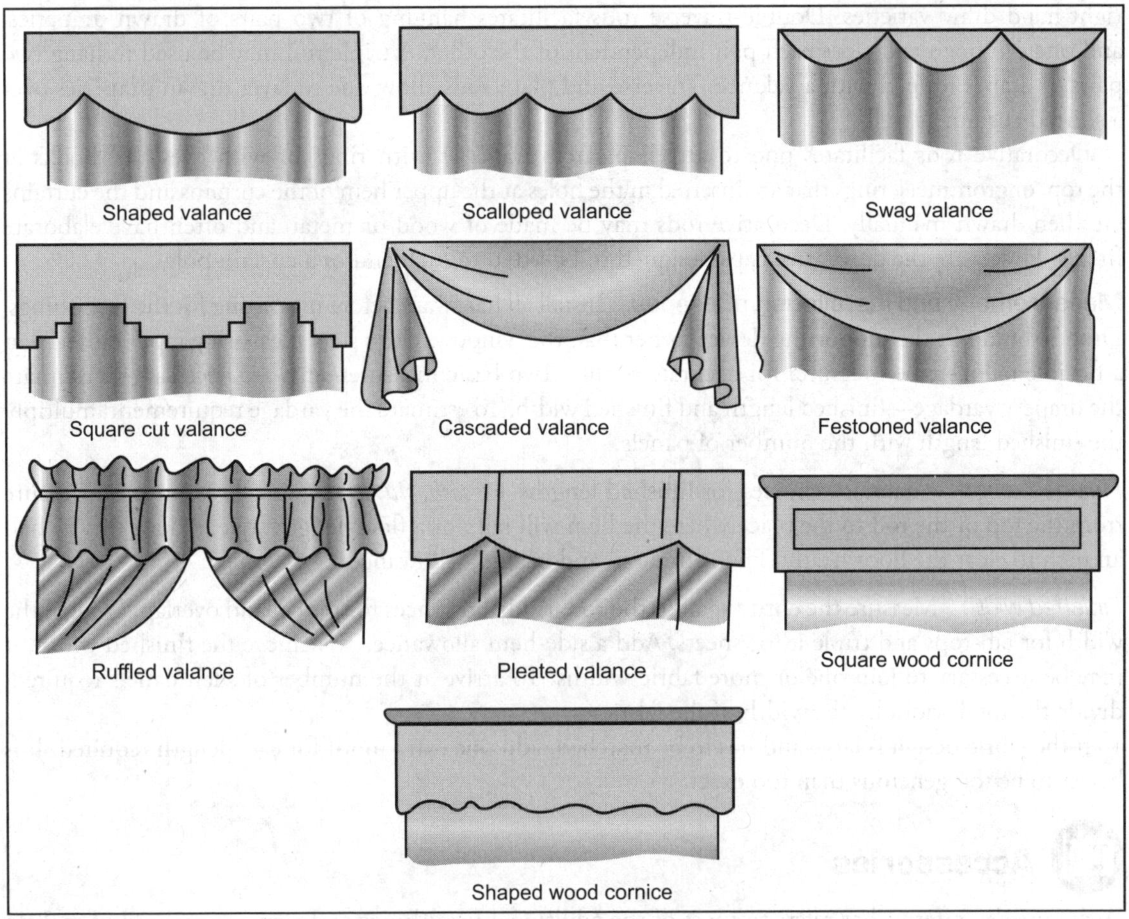

Shaped valance
Scalloped valance
Swag valance
Square cut valance
Cascaded valance
Festooned valance
Ruffled valance
Pleated valance
Square wood cornice
Shaped wood cornice

Fig. 27.17 Types of valances and cornices

The length of the cascade should be 2½ to 3 times its finished width. Swags and cascades are illustrated in Figure 27.18.

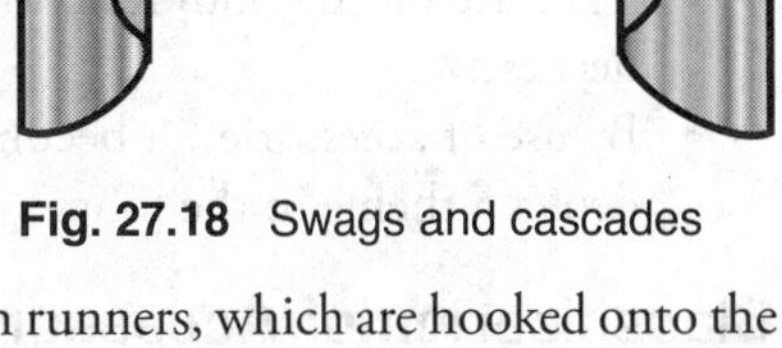

Curtain rods Finding the right hardware is essential to the success of the window treatment. Curtain rods are generally used for shirred curtains or simple cafés. Most rods now come in adjustable lengths.

Drapery cranes These are the appropriate hardware to use where installations have to be flexible. On French windows or swinging casement windows, this type of drapery rod, with its hinged bracket, allows the free edge to swing away from the door or window with the casement.

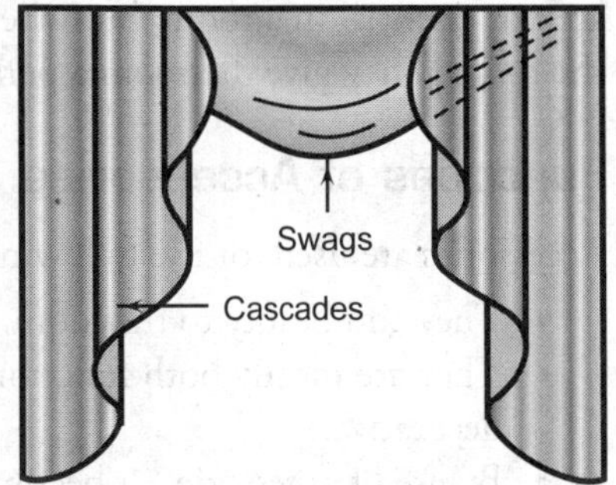

Fig. 27.18 Swags and cascades

Traverse and decorative rods These are used in conjunction with runners, which are hooked onto the curtain. They come in many types. The conventional traverse rod is used with classic pleated draperies that pull away from the centre to either side. A one-way draw traverse lets one pull the drapery back to either side of the window. Ideal for corner windows, one-way traverse rods are available in a left- or right-hand draw varieties. Double-traverse rods facilitates hanging of two pairs of drawn draperies, and one can open and close each pair independent of the other. A triple rod may be used to hang two pairs of drapes topped with a valance. Traverse and plain rods allow one to layer drawn draperies over a shirred curtain as well.

Decorative rods facilitates one to attach pleated draperies with rings or with eyes and hooks at the top, or grommets, rings that are inserted in the holes at the upper hem of the curtains and the curtains are then drawn manually. Decorative rods may be made of wood or metal, and often have elaborate finials. Finials are the decorative caps designed to be fitted to each end of a curtain pole.

Measurement and installation of drapes Install all hardware before measuring for the furnishings. Drapes should fit the supporting device rather than the window. Use a steel measuring tape (rather than a flexible tailor's tape-measure) for accurate results. Two basic measurements are necessary to estimate the drapery yardage—finished length and finished width. To estimate the yardage requirement, multiply the finished length with the number of panels.

Finished length Standard choices for finished lengths are *sash, sill, apron,* and *floor* lengths. Measure from the top of the rod to the place where the hem will fall; for a floor-length style, reduce this by half an inch to clear the floor neatly. Then add hem and heading allowances.

Finished width Measure the entire span of the rod. Add allowances for return and overlap. Double the width for tab-tops and triple it for sheers. Add a side-hem allowance. To achieve the finished width, it may be necessary to join one or more fabric widths. To arrive at the number of such panels required, divide the total width by the width of the fabric.

If the fabric design is large and has to be matched, add one extra motif for each length required. It is better to be too generous than too exact.

 Accessories

'Accessories' is a term that refers to most of the additional furnishings and elements needed to make a room viable in all senses. Accessories are decorative and functional articles that enhance the beauty of a room and bring in charm. The right accessories help to stress the decorative theme of the room. They are not essential in a room, but when used, they help to bring out the individuality and add vitality to the room. They give the room a personal touch and make it look more lived-in.

Functions of Accessories

Accessories are used for the following reasons:

- They add beauty to the room.
- They are mostly both functional as well as decorative.
- By use of accessories, it becomes easier to depict a theme in the room.
- The room looks livelier and not bare.
- They give a personal touch to the room.
- They lend a lived-in look to the room.
- They are a medium to show artistic expression.

Classification of Accessories

Common accessories in a guestroom include the following.

Functional accessories Table calendars, ash trays, pen stands, and lampshades are functional accessories. These articles are mainly functional but can be highly decorative too.

Object d' art Paintings, ornamental mirrors, crystals, candle stands, sculptures in bronze, brass, stone, ceramics, and antique articles are mainly decorative articles.

Decorative accents This is a distinct class of accessories. These are not separate articles but decorative accents that bring charm and beauty to a room. Examples are piping on cushions, tassels on curtains, tessellated tiles on walls and floors, and so on. Refer to the scan code for pictures of more accessories.

Selection and Placement of Accessories

The following should be taken care of in selection and placement of accessories:

1. Accessories should be chosen not only for their beauty, but also to promote the appearance of a room as a unit and to project a theme.
2. Accessories should be selected to scale with the size of the room.
3. Accessories may be chosen according to the season. Richly coloured vases and pieces of pottery, warm-coloured lampshades, and rich oil paintings look good in winter. Fragile vases and vivid watercolours look good in the summer. Another way to obtain a cool look in the summer is to minimize the number of accessories, since a sense of bareness is also a sense of coolness.
4. Accessories should not be overdone. Too many accessories should not be used in a room else it may look crowded and the beauty of individual accessories will be lost.
5. Too little accessories also will not be noticed in a large room, especially if the accessories are small and delicate. In such cases a small group of accessories can be placed together.
6. Accessories should be placed or hung in a variety of areas, both vertical and horizontal, in a room. Walls, tables, tops of fireplace, floors, and ceilings should be utilized.
7. Accessories should not hamper or come in the way of the primary function of the place.
8. Ample plain background should be ensured to emphasize the accessories so that they create focal points to give the eyes a pleasant resting place, holding the attention at the point of interest.
9. Before finally placing the accessory, it should be tested out in different places to achieve maximum beauty.
10. All accessories should not generate the same level of interest. Some should be subdued, some more attractive.

SUMMARY

Interior decoration is a highly personal expression of the sum of the interests of an individual or a group, a practical statement created by combining various elements of aesthetics using certain design principles. Though it is a matter of personal taste, the use of the formal elements of art according to certain principles of design ensure success in decoration.

For a decorator, colour is an important tool. It can be used in various ways, in its various tints and shades, on different surfaces to create beauty. Colour has a definite psychological effect. In using colour, it is important to understand the dimensions of colour—hues, values, and chroma. Equally significant is the feel of the colour when applied to a room, in terms of its warmth or coolness. Colour has a special impact in this way, with warm hues making a room seem to advance and cool hues making it seem to recede. Prang's colour system, based on 12 hues, has been explained in detail in this chapter. Designers commonly use Prang's colour wheel as a basis for developing colour schemes. Further, various colour schemes of related and contrasting hues have been described.

Another important aspect of decoration is lighting. Lighting has both functional and aesthetic significance. It can be classified in various ways. With many hotels becoming eco-sensitive, the trend is to utilize natural lighting in the interiors to the maximum. Various methods of using artificial lights have been discussed. Different types of lighting fixtures used in hotels have been illustrated. How lighting is planned for various areas of a hotel has been described.

The chapter next dealt with floor finishes. Because of the amount of interior area they cover, floor finishes play an important role in interior decoration. The various factors to be considered in the selection of flooring have been discussed. The types of floor finishes available today offer a large range to choose from. Appearance, safety, and ease of maintenance are major factors governing the selection of flooring for hotels. The various types of floor coverings available and their properties have thus been described.

A separate section has been devoted to the soft floor coverings—mainly carpets. There is a wide selection of carpets available nowadays. However, due to the maintenance and care they require, many hotels are doing away with carpets, especially in guestrooms. If a carpet is installed, it is important that it be cleaned and maintained as per a regular schedule. The practice of delaying cleaning until the carpet is visibly dirty is detrimental to the life and appeal of a carpet.

The chapter then discussed ceiling and wall coverings. Various types of ceiling and wall coverings, their maintenance needs, and cleaning techniques have been dealt with.

Windows and window treatments have been described in the concluding section. The function of various types of windows has been outlined. The various stiff and soft window treatments have been discussed in detail as well. The chapter concludes with a discussion on functions, classification, selection and placement of accessories.

KEY TERMS

Acoustics The sound absorption quality of certain materials, usually in ceilings, walls, and floors.

Anaglypta A type of wallpaper produced by bonding together two layers of paper and cotton fibres and then embossing them.

Anglepoise A type of desk lamp that allows the angle of the light to be adjusted without moving the base.

Average pile density This is the weight of pile yarn in a cubic yard of carpet. It is calculated by multiplying the pile weight by 36 and dividing the product by the pile height (in inches).

Black lacquer A lacquer with a durable, glossy, black finish, originally from the Orient.

Bleeding The loss of colour when a fabric or textile product is wet, usually due to improper dyeing, addition of too little mordant, or the poor quality of the dyestuffs used.

Burlap Jute canvas.

Chamois Originally, leather from the hide of the chamois antelope, used mainly in cleaning and polishing. Now these are usually skivers—that is, split sheepskins—or simulated skins. Chamois leather is used wet for cleaning windows and mirrors. It is also used dry as a polishing cloth for silver.

Chroma Also known as intensity, this refers to the brightness or dullness of a colour.

Cornices These are 4–7 inches deep, box-like shapes used at the top, horizontal portion of the drapery treatment on a window to hide the poles and other hardware.

Concrete A mixture of cement and various fillers, such as sand, gravel, crushed stone, and seashells. The elements are mixed together in dry form and then combined with water, reacting chemically to form the hard, stone-like construction material.

Crocking This refers to the colour of a fabric rubbing off as a result of improper dye penetration or fixation.

Dado A stronger, more easily cleaned material used to surface the lower part of a wall, approximately upto 150 cm height from the floor. A dado is essential to prevent damage caused by banging of trolleys, luggage, and rubbing and scratching that may be caused by people in hotels.

Decal (short for decalcomania) The art of transferring decorative designs or pictures printed on specially prepared paper to glass, wood, or other materials.

Fade-o-meter Standard laboratory device for testing a fabric's colour-fastness when exposed to sunlight.

Face weight The amount of fibre (per square yard) that is in the face of a carpet (total weight less the weight of the backing).

Gauge In tufted carpets, the number of warp-pile yarns (ends) across the width is expressed by the gauge. A medium-weight carpet has a gauge of 1/8 and a heavy-duty carpet has a gauge of 5/64. Gauge is based on the number of needles or tufts per widthwise inch, expressed as a fraction.

GLS lamps General lighting service lamps.

Grommets Metal rings inserted in the holes in the upper hem of curtains to reinforce the material so that it may be hung on the rods without danger of tearing.

Grout (also grouting) A term used to describe the areas or binding material between raised or filling elements of flooring or wall treatments (such as tiles).

Gypsum Used to make plaster of Paris, this is chemically hydrated calcium sulphate.

Hessian Strong coarse cloth of hemp or jute.

HPMV lamps High-pressure mercury-vapour lamps.

HPSV lamps High-pressure sodium-vapour lamps.

Hue The specific term used to indicate the name of an exact colour, such as crimson red, Turkish blue, sea green, and so on.

Lincrusta Linseed oil and fillers are bonded to backing paper to make a type of wallpaper called lincrusta. It is supplied in simulating wood effects or making up textured designs.

Lithopone A white pigment made of zinc sulphide and barium sulphate.

Louvres Slats of plastic, wood, or glass inset in windows or shutters, sometimes revolving to control passage of air and light.

Nitrocotton Refers to cellulose nitrate.

Noise reduction coefficient (NRC) A scale that indicates the amount of sound waves a material or surface absorbs.

Mordant A substance added to dye solutions to make the dye fast to the fabric.

Parquet A type of high-quality hardwood flooring in which decorative hardwoods are cut into blocks and formed into panels, permitting elaborate geometric designs such as herringbone, basket weaves, and strip patterns.

Pile height The measurement (usually in fractions of an inch) of the pile of a carpet from the base of the primary backing to the tip of the yarn.

Pitch In woven goods, the number of warp yarns in a 27-inch width. For instance, the standard pitch for a Wilton carpet is 256.

Primary colours The basic colour pigments that cannot be obtained by mixing other hues. Red, yellow, and blue are the fundamental or primary colours.

PVC Polyvinyl chloride.

Quarry tiles Hard-wearing tiles made from a blend of unrefined clays that have been fired under pressure to make them hard and durable.

Resilience The term refers to the ability of a surface to recover its original appearance and thickness after being subjected to compressive forces or crushing under traffic.

Secondary colours (also binary colours) Those that result when two primary colour pigments are mixed in equal quantities. The three secondary colours are purple, orange, and green.

Shade A value that is darker than the normal colour of a pure pigment is called a shade.

Shading The twisting of carpet pile caused by feet or the moving of furniture across it, which shows up as dark patches.

Shoji screens Japanese screens originally made of rice paper mounted on a wooden frame coated with black lacquer, but now available in translucent plastic materials.

Sisal A fibre obtained from the leaves of a plant resembling cactus. The fibre is used for making twine, rope, and sacking. Sisal is also commonly used for making mats. It tends to rot in water, however.

Standard colours The primary and secondary colours are together called the six standard colours. Thus, the six standard colours in pigments are red, yellow, blue, purple, green, and orange.

Stucco Plaster or cement used for coating wall surfaces or moulding into architectural decorations.

Supaglypta This is a strong, deeply moulded cotton-based wallpaper, good for covering badly cracked walls and ceilings. Supaglypta looks like plaster and can be emulsion-painted.

Swags Decorative drapery treatments meant to hide the curtain headings and usually tapering to a cascade (or tail).

Tessellated tiles Small ceramic tiles often used in mosaic patterns to give a highly decorative floor.

Tertiary colours (also intermediate colours) These are formed by mixing a primary colour with its neighbouring secondary colour in equal amounts. There are 6 intermediate pigment hues—yellow-green, red-purple, blue-green, red-orange, blue-purple, and yellow-orange.

Textiles The term was derived from a French word literally meaning 'to weave', but is now used to refer to all types of fibres, yarns, and fabrics.

Tint A value that is lighter than the normal colour of a pigment is called a tint.

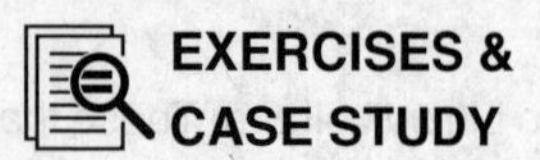

Tracking The smoothing down of a carpet in heavily used areas.

Tuft An individual yarn (either a cut length or one half of a loop) resulting from a single penetration of the primary backing of a carpet by a threaded needle.

Valances This is a decorative heading made of frilled or pleated material that hangs from a valance rail, fixed over the top of a curtain to hide the hardware and to add decoration.

Value This term describes the lightness or darkness of a colour. There are a total of nine values for each pigment, ranging from white to black.

Wainscoting A continuous type of wall panelling that extends from the floor to halfway up the wall.

Facilities Planning and Facilities Management

Learning Objectives

After reading this chapter, you should be able to

- understand the meaning and importance of planning and managing facilities
- list the factors to be considered in planning and designing of hospitality facilities
- describe the stages in developing a hospitality property
- discuss the hotel design process
- explain the planning of guestrooms and en-suite bathrooms
- appreciate the importance of mood boards in planning and designing facilities
- understand the requirements in designing for the physically challenged
- enumerate the role of a facilities manager
- enlist and discuss the components of facilities management

Introduction to Facility Planning

Facility planning is the planning of design, layout, and accommodation of any area including site selection, space requirement, menu, equipment requirement, and other planning functions that guide the project into reality. It refers to the process of arranging the physical facilities such that the optimum operational efficiency is achieved. Planning and designing of facilities are discussed in brief in this chapter since this is a fundamental task of consultants and designers and not the housekeeper. However, the housekeeper will have to maintain the areas after the handover of the projects, hence this overview. Planning and designing of guestrooms and en-suite bathrooms are discussed. Planning food and beverage (F&B) and other areas are not in the scope of this book.

Factors Considered in Planning and Designing of Hospitality Facilities

The factors to be taken into account while planning and designing hospitality facilities are as follows.

Location The location of the site of the hospitality property has an effect on the type of premises, surroundings, and constraints. Accessibility, proximity to city centre, subsoil conditions, and financial aspects need to be kept in mind.

Image and style Both image and style project the way in which the organization communicates messages such as brand identity or quality through its facility. Architectural styles in sync with the concept have to be chosen.

Concept The concept is developed keeping in mind the objectives and market orientation, which the hotel company would like to achieve.

Company policy Planning and designing is done in accordance with the policies of the company regarding product style, brand, and future development strategy.

Functional and operational efficiency This includes optimum space utilization, seating capacity, and operational needs. The designer plans for space, form and colour, lighting and audio-visual systems, integration of technology and finishes, and durability.

Aesthetics These include style, character, and design features, which will appeal to the target clientele. Themes are developed to express mood, historical period, fashion, or ethnic origin. There is also a trend towards cleaner, simpler, less fussy lines, with more emphasis on space, which reflect contemporary lifestyle.

Customer comfort This is the most important consideration in designing hospitality facilities. From location of guestroom and public areas to details of comfort factor in furniture and bedding in guestrooms, all need to be considered.

Financing Budget considerations involve investment criteria, payback, financing, and resources.

Business planning This considers planned life cycle of the business and future changes.

Logistics This involves planning critical dates, stages, resources, and contractors.

Stages in Developing Hospitality Property

The development of lodging properties can be divided into several stages, which are as follows.

Conceptualization This is the stage when the hotel is first envisioned. The conceptualization stage follows a proven demand and includes the resources to develop the hotel and the development process continues until the hotel finally opens.

Assistance of specialists The owner and the developer require the assistance of legal and financial experts and marketing consultants. They also assemble a development team that includes architects, engineers, as well as interior, kitchen, and other design consultants.

Feasibility study This is prepared by a consulting firm for the hotel management company for review. This study provides the following details:

- A description of the local area around the proposed hotel property, potential markets, economic vitality of the city or region, and suitability of the project site and recommends proposed facilities.
- An assessment of the current and future demand for the accommodation, F&B, hotel facilities, and other revenue generators such as types and number of guestrooms, convention rooms, restaurants, lounges and recreational facilities. It also identifies the competitive properties and their growth.
- An estimate of the hotel's operating income, the projection of cash flow, and expenses for at least a period of five years.
- A help to the owners to obtain finances since a feasibility study helps enhance the confidence of financers and franchisers.

Feasibility report After conducting the study, the consultant prepares a feasibility report that covers the following components:

- Local area evaluation
- Lodging market analysis
- Proposed facilities
- Financial analysis

Contract with construction firm A contract is then signed with a construction firm to build the property.

The project brief A project brief, which is an important document that establishes the project's objectives and parameters for all the parties concerned, including owners, managers/operators, and the design team, is then prepared. A project brief must include both fundamental matters and the required attributes. It includes the following.

Objectives of development This defines the goal in establishing the property.

Budget for development This specifies the spending limits and the required rate of return.

Time frames for development These state the commencement and finish date to maximize selling opportunities.

Quality specifications This lays down the standards and durability required from the development.

Hotel design process

The hotel design process involves the various phases as explained here.

The pre-design phase This phase includes the following.

Owner/Developer Sets the project objectives, convenes the development team, commissions the feasibility study, plans the project budget, scouts for site options, secures the site approvals, organizes the schedule, researches for financing, negotiates joint venture, outlines managing board agreements, and makes ready the project brief.

Feasibility consultant Conducts market analysis and formulates financial projections.

Hotel management company Appraises and reaffirms feasibility recommendations, proposes consultants and architectural firm, creates design program, and determines design and operating criteria.

Architect Analyses site and location, prepares initial conceptual design, and assesses budget.

The design phase This phase includes the following.

Owner/Developer Apprises all members of the development team, critically appraises and approves the design teams' proposals, and establishes design schedule.

Architect Prepares schematic designs (architectural, engineering, sites etc.), outline specification, and preliminary budget; completes design development, prepares draft of construction specifications, and updates budget; and completes contract documents including all drawings, specifications, and bid documents. Through all stages the architects coordinate with engineers, other design consultants, as well as the management company.

Hotel management company Reviews architectural and design submittals, prepares designs for such back-of-the-house areas as employee locker and storage areas, prepares cost estimates of operating equipment and supplies, and reviews mock-up guestroom. It also establishes purchasing procedures.

Interior designer They design interiors of all guestrooms, public areas, and administrative office designs and specifications, and lists complete specifications for mock-up room and schedule review.

Food service consultant They prepare all kitchen, bar, and related designs and specifications. Food service consultants also coordinate with other back-of-the-house consultants and management staff.

Planning space Each hotel will have specific space requirements depending on the following factors:

- Type of hotel, its location, and its intended market segment
- Areas of site, features, and planning constraints
- Number of rooms, principal facilities, and nature of use
- Broad concept of architectural design
- Site condition
- Access requirements for guests, special groups, and services
- Parking, basement, and construction implications
- Provision for phased expansion as well as future changes
- Landscape and recreational areas
- Number of rooms of each category, including the requirements of guests with special needs
- Space standards with significant minimum dimension
- Main furniture and fittings

Lobby Space considerations in the lobby include

- Architectural design
- Entrances, elevators, and main circulation within the lobby
- Space allocation for the front desk and other uniformed guest services
- Hotel shop, retail shops, lounges, and other public facilities
- F&B areas such as patisserie and lobby bar
- Seating capacities and nominal space allocation
- Circulation to F&B areas such as restaurants and bar

Function and conference areas Space considerations for these include

- Ballroom and banquet hall seating and space provisions
- Convention and function halls—number, sizes, and specific requirements
- Foyers, lounges reception rooms—numbers, sizes, and specific requirements
- Business centre and special requirements

Recreational areas Space considerations for recreational areas include

- Range of internal and external recreational facilities
- Swimming pool location, size, character, and ancillary requirements
- Gymnasium, sports, and other leisure areas
- Facilities for children
- Spa

Administration Space considerations for administrative areas include

- Areas for heads of department in administration
- Space allocation for accounts department and marketing offices
- Circulation and ancillary areas
- Provisions for human resources and training
- Separate plant for engineering and maintenance

- Engineering offices, plant rooms, and maintenance workshops
- Back of the house and service areas
- Loading dock: receiving areas, general storage, and garbage disposal
- Main and subsidiary kitchen areas and food storage requirements
- Housekeeping, laundry, and valet areas' circulation arrangements
- Employee changing and toilet areas, and dining room

Public areas The extent of public areas is largely dictated by the grade, location, and the market segment the hotel caters to.

Budget hotels Space allocation to public and support areas are kept to less than 20%.

Mid-range hotels Rationalization of space is necessary. Function areas are generally kept to small meeting/party rooms.

Luxury hotels Space requirements depend on location and market emphasis.

Planning of Guestrooms

Most hotels offer a mixture of room types including double rooms with two double or queen-sized beds, single rooms with a queen-sized bed, and rooms with a king-sized bed plus a convertible sofa. Other combinations called suites or parlour room plans can include living rooms, dining rooms, and multiple bathrooms. There are two common models for suites, with many variations in each.

Front-to-back or shotgun arrangement It is a narrow suite in which the living room faces an atrium or outside corridor; the bathroom is in the middle of the bay; and the bedroom is in the rear, with an exterior orientation.

Side-by-side model This suite consists of two small bays, each with windows to the outside.

Guestroom floor configurations include the following:

The double loaded slab The guestrooms are laid out on both sides of a central corridor. In general, it is the most efficient, with about 70% of the gross floor area devoted to guestrooms.

The tower The rooms are grouped around a central vertical core.

The atrium This features guestrooms off a single-loaded corridor encircling a multi-storey lobby space.

Factors in planning guestrooms There are certain important factors that are to be kept in mind while planning guestrooms.

Planning rooms pace Rooms that are too small are congested and therefore more difficult to clean by housekeepers. Space and circulation in the guestroom should be well planned. Rooms are planned to provide zoned areas for various functions, each with sufficient activity space for convenient use and cleaning. For economy, zones should overlap to serve more than one purpose. Minimum functional spaces include the following areas.

Lounge area Provides soft seating group, considers comfort, lighting, coffee and side tables, TV viewing angle, and sofas in suites.

Work area Locates these near windows, provides adequate artificial task lighting, movable furniture and desk or work table, comfortable chair with proportional height to the table, and provides a phone.

Sleep area Provides comfortable beds in a quiet area, away from window, screened from entrance, and provides nightstand and a telephone.

Dressing area Provides full length mirror with proper lighting, upholstered chair/stool, multiple use, and provides a couple of drawers in the dresser to store amenities.

Storage area Provides a cupboard with ample storage area for guest clothes, amenities, personal safe, and a folded ironing board, and provides a luggage rack near the entrance and cupboard.

F&B utility area Provides a minibar and a counter space above it for coffee kettle, tea, coffee and sugar sachet tray, crockery, and cutlery.

Bathroom Provides acoustic design to dampen internal noise, functional and aesthetic sanitary fixtures, diffused lighting at the vanitory counter and shower area, and plans for ample ventilation.

Factors like room dimensions are important considerations in guestroom planning.

Room dimensions The sleeping area extends about 8 ft. in length for a twin bed, 9 ft. 6 in. for a queen bed, and 12 ft. 2 in. for a double bed allowing for side access. The width for single beds should be 10–12 ft. In suites, the width should be minimum 19 ft. 8 in. The comfortable day use area with two easy chairs and coffee table takes up about 5 ft. 6 in. A space with similar dimensions provides a good work area. A separate dressing area may be provided in a luxury hotel. Bathroom dimensions are dictated by the number and spacing of fitments.

Standardization In most hotels, rooms of a particular category are repetitive in layout and size with some variations in furniture arrangement. This standardization in rooms is advantageous in that it saves on construction cost and time and allows prefabrication. It also aids in cost saving in bulk purchase of equipment, furniture, furnishings, and amenities. It also facilitates organization of guestroom cleaning and maintenance. It leads to uniform offering in quality across chain properties.

Planning en-suite bathrooms The following factors are considered in planning bathrooms in guestrooms.

Location Bathroom location should be planned between two guestrooms as it gives constructional advantages. There should be service access from entrance and mechanical ventilation. In case there is an external wall, plan for natural light and ventilation.

Dimensions A standard room should have minimum bathroom space of 5 ft. 6 in. × 2 ft. 6 in.

Fixtures and fittings Depending on the extent of luxury, 5–7 featured bathrooms may be planned.

Vanitory unit Provides dual counters for twin rooms, and colour-coded water taps for hot and cold water. Wash basin is usually recessed in the counter. It provides a good mirror with diffused lighting.

Water closet Provides partially screened siphonic closets, wall mounted, with enclosed flushing cisterns, and provides hygiene hand shower and toilet roll holder.

Bidet Provided in luxury properties, they should have thermostatic mixing units.

Bath tub Standard dimensions are 5 ft. 6 in. × 2 ft. 6 in., they may have whirlpools or Jacuzzis in luxury properties. It provides colour-coded faucets, adjustable shower extension, grab bars, recessed soap holders, and retractable drying line above bath area.

Shower cubicle Provides glass cubicle fitted with adjustable shower extension, provides screening, colour-coded taps, and recessed soap holder.

Other fixtures Include towel rail, overhead rack, clothes hook, dressing robe, shaving mirrors on swivel bracket, emergency telephone, music speaker, fitted hair dryers, recessed soap trays, glass holder, waste bin, weighing scale (in luxury properties), both general and diffused lighting, and floor drainage.

Creating Mood Boards

A part of the planning process of a hotel is the creation of mood boards. A mood board refers to a creative visual representation of ideas and concepts on a planned project in the form of a collage of images and sample swatches of décor materials detailed by the interior designer. The designer creates a mood board by amalgamating ideas of the client, adding his or her creative inputs and translates it into feasible suggestions. Once mood boards are agreed upon and approved sample rooms can be prepared.

Significance of mood boards

Creation and approval of mood boards is a necessary process in planning and designing a hotel project. It serves vital purposes,

- It establishes a clear direction on a project before the actual design work starts.
- It helps explore ideas to figure out the general style and atmosphere of an interior space.
- It assists the designer to be organised by placing visual ideas together in one board.
- It enables the designer to convey options to clients through visual illustrations of designs.
- As a visual tool, it is instrumental in effectively communicating the designers' vision, ideas, and concepts to clients and get approvals.
- It helps eliminate multiple review cycles as the client and the designer are on the same page on an agreed mood board.

Mood board elements

The essential components that make up an effective mood board are as follows.

- Ideas, inspirations of concept defining the style or overall feel of the space or room with images.
- Colour palettes and their combination in the form of paint swatches and coloured images.
- Sample swatches of materials giving concrete idea of textures and pattern of fabrics, floorings, wall coverings, and so on.
- Pictures and illustrations offering options to clients on window treatments, furniture, soft furnishings, and artwork, artefacts, and other accessories.

Designing for the Differently-Abled

All establishments have a responsibility towards accommodating differently-abled guests. Statutory provisions must be made to enable easy access to designated rooms for users who are differently abled—usually 1–2% of the total number of guestrooms—as well as to the public areas. All areas and adjuncts of the property—be they vans and buses, parking areas, the front door, the reservation area, the guestrooms and associated amenities, the restaurants and bars, the exercise and health facilities, the meeting rooms, the restrooms, the telephones, or the shops—should be accessible to and designed universally to suit such guests. Center for Universal Design defines universal design as the design of products and environments to be usable by all people, to the greatest extent possible, without the need for adaptation or specialized design. Specific physical requirements for differently-abled guests are mentioned in Table 28.1.

Table 28.1 Specific physical requirements for differently-abled guests

Feature	Requirement
Ramps	1:20 – 1:15 ramp gradient, minimum clear width of 1500 mm between handrails
Corridors	At least 1500 mm wide with wheelchair turning space of 1800 mm x 1800 mm at regular intervals
Doors	900 mm clear opening
Lobbies	460 mm wider than the door on the latch side
Bathrooms	1520 mm central turning space and 2700 mm width; specially designed fittings and grab bars
Beds and furniture	Space between beds and furniture more than 910 mm, with knee room of 685 mm
Switches	Set at 750 mm – 1100 mm height from the floor
Windowsills and mirrors	Eye level for a person in a wheelchair is assumed to be about 1070 mm – 1370 mm from the floor

Parking

At least one designated accessible parking space, closest to the entrance, is to be provided for differently-abled guests, in every 25 parking spaces. The accessible route should be level or gently sloping with a minimum width of 1200 mm. In case of basement parking, accessible parking bays should be located closest to the lobby elevator. The accessible parking bay should be 4800 mm wide, out of which at least 1200 mm is used as transfer zone on both sides and 6000 mm long, including 1200 mm wide transfer zone at the rear to allow for wheelchair loading. The transfer zones should have yellow or white markings. International symbol of accessibility should be clearly painted on the 2400 mm wide area where the vehicle is to be parked. A signboard with the same symbol should also be displayed at a height of 1200 mm from the floor level at the end of the bay.

Transportation

Van or bus shuttle services should be accessible to people with physical impairments. It should be ensured that vehicles that are accessible to the physically challenged are used for transporting them and there should be no discrimination against such guests. Any policies that unintentionally discriminate against these guests should be altered. For instance, if the transport provider has a policy for not allowing animals on the vehicles, it may be altered for a visually impaired guest who has a guide dog as his or her companion.

Entrances

The surfaces at the entrance should be firm, even and slip-resistant in all weather conditions. Gently sloping ramps and grab rails must be provided. Automatic or semiautomatic doors without thresholds are favourable to universal design. Doors should be clearly distinguishable from the surrounding walls. A landing area of minimum 1800 mm × 1800 mm should be provided immediately after the door.

Lobby

A lobby that is split levelled is not an accessible feature. A levelled lobby is preferable for accessibility. Adequate circulation space for wheelchair bound individuals with their guides must be provided.

The lobby lounge should offer seating both with and without armrests. Lobby centrepieces should be easily detectable by vision impaired guests.

Reception

The location of the reception counter must be clearly demarcated in the lobby and the route from entrance to the counter should be obstacle-free. Many reception counters are too high for business to be conducted appropriately with guests who are short or use wheelchairs. A universal design calls for a reception designed to accommodate both standing and sitting guests. Provide a minimum clear floor area of 1200 mm × 1800 mm in front of the reception desk with a provision of 500 mm deep knee recess for manoeuvring wheelchairs. If knee recess is not provided, then the minimum manoeuvring space provided should be 1400 mm deep and 2200 mm wide. The reception counter surface must be non-reflective and for hearing impaired guests, hearing enhancement system should be provided and the availability of the same shall be indicated with a symbol at the reception.

Reservations

The management of a hotel needs to provide solutions for differently abled guests to enable them to make reservations for themselves. For instance, for a guest who has a hearing impairment or a speech impairment, places of lodging should provide effective means of communication. The reservations desk should have a tele-typewriter (TTY) installed. The person taking reservations should be trained in the use of a TTY.

A TTY is also known as a 'telecommunications device for the deaf' or TDD. This device 'rings' by way of a flashing light or in more recent models, a vibrating wristband that resembles a watch. The TTY also has a keyboard that holds from 20 to 30 character keys, a display screen, and a modem. The letters that the TTY user types into the machine are turned into electrical signals that can travel over regular telephone lines. When the signals reach their destination (in this case, another TTY), they are converted back into letters that appear on a display screen, are printed out on paper, or both. Some of the newer TTYs are even equipped with answering machines.

Another method of communicating reservations nowadays is via the Internet through computers for the physically impaired, now that many hotels have an online reservation option on their websites.

Elevators

Elevators should have a minimum width and depth of 1200 mm and 1400 mm respectively with a clear door opening of not less than 900 mm. There must be provision of horizontally place grab bars at a height of 900 mm from the elevator floor level. On the external side, illuminated call buttons, contrasting in colour from surrounding wall surface, should be installed at a height between 800 mm – 1100 mm from the furnished floor surface. In the elevator cabin, the control panel should be placed at a height of 800 mm to 1200 mm from the elevator floor level. Letterings on external call buttons and internal control panel should be raised and available in Braille too. elevators should have a voice announcement system too along with the visual display for floor indication. A mirror on the rear wall is advisable so a wheelchair-bound person may see behind.

Public Restrooms

Accessible toilets must be provided in public restrooms near lobby and banquet areas. These toilets should be minimum 1800 mm × 2550 mm where a floor mounted WC is used. All fixtures and utilities should provide a clearance area of 750 mm × 1200 mm for wheelchair access. The toilet door should be sliding type and a 600 mm long horizontal pull bar should be provided on the inside of the door. The locking device should be operable single handily. Horizontal grab bars mounted at a height of 200 mm on the side wall near the WC seat must have a circular diameter of 30–45 mm and be free of hazardous elements. A 750 mm long horizontal grab bar must be provided on the rear wall of the WC. Top of the WC seat should be 450 mm to 480 mm from the floor level. A clearance of 750 mm from the front edge of the WC to the rear wall should be provided to facilitate side transfer. Flush control should be located not more than 1100 mm from the floor level. Vanitory units should have a clearance space of minimum 750 mm × 1200 mm, of which a maximum of 480 mm in depth may be under the unit. The unit should be mounted such that the top edge is between 800 mm and 840 mm from the floor, with a knee space at least 740 mm wide, 200 mm deep and 750 mm high. Lever type of automatic faucets are preferable. Two vertical grab bars of 600 mm length on either side of the unit should be installed. All accessories such as soap dispensers and hand dryers should be at a height of 800 mm and 1100 mm from the floor surface. An emergency alarm should be provided.

Guest Corridors

Minimum width of the corridor for universal accessibility should be 1500 mm. A distinct colour contract between the colour of walls and flooring should be provided to aid visually impaired guests. Corridors must be maintained obstruction-free and should be at one level. There should not be any protruding devices upto a height of 2 metres from the flooring. Minimum lighting of 100 lux must be available. Anti-slip and anti-glare flooring is to be provided.

Guestrooms

All hotel properties need to have some guestrooms accessible to the differently abled guests and adapted to their needs; one universal room for every twenty rooms is advisable. A physically accessible room should have the following features:

- Provision of accessible route from the lobby
- Room number in Braille embossed on the wall beside the door
- Doorway push-and-pull clearance, with a minimum 900 mm clear opening in the door width
- Accessible door hardware and security features
- The card entry system and peephole mounted between 900 mm and 1000 mm height
- Controls and light switches mounted between 750 mm to 1100 mm height from the floor
- An unobstructed route of 900 mm width to all furniture, with a turning radius of 1800 mm × 1800 mm somewhere in the room
- Distinct colour contrast between flooring and wall surfaces and furniture
- Bed height of 500 mm, including the mattress, from the floor
- In case of twin beds, a minimum space in between, of 900 mm
- Emergency assistance alarm operable from the bed and the adjacent floor area
- Clear space of 1100 mm in front of an open wardrobe
- Adjustable rails provided at a height of 1000 mm and 1400 mm from the floor level, in wardrobe

- Study table of minimum 900 mm width, 700 mm deep, and 760 mm height. Clear knee recess 700 mm high, under the table
- Minibar counter not higher than 850 mm
- En-suite bathroom of at least 2700 mm × 2500 mm dimensions, with minimum 900 mm wide clear opening to the bathroom door
- Accessible sinks and faucets
- Grab bars for the WC
- Toilet seat at 432 mm to 480 mm height above the floor
- Adequate manoeuvring space in front of the toilet, tub, and shower for a wheelchair
- Bath tub of dimensions 700 mm width, 1600–1700 mm length and 480 mm height
- Grab bars and transfer seat for the tub at a height of 555 mm to 580 mm from the finished floor surface
- Towel rails installed at a height of 900 mm and 1100 mm from floor level, reachable from the tap side of the bath tub

A room adapted to guests with hearing impairment may include the following facilities:

- A text telephone
- Audio-visual emergency-warning devices
- Notification devices for door knocking and telephone ringing
- Vibrating pillows for alarm or wake-up call

Exercise and Health Facilities

These should be located on an accessible path of travel and be equally accessible to guests with physical impairments. There should be at least one means of access to the pool for such guests, whether in the form of a ramp, transfer tier, or lift.

Facilities Management

Facilities management is the integration of processes within an organization to maintain and develop the agreed services that support and improve the effectiveness of its primary activity. It is an interdisciplinary field that involves guiding and managing the operations and maintenance of commercial, residential, or institutional buildings, such as hotels, malls, airports, railways, hospitals, schools, gated housing communities, office complexes, and so on, on behalf of the property owners. The services provided by the facilities management companies are usually the non-core, support services.

Role of Facilities Manager

The facilities manager organizes, controls, and coordinates the strategic and operational management of buildings and facilities in order to ensure the proper and efficient operation of all physical aspects, in accordance with legislation in the field, creating and sustaining safe and productive environment for guests, employees, or residents. He facilitates services and support to create safe and comfortable accommodation and work areas. The managers deal with various contractors and suppliers to carry out property maintenance tasks and services such as security, area cleaning, and so on. The facilities manager should be adept in manpower planning, time management, crisis management, and have knowledge of technical operations. The manager should have good organizational and people management skills so as to get the staff to do efficient work. The main areas of legislation in this sector are health and safety, employment, or contract casual workers, and property law.

Common Services Provided by Facilities Management Companies

Services provided by facilities management companies may include maintenance of heating, ventilation, and air conditioning (HVAC), plumbing systems, lighting systems, public area cleaning, decoration, grounds keeping, security, and so on. It is the role of facility management companies to coordinate and oversee the safe, secure, and environmentally sound operations and maintenance of these assets in a cost-effective manner and aimed at long-term preservation of the asset value, and also other janitorial duties such as making sure the environment is properly cleaned and sanitized for its guests. In those cases where the operation of the facility directly involves the occupants and/or customers of the owner organization, the satisfactory delivery of facility-related services to these people will be an important consideration too, hence the term 'end-user satisfaction' is often used both as a goal and a measure of performance.

Components of Facilities Management

The components of facilities management (Figure 28.1) are as follows.

Asset management Assets mainly include the physical infrastructure such as the elevator and its components, furniture, safety, and security equipment, and so on. Management of assets is essential for efficient operations and optimum building performance.

Building management control systems Building management systems help to integrate functions, performance, and output.

Building code and regulatory compliance Facility managers must keep abreast of legislations and building codes and ensure compliance to them.

Fig. 28.1 Components of facilities management

Building repairs and maintenance Planned and unplanned (breakdowns) maintenance activities optimize the performance of a building and ensure its financial and environmental sustainability.

Cleaning and general maintenance Cleaning and property maintenance are the responsibilities of a facility manager and these are carried out with the help of a contract or in-house staff.

Contract and contractor management Contracts and outsourcing are fundamental components of facilities management and elementary to this is the identification and selection of a good network of contractors and suppliers.

Energy and water management Improving energy efficiency and management is the key action, which can be undertaken to reduce energy costs and make the building sustainable. Water consumption and utilization are key indicators of the facility's performance and provide significant operational savings. Energy and water management should be considered together and integrated solutions should be developed.

Enhancing comfort for facility users This aspect includes the components that contribute to the comfort and health of occupants of a building such as indoor air quality (IAQ), thermal comfort, optimum lighting, acoustics, check on pollutants, and so on.

Essential health and safety services provision and compliance The essential services include the fire and life safety protection items installed or constructed in a building.

IT management This includes a gamut of technology enablement and integration in all spheres of the facility.

Human resource management The function of managing the workforce involved in servicing the facility and related administration staff is under the purview of the facility management.

Project management All construction and renovation projects are to be managed as a component of facility management.

Procurement and supplies management Responsible procurement of materials and supplies required to run the facility smoothly is an important function.

Landscaping and grounds maintenance This function may include care of potted plants, gardens, roof top gardens, composting, and so on.

Improving building performance This involves a whole-facility approach to improve comfort and energy efficiency and fix problems to enhance performance of the building.

Maintaining safety and security for occupants and assets Owners and facility managers have a legal and moral obligation to provide a safe and secure physical environment for occupants and guests.

Documentation and monitoring Records of all works pertaining to maintenance and regulations should be kept.

Risk management Risk assessment is to be conducted on each asset. Threats may include fire, flood, vandalism, and so on. Credible threats to the performance of each asset should be documented. Evacuation procedures should be in place.

Sustainability projects and implementation A sustainable building not only uses resources efficiently, but creates healthier environments for people to live and work in.

Waste management Waste minimization, effective waste segregation, and management of waste represent efficient use of resources and energy.

SUMMARY

A lot of thought and deliberation goes into planning and designing hotel facilities. The success of the hospitality enterprise depends on the meticulous planning tasks undertaken by the management of the hotel business. This chapter discusses two aspects of facilities, namely planning and management. A housekeeper will find this information of much help since the onus of maintaining the property is on the housekeeping department. Moreover, many a time, it is the hotel housekeepers who opt for working as facilities managers for corporate giants and other large facilities. This chapter defines both facilities planning and facilities management. It goes on to explain the factors considered in the planning and designing of facilities including the feasibility study and the project brief. The stages in developing a hospitality property are considered next. The hotel design stages namely, pre-design and the design phase, are explained. Considerations for planning of space for various areas and functions in a hotel are enlisted. Planning of guestrooms including the common suite models, floor configurations and factors considered for the same and planning of en-suite bathrooms are also discussed.

Designing for the differently-abled has attracted a lot of attention in some countries and there are rules laid out for designing for disabled guests. In India too, many hotels provide accessible rooms and surrounds for disabled guests. The chapter discusses the requirements of designing in various areas of hotels, for people with different abilities.

The second part of the chapter discusses facilities management. The role of facilities manager is to take care of all the operations within a building system for a smooth and effective functioning. The components of facilities management system are elaborated upon.

KEY TERMS

Atrium A configuration of guestrooms where the guestrooms overlook a spectacular lobby with a high spread ceiling.

Double loaded slab A configuration of guestrooms in which the guestrooms are laid out on both sides of a central corridor.

Facilities management An interdisciplinary field that involves guiding and managing the operations and maintenance of commercial, residential or, institutional buildings, such as hotels, malls, airports, railways, hospitals, schools, gated housing communities, office complexes, and so on, on behalf of the property owners.

Facilities planning The planning of design, layout, and accommodation of any area including site selection, space requirement, menu, equipment requirement, and other planning functions that guide the project into reality.

Feasibility study It assesses present and future demand for lodging and hotel facilities such as meeting rooms, restaurants, lounges, and recreational facilities. It provides a description of the local area and potential markets and recommends proposed facilities and estimates the proposed hotel's operating income and expenses for several years after it opens.

HVAC Heating, ventilation, and air conditioning.

Mood board Refers to a creative visual representation of ideas and concepts on a planned project in the form of a collage of images and sample swatches of décor materials detailed by the interior designer.

Project brief An important document that establishes the project's objectives and parameters for all the parties concerned, including owners, managers/ operators, and the design team.

Shotgun arrangement Also called the front-to-back arrangement, this guestroom model features a narrow suite in which the living room faces an atrium or outside corridor, the bathroom is in the middle of the bay, and the bedroom is in the rear, with an exterior orientation.

Side by side model A common guestroom suite model that consists of two small bays, each with windows to the outside.

Tower configuration A configuration of guestrooms where the rooms are grouped around a central vertical core.

TDD Telecommunications device for the deaf. See also TTY.

TTY Teletypewriter—a telecommunications device for the deaf. It is also known as a TDD.

Universal design refers to the design of products and environments to be usable by all people, to the greatest extent possible, without the need for adaptation or specialized design.

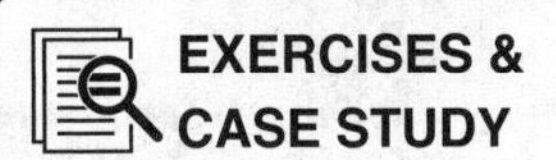

29

Hotel Renovation

Learning Objectives

After reading this chapter, you should be able to

- explain the technical terms and jargon used in renovation activities
- describe the procedures and tasks involved in renovation
- develop a snag list prior to hotel renovations
- distinguish, at length, between refurbishing and redecoration

Introduction

The process of renewing and updating a hospitality property to offset the ravages of use and to modify spaces to meet the needs of changing markets constitutes renovation.

Renovation freshens up the look and feel of the interior spaces; provides a means to update and modernize the systems that provide a safe, comfortable, and convenient interior environment; and allows managers to change the types of services and facilities offered to the public.

Technological, functional, and stylistic obsolescence force most managers to introduce changes within five years of opening a new facility, with extensive changes taking place typically over a 12–15-year cycle.

Reasons to Renovate

The most common reasons why hotels renovate their properties are as follows:

- The furnishings and finishes within the facility are worn out.
- The interior design is out of date and this is directly linked to declining revenues.
- The market for the mix of facilities offered by the hotel has changed and new opportunities can be made available only by renovating under-utilized facilities to meet changing guest demands, the latest trends, and competition from other hotels.
- The current or previous owner has not spent the funds necessary to keep the hotel in a fully updated condition, and the physical property has deteriorated. As a direct result, business volume has declined to a point where revenues do not support the hotel's level of debt.
- Acquiring and renovating an existing hotel presents an opportunity that is superior to constructing a new hotel in terms of location, time, and costs.

Types of Renovation

Renovation projects fall into one of the three categories: minor renovations, major renovations, and restoration.

Minor renovation (5–7-year cycle) The scope of a minor renovation is to replace or renew the non-durable furnishings and finishes within a space, without changing the space's use or physical layout. For instance, a minor renovation of a guestroom might include replacing carpets and wall coverings, drapery, bedspreads, minor paintwork, and touching up of the furniture finishes.

Major renovation (12–15-year cycle) The scope of a major renovation is to replace or renew all furnishings and finishes within a space and may include extensive modifications to the physical layout and utilization of the space itself. A major renovation of a guestroom might include everything described as a minor renovation, plus the replacement of furniture, bedding, lighting, and accessories. In many cases, the bathroom is upgraded too, which might include replacing vinyl flooring with ceramic tiles or replacing the vanity and lavatory units.

Restoration (25–50-year cycle) The scope of a restoration typically allows for a complete gutting of a space and replacing of all systems that are technically and functionally obsolete, while restoring furnishings and systems that can still be used, given the current needs of the facility. It may, for instance, include wholesale replacement of kitchen and laundry facilities, interior demolition of entire guestroom floors to reconfigure the mix of rooms and/or the placement of bathrooms, the replacement of all mechanical, electrical, and plumbing systems, and so on.

Subsidiary Processes in Renovation

The renovation project typically comprises four sub-processes.

Refurbishing This is just the freshening up of a property. This includes cosmetic changes such as changing the draperies, upholstery, and so on.

Redecoration This involves the renewal of paintwork, touching up of furniture and finishes, renewal of soft furnishings, and spring-cleaning. This is also done annually in order to maintain the standard of rooms.

Restoration This is the restoring of a property to its exact original design with authentic materials.

Remodelling This is the altering of the physical structure of the property.

We shall now look at the refurbishing and redecoration processes in detail.

Refurbishing

This process entails renovating a property so as to give it a fresh look and includes replacing furniture, fittings, and soft furnishings that have become worn out or obsolete. This is usually carried out in every hotel once in 5–7 years, depending upon the budget of the hotel and also on the amount of wear and tear the interiors face. The following are the steps in a typical refurbishment programme.

Evaluation (physical inspection) The physical inspection is necessary to ascertain whether such a project is really necessary. It is done by an authorized person in housekeeping, such as the executive or assistant housekeeper, and involves checking every room and area in the hotel for necessary renovations. A worksheet is prepared on the basis of the physical inspection sheet, which gives details of the areas and estimated costs of renovation. A sample format of a renovation worksheet is given in Exhibit 29.1.

Exhibit 29.1 Sample renovation worksheet

	Areas and renovation requirements	Specifications	Costs per module
	Renovation module		
	Rooms		
A	**Guest rooms** *Major renovation*—Wall vinyl, flooring, all case goods, bath tiles, and lighting replacement. *Minor renovation*—Soft-goods replacement (carpet, spreads, drapes, minor accessories, upholstered goods); lampshades and artwork.		
	Food and beverages		
A	**Coffee shop** *Major renovation*—Total renovation of space, carpet vinyl, furniture, counters, lighting, electrical & mechanical fittings, minor construction, ceiling work, uniforms, menus & graphics concept change. *Minor renovation*—Replacement of carpet, chairs and tables; re-upholstering of banquet facilities; decorative lighting.		
	Public areas		
A	**Lounge** Create a new two module lounge from existing guestrooms. Renovate existing two module lounge areas.		
B	**Ballroom** *Major renovation*—Total renovation of space, including carpet, vinyl flooring, lighting, ceiling, doors/hardware, graphics, electrical/mechanical work; repair/re-levelling/re-covering of movable walls/partitions.		

Allocation of time The expected completion date must also be taken into account when estimating the work and costs involved. A refurbishment programme should preferably be conducted during periods of low occupancy or at whatever is the most convenient time for the hotel.

Budgeting At this stage, how much money is going to be made available for the project is decided. An action plan for expenditure to be incurred in future is drawn up, which acts as a guideline in controlling the expenditure pattern.

Thematic choice This involves taking a decision as to whether the original theme of the area should be changed or retained. If a change of theme is decided upon, then the suitability of the newly chosen theme should be researched and a feasibility study carried out to find out whether it is financially viable.

Design feasibility studies The project should be ergonomically sound and should meet all the practicalities of hygiene, cleanliness, and comfort. Once the finances have been worked out, work studies should be carried out to ascertain if these parameters can be optimally met.

Décor preliminaries Suitable fabrics, finishes, and colours should be selected. As far as possible, they should be in durable, easy-to-clean, fire-resistant materials, and should contribute to the ambience of the property.

Staffing budget The refurbishing project can be carried out either by hotel employees or by contractors. A cost comparison has to be made to ascertain which is more viable and also the necessity, if any, of recruiting new staff. Considerations of preparing new uniforms, training programmes, and so on also need to be taken into account.

Equipment inventory These may need to be purchased or hired if not available on the premises.

Raw materials inventory and warehousing Sufficient supplies should be ordered and systems put in place to ensure reordering at the best possible purchase prices. Storage space should be set aside for the supplies as well.

Adjusting for inconvenience to guests, staff, and suppliers Alternate arrangements should be made to minimize the inevitable inconveniences caused to guests, staff, and suppliers while the project is in progress. Temporary operational adjustments should be made, if necessary, and guests should be informed that a renovation is in progress.

Procedural guidelines All the company and statutory procedures to be adhered to must be enumerated and the project evaluated in light of these. They may include

- planning permissions;
- fire regulations;
- health and safety aspects;
- licensing laws; and
- company policies.

Controls All aspects where control must be exercised should be tabulated. These include

- financial control;
- purchasing control;
- contracts;
- insurance;
- inspection; and
- records.

These are the most important aspects of control. Complete documentation in the form of a room history card should be made available, so that all the details of the project carried out are made available for future planning.

Takeover from contractors This stage entails handover of the completed renovation project by the contractor to the housekeeping department. A detailed snag list is prepared by the housekeeping supervisor. A detailed list is prepared on the basis of a physical inspection referred to as snagging, in which all possible pending construction and maintenance requirements in a room or area are mentioned. It is normally prepared by the housekeeper during takeover of a renovated area or a new property. A sample snag list format is given in Exhibit 29.2. Once the contractors rectify the snags pointed out in the original snag list, the housekeepers again inspect the area for the correction of the snags, any further

Exhibit 29.2 A sample snag list format

HOTEL XYZ
SNAG LIST

Date: ____________ **Time:** ____________ **Prepared by:** ____________

SL NO.	AREA/ ROOM NO.	ELECTRICAL	MASONRY	PLUMBING	CARPENTRY	HOUSEKEEPING	MISCELLANEOUS
1.	302	TV power socket not working	Paint above the wall skirting near window chipped	Leak in the hygiene shower	Laminate chipped in inner part of the wardrobe	Smudge on wall below the window	
2.	305	Recess light in far right corner not working	Small cracks have developed on the wall near bathroom after repainting	Water is not getting drained rapidly in bath tub	The coffee table is wobbling	Cement marks in bathroom to be removed	

Signature of Executive Housekeeper: ....

damages while carrying out remedial work or any other pending defects, second time around, and this process is called *desnagging*.

Redecoration

This can involve the renewal of paintwork, touching up of furniture and accessories, renewal of soft furnishings, and spring-cleaning. It is also done annually in order to maintain the standards of the rooms in a property. In many hotels, where the budget does not allow for annual refurbishment programmes, redecoration is carried out instead. The executive housekeeper should ensure that a high standard of work is maintained and should decide whether the tasks are to be contracted to an interior decorator or carried out by the housekeeping department itself. The contract, if that is the mode of operation chosen, should specify the commencement and completion days and the quanta of work to be carried out.

Procedures undertaken prior to redecoration

Before the rooms are handed over to the contractors, the following procedures need to be carried out:

- Inform the front office and the engineering and maintenance departments of the programme.
- Remove curtains, lampshades, bed covers, linen, and guest supplies from the area and store them in the floor pantry.
- Get telephones disconnected.
- Disconnect and store television sets separately.
- Upholstered furniture should be sent to the upholstery yard for shampooing or repair.
- Roll up and remove all carpets and send for shampooing.
- Seal bathtubs, wash basins, and other ceramic fixtures.
- Cover remaining items of furniture and fixtures with dust sheets.

Post redecoration procedures

Once the redecoration is complete and the rooms are handed over, thorough cleaning has to be done before they are made ready for sale. All preventive maintenance should be carried out during this period.

SUMMARY

An executive housekeeper may, in the course of his or her career, be involved in the hotel renovation process. All housekeepers should know and understand renovation terms such as refurbishing, redecoration, restoration, re-modelling, and minor and major renovations. The responsibility and involvement of the housekeeper in the renovation process may vary across different properties. In some properties, the management may not believe in involving housekeepers in the selection of furnishings, floorings, or other aspects of renovation at all; some may simply contract out this function to a consultant; others will want every aspect undertaken and supervised by in-house personnel. The management must realize that a qualified, experienced, and professional housekeeper is an asset and has the potential to handle minor renovations, refurbishing, and redecoration on his or her own.

This chapter has explained the various types of renovation projects and the tasks and procedures involved in each. The snag list has been described, with a sample format by way of example. The snag list serves as an important document tool while carrying out renovation. Desnagging has also been discussed.

Renovation calls for a good deal of market research and creativity on the part of the management as well as the executive housekeeper. It is important to recognize the target clientele and arrive at an ideal mix of facilities for them, such that they are either at par with or much better than those offered by the competitors.

KEY TERMS

Desnagging Refers to physically inspecting the rectification of all the defects from the original snag list by the contractors to desired standards and checking that nothing has been further damaged while carrying out the remedial work.

Ergonomics The study of people's efficiency in relation to their working environment.

Major renovation This is the extent of renovation that entails replacing or renewing all furnishings and finishes within an area and may include extensive modifications to the use and physical layout of the space itself.

Minor renovation This is the extent of renovation that entails replacing or renewing the non-durable furnishings and finishes within an area without changing the space's use or physical layout.

Redecoration This involves renewing paintwork, touch-ups, replacing soft furnishings, and spring-cleaning. It is often undertaken annually, in order to maintain rooms to a certain standard.

Refurnishing This is the extent of renovation that entails giving a property a fresh look and includes replacing furniture, fittings, and soft furnishings that have become worn out or obsolete.

Re-modelling This renovation process involves altering the structure of the existing property in part or as a whole.

Renovation This is the process of renewing and updating a hospitality property to offset the ravages of use and modify spaces to meet the needs of changing markets.

Restoration This is the process of restoring a property to its exact original design using authentic materials.

Snag list A detailed list prepared on the basis of a physical inspection, in which all possible pending construction and maintenance requirements in a room or area are mentioned. It is normally prepared by the housekeeper during takeover of the renovated area from the contractor handling renovation or of a new property from the projects team.

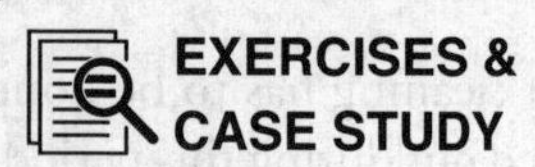

Flower Arrangements and Themed Decorations

Learning Objectives

After reading this chapter, you should be able to
- appreciate the importance of flower arrangements in enhancing the beauty of a hotel's interiors
- enumerate the basic ingredients required for making up an aesthetic floral arrangement
- choose the best cut flowers and undertake their care and conditioning, before arranging them
- apply the eight features of good design in designing flower arrangements
- categorize arrangements by the different aesthetic styles
- discuss the principles of the popular Japanese style of flower arrangement called *ikebana*
- list the common flowers and foliage species used for floral arrangements
- get an insight into themed decorations for festive and special occasions

Introduction

Flower arrangement is a very old art. In India, flowers were earlier arranged in temples and during festivities. The first rules of *ikebana* were laid down in Japan more than a thousand years ago. Yet, before the 1930s, flower arrangement was considered neither a serious craft with set rules nor a recognized art form in much of the West. Flowers were widely used for interior decoration, but they were cut from the garden and simply massed into water-filled containers to brighten the home. The beauty of the display relied upon the blooms themselves rather than the aesthetic appeal of the design. Only later was this practice modified so that floral arrangements became a more stylized affair.

After the 1930s, rules and guidelines were formulated for amateur florists, following which the first flower-arranging experts made their appearance on the scene professionally. Now this art is used in hotels, offices, and hospitals on an everyday basis. Even at homes and venues of festivities on auspicious occasions, flowers are used in a big way in the form of garlands, wall hangings, and floor decorations. Flower arrangements grace tabletops, window sills, corners, fireplaces, banisters, and so on to suit the occasion.

Today, flower arrangement may be defined as the art of organizing and grouping together plant materials (flowers, foliage, fruits, twigs, and so on) to achieve harmony of form, colour, and texture, thereby adding cheer, life, and beauty to the surroundings.

Flower Arrangement in Hotels

In hotels, flowers are used extensively. There may be a large arrangement of flowers in the foyer and in lounges and restaurants, as well as smaller arrangements in the suites. Some hotels provide a bud vase in every room. VIP rooms may even have more than one arrangement.

Figure 30.1 shows a contemporary arrangement suitable for lobbies. Guests appreciate the time and trouble spent on the arrangements and the pleasing atmosphere they create.

Fig. 30.1 Contemporary arrangement for lobbies

Various types of arrangements are chosen, as appropriate to the area and occasion. Medium-sized 'round' arrangements are often provided at the guest relations executives' desk in the lobby and on coffee tables in the lounges. In most five-star hotels, one can see huge, spectacular arrangements in the lobbies. Restaurants generally have bud vases on each table, with one or two flowers in them. Table arrangements for conferences must be low so that guests may see over them. At informal banquets, large arrangements may be seen. At wedding banquets, wall arrangements using gerberas and carnations are very popular nowadays. On special occasions and festivals, a large amount of flowers is required for making up various types of arrangements—some hotels even make beautiful traditional flower carpets for the lobby. The extent to which flowers are used in hotel interiors depends on the degree of luxury provided, the number of special functions held there and, of course, the hotel policy.

The housekeeper is responsible for all flower arrangements and their placement in most hotels. He or she may arrange them personally or delegate the task to an assistant. Another possibility is employing a part-time or full-time florist. Simple arrangements such as a bud in a vase can be done by room attendants themselves. Alternatively, flower arrangements may be provided on contract, in which case the arrangements are brought in and taken away at agreed times and little or no floral work is carried out on the premises.

Unless the decorations are provided by a contractor, the housekeeping department needs to have a flower room equipped with all the necessities for making up arrangements, including a sink with running water, containers, buckets, vases, scissors, and so on.

Flower Arrangement Basics

Making up a good flower arrangement requires a lot of creativity on the part of the arranger, and beginners can develop this art through study and experimentation with different plant materials. Studying pictures of interesting arrangements in books and magazines for ideas is one way of learning this art, but actual practice is essential for developing skill in flower arrangement. Scan the code for viewing a video showcasing creation of two flower arrangements, a basic all round and another a contemporary one.

Basic Ingredients

The materials used for making flower arrangements are not necessarily expensive or elaborate (compared to other crafts); but as with all other crafts, they are a necessity. The following groups of ingredients and aids are essential to flower arrangement:

- Mechanics
- Equipment
- Containers
- Bases
- Accessories
- Plant material
- Support

Mechanics

These are items used to keep the flowers, foliage, and stems in place within the container. Mechanics must be fixed securely and should be hidden from view. The most popular and basic mechanics are florists' foam, pin holders, and chicken wire. Many of the mechanics listed below are not necessary for a beginner. The various mechanics used in flower arrangement are shown in Figure 30.2.

Floral foam This is also called 'oasis'. It is a cellular plastic material. However, few plants, such as tulips, find water intake difficult when set in foam. There are two types available—green foam and brown/grey foam.

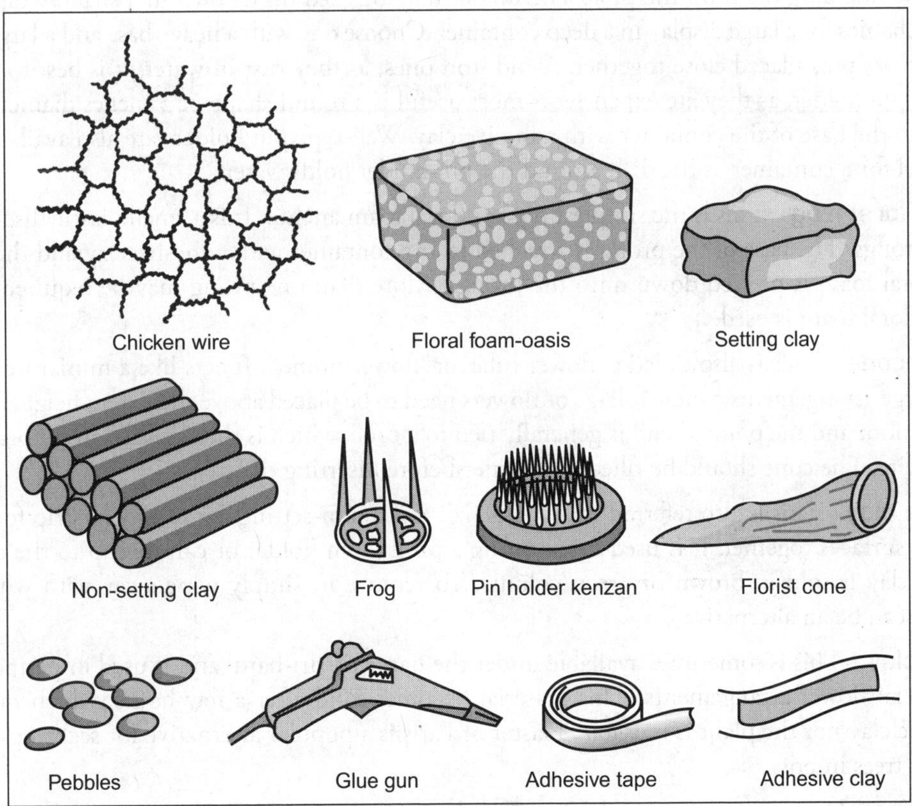

Fig. 30.2 Mechanics used in flower arrangement

Green foam This needs to be soaked in water for at least half an hour and then fresh plant material may be inserted into it. The popular shapes for green foam are 'rounds' and 'blocks'. This type of foam is extremely light when dry, but its weight increases by over 30 times when saturated with water. The green foam should be stored wrapped in plastic or foil after use to prevent degradation from atmospheric moisture.

Brown/grey foam This is used only for dry plant material or artificial display materials. The advantage of this type of foam is that stems can be held at any angle in both shallow and deep containers. The problem of smelly water is also eliminated for longer-lasting arrangements. In case of large arrangements, however, extra support with chicken wire is required.

Chicken wire This is also called 'wire mesh' or 'wire netting'. A fine-gauge wire should be selected. To begin with, a 2-inch mesh may be bought. To use, you cut off the thicker, firm edge and roll the wire into a tube or crumple into a ball to fit the container. This is the preferred type of mechanics for tall or heavy stems. The 1-inch mesh grade is used to cover floral foam blocks in large displays. Florists' wires may be of two kinds: galvanized wire and plastic-coated wire. However, all types of chicken wire should be dried before storing for later use.

Pin-holders These are also called *kenzan* or needle-point holders. A series of sharply pointed pins are firmly held in a solid lead base, which may be circular or rectangular. It holds thick and heavy stems securely by impaling them on the pins. The holder may be used on its own in a shallow dish or with other mechanics for a large display in a deep container. Choose one with a heavy base and a large number of sharp brass pins placed close together. Avoid iron ones, as they rust in water. It is best to start with one basic pin holder, as they are expensive—most useful is a round shape of 3 inches diameter. It may be stuck to the base of the container with adhesive clay. Well-type pin holders are also available, which do not call for a container as the dish around the pin holder holds water.

Prong/Floral frog This is the simplest type of floral foam anchor. It is a small plastic disc with four vertical prongs. The base of the prong is attached to the container with adhesive clay and the block or round floral foam is pressed down onto the prongs. More than one prong may be required if a large block of floral foam is used.

Florist's cone This is also called a 'flower tube' or 'flower funnel'. It acts like a miniature vase. It is used in large arrangements, where foliage or flowers need to be placed above their stem height. Its length is about 1 foot and the pointed end is generally tied to a cane, which is then pushed into floral foam or chicken wire. The cone should be filled with water before inserting the stem.

Adhesive clay This is also referred to as 'oasis fix'. It is a non-setting sticky clay in strip form which holds dry surfaces together. It is used for securing a prong, pin holder or candle cup to the container. Adhesive clay is sold in brown or green colours. To remove it, simply wipe away with white spirit. Plasticine can be an alternative.

Setting clay This is sometimes available under the name of 'dri-hard' and is used in permanent dry and artificial flower arrangements. This material becomes solid after a few hours, which means that neither the clay nor the plant is reusable. Plaster of Paris is a popular alternative for securing the stems of topiary trees in pots.

Non-setting clay This is also available under the name 'stay-soft'. It is used for dry and artificial flower arrangements, where the plant material is to be removed and reused at a later date or where non-permanent accessories such as candles are to be inserted. Plasticine can be used as an alternative.

Adhesive tape This is also called 'oasis tape'. This strong sticky tape may be wide or narrow and is used mainly to secure floral foam or chicken wire to the container. Narrow tape is occasionally stretched across the top of a shallow wide-mouthed container in criss-cross fashion to form a grid to hold plants.

Glue Quick-drying glue is used in dried flower arrangements to attach flowers or leaves to the container or to other plant materials. The most convenient way to apply the glue is using a glue gun.

Pebbles and marbles Small pebbles have long been used to hold the stems of cut flowers. Round marbles or flattened glass nuggets in a glass vase can also add to the attractiveness of the display.

Equipment

This includes tools or other aids used to ensure that a satisfactory arrangement of plant material is created within the container. Only a few pieces of equipment out of all those listed below are essential for a beginner—bucket, scissors, knife, and watering can (Figure 30.3).

Bucket A water-filled bucket is a vital piece of equipment for collecting flowers from the garden and for conditioning the blooms before making an arrangement. Choose the type with side handles, as the standard free-swinging single handle can damage flowers during transport.

Florist's scissors Ordinary scissors are not suitable for cutting plant stems—they tend to crush the tissues. Choose a pair of florist's scissors instead. In these, the blades are short and one is serrated. At the base, there may be a notch to be used for cutting thin wires (but not woody stems or heavy gauge wire).

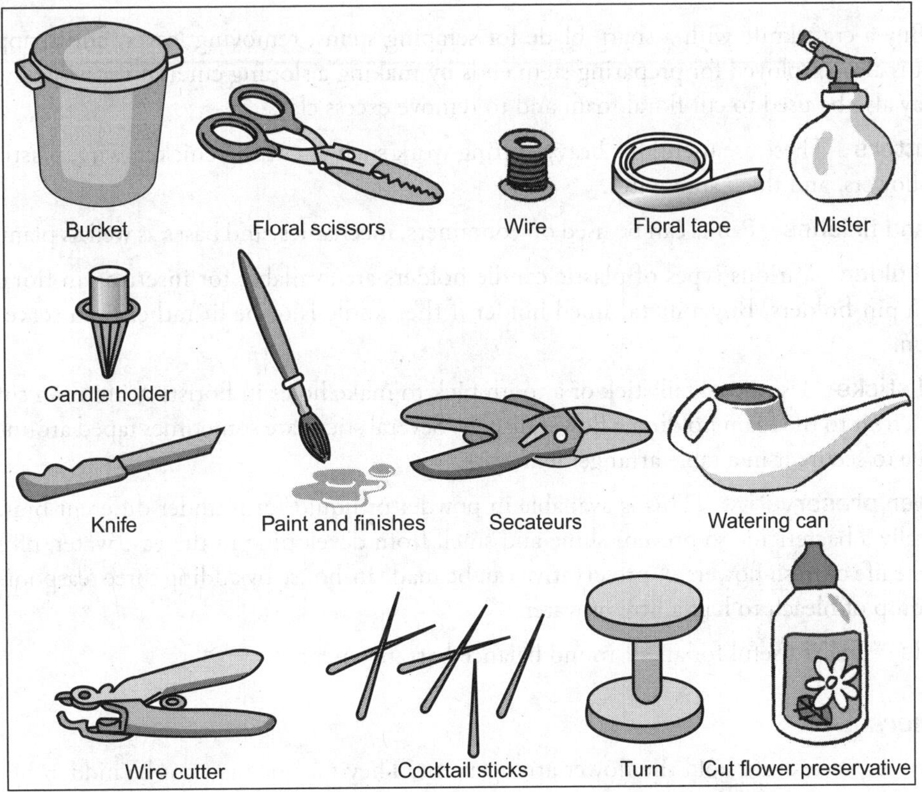

Fig. 30.3 Equipment used in flower arrangement

Mister A hand-held spray bottle to produce a fine mist of water droplets is an aid to keeping an arrangement looking fresh in warm weather. Spray the mist slightly above the top of the display as soon as the arrangement is done and then repeat daily.

Secateurs These are used to cut through thick and woody stems. The garden type is commonly available, but there are narrower ones made especially for the florist.

Watering can This is used for topping up the water supply in the container or re-wetting the florists' foam for holding a fresh flower arrangement. Buy a plastic one and look for two important features—the spout should be long and narrow and it should arise from the base of the can.

Floral tape This stem-binding tape made of plastic and waxed paper is ½ inch wide and is used to cover artificial stems made of wire. It stretches slightly when wound around the item to be covered and sticks to itself when warmed in the hands.

Wire This is used to support drooping stems and for making posies, corsages, and so on. It is also used to make false stems for dried and artificial flowers and to bind clumps of blooms together. Three types of wires are used:

Stub wire Strongest; available in green, blue, and black colours.

Rose wire Thinner silver wire for fine work.

Reel wire Available in blue, green, silver, and black; wound on a bobbin; extensively used for binding plant material.

Knife Buy a craft knife with a sharp blade for scraping stems, removing leaves, and stripping away thorns. It is also employed for preparing stem ends by making a sloping cut and occasionally a vertical slit. It may also be used to cut floral foam and to remove excess clay.

Wire cutters These are useful for heavy cutting work such as cutting chicken wire, plastic stems of artificial flowers, and thick stub wires.

Paints and finishes Paints can be used on containers, mechanics, and bases as well as plant material.

Candle holder Various types of plastic candle holders are available for inserting in floral foam or placing in pin-holders. Buy a metal-lined holder if the candle is to be lit rather than serve purely as decoration.

Cocktail sticks Use a cocktail stick or a tooth pick to make holes in florists' foam for a soft stem or to attach a fruit to the foam holding a flower display. Several sticks are sometimes taped around the base of a candle to secure it in a table arrangement.

Cut flower preservative This is available in powder or liquid form under different brand names. It is basically a bactericide to prevent slime and smell from developing in the vase water, plus sugar to prolong the life of fresh flowers. A preservative can be made in-house by adding three teaspoons of sugar and one drop of bleach to half a litre of water.

Turntable This is useful for an all-round balanced arrangement.

Containers

These are receptacles that hold the flower arrangement. They may or may not be hidden by the plant material. The container must be waterproof if fresh flowers are used. The base material from which the container is made determines its texture. Neutral colours such as soft grey, dull brown, off-white, or earth colours are most suitable because they are inconspicuous and do not detract attention from the flowers displayed. Elaborately decorated containers are unsuitable. Theme and simplicity should be kept in mind while choosing the design of the container.

Vase and jug A vase is a container that is at least as tall as it is wide and is often quite narrow, with a restricted mouth. It is a favourite container for cut flowers. If a glass vase is used, it is best to partly fill it with glass nuggets or marbles so that underwater stems do not look unattractive. A bud vase is a tall, thin vase that holds a single specimen of rose, tulip, or orchid. Metal vases were once very popular, but now pottery and plastic ones are common.

A jug is a lipped container with a single handle and is useful for old-world and 'natural' arrangements.

Basket This is a popular container for dried flower arrangements. Willow and bamboo baskets are easily available. Colours range from pale cream to near black. It is wise to choose a closely woven one so that the mechanics are hidden from view. A good all-purpose selection is a shallow, wide basket with a high handle.

For fresh flower arrangements, it is necessary to have a waterproof container within perhaps a hamper, a square or rectangular lidded basket.

Bowls and trays These are shallow containers. Cups and dishes are shallower than the fishbowl type and are widely used for tabletop arrangements. A tazza is a cup borne on a tall and narrow stem. An urn is a robust cup in pottery, stone, or plastic, borne on a short, stout stem and often with handles and a square base. A tray is a flat container with raised sides, used for dried and artificial flower displays and also for line arrangements with fresh plant materials. A board is a piece of cork, decorative wood, or similar, used as a container without any sides; on this, some florists' foam or clay is placed and dried or artificial plant materials are inserted into it.

Rose bowl This used to be a popular container for table decorations. The low cylindrical base of pottery or glass holds water and the plant-holding lid consists of either a criss-cross frame of thick silvered wire or a series of round holes for the stem. It is useful for a posy-type arrangement.

Wreath frame Wreaths bedecked with seasonal flowers, berries, and foliage are favourite features for the table and door at festivities such as Christmas. Choices may be made from a woven cane ring, a wire frame in which moss has been inserted, a frame covered with real or artificial conifer foliage, and a florists' foam ring.

Candle cup This is a shallow dish of plastic or metal that holds a block or round of florists' foam and has a short stem at the base. This stem is fixed in a candlestick with adhesive clay and taped in place before beginning the arrangement.

Florists' foam container This is a plastic container which has internal projections designed to hold a block or round of florists' foam.

Miscellaneous objects Common items of daily use, such as wine glasses, jelly moulds, decanters, kettles, saucepans, coffeepots, and so on may be used as containers as well. Other objects, such as shells and driftwood, also can serve as containers. Hollowed-out vegetable marrows and melons are eye-catching, but the gas emitted by the living container shortens the life of the cut flowers.

Various types of containers are shown in Figure 30.4.

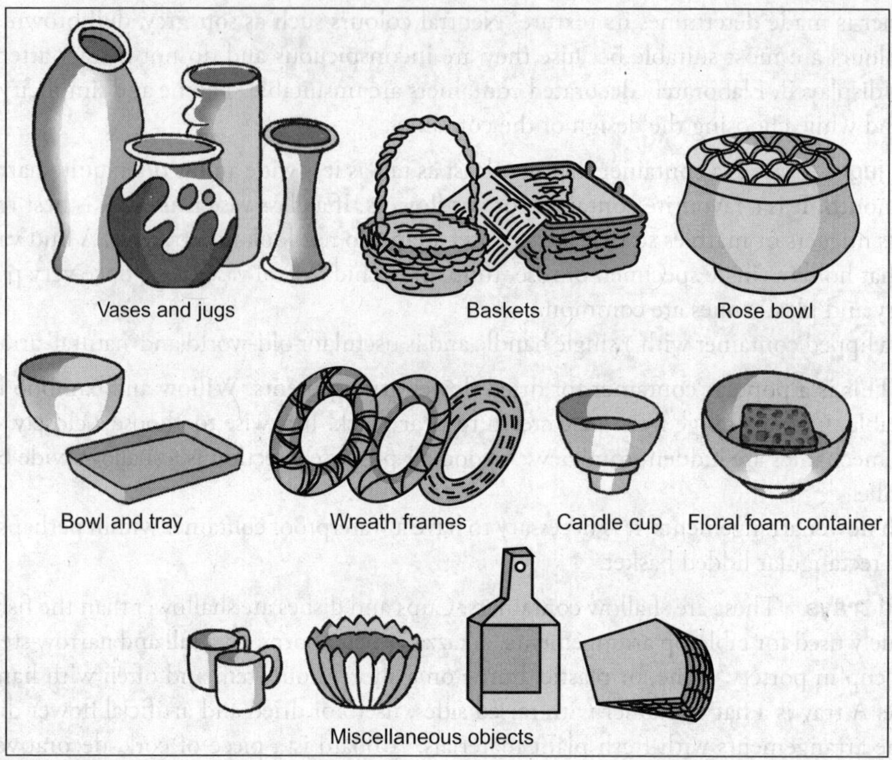

Fig. 30.4 Containers used in flower arrangement

Bases

An object that is placed underneath the container to protect the surface of the support and/or to add to the beauty of the display is called a base. It is often used to link the arrangement with accessories and can be employed to improve both the visual appeal and sense of balance.

Table mat A straw, bamboo, or plastic table mat is the most popular base. Shiny and highly decorated surfaces should be avoided and the smallest practical size should be used.

Tree section A cross-cut section of a tree trunk, with or without bark, makes an excellent decorative base for some arrangements. An oval section is ideal for holding containers with landscape exhibits or line arrangements. The container is usually set at one side rather than at the centre of the base. The tree section can be left untreated or be stained with a wood dye, and is often coated with furniture wax or varnish.

Wood base Rectangles or rounds made out of plywood, block board, chipboard, or fibreboard can be used, but a cork base is the most popular.

Stone base Pieces of marble, slate, limestone, and so on make excellent decorative bases in the right set-up. Stone gives a feeling of solidity and a section that has a hollow designed in it to hold a small container is very useful.

Covered base Plain rounds of wood may be covered with felt or nylon to make them more suitable as bases. The cloth is either cut and glued to the board or tailored into an elasticized slipcover in which the board is placed.

Oriental base Carved, fancy, trivet-type bases are used in some Chinese arrangements and may be used in similar arrangements.

The types of bases commonly used are shown in Figure 30.5.

Fig. 30.5 Bases used in flower arrangement

Support

This refers to the structure on which the container stands. The usual supports are tables, sideboards, alcoves, and shelves. With the exception of fireplace displays and large floating arrangements, floral displays are rarely placed at ground level. A pedestal made of wood, stone, or metal acts as a good support.

Plant materials

These can be divided into three basic types. Most arrangements use all the three types of plant materials.

Line material This consists of tall stems, flowering spikes, or bold leaves that are used to create the basic framework or skeleton. This line material may be straight or curved and it sets the height and width of the finished arrangement. Examples: Gladioli, birds of paradise, golden rods, larkspur, asparagus ferns, palms, tuberoses, and Peruvian lilies.

Dominant/focal/point material This consists of bold flowers or clusters of small showy blooms. Eye-catching foliage is occasionally used. The dominant material provides a centre of interest. Examples: Gerbera, chrysanthemum, lilies, anthurium, tulips, poppies, roses, dahlias, and daffodils.

Filler/secondary material This consists of smaller flowers or all sorts of leaves and foliage that are used to cover the mechanics and edges of the container and also provide added interest and colour to the display. Unwanted bare spots are filled by these. Examples: Asters, ivy, marguerites, button chrysanthemums, carnations, *Gypsophila* (baby's breath), and *Limonium*.

Accessories

These are non-plant materials included in or placed alongside the arrangement. Their purpose is generally decorative but could be functional at times. Accessories are added to the design for extra interest or to 'stretch' the flowers when they are in short supply. With careful use, they can enhance an arrangement considerably. Some versatile accessories are: baskets; bronze lamps; miniature dolls; hats; baby shoes; grain scoops; wooden shapes; ribbons; pottery items; artificial glitter; beads; wooden fruit shapes; painted wire; silk flowers and foliage; candles; driftwood; shells; idols; carved objects; tree barks; and interesting pebbles.

Buying Cut Flowers

The person incharge of buying flowers in a hotel must know where and how to buy cut flowers. Flowers are a highly perishable commodity and if the vendors themselves have not kept them in good condition, they will not last long. Exotic flowers are expensive and it is best to buy them from a wholesale market, where one can get a lot of variety at a reasonable price. The following points should be kept in mind while buying cut flowers:

- Look at the flower buckets first. They should be placed out of direct sunlight and the water should be clean and not smelly.
- Foliage should be firm and the cut ends properly immersed in water.
- Choose blooms at the just-open stage and not the full-bloom stage for a long-lasting display. The bud stage is too early—closed, green buds do not often open indoors. The problem with the full-blown stage, though it seems ripe for display, is that all the flowers are fully open and so the display will be short-lived.

Care and Conditioning of Flowers

A flower or leaf cut from a plant has a short, though beautiful, life. It is possible to prolong this for a little while by a few methods. This is well worth doing, as having spent time and money on a flower arrangement, it is gratifying to have it last as long as possible. Flower arrangers use the term 'conditioning' to refer to the preparation of cut plant materials for a long life, the filling of stems with water, and prevention of wilting. Cut flowers can be cared for and kept fresh for longer if the points discussed here are kept in mind.

Preparation

While preparing flower arrangements, adhere to the following guidelines:

- Plant materials should be cut at a slant, using sharp scissors or knife, either early in the morning or after sunset. At this time, they are crisp and filled with moisture.
- As a general rule, it is best to cut flowers before they reach maturity.
- Carry cut flowers in a heads-down position so that heavy-headed flowers will not snap off.
- Wrap the flowers in newspaper till the neck of the flowers. Plunge this bunch into a bucket of water for 3–4 hours or overnight to condition. In case of foliage, submerge them in water for about two hours.
- Use a good pruning knife or scissors to make clean, slanting cuts, causing minimal damage or bruising to the little ducts in the stem which carry water.
- Make slanting cuts in stems rather than straight ones—preferably underwater, to avoid the introduction of air bubbles—immediately before putting the stems in water, as this helps expose a larger surface area for water suction by the stems.
- To revive wilting flowers, snip off half an inch of the stem underwater and plunge in a deep container of water. Dead flowers should be cut off.
- Remove all leaves from the stems of flowers that have shorter lives than most.
- Re-cut any stem that has been left out of water, doing this underwater if possible and removing about 2 inches of the stem.

- Shape a leaf to resemble its original proportions when trimming away a brown spot along its margin.
- Preserve or revive woody stems by pounding the bottom 2 inches of the stems before plunging in water.
- Ensure enough water for woody stems by paring 2 inches off the ends and making a cross-shaped cut in the end.
- To reduce underwater decay, strip the stems of all foliage and thorns that fall below the waterline. However, de-thorning roses may shorten their life.
- Flowers with hollow stems, such as dahlias and marigolds, should have the stem ends seared over a candle flame to coagulate the sap at the ends, thus preventing the sap from bleeding out.
- Dribbling candle wax at the base of the flower heads keeps the bottom petals from falling off flowers such as chrysanthemums.
- Some plant materials are longer lasting when mature, such as stems of pomegranate, sweet lime, and sapota. These could be used as basic line material.

Aftercare

The following guidelines should be kept in mind for aftercare:

- Never place a fresh flower arrangement where it will be exposed to direct draughts from a fan or window. To prevent dehydration, keep cut flowers away from direct sunlight and large appliances as well.
- Do not put flowers near a bowl of fruit, especially apples, pears, and plums. They emit ethylene gas when ripening, which causes wilting of flowers.
- Prolong the freshness of the arrangement by spraying with lukewarm water from a mister morning and night.
- Change the water every day if the arrangement is meant to last a while. Never use chilled water, as cut stems fare best in warm water of about 45°C.
- Listerine, ammonia, charcoal, salt, lemonade, sugar, camphor, or aspirin added in small amounts to the water slows down bacterial growth, thus prolonging the life of flowers. Alternatively, use commercial cut-flower preservatives available in the market.
- Use clean containers to prevent premature fouling and bacterial growth. Use coloured glass containers if possible—the darker the glass, the harder it is for nasty green algae to grow. Do not use aluminium containers for flowers.
- Every three days, re-cut the stems, clean the vase, completely replace the water, and add more preservative.

Designing Flower Arrangements

Decorating with flowers is a creative and stimulating art, which often carries a message or theme and expresses the mood or emotions of the arranger. Blending together the eight features of good design helps in creating beautiful flower arrangements (see Figure 30.6). An arrangement made keeping these features in mind will turn out to be a beautiful piece of floral art. These have been discussed in detail in this section.

Style

Following styles already established by experts ensures a beautiful flower arrangement. There are many styles in flower arrangement and new ones are constantly being added, as this is now a professional art. Styles can be of various kinds.

Based on the angle from which they are seen, the style could be an all-around arrangement or a facing arrangement.

Based on the amount of space present in the arrangement, style could be the massed style; line style; or miscellaneous style.

Based on the type of plant material used, it could be a foliage arrangement or dried flower arrangement.

Based on the effect of the arrangement, it could be formal; semi-formal; informal; or modern/abstract/free-style.

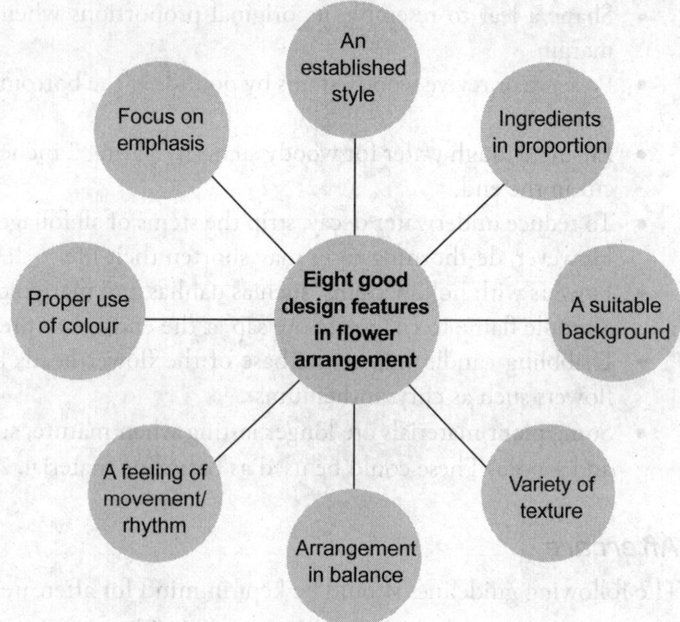

Fig. 30.6 Features of a good design

Let us now discuss each of these styles in detail. The various styles of flower arrangement are shown in Figures 30.7–30.21.

Based on the angle

On the basis of the angle from which a flower arrangement is viewed, it can be classified as follows.

All-around arrangement This arrangement is designed to be seen from all sides and is therefore chosen for a table or a room centrepiece. When seen from above, it is usually circular, but may be broadly oval or square as well (see Figure 30.7).

Facing arrangement This is also called the 'flat-back arrangement' and is designed to be seen only from the front and perhaps the sides. It is therefore chosen for placement on a shelf or sideboard (see Figure 30.8). It should not be placed too close to the wall, however.

Fig. 30.7 All-around arrangement

Based on the space present in the arrangement

On the basis of the space present in the arrangement, flower arrangements can be classified in the following ways.

Mass style Little or no space is enclosed within the boundary of the arrangement. This style originated in Europe, beginning according to tradition with the Renaissance. The mass style has several basic features:

- Generally the arrangement is an all-around one and line material is used to create a skeleton consisting of an upright axis and several horizontal laterals.
- The framework is more or less completely covered with flowers and/or other plant material.
- There is usually no attempt to make any particular part a distinct focal point and transition is considered important.
- Colours, shapes, and other features of neighbouring blooms tend to blend together rather than stand out in sharp contrast.

Fig. 30.8 Facing arrangement

Popular mass-style arrangements are as follows.

Bunch in a vase This is the simplest arrangement. The stem bases of the bunch are cut and then the flowers are put in a vase half-filled with water.

Biedermeier This is a flat or domed mass in a round and shallow container. The flowers may be fresh, dried, or artificial. The blooms are arranged to give concentric circles of different colours and there is an outer collar of foliage. The term nowadays is used for any low circular arrangement where the stems are almost completely hidden. The other names for this are *posy* and *domed display*.

Traditional mass This is the term for the classic massed arrangement that is held in place by florists' foam or crumpled chicken wire. The first step should be to create a central upright axis with line material and then the dominant flowers should be inserted. The final step is to use filler material to cover nearly all of the line material.

Byzantine cone This is an ancient style of arrangement. It is not recommended for the display of fresh flowers since it is difficult to keep moist and the effect is extremely formal. Furthermore, a lot of plant material is required. The mechanic is traditionally a moss-filled wire frame, but now a cone of florists' foam is used. Dried or artificial flowers are best used. The surface of the brown florists' foam is first covered with leafy sprigs and then a variety of short-stemmed blooms, fruits, berries, accessories, and so on are added to provide interest and colour.

Line style In this style, open spaces within the boundary of the arrangement are the main feature. Most of the display is line material. The line concept originated in the East and the rules were laid down in China and Japan more than thousands of years ago. The basic feature of a line design is limited use of plant material with support often provided by a pin-holder.

Each element of the design is important and the airy spaces contained within the framing line material are vital to the overall effect of the display. It is the lines and not the mass that are the main source of appeal. Here, transition is not important.

Ikebana The word literally means 'making flowers live' in Japanese. This Japanese style has been practised for thousands of years. These arrangements are more than an aesthetic grouping of plant materials.

They are symbolic representations of an ideal harmony that exists between earthly and eternal life. In each arrangement, there is an imaginary triangle. Its tallest line represents 'heaven'. Facing and looking towards heaven is 'man'. The lowest line, looking up to both, is 'earth' (see Figure 30.20). For further details of this art, refer to the section on 'Japanese flower arrangement'.

Vertical line This type of line style is formal, geometric, and defined by clear-cut rules. The important feature is the bold line material set vertically to form a central axis. At the base are short wings of foliage to cover the mechanics. The third plant element is the single bloom or small group of dominant flowers placed along the axis or close to the base of the arrangement (see Figure 30.9). Little or no filler material is required.

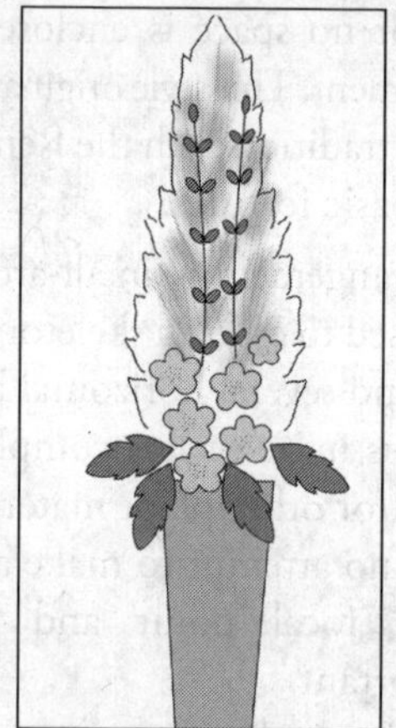

Fig. 30.9 A vertical line shaped flower arrangement

Line-mass style In this style, some open space is present within the boundary of the arrangement. Only part of the area between the framework of the line material is filled with leaves and/or flowers. The skeleton is formed by the line material and it is clothed but not covered by other flowers and foliage. There are many shapes in the line-mass style.

Triangular shape The triangle is a popular shape for symmetrical arrangements. The first step is to establish lines of height and width, usually with flowers or foliage of finer form or paler colour. The next step is to establish a focal point of interest with large or darker-coloured flowers. Fill in with flowers of varied stem lengths, grouping colours rather than dotting them about at random (see Figure 30.10).

Circular shape The circular or round shape is loved by nature since a majority of flowers fall into that shape. Arranging flowers in circular designs adds a pleasing element of repetition that is satisfying to the viewer's eye. Monotony should be avoided by using foliage that offers contrast to the dominant round forms (see Figure 30.11).

Fig. 30.10 A triangular shaped flower arrangement

Fig. 30.11 A circular shaped flower arrangement

Crescent shape The crescent is asymmetrical and formal in character. It requires more skill and experience on the part of the arranger than other basic styles. For this arrangement, choose plant materials with pliable stems (see Figure 30.12).

Fig. 30.12 A crescent shaped flower arrangement

Fan shape The fan or horizontal shape is a good line to follow when designing flowers for the centre of the table. It does not need to be a tall arrangement to be effective. It is a low arrangement and thus does not interfere with conversation across the table. It is symmetrical and thus attractive from every angle (see Figure 30.13).

Hogarth or 'S' shape This style was pioneered by an eighteenth-century painter, William Hogarth. This is a very graceful style of line arrangement and is a favourite at flower shows. It is easier to make when curved branches and pliable stems are used. After establishing the S shape with these, flowers are filled in at the centre and just above and below the rim of the tall container (see Figure 30.14).

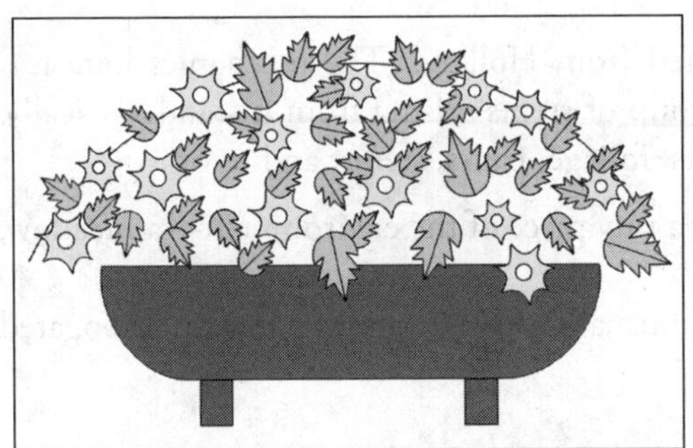

Fig. 30.13 A fan shaped flower arrangement

Fig. 30.14 A hogarth shaped flower arrangement

Right- or left-faced triangles These asymmetrical arrangements are most effective in low rectangular containers (see Figure 30.15).

Fig. 30.15 A right-faced triangle shaped flower arrangement

Miscellaneous style These arrangements do not belong to any of the basic styles. They may be a combination of two or three of the other styles mentioned. There are miscellaneous styles that are defined by their size—the miniature and petite are at one extreme and the grand displays at the other. Miniatures and petites are small-scale arrangements requiring less material but a lot of skill. The size of a miniature is 4 inches height, width, and depth maximum. The petite should not exceed 9 inches in height, width, or depth. On the other hand, the grand displays stand at least 3 feet high and are seen in churches, hotel foyers, and so on.

Chicken wire is the preferred mechanic here and a large high container is essential. In some miscellaneous arrangements, the plant material does not appear to radiate from a single point as in landscape and parallel styles.

Parallel style Also called the *European style*, it originated from Holland. The mechanics here is a rectangular block of florists' foam in a shallow dish. A group of stems arising from it stand vertically. The foam is hidden by a horizontal groundwork of flowers, foliage, fruits, stems, and so on.

Landscape style The goal is to create a representative of a tiny piece of the environment—a meadow, woods, beach, or another.

Other miscellaneous styles are massed arrangements in unusual forms—round wreaths, the elongated swags, garlands, and topiary trees.

Based on the type of plant material used

On the basis of the type of plant material used in the arrangement, it can be classified in the following ways.

Foliage arrangement Nothing does more than cut green foliage to freshen up a room at a minimum expenditure of both time and money. Foliage is easy to come by. Use branches of interesting form and foliage of many shapes and colours (see Figure 30.16). Foliage arrangements have a natural affinity for modern furnishings and contemporary architecture. They do take to a traditional setting also if styled properly and placed in a suitable container.

Fig. 30.16 A foliage arrangement

Dried flower arrangement Preserved or dried plant material can be arranged in containers either on its own or combined with fresh plant materials. These can be used for permanent or semi-permanent décor. During those months when little is available from the garden and flower prices shoot up in the markets, an arrangement of dried flowers and foliage is extremely useful. From a florist one can obtain a great variety of dried materials, such as wood roses, wood berries, cones, poppy heads, bulrushes, firs, beeches, eucalyptus, ferns, and so on. Even brooms, grass, and reeds could be used.

The base is invariably provided by driftwood. Fresh flowers could be added and held in place by the use of wires, test tubes, florist's cones, cello tape, plasticine, and so on.

To prepare your own materials, gather them in the summer or autumn. Hang them head downward until they are thoroughly dried. For drying flowers and foliage, first place the stems in a solution of two parts of water to one part glycerine for two weeks. Dried materials may be painted silver, white, black, or gold (see Figure 30.17).

Fig. 30.17 A dried flower arrangement

Based on the effect

The flower arrangement styles discussed so far could be formal, semi-formal, or informal, based on the effect they create.

Formal arrangement This is symmetrical and precise.

Semi-formal arrangement This is more or less symmetrical in outline, but not in the details of arrangement.

Informal arrangement This is asymmetrical and 'free'.

Modern or abstract or free-style arrangement These have no fixed rules or formulas for correct proportions. These arrangements do not have a definite geometric outline; instead the emphasis is on line and space. The individual beauty of each piece of plant material is emphasized instead of the beauty of an outline shape or a mass (see Figure 30.18).

Fig. 30.18 An abstract arrangement

Proportion

As in all forms of art, the classic good proportion—the 'golden ratio'—is important in flower arrangements. For centuries, the golden ratio has been used as the yardstick for perfect proportion. Good proportion means the size of each element—container, plant material, base, and accessories—should result in a pleasing, harmonious appearance. For the arrangement as a whole, everything should be in scale.

Background

The arrangement may have good style and proportion, but if the background or setting in which it has been placed is unsuitable, it may lose its charm. The various aspects to consider are as follows.

Style of the room For example, an abstract arrangement would look out of place in a chintzy cottage setting.

Size of the room For example, a petite arrangement in a large, lofty hall can look pathetic.

Type of wall surface For example, an ornately patterned wallpaper makes a poor backdrop for a facing arrangement placed against it and so does a white or cream wall for an arrangement filled with very pale-coloured flowers.

Practicality For example, dining-table arrangements that obstruct conversation across the table and hall arrangements that obstruct free passage are unsuitable.

Texture

Plant material comes in various textures—glossy, velvety, dull, prickly, and so on. It is up to the skill of the arranger how she or he combines textures to achieve beauty in arrangements. A glossy flower is brightened when placed next to matt foliage, and shiny leaves in strong lighting make the arrangement sparkle. A variety of textures within the arrangement increases interest by avoiding monotony.

Balance

Here, physical as well as visual balance needs to be considered.

Physical balance This is vital for any arrangement. If it is too asymmetrical, then there is a danger that the whole arrangement will tip over. The mechanics must always be securely fixed and the container should always be heavy enough to support the plant material. The more one-sided the display, the heavier the container should be. Sand and gravel can be added to achieve this.

Visual balance This calls for the arrangement to look stable even if it is one-sided. To increase the visual weight of the lighter side, keep in mind that:

- Dark flowers look heavier than pale ones.
- Round flowers look heavier than trumpets and conical ones.

Top to bottom balance also needs to be considered. Large flowers placed centrally and close to the bottom of the arrangement give a feeling of good balance.

Rhythm or Movement

This involves using techniques and materials that guide the eye from one part of the display to another. Rhythm in flower arrangements may be achieved by:

- Using curved stems.
- Hiding all or part of any tall, straight stems.
- Placing flowers 'in and out' through the arrangement.
- Having flowers at various stages of development in the arrangement.
- Using foliage of various sizes and contrasting shapes.
- Having an irregular line of various-sized blooms.

Colour

This is one of the first things noticed when we look at a flower arrangement. Colour is a matter of personal taste, but the application of some general rules results in arrangements with good colour combinations. The basis of the use of colours is the colour wheel.

Colour schemes in flower arrangements The major families are given below:

Monochromatic Here, various tints and shades of a single hue are used. Red can be chosen for a dramatic effect, yellow for brightness, blue for a restful effect, and so on. An assortment of shapes, sizes, and textures should be used to avoid monotony. Also, a wide range of the base colour, varying from pale tints to the darkest shades should be used (see Figure 30.19).

Fig. 30.19 Monochromatic colour

Analogous Two, three, or four hues next to each other on a colour wheel are used. It has the subdued charm of monochromatic schemes and there is a much larger range of plants to choose from. Tints and shades are important here and add to the interest of the display. The colours used should not occur in equal amounts—one should dominate.

Contrasting/complimentary Here, colours directly across each other on the colour wheel are used. For example, blue iris with orange gerbera. Contrasting schemes are always lively, but they should not be over-bright. Use tints of the basic colours to make a pastel arrangement. For example, pink with powder blue. In this way, a contrasting scheme can be subdued. Another way is to use a tint of one colour and a shade of the contrasting one (see Figure 30.13).

Polychromatic/rainbow/scattered Colours from all parts of the colour wheel are used here. If carefully arranged for a harmonious effect through other elements, this can be pleasing, especially in summers. If not, the effect may be too bright or too spotty.

Emphasis/Dominance

This involves having one or more areas in the arrangement to which the eye is drawn and on which it rests for a short time. This point is known as a 'focal point' or 'centre of interest'. Emphasis may not be an important feature for a traditional, all-around arrangement, but it is essential in facing line-mass and most freestyle arrangements. The usual methods to achieve emphasis are as follows.

- Include a small group of bold flowers (dominant material).
- Use an unusual container.
- Use striking foliage.
- Have sufficient plain background.

General Guidelines for Flower Arrangements

The following are some general guidelines for flower arrangement.

- Make a definite plan for any flower arrangement based on the purpose, room area, and location of the arrangement in the room.

- Select containers, flowers, and foliage that express the mood of the room, the occasion, and the colour scheme of the interiors.
- Use flowers with stems of different sizes and select flowers according to the size of the vase.
- Arrange the tallest stems first and then others according to the type of arrangement, namely mass, line, line-mass, Japanese, and so on.
- Large flowers with bright, bold colours can be used in small numbers and at the centre in tall vases. Small, short-stemmed flowers may be easily arranged in groups in low vases.
- Avoid mixing up fresh flowers and artificial flowers.
- Extend some low material forward to create depth.
- Avoid regular spacing and stair-step sequences.
- Distinctive flowers should usually be placed alone.
- Small flowers such as violets may be in tight bunches.
- Use large, medium, and small leaves or flowers together instead of having them in the same sizes.
- Low containers are suitable for all types of arrangements.
- Practice using bases under containers.
- Small arrangements look good grouped with other objects and accessories.
- Always cover the stem holders.
- Pour enough water into the vases.
- Follow the points given for the care and conditioning of flowers.

Placing Flower Arrangements

After creating a good flower arrangement, its placement should be apt; otherwise it may lose its charm. Arrangements can be placed at the following levels.

Eye level These can be prominently seen. Television tops, alcoves, pedestals, and so on may be used. Flower arrangements are typically placed at heights from 18 inches to 4 feet, depending on whether viewers are likely to be seated or standing when they happen upon the arrangement.

High level For anything placed well above eye level, the flowers used must be long. The arrangement can also be suspended from the ceiling.

Low level Flowers and vases must be large and decorative. Floating arrangements look better when placed low.

Most flower arrangements should be placed at eye level, permitting one to look into the arrangement and to see the tops of all the flowers. Tall arrangements are best enjoyed below eye level. If they are placed too high or the arrangements themselves are too high, they will carry the eye up towards the ceiling. If placing arrangements above eye level, some drooping lines must be introduced in the arrangements so that the eye is carried downwards.

Arrangements should be grouped with something else in the room. It should become an essential part of the interior scheme. At the same time, flower arrangements look good when placed against plain backgrounds. Similarly, a vase with decorative patterns detracts from the effect of the arrangement.

Tall arrangements look good when placed on a tall table to fit in with the composition of other furniture and accessories in the room. Miniature arrangements are scaled to small objects and go well on a tea tray. They would appear lost if placed next to large objects or on a large table. If arrangements are to be used on the dining table, they should not disturb the people sitting at the table. Low or floating arrangements are advisable for the dining table. When flower arrangements are complete, it is advisable to leave them on for a few moments. When seen with a fresh vision, it may be found that some of the flowers should be removed or shortened, or a change made in the position of flowers or leaves, to achieve a better arrangement.

Flower Arrangements for Various Hotel Areas

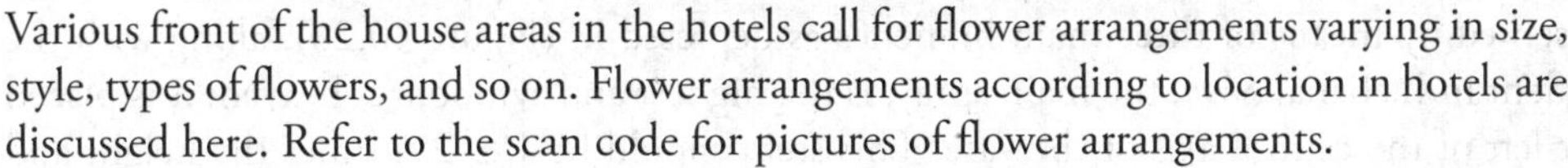

Various front of the house areas in the hotels call for flower arrangements varying in size, style, types of flowers, and so on. Flower arrangements according to location in hotels are discussed here. Refer to the scan code for pictures of flower arrangements.

Lobby A lobby calls for a spectacular arrangement with exotic flowers in large containers. Since the area is large, an all-round mass arrangement on a round table is ideal. The height should be at least 2½ ft. for it to be visible as soon as guests enter the lobby and also from any part of the lobby. Apart from this main arrangement, very small arrangements carrying the same theme and flowers may be placed at the centre tables in the lobby seating area.

Front desk A one- or two-sided arrangement is usually kept at one end of the front desk. A medium-sized arrangement using bright coloured flowers is usually seen. The shapes that work well here are triangular or one-sided triangular arrangements. It is a good idea to extend the theme and colour of the lobby arrangement to the flower arrangements too.

Conference rooms and halls In a conference room, the most suitable arrangement is a low horizontal or fan-shaped arrangement, which will not hamper discussions across the table. In a conference hall, where there may be a frill-covered dais on stage, low oval-shaped arrangements are placed equidistantly on the dais.

VIP rooms Medium-sized mass arrangements in geometric shapes are placed in VIP rooms. Ikebana arrangement is also placed in such rooms in many properties.

Restaurants The arrangements in restaurants are traditionally in the form of bud vases with one or two flowers placed in them on each table. However, nowadays, small and low all-round arrangements too are seen at many fine-dining restaurants. A single large floating flower in a goblet of water is also a trendy arrangement. A low arrangement is advisable as it allows unhindered conversation across the table. The flowers used should not be strong smelling ones as the fragrance would clash with the aroma of food and wine.

Buffets A traditional mass arrangement such as a large triangular or one-sided triangular arrangement is suitable at the end of a buffet counter. Large mass arrangements are also placed at the centre of the salad display. These arrangements may include fruits. Wall arrangements are also seen at wedding banquets.

Public restrooms In washrooms, an arrangement with one or two large blooms in a tall container is usually found at one end of the vanitory counter.

Health club Tall contemporary arrangements with minimal flowers are usually placed in health clubs as they suggest action. In traditional arrangements, Ikebana in Nageire style is ideal.

Spa An elegant floating arrangement done with locally available flowers in traditional large shallow containers is ideal to be placed at the floor level in the spa. Floating candles in the arrangements add to their charm and gel beautifully with the spa theme.

Japanese/Oriental Flower Arrangement

The Japanese lay great emphasis on the art of flower arrangement. People in Japan use flowers to symbolize seasons or particular occasions. In all their arrangements, a single principle is followed, and the most striking characteristic is that they give the impression of naturally growing plants.

Ikebana literally means 'making flowers live' in Japanese. In all such arrangements, Heaven, Man, and Earth are represented by means of three main branches as depicted in (Figure 30.20), along with the angles of placement in Ikebana. *Shin*, the main spray, is the highest and symbolizes heaven; it is placed 10–15° right or left of the central axis of the vase. This stem should be 1½–2½ times the height and width of the container. *Soe*, the second highest stem, represents man. It provides width to the arrangement and is about three-fourth the height of the tallest spray. This stem forms an angle of about 45° with the rim of the container. *Hikae* or *Tai*, the lowest spray, denotes earth. This branch is about half as tall as the one signifying man and extends very little beyond the diameter of the container, forming an angle of about 75° with the rim of the container. It is placed opposite the branch signifying man and is used to balance the arrangement.

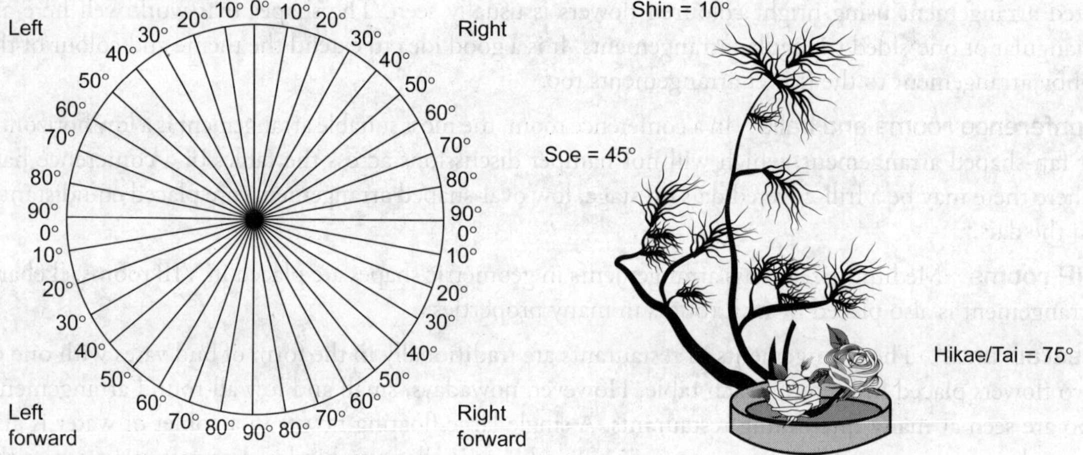

Fig. 30.20 Angles and three main lines in Ikebana

The Japanese use tall vases as well as low bowls. Tall vases are usually made of bamboo, bronze, or pottery. Sometimes the bamboo ones are painted with black lacquer. Low bowls are made of bronze and pottery. For holding flowers, metal holders are used in vases and bowls. A naturally forked branch is also used to hold the stems in place.

Another important aspect in their arrangements is that they always use an odd number of flowers, as they believe that odd numbers are lucky as well as more aesthetic. Thus, in all arrangements, three, five, or seven flower sprays are used. There is no overcrowding and all plant materials are seen as separate units, but as a part of the whole.

There are various schools of oriental flower arrangement, *Ohara* and *Sogetsu* being the popular ones. In the *Ohara* school, when a flat or low container is used, it is called a *moribana* style. *Moribana* is an informal arrangement in a shallow container in which a pin-holder is used as mechanics. Landscapes are portrayed or large, colourful flowers are displayed.

When a tall vase without a pin-holder is used, the arrangement is said to be in the *hikae* style.

A formal arrangement called the *seika* style has strict rules governing the lengths and angles of the stems. It is basically a triangular arrangement and usually stiff so that all stems arise from a single point.

A floating arrangement is called *ukibana* and a basket arrangement with fruits and flowers is *morimano*.

Nonohana is a type of oriental flower arrangement in which dried flowers, branches, and leaves are used. Another classical arrangement in a tall cylindrical vase with a flowing and natural effect is called *Nagerie* (see Figure 30.21).

Fig. 30.21 *Ikebana* style—*Nagerie* arrangement

Common Flowers and Foliage

Let us now take a look at some common flowers and foliage used in various flower arrangements. Figures 30.22 and 30.23 show some of these flowers and foliage.

Flowers

Some common varieties of flowers used in arrangements are: Roses, Arum lilies, Gladioli, Dahlias, Chrysanthemums, Gerberas, Tulips, Asters, Carnations, Freesias, Tuberoses, Lotuses, *Anthurium*, Birds of paradise, Marigold, Orchids, Irises, Petunias, *Hibiscus*, Poppies, *Camellia*, Peonies, *Hydrangea*, Snowdrops, *Gypsophila* (baby's breath), Bottle brush, Hollyhocks, Cannas, Geraniums, Daisies, Larkspurs, Spider lilies, Water lilies, Zinnias, Marguerites, and Lady's lace.

Ginger lily
Alstromeria
Tuberose
Anthurium
Heliconia
Gladioli
Allium
Gypsophila
Golden rods
Orchids
Cymbidium orchids
Bird of paradise

Fig. 30.22 Some common flowers used in arrangements

Areca palm

Fishtail palm

Asparagus ferns

Foxtail asparagus ferns

Cypress leaves

Dracaena

Bottlebrush

Murraya paniculata - Kaamini

Philodendron

Sword ferns

Xanadu

Ivy

Jerusalem sage

Mountain lily

Iron bark/Eucalyptus fern

Buttercups

Coral bells

Plantain lily/Hosta

Variegated privet

Coral bells

Fig. 30.23 Commonly used foliage in flower decoration

Foliage

The commonly used varieties of foliage are: True ferns, Asparagus ferns, Palm leaves, Umbrella palms, Bamboos, Pine, Cypress, Goldenrods, Citrus branches, Crotons, Copper beech, Boxwood, Oleander, Ivy, and *Caladium*.

Themed Decorations in Hotels

The arrangements for the themed décor for a festive event or a convention is under the purview of the housekeeping department. Housekeepers keep in mind the specifications of the client for the event and depending on the extent of arrangements and décor, either hire contractors or carry out the decoration work in-house.

Festive/Convention Theme Décor

The scope of theme décor may vary based on the type of event. For instance, where a Christmas Ball requires extensive planning for festive materials, lighting, feast table decorations and colour scheme coordination, a medical conference may call for a very formal set up with minimal add-ons in terms of theme decoration. Where extensive theme coordinated décor is called for, the following elements must be catered to:

Stage design Temporary stages are erected as per size dimensions required by the client. Steps should be carefully fitted to avoid mishaps. Poles and drapes, balloons, floral decors, hanging LED lamps, statement pieces of furniture can be used to match the theme and draw attention to the central ceremony.

Decorative backdrops These add tremendous visual stimulation at the backdrop of the stage, complementing the stage ceremony. Digital LED backdrops are a popular and versatile option to create animated effects, if the budget of the client permits.

Fabric drapings Lengths of voile or satin fabrics in theme coordinated colours draped elegantly as swags and cascades give a luxurious feel to the décor. Organza material is used for stretch designs on backdrops and ceilings.

Flower arrangements With a wide array of containers, holders, wire mesh and floral foam shapes available, it is now possible to create floral arrangements at any possible place in the venue, be it flowers lining the ceiling or hanging in globes. Fresh and artificial flowers are used to create themes and effects in the form of pedestal arrangements, posies or bouquets.

Table decorations Theme-based centrepieces, interesting floral arrangements, elegant table linen and decorative napkin folds attract attention to festive feast tables. Table linen uplift the décor; they may be in the form of white or coloured brocade with runners, white cotton underlay with a colour-coordinated organza or damask overlay. Table centrepieces may vary from petals and dainty floating candles in a glass bowl, small candelabra, flowers on a wrought iron stand, flower arrangements with candles, foliage and floral garlands, fish bowls with gold fish, and so on.

Props Carefully chosen props help build the theme of the décor. Paper lanterns, terracotta pots, pillars and urns, decorative umbrellas, artefacts, decorative screens, canvas frames with floral décor and such props are commonly used.

Seating arrangements Chairs with satin covers and bows in theme colours are usually grouped around frilled tables covered in satin damask for seated banquets. Generally, theatre style arrangements are done in halls where a stage is set. Two types of chair covers are used, the fitted ones and the sack style.

Ceiling décor Ceilings lend themselves very well to creating dramatic lighting and visual effects. Creative hangings and drapes used on ceilings as decoration reduce the need for floor décor, leaving it free for movement.

Lighting Dramatic lighting can uplift the ambience of a venue like no other element. LED lighting provides many options nowdays and requires minimum wiring. Various kinds include fairy lights, rope lights, joy lights, strip lights, rice lights, curtain lights, and so on. The amount of lighting depends on the kind of event; for instance a conference calls for simple but ample lighting for attendees to take notes at the table, but at the same time subdued enough for the presentation on the stage to be projected effectively.

Rangoli

The folk art of rangoli used to beautify exterior and interior floor spaces with designs in coarse coloured powder is an ancient one in India. It is known by various names throughout India, such as *Chowkpurana* in North India, *Alpana* in West Bengal, *Aripana* in Bihar, *Jhoti* in Odisha, *Mandana* in Rajasthan, *Kolam* in South India, *Muggu* in Andhra Pradesh, and so on. The primary objective of making rangoli in earlier times was to extend a creative, colourful, warm welcome to a visitor, and as an auspicious symbol during festivals. Every morning, as a daily ritual, the lady of the house decorated the entrance area of the house with a rangoli. Now a days, rangoli is used as a decorative expression of traditional festive cheer. Very often, lit earthen oil lamps are placed as part of the design as an auspicious element. Rangolis are drawn for weddings, births, and religious festivals.

In hotels too, whenever a traditional theme is to be portrayed, rangolis are made by housekeeping staff to create the desired ambience. A rangoli is prepared free-hand with coloured powder in various hues applied in traditional designs on the cleaned floor. The raw materials used for making the coloured powder are rice flour, rice paste, coloured rice, powdered pulses, chalk powder, coloured sawdust, coloured sand, brick powder, marble dust, and for colouring, vermillion, turmeric, and food colour. Petals of flowers and leaves add interest to rangoli designs.

The designs, first drawn with chalk, are usually geometrical and vary from simple to large complicated ones. Some basic designs are depicted in Figure 30.24. Those proficient in the art are adept at starting straight by making dot markings with the powder. The knack is to let the powder flow freely through a gap formed in between the pinched thumb and index finger. Rangoli designs are generally symmetrical and common motifs are that of a geometrical shape, lotus, mango, flowers, leaves, creepers, trees, peacock, swans, conch, shell, pot, celestial symbols, religious symbols, and footprints.

Fig.30.24 Basic rangoli designs

A discussion on rangoli is incomplete without the mention of flower carpet or *pookalam*, made during the harvest festival of Onam. Petals of fresh flowers in various colours and leaves are used to create intricate designs within a circle, in front of houses to celebrate the festival.

SUMMARY

Flower arrangement is a very personal and relaxing art. Any plant material bunched up in a container will be pleasing, but an art form is created when certain guidelines are followed. An exhaustive discussion in this chapter has been supported by suitable illustrations and pictures, so that it is beneficial for both a beginner and an enthusiast. It should of course be kept in mind that with the hotel industry going the eco-sensitive way, indoor plants, bonsai, and artificial or dried flower arrangements have replaced the once extensive use of fresh-flower arrangements in many hotels.

The important section on the basic ingredients for flower arrangement is detailed. Of the various types of equipment and mechanics discussed, not all are essential for all arrangements or for a beginner.

Once cut, plant materials have a short though beautiful life as part of a flower arrangement. It should be every arranger's goal to prolong the life of this plant material. Many tips on the buying, care, and conditioning of plant material are given. General guidelines are chalked out to help every step of the way. The placement of arrangements to get the best out of them has been discussed .

A separate section is reserved for the popular style of Japanese flower arrangement—ikebana. This is followed by the names and pictures of several types of flowers and foliage commonly used in flower arrangements.

Themed decorations in hotels for various events, special occasions and festivals are under the purview of the housekeeping department and the same is covered in the last section of the chapter.

KEY TERMS

Accessories An accessory is an item of non-plant material that is included with or alongside the arrangement. It could be decorative or sometimes functional. Examples are idols, wooden blocks, and so on.

Base An object that is placed underneath the container to protect the surface of the support and/or to add to the beauty of the display is called a base. They could be thin tree sections, table mats, or salvers.

Biedermeier This is a flat or domed massed floral display in a round, shallow container in which fresh, dried, or artificial flowers are arranged in concentric circles of different colours with an outer collar of foliage. The term is nowadays applied to any low circular arrangements where the stems are almost completely hidden. The other names for this are 'posy' and 'domed display'.

Byzantine cone This is an ancient style of high conical arrangement, comprising mainly dried or artificial flowers, where the effect is extremely formal.

Conditioning This refers to the preparation of cut plant materials for a longer life, the filling of stems with water, and the prevention of wilting.

Fillers These are plant materials used to hide plant stems, the container edges, and, most importantly, the oasis.

Foliage This usually refers to leafy plant materials in flower arrangements.

Foyer Lobby.

Golden ratio The ratio 2:3 as applied to design, where the shorter side measures two units and the longer three units. It is also called the Greek oblong.

Hikae This is an oriental arrangement where a tall vase without a pin-holder is used. The word '*hikae*' also represents the lowest spray in *ikebana*, denoting the Earth. This branch is about half as tall as the stem signifying man and extends very little beyond the diameter of the container, forming an angle of about 75° with the rim of the container.

Hogarth This is a very graceful style of S-shaped line arrangement in a tall container that was pioneered by an eighteenth-century painter, William Hogarth.

Ikebana The word literally means 'making flowers live' in Japanese. These Japanese arrangements are more than aesthetic grouping of plant materials. In each arrangement, there is an imaginary triangle depicting the relationship between heaven, man, and earth.

Kenzan These mechanics in flower arrangements are also called pin-holders or needle-point holders. A series of sharply pointed pins are firmly held in a solid lead base, which may be circular or rectangular. It holds thick and heavy stems securely.

Mechanics These are items used to keep the flowers, foliage, and stems in place within the container. The most popular and basic mechanics are floral foam, pin-holders, and chicken wire.

Miniatures These are small-scale flower arrangements measuring a maximum of 4 inches in height, width, and depth, thus requiring less material but a lot of skill.

Moribana This is an informal oriental flower arrangement in a shallow container, in which a pin-holder is used to portray landscapes or display large, colourful flowers.

Morimano A type of oriental flower arrangement done in a basket with fruits and flowers.

Nagerie A classical oriental flower arrangement in a tall cylindrical vase with a flowing and natural effect.

Nonohana A type of oriental flower arrangement in which dried flowers, branches, and leaves are used.

Oasis This is another name for florists' foam.

Petites These are small-scale arrangements measuring a maximum of 9 inches in height, width, and depth, thus requiring less material but a lot of skill.

Prong This is the simplest type of floral-foam anchor. It is a small plastic disc with four vertical prongs. The base of the prong is attached to the container with adhesive clay and the block or round of floral foam

is pressed down onto the prongs. It is also called floral frog.

Seika This is a formal oriental flower arrangement that has strict rules governing the lengths and angles of the stems. It is basically a triangular and usually stiff style in which all stems arise from a single point.

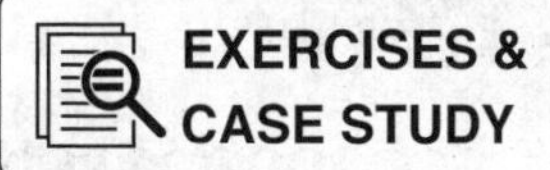

Tazza A cup borne on a tall and narrow stem.

Ukibana A floating Oriental flower arrangement.

Urn A robust cup in pottery, stone, or plastic, borne on a short, stout stem and often with handles and a square base.

31 Horticulture

Learning Objectives

After reading this chapter, you should be able to

- explain the importance of horticulture as an aspect of housekeeping
- describe the essential components of horticulture
- gain insight into popular garden styles in hotels
- identify the various types of indoor plants and prescribe general horticultural maintenance programmes for them
- discuss the trend of creative use of bonsai plants in hotels
- understand the principles and use of hydroponics and aquaponics in hotels
- appreciate the trend of placing terrariums in hotels
- assess the advantages and disadvantages of using artificial plants in hotels

Introduction

It is essential to appreciate the contribution of horticulture, landscaping, and gardening in the hospitality industry. Aesthetic use of horticulture freshens up the atmosphere, enhances the look of the property, and creates a lasting impression on guests. It also has a beneficial effect on the health of guests and, even more, the staff.

In a five-star hotel, the housekeeping department usually has a full-time horticulturist either on the payroll or on a contract agreement. Before the actual inception of the hotel, the area for landscaping should be clearly earmarked so that it can be planned well in advance, such that, when the hotel commences operations, a lush, green garden is ready to welcome guests.

A housekeeper must realize the importance of horticulture as an aspect of housekeeping that makes guests feel they are in touch with nature, away from today's frenzied urban lifestyle. Plants greatly complement the decorative aspects of a bedroom and public area, according freshness and charm while breaking the monotony of static furniture and fixtures.

The executive housekeeper should have basic knowledge of soils, watering, manures, perennials, and seasonal plants, and so on. He or she should know about the climatic conditions prevalent at the property's location and be aware of the types of plants suitable for these conditions. In the area of landscaping, it is beneficial to know about groundcovers, hedging plants, and focus plants that will complement one another.

Horticulture is the science of growing plants or of gardening. A garden, by definition, is a piece of land devoted to growing flowers, fruits, vegetables, shrubbery, and turf. Gardens brighten their surroundings; they add to the beauty of the landscape. There can be gardens devoted solely to one species of a flowering plant—for example, a rose garden; but most gardens are a conglomeration of various types of plants. Flowers, colourful leaves, and sometimes attractive stems may become the centre of attraction in the garden design. The types of flowers that can be grown in a garden depend on the size of the garden, its location, and the amount of sunshine and shade it gets. At the inception of a hotel, when the types of plants to be used are decided, the selected varieties should be bought and nurtured in the property's greenhouse so that they are ready to be planted as soon as construction of the property is over; it is not wise to plant while construction is in progress.

Essential Components of Horticulture

The essential components of horticulture are discussed in this section.

Hedges

A garden becomes much more attractive when its boundary is delineated by a hedge rather than a wall. The two most common shrubs used for making up hedges in Indian gardens are henna and hibiscus. Periodic trimming of the hedges is essential with both these species. A hibiscus hedge takes up more space than the slim and straight henna. Nowadays, the yellowish-green foliage of the shrub duranta is making it a very popular choice as a hedgerow plant. Bougainvillea plants also make good hedges, plus they bear magnificent bunches of flowers in various hues.

Lawns

A lawn is an expanse of closely mown, grass-covered land. Apart from its visual appeal, lawns absorb and hold water, which helps reduce water run-off and improves water quality in the garden soil. Lawns also have a significant cooling effect, provide oxygen, trap dust and dirt, promote healthful microorganisms, prevent soil erosion, and filter out rainwater contaminants. The basics of maintaining a healthy lawn are outlined here:

The soil The soil's pH, checked with a pH tester, should be between 6.5 and 7.0, which is just slightly acidic. If the soil is too acidic, it will need a sprinkling of lime. Sulphur can be added to soil which is not acidic enough. Lawns grow best in loamy soils that have a mix of clay, silt, and sand. Addition of organic matter, such as compost and grass clippings, benefits any type of soil.

Selecting the grass Choose a locally adapted grass. Grasses vary in the type of climate they prefer, the amount of water and nutrients required, shade tolerance, and the degree of wear they can withstand. An experienced gardener can recommend the grass best adapted for use in a given area.

Mowing This should be done often, but the grass should not be shorn too short. In mowing very short, the surface roots become exposed, the soil dries out faster, and surface aeration is reduced. As a general rule, the grass should not be cut off by more than one-third of its length at any time. Most turf species are healthiest when kept between 2.5 and 3.5 inches tall. Leave the grass clippings on the lawn—this method is known as 'grass cycling'—to provide nutrients equivalent to one application of fertilizer. If the lawn is mowed before the grass gets too tall, the clippings left on the lawn will quickly disappear from view. This technique also saves hauling away all the cuttings for disposal.

Watering Water deeply but not too often. Thorough watering encourages the lawn to develop deep root systems, which make the lawn hardier and more draught-resistant. Avoid over-watering, which can in fact be more damaging than under-watering. Let the lawn dry out reasonably before re-watering. As a rule of thumb, the colour of the grass should be dull and footprints should stay compressed for more than a few seconds before a lawn needs to be watered. To gauge the optimal duration of watering, put a cup in the sprinkler zone before turning it on—it should get filled with water to a height of at least 2.5 cm for adequate watering to have happened. The best time for watering is in the early morning, so that less water will be lost through evaporation. How long gardeners should wait between successive waterings (before the lawn dries out) is outlined in Table 31.1.

Table 31.1 Different grass types and their watering needs

Type of grass	Watering interval
Bahia grass, buffalo grass, Bermuda grass, St. Augustine grass, and centipede grass	12–21 days
Carpet grass, fine fescue, kikuyu grass, seashore paspalum, tall fescue, and Zoysia	8–12 days
Ryegrass, Kentucky bluegrass, and bentgrass	5–7 days

Controlling thatch Thatch is the accumulation of above-soil runners put out by the grasses. This layer should be about 1.25 cm on a healthy lawn. The proportion of thatch-to-lawn should be kept in balance by natural decomposition, earthworms, and microorganisms. Too much thatch prevents water and nutrients from reaching the grass roots. If necessary, excess thatching can be reduced by harrowing with a steel rake.

Fertilizing The lawn should be fertilized once or twice a year. This is sufficient for an attractive lawn. Avoid using fast-acting fertilizers, as some nutrients may get washed away with watering or rain and the wasted fertilizer then pollutes groundwater supplies. Compost is the best option.

Controlling weeds A non-toxic by-product of corn processing, corn gluten kills weed seedlings within days of application. It also adds nitrogen to the soil, thus acting as a fertilizer.

Minimizing chemical pesticides Along with killing harmful pests, chemical pesticides also kill the soil organisms that contribute to a healthy lawn. Use neem-based natural pesticides instead for best results in Indian conditions.

Flowerbeds, Shrubbery, and Trees

It is always advisable to keep one type of flowering plant confined to one bed or one set of pots, arranged in an attractive pattern, and kept well-trimmed. Planting annually flowering varieties in beds and seasonals in pots that can be displayed only when in full bloom (and returned to the greenhouse when dormant) is a practical option. It saves manpower and the flowerbed remains in full bloom throughout the year.

Arrangement of flowerbeds The spacing of different flowering plants is of vital importance. A garden can be made more attractive if instead of treating all flowering plants equally, prominence is given to one variety—for instance, chrysanthemum or rose—with all other flowering plants chosen to add emphasis to these main plants. The intermingling of flowering plants at random, without any pattern to the arrangement, will mar the beauty of the garden.

In selecting larger trees for the garden, instead of the usual *Ashoka* and *gulmohur*, one can plant frangipani, *Nycanthes* (parijat), *Compaita guencensis, Michelia champaca*, and so on, all of which have fragrant blossoms. Another good option is *Lagerstroemia speciosa* (also known as 'pride of India'), whose purple flowers are a treat for the eyes. If creepers are preferred, jasmine and *Passiflora* are a sensible option.

Pathways Where the garden is fairly large, as in most hotel properties, care should be taken to provide pathways among the flowerbeds. These afford more visibility to the flowers as well as making the approach to the plants easier for visitors. Small shrubs with attractive flowers or leaves should be grown on either sides of the pathways so as to act as a border for both the flowerbeds and the pathways.

Groundcover An important consideration in some pathways are groundcover vegetation in the grout spaces between the paver flags or the stepping stones. Groundcover plant varieties that are mat-forming and robust enough to tolerate moderate foot traffic are ideal. Those that have dainty flowers or release fragrance on light abrasion add interest. Ideal groundcover plants include creeping Jenny, dwarf mondo grass, creeping phlox, soapwort, isotoma, pearlwort, stonecrop, baby's tears or pearl grass, Corsican mint, and wedelia or creeping daisy.

Selection and sowing of seeds Seeds that are older than one season can become inferior in quality and should not be used; check the date of packaging on the container. Seeds sold by a reputed supplier or nursery should be preferred, of course.

Never wash roughly or 'treat' the seeds unless instructed by the supplier. Sow seeds in a shallow trough or tray, lightly mixed with soil in such a way that some seeds are exposed and some buried. Dampen the soil when sowing; do not water until the next day, when a slight sprinkling of water should suffice. Water the soil fully only when the surface soil begins to lose its dampness; but do not let the soil dry up either.

When the seedlings have grown to nearly 1 inch, replant them in another trough, separating the seedlings into regular, spaced rows, with a gap of at least 2 inches between seedlings. Before attempting to uproot the seedlings, make sure that the soil is damp. While handling the seedlings, pull them by the leaf and not by the stem, since the tender stem can break beyond repair. In areas where there is a menace of locusts or birds, it is advisable to cover the seedlings with wire netting or other appropriate coverings that do not hinder light and air.

When the seedlings grow to about 4 inches in height, they can be replanted in garden beds or pots, singly or in twos.

Pots and containers Pots to grow plants in should be scientifically apt for the purpose. Ideally, they should be prepared as shown in Figure 31.1.

Three following layers should be laid down inside the pot:

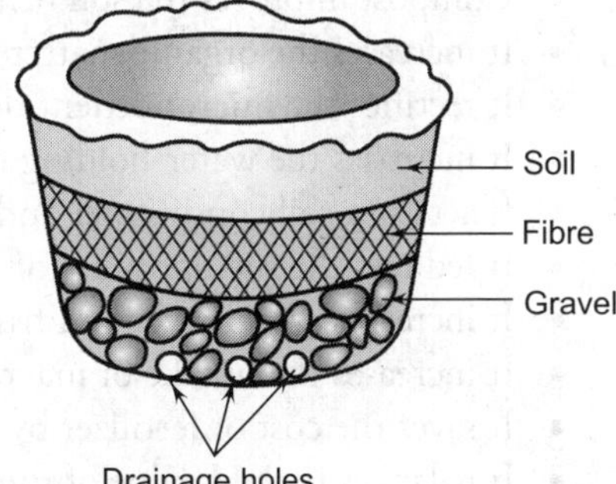

Fig. 31.1 Filling a pot

Gravel The lowest layer should be filled with gravel, consisting of largish stones. This is to avoid waterlogging. The gravel, in conjunction with the drainage hole, helps to remove excess water from the pot.

Fibrous layer Just above the gravel layer, there should be a layer of plant fibre, ideally coconut husk. The fibre layer stores a fair amount of water, but does not allow waterlogging. Its function is to act as a filter for the excess water in the soil above it.

Soil Above the fibrous layer comes the soil in which the sapling is planted. The soil should always be moist and loose. A sufficient amount of sand should be mixed into the soil layer. To this, an ample amount of manure should be added to get an ideal pot.

Selection of saplings While buying potted saplings, one should aim to buy those that are neither too small nor too big for their pots. Never buy a sapling that has roots growing out of the drainage hole in the pot—this means it has already outgrown its pot and the root ball is too dense. Also avoid any plant whose foliage is spilling over the rim of the pot.

When buying a sapling in a polythene bag, check the quality of the soil in it—it should not be too wet or too dry. Make sure that there is no fungus on the sapling or on the surface of the soil. There should not be any green 'film' on the soil surface either.

Buy saplings and plants from a reputed nursery. In case of any doubt, consult an experienced, reliable gardener or have him select the saplings.

Soil maintenance Any harm to the soil will affect the plants growing in it too. Therefore, soil maintenance is all-important in gardening.

The soil should not be too firm or too waterlogged. The desirable degree of sand in the soil often depends on the plants to be grown in it. Very tender plants like balsam need more sand content than, for example, the rose plant does.

Tilling of the soil is equally important. This provides adequate aeration, which is necessary for the roots of the plants to breathe. While tilling soil on which plants are already standing, utmost care should be taken so as not to harm the roots of the standing plants. To ensure this, first of all make sure to water the soil before tilling. Secondly, do not use a large spade or rake close to a standing plant.

Manuring Compost and cow dung make ideal manure for gardens. The urine of the cow is also ideal for plants. The natural urea contained in it acts as a fertilizer, without any of the ill-effects of artificially manufactured fertilizers. The use of chemical fertilizers should be discouraged. It has been proved that these fertilizers in the long run 'harden' the soil. Tea strainings, powdered goat dung, and powdered eggshells are good natural manure for most plants, especially rose and balsam.

Compost It is formed by the decomposition of organic matter by the action of a mixed population of microorganisms in a warm, moist, and aerobic environment over a period of time. The use of compost should be encouraged in preference to chemical fertilizers. The benefits of using compost are outlined in this section.

- Compost improves the soil texture and structure of both clayey and sandy soils.
- It increases the organic matter (humus) in the soil.
- It rectifies the micronutrient deficiency in the soil.
- It increases the water-holding capacity of the soil.
- It acts as a soil conditioner and maintains soil health.
- It reduces the susceptibility of topsoil to wind and water erosion.
- It increases crop flower and fruit yields.
- It increases the uptake of macro- and micro-nutrients by the plants.
- It saves the cost of fertilizer by more than 10%.
- It balances the pH value of the soil.
- It is eco-friendly.

Vermicompost Another eco-friendly option is the use of vermicompost. Vermicompost or vermicast is a natural organic manure composed of the excreta of earthworms fed on scientifically decomposed organic wastes such as the dung of cattle and other animals, coir pith, farm wastes, urban garbage such as paper and rags, and a variety of agro-industrial waste. It enriches the soil as well as promoting plant growth, and confers on the plants all the benefits of the more common garden compost.

Bio-fertilizers The use of bio-fertilizers is also beneficial to plants. These are distinct strains of microorganisms that enhance the productivity of the soil—whether by fixing atmospheric nitrogen, or by dissolving soil phosphorus so as to make it available to plants, or stimulating plant growth through the synthesis of growth-promoting substances. Bio-fertilizers have the ability to mobilize nutritionally important elements from non-usable forms into usable ones. Indian soils normally have a low population of nitrogen-fixing bacteria. Hence, the introduction of plant-specific and soil-specific microorganisms to overcome this limitation is recommended.

Pest control The pest menace is a serious problem for gardeners. Most people adopt the shortcut of using chemical insecticides in liquid or powder form. However, chemical insecticides are undesirable—they do destroy pests, but they also harm the plants and the garden in the long run. Moreover, since all insecticides are toxic, they pose a serious threat to human beings and animals coming into contact with the plants and flowers onto which they have been sprayed or applied. The more viable alternative is to use powdered neem oil-cake, tobacco lotion, powdered custard-apple seeds, and such other natural insecticides.

Most plant disorders result from infections in the soil. Keeping the soil healthy is the best preventive measure in keeping plants free from diseases. Before cultivation, take care to burn a good amount of dry leaves and twigs on the soil surface. This will destroy pests in the soil and renew the soil nutrients.

Watering Different plants need different quantities of water. Furthermore, the water requirements of a plant are not the same throughout its life. Here are some rules of thumb regarding the watering of plants:

Check the soil humidity If a slight pressure on the soil surface leaves a finger imprint on the soil and if the soil looks damp and dark, watering can be avoided for that day. On the other hand, if the soil surface crumbles at the touch and if the surface looks cracked and light-coloured, it shows that watering is needed.

Be consistent in watering Water deficiency, even if acute, cannot be made up in one day by over-watering. Too much water will only result in flooding and the washing away of manure and nutrients. Adequate and consistent watering for nearly a week is the only way to reliably restore plant health.

Water just enough, and not more The water requirement of a plant is indicated by its leaves. When a plant is over-watered, its roots begin to rot and the situation is indicated by the yellowing of the leaves. When a plant is under-watered, its leaves begin to crumble and dry up. Not all plants need daily watering. Plants such as cacti, for example, need only a sprinkling of water twice a week. If a cactus is placed in a humid spot such as a bathroom, watering may not be needed at all. In case of potted plants, care should be taken to sprinkle only as much water on the soil surface as will penetrate the soil in the pot to a halfway depth and not reach the bottom.

Water gently As regards the manner of watering, water should be sprinkled and never poured. Pouring water on the plant will create gorges in the soil, which will spoil the roots of the plant. A sprinkler should be used for watering plants. For larger gardens, mechanical tap sprinklers are available.

Water leaves in the evening When plants are watered in the morning, avoid spraying water on the leaves. Water droplets left on the leaf act as a convex lens in the sun and cause convergence of sunrays onto the leaf surface. As a result, the leaves become burnt and brittle. Spraying of leaves must be done only in the evening.

Sunshine Different plants require different degrees of sunshine as well. Most flowering plants need direct sunshine. Some leafy plants, however, can grow even in shade or indirect sunlight. Where direct and strong sunlight poses a threat to plants, adequate arrangements should be made to give them enough shade. Exposure to strong sunlight for a prolonged period may prove harmful to delicate plants.

Plant Nursery

Hotels with extensive lawns and gardens necessarily manage a small nursery too on their premises, typically in the outdoor area at the back of the house. It is essentially a place where saplings are grown before they are transplanted into the gardens. The nursery also houses the horticulture shed, compost area, and storage space for plants and saplings. The nursery should be maintained neat and clean; it is wise to have a thick hedge around it to keep it away from view.

Horticulture Equipment and Tools

A landscaped hotel garden is maintained with the help of machines and tools and the primary equipment are discussed in this section with depiction in Figure 31.2.

Wheelbarrow This equipment is used to collect and translocate heavy things, soil, trash, and other materials in garden areas.

Lawn mower This is an equipment with high-carbon steel disc-blades used for cutting grass and weeds in lawns; the grass box at the rear of the equipment collects the cut grass as the operator moves the machine ahead.

Garden plough/Tiller This equipment is designed to break and cut forward through the hard ground and loosen up the firm, rocky soil. Their action combines digging and mixing up of soil into a loose, nutrient- rich bed for cultivation.

Mechanical hedge trimmer This mechanical gardening machine, either electric or gasoline operated, assists in pruning and shaping solitary shrubs and hedges, keeping them neat.

Garden shovel This hand tool with a flat bottom edge and a long wooden shaft works best with already loosened soil. It is used for digging shallow trenches, planting and transplanting, stripping grass in small areas, and removing dirt and debris in the garden.

Garden trowel This hand-held gardening tool, available in different widths, either a wooden or rubber handle and stainless steel blades, are used for digging small holes for planting seeds and saplings, dig out weeds, and scooping up soil when potting plants.

Garden hoe Designed with a flat steel blade attached perpendicular to a long wooden shaft, a garden hoe is primarily meant for tilling, weeding, digging narrow furrows for planting and loosening soil around shallow-rooted plants.

Pitch fork This hand implement has a long shaft with three to four thin, sharp, widely spaced prongs or tines. Pitch fork is utilised in lifting and moving bunches of long, loose vegetation, grass, weeds, and hay. It also turns compost piles effectively.

Rake This hand tool has a long shaft and multi-pronged head. The length, shape, and number of prongs vary in different types of rakes meant for varied purposes such as scraping, breaking, loosening, and levelling soil or gathering materials such as fallen leaves, weeds, mulch, and soil.

Garden shears These are manual tools with long sharp metal blades used to trim hedges, shrubs, and small patches of tall decorative grasses.

Secateurs These are used for hand pruning of hard and thorny branches of shrubs, and cutting foliage and flowers with their stalks for floral arrangements and harvesting fruits and vegetables that have thicker stalks.

Fig. 31.2 Horticulture equipment and tools

Pruning saw A pruning saw is a hand tool used to cut large woody branches of 1½ to 5 inches diameter. It has sharp, foldable serrated blades, usually of stainless steel. A **tree pruner** is a curved pruning saw mounted on a telescopic pole for pruning the high branches on trees.

Hand cultivator This hand tool with a wooden handle and three-four bent stainless steel prongs helps to till, loosen and aerate the soil, and remove the weeds around plants in small patches of the garden.

Backpack sprayer A backpack tank-type pressure sprayer is very useful to a gardener in applying treatment solutions of fertilisers, insecticides, fungicides, and herbicides as a fine mist in lawns and gardens.

Watering can A galvanised metal or plastic container with an elongated sprinkler spout is used for watering indoor and outdoor plants with a gentle flow so as not to damage the leaves or displace the soil around the plants.

Watering hose A garden hose is available in internal pipe diameters of ½", ¾" or 1"and has an inner layer made of polyurethane and outer layer made of PVC to withstand abrasion and pressure. To connect the watering hose to a valve or faucet, snap-fit couplings or connectors are used. The length of the hose should be considered as per the reach required.

Lawn sprinkler A lawn sprinkler is a mechanism that consists of a sprinkler head working on a pressure system through which water is sprayed evenly to irrigate a lawn. Sprinklers should be placed strategically to distribute water evenly to the grass areas. Those with timer mechanism are convenient, or a rain guage to check moisture level may be used.

Landscaping

This entails the creation of an area where trees, plants, turf, decks, walks, ponds, and other features are used to create an outdoor space that is functional as well as visually appealing. See Figures 31.3 (a), (b), and (c) for some examples of landscaped areas. There are five considerations in planning a good landscape. The landscape should be: (1) functional, (2) maintainable, (3) environmentally sound, (4) cost-effective, and (5) visually pleasing.

A variety of features may be used to make landscapes attractive:

Living elements Flora and fauna including plants—both flowering and non-flowering—and trees; and animals like geese, fishes, and turtles

Natural elements Bodies of water including fountains, cascades, lagoons, and landforms

Built elements Fences, buildings, and statues

(a)

(b)

(c)

Fig. 31.3 Landscaped areas in various hotels: (a) trees, shrubs, and lawns; (b) a patio garden; and (c) perennial flowering plants in the landscape

Base Plan

Landscaping starts with a base plan, which is developed from the information collected about the site. Information is obtained from many sources and involves communicating with many people. The base planning process includes interviews; site surveys; site analysis; and the study of site plans and structural and utility blueprints. All this information is incorporated into one final drawing, called the base plan.

Landscape Design

Once the base plan is ready, the landscape designing sequence begins. There are four steps in the landscape designing sequence: (1) bubble diagrams, (2) concept plans, (3) draft designs, and (4) final landscape design.

Bubble diagrams

A bubble diagram defines the spaces that are identified on the base plan. Initially, the bubbles on it roughly correspond to what will eventually be a specific physical space in the landscape, but they are not specific and are without detail. A designer may sketch many bubble diagrams before the most suitable one is identified. Once a bubble diagram has been chosen, it will continue to be refined and the sizes and shapes of the bubbles will change. Spaces that need to be located on the bubble diagram include patios and decks, entryways and patio gardens, ponds and water features, lawns or turf, shrubbery and flower beds, container groupings, and so on. A sample bubble diagram is shown in Figure 31.4.

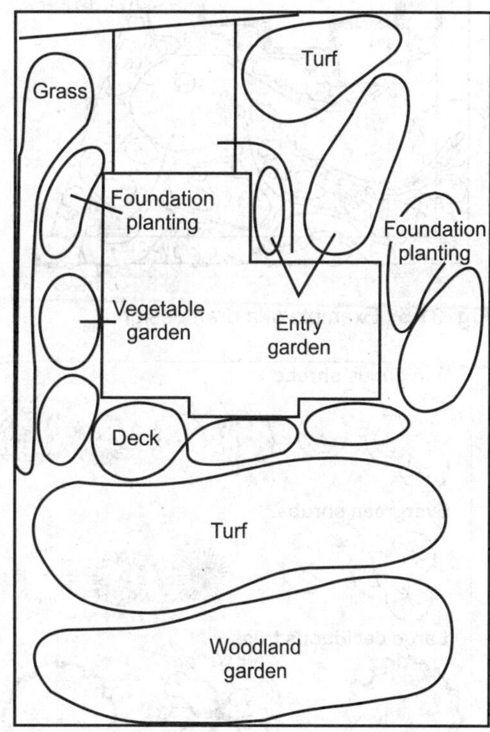

Fig. 31.4 Example of a bubble design

Concept plans

At this stage, where the bubbles each begin to take on a specific character, the process enters the concept-planning stage. Part of the process is a visualization exercise and part of it takes place on paper. Concept plans are more detailed than bubble diagrams; the shapes of the spaces now begin to look like what the actual spaces in the completed landscape will look like. While developing effective spaces in a concept plan, large spaces should be planned first. This ensures that these spaces will be well designed and make the designing of the corresponding smaller spaces easier. The larger spaces that should be considered first in a concept plan are ponds, woods, lawns, large areas of ground cover, and parking lots. Smaller spaces that are impacted by these larger spaces include decks and patios, walkways and paths, pools, plant beds and borders.

Draft designs

This stage continues to define in greater specificity what has been envisaged in the concept plan. The rough draft is reviewed and revised until the designer is satisfied with the results. The spaces created in the

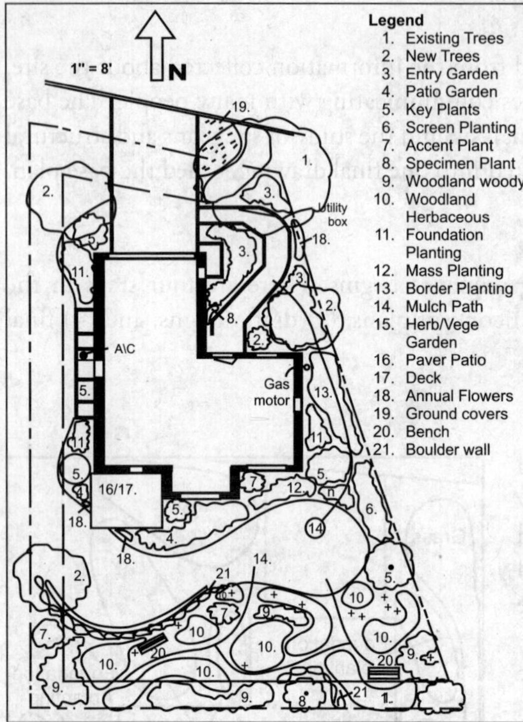

Fig. 31.5 Example of a draft design

concept plan now have specific forms and functions. It is important to assign specific spaces to the plants to be used in the draft design. The plant spaces are usually identified by a specific classification (tree, shrub, annual flowers, and so on) or by their function (screen planting, foundation plants, patio gardens, and similar). The location of these plant spaces on the draft design helps determine the types of plants or plant groupings. Plants with important functions and larger trees are usually located first on the draft design. A sample draft design is shown in Figure 31.5.

Final landscape design

In finalizing the completed landscape design, the designers use graphics and symbols rather than words. Different symbols are used to indicate different types of plants—evergreens, deciduous trees, groundcover, and so on. Hardscape materials such as brick and decking are also depicted graphically. Some of the most common symbols in use are illustrated in Figures 31.6 and 31.7.

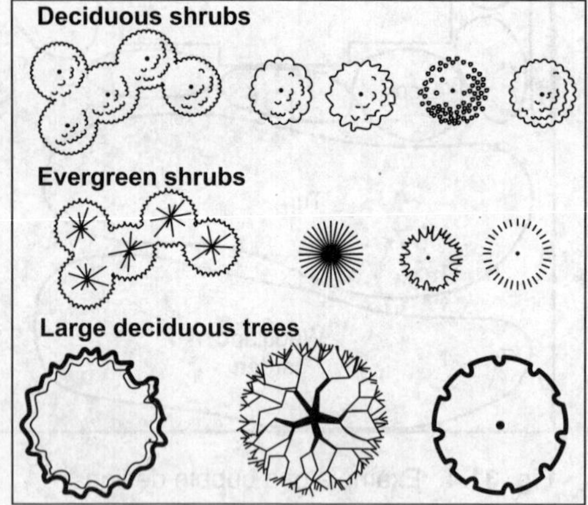

Fig. 31.6 Symbols used for shrubs and trees

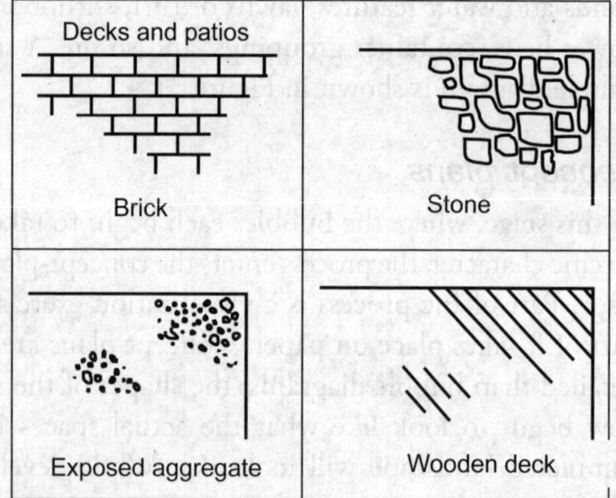

Fig. 31.7 Symbols used for hardscape materials

Garden Styles

Gardens and green spaces enliven the surroundings and enhance the aesthetics of a hospitality property. They lower both outdoor and indoor temperature and provide healthier air quality. Various properties have different types of gardens going with their theme and the primary types are discussed here.

Traditional formal gardens These gardens, often seen in luxury hotels, focus on the principles of symmetry and balance and feature formal elements with architectural themes such as manicured lawns, clipped hedges and neatly edged pathways. Symmetry is achieved by repetition of similar shaped plantings and hedges on either side of architectural features of the garden. There is dominance of geometrical shapes in designing. Another feature is the usage of classical sculpted pedestal urns as planters. Also common is the placement at focal points of the classic circular stone fountains. Emphasis on colours is absent, and coloured flowers and shrubs are few but balanced and symmetrically planted. There is predominance of green trees such as cypress and palms and hedge shrubs like boxwood and duranta along with the vast expanse of a grass lawn.

Contemporary gardens These gardens, usually a part of business hotels, are characterised by minimalism, non-symmetrical design, use of concrete and metal, focusing mainly on practical functionality rather than nature. The emphasis is on open hard-surfaced spaces meant for leisure. Clean, contemporary look is added with use of metal grids and sheeting and geometrically shaped concrete or resin stepping stones, architectural elements, planters and fountains. Structured trees such as Ashoka and palms and cacti with clean lines are suitable for these types of gardens.

Cottage gardens These gardens are common in front of cottages and villas in hotels, where the horizontal, informal garden spills over on pathways and small lawns creating softer edges. Easily maintained, colourful ornamental flowering plants, herbs, edible, and medicinal plants are common features here, mingling together to create an organised mess style. Additional elements include randomly scattered terracotta pots, paver stones with groundcover plants growing between them, white or wood brown picket or bamboo fences, lattice trellises, arbour gates, and walls with flowering creepers and climbers. Natural theme is emphasised with materials such as brick, weathered stones, grit and gravel and mulch.

Natural gardens Such garden styles are found surrounding homestay accommodations and reflect the natural landscape surrounding them. The choice of plantings depends entirely on the region and its native robust vegetation, which does not require much maintenance. There is no particular structure to the garden, which blends smoothly with its surrounding. Rustic materials are used to bring out the expression of naturalism.

Woodland gardens These gardens are dominated by huge trees with an expanse of canopy cover. Thus, the shrubs growing underneath need to be shade tolerant. The garden has a informal style more on the lines of a forest with a variety in vegetation textures and colours. Typically, mulch-covered or gravel walkways course through the garden to lead to rustic wrought iron benches. Ferns and climbing vines enhance the woodland ambience.

Courtyard gardens These gardens are typically found in hotel courtyards and open lounges. The challenge with these is the limited space and enclosing walled surfaces which makes for shaded areas, ideal for relaxation but a complication for choice of plantings. Often, plantings are taken vertically up the walls and use of tall planters and hanging containers are common.

Vertical gardens Vertical gardening is an alternative method of gardening for growing plants in a vertical space such as walls and roofs in urban areas where horizontal garden space is limited. Ideal plants for vertical gardens are slow growing, dense, low, and compact. Plants should also be chosen according to the facing aspect of the wall, whether sunny or in shade. Sunny walls will necessitate drought-tolerant plants and walls in shaded areas call for shade-loving plants. Common plants suitable for vertical gardening are syngonium, begonia, peperomia, philodendron, anthurium, asparagus, jade, sedum, sword ferns, lantana, chlorophytum, and fittonia. Vertical gardens may be designed in two different ways.

- *Green façade* In these systems, climbing plants or cascading groundcovers grown in the ground soil or elevated containers are trained to cover specially designed support structures. The ground or the containers are kept watered and fertilised. The green façade may be anchored to existing walls or created as a freestanding column or fence.
- *Living walls/Green walls* These systems consist of pre-vegetated, polypropylene or polystyrene vertical panels, modules or blankets fixed to a vertical wall structure or frame. These are higher maintenance systems than green façade. Living walls come in two forms – modular green walls and vegetated mat walls. In modular green walls, small, detachable, and durable, cup-like recycled polypropylene containers with plants are installed into frames with receptacles. On the other hand, vegetated mat walls are composed of two layers of synthetic fabric with pockets filled with nutrient media and plants. The mats are mounted on a frame against the building wall with a waterproof membrane in between. Water and nutrients are delivered through an irrigation system atop the wall.

Zen gardens These are a Japanese concept of uncluttered landscaped gardens meant to provide tranquillity and reflect a meditative outlook. They were originally created as spaces of self-reflection and to connect with one's inner self. They mainly consist of immaculately raked white gravel in concentric, wavy or straight lines, broken by strategically placed materials such as stones, rocks, clumps of moss a few shrubs pruned into discipline. Though white gravel and sand represent water in these gardens, sometimes water flowing under arched natural bridges too forms a part of the pristine landscape. When present, waterbodies have small water plants and koi fishes in them as flora and fauna respectively.

Rock garden/rockery These gardens are dominated by rocks, boulders and gravel with vegetation placed in small clusters amongst them to achieve a natural look. Alpines such as the flowering saxifrages or rockfoil and sedum or stonecrop species are highly suitable as they have very less water needs and the flowers look ornamental against rocky boulders.

Xeriscapes These are landscaped areas which are designed to eliminate or significantly reduce the need for water other than what the natural climate of the region provides. Xeriscape gardens are favoured in arid regions and feature drought-tolerant native vegetation or xerophytes such as cacti, agave, succulents, juniper, thyme, and sage. Trees such as the acacia, sapodilla, oleander and crown of thorns, poinsettia and pine are suitable for xeriscapes. Typically, xeriscapes feature rocks and pebbles to cover the soil surface in order to avoid evaporation of moisture from it. Xeriscapes are cost effective and environment-friendly and look unique when part of a hotel's landscaped area.

Aquatic gardens These are gardens dominated by waterbodies, usually ponds and springs that were already natural part of the landscape and extended with artificial ones such as water fountains, cascades and waterways. Aquatic plants, fishes and freshwater turtles are grown to maintain the water refreshed and clean of algal blooms. Suitable plants are hydrilla, water lily, lotus, pond taro, horsetail reed, water lettuce, and creeping Jenny.

Kitchen gardens Many hotels have kitchen gardens and encourage their guests to experience gardening and harvesting the produce from these. These gardens grow vegetables, fruits, and herbs. Herbs such as rosemary, sage, lavender, anise, mint, lemongrass, lemon balm, thyme, and basil not only lend visual appeal but fragrance to the surroundings too. Trays of microgreens of beetroot, red amaranth, radish, coriander, mustard, and many other edible plants grown in shade add interest to kitchen gardens.

Indoor Plants

In hotel properties, indoor plants are appreciated for their ability to add charm and liveliness to hotel guestrooms and public areas such as lobbies and corridors. They should be chosen with care, so that their colours, shapes, and size fit in with the décor of the space. For example, it would be a mistake to have a plant that climbs to a great height in a low-ceilinged room, or a very large, bushy plant in a small or narrow room. The temperature, the type of heating in the room, and the amount of light available there must also be taken into account. Whenever in doubt, one should not hesitate to take advice from an expert horticulturist, gardener, or nursery manager on matters such as the suitable types of plants for a space or any special treatment they may require.

Care of Indoor Plants

Most indoor plants require regular attention—watering, re-potting, cleaning, and in some cases feeding. In addition, indoor plants should generally be placed away from draughts as far as possible and never left near a window or doorway on cold nights without placing a layer of newspaper between the plant and the glass panes.

Watering The amount and frequency of watering depends on the kind of plant, the weather, the type of heating in the room, and so on. During winter, a week or even a fortnight may pass without the plant needing water; but it will need more during spring and summer. Always use water that is neither too chill nor too warm—preferably rainwater—and pour it into the soil, not onto the foliage. Too much water can be dangerous to many plants and it is a good idea to help drain the soil by putting a few stones at the bottom of the pot. On the other hand, the soil should never be allowed to become dry and powdery either.

Potting and re-potting It is best to consult experts and to refer to a reliable book on these important points. In general, use a light soil mix for potting plants—a good mixture is made of equal quantities of leaf mould and a peaty soil containing plenty of fibre with half the quantity of sharp sand.

If the roots form a close network within the soil and begin to come out of the pot, the plant probably needs re-potting in a larger container. This is best done in the spring, and good quality soil or potting compost should be used. Some plants, however, prefer a top dressing of rich soil to re-potting.

Cleaning Ferns, ivies, and other plants prized for their green foliage require regular cleaning, so that the pores do not become clogged with dust; it also reduces the risk of attack by insects. Spray or sponge the leaves with water and dry them afterwards. Large-leafed plants may be treated with a special plant insecticide, which also gives them a fine sheen.

Feeding A good propriety plant food is the best means of giving the necessary foods to plants.

Placement of Indoor Plants

Plants do not like to be moved, so decide on a satisfactory position and leave them there. Small plants look nice grouped together in a metal-lined jardinière, which can be placed near a window. For more exotic plants, a shelf in a warm place is ideal. Attractive and inexpensive jardinières are available in metal and cane. Many of these can be fixed to a wall or hung from the ceiling to show off the plants to their best advantage. Climbing plants can often be trained across a wall or up a frame made of cane and bamboo. An ordinary garden trellis can be used as a room-dividing screen, with plants trained up on it or hung from it in holders.

Popular indoor plants

Whenever one thinks of an indoor plant, a palm is what comes to mind first. Areca palms are widely used everywhere. However, this trend should be changed to avoid an impression of not enough thought having given to the greenery—even other plants from the palm family Arecaceae (*Raphis*, *Livistona* and Nalina) are preferable; better still, plants from the genera *Philodendron* (varieties such as Florida or Burle Marx's fantasy), *Schefflera* (green or variegated varieties), and *Brassia* may be used.

Some popular flowering and non-flowering indoor plants are discussed in this section.

Climbing plants Some common climbing plants are as follows.

Cissus antarctica 'grandidentata' and Cissus striata These are fast-growing plants with notched, oval leaves. They need a cool room, rich soil, and good light.

Philodendron Most species in this genus are well adapted to growing indoors. They have glossy, leathery leaves and aerial roots that can be trained up a wall or trellis. These plants prefer warmth, but will stand cool conditions; they like plenty of water.

Plumbago capensis This quick-growing plant has small, oval leaves and blue flowers. It does not tolerate temperatures below 7°C.

Rhoicissus rhomboidea (grape ivy) This tendril-climber with glossy leaves arranged in threes requires a fair amount of water and rich soil.

Trailing or spreading plants Let us now look at some trailing and spreading plants used in hotels.

Chlorophytum elatum 'variegatum' (spider plant) The rosettes of long, narrow, pale-green leaves striped with white or silver are very adaptable, and particularly good for a north-facing aspect.

Hedera (ivy) These trail very gracefully and can also be made to climb. The species *H. helix* is hardier than many others of this genus and is best for an unheated room—but all the ivies are very easy to manage.

Peperomia glabberima This plant has red stems and long, fleshy flowers with spikes; other varieties have trailing stems with small leaves. In a warm, moist atmosphere, they produce flowers, but also thrive in cooler conditions. Low-growing and bushy varieties of *Peperomia* are also available.

Tradescantia (silver queen and wandering Jew species) Excellent trailer and easily grown in baskets, this plant has pale green leaves with silver-white veins.

Low-growing plants Low growing plants are discussed here.

Begonia rex Its attractive foliage needs constant warmth, humidity, and frequent spraying, and grows best in country districts.

X Fatshedera lizei A hybrid of Japanese fatsia and Irish ivy, this plant with pointed leaves is hardy and easy to grow.

Maranta The attractively marked leaves of these plants need heat and moisture; but if kept in a constant temperature, can survive fairly cool conditions.

Tolmiea menziesii (piggyback plant) This plant has pale green, heart-shaped leaves. Given some shade and plenty of water, it is very easy to grow.

India-rubber plants These popular indoor plants have become a part of the contemporary interiors owing to their statuesque appearance and undemanding habit of growth.

Ficus elastica This typically has shiny oval leaves; the *F. elastica 'decora'* has larger leaves with red undersides. Other plants in the genus are *F. elastica 'variegata'*, with yellow markings, and *F. chauvieri*,

which has wavy-edged leaves with yellow veins. They prefer warmth, but will bear cool conditions. They need plenty of water in spring and summer but very little in winter.

Cacti and other succulents These can be grown successfully without constant warmth, but they do need as much sun as possible, so keep them in a south-facing window. They like dry air and a minimum of watering.

Greenhouse and florists' plants Lovely as these are, these hothouse types are not easy to manage. Their period of flowering is usually fairly short and, failing a greenhouse, they cannot be easily made to flower again. Their short lives can, however, be prolonged by proper care.

Azalea Keep the root ball moist by standing the pot in a bowl of water. Stand it in an evenly warm temperature, out of draughts. On no account give it water containing lime.

Begonia Water frequently and spray.

Cineraria Water frequently. It will stand fairly cool temperatures.

Cyclamen Best bought in early autumn. Avoid wetting the tuber when watering. To revive a flagging plant, stand the pot on a block of wood in a large bowl and pour boiling water round the block; the steam will revive the plant, which can then be watered thoroughly. Pull out any decayed leaves and flower stalks by their sockets.

Hydrangea This set of plants need plenty of water and overhead spraying; but they like dry air, yet hate draughts.

Primula These comparatively long-flowering plants may survive from year to year if kept at a cool temperature; watered frequently but drained well; and, if necessary, transferred to a large pot.

Pests and diseases

Some insects are so small that their presence is not noticed until the plant shows signs of ill health. Suspicious symptoms are: mottling or yellowing of leaves; a fine white network like a cobweb; or mildew which produces a whitish powder on the leaves.

Professional Maintenance of Indoor Plants

The executive housekeeper must ensure that the following factors are kept in mind for the professional maintenance of indoor plants:

Arrangement Plants and flowers should be arranged according to the original plan, which should include a detailed description of which plants go where. The light and heat requirements of the plants should be considered at the initial stage. Foliage textures should be specified and each plant should have the structure, shape, appearance, size, and edging that had been specified.

Correct Height Selection of plants of the correct height is important. In case of groupings, the shorter plants should be in front. If the grouping can be seen from all sides, it must be well balanced throughout and built up at the centre. Keep the scale of the surroundings in mind when choosing the plant heights—a three-foot plant is good for a position next to a desk, but a plant of at least six-feet height must be chosen if it is meant to be viewed from the point of entry into a room or restaurant across the room.

Containers Plant containers must be appropriately selected to blend with the overall design of the area. While choosing containers for different areas, the light, temperature, humidity, and desired soil condition must be considered. Large containers, with big plants inside, must be top-dressed with moss or grass covering so as to avoid soil exposure.

Watering schedules Separate schedules for watering in winter and summer are required to keep plants in good condition. Contrary to popular belief, even the watering of plants requires specific skills and knowledge. Choose a can with a long, thin spout so that the water can be directed onto the soil without splashing the plant itself.

Misting and spraying Misting is beneficial for a lot of plants. A small hand-held spray bottle with nozzle should be good enough to do the job of keeping them healthy.

Reconditioning schedules Feeding is important to all plants. For this, they need to be taken back to the greenhouse and exchanged with another set of plants. After each set of plants has been indoors for around two weeks, it needs to be taken to the greenhouse and reconditioned to keep it healthy and growing.

Trimming and dead-heading The regular grooming of plants is very important in a hospitality property. All dead flowers and leaves need to be removed regularly.

Treating An occasional light spray of eco-friendly pesticides will keep plants safe from pests.

Bonsai in Hotel Properties

The use of bonsais to beautify hotel interiors is an innovative trend—these may now be found adorning lobbies and restaurants in many hotels.

Bonsai is a horticultural art that is believed by some authorities to have originated in China, from where Buddhist monks spread this art to Korea and then to Japan. But another school of thought says that it originated in Japan. Though potted plants were grown in China as early as 1000 BC, the art of true bonsai-making started only around 600 BC. The ancient proponents of this art believed that the miniaturization and training into auspicious shapes of trees and plants conferred certain divine powers on them. This may be due to the influence of the Zen religion.

Bonsai literally means 'a plant in a tray'. It is a creative art where the raw material is a living thing—a tree or a plant. The art of bonsai differs from the simple growing of potted plants in many aspects. In the bonsai school, the shape and properties of a full-grown tree or a plant, as found in nature, are sought to be copied exactly in miniature. Simple container gardening does not need such exactness—plants are left to grow naturally to the extent they will within the restrictions of the pot and the question of miniaturization does not arise.

Elements of Bonsai

The three elements that make a good bonsai form are the pot, the soil, and the plant. These should be in the proper proportion and should complement each other.

The pot Pots for holding bonsai should be chosen carefully. Both ceramic and terracotta pots are available. In Japan and China, ceramic pots are used for bonsai-making. These pots come in various shapes—round, oval, square, triangular, hexagonal, and so on. The pot selected should suit the tree that is to be made into a bonsai. If the tree is tall and slender, the length of the pot should be two-third or three-fourth the height of the tree. If the tree is short, with low, spreading branches, then the pot should be three quarters of the width of the tree. Upright and gently slanting trees are often placed in a rectangular or oval pot. Thick-trunked trees and those with dark foliage look best in heavy pots, whereas slender-framed trees look better in delicate pots.

The soil The ideal potting mixture for bonsai is river sand, red soil, and compost in the proportion 2:1:4.

The tree/plant This is the most important element in bonsai-making. Any tree or shrub can be made into a bonsai, but those with small leaves look better as bonsai. Even succulents can be made into bonsai. For example, members of the *Adenium* genus can be made into bonsai within a very short time and their crooked, tangled trunks and beautiful flowers give an added attraction to these plants. Plants of the Ficus genus also give early results. *Ficus benjamina*, *Ficus bengalensis*, and *Ficus nuda* from this family are some of the popular species for bonsai. Junipers make excellent bonsai, with their beautiful foliage. Fruit-bearing and flowering plants are also good for bonsai-making. Tamarind and cherry, when converted into bonsai, can be a feast for the eye.

Converting a Tree into a Bonsai

With some aesthetic sense, patience, and a pinch of common sense, anybody can make a bonsai of any tree that is common in that geographical region. The aesthetics of scale call for relatively short leaves on trees that shed leaves annually and short needles on conifers. In addition, trees with small flowers and fruits are favoured. Open spaces between the branches and between masses of foliage are also aesthetically necessary.

Under certain conditions, trees growing in the wild may be stunted by nature. Such trees can be transplanted into bonsai containers and then pruned and cut into attractive shapes.

Another method is *air-layering*. This gives excellent results. Other methods are those of making bonsai include cutting or by planting; but this takes a long time.

Care of Bonsai

Once the tree has been planted in the container, it needs constant attention. Watering is very important—even for succulents, which generally need less water. The pot being shallow, ideally watering should be done three times a day during summer; otherwise reverse osmosis will take place and the plant will perish. Some people think that starving the plant will give good results; but nothing can be more incorrect, as the plant will die of starvation. As far as possible, chemical fertilizers should be avoided. Dried and powdered cow dung, bone meal, and neem cake are ideal food for bonsai.

For a fruit-bearing or a flowering bonsai, an NPK mixture—1 spoonful in 1 litre of water—sprayed once in a month gives good results.

When the bonsai becomes pot-bound—that is, the pot is filled with excess roots—the plant should be re-potted after pruning the excess roots. The pot should be filled with a new potting mixture, surrounded by a layer of sand so that the new roots can grow easily. It is a sign that the bonsai has become pot-bound when the leaves turn yellow, the plant looks unhealthy, and new roots are not coming up.

Re-potting can be done once or twice a year. The first re-potting can be in June–July and the next in January–February.

Wiring for Shape

The bonsai can be shaped according to one's own imagination. For this, anodized-aluminium wires or copper wires can be used. Wiring helps the tree to look naturally 'weathered', though it needs much time and patience.

Styles of Bonsai

Bonsai can be arranged in different styles. Some of the popular styles are listed here. The corresponding illustrations are presented in Figures 31.8(a) to 31.8(g).

(a)

(b)

(c)

(d)

(e)

(f)

(g)

Fig. 31.8 Styles of bonsai: (a) informal upright style; (b) windswept style; (c) roots-over-rock style; (d) cascade style; (e) multiple-trunk style; (f) forest style; (g) broom style

Informal upright style In this style, a single tree grows straight up.

Windswept style In this style, the bonsai appears like a tree that grows near the coastline and has been constantly battered by the wind.

Root-over-rock style Trees growing over rocks, exposing some of their root structure, are always fascinating. Members of the *Ficus* genus are more suited to this style of arrangement.

Exposed-root style Here, the roots can be seen above the pot rim. *Adenium*, though a succulent, is best suited to this style.

Clump style Here, the roots of the trees look clumped together. Plants of the *Nandina* genus look better in this style.

Cascade style In this style, tall pots are used so that the branches are hanging down below the rim.

Multiple-trunk style This can be created in a number of ways. For instance, it may be achieved by cutting a deciduous tree almost down to the ground and letting it spring up again and again (each time it will tend to put out a fresh shoot).

Forest style Here, six or seven trees are planted together in the pot and the arrangement gives the look of a forest. *Chamaecyparis pisifera* can be used very effectively for this arrangement.

Broom style This style looks like a broom when the plant is denuded of all its leaves in winter.

There are many other styles and with some aesthetic sense, one can experiment with creating new styles, as there are no hard and fast rules.

Hydroponics and Aquaponics in Hotel Properties

Hydroponics is a new age agricultural system where crop plants are grown in nutrient-rich medium instead of soil. Many hotels around the globe now feature in-house hydroponics farms to supply fresh produce to the table, grow exotic produce and provide farming experience to their customers who are exponents of eco-friendliness and add to their sustainability quotient. These farms can be installed in hotel basements or their shaded rooftops. When hotels are able to grow their own food ingredients, chefs are able to use them fresh and also lower their food costs.

In aquaponics system, the plants are grown without soil too, but the difference is that fishes too are cultured in the aquatic medium, creating a symbiotic environment. The excreted waste of fishes are converted by microbes to rich, organic nutrients which are taken up by the plants. The plants in turn filter and purify the water naturally for the fishes and microbes in the aquatic system.

Working of Hydroponics System

A natural plant draws essential nutrients and water from the soil, and manufactures its own food through chlorophyll in presence of sunlight. When plants are hydroponically grown, these essential components are supplemented by nutrient-charged aqueous solution supplied directly to the plant roots and augmented lighting. The brightness of supplemental lighting is controlled to mimic natural cycles of day and night. The plants are either suspended in the aqueous nutrient-rich solution or anchored in soil-free medium composed of perlite, coco peat and vermiculite, or their combinations. The roots in such cases receive their nutrients through an active or passive system. In the active system, pumps are used to circulate and aerate nutrient solutions to the roots. In the passive system, nutrient solutions are fed to the root zone through gravity or capillary action.

Advantages and Disadvantages of Hydroponics System

The advantages rendered through application of hydroponics are:

- Nutrient efficiency
- Drastic reduction – up to 80–90%, in irrigation water
- Doubled growth rate and yield of plants
- Extended growing season
- Soilless operations
- Minimal pesticide usage
- No problem of weeds
- Optimum space utilisation due to higher plant density
- Convenient harvesting from counters, tables and benches

Despite the numerous advantages, it is vital to consider the disadvantages too.

- Expensive installation
- Need of constant monitoring and maintenance
- Affected adversely with power outages
- Susceptible to waterborne infections

Common Plants Grown with Hydroponics System in Hotels

Plants that grow well hydroponically are those that do not have tall growth, deep taproots, and vining tendency. Thus, plants such as strawberries, lettuce, greens, herbs, tomatoes, and peppers grow very well in hydroponics.

 Terrariums in Hotel Properties

Terrariums are increasingly becoming a regular feature in hotel lobbies, lounges and restrooms. A terrarium may be defined as an open or enclosed transparent container, usually a glass or acrylic vessel that contains growing medium and plants in its interior, creating a miniature ecosystem.

Advantages of Creating Terrariums

Creating terrariums makes for easy indoor gardening of tropical plants. It is an effective way of bringing in nature and express it in different themes, without it occupying too much space. When created scientifically, terrariums are low maintenance and need very less water. Terrariums offer health benefits to people by increasing relative humidity of a space due to transpiration and purify air due to phytoremediation. They also serve as a hobby for healing. With a wide variety of themes to create, they enhance creativity. A terrarium acts as a comprehensive tool to learn natural processes hands on.

Working Principle of Terrariums

Terrariums work as miniature greenhouses as depicted in Figure 31.9. The plants in the terrarium take up moisture from the soil, transpire and release water vapour. The water vapour condenses on the walls of the terrarium and trickles down back to the soil, thus, effectively establishing a water cycle. Plants also give out oxygen and absorb carbon dioxide during their metabolic processes in the terrarium. The microbes in the soil release carbon dioxide. Terrariums are self-nourishing ecosystems and support slow growing plants.

Types of Terrariums

Terrariums may primarily be of two types, sealed or open.

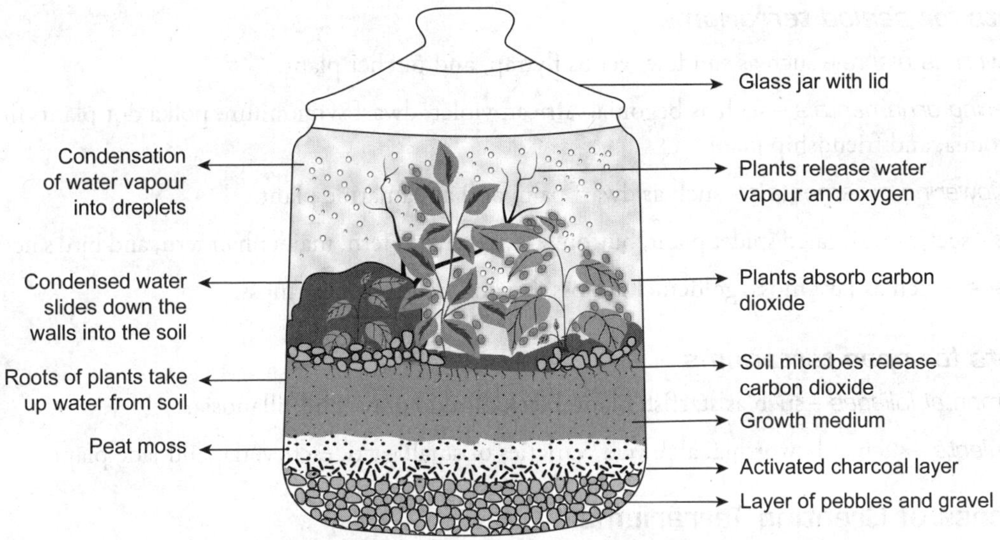

Fig. 31.9 Working principle of a terrarium

Sealed terrariums These terrariums have a removable lid and are self-sufficient miniature landscapes with their own water and nutrient cycles.

Open terrariums These are uncovered terrariums, open on one end and feature artistic mini-landscapes of plants that do not require much humidity. The main feature of open terrariums is that they are not self-sufficient in their watering needs.

Materials Required to Create Terrariums

To build a terrarium from scratch and maintain it, the following materials are required:

- A glass container (with a lid in case of sealed terrarium)
- Pebbles, rocks and gravel (to act as a drainage layer for excess water)
- Activated charcoal (to retard growth of mould and mildew, cleanse the water and deodourise the terrarium)
- Peat moss (to acts as a water reservoir bed between the growing medium and gravel)
- Growing medium (such as combinations of perlite, vermiculite, red soil, and coco peat)
- Suitable plants
- Spatula (to work the contents into layers and make small holes for planting)
- Long tweezers (to insert plants)
- Syringe (to water the plants in small, measured amounts)
- Small quantity of water

Plants Suitable for Terrariums

Ideal plants for terrariums are foliage plants that grow slow, mainly dwarf varieties. It is wise to combine in one terrarium plant varieties that have similar requirements of moisture and light. As a general rule of thumb, tropical plans flourish in sealed terrariums, whereas succulents thrive in open terrariums.

Plants for sealed terrariums

Carnivorous plants – such as sundew, Venus flytrap, and pitcher plant.

Flowering ornamentals – such as begonia, African violet, dwarf syngonium, polka dot plant, fittonia, peperomia, and friendship plant.

Non-flowering ornamentals – such as dwarf palm and aquamarine plant.

Ferns – such as variegated spider plant, button fern, asparagus fern, maidenhair fern, and bird's nest fern.

Mosses – such as Java moss, golden clubmoss, bryophyte moss, peat moss.

Plants for open terrariums

Ornamental foliages – such as starfish plant, black mondo grass, and tillandsia.

Succulents – such as haworthia, aloe vera, varieties of small cacti, escheveria, and jade plant.

Process of Creating Terrariums

The process of creating a terrarium is scientific, with each step to be followed stringently as it has scientific bearing. The process is outlined in Figure 31.10.

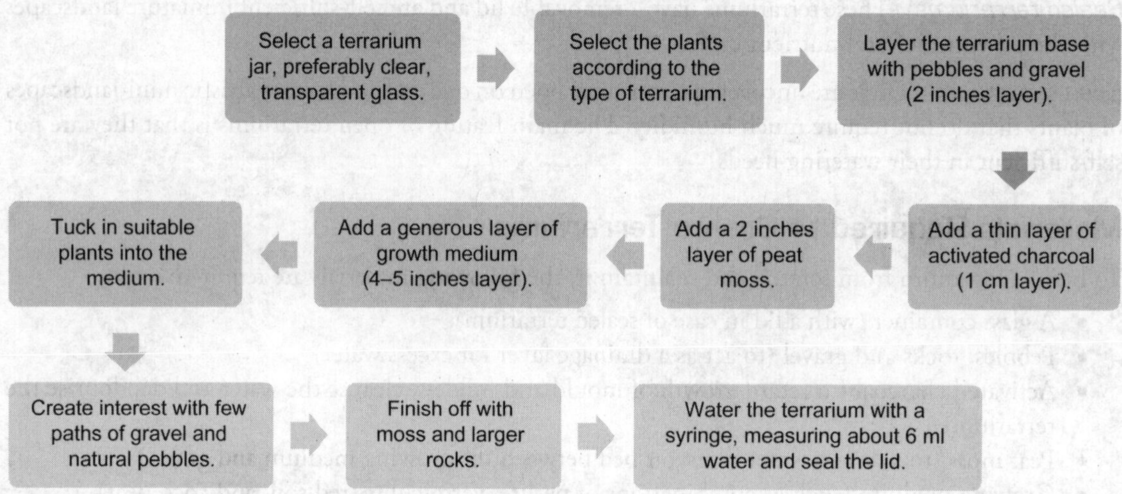

Fig. 31.10 Process of creating a terrarium

Care of Terrariums

Terrariums can be maintained healthy for years when well cared for. A terrarium should be watered once a month with very small amount of non-chlorinated water with a syringe as excess water is detrimental to the terrarium ecosystem. A balanced terrarium shows some amount of condensation on walls. Check the terrarium frequently for appearance of large water droplets condensation on terrarium walls as these need to be wiped away. The external glass walls of terrariums need to be cleaned regularly to allow maximum light penetration. Place it indoors near indirect sunlight. Remove the lid of a sealed terrarium once a week for an hour to refresh the interior air. Trim away dried and yellowed plant parts. Replace dead plants immediately.

Artificial Plants

Artificial plants are non-living replicas of real plants and are typically made from plastics now days. Materials such as paper, cotton, silk, rayon and polyester too are widely used. Ornamental parts like berries and seeds are moulded from plastic and painted with colours to simulate the real plant constituents. Adhesive and wires are used to bind artificial plants and flowers together.

Advantages of using Artificial Plants

The main benefits of artificial plants for hotels, hospitals, office buildings, and other busy public spaces are,

- they do not require watering at all.
- they don't need to be kept in sunlight to survive, enabling their placement more creatively at venues.
- their maintenance is easier and less time consuming than that required for natural ones.

Disadvantages of using Artificial Plants

The significant drawbacks in use of artificial plants are,

- because of the synthetic materials used, they tend to attract dust and dirt due to static.
- they have no role in cleaning the air of the surroundings.
- they may appear cheap imitations to guests and thus affect brand image negatively.
- manufactured mainly from synthetic plastics, they are non-biodegradable and a jarring note in the sustainability concept.

Care of Artificial Plants

- Routine cleaning of artificial plants should be done once a week and involves light dusting with a soft-bristled paintbrush. Begin at the top of the plant, and work downwards to ensure no debris falls onto clean areas of the plant.
- For removal of ingrained dirt and marks, artificial plants should be wiped down with a wet cloth dampened with warm water. Use of chemical cleaning solutions is to be avoided as this could cause the plant's colours to run, especially if it is made from delicate material like silk.
- For artificial plants made of silk, it is essential to test a small hidden area of the plant first.
- After wet cleaning, dry the plant gently to avoid breakage.

SUMMARY

In recent times, horticulture has become an important trend as more and more hospitality establishments have begun utilizing the beauty of nature extensively to enhance the aesthetics of their properties. Due to the only recent popularity of this trend, we come across many self-made horticulturists who may not have thorough knowledge and experience in the field. They try to earn a quick buck by selling hotels some expensive plants that may not suit the needs of the individual properties. Rather, gardens and landscapes need to be planned carefully and though most five-star hotels have either a full-time horticulturist or one on contract, the executive housekeeper should be in a position to recommend ideas, advise, and understand the horticulturist and gardeners. After all, horticulture does come under the purview of the housekeeping department.

The science of growing plants has been briefly dealt with under this chapter. The chapter began with a

discussion of the importance of horticulture. Essential components of horticulture—such as hedges, spacing of plants, pathways, groundcover, selection of seeds and saplings, soil maintenance, manure, pest control, potting, watering, and sunshine—have been discussed in detail. A lot of stress has been laid on eco-friendly options in the use of manure. The landscaping of hotel grounds has been dealt with in brief. There are a number of illustrations in this section so that the reader can easily comprehend certain technical terms used. The all-important topic of indoor plants has been presented as a separate section, with examples and pictures. Another section has been devoted to the art of bonsai, as it is the latest rage in beautification of hotel lobbies and restaurants.

The new age trends of growing crops through hydroponics and maintaining an indoor garden and terrariums have been discussed at length in the next section. The chapter ends with notes on usage of artificial plants, its advantages, disadvantages and care.

KEY TERMS

Activated charcoal refers to charcoal chunks or powder that have been heated or otherwise treated to increase their adsorptive power.

Aquaponics In aquaponics system, the plants are grown without soil in aquatic medium and fishes too are cultured in the same, creating a symbiotic environment.

Bio-fertilizers These are certain strains of microorganisms that enhance the productivity of the soil, whether by fixing atmospheric nitrogen or by dissolving soil phosphorus, or by stimulating plant growth through the synthesis of growth-promoting substances.

Bonsai Literally meaning 'a plant in a tray', this refers to a tree or a plant whose typical growth in nature has been copied exactly in a miniature style within the confines of a container.

Coco peat A light-weight growing medium for plants derived from the non-fibrous, spongy pith that holds together coir fibres in coconut husk.

Compost Manure formed by the decomposition of organic matter by a mixed population of microorganisms in a warm, moist, and aerobic environment over a period of time.

Deciduous Trees and shrubs that shed their leaves periodically.

Deck An exterior platform of wooden planks or wood-covered iron frames adjoining an interior living area. It may be used as a sit-out or a space for sunbathing. The term is also used interchangeably with 'patio'.

Evergreens Trees and shrubs that keep their leaves all the year round.

Groundcover Grass or low-growing plants spread over a large area to 'carpet' the ground.

Hardscape The non-living structures and materials incorporated in a planned landscape.

Horticulture The science of growing plants or of gardening.

Hydroponics A new age agricultural system where crop plants are grown in nutrient-rich medium instead of soil.

Landscaped area An area where trees, plants, turf, decks, walks, ponds, and so on have been used to create a natural-looking outdoor space that is functional and visually appealing.

Manure Any substance, natural or artificial, to be spread over or mixed with soil to fertilize it.

Patio An exterior, paved, usually roofless area adjoining interior living areas. The term is also used interchangeably with 'deck'.

Peat moss Dead fibrous material formed in peat bogs due to decomposition of mosses and other vegetation. It is used as soil amendment and growing medium for seeds.

Perennials Plants that flower throughout the year.

Perlite An amorphous, porous, and lightweight mineral in the form of minute white rocks, derived from volcanic glass and used as a hydroponic substrate and to improve soil drainage and aeration.

Succulents Plants that have thick, fleshy stems and leaves due to their high water content.

Terrarium An open or enclosed transparent container, usually a glass or acrylic vessel that contains growing medium and plants in its interior, creating a miniature ecosystem.

Trellis Metal grilles or cane or bamboo frameworks used in the garden to train climbers or to hang pots from.

Turf Grass together with the surface layer of soil held together by their roots.

Vermicompost/vermicasts A natural organic manure consisting of the excreta of earthworms fed on decomposed organic wastes such as the dung of cattle and other animals, coir pith, farm wastes, urban garbage such as paper and rags, and various agro-industrial wastes.

Vermiculite Naturally occurring mineral flakes of hydrated magnesium iron aluminum silicate added to growing mediums for better aeration, and moisture and nutrient retention. Also acts as a soil improvement agent.

Vertical gardens Gardens featuring plants growing in a vertical space such as walls and roofs in urban areas where horizontal garden space is limited.

Xeriscapes Landscaped areas designed to eliminate or significantly reduce the need for water other than what the natural climate of the region provides.

Sustainability Concepts in Hospitality Properties

Learning Objectives

After reading this chapter, you should be able to

- define the concept of sustainability in hotels
- get insights into certification of eco-sensitive/green hotels
- discuss the points of consideration in choosing a site, building specifications, and construction parameters for an eco-sensitive hotel
- explain the importance and methods of energy and water conservation
- explain the importance of waste management and various methods of managing waste
- understand the benefits of using environment-friendly guest supplies and stationery

Introduction

Hotels, those existing and the new entrants, have made efforts to imbibe the concept of environment sensitivity in their day to day operations. Sustainability in hotel operations is achieved when a hospitality venture is able to balance financial, social and environmental factors to facilitate responsible business decision making. The United Nations Commission on Sustainable Development defines the concept of sustainability as 'the development that meets the needs of the present without compromising the ability of future generations to meet their own needs.' Prominent hotel chains have initiated efforts to align their initiatives with the UN Sustainability Development Goals (UNSDG) 2030.

Unlike most hospitality products, sustainability is difficult to quantify. Many hotels blindly implement hearsay knowledge about eco-friendly practices and end up spending surplus rather than saving on capital. The need of the hour is to strike a balance between eco-sensitivity and luxury. For a hotel to be truly eco-sensitive, each and every managerial staff should have in-depth knowledge about how to go about making their department eco-friendly. Above all, it is imperative that the stakeholders at the hotel have a serious commitment towards turning eco-sensitive.

Tourism and hospitality consumers are increasingly seeking sustainable destinations. According to the findings of a survey of 29,000 travellers across 30 countries in 'The Sustainable Travel Report 2021' by Bookings.com, 81% global travellers intended to stay in a sustainable accommodation at least once in the upcoming year. For today's intelligent, pro-environment guests to be convinced that the hotel they are staying in, truly cares for the environment, each and every staff of the hotel needs to be an ambassador of the green initiatives of the hotel.

Advantages of Adopting Sustainability Concepts for Hotels

- Leads to optimum utilization of resources such as energy, water and so on.
- Promotes resource conservation.
- Steers hotels towards harnessing renewable energy sources.
- Significantly reduces operations and maintenance costs.
- Ensures minimisation and effective management of wastes.
- Applying green design in buildings creates a safe, healthy environment and enhances comfort and productivity for its occupants - staff and guests.
- Enhances the hotel's brand image, becomes a USP and draws appreciation and loyalty from environmentally-concerned guests.
- Assists hotels in delivering sound corporate social responsibility.
- Encourages acceptance of the hospitality business by the local community of the area and builds their trust.
- Enables the hospitality property to adhere to regulatory compliances.
- Results in hotels' carbon footprints becoming potentially carbon neutral and achieving net zero emissions.
- Makes the hotel eligible for government incentives, where such schemes exist.
- Reduces overall negative impact on environment.

Eco-sensitive/Green Hotels

Eco-sensitive hotels, also called 'green hotels', are earth-friendly hotels that feature implementation of environmental policies and standards, innovative and imaginative programmes for conserving natural resources, reducing waste, minimizing pollution, and maximizing sustainability.

Many of these properties are designed and constructed with a concern for environmental quality. Most of them consist of recycled or renovated buildings with upgrades to conserve energy and water, minimize waste and green house gas emissions, incorporate natural landscaping, or utilize recovered building materials. Other properties support local environmental efforts or groups and/or offer environmental education or excursions.

Certification of Eco-sensitive Properties

Awareness about sustainability and environment concerns is leading to many hotel properties going in for green certification. India is home to the largest hotel achieving the LEED Platinum rating globally – the ITC Grand Chola, Chennai. ITC Hotels also have the distinction of being the hotel chain with maximum LEED Platinum certified properties in the world. India also has the first Ecotel in Asia – The Orchid, Mumbai. This section discusses briefly, the various green certifications hotels may apply for.

LEED Certification

LEED or Leadership in Energy and Environmental Design certification is a globally recognised green rating and certification programme devised by the US Green Building Council. In India, the LEED certification is driven by Green Business Certification Inc. (GBCI), India. It takes up rating of both existing and new projects by awarding points for compliance on specific parameters in six categories - sustainable sites, water efficiency, energy and atmosphere, materials and resources, indoor environmental quality, and innovation in design. The certification is awarded up to 110 points in the following four levels based on the points earned,

40 – 49 points: LEED Certified
50 – 59 points: LEED Silver Certification
60 – 70 points: LEED Gold Certification
80 + points: LEED Platinum Certification

Ecotel Certification

Ecotel certification is based on five separate inspections, each with a three-tiered numerical scoring system carried out by HVS International (Hospitality Valuation Services International). The five inspections correspond with the five globe awards for the five cornerstones of environmental responsibility - energy efficiency, water conservation, solid waste management, environmental commitment, employee education, and community development.

Within each globe inspection there are three levels of criteria and scoring: primary, secondary, and tertiary scores. Hotels that achieve the globes qualify as Ecotel certified hotels for a period of two years and must agree to re-inspections at any time during that period.

GRIHA Certification

Green Rating for Integrated Habitat Assessment (GRIHA) system is the national rating system adopted by India for green buildings. It was developed by The Energy and Resources Institute (TERI) and endorsed by The Ministry of New and Renewable Energy. GRIHA system encourages buildings to adopt a 5 'R' philosophy of sustainable development.

i. *Refuse* to blindly adopt international trends, materials, technologies, products, and so on, especially where local substitutes or equivalents are available.
ii. *Reduce* dependence on high energy products, systems and processes
iii. *Reuse* materials, products, traditional technologies, so as to reduce the cost incurred in designing buildings as well as in operating them
iv. *Recycle* all possible waste generated from the building site during construction, operation, and demolition
v. *Reinvent* engineering systems, designs, and practices

In its rating systems, GRIHA assesses a building on 34 criteria and awards points on a scale of 100. It also quantifies energy/power consumption, water consumption, waste generation, and renewable energy integration. GRIHA certification is awarded as follows based on scores attained by the buildings.

50 – 60 points: 1 star GRIHA rated building
61 – 70 points: 2 star GRIHA rated building
71 – 80 points: 3 star GRIHA rated building
81 – 90 points: 4 star GRIHA rated building
91 – 100 points: 5 star GRIHA rated building

IGBC Green Resorts Certification

The Indian Green Building Council (IGBC) launched the IGBC Green Resorts rating system to address the pertinent need to address sustainable development in the hospitality sector. The rating programme awards credits on five criteria - guest experience, resort design and infrastructure, sustainable landscape, resort facility management, societal contribution, and innovation and development. The certification levels awarded based on total credits earned are,

40 – 49 credits: Certified for best practices
50 – 59 credits: Silver certification for outstanding performance
60 – 74 credits: Gold certification for national excellence
75 – 100 credits: Platinum certification for global leadership

ISO 14001:2015 Certification

This certification enables hotels to get guidance on and certified for their environment management systems (EMS). It provides organisations with a systematic framework to protect the environment and respond to changing environmental conditions in balance with socio-economic needs. Its implementation directs the organisation's environmental policy, plans and actions. It specifies the strategic requirements that enable an organisation to achieve the intended outcomes it sets for its EMS.

Green Globe Certification

Green Globe certification measures sustainability performance of travel and tourism businesses and their suppliers. The certification has a 360 degree assessment approach and uses 44 point crieteria and over 380 compliance indicators in four key areas – sustainable management, social and economic sustainability, cultural heritage, and environment. The Green Globe logo is issued only when the operation has been successfully benchmarked and has passed an on-site audit. To retain the use of the logo, the business has to get certified annually.

Green Seal Certification

Green Seal's GS-33 offers certification for lodging properties in three levels, bronze, silver, and gold, based on the scores achieved by them in the evaluation categories of – waste minimisation, energy conservation and management, management of fresh water resources, and waste water management, pollution prevention and environmentally sensitive purchasing.

EarthCheck Certification

EarthCheck certification for sustainable design and operations is offered to the tourism sector, including hotels, airports and airlines, convention centres, theme parks, golf courses, and destinations. The aspects of sustainability are awarded based on the KPI that include – energy efficiency, conservation and management, greenhouse gases emission, management of drinking water and rainwater resources, preservation and management of ecosystems, social and cultural affairs, air quality and noise control, wastewater management, solid waste management and storage of substances harmful to the environment.

BREEAM Certification

Building Research Establishment Environmental Assessment Method (BREEAM) is a sustainability rating system for assessing environmental performance of new and in-use buildings in terms of best practices in sustainable design, construction and operation. BREEAM assessment is based on evaluation of criteria such as energy, water use, health and wellbeing, pollution, transport, materials, waste, ecology

and management processes. As per the percentage scores, ratings are provided on a scale of pass to outstanding, depicted with stars on the BREEAM certificate as follows.

≥ 85: Outstanding (5 stars)
≥ 70: Excellent (4 stars)
≥ 55: Very good (3 stars)
≥ 45: Good (2 stars)
≥ 30: Pass (1 star)
> 30: Unclassified

Choosing an Eco-friendly Site

The building site chosen for a property can greatly affect the comfort and energy-efficiency of the hotel built upon it. A south-facing slope or good southern exposure on a plot that allows for the long sides of the building to face north–south will facilitate the utilization of prevailing summer breezes for cooling and the gain of solar heat desirable in winter. A hot, bare site will require a greater investment in wide overhangs, shading devices such as awnings or pergolas, and shade trees to keep utility bills down and comfort levels up.

The prospective building site should be examined for existing tree groupings, landforms, and structures that will aid in creating pleasant, usable outdoor spaces. Off-site conditions that may affect outdoor activities or indoor living with open windows—such as traffic noises, odours, or pollution—should be considered before selecting a site.

Examination of the particular site's unique characteristics is important. The top of a hill may be too windy, dry, and exposed to the hot sun. A valley may be too damp, windless, foggy, or subject to flooding. The location and type of trees in the area should be evaluated for their suitability by way of providing shade in summer, channelling or blocking summer breezes to and through the property, and hindering or encouraging the penetration of solar heat in winter.

A plot that allows for the siting of the hotel on a relatively flat area and in a natural clearing will minimize the disruption to the natural vegetation. This will avoid erosion, discourage the growth of invasive exotic vegetation, and be less expensive than massive landscaping exercises. Also, minimizing the disruption of natural drainage patterns is generally less expensive upfront and avoids the costly maintenance of elaborate artificial drainage systems. When native trees and vegetation must be removed, they can often be replanted elsewhere, on or off the site. Respecting existing wildlife trails and habitats will enhance the enjoyment of wildlife observation.

Every attempt must be made to protect and retain existing landscaping and natural features. Select plants that have low water and pesticide needs, and generate minimal 'trimmings'. Use compost and mulch optimally to save both water and time.

Sustainable sites should also allow for alternative transportation—such as parking, showering, and changing facilities for bicyclists, pool cars, and charging facilities for electrically or solar-powered vehicles.

The site should also facilitate the management of storm water. Rainwater recharge pits ensure zero discharge into municipal drainage systems.

The 'heat island effect', which occurs when developed urban areas have significantly higher average temperatures than the rural areas surrounding them, should be minimized as well. To achieve this, environmental agencies recommend that 80% of the parking be underground and that more than 75% of the terrace area be insulated and coated with reflective, high-albedo roof paint.

Minimal exterior lighting helps to limit night-sky pollution.

Sustainable Hotel Design and Construction

An eco-sensitive hotel should be a 'green' building, also known as an 'ecologically sustainable building'. The structure should be designed, built, renovated, operated, or reused in an eco-friendly and resource-efficient manner. 'Green' buildings are designed to meet certain objectives—such as protecting occupants' health; improving employee productivity; using energy, water, and other resources more efficiently; and reducing the overall impact on the environment. Therefore, a 'green' building can be defined as any building that is sited, designed, constructed, operated, and maintained for the health and well-being of the occupants, while minimizing its impact on the environment.

'Green' building practices offer an opportunity to create environmentally sound and resource-efficient buildings by using an integrated approach to design. Such buildings promote resource conservation by including design features that encourage energy efficiency, use of renewable energy, and water conservation. By promoting resource conservation, 'green' building design creates healthy and comfortable environments, reduces operation and maintenance costs, regulates the environmental impact of building construction to ensure retrofit, and emphasizes waste minimization. In addition, 'green' building design also addresses such issues as historical preservation and access to public transportation and other community infrastructure systems. The entire life cycle of the building and its components is considered, as well as the building's immediate economic and environmental impact and performance.

A trend in sustainable design of buildings is biophilic design in which architects and designers incorporate nature into building spaces to enhance the wellbeing of its occupants. Biophilia means 'affinity to nature' and thus biophilic interiors feature courtyard gardens, living walls, potted plants, aquariums, fountains and water features, bird feeders, butterfly gardens, and so on.

Cost

A 'green' building may cost more to build upfront (it is about 15% more expensive and the fee for certification is high as well), but it saves in the long run through lower operating costs over the life of the building. The 'green'-building approach applies life cycle cost analysis for the project to determine the appropriate upfront expenditure. This analytical method calculates the costs over the entire useful life of the asset and uses this figure to set off initial investments.

These and other cost savings can only be fully realized when they are incorporated at the conceptual phase of the project's design with the assistance of an integrated team of professionals. The integrated-systems approach ensures that the building is designed as one system rather than a collection of standalone systems.

Some benefits—such as improving occupants' health, comfort, and productivity or reducing pollution and landfill waste—are not easily quantified. Consequently, they are often not adequately considered in cost analysis. Even with a tight budget, many 'green' building measures can be incorporated with minimal or zero increase in upfront costs and yet they can yield enormous savings.

Materials

One of the best ways to minimize the use of raw materials, for instance, is to select a site that already has a building on it and remodel the same as necessary—needless to say, this is also a huge saving in terms of costs. The building's orientation should be such that there is a minimization of heat gain in summers and maximization during winters. The location of cooling towers should be away from boilers, generator units, kitchen, and laundry exhausts.

Also, select sustainable construction materials and products by evaluating several characteristics—such as reused and recycled content; zero or low harmful emissions; zero or low toxicity; sustainably harvested materials; high recyclability; durability and longevity; and local production. Products that meet at least some of these criteria promote resource conservation and efficiency.

Recycle and reuse Using products with a significant proportion of recycled content also helps develop markets for recycled materials.

'Trash is cash', and fly ash, for instance, is a good example of it. *Fly ash* is the waste product of the thermal power industry. Fly ash-based cement and AAC blocks for construction are ideal options for a 'green' building. Similarly, by using certified wood, the unnecessary felling of trees is avoided. All new wood used should come from trees that are pre-selected and felled without damage to adjoining trees; wood from old furniture should be simultaneously reused.

Check emissions Choose construction materials and interior-finish products with zero or low emissions to improve indoor air quality and achieve net zero. Many building materials as well as cleaning and maintenance products emit toxic gases, such as volatile organic compounds (VOC) and formaldehyde. These gases can have a detrimental impact on occupants' health and productivity. All HVAC equipment should be free from chlorofluorocarbons (CFCs), which are implicated in the depletion of the ozone layer.

Regulate interior environment Provide adequate ventilation and a high-efficiency, in-duct filtration system. Heating and cooling systems that ensure adequate ventilation and proper filtration can have a dramatic positive impact on indoor air quality. Use low-emission glass for windows. *Low e-glass* is unique in that it deflects heat whilst allowing light to pass through. Double- or triple-glazed windows, whatever the material, generally insulate the room from the outside heat or cold.

Fight germs Prevent microbial contamination indoors with a selection of materials resistant to microbial growth; provide effective drainage from the roof and through the surrounding landscape; install adequate ventilation in bathrooms; allow proper drainage of air-conditioning coils; and design building systems to control humidity.

Design 'efficiently' Use dimensional planning and other material-efficiency strategies. These strategies reduce the amount of building materials needed and cut construction costs. For example, design rooms on 4-foot multiples to conform to standard-sized wallboard and plywood sheets. Reuse and recycle construction and demolition materials. For example, using inert demolition materials as a base for a parking lot keeps these materials out of landfills and costs less. Design with adequate space to facilitate collection of recyclables and to incorporate a solid-waste management programme that prevents waste generation.

Resource efficiency This can be accomplished by utilizing materials that feature the following:

Recycled content Products with identifiable recycled content, including post-industrial content (with a preference for post-consumer content). In the building itself, adequate storage and collection of recyclables should be provided for. Separate storage bins need to be provided at each floor/level for different recyclable materials such as paper, cardboard, glass, plastic, and metals.

Natural, plentiful, or renewable sources Materials harvested from sustainably managed sources and preferably certified by an independent third party (for example, certified wood from the forest department) should be preferred. Rapidly renewable materials such as medium-density fibre board (MDF), especially the kind made from quickly renewable woods such as eucalyptus, should be used for storage shelves and cabinets. MDF is a composite wood product similar to particleboard, made from waste wood fibres that have been glued together with resin using heat and pressure. This material is

smooth, uniform, and does not warp. MDF is solely made from waste products, the leftover scraps that would otherwise be dumped in a landfill.

Resource-efficient manufacturing process Products manufactured by resource-efficient processes—including reduced energy consumption, minimized waste (say with recycled, recyclable, and/or source-reduced packaging), and reduced emission of greenhouse gases—are better for the environment.

Locally available raw materials and processes Building materials, components, and systems found locally or regionally save energy and resources expended in transportation to the project site. At least 40% of the building materials should come from within 500 miles of the project site.

Salvaged, refurbished, or re-manufactured products Use of these could include saving products and materials from disposal and renovating, repairing, restoring, or generally improving their appearance, performance, quality, functionality, or value. At least 10% of the building materials should be salvaged from other sites.

Reusability or recyclability Select materials that can be easily dismantled and reused or recycled at the end of their useful life.

Recycled or recyclable product packaging Products enclosed in recycled content or recyclable packaging do not add to the environmental burden.

Durability Materials that are longer-lasting or are comparable to conventional products with long-life expectancies cut down on replacement costs as well as procurement of raw materials a second time.

Indoor air quality (IAQ) is enhanced by utilizing materials that have the following features:

Low toxicity or non-toxicity Materials that emit few or no carcinogens, reproductive toxicants, or irritants—as demonstrated by the manufacturer through appropriate testing—should be chosen for indoor use in particular.

Minimal chemical emissions Products that produce minimal emissions of volatile organic compounds (VOCs) are best; better still if they also maximize resource and energy efficiency.

Low-VOC assembly Materials installed with minimal VOC-producing compounds or no-VOC (mechanical) attachment methods and minimal hazards are preferred. Low-VOC adhesives and sealants should be used for carpets, composite wood products, and paints.

Moisture resistance Products and systems that resist moisture or inhibit the growth of biological contaminants in buildings should be chosen.

Healthful maintenance Materials, components, and systems that employ simple, non-toxic, or low-VOC methods of cleaning are required indoors.

Monitoring Products that promote healthy IAQ by identifying indoor air pollutants or enhancing the air quality are a bonus. Also, for the maintenance of indoor air quality, there should be effective control of tobacco smoke. Designated smoking rooms need to be provided at convenient locations with separate exhaust systems.

Energy Conservation

Due to indiscriminate use, insufficient energy sources have become a global problem, though the impact of the crisis differs from country to country. The global energy demand is increasing due to the increase in population, industrial development, and changing lifestyles. On an average, 80% of the energy used worldwide is procured from fossil fuels such as coal and petroleum. These fuels are depleting at an alarming rate.

The hotel industry consumes energy in different forms—electricity, heat, petrol, and so on. Each organization invests a huge amount of money to acquire all these sources of energy. For instance, a 500-room, 5-star property with all facilities operating during a power crisis pays an energy bill of ₹12 lakh per month. It is possible to save 15–20% of this cost by using energy conservation methods. Even if we keep a modest target of 7%, the hotel can save up to ₹10 lakh per annum. What is more, the implementation of energy conservation mechanisms will not only help the hotel, but also society and the nation as a whole.

Energy Monitoring

Each and every member of the hotel's staff, therefore, should be made aware of the organization's concern regarding the consumption of energy. Before implementing such a system, it is important to conduct a thorough study of various energy conservation systems practised in different hotels. All the representatives of the various departments should work together to formulate the guidelines for conserving energy in the hotel. These guidelines should clearly mention the dos and don'ts in order to maintain strict control over the consumption of energy. The following areas are of particular importance:

Guestrooms These account for a major portion of a hotel's total energy consumption. Energy used for air-conditioning, ventilation, and heating changes with weather conditions, but lighting is directly proportional to the occupancy.

Laundry This facility utilizes a large amount of energy for washing as well as 'finishing' processes. The amount of energy consumption within the department depends largely on the type of equipment in use and, to a lesser extent, the type of fabrics.

Lighting This accounts for 10–25% of the hotel's electricity consumption. Different types of lighting are used in different areas, according to the requirements for illumination there. However, while lighting uses the lion's share of energy, it should be remembered that heating, ventilation, air-conditioning, and other over-sized equipment operate less efficiently.

Tips for Energy Conservation

We shall now look at some general tips for energy conservation in hotels. Passive design strategies can dramatically affect a building's energy performance. These may encompass the building's shape and orientation, passive use of solar energy, and the use of natural lighting.

Natural light Develop strategies to optimise natural lighting. Studies have shown that it has a positive impact on productivity and well-being as well. Consider installing skylights if needed. Clean all the glass panes on the north face periodically to improve natural lighting.

Artificial lighting Install high-efficiency lighting systems with advanced controls, including motion sensors tied to dimmers. Consider the use of timer switch to switch off lights during hours when they are unlikely to be used.

Task lighting reduces the level of general overhead lighting required. Use translucent shades and keep them clean to obtain maximum illumination. Use light-coloured paints on the walls and smooth surfaces to maximize the intensity of the available light.

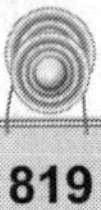

In guestrooms, have a lighting system that is activated only after inserting the key tag into the energy-saver slot. Replace incandescent bulbs with energy-saving CFLs and LED lamps.

Place light fixtures at the right height. Lower the height of fixtures in high-ceilinged areas wherever possible. Install chandeliers and other decorative fixtures only in public areas such as banquet halls, as they consume more energy.

Temperature control Use an energy-efficient heating/cooling system of the proper size in conjunction with a thermally efficient building shell. Maximize the use of light colours for roofing and wall finishes; install high R-value walls and ceilings; and use minimal glassed areas on the east and west exposures. Use draperies and sun films on window panes to cut down on air-conditioning costs.

Use heat-reclaiming equipment in air-conditioning plants. The heat displaced while cooling the air can be used to heat water, which can be used in guestrooms as well as the laundry and kitchens.

Hot-water pipes should be well insulated. Indeed, leakage of both air and water should be avoided. Damaged insulation should be changed as early as possible. Filters should be cleaned regularly. The temperature of the heated water should not exceed the recommended levels for the various areas. For instance, in baths it should be 30–43°C, in showers 32–35°C, and in sinks 43–49°C.

Appliances Minimize the electric loads from appliances and other electrical equipment as well as lighting by ensuring that the removal of the key-tag from its slot invokes the energy-saver settings. Turn off lights and fans in rooms that are physically unoccupied.

All equipment should be maintained and kept clean for the highest possible efficiency.

Computer modelling is an extremely useful tool in optimizing the design of electrical and mechanical systems as well as the building shell.

Ensure appliances with energy star label for maximum energy savings. Globally recognised Energy Star certification by US Environment Protection Agency (EPA), provides labelling of products that pass stringent standards for energy efficiency, see Figure 32.1. Star labelling of appliances is mandated in India for most electronic appliances by the Bureau of Energy Efficiency (BEE), Ministry of Power, GoI. Use of such appliances guarantee energy efficiency and reduced energy costs. The more the stars, more energy efficient the appliance. A representative energy star label for washing machines is shown in Figure 32.2.

Fig. 32.1 Energy star label of the US EPA

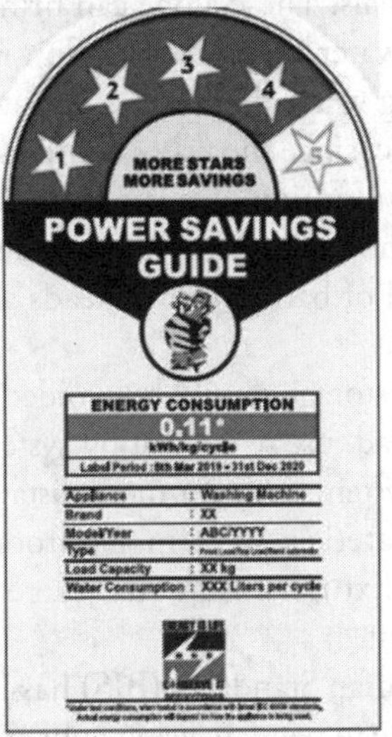

Fig. 32.2 A sample BEE star label for washing machines

Alternative sources Consider alternative energy sources such as photovoltaic and fuel cells, which are now available for new products and applications. Renewable energy sources provide a great symbol of emerging technologies for the future.

Use solar energy that is abundantly available naturally and save on electricity costs. Solar energy can be used for lighting and heating water.

Cooking fuel Biogas can be used to cook staff meals. A biogas plant may be installed and the organic waste generated in the hotel can be used for the production of biogas.

Transport Provide guests with bicycles, walking maps, and information on public transportation. Small solar-powered vehicles can be used to ferry guests within the property's premises.

Water Conservation

Water is the most basic component of all life on earth. However, the 'enrichment' of water with chemicals and waste has become a universal problem. Since freshwater shortage is a reality, effective water management procedures are essential for the success of any establishment.

General Tips for Water Conservation

Let us now look at some general guidelines for water conservation.

Bathrooms Opt for sustainable bathroom design which saves significant amount of water. Install pressure reducing valves in the main plumbing lines to reduce water output from fixtures. Auto-sensing faucets and flow regulating fixtures are vital in sustainable bathroom design. Employ a dual plumbing in the design to use recycled water for flushing toilets or a 'grey-water' system that recovers rainwater or other non-potable water for on-site irrigation.

Minimize wastage of water by using ultra low-flush toilets, low-flow showerheads, and other water-conserving fixtures. Low-flushing WCs require a maximum of 6 litres of water, as compared to traditional WCs that require 10–12 litres. Automatic flushes activated by infra-red sensors are ideal for use in public-area urinals. These alone can bring about a 30% reduction in total water usage.

Use aerated water taps and water-flow restrictors. Aerated taps mix air bubbles into the water, providing white, sparkling water that gushes out at a higher pressure. Thus, the amount of water used is less and at the same time, since the water comes at pressure, it is more effective in cleaning. Aerators in taps may reduce the consumption of water from 200 litres per shower to 110 litres.

In general, showers use less water than baths, hence most guestrooms may be planned to have shower cubicles instead of baths. Showerheads are available nowdays with spray technology that reduce water usage by 30%.

Excess water storage should be avoided, especially hot water, which loses heat easily in annulated pipes and tanks. Instead, use re-circulating systems for centralized distribution of hot water. Install point-of-use water-heating systems only for more distant locations.

New age materials used in bathroom surfaces enhance ease of cleaning employing less water usage. Rimless fixtures ensure that there are no breeding grounds available for microbes, thus making cleaning efficient.

Bureau of Indian Standards (BIS) has introduced water efficiency rating system for plumbing fixtures and sanitaryware to regulate water consumption, as shown in Table 32.1 and based on the rating criteria, issues labels as depicted in Figure 32.3 to be displayed on the products.

Table 32.1 BIS water efficiency star rating criteria for sanitaryware

Sanitaryware Product	Water consumption per unit	Star rating criteria		
		1 star	2 stars	3 stars
Water closets	Full flush (litres/flush)	Not more than 6.0	Not more than 4.8	Not more than 4.0
	Reduced flush (litres/flush)	Not more than 3.0	Not more than 2.8	Not more than 2.0
Urinals	Litres/flush	Not more than 3.0	Not more than 2.0	Not more than 1.0

Fig. 32.3 BIS water efficiency star rating label for sanitaryware

Waste management Use recycled waste water for horticultural purposes, flushing toilets, and air-conditioning through separate pipe systems. A sewage treatment plant should be installed for recycling waste water generated by the hotel.

Rainwater harvesting Replenish ground water by rainwater harvesting. The total daily water requirement of a hotel is approximately 250 kilolitres a day. This comes to about 90 million litres a year. This includes both fresh water use (around 80%) and 'grey-water' reuse (around 20%) for horticulture. By using rainwater harvesting, nearly 25% of the water used within the premises is saved and an unaccounted-for amount of storm water from surrounding areas is directed through proper channels into rainwater-harvesting wells to recharge the ground water.

Horticulture Use timer-controlled sprinkler systems and self-closing nozzles on hoses. The sprinkler system may be timed to operate during the early morning or late evening hours, when the sun is not at its peak. This minimizes the evaporation of water.

Alternatively, use the drip-irrigation method for watering plants in the gardens as well. Plants need water only at the roots. In drip irrigation, pipes with small openings are spread out along the ground near the plants. Water from these openings irrigates only the roots and does not drench the whole plant.

Switch to drought-resistant, indigenous plants. Replace mowed landscaping with native groundcover species.

Table 32.2 presents some statistics on the unintentional wastage of water.

Table 32.2 Unintentional wastage of water

Activity	Wasteful method	Quantity of water used (in litres)	Water-saving method	Quantity of water required (in litres)	Quantity of water saved (in litres)
Brushing teeth	Running tap for 5 minutes	45	Tumbler/glass	0.5	44.5
Washing hands	Running tap for 2 minutes	18	Half-filled bowl or basin	2	16
Shaving	Running tap	18	Shaving mug	0.25	17.75
Shower	Letting the shower run while soaping and staying too long under the shower	90	Wet down, turn shower off, soap up, and rinse off	20	70
Flushing toilet	Using traditional large-capacity cistern	13.5 or more	Dual-system—short flush for liquid waste; full flush for solid waste	4.59	4.5 or more
Watering plants	Running hose for 5 minutes (at low pressure)	120	Watering can	5	115
Washing floor	Running hose for 5 minutes (at full pressure)	200	Mop and bucket	18	182

Waste Management

This is an integral part of green hotel operations. The waste generated by the property should, as far as possible, be recycled.

Linen and other textiles Condemned bed-linen, towels, and curtains should be reused for making dusters, face cloths, scarves, swab cloths, waiter's cloths, and so on.

Garbage reuse and recycling Segregation of wet and dry garbage should be adopted for recycling, reusing, and recovering waste. Provide recycle baskets for newspaper, white paper, glass, aluminium, cardboard, and plastic in guestrooms—make recycling as easy as possible.

Leftover cooking oil may be sold to manufacturers of soap. Leftovers from guest plates and other food wastes can be recycled in a compost bin or vermi-compost pit to procure manure or in a biogas plant to obtain biogas as fuel.

Sewage A sewage treatment plant is an effective way of recycling waste water generated in the hotel. The recycled water thus produced may be used in gardening and for flushing toilets.

Environment-friendly Housekeeping

The housekeeping department can contribute in a big way to making a hotel eco-sensitive. The department can do so in the following ways:

- Many hotels wash bed linen on a daily basis. Since the linen is almost always very lightly soiled, the department may—in consultation with the management—draw up a policy for laundering bed linen only once in 2–3 days unless perceptibly soiled. This practice can save a large amount of water. The ideal way to introduce this policy would be to leave the option to guests. A tent card as shown in Exhibit 32.1, that states the purpose behind the same will always encourage the guests to oblige. Providing relevant water conservation statistics, such as those presented in Table 32.2, will reinforce the guest's decision.

Exhibit 32.1 Eco card

Hotel Spring Leaves International

ECO CARD

Dear Guest,

As part of our sustainability efforts, we change your bed linen every third day of your stay and again at check-out. Should you want your bed linen changed sooner, you are requested to place this card on the pillow and we shall gladly do so.

A towel left hanging on the towel rack means "I shall use it again."

A towel on the floor means "Please replace."

- During low-occupancy seasons, operate rooms on selected floors, closing off certain floors.
- Employees should switch off lights and fans that are not in use.
- Employees should immediately report any leaky faucets or pipes.
- Employees should ensure that only the correct wattage of bulbs is used and that light shades are clean.
- Opt for rechargeable batteries for battery operated electronic devices such as TV remotes, clocks, and torches.
- Employees should ensure that drapes are closed to maximize the effect of air-conditioning or heating.
- The usage of cold-water detergents in the laundry reduces the need for hot water.
- The final rinse water should be used for the first wash of the next batch of soiled linen.
- Ensure preventive maintenance of laundry equipment.
- Optimize laundry equipment operating hours by managing laundry flow and shut down equipment when not in use, instead of keeping on standby mode.
- Feed in customised wash formulas in washers for sheets, duvets, towels, F&B linen and uniforms to increase linen lifespan, reduce utility consumption and bring down overall HLP costs.
- Incorporate water reclamation programmes, such as Ecolab's Aquamiser, in the laundry which are designed to reuse water, providing significant water savings.
- Track the performance of lint collector in the dryers at the laundry with daily logs and monitoring to maintain proper drying time, prevent linen damage and reduce utility costs.

- Install sub-metering system to measure utility consumption in the laundry, thus identifying areas for laundry efficiency optimization.
- Consider using fabric blends with synthetic fibres, as they require lower temperatures for washing, drying, and ironing.
- Biodegradable detergents should be used.
- Use biodegradable and eco-friendly chemicals in all cleaning and laundry operations. Use non-toxic cleaners, sanitizers, paints, pesticides, and so on throughout the hotel.
- No aerosol dispensers should be used in dispensing or applying cleaning materials and air fresheners.
- Guest supplies and amenities, provided by the housekeeping department for guests should be biodegradable and eco-friendly.
- Minimize the amount of paper used for each guest—that is, reduce the size of paper invoices and similar documents.
- Provide potable water in reusable glass bottles in guestrooms and at conferences, instead of sealed plastic bottles of water.
- Tie up with recycling programmes such as used soap recycling and pillow-filling recycling.
- The housekeeping department can source and purchase linen made from organically grown produce.
- Water from the laundry can be treated and used for watering plants.
- The executive housekeeper should create an incentive programme to encourage staff to participate in and improve upon environment-friendly practices.

Eco-friendly guest supplies and stationery

The use of eco-friendly stationery goes a long way in promoting environmental-friendly practices. The following practices can be followed in the purchase and use of guest supplies and stationery in hotels.

- Whenever possible, buy guest amenities in bulk. Use refillable dispensers for hair and skincare products.
- Buy guest products that contain recycled materials.
- For guest stationery, use recycled-paper products (with a high post-consumer recycled content) that are either unbleached or bleached using a chlorine-free process.
- All guest supplies—soaps, shampoos, and foaming bath liquids—should be biodegradable.
- Reusable, non-disposable cups and mugs should be provided to guests for in-room beverages. Place cups and mugs upside down on paper doilies instead of covering them with plastic wrapping. Provide cloth napkins and ceramic dishes too, as these are reusable.
- Provide morning newspapers in public areas for community access instead of individual room distribution. This reduces paper waste by 60%.
- Replace paper hand towels with air dryers in restrooms.
- Consider the use of bamboo and hemp fabrics for duvets, pillowcases, dust ruffles, and bath curtains.
- Donate leftover guest amenities, mattresses, old furniture, and so on to charities.

SUMMARY

Nothing is a waste in nature because nature knows how to reuse and recycle. Eco-sensitive or green hotels follow the same principle— reuse and recycle whatever possible. In the current scenario the world finds itself in, sustainability underlines all operations and decisions at hospitality properties. Hotels in India are pursuing sustainability certifications and some which are certified for their sustainability efforts include those part of the ITC Hotels chain, The Orchid, Mumbai; RODAS, Mumbai; and The Raintree, Chennai, to name a few. There are other hotels in India which, though not certified, have been following eco-friendly practices, such as the CGH Earth Group properties.

There are many international and national agencies certifying eco-sensitive hotels, and all require few criteria to be met for certification to be granted. The usual criteria are: sustainable infrastructure, energy conservation; water conservation; waste management; environmental commitment; community involvement and employee education. Important certifying agencies have been presented in brief.

An green hotel's success story begins with the siting of the building itself. The site should be such that it facilitates shade in summer, channels or blocks summer breezes, and encourages penetration of solar heat in winter. Steps should be taken to minimize the 'heat island' effect. This chapter discussed in detail many aspects of siting green hotels optimally.

The chapter then dealt with the design and construction of the buildings. A sustainability-centric hotel should be a 'green' building, sited, designed, constructed, operated, and maintained for the health and well-being of the occupants while minimizing the impact on the environment. Many points of consideration have been discussed with regard to the building design and construction.

Energy and water conservation are integral parts of environmental sensitivity. Both resources are depleting rapidly and alternative, renewable resources need to be sourced and utilized. This chapter outlined many methods for the conservation of energy and water.

Waste management primarily involves recycling wastes generated on the property's premises and many tips have been given for the same.

The concluding section dealt with eco-friendly housekeeping, with the stress on eco-friendly guest supplies and stationery. Innovations in products and procedures have made possible immense variety in eco-friendly materials and methods. Hotels with a commitment to the environment need to be on the lookout for these innovations and generate their own creative ideas too.

KEY TERMS

AAC blocks Autoclaved aerated concrete blocks.

BEE Bureau of Energy Efficiency.

Biodegradable Substances capable of being decomposed by living organisms.

Biogas A mixture of methane and carbon dioxide produced by bacterial degradation of organic matter, and used as fuel.

Biophilic design Design of building exterior and interior in which architects and designers incorporate nature into building spaces to enhance the wellbeing of its occupants.

BIS Bureau of Indian Standards.

BREEAM Building Research Establishment Environmental Assessment Method.

Carbon neutral Carbon neutrality means achieving an equivalent balance between emitting carbon and absorbing carbon from the atmosphere in carbon sinks.

CFCs Chlorofluorocarbons. These are compounds responsible for ozone-layer depletion.

CFLs Compact fluorescent lamps.

Compost Manure formed by the decomposition of organic matter by a mixed population of microorganisms in warm, moist, and aerobic conditions over a specific period of time.

Eco card Also termed as linen reuse card, conservation card, or sustainability card, it indicates a choice to guests to opt for change of linen once in 2–3 days, in line with the hotel's sustainability programme.

EMS Environment Management System.

EPA Environmental Protection Agency (USA).

Green hotels These are earth-friendly or eco-sensitive hotels that feature implementation of environmental policies and standards, innovative and imaginative programmes for conserving natural resources, reducing waste, minimizing pollution, and maximizing sustainability.

Fly ash A waste product of the thermal power industry, it is used to make cement and AAC blocks which are ideal materials for a 'green' building.

Greenhouse gases Gases such as carbon dioxide, which contribute to the 'greenhouse effect' by trapping the infra-red radiation of the sun.

'Green' building Any building that is sited, designed, constructed, operated, and maintained for the health and well-being of the occupants while minimizing the impact on the environment.

Grey water Waste water from baths, washing machines, and so on that is treated and recycled, especially for use in gardening and for flushing toilets.

GRIHA Green Rating for Integrated Habitat Assessment.

Heat island effect This occurs when developed urban areas have significantly higher average temperatures than the rural areas surrounding them.

High-albedo paint Albedo is the measure of reflectivity of a surface. Thus a high-albedo paint refers to a paint having high reflectivity.

HLP Heat Light and Power, the most significant costs in laundry.

HVAC Heating, ventilation, and air-conditioning.

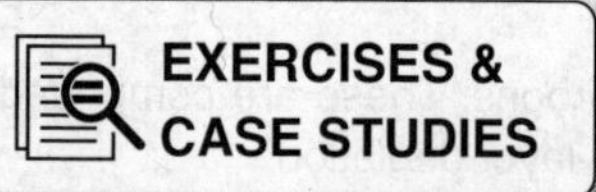

IGBC Indian Green Building Council.

LEED Leadership in Energy and Environmental Design.

Low-emission glass A type of glass that deflects heat whilst allowing light to pass through.

MDF Medium density fibreboard, a composite wood product similar to particleboard. It is made out of waste wood fibres glued together with resin through the application of heat and pressure.

Mulch Protective ground coverings of rotting vegetable matter spread upon garden and planter soil to reduce evaporation and soil erosion. Decomposing mulches also act as manure for the plants.

Net zero It implies cutting greenhouse gas emissions to as close to zero as possible, with any remaining emissions re-absorbed from the atmosphere by oceans and forests. As per The Paris Agreement, emissions need to be reduced by 45% by 2030 and reach net zero by 2050 to contain global warming.

R-value The measure of a material's resistance to heat flow. The higher the R-value of a material, the greater its insulating capability.

SDG 2030 Sustainable Development Goals 2030 developed by the United Nations.

Trellises Grilles or latticed frames used in gardens to train climbers (plants) or hang pots from.

Vermicompost A natural organic manure comprising the excreta of earthworms fed on decomposed organic wastes such as the dung of cattle and other animals, coir pith, farm wastes, urban garbage such as paper and rags, and various agro-industrial wastes.

VOCs Volatile organic compounds.

New Property Operations

Learning Objectives

After reading this chapter, you should be able to
- enumerate the tasks involved in setting up a housekeeping department in a soon-to-be-opened property
- list the responsibilities of the housekeeping department in a soon-to-be-opened property
- plan and organize staff, material resources, and housekeeping procedures for a new property

Introduction

Being involved in a soon-to-be-launched property in which department planning has yet to be undertaken gives an executive housekeeper the opportunity to influence how a department will be set up. Involvement in such an experience is rewarding, enlightening, and challenging. At this juncture, however, it is wise to remember that 'good results without planning is good luck, not good management'.

Starting up Housekeeping

When the housekeeping department starts from scratch, it consists of only one employee—the executive housekeeper. The executive housekeeper's position within the organization should be clearly defined. Most executive housekeepers are department heads, but many do reach corporate levels as well. It should be made known to the incumbent whether he/she has to report to the rooms division manager, the resident manager, or the general manager.

Housekeeper in a New Property

For a housekeeper in a soon-to-be opened property, the following are some initial steps in the process of starting up the property.

Finding your place The executive housekeeper will have many occasions to relate to other members of the organization. Therefore, it is important for him or her to get to know—and become known to—each of these managers; and respect and understanding need to be developed between each of these roles for each person and their functions. Managers of other departments, too, should in their turn develop an understanding and respect for the functions of the housekeeping department and its significance in the total operation. The organization chart is a tool that is useful here for gleaning information on reporting relationships and coordination within the organization.

Getting acquainted The next priority for the housekeeper is to become acquainted with the new surroundings. The executive housekeeper should consult a set of the working architectural drawings of the rooms in the property. These will allow him or her to study the physical layout of the facility thoroughly and provide the basis for determining the scope of involvement and delineation of responsibilities of the various managers' areas. These working drawings will also assist the housekeeper when on-site inspections begin, as well as help to put the manpower planning into perspective. The executive housekeeper must also take a look at the temporary working area out of which departmental planning may begin.

Planning, organizing, and priority recruiting The housekeeper needs to use his or her time efficiently in planning, organizing, and recruiting. Planning and organizing have to be done for the necessary minimum manpower, as well as the designing of systems, establishment of procedures, determination of supply and equipment needs, and devising of reporting and coordinating relationships within the department. The housekeeper must establish the requisite qualifications for his or her two principal assistants—the deputy housekeeper and the laundry manager—and specify these requirements to the personnel manager as soon as possible. Advertisements need to be placed and recruitment begun and completed within 10–15 days. Until at least these two managers are present, the entire planning, organizing, and staffing functions rests on the shoulders of the executive housekeeper, which leaves him or her with less time for other supervisory and planning duties so essential at this initial stage.

Material Resources

Before getting the workforce ready and going, the executive housekeeper needs to plan the procurement of the material resources the staff will require to accomplish their tasks. Market surveys should be carried out to identify the best supplies and equipment available, with an eye to the needs of the hotel as well as the cost factor. Cleaning supplies, guest supplies, linen, uniforms, and various pieces of equipment need to be procured in coordination with the purchase department.

Systems and Procedures

By this stage, the executive housekeeper should have established at least a mental plan of daily operations as they should be conducted. Procedures and daily routines now need to be standardized for the new property. Standard operating procedures, task lists, and the duties and responsibilities of specific positions should be formally in place before the new employees' induction into the property. This is a very crucial stage, as the effectiveness of procedures established now will directly show up in the results achieved. Standard operating procedures for reporting to work, preparing to clean various areas, cleaning procedures, key control, and security and safety procedures must be established.

Division of Work

At the next stage, once recruitment has begun, the housekeeping responsibilities for the entire property need to be identified. The executive housekeeper should make regular tours of the property while it is under construction and draw up a division-of-work document. It is important to know the location of service areas and storerooms to optimize this process.

The executive housekeeper should include in the division-of-work document all the areas and sub-areas that the housekeeping department is collectively responsible for and identify the person to whom

the cleaning of each area is to be allotted. This document should be reviewed and approved by the executive committee of the property. All other departments in the hotel also need to be made aware of this division of work, so that coordination after opening is easier. (Refer to Chapter 2 for details on the various areas housekeeping is responsible for cleaning and maintaining.)

Area Responsibility Plan

This document goes on to fix responsibility for the areas mentioned in the division-of-work document and shows the boundaries of the various areas on a copy of the floor plan or blueprint. This helps to ensure that not a single area has been left out in assigning responsibilities and also that there is no overlap in cleaning responsibilities.

The executive housekeeper prepares this plan and gives it for finalization and amendment to the hotel's executive committee.

Organizing the New Workforce

Once the area responsibility plan is in order, the departmental organization chart needs to be finalized. This indicates the assigned responsibilities. Supervisors are decided upon for the various areas—for example, floor supervisors, a public area supervisor, a desk control supervisor, a linen room supervisor, and so on.

The task of organizing the laundry workforce in a similar manner may be delegated to the laundry manager.

At this stage, the executive housekeeper must also plan for zero-base scheduling—hiring employees taking into account the actual occupancy for specified periods of the year. (Refer to Chapter 3 to refresh your understanding of zero-base scheduling.)

House Break-up

A house break-up is a pictorial representation of the location of all guestrooms as given in the physical layout plan of the hotel. It consists of a line drawing of the guestroom section of the hotel, showing the relative positions of guestrooms, guest corridors, floor pantries, and other areas significant to guestroom cleaning; though not necessarily accurate in terms of exact direction headings or scale.

Further, room sections of 13–20 rooms at a time, as close to each other as possible, need to be marked out on the house break-up so that individual GRAs or teams of GRAs can be assigned to a particular section each. Room sections can be assigned numbers for convenience.

Finally, house divisions need to be marked for supervisors. House divisions are groups of 4–6 room sections along with the associated corridors, elevators, stairways, service areas, and storage areas. House divisions can be named as per the theme of the hotel, though it is primarily meant for the reference of the housekeeping department staff.

Workload of GRAs and Supervisors

The housekeeper then decides on the number of rooms to be assigned to each GRA and to each of their supervisors. The number of rooms to be cleaned by a single GRA may range from 13 to 20 rooms per day. This range depends on various factors, such as the size of the guestrooms, the types of guestrooms, the kinds of fixtures, furniture, and other contents in the guestroom, the distance between the guestrooms in the property, whether assignments are made for team cleaning or individual cleaning, and so on.

Staffing Considerations

The various documents that act as tools in the management of personnel need to be in place before recruitment is completed. The important tools at this stage are job descriptions, position descriptions, and job specifications. The departmental staffing guide also needs to be developed and staff hired on the basis of zero-base scheduling. Staff requirements for particular occupancy periods should be worked out in a tabular form and filed for reference. This table is referred to as the *staffing guide* and serves as an important tool for achieving zero-base scheduling (refer to Chapter 3 for details). The executive housekeeper can refer to this table in preparing daily schedules for the housekeeping staff later as well.

Orientation and Training

Orientation or induction is the guided adjustment of new employees to the organization, the work environment, and the job. The process communicates the organization's basic philosophy, policies, rules, and procedures. This is the stage where new employees are given an employee handbook with relevant details of the organization's history, policies and practices, rules and regulations, departments, staff benefits, and safety regulations. The executive housekeeper may orient the new employees personally or may delegate the responsibility to an assistant housekeeper.

Either way, training is a must for the newly hired employees to develop the skills needed for performing their job well. At this stage, a procedure manual is handed to the employees, which lists the standard operating procedures (SOPs) in simple words. The task of training may be delegated to supervisors, but the executive housekeeper is ultimately responsible for the training programmes. Of course, it should be ensured that training becomes an ongoing process.

Scheduling of New Employees

GRAs, supervisors, and housemen need to be scheduled once the workloads have been decided and the duty rota has been drawn up. Here, the executive housekeeper needs to consider the benefits of team scheduling. New employees may not be confident enough in the first few weeks of performing their tasks to operate singly. Team staffing may come to the rescue here. For example, a new GRA may be paired with another experienced GRA in servicing a guestroom. This is sometimes referred to as the 'buddy system'.

Countdown

Here is a checklist of the housekeeping responsibilities to be met while inaugurating a new property:

Three Months before the Opening

The following activities need to be carried out three months prior to the opening.

1. Check the blueprints for the housekeeping department.
2. Check the layout of the linen and uniform rooms.
3. Check the layout of the laundry.
4. Check the location and layout of the floor pantries.
5. Check the layout of the different types of guestrooms.
6. Appoint a horticulturist in coordination with the personnel department and initiate the setting up of a plant nursery and greenhouse. Look into the purchasing of saplings and seeds.
7. Consider the space allocation for all these areas in accordance with the total front-of-the-house area.

8. Evaluate the function and maintenance of furniture and other hard surfaces.
9. Work in coordination with the interior designers and architects to plan the indoor spaces.
10. Undertake a market survey to identify the best equipment, cleaning supplies, linen, and guest supplies available and work out the costs. Evaluate the quality and quantity required, set up par stock levels and then contact the suppliers of each item or product to get specifications.
11. Obtain required approvals and coordinate the purchase of equipment, cleaning supplies, linen, and guest supplies with the purchase department, keeping in mind the lead time available (well before the inauguration) for the delivery of the goods.
12. Manpower planning needs to be initiated in coordination with the other departments.
13. Discuss uniform requirements and designs with the various departmental heads.

Two Months in Advance

Two months ahead of the opening, the following activities need to be carried out.

1. Fine-tune the manpower requirement. Hire only the minimum staff required. Consider contracted services to compensate for a possible high turnover of staff at this initial stage of adjustments and learning.
2. Consider contracted services for pest control, florists, and so on so that specifications, terms, and conditions can be worked out. Consider the feasibility of these contracted services in terms of needs versus costs.
3. Orientation and training of staff should be started on a continuous basis.
4. Follow up with the purchase department regarding the indented items and delivery dates.
5. Look into set up of the linen room and sewing room.
6. Check floor pantry layout on all floors and their set up requirements.
7. Decide on customisation of GRA carts, their placement etc., and procure them.
8. Draw up staffing guide and job descriptions and coordinate with HR for recruitment.
9. Create housekeeping manual, incorporating policies, SOPs, and safety norms.
10. Create forms and formats and place order for stationery.

Six Weeks in Advance

When there are about six weeks to go, the following activities need to be taken care of:

1. Hire the necessary supervisory and lower-rung staff. An assistant housekeeper must be on-board now to look into training needs and train staff.
2. Clean up all the newly constructed areas and carry out a thorough inspection before takeover from projects. Snag lists should be prepared for all areas and snags rectified by the project team or the concerned staff. A sample snag list is given in Exhibit 29.2 of Chapter 29.
3. After the entire construction is over, initiate actual horticulture activities such as landscaping and gardening.
4. Organize the storage of all items purchased.
5. Work out systems and procedures.
6. Check the standard operating procedures (SOPs).
7. Begin the purchasing of uniforms after getting relevant inputs regarding the staff of all the hotel departments.
8. Organize orientation and training for the new staff and continue the training schedule for the older staff.

Four Weeks to Go

With four weeks left for the opening, the following areas need to be looked at:

1. Check the cleanliness of all areas under the housekeeping department's purview.
2. Check the quality and quantity of all the equipment and supplies delivered.
3. Ensure that lower-rung staff have had basic training in handling guests.
4. Move in and set up the department physically.
5. Redefine and fine-tune the systems and procedures as necessary.
6. Begin the stitching and issuing of staff uniforms.

One Week to Go

Finally, a week in advance of the opening, the following activities must be carried out:

1. Draw up duty rotas and schedule staff accordingly.
2. Set up the relevant work areas and ensure their cleanliness.
3. Work out frequency schedules for the cleaning up of various areas of the property.
4. Constantly tour the property and be available to the housekeeping staff for last-minute queries and changes.

SUMMARY

In this chapter, we discussed the planning and implementation of all departmental activities by the newly appointed executive housekeeper at a soon-to-be-opened property. The executive housekeeper must prioritize his or her work carefully at this stage, since there is a lot to be accomplished in relatively little time.

The housekeeper starts by getting acquainted with the layouts of the various areas, making regular tours of the newly constructed property, and then embarking on the planning required to set up the department.

The process of recruitment happens stage by stage, as and when personnel become necessary for various tasks. The immediate assistants to the executive housekeeper are recruited in the first phase. The procurement process for material resources is initiated by the executive housekeeper simultaneously.

While their arrival is awaited and before the recruitment of the lower-rung employees, systems and procedures must be put in place. Standard operating procedures are formulated so that the training of new employees becomes simpler.

Next, the division-of-work document and area responsibility plans are prepared. Organizing the man-power is a critical stage in the countdown to the opening of a new property. To assist in this, a departmental staffing guide is prepared by the executive housekeeper, which further helps in preparing the table of personnel requirements for every occupancy level anticipated. The housekeeper then undertakes the zero-base scheduling with this documentation. Side by side with this process, supervisors are hired and areas of responsibility delegated; the laundry is handed over to the laundry manager.

The house break-up plan is discussed next. This plan helps in the efficient assignment of guestrooms and associated areas for cleaning. Subdivision of the house break-up into room sections and house divisions helps in scheduling the work of GRAs and supervisors respectively. At this time, the housekeeper needs to consider the advantages of using team-cleaning systems.

The chapter then went on to discuss other aspects of manpower planning essential through the countdown. Job descriptions and specifications have to be finalized and staff recruited for the whole operation. Their orientation and training in time for the opening become the executive housekeeper's chief responsibility now. The employee handbook and procedure manuals are handed over to new staff at this stage.

The final scheduling of staff is done by the executive housekeeper, keeping in mind the house break-up plan, room sections, and house divisions. Since the property under discussion is new, team scheduling is highly recommended to accomplish housekeeping tasks.

The concluding section of the chapter gave a checklist specifying the housekeeping responsibilities just prior to the opening of a new hotel.

KEY TERMS

Area responsibility plan This document assigns responsibility for all the areas mentioned in the division-of-work document to the relevant members of staff and shows the boundaries of the various areas to be cleaned or maintained on a copy of a floor plan or blueprint of the property.

Buddy system A system of scheduling where a new GRA is paired with another who is more experienced for the servicing of a guestroom.

Cleaning supplies Cleaning agents and smaller pieces of cleaning equipment.

Division-of-work document A document that details all the areas and sub-areas that the housekeeping department is responsible for and the person responsible for the cleaning of each area.

Guest supplies Items placed in the guestroom free of cost for the use and comfort of guests.

Horticulture The science of growing plants or of gardening.

House break-up A pictorial representation of the location of all guestrooms as given in the physical layout plan of the hotel. It consists of a line drawing of the guestroom sections of the hotel, showing the approximate positions of guestrooms, guest corridors, floor pantries, and other areas significant to guestroom cleaning relative to each other.

House divisions A group of 4- to 6-room sections, along with the associated corridors, elevators, stairways, service areas, and storage areas. They are each allotted to a supervisor for inspection.

Job description A detailed document identifying all the likely duties of a job position as well as reporting relationships, additional responsibilities, working conditions, and any knowhow about equipment and materials necessary.

Job specification A document detailing the minimum qualities or traits required by an individual to perform a particular job.

Key control The procedure of carefully monitoring, controlling, and tracking the use of keys in a hospitality operation.

Linen Specifically, material woven from flax; though now the term is often used loosely to refer to soft furnishings which were originally made typically of linen. Actual linen material is less elastic and more absorbent than cotton.

Organization chart A schematic representation of the relationships between positions within an organization, showing where each position fits into the overall organization and illustrating the divisions of responsibility and the lines of authority.

Orientation Also called 'induction', this is the guided initiation and adjustment of a new employee to the organization, the work environment, and the job. The process communicates the organization's basic philosophy, policies, rules, and procedures to the new recruit.

Position description Documents written for employees to enumerate the management prerogatives and give the basic function, scope, and specific responsibilities of a position.

Rooms division manager The person who heads the organizational division responsible for the allocation of guestrooms—including the front office and the housekeeping department.

Room section A group of 13–20 guestrooms, as close together as possible, that is allotted for cleaning and servicing to an individual GRA or a single GRA team in an eight-hour shift.

Resident manager The person in charge of hotel operations exclusive of food-and-beverage operations who is resident on the hotel premises. He or she acts as the principle assistant to the general manager.

Snag list A detailed list prepared on the basis of a physical inspection, in which all possible maintenance requirements in a room are mentioned. It is normally prepared by the housekeeper during takeover of the renovated area from the contractor handling renovation or of a new property from the project team.

Staffing guide A document that serves as a scheduling and control tool that enables the executive housekeeper to determine the total work hours and number of employees required to operate the housekeeping department at specific occupancy levels of the hotel.

Standard operating procedure (SOP) A document of a standing nature that specifies a certain method of operating or a specific procedure for the accomplishment of a task. SOPs can be developed for all important housekeeping activities and tasks.

Team cleaning This is a system of scheduling cleaning where a pair or a group of employees are

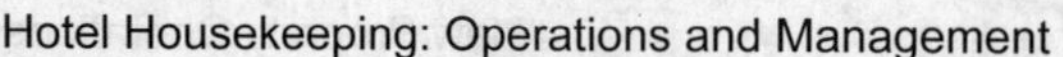

organized into a permanent team and are scheduled to perform cleaning tasks as a single unit.

Zero based budgeting Zero based budgets are developed from level zero, i.e., commencing right at the beginning of the budget process, where all accounts have a value of zero, unlike the usual process where accounts start with the previous year's balance.

Zero-base scheduling This refers to the hiring of employees while taking into account the actual occupancy for a specified period of time.

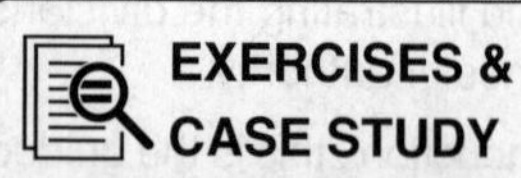

34

Changing Trends in Housekeeping

Learning Objectives

After reading this chapter, you should be able to

- describe the emerging trends in housekeeping at hospitality properties
- list the applications of information technology in the housekeeping department

Introduction

Hotel housekeeping is changing dynamically. All aspects of housekeeping - cleanliness, safety and aesthetics have taken on higher standards. Where earlier hotel cleanliness standards were elevated to hygienically clean, now clinically clean standards are here to stay. Outsourcing of services has become common in the hospitality industry. Recruiting, training, motivating, and retaining quality staff has become a major challenge in housekeeping today. There is conscious effort made by housekeepers to adopt sustainable practices and products. In addition to these changes, housekeepers are now increasingly relying on use of information technology in daily housekeeping operations, IT enabled equipment, and new scientific techniques.

From Cleanliness to Hygienically Clean to Clinically Clean Standards

Housekeepers had earlier taken the standards of cleanliness to 'hygienically clean'; which is now further enhanced to 'clinically clean' during and after the COVID-19 pandemic. Housekeepers came to the forefront taking on the role of hygiene and safety managers entrusted with the responsibility of developing SOPs for clinically clean standards and training employees to implement them.

Clinically Clean Standards

Clinically clean standards facilitate cleaning and disinfection, eliminating pathogens and are followed routinely in health care facilities. During the 2019–2020 pandemic, hotels adopted these stringent standards and housekeepers came into front line to implement them. Refer Chapter 14 for more details on clinically clean standards.

Use of disinfectant cleaners

To achieve clinically clean standards, brands offering cleaning solutions for hotels have come up with disinfectant cleaners. Two types of disinfectant cleaners are available, one step disinfectant cleaners and two-step disinfectant cleaners. One step disinfectant cleaners take care of removal of organic soil, dust and dirt along with pathogens. Two step disinfectant cleaners need to be applied twice, once to remove organic soil and second time, to carry out the disinfection function.

Stringent Operational and Hygiene Audits

An operational audit in a hotel is essentially a management tool for a structured review of a department's operating procedures and the results they provide, to use the outcome to iron out deficiencies and improve efficiency and effectiveness. Hygiene audits on the other hand review the implementation and effectiveness of a facility's hygiene and cleanliness standards. In mystery audits, the auditee are not informed of the audit schedule and details as opposed to inspection audits where the auditee are kept aware of the audit parameters, schedule and other details. Operational and hygiene audits are now a regular occurrence in hotels and internal auditors carry out scheduled audits.

Chain hotels, as a general practice are subject to audits by the corporate office or franchise inspection team assessing adherence to company standards. Hotels may also engage an external, third party auditor to carry out mystery audits. Cleaning partners of hospitality businesses, such as Diversey and Ecolab too assist hotels by undertaking hygiene audits. Hotel groups also coordinate with hygiene certification organisations such as Bureau Veritas or Det Norske Veritas (DNV) to not only assist them in establishing standards but also in carrying out extensive hygiene audits. Ministry of Tourism, Government of India, introduced an initiative called Saathi – System for Assessment Awareness and Training for Hospitality Industry which assists hotels to conduct audits and undertake self-certification.

Housekeeping managers should treat audits as a fact-finding exercise and not a blame- game activity. The functions of an audit are:

- Providing an objective assessment of operations.
- Identifying areas of limitations, inefficiency and waste, their causes and recommending alternatives.
- Gauging anomalies in implementation of policies, standards, and procedures
- Assessing observance of legal compliances.
- Evaluating performance of staff on set standards
- Uncovering unauthorised practices and irregular activities.
- Discovering areas of income enhancement.
- Documenting current practice and suggested improvements.
- Enabling enhanced communication between management and employees.

A brief operational audit checklist of the housekeeping department is provided in Table 34.1.

Table 34.1 Sample audit checklist for hotel housekeeping operations

Hotel operations audit (Housekeeping)					
S. No.	**Parameter**	**✓**	**×**	**NA**	**Recommendations**
	Managerial operations				
1.	Availability of departmental manual with policies and SOPs				
2.	Communication of hotel and departmental organisation structure/chart				
3.	Communication of job descriptions and specifications				

(Contd.)

Table 34.1 *Contd.*

Hotel operations audit (Housekeeping)					
S. No.	**Parameter**	**✓**	**×**	**NA**	**Recommendations**
4.	Set standards of productivity and performance				
5.	Availability of staffing guide				
6.	Effective employee orientation				
7.	Communication of company policies and procedures				
8.	Workplace diversity implementation				
9.	Display of weekly duty roster				
10.	Documentation of employee attendance				

Advances in Operations and Cleaning Technology

Smart Guestrooms

Hotels were always guest-centric, and with application of technology the guest experience management (GEM) has been now taken to another level. Hotels now feature smart guestrooms that are enabled with Artificial Intelligence (AI) powered Guest Room Management System (GRMS) which brings about automation of guestroom functions such as control on lighting, HVAC, curtains, door operations, television, music, and hotel guest services through touchscreen interfaces. These systems can also be integrated with mobile phone apps for further convenience. Technology-enabled smart guestrooms not only manage room energy consumption, but enhance in-room guest comfort, experience, and satisfaction. Different scenes can be set by the guests or hotel staff in each guestroom with AI integrated interactive walls or mirrors and GRMS that also allow display of world news, weather forecasts, maps, and much more. With AI and Voice recognition technology, guests can enjoy personalised virtual assistance such as requesting a particular thermostat setting, curtains to be closed, directions to a local restaurant or the hotel spa, all with voice command in their native language. Sensors installed in the guestrooms suggest occupancy or non-occupancy to housekeepers. When the GRMS is linked to the Property Management System (PMS) of the hotel, it makes it possible to capture and store guest preferences that are later used to surprise and delight guest with an already customised room experience on their subsequent visit to the hotel. See the section on features of mobile phone, PDA and tab-based apps for guests in this chapter for more information on applications of these apps when integrated with GRMS in smart guestrooms.

IT Savvy Housekeeping Operations

Many housekeepers have strived to make their department computer-savvy. Computers are now being used in many housekeeping departments for rooms management, inventory control, linen management, and so on, to varying extents. Computers can now be linked to the telephone system in each guestroom. This technology greatly reduces the cost of individual wiring in each guestroom. For instance, an interface can be created between the telephone system and the CPU of the hotel's computer network by the GRA dialling a specific sequence of numbers on the phone from a specific guestroom. Once connected, the computer immediately recognizes the room number to which it is being connected. After the connection is established, a specific list of dial-up codes become available to the GRA, by way of which he or she can now transmit information to the computer system directly without the need for additional input devices in the rooms. Refer Chapter 14 to learn more about the surge in technology applications during the pandemic scenario.

Use of mobile phone, PDA and tab-based apps and cloud based real time information

With the advent of myriad housekeeping organisation apps on mobile phones, Personal Digital Assistant (PDA) or tabs integrated with GRMS, housekeepers are able to access cloud based, real time information and manage operations efficiently, on the go. Most mobile phone apps such as Opera Mobile Cloud Service, 1Check, DigiValet, Beekeeper, Optii, HotelKey, Hotelogix, Alice, eZeeAbsolute, Flexkeeping, and so on offer a variety of features.

Features of mobile phone and tab apps for housekeeping operations:

- Integration with PMS for drawing real time data to allocate rooms for cleaning, create room assignments, assign tasks, make duty rosters, and track cleaning progress.
- Availability of floor plans and layout for zoning and allocation
- Information on average cleaning and turnaround time of each room via analytics dashboard.
- Automatic updation of PMS when data is fed through mobile due to mobile-PMS interface.
- Availability of real time room status on mobile for supervisors, front desk executive and management.
- Instant updation of room status by supervisors as they are alerted on mobile to inspect rooms. The supervisors can release rooms for sale to front office immediately through the mobile app after inspection.
- Availability of inspection checklists on mobile.
- Obtaining cleaning history of rooms and areas.
- Posting of work order requests for maintenance directly by room attendants as soon as a maintenance issue is observed while cleaning.
- Real time access to guest special requests and pending tasks.
- Instant communication between supervisors and associates, notifying runners of items required.
- Allowing guests to determine convenient cleaning and turn down service times.
- Notification to guests as soon as their room is cleaned.
- Making training needs analysis report
- Delivering training modules to entire team in their own language.
- Analysis of room costs amalgamating housekeeping and maintenance costs and energy consumption.

Features of mobile phone and tab-based apps for guests:

- Display of welcome letter
- Access to hotel's Wi-Fi
- Access to view guest folio anytime during the stay
- Virtual guestroom key enablement through mobile
- Message communication with hotel staff
- Presentations on hotel's features, safety document, information about other properties under the group's portfolio.
- Storage of relevant guest data in PMS as guest preferences.

- Activation of movies, internet, spa, and IRD upon check-in.
- Offers control of in-room lighting and mood lighting. Micro control over lighting via placing of light icons on the displayed actual picture of room
- Setting of temperature controls, with the provision of an alert to the maintenance team if the actual temperature didn't match the one set in the app within stipulated time.
- Control of blackouts and sheer curtains to open, close or hold them at the current position.
- Services such as collect and deliver laundry, request loan items
- Choice of online newspapers in various languages and from different countries.
- Access to internet browser with option to use on app or TV.
- Display of details on and reservations for local attractions and tours.
- Control over entertainment such as television control, electronic programme guide, selection of favourite channels, display of categorised movie catalogue, HD playback of movies on TV, option to search and play content from YouTube, also stream it on TV, stream content from guest devices on TV, music on demand with display of categorised music catalogue, selection of playlist, display of radio channels
- Enablement of door camera to live stream the feed captured and operation of door lock via the app. Door bell operation too integrated with door camera activation.
- Activation of privacy/DND and make my room requests with PMS interface.
- Display of IRD menu and booking options.
- Access to service directory, alarm set up, flight status, location map, weather forecasts, and currency exchange rates.
- Solicit feedback of guests with pictorial stages of satisfaction, and text and voice message.

Use of housekeeping software

Housekeeping operations modules are an integral part of integrated hotel management software or PMS such as Oracle Hospitality's Opera, Cloudbeds, Mews, HotelTime, RMS, IDS Next and so on. See information box in Chapter 16 for housekeeping features of Opera PMS.

Many software packages are now available in India that provide specific applications for housekeeping operations. For a detailed discussion on the applications of housekeeping software refer Chapter 16.

Tracking guest feedback

All department heads and managers track guest feedback to take action on the negative ones, so that their department and the hotel's performance is at the top of the business. Guest feedback is collected through the internal feedback system, a part of Guest Experience Management System (GEMS) and social media platforms. In these systems, feedback is usually classified into that on people, product and process. Housekeepers then carry out analysis of the root cause, people involved, and action taken. Service recovery is the prime part of handling negative feedback and involves preventive measures, standardised recovery and closing the loop. Effective training in recognised areas where negative feedback is high is part of recovery. Positive feedback needs to be communicated to and celebrated with the team.

Applications of Robotics and Artificial Intelligence (AI)

Robots are machines programmed to carry out simple or complex tasks automatically, with great precision. Robots may be either totally autonomous or semi-autonomous. Some may apply AI and speech recognition technology. Use of robots for specific functions may lead to cost-effectiveness, time-saving, and accuracy. Especially during the pandemic, when social distancing became the mandatory norm, use of robots in cleaning and disinfection saved the day for housekeepers in many hotels and the trend is here to stay. Refer Chapter 7 for details on robotic cleaning equipment.

Artificial Intelligence refers to the ability of a computer system to imitate the abilities of the human mind, grasping from examples, experiences, identifying objects, figuring out solutions to problems, comprehending and responding to languages, making decisions, and combining such capabilities to execute functions like a human. Cobots or collaborative robots equipped with AI features operate in responsive coordination with humans, interacting with them in a shared workspace to perform their tasks. They synergistically enhance human capabilities with their robust strength and flexibility, precision, and data capabilities. Many hotels have cobots delivering minibar items and extra or requested supplies to guests, collecting linen from floors, delivering linen to guests, cleaning washrooms, and so on.

Applications of RFID

Radio Frequency Identification (RFID) technology has found applications in housekeeping operations in the way linen and uniforms are organised and accounted. All linen items are tagged with water and heat resistant RFID tags by the manufacturer or at the housekeeping department. Each tag identity is scanned into the system and added to inventory. At every stage of handling, whether on floors or laundry, the process of linen accounting is eased with scanning by the tags being read by linen & laundry carts installed with RFID readers. Thus, manual counting and segregation is done away with and linen losses are curtailed due to RFID-based tracking.

In many hotels, RFID tags are sewn on the uniform labels and registered in the computer database with the garment's information. An RFID reader recognises the code on the returned soiled uniform and the conveyor automatically brings forth the corresponding fresh uniform on hanger to the front for delivery. The tags make tracking and inventory of uniforms highly efficient.

Sustainable Cleaning Solutions

Whether products or processes, housekeepers are going in for sustainable options that are safe for the planet and its people.

Use of sustainable cleaning products

Cleaning solutions brands such as Diversey, Ecolab and Scheveran offer sustainable, green-certified (usually EPA or Green Seal certified) cleaning products that have environment-friendly features such as biodegradability, low-toxicity, low-VOC and recyclable packaging. Further, these companies partner with housekeepers in implementing sustainable cleaning solutions which lead to savings in water, energy, and costs. In laundry, cold water-based cleaning chemicals are helping to save on energy costs. The hazardous chemical PERC is being replaced by hydrocarbons and pressurised liquid carbon dioxide.

Use of microfibre cleaning aids

Another revolutionary trend in hygiene in hotels is the advent of microfiber cleaning technology into housekeeping. Microfibers are made of ultra-fine polyester and polyamide blended microfibres, which have extremely minute strands that attract, capture and hold dust, dirt and microbes effectively.

The positively charges microfibers attract dust and dirt particles that tend to have a negative charge. The use of colour-coded microfiber dusters and mops results in much more effective dirt and germ control than their traditional counterparts. It is an eco-friendly change due to the negligible usage of chemicals and being low cost.

Application of nanotechnology

Nanotechnology enabled cleaning solutions are a boon for housekeepers. Nanotechnology refers to the science of application of extremely minute particles of matter; 1 nanometre is 1 billionth of a meter. Surfaces and fixtures coated with nano finishes such as silver nano are easier and quicker to clean, requiring significantly lesser usage of chemicals. Nanoparticles incorporated in thin polymer layers allow it to bond as a strong, transparent film on glass surfaces rendering them scratch free and water and dirt repellent. Silver nano makes the surface germicidal and inhibits further microbial growth. The technology is especially useful in developing self-cleaning coatings, where the titanium oxide nanoparticles, referred to as photocatalysts, coated on surfaces are activated with light energy and disinfect surfaces in minutes. Silver nanoparticle technology is also used in the laundry; it is used in washing machines to clean and disinfect linen. Silver or copper nanoparticles coated on fabrics and furnishings can repel stains, degrade odour-causing chemicals and retard microbe growth.

Use of PPE

Use of personal protective equipment was always a precautionary measure in certain housekeeping tasks, but the same has now been adopted very stringently. Since the COVID-19 pandemic, there has been advent of a variety of PPE, which have become part of housekeeping operations, as much as uniforms, to safeguard the staff. Housekeepers tie up with PPE vendors to customise PPE kits which are comfortable to wear while performing housekeeping tasks. In fact, housekeepers are now also custodians of PPE kits for the entire hotel's staff. Refer Chapter 7 for a detailed discussion on PPE.

Sustainable Amenities, Products and Processes

Guest amenities too are going sustainable, where possible. As competition is increasing, special amenities for wellbeing are being offered by hotels to woo guests. Housekeepers are substituting all single use plastic amenity and products in guestrooms with sustainable alternatives. The trend of using mineral water bottles is being substituted by placing customised, reusable glass bottles with RO-treated potable water. Many hotels have installed RO plants for this sustainability step. Products and processes are becoming green-oriented. Refer Chapter 32 for more details on eco-friendly amenities, products, and processes.

Responsible Procurement

Responsible procurement involves choosing products and services that have a reduced effect on the environment and society when compared to similar items that serve the same purpose. Procurement decisions in housekeeping have a significant impact on the environment as significant number of products are imported from far-off countries to cater to guest demands, thus increasing the carbon footprint. Housekeepers are now increasingly moving towards responsible procurement in tandem with the hotel's sustainability commitment. They look for ecolabels in products and go into their life cycle costs (LCC) with vendors before making purchasing decisions. Refer Chapter 17 for a detailed discussion on responsible procurement.

Sustainable Toiletries

More and more hotels are opting for toiletry ranges evolved after research and experimentation on the potent healing, curative, and therapeutic properties of herbs, their extracts, and essential oils on the skin and hair, especially as laid down in Ayurveda. These products are also not tested upon animals and tend to be biodegradable. Some of the herbs and natural substances frequently used in toiletries such as shampoos, conditioners, creams, lotions, and so on are aloe vera, liquorice, citrus fruit, Indian gooseberry, *neem*, sunflower, basil, pumpkin, cucumber, turmeric, sandalwood, apricot, mace, clove, nutmeg, coriander, rose, *henna*, clay, alum, and honey. Hotels are going for world-class, designer label toiletries and cosmetics to be placed in guest bathrooms, partnering with vendors to customise toiletries with herbal and natural ingredients. Hotel amenities such as soaps, shampoos, and conditioners are nowadays coming in new biodegradable packaging.

Partnering with Recycling Programmes

More and more housekeepers are partnering with recycling vendors who run programmes for collection and recycling of used supplies and materials. Used soap bars from guestrooms are collected and handed over to such vendors, who in turn recycle them and the resulting soap cakes are distributed to needy communities through NGOs. Programmes such as Clean the World, Soap Cycling and Soap for Hope are some such initiatives. Housekeepers also partner with linen mills to recycle pillows that have lost their plushness. Such mills rework the filling material and incorporate them in new scatter cushions. Many hotels also partner in carpet recycling programmes by donating out of condition carpets to vendors who use post-consumer carpet fibres to manufacture carpet cushions or paddings. Quite a few hotels go in for these recycled carpet cushions as part of their sustainability efforts.

Sustainable Textiles

Some international chains are experimenting with textiles made of bamboo fibres as an environmentally sustainable material for bed and bath linen and uniforms. Bamboo is one of the world's most prolific, regenerative crops and is grown without the use of any pesticides or fertilizers. Fabrics made of bamboo are naturally antibacterial and hypoallergenic. Bamboo fibres are usually blended with cotton (65%:35% or 40%:60%) to yield more absorbent, softer, and smell-resistant luxury bath linen than normal ones. Bamboo fabrics have a unique silky texture and are superior to cotton in terms of softness, durability, and comfort, and are therefore, ideal for the manufacture of bed linen. The fabrics do not pill. The bamboo fibre under microscope shows various gaps and holes and hence the fabrics made out of it can rapidly absorb and evaporate moisture, making them exceptionally comfortable. Moreover, bamboo is cool in summer and warm in winter.

Many hotel groups have programmes to support artisan weavers and have tie ups with them to procure traditional textiles and weaves for furnishings, tapestries, and so on. For a detailed discussion on such traditional textiles, refer Chapter 18.

Energy and Water Conserving Products

Housekeepers are now opting for products and equipment that help conserve energy. Appliances with energy star ratings are preferred (refer Chapter 32). Automated energy management systems integrated with the guestroom key card or micro door sensor manage light and air conditioning as guests enter or leave their room, saving 25–40% on HVAC costs. Some hotels have heat sensors installed in the rooms so that housekeeping knows when the guests are in the room. Housekeepers and interior designers today also have at their disposal energy-efficient lamps that consume a mere 9W of power and give the same light output as a 60W bulb. This can reduce power tariffs by as much as 80% without taking away the aesthetic appeal of the property. Some trends in lighting that have been gaining momentum in hotels are the use of luminaries and LEDs with sensor technology, compact luminaries, and compact halogen lamps. Hotels are also going in for application of solar power in a big way, some are even harnessing wind energy. In laundries, washers with electric water heating system are preferable so that passive steam heating that consumes more energy is eliminated. Hotels have very high consumption of water and to reduce water wastage and consumption, water efficiency rated fixtures and appliances are preferred by housekeepers. For more details on these, refer Chapter 32.

Ozone Treatment

Ozone treatment has emerged as a clean and environment-friendly technique that has a wide variety of applications in the housekeeping department. Ozone is a form of oxygen molecule composed of three atoms of oxygen instead of the usual two. It decomposes quickly and turns into regular oxygen easily. However, when the extra oxygen atom splits away from the ozone molecule. This extra oxygen atom then tends to oxidize substances it comes into contact with. Thus, ozone can act as a disinfectant that is safer and more effective than chlorine since it purifies water and air leaving behind no harmful by-products.

Air treatment with ozone Ozonizers can be used to treat the air in hotel rooms and public areas.

Room ozonizer This is a compact device that can be used to disinfect and deodourize air-conditioned rooms, thus, improving the indoor air quality. Room ozonizers effectively remove the smell of smoke and other foul odours that have built up in course of everyday use.

Ozonizers for lobbies and corridors Ozonizers can also be placed in lobbies and corridors or passages to disinfect the air and effectively remove all foul odours. Small-capacity ozonizers, such as the 1-gram models, can be enough to minimize the odour in such areas.

Ozonizing air-scrubbers in bars and pubs These are generally smoky areas, and many people—both smokers and non-smokers—experience discomfort in such crowded places when the smell of food mingles with these smoky odours indoors. Specially designed scrubbers can draw the foul air out, treat it with ozone to disinfect and clean the air, and then return it through the air-handling unit.

Water treatment with ozone Ozone can also be used to treat drinking water, swimming pools, recirculated water, and laundry operations.

Disinfection of drinking water Ozone is an all-pervasive anti-bacterial and anti-viral agent. It needs only a short reaction time of a few seconds to effectively kill all germs, including viruses, within a few seconds. Ozonizers disinfect, remove turbidity, and unpleasant tastes and odours from water to provide safe drinking water.

Swimming pool treatment Here, ozone is injected at the water entry point of the pool to disinfect the water. This treatment makes the water clear, sparkling, and appealing. It is safer for swimmers as well compared to chlorine, which is accompanied by certain health hazards—eye irritation, hair loss, and skin rashes.

Ozonization of recirculated water Ozonization of recirculated water in cooling towers dramatically enhances its performance, reducing the operating costs by eliminating the use of chemicals and considerably lowering the make-up water requirement. Its disinfection properties effectively prevent bacteria build-up, as well as destroying organic binding matter such as slime and algae. It thus increases the efficiency of the cooling tower and reduces power consumption as well.

Ozone in laundries Ozone is an effective cleaning agent in all single-colour laundry operations since it improves the efficiency of the washing process by reacting with the dirt molecules and converting them to oxides that are easier to treat. Ozone substantially reduces or eliminates the need for laundering chemicals. Its deodorizing properties also help to eliminate any odour from the laundered clothes.

Additional Amenities for Guest Convenience, Comfort, and Wellbeing

- For today's tech-savvy guest, rooms now have a docking station where all sorts of electronic devices may be charged together at one platform.
- Hotels provide free wireless access throughout their property. High speed internet connectivity is provided to guests.
- Hotels are offering streaming content on OTT with guests using personal accounts with hotel TVs.
- Bathrooms are getting more spacious with both shower cubicle and a bath tub.
- Where a decade earlier, ironing board, iron box, and coffee making machines were only guest loan items, now they are to be found placed in every room.
- Various kinds of teas, coffees, sugars in sachets are now found placed in tea trays.
- More layers of padding are added to beds above the mattress to provide additional comfort in the form of a mattress pad.
- Many hotels offer a pillow menu for guests, providing a choice of pillows such as slim soft pillow, super soft pillow, cotton comfort pillow, latex pillow, poly-fill pillow, feather-fill pillow/feather-down pillow, tranquillity pillow, baby pillow, energy pillow, silk cotton pillow, relax support pillow, ortho-care pillow, air-care pillow, bath comfort pillow, aromatherapy pillow, cervical pillow, body pillow, and meditation pillow.
- A slumber/sleep kit, which may contain eye mask, ear plugs, aroma roll-ons, and blackout eye bands for guests with jet lag, is placed in the drawer of the nightstand.
- A yoga kit can also be found as an amenity in guestrooms. It contains a yoga mat, oil diffusers and aroma oils, yoga hand book, and free-size yoga apparel.
- Small attractive indoor plants are placed in guest bathrooms.

New Scientific Techniques and Equipment

The use of new scientific techniques such as work studies and ergonomics is a new trend in housekeeping.

Work Studies

These are analyses of the tasks, equipment, and time taken to do specific jobs. They can be an important tool in determining the hotel's standard operating procedures. Many housekeepers have realised this value of work studies and are developing SOPs based on work studies done at their properties. For more details on work study refer Chapter 3.

Ergonomics

This scientific discipline is concerned with the understanding of interactions between humans and the elements of a system they work in or with in terms of the impact on efficiency and comfort. Work studies

of the ergonomic efficiency of each task and the equipment, processes, and products used in it is necessary for the well-being of the housekeeping staff because of the physically demanding profession that it is. Refer Chapter 23 for a detailed discussion on ergonomics.

Application of ergonomic principles can be seen in the way housekeepers are customising the room attendant's carts to make them more efficient and at the same time ergonomically much easier and safer to work with, as represented in the case study in Chapter 23.

Scientific Equipment for Quality Checks

Scientific equipment aid housekeepers to achieve high standards of cleaning and maintenance.

- Decibel meters are used to check sound levels. Sound decibel level on and near bed is to be maintained at 35 dB.
- Luxmeters are used to check illumination in an area. The overall lux level of the room should be maintained at 100 lux.
- Glossmeters are used to check gloss level of flooring. Gloss level in guestroom should be maintained at 90 and reflectance at 95.
- IAQ sensors are used to detect imbalances in indoor air quality. It is a norm now in many hotels to display the IAQ parameters in the lobby for guests' reference.
- Reflectometers are used to check the brightness of hotel linen. The following reflectometer readings are recommended, bed linen—95, bath linen—94, table linen—95, uniforms—92.

Outsourcing Becomes a Necessity

The realm of housekeeping continues to witness a huge growth in the trend of outsourced services. Housekeeping being a work-intensive department, housekeepers perceive outsourcing as an effective business strategy, especially for the continual maintenance of the public areas of their properties. Most hotel chains, across all segments, have resorted to outsourcing nowadays.

Today, housekeeping demands skilled specialization, which in turn requires a sizeable investment in terms of the infrastructure and equipment required to achieve superior results. Housekeeping experts opine that outsourcing proves to be the best solution for many specialized tasks as it is highly cost-effective, makes better business sense, and at the same time meets the demand of quality standards. It brings in 'specialists' both in terms of man and machine to deliver quality as per the standard norms and philosophy laid down by the individual property.

Outsourcing cuts down on the training needed for operating these machines and the safety hazards that are often involved, as well as the need for investment in machinery that is not used frequently. Outsourcing and contracting works well for hotels as it also minimizes manpower-related issues such as filling the need-gap caused due to attrition of manpower, unavailability of suitable personnel to fill the need, and unionization. Refer Chapter 4 for detailed discussion on outsourcing.

Enhanced Need of Training and Motivation

The biggest challenge in hotel housekeeping in the present scenario is finding, training, retraining, and continuously motivating quality staff. Increased mechanization of housekeeping operations has placed housekeeping managers in a position to train staff on optimum usage of equipment, supplies, and energy to increase efficiency in operations. This is crucial to minimizing wasteful expenditure. For training in the use of equipment, many housekeepers are tying up with companies that supply the equipment to the hospitality industry. Hotels are also promoting cross-training, thereby reducing the worry of staff requirements by making it possible to rotate inter-department shifts during high-pressure situations. Another upcoming training trend is that of housekeepers collaborating with hotel management institutions for theoretical knowledge, where the institution's faculty deliver lecture sessions to the housekeeping staff. Training for housekeeping staff has to be divided into four parts—attitudinal, technical, soft skills, and SOPs. The first two aspects are usually grossly neglected in training modules and the latter have to be learnt on the job. The quality of on-the-job training available to staff at a property depends on the managerial mindset. Some hotels may not choose to invest in training staff and prefer to save money. In the long run, though, they often end up losing money due to lack of trained staff. One way or the other, the hotels ultimately end up paying for training, so it is best to get it right at the start.

Retaining and motivating staff is crucial for the success of any organization. This is especially true in the hospitality industry, where the housekeeping team members are involved in unglamorous tasks that are very often taken for granted and go unappreciated. Described as an extremely monotonous and thankless job even by veterans of the industry, housekeeping is still in need of recognition and innovation. It is not incentivized in the same way as some other departments in a hotel. In addition, lack of communication between the managerial and grassroot levels leaves employees frustrated and overworked. And of course, unskilled and untrained employees can become a challenge, coupled with the massive attrition rates of trained personnel due to more lucrative options coming up.

Employee engagement, skill enhancement, multiskilling and rewarding options to break the veritable monotony by way of outings, forums in which to exchange views and facilitate an exchange of dialogue, or recognition of employees by name go a long way towards ensuring job satisfaction. Team parties, public appreciation, and taking suggestions from employees are all good tools for motivation. A departmental performance review not only serves an operational purpose but is essential as a team building tool. Housekeeping managers must also assist their employees in achieving an ideal work-life balance. Refer to Chapter 3 for more details on training and motivation.

Women-Only Floors

Many luxury hotels now offer exclusive women-only floors due to a surge in the number of women business travellers, especially single lady travellers. The trend started in India with the ITC hotels and has now been implemented by many other hotels. These floors, popularly called the eva floor or duchesse floors offer rooms and services exclusively to women travellers, emphasising on safety and feminine pampering products.

- They can be exclusively accessed only by women; no male staff is allotted to the floor and no male guest is allowed access to the floor.
- The entire operations on the floor are managed by a female crew.
- Additional safety features on such floors and rooms include, female security guards and butlers, lady chauffeurs, dedicated female concierge, in-room video phones and pepper spray.
- The décor of the rooms and amenities placed too emphasize feminity, for example, soft, pastel colour schemes, fresh flowers, fruit bowls, chocolate platter, pink or lavender linen, ladies grooming kit, yoga kit, jewellery box, glossy magazines, facial steamer, hair dryers, hair curling

and straightening irons, manicure sets, pedicure machines, silk curtains, super soft furry cushions, soft fur rugs, aromatherapy oils and diffusers, fresh flower arrangements, and so on.

- Feminine needs such as full-length mirrors, padded hangers, sanitary products kit, makeup mirrors, makeup fridges, and extra bath and body cosmetics are placed as standard contents.

Luxury Process Trends

Turndown service is now being delivered in a more creative way with GRAs placing towel art, flower petal art, paper art, and small good night goodies on the bed. Pillows are sprayed with relaxing sprays and sleep kit with sleep accessories is placed on the bed. Innovation and creativity is also seen in customising the turndown such as dessert turndown, tropical fruit turndown, chocolate turndown, champagne turndown, wine turndown, cognac or liquor turndown, flavoured Gin turndown, ginger beer turndown or chamomile green tea turndown. Some hotels offer art turndown where colouring pencils and a colouring book, miniature folk art sculptures as keepsakes made by local artisans portraying the culture of the place are placed on the bed.

Another area where creativity is being seen is in the provision of a bath butler service. In this service, a personal valet makes up a relaxing bath with a preferred essence, floral petals, herbs, and bath salts. A choice of beverage and appetisers too are kept ready at arm's length.

Design Trends

Design trends are being applied in hotels with the underlying concept of sustainability. The Covid-19 pandemic too has necessitated introduction of minimalism in design and emphasis on microbe-retarding surfaces and designing. Read more about designing with sustainability in Chapter 32 and designing for infection prevention in Chapter 14.

Design Trends in Public Areas

- Trends in landscaping are towards having more outdoor seating and dining areas and open-air spaces designed for wellness, recreation, and entertainment activities.
- Architectural spaces are designed to blend in infection control equipment, such as UV machines and IAQ sensors, aesthetically.
- With hotel reception increasingly going the online way, reception areas are being reduced and more area being allocated to other functions. Thus, many hotels feature dynamic, functional lobbies with new multi-use spaces such as lobby bar, patisserie area, social zones, and co-working spaces.
- Biophilic design is being integrated in hotel exterior and interior spaces by architects and designers to incorporate nature into the building to enhance the wellbeing of its occupants. Vertical gardens, active green walls, and hydroponics are thus, a sustainable trend. Use of small and large indoor plants, bonsai and terrariums in interiors rather than elaborate flower arrangements is another sustainable initiative. Refer Chapter 32 to learn more about biophilic design, and Chapter 31 for details on bonsai, terrariums and hydroponics.
- New concepts in flower arrangements are seen with minimal flowers and more foliage and dried plant material being used. Aesthetic vases are used.

- Increased use of low emissive glass for exterior walls, doors, and windows of main building of hotels. This glass is treated with an invisible metallic oxide coating, creating a surface that allows light to pass through, while reflecting the heat. Use of this glass reduces energy consumption, decreases fading of window treatment fabrics, and enhances the comfort factor in residential buildings.
- Contemporary state-of-the-art, energy saving lighting fixtures with LED are used in elaborate chandeliers.
- Hotel designers are integrating local art in interiors. From use of local, ethnic weaves in furnishings, displaying local artwork and handicrafts, to incorporating locally traditional architectural materials and elements, emphasis is on giving guests glimpses of local culture and tradition.
- Contemporary hotel designing lays emphasis on texture, fragrance and colour to stimulate guest's senses and at the same time, use of detailed patterns is avoided to create clean, soothing spaces.

Design Trends in Guestrooms

- Technology is being integrated in all functional aspects of guestrooms be it in the form of motorised curtains, interactive walls and TV, mood lighting, energy saving fixtures and systems, or enablement of artificial intelligence features.
- Interiors are turning stylish in elements of texture, form, light, and colour.
- Vibrant colours are being experimented with in guestroom interiors.
- Hotels are investing in beds with thick plush mattresses, which offer high degree of comfort and are hypoallergenic too.
- Themed guestrooms, with themes such as desert, tropics, rainforests are gaining popularity.
- Exposed bathrooms are a fast catching up trend especially in guestrooms at resorts and spas. These bathrooms are exposed to the sky as there is no roof. Flooring has pebbled areas and typically some outdoor plants can be found in exposed bathrooms.
- Spacious bathrooms are in vogue with both shower cubicle and bath tub.
- Contemporary sleek bathroom fixtures with sensors to control flow of water are a trend.
- Personal Jacuzzi and whirlpools can be found in contemporary luxury guestrooms.

SUMMARY

Housekeeping operations have seen a surge of innovations and trends, the principal ones being sustainability and technology based. Professional housekeepers are striving to get housekeeping its due recognition in the hospitality industry. After all, this department is responsible for bringing in the largest share of profit to an accommodation operation, but this fact is hardly acknowledged and veterans of the industry too often consider it a thankless job.

Advances in cleaning technology is discussed in great detail. This chapter discussed information technology in housekeeping at length, mentioning guestroom management systems, mobile phone, PDA and tab based housekeeping apps. Many hospitality-specific softwares having comprehensive housekeeping applications are on offer in the market now. Hotels in developed countries have utilized IT in a big way in housekeeping, which is not yet the case in the Indian scenario, however. Thus, housekeepers need to become more IT-savvy and collaborate with software professionals in developing modules for various applications in housekeeping operations. Almost all subroutines in housekeeping tasks are amenable to being adapted to IT systems.

Sustainable solutions in cleaning operations such as use of green chemicals, recycling partnerships, and responsible procurement are also discussed.

Housekeeping operations are increasingly becoming scientific and mechanized. Scientific equipment and techniques have enabled housekeepers

to enhance worker comfort and efficiency, and help carry out stringent quality checks. However, the fact remains that the majority of the lower-rung housekeeping workforce are unskilled. Hence, training in housekeeping procedures and equipment is essential and this should be a continuous process. When the department spends time, energy, and resources on training employees, all efforts should be made to motivate and retain them as well. This chapter has also discussed the training and motivation issues in housekeeping today.

A major trend in hotels is towards becoming more eco-sensitive. This trend is influencing the housekeeping departments in the hotels too. Housekeepers are developing and adopting new ways to conserve water and energy and opting for eco-friendly amenities and products. The last section of the chapter discusses the various design trends in hotels.

KEY TERMS

AI Artificial Intelligence, refers to machines performing intelligent tasks with reasoning, problem solving, human speech recognition, and autonomous navigation, all elements mimicking human cognitive functions.

Amenity A service or item offered to guests or placed in guestrooms for their convenience and comfort at no extra cost.

Aromatherapy The use of aromatic plant extracts and essential oils for healing and cosmetic purposes.

Ayurveda A Sanskrit term made up of the words *ayu* ('life') and *veda* ('knowledge' or 'science'), this refers to a system of using the inherent principles of nature to maintain health in a person by keeping the individual's body, mind, and spirit in perfect equilibrium with nature.

Biodegradable Substances capable of being decomposed by living organisms.

Biophilic design Design of building exterior and interior in which architects and designers incorporate nature into building spaces to enhance the wellbeing of its occupants.

Bonsai Literally meaning 'a plant in a tray', this refers to a tree or a plant whose typical growth in nature has been copied exactly in a miniature style within the confines of a container.

Clinically clean standards Standards of cleanliness that facilitate cleaning and disinfection, eliminating pathogens. It is followed routinely in health care facilities.

Cobots or collaborative robots operate in responsive coordination with humans, interacting with them in a shared workspace to perform their tasks. They synergistically enhance human capabilities with their robust strength and flexibility, precision, and data capabilities.

CPU Central processing unit of a computer system.

Cross-training Training employees to work in departments other than their speciality during periods of staff shortage.

Diffusers Small devices that are used in aromatherapy to disperse essential oils so that the fragrance disperses in the surrounding air.

EPA Environmental Protection Agency (USA).

Ergonomics The study of the efficiency of people in relation to their working environment.

Eva floors An exclusive women's-only floor in hotels, offering rooms and services exclusively to women clientele. Also called Duchesse floors.

Exposed bathrooms These bathrooms usually found in resorts and spas are exposed to the sky as there is no roof.

GEM Guest Experience Management.

Glossmeter A glossmeter is an instrument used to measure the level of gloss of a surface.

GRMS Guest Room Management System.

GRA Guestroom Associate/attendant.

Hydroponics A new age agricultural system where crop plants are grown in nutrient-rich medium instead of soil.

Hygiene The science that deals with the preservation of health by maintaining high standards of cleanliness.

Hygiene audit A structured review of implementation and effectiveness of a facility's hygiene and cleanliness standards.

Hypoallergenic Refers to substances or surfaces least likely to cause allergic reactions.

IT Information technology.

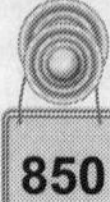

Jacuzzi A bath with a system of underwater jets of water to massage the body.

LCC Life cycle costing, a technique of costing in responsible procurement that establishes the total costs of purchasing a product or service from 'cradle to grave' by posing questions related to each stage of its life cycle.

LED Light emitting diode.

Low emissive glass This glass is treated with an invisible metallic oxide coating, creating a surface that allows light to pass through, while reflecting the heat. This results in substantial energy conservation in buildings where it is used.

Luxmeter A luxmeter is a device used to measure the illumination on a surface.

Microfiber Cloth made of ultra-fine polyester and polyamide blended fibres, which have extremely minute strands that attract, capture and hold dust, dirt and microbes effectively. The positively charged microfibres attract dust and dirt particles that tend to have a negative charge.

Nanotechnology A field of research, innovation and subsequent application concerned with creating materials on the scale of atoms and molecules (nanoparticles). A nanometre is one-billionth of a metre. The technology is especially useful in developing self-cleaning coatings.

Net Promoter Score NPS is a metric to measure customer loyalty and satisfaction derived from asking customers how likely they are to recommend the product or service to friends and colleagues on a scale of 0–10.

Operational audit A management tool for a structured review of a department's operating procedures and the results they provide, to use the outcome to iron out deficiencies and improve efficiency and effectiveness.

Outsourcing A conscious business decision to move internal work to an external provider.

Ozone A form of oxygen where each molecule is composed of three atoms of oxygen instead of the more usual. It decomposes quickly and easily, turning into regular oxygen when the extra oxygen atom splits away from the ozone molecule.

Patisserie Refers to an outlet where pastries and cakes are sold.

Pedicure machines Machines used for cosmetic treatment of feet and toenails.

PERC Perchloroethylene; a carcinogenic dry cleaning solvent.

Performance standards A required level of performance to meet the quality standards set by the organization.

PDA Personal digital assistant—a handheld computer that serves as an organizer for personal information; it may be also combined with a cell phone and other wireless technologies, providing a mobile office for people on the go.

Pillow menu A list of available pillows provided by a hotel to guests, usually free of charge. It allows guests to make an alternative pillow choice. Some common pillow alternatives are memory foam, buckwheat hull, and hypoallergenic. Some hotels offer pillows to treat specific conditions such as headaches or stress.

PPE Personal Protective Equipment.

Productivity standards An acceptable amount of work to be done within a specific time frame according to an established level of performance.

Reflectometers A device to measure the level of reflectance of a reflective surface.

RFID Radio Frequency Identification; A wireless technology that employs radio waves to read and capture information stored on a tag attached to an object.

RO Reverse Osmosis.

Slumber/sleep kit A slumber/sleep kit may contain eye mask, ear plugs, aroma roll-ons, and blackout eye bands for jet lag; it is placed in the drawer of the nightstand.

SOPs Documents of a standing nature that specify a certain method of operating or specific procedures for the accomplishment of a task. SOPs can be developed for all important housekeeping activities and tasks.

Terrarium An open or enclosed transparent container, usually a glass or acrylic vessel that contains growing medium and plants in its interior, creating a miniature ecosystem.

Towel art The art of folding towels to resemble natural things such as flowers, animals, etc. In hotels it is usually done by a housekeeper and placed on beds in guestrooms.

Vertical gardens Also called green walls, these are gardens that scale the walls vertically and help conserve space and water. The set up involves plants grown in a medium like soil and features an integrated water delivery system.

VOC Volatile Organic Compounds.

Wi-Fi Wireless fidelity—an amenity provided nowadays by most world-class hotels, this technology enables guests to access a wide range of information, applications, and computing resources without having to worry about connectivity issues.

Whirlpool A heated pool in which hot aerated water is continuously circulated.

Work study An analysis of the tasks, the equipment, and the time taken to do a specific job. This is an important tool for determining standard operating procedures.

Yoga kit Contains a yoga mat, oil diffusers and aroma oils, CDs on basic yogasanas, yoga hand book, and yoga apparel. It is placed as a guestroom amenity.

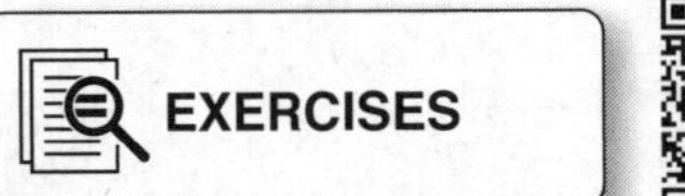

About the Authors

G Raghubalan is a consultant, trainer and entrepreneur in the hospitality industry. He is a seasoned professional with more than 33 years, including stints in hotel operations, academics, training, consulting, international recruitment and human resources, before venturing as an entrepreneur.

After having passed out of the premier hospitality Institute of the country, IHM Mumbai, Raghubalan has had stints with leading hospitality brands, including the Central Park Hotel (formerly a Welcomgroup property at Bangalore), CGH Earth (Kerala), Novotel & HICC (Hyderabad) and Citymax Hotels (India). His international experience includes handling Human Resources and Training functions at Abu Dhabi, UAE, with the Hospitality division of Al Ahlia General Trading company and Jananah Investments LLC for leading restaurant brands such as La Brioche, Applebees and the Rocky Mountain Chocolate Factory.

His academic experience includes teaching at the Christ College (now Christ University), KKRM (Woodlands) College of Hotel Management, Bangalore, as well as the Principal at the R N Shetty College of Hotel Management, Hubli and the PES Institute of Hotel Management, Bangalore. He continues his association with hotel management education and the industry as an adjunct faculty at Welcomgroup Graduate School of Hotel Administration, Manipal, and as a resource person for various national and international seminars and webinars. He is an Article reviewer for the Research Journal of the Silver Mountain School of Hotel Management, Nepal.

With his extensive experience, Raghubalan has turned an entrepreneur as a partner at SRJ Services, a venture catering for special interest travelers and unique handcrafted products, within India and outside. He is also a certified Image Consultant, from the Conselle Institute of Image Management, USA, and a Certified Soft skill trainer from NABET (National accreditation board for education and training). He is a keen fitness enthusiast and an Ultra runner.

Smritee Raghubalan is a Bengaluru-based hospitality educator and consultant. She has a professional experience of 23 years, out of which 19 years have been in the academia. She has done her Masters in Home Science and holds the UGC – NET qualification. As an Associate Professor, she has taught and contributed in the field of Accommodation Management in various universities. In addition to her academic post, she has also held administrative posts of Assistant Registrar and NAAC Coordinator. She was a part of the syllabus review committee for Accommodation Management at NCHMCT in 2020. She has presented and published papers in various seminars and journals and has delivered many invited guest lectures on innovative topics in the field of Accommodation Management.

She is an Executive Committee member of Professional Housekeepers Association (PHA) and holds the portfolio of Managing Editor of the PHA bi-annual e-infozine, 'Voice of Housekeepers'. She is also the Chief Mentor of PHA YUVA, the youth chapter of PHA. She has completed the basic course in Ikebana from the Japanese Language School, Bengaluru. She is also pursuing a parallel career as a novelist, having self-published her first novel in 2021– The Call of The Mahua in the medical romance genre.

Ms. Raghubalan has been an invited judge for housekeeping competitions and moderator at many panel discussions organized by various hospitality expos. She has been honoured by International Hospitality Council as a celebrity author and novelist in 2022 and as an outstanding hospitality educator in 2019. She was also honoured as a celebrity author at LPU Authors' Conclave in 2016. She has been featured on the web platform 'Indian Women in Hospitality'.

Related Titles

Food and Beverage Service [9780199464685]

R. Singaravelavan, *State Institute of Hospitality Management, Kozhikode*

The second edition of *Food and Beverage Service* is specifically tailored to meet the requirements of the students of hotel management courses. Each of the six sections—introduction to food and beverage service, menu knowledge and planning, food service, beverages and tobacco, bar operations and control, and ancillary functions—have been thoroughly updated to cover all the aspects of the food service industry.

Key Features

- llustrates the key concepts with the help of photographs of various table layouts and other services, sample menus, and side bars
- Provides a detailed description of the various types of wines, non-alcoholic beverages, guéridon service, and specialized service skills for breakfast, afternoon tea, brunch, and so on
- Includes the French terms used for the various staff members, menu, and dishes
- Includes well-illustrated chapters with numerous photographs, flowcharts, illustrations, tables, and examples
- Contains cases to enhance critical thinking and relate concepts to real-life situations

Food Production Operations 4e [9780190124793]

Parvinder S Bali In its third edition, Food Production Operations, is a comprehensive text designed for students of degree and diploma courses in hotel management. The book introduces students to the world of professional cookery and covers all aspects of food production.

Key Features

- Introduces the basics of Indian and Western cuisines
- Includes sections on food safety, new concepts in wine and food pairing, and game and poultry
- Throws light on the role of FSSAI in food industry and the importance of grooming in kitchen

Hotel Front Office: Operations and Management 2e [9780199464692]

Jatashankar R. Tewari, *Uttarakhand Open University*

The second edition of Hotel Front Office is specifically tailored to meet the requirements of the students pursuing hotel management courses. The book aims to explore all the relevant aspects and issues related to front office operations and management with the help of numerous industryrelated examples, cases, and project assignments.

Key Features

- Discusses the functions of front office operations, and suggests ways and means to make them more effective

Food Science and Nutrition 3e [9780199489084]

Sunetra Roday, *Maharashtra State Institute of Hotel Management and Catering Technology (MSIHMCT), Pune*

The third edition of Food Science and Nutrition provides complete and exhaustive coverage of topics related to food science, food safety, and nutrition. It is aimed at students of undergraduate, diploma, or certificate courses in hotel management, hospitality studies, and catering technology.

Key Features

- Covers subjects taught in hospitality and hotel administration, food technology, applied sciences, home science, and nursing courses
- Provides ample examples, review questions, analytical thinking exercises, and updated reference charts and tables

Other Related Titles

9780198062912 Ghoshal: *Hotel Engineering*
9780199458844 Devendra: *Soft Skills for Hospitality*
9780199469833 Seal: *Food & Beverage Management*
9780198084013 Devendra: *Hotel Law*
9780195694468 Iyengar: *Hotel Finance*
9780198084013 Devendra: *Hotel Law*
9780198064633 Bansal: *Hotel Facility Planning*
9780198084006 Seal: *Computers in Hotels: Concepts and Applications*
9780198073895 Bali: *International Cuisine and Food Production Management*
9780198068495 Bali: *Quantity Food Production Operations and Indian Cuisine*
9780199474448 Bali: *Theory of Cookery*
9780199488797 Bali: *Theory of Bakery*